THE TIMES

QUOTATIONS

THE TIMES

Quotations

TIMES BOOKS

First published in 2006 by Times Books

HarperCollins Publishers
77–85 Fulham Palace Road
London w6 8jb
www.collins.co.uk

© 2006 Times Newspapers Ltd 2006

10 9 8 7 6 5 4 3 2 1 0

The Times is a registered trademark of Times Newspapers Ltd

ISBN 13: 978–0–00–724048–7
ISBN 10: 0–00–724048–1

A catalogue record for this book is available from the
British Library.

Art direction: Mark Thomson
Designed by Richard Marston

Typeset in FF Nexus

Printed and bound in Great Britain by
Clays Ltd, St Ives plc

CONTENTS

INTRODUCTION

QUOTATION IS OUR national vice (*Evelyn Waugh*), the parole
of literary men all over the world (*Sam Johnson*), and the act of
repeating erroneously the words of another (*Ambrose Bierce*).
But quotation is also the most enduring form of immortality.

Quotable lines bring to pass a monument with a longer
shelf-life than brass (the poet Horace, coarsely translated).
Every hour of every day, billions of words are spoken and
written. And those are just in English, the world language.
Almost all of these words have been said many times
before. Most language is repetition, slop, pudder, jargon –
conventional noises that pass through the ears of the audience
without creating a ripple. It is almost impossible to think
a new thought or make an original statement that has not
been thought or made many times before. Originality is the
business of poets and philosophers. It is the last thing we
expect (or want?) from our politicians, football managers, pop

stars, television readers of the autocue, and other celebrities who are famous for being famous, not for being original.

But in the ceaseless chatter of language, just occasionally something original is said. And the astonishing revolution in communication that rages around us means that Everyman (and Everywoman) can at last get their voices heard. Until this generation, politicians and ruling elites in other fields were those who were heard and published. In the future everyone will be famous for fifteen minutes (*Andy Warhol*). I'm bored with that line. My new line is, 'In fifteen minutes everybody will be famous.' Today everybody can be quoted. And is.

There are already many excellent quotation dictionaries, from Oxford and Collins to Penguin and Bartletts. So why do we need another one? The distinctive feature of *The Times Quotations* is that it catches the rascal quotations when they are just hatched. Other dictionaries record the great sayings of the past. One of my favourite bits in *The Times* is the 'Quotes of the Week' at the back of the Weekend section. My observation suggests that other people also turn to them first on Saturdays. They are included. So here we find the witty, wise and weird sayings made yesterday by the famous and the infamous, by Everyman and (that oxymoronic newspaper construct) the Ordinary Man. The surest way to make a monkey of a man is to quote him (*Benchley*).

There are many uses for a quotation dictionary. A bad one is for a hack in a hurry to decorate his prose with other men's flowers (*Archie Wavell*). A good one is to verify your references, sir (*Routh*). But the best is to open the door we never opened into the rose-garden (*Eliot*, Thomas Stearns, not George).

The best choice of a single book for a desert island (perhaps even before Shakespeare and the Authorized Version) is a good dictionary of quotations. With it you can remember old friends and meet new ones. It is an immortal possession (*Thucydides*). Words are a man's defining characteristic and our only true immortality. *The Times Quotations* is a running commentary on current affairs, as well as a treasury of the past, and a window into future reading. And it is also, of course, the best book yet published for browsing like a butterfly and stinging like a bee.

PHILIP HOWARD

LIST OF THEMES

ABSENCE

1 My life will be sour grapes and ashes
without you.
The Young Visiters (1919) **Ashford, Daisy** (1881–
1972) English child author

2 Absence makes the heart grow fonder,
Isle of Beauty, Fare thee well!
'Isle of Beauty' (song, 1830) **Bayly, Thomas
Haynes** (1797–1839) English songwriter, writer
and dramatist

3 When I came back to Dublin, I was
courtmartialled in my absence and
sentenced to death in my absence, so I said
they could shoot me in my absence.
The Hostage (1958) **Behan, Brendan** (1923–1964)
Irish dramatist, writer and Republican

4 The heart may think it knows better: the
senses know that absence blots people out.
We have really no absent friends.
The Death of the Heart **Bowen, Elizabeth** (1899–
1973) Irish writer

5 I am shut out of mine own heart
because my love is far from me.
'I Am Shut Out of Mine Own Heart' (1914)
Brennan, Christopher (1870–1932) Australian
poet

6 Now that we've done our best and worst,
and parted.
'The Busy Heart' (1913) **Brooke, Rupert** (1887–
1915) English poet

7 Absence is to love what the wind is to fire;
it extinguishes the small, it kindles the
great.
Histoire Amoureuse des Gaules (1665) **Bussy-
Rabutin, Comte de** (1618–1693) French soldier
and writer

8 That out of sight is out of mind
Is true of most we leave behind.
Songs in Absence (1849) **Clough, Arthur Hugh**
(1819–1861) English poet and letter writer

9 Absence from whom we love is worse than
death.
'Hope, like the Short-lived Ray' (1791) **Cowper,
William** (1731–1800) English poet, hymn
writer and letter writer

10 The absent are always in the wrong.
L'Obstacle Imprévu (1717) **Destouches, Philippe
Néricault** (1680–1754) French dramatist

11 My life closed twice before its close –
It yet remains to see
If Immortality unveil
A third event to me
So huge, so hopeless to conceive
As these that twice befell.
Parting is all we know of heaven,
And all we need of hell.
'My life closed twice before its close' (1896)
Dickinson, Emily (1830–1886) US poet

12 When I died last, and, Dear I die
As often as from thee I go,
Though it be but an hour ago,
And Lovers' hours be full eternity.
Songs and Sonnets (1611) **Donne, John** (1572–
1631) English poet

13 O what pain it is to part!
The Beggar's Opera (1728) **Gay, John** (1685–1732)
English poet, dramatist and librettist

14 Leaving is dying a little,
Dying to one's loves:
One leaves behind a little of oneself
At every moment, everywhere.
Seul (1891) **Haraucourt, Edmond** (1856–1941)

15 With leaden foot time creeps along
While Delia is away.
Absence **Jago, Rev. Richard** (1715–1781) English
poet

16 What's this dull town to me?
Robin's not near.
He whom I wished to see,
Wished for to hear;
Where's all the joy and mirth
Made life a heaven on earth?
O! they're all fled with thee,
Robin Adair.
'Robin Adair' (c.1750) **Keppel, Lady Caroline**
(b. 1735)

17 Absence diminishes mediocre passions and
increases great ones, as the wind
extinguishes candles and kindles fire.
Maximes (1678) **La Rochefoucauld** (1613–1680)
French writer

18 I do not love thee! – no! I do not love thee!
And yet when thou art absent I am sad;
And envy even the bright blue sky above thee,
Whose quiet stars may see thee and be glad.
The Sorrows of Rosalie (1829) **Norton, Caroline** (1808–1877) English poet

19 With all my will, but much against my heart,
We two now part.
My Very Dear,
Our solace is, the sad road lies so clear.
It needs no art,
With faint, averted feet
And many a tear,
In our opposed paths to persevere.
The Unknown Eros (1877) **Patmore, Coventry** (1823–1896) English poet

20 And if you ask how I regret that parting:
It is like the flowers falling at Spring's end
Confused, whirled in a tangle.
What is the use of talking, and there is no end of talking,
There is no end of things in the heart.
'Exile's Letter' (1915) **Pound, Ezra** (1885–1972) US poet

21 And oft the pangs of absence to remove
By letters, soft interpreters of love.
'Henry and Emma' (1708) **Prior, Matthew** (1664–1721) English poet

22 Long absent, soon forgotten.
Out of sight, out of mind.
When the cat's away, the mice will play.
Proverb

23 Remember me when I am gone away,
Gone far away into the silent land …
Better by far you should forget and smile
Than you should remember and be sad.
'Remember' (1862) **Rossetti, Christina** (1830–1894) English poet

24 Most of what matters in your life takes place in your absence.
Midnight's Children (1981) **Rushdie, Salman** (1947–) Indian-born English author

25 Give me to drink mandragora
That I might sleep out this great gap of time
My Antony is away.
Antony and Cleopatra

26 How like a winter hath my absence been
From thee, the pleasure of the fleeting year!
What freezings have I felt, what dark days seen!
What old December's bareness everywhere!
Sonnet 97 **Shakespeare, William** (1564–1616) English dramatist, poet and actor

27 Every time I kiss thy hand to bid adieu, and every absence which follows it, are preludes to that eternal separation which we are shortly to make.
Tristram Shandy (1759–1767) **Sterne, Laurence** (1713–1768) Irish-born English writer and clergyman

28 To think of one's absent love is very sweet; but it becomes monotonous after a mile or two of a towing-path, and the mind will turn away to Aunt Sally, the Cremorne Gardens, and financial questions. I doubt whether any girl would be satisfied with her lover's mind if she knew the whole of it.
The Small House at Allington (1864) **Trollope, Anthony** (1815–1882) English writer, traveller and post office official

29 Sweetest Melodies
Are those by distance made more sweet.
Personal Talk (1807) **Wordsworth, William** (1770–1850) English poet
See also change; grief; suffering; travel

ACTING

1 Laugh at yourself, but don't ever aim your doubt at yourself. Be bold. When you embark for strange places, don't leave any of yourself safely on shore. Have the nerve to go into unexplored territory.
Connecticut College News, (1980) **Alda, Alan** (1936–) US actor and director

2 How different, how very different from the home life of our own dear Queen!
Remark. On a performance of Cleopatra by Sarah Bernhardt

3 The whole world plays the actor. (*Totus mundus agit histrionem*)

Motto of Globe playhouse

4 Can't act, can't sing, slightly bald. Can dance a little.
Comment by a Hollywood executive on Fred Astaire's first screen test **Anonymous**

5 A painter paints, a musician plays, a writer writes – but a movie actor waits.
A Life on Film (1967) **Astor, Mary** (1906–1987) US actress

6 There are two kinds of talents, man-made talent and God-given talent. With man-made talent you have to work very hard. With God-given talent, you just touch it up once in a while.
Newsweek, (1967) **Bailey, Pearl** (1918–1990) US singer and actress

7 Acting is a form of confusion.
Tallulah (1952) **Bankhead, Tallulah** (1903–1968) US actress

8 There is as much difference between the stage and the film as between a piano and a violin. Normally you can't become a virtuoso in both.
The New York Post, (1956) **Barrymore, Ethel** (1879–1959) US actress

9 The fellow is the world's greatest actor. He can do with no effort what the rest of us spent years trying to learn; to be perfectly natural.
In Jane Mercer, *Great Lovers of the Movies*, (1975) **Barrymore, John** (1882–1942) US actor. On Gary Cooper

10 O God, send me some good actors – cheap.
The Guardian, (1976) **Baylis, Lilian** (1874–1937) English theatrical manager

11 She sleeps alone at last.
Attr. **Benchley, Robert** (1889–1945) US essayist, humorist and actor. Suggesting an epitaph for an actress

12 For the theatre one needs long arms; it is better to have them too long than too short. An artiste with short arms can never, never make a fine gesture.
Attr. **Bernhardt, Sarah** (1844–1923) French actress

13 Actors speak of things imaginary as if they were real, while you preachers too often speak of things real as if they were imaginary.
Attr. **Betterton, Thomas** (1635–1710) English actor and dramatist. Reply to the Archbishop of Canterbury

14 An actor's a guy who, if you ain't talking about him, ain't listening.
The Observer, (1956)

15 To grasp the full significance of life is the actor's duty, to interpret it is his problem, and to express it his dedication.
In David Shipman, *Marlon Brando* (1974) **Brando, Marlon** (1924–2004) US actor

16 If it's a good script I'll do it. And if it's a bad script, and they pay me enough, I'll do it.
International Herald Tribune, (1988) **Burns, George** (1896–1996) US comedian

17 I'm shocked. My career must have slipped. This is the first time I've been able to pick up an award.
The Times, (1999) Comment at the Golden Globe awards ceremony

18 I'm every bourgeois' nightmare. A Cockney with intelligence and a million dollars. They think they should have done it – but then why didn't they, if they were so much smarter and more intelligent than this stupid Cockney git?
The Times, (2000) Commenting on the patronizing attitude of the British press to his work as an actor **Caine, Michael** (1933–) English actor

19 Watching Tallulah Bankhead on stage is like watching somebody skating over very thin ice – and the English want to be there when she falls through.
In Gavin Lambert, *On Cukor* **Campbell, Mrs Patrick** (1865–1940) English actress

20 You have to believe in yourself, that's the secret. Even when I was in the orphanage, when I was roaming the street trying to find enough to eat, even then I thought of myself as the greatest actor in the world.
Reader's Digest, (1982) **Chaplin, Charlie** (1889–1977) English comedian, actor, director and satirist

21 I still prefer a good juggler to a bad Hamlet.
The Observer, (1943) **Cochran, Charles B.** (1872–1951) English showman and theatrical producer

22 To see him act is like reading Shakespeare by flashes of lightning.
Table Talk (1835) **Coleridge, Samuel Taylor** (1772–1834) English poet, philosopher and critic. Of Edmund Kean

23 When I took the role in Harry Potter, my kids sat me down and told me I had better be careful to get my character right. They warned me that kids would write and let me know if I wasn't successful. Boy, talk about pressure.
Attr. (2001) On accepting the role of Hagrid

24 If anyone asked me what I was doing, I'd say 'I've come 1500 miles to a foreign country to pretend to be someone else in front of a machine'.
Arena, (1991) On film acting **Coltrane, Robbie** (1950–) Scottish comedian and actor

25 Acting should be like punk in the best way. It should be a full-on expression of self – only without the broken bottles.
Uncut magazine, (2000) **Cusack, John** (1966–) US actor

26 Without wonder and insight, acting is just a trade. With it, it becomes creation.
The Lonely Life (1962) **Davis, Bette** (1908–1989) US actress

27 Acting is not the things you say, it's the things you don't say
Attr. **Dench, Judi** (1934–) English actress

28 He has so many muscles that he has to make an appointment to move his fingers.
Attr. **Diller, Phyllis** (1917–1974) US comedian. Of Arnold Schwarzenegger

29 The question actors most often get asked is how they can bear saying the same things over and over again night after night, but God knows the answer to that is, don't we all anyway; might as well get paid for it.
The Dud Avocado (1958) **Dundy, Elaine** (1927–) US writer

30 Acting doesn't bring anything to a text. On the contrary, it detracts from it.
International Herald Tribune, (1990) **Duras, Marguerite** (1914–1996) French author and filmmaker

31 The king for my money! He speaks all his words distinctly, half as loud again as the other. Anybody may see he is an actor.
Tom Jones (1749) **Fielding, Henry** (1707–1754) English writer, dramatist and journalist

32 You spend all your life trying to do something they put people in asylums for.
In Halliwell, *Filmgoer's Book of Quotes* (1973) **Fonda, Jane** (1937–) US actress and political activist

33 It is easier to get an actor to be a cowboy than to get a cowboy to be an actor.
Attr. **Ford, John** (1895–1973) Irish-American film director

34 I'll tell you what really turns my toes up – love scenes with 68-year-old men and young actresses. I promise you, when I get to that age I will say no.
The Observer, (1999) **Gibson, Mel** (1956–) Australian actor

35 Being another character is more interesting than being yourself.
Attr. **Gielgud, Sir John** (1904–2000) English actor

36 I have yet to see one completely unspoiled star, except for the animals – like Lassie.
Saturday Evening Post, (1963) **Head, Edith** (1898–1981) US costume designer

37 That's what show business is – sincere insincerity.
The Observer, (1977) **Hill, Benny** (1924–1992) English comedian

38 I deny that I ever said that actors are cattle. What I said was, 'Actors should be treated like cattle'.
Attr.

39 Nobody can really like an actor.
The New Yorker, (1992) **Hitchcock, Alfred** (1899–1980) English film director

40 At one time I thought he wanted to be an actor. He had certain qualifications, including no money and a total lack of responsibility.
From Under My Hat (1953) **Hopper, Hedda** (1890–1966) US actress and writer

41 Playing Shakespeare is very tiring. You never get to sit down, unless you're a King.
In Cooper and Hartman, *Violets and Vinegar* (1980) **Hull, Josephine** (1886–1957) US actress

42 Acting is not about dressing up. Acting is about stripping bare. The whole essence of learning lines is to forget them so you can make them sound like you thought of them that instant.
Sunday Telegraph, (1992) **Jackson, Glenda** (1936–) English actress and Labour politician

43 Players, Sir! I look upon them as no better than creatures set upon tables and joint stools to make faces and produce laughter, like dancing dogs.
In Boswell, *The Life of Samuel Johnson* (1791)

44 I'll come no more behind your scenes, David: for the silk stockings and white bosoms of your actresses excite my amorous propensities.
In Boswell, *The Life of Samuel Johnson* (1791) To Garrick **Johnson, Samuel** (1709–1784) English lexicographer, poet, critic, conversationalist and essayist

45 Massey won't be satisfied until somebody assassinates him.
In Meredith, George S. Kaufman and the Algonquin Round Table (1974) **Kaufman, George S.** (1889–1961) US scriptwriter, librettist and journalist. On Raymond Massey's interpretation of Abraham Lincoln

46 In America it is considered a lot more important to be a great Batman than a great Hamlet.
Attr. **Kline, Kevin** (1947–) US film actor

47 She looked as though butter wouldn't melt in her mouth – or anywhere else.
Attr. **Lanchester, Elsa** (1902–1986) US film actress. Of Maureen O'Hara

48 *Romance on the High Seas* was Doris Day's first picture; that was before she became a virgin.

Memoirs of an Amnesiac (1965) **Levant, Oscar** (1906–1972) US pianist and autobiographer

49 Who teach the mind its proper face to scan,
And hold the faithful mirror up to man.
'The Actor' **Lloyd, Robert** (1733–1764) English poet

50 Speak in a loud clear voice and try not to bump into the furniture.
In Halliwell, *Filmgoer's Book of Quotes* (1973) **Lunt, Alfred** (1892–1977) US actor. On acting

51 I've made so many movies playing a hooker that they don't pay me in the regular way any more. They leave it on the dresser.
Out on a Limb (1983) **Maclaine, Shirley** (1934–) US actress

52 Actors don't pretend to be other people; they become themselves by finding other people inside them.
Harland's Half Acre (1984) **Malouf, David** (1934–) Australian writer and poet

53 Acting is therefore the lowest of the arts, if it is an art at all.
Impressions and Opinions (1891) **Moore, George** (1852–1933) Irish writer, dramatist and critic

54 In the act of imitation there is the level of no-imitation. When the act of imitation is perfectly accomplished and the actor becomes the thing itself, the actor will no longer have the desire to imitate.
Fúshi kaden (1400–1418) **Motokiyo, Zeami** (1363–1443) Japanese actor and playwright

55 Acting is a question of absorbing other people's personalities and adding some of your own experience.
In Halliwell, *Filmgoer's Companion* (1984) **Newman, Paul** (1925–) US actor

56 I always knew that if all else failed I can become an actor. And all else failed.
Attr. **Niven, David** (1909–1983) English actor

57 Why not try acting? It's much easier.
Said to Dustin Hoffman, who had stayed up all night to play a character in the film *Marathon Man* (1976)

58 The actor should be able to create the universe in the palm of his hand.

New York Times, (1986) **Olivier, Sir Laurence** (1907–1989) English actor and director

59 Rumours of Ralph Fiennes's acting ability are wildly exaggerated. He is as asexual as an adenoid.
The Times, (1998) **Paglia, Camille** (1947–) US academic and writer

60 She ran the whole gamut of the emotions from A to B.
In Carey, *Katherine Hepburn* (1985). Remark on a performance by Katherine Hepburn

61 Scratch an actor and you'll find an actress.
Attr. **Parker, Dorothy** (1893–1967) US writer, poet, critic and wit

62 Actors marrying actors play a dangerous game. They're always fighting over the mirror.
Attr. **Reynolds, Burt** (1936–) US actor

63 There are lots of reasons why people become actors. Some to hide themselves, and some to show themselves.
In Tynan, *Show People*

64 The art of acting consists in keeping people from coughing.
The Observer

65 The most precious things in speech are pauses.
Attr. **Richardson, Sir Ralph** (1902–1983) English actor

66 I live a privileged life. I'm rich. I'm happy. I have a great job. It would be absurd to pretend that it's anything different. I'm like a pig in shit.
Attr. **Roberts, Julia** (1967–) US film actress

67 Acting is standing up naked and turning around slowly.
Life is a Banquet (1977) **Russell, Rosalind** (1911–1976) US actress

68 Like a dull actor now, I have forgot my part and I am out,
Even to a full disgrace.
Coriolanus, V.iii

69 He would drown the stage with tears,
And cleave the general ear with horrid speech;
Make mad the guilty, and appal the free,
Confound the ignorant, and amaze indeed
The very faculties of eyes and ears.
Hamlet, II.ii. On the power of acting
Shakespeare, William (1564–1616) English dramatist, poet and actor

70 *Burleigh comes forward, shakes his head, and exit.*
Sneer: He is very perfect indeed. Now pray, what did he mean by that?
Puff: Why, by that shake of the head, he gave you to understand that even though they had more justice in their cause and wisdom in their measures, yet, if there was not a greater spirit shown on the part of the people, the country would at last fall a sacrifice to the hostile ambition of the Spanish monarchy.
Sneer: The devil! – did he mean all that by shaking his head?
Puff: Every word of it. If he shook his head as I taught him.
The Critic (1779)

71 I wish, sir, you would practise this without me. I can't stay dying here all night.
The Critic (1779) **Sheridan, Richard Brinsley** (1751–1816) Irish dramatist, politician and orator

72 Talent is nothing but a prolonged period of attention and a shortened period of mental assimilation.
The Art of the Stage (1950) **Stanislavsky, Konstantin** (1863–1938) Russian actor and director; developed the 'method' theory of acting in which the actor identifies with the role

73 Imagination! imagination! I put it first years ago, when I was asked what qualities I thought necessary for success upon the stage.
The Story of My Life (1933) **Terry, Dame Ellen** (1847–1928) English actress, theatrical manager and memoirist

74 Ladies, just a little more virginity, if you don't mind.
In H. Teichmann, *Smart Alec*. Directing a group of sophisticated actresses

75 Take that black box away. I can't act in front of it.
In K. Brownlow, *Hollywood: The Pioneers*. Objecting to the presence of a camera while performing in a silent film **Tree, Sir Herbert Beerbohm** (1853–1917) English actor and theatre manager

76 I am a just an ordinary goddamn American and I talk for all the ordinary goddamn Americans, the butchers and bakers and plumbers. I know these people; I know what they think.
In Barry Norman, *The Film Greats* (1985)

77 I've spent my whole career playing myself.
In Barry Norman, *The Film Greats* (1985) **Wayne, John** (1907–1979) US actor

78 Ah, every day dear Herbert becomes *de plus en plus Oscarié*. It is a wonderful case of nature imitating art.
Attr. **Wilde, Oscar** (1854–1900) Irish poet, dramatist, writer, critic and wit. Referring to Beerbohm Tree's unconscious adoption of some of the mannerisms of a character he was playing in one of Wilde's plays

79 Guys like him and Caine talk about acting as if they knew what it was.
Interview, *Daily Mail*, (1996) **Williamson, Nicol** (1938–) Scottish actor. Of Sean Connery

80 They say an actor is only as good as his parts. Well, my parts have done me pretty well, darling.
The Times, (1999) **Windsor, Barbara** (1937–) English actress. Comment on being named a top BBC personality
See also cinema; criticism; film quotes; television; theatre and dance

ACTION

1 Action is but coarsened thought – thought become concrete, obscure, and unconscious.
Journal, (1850) **Amiel, Henri-Frédéric** (1821–1881) Swiss philosopher and writer

2 Under conditions of tyranny it is far easier to act than to think.
In Auden, *A Certain World* (1970) **Arendt, Hannah** (1906–1975) German-born US theorist

3 Our actions determine our dispositions.
Nicomachean Ethics

4 What we have to learn to do, we learn by doing.
Nicomachean Ethics **Aristotle** (384–322 BC) Greek philosopher

5 And you will give yourself peace if you perform each act as if it were your last.
Meditations **Aurelius, Marcus** (121–180) Roman emperor and Stoic philosopher

6 One should try everything once, except incest and folk-dancing.
Farewell my Youth (1943) **Bax, Sir Arnold** (1883–1953) English composer

7 Anything that is worth doing has been done frequently. Things hitherto undone should be given, I suspect, a wide berth.
Mainly on the Air (1946) **Beerbohm, Sir Max** (1872–1956) English satirist, cartoonist, critic and essayist

8 Take therefore no thought for the morrow: for the morrow shall take thought for the things of itself. Sufficient unto the day is the evil thereof.
Matthew, 6:34

9 But be ye doers of the word, and not hearers only.
James, 1:22 **The Bible (King James Version)**

10 It has been said that there are few situations in life that cannot be honourably settled, and without loss of time, either by suicide, a bag of gold, or by thrusting a despised antagonist over the edge of a precipice upon a dark night.
Kai Lung's Golden Hours (1922) **Bramah, Ernest** (1868–1942) British author

11 Madam, if it is possible, it has been done; impossible? It will be done.
In J. Michelet, *Histoire de la Révolution Française* (1847) **Calonne, Charles Alexandre de** (1734–1802) French statesman

12 Every decision is liberating, even if it leads to disaster. Otherwise, why do so many people walk upright and with open eyes into their misfortune?
The Secret Heart of the Clock: Notes, Aphorisms, Fragments 1973-1985 (1991)

13 Whatever their activity is, the active think they are better.
The Human Province (1969) **Canetti, Elias** (1905–1994) Bulgarian-born English writer, dramatist and critic

14 The end of man is an Action and not a Thought, though it were the noblest.
Sartor Resartus (1834) **Carlyle, Thomas** (1795–1881) Scottish historian, biographer, critic, and essayist

15 'Why,' said the Dodo, 'the best way to explain it is to do it.'
Alice's Adventures in Wonderland (1865) **Carroll, Lewis** (1832–1898) English writer and photographer

16 Is every human action, as you now think, The fruit of imitation and thoughtlessness?
La realidad y el deseo (1964) **Cernuda, Luis** (1902–1963) Spanish poet

17 It is an undoubted truth, that the less one has to do, the less time one finds to do it in. One yawns, one procrastinates, one can do it when one will, and therefore one seldom does it at all.
Letter **Chesterfield, Lord** (1694–1773) English politician and letter writer

18 Chi Wen Tzu always thought three times before taking action. Twice would have been quite enough.
Analects **Confucius** (c.550–c.478 BC) Chinese philosopher and teacher of ethics

19 Every public action which is not customary, either is wrong or, if it is right, is a dangerous precedent. It follows that nothing should ever be done for the first time.
Microcosmographia Academica (1908) **Cornford, F.M.** (1874–1943) English Platonic scholar

20 Deliberation is the work of many men. Action, of one alone.
War Memoirs **De Gaulle, Charles** (1890–1970) French general and statesman

21 There must be a beginning of any great matter, but the continuing unto the end until it be thoroughly finished yields the true glory.
Dispatch to Sir Francis Walsingham, (1587) **Drake, Sir Francis** (c.1540–1596) English navigator

22 But now the world's o'er stocked with prudent men.
The Medal (1682) **Dryden, John** (1631–1700) English poet, satirist, dramatist and critic

23 The distance isn't important; it is only the first step that is difficult.
Letter to d'Alembert, (1763) **Du Deffand, Marquise** (1697–1780) French noblewoman. Commenting on the legend of St Denis, who is believed to have carried his severed head for six miles after his execution

24 Adventure must be held in delicate fingers. It should be handled, not embraced. It should be sipped, not swallowed at a gulp.
The Man with a Load of Mischief (1924) **Dukes, Ashley** (1885–1959)

25 Our deeds determine us, as much as we determine our deeds.
Adam Bede (1859) **Eliot, George** (1819–1880) English writer and poet

26 We are taught by great actions that the universe is the property of every individual in it.
Nature (1836)

27 The reward of a thing well done, is to have done it.
'New England Reformers' (1844)

28 The manly part is to do with might and main what you can do.
Conduct of Life (1860)

29 In skating over thin ice, our safety is in our speed.
Essays (1860) **Emerson, Ralph Waldo** (1803–1882) US poet, essayist, transcendentalist and teacher

30 Deeds, not words shall speak me.
The Lover's Progress (1647) **Fletcher, John** (1579–1625) English dramatist

31 I believe ... that profit is not always what motivates man; that there are disinterested actions. ... By disinterested I mean: gratuitous. And that evil acts, what people call evil, can be as gratuitous as good acts.
Les Caves du Vatican (1914) **Gide, André** (1869–1951) French writer, critic, dramatist and poet

32 We never do anything well till we cease to think about the manner of doing it.
Atlas (1830) **Hazlitt, William** (1778–1830) English writer and critic

33 Let's find out what everyone is doing, And then stop everyone from doing it.
Ballads for Broadbrows (1930) **Herbert, Sir A.P.** (1890–1971) English humorist, writer, dramatist and politician

34 Believe every day that has dawned is your last.
Epistles

35 Carpe diem. *(Seize the day)*
Odes **Horace** (65–8 BC) Roman lyric poet and satirist

36 The great end of life is not knowledge but action.
Science and Culture (1877) **Huxley, T.H.** (1825–1895) English biologist, Darwinist and agnostic

37 There is no more miserable human being than one in whom nothing is habitual but indecision.
Principles of Psychology (1890) **James, William** (1842–1910) US psychologist and philosopher

38 The love of life is necessary to the vigorous prosecution of any undertaking.
The Rambler (1750–1752) **Johnson, Samuel** (1709–1784) English lexicographer, poet, critic, conversationalist and essayist

39 The way to get things done is not to mind who gets the credit for doing them.
Attr. **Jowett, Benjamin** (1817–1893) English scholar, translator, essayist and priest

40 I should always act in such a way that I may want my maxim to become a general law.
Outline of the Metaphysics of Morals (1785) **Kant, Immanuel** (1724–1804) German idealist philosopher

41 Truly, when the day of judgement comes, it will not be a question of what we have read, but what we have done.
De Imitatione Christi (1892) **Kempis, Thomas à** (c.1380–1471) German mystic, monk and writer

42 If the creator had a purpose in equipping us with a neck, he surely meant us to stick it out.
Encounter, (1970) **Koestler, Arthur** (1905–1983) British writer, essayist and political refugee

43 A journey of a thousand miles must begin with a single step.
Tao Te Ching **Lao-Tzu** (c.604–531 BC) Chinese philosopher

44 In harsh circumstances when there is little hope, the boldest measures are the safest.
History **Livy** (59 BC–AD 17) Roman historian

45 Because it is there.
New York Times, (1923) **Mallory, George Leigh** (1886–1924) English mountaineer. Asked why he wished to climb Mt Everest

46 If you take no risks, you will suffer no defeats. But if you take no risks, you win no victories.
US News & World Report, (1987) **Nixon, Richard** (1913–1994) US Republican politician and President

47 The man of reflection discovers Truth; but the one who enjoys it and makes use of its heavenly gifts is the man of action.
Friend Manso (1882) **Pérez Galdos, Benito** (1843–1920)

48 Our remedies oft in ourselves do lie, Which we ascribe to heaven.
All's Well That Ends Well, I.i **Shakespeare, William** (1564–1616) English dramatist, poet and actor

49 Activity is the only road to knowledge.
Man and Superman (1903)

50 Assassination is the extreme form of censorship.
The Showing-Up of Blanco Posnet (1911) **Shaw, George Bernard** (1856–1950) Irish socialist, writer, dramatist and critic

51 I have taken great care not to laugh at human actions, not to weep at them, nor to hate them, but to understand them.

Tractatus Politicus (1677) **Spinoza, Baruch** (1632–1677) Dutch philosopher and theologian

52 Men are rewarded and punished not for what they do, but rather for how their acts are defined. This is why men are more interested in better justifying themselves than in better behaving themselves.
The Second Sin (1973) **Szasz, Thomas** (1920–) Hungarian-born US psychiatrist and writer

53 Recalling once after dinner that he had done nothing to help anyone all that day, he gave voice to that memorable and praiseworthy remark: 'Friends, I have lost a day.'
In Suetonius, *Lives of the Caesars* **Titus Vespasianus** (AD 39–81)

54 Where force is necessary, one should make use of it boldly, resolutely, and right to the end. But it is as well to know the limitations of force; to know where to combine force with manoeuvre, assault with conciliation.
What Next? (1932) **Trotsky, Leon** (1879–1940) Russian revolutionary and Communist theorist

55 Fortune helps those who dare.
Aeneid **Virgil** (70–19 BC) Roman poet

56 I had rather wear out than rust out.
Attr. **Whitefield, George** (1714–1770) English evangelist
See also change

ADVERTISING

1 Time spent in the advertising business seems to create a permanent deformity like the Chinese habit of foot-binding.
In David S. McLellan and David C. Acheson, *Among Friends* (1980) **Acheson, Dean** (1893–1971) US Democrat politician

2 An advertising agency is 85 per cent confusion and 15 per cent commission.
Treadmill to Oblivion (1954) **Allen, Fred** (1894–1956) US vaudeville performer and comedian

3 In good times, people want to advertise; in bad times, they have to.
Town & Country, (1955) **Barton, Bruce** (1886–1967) US advertising agent and writer

4 When you mutilate movies for mass media, you tamper with the hearts and minds of America.
New York Times, (1985) **Beatty, Warren** (1937–) US actor and director. On refusing to grant television rights for his films because of cuts made for commercial breaks

5 Doing business without advertising is like winking at a girl in the dark. You know what you are doing, but nobody else does.
New York Herald Tribune, (1956) **Britt, Steuart Henderson** (1907–1979) US social psychologist

6 You can tell the ideals of a nation by its advertisements.
South Wind (1917) **Douglas, Norman** (1868–1952) Austrian-born Scottish writer

7 Advertising has us chasing cars and clothes, working jobs we hate, so we can buy shit we don't need.
Fight Club (film, 1999) **Fincher, David** (1963–) US film director

8 We grew up founding our dreams on the infinite promise of American advertising. I still believe that one can learn to play the piano by mail and that mud will give you a perfect complexion.
Save Me the Waltz (1932) **Fitzgerald, Zelda** (1900–1948) US writer

9 People can have it any colour – so long as it's black.
In Allan Nevins, *Ford* (1957), although it is unclear whether Ford actually uttered these precise words **Ford, Henry** (1863–1947) US car manufacturer. On the Model T Ford motor car

10 It is far easier to write ten passably effective Sonnets, good enough to take in the not too inquiring critic, than one effective advertisement that will take in a few thousand of the uncritical buying public.
On the Margin (1923) **Huxley, Aldous** (1894–1963) English writer, poet and critic

11 Advertisements contain the only truths to be relied on in a newspaper.
Letter, (1819) **Jefferson, Thomas** (1743–1826) US Democrat statesman and President

12 Promise, large promise, is the soul of an advertisement.

The Idler (1758–1760) **Johnson, Samuel** (1709–1784) English lexicographer, poet, critic, conversationalist and essayist

13 Society drives people crazy with lust and calls it advertising.
The Guardian, (1989) **Lahr, John** (1941–)

14 Advertising may be described as the science of arresting the human intelligence long enough to get money from it.
In Prochow, *The Public Speaker's Treasure Chest* **Leacock, Stephen** (1869–1944) English-born Canadian humorist, writer and economist

15 Half the money I spend on advertising is wasted, and the trouble is I don't know which half.
In Ogilvy, *Confessions of an Advertising Man* (1963) **Leverhulme, Lord** (1851–1925) English soap manufacturer and philanthropist

16 Ninety-Mile Beach was obviously named by one of New Zealand's first advertising copywriters … It is fifty-six miles long.
How to Get Lost and Found in New Zealand (1976) **McDermott, John W.** (1937–) Hawaiian travel writer

17 Ads are the cave art of the twentieth century.
Culture Is Our Business (1970) **McLuhan, Marshall** (1911–1980) Canadian communications theorist

18 Beneath this slab
John Brown is stowed.
He watched the ads,
And not the road.
'Lather as You Go' (1942) **Nash, Ogden** (1902–1971) US poet
See also business

ADVICE

1 Don't panic.
The Hitch Hiker's Guide to the Galaxy (1979) **Adams, Douglas** (1952–2001) English writer

2 There are very few personal problems that cannot be solved through a suitable application of high explosives.
The Dilbert Principle

3 On the keyboard of life, always keep one finger on the escape key.
The Dilbert Principle **Adams, Scott** (1957–) US cartoonist

4 A woman seldom asks advice before she has bought her wedding clothes.
The Spectator, (September 1712) **Addison, Joseph** (1672–1719) English essayist, poet, playwright and statesman

5 The best defence against the atom bomb is not to be there when it goes off.
The British Army Journal, quoted in *The Observer*, (1949)

6 Whatever you do, do it warily, and take account of the end.
Gesta Romanorum **Anonymous**

7 Distrust yourself, and sleep before you fight.
'Tis not too late tomorrow to be brave.
The Art of Preserving Health (1744) **Armstrong, Dr John** (1709–1779) Scottish physician, poet and writer

8 Read *The New Yorker*, trust in God;
And take short views.
Collected Poems, (1939–1947)

9 Thou shalt not sit
With statisticians nor commit
A social science.
Collected Poems, 1939–1947, 'Under Which Lyre' **Auden, W.H.** (1907–1973) English poet, essayist, critic, teacher and dramatist

10 Whenever you fall, pick up something.
Attr. **Avery, Oswald Theodore** (1877–1955) Canadian bacteriologist

11 A man ought warily to begin charges which once begun will continue.
'Of Expense' (1625) **Bacon, Francis** (1561–1626) English philosopher, essayist, politician and courtier

12 Never ascribe to an opponent motives meaner than your own.
Address, St Andrews University, (1922) **Barrie, Sir J.M.** (1860–1937) Scottish dramatist and writer

13 My only solution for the problem of habitual accidents is for everybody to stay in bed all day. Even then, there is always the chance that you will fall out.
Chips off the Old Bentley **Benchley, Robert** (1889–1945) US essayist, humorist and actor

14 Be not curious in unnecessary matters: for more things are shewed unto thee than men understand.
Apocrypha, *Ecclesiasticus, 3:23* **The Bible (King James Version)**

15 *Advice*: The smallest current coin.
The Cynic's Word Book (1906). **Bierce, Ambrose** (1842–c.1914) US writer, verse writer and soldier

16 Fear God, and take your own part.
The Romany Rye (1857) **Borrow, George** (1803–1881) English writer and linguist

17 Ah! gentle dames, it gars me greet,
To think how monie counsels sweet,
How monie lengthen'd, sage advices
The husband frae the wife despises!
'Tam o' Shanter' (1790) **Burns, Robert** (1759–1796) Scottish poet and song writer

18 Who cannot give good counsel? 'tis cheap, it costs them nothing.
Anatomy of Melancholy (1621) **Burton, Robert** (1577–1640) English clergyman and writer

19 Never trust anyone who wears a beard, a bow tie, two-toned shoes, sandals or sunglasses.
The Times, (1992) **Caine, Michael** (1933–) English actor. Quoting his father

20 Do not buy what you want, but what you need; what you do not need is dear at a farthing.
Reliquiae (Remains) **Cato the Elder** (234–149 BC) Roman statesman

21 Stop wishing to merit anyone's gratitude or thinking that anyone can become grateful.
Carmina **Catullus** (84–c.54 BC) Roman poet

22 I will end with a rule that may serve for a statesman, a courtier, or a lover – never make a defence or apology before you be accused.
Letter to Wentworth, (1636) **Charles I** (1600–1649) King of Great Britain and Ireland

23 Be wiser than other people if you can; but do not tell them so.
Letter to his son, (1745)

24 Take the tone of the company you are in.
Letter to his son, (1747)

25 Advice is seldom welcome; and those who want it the most, always like it the least.
Letter to his son, (1748)

26 In matters of religion and matrimony I never give any advice; because I will not have anybody's torments in this world or the next laid to my charge.
Letter to A.C. Stanhope, (1765) **Chesterfield, Lord** (1694–1773) English politician and letter writer

27 Stay out all night, but take especial care
That Prudence bring thee back to early prayer
As one with watching and with study faint,
Reel in a drunkard, and reel out a saint.
'Night' (1761) **Churchill, Charles** (1731–1764) English poet, political writer and clergyman

28 No sober man dances, unless he happens to be mad.
Pro Murena **Cicero** (106–43 BC) Roman orator, statesman, essayist and letter writer

29 To ask advice is in nine cases out of ten to tout for flattery.
In L.C. Collins, *Life of John Churton Collins* (1912) **Collins, John Churton** (1848–1908) English scholar, critic and essayist

30 When you have faults, do not fear to abandon them.
Analects **Confucius** (c.550–c.478 BC) Chinese philosopher and teacher of ethics

31 'But suppose there are two mobs?' suggested Mr Snodgrass. 'Shout with the largest,' replied Mr Pickwick.
The Pickwick Papers (1837) **Dickens, Charles** (1812–1870) English writer

32 Come when you're call'd;
And do as you're bid;
Shut the door after you;
And you'll never be chid.
Popular Tales (1804), 'The Contrast'
Edgeworth, Maria (1767–1849) English-born Irish writer

33 It was a high counsel that I once heard given to a young person, – 'Always do what you are afraid to do.'
Essays, First Series (1841) **Emerson, Ralph Waldo** (1803–1882) US poet, essayist, transcendentalist and teacher

34 Never trust the man who hath reason to suspect that you know that he hath injured you.
Jonathan Wild (1743) **Fielding, Henry** (1707–1754) English writer, dramatist and journalist

35 Early to bed and early to rise,
Makes a man healthy, wealthy and wise.
Poor Richard's Almanac (1758) **Franklin, Benjamin** (1706–1790) US statesman, scientist, political critic and printer

36 Never explain: your friends don't need it and your enemies won't believe it.
Attr. **Grayson, Victor** (1881–c.1920) British Labour politician

37 Keep looking shocked and move slowly towards the cakes.
The Simpsons, TV cartoon series **Groening, Matt** (1954–) US cartoonist. Instruction in Homer Simpson's brain to Homer during communal crisis

38 I intended to give you some advice but now I remember how much is left over from last year unused.
In Braude, *Braude's Second Encyclopedia* (1957) **Harris, George** (1844–1922) US churchman and educator. In his address to students at the start of a new academic year

39 Calmnesse is great advantage. He that lets
Another chafe, may warm him at his fire.
The Temple (1633), 'The Church-Porch' **Herbert, George** (1593–1633) English poet and priest

40 'Tis a lesson you should heed,
Try, try again.
If at first you don't succeed,
Try, try again.
'Try and Try Again' **Hickson, William Edward** (1803–1870) English educationist

41 And, when you stick on conversation's burrs,
Don't strew your pathway with those dreadful urs.

'A Rhymed Lesson' (1848) **Holmes, Oliver Wendell** (1809–1894) US physician, poet, writer and scientist

42 I have, all my life long, been lying till noon; yet I tell all young men, and tell them with great sincerity, that nobody who does not rise early will ever do any good.
In Boswell, *Journal of a Tour to the Hebrides* (1785) **Johnson, Samuel** (1709–1784) English lexicographer, poet, critic, conversationalist and essayist

43 Advice is what we ask for when we already know the answer but wish we didn't.
How to Save Your Own Life (1977) **Jong, Erica** (1942–) US writer

44 He told me never to sell the bear's skin before killing the beast.
Fables, 'L'ours et les deux compagnons' **La Fontaine, Jean de** (1621–1695) French poet and fabulist

45 One gives nothing so generously as advice.
Maximes (1678) **La Rochefoucauld** (1613–1680) French writer

46 When you have got an elephant by the hind leg, and he is trying to run away, it's best to let him run.
Remark, (1865) **Lincoln, Abraham** (1809–1865) US statesman and President

47 In harsh circumstances when there is little hope, the boldest measures are the safest.
History **Livy** (59 BC–AD 17) Roman historian

48 And they are right, those who say that bad company leads to the gallows.
The Mandrake (1518) **Machiavelli** (1469–1527) Florentine statesman, political theorist and historian

49 He that would govern others, first should be
The master of himself.
The Bondman: an Antient Story (1624) **Massinger, Philip** (1583–1640) English dramatist and poet

50 Be plain in dress, and sober in your diet;
In short, my deary! kiss me, and be quiet.
Summary of Lord Lyttleton's Advice **Montagu, Lady Mary Wortley** (1689–1762) English letter writer, poet, traveller and introducer of smallpox inoculation

51 You may go into the field or down the lane, but don't go into Mr McGregor's garden: your Father had an accident there; he was put in a pie by Mrs McGregor.
The Tale of Peter Rabbit (1902) **Potter, Beatrix** (1866–1943) English children's writer

52 Abstain from beans.
Attr. **Pythagoras** (6th century BC) Greek philosopher and mathematician

53 My advice was delicately poised between the cliché and the indiscretion.
The Times, (1981) **Runcie, Robert** (1921–2000) On his discussions with the Prince and Princess of Wales prior to marrying them

54 In baiting a mouse-trap with cheese, always leave room for the mouse.
The Square Egg (1924), 'The Infernal Parliament' **Saki** (1870–1916) Burmese-born British writer

55 Trust the man who hesitates in his speech and is quick and steady in action, but beware of long arguments and long beards.
Soliloquies in England (1922) **Santayana, George** (1863–1952) Spanish-born US philosopher and writer

56 Neither a borrower nor a lender be;
For loan oft loses both itself and friend,
And borrowing dulls the edge of husbandry.
Hamlet, I.iii **Shakespeare, William** (1564–1616) English dramatist, poet and actor

57 Take short views, hope for the best, and trust in God.
In Holland, *A Memoir of the Reverend Sydney Smith* (1855) **Smith, Sydney** (1771–1845) English clergyman, essayist, journalist and wit

58 Gifts from enemies are no gifts, and bring no good.
Ajax, line 665 **Sophocles** (496–406 BC) Greek dramatist

59 Walk softly and carry an armoured tank division, I always say.
A Few Good Men (film, 1992) **Sorkin, Aaron** (1961–) US screenwriter

60 And as she lookt about, she did behold,
How over that same dore was likewise writ,
Be bold, be bold, and every where Be bold
...
At last she spyde at that roome's upper end,
Another yron dore, on which was writ,
Be not too bold.
The Faerie Queene (1596) **Spenser, Edmund** (c.1522–1599) English poet

61 No one wants advice – only corroboration.
Attr. **Steinbeck, John** (1902–1968) US writer

62 It's queer how ready people always are with advice in any real or imaginary emergency, and no matter how many times experience has shown them to be wrong, they continue to set forth their opinions, as if they had received them from the Almighty!
Letter, (1887) **Sullivan, Annie** (1866–1936) US lecturer, writer and teacher

63 Don't trust first impulses; they are always generous.
Attr. **Talleyrand, Charles-Maurice de** (1754–1838) French statesman, memoirist and prelate

64 They tell me not to drink, and I do drink ...
They tell me not to eat, and I do eat.
The Letters and Private Papers of William Makepeace Thackeray (1946) **Thackeray, William Makepeace** (1811–1863) Indian-born English writer

65 I have lived some thirty years on this planet, and I have yet to hear the first syllable of valuable or even earnest advice from my seniors.
Walden (1854) **Thoreau, Henry David** (1817–1862) US essayist, social critic and writer

66 Early to rise and early to bed makes a male healthy and wealthy and dead.
The New Yorker, (1939) **Thurber, James** (1894–1961) US humorist, writer and dramatist

67 Who goeth a borrowing
Goeth a sorrowing.
Few lend (but fools)
Their working tools.
Five Hundred Points of Good Husbandry (1557) **Tusser, Thomas** (c.1524–1580) English writer, poet and musician

68 Trust not the horse, Trojans. Whatever it is,
I fear the Greeks even when they bring
gifts.
Aeneid **Virgil** (70–19 BC) Roman poet

69 Sparrowhawks, Ma'am.
Attr. **Wellington, Duke of** (1769–1852) Irish-
born British military commander and
statesman. Advice when asked by Queen
Victoria how to remove sparrows from the
Crystal Palace

70 Are you in trouble? Do you need advice?
Write to Miss Lonelyhearts and she will
help.
Miss Lonelyhearts (1933) **West, Nathaniel** (1903–
1940) US novelist

71 A man cannot be too careful in the choice
of his enemies.
The Picture of Dorian Gray (1891)

72 It is always a silly thing to give advice, but
to give good advice is absolutely fatal.
Attr. **Wilde, Oscar** (1854–1900) Irish poet,
dramatist, writer, critic and wit

73 It is a good rule in life never to apologize.
The right sort of people do not want
apologies, and the wrong sort take a mean
advantage of them.
The Man Upstairs (1914) **Wodehouse, P.G.**
(1881–1975) English humorist and writer
See also life; proverbs

AGE

1 When old people speak it is not because of
the sweetness of words in our mouths; it is
because we see something which you do
not see.
No Longer At Ease (1961) **Achebe, Chinua**
(1930–) Nigerian writer, poet and critic

2 I inhabit a weak, frail, decayed tenement;
battered by the winds and broken in on by
the storms, and, from all I can learn, the
landlord does not intend to repair.
Attr.

3 Old minds are like old horses; you must
exercise them if you wish to keep them in
working order.
Attr. **Adams, John Quincy** (1767–1848) US
lawyer, diplomat and President

4 You can only perceive real beauty in a
person as they get older.
The Guardian, (1988) **Aimeé, Anouk** (1932–)
French actress

5 I still think of myself as I was 25 years ago.
Then I look in a mirror and see an old
bastard and I realise it's me.
The Independent, (1993) **Allen, Dave** (1936–2005)
Irish comedian and television personality

6 I recently turned sixty. Practically a third of
my life is over.
The Observer Review, (1996) **Allen, Woody**
(1935–) US film director, writer, actor and
comedian

7 Old age is a second childhood.
Clouds (1417) **Aristophanes** (c.445–385 BC) Greek
playwright

8 I am past thirty, and three parts iced over.
Letter to A.H. Clough, (1853) **Arnold, Matthew**
(1822–1888) English poet, critic, essayist and
educationist

9 Ageing seems to be the only available way
to live a long time.
Attr. **Auber, Daniel François Esprit** (1782–1871)
French opera composer

10 The older one becomes the quicker the
present fades into sepia and the past looms
up in glorious technicolour.
The Observer, (1998) **Bainbridge, Beryl** (1934–)
English novelist

11 I am saving up for my own hospital trolley.
The Times, (1999) **Baker, Tom** (1934–) English
actor and writer. On becoming a pensioner

12 I will never be an old man. To me, old age
is always fifteen years older than I am.
The Observer, (1955) **Baruch, Bernard** (1870–
1965) US financier, government advisor and
writer

13 If you live long enough, you'll see that
every victory turns into a defeat.
All Men are Mortal (1946)

14 Since it is the Other within us who is old, it
is natural that the revelation of our age
should come to us from outside – from
others. We do not accept it willingly.

The Coming of Age (1970) **Beauvoir, Simone de** (1908–1986) French writer, feminist critic and philosopher

15 Most women are not so young as they are painted.
The Works of Max Beerbohm (1896) **Beerbohm, Sir Max** (1872–1956) English satirist, cartoonist, critic and essayist

16 Age is strictly a case of mind over matter. If you don't mind, it doesn't matter.
New York Times, (1974) **Benny, Jack** (1894–1974) US comedian

17 He then shuffled out on to the big lawn, with a stick in his hand, and he prodded with it at the worms in the grass, muttering to himself, 'Ah, damn ye: haven't got me yet.'
As We Were (1930) **Benson, E.F.** (1867–1940) English writer. Speaking of a fellow of King's College, Cambridge, who never emerged from his rooms except in the evening gloaming

18 If I'd known I was gonna live this long, I'd have taken better care of myself.
The Observer, (1983) **Blake, Eubie** (1883–1983) US jazz performer and songwriter who died five days after his hundredth birthday

19 To be old is to be part of a huge and ordinary multitude … the reason why old age was venerated in the past was because it was extraordinary.
The View in Winter (1979) **Blythe, Ronald** (1922–) English writer

20 Only the old are innocent. That is what the Victorians understood, and the Christians. Original sin is a property of the young. The old grow beyond corruption very quickly.
Stepping Westward (1965) **Bradbury, Malcolm** (1932–) English writer, critic and academic

21 When your grape was green you denied me.
When your grape was ripe you despised me.
Can I have a nibble at the old sultana?
'After Long Absence' **Bray, John Jefferson** (1912–1995) Australian lawyer and poet

22 Old age takes away from us what we have inherited and gives us what we have earned.

Thoughts in a Dry Season (1978) **Brenan, Gerald** (1894–1987) English writer

23 Grow old along with me!
The best is yet to be,
The last of life for which the first was made:
Our times are in His hand
Who saith, 'A whole I planned,
Youth shows but half; trust God: see all, nor be afraid!'
'Rabbi Ben Ezra' (1864) **Browning, Robert** (1812–1889) English poet

24 Ah well, perhaps one has to be very old before one learns how to be amused rather than shocked.
China, Past and Present (1972) **Buck, Pearl S.** (1892–1973) US writer and dramatist

25 Fame is no sanctuary from the passing of youth … suicide is much easier and more acceptable in Hollywood than growing old gracefully.
Girls on Film (1986) **Burchill, Julie** (1960–) English writer

26 The arrogance of age must submit to be taught by youth.
Letter to Fanny Burney, (1782) **Burke, Edmund** (1729–1797) Irish-born British statesman and philosopher

27 What is the worst of woes that wait on age?
What stamps the wrinkle deeper on the brow?
To view each loved one blotted from life's page,
And be alone on earth, as I am now.
Childe Harold's Pilgrimage (1818)

28 Years steal
Fire from the mind as vigour from the limb;
And life's enchanted cup but sparkles near the brim.
Childe Harold's Pilgrimage (1818)

29 I am ashes where once I was fire.
'To the Countess of Blessington' (1823) **Byron, Lord** (1788–1824) English poet, satirist and traveller

30 Respect.

The Mail on Sunday, (1996) **Calment, Jeanne** (1875–1997) Frenchwoman, renowned for her longevity. Reply to someone who asked what she would like for her 121st birthday

31 As a white candle
In a holy place,
So is the beauty
Of an aged face.
'The Old Woman' (1913) **Campbell, Joseph** (1879–1944) Irish poet and republican

32 Alas! after a certain age every man is responsible for the face he has.
The Fall, (1956) **Camus, Albert** (1913–1960) Algerian-born French writer

33 'You are old, Father William,' the young man said,
'And your hair has become very white;
And yet you incessantly stand on your head –
Do you think, at your age, it is right?'
'In my youth,' Father William replied to his son,
'I feared it might injure the brain;
But now that I'm perfectly sure I have none,
Why, I do it again and again.'
Alice's Adventures in Wonderland (1865) **Carroll, Lewis** (1832–1898) English writer and photographer

34 I'm over eighty in a world where the young reject the old with more intensity than ever before ... Now I'd like my old age to be my best performance. Death is the best exit.
In Behr, *Thank Heaven for Little Girls* (1993) **Chevalier, Maurice** (1888–1972) French singer and actor

35 We grow old more through indolence, than through age.
Pensées de Christine, reine de Suede (1825) **Christina of Sweden** (1626–1689) Queen of Sweden

36 Old-age, a second child, by Nature curs'd
With more and greater evils than the first,
Weak, sickly, full of pains; in ev'ry breath
Railing at life, and yet afraid of death.
Gotham (1764) **Churchill, Charles** (1731–1764) English poet, political writer and clergyman

37 No man is so old as to think he cannot live one more year.
Attr. **Cicero** (106–43 BC) Roman orator, statesman, essayist and letter writer

38 Like some poor nigh-related guest,
That may not rudely be dismist;
Yet hath outstay'd his welcome while,
And tells the jest without the smile.
'Youth and Age' (1834) **Coleridge, Samuel Taylor** (1772–1834) English poet, philosopher and critic

39 A man is as old as he's feeling,
A woman as old as she looks.
'The Unknown Quantity' **Collins, Mortimer** (1827–1876) English poet and writer

40 Pushing forty? She's clinging on to it for dear life.
Attr. **Compton-Burnett, Dame Ivy** (1884–1969) English novelist. Describing a certain woman's age

41 The really frightening thing about middle age is the knowledge that you'll grow out of it.
In A. E. Hotchner, *Doris Day: Her Own Story* (1976) **Day, Doris** (1924–) US singer and actress

42 At twenty you have many desires which hide the truth, but beyond forty there are only real and fragile truths – your abilities and your failings.
The Daily Mail, (1991) **Depardieu, Gérard** (1948–) French actor

43 It is strange that the one thing that every person looks forward to, namely old age, is the one thing for which no preparation is made.
Attr. **Dewey, John** (1859–1952) US educationist, philosopher and reformer

44 When a man fell into his anecdotage it was a sign for him to retire from the world.
Lothair (1870) **Disraeli, Benjamin** (1804–1881) English statesman and writer

45 Old age is an insult. It's like being smacked.
The Sunday Times, (1988) **Durrell, Lawrence** (1912–1990) Indian-born British poet and writer

46 We walk along the gas-lit street in a
dreadful row, we three,
The woman I was, the woman I am, and
the woman I'll one day be.
In Moore, *The Story of Australian Art* **Edmond,
James** (1859–1933) Scottish-born Australian
writer and editor. Caption to a drawing of
three women by Norman Lindsay

47 I would not want it to be thought that I had
lived for all these years without having
anything to show for it.
On the retouching of a photograph to
disguise wrinkles

48 The years between fifty and seventy are the
hardest You are always being asked to do
things, and you are not yet decrepit
enough to turn them down.
In *The Guardian*, (2000) **Elizabeth, the Queen
Mother** (1900–2002) Queen of the United
Kingdom and mother of Elizabeth II

49 Spring still makes spring in the mind,
When sixty years are told.
Poems (1847) **Emerson, Ralph Waldo** (1803–
1882) US poet, essayist, transcendentalist and
teacher

50 The age of a woman doesn't mean a thing.
The best tunes are played on the oldest
fiddles.
Newsweek, (1949) **Engel, Sigmund** (b.1869)

51 If only youth knew; if only age could.
Les Prémices (1594) **Estienne, Henri** (1531–1598)
French scholar, lexicographer and publisher

52 The years have stolen
all her loveliness,
her days are fallen
in the long wet grass
like petals shaken
from the lilac's bosom.
Collected Poems (1966) **Fairburn, A.R.D.** (1904–
1957) New Zealand poet

53 At sixteen I was stupid, confused, insecure
and indecisive. At twenty-five I was wise,
self-confident, prepossessing and assertive.
At forty-five I am stupid, confused,
insecure and indecisive. Who would have
supposed that maturity is only a short
break in adolescence?
The Observer, (1974) **Feiffer, Jules** (1929–) US
cartoonist

54 Being an old maid is like death by
drowning, a really delightful sensation
after you cease to struggle.
In R.E. Drennan, *Wit's End* (1973), 'Completing
the Circle' **Ferber, Edna** (1887–1968)

55 At twenty years of age, the will reigns; at
thirty, the wit; and at forty, the judgement.
Poor Richard's Almanac (1741)

56 Old boys have their playthings as well as
young ones; the difference is only in price.
Poor Richard's Almanac (1752) **Franklin,
Benjamin** (1706–1790) US statesman, scientist,
political critic and printer

57 I must reluctantly observe that two causes,
the abbreviation of time, and the failure of
hope, will always tinge with a browner
shade the evening of life.
Memoirs of My Life and Writings (1796) **Gibbon,
Edward** (1737–1794) English historian,
politician and memoirist

58 When you're my age, you just never risk
being ill – because then everyone says: Oh,
he's done for.
Sunday Express Magazine, (1988) **Gielgud, Sir
John** (1904–2000) English actor

59 Threatening, terrifying is oncoming old
age, but nothing will reverse and return!
Dead Souls (1835–1842) **Gogol, Nicolai
Vasilyevich** (1809–1852) Russian writer and
soldier

60 I love every thing that's old: old friends, old
times, old manners, old books, old wine.
She Stoops to Conquer (1773) **Goldsmith, Oliver**
(c.1728–1774) Irish dramatist, poet and writer

61 Oh how you hate old age – well so do I …
but I, who am more a rebel against man
than you, rebel less against nature, and
accept the inevitable and go with it gently
into the unknown.
Letter to W.B. Yeats **Gonne, Maud** (1865–1953)
Irish patriot and philanthropist

62 'Old Cary Grant fine. How you?'
In Halliwell, *Filmgoer's Book of Quotes* (1973)
Grant, Cary (1904–1986) English-born US film
actor. Responding to a telegram received by
his agent inquiring: 'How old Cary Grant?'

63 We do not necessarily improve with age: for better or worse we become more like ourselves.
The Observer, (1988) **Hall, Sir Peter** (1930–) English theatre director

64 With expectation beating high,
Myself I now desired to spy;
And straight I in a glass surveyed
An antique lady, much decayed.
In Sarah Hale, *Biography of Distinguished Women* (1876) **Hamilton, Elizabeth** (1758–1816) Scottish poet and novelist

65 Perhaps with age I've learned to let go of things and people, not to possess or confine them.
Attr. **Harrison, Tony** (1937–) English poet

66 You will recognize, my boy, the first sign of old age: it is when you go out into the streets of London and realize for the first time how young the policemen look.
In Pulling, *They Were Singing* (1952) **Hicks, Sir Seymour** (1871–1949) English actor-manager

67 Anno domini … that's the most fatal complaint of all, in the end.
Goodbye, Mr Chips (1934) **Hilton, James** (1900–1954) English writer and screenwriter

68 For him in vain the envious seasons roll
Who bears eternal summer in his soul.
'The Old Player' (1861)

69 To be seventy years young is sometimes far more cheerful and hopeful than to be forty years old.
'On the Seventieth Birthday of Julia Ward Howe' (1889) **Holmes, Oliver Wendell** (1809–1894) US physician, poet, writer and scientist

70 Oh, to be seventy again!
In Fadiman, *The American Treasury* **Holmes, Oliver Wendell, Jr** (1841–1935) US jurist and judge. At the age of 86, on seeing a pretty girl

71 I don't generally feel anything until noon, then it's time for my nap.
International Herald Tribune, (1990) **Hope, Bob** (1903–2003) US comedian

72 Whenever a man's friends begin to compliment him about looking young, he may be sure that they think he is growing old.

Bracebridge Hall (1822) **Irving, Washington** (1783–1859) US writer and diplomat

73 It is so comic to hear oneself called old, even at ninety I suppose!
In Leon Edel (ed.), *The Diary of Alice James* (1889) **James, Alice** (1848–1892) US diarist

74 And time itself's a feather
Touching them gently. Do they know they're old,
These two who are my father and my mother
Whose fire from which I came, has now grown cold?
The Mind has Mountains (1966) **Jennings, Elizabeth** (1926–2001) English poet

75 At seventy-seven it is time to be in earnest.
A Journey to the Western Islands of Scotland (1775)

76 There is a wicked inclination in most people to suppose an old man decayed in his intellects. If a young or middle-aged man, when leaving a company, does not recollect where he laid his hat, it is nothing; but if the same inattention is discovered in an old man, people will shrug up their shoulders, and say, 'His memory is going.'
In Boswell, *The Life of Samuel Johnson* (1791) **Johnson, Samuel** (1709–1784) English lexicographer, poet, critic, conversationalist and essayist

77 Our hearts are young 'neath wrinkled rind: Life's more amusing than we thought.
'Ballade of Middle Age' **Lang, Andrew** (1844–1912) Scottish poet, writer, mythologist and anthropologist

78 Perhaps being old is having lighted rooms Inside your head, and people in them, acting.
People you know, yet can't quite name.
'The Old Fools' (1974) **Larkin, Philip** (1922–1985) English poet, writer and librarian

79 If, as you grow older, you feel you are also growing stupider, do not worry. This is normal, and usually occurs around the time when your children, now grown, are discovering the opposite – they now see that you aren't nearly as stupid as they had believed when they were young teenagers. Take heart from that.

Quoted in *The Globe and Mail*, (1989)
Laurence, Margaret (1926–1987) Canadian
novelist. Address at Trent University, 1983

80 Old age is woman's hell.
Attr. **Lenclos, Ninon de** (1620–1705) French
courtesan

81 Will you still need me, will you still feed
me,
When I'm sixty-four?
'When I'm Sixty Four' (song, 1967) **Lennon,
John** (1940–1980) and **McCartney, Paul**
(1942–) English rock musicians, songwriters,
peace campaigners and cultural icons

82 I am just turning forty and taking my time
about it.
The Times, (1970) **Lloyd, Harold** (1893–1971)
Film comedian. Reply when, aged 77, he was
asked his age

83 Each of us feels the good days hasten and
depart, our days that perish and are
counted against us.
Epigrammata **Martial** (c.AD 40–c.104) Spanish-
born Latin epigrammatist and poet

84 Age is not a particularly interesting subject.
Anyone can get old. All you have to do is
live long enough.
Groucho and Me (1959) **Marx, Groucho** (1895–
1977) US comedian

85 From the earliest times the old have
rubbed it into the young that they are wiser
than they, and before the young had
discovered what nonsense this was they
were old too, and it profited them to carry
on the imposture.
Cakes and Ale (1930)

86 I am sick of this way of life. The weariness
and sadness of old age make it intolerable.
I have walked with death in hand, and
death's own hand is warmer than my own.
I don't wish to live any longer.
In M.B. Strauss, *Familiar Medical Quotations*
Said on his 90th birthday **Maugham, William
Somerset** (1874–1965) English writer,
dramatist and physician

87 Being seventy is not a sin.
Reader's Digest, (1971) **Meir, Golda** (1898–1978)
Russian-born Israeli stateswoman and Prime
Minister

88 The best years are the forties. After fifty a
man begins to deteriorate, but in his
forties he is at the maximum of his villainy.
In Lieberman, *3,500 Good Quotes for Speakers*
(1983) **Mencken, H.L.** (1880–1956) US writer,
critic, philologist and satirist

89 Everything comes with age, and everyone
knows, Madame, that twenty is not the
time to be a prude.
Le Misanthrope (1666) **Molière** (1622–1673)
French dramatist, actor and director

90 So the years hang like old clothes,
forgotten in the wardrobe of our minds.
Did I wear that? Who was I then?
No Other Life (1993) **Moore, Brian** (1921–1999)
Canadian writer

91 Do you think my mind is maturing late,
Or simply rotted early?
'Lines on Facing Forty' (1942)

92 I prefer to forget both pairs of glasses and
pass my declining years
Saluting strange women and grandfather
clocks.
The Private Dining Room and Other New Verses
(1952) **Nash, Ogden** (1902–1971) US poet

93 King David and King Solomon
Led merry, merry lives,
With many, many lady friends
And many, many wives;
But when old age crept over them,
With many, many qualms,
King Solomon wrote the Proverbs
And King David wrote the Psalms.
'King David and King Solomon' (1935) **Naylor,
James Ball** (1860–1945) US physician and
writer

94 At 50, everyone has the face he deserves.
Notebook (1949) **Orwell, George** (1903–1950)
English writer and critic

95 At 70, I'm in fine fettle for my age, sleep
like a babe and feel around 12. The secret?
Lots of meat, drink and cigarettes and not
giving in to things.
The Times, (1998) **Paterson, Jennifer** (1928–
1999) English food writer and TV chef

96 Mr Old Age, would catch you in his deadly
trap
And come finally to polish you off,
His machine-gun dripping with years.
'Where are you now, Batman?' **Patten, Brian**
(1946–) British poet

97 *Rab C. Nesbitt*: I hate middle age. Too
young for the bowling green, too old for
Ecstasy.
Rab C. Nesbitt, television series **Pattison, Ian**
(1950–) Scottish actor

98 Goddess, allow this aged man his right,
To be your beadsman now that was your
knight.
'Sonnet. A Farewell to Arms' (1590) **Peele,
George** (c.1558–c.1597) English dramatist and
poet

99 A man not old, but mellow, like good wine.
Ulysses (1902) **Phillips, Stephen** (1864–1915)
English poet

100 Age only matters when one is ageing. Now
that I have arrived at a great age, I might
just as well be twenty.
In J. Richardson, *The Observer, Shouts and
Murmurs*

101 One starts to get young at the age of sixty
and then it is too late.
The Sunday Times, (1963) **Picasso, Pablo** (1881–
1973) Spanish painter, sculptor and graphic
artist

102 One of the pleasures of middle age is to
find out that one WAS right, and that one
was much righter than one knew at say 17
or 23.
ABC of Reading (1934) **Pound, Ezra** (1885–1972)
US poet

103 Growing old is like being increasingly
penalized for a crime you haven't
committed.
A Dance to the Music of Time (1973) **Powell,
Anthony** (1905–2000) English writer and critic

104 It is better to die young than to outlive all
one loved, and all that rendered one
lovable.
The Confessions of an Elderly Gentleman (1836)

105 Tears fell from my eyes – yes, weak and
foolish as it now appears to me, I wept for
my departed youth; and for that beauty of
which the faithful mirror too plainly
assured me, no remnant existed.
The Confessions of an Elderly Lady (1838) **Power,
Marguerite, Countess of Blessington** (1789–
1849) English writer

106 I will not make age an issue of this
campaign. I am not going to exploit for
political purposes my opponent's youth
and inexperience.
TV debate, (1984) On his challenger, Walter
Mondale, in the 1984 election campaign

107 I am delighted to be with you. In fact, at
my age, I am delighted to be anywhere.
Speech at the Oxford Union, (1992) **Reagan,
Ronald** (1911–2004) US actor, Republican
statesman and President

108 As we get older we do not get any younger.
Seasons return, and today I am fifty-five,
And this time last year I was fifty-four,
And this time next year I shall be sixty-two.
'Chard Whitlow (Mr Eliot's Sunday Evening
Postscript)' (1941) **Reed, Henry** (1914–1986)
English poet, radio dramatist and translator

109 Darling, I am growing old,
Silver threads among the gold.
'Silver Threads Among the Gold' (1873)
Rexford, Eben (1848–1916) English songwriter

110 Ancient person, for whom I
All the flattering youth defy,
Long be it ere thou grow old,
Aching, shaking, crazy, cold;
But still continue as thou art,
Ancient person of my heart.
'A Song of a Young Lady to her Ancient Lover'
(1691) **Rochester, Earl of** (1647–1680) English
poet, satirist, courtier and libertine

111 When you are very old, at night, in the
candle-light, sitting spinning by the fire,
you will say as you sing my verses,
marvelling, 'Ronsard sang of me in the
time of my beauty.'
Sonnets pour Hélène (1578) **Ronsard, Pierre de**
(1524–1585)

112 It is fun to be in the same decade with you.

In Winston S. Churchill, *The Hinge of Fate*
Roosevelt, Franklin Delano (1882–1945) US
Democrat statesman and President. After
Churchill had congratulated him on his 60th
birthday

113 Don't trust anyone over thirty.
In S.B. Flexner, *Listening to America* **Rubin,
Jerry** (1936–) US political activist

114 I have always felt that a woman has a right
to treat the subject of her age with
ambiguity until, perhaps, she passes into
the realm of over ninety. Then it is better
she be candid with herself and with the
world.
My Life for Beauty (1965) **Rubinstein, Helena**
(1872–1965) Polish-born US cosmetician and
businesswoman

115 The young have aspirations that never
come to pass, the old have reminiscences
of what never happened. It's only the
middle-aged who are really conscious of
their limitations.
Reginald (1904) **Saki** (1870–1916) Burmese-born
British writer

116 The young man who has not wept is a
savage, and the old man who will not
laugh is a fool.
Dialogues in Limbo (1925) **Santayana, George**
(1863–1952) Spanish-born US philosopher and
writer

117 Old age is not an illness, it is a timeless
ascent. As power diminishes, we grow
toward the light.
Ms magazine, (1982) **Sarton, May** (1912–1995)
US poet and writer

118 When I was young, I was told: 'You'll see,
when you're fifty.' I am fifty and I haven't
seen a thing.
In Pierre-Daniel Templier, *Erik Satie*, 2, Letter
to his brother **Satie, Erik** (1866–1925) French
composer

119 As I grow older and older,
And totter towards the tomb,
I find that I care less and less
Who goes to bed with whom.
In Hitchman, *Such a Strange Lady* (1975) **Sayers,
Dorothy L.** (1893–1957) English writer,
dramatist and translator

120 In a dream you are never eighty.
'Old' (1962) **Sexton, Anne** (1928–1974) US poet

121 Though age from folly could not give me
freedom,
It does from childishness.
Antony and Cleopatra, I.iii

122 Age cannot wither her, nor custom stale
Her infinite variety. Other women cloy
The appetites they feed, but she makes
hungry
Where most she satisfies.
Antony and Cleopatra, II.ii

123 Unregarded age in corners thrown.
As You Like It, II.iii

124 Therefore my age is as a lusty winter,
Frosty, but kindly.
As You Like It, II.iii

125 And so, from hour to hour, we ripe and
ripe,
And then, from hour to hour, we rot and
rot;
And thereby hangs a tale.
As You Like It, II.vii

126 The satirical rogue says here that old men
have grey beards; that their faces are
wrinkled; their eyes purging thick amber
and plum-tree gum; and that they have a
plentiful lack of wit, together with most
weak hams – all of which, sir, though I
most powerfully and potently believe, yet I
hold it not honesty to have it thus set
down.
Hamlet, II.ii

127 Is it not strange that desire should so many
years outlive performance?
Henry IV, Part 2, II.iv

128 O, sir, you are old;
Nature in you stands on the very verge
Of her confine.
King Lear, II.iv

129 A good old man, sir, he will be talking; as
they say 'When the age is in the wit is out.'
Much Ado About Nothing, III.v

130 You and I are past our dancing days.
Romeo and Juliet, I.v

131 That time of year thou mayst in me behold
When yellow leaves, or none, or few, do
hang
Upon those boughs which shake against
the cold,
Bare ruin'd choirs where late the sweet
birds sang.
In me thou seest the twilight of such day
As after sunset fadeth in the west,
Which by and by black night doth take
away,
Death's second self, that seals up all in
rest.
Sonnet 73

132 Crabbed age and youth cannot live
together:
Youth is full of pleasance, age is full of
care …
Age, I do abhor thee; youth, I do adore
thee.
The Passionate Pilgrim, xii **Shakespeare,
William** (1564–1616) English dramatist, poet
and actor

133 Old men are dangerous: it doesn't matter
to them what is going to happen to the
world.
Heartbreak House (1919)

134 Every man over forty is a scoundrel.
Man and Superman (1903) **Shaw, George
Bernard** (1856–1950) Irish socialist, writer,
dramatist and critic

135 There is more felicity on the far side of
baldness than young men can possibly
imagine.
'Last Words' (1933) **Smith, Logan Pearsall**
(1865–1946) US-born British epigrammatist,
critic and writer

136 I grow old ever learning many things.
In Bergk (ed.), *Poetae Lyrici Graeci* **Solon** (c.638–
c.559 BC) Athenian statesman, reformer and
poet

137 You are old, Father William, the young
man cried,
The few locks which are left you are grey;
You are hale, Father William, a hearty old
man,
Now tell me the reason, I pray …
In the days of my youth I remembered my
God!
And He hath not forgotten my age.

'The Old Man's Comforts, and how he Gained
them' (1799) **Southey, Robert** (1774–1843)
English poet, essayist, historian and letter
writer

138 Being over seventy is like being engaged in
a war. All our friends are going or gone
and we survive amongst the dead and the
dying as on a battlefield.
Memento Mori **Spark, Muriel** (1918–2006)
Scottish writer, poet and dramatist

139 Chill on the brow and in the breast
The frost of years is spread –
Soon we shall take our endless rest
With the unfeeling dead.
Insensibly, ere we depart,
We grow more cold, more kind:
Age makes a winter in the heart,
An autumn in the mind.
'Grave Epigrams' **Sparrow, John** (1906–1992)
English lawyer and writer

140 There are so few who can grow old with a
good grace.
The Spectator, 263, (1712) **Steele, Sir Richard**
(1672–1729) Irish-born English writer,
dramatist and politician

141 Men come of age at sixty, women at
fifteen.
The Observer, (1944) **Stephens, James** (1882–
1950) Irish poet and writer

142 By the time a man gets well into the
seventies his continued existence is a mere
miracle.
Virginibus Puerisque (1881)

143 Our frailties are invincible, our virtues
barren; the battle goes sore against us to
the going down of the sun.
Across the Plains (1892) **Stevenson, Robert
Louis** (1850–1894) Scottish writer, poet and
essayist

144 If you live long enough, the venerability
factor creeps in; you get accused of things
you never did and praised for virtues you
never had.
In Laurence J. Peter, *Peter's Quotations* **Stone,
I.F.** (1907–1989) US writer

145 Old men and comets have been reverenced
for the same reason; their long beards, and
pretences to foretell events.
Thoughts on Various Subjects (1711)

146 Every man desires to live long; but no man would be old.
Thoughts on Various Subjects (1711)

147 I'm as old as my tongue, and a little older than my teeth.
Polite Conversation (1738) **Swift, Jonathan** (1667–1745) Irish satirist, poet, essayist and cleric

148 What a sad old age you are preparing for yourself.
In J. Amédée Pichot, *Souvenirs intimes sur M. de Talleyrand* (1870) **Talleyrand, Charles-Maurice de** (1754–1838) French statesman, memoirist and prelate. Remark to young man who boasted that he did not play whist

149 The force that through the green fuse drives the flower
Drives my green age; that blasts the roots of trees
Is my destroyer.
And I am dumb to tell the crooked rose
My youth is bent by the same wintry fever.
'The force that through the green fuse drives the flower' (1934)

150 Do not go gentle into that good night,
Old age should burn and rave at close of day;
Rage, rage against the dying of the light.
'Do Not Go Gentle into that Good Night' (1952) **Thomas, Dylan** (1914–1953) Welsh poet, writer and radio dramatist

151 Her own mother lived the latter years of her life in the horrible suspicion that electricity was dripping invisibly all over the house.
My Life and Hard Times (1933) **Thurber, James** (1894–1961) US humorist, writer and dramatist

152 Old age is the most unexpected of all the things that happen to a man.
Diary in Exile, (8 May 1935) **Trotsky, Leon** (1879–1940) Russian revolutionary and Communist theorist

153 Keep breathing.
Attr. **Tucker, Sophie** (1884–1966) Russian-born US vaudeville singer. Asked, when 80, the secret of longevity

154 There are no old men any more. *Playboy* and *Penthouse* have between them made an ideal of eternal adolescence, sunburnt and saunaed, with the grey dorianed out of it.
Dear Me (1977) **Ustinov, Sir Peter** (1921–2004) English actor, director, dramatist, writer and raconteur

155 To me Adler will always be Jung.
Telegram to Larry Adler on his 60th birthday **Wall, Max** (1908–1990) English comedian

156 What has one to do, when one grows tired of the world, as we both do, but to draw nearer and nearer, and gently waste the remains of life with friends with whom one began it?
Letter to George Montagu, (1765)

157 Old age is no such uncomfortable thing if one gives oneself up to it with a good grace, and doesn't drag it about 'To midnight dances and the public show'.
Letter, (1774) **Walpole, Horace** (1717–1797) English writer and politician

158 Is not old wine wholesomest, old pippins toothsomest? Does not old wood burn brightest, old linen wash whitest? Old soldiers, sweethearts, are surest, and old lovers are soundest.
Westward Hoe (1607) **Webster, John** (c.1580–c.1625) English dramatist

159 The aged are usually tougher and more calculating than the young, provided they keep enough of their wits about them. How could they have lived so long if there weren't steel buried inside them?
The Eye of the Storm (1973) **White, Patrick** (1912–1990) English-born Australian writer and dramatist

160 Women sit or move to and fro, some old, some young.
The young are beautiful – but the old are more beautiful than the young.
'Beautiful Women' (1871) **Whitman, Walt** (1819–1892) US poet and writer

161 One should never trust a woman who tells one her real age. A woman who would tell one that would tell one anything.
A Woman of No Importance (1893)

162 *Mrs Allonby*: I delight in men over seventy. They always offer one the devotion of a lifetime.
A Woman of No Importance (1893)

163 The old believe everything: the middle-aged suspect everything: the young know everything.
The Chameleon (1894)

164 No woman should ever be quite accurate about her age. It looks so calculating.
The Importance of Being Earnest (1895), IV
Wilde, Oscar (1854–1900) Irish poet, dramatist, writer, critic and wit

165 In old age
the mind
casts off
rebelliously
an eagle
from its crag.
Paterson (1946–1958) **Williams, William Carlos** (1883–1963) US poet, writer and paediatrician

166 He was either a man of about a hundred and fifty who was rather young for his years or a man of about a hundred and ten who had been aged by trouble.
In Usborne, *Wodehouse at Work to the End* (1976) **Wodehouse, P.G.** (1881–1975) English humorist and writer

167 The wiser mind
Mourns less for what age takes away
Than what it leaves behind.
'The Fountain' (1800) **Wordsworth, William** (1770–1850) English poet

168 Out-worn heart, in a time out-worn,
Come clear of the nets of wrong and right;
Laugh, heart, again in the grey twilight,
Sigh, heart, again in the dew of the morn.
In the *National Observer*, (1893), 'Into the Twilight'

169 I thought no more was needed
Youth to prolong
Than dumb-bell and foil
To keep the body young.
O who could have foretold
That the heart grows old?
'A Song' (1918)

170 An aged man is but a paltry thing,
A tattered coat upon a stick, unless
Soul clap its hands and sing, and louder sing
For every tatter in its mortal dress.
'Sailing to Byzantium' (1927)

171 The innocent and the beautiful
Have no enemy but time.
The Winding Stair and Other Poems (1933)

172 You think it horrible that lust and rage
Should dance attention upon my old age;
They were not such a plague when I was young;
What else have I to spur me into song?
In the *London Mercury*, (1938) **Yeats, W.B.** (1865–1939) Irish poet, dramatist, editor, writer and senator

173 At thirty man suspects himself a Fool;
Knows it at forty, and reforms his Plan;
At fifty chides his infamous Delay,
Pushes his prudent Purpose to Resolve;
In all the magnanimity of Thought
Resolves; and re-resolves; then dies the same.
Night-Thoughts on Life, Death and Immortality (1742–1746) **Young, Edward** (1683–1765) English poet, dramatist, satirist and clergyman
See also experience; life; memory; wisdom; youth

AMERICA

1 A man went looking for America and couldn't find it anywhere.
Advertisement for the film *Easy Rider*, (1969)

2 American society is a sort of flat, fresh-water pond which absorbs silently, without reaction, anything which is thrown into it.
Letter, (1911) **Adams, Henry** (1838–1918) US historian and memoirist

3 I always consider the settlement of America with reverence and wonder, as the opening of a grand scene and design in providence, for the illumination of the ignorant and the emancipation of the slavish part of mankind all over the earth.
Notes for *A Dissertation on the Canon and Feudal Law* (1765)

4 The Revolution was effected before the War commenced. The Revolution was in the minds and hearts of the people; a change in their religious sentiments of their duties and obligations.
The Works of John Adams (1856), letter, (1818) **Adams, John** (1735–1826) US lawyer, diplomat and President

5 Think of your forefathers! Think of your posterity!
Speech, (December 1802) **Adams, John Quincy** (1767–1848) US lawyer, diplomat and President

6 A spirit of national masochism prevails, encouraged by an effete corps of impudent snobs who characterize themselves as intellectuals.
New York Times, (1969) **Agnew, Spiro T.** (1918–1996) US Vice President

7 Good Americans, when they die, go to Paris.
In Oliver Wendell Holmes, *The Autocrat of the Breakfast Table* (1858)

8 A Boston man is the east wind made flesh.
Attr. **Appleton, Thomas Gold** (1812–1884) US epigrammatist

9 Our society distributes itself into Barbarians, Philistines, and Populace; and America is just ourselves, with the Barbarians quite left out, and the Populace nearly.
Culture and Anarchy (1869) **Arnold, Matthew** (1822–1888) English poet, critic, essayist and educationist

10 God bless the U.S.A., so large,
So friendly, and so rich.
'On the Circuit' **Auden, W.H.** (1907–1973) English poet, essayist, critic, teacher and dramatist

11 What the American public doesn't know is what makes it the American public.
Tommy Boy (film, 1995) **Aykroyd, Dan** (1952–) US film actor

12 America, thou half-brother of the world;
With something good and bad of every land.
Festus (1839) **Bailey, Philip James** (1816–1902)

13 In America nothing dies easier than tradition.
New York Times, (1991) **Baker, Russell** (1925–) US writer

14 America! America!
God shed His grace on thee
And crown thy good with brotherhood
From sea to shining sea!
'America the Beautiful', (song, 1895) **Bates, Katherine Lee** (1859–1929) US writer and poet

15 I have fallen in love with American names,
The sharp gaunt names that never get fat,
The snakeskin-titles of mining-claims,
The plumed war-bonnet of Medicine Hat,
Tucson and Deadwood and Lost Mule Flat.
'American Names' (1927) **Benét, Stephen Vincent** (1898–1943) US poet

16 And this is good old Boston,
The home of the bean and the cod,
Where the Lowells talk only to Cabots,
And the Cabots talk only to God.
Toast at Harvard dinner, (1910) **Bossidy, John Collins** (1860–1928) US oculist

17 America is not a young land: it is old and dirty and evil before the settlers, before the Indians. The evil is there waiting.
Naked Lunch (1959) **Burroughs, William S.** (1914–1999) US writer

18 America needs to be more like The Waltons and less like The Simpsons.
Speech, (January 1992) **Bush, George H.W.** (1924–) US Republican President; father of US President George W. Bush

19 ... a society like ours [the USA] of which it is truly said to be often but three generations 'from shirt-sleeves to shirt-sleeves'.
True and False Democracy **Butler, Nicholas Murray** (1862–1947) US teacher, lecturer, politican and writer

20 I called the New World into existence, to redress the balance of the Old.
Speech, (1826) **Canning, George** (1770–1827) English Prime Minister, orator and poet

21 This is virgin territory for whorehouses.
In Kenneth Allsop, The Bootleggers (1961) **Capone, Al** (1899–1947) Chicago gangster. Talking about suburban Chicago

22 Over increasingly large areas of the United States, spring now comes unheralded by the return of the birds, and the early mornings are strangely silent where once they were filled with the beauty of bird song.
The Silent Spring (1962) **Carson, Rachel Louise** (1907–1964) US marine biologist and writer

23 A big hard-boiled city with no more personality than a paper cup.
The Little Sister (1949) **Chandler, Raymond** (1888–1959) US crime novelist. Of Los Angeles

24 We travel by plane, oftener than not, and yet the spirit of our country seems to have remained a country of railroads.
Bullet Park (1969) **Cheever, John** (1912–1982) US novelist

25 America is the only nation in history which miraculously has gone directly from barbarism to degeneration without the usual interval of civilization.
Attr. **Clemenceau, Georges** (1841–1929) French Prime Minister and journalist

26 Part of growing up is learning how to control your impulses.
The Times, (1999) **Clinton, Hillary** (1947–) US Democrat politician. Introducing her husband President Clinton at a gun-control rally

27 Any President that lies to the American people should resign.
Speech as Governor of Arkansas, (1974)

28 Though our challenges are fearsome, so are our strengths. Americans have ever been a relentless, questioning, hopeful people.
Inauguration speech, (20 January 1993) **Clinton, William ('Bill')** (1946–) US Democrat President

29 Only America makes you feel that everybody wants to be like you. That's what success is: everybody wants to be like you.
In Arthur Taylor, *Notes and Tones* (1977) **Coleman, Ornette** (1930–) US jazz musician

30 The governments of the past could fairly be characterized as devices for maintaining in perpetuity the place and position of certain privileged classes ... The Government of the United States is a device for maintaining in perpetuity the rights of the people, with the ultimate extinction of all privileged classes.
Speech, (1924) **Coolidge, Calvin** (1872–1933) US President

31 Gentlemen, get the thing straight once and for all. The policeman isn't there to create disorder, the policeman is there to preserve disorder.
Attr. **Daley, Richard J.** (1902–1976) US politician and Mayor of Chicago. To the press, concerning riots during Democratic Convention, 1968

32 What this country needs is more unemployed politicians.
Speech, (1967) **Davis, Angela** (1944–) US political activist, revolutionary and author

33 Poor Mexico, so far from God and so near to the United States!
Attr. **Díaz, Porfirio** (1830–1915) Mexican general and statesman

34 The thing that impresses me most about America is the way parents obey their children.
In *Look*, (1957) **Edward VIII** (later Duke of Windsor) (1894–1972) King of the United Kingdom; abdicated 11 December 1936

35 Whatever America hopes to bring to pass in this world must first come to pass in the heart of America.
Inaugural address, (1953) **Eisenhower, Dwight D.** (1890–1969) US Republican President and general

36 The Americans have little faith. They rely on the power of a dollar.
Lecture (1841), 'Man the Reformer'

37 We say the cows laid out Boston. Well, there are worse surveyors.
Conduct of Life (1860)

38 America is a country of young men.
Society and Solitude (1870)

39 There is a little formula, couched in pure Saxon, which you may hear in the corners of the streets and in the yard of the dame's school, from very little republicans: 'I'm as good as you be,' which contains the essence of the Massachusetts Bill of Rights and of the American Declaration of Independence.
Natural History of Intellect (1893) **Emerson, Ralph Waldo** (1803–1882) US poet, essayist, transcendentalist and teacher

40 I really believe that the pagans, and the abortionists, and the feminists, and the gays and lesbians who are actively trying to make that an alternative lifestyle, the ACLU, People for the American Way, all of them who have tried to secularize America, I point the finger in their face and say, you helped this to happen – the abortionists have got to bear some burden for this because God will not be mocked.
The 700 Club (13 September 2001) **Falwell, Reverend Jerry** (1933–) Right-wing US tele-evangelist. On the terrorist attacks of 11 September 2001. He later apologized.

41 Americans, while willing, even eager, to be serfs, have always been obstinate about being peasantry.
The Great Gatsby (1926) **Fitzgerald, F. Scott** (1896–1940) US writer

42 I guess it proves that in America anyone can be President.
In Reeves, *A Ford Not a Lincoln* **Ford, Gerald R.** (1913–) US Republican President. Referring to his own appointment as President

43 When a society fosters as much crime and destitution as ours, with ample resources to meet the actual necessities of every one, there must be something radically wrong, not in the society but in the foundation upon which society is reared.
Black and White: Land, Labor and Politics in the South (1884) **Fortune, T. Thomas** (1856–1928) US journalist and editor

44 Yes, America is gigantic, but a gigantic mistake.
In Peter Gay, *Freud: A Life for Our Time* (1988) **Freud, Sigmund** (1856–1939) Austrian physicist; founder of psychoanalysis

45 What America does best is to understand itself. What it does worst is to understand others.
Time, (1986) **Fuentes, Carlos** (1928–) Mexican novelist and playwright

46 The compact which exists between the North and the South is 'a covenant with death and an agreement with hell'.
Resolution adopted by the Massachusetts Anti-Slavery Society, (1843) **Garrison, William Lloyd** (1805–1879) US abolitionist and newspaper editor

47 When the white man came we had the land and they had the Bibles; now they have the land and we have the Bibles.
Attr. **George, Dan** (1899–1982) Canadian Indian chief

48 The Americans cannot build aeroplanes. They are very good at refrigerators and razor blades.
In Alistair Cooke, *America* **Goering, Hermann** (1893–1946) Nazi leader and military commander. Assurance to Hitler

49 New York ... that unnatural city where every one is an exile, none more so than the American.
The Living of Charlotte Perkins Gilman (1935) **Gilman, Charlotte Perkins** (1860–1935) US writer, social reformer and feminist

50 The United States is like a gigantic boiler. Once the fire is lighted under it there is no limit to the power it can generate.
In Winston S. Churchill, *Their Finest Hour* **Grey, Edward, Viscount of Fallodon** (1862–1933) English statesman and writer

51 'Do you pray for the senators, Dr Hale?' 'No, I look at the senators and I pray for the country.'
In Van Wyck Brooks, *New England Indian Summer* (1940) **Hale, Edward Everett** (1822–1909) Chaplain to the US Senate

52 Before he [Gilbert Harding] could go to New York he had to get a US visa at the American consulate in Toronto. He was called upon to fill in a long form with many questions, including 'Is it your intention to overthrow the Government of the United States by force?' By the time Harding got to that one he was so irritated that he answered: 'Sole purpose of visit.'

In W. Reyburn, *Gilbert Harding* (1978)
Harding, Gilbert (1907–1960) English writer and broadcaster

53 America's present need is not heroics but healing, not nostrums but normalcy.
Speech, Boston, (May 1920) **Harding, Warren G.** (1865–1923) US statesman and Republican President

54 The United States, I believe, are under the impression that they are twenty years in advance of this country; whilst, as a matter of actual verifiable fact, of course, they are just about six hours behind it.
The Devil in Woodford Wells **Hobson, Sir Harold** (1904–1992) British critic and writer

55 It created in me a yearning for all that is wide and open and expansive. Something that will never allow me to fit in in my own country, with its narrow towns and narrow roads and narrow kindnesses and narrow reprimands.
Independent, (1994) **Hopkins, Anthony** (1937–) Welsh actor

56 Democrats make up plans and then do something else. Republicans follow the plans their grandfathers made ... Republican boys date democratic girls. They plan to marry Republican girls, but feel they're entitled to a little fun first.
House debate, (1983) **Jacobs, Andrew** (1932–) Lawyer and Democrat Congressman

57 It's a complex fate, being an American.
Letter, (1872) **James, Henry** (1843–1916) US-born British writer, critic and letter writer

58 We hold these truths to be self-evident: that all men are created equal; that they are endowed by their Creator with certain unalienable rights; that among these are life, liberty, and the pursuit of happiness.
Declaration of Independence, (1776)

59 To attain all this universal republicanism, however, rivers of blood must yet flow, and years of desolation pass over; yet the object is worth rivers of blood, and years of desolation.
Letter to John Adams, (1823) **Jefferson, Thomas** (1743–1826) US Democrat statesman and President

60 I am willing to love all mankind, except an American.
In Boswell, *The Life of Samuel Johnson* (1791)
Johnson, Samuel (1709–1784) English lexicographer, poet, critic, conversationalist and essayist

61 Where is Hollywood located? Chiefly between the ears. In that part of the American brain lately vacated by God.
How To Save Your Own Life (1977) **Jong, Erica** (1942–) US writer

62 And so, my fellow Americans: ask not what your country can do for you – ask what you can do for your country. My fellow citizens of the world: ask not what America will do for you, but what together we can do for the freedom of man.
Inaugural address, (1961)

63 The United States has to move very fast to even stand still.
The Observer, (1963)

64 The worse I do, the more popular I get.
Attr. Of his popularity after the failure of the US invasion of Cuba **Kennedy, John F.** (1917–1963) US Democrat President

65 America is a melting pot, the people at the bottom get burned while all the scum floats to the top.
King, Charles (1844–1933) US general and writer

66 Being a New Yorker is a state of mind. If, after living there for six months, you find that you walk faster, talk faster and think faster, you are a New Yorker.
The Observer, (1999) **Koch, Ed** (1924–) US politician and jurist; Mayor of New York 1978–89

67 And suddenly she craved again for the more absolute silence of America. English stillness was so soft, like an inaudible murmur of voices, of presences.
St Mawr (1925) **Lawrence, D.H.** (1885–1930) English writer, poet and critic

68 In other countries, art and literature are left to a lot of shabby bums living in attics and feeding on booze and spaghetti, but in America the successful writer or picture-painter is indistinguishable from any other decent business man.
Babbit (1922) **Lewis, Sinclair** (1885–1951) US writer

69 There won't be any revolution in America ... The people are too clean. They spend all their time changing their shirts and washing themselves. You can't feel fierce and revolutionary in a bathroom.
Juan in America (1931) **Linklater, Eric** (1899–1974) Welsh-born Scottish writer and satirist

70 The only things that the United States has given to the world are skyscrapers, jazz, and cocktails. That is all. And in Cuba, in our America, they make much better cocktails.
Poet in New York (1940, trans. 1988) **Lorca, Federico García** (1898–1936) Spanish poet and dramatist

71 Here too in Maine things bend to the wind forever.
After two years away, one must get used to the painted soft wood staying bright and clean,
to the air blasting an all-white wall whiter, as it blows through curtain and screen touched with salt and evergreen.
For the Union Dead (1964), 'Soft Wood' **Lowell, Robert** (1917–1977) US poet and writer

72 First, the sweetheart of the nation, then her aunt, woman governs America because America is a land where boys refuse to grow up.
'Americans are Boys' **Madariaga, Salvador de** (1886–1978) Spanish writer, diplomat and teacher

73 Canadians are Americans with no Disneyland.
The Changeover (1984) **Mahy, Margaret** (1936–) New Zealand writer

74 All the security around the American President is just to make sure the man who shoots him gets caught.
Sunday Telegraph, (1990) **Mailer, Norman** (1923–) US writer

75 Sitting at the table doesn't make you a diner, unless you eat some of what's on that plate. Being here in America doesn't make you an American. Being born here in America doesn't make you an American.
Malcolm X Speaks, (1965) **Malcolm X** (1925–1965) US black leader

76 If there is any country on earth where the course of true love may be expected to run smooth, it is America.
Society in America (1837) **Martineau, Harriet** (1802–1876) English writer

77 There are only about four hundred people in New York society.
Interview with Charles H. Crandall in the *New York Tribune*, (1888) **McAllister, Ward** (1827–1895)

78 McCarthyism is Americanism with its sleeves rolled.
Speech, (1952) **McCarthy, Joseph** (1908–1957) US Republican politician

79 The happy ending is our national belief.
Attr.

80 An interviewer asked me what book I thought best represented the modern American woman. All I could think of to answer was: *Madame Bovary*.
On the Contrary (1961) **McCarthy, Mary** (1912–1989) US writer and critic

81 All Native American orators, whatever their language group, are translated to sound either like Dr. Johnson, the prophet Isaiah, or ... the Sioux wise man Black Elk.
The New York Review of Books, (1999) **McMurtry, Larry** (1936–) US author and screenwriter

82 No one ever went broke underestimating the intelligence of the American people.
Attr. **Mencken, H.L.** (1880–1956) US writer, critic, philologist and satirist

83 The United States is the glory, jest, and terror of mankind.
In Purdy (ed.), *The New Romans* (1988) **Minifie, James M.** (1900–1974) Canadian broadcaster

84 Things on the whole are much faster in America; people don't 'stand for election', they 'run for office.'

Sons and Rebels (1960) **Mitford, Jessica** (1917–1996) English writer

85 Americans are possibly the dumbest people on the planet ... We Americans suffer from an enforced ignorance. We don't know about anything that's happening outside our country. Our stupidity is embarrassing.
Speech in Germany, (2004) **Moore, Michael** (1954–) US activist and writer

86 Our manifest destiny to overspread the continent allotted by Providence for the free development of our yearly multiplying millions.
United States Magazine and Democratic Review, (1837) **O'Sullivan, John L.** (1813–1895) US editor and diplomat

87 I rejoice that America has resisted. Three millions of people, so dead to all the feelings of liberty, as voluntarily to submit to be slaves, would have been fit instruments to make slaves of the rest.
Speech, House of Commons, (1766) **Pitt, William** (1708–1778) English politician and Prime Minister

88 Rural Americans are real Americans. There's no doubt about that. You can't always be sure with other Americans. Not all of them are real.
Remark during the 1992 Presidential campaign **Quayle, Dan** (1947–) US politician

89 And furthermore did you know that behind the discovery of America there was a Jewish financier?
Cocksure (1968) **Richler, Mordecai** (1931–2001) Canadian novelist

90 This country has come to feel the same when Congress is in session as we do when the baby gets hold of the hammer. It's just a question of how much damage he can do with it before we can take it away from him.
Will Rogers: His Life and Times, (1973) **Rogers, Will** (1879–1935) US comedian

91 I think if the people of this country can be reached with the truth, their judgment will be in favour of the many, as against the privileged few.
Ladies' Home Journal **Roosevelt, Eleanor** (1884–1962) US writer and lecturer

92 We have room in this country for but one flag, the Stars and Stripes ... We have room for but one loyalty, loyalty to the United States ... We have room for but one language, the language of the Declaration of Independence and the Gettysburg speech.
Speech, (1918)

93 There can be no fifty-fifty Americanism in this country. There is room here for only hundred per cent Americanism, only for those who are Americans and nothing else.
In Lord Charnwood, *Theodore Roosevelt* (1923) **Roosevelt, Theodore** (1858–1919) US Republican President

94 America ... where law and custom alike are based upon the dreams of spinsters.
Marriage and Morals (1929)

95 In America everybody is of the opinion that he has no social superiors, since all men are equal, but he does not admit that he has no social inferiors.
'Ideas that have harmed mankind' (1950) **Russell, Bertrand** (1872–1970) English philosopher, mathematician, essayist and social reformer

96 We've got the kind of President who thinks arms control means some kind of deodorant.
The Observer, (1987) **Schroeder, Patricia** (1940–) US politician

97 I expect no very violent transition.
Attr. **Sedgwick, Catharine Maria** (1789–1867) US writer and feminist. Comparing heaven with her home town of Stockbridge, Massachussetts

98 A Bad Thing: America was thus clearly top nation, and History came to a .
1066 And All That (1930) **Sellar, Walter** (1898–1951) and **Yeatman, Robert Julian** (1897–1968) British writers

99 New York ... is not Mecca. It just smells like it.
California Suite (1976) **Simon, Neil** (1927–) US playwright

100 My country, 'tis of thee,
Sweet land of liberty,
Of thee I sing:
Land where my fathers died,
Land of the pilgrims' pride,
From every mountain-side
Let freedom ring.
'America' (1832) **Smith, Samuel Francis** (1808–1895) American Baptist clergyman and poet

101 That strange blend of the commercial traveller, the missionary, and the barbarian conqueror, which was the American abroad.
Last and First Men (1930) **Stapledon, Olaf** (1886–1950) British philosopher and writer

102 In the United States there is more space where nobody is than where anybody is. That is what makes America what it is.
The Geographical History of America (1936) **Stein, Gertrude** (1874–1946) US writer, dramatist, poet and critic

103 Cannery Row in Monterey in California is a poem, a stink, a grating noise, a quality of light, a tone, a habit, a nostalgia, a dream.
Cannery Row (1939) **Steinbeck, John** (1902–1968) US writer

104 The trouble with this country is that it has a two-party system and a one-party press.
Speech, (1952)

105 In America any boy may become President and I suppose it's just one of the risks he takes!
Speech, (1952) **Stevenson, Adlai** (1900–1965) US lawyer, statesman and United Nations ambassador

106 I like to walk around Manhattan, catching glimpses of its wild life, the pigeons and cats and girls.
Three Witnesses, 'When a Man Murders' **Stout, Rex** (1886–1975)

107 I found there a country with thirty-two religions and only one sauce.
In Pedrazzini, *Autant en apportent les mots* **Talleyrand, Charles-Maurice de** (1754–1838) French statesman, memoirist and prelate. Of America

108 America ... just a nation of two hundred million used-car salesman with all the money we need to buy guns and no qualms about killing anybody else in the world who tries to make us uncomfortable.
Attr. **Thompson, Hunter S.** (1937–2005) US author

109 America is a large, friendly dog in a very small room. Ever time it wags its tail it knocks over a chair.
Broadcast news summary, (1954) **Toynbee, Arnold** (1889–1975) English historian

110 Overpaid, overfed, oversexed and over here.
The Sunday Times, (1976) **Trinder, Tommy** (1909–1989) English comedian and actor. Referring to the GIs in World War II

111 What though people had plenty to eat and clothes to wear, if they put their feet upon the tables and did not reverence their betters? The Americans were to her rough, uncouth, and vulgar, – and she told them so.
An Autobiography (1883) **Trollope, Anthony** (1815–1882) English writer, traveller and post office official. On Frances Trollope's *Domestic Manners of the Americans*

112 All the president is, is a glorified public relations man who spends his time flattering, kissing and kicking people to get them to do what they are supposed to do anyway.
Letter to his sister, (1947)

113 The buck stops here.
Sign on his desk **Truman, Harry S.** (1884–1972) US Democrat President

114 The land of the dull and the home of the literal.
Reflections upon a Sinking Ship (1969)

115 In America, the race goes to the loud, the solemn, the hustler. If you think you are a great writer, you must say that you are.
In George Plimpton, *Writers at Work* (1981)

116 Half of American people have never read a newspaper. Half never voted for President. One hopes it is the same half.
Screening History (1992) **Vidal, Gore** (1925–) US writer, critic and poet

117 The next Augustan age will dawn on the other side of the Atlantic. There will, perhaps, be a Thucydides at Boston, a Xenophon at New York, and, in time, a Virgil at Mexico, and a Newton at Peru. At last, some curious traveller from Lima will visit England and give a description of the ruins of St Paul's, like the editions of Balbec and Palmyra.
Letter to Sir Horace Mann, (1774) **Walpole, Horace** (1717–1797) English writer and politician

118 I moved to New York City for my health. I'm paranoid and New York was the only place where my fears were justified.
Attr. **Weiss, Anita**

119 Every time Europe looks across the Atlantic to see the American eagle, it observes only the rear end of an ostrich.
America **Wells, H.G.** (1866–1946) English writer

120 The United States themselves are essentially the greatest poem.
Leaves of Grass (1855 edition), Preface **Whitman, Walt** (1819–1892) US poet and writer

121 Of course, America had often been discovered before, but it had always been hushed up.
Personal Impressions of America (1883)

122 The youth of America is their oldest tradition. It has been going on now for three hundred years.
A Woman of No Importance (1893) **Wilde, Oscar** (1854–1900) Irish poet, dramatist, writer, critic and wit

123 The Constitution does not provide for first and second class citizens.
An American Program (1944) **Willkie, Wendell** (1892–1944)

124 America lives in the heart of every man everywhere who wishes to find a region where he will be free to work out his destiny as he chooses.
Speech, (1912)

125 America ... is the prize amateur nation of the world. Germany is the prize professional nation.

Speech, (1917)

126 America is the only idealistic nation in the world.
Speech, (1919) **Wilson, Woodrow** (1856–1924) US Democrat President

127 Like so many substantial Americans, he had married young and kept on marrying, springing from blonde to blonde like the chamois of the Alps leaping from crag to crag.
In Usborne, *Wodehouse at Work to the End* (1976) **Wodehouse, P.G.** (1881–1975) English humorist and writer

128 America is God's Crucible, the great Melting-Pot where all the races of Europe are melting and re-forming!
The Melting Pot (1908) **Zangwill, Israel** (1864–1926) English writer and Jewish spokesman
See also global affairs; politics

ANGER

1 The angry man always thinks he can do more than he can.
Liber Consolationis **Albertano of Brescia** (c.1190–c.1270) Jurist, philosopher and politician

2 The man who is angry on the right grounds and with the right people, and in the right manner and at the right moment and for the right length of time, is to be praised.
Nicomachean Ethics **Aristotle** (384–322 BC) Greek philosopher

3 Anger makes dull men witty, but it keeps them poor.
'Apophthegms' (1679) **Bacon, Francis** (1561–1626) English philosopher, essayist, politician and courtier

4 When he was angry, one of his eyes became so terrible, that no person could bear to behold it; and the wretch upon whom it was fixed, instantly fell backward, and sometimes expired. For fear, however, of depopulating his dominions and making his palace desolate, he but rarely gave way to his anger.

Vathek (1787) **Beckford, William** (1760–1844) English writer, collector and politician

5 A soft answer turneth away wrath.
Proverbs, 15:1

6 Be ye angry, and sin not; let not the sun go down upon your wrath.
Ephesians, 4:26 **The Bible (King James Version)**

7 The tygers of wrath are wiser than the horses of instruction.
The Marriage of Heaven and Hell (c.1790–1793)

8 I was angry with my friend:
I told my wrath, my wrath did end.
I was angry with my foe:
I told it not, my wrath did grow.
Songs of Experience (1794) **Blake, William** (1757–1827) English poet, engraver, painter and mystic

9 We think na on the lang Scots miles,
The mosses, waters, slaps, and styles,
That lie between us and our hame,
Whare sits our sulky, sullen dame,
Gathering her brows like gathering storm,
Nursing her wrath to keep it warm.
'Tam o' Shanter' (1790) **Burns, Robert** (1759–1796) Scottish poet and songwriter

10 Beware the fury of a patient man.
Absalom and Achitophel (1681) **Dryden, John** (1631–1700) English poet, satirist, dramatist and critic

11 Anger is one of the sinews of the soul; he that wants it hath a maimed mind.
The Holy State and the Profane State (1642) **Fuller, Thomas** (1608–1661) English churchman and antiquary

12 Anger is never without an Argument, but seldom with a good one.
Thoughts and Reflections (1750) **Halifax, Lord** (1633–1695) English politician, courtier, pamphleteer and epigrammatist

13 Spleen can subsist on any kind of food.
'On Wit and Humour' (1819) **Hazlitt, William** (1778–1830) English writer and critic

14 A tart temper never mellows with age, and a sharp tongue is the only edged tool that grows keener with constant use.
'Rip Van Winkle' (1820) **Irving, Washington** (1783–1859) US writer and diplomat

15 Beware of the man who does not return your blow: he neither forgives you nor allows you to forgive yourself.
Man and Superman (1903) **Shaw, George Bernard** (1856–1950) Irish socialist, writer, dramatist and critic

16 O heavenly Foole, thy most kisse worthy face
Anger invests with such a lovely grace,
That Anger's selfe I needes must kisse againe.
Astrophel and Stella (1591) **Sidney, Sir Philip** (1554–1586) English poet, critic, soldier, courtier and diplomat

17 Anger has overpowered him, and driven him to a revenge which was rather a stupid one, I must acknowledge, but anger makes us all stupid.
Heidi (1880) **Spyri, Johanna** (1827–1901) Swiss writer

18 When angry count four; when very angry swear.
Pudd'nhead Wilson's Calendar (1894) **Twain, Mark** (1835–1910) US humorist, writer, journalist and lecturer

19 Man is a rational animal who always loses his temper when he is called upon to act in accordance with the dictates of reason.
Intentions (1891) **Wilde, Oscar** (1854–1900) Irish poet, dramatist, writer, critic and wit
See also argument; revenge; spite

ANIMALS

1 The rabbit has a charming face;
Its private life is a disgrace.
La Ménagerie (1968), 'The Rabbit' **Anonymous**

2 The fox knows many things but the hedgehog one big one.
In Plutarch, *Moralia* **Archilochus** (fl. c.650 BC) Greek poet

3 Tyger Tyger, burning bright
In the forests of the night:
What immortal hand or eye
Could frame thy fearful symmetry?
'The Tyger' (1794) **Blake, William** (1757–1827) English poet, engraver, painter and mystic

4 Whenever you observe an animal closely,
you have the feeling that a person sitting
inside is making fun of you.
The Human Province **Canetti, Elias** (1905–1994)
Bulgarian-born English writer, dramatist and
critic

5 Poor little Foal of an oppressed race!
I love the languid patience of thy face.
'To a Young Ass' (1794) **Coleridge, Samuel
Taylor** (1772–1834) English poet, philosopher
and critic

6 Cows are my passion.
Dombey and Son (1848) **Dickens, Charles** (1812–
1870) English writer

7 Nature's great masterpiece, an Elephant,
The only harmless great thing –
Still sleeping stood; vexed not his fantasy
Black dreams; like an unbent bow,
carelessly,
His sinewy proboscis did remissly lie.
'The Progress of the Soul' (1601) **Donne, John**
(1572–1631) English poet

8 Animals are such agreeable friends – they
ask no questions, they pass no criticisms.
Scenes of Clerical Life (1858) **Eliot, George** (1819–
1880) English writer and poet

9 How like us is the ape, most horrible of
beasts.
In Cicero, *De Natura Deorum* **Ennius, Quintus**
(239–169 BC)

10 A horse is dangerous at both ends and
uncomfortable in the middle.
The Sunday Times, (1966) **Fleming, Ian** (1908–
1964) English writer

11 Animals are always loyal and love you,
whereas with children you never know
where you are.
The Times, (1993) **Foyle, Christina** (1911–1999)
Member of famous British bookselling family

12 Brutes never meet in bloody fray,
Nor cut each other's throats, for pay.
'Logicians Refuted' (1759) **Goldsmith, Oliver**
(c.1728–1774) Irish dramatist, poet and writer

13 I go among the Fields and catch a glimpse
of a Stoat or a fieldmouse peeping out of
the withered grass – the creature hath a
purpose and its eyes are bright with it. I go
amongst the buildings of a city and I see a
Man hurrying along – to what? the
Creature has a purpose and his eyes are
bright with it.
Letter to George and Georgiana Keats, (14
February–3 May 1819) **Keats, John** (1795–1821)
English poet

14 Be a good animal, true to your animal
instincts.
The White Peacock (1911) **Lawrence, D.H.** (1885–
1930) English writer, poet and critic

15 When the land is cultivated entirely by the
spade and no horses are kept, a cow is kept
for every three acres of land.
Principles of Political Economy (1848) **Mill, John
Stuart** (1806–1873) English philosopher,
economist and reformer

16 The cow is of the bovine ilk;
One end is moo, the other, milk.
Free Wheeling (1931)

17 The turtle lives 'twixt plated decks
Which practically conceal its sex.
I think it clever of the turtle
In such a fix to be so fertile.
Hard Lines (1931) **Nash, Ogden** (1902–1971) US
poet

18 Why is a lobster any more ridiculous than a
dog – or any other creature one chooses to
take for a walk? I have a liking for lobsters:
they are peaceful and solemn, they know
the secrets of the sea, they do not bark,
and they do not eat into the essential
privacy of one's soul the way dogs do. And
Goethe had an aversion to dogs, and he
was not mad.
In T. Gautier, *Portraits et Souvenirs Littéraires*
(1875) **Nerval, Gérard de** (1808–1855) French
poet and writer. Justifying his habit of
walking a lobster, on a lead, in the gardens of
the Palais Royal

19 The spider's touch, how exquisitely fine!
Feels at each thread, and lives along the
line.
An Essay on Man (1733) **Pope, Alexander** (1688–
1744) English poet, translator and editor

20 Cats is 'dogs' and rabbits is 'dogs' and so's
   Parrats, but this 'ere 'Tortis' is an insect,
   and there ain't no charge for it.
   (1869) **Punch**

21 The lion is the beast to fight:
   He leaps along the plain,
   And if you run with all your might,
   He runs with all his mane.
   'Sage Counsel' **Quiller-Couch, Sir Arthur ('Q')**
   (1863–1944) English man of letters

22 To confess that you are totally Ignorant
   about the Horse, is social suicide: you will
   be despised by everybody, especially the
   horse.
   Horse Nonsense (1933) **Sellar, Walter** (1898–1951)
   and **Yeatman, Robert Julian** (1897–1968)
   British writers

23 No beast so fierce but knows some touch
   of pity.
   Richard III, I.ii **Shakespeare, William** (1564–
   1616) English dramatist, poet and actor

24 Nowadays we don't think much of a man's
   love for an animal; we mock people who
   are attached to cats. But if we stop loving
   animals, aren't we bound to stop loving
   humans too?
   Cancer Ward (1968) **Solzhenitsyn, Alexander**
   (1918–) Russian writer, dramatist and
   historian

25 People are beginning to see that the first
   requisite to success in life, is to be a good
   animal.
   Education (1861) **Spencer, Herbert** (1820–1903)
   English philosopher and journalist

26 The leopard follows his nature as the lamb
   does, and acts after leopard law; she can
   neither help her beauty, nor her courage,
   nor her cruelty; nor a single spot on her
   shining coat; nor the conquering spirit
   which impels her; nor the shot which
   brings her down.
   The History of Henry Esmond (1852) **Thackeray,**
   William Makepeace (1811–1863) Indian-born
   English writer

27 There are two things for which animals are
   to be envied: they know nothing of future
   evils, or of what people say about them.

Letter, (1739) **Voltaire** (1694–1778) French
philosopher, dramatist, poet, historian, writer
and critic

28 I think I could turn and live with animals,
   they are so placid and self-contain'd,
   I stand and look at them long and long.
   They do not sweat and whine about their
   condition,
   They do not lie awake in the dark and weep
   for their sins,
   They do not make me sick discussing their
   duty to God,
   Not one is dissatisfied, not one is
   demented with the mania of owning
   things,
   Not one kneels to another, nor to his kind
   that lived thousands of years ago,
   Not one is respectable or unhappy over the
   whole earth.
   'Song of Myself' (1855) **Whitman, Walt** (1819–
   1892) US poet and writer
   See also birds; pets

APPEARANCE

1 My dear, my dear, you never know when
   any beautiful young lady may not blossom
   into a Duchess!
   In Portland, *Men, Women, and Things* (1937)
   Ailesbury, Maria, Marchioness of (d. 1893)
   English aristocrat

2 Outside every fat man there was an even
   fatter man trying to close in.
   One Fat Englishman (1963) **Amis, Kingsley**
   (1922–1995) English writer, poet and critic

3 You look rather rash my dear your colors
   don't quite match your face.
   The Young Visiters (1919)

4 Ethel patted her hair and looked very
   sneery.
   The Young Visiters (1919) **Ashford, Daisy** (1881–
   1972) English child author

5 Take a close-up of a woman past sixty! You
   might as well use a picture of a relief map
   of Ireland!
   Attr. **Astor, Nancy, Viscountess** (1879–1964)
   US-born British Conservative politician and
   hostess. Refusing to pose for a close-up
   photograph

6 It's a sort of bloom on a woman. If you have it, you don't need to have anything else; and if you don't have it, it doesn't much matter what else you have.
What Every Woman Knows (1908) **Barrie, Sir J.M.** (1860–1937) Scottish dramatist and writer. On charm

7 O why was I born with a different face? Why was I not born like the rest of my race?
'Letter to Thomas Butts' (1803) **Blake, William** (1757–1827) English poet, engraver, painter and mystic

8 Hair is the first thing. And teeth the second. Hair and teeth. A man got those two things he's got it all.
The Godfather of Soul (1986) **Brown, James** (1933–) US singer

9 It is the common wonder of all men, how among so many millions of faces, there should be none alike.
Religio Medici (1643) **Browne, Sir Thomas** (1605–1682) English physician, author and antiquary

10 She just wore
Enough for modesty – no more.
'White Rose and Red' (1873) **Buchanan, Robert Williams** (1841–1901) British poet, writer and dramatist

11 Style, like sheer silk, too often hides eczema.
The Fall (1956) **Camus, Albert** (1913–1960) Algerian-born French writer

12 Ears like bombs and teeth like splinters: A blitz of a boy is Timothy Winters.
Union Street (1957), 'Timothy Winters' **Causley, Charles** (1917–2003) English poet and teacher

13 Sunburn is very becoming – but only when it is even – one must be careful not to look like a mixed grill.
Lido Beach **Coward, Sir Noël** (1899–1973) English dramatist, actor, producer and composer

14 A pretty girl who naked is
is worth a million statues.
Collected Poems, 133 (1938) **Cummings, E. E.** (1894–1962) US poet, noted for his typography, and painter

15 I have no dress except the one I wear every day. If you are going to be kind enough to give me one, please let it be practical and dark so that I can put it on afterwards to go to the laboratory.
Letter to a friend, (1894) **Curie, Marie** (1867–1934) Polish-born French physicist. Referring to a wedding dress

16 The most delightful advantage of being bald – one can hear snowflakes.
The Observer, (1976) **Daniels, R.G.** (1916–1993) English magistrate

17 He might have brought an action against his countenance for libel, and won heavy damages.
Oliver Twist (1838)

18 If you could see my legs when I take my boots off, you'd form some idea of what unrequited affection is.
Dombey and Son (1848)

19 It was not a bosom to repose upon, but it was a capital bosom to hang jewels upon.
Little Dorrit (1857) **Dickens, Charles** (1812–1870) English writer

20 Is it one of my well looking days, child? Am I in face to-day?
She Stoops to Conquer (1773) **Goldsmith, Oliver** (c.1728–1774) Irish dramatist, poet and writer

21 There are two reasons why I'm in show business, and I'm standing on both of them.
Attr. **Grable, Betty** (1916–1973) US film actress and wartime 'pin-up'

22 His smile explained everything; he carried it always with him as a leper carried his bell; it was a perpetual warning that he was not to be trusted.
England Made Me (1935) **Greene, Graham** (1904–1991) English writer and dramatist

23 Grass doesn't grow on a busy street.
Hague, William (1961–) British Conservative politician. Defending his premature baldness

24 Oh, she's a splendid girl. Wonderfully pneumatic.
Brave New World (1932) **Huxley, Aldous** (1894–1963) English writer, poet and critic

25 Barbara Cartland's eyes were twin miracles of mascara and looked like the corpses of two small crows that had crashed into a chalk cliff.
Attr.

26 Arnold Schwarzenegger's body is like a condom full of walnuts.
TV column **James, Clive** (1939–) Australian-born, UK-based TV critic and presenter

27 Being kissed – by a man who didn't wax his moustache was – like eating an egg without salt.
The Story of the Gadsbys (1888), 'Poor Dear Mamma' **Kipling, Rudyard** (1865–1936) Indian-born British poet and writer

28 How do you look when I'm sober?
In J. Yardley, *Ring* **Lardner, Ring** (1885–1933) US humorist and writer. Speaking to a flamboyantly dressed stranger who walked into the club where he was drinking

29 I have a face that would stop a sundial.
Attr. **Laughton, Charles** (1899–1962) English actor

30 The landlady of a boarding-house is a parallelogram – that is, an oblong angular figure, which cannot be described, but which is equal to anything.
Literary Lapses (1910) **Leacock, Stephen** (1869–1944) English-born Canadian humorist, writer and economist

31 Should you be a teenager blessed with uncommon good looks, document this state of affairs by the taking of photographs. It is the only way anyone will ever believe you in years to come.
Tips For Teens, Social Studies, (1981) **Lebowitz, Fran** (1950–) US satirist

32 The Lord prefers common-looking people. That is why he makes so many of them.
In James Morgan, *Our President* (1928) **Lincoln, Abraham** (1809–1865) US statesman and President

33 Even respectable girls delight in hearing their beauty praised; even the innocent are worried and pleased by their appearance.
Ars Amatoria, I, line 623 **Ovid** (43 BC–AD 18) Roman poet

34 Edith Evans looks like something that would eat its young.
Parker, Dorothy (1893–1967) US writer, poet, critic and wit

35 I'm not offended by dumb blonde jokes because I know I'm not dumb, and I know I'm not blonde.
TV interview **Parton, Dolly** (1946–) US country singer and actress

36 The imitator or maker of the images knows nothing of true existence; he knows appearances only.
The Republic, X **Plato** (c.429–347 BC) Greek philosopher

37 Certain people are born with natural false teeth.
Stop the Week, (BBC radio programme, 1977) **Robinson, Robert** (1927–) English broadcaster

38 All the American women had purple noses and gray lips and their faces were chalk white from terrible powder. I recognized that the United States could be my life's work.
In *Time,* (1965) **Rubinstein, Helena** (1872–1965) Polish-born US cosmetician and businesswoman. Recalling her arrival in America on a cold day in 1914

39 Things are entirely what they appear to be and behind them ... there is nothing.
La Nausée (1938) **Sartre, Jean-Paul** (1905–1980) French philosopher, writer, dramatist and critic

40 Cruel he looks, but calm and strong,
Like one who does, not suffers wrong.
Prometheus Unbound (1820) **Shelley, Percy Bysshe** (1792–1822) English poet, dramatist and essayist

41 There is no trusting appearances.
The School for Scandal (1777) **Sheridan, Richard Brinsley** (1751–1816) Irish dramatist, politician and orator

42 This Englishwoman is so refined
She has no bosom and no behind.
'This Englishwoman' (1937) **Smith, Stevie** (1902–1971) English poet and writer

43 A short neck denotes a good mind ... You see, the messages go quicker to the brain because they've shorter to go.

The Ballad of Peckham Rye (1960) **Spark, Muriel** (1918–2006) Scottish writer, poet and dramatist

44 But there are other things than dissipation that thicken the features. Tears, for example.
Black Lamb and Grey Falcon (1942) **West, Dame Rebecca** (1892–1983) English writer, critic and feminist

45 If anything is sacred the human body is sacred.
'I Sing the Body Electric' (1855) **Whitman, Walt** (1819–1892) US poet and writer

46 It is only shallow people who do not judge by appearances.
The Picture of Dorian Gray (1891)

47 Good looks are a snare that every sensible man would like to be caught in.
The Importance of Being Earnest, (1895) **Wilde, Oscar** (1854–1900) Irish poet, dramatist, writer, critic and wit

48 One can never be too thin or too rich.
Attr. **Windsor, Duchess of** (**Wallis Simpson**) (1896–1986) Wife of Duke of Windsor (formerly Edward VIII)
See also beauty; deception; eyes

ARCHITECTURE

1 Nothing can be said in his vindication, but that his abolishing Religious Houses and leaving them to the ruinous depredations of time has been of infinite use to the landscape of England in general.
The History of England (1791) **Austen, Jane** (1775–1817) English writer

2 Houses are built to live in and not to look on; therefore let use be preferred before uniformity, except where both may be had.
Essays (1625) **Bacon, Francis** (1561–1626) English philosopher, essayist, politician and courtier

3 I think that cars today are almost the exact equivalent of the great Gothic cathedrals ... the supreme creation of an era, conceived with passion by unknown artists.
Attr. **Barthes, Roland** (1915–1980) French writer, critic and teacher

4 'Where do architects and designers get their ideas?' The answer, of course, is mainly from other architects and designers, so is it mere casuistry to distinguish between tradition and plagiarism?
Commerce and Culture (1989)

5 Interior design is a travesty of the architectural process and a frightening condemnation of the credulity, helplessness and gullibilty of the most formidable consumers – the rich.
Taste (1991) **Bayley, Stephen** (1951–) English designer and critic

6 Sir Christopher Wren
Said, 'I am going to dine with some men.
If anybody calls
Say I am designing St Paul's.'
Biography for Beginners **Bentley, Edmund Clerihew** (1875–1956) English writer

7 Ghastly Good Taste, or A Depressing Story of the Rise and Fall of English Architecture.
Title of book, (1933)

8 Come, friendly bombs, and fall on Slough
It isn't fit for humans now,
There isn't grass to graze a cow
Swarm over, Death!
Continual Dew (1937) **Betjeman, Sir John** (1906–1984) English poet laureate

9 Let architects sing of aesthetics that bring
Rich clients in hordes to their knees;
Just give me a home, in a great circle dome
Where stresses and strains are at ease.
Time, (1964) **Buckminster Fuller, Richard** (1895–1983) US architect and engineer. Lines to the tune of 'Home on the Range'

10 A kind of vast municipal fire station ... like a monstrous carbuncle on the face of a much-loved and elegant friend.
Speech to the Royal Institute of British Architects, (1984) **Charles, Prince of Wales** (1948–) Son and heir of Elizabeth II and Prince Philip. On the proposed extension to the National Gallery

11 It didn't look like a biscuit box did it? I've always felt that it might.
Private Lives (1930) **Coward, Sir Noël** (1899–1973) English dramatist, actor, producer and composer. Of the Taj Mahal

12 It's beige! My color!
In J. Smith, *Elsie De Wolfe* **De Wolfe, Elsie** (1865–1950) US interior designer. On first sighting the Acropolis

13 Light (God's eldest daughter) is a principal beauty in building.
The Holy State and the Profane State (1642) **Fuller, Thomas** (1608–1661) English churchman and antiquary

14 I always feel sad when I look at new buildings which are constantly being built and on which millions are spent ... Has the age of architecture passed without hope of return?
Attr. **Gogol, Nicolai Vasilyevich** (1809–1852) Russian writer and soldier

15 'Fan vaulting' ... an architectural device which arouses enormous enthusiasm on account of the difficulties it has all too obviously involved but which from an aesthetic standpoint frequently belongs to the 'Last-supper-carved-on-a-peach-stone' class of masterpiece.
Pillar to Post (1938) **Lancaster, Sir Osbert** (1908–1986) English writer, cartoonist and stage designer

16 A house is a machine for living in.
Vers une architecture (1923) **Le Corbusier** (1887–1965) French architect

17 I prefer drawing to talking. Drawing is faster, and allows less room for lies.
Time, (1961) **Le Corbusier** (1887–1965) Swiss architect

18 Inner-city council estates make you believe the world was really built in six days.
Mad Cows (1996) **Lette, Kathy** (1959–) Australian novelist

19 What has happened to architecture since the second world war that the only passers-by who can contemplate it without pain are those equipped with a white stick and a dog?
The Times, (1983) **Levin, Bernard** (1928–) British author and journalist

20 A house is a machine for loving in.
In Ian McKay et al., *Living and Partly Living* **McGregor, Craig** (1933–) Australian writer

21 A chair is a very difficult object. A skyscraper is almost easier. That is why Chippendale is famous.
Time, (1957)

22 Less is more.
New York Herald Tribune, (1959)

23 Architecture starts when you carefully put two bricks together. There it begins.
New York Herald Tribune, (1959) **Mies van der Rohe, Ludwig** (1886–1969) German-born US architect and designer

24 If what is called development is allowed to multiply at the present rate, then by the end of the century Great Britain will consist of isolated oases of preserved monuments in a desert of wire, concrete roads, cosy plots and bungalows ... Upon this new Britain the Review bestows a name in the hope that it will stick – SUBTOPIA.
Architectural Review, (1955) **Nairn, Ian** (1930–1983) English writer on architecture and journalist

25 There it stands, like Santa Maria della Salute on the lagoon in Venice, a perfect symbol linking the city to the sea ... I believe it is a building of which all Australians may rightly be proud, perhaps the only true work of architecture on this continent.
On Second Thoughts (1971) **Pringle, John Martin Douglas** (1912–1999) Scottish-born Australian writer. On Sydney Opera House

26 They're all made out of ticky-tacky, And they all look just the same.
'Little Boxes' (song, 1962) **Reynolds, Malvina** (1900–1978) US singer-songwriter. Describing newly built houses south of San Francisco

27 Better the rudest work that tells a story or records a fact, than the richest without meaning. There should not be a single ornament put upon great civic buildings, without some intellectual intention.
The Seven Lamps of Architecture (1849)

28 When we build, let us think that we build for ever.
The Seven Lamps of Architecture (1849)

29 No person who is not a great sculptor or painter can be an architect. If he is not a sculptor or painter, he can only be a builder.
Lectures on Architecture and Painting (1854)

30 You know there are a great many odd styles of architecture about; you don't want to do anything ridiculous; you hear of me, among others, as a respectable architectural man-milliner; and you send for me, that I may tell you the leading fashion.
The Crown of Wild Olive (1866) **Ruskin, John** (1819–1900) English art critic, philosopher and reformer

31 Architecture is, as it were, petrified music.
Philosophy of Art (1803) **Schelling, Friedrich von** (1775–1854) German philosopher

32 In Architecture as in all other Operative Arts, the end must direct the Operation. The end is to build well. Well building hath three Conditions: Commodity, Firmness, and Delight.
Elements of Architecture (1624) **Wotton, Sir Henry** (1568–1639) English diplomat, traveller and poet

33 The physician can bury his mistakes, but the architect can only advise his client to plant vines.
New York Times Magazine, (1953) **Wright, Frank Lloyd** (1869–1959) US architect and writer
See also art; cities; cities: London

ARGUMENT

1 Our disputants put me in mind of the skuttle fish, that when he is unable to extricate himself, blackens all the water about him, till he becomes invisible.
The Spectator, 1712

2 Arguments out of a pretty mouth are unanswerable.
Women and Liberty **Addison, Joseph** (1672–1719) English essayist, poet, playwright and statesman

3 This is a rotten argument, but it should be good enough for their lordships on a hot summer afternoon.
Annotation in ministerial brief **Anonymous**

4 Thrice is he armed that hath his quarrel just,
But four times he who gets his blow in fust.
Josh Billings, his Sayings (1865) **Billings, Josh** (1818–1885) US writer, philosopher and lecturer

5 Reasons are not like garments, the worse for wearing.
Attr. (c.1599) **Essex, Robert Devereux, Earl of** (1566–1601) Elizabethan soldier and courtier. To Lord Willoughby

6 I have heard many arguments which influenced my opinion, but never one which influenced my vote.
Attr. **Fergusson, Sir James** (1832–1907) Scottish Conservative statesman

7 Myself when young did eagerly frequent Doctor and Saint, and heard great argument
About it and about: but evermore
Came out by the same Door as in I went.
The Rubáiyát of Omar Khayyám (1859) **Fitzgerald, Edward** (1809–1883) English poet, translator and letter writer

8 Those, who in quarrels interpose,
Must often wipe a bloody nose.
Fables (1727) **Gay, John** (1685–1732) English poet, dramatist and librettist

9 Disagreement may be the shortest cut between two minds.
Sand and Foam (1926) **Gibran, Kahlil** (1883–1931) Lebanese poet, mystic and painter

10 It's possible to disagree with someone about the ethics of non-violence without wanting to kick his face in.
Treats (1976), Scene iv **Hampton, Christopher** (1946–) English dramatist

11 Be calm in arguing; for fiercenesse makes Errour a fault, and truth discourtesie.
The Temple (1633) **Herbert, George** (1593–1633) English poet and priest

12 It takes in reality only one to make a quarrel. It is useless for the sheep to pass resolutions in favour of vegetarianism while the wolf remains of a different opinion.

Outspoken Essays (1919) **Inge, William Ralph** (1860–1954) English divine, writer and teacher

13 I dogmatize and am contradicted, and in this conflict of opinions and sentiments I find delight.
In Sir John Hawkins, *Life of Samuel Johnson* (1787)

14 Though we cannot out-vote them we will out-argue them.
In Boswell, *The Life of Samuel Johnson* (1791) **Johnson, Samuel** (1709–1784) English lexicographer, poet, critic, conversationalist and essayist

15 There is no good in arguing with the inevitable. The only argument available with an east wind is to put on your overcoat.
Democracy and Other Addresses (1887) **Lowell, James Russell** (1819–1891) US poet, editor, abolitionist and diplomat

16 'Yes, but not in the South', with slight adjustments, will do for any argument about any place, if not about any person.
Lifemanship (1950) **Potter, Stephen** (1900–1969) English writer, critic and lecturer. A blocking phrase for conversation

17 A married couple are well suited when both partners usually feel the need for a quarrel at the same time.
Le Mariage **Rostand, Jean** (1894–1977) French biologist

18 In a false quarrel there is no true valour.
Much Ado About Nothing, V.i **Shakespeare, William** (1564–1616) English dramatist, poet and actor

19 The quarrel is a very pretty quarrel as it stands – we should only spoil it by trying to explain it.
The Rivals (1775) **Sheridan, Richard Brinsley** (1751–1816) Irish dramatist, politician and orator

20 Heat is in proportion to the want of true knowledge.
Tristram Shandy (1759–1767) **Sterne, Laurence** (1713–1768) Irish-born English writer and clergyman

21 I love argument, I love debate. I don't expect anyone just to sit there and agree with me, that's not their job.
The Times, (1980) **Thatcher, Margaret** (1925–) English Conservative Prime Minister

22 Ah! Don't say that you agree with me. When people agree with me I always feel that I must be wrong.
Intentions (1891) **Wilde, Oscar** (1854–1900) Irish poet, dramatist, writer, critic and wit

23 We make out of the quarrel with others, rhetoric; but of the quarrel with ourselves, poetry.
'Anima Hominis' (1917) **Yeats, W.B.** (1865–1939) Irish poet, dramatist, editor, writer and senator
See also anger; revenge; right and wrong; spite

ART

1 Photography can never grow up if it imitates some other medium. It has to walk alone; it has to be itself.
Infinity, (1951) **Abbott, Berenice** (1898–1991) US photographer

2 Sometimes I do get to places just when God's ready to have somebody click the shutter.
American Way (1974)

3 There are always two people in every picture: the photographer and the viewer.
Playboy, (1983) **Adams, Ansel** (1902–1984) US photographer

4 Creativity is allowing yourself to make mistakes. Art is knowing which ones to keep.
The Dilbert Principle **Adams, Scott** (1957–) US cartoonist

5 The works of art, by being publicly exhibited and offered for sale, are becoming articles of trade, following as such the unreasoning laws of markets and fashion; and public and even private patronage is swayed by their tyrannical influence.
Speech to the Royal Academy, (May 1851) **Albert, Prince Consort** (1819–1861) German-born husband of Queen Victoria

6 To the accountants, a true work of art is an investment that hangs on the wall.
Sunday Telegraph, (1993) **Alexander, Hilary** (1818–1895)

7 We would prefer to see the Royal Opera House run by a philistine with the requisite financial acumen than by the succession of opera and ballet lovers who have brought a great and valuable institution to its knees.
Select Committe Report into the Royal Opera House, (1997) **Anonymous**

8 Life is very nice, but it has no shape. It is the purpose of art to give it shape.
The Rehearsal (1950) **Anouilh, Jean** (1910–1987) French dramatist and screenwriter

9 A photograph is a secret about a secret. The more it tells you the less you know.
In Patricia Bosworth, *Diane Arbus: a Biography* (1985) **Arbus, Diane** (1923–1971) US photographer

10 No one has ever written, painted, sculpted, modelled, built or invented except literally to get out of hell.
In Lewis Wolpert, *Malignant Sadness* (1999) **Artaud, Antonin** (1896–1948) French actor, dramatist and theorist

11 The job of the artist is always to deepen the mystery.
Sunday Telegraph, (1964) **Bacon, Francis (artist)** (1909–1992) Irish-born expressionist painter

12 The essence of all art is to have pleasure in giving pleasure.
Time, (1975) **Baryshnikov, Mikhail** (1948–) Latvian-born ballet dancer

13 The lower one's vitality, the more sensitive one is to great art.
'Enoch Soames' (1912) **Beerbohm, Sir Max** (1872–1956) English satirist, cartoonist, critic and essayist

14 It would follow that 'significant form' was form behind which we catch a sense of ultimate reality.
Art (1914) **Bell, Clive** (1881–1964) English art critic

15 I feel that art has something to do with the achievement of stillness in the midst of chaos. A stillness which characterizes prayer, too, and the eye of the storm. I think that art has something to do with an arrest of attention in the midst of distraction.
In Plimpton (ed.), *Writers at Work* (1967)

16 Art is one rescue from this chaotic acceleration. Metre in poetry, tempo in music, form and colour in painting. But we do feel that we are speeding earthward, crashing into our graves.
Ravelstein (2000) On the perception that time seems to speed up as we grow older **Bellow, Saul** (1915–2005) Canadian-born US Jewish writer

17 Art is mind and heart and touch as much and more than it is mere instrument, technique – without which however it cannot exist at all.
The Bernard Berenson Treasury (1962) **Berenson, Bernard** (1865–1959) Lithuanian-born US art critic

18 After years of playing with images of life and death, life has made me shy.
The Observer, (1997) **Bergman, Ingmar** (1918–) Swedish film director

19 Any great work of art … revives and readapts time and space, and the measure of its success is the extent to which it makes you an inhabitant of that world – the extent to which it invites you in and lets you breathe its strange, special air.
Vogue, (1958) **Bernstein, Leonard** (1918–1990) US composer and conductor

20 It is so much worse to be a mediocre artist than to be a mediocre post office clerk.
5000 Nights at the Opera (1972) **Bing, Rudolf** (1902–1997) Director of the New York Metropolitan Opera

21 When Sr Joshua Reynolds died
All Nature was degraded:
The King dropd a tear into the Queens Ear:
And all his Pictures Faded.
Annotations to Sir Joshua Reynolds' Works (c.1808) **Blake, William** (1757–1827) English poet, engraver, painter and mystic

22 It is usually better to permit a piece of trash than to suppress a work of art.
When Freedoms Collide (1988) **Borovoy, A. Alan** (1932–) Canadian writer and civil liberties advocate

23 Art is the only thing that can go on mattering once it has stopped hurting.
The Heat of the Day (1949) **Bowen, Elizabeth** (1899–1973) Irish writer

24 Any artist knows that after a good bout of work one is both too tired and too excited to be of any use to anyone. ... What one wants ... is for other people to occupy themselves with one's own moods and requirements; to lie on a sofa and listen to music, and to have things brought to one on a tray!
Drawn from Life (1941) **Bowen, Stella** (1893–1947) Australian writer

25 I know all about art, but I don't know what I like.
In Stephen Murray-Smith (ed.), *The Dictionary of Australian Quotations* **Brack, (Cecil) John** (1920–1999) Australian artist

26 Art is meant to disturb, science reassures.
Day and Night, Notebooks (1952) **Braque, Georges** (1882–1963) French painter

27 A hundred canvasses and seven sons
He left, and never got a likeness once.
'*Epitaph on a Portrait Painter*' **Bray, John Jefferson** (1912–1995) Australian lawyer and poet

28 Nothing grows well in the shade of a big tree.
Attr. **Brancusi, Constantin** (1876–1957) Romanian sculptor. Refusing Rodin's invitation to work in his studio

29 Art is not a better, but an alternative existence; it is not an attempt to escape reality but the opposite, an attempt to animate it. It is a spirit seeking flesh but finding words.
Less Than One (1986) **Brodsky, Joseph** (1940–1996) Russian poet, essayist, critic and exile

30 In any society, the artist has a responsibility. His effectiveness is certainly limited and a painter or writer cannot change the world. But they can keep an essential margin of non-conformity alive. Thanks to them, the powerful can never affirm that everyone agrees with their acts. That small difference is very important.
In Anthony Hill, *Contemporary Artists* (1977) **Buñuel, Luis** (1900–1983) Spanish film director

31 An art can only be learned in the workshop of those who are winning their bread by it.
Erewhon (1872) **Butler, Samuel** (1835–1902) English writer, painter, philosopher and scholar

32 Yes, but it takes courage for an adult to draw as badly as that.
The Independent, (1994) **Calman, Mel** (1931–1994) English cartoonist. In answer to the criticism of his cartoons that 'any child could do better'

33 Remember I'm an artist. And you know what that means in a court of law. Next worst to an actress.
The Horse's Mouth (1944) **Cary, Joyce** (1888–1957) English novelist

34 I say that good painters imitated nature; but that bad ones vomited it.
Exemplary Novels, (1613) **Cervantes, Miguel de** (1547–1616) Spanish writer and dramatist

35 The day is coming when a single carrot, freshly observed, will set off a revolution.
Attr. **Cezanne, Paul** (1839–1906) French painter

36 When I'm finishing a picture I hold some God-made object up to it – a rock, a flower, or a tree branch – as a final test. If the painting stands up beside a thing man cannot make, the painting is authentic. If there's a clash, it's bad art.
Saturday Evening Post (2 December 1962)

37 Great art picks up where nature ends.
Time, (1985)

38 Art is the unceasing effort to compete with the beauty of flowers – and never succeeding.

In Frank S. Pepper, *The Wit and Wisdom of the 20th Century* (1987) **Chagall, Marc** (1887–1985) Russian-born French painter

39 The artist may not be a judge of his characters, only a dispassionate witness.
Attr. **Chekhov, Anton** (1860–1904) Russian writer, dramatist and doctor

40 The artistic temperament is a disease that afflicts amateurs.
Heretics (1905)

41 Art, like morality, consists in drawing the line somewhere.
Orthodoxy (1908) **Chesterton, G.K.** (1874–1936) English writer, poet and critic

42 There is no more sombre enemy of good art than the pram in the hall.
Enemies of Promise (1938)

43 It is closing time in the gardens of the West and from now on an artist will be judged only by the resonance of his solitude or the quality of his despair.
Horizon (1949–1950) **Connolly, Cyril** (1903–1974) English literary editor, writer and critic

44 A work that aspires, however humbly, to the condition of art should carry its justification in every line.
The Nigger of the Narcissus (1897) **Conrad, Joseph** (1857–1924) Polish-born British writer, sailor and explorer

45 The sound of water escaping from mill-dams, etc, willows, old rotten planks, slimy posts, and brickwork, I love such things ... those scenes made me a painter and I am grateful.
Letter to John Fisher, (1821)

46 In Claude's landscape all is lovely – all amiable – all is amenity and repose; – the calm sunshine of the heart.
In C.R. Leslie, *Memoirs of the Life of John Constable* (1843)

47 The amiable but eccentric Blake ... said of a beautiful drawing of an avenue of fir trees ... 'Why, this is not drawing, but inspiration.' ... Constable replied, 'I never knew it before; I meant it for drawing'.
In C.R. Leslie, *Memoirs of the Life of John Constable* (1843)

48 As if painted in honey.
In *The Times Literary Supplement*, (1993) Description of Watteau's 'Plaisirs du Bal' **Constable, John** (1776–1837) English painter

49 Dinner with Robinson, a pupil of Schelling. His work on the aesthetics of that man Kant. Very ingenious ideas. Art for art's sake, without a purpose; every purpose distorts the true nature of art. But art achieves a purpose which it does not have.
Journal Intime, (1804) **Constant, Benjamin** (1767–1834) Swiss-born French writer and politician

50 Art is ruled uniquely by the imagination.
Esthetic **Croce, Benedetto** (1866–1952) Italian philosopher, historian and critic

51 Mr Lely, I desire you would use all your skill to paint my picture freely like me, and not flatter me at all; but remark all these roughnesses, pimples, warts, and everything as you see me, otherwise I will never pay a farthing for it.
In Horace Walpole, *Anecdotes of Painting in England* (1763) **Cromwell, Oliver** (1599–1658) English general, statesman and Puritan leader

52 At the age of six I wanted to be a cook. At seven I wanted to be Napoleon. And my ambition has been growing steadily ever since.
The Secret Life of Salvador Dali (1948)

53 It is good taste, and good taste alone, that possesses the power to sterilize and is always the first handicap to any creative functioning.
Diary of a Genius (1966)

54 I'm going to live forever. Geniuses don't die.
The Observer, (1986)

55 Have no fear of perfection – you'll never reach it.
Attr. **Dali, Salvador** (1904–1989) Spanish painter and writer

56 The finest collection of frames I ever saw.
Attr. **Davy, Sir Humphry** (1778–1829) English chemist and inventor. His opinion of the art galleries in Paris

57 Art is the most beautiful of all lies.
Monsieur Croche, antidilettante **Debussy, Claude** (1862–1918) French composer and critic

58 Art is vice. You don't marry it legitimately, you rape it.
In Paul Lafond, *Degas* (1918)

59 Everybody has talent at twenty-five. The difficult thing is to have it at fifty.
In Gammell, *The Shop-Talk of Edgar Degas* (1961) **Degas, Edgar** (1834–1917) French painter and sculptor

60 Art is for everyone – paint, like a piece of music, is the most international thing I know.
Attr. **Demarco, Richard** (1930–) Scottish exhibition and theatre director, art patron and teacher

61 I don't believe in art. I believe in artists.
The World of Marcel Duchamp (1966) **Duchamp, Marcel** (1887–1968) French-born US artist

62 The only way of expressing emotion in the form of art is by finding an 'objective correlative'; in other words, a set of objects, a situation, a chain of events which shall be the formula of that particular emotion; such that when the external facts, which must terminate in sensory experience, are given, the emotion is immediately evoked.
'Hamlet' (1919)

63 No poet, no artist of any sort, has his complete meaning alone. His significance, his appreciation is the appreciation of his relation to the dead poets and artists.
'Tradition and the Individual Talent' (1919)

64 No artist produces great art by a deliberate attempt to express his own personality.
'Four Elizabethan Dramatists' (1924) **Eliot, T.S.** (1888–1965) US-born British poet, verse dramatist and critic

65 Every artist writes his own autobiography.
The New Spirit (1890) **Ellis, Havelock** (1859–1939) English sexologist and essayist

66 Art is a jealous mistress, and, if a man have a genius for painting, poetry, music, architecture, or philosophy, he makes a bad husband and an ill provider.
Conduct of Life (1860)

67 Artists must be sacrificed to their art. Like bees, they must put their lives into the sting they give.
Letters and Social Aims (1875) **Emerson, Ralph Waldo** (1803–1882) US poet, essayist, transcendentalist and teacher

68 Art is all the things that politics isn't: it's passionate, ambiguous, complex, mysterious and thrilling. It's our means of redemption, it's the image of our humanity.
The Observer, (1996) Commenting on the Government's decision to freeze spending on the arts

69 I would like to see the good in art made popular and the popular made good.
BBC radio interview, (1998) **Eyre, Richard** (1943–) English film, theatre and television director

70 I encountered the mama of dada again.
Appreciations (1955) **Fadiman, Clifton** (1904–1999) US writer, editor and broadcaster. Of Gertrude Stein

71 All art is autobiographical; the pearl is the oyster's autobiography.
Atlantic, (1965) **Fellini, Federico** (1920–1993) Italian film director

72 It hath been thought a vast commendation of a painter to say his figures seem to breathe; but surely it is much greater and nobler applause, that they appear to think.
Joseph Andrews (1742) **Fielding, Henry** (1707–1754) English writer, dramatist and journalist

73 The artist must be in his work as God is in creation, invisible and all-powerful; his presence should be felt everywhere, but he should never be seen.
Letter to Mlle Leroyer de Chantepie, (1857) **Flaubert, Gustave** (1821–1880) French writer

74 Great artists are people who find the way to be themselves in their art. Any sort of pretension induces mediocrity in art and life alike.
Margot Fonteyn: Autobiography (1976) **Fonteyn, Margot** (1919–1991) English dancer

75 Works of art, in my opinion, are the only
objects in the material universe to possess
internal order, and that is why, though I
don't believe that only art matters, I do
believe in Art for Art's sake.
Two Cheers for Democracy (1951)

76 To make us feel small in the right way is a
function of art. Men can only make us feel
small in the wrong way.
Attr. **Forster, E.M.** (1879–1970) English writer,
essayist and literary critic

77 The hell of it seems to be, when an artist
starts saving the world, he starts losing
himself.
Extracts from a Sporadic Diary **Friel, Brian**
(1929–) Irish dramatist and writer

78 Mr Fry ... brought out a screen upon which
there was a picture of a circus. The
interviewer was puzzled by the long waists,
bulging necks and short legs of the figures.
'But how much wit there is in those
figures,' said Mr Fry. 'Art is significant
deformity.'
In Virginia Woolf, *Roger Fry* (1940) **Fry, Roger**
(1866–1934) English art critic, philosopher and
painter

79 Art is either a plagiarist or a revolutionist.
In Huneker, *Pathos of Distance* (1913)

80 Civilization is paralysis.
In Cournos, *Modern Plutarch* (1928) **Gauguin,
Paul** (1848–1903) French Post-Impressionist
painter

81 I hate all Boets and Bainters.
In Campbell, *Lives of the Chief Justices* (1849)
George I (1660–1727) King of Great Britain
and Ireland

82 If it is a joy to enjoy what is good, then it is
a greater one to feel what is better, and in
art only the best is good enough. Naples,
3rd March, 1787.
Italian Journey (1816–17)

83 Incidentally, however, ultimately the
greatest art is in limiting and isolating
oneself.
Gespräche mit Eckermann, (1825)

84 Classicism I call health, and romanticism
disease.

Gespräche mit Eckermann, (1829) **Goethe** (1749–
1832) German poet, writer, dramatist and
scientist

85 I rarely draw what I see. I draw what I feel
in my body.
Attr. **Hepworth, Dame Barbara** (1903–1975)
English sculptor

86 As my poor father used to say
In 1863,
Once people start on all this Art
Good-bye, moralitee!
And what my father used to say
Is good enough for me.
'*Lines for a Worthy Person*' (1930)

87 A highbrow is the kind of person who looks
at a sausage and thinks of Picasso.
Attr. **Herbert, Sir A.P.** (1890–1971) English
humorist, writer, dramatist and politician

88 A coo and a cauf
Cut in hauf.
The Cowdenbeath Man **Hershaw, William**
(1957–) Scottish poet. On Damien Hirst's
entry for the Turner Prize for contemporary
art

89 Why don't they draw, draw and draw?
Their one idea is to cultivate the emotional
sense, under the plea that they are
expressing their personality.
In Colin Thiele, *Heysen of Hahndorf* **Heysen,
Sir Hans William** (1877–1968) German-born
Australian artist

90 I sometimes feel that I have nothing to say
and I want to communicate this.
The Observer Review, (1995) On winning the
Turner Prize

91 It's amazing what you can do with an E in
A-level art, twisted imagination and a
chainsaw.
Attr. **Hirst, Damien** (1965–) British artist

92 Once you can manipulate pictures on a
computer you can't believe them any more.
There will be no more Cartier-Bressons.
Interview, *The Observer*, May 1999 **Hockney,
David** (1937–) English artist. On the death of
photography

93 In the upper and the lower churches of St Francis, Giotto and Cimabue showed that art had once worshipped something other than itself.
Those Barren Leaves (1925) **Huxley, Aldous** (1894–1963) English writer, poet and critic

94 Drawing is the true test of art.
Pensées d'Ingres (1922) **Ingres, J.A.D.** (1780–1867) French painter

95 It is art that makes life, makes interest, makes importance, for our consideration and application of these things, and I know of no substitute whatever for the force and beauty of its process.
Letter to H.G. Wells, (1915) **James, Henry** (1843–1916) US-born British writer, critic and letter writer

96 The artist, like the God of creation, remains within or behind or beyond or above his handiwork, invisible, refined out of existence, indifferent, paring his fingernails.
A Portrait of the Artist as a Young Man (1916) **Joyce, James** (1882–1941) Irish writer

97 The excellence of every art is its intensity, capable of making all disagreeables evaporate, from their being in close relationship with Beauty and Truth.
Letter to George and Tom Keats, 21 December 1817 **Keats, John** (1795–1821) English poet

98 In free society art is not a weapon ... Artists are not engineers of the soul.
Speech, (1963) **Kennedy, John F.** (1917–1963) US Democrat President

99 Till the Devil whispered behind the leaves, 'It's pretty, but is it Art?' ...
We know that the tail must wag the dog, for the horse is drawn by the cart;
But the Devil whoops, as he whooped of old: 'It's clever, but is it Art?'
'The Conundrum of the Workshops' (1890) **Kipling, Rudyard** (1865–1936) Indian-born British poet and writer

100 Art does not reproduce what is visible; it makes things visible.
'Creative Credo' (1920)

101 An active line going for a stroll, freely, aimlessly, a walk for its own sake. The agent is a point which moves around.
Pedagogical Sketchbook, (1925) **Klee, Paul** (1879–1940) Swiss painter, engraver and teacher

102 The only person who is an artist is the one that can make a puzzle out of the solution.
By Night (1919) **Kraus, Karl** (1874–1936) Austrian scientist, critic and poet

103 If people only knew as much about painting as I do, they would never buy my pictures.
In Campbell Lennie, *Landseer the Victorian Paragon* **Landseer, Sir Edwin Henry** (1802–1873) English painter, engraver and sculptor

104 Never trust the artist. Trust the tale. The proper function of a critic is to save the tale from the artist who created it.
Studies in Classic American Literature (1923) **Lawrence, D.H.** (1885–1930) English writer, poet and critic

105 I do not know whether he draws a line himself. But I assume that his is the direction ... It makes Disney the most significant figure in graphic art since Leonardo.
In R. Schickel, *Walt Disney* **Low, Sir David** (1891–1963) New Zealand-born British political cartoonist

106 For painters, poets and builders have very high flights, but they must be kept down.
Letter to the Duchess of Bedford, (1734) **Marlborough, Sarah, First Duchess of** (1660–1744) Wife of John Churchill, First Duke of Marlborough

107 The artist as a citizen can be a democrat, just as well and as badly as everybody else. The artist as an artist may not be a democrat.
Interview in *Der Spiegel*, (1994) **Maron, Monika** (1941–) German writer

108 There is nothing more difficult for a truly creative painter than to paint a rose, because before he can do so he has first to forget all the roses that were ever painted.
Attr. **Matisse, Henri** (1869–1954) French artist and author

109 Art is not a mirror to reflect the world, but a hammer with which to shape it.
The Guardian, (1974) **Mayakovsky, Vladimir** (1893–1930) Russian poet, dramatist and artist

110 One day the inspiration comes, and then it goes. It's all stomach.
Attr. **Millais, Sir John Everett** (1829–1896) English painter

111 Art must be parochial in the beginning to be cosmopolitan in the end.
Hail and Farewell: Ave (1911) **Moore, George** (1852–1933) Irish writer, dramatist and critic

112 If I didn't start painting, I would have raised chickens.
In Aotto Kallir (ed.), *Grandma Moses, My Life's History*

113 I don't advise any one to take it up as a business proposition, unless they really have talent, and are crippled so as to deprive them of physical labor.
Attr. Of painting **Moses, Grandma** (1860–1961) US painter

114 The artist has a special task and duty – the task of reminding men of their humanity and the promise of their creativity.
Attr. **Mumford, Lewis** (1895–1990) US sociologist and writer

115 All art deals with the absurd and aims at the simple. Good art speaks truth, indeed is truth, perhaps the only truth.
The Black Prince (1989) **Murdoch, Iris** (1919–1999) Irish-born British writer, philosopher and dramatist

116 Great artists have no homeland.
Lorenzaccio (1834) **Musset, Alfred de** (1810–1857) French dramatist and poet

117 As an artist, one has no home in Europe except Paris.
Ecco Homo (1888) **Nietzsche, Friedrich Wilhelm** (1844–1900) German philosopher, critic and poet

118 There's no environment where you can do wacky things that end up being creative ... If you're different, you're a minus ... That nips originality in the bud.

In *Created in Japan* **Nishimura, Yoshifumi** Japanese chemist. In conversation with Stephen Kreider Yoder, former Tokyo correspondent of the *Wall Street Journal*

119 A successful artist would have no trouble being a successful member of the Mafia.
Good Weekend, (1985) **Nolan, Sir Sidney Robert** (1917–1992) Australian artist

120 When you take a flower in your hand and really look at it, it's your world for the moment.
New York Post, (1946)

121 I hate flowers – I paint them because they're cheaper than models and they don't move.
New York Herald Tribune, (1954) **O'Keeffe, Georgia** (1887–1986) US artist

122 I mix them with my brains, sir.
In Samuel Smiles, *Self-Help* (1859) **Opie, John** (1761–1807) Asked how he mixed his colours

123 Art is incapable of bearing the burden of our lives. When it tries, it fails, losing its essential grace.
The Theme of our Time, (1923) **Ortega y Gasset, José** (1883–1955)

124 A picture has been said to be something between a thing and a thought.
In Arthur Symons, *Life of Blake* **Palmer, Samuel** (1805–1881) English landscape painter

125 Modernism is the acceptance of the concrete landscape and the destruction of the human soul.
Junk and the new Arts and Crafts Movement **Paolozzi, Eduardo** (1924–2005) Scottish sculptor

126 The love of art for art's sake.
Studies in the History of the Renaissance (1873)

127 All art constantly aspires towards the condition of music.
Studies in the History of the Renaissance (1873) **Pater, Walter** (1839–1894) English critic, writer and lecturer

128 Painting is a blind man's profession. He paints not what he sees, but what he feels, what he tells himself about what he has seen.
In Jean Cocteau, *Journals* (1929), 'Childhood'

129 It's better like that, if you want to kill a picture all you have to do is to hang it beautifully on a nail and soon you will see nothing of it but the frame. When it's out of place you see it better.
In Roland Penrose, *Picasso: His Life and Work* (1958) Explaining why a Renoir in his apartment was hung crooked

130 When I was their age, I could draw like Raphael, but it took me a lifetime to learn to draw like them.
In Penrose, *Picasso: His Life and Work* (1958) Remark made at an exhibition of children's drawings

131 There's no such thing as a bad Picasso, but some are less good than others.
In A. Whitman, *Come to Judgement* **Picasso, Pablo** (1881–1973) Spanish painter, sculptor and graphic artist

132 Joy is a well-made object.
Maclean's, (1989) **Reid, Bill** (1920–1998) Canadian sculptor and jeweller

133 They were madmen; but they had in them that little flame which does not go out.
In Jean Renoir, *Renoir, My Father* (1962) Of the men of the French Commune

134 The pain passes, but the beauty remains.
Attr. On why he still painted although he had arthritis of his hands

135 I just keep painting till I feel like pinching. Then I know it's right.
Attr. Of the lifelike flesh tones of his nudes **Renoir, Pierre Auguste** (1841–1919) French painter

136 A mere copier of nature can never produce anything great.
Discourses on Art (1770)

137 Taste does not come by chance: it is a long and laborious task to acquire it.
In Northcote, *Life of Sir Joshua Reynolds* (1818) **Reynolds, Sir Joshua** (1723–1792) English portrait painter

138 I've never been in there [the Louvre] ... but there are only three things to see, and I've seen colour reproductions of all of them.
In Ernest Hemingway, *A Farewell to Arms* (1929) **Ross, Harold W.** (1892–1951) US editor

139 Burning of people and (what was more valuable) works of art.
In H.R. Trevor-Roper, *Historical Essays* **Rowse, A.L.** (1903–1997) English historian, writer and poet

140 People don't want art, they want football.
Scala, (1992) **Rückriem, Ulrich** (1938–) German sculptor

141 I believe the right question to ask, respecting all ornament, is simply this: Was it done with enjoyment – was the carver happy while he was about it?
The Seven Lamps of Architecture (1849)

142 The purest and most thoughtful minds are those which love colour the most.
The Stones of Venice (1853)

143 Nobody cares much at heart about Titian; only there is a strange undercurrent of everlasting murmur about his name, which means the deep consent of all great men that he is greater than they.
The Two Paths (1859)

144 Fine art is that in which the hand, the head, and the heart of man go together.
The Two Paths (1859)

145 I have seen, and heard, much of Cockney impudence before now; but never expected to hear a coxcomb ask two hundred guineas for flinging a pot of paint in the public's face.
Fors Clavigera, Letter 79, (1877) Of one of Whistler's works **Ruskin, John** (1819–1900) English art critic, philosopher and reformer

146 Ninety per cent of the art I buy will probably be worthless in ten years' time.
The Observer, (1997) **Saatchi, Charles** (1943–) Co-founder of Saatchi & Saatchi advertising agency

147 Art is not a study of positive reality; it is a search for ideal truth.
The Devil's Pond (1846)

148 Art is a demonstration of which nature is the proof.
François le Champi **Sand, George** (1804–1876) French writer and dramatist

149 Nothing is really so poor and melancholy as art that is interested in itself and not in its subject.
The Life of Reason (1906) **Santayana, George** (1863–1952) Spanish-born US philosopher and writer

150 Every time I paint a portrait I lose a friend.
In Bentley and Esar, *Treasury of Humorous Quotations* (1951) **Sargent, John Singer** (1856–1925) US painter

151 Life is serious, art is serene.
Wallenstein I (1798–1801), Prologue **Schiller, Johann Christoph Friedrich** (1759–1805) German writer, dramatist, poet and historian

152 An amateur is an artist who supports himself with outside jobs which enable him to paint. A professional is someone whose wife works to enable him to paint.
Attr. **Shahn, Ben** (1898–1969) Lithuanian-born US painter and muralist. Outlining the difference between professional and amateur painters

153 The true artist will let his wife starve, his children go barefoot, his mother drudge for his living at seventy, sooner than work at anything but his art.
Man and Superman (1903)

154 I believe in Michael Angelo, Velasquez, and Rembrandt; in the might of design, the mystery of colour, the redemption of all things by Beauty everlasting, and the message of Art that has made these hands blessed. Amen.
The Doctor's Dilemma (1908) **Shaw, George Bernard** (1856–1950) Irish socialist, writer, dramatist and critic

155 How often my soul visits the National Gallery, and how seldom I go there myself!
Afterthoughts (1931) **Smith, Logan Pearsall** (1865–1946) US-born British epigrammatist, critic and writer

156 Interpretation is the revenge of the intellect upon art.
Evergreen Review, (1964)

157 A photograph is not only an image (as a painting is an image), an interpretation of the real; it is also a trace, something directly stencilled off the real, like a footprint or a death mask.
New York Review of Books, (1977) **Sontag, Susan** (1933–) US critic and writer

158 The professional art world is becoming a conspiracy against the public.
The Daily Mail, (1996) **Spalding, Julian** (1948–) English art administrator

159 Finality is death. Perfection is finality. Nothing is perfect. There are lumps in it.
The Crock of Gold (1912) **Stephens, James** (1882–1950) Irish poet and writer

160 A little amateur painting in water-colours shows the innocent and quiet mind.
Virginibus Puerisque (1881) **Stevenson, Robert Louis** (1850–1894) Scottish writer, poet and essayist

161 Skill without imagination is craftsmanship and gives us many useful objects such as wickerwork picnic baskets. Imagination without skill gives us modern art.
Artist Descending a Staircase (1973)

162 What is an artist? For every thousand people there's nine hundred doing the work, ninety doing well, nine doing good, and one lucky bastard who's the artist.
Travesties (1975)

163 I doubt that art needed Ruskin any more than a moving train needs one of its passengers to shove it.
The Times Literary Supplement, (1977) **Stoppard, Tom** (1937–) British dramatist

164 Grant me paradise in this world; I'm not so sure I'll reach it in the next.
Attr. **Tintoretto** (1518–1594) Venetian painter. Arguing that he be allowed to paint the Paradiso at the Doge's palace in Venice, despite his advanced age

165 Art is not a handicraft, it is a transmission of feeling which the artist has experienced.
What is Art? (1898)

166 Art is a human activity which has as its purpose the transmission to others of the highest and best feelings to which men have risen.

What is Art? (1898) **Tolstoy, Leo** (1828–1910) Russian writer, essayist, philosopher and moralist

167 I've lost one of my children this week.
In E. Chubb, *Sketches of Great Painters* His customary remark following the sale of one of his paintings

168 My business is to paint not what I know, but what I see.
In E. Chubb, *Sketches of Great Painters* Responding to a criticism of the fact that he had painted no portholes on the ships in a view of Plymouth **Turner, Joseph Mallord William** (1775–1851) English painter

169 If Botticelli were alive today he'd be working for Vogue.
The Observer, (1962) **Ustinov, Sir Peter** (1921–2004) English actor, director, dramatist, writer and raconteur

170 He will lie even when it is inconvenient, the sign of the true artist.
Two Sisters (1970)

171 As much of an art form as interior decorating.
Attr. Of photography

172 The only genius with an IQ of 60.
Attr. On Andy Warhol **Vidal, Gore** (1925–) US writer, critic and poet

173 An artist is someone who produces things that people don't need to have but that he – for some reason – thinks it would be a good idea to give them.
From A to B and Back Again (1975) **Warhol, Andy** (c.1926–1987) US painter, graphic designer and filmmaker

174 Any authentic work of art must start an argument between the artist and his audience.
The Court and the Castle (1958) **West, Dame Rebecca** (1892–1983) English writer, critic and feminist

175 Another unsettling element in modern art is that common symptom of immaturity, the dread of doing what has been done before.
The Writing of Fiction (1925) **Wharton, Edith** (1862–1937) US writer

176 Listen! There never was an artistic period. There never was an Art-loving nation.
Mr Whistler's 'Ten O'Clock' (1885)

177 Yes, madam, Nature is creeping up.
In Seitz, *Whistler Stories* (1913) To a lady who told him a landscape reminded her of his work

178 I cannot tell you that, madam. Heaven has granted me no offspring.
In Seitz, *Whistler Stories* (1913) Replying to a lady inquiring whether he thought genius hereditary

179 No, I ask it for the knowledge of a lifetime.
In Seitz, *Whistler Stories* (1913) Replying to the question 'For two days' labour, you ask two hundred guineas?'

180 'Why,' answered Whistler in dulcet tones, 'why drag in Velasquez?'.
In Seitz, *Whistler Stories* (1913) To a lady who said the two greatest painters were himself and Velasquez **Whistler, James McNeill** (1834–1903) US painter, etcher and pamphleteer

181 Art is the imposing of a pattern on experience, and our aesthetic enjoyment is recognition of the pattern.
Dialogues (1954) **Whitehead, A.N.** (1861–1947) English mathematician and philosopher

182 Art is the most intense mode of individualism that the world has known.
The Nineteenth Century, (1889)

183 The final revelation is that Lying, the telling of beautiful untrue things, is the proper aim of Art.
'The Decay of Lying' (1889)

184 All art is quite useless.
The Fortnightly Review, 1891, 'The Soul of Man under Socialism' **Wilde, Oscar** (1854–1900) Irish poet, dramatist, writer, critic and wit

185 Art is like soup. There will be some vegetables you don't like but as long as you get some soup down you it doesn't matter.
The Daily Mail, (1996) On modern art

186 Public art is art that the public can't avoid.
Attr. **Wyllie, George** (1921–) Scottish artist

187 A tremendous part in strengthening
friendship between our peoples must be
played by art, whose eternal role is the
uniting of human hearts in the name of
goodness and justice.
Yevtushenko Poems (1966) **Yevtushenko,
Yevgeny** (1933–) Russian poet
See also architecture; criticism; nature; theatre
and dance

AUSTRALIA

1 And while we don't exactly hate New
Zealanders, we're not exactly fond of each
other. While they regard us as vulgar
yobboes, almost Yank-like, we think of
them as second-hand, recycled Poms.
Age, (1977) **Adams, Phillip** (1939–) On attitudes
to New Zealanders

2 The Australian native can withstand all the
reverses of nature, fiendish droughts and
sweeping floods, horrors of thirst and
enforced starvation – but he cannot
withstand civilisation.
The Passing of the Aborigines … (1938) **Bates,
Daisy May** (1863–1951) Irish-born journalist,
anthropologist and reformer

3 We had intended you to be
The next Prime Minister but three:
The stocks were sold; the Press was
squared;
The Middle Class was quite prepared.
But as it is! –
My language fails!
Go out and govern New South Wales!
Cautionary Tales (1907), 'Lord Lundy' **Belloc,
Hilaire** (1870–1953) English writer of verse,
essayist and critic; Liberal MP

4 The people of Melbourne
Are frightfully well-born.
'Observation Sociologique' **Beven, Rodney
Allan** (1916–1982)

5 The physical mastering of Australia was
swift and often dramatic, but the
emotional conquest was slow.
Title of book, (1966) **Blainey, Geoffrey
Norman** (1930–) Australian writer

6 The Australian town-dweller spent a
century in the acquisition of his toy: an
emasculated garden, a five-roomed cottage
of his very own, different from its
neighbours by a minor contortion of
window or porch – its difference significant
to no-one but himself.
Australia's Home (1952)

7 The ugliness I mean is skin deep. If the
visitor to Australia fails to notice it
immediately, fails to respond to the surfeit
of colour, the love of advertisements, the
dreadful language, the ladylike
euphemisms outside public lavatory doors,
the technical competence, but the almost
uncanny misjudgement in floral
arrangements, or if he thinks that things of
this sort are too trivial to dwell on, then he
is unlikely to enjoy modern Australia.
The Australian Ugliness (1960) **Boyd, Robin
Gerard Penleigh** (1919–1971) Australian
architect

8 Going to Australia was like sunshine and
fresh invigorating air.
In G.M. Caroe, *William Henry Bragg* (1978)
Bragg, William Henry (1862–1942) English
scientist and academic

9 I've always wanted to see a ghost town.
You couldn't even get a parachute to open
here after 10 p.m.
Melbourne Sun, (1965) **Bygraves, Max** (1922–)
English singer and entertainer

10 In Australia alone is to be found the
Grotesque, the Weird, the strange
scribblings of nature learning how to write.
Preface to A.L. Gordon, *Sea Spray and Smoke
Drift* (1867) **Clarke, Marcus** (1846–1881)
English-born Australian writer

11 If the Spirit of the Bush walked down
Martin Place it would be raped before it
got ten feet.
Remark at the Adelaide Arts Festival, March
1964 **Cusack, Dymphna** (1902–1981)

12 It is all very well to call him a white-livered
cur, a bully, a coward, a liar and a psychotic
murderer but to actually name him as a
queer is going too far.

Knockers (1972) **Dunstan, Keith** (1925–)
Australian journalist. On the opinion that
Ned Kelly and his gang were homosexuals,
expressed by Sidney Baker in *The Australian
Language*, 1966

13 But for my everlasting good fortune I was
flung into the wide sea of Australian bush
alone, to sink or to swim.
My Life (1940) **Ellis, Havelock** (1859–1939)
English sexologist and essayist

14 Australia is the only country in the world
where the peasantry make the laws.
The Time Is Not Yet Ripe (1912) **Esson, Louis**
(1879–1943) Scots-born Australian dramatist

15 Ah, yes, but they will make fine ancestors.
Attr. **Forro, (Rev. Fr) Francis Stephen** (1914–
1974) Response to a journalist's comment on
the scruffiness of Hungarian refugees
arriving at Mascot aerodrome, Australia, in
1956

16 In Canberra, even the mistakes are planned
by the National Capital Development
Commission.
Life in Canberra **Fitzgerald, Alan John** (1935–)
Australian writer and Director of Planning

17 The Australians were wise to choose such a
large country, for of all the people in the
world they clearly require the most space.
Annals of an Abiding Liberal (1980) **Galbraith,
J.K.** (1908–2006) Canadian-born US
economist, diplomat and writer

18 I recall at least two Australian ambassadors
who complained to me in the past about
the constraints which the inherited British
style placed on Australian diplomacy, but,
when their time came to resist the
invitation of knighthood, their resolve
buckled under the terrible strain.
Gods and Politicians (1982) **Grant, Bruce
Alexander** (1925–) Australian writer, critic and
civil servant

19 Lyndon B. Johnson always thought that
Australia was the next large rectangular
State beyond El Paso, and treated it
accordingly.
Interview in film *Allies* **Green, Marshall**
(1916–)

20 The little exclusive circles, which in
Melbourne and Sydney had politely
imitated English gentility, looked askance
at the lucky upstarts – and intermarried
with them. In the second half of the
nineteenth century Australia became
familiar with a new vulgarity and a new
vigour.
Australia (1930) **Hancock, Sir William Keith**
(1898–1988) Australian historian

21 In an atmosphere of reciprocal banter or
rubbishing, Australians can express mutual
affection without running into risk of
indecently exposing states of feeling.
In Keith Dunstan, *Knockers* (1972)

22 The Australian world is peopled with good
blokes and bastards, but not heroes.
In Coleman (ed.), *Australian Civilization*
Harris, Max (1921–1995) Australian critic, poet
and publisher

23 We are still prisoners of our colonial
history.
The Resolution of Conflict (1979) **Hawke, Bob**
(1929–) Australian Premier

24 Gough Whitlam had many geniuses and
one of them was that when he decided we
were going to embark on one of the great
national disasters, it was done with flair.
Sydney Morning Herald, (1988) **Hayden, Bill**
(1933–) Australian statesman

25 I don't despair about the cultural scene in
Australia because there isn't one here to
despair about.
In Dunstan, *Knockers* (1972) **Helpman, Sir
Robert Murray** (1909–1986) Australian
choreographer and director

26 There's no place like home, Mum. Have
me head read if ever I leave this gawd's
own lovely land again. You dunno what a
lovely land it is till you've seen them other
crowded, foggy, frozen, furrin holes.
Capricornia (1938) On returning from the war

27 Until we give back to the Blackman just a
bit of the land that was his and give it back
without provisos, without strings to snatch
it back, without anything but complete
generosity of spirit in concession for the
evil we have done him – until we do that,
we shall remain what we have always been
so far, a people without integrity; not a
nation but a community of thieves.

Poor Fellow My Country (1975) On the plight of the Aborigines **Herbert, Xavier** (1901–1984) Australian writer, poet and social critic

28 We're a nation of punters and party-goers.
Bicentenary television programme, '*Australia Live*', 1988 **Hogan, Paul** (1939–) Australian actor

29 And her five cities, like teeming sores,
Each drains her: a vast parasite robber-state
Where second-hand Europeans pullulate
Timidly on the edge of alien shores.
'Australia' (1939) **Hope, Alec (Derwent)** (1907–) Australian poet and critic

30 Australia is a lucky country run mainly by second-rate people who share its luck.
The Lucky Country: Australia in the Sixties (1964) **Horne, Donald Richmond** (1921–) Australian novelist

31 I think one of the highest compliments ever paid to Australia was the imminent Japanese invasion. To think the Japanese would [think] of coming to Australia [to] live! They did change their mind, with a little persuasion.
Men in Vogue, (1976)

32 The only people really keeping the spirit of irony alive in Australia are taxi-drivers and homosexuals.
Australian Women's Weekly, (1983) **Humphries, Barry** (1934–) Australian entertainer

33 *On the Beach* is a story about the end of the world, and Melbourne sure is the right place to film it.
Attr. **Jillett, Neil** (1933–) A phrase wrongly attributed to Ava Gardner, who starred in the film *On the Beach*, adapted from Nevil Shute's novel of that name (1957)

34 And all lying mysteriously within the Australian underdark, that peculiar, lost weary aloofness of Australia. There was the vast town of Sydney. And it didn't seem to be real, it seemed to be sprinkled on the surface of a darkness into which it never penetrated.
Kangaroo (1923) **Lawrence, D.H.** (1885–1930) English writer, poet and critic

35 And the sun sank on the grand Australian bush – the nurse and tutor of eccentric minds, the home of the weird, and of much that is different from things in other lands.
'Rats' (1893) **Lawson, Henry** (1867–1922) Australian writer and poet

36 What sort of peculiar capitalist country is this, in which the workers' representatives predominate in the Upper House and, till recently, did so in the Lower House as well, and yet the capitalist system is in no danger?
Collected Works (1963) **Lenin, V.I.** (1870–1924) Russian revolutionary, Marxist theoretician and first leader of the USSR. On Australia

37 Until we partially abolish poverty at home we have no right to burden ourselves with millions of paupers from abroad. What we have, we hold. AUSTRALIA FOR THE AUSTRALIANS.
The Pleasant Career of a Spendthrift in London (1929) **Meudell, George Dick** (1860–1936) Australian writer, traveller and social commentator

38 The Australian's loving relationship with his car has become a commonplace: he fondles each nut and bolt in interminable conversations in the pub; strips it, lays it on the lawn, and greases its nipples while his wife wonders whether he will ever better his indoor average of one-a-month.
The U-Jack Society (1972) **Moffitt, Ian Lawson** (1929–) Australian journalist and novelist

39 Much of the hostility to Australia ... shown by English people above a certain class can be traced to the fact that we are, to a large extent, the poor who got away.
Sydney Morning Herald, (1974) **Murray, Les A.** (1938–) Australian poet and writer

40 I believe we will survive; that what is significant in us will survive; that we will come out of this struggle battered, stripped to the bone, but spiritually sounder than we went in, surer of our essential character, adults in a wider world than the one we lived in hitherto. These are great, tragic days. Let us accept them stoically, and make every yard of Australian earth a battle-station.

Meanjin Papers, (1942) **Palmer, Vance** (1885–1959) Australian writer. On Australia in the Second World War

41 Nor do I doubt but that this country will prove the most valuable acquisition Great Britain ever made.
Historical Records of New South Wales **Phillip, Arthur** (1738–1814) English naval officer and Colonial Governor. From a letter to Lord Sydney, 1788

42 Above our writers – and other artists – looms the intimidating mass of Anglo-Saxon culture. Such a situation almost inevitably produces the characteristic Australian Cultural Cringe – appearing either as the Cringe Direct, or as the Cringe Inverted, in the attitude of the Blatant Blatherskite, the God's-Own-Country and I'm-a-better-man-than-you-are Australian bore.
Meanjin, 1950, 'The Cultural Cringe' **Phillips, Arthur Angell** (1900–1985) Australian critic

43 Only one profound book has been written about Australia. It is D. H. Lawrence's novel *Kangaroo.* ... Most of it is as true today as when it was written thirty-five years ago. I can think of no more convincing proof of the superiority of the creative writer over the journalist or historian.
Australian Accent **Pringle, John Martin Douglas** (1912–) Scottish-born Australian writer

44 ... as an Australian I was brought up in an Anglo-Irish country – part of the weirdness of our personality is that inside every Australian there's an Irishman fighting an Englishman.
The Independent, (1992) **Royce, Phillip** (1903–)

45 At sunset, when the Harbour is glazed with pebbles of gold and white, and the sun is burning out like a bushfire behind Balmain, the ferry-boats put on their lights. They turn into luminous water-beetles, filled with a gliding, sliding reflected glitter that bubbles on the water like phosphorus.
Bread and Wine (1970) On Sydney's ferry-boats

46 The character and the life of Sydney are shaped continually and imperceptibly by the fingers of the Harbour, groping across the piers and jetties, clutching deeply into the hills, the water dyed a whole paint-box's armoury of colour with every breath of air, every shift of light or shade, according to the tide, the clock, the weather and the state of the moon. The water is like silk, like pewter, like blood, like a leopard's skin, and occasionally merely like water.
Bread and Wine (1970) **Slessor, Kenneth** (1901–1971) Australian poet and journalist

47 The ideal Australia I visualised during any exile and which drew me back, was always, I realise, a landscape without figures.
Flaws in the Glass (1981) **White, Patrick** (1912–1990) English-born Australian writer and dramatist

48 Do you know, Mr Hopper, dear Agatha and I are so much interested in Australia. It must be so pretty with all the dear little kangaroos flying about.
Lady Windermere's Fan (1892) **Wilde, Oscar** (1854–1900) Irish poet, dramatist, writer, critic and wit

BEAUTY

1 There is no excellent beauty, that hath not some strangeness in the proportion.
Essays (1625) **Bacon, Francis** (1561–1626) English philosopher, essayist, politician and courtier

2 Beauty and the lust for learning have yet to be allied.
Zuleika Dobson (1911) **Beerbohm, Sir Max** (1872–1956) English satirist, cartoonist, critic and essayist

3 Exuberance is Beauty.
'Proverbs of Hell' (1793) **Blake, William** (1757–1827) English poet, engraver, painter and mystic

4 For beauty being the best of all we know
Sums up the unsearchable and secret aims
Of nature.
'The Growth of Love' (1876)

5 I love all beauteous things,
I seek and adore them.
'I Love All Beauteous Things' (1890) **Bridges,
Robert** (1844–1930) English poet, dramatist,
essayist and doctor

6 Beauty and Truth, though never found, are
worthy to be sought.
'To David in Heaven' (1865)

7 All that is beautiful shall abide,
All that is base shall die.
'Balder the Beautiful' (1877) **Buchanan, Robert
Williams** (1841–1901) British poet, writer and
dramatist

8 It is better to be first with an ugly woman
than the hundredth with a beauty.
The Good Earth (1931) **Buck, Pearl S.** (1892–
1973) US writer and dramatist

9 It has been said that a pretty face is a
passport. But it's not, it's a visa, and it runs
out fast.
Mail on Sunday, (1988) **Burchill, Julie** (1960–)
English writer

10 Beauty in distress is much the most
affecting beauty.
*A Philosophical Enquiry into the Origin of our
Ideas of the Sublime and Beautiful* (1757) **Burke,
Edmund** (1729–1797) Irish-born British
statesman and philosopher

11 Glory, like the phoenix 'midst her fires,
Exhales her odours, blazes, and expires.
English Bards and Scotch Reviewers (1809)

12 She walks in beauty, like the night
Of cloudless climes and starry skies;
And all that's best of dark and bright
Meet in her aspect and her eyes.
'She Walks in Beauty' (1815) **Byron, Lord**
(1788–1824) English poet, satirist and traveller

13 The cruel girls we loved
Are over forty,
Their subtle daughters
Have stolen their beauty;
And with a blue stare
Of cool surprise
They mock their anxious mothers
With their mothers' eyes.
'Mothers and Daughters' (c.1965) **Campbell,
David** (1915–1979) Australian poet, rugby
player and wartime pilot

14 Everything has its beauty but not everyone
sees it.
Analects **Confucius** (c.550–c.478 BC) Chinese
philosopher and teacher of ethics

15 Beauty is the lover's gift.
The Way of the World (1700) **Congreve, William**
(1670–1729) English dramatist

16 There is nothing ugly; I never saw an ugly
thing in my life: for let the form of an
object be what it may, – light, shade, and
perspective will always make it beautiful.
In C.R. Leslie, *Memoirs of the Life of John
Constable* (1843) **Constable, John** (1776–1837)
English painter

17 There must be religion for religion's sake,
morality for morality's sake, as there is art
for art's sake ... the beautiful cannot be the
way to what is useful, nor to what is good,
nor to what is holy; it leads only to itself.
Lecture, (1818) **Cousin, Victor** (1792–1867)

18 When beauty fires the blood, how love
exalts the mind.
Cymon and Iphigenia (1700) **Dryden, John**
(1631–1700) English poet, satirist, dramatist
and critic

19 Beauty is the child of love.
The New Spirit (1890)

20 The absence of flaw in beauty is itself a
flaw.
Impressions and Comments (1914) **Ellis,
Havelock** (1859–1939) English sexologist and
essayist

21 Though we travel the world over to find the
beautiful we must carry it with us or we
find it not.
Essays, First Series (1841) **Emerson, Ralph
Waldo** (1803–1882) US poet, essayist,
transcendentalist and teacher

22 No woman can be a beauty without a
fortune.
The Beaux' Stratagem (1707) **Farquhar, George**
(1678–1707) Irish dramatist

23 Ugliness is, in a way, superior to beauty
because it lasts.
The Scotsman, (1998) **Gainsbourg, Serge** (1928–
1991) French singer, songwriter and director

24 He [Jolyon] was afflicted by the thought that where Beauty was, nothing ever ran quite straight, which, no doubt, was why so many people looked on it as immoral.
In Chancery (1920) **Galsworthy, John** (1867–1933) English writer and dramatist

25 Beauty is as useful as usefulness. Maybe more so.
Les Misérables (1862) **Hugo, Victor** (1802–1885) French poet, writer, dramatist and politician

26 Beauty is no quality in things themselves: It exists merely in the mind which contemplates them; and each mind perceives a different beauty.
Essays, Moral, Political, and Literary (1742) **Hume, David** (1711–1776) Scottish philosopher and political economist

27 Beauty is altogether in the eye of the beholder.
Molly Bawn (1878) **Hungerford, Margaret Wolfe** (c.1855–1897) Irish novelist

28 What ills from beauty spring.
The Vanity of Human Wishes (1749) **Johnson, Samuel** (1709–1784) English lexicographer, poet, critic, conversationalist and essayist

29 A thing of beauty is a joy for ever: Its loveliness increases; it will never Pass into nothingness; but still will keep A bower quiet for us, and a sleep Full of sweet dreams, and health, and quiet breathing.
'Endymion' (1818)

30 I have two luxuries to brood over in my walks, your Loveliness and the hour of my death. O that I could have possession of them both in the same minute.
Letter to Fanny Brawne, 25 July 1819

31 'Beauty is truth, truth beauty,' – that is all Ye know on earth, and all ye need to know.
'Ode on a Grecian Urn' (1819)

32 I never can feel certain of any truth but from a clear perception of its Beauty.
Letter to George and Georgiana Keats, 16 December 1818–4 January 1819 **Keats, John** (1795–1821) English poet

33 Beauty from order springs.
Art of Cookery (1708) **King, William** (1663–1712) English judge and writer

34 Why do progress and beauty have to be so opposed?
Hour of Gold, Hour of Lead (1973) **Lindbergh, Anne Morrow** (1906–2001) US aviator, poet and writer

35 On Richmond Hill there lives a lass, More sweet than May day morn, Whose charms all other maids surpass, A rose without a thorn.
'The Lass of Richmond Hill' (1789) **Macnally, Leonard** (1752–1820) Irish lawyer, dramatist and political informer

36 Was this the face that launch'd a thousand ships, And burnt the topless towers of Ilium?
Doctor Faustus (1604)

37 O, thou art fairer than the evening's air Clad in the beauty of a thousand stars.
Doctor Faustus (1604) **Marlowe, Christopher** (1564–1593) English poet and dramatist

38 The beauty of a face is a frail ornament, a passing flower, a moment's brightness belonging only to the skin.
Les Femmes savantes (1672) **Molière** (1622–1673) French dramatist, actor and director

39 Beauty is handed out as undemocratically as inherited peerages, and beautiful people have done nothing to deserve their astonishing reward.
The Observer, (1999) **Mortimer, John** (1923–) English lawyer, dramatist and writer

40 If Cleopatra's nose had been shorter the whole face of the earth would have changed.
Pensées (1670) **Pascal, Blaise** (1623–1662) French philosopher and scientist

41 The flowers anew, returning seasons bring! But beauty faded has no second spring.
The First Pastoral (1710) **Philips, Ambrose** (c.1675–1749) English poet and politician

42 I hate that aesthetic game of the eye and the mind, played by these connoisseurs, these mandarins who 'appreciate' beauty. What is beauty, anyway? There's no such thing. I never 'appreciate', any more than I 'like'. I love or I hate.

In Françoise Gilot and Carlton Lake, *Life with Picasso* (1964) **Picasso, Pablo** (1881–1973) Spanish painter, sculptor and graphic artist

43 So many thousand beauties are gone down to Avernus,
Ye might let one remain above with us.
'Prayer for his Lady's Life' (1908) **Pound, Ezra** (1885–1972) US poet

44 I remember a wonderful moment:
Before me you appeared,
Like a fleeting apparition,
Like a spirit of pure beauty.
'To –' (1825) **Pushkin, Aleksandr** (1799–1837) Russian poet, novelist and playwright

45 What is beautiful has its origin in the death of what is useful; what is useful becomes beautiful when it has outlived its usefulness.
Letter to Miguel de Unamuno, 19 July 1903 **Rodó, José Enrique** (1872–1917)

46 And when I told them how beautiful you are
They didn't believe me! They didn't believe me!
'They Didn't Believe Me' (song, 1914) **Rourke, M.E.** (20th century) US songwriter

47 There are no ugly women, only lazy ones.
My Life for Beauty (1965) **Rubinstein, Helena** (1872–1965) Polish-born US cosmetician and businesswoman

48 Remember that the most beautiful things in the world are the most useless; peacocks and lilies for instance.
The Stones of Venice (1851) **Ruskin, John** (1819–1900) English art critic, philosopher and reformer

49 Mathematics, rightly viewed, possesses not only truth, but supreme beauty – a beauty cold and austere, like that of sculpture.
Mysticism and Logic (1918) **Russell, Bertrand** (1872–1970) English philosopher, mathematician, essayist and social reformer

50 One of the greatest satisfactions for a man is when the woman he passionately desired and who obstinately refused to give herself to him ceases to be beautiful.
Notebooks (1834–1847) **Sainte-Beuve, Charles-Augustin** (1804–1869) French writer and critic

51 I always say beauty is only sin deep.
'Reginald's Choir Treat' (1904) **Saki** (1870–1916) Burmese-born British writer

52 Beauty endures for only as long as it can be seen; goodness, beautiful today, will remain so tomorrow.
In Naim Attallah, *Women* (1987) **Sappho** (fl. 7th–6th centuries BC) Greek poet

53 Beauty is the product of harmony between the mind and the senses.
'On Naive and Sentimental Poetry' (1795–1796) **Schiller, Johann Christoph Friedrich** (1759–1805) German writer, dramatist, poet and historian

54 Beauty itself doth of itself persuade
The eyes of men without an orator.
'The Rape of Lucrece' **Shakespeare, William** (1564–1616) English dramatist, poet and actor

55 That Beautie is not, as fond men misdeeme,
An outward shew of things, that onely seeme ...
For of the soule the bodie forme doth take:
For soule is forme, and doth the bodie make.
Fowre Hymnes (1596) **Spenser, Edmund** (c.1522–1599) English poet

56 Beauty is momentary in the mind –
The fitful tracing of a portal;
But in the flesh it is immortal.
The body dies; the body's beauty lives.
So evenings die, in their green going,
Aware, interminably flowing.
'Peter Quince at the Clavier' (1923)

57 I do not know which to prefer,
The beauty of inflections
Or the beauty of innuendoes,
The blackbird whistling
Or just after.
'Thirteen Ways of Looking at a Blackbird' (1923) **Stevens, Wallace** (1879–1955) US poet, essayist, dramatist and lawyer

58 It is amazing how complete is the delusion that beauty is goodness.
The Kreutzer Sonata (1890) **Tolstoy, Leo** (1828–1910) Russian writer, essayist, philosopher and moralist

59 O beautiful boy, do not put too much trust in your beauty.
Eclogues, II, line 17 **Virgil** (70–19 BC) Roman poet

60 Would you think Heaven could be so small a thing
As a lit window on the hills at night.
'I Shall Not Go To Heaven' **Waddell, Helen Jane** (1889–1965) Irish scholar and writer

61 Beauty is altogether in the eye of the beholder.
The Prince of India (1893) **Wallace, Lew** (1827–1905) US novelist and statesman

62 Taught from their infancy that beauty is woman's sceptre, the mind shapes itself to the body, and roaming round its gilt cage, only seeks to adorn its prison.
A Vindication of the Rights of Woman (1792) **Wollstonecraft, Mary** (1759–1797) English feminist, writer and teacher

63 She bore about with her, she could not help knowing it, the torch of her beauty; she carried it erect into any room that she entered; and after all, veil it as she might, and shrink from the monotony of bearing that it imposed on her, her beauty was apparent. She had been admired. She had been loved.
To the Lighthouse (1927) **Woolf, Virginia** (1882–1941) English writer and critic

64 O heart, we are old;
The living beauty is for younger men:
We cannot pay its tribute of wild tears.
In the Little Review, (1918) **Yeats, W.B.** (1865–1939) Irish poet, dramatist, editor, writer and senator
See also appearance; eyes

BELIEF

1 A belief is not true because it is useful.
Journal, (1876) **Amiel, Henri-Frédéric** (1821–1881) Swiss philosopher and writer

2 Unless you believe, you will not understand.
De Libero Arbitrio **Augustine, Saint** (354–430) Numidian-born Christian theologian and philosopher

3 So long as there are earnest believers in the world, they will always wish to punish opinions, even if their judgement tells them it is unwise, and their conscience that it is wrong.
Literary Studies (1879) **Bagehot, Walter** (1826–1877) English economist and political philosopher

4 Lord, I believe; help thou mine unbelief.
Mark, 9:24

5 Blessed are they that have not seen, and yet have believed.
John, 20:29 **The Bible (King James Version)**

6 Men generally believe what they wish.
De Bello Gallico **Caesar, Gaius Julius** (c.102–44 BC) Roman statesman, historian and army commander

7 The difference between Orthodoxy or My-doxy and Heterodoxy or Thy-doxy.
History of the French Revolution (1837) **Carlyle, Thomas** (1795–1881) Scottish historian, biographer, critic, and essayist

8 If you'll believe in me, I'll believe in you.
Through the Looking-Glass (1872) **Carroll, Lewis** (1832–1898) English writer and photographer

9 The men who really believe in themselves are all in lunatic asylums.
Orthodoxy (1908) **Chesterton, G.K.** (1874–1936) English writer, poet and critic

10 A man must not swallow more beliefs than he can digest.
The Dance of Life **Ellis, Havelock** (1859–1939) English sexologist and essayist

11 I do not believe in Belief … Lord I disbelieve – help thou my unbelief.
Two Cheers for Democracy (1951) **Forster, E.M.** (1879–1970) English writer, essayist and literary critic

12 In spite of everything I still believe that people are good at heart.
The Diary of Anne Frank (1947) **Frank, Anne** (1929–1945) Jewish diarist; died in Nazi concentration camp

13 We listen to others to discover what we ourselves believe.

CBC Times, (1959) **Grant, George** (1918–1988) Canadian philosopher and political commentator

14 My belief certainly seems to get stronger in the presence of people whose goodness seems of almost supernatural origin.
Attr. **Greene, Graham** (1904–1991) English writer and dramatist

15 And I said to a man who stood at the gate of the year: 'Give me a light that I may tread safely into the unknown.' And he replied: 'Go out into the darkness and put your hand into the hand of God. That shall be to you better than a light, and safer than a known way.'
The Desert (1908) **Haskins, Minnie Louise** (1875–1957) English teacher and writer. Quoted by King George VI in his Christmas broadcast, 1939

16 As I get older I seem to believe less and less and yet to believe what I do believe more and more.
The Observer, (1988) **Jenkins, David** (1925–) English Bishop of Durham

17 My dear child, you must believe in God in spite of what the clergy tell you.
In M. Asquith, *Autobiography* (1922) **Jowett, Benjamin** (1817–1893) English scholar, translator, essayist and priest

18 There is only one (true) religion; but there can be many different kinds of belief.
Religion within the Boundaries of Mere Reason (1793) **Kant, Immanuel** (1724–1804) German idealist philosopher

19 Credulity is the man's weakness, but the child's strength.
Essays of Elia (1823) **Lamb, Charles** (1775–1834) English essayist, critic and letter writer

20 The dust of exploded beliefs may make a fine sunset.
Livre sans nom: Twelve Reflections (1934) **Madan, Geoffrey** (1895–1947) English bibliophile

21 It is as absurd to argue men, as to torture them, into believing.
Sermon, (1831)

22 Though you can believe what you choose, you must believe what you ought.

Letter, (1848)

23 We can believe what we choose. We are answerable for what we choose to believe.
Letter to Mrs Froude, (1848) **Newman, John Henry, Cardinal** (1801–1890) English Cardinal, theologian and poet

24 Doublethink means the power of holding two contradictory beliefs in one's mind simultaneously, and accepting both of them.
Nineteen Eighty-Four (1949) **Orwell, George** (1903–1950) English writer and critic

25 You can't teach an old dogma new tricks.
In R. E. Drennan, *Wit's End* **Parker, Dorothy** (1893–1967) US writer, poet, critic and wit

26 The most positive men are the most credulous.
Miscellanies (1727) **Pope, Alexander** (1688–1744) English poet, translator and editor

27 Every man, wherever he goes, is encompassed by a cloud of comforting convictions, which move with him like flies on a summer day.
Sceptical Essays (1928)

28 Of course not. After all, I may be wrong.
Attr. On being asked if he would be willing to die for his beliefs **Russell, Bertrand** (1872–1970) English philosopher, mathematician, essayist and social reformer

29 During the writing ... of this book, I realized that the public will believe anything – so long as it is not founded on truth.
Taken Care Of (1965), Preface **Sitwell, Dame Edith** (1887–1964) English poet, anthologist, critic and biographer

30 The courage to believe in nothing.
Fathers and Sons (1862) **Turgenev, Ivan** (1818–1883) Russian writer and dramatist

31 To believe in God is to yearn for his existence and, moreover, it is to behave as if he did exist.
The Tragic Sense of Life (1913) **Unamuno, Miguel de** (1864–1936) Spanish philosopher, poet and writer

32 What has always been believed by everyone, everywhere, will most likely turn out to be false.
Moralities, (1932) **Valéry, Paul** (1871–1945) French poet, mathematician and philosopher

33 Orthodoxy is my doxy; heterodoxy is another man's doxy.
In Joseph Priestley, *Memoirs* (1807) **Warburton, William** (1698–1779) English cleric and controversialist
See also faith; God; philosophy; religion; thought

BIRDS

1 What do you think of 'Cloudcuckooland'?
Birds **Aristophanes** (c.445–385 BC) Greek playwright. Suggestion for the name of the Birds' capital city

2 There is a tale that is told in London about a nightingale, how it did this and that and, finally for no apparent reason, rested and sang in Berkeley Square.
These Charming People (1924) **Arlen, Michael** (1895–1956)

3 I heard a linnet courting
His lady in the spring.
'I heard a linnet' (1890) **Bridges, Robert** (1844–1930) English poet, dramatist, essayist and doctor

4 Near all the birds
Will sing at dawn, – and yet we do not take
The chaffering swallow for the holy lark.
Aurora Leigh (1857) **Browning, Elizabeth Barrett** (1806–1861) English poet; wife of Robert Browning

5 When asked to name my favourite bird I usually name the bar-tailed godwit.
The Times, (1999) **Clarke, Kenneth** (1940–) English Conservative politican

6 The crow will tumble up and down
At the first sight of spring
And in old trees around the town
Brush winter from its wing.
'Crows in Spring' **Clare, John** (1793–1864) English rural poet; died in an asylum

7 The Dodo never had a chance. He seems to have been invented for the sole purpose of becoming extinct and that was all he was good for.
How to Become Extinct (1941) **Cuppy, Will** (1884–1949) US humorist

8 The silver swan, who, living had no note,
When death approached unlocked her silent throat.
'The Silver Swan' (1612) **Gibbons, Orlando** (1583–1625) English organist and composer of church music

9 I never knew how wide the dark,
I never knew the depth of space,
I never knew how frail a bark,
How small is man within his place,
Not till I heard the swans go by,
Not till I marked their haunting cry,
Not till, within the vague on high,
I watched them pass across the sky.
'Swans at Night' **Gilmore, Dame Mary** (1865–1962) Australian poet and journalist

10 A little ball of feather and bone.
'Shelley's Skylark' (1887)

11 At once a voice arose among
The bleak twigs overhead
In a full-hearted evensong
Of joy illimited;
An aged thrush, frail, gaunt, and small,
In blast-beruffled plume,
Had chosen thus to fling his soul
Upon the growing gloom.
So little cause for carolings
Of such ecstatic sound
Was written on terrestrial things
Afar or nigh around,
That I could think there trembled through
His happy good-night air
Some blessed Hope, whereof he knew
And I was unaware.
'The Darkling Thrush' (1900) **Hardy, Thomas** (1840–1928) English writer and poet

12 Whan the lytell byrdes swetely dyde synge
Laudes to theyr maker erly in the mornynge.
The Passetyme of Pleasure (1509) **Hawes, Stephen** (d. c.1523) English allegorical poet

13 The common cormorant or shag
   Lays eggs inside a paper bag
   The reason you will see no doubt
   It is to keep the lightning out.
   But what these unobservant birds
   Have never noticed is that herds
   Of wandering bears may come with buns
   And steal the bags to hold the crumbs.
   'The Common Cormorant' (c.1925)
   Isherwood, Christopher (1904–1986) English
   novelist

14 … I gave him the lead gift in the twilight.
   What fell was relaxed,
   Owl-downy, soft feminine feathers; but
   what
   Soared: the fierce rush: the night-heron by
   the flooded river cries fear at its rising
   Before it was quite unsheathed from
   reality.
   Hurt Hawks (1928) **Jeffers, Robinson** (1887–
   1962) US poet

15 Where the nightingale doth sing
   Not a senseless, trancèd thing,
   But divine melodious truth.
   'Ode' (1818)

16 Thou wast not born for death, immortal
   Bird!
   No hungry generations tread thee down;
   The voice I hear this passing night was
   heard
   In ancient days by emperor and clown:
   Perhaps the self-same song that found a
   path
   Through the sad heart of Ruth, when sick
   for home,
   She stood in tears amid the alien corn;
   The same that oft-times hath
   Charm'd magic casements, opening on the
   foam
   Of perilous seas, in faery lands forlorn.
   'Ode to a Nightingale' (1819) **Keats, John**
   (1795–1821) English poet

17 There was an Old Man with a beard,
   Who said, 'It is just as I feared! –
   Two Owls and a Hen,
   Four Larks and a Wren,
   Have all built their nests in my beard!'
   A Book of Nonsense (1846) **Lear, Edward** (1812–
   1888) English artist and writer

18 Shoot all the bluejays you want, if you can
   hit 'em, but remember it's a sin to kill a
   mockingbird.
   To Kill a Mockingbird (1960) **Lee, Harper**
   (1926–) US writer

19 What bird so sings, yet does so wail?
   O 'tis the ravish'd nightingale.
   Jug, jug, jug, jug, tereu, she cries,
   And still her woes at midnight rise.
   Campaspe (1584)

20 How at heaven's gates she claps her wings,
   The morn not waking till she sings.
   Campaspe (1584) Of the lark **Lyly, John** (c.1554–
   1606) English dramatist and politician

21 The ostrich burying its head in the sand
   does at any rate wish to convey the
   impression that its head is the most
   important part of it.
   Journal of Katherine Mansfield (1954) **Mansfield,
   Katherine** (1888–1923) New Zealand writer

22 Lovely are the curves of the white owl
   sweeping
   Wavy in the dusk lit by one large star.
   Lone in the fir-branch, his rattle-note
   unvaried,
   Brooding o'er the gloom, spins the brown
   eve-jar.
   'Love in the Valley' (1883) **Meredith, George**
   (1828–1909) English writer, poet and critic

23 A wonderful bird is the pelican,
   His bill will hold more than his belican.
   He can take in his beak
   Food enough for a week,
   But I'm damned if I see how the helican.
   Nashville Banner, (1913) **Merritt, Dixon Lanier**
   (1879–1972) US editor

24 The song of canaries
   Never varies,
   And when they're moulting
   They're pretty revolting.
   The Face is Familiar (1940) **Nash, Ogden** (1902–
   1971) US poet

25 He regretted that he was not a bird, and
   could not be in two places at once.
   Attr. **Roche, Sir Boyle** (1743–1807) Irish
   politician

26 And now this pale swan in her wat'ry nest
   Begins the sad dirge of her certain ending.

'The Rape of Lucrece' **Shakespeare, William** (1564–1616) English dramatist, poet and actor

27 Hail to thee, blithe Spirit!
Bird thou never wert,
That from Heaven, or near it,
Pourest thy full heart
In profuse strains of unpremeditated art.
'To a Skylark' (1820) **Shelley, Percy Bysshe** (1792–1822) English poet, dramatist and essayist

28 The merry Cuckow, messenger of Spring,
His trumpet shrill hath thrise already sounded.
Amoretti and Epithalamion (1595), Sonnet 19 **Spenser, Edmund** (c.1522–1599) English poet

29 I once had a sparrow alight upon my shoulder for a moment while I was hoeing in a village garden, and I felt that I was more distinguished by that circumstance than I should have been by any epaulet I could have worn.
Walden (1854) **Thoreau, Henry David** (1817–1862) US essayist, social critic and writer

30 We think caged birds sing, when indeed they cry.
The White Devil (1612)

31 Call for the robin redbreast and the wren,
Since o'er shady groves they hover,
And with leaves and flowers do cover
The friendless bodies of unburied men.
The White Devil (1612) **Webster, John** (c.1580–c.1625) English dramatist

32 Caged birds accept each other but flight is what they long for.
Camino Real (1953) **Williams, Tennessee** (1911–1983) US dramatist and writer

33 On a tissue-thin monotone of blue-grey buds
two blue-grey birds, chasing a third,
at full cry! Now they are
flung outward and up – disappearing suddenly!
'*Spring Strains*' (1917) **Williams, William Carlos** (1883–1963) US poet, writer and paediatrician

34 O blithe new-comer! I have heard,
I hear thee and rejoice.
O Cuckoo! Shall I call thee bird,
Or but a wandering voice?

'To the Cuckoo' (1807) **Wordsworth, William** (1770–1850) English poet
See also animals; pets

BIRTH

1 The best contraceptive is a glass of cold water: not before or after, but instead.
Remark by a delegate at the International Planned Parenthood Federation Conference **Anonymous**

2 The stain of illegitimacy, unbleached by nobility or wealth, would have been a stain indeed.
Emma (1816) **Austen, Jane** (1775–1817) English writer

3 For that which is born death is certain, and for the dead birth is certain. Therefore grieve not over that which is unavoidable.
Ch. II **Bhagavadgita**

4 Joys impregnate. Sorrows bring forth.
The Marriage of Heaven and Hell (c.1790–1793)

5 My mother groand! my father wept.
Into the dangerous world I leapt:
Helpless, naked, piping loud:
Like a fiend hid in a cloud.
Struggling in my father's hands:
Striving against my swaddling bands:
Bound and weary I thought best
To sulk upon by mothers breast.
Songs of Experience (1794) **Blake, William** (1757–1827) English poet, engraver, painter and mystic

6 Abortions will not let you forget
You remember the children you got that you did not get.
Selected Poems (1963) **Brooks, Gwendolyn** (1917–2000) US poet

7 For man's greatest offence is to have been born.
Life is a Dream (1636) **Calderón de la Barca, Pedro** (1600–1681) Spanish dramatist and poet

8 I came upstairs into the world; for I was born in a cellar.
Love for Love (1695) **Congreve, William** (1670–1729) English dramatist

9 Claudia ... remembered that when she'd
had her first baby she had realised with
astonishment that the perfect couple
consisted of a mother and child and not, as
she had always supposed, a man and
woman.
The Other Side of the Fire **Ellis, Alice Thomas**
(1932–2005) British writer

10 Every year, in the fulness o' summer, when
the sukebind hangs heavy from the wains
... 'tes the same. And when the spring
comes her hour is upon her again. 'Tes the
hand of Nature, and we women cannot
escape it.
Cold Comfort Farm (1932) **Gibbons, Stella**
(1902–1989) English poet and novelist

11 Childbirth was the moment of truth in my
life. Suddenly you realise that you are
having the greatest love affair of your life
(but you also realise that God's a bloke).
The Observer (June 1999) **Lette, Kathy** (1959–)
Australian novelist

12 I'll simply say here that I was born Beatrice
Gladys Lillie at an extremely tender age
because my mother needed a fourth at
meals.
Every Other Inch a Lady (1973) **Lillie, Beatrice**
(1894–1989) Canadian-born English actress

13 Where are the children I might have had?
You may suppose I might have wanted
them. Drowned to the accompaniment of
the rattling of a thousand douche bags.
Under the Volcano (1947) **Lowry, Malcolm**
(1909–1957) English writer and poet

14 I'm not interested in being Wonder
Woman in the delivery room. Give me
drugs.
Attr. **Madonna** (1958–) US singer. Requesting
an epidural in advance of childbirth, 1996

15 In the dark womb where I began
My mother's life made me a man.
Through all the months of human birth
Her beauty fed my common earth.
I cannot see, nor breathe, nor stir,
But through the death of some of her.
'C.L.M.' (1910) **Masefield, John** (1878–1967)
English poet, writer and critic

16 Death and taxes and childbirth! There's
never any convenient time for any of them.
Gone with the Wind (1936) **Mitchell, Margaret**
(1900–1949) US author

17 'One advantage of being pregnant,' says a
wife in one of my television plays, 'you
don't have to worry about getting
pregnant.'
Feeling You're Behind (1984) **Nicholls, Peter**
(1927–) English dramatist

18 It serves me right for putting all my eggs
in one bastard.
You Might As Well Live **Parker, Dorothy** (1893–
1967) US writer, poet, critic and wit

19 We want far better reasons for having
children than not knowing how to prevent
them.
Hypatia **Russell, Dora** (1894–1986) British
author and campaigner

20 *Don Pedro*: Out o' question, you were born
in a merry hour.
Beatrice: No, sure, my lord, my mother
cried; but then there was a star danc'd, and
under that was I born.
Much Ado About Nothing, II.i **Shakespeare,
William** (1564–1616) English dramatist, poet
and actor

21 Not to be born is the best of all; next best
is, having been born, to return as quickly
as possible whence we came.
Oedipus at Colonus, line 1225 **Sophocles** (496–
406 BC) Greek dramatist

22 'Who was your mother?' 'Never had none!'
said the child, with another grin. 'Never
had any mother? What do you mean?
Where were you born?' 'Never was born!'
persisted Topsy.
Uncle Tom's Cabin (1852) **Stowe, Harriet
Beecher** (1811–1896) US writer and reformer

23 I was born in very sorry circumstances. My
mother was sorry and my father was sorry
as well.
The Observer, (1998) **Wisdom, Norman** (1915–)
English comic actor

24 Our birth is but a sleep and a forgetting.
The Soul that rises with us, our life's Star,
Hath had elsewhere its setting,
And cometh from afar;
Not in entire forgetfulness,
And not in utter nakedness,
But trailing clouds of glory do we come
From God, who is our home:
Heaven lies about us in our infancy!
'Ode: Intimations of Immortality' (1807)
Wordsworth, William (1770–1850) English
poet
See also childhood and children; families;
parenthood

BOOKS

1 A reader seldom peruses a book with
pleasure until he knows whether the writer
of it be a black man or a fair man, of a mild
or choleric disposition, married or a
bachelor.
The Spectator, (1711)

2 Of all the diversions of life, there is none so
proper to fill up its empty spaces as the
reading of useful and entertaining authors.
The Spectator, (1711) **Addison, Joseph** (1672–
1719) English essayist, poet, playwright and
statesman

3 Two men wrote a lexicon, Liddell and
Scott;
Some parts were clever, but some parts
were not.
Hear, all ye learned, and read me this
riddle,
How the wrong part wrote Scott, and the
right part wrote Liddell.
On Henry Liddell and Robert Scott, co-
authors of the Greek Lexicon (1843)
Anonymous

4 He [the translator] will find one English
book and one only, where, as in the Iliad
itself, perfect plainness of speech is allied
with perfect nobleness; and that book is
the Bible.
On Translating Homer (1861) **Arnold, Matthew**
(1822–1888) English poet, critic, essayist and
educationist

5 Some books are undeservedly forgotten;
none are undeservedly remembered.
The Dyer's Hand (1963) **Auden, W.H.** (1907–
1973) English poet, essayist, critic, teacher and
dramatist

6 Take up and read, take up and read!
Confessions (397–398) **Augustine, Saint** (354–430)
Numidian-born Christian theologian and
philosopher

7 Oh, Lord! not I; I never read much; I have
something else to do.
Northanger Abbey (1818) **Austen, Jane** (1775–
1817) English writer

8 If I had been someone not very clever, I
would have done an easier job like
publishing. That's the easiest job I can
think of.
Attr. **Ayer, A.J.** (1910–1989) English
philosopher

9 Books will speak plain when counsellors
blanch.
'Of Counsel' (1625)

10 Some books are to be tasted, others to be
swallowed, and some few to be chewed
and digested; that is, some books are to be
read only in parts; others to be read but
not curiously; and some few to be read
wholly, and with diligence and attention.
'Of Studies' (1625) **Bacon, Francis** (1561–1626)
English philosopher, essayist, politician and
courtier

11 Books say: she did this because. Life says:
she did this. Books are where things are
explained to you; life is where things aren't.
Flaubert's Parrot (1984) **Barnes, Julian** (1946–)
English writer

12 Few books are more thrilling than certain
confessions, but they must be honest, and
the author must have something to
confess.
The Second Sex (1953) **Beauvoir, Simone de**
(1908–1986) French writer, feminist critic and
philosopher

13 Books are not made for furniture, but there
is nothing else that so beautifully furnishes
a house.

Life Thoughts (1858) **Beecher, Henry Ward** (1813–1887) US clergyman, lecturer, editor and writer

14 When I am dead, I hope it may be said: 'His sins were scarlet, but his books were read.'
Sonnets and Verse (1923) **Belloc, Hilaire** (1870–1953) English writer of verse, essayist and critic; Liberal MP

15 Definition of a classic: a book everyone is assumed to have read and often thinks they have.
Independent on Sunday, 1991 **Bennett, Alan** (1934–) English dramatist, actor and diarist

16 Of making many books there is no end; and much study is a weariness of the flesh.
Ecclesiastes, 12:12 **The Bible (King James Version)**

17 Reading is not a duty, and has consequently no business to be made disagreeable.
Obiter Dicta (second series, 1887) **Birrell, Augustine** (1850–1933) English politician

18 The original is not faithful to the translation.
Sobre el 'Vathek' de William Beckford (1943) **Borges, Jorge Luis** (1899–1986) Argentinian writer, poet and librarian. On Henley's translation of Beckford's Vathek

19 A best-seller was a book which somehow sold well simply because it was selling well.
The Image (1962) **Boorstin, Daniel** (1914–2004) US librarian, historian, lawyer and writer

20 I take the view, and always have done, that if you cannot say what you have to say in twenty minutes, you should go away and write a book about it.
Attr. **Brabazon of Tara, Lord** (1910–1974) English businessman and Conservative politician

21 You don't have to burn books to destroy a culture. Just get people to stop reading them.
Reader's Digest, (1994) **Bradbury, Ray** (1920–) US science fiction writer

22 There are worse crimes than burning books. One of them is not reading them.

Remark, (1991) **Brodsky, Joseph** (1940–1996) Russian poet, essayist, critic and exile

23 They do most by Books, who could do much without them, and he that chiefly owes himself unto himself, is the substantial man.
Christian Morals (1716) **Browne, Sir Thomas** (1605–1682) English physician, author and antiquary

24 The possession of a book becomes a substitute for reading it.
New York Times Book Review **Burgess, Anthony** (1917–1993) English writer, linguist and composer

25 'Tis pleasant, sure, to see one's name in print;
A Book's a Book, altho' there is nothing in't.
English Bards and Scotch Reviewers (1809) **Byron, Lord** (1788–1824) English poet, satirist and traveller

26 A great book is like great evil.
In R. Pfeiffer (ed.), *Fragments* **Callimachus** (c.305–c.240 BC) Cyrene-born Alexandrian poet and epigrammatist

27 A classic is a book that has never finished saying what it has to say.
The Literature Machine (1987) **Calvino, Italo** (1923–1985) Italian writer

28 So essential did I consider an Index to be to every book, that I proposed to bring a Bill into parliament to deprive an author who publishes a book without an Index of the privilege of copyright; and, moreover, to subject him, for his offence, to a pecuniary penalty.
Lives of the Chief Justices, Preface to Vol. III **Campbell, Baron** (1799–1861) Scottish lawyer and politician

29 Gentlemen you must not mistake me. I admit that the French Emperor is a tyrant. I admit that he is a monster. I admit that he is the sworn foe of our own nation, and, if you will, of the whole human race. But, gentlemen, we must be just to our great enemy. We must not forget that he once shot a bookseller.

Attr. in a footnote in G.O. Trevelyan, *The Life and Letters of Lord Macaulay* (1876) **Campbell, Thomas** (1777–1844) Scottish poet, ballad writer and journalist. Excusing himself in proposing a toast to Napoleon at a literary dinner

30 He who first shortened the labour of Copyists by device of Movable Types was disbanding hired Armies, and cashiering most Kings and Senates, and creating a whole new Democratic world: he had invented the Art of Printing.
Sartor Resartus (1834)

31 The true University of these days is a Collection of Books.
On Heroes, Hero-Worship, and the Heroic in History (1841) **Carlyle, Thomas** (1795–1881) Scottish historian, biographer, critic, and essayist

32 'What is the use of a book,' thought Alice, 'without pictures or conversations?'
Alice's Adventures in Wonderland (1865) **Carroll, Lewis** (1832–1898) English writer and photographer

33 The success of many books is due to the affinity between the mediocrity of the author's ideas and those of the public.
In J. R. Solly, *A Cynic's Breviary* (1925) **Chamfort, Nicolas** (1741–1794) French writer

34 All men who read escape from something else ... they must escape at times from the deadly rhythm of their private thoughts.
Atlantic Monthly (1944)

35 If my books had been any worse I should not have been invited to Hollywood, and ... if they had been any better, I should not have come.
Letter to C.W. Morton, (1945) **Chandler, Raymond** (1888–1959) US crime writer

36 Due attention to the inside of books, and due contempt for the outside, is the proper relation between a man of sense and his books.
Letter to his son, (1749) **Chesterfield, Lord** (1694–1773) English politician and letter writer

37 It is a good thing for an uneducated man to read books of quotations.

My Early Life (1930) **Churchill, Sir Winston** (1874–1965) English Conservative Prime Minister

38 Some read to think, – these are rare; some to unite, – these are common; and some to talk, – and these form the great majority.
Lacon (1820) **Colton, Charles Caleb** (c.1780–1832) English clergyman and satirist

39 As repressed sadists are supposed to become policemen or butchers so those with irrational fear of life become publishers.
Enemies of Promise (1938) **Connolly, Cyril** (1903–1974) English literary editor, writer and critic

40 University printing presses exist for the purpose of producing books which no one can read, and they are true to their high calling.
Attr. **Cornford, F.M.** (1874–1943) English Platonic scholar

41 Books are not seldom talismans and spells.
The Task (1785) **Cowper, William** (1731–1800) English poet, hymn writer and letter writer

42 With awe around these silent walks I tread: These are the lasting mansions of the dead.
The Library (1808)

43 This, books can do – nor this alone: they give
New views to life, and teach us how to live;
They soothe the grieved, the stubborn they chastise;
Fools they admonish, and confirm the wise,
Their aid they yield to all: they never shun
The man of sorrow, nor the wretch undone;
Unlike the hard, the selfish, and the proud,
They fly not from the suppliant crowd;
Nor tell to various people various things,
But show to subjects, what they show to kings.
The Library (1808)

44 Books cannot always please, however good;
Minds are not ever craving for their food.
The Borough (1810) **Crabbe, George** (1754–1832) English poet, clergyman, surgeon and botanist

45 A truly great book should be read in youth, again in maturity, and once more in old age, as a fine building should be seen by morning light, at noon, and by moonlight.
In Grant, *The Enthusiasms of Robertson Davies* **Davies, Robertson** (1913–1995) Canadian playwright, writer and critic

46 Such is our pride, our folly, or our fate, That few, but such as cannot write, translate.
'To Richard Fanshaw' (1648) **Denham, Sir John** (1615–1669) English poet, royalist and Surveyor-General

47 The reading of all good books is like a conversation with the finest men of past centuries.
Discours de la Méthode (1637) **Descartes, René** (1596–1650) French philosopher and mathematician

48 Medicine for the soul.
History **Diodorus Siculus** (c.1st century BC) Greek historian. Inscription over library door in Alexandria

49 There is an art of reading, as well as an art of thinking, and an art of writing.
Literary Character (1795) **D'Israeli, Isaac** (1766–1848) English literary critic; father of Benjamin Disraeli

50 If an army of monkeys were strumming on typewriters they might write all the books in the British Museum.
The Nature of the Physical World (1928) **Eddington, Sir Arthur** (1882–1944) English astronomer, physicist and mathematician

51 Tis the good reader that makes the good book.
Society and Solitude (1870)

52 The book written against fame and learning has the author's name on the title-page.
Journals **Emerson, Ralph Waldo** (1803–1882) US poet, essayist, transcendentalist and teacher

53 Oh really. What exactly is she reading?
Attr. **Evans, Dame Edith** (1888–1976) English actress. On being told that Nancy Mitford had been lent a villa to enable her to finish a book

54 Books are made not like children but like the pyramids ... and they're good for nothing! and they stay in the desert! Jackals piss at their foot and the bourgeois climb up on them.
Letter to Ernest Feydeau, (1857)

55 Do not read, as children do, for the sake of entertainment, or like the ambitious, for the purpose of instruction. No, read in order to live.
Letter to Mlle Leroyer de Chantepie, (1857) **Flaubert, Gustave** (1821–1880) French writer

56 This is the saddest story I have ever heard.
The Good Soldier (1915), first sentence **Ford, Ford Madox** (1873–1939) English novelist

57 I suggest that the only books that influence us are those for which we are ready, and which have gone a little farther down our particular path than we have yet got ourselves.
Two Cheers for Democracy (1951) **Forster, E.M.** (1879–1970) English writer, essayist and literary critic

58 If I read a book that impresses me, I have to take myself firmly in hand before I mix with other people; otherwise they would think my mind rather queer.
The Diary of Anne Frank (1947) **Frank, Anne** (1929–1945) Jewish diarist; died in Nazi concentration camp

59 A lonesome man on a rainy day who does not know how to read.
In Shriner, *Wit, Wisdom, and Foibles of the Great* **Franklin, Benjamin** (1706–1790) US statesman, scientist, political critic and printer. On being asked what condition of man he considered the most pitiable

60 The book is the world's most patient medium.
The Scholar in Society (film, 1984) **Frye, Northrop** (1912–1991) Canadian critic and academic

61 Learning hath gained most by those books by which the printers have lost.
The Holy State and the Profane State (1642) **Fuller, Thomas** (1608–1661) English churchman and antiquary

62 My early and invincible love of reading, which I would not exchange for the treasures of India.
Memoirs of My Life and Writings (1796) **Gibbon, Edward** (1737–1794) English historian, politician and memoirist

63 Another damned, thick, square book. Always scribble, scribble, scribble! Eh! Mr. Gibbon?
In Henry Best, *Personal and Literary Memorials* (1829) **Gloucester, William, Duke of** (1743–1805) English Field Marshal; brother of George III

64 I … shewed her that books were sweet unreproaching companions to the miserable, and that if they could not bring us to enjoy life, they would at least teach us to endure it.
The Vicar of Wakefield (1766)

65 A book may be amusing with numerous errors, or it may be very dull without a single absurdity.
The Vicar of Wakefield (1766) **Goldsmith, Oliver** (c.1728–1774) Irish dramatist, poet and writer

66 Libraries are reservoirs of strength, grace and wit, reminders of order, calm and continuity, lakes of mental energy, neither warm nor cold, light nor dark. The pleasure they give is steady, unorgiastic, reliable, deep and long-lasting.
Daddy, We Hardly Knew You (1989) **Greer, Germaine** (1939–) Australian feminist, critic, English scholar and writer

67 The art of reading is to skip judiciously.
The Intellectual Life (1873) **Hamerton, P.G.** (1834–1894) British artist and writer

68 It is there, where they
Burn books, that eventually they burn people too.
Almansor: A Tragedy (1821)

69 It is an old story, yet it remains forever new.
Book of Songs (1822–1823) **Heine, Heinrich** (1797–1856) German lyric poet, essayist and journalist

70 Reading is sometimes an ingenious device for avoiding thought.

Friends in Council (1849) **Helps, Sir Arthur** (1813–1875) English historian and writer

71 For a true writer each book should be a new beginning, where he tries again for something that is beyond attainment.
Speech for the presentation of the Nobel Prize, (1954) **Hemingway, Ernest** (1898–1961) US author

72 He was wont to say that if he had read as much as other men, he should have knowne no more than other men.
In Aubrey, *Brief Lives* (c.1693) **Hobbes, Thomas** (1588–1679) Political philosopher

73 You can destroy what you haven't published; the word once out cannot be recalled.
Ars Poetica **Horace** (65–8 BC) Roman poet

74 The arsenals of divine vengeance, if I may so describe the Bodleian library.
D. Iunii Iuvenalis Saturae (1905), Preface **Housman, A.E.** (1859–1936) English poet and scholar

75 The Reason why there is no table or Index added hereunto, is, that every Page in this Work is so full of Signal Remarks, that were they couched in an Index, it would make a volume as big as the Book, and so make the Postern Gate bear no proportion with the Building.
Note in the front of *Proedria Basilike* (1664) **Howell, John**

76 The proper study of mankind is books.
Crome Yellow (1921)

77 A bad book is as much of a labour to write as a good one; it comes as sincerely from the author's soul … its sincerities will be … uninterestingly expressed, and the labour expended on the expression will be wasted. Nature is monstrously unjust. There is no substitute for talent. Industry and all the virtues are of no avail.
Point Counter Point (1928) **Huxley, Aldous** (1894–1963) English writer, poet and critic

78 I'm replacing some of the timber used up by my books. Books are just trees with squiggles on them.
Radio Times, (1984) **Innes, Hammond** (1913–1998) English novelist. On growing trees

79 The book of my enemy has been
remaindered
And I am pleased.
'The Book of My Enemy Has Been
Remaindered' **James, Brian** (1892–1972)
Australian writer

80 But these were the dreams of a poet
doomed at last to wake a lexicographer.
A Dictionary of the English Language (1755),
Preface

81 Books that you may carry to the fire, and
hold readily in your hand, are the most
useful after all.
In Sir John Hawkins, *Life of Samuel Johnson*
(1787)

82 A man ought to read just as inclination
leads him; for what he reads as a task will
do him little good.
In Boswell, *The Life of Samuel Johnson* (1791)

83 A translator is to be like his author; it is not
his business to excel him.
Attr. **Johnson, Samuel** (1709–1784) English
lexicographer, poet, critic, conversationalist
and essayist

84 One man is as good as another until he
has written a book.
In E. Abbott and L. Campbell (eds), *Life and
Letters of Benjamin Jowett* (1897) **Jowett,
Benjamin** (1817–1893) English scholar,
translator, essayist and priest

85 I think you should only read those books
which bite and sting you.
Letter to Oskar Pollak, (1904)

86 A book must be the axe for the frozen sea
within us.
Letter to Oskar Pollak, (1904) **Kafka, Franz**
(1883–1924) Czech-born German-speaking
writer

87 Book learning certainly increases
knowledge, but does not broaden one's
ideas and insight when it is not
accompanied by reason.
Pragmatic Anthropology (1800) **Kant, Immanuel**
(1724–1804) German idealist philosopher

88 Much have I travell'd in the realms of gold,
And many goodly states and kingdoms
seen …
Then felt I like some watcher of the skies
When a new planet swims into his ken;
Or like stout Cortez when with eagle eyes
He star'd at the Pacific – and all his men
Look'd at each other with a wild surmise –
Silent, upon a peak in Darien.
'On First Looking into Chapman's Homer'
(1816) **Keats, John** (1795–1821) English poet

89 … a book which in some manner
celebrates and encourages the human
imagination, which renders possible the
impossible, which sustains the interior life
of the reader and which speaks to and of
the human spirit.
What makes a classic a classic? The test of time
Kennedy, A.L. (1965–) Scottish novelist.
Definition of a classic

90 Every age hath its book.
Chapter 13 **Koran**

91 The making of a book, like the making of a
clock, is a craft; it takes more than wit to be
an author.
Les caractères ou les moeurs de ce siècle (1688) **La
Bruyère, Jean de** (1645–1696) French satirist

92 But the shortest works are always the best.
Fables, 'Les lapins' **La Fontaine, Jean de** (1621–
1695) French poet and fabulist

93 Few books today are forgivable.
The Politics of Experience (1967) **Laing, R.D.**
(1927–1989) Scottish psychiatrist,
psychoanalyst and poet

94 I mean your borrowers of books – those
mutilators of collections, spoilers of the
symmetry of shelves, and creators of odd
volumes.
Essays of Elia (1823)

95 Why have we none [i.e. no grace] for books,
those spiritual repasts – a grace before
Milton – a grace before Shakespeare – a
devotional exercise proper to be said before
reading the Faerie Queene?
Essays of Elia (1823)

96 I love to lose myself in other men's minds.
When I am not walking, I am reading; I
cannot sit and think. Books think for me.

Last Essays of Elia (1833) **Lamb, Charles** (1775–1834) English essayist, critic and letter writer

97 It is often said that one has but one life to live, but that is nonsense. For one who reads, there is no limit to the number of lives that may be lived, for fiction, biography and history offer an inexhaustible number of lives in all periods of time.
Reader's Digest, (1993) **L'Amour, Louis** (1908–1988) US author

98 Never judge a book by its cover.
Metropolitan Life (1978)

99 Wealth and power are much more likely to be the result of breeding than they are of reading.
Social Studies (1981) On self-help books
Lebowitz, Fran (1946–) US writer

100 There can hardly be a stranger commodity in the world than books. Printed by people who don't understand them; sold by people who don't understand them; bound, criticized and read by people who don't understand them, and now even written by people who don't understand them.
A Doctrine of Scattered Occasions **Lichtenberg, Georg** (1742–1799) German physicist, satirist and writer

101 The book is the greatest interactive medium of all time. You can underline it, write in the margins, fold down a page, skip ahead. And you can take it anywhere.
Daily Telegraph, (1996) **Lynton, Michael** British publishing executive

102 It was a book to kill time for those who like it better dead.
Attr. **Macaulay, Dame Rose** (1881–1958) English writer

103 Everyone probably thinks that I'm a raving nymphomaniac, that I have an insatiable sexual appetite, when the truth is I'd rather read a book.
Q Magazine, (1991) **Madonna** (1958–) US singer and actress

104 The pleasure of all reading is doubled when one lives with another who shares the same books.

Letter, (1928) **Mansfield, Katherine** (1888–1923) New Zealand writer

105 To read too many books is harmful.
The New Yorker, (1977) **Mao Tse-Tung** (1893–1976) Chinese Communist leader

106 I did toy with the idea of doing a cook-book ... I think a lot of people who hate literature but love fried eggs would buy it if the price was right.
Groucho and Me (1959) **Marx, Groucho** (1895–1977) US comedian

107 My book is licentious, but my life is pure.
Epigrammata **Martial** (c.AD 40–c.104) Spanish-born Latin epigrammatist and poet

108 There is an impression abroad that everyone had it in him to write one book; but if by this is implied a good book the impression is false.
The Summing Up (1938) **Maugham, William Somerset** (1874–1965) English writer, dramatist and physician

109 As good almost kill a Man as kill a good Booke; who kills a Man kills a reasonable creature, God's Image; but hee who destroyes a good Booke, kills reason it selfe, kills the Image of God, as it were in the eye. Many a man lives a burden to the Earth; but a good Booke is the pretious life-blood of a master spirit, imbalm'd and treasur'd up on purpose to a life beyond life.
Areopagitica (1644) **Milton, John** (1608–1674) English poet, libertarian and pamphleteer

110 A second-hand bookshop is the sign and symbol of a civilized community ... and the number and quality of these shops give you the exact measure of a city's right to be counted among the great cities of the world ... Show me a city's second-hand bookshops, and I will tell you what manner of citizens dwell there, and of what ancestry sprung.
Collected Essays (1940) **Murdoch, Sir Walter Logie Forbes** (1874–1970) Australian writer and broadcaster

111 Reading isn't an occupation we encourage among police officers. We try to keep the paper work down to a minimum.

Loot (1967) **Orton, Joe** (1933–1967) English dramatist and writer

112 A book that furnishes no quotations is, me judice, no book – it is a plaything.
Crotchet Castle (1831) **Peacock, Thomas Love** (1785–1866) English writer and poet

113 Much reading is an oppression of the mind, and extinguishes the natural candle, which is the reason of so many senseless scholars in the world.
'Advice to His Children' (1699) **Penn, William** (1644–1718) English Quaker, founder of state of Pennsylvania

114 We know that you are mad with too much reading.
Satyricon **Petronius Arbiter** (d. AD 66) Roman satirist

115 *Books Do Furnish a Room.*
Title of novel, (1971) **Powell, Anthony** (1905–2000) English writer and critic

116 An anthology is like all the plums and orange peel picked out of a cake.
Letter to Mrs Robert Bridges, (1915) **Raleigh, Sir Walter A.** (1861–1922) English scholar, critic and essayist

117 I have known her pass the whole evening without mentioning a single book, or in fact anything unpleasant, at all.
A Very Great Man Indeed (1953) **Reed, Henry** (1914–1986) English poet, radio dramatist and translator

118 When a new book is published, read an old one.
Attr. **Rogers, Samuel** (1763–1855) British poet

119 We all know that books burn – yet we have the greater knowledge that books cannot be killed by fire. People die, but books never die. No man and no force can abolish memory ... In this war, we know, books are weapons.
Publisher's Weekly, 1942, 'Message to the American Booksellers Association' **Roosevelt, Franklin Delano** (1882–1945) US Democrat President

120 A book is a version of the world. If you do not like it, ignore it; or offer your own version in return.

Independent on Sunday, (1990) **Rushdie, Salman** (1947–) Indian-born English author

121 All books are divisible into two classes: the books of the hour, and the books of all time.
Sesame and Lilies (1865)

122 If a book is worth reading, it is worth buying.
Sesame and Lilies (1865)

123 We call ourselves a rich nation, and we are filthy and foolish enough to thumb each other's books out of circulating libraries!
Sesame and Lilies (1865), 'Of Kings' Treasuries' **Ruskin, John** (1819–1900) English art critic, philosopher and reformer

124 There are two motives for reading a book: one, that you enjoy it, the other that you can boast about it.
The Conquest of Happiness (1930) **Russell, Bertrand** (1872–1970) English philosopher, mathematician, essayist and social reformer

125 A library is thought in cold storage.
A Book of Quotations (1947) **Samuel, Lord** (1870–1963) English Liberal statesman, philosopher and administrator

126 An honest tale speeds best being plainly told.
Richard III, IV.iv

127 Come and take choice of all my library, And so beguile thy sorrow.
Titus Andronicus, IV.i

128 My library
Was dukedom large enough.
The Tempest, I.ii **Shakespeare, William** (1564–1616) English dramatist, poet and actor

129 With a tale forsooth he commeth unto you, with a tale, which holdeth children from play, and olde men from the Chimney corner.
The Defence of Poesie (1595) **Sidney, Sir Philip** (1554–1586) English poet, critic, soldier, courtier and diplomat

130 A best-seller is the gilded tomb of a mediocre talent.
Afterthoughts (1931) **Smith, Logan Pearsall** (1865–1946) US-born British epigrammatist, critic and writer

131 No furniture so charming as books, even if you never open them, or read a single word.
In Holland, *A Memoir of the Reverend Sydney Smith* (1855)

132 Live always in the best company when you read.
In Holland, *A Memoir of the Reverend Sydney Smith* (1855) **Smith, Sydney** (1771–1845) English clergyman, essayist, journalist and wit

133 The generall end therefore of all the booke is to fashion a gentleman or noble person in vertuous and gentle discipline.
The Faerie Queene (1596) **Spenser, Edmund** (c.1522–1599) English poet

134 Reading is to the Mind, what Exercise is to the Body … But as Exercise becomes tedious and painful when we make use of it only as the Means of Health, so Reading is apt to grow uneasy and burdensome, when we apply our selves to it only for our Improvement in Virtue.
The Tatler, 47, (1710) **Steele, Sir Richard** (1672–1729) Irish-born English writer, dramatist and politician

135 It is wonderful that even today, with all the competition of radio, television, films, and records, the book has kept its precious character. A book is somehow sacred. A dictator can kill and maim people, can sink to any kind of tyranny, and only be hated. But when books are burnt the ultimate in tyranny has happened. This we cannot forgive.
Attr. **Steinbeck, John** (1902–1968) US writer

136 Digressions, incontestably, are the sunshine; – they are the life, the soul of reading; – take them out of this book for instance, – you might as well take the book along with them.
Tristram Shandy **Sterne, Laurence** (1713–1768) Irish-born English writer and clergyman

137 Books are good enough in their own way, but they are a mighty bloodless substitute for life.
Virginibus Puerisque (1881) **Stevenson, Robert Louis** (1850–1894) Scottish writer, poet and essayist

138 It is a librarian's duty to distinguish between poetry and a sort of belle-litter.
Travesties (1975) **Stoppard, Tom** (1937–) British dramatist

139 Books, like men their authors, have no more than one way of coming into the world, but there are ten thousand to go out of it, and return no more.
A Tale of a Tub (1704) **Swift, Jonathan** (1667–1745) Irish satirist, poet, essayist and cleric

140 What is a diary as a rule? A document useful to the person who keeps it, dull to the contemporary who reads it, invaluable to the student, centuries afterwards, who treasures it!
The Story of My Life (1933) **Terry, Dame Ellen** (1847–1928) English actress, theatrical manager and memoirist

141 Of all the needs a book has the chief need is that it be readable.
Autobiography (1883) **Trollope, Anthony** (1815–1882) English writer, traveller and post office official

142 A good book is the best of friends, the same today and for ever.
Proverbial Philosophy (1838) **Tupper, Martin** (1810–1889) English writer, lawyer and inventor

143 Books have the same enemies as man: fire, damp, animals, time; and their own contents.
Littérature **Valéry, Paul** (1871–1945) French poet, mathematician and philosopher

144 Particularly against books the Home Secretary is. If we can't stamp out literature in the country, we can at least stop it being brought in from outside.
Vile Bodies (1930) **Waugh, Evelyn** (1903–1966) English writer and diarist

145 Beware you be not swallowed up in books! An ounce of love is worth a pound of knowledge.
In Southey, *Life of Wesley* (1820) **Wesley, John** (1703–1791) English theologian and preacher

146 God forbid that any book should be banned. The practice is as indefensible as infanticide.

The Strange Necessity (1928) **West, Dame Rebecca** (1892–1983) English writer, critic and feminist

147 There is no such thing as a moral or an immoral book. Books are well written, or badly written. That is all.
The Picture of Dorian Gray (1891)

148 Oh! it is absurd to have a hard-and-fast rule about what one should read and what one shouldn't. More than half of modern culture depends upon what one shouldn't read.
The Importance of Being Earnest (1895) **Wilde, Oscar** (1854–1900) Irish poet, dramatist, writer, critic and wit

149 To my daughter Leonora without whose never-failing sympathy and encouragement this book would have been finished in half the time.
The Heart of a Goof (1926) **Wodehouse, P.G.** (1881–1975) English humorist and writer. Dedication

150 Up! up! my friend, and quit your books;
Or surely you'll grow double –
Books! 'tis a dull and endless strife:
Come, hear the woodland linnet,
How sweet his music! on my life,
There's more of wisdom in it.
'The Tables Turned' (1798) **Wordsworth, William** (1770–1850) English poet
See also literature; poetry; writing

BOREDOM

1 Idle people are often bored and bored people, unless they sleep a lot, are cruel. It is not accident that boredom and cruelty are great preoccupations in our time.
Speedboat (1976) **Adler, Renata** (1938–) US film critic and writer

2 Perhaps the world's second-worst crime is boredom; the first is being a bore.
Attr. **Beaton, Cecil** (1904–1980) English photographer

3 The world is eaten up by boredom ... It is like dust. You go about and never notice, you breathe it in ... It is sifted so fine, it doesn't even grit on your teeth. But stand still for an instant and there it is, coating your face and hands.
The Diary of a Country Priest (1936) **Bernanos, Georges** (1888–1948) French novelist and essayist

4 Bore: A person who talks when you wish him to listen.
The Cynic's Word Book (1906) **Bierce, Ambrose** (1842–c.1914) US writer, verse writer and soldier

5 Boredom is a sign of satisfied ignorance, blunted apprehension, crass sympathies, dull understanding, feeble powers of attention and irreclaimable weakness of character.
Mr Bolfry (1943) **Bridie, James** (1888–1951) Scottish dramatist, writer and physician

6 I mused for a few moments on the question of which was worse, to lead a life so boring that you are easily enchanted or a life so full of stimulus that you are easily bored.
The Lost Continent (1989) **Bryson, Bill** (1951–) US travel writer

7 Society is now one polish'd horde,
Form'd of two mighty tribes, the Bores and Bored.
Don Juan (1819–1824) **Byron, Lord** (1788–1824) English poet, satirist and traveller

8 He loved to be bored; don't think he was contemptuously dismissive of the element of boredom inherent in sexual activity. He adored and venerated boredom. He said that dogs, for example, were never bored, nor birds, so, obviously, the capacity that distinguished man from the other higher mammals, from the scaled and feathered things, was that of boredom. The more bored one was, the more one expressed one's humanity.
'The Quilt Maker' (1981) **Carter, Angela** (1940–1992) English writer. Rationalization of the Japanese veneration of boredom

9 There is no such thing on earth as an uninteresting subject; the only thing that can exist is an uninterested person.
Heretics (1905) **Chesterton, G.K.** (1874–1936) English writer, poet and critic

10 I wanted to be bored to death, as good a way to go as any.
Comfort me with Apples (1956) **De Vries, Peter** (1910–1993) US novelist

11 No more about sex, it's too boring.
Tunc (1968) **Durrell, Lawrence** (1912–1990) Indian-born British poet and writer

12 Every hero becomes a bore at last.
Representative Men (1850) **Emerson, Ralph Waldo** (1803–1882) US poet, essayist, transcendentalist and teacher

13 Sooner barbarity than boredom.
Attr. **Gautier, Théophile** (1811–1872) French poet, writer and critic

14 Some people can stay longer in an hour than others can in a week.
In Esar, *Treasury of Humorous Quotations* (1951) **Howells, W.D.** (1837–1920) US writer, critic, editor and poet

15 Symmetry is boredom, and boredom is the very source of death. Despair yawns.
Les Misérables (1862) **Hugo, Victor** (1802–1885) French poet, writer, dramatist and politician

16 I can sympathize with people's pains, but not with their pleasures. There is something curiously boring about somebody else's happiness.
Limbo (1920) **Huxley, Aldous** (1894–1963) English writer, poet and critic

17 The effect of boredom on a large scale in history is underestimated. It is a main cause of revolutions, and would soon bring to an end all the static Utopias and the farmyard civilization of the Fabians.
End of an Age (1948) **Inge, William Ralph** (1860–1954) English divine, writer and teacher

18 Sir, you are like a pin, but without either its head or its point.
Attr. **Jerrold, Douglas William** (1803–1857) English dramatist, writer and wit. Remark to a small thin man who was boring him

19 We are almost always bored by the very people whom we are not allowed to find boring.
Maximes (1678) **La Rochefoucauld** (1613–1680) French writer

20 Is life not a hundred times too short – to get bored?
Beyond Good and Evil (1886) **Nietzsche, Friedrich Wilhelm** (1844–1900) German philosopher, critic and poet

21 'I believe I take precedence,' he said coldly; 'you are merely the club Bore; I am the club Liar.'
Beasts and Super-Beasts (1914) **Saki** (1870–1916) Burmese-born British writer

22 O, he is as tedious
As a tired horse, a railing wife;
Worse than a smoky house; I had rather live
With cheese and garlic in a windmill, far,
Than feed on cates and have him talk to me
In any summer house in Christendom.
Henry IV, Part 1, III.i

23 Life is as tedious as a twice-told tale
Vexing the dull ear of a drowsy man.
King John, III.iv **Shakespeare, William** (1564–1616) English dramatist, poet and actor

24 It is to be noted, That when any Part of this Paper appears dull, there is a Design in it.
The Tatler, 38, (1709) **Steele, Sir Richard** (1672–1729) Irish-born English writer, dramatist and politician

25 A bore is a man who, when you ask him how he is, tells you.
The So-Called Human Race (1922) **Taylor, Bert Leston** (1866–1921) US journalist

26 Dylan talked copiously, then stopped. 'Somebody's boring me,' he said, 'I think it's me.'
In Heppenstall, *Four Absentees* (1960) **Thomas, Dylan** (1914–1953) Welsh poet, writer and radio dramatist

27 He is an old bore; even the grave yawns for him.
In Pearson, *Beerbohm Tree* (1956) **Tree, Sir Herbert Beerbohm** (1853–1917) English actor and theatre manager. Of Israel Zangwill

28 A healthy male adult bore consumes one and a half times his own weight in other people's patience.
Assorted Prose (1965) **Updike, John** (1932–) US writer, poet and critic

29 The secret of being boring is to say everything.
Discours en vers sur l'homme (1737) **Voltaire** (1694–1778) French philosopher, dramatist, poet, historian, writer and critic
See also idleness and unemployment

BRITAIN

1 Great Britain ... has lost an Empire and not yet found a role. The attempt to play a separate power role – that is, a role apart from Europe, a role based on a 'special relationship' with the United States, a role based on being the head of a Commonwealth ... this role is about to be played out ... Her Majesty's Government is now attempting, wisely in my opinion, to re-enter Europe.
Speech, (1962) **Acheson, Dean** (1893–1971) US Democrat politician

2 This is not 'polite and tidy Britain' ... It's Widow Twankey's Nuclear Laundry.
In Britain in the Eighties (1989) **Artley, Alexandra** British writer. On the reprocessing of foreign nuclear waste in Britain

3 I think the British have the distinction above all other nations of being able to put new wine into old bottles without bursting them.
Hansard, (1950) **Attlee, Clement** (1883–1967) English statesman and Prime Minister

4 Britain today is suffering from galloping obsolescence.
Speech, (1963) **Benn, Tony** (1925–) English Labour politician

5 There are no countries in the world less known by the British than these selfsame British Islands.
Lavengro (1851) **Borrow, George** (1803–1881) English writer and linguist

6 One of the reasons Britain is such a steady and gracious place is the calming influence of the football results and shipping forecasts.
Notes from a Small Island, (1996) **Bryson, Bill** (1951–) US travel writer

7 The people Hitler never understood, and whose actions continued to exasperate him to the end of his life, were the British.
Hitler, A Study in Tyranny (1952) **Bullock, Alan, Baron** (1914–2004) English historian

8 Britain has lived for too long on borrowed time, borrowed money and even borrowed ideas.
The Observer, (1976) **Callaghan, James** (1912–2005) English Labour statesman and Prime Minister

9 What annoys me about Britain is the rugged will to lose.
Attr. **Camp, William** (1926–)

10 The British love permanence more than they love beauty.
The Observer, (1964) **Casson, Sir Hugh** (1910–1999) English architect and writer

11 The maxim of the British people is 'Business as usual'.
Speech, November 1914

12 They are the only people who like to be told how bad things are – who like to be told the worst.
Speech, (1921) Of the British

13 The British Empire and the United States will have to be somewhat mixed up together in some of their affairs for mutual and general advantage. For my own part, looking out for the future, I do not view the process with any misgivings. I could not stop it if I wished; no one can stop it. Like the Mississippi, it just keeps rolling along. Let it roll. Let it roll on full flood, inexorable, irresistible, benignant, to broader lands and better days.
Speech, House of Commons, August 1940

14 When I warned them [the French Government] that Britain would fight on alone whatever they did, their Generals told their Prime Minister and his divided Cabinet, 'In three weeks England will have her neck wrung like a chicken'. Some chicken! Some neck!
Speech, December 1941

15 I have not become the King's First Minister in order to preside over the liquidation of the British Empire.
Speech, Mansion House, November 1942 **Churchill, Sir Winston** (1874–1965) English Conservative Prime Minister

16 A vain, speech-mouthing, speech-reporting guild,
One benefit-club for mutual flattery.
'Fears in Solitude' (1798) **Coleridge, Samuel Taylor** (1772–1834) English poet, philosopher and critic. Of Britain

17 You are not going, I hope, to leave the destinies of the British Empire to prigs and pedants.
Speech, House of Commons, 1863 **Disraeli, Benjamin** (1804–1881) English statesman and writer

18 Courtesy is not dead – it has merely taken refuge in Great Britain.
The Observer, (1953) **Duhamel, Georges** (1884–1966) French writer, poet, dramatist and physician

19 I had been told by Jimmy Edmond in Australia that there were only three things against living in Britain: the place, the climate and the people.
In Low, Low Autobiography **Edmond, James** (1859–1933) Scottish-born Australian writer and editor

20 It does mean, if this is the idea, the end of Britain as an independent European state … it means the end of a thousand years of history.
Speech, 1962 **Gaitskell, Hugh** (1906–1963) English Labour politician. On Britain's joining the European Community

21 My father used to say that the reason the sun never set on the British Empire is because God would never trust the British in the dark.
Glasgow Herald, April 2000 **Galloway, George** (1954–) Scottish Labour politician

22 Britain is not a country that is easily rocked by revolution … In Britain our institutions evolve. We are a Fabian Society writ large.
My Queen and I (1975) **Hamilton, William (Willie)** (1917–2000) English politician, teacher and antiroyalist

23 In the end it may well be that Britain will be honoured by historians more for the way she disposed of an empire than for the way in which she acquired it.
New York Times, (1962) **Harlech, Lord** (1918–1985) English politician, and TV company chairman

24 Once, when a British Prime Minister sneezed, men half a world away would blow their noses. Now when a British Prime Minister sneezes nobody else will even say 'Bless You'.
The Times, (1976) **Levin, Bernard** (1928–2004) British writer

25 What is our task? To make Britain a fit country for heroes to live in.
Speech, (1918) **Lloyd George, David** (1863–1945) British Liberal statesman

26 His Majesty's dominions, on which the sun never sets.
Blackwood's Edinburgh Magazine, (1829) **North, Christopher** (1785–1854) Scottish poet, writer, editor and critic

27 The Empire is a Commonwealth of Nations.
Speech, Adelaide, 1884 **Rosebery, Earl of** (1847–1929) English statesman

28 He [the Briton] is a barbarian, and thinks that the customs of his tribe and island are the laws of nature.
Caesar and Cleopatra (1901) **Shaw, George Bernard** (1856–1950) Irish socialist, writer, dramatist and critic

29 If any of the provinces of the British empire cannot be made to contribute towards the support of the whole empire, it is surely time that Great Britain should free herself from the expense of defending those provinces in time of war, and of supporting any part of their civil or military

establishments in time of peace, and endeavour to accommodate her future views and designs to the real mediocrity of her circumstances.
Wealth of Nations (1776) **Smith, Adam** (1723–1790) Scottish economist, philosopher and essayist

30 Hail, happy Britain! highly favoured isle,
And Heaven's peculiar care!
The Chase (1735) **Somerville, William** (1675–1742) English poet

31 When Britain first, at heaven's command,
Arose from out the azure main,
This was the charter of the land,
And guardian angels sung this strain:
'Rule, Britannia, rule the waves;
Britons never will be slaves.'
Alfred: A Masque (1740) **Thomson, James** (1700–1748) Scottish poet and dramatist

32 The government of the world I live in was not framed, like that of Britain, in after-dinner conversations over the wine.
Walden (1854), 'Economy' **Thoreau, Henry David** (1817–1862) US essayist, social critic and writer
See also cities: London; England; Ireland; patriotism; Scotland

BUSINESS

1 A memorandum is written not to inform the reader but to protect the writer.
Attr. **Acheson, Dean** (1893–1971) US Democrat politician

2 It's just called 'The Bible' now. We dropped the word 'Holy' to give it a more mass-market appeal.
Editor at Hodder & Stoughton quoted in *Daily Telegraph*, (1989)

3 Change imposed is change opposed.
Management slogan, Deloitte and Touche, (1999)

4 A Company for carrying on an undertaking of Great Advantage, but no one to know what it is.
The South Sea Company Prospectus
Anonymous

5 Business, you know, may bring money, but friendship hardly ever does.
Emma (1816) **Austen, Jane** (1775–1817) English writer

6 Business is really more agreeable than pleasure; it interests the whole mind, the aggregate nature of man more continuously, and more deeply. But it does not look as if it did.
The English Constitution (1867) **Bagehot, Walter** (1826–1877) English economist and political philosopher

7 Generous people make bad shopkeepers.
Illusions perdues (1843) **Balzac, Honoré de** (1799–1850) French writer

8 Every man's occupation should be beneficial to his fellow-man as well as profitable to himself. All else is vanity and folly.
The Humbugs of the World (1866)

9 Every crowd has a silver lining.
Attr. **Barnum, Phineas T.** (1810–1891) US showman and writer

10 Jesus picked up twelve men from the bottom ranks of business and forged them into an organization that conquered the world.
The Man Nobody Knows: A Discovery of the Real Jesus (1924) **Barton, Bruce** (1886–1967) US advertising agent and writer

11 Committee – a group of men who keep minutes and waste hours.
Attr. **Berle, Milton** (1908–2002) US comedian

12 You ask me what it is I do. Well actually, you know,
I'm partly a liaison man and partly P.R.O.
Essentially I integrate the current export drive
And basically I'm viable from ten o'clock till five.
'Executive' (1974) **Betjeman, Sir John** (1906–1984) English poet laureate

13 In matters of commerce the fault of the Dutch
Is offering too little and asking too much.
The French are with equal advantage content,
So we clap on Dutch bottoms just twenty per cent.

Coded dispatch to Sir Charles Bagot, English Ambassador to the Hague, (1826) **Canning, George** (1770–1827) English Prime Minister, orator and poet

14 British management doesn't seem to understand the importance of the human factor.
Speech, (1979) **Charles, Prince of Wales** (1948–) Son and heir of Elizabeth II and Prince Philip

15 Pile it high, sell it cheap.
Business motto **Cohen, Sir Jack** (1898–1979) Supermarket magnate

16 I have found some of the best reasons I ever had for remaining at the bottom simply by looking at the men at the top.
Essays **Colby, Frank Moore** (1865–1925) US editor, historian and economist

17 The business of America is business.
Speech, (1925) **Coolidge, Calvin** (1872–1933) US President

18 It takes one hen to lay an egg,
But seven men to sell it.
'The Regimental Hen' **Dennis, C.J.** (1876–1938) Australian writer and poet

19 Here's the rule for bargains. 'Do other men, for they would do you.' That's the true business precept. All others are counterfeit.
Martin Chuzzlewit (1844) **Dickens, Charles** (1812–1870) English writer

20 A company director who takes a pay rise of £50,000 when the rest of the workforce is getting a few hundred is not part of some general trend. He is a greedy bastard.
Speaking at the TUC conference, (1998) **Edmonds, John** (1944–) British trade unionist

21 Nothing astonishes men so much as common-sense and plain dealing.
'Art' (1841) **Emerson, Ralph Waldo** (1803–1882) US poet, essayist, transcendentalist and teacher

22 You can run the office without a boss, but you can't run an office without the secretaries.
The Observer, (1981) **Fonda, Jane** (1937–) US actress and activist

23 A business that makes nothing but money is a poor kind of business.
Interview **Ford, Henry** (1863–1947) US car manufacturer

24 No nation was ever ruined by trade.
Essays **Franklin, Benjamin** (1706–1790) US statesman, scientist, political critic and printer

25 In a community where public services have failed to keep abreast of private consumption things are very different. Here, in an atmosphere of private opulence and public squalor, the private goods have full sway.
The Affluent Society (1958)

26 The salary of the chief executive of the large corporation is not a market award for achievement. It is frequently in the nature of a warm personal gesture by the individual to himself.
Annals of an Abiding Liberal (1980)

27 You must now speak always of the market system. The word 'capitalism', once the common reference, has acquired a deleterious Marxist sound.
The Observer, (1998) **Galbraith, J.K.** (1908–2006) Canadian-born US economist, diplomat and writer

28 It is difficult but not impossible to conduct strictly honest business. What is true is that honesty is incompatible with the amassing of a large fortune.
Non-Violence in Peace and War (1948) **Gandhi, Mohandas** (1869–1948) Indian political leader

29 No one can possibly achieve any real and lasting success or 'get rich' in business by being a conformist.
International Herald Tribune, (1961)

30 The meek shall inherit the earth, but not the mineral rights.
In Robert Lenzner, *The Great Getty* (1985) **Getty, John Paul** (1892–1976) US oil billionaire and art collector

31 There is a misunderstanding by marketers in our culture about what freedom of choice is. In the market, it is equated with multiplying choice. This is a misconception. If you have infinite choice, people are reduced to passivity.
New York Times, (1990) **Gitlin, Todd** (1943–) US sociologist

32 Chaplin is no business man – all he knows is that he can't take anything less.
Attr. **Goldwyn, Samuel** (1882–1974) Polish-born US film producer

33 The art of management is the art of taking credit for other people's work.
The Daily Telegraph, (2003) **Greer, Germaine** (1939–) Australian feminist writer

34 The art of publicity is a black art; but it has come to stay, and every year adds to its potency.
Speech, (1951) **Hand, Learned** (1872–1961) US judge

35 Someone who can't see something working in practice without asking whether it would work in theory.
Attr. **Heller, Walter** (1915–1987) US economist. Definition of an economist

36 The grass will grow in the streets of a hundred cities, a thousand towns; the weeds will overrun the fields of millions of farms if that protection is taken away.
Speech, (1932) **Hoover, Herbert Clark** (1874–1964) US Republican President. Predicting the outcome if tariff protection were removed

37 People want economy and they will pay any price to get it.
New York Times, (1974) **Iacocca, Lee** (1924–) US businessman; President of Ford Motor Company

38 In both rich and poor nations consumption is polarized while expectation is equalized.
Celebration of Awareness (1970) **Illich, Ivan** (1926–) Austrian-born US educator, sociologist, writer and priest

39 The last stage of fitting the product to the market is fitting the market to the product.
The Observer, (1989) **James, Clive** (1939–) Australian writer and broadcaster

40 O dome gigantic, dome immense;
Built in defiance of common sense.
In *The Observer,* (1999) **James, P.D.** (1920–) English crime writer. Comment on the Millennium Dome

41 If you can keep your head when all about you are losing theirs, it's just possible you haven't grasped the situation.
Please Don't Eat the Daisies, (1957) **Kerr, Jean** (1923–2003) US playwright, born Bridget Collins

42 I think that Capitalism, wisely managed, can probably be made more efficient for attaining economic ends than any alternative system yet in sight, but that in itself it is in many ways extremely objectionable.
'The End of Laissez-Faire' (1926)

43 Wordly wisdom teaches that it is better for the reputation to fail conventionally than to succeed unconventionally.
The General Theory of Employment, Interest and Money (1936) **Keynes, John Maynard** (1883–1946) English economist

44 When you are skinning your customers, you should leave some skin on to heal so that you can skin them again.
The Observer, (1961) **Khrushchev, Nikita** (1894–1971) Russian statesman and Premier of the USSR. Remark to British businessmen

45 Love your neighbour is not merely sound Christianity; it is good business.
The Observer, (1921) **Lloyd George, David** (1863–1945) British Liberal statesman

46 Macmillan and Company Limited propose to carry on their business at St Martin's Street, London W.C.2 until they are either taxed, insured, ARP'd or bombed out of existence.
Announcement, 17 September 1939 **Macmillan, Harold** (1894–1986) British Conservative Prime Minister

47 The people recognize themselves in their commodities; they find their soul in their automobile, hi-fi set, split-level home, kitchen equipment.
One-Dimensional Man (1964) **Marcuse, Herbert** (1898–1979) German-born US philosopher

48 He is the only man who is ever apologizing for his occupation.
Prejudices (1927) **Mencken, H.L.** (1880–1956) US writer, critic, philologist and satirist. Referring to the businessman

49 When any creativity becomes useful, it is sucked into the vortex of commercialism, and when a thing becomes commercial, it becomes the enemy of man.
The New Yorker, (1961) **Miller, Arthur** (1915–2005) US dramatist and screenwriter

50 Nobody talks more of free enterprise and competition and of the best man winning than the man who inherited his father's store or farm.
Attr. **Mills, C. Wright** (1916–1962) US sociologist

51 Although it is interesting as a novelty, the telephone has no commercial application.
Morgan, John Pierpoint (1837–1913) US financier and banker. Rejecting Alexander Graham Bell's new invention

52 Curiosity is the key to creativity.
Made in Japan (1986) **Morita, Akio** (1921–1999) Japanese businessman, chief executive of Sony

53 Monopoly is a terrible thing, till you have it.
The New Yorker, (1979) **Murdoch, Rupert** (1931–) Australian-born publisher and international businessman

54 England is a nation of shopkeepers.
In O'Meara, *Napoleon in Exile* (1822) **Napoleon I** (1769–1821) French emperor

55 No praying, it spoils business.
Venice Preserv'd (1682) **Otway, Thomas** (1652–1685) English dramatist and poet

56 The secret of business is to know something that nobody else knows.
The Economist, (1991) **Onassis, Aristotle** (1906–1975) Turkish-born Greek shipping magnate

57 Expenditure rises to meet income.
Attr. **Parkinson, C. Northcote** (1909–1993) English political scientist and historian

58 The Peter Principle: In a hierarchy every employee tends to rise to his level of incompetence.

The Peter Principle, (1969) **Peter, Laurence J.** (1919–1990) US educationist

59 You pays your money and you takes your choice.
(1846) **Punch**

60 He's a businessman. I'll make him an offer he can't refuse.
The Godfather (1969) **Puzo, Mario** (1920–) US writer

61 We even sell a pair of earrings for under £1, which is cheaper than a prawn sandwich from Marks & Spencers. But I have to say the earrings probably won't last as long.
Speech to the Institute of Directors at the Albert Hall, (1991) **Ratner, Gerald** (1949–) British businessman

62 I have my veto pen drawn and ready for any tax increase that Congress might even think of sending up. And I have only one thing to say to the tax increasers. Go ahead – make my day.
Time, (1985) **Reagan, Ronald** (1911–2004) US actor, Republican statesman and President. To the American Business Conference

63 In the factory we make cosmetics. In the store we sell hope.
In Tobias, *Fire and Ice* (1976) **Revson, Charles** (1906–1975) US cosmetic company executive

64 A friendship founded on business is better than a business founded on friendship.
Attr. **Rockefeller, John D.** (1839–1937) US oil magnate and philanthropist

65 I am still looking for the modern equivalent of those Quakers who ran successful businesses, made money because they offered honest products and treated their people decently ... This business creed, sadly, seems long forgotten.
Body and Soul (1991)

66 I think that business practices would improve immeasurably if they were guided by 'feminine' principles and qualities like love and care and intuition.
Body & Soul (1991) **Roddick, Anita** (1942–) British businesswoman, founder of The Body Shop

67 We demand that big business give the people a square deal; in return we must insist that when any one engaged in big business honestly endeavors to do right he shall himself be given a square deal.
Theodore Roosevelt: an Autobiography (1913) **Roosevelt, Theodore** (1858–1919) US Republican President

68 Small is Beautiful. A study of economics as if people mattered.
Title of book, (1973) **Schumacher, E.F.** (1911–1977) German-born British economist and essayist

69 A dinner lubricates business.
In Boswell, *The Life of Samuel Johnson* (1791) **Scott, William** (1745–1836) English lawyer

70 The customer is always right.
Slogan adopted at his shops **Selfridge, Harry Gordon** (1858–1947) US-born British merchant

71 The big print giveth and the fine print taketh away.
Attr. **Sheen, J. Fulton** (1895–1979) US Catholic bishop, broadcaster and writer. Referring to his contract for a television appearance

72 Cecil's despatch of business was extraordinary, his maxim being, 'The shortest way to do many things is to do only one thing at once.'
Self-Help (1859) **Smiles, Samuel** (1812–1904) English writer

73 People of the same trade seldom meet together, even for merriment and diversion, but the conversation ends in a conspiracy against the public, or in some contrivance to raise prices.
Wealth of Nations (1776)

74 To found a great empire for the sole purpose of raising up a people of customers, may at first sight appear a project fit only for a nation of shopkeepers. It is, however, a project altogether unfit for a nation of shopkeepers; but extremely fit for a nation whose government is influenced by shopkeepers.
Wealth of Nations (1776) **Smith, Adam** (1723–1790) Scottish economist, philosopher and essayist

75 Everyone lives by selling something.
Across the Plains (1892), 'Beggars' **Stevenson, Robert Louis** (1850–1894) Scottish writer, poet and essayist

76 Is it really good for policy-makers to act as if everything has its price, and as if policies should be judged chiefly by their effects in delivering material benefits to selfish citizens? … It does not ask those individuals whether they also have other values which are not revealed by their shopping.
Capitalism, Socialism and the Environment (1976) **Stretton, Hugh** (1924–) Australian political scientist and historian

77 My life's been a meeting, Dad, one long meeting. Even on the few committees I don't yet belong to, the agenda winks at me when I pass.
The Keep (1961) **Thomas, Gwyn** (1913–1981) Welsh writer, dramatist and teacher

78 Did you ever expect a corporation to have a conscience, when it has no soul to be damned, and no body to be kicked?
Attr. **Thurlow, Edward, First Baron** (1731–1806) English lawyer, politician and Lord Chancellor

79 A committee should consist of three men, two of whom are absent.
In Pearson, *Beerbohm Tree* **Tree, Sir Herbert Beerbohm** (1853–1917) English actor and theatre manager

80 Deals are my art form. Other people paint beautifully on canvas or write wonderful poetry. I like making deals, preferably big deals. That's how I get my kicks.
Trump: The Art of the Deal (1987)

81 I love real estate. It is tangible, it's solid, it's beautiful. It's artistic, from my standpoint, and I just love real estate.
Interview on Wall Street with *Fortune*, (2002) **Trump, Donald** (1946–) US billionaire property developer

82 The public be damned! I'm working for my stockholders.
Remark, (1883) **Vanderbilt, William H.** (1821–1885) US financier and railway magnate. When asked whether the public should be consulted about luxury trains

83 Conspicuous consumption of valuable goods is a means of reputability to the gentleman of leisure.
The Theory of the Leisure Class (1899) **Veblen, Thorstein** (1857–1929) US economist and sociologist

84 Commercialism is doing well that which should not be done at all.
Listener (1975) **Vidal, Gore** (1925–) US writer, critic and poet

85 Being good in business is the most fascinating kind of art.
The Observer, (1987) **Warhol, Andy** (c.1926–1987) US painter, graphic designer and filmmaker

86 If Max gets to Heaven he won't last long. He will be chucked out for trying to pull off a merger between Heaven and Hell ... after having secured a controlling interest in key subsidiary compames in both places, of course.
In A.J.P. Taylor, *Beaverbrook* (1972) **Wells, H.G.** (1866–1946) English writer. Of Max Beaverbrook

87 A living is made, Mr Kemper, by selling something that everybody needs at least once a year. Yes, sir! And a million is made by producing something that everybody needs every day. You artists produce something that nobody needs at any time.
The Merchant of Yonkers (1939) **Wilder, Thornton** (1897–1975) US author and playwright

88 What is good for the country is good for General Motors, and vice versa.
Remark to Congressional Committee, (1953) **Wilson, Charles E.** (1890–1961) US industrialist, car manufacturer and politician

89 Business underlies everything in our national life, including our spiritual life. Witness the fact that in the Lord's Prayer the first petition is for daily bread. No one can worship God or love his neighbour on an empty stomach.
Speech, (1912) **Wilson, Woodrow** (1856–1924) US Democrat President

90 Nothing is illegal if one hundred businessmen decide to do it.

Attr. **Young, Andrew** (1932–) US politician and civil rights campaigner
See also advertising; money and wealth

CHANGE

1 Times change, and we change with them.
In Harrison, *Description of Britain* (1577) **Anonymous**

2 The universe is change; life is what thinking makes of it.
Meditations **Aurelius, Marcus** (121–180) Roman emperor and Stoic philosopher

3 That all things are changed, and that nothing really perishes, and that the sum of matter remains exactly the same, is sufficiently certain.
Thoughts on the Nature of Things (1604) **Bacon, Francis** (1561–1626) English philosopher, essayist, politician and courtier

4 Consistency requires you to be as ignorant today as you were a year ago.
Notebook (1892) **Berenson, Bernard** (1865–1959) Lithuanian-born US art critic

5 It is said I am against change. I am not against change. I am in favour of change in the right circumstances. And those circumstances are when it can no longer be resisted.
Attr. by Paul Johnson in *The Spectator*, May 1996 **Brittain, Vera** (1893–1970) English writer and pacifist

6 A state without the means of some change is without the means of its conservation.
Reflections on the Revolution in France (1790) **Burke, Edmund** (1729–1797) Irish-born British statesman and philosopher

7 All conservatism is based upon the idea that if you leave things alone you leave them as they are. But you do not. If you leave a thing alone you leave it to a torrent of change.
Orthodoxy (1908) **Chesterton, G.K.** (1874–1936) English writer, poet and critic

8 They must often change who would be constant in happiness or wisdom.
Analects **Confucius** (c.550–c.478 BC) Chinese philosopher and teacher of ethics

9 The world's a scene of changes, and to be Constant, in Nature were inconstancy.
The Mistress (1647) **Cowley, Abraham** (1618–1667) English poet and dramatist

10 Change is inevitable. In a progressive country change is constant.
Speech, Edinburgh, (1867) **Disraeli, Benjamin** (1804–1881) English statesman and writer

11 When it is not necessary to change, it is necessary not to change.
Speech concerning Episcopacy, (1641) **Falkland, Viscount** (c.1610–1643) English politician and writer

12 You cannot step twice into the same river.
In Plato, *Cratylus* **Heraclitus** (c.540–c.480 BC) Greek philosopher

13 Change is not made without inconvenience, even from worse to better.
In Johnson, *Dictionary of the English Language* (1755) **Hooker, Richard** (c.1554–1600) English theologian and churchman

14 There is a certain relief in change, even though it be from bad to worse; as I have found in travelling in a stage-coach, that it is often a comfort to shift one's position and be bruised in a new place.
Tales of a Traveller (1824) **Irving, Washington** (1783–1859) US writer and diplomat

15 The more things change the more they remain the same.
Les Guêpes (1849) **Karr, Alphonse** (1808–1890) French writer and editor. (*Plus ça change, plus c'est la même chose*)

16 There is nothing stable in the world; uproar's your only music.
Letter to George and Tom Keats, (13 January 1818) **Keats, John** (1795–1821) English poet

17 What is conservatism? Is it not adherence to the old and tried, against the new and untried?
Speech, (1860) **Lincoln, Abraham** (1809–1865) US statesman and President

18 Well, I find that a change of nuisances is as good as a vacation.
Attr. **Lloyd George, David** (1863–1945) British Liberal statesman. On being asked how he maintained his cheerfulness when beset by numerous political obstacles

19 Some groups increase, others diminish, and in a short space the generations of living creatures are changed and like runners pass on the torch of life.
De Rerum Natura **Lucretius** (c.95–55 BC) Roman philosopher

20 The philosophers have merely interpreted the world in various ways; the point, however, is to change it.
Theses on Feuerbach (1845, published 1888) **Marx, Karl** (1818–1883) German political philosopher and economist; founder of Communism

21 Like all weak men he laid an exaggerated stress on not changing one's mind.
Of Human Bondage (1915) **Maugham, William Somerset** (1874–1965) English writer, dramatist and physician

22 There is, in public affairs, no state so bad, provided it has age and stability on its side, that is not preferable to change and disturbance.
Essais (1580) **Montaigne, Michel de** (1533–1592) French essayist and moralist

23 Since 'tis Nature's law to change, Constancy alone is strange.
'A Dialogue between Strephon and Daphne' (1691) **Rochester, Earl of** (1647–1680) English poet, satirist, courtier and libertine

24 'Change' is scientific, 'progress' is ethical; change is indubitable, whereas progress is a matter of controversy.
Unpopular Essays (1950) **Russell, Bertrand** (1872–1970) English philosopher, mathematician, essayist and social reformer

25 Now the melancholy god protect thee; and the tailor make thy doublet of changeable taffeta, for thy mind is a very opal.
Twelfth Night, II.iv **Shakespeare, William** (1564–1616) English dramatist, poet and actor

26 Times go by turns, and chances change by course,
From foul to fair, from better hap to worse.
'Times go by Turns' (1595) **Southwell, Robert** (1561–1595) English poet and Jesuit martyr

27 What man that sees the ever-whirling
wheele
Of Change, the which all mortall things
doth sway,
But that therby doth find, and plainly feele,
How Mutability in them doth play
Her cruell sports, to many men's decay?
The Faerie Queene (1596) **Spenser, Edmund**
(c.1522–1599) English poet

28 There is nothing in this world constant, but
inconstancy.
A Critical Essay upon the Faculties of the Mind
(1709) **Swift, Jonathan** (1667–1745) Irish satirist,
poet, essayist and cleric

29 Forward, forward let us range,
Let the great world spin for ever down the
ringing grooves of change.
'Locksley Hall' (1838)

30 The old order changeth, yielding place to
new,
And God fulfils himself in many ways,
Lest one good custom should corrupt the
world.
The Idylls of the King **Tennyson, Alfred, Lord**
(1809–1892) English lyric poet

31 Things do not change; we change.
Walden (1854) **Thoreau, Henry David** (1817–
1862) US essayist, social critic and writer

32 Future shock ... the shattering stress and
disorientation that we induce in individuals
by subjecting them to too much change in
too short a time.
Future Shock (1970) **Toffler, Alvin** (1928–) US
writer and futurist

33 The stone that is rolling can gather no
moss;
For master and servant oft changing is
loss.
Five Hundred Points of Good Husbandry (1557)
Tusser, Thomas (c.1524–1580) English writer,
poet and musician
See also action; time

CHARITY

1 The living need charity more than the
dead.
The Jolly Old Pedagogue (1866) **Arnold, George**
(1834–1865) US poet

2 In charity there is no excess.
'Of Goodness, and Goodness of Nature' (1625)
Bacon, Francis (1561–1626) English
philosopher, essayist, politician and courtier

3 Don't bother to thank me. I know what a
perfectly ghastly season it's been for you
Spanish dancers.
Attr. **Bankhead, Tallulah** (1903–1968) US
actress. Said on dropping fifty dollars into a
tambourine held out by a Salvation Army
collector

4 It is more blessed to give than to receive.
Acts of the Apostles, 20:35

5 God loveth a cheerful giver.
II Corinthians, 9:7 **The Bible (King James
Version)**

6 Charity begins at home, is the voice of the
world.
Religio Medici (1643) **Browne, Sir Thomas**
(1605–1682) English physician, author and
antiquary

7 Of every thousand dollars spent in so-
called charity today, it is probable that nine
hundred and fifty dollars is unwisely spent.
'Wealth' (1889) **Carnegie, Andrew** (1835–1919)
Scottish-born US millionaire and
philanthropist

8 The manner of giving is worth more than
the gift.
Le Menteur (1643) **Corneille, Pierre** (1606–1684)
French dramatist, poet and lawyer

9 He that feeds upon charity has a cold
dinner and no supper.
Attr. **Fuller, Thomas** (1608–1661) English
churchman and antiquary

10 Give us your fucking money.
BBC TV broadcast, 3 July 1985 **Geldof, Bob**
(1954–) Irish rock musician. Emotional appeal
during the Live Aid concert to raise funds for
famine victims in Ethiopia

11 I have learned more about love,
selflessness and human understanding in
this great adventure in the world of Aids
than I ever did in the cutthroat,
competitive world in which I spent my life.
Independent on Sunday, (1992) **Perkins,
Anthony** (1932–1992) US actor

12 Keeping books on charity is capitalist nonsense! I just use the money for the poor. I can't stop to count it.
In Fleur Cowles, Bloody Precedent: the Peron Story (1952) **Peron, Eva** (1919–1952) Argentinian actress and politician

13 For Forms of Government let fools contest;
Whate'er is best administer'd is best:
For Modes of Faith, let graceless zealots fight;
His can't be wrong whose life is in the right:
In Faith and Hope the world will disagree,
But all Mankind's concern is Charity.
Essay on Man (1733) **Pope, Alexander** (1688–1744) English poet, translator and editor

14 Charity begins at home.
Proverb

15 He does the poor man two favours who gives quickly.
Sententiae **Publilius, Syrus** (1st century BC) Roman writer

16 The feigned charity of the rich man is for him no more than another luxury; he feeds the poor as he feeds dogs and horses.
Letter to M. Moulton **Rousseau, Jean-Jacques** (1712–1778) Swiss-born French philosopher, educationist and essayist

17 *Rowley*: I believe there is no sentiment he has more faith in than that 'charity begins at home'.
Sir Oliver Surface: And his, I presume, is of that domestic sort which never stirs abroad at all.
The School for Scandal (1777) **Sheridan, Richard Brinsley** (1751–1816) Irish dramatist, politician and orator

18 Charity is cold in the multitude of possessions, and the rich are covetous of their crumbs.
Jubilate Agno (c.1758–63) **Smart, Christopher** (1722–1771) English poet and translator

19 The man who leaves money to charity in his will is only giving away what no longer belongs to him.
Letter, (1769) **Voltaire** (1694–1778) French philosopher, dramatist, poet, historian, writer and critic

20 It is an ugly trick. It is a virtue grown by the rich on the graves of the poor. Unless it is accompanied by sincere revolt against the present social system, it is cheap moral swagger.
The Clarion **West, Dame Rebecca** (1892–1983) English writer, critic and feminist. Of charity *See also* compassion; goodness; kindness; suffering

CHILDHOOD AND CHILDREN

1 In every child who is born, under no matter what circumstances, and no matter what parents, the potentiality of the human race is born again.
Let Us Now Praise Famous Men (1941) **Agee, James** (1909–1955) US novelist and poet

2 It was no wonder that people were so horrible when they started life as children.
One Fat Englishman (1963) **Amis, Kingsley** (1922–1995) English writer, poet and critic

3 Children need to get into trouble to learn how to get out of trouble.
The Mental Health Foundation, in *The Times*, (1999) **Anonymous** Commenting on over-protective parents

4 Children are natural mimics who act like their parents despite every effort to teach them good manners.
Anonymous

5 Only those in the last stages of disease could believe that children are true judges of character.
The Orators (1932) **Auden, W.H.** (1907–1973) English poet, essayist, critic, teacher and dramatist

6 On every formal visit a child ought to be of the party, by way of provision for discourse.
Sense and Sensibility (1811) **Austen, Jane** (1775–1817) English writer

7 Children sweeten labours, but they make misfortunes more bitter.
Essays (1625) **Bacon, Francis** (1561–1626) English philosopher, essayist, politician and courtier

8 Children have never been very good at listening to their elders, but they have never failed to imitate them. They must, they have no other models.
Nobody Knows My Name (1961) **Baldwin, James** (1924–1987) US writer, dramatist, poet and civil rights activist

9 What is an adult? A child blown up by age.
The Woman Destroyed (1969) **Beauvoir, Simone de** (1908–1986) French writer, feminist critic and philosopher

10 I am married to Beatrice Salkeld, a painter. We have no children, except me.
Attr. **Behan, Brendan** (1923–1964) Irish dramatist, writer and Republican

11 I call you bad, my little child, upon the title page,
Because a manner rude and wild is common at your age.
Introduction to A Bad Child's Book of Beasts (1896)

12 And always keep a-hold of Nurse
For fear of finding something worse.
Cautionary Tales (1907)

13 The Chief Defect of Henry King
Was chewing little bits of String.
Cautionary Tales (1907), 'Henry King' **Belloc, Hilaire** (1870–1953) English writer of verse, essayist and critic; Liberal MP

14 Maud was my hateful nurse who smelt of soap ...
She rubbed my face in messes I had made
And was the first to tell me about Hell,
Admitting she was going there herself.
Summoned by Bells (1960) **Betjeman, Sir John** (1906–1984) English poet laureate

15 Train up a child in the way he should go: and when he is old, he will not depart from it.
Proverbs, 22:6

16 Suffer the little children to come unto me, and forbid them not: for of such is the kingdom of God.
Mark, 10:14 **The Bible (King James Version)**

17 '... I have no name
I am but two days old – '
What shall I call thee?
'... I happy am,
Joy is my name, – '
Sweet joy befall thee!
Songs of Innocence (1789) **Blake, William** (1757–1827) English poet, engraver, painter and mystic

18 There is no end to the violations committed by children on children, quietly talking alone.
The House in Paris (1935) **Bowen, Elizabeth** (1899–1973) Irish writer

19 Do you hear the children weeping, O my brothers,
Ere the sorrow comes with years?
'The Cry of the Children' (1844) **Browning, Elizabeth Barrett** (1806–1861) English poet; wife of Robert Browning

20 Ah! happy years! once more who would not be a boy?
Childe Harold's Pilgrimage (1818) **Byron, Lord** (1788–1824) English poet, satirist and traveller

21 In the heart of dew we lie
Drowned in brief immortality
And watch our fair-haired children play.
'Hearts and Children' **Campbell, David** (1915–1979) Australian poet, rugby player and wartime pilot

22 I am fond of children (except boys).
Letter to Kathleen Eschwege, (1879) **Carroll, Lewis** (1832–1898) English writer and photographer

23 Boys do not grow up gradually. They move forward in spurts like the hands of clocks in railway stations.
Enemies of Promise (1938) **Connolly, Cyril** (1903–1974) English literary editor, writer and critic

24 Violet Elizabeth dried her tears. She saw that they were useless and she did not believe in wasting her effects. 'All right,' she said calmly, 'I'll thcream then. I'll thcream, an' thcream, an' thcream till I'm thick.'
Still William (1925)

25 'I don't play little girls' games,' [William] said scathingly. But Violet Elizabeth did not appear to be scathed. 'Don't you know any little girlth?' she said pityingly. 'I'll teach you little girlth gameth,' she added pleasantly. 'I don't want to,' said William. 'I don't like them. I don't like little girls' games. I don't want to know 'em.'
The Just William Collection (1991), 'The Sweet Little Girl in White' **Crompton, Richmal** (1890–1969) English writer and teacher

26 Angel of Words, in vain I have striven with thee,
Nor plead a lifetime's love and loyalty;
Only, with envy, bid thee watch this face,
That says so much, so flawlessly,
And in how small a space!
'A Child Asleep' **De La Mare, Walter** (1873–1956) English Poet

27 'It opens the lungs, washes the countenance, exercises the eyes, and softens down the temper', said Mr Bumble. 'So cry away.'
Oliver Twist (1838)

28 In the little world in which children have their existence ... there is nothing so finely perceived and so finely felt as injustice.
Great Expectations (1861) **Dickens, Charles** (1812–1870) English writer

29 We spend the first twelve months of our children's lives teaching them to walk and talk and the next twelve telling them to sit down and shut up.
Attr. **Diller, Phyllis** (1917–1974) US comedian

30 It is only rarely that one can see in a little boy the promise of a man, but one can almost always see in a little girl the threat of a woman.
Attr. **Dumas, Alexandre (Fils)** (1824–1895) French author

31 I think what is happening to me is so wonderful, and not only what can be seen on my body, but all that is taking place inside. I never discuss myself or any of these things with anybody; that is why I have to talk to myself about them.
Diary of a Young Girl **Frank, Anne** (1929–1945) Jewish diarist; died in Nazi concentration camp

32 To bear many children is considered not only a religious blessing but also an investment. The greater their number, some Indians reason, the more alms they can beg.
In Fallaci, *New York Review of Books* **Gandhi, Indira** (1917–1984) Indian statesman and Prime Minister

33 My father was frightened of his mother. I was frightened of my father, and I'm damned well going to make sure that my children are frightened of me.
In R. Churchill, *Lord Derby – 'King of Lancashire'* (1959) **George V** (1865–1936) King of the United Kingdom

34 Few, perhaps, are the children who, after the expiration of some months or years, would sincerely rejoice in the resurrection of their parents.
Memoirs of My Life and Writings (1796) **Gibbon, Edward** (1737–1794) English historian, politician and memoirist

35 Your children are not your children.
They are the sons and daughters of Life's longing for itself.
They came through you but not from you,
And though they are with you yet they belong not to you.
The Prophet (1923) **Gibran, Kahlil** (1883–1931) Lebanese poet, mystic and painter

36 Billy, in one of his nice new sashes,
Fell in the fire and was burnt to ashes;
Now, although the room grows chilly,
I haven't the heart to poke poor Billy.
Ruthless Rhymes for Heartless Homes (1899) **Graham, Harry** (1874–1936) English writer

37 'It's so sweet
to hear their chatter, watch them grow and thrive,'
she says to his departing smile. Then, nursing
the youngest child, sits staring at her feet.
To the wind she says, 'They have eaten me alive.'
Poems (1968) **Harwood, Gwen** (1920–1995) Australian poet and music teacher

38 The proper time to influence the character of a child is about a hundred years before he is born.

The Observer, (1929) **Inge, William Ralph** (1860–1954) English divine, writer and teacher

39 I suppose one of the reasons why I grew up feeling the need to cause laughter was perpetual fear of being its unwitting object.
Unreliable Memoirs (1980) **James, Clive** (1939–) Australian-born, UK-based TV critic and presenter

40 Rest in soft peace, and, ask'd, say here doth lye
Ben Jonson his best piece of poetrie.
'On My First Son' (1616) **Jonson, Ben** (1572–1637) English dramatist and poet

41 At every step the child should be allowed to meet the real experiences of life; the thorns should never be plucked from his roses.
The Century of the Child (1909) **Key, Ellen** (1849–1926) Swedish feminist, writer and lecturer

42 A loud noise at one end and no sense of responsibility at the other.
Attr. **Knox, Ronald** (1888–1957) English Catholic priest and biblical translator. Definition of a baby

43 Boys are capital fellows in their own way, among their mates; but they are unwholesome companions for grown people.
Essays of Elia (1823)

44 Riddle of destiny, who can show
What thy short visit meant, or know
What thy errand here below?
'On an Infant Dying as soon as Born' **Lamb, Charles** (1775–1834) English essayist, critic and letter writer

45 A child's a plaything for an hour.
Parental Recollections **Lamb, Mary** (1764–1847) English prose writer

46 Remember that as a teenager you are at the last stage in your life when you will be happy to hear that the phone is for you.
Social Studies (1981) **Lebowitz, Fran** (1946–) US writer

47 You are better than all the ballads
That ever were sung or said;
For ye are living poems,
And all the rest are dead.
'Children' (1849)

48 There was a little girl
Who had a little curl
Right in the middle of her forehead,
When she was good
She was very, very good,
But when she was bad she was horrid.
'There was a Little Girl' (1882) Written for his second daughter when she was a baby
Longfellow, Henry Wadsworth (1807–1882) US poet and writer

49 Was it for this I uttered prayers,
And sobbed and cursed and kicked the stairs,
That now, domestic as a plate,
I should retire at half-past eight?
'Grown-up' (1920)

50 Childhood is not from birth to a certain age and at a certain age
The child is grown, and puts away childish things,
Childhood is the kingdom where nobody dies.
Nobody that matters, that is.
Wine from these Grapes (1934) **Millay, Edna St Vincent** (1892–1950) US poet and dramatist

51 Society chooses to disregard the mistreatment of children, judging it to be altogether normal because it is so commonplace.
Pictures of a Childhood (1986) **Miller, Alice** Swiss-born US psychotherapist and writer

52 I love children – especially when they cry, for then someone takes them away.
Attr. **Mitford, Nancy** (1904–1973) English writer

53 It should be noted that children at play are not merely playing; their games should be seen as their most serious actions.
Essais (1580) **Montaigne, Michel de** (1533–1592) French essayist and moralist

54 Children aren't happy with nothing to ignore,
And that's what parents were created for.
'The Parent' (1933) **Nash, Ogden** (1902–1971) US poet

55 Do engine drivers, I wonder, eternally wish they were small boys?

The Best of Myles Na Gopaleen (1990) **O'Brien, Flann** (1911–1966) Irish novelist and journalist

56 Anybody who has survived his childhood has enough information about life to last him the rest of his days.
In New York Times Book Review, (1989) **O'Connor, Flannery** (1925–1964) US writer

57 I'd the upbringing a nun would envy and that's the truth. Until I was fifteen I was more familiar with Africa than my own body.
Entertaining Mr Sloane (1964) **Orton, Joe** (1933–1967) English dramatist and writer

58 Growing up's wonderful if you keep your eyes closed tightly,
and, if you manage to grow,
take your soul with you,
nobody wants it.
Grinning Jack (1990) **Patten, Brian** (1946–) British poet

59 One stops being a child when one realizes that telling one's trouble does not make it better.
The Business of Living: Diaries 1935–50 **Pavese, Cesare** (1908–1950) Italian writer and translator

60 Men are generally more careful of the breed of their horses and dogs than of their children.
Some Fruits of Solitude, in Reflections and Maxims relating to the Conduct of Humane Life (1693) **Penn, William** (1644–1718) English Quaker, founder of state of Pennsylvania

61 Behold the child, by Nature's kindly law, Pleas'd with a rattle, tickled with a straw.
An Essay on Man (1733) **Pope, Alexander** (1688–1744) English poet, translator and editor

62 If one doesn't get birthday presents it can remobilize very painfully the persecutory anxiety which usually follows birth.
The Primal Scene, as it were (1958) **Reed, Henry** (1914–1986) English poet, radio dramatist and translator

63 Grown-ups never understand anything for themselves, and it is tiresome for children to be always and forever explaining things to them.

The Little Prince (1943) **Saint-Exupéry, Antoine de** (1900–1944) French author and aviator

64 Children with Hyacinth's temperament don't know better as they grow older; they merely know more.
The Toys of Peace (1919) **Saki** (1870–1916) Burmese-born British writer

65 How sharper than a serpent's tooth it is To have a thankless child.
King Lear, I.iv **Shakespeare, William** (1564–1616) English dramatist, poet and actor

66 Children... have no use for psychology. They detest sociology. They still believe in God, the family, angels, devils, witches, goblins, logic, clarity, punctuation, and other such obsolete stuff ... When a book is boring, they yawn openly. They don't expect their writer to redeem humanity, but leave to adults such childish illusions.
Nobel Prize acceptance speech, (1978) **Singer, Isaac Bashevis** (1904–1991) Polish-born US Yiddish writer

67 No child is born a criminal: no child is born an angel: he's just born.
Remark **Smith, Sir Sydney** (1883–1969) New Zealand-born British forensic scientist and writer

68 There are only two things a child will share willingly – communicable diseases and his mother's age.
Attr. **Spock, Dr Benjamin** (1903–1998) US paediatrician and psychiatrist

69 The child that is not clean and neat, With lots of toys and things to eat, He is a naughty child, I'm sure – Or else his dear papa is poor.
A Child's Garden of Verses (1885)

70 A child should always say what's true, And speak when he is spoken to, And behave mannerly at table: At least as far as he is able.
A Child's Garden of Verses (1885)

71 Must we to bed indeed? Well then, Let us arise and go like men, And face with an undaunted tread The long black passage up to bed.

A *Child's Garden of Verses* (1885) **Stevenson, Robert Louis** (1850–1894) Scottish writer, poet and essayist

72 I have been assured by a very knowing American of my acquaintance in London, that a young healthy child well nursed is, at a year old, a most delicious, nourishing, and wholesome food, whether stewed, roasted, baked, or boiled; and I make no doubt that it will equally serve in a fricassee, or a ragout.
A *Modest Proposal for Preventing the Children of Ireland from being a Burden to their Parents or Country* (1729) **Swift, Jonathan** (1667–1745) Irish satirist, poet, essayist and cleric

73 A child becomes an adult when he realizes that he has a right not only to be right but also to be wrong.
The Second Sin (1973) **Szasz, Thomas** (1920–) Hungarian-born US psychiatrist and writer

74 No man can tell but he that loves his children, how many delicious accents make a man's heart dance in the pretty conversation of those dear pledges; their childishness, their stammering, their little angers, their innocence, their imperfections, their necessities are so many little emanations of joy and comfort to him that delights in their persons and society.
XXV Sermons Preached at Golden Grove (1653) **Taylor, Bishop Jeremy** (1613–1667) English divine and writer

75 And the wild boys as innocent as strawberries.
'The Hunchback in the Park' **Thomas, Dylan** (1914–1953) Welsh poet, writer and radio dramatist

76 Hypocrisy in anything whatever may deceive the cleverest and most penetrating man, but the least wide-awake of children recognizes it, and is revolted by it, however ingeniously it may be disguised.
Attr. **Tolstoy, Leo** (1828–1910) Russian writer, essayist, philosopher and moralist

77 There's plenty of boys that will come hankering and gruvvelling around when you've got an apple, and beg the core off you; but when they've got one, and you beg for the core and remind them how you give them a core one time, they make a mouth at you and say thank you 'most to death, but there ain't-a-going to be no core.
The Adventures of Tom Sawyer (1876) **Twain, Mark** (1835–1910) US humorist, writer, journalist and lecturer

78 It seems to me that since I've had children, I've grown richer and deeper. They may have slowed down my writing for a while, but when I did write, I had more of a self to speak from.
Attr. **Tyler, Anne** (1941–) US writer

79 Never have children, only grandchildren.
Two Sisters (1970) **Vidal, Gore** (1925–) US writer, critic and poet

80 Birds in their little nests agree
And 'tis a shameful sight,
When children of one family
Fall out, and chide, and fight.
Divine Songs for Children (1715) **Watts, Isaac** (1674–1748) English hymn writer, poet and minister

81 Children begin by loving their parents. After a time they judge them. Rarely, if ever, do they forgive them.
A Woman of No Importance (1893) **Wilde, Oscar** (1854–1900) Irish poet, dramatist, writer, critic and wit

82 We are gearing our programmes at two to eight-year-olds. We feel that nine-year-olds can no longer be considered children.
The Times, 'Quotes of the Week', (1999) **Wood, Anne** British television producer

83 Sweet childish days, that were as long
As twenty days are now.
'To a Butterfly' (1807) **Wordsworth, William** (1770–1850) English poet

84 There are no illegitimate children – only illegitimate parents.

Decision, State District Court, Southern District of California (June 1928) **Yankwich, Léon R.** (1888–1975) US district court judge. Quoting columnist O.O. McIntyre
See also birth; families; parenthood; youth

CHRISTIANITY

1 Where Peter is, there of necessity is the Church.
Explanatio psalmi 40 **Ambrose, Saint** (c.340–397) French-born churchman; writer of music and hymns. *(Ubi Petrus, ibi ergo ecclesia)*

2 The nearer the Church the further from God.
Sermon 15, Of the Nativity (1629) **Andrewes, Bishop Lancelot** (1555–1626) English churchman

3 Archbishop@demon.net.
The Times, (1999) **Anonymous** E-mail address offered to and rejected by the Archbishop of Wales

4 But there remains the question: what righteousness really is. The method and secret and sweet reasonableness of Jesus.
Literature and Dogma (1873) **Arnold, Matthew** (1822–1888) English poet, critic, essayist and educationist

5 My object will be, if possible, to form Christian men, for Christian boys I can scarcely hope to make.
Letter, (1828) **Arnold, Thomas** (1795–1842) English historian and educator

6 The good Christian should beware of mathematicians and all those who make empty prophecies. The danger already exists that mathematicians have made a covenant with the devil to darken the spirit and confine man in the bonds of Hell.
Attr.

7 Outside the church there is no salvation.
De Baptismo **Augustine, Saint** (354–430) Numidian-born Christian theologian and philosopher

8 Where Christ erecteth his Church, the devil in the same churchyard will have his chapel.

Sermon, (1588) **Bancroft, Richard** (1544–1610) English churchman

9 I always like to associate with a lot of priests because it makes me understand anti-clerical things so well.
Attr. **Belloc, Hilaire** (1870–1953) English writer of verse, essayist and critic; Liberal MP

10 Thou art Peter, and upon this rock I will build my church; and the gates of hell shall not prevail against it.
Matthew, 16:18 **The Bible (King James Version)**

11 But if at the Church they would give us some Ale,
And a pleasant fire our souls to regale:
We'd sing and we'd pray all the live-long day;
Nor ever once wish from the Church to stray.
Songs of Experience (1794) **Blake, William** (1757–1827) English poet, engraver, painter and mystic

12 As for the British churchman, he goes to church as he goes to the bathroom, with the minimum of fuss and no explanation if he can help it.
The Age of Illusion (1963) **Blythe, Ronald** (1922–) English writer

13 Of late years an abundant shower of curates has fallen upon the North of England.
Shirley (1849) **Brontë, Charlotte** (1816–1855) English writer

14 Every day, people are straying away from the church and going back to God.
In John Cohen, *The Essential Lenny Bruce* (1967)

15 It was just one of those parties which got out of hand.
The Guardian, (1979) Referring to the Crucifixion **Bruce, Lenny** (1925–1966) US comedian

16 Politics and the pulpit are terms that have little agreement. No sound ought to be heard in the church but the healing voice of Christian charity.
Reflections on the Revolution in France ... (1790) **Burke, Edmund** (1729–1797) Irish-born British statesman and philosopher

17 They would have been equally horrified at hearing the Christian religion doubted, and at seeing it practised.
The Way of All Flesh (1903) **Butler, Samuel** (1835–1902) English writer, painter, philosopher and scholar

18 The trouble with born-again Christians is that they are an even bigger pain the second time around.
San Francisco Chronicle, (1981) **Caen, Herb** (1916–1997)

19 If Jesus Christ were to come to-day, people would not even crucify him. They would ask him to dinner, and hear what he had to say, and make fun of it.
In Wilson, Carlyle at his Zenith (1927) **Carlyle, Thomas** (1795–1881) Scottish historian, biographer, critic, and essayist

20 Carlyle said that men were mostly fools. Christianity, with a surer and more reverend realism, says that they are all fools.
Heretics (1905)

21 The Christian ideal has not been tried and found wanting. It has been found difficult; and left untried.
What's Wrong with the World (1910) **Chesterton, G.K.** (1874–1936) English writer, poet and critic

22 He who begins by loving Christianity better than Truth will proceed by loving his own sect or church better than Christianity, and end by loving himself better than all.
Aids to Reflection (1825) **Coleridge, Samuel Taylor** (1772–1834) English poet, philosopher and critic

23 In this sign thou shalt conquer.
In Eusebius, Vita Constantini **Constantine, Emperor** (c.288–337) Roman Emperor. His motto, in memory of a vision of the Cross which appeared to him on the eve of his defeat of Maxentius and victorious entry into Rome, 312

24 Who has not the Church as his mother cannot have God as his father.
De Unitate Ecclesiae

25 There is no salvation outside the Church.
Letter **Cyprian, Saint** (c.200–258) Carthaginian churchman, theological writer and martyr

26 Among the best traitors Ireland has ever had, Mother Church ranks at the very top, a massive obstacle in the path to equality and freedom.
The Price of My Soul (1969) **Devlin, Bernadette** (1947–) Irish politician

27 A Protestant, if he wants aid or advice on any matter, can only go to his solicitor.
Lothair (1870)

28 His Christianity was muscular.
Endymion (1880) **Disraeli, Benjamin** (1804–1881) English statesman and writer

29 Done is a battell on the dragon blak;
Our campioun Christ counfoundit hes his force;
The yettis of hell ar brokin with a crak,
The signe triumphall rasit is of the croce.
'On the Resurrection of Christ' **Dunbar, William** (c.1460–c.1525) Scottish poet, satirist and courtier

30 I like the silent church before the service begins, better than any preaching.
Essays, First Series (1841) **Emerson, Ralph Waldo** (1803–1882) US poet, essayist, transcendentalist and teacher

31 For clergy are men as well as other folks.
Joseph Andrews (1742)

32 There is not in the universe a more ridiculous, nor a more contemptible animal, than a proud clergyman.
Amelia (1751) **Fielding, Henry** (1707–1754) English writer, dramatist and journalist

33 Drop, drop, slow tears,
And bathe those beauteous feet,
Which brought from Heav'n
The news and Prince of Peace.
Poetical Miscellanies (1633), 'An Hymn' **Fletcher, Phineas** (1582–1650) English poet and clergyman

34 I wouldn't recommend anyone to be a Catholic, unless they had to be.
Attr. **Greene, Graham** (1904–1991) English writer and dramatist

35 Christianity is part of the laws of England.

In Blackstone, *Commentaries on the Laws of England* (1769) **Hale, Sir Matthew** (1609–1676) English judge and writer

36 A local cult called Christianity.
The Dynasts, Part I (1903) **Hardy, Thomas** (1840–1928) English writer and poet

37 It is in defeat that we become Christian.
A Farewell to Arms (1929) **Hemingway, Ernest** (1898–1961) US author

38 Kneeling ne're spoil'd silk stocking. Quit thy state.
All equall are within the churches gate.
The Temple (1633) **Herbert, George** (1593–1633) English poet and priest

39 The church is not a mere ecclesiastical wing of the state which benignly blesses what an increasingly secular society does. Its function is primarily to represent God to the nation.
The Times, (1992) **Higton, Tony** (19th century) Church of England evangelical

40 The sedate, sober, silent, serious, sad-coloured sect.
The Comic Annual (1839) **Hood, Thomas** (1799–1845) English poet, editor and humorist. Of Quakers

41 No testimony is sufficient to establish a miracle, unless the testimony be of such a kind that its falsehood would be more miraculous than the fact which it endeavours to establish.
Philosophical Essays Concerning Human Understanding (1748) **Hume, David** (1711–1776) Scottish philosopher and political economist

42 Christianity accepted as given a metaphysical system derived from several already existing and mutually incompatible systems.
Grey Eminence (1941) **Huxley, Aldous** (1894–1963) English writer, poet and critic

43 Nowhere probably is there more true feeling, and nowhere worse taste, than in a churchyard – both as regards the monuments and the inscriptions. Scarcely a word of the true poetry anywhere.

In E. Abbott and L. Campbell (eds), *Life and Letters of Benjamin Jowett* (1897) **Jowett, Benjamin** (1817–1893) English scholar, translator, essayist and priest

44 We have used the Bible as if it was a constable's handbook – an opium-dose for keeping beasts of burden patient while they are being overloaded.
'Letters to Chartists' (1848) **Kingsley, Charles** (1819–1875) English writer, poet, lecturer and clergyman

45 The Three in One, the One in Three? Not so!
To my own Gods I go.
It may be they shall give me greater ease
Than your cold Christ and tangled Trinities.
Plain Tales from the Hills (1888) **Kipling, Rudyard** (1865–1936) Indian-born British poet and writer

46 While I cannot be regarded as a pillar, I must be regarded as a buttress of the church, because I support it from the outside.
Attr. **Lamb, William, Lord** (1779–1848) British prime minister

47 Be a sinner and sin strongly, but believe and rejoice in Christ even more strongly.
Letter to Melanchthon **Luther, Martin** (1483–1546) German Protestant theologian and reformer

48 She may still exist in undiminished vigour when some traveller from New Zealand shall, in the midst of a vast solitude, take his stand on a broken arch of London Bridge to sketch the ruins of St Paul's.
Collected Essays (1843) **Macaulay, Lord** (1800–1859) English Liberal statesman, essayist and poet. Of the Roman Catholic Church

49 I don't believe in God – that's just a fact, it's not an act of will … But ethics came to me in the frame of Christian teaching, and even though I don't believe in an afterlife, I'm still concerned with the salvation of my soul.
In Carol Gelderman, *Mary McCarthy* (1988) **McCarthy, Mary** (1912–1989) US writer and critic

50 Better sleep with a sober cannibal than a drunken Christian.
Moby Dick (1851) **Melville, Herman** (1819–1891) US writer and poet

51 Puritanism – The haunting fear that someone, somewhere, may be happy.
A Mencken Chrestomathy (1949)

52 The chief contribution of Protestantism to human thought is its massive proof that God is a bore.
Notebooks (1956) **Mencken, H.L.** (1880–1956) US writer, critic, philologist and satirist

53 There are many who stay away from church these days because you hardly ever mention God any more.
The Crucible (1952) **Miller, Arthur** (1915–2005) US dramatist and screenwriter

54 No kingdom has ever had as many civil wars as the kingdom of Christ.
Lettres persanes (1721) **Montesquieu, Charles** (1689–1755) French philosopher and jurist

55 Very much like the Church of England. It is doctrinally inexplicable but it goes on.
Attr. **Muggeridge, Malcolm** (1903–1990) English writer. On *Punch*, which he once edited

56 The Christian decision to find the world ugly and bad has made the world ugly and bad.
The Gay Science (1887)

57 I call Christianity the one great curse, the one great innermost form of depravity, the one great instinct for revenge, for which no means is poisonous, furtive, underground, petty enough – I call it the one immortal blemish of humanity.
Der Antichrist (1888) **Nietzsche, Friedrich Wilhelm** (1844–1900) German philosopher, critic and poet

58 The Roman Catholic Church is getting nearer to communism every day.
The Irish Times, (1969) **Paisley, Rev. Ian** (1926–) Northern Irish politician and church leader

59 No pain, no palm; no thorns, no throne; no gall, no glory; no cross, no crown.

No Cross, No Crown (1669) **Penn, William** (1644–1718) English Quaker, founder of state of Pennsylvania

60 It is hard to tell where the MCC ends and the Church of England begins.
New Statesman, (1962) **Priestley, J.B.** (1894–1984) English writer, dramatist and critic

61 I hope I can persuade the church to loosen its stays a bit and perhaps rock the boat a little.
In *The Guardian*, (2000) **Runcie, Robert** (1921–2000) Archbishop of Canterbury 1980–1991

62 People may say what they like about the decay of Christianity; the religious system that produced green Chartreuse can never really die.
Reginald (1904) **Saki** (1870–1916) Burmese-born British writer

63 The Bible is literature, not dogma.
Introduction to Spinoza's *Ethics* **Santayana, George** (1863–1952) Spanish-born US philosopher and writer

64 It is the protest of the individual soul against the interference of priest or peer between the private man and his God. I should call it Protestantism if I had to find a name for it.
Saint Joan (1924) **Shaw, George Bernard** (1856–1950) Irish socialist, writer, dramatist and critic

65 'The Church of England,' I said, seeing that Mr Inglesant paused, 'is no doubt a compromise.'
John Inglesant (1880) **Shorthouse, J.H.** (1834–1903) English novelist

66 Who dreamed that Christ has died in vain? He walks again on the Seas of Blood, he comes in the terrible Rain.
The Shadow of Cain (1947) **Sitwell, Dame Edith** (1887–1964) English poet, anthologist, critic and biographer

67 A Curate – there is something which excites compassion in the very name of a Curate!!!
Edinburgh Review, (1822)

68 What Bishops like best in their Clergy is a dropping-down deadness of manner.

The Works of the Rev. Sydney Smith (1839)

69 I have seen nobody since I saw you, but persons in orders. My only varieties are vicars, rectors, curates, and every now and then (by way of turbot) an archdeacon.
Letters, to Miss Berry (1843)

70 As the French say, there are three sexes – men, women, and clergymen.
In Holland, *A Memoir of the Reverend Sydney Smith* (1855) **Smith, Sydney** (1771–1845) English clergyman, essayist, journalist and wit

71 Becoming an Anglo-Catholic must surely be a sad business – rather like becoming an amateur conjurer.
The Coming Struggle for Power **Strachey, John St Loe** (1901–1963) English politican

72 I conceive some scattered notions about a superior power to be of singular use for the common people, as furnishing excellent materials to keep children quiet when they grow peevish, and providing topics of amusement in a tedious winter-night.
An Argument Against Abolishing Christianity (1708)

73 I never saw, heard, nor read, that the clergy were beloved in any nation where Christianity was the religion of the country. Nothing can render them popular, but some degree of persecution.
Thoughts on Religion (1765) **Swift, Jonathan** (1667–1745) Irish satirist, poet, essayist and cleric

74 There is a certain class of clergyman whose mendicity is only equalled by their mendacity.
Attr. **Temple, Frederick, Archbishop** (1821–1902) English churchman

75 Christianity is the most materialistic of all great religions.
Readings in St John's Gospel (1939)

76 The Church exists for the sake of those outside it.
Attr.

77 I believe in the Church, One Holy, Catholic and Apostolic, and I regret that it nowhere exists.
Attr. **Temple, William** (1881–1944) Anglican prelate, social reformer and writer

78 As often as we are mown down by you, the more we grow in numbers; the blood of Christians is the seed.
Apologeticus **Tertullian** (c.AD 160–c.225) Carthaginian theologian

79 What the church can't prevent, it blesses.
Scraps (1973) **Tucholsky, Kurt** (1890–1935) German satirist and writer

80 Most people are bothered by those passages in Scripture which they cannot understand; but as for me, I always noticed that the passages in Scripture which trouble me most are those that I do understand.
In Simcox, *Treasury of Quotations on Christian Themes* **Twain, Mark** (1835–1910) US humorist, writer, journalist and lecturer

81 In general the churches, visited by me too often on weekdays ... bore for me the same relation to God that billboards did to Coca-Cola: they promoted thirst without quenching it.
A Month of Sundays (1975) **Updike, John** (1932–) US writer, poet and critic

82 Organized religion is making Christianity political rather than making politics Christian.
The Observer, (1986) **Van der Post, Sir Laurens** (1906–1996) South African explorer and writer

83 There is a species of person called a 'Modern Churchman' who draws the full salary of a beneficed clergyman and need not commit himself to any religious belief.
Decline and Fall (1928)

84 I have noticed again and again since I have been in the Church that lay interest in ecclesiastical matters is often a prelude to insanity.
Decline and Fall (1928) **Waugh, Evelyn** (1903–1966) English writer and diarist

85 Yes, about ten minutes.
Attr. **Wellington, Duke of** (1769–1852) Irish-born British military commander and statesman. Responding to a vicar's enquiry as to whether there was anything he would like his forthcoming sermon to be about

86 'God knows how you Protestants can be expected to have any sense of direction,' she said. 'It's different with us. I haven't been to mass for years, I've got every mortal sin on my conscience, but I know when I'm doing wrong. I'm still a Catholic.'
The Wrong Set (1949) **Wilson, Sir Angus** (1913–1991) English novelist and critic

87 The itch of disputing will prove the scab of churches.
A Panegyric to King Charles (1651) **Wotton, Sir Henry** (1568–1639) English diplomat, traveller and poet

88 A Christian is a man who feels
Repentance on a Sunday
For what he did on Saturday
And is going to do on Monday.
'The Christian' (1909) **Ybarra, Thomas Russell** (1880–1971) US writer and poet

89 Scratch the Christian and you find the pagan – spoiled.
Children of the Ghetto (1892) **Zangwill, Israel** (1864–1926) English writer and Jewish spokesman
See also belief; Christmas; the devil; faith; God; religion

CHRISTMAS

1 I have often thought, says Sir Roger, it happens very well that Christmas should fall out in the Middle of Winter.
The Spectator, January 1712 **Addison, Joseph** (1672–1719) English essayist, poet, playwright and statesman

2 In the old days, it was not called the Holiday Season; the Christians called it 'Christmas' and went to church; the Jews called it 'Hanukka' and went to synagogue; the atheists went to parties and drank. People passing each other on the street would say 'Merry Christmas!' or 'Happy Hanukka!' or (to the atheists) 'Look out for the wall!'
Christmas Shopping: A Survivor's Guide **Barry, Dave** (1947–) US columnist and journalist

3 I'm dreaming of a white Christmas, just like the ones I used to know.

'White Christmas' (song, 1942) **Berlin, Irving** (1888–1989) Russian-born US composer and songwriter

4 And girls in slacks remember Dad,
And oafish louts remember Mum,
And sleepless children's hearts are glad,
And Christmas morning bells say 'Come!'
Even to shining ones who dwell
Safe in the Dorchester Hotel.
And is it true? And is it true,
This most tremendous tale of all,
Seen in a stained-glass window's hue,
A Baby in an ox's stall?
A Few Late Chrysanthemums (1954) **Betjeman, Sir John** (1906–1984) English poet laureate

5 The leading symbol of the hagiography of US mercantilism.
The Times, (1998) **Castro, Fidel** (1927–) President of Cuba. On Santa Claus

6 A very merry Christmas, with roast beef in a violent perspiration, and the thermometer 110° in the shade!
Australasian, (1868) **Clarke, Marcus** (1846–1881) English-born Australian writer

7 Bloody Christmas, here again,
Let us raise a loving cup:
Peace on earth, goodwill to men,
And make them do the washing-up.
'Another Christmas Poem' **Cope, Wendy** (1945–) English poet

8 Christmas is the Disneyfication of Christianity.
Independent, (1996) **Cupitt, Don** (1934–) English theologian

9 How many observe Christ's birthday! How few, his precepts! O! 'tis easier to keep holidays than commandments.
Poor Richard's Almanack, 1732–57 **Franklin, Benjamin** (1706–1790) US statesman, scientist, political critic and printer

10 Christmas to a child is the first terrible proof that to travel hopefully is better than to arrive.
Paperweight **Fry, Stephen** (1957–) British comedian and writer

11 If someone said on Christmas Eve,
   'Come; see the oxen kneel
   In the lonely barton by yonder coomb
   Our childhood used to know,'
   I should go with him in the gloom,
   Hoping it might be so.
   'The Oxen' (1915) **Hardy, Thomas** (1840–1928)
   English writer and poet

12 I'm walking backwards for Christmas.
   The Goon Show **Milligan, Spike** (1918–2002)
   Irish comedian and writer

13 'Twas the night before Christmas, when all
   through the house
   Not a creature was stirring, not even a
   mouse;
   The stockings were hung by the chimney
   with care,
   In hopes that St Nicholas soon would be
   there ...
   'Happy Christmas to all, and to all a
   goodnight!'
   'A Visit from St Nicholas' (1823) **Moore,
   Clement C.** (1779–1863) US poet and writer

14 People can't concentrate properly on
   blowing other people to pieces properly if
   their minds are poisoned by thoughts
   suitable to the twenty-fifth of December.
   'I'm a Stranger Here Myself' (1938) **Nash,
   Ogden** (1902–1971) US poet

15 Christmas comes but once a year.
   Proverb

16 Heap on more wood! – the wind is chill;
   But let it whistle as it will,
   We'll keep our Christmas merry still ...
   England was merry England, when
   Old Christmas brought his sports again.
   'Twas Christmas broach'd the mightiest
   ale;
   'Twas Christmas told the merriest tale;
   A Christmas gambol oft could cheer
   The poor man's heart through half the
   year.
   Marmion (1808) **Scott, Sir Walter** (1771–1832)
   Scottish writer and historian

17 It is Christmas Day in the Workhouse.
   'In the Workhouse – Christmas Day' (1879)
   Sims, George R. (1847–1922) English
   dramatist and novelist

18 At Christmas play and make good cheer,
   For Christmas comes but once a year.
   Five Hundred Points of Good Husbandry (1557)
   Tusser, Thomas (c.1524–1580) English writer,
   poet and musician

19 To perceive Christmas through its
   wrapping becomes more difficult with
   every year.
   The Second Tree from the Corner (1954) **White,
   E.B.** (1899–1985) US humorist and writer

20 O Christmas tree, O Christmas tree,
   How faithful are thy branches!
   Adaptation of an old folk-song, (1820)
   Zarnack, Joachim August (1777–1827) German
   preacher and pedagogue
   See also Christianity; faith; God

CINEMA

1 People have been modelling their lives
  after films for years, but the medium is
  somehow unsuited to moral lessons,
  cautionary tales or polemics of any kind.
  *A Year in the Dark: A Year in the Life of a Film
  Critic* (1971) **Adler, Renata** (1938–) US film
  critic and writer

2 What's a cult? It just means not enough
  people to make a minority.
  The Observer, (1981) **Altman, Robert** (1922–) US
  film director

3 We made films at Ealing that were good,
  bad and indifferent, but they were
  indisputably British. They were rooted in
  the soil of the country.
  Attr. **Balcon, Michael** (1896–1977) British film
  producer, head of Ealing Studios

4 Does this prove, once and for all, that size
  does matter?
  The Observer, (1998) **Cameron, James** (1954–)
  US film director. Accepting the Oscars won
  by the film *Titanic*

5 There are no rules in film-making. Only
  sins; and the cardinal sin is dullness.
  People magazine, obituary, (1991) **Capra, Frank
  (Fritjof)** (1897–1991) US film director

6 You can live a long time in Hollywood and
  never see the part they use in pictures.
  The Little Sister (1949)

7 When in doubt, have two guys come through the door with guns.
Attr. **Chandler, Raymond** (1888–1959) US crime novelist

8 All I need to make a comedy is a park, a policeman and a pretty girl.
My Autobiography (1964) **Chaplin, Charlie** (1889–1977) English comedian, film actor, director and satirist

9 Bogart's a hell of a nice guy till 11:30 p.m. After that he thinks he's Bogart.
Attr. **Chasen, Dave** (1899–1973) US restaurateur

10 A film is a petrified fountain of thought.
Esquire magazine, (1961) **Cocteau, Jean** (1889–1963) French film director

11 I didn't do it because your prestige in cinema tends to drop if you do television.
The Times, (1998) **Connery, Sean** (1930–) Scottish actor. On turning down a part in US sitcom *Friends*

12 Censors tend to do what only psychotics do: they confuse reality with illusion.
Cronenberg on Cronenberg (1992) **Cronenberg, David** (1943–) Canadian film director

13 The public is always right.
In Colombo, *Wit and Wisdom of the Moviemakers* **De Mille, Cecil B.** (1881–1959) US filmmaker

14 Girls bored me – they still do. I love Mickey Mouse more than any woman I've ever known.
In Wagner, *You Must Remember This* **Disney, Walt** (1901–1966) US filmmaker and pioneer of animated films

15 There's a big trend in Hollywood of taking very good European films and turning them into very bad American films. I've been offered a few of those, but it's really a peverse activity, I'd rather go on the dole.
The Independent, (1994) **Doyle, Roddy** (1958–) Irish writer

16 Photography is truth. Cinema is truth twenty-four times a second.
Le Petit Soldat (film, 1960)

17 All you need for a movie are a gun and a girl.

Supposed diary entry, (1991)

18 Of course a film should have a beginning, a middle and an end. But not necessarily in that order.
Attr. **Godard, Jean-Luc** (1930–) Franco-Swiss film director and writer

19 If it's well done, it's ignored. If it's badly done, people call attention to it.
Attr. **Goldman, William** (1931–) US screenwriter. On screenwriting

20 Why should people go out and pay money to see bad films when they can stay at home and see bad television for nothing?
The Observer, (1956)

21 Directors are always biting the hand that lays the golden egg.
In Zierold, *Moguls* (1969)

22 To hell with the cost. If it's a sound story, we'll make a picture of it.
In Zierold, *Moguls* (1969) On being warned that a story was too caustic

23 I don't care if it doesn't make a nickel, I just want every man, woman, and child in America to see it.
In Zierold, *Moguls* (1969) Before the opening of his film *The Best Years of Our Lives* in 1946 **Goldwyn, Samuel** (1882–1974) Polish-born US film producer

24 Twelve! So who needs twelve! Couldn't we make do with six?
Radio Times, (1983) **Grade, Lew** (1906–1994) Russian-born British film, TV and theatrical producer. To Franco Zeffirelli who had explained that the high cost of the film *Jesus of Nazareth* was partly because there had to be twelve apostles

25 We have our factory, which is called a stage. We make a product, we color it, we title it and we ship it out in cans.
Newsweek, (1969) **Grant, Cary** (1904–1986) English-born US actor

26 There are only three ages for women in Hollywood – Babe, District Attorney, and Driving Miss Daisy.
Attr. **Hawn, Goldie** (1945–) US film actress

27 Complete nudity is never permitted. This includes nudity in fact or in silhouette, or any lecherous or licentious notice thereof by other characters in the picture.
Code of conduct established for the American film industry, (1930) **The Hays Code**

28 The length of a film should be directly related to the endurance of the human bladder.
In Simon Rose, *Classic Film Guide* (1995)

29 Cinema is life with the dull bits cut out.
In Simon Rose, *Classic Film Guide* (1995)

30 You can't direct a Laughton picture. The best you can hope for is to referee.
Attr. On the notoriously difficult English actor, Charles Laughton

31 A good film is when the price of the dinner, the theatre admission and the babysitter were worth it.
Attr.

32 If I made Cinderella people would be looking for the body in the coach.
Attr. **Hitchcock, Alfred** (1899–1980) English film director

33 Clint Eastwood is a man who walks softly and carries a big percentage of the gross.
In Simon Rose, *Classic Film Guide* (1995) **Hope, Bob** (1903–2003) English-born US comedian

34 I can't see what Jack Warner can do with an Oscar; it can't say yes.
Attr. **Jolson, Al** (c.1885–1950) US singer and actor

35 Movies are so rarely great art that if we cannot appreciate the great trash we have very little reason to be interested in them.
Kiss Kiss Bang Bang, (1968) **Kael, Pauline** (1919–2001) US critic

36 The son-in-law also rises.
In Colombo, *Wit and Wisdom of the Moviemakers* **Knopf, Edwin H.** (1899–) US actor, director and screenwriter. Said when Louis B. Mayer promoted his daughter's husband (David O. Selznick), c.1933

37 Strip the phoney tinsel off Hollywood and you'll find the real tinsel underneath.
Attr. **Levant, Oscar** (1906–1972) US pianist and autobiographer

38 If the boy and girl walk off into the sunset hand-in-hand in the last scene, it adds 10 million to the box office.
Attr. **Lucas, George** (1944–) US film director. Advice to Steven Spielberg

39 Talking films are a very interesting invention, but I do not believe that they will remain long in fashion.
Films Sonores Avant, (1928) **Lumiere, Jean-Louis** (1864–1948) French inventor

40 Hollywood: Where the stars twinkle until they wrinkle.
Attr. **Mature, Victor** (1913–1999) US film actor

41 Cinema should make you forget you're sitting in a theatre.
Attr. **Polanski, Roman** (1933–) Polish-born, US and French-based film director

42 James Bond is a man of honor, a symbol of real value to the free world.
Attr. **Reagan, Ronald** (1911–2004) US actor, later US President

43 Cannes is where you lie on the beach and stare at the stars – or vice versa.
Attr. **Reed, Rex** (1938–) US film and music critic and columnist

44 The movies are the only business where you can go out front and applaud yourself.
In Halliwell, *Filmgoer's Book of Quotes* (1973) **Rogers, Will** (1879–1935) US humorist, actor, rancher, writer and wit

45 Violence in real life is terrible; violence in the movies can be cool. It's just another colour to work with.
The Observer, Sayings of the Week, (1994)

46 I steal from every single movie ever made. I love it – if my work has anything it's that I'm taking this from this and that from that and mixing them together.
In Jami Bernard, *Tarantino, the Man and his Movies* (1995) **Tarantino, Quentin** (1963–) US film director and scriptwriter

47 Forrest Gump is roughly as truthful about the world of intellectual handicap as the Little Mermaid is about fish.
Attr. **Tookey, Christopher** (1950–) English film critic, *Daily Mail*

48 Thanks to the movies, gunfire has always sounded unreal to me, even when being fired at.
Dear Me (1977) **Ustinov, Sir Peter** (1921–2004) English actor, director, dramatist, writer and raconteur

49 We fight wars which we lose, then we make films showing how we won them, and the films make more money than the wars lost.
Attr. **Vidal, Gore** (1925–) US writer, critic and poet

50 The cinema has no boundaries. It's a ribbon of dream.
In Kenneth Tynan, *Show People: Profiles in Entertainment* (1979)

51 Everybody denies I am a genius – but nobody ever called me one!
In Halliwell, *Filmgoer's Companion* (1984)

52 I began at the top and I've been working my way down ever since.
In Colombo, *Wit and Wisdom of the Moviemakers* **Welles, Orson** (1915–1985) US actor, director and producer

53 It used to be that we in film were the lowest form of art. Now we have something to look down on.
In A. Madsen, *Billy Wilder* (1968) **Wilder, Billy** (1906–2002) Austrian-born US fllm director, producer and screenwriter
See also acting; film quotes; television

CITIES

1 Happy is that city which in time of peace thinks of war.
In Robert Burton, *Anatomy of Melancholy* (1621–1651) **Anonymous** Inscription in the armoury of Venice

2 Match me such marvel save in Eastern clime,
A rose-red city 'half as old as Time'!
'Petra' (1845) **Burgon, John William** (1813–1888) English churchman

3 He so beautified the city that he justly boasted that he found it brick and left it marble.
In Suetonius, *Lives of the Caesars* **Caesar, Augustus** (63 BC–AD 14) First Roman emperor

4 If you would be known, and not know, vegetate in a village; if you would know, and not be known, live in a city.
Lacon (1820) **Colton, Charles Caleb** (c.1780–1832) English clergyman and satirist

5 God made the country, and man made the town.
The Task (1785) **Cowper, William** (1731–1800) English poet, hymn writer and letter writer

6 To one who has been long in city pent,
'Tis very sweet to look into the fair
And open face of heaven.
'To one who has been long in city pent' (1816) **Keats, John** (1795–1821) English poet

7 Cities and Thrones and Powers,
Stand in Time's eye,
Almost as long as flowers,
Which daily die:
But, as new buds put forth,
To glad new men,
Out of the spent and unconsidered Earth,
The Cities rise again.
'Cities and Thrones and Powers' (1906) **Kipling, Rudyard** (1865–1936) Indian-born British poet and writer

8 The two elements the traveller first captures in the big city are extrahuman architecture and furious rhythm. Geometry and anguish.
Poet in New York (1940, trans. 1988) **Lorca, Federico García** (1898–1936) Spanish poet and dramatist

9 Towred Cities please us then,
And the busie humm of men.
'L'Allegro' (1645) **Milton, John** (1608–1674) English poet, libertarian and pamphleteer

10 This city was full of lunatics, people who went into muttering fits on the bus, others who shouted obscenities in automats, lost souls who walked the pavements alone, caught up in imaginary conversations.
An Answer From Limbo (1994) **Moore, Brian** (1921–1999) Irish-American writer

11 A house is much more to my taste than a tree,
And for groves, oh! a good grove of chimneys for me.

'Country and Town' (song, 1840) **Morris, Charles** (1745–1838) English songwriter and soldier

12 Clearly, then, the city is not a concrete jungle, it is a human zoo.
The Human Zoo (1969) **Morris, Desmond** (1928–) English anthropologist and broadcaster

13 The city is a fact in nature, like a cave, a run of mackerel or an ant-heap. But it is also a conscious work of art, and it holds within its communal framework many simpler and more personal forms of art.
The Culture of Cities (1938) **Mumford, Lewis** (1895–1990) US sociologist and writer

14 The City is of Night; perchance of Death,
But certainly of Night; for never there
Can come the lucid morning's fragrant breath
After the dewy dawning's cold grey air …
The City is of Night, but not of Sleep;
There sweet sleep is not for the weary brain;
The pitiless hours like years and ages creep,
A night seems termless hell.
The City of Dreadful Night (1880) **Thomson, James** (1834–1882) Scottish poet and dramatist

15 Jealousy's a city passion; 'tis a thing unknown amongst people of quality.
The Confederacy (1705) **Vanbrugh, Sir John** (1664–1726) English dramatist and baroque architect

16 The screech and mechanical uproar of the big city turns the citified head, fills citified ears – as the song of birds, wind in the trees, animal cries, or as the voices and songs of his loved ones once filled his heart. He is sidewalk-happy.
The Living City (1958) **Wright, Frank Lloyd** (1869–1959) US architect and writer
See also the country

CITIES: LONDON

1 Nobody is healthy in London. Nobody can be.
Emma (1816) **Austen, Jane** (1775–1817) English writer

2 I wander thro' each charter'd street,
Near where the charter'd Thames does flow
And mark in every face I meet
Marks of weakness, marks of woe.
'London' (1794) **Blake, William** (1757–1827) English poet, engraver, painter and mystic

3 London! Pompous Ignorance sits enthroned there and welcomes Pretentious Mediocrity with flattery and gifts. Oh, dull and witless city! Very hell for the restless, inquiring, sensitive soul. Paradise for the snob, the parasite and the prig; the pimp, the placeman and the cheapjack.
The Anatomist (1931) **Bridie, James** (1888–1951) Scottish dramatist, writer and physician

4 Some new neighbours, that came a month or two ago, brought with them an accumulation of all the things to be guarded against in a London neighbourhood, viz, a pianoforte, a lap-dog, and a parrot.
Letter to Mrs Carlyle, (1839) **Carlyle, Jane Welsh** (1801–1866) Scottish letter writer, literary hostess and poet

5 Provided that the City of London remains as it is at present, the clearing-house of the world, any other nation may be its workshop.
Speech, London, (1904) **Chamberlain, Joseph** (1836–1914) English politician

6 But what is to be the fate of the great wen of all? The monster, called … 'the metropolis of the empire'?
'Rural Rides', (1822) **Cobbett, William** (1762–1835) English politician, reformer, writer, farmer and army officer. Of London

7 Oh, London is a fine town,
A very famous city,
Where all the streets are paved with gold,
And all the maidens pretty.
The Heir at Law (1797) **Colman, the Younger, George** (1762–1836) English dramatist and Examiner of Plays

8 It was a Sunday afternoon, wet and cheerless: and a duller spectacle this earth of ours has not to show than a rainy Sunday in London.
Confessions of an English Opium Eater (1822) **De Quincey, Thomas** (1785–1859) English writer

9 London; a nation, not a city.
Lothair (1870) **Disraeli, Benjamin** (1804–1881)
English statesman and writer

10 London, that great cesspool into which all
the loungers of the Empire are irresistibly
drained.
A Study in Scarlet (1887) **Doyle, Sir Arthur
Conan** (1859–1930) Scottish writer and war
correspondent

11 London, thou art the flower of cities all!
Gemme of all joy, jasper of jocunditie.
'London' (1834) **Dunbar, William** (c.1460–
c.1525) Scottish poet, satirist and courtier

12 Crowds without company, and dissipation
without pleasure.
Memoirs of My Life and Writings (1796) **Gibbon,
Edward** (1737–1794) English historian,
politician and memoirist

13 Maybe it's because I'm a Londoner
That I love London so.
'Maybe It's Because I'm a Londoner' (song,
1947) **Gregg, Hubert** (1914–2004) British
broadcaster and actor

14 By seeing London, I have seen as much of
life as the world can show.
In Boswell, *Journal of a Tour to the Hebrides*
(1785)

15 When a man is tired of London, he is tired
of life; for there is in London all that life
can afford.
In Boswell, *The Life of Samuel Johnson* (1791)
Johnson, Samuel (1709–1784) English
lexicographer, poet, critic, conversationalist
and essayist

16 The chief advantage of London is, that a
man is always so near his burrow.
In Boswell, *The Life of Samuel Johnson* (1791)
Meynell, Hugo (1727–1780) Frequenter of
London society, acquaintance of Dr Johnson

17 If one must have a villa in summer to
dwell,
Oh, give me the sweet shady side of Pall
Mall!
'The Contrast' (song, 1840) **Morris, Charles**
(1745–1838) English songwriter and soldier

18 Forget six counties overhung with smoke,
Forget the snorting steam and piston
stroke,
Forget the spreading of the hideous town;
Think rather of the pack-horse on the
down,
And dream of London, small and white and
clean,
The clear Thames bordered by its gardens
green.
The Earthly Paradise (1868–1870) **Morris,
William** (1834–1896) English poet, designer,
craftsman, artist and socialist

19 It is the folly of too many to mistake the
echo of a London coffee house for the voice
of the kingdom.
The Conduct of the Allies (1711) **Swift, Jonathan**
(1667–1745) Irish satirist, poet, essayist and
cleric

20 Earth has not anything to show more fair;
Dull would he be of soul who could pass by
A sight so touching in its majesty:
This city now doth, like a garment, wear
The beauty of the morning; silent, bare,
Ships, towers, domes, theatres, and
temples lie
Open unto the fields, and to the sky,
All bright and glittering in the smokeless
air ...
Dear God! the very houses seem asleep;
And all that mighty heart is lying still!
'Sonnet composed upon Westminster Bridge'
(1807) **Wordsworth, William** (1770–1850)
English poet
See also England

CLASS

1 The rich man in his castle,
The poor man at his gate,
God made them, high or lowly,
And order'd their estate.
Hymn, (1848) **Alexander, Cecil Frances** (1818–
1895) Irish poet and hymn writer

2 The working class can kiss my arse –
I've got the boss's job at last.
Australian Labor movement, traditional folk
saying, sung to the tune of the 'Red Flag'
Anonymous

3 I have nothing against Oxford men. Some of our best shearers' cooks are Oxford men.
In R. H. Croll, *I Recall* ... **Archibald, John Feltham** (1856–1919) Australian journalist and publisher

4 *Philistine* gives the notion of something particularly stiff-necked and perverse in the resistance to light and its children; and therein it specially suits our middle class.
Culture and Anarchy (1869)

5 I often, therefore, when I want to distinguish clearly the aristocratic class from the Philistines proper, or middle class, name the former, in my own mind, the Barbarians.
Culture and Anarchy (1869)

6 One has often wondered whether upon the whole earth there is anything so unintelligent, so unapt to perceive how the world is really going, as an ordinary young Englishman of our upper class.
Culture and Anarchy (1869) **Arnold, Matthew** (1822–1888) English poet, critic, essayist and educationist

7 My dear Clincham, The bearer of this letter is an old friend of mine not quite the right side of the blanket as they say in fact he is the son of a first rate butcher but his mother was a decent family called Hyssopps of the Glen so you see he is not so bad and is desireus of being the correct article.
The Young Visiters (1919) **Ashford, Daisy** (1881–1972) English child author

8 Sir Walter Elliot, of Kellynch Hall, in Somersetshire, was a man who, for his own amusement, never took up any book but the Baronetage; there he found occupation for an idle hour and consolation in a distressed one ... this was the page at which the favourite volume always opened:
– ELLIOT OF KELLYNCH-HALL.
Persuasion (1818) **Austen, Jane** (1775–1817) English writer

9 The House of Peers has never been a House where the most important peers were most important.

The English Constitution (1867) **Bagehot, Walter** (1826–1877) English economist and political philosopher

10 Equality may perhaps be a right, but no power on earth can ever turn it into a fact.
La Duchesse de Langeais (1834) **Balzac, Honoré de** (1799–1850) French writer

11 His Lordship may compel us to be equal upstairs, but there will never be equality in the servants' hall.
The Admirable Crichton (1902) **Barrie, Sir J.M.** (1860–1937) Scottish dramatist and writer

12 One must shock the bourgeois.
Attr. **Baudelaire, Charles** (1821–1867) French poet, translator and critic

13 Because you are a great lord, you think yourself a great genius! You took the trouble to be born, but nothing more.
Mariage de Figaro (1784) **Beaumarchais** (1732–1799) French dramatist

14 In my opinion, Butlers ought
To know their place, and not to play
The Old Retainer night and day.
Cautionary Tales (1907)

15 Godolphin Horne was Nobly Born;
He held the Human Race in Scorn –
Alas! That such Affected Tricks
Should flourish in a Child of Six!
Cautionary Tales (1907), 'Godolphin Horne'

16 Like many of the Upper Class
He liked the Sound of Broken Glass.
New Cautionary Tales (1930) **Belloc, Hilaire** (1870–1953) English writer of verse, essayist and critic; Liberal MP

17 The vices of the rich and great are mistaken for error; and those of the poor and lowly, for crimes.
Desultory Thoughts and Reflections (1839) **Blessington, Lady Marguerite** (1789–1849) Irish-born writer and socialite

18 Victories and defeats for the bigshots at the top aren't always victories and defeats for those at the bottom.
Mother Courage and her Children (1941) **Brecht, Bertolt** (1898–1956) German dramatist

19 Poets and painters are outside the class system, or rather they constitute a special class of their own, like the circus people and the gipsies.
Thoughts in a Dry Season (1978) **Brenan, Gerald** (1894–1987) English writer

20 I am a gentleman, though spoiled i' the breeding. The Buzzards are all gentlemen. We came in with the Conqueror.
English Moor (1637) **Brome, Richard** (c.1590–1652) English dramatist

21 My Lord Tomnoddy is thirty-four;
The Earl can last but a few years more.
My Lord in the Peers will take his place:
Her Majesty's councils his words will grace.
Office he'll hold and patronage sway;
Fortunes and lives he will vote away;
And what are his qualifications? – ONE!
He's the Earl of Fitzdotterel's eldest son.
'My Lord Tomnoddy' (1855) **Brough, Robert Barnabas** (1828–1860) English journalist and writer

22 The great Unwashed.
Attr. **Brougham, Lord Henry** (1778–1868) Scottish politician, abolitionist and journalist

23 Without class differences, England would cease to be the living theatre it is.
Remark, (1985) **Burgess, Anthony** (1917–1993) English writer, linguist and composer

24 Somebody has said, that a king may make a nobleman but he cannot make a Gentleman.
Letter to William Smith, (1795) **Burke, Edmund** (1729–1797) Irish-born British statesman and philosopher

25 The basic rule of human nature is that powerful people speak slowly and subservient people quickly – because if they don't speak fast nobody will listen to them.
The Times, (1992) **Caine, Michael** (1933–) English actor

26 Of course they have, or I wouldn't be sitting here talking to someone like you.
In J. Cooper, *Class* (1979) **Cartland, Barbara** (1902–2000) English writer. When asked in a radio interview whether she thought that British class barriers had broken down

27 So many people don't know how to behave at a shooting party.
The Observer, (1998) **Chelsea, Jenny, Viscountess** Introducing a seminar on upper class behaviour

28 Thanks to Mr Blair, my family and I will be leaving British politics after a limited period of involvement.
The Observer, (1998) **Cranborne, Robert Cecil, Lord** (1946–) English critic and writer. Member of the Cecil family, represented in the House of Lords since 1603

29 I never knew the lower classes had such white skins.
Attr. **Curzon, Lord** (1859–1925) English statesman and scholar. On seeing some soldiers bathing

30 While there is a lower class, I am in it. While there is a criminal class I am of it. While there is a soul in prison, I am not free.
Remark made during his trial for sedition, (1918) **Debs, Eugene Victor** (1855–1926) US radical politician and trade union leader

31 He bid me observe ... that the calamities of life were shared among the upper and lower part of mankind; but that the middle station had the fewest disasters.
The Life and Adventures of Robinson Crusoe (1719) **Defoe, Daniel** (c.1661–1731) English writer and critic

32 'Two nations; between whom there is no intercourse and no sympathy; who are as ignorant of each other's habits, thoughts, and feelings, as if they were dwellers in different zones, or inhabitants of different planets; who are formed by a different breeding, are fed by a different food, are ordered by different manners, and are not governed by the same laws.'
'You speak of –' said Egremont, hesitatingly.
'THE RICH AND THE POOR.'
Sybil (1845) **Disraeli, Benjamin** (1804–1881) English statesman and writer

33 He is used to dealing with estate workers. I cannot see how anyone can say he is out of touch.

Daily Herald, (1963) **Douglas-Home, Lady Caroline** (1937–) Daughter of Sir Alec Douglas-Home; Lady-in-Waiting. Referring to her father's suitability for his new role as prime minister

34 Property has its duties as well as its rights.
Letter to the Earl of Donoughmore, (1838) **Drummond, Thomas** (1797–1840) Scottish statesman and engineer

35 If by the people you understand the multitude, the hoi polloi, 'tis no matter what they think; they are sometimes in the right, sometimes in the wrong: their judgement is a mere lottery.
Essay of Dramatic Poesy (1668) **Dryden, John** (1631–1700) English poet, satirist, dramatist and critic

36 We are forever being told we have a rigid class structure. That's a load of codswallop.
Daily Mail, (1996) **Edward, Prince** (1964–) Son of Queen Elizabeth II

37 My favourite programme is 'Mrs Dale's Diary'. I try never to miss it because it is the only way of knowing what goes on in a middle-class family.
Attr. **Elizabeth, the Queen Mother** (1900–2002) Queen of the United Kingdom and mother of Elizabeth II

38 Name-dropping is so vulgar, as I was telling the Queen last week.
In *The Observer*, (1999) **Fawsley, Lord St John of** (1929–) British Conservative politician and constitutional expert

39 The result is that people with a culture of poverty suffer much less repression than we of the middle-class suffer and indeed, if I may make the suggestion with due qualification, they often have a lot more fun than we have.
The Freedom of the City (1973) **Friel, Brian** (1929–) Irish dramatist and writer

40 All men are equal – all men, that is to say, who possess umbrellas.
Howard's End (1910) **Forster, E.M.** (1879–1970) English writer, essayist and literary critic

41 They all shall equal be!
The Earl, the Marquis, and the Dook,
The Groom, the Butler, and the Cook,
The Aristocrat who banks with Coutts,
The Aristocrat who cleans the boots.
The Gondoliers (1889) **Gilbert, W.S.** (1836–1911) English dramatist, humorist and librettist

42 All the world over, I will back the masses against the classes.
Speech, Liverpool, (1886) **Gladstone, William** (1809–1898) English statesman and reformer

43 Ye friends to truth, ye statesmen, who survey
The rich man's joys increase, the poor's decay,
'Tis yours to judge, how wide the limits stand
Between a splendid and a happy land.
The Deserted Village (1770) **Goldsmith, Oliver** (c.1728–1774) Irish dramatist, poet and writer

44 I don't see any harm in being middle class, I've been middle class all my life and have benefited from it.
The Observer, (1983) **Hailsham, Quintin Hogg, Baron** (1907–2001) English Conservative politician and Lord Chancellor

45 … it takes a great deal to produce ennui in an Englishman and if you do, he only takes it as convincing proof that you are well-bred.
With Malice Toward Some (1938) **Halsey, Margaret** (1910–1997) US writer

46 'Bourgeois,' I observed, 'is an epithet which the riff-raff apply to what is respectable, and the aristocracy to what is decent.'
The Dolly Dialogues (1894) **Hope, Anthony** (1863–1933) English writer, dramatist and lawyer

47 Every time an Englishman opens his mouth, he enables other Englishmen if not to despise him, at any rate to place him in some social and class pigeonhole.
The Times, (1992) **Howard, Philip** (1933–) English journalist

48 This man I thought had been a Lord among wits; but, I find, he is only a wit among Lords.

In Boswell, *The Life of Samuel Johnson* (1791) **Johnson, Samuel** (1709–1784) English lexicographer, poet, critic, conversationalist and essayist. Of Lord Chesterfield

49 The people have little intelligence, the great no heart … if I had to choose I should not hesitate: I would be of the people.
Les caractères ou les moeurs de ce siècle (1688) **La Bruyère, Jean de** (1645–1696) French satirist

50 How beastly the bourgeois is especially the male of the species.
Pansies (1929), 'How Beastly the Bourgeois Is' **Lawrence, D.H.** (1885–1930) English writer, poet and critic

51 An Englishman's way of speaking absolutely classifies him.
My Fair Lady (1956) **Lerner, Alan Jay** (1918–1986) US lyricist and screenwriter

52 I'm not interested in classes … Far be it from me to foster inferiority complexes among the workers by trying to make them think they belong to some special class. That has happened in Europe but it hasn't happened here yet.
In A.M. Schlesinger Jr., *The Coming of the New Deal* **Lewis, John Llewellyn** (1880–1969) US union leader

53 The ascent of the privileged, not only in the Lager but in all human coexistence, is an anguishing but unfailing phenomenon: only in Utopias are they absent. It is the duty of righteous men to make war on all undeserved privilege, but one must not forget that this is a war without end.
The Drowned and the Saved (1988) **Levi, Primo** (1919–1987) Italian writer, poet and chemist; survivor of Auschwitz

54 Noblesse oblige.
Maximes et réflexions (1812) **Lévis, Duc de** (1764–1830) French writer and soldier

55 We were located half way up the social ladder. Or half way down. It depends on which way you're looking.
The Toronto Star, (1989) **Lillie, Beatrice** (1894–1989) Canadian-born English actress. Commenting on her childhood in Toronto

56 A fully equipped duke costs as much to keep up as two Dreadnoughts; and dukes are just as great a terror and they last longer.
Speech, (1909)

57 Every man has a House of Lords in his own head. Fears, prejudices, misconceptions – those are the peers, and they are hereditary.
Speech, Cambridge, (1927) **Lloyd George, David** (1863–1945) British Liberal statesman

58 There were gentlemen and there were seamen in the navy of Charles the Second. But the seamen were not gentlemen; and the gentlemen were not seamen.
History of England (1849) **Macaulay, Lord** (1800–1859) English Liberal statesman, essayist and poet

59 For titles do not reflect honour on men, but rather men on their titles.
Dei Discorsi **Machiavelli** (1469–1527) Florentine statesman, political theorist and historian

60 The slavery of being waited upon that is more deadening than the slavery of waiting upon other people.
The Adventures of Sylvia Scarlett (1918) **Mackenzie, Sir Compton** (1883–1972) Scottish writer and broadcaster

61 Take, for instance, the question of class. There were many undergraduates like myself who theoretically conceded that all men were equal, but who, in practice, while only too willing to converse, or attempt to, with say Normandy peasants or shopkeepers, would wince away in their own college halls from those old grammar school boys who with impure vowels kept admiring Bernard Shaw or Noël Coward while grabbing their knives and forks like dumb-bells.
The Saturday Book (1961) **MacNeice, Louis** (1907–1963) Belfast-born poet, writer, radio producer, translator and critic

62 The one class you do not belong to and are not proud of at all is the lower-middle class. No one ever describes himself as belonging to the lower-middle class.
How to be an Inimitable **Mikes, George** (1912–1987) Hungarian-born British writer

63 Persons require to possess a title, or some other badge of rank, or of the consideration of people of rank, to be able to indulge somewhat in the luxury of doing as they like without detriment to their estimation.
On Liberty (1859) **Mill, John Stuart** (1806–1873) English philosopher, economist and reformer

64 An aristocracy in a republic is like a chicken whose head had been cut off: it may run about in a lively way, but in fact it is dead.
Noblesse Oblige (1956) **Mitford, Nancy** (1904–1973) English writer

65 Great lords have pleasures, but the people have fun.
Pensées et fragments inédits (1899) **Montesquieu, Charles** (1689–1755) French philosopher and jurist

66 Wherever I found talent and courage, I rewarded it ... without asking whether there were any quarters of nobility to show.
In O'Meara, *Napoleon in Exile* (1822) **Napoleon I** (1769–1821) French emperor. Of his generals

67 England is the most class-ridden country under the sun. It is a land of snobbery and privilege, ruled largely by the old and silly.
The Lion and The Unicorn, (1941) **Orwell, George** (1903–1950) English author

68 The working class has come a long way in recent years, all of it downhill. They look like one big Manson family.
Arena, (1989)

69 They are the real class traitors, betrayers of the men who fought the Second World War, those men who fought for Churchill but voted for Clement Attlee. But in the tattooed jungle they have no sense of history. The true unruly children of Thatcherism, they know their place and wallow in their peasanthood.
Arena, (1989) Of the working class in the 1980s **Parsons, Tony** (1953–) British journalist and author

70 It is a reproach to religion and government to suffer so much poverty and excess.
Some Fruits of Solitude, in Reflections and Maxims relating to the Conduct of Humane Life (1693) **Penn, William** (1644–1718) English Quaker, founder of state of Pennsylvania

71 Come, let us pity those who are better off than we are.
Come, my friend, and remember that the rich have butlers and no friends,
And we have friends and no butlers.
'The Garret' (1916) **Pound, Ezra** (1885–1972) US poet

72 You can be in the Horse Guards and still be common, dear.
Separate Tables (1955) **Rattigan, Terence** (1911–1977) English dramatist and screenwriter

73 The bourgeois are other people.
Journal, (1890) **Renard, Jules** (1864–1910) French writer and dramatist

74 It ought to be quite as natural and straightforward a matter for a labourer to take his pension from his parish, because he has deserved well of his parish, as for a man in higher rank to take his pension from his country, because he has deserved well of his country.
Unto this Last (1862), Preface **Ruskin, John** (1819–1900) English art critic, philosopher and reformer

75 I have little or no time for people who aspire to be members of the middle class.
Remark at the launch of the Socialist Labour Party, (1996) **Scargill, Arthur** (1941–) English trade union leader. On John Prescott's description of himself as middle class

76 This is 95 per cent about class warfare and 5 per cent animal welfare.
In *The Observer*, (1999) **Scott, Walter-Montagu-Douglas, Duke of Buccleuch** (1923–) British Conservative politician and landowner. On the proposal to ban hunting in Scotland

77 Skullion had little use for contraceptives at the best of times. Unnatural, he called them, and placed them in the lower social category of things along with elastic-sided boots and made-up bow ties. Not the sort of attire for a gentleman.
Porterhouse Blue (1974) **Sharpe, Tom** (1928–) English writer

78 When domestic servants are treated as human beings it is not worth while to keep them.

Man and Superman (1903) **Shaw, George Bernard** (1856–1950) Irish socialist, writer, dramatist and critic

79 Many faint with toil,
That few may know the cares and woe of sloth.
Queen Mab (1813)

80 The rich have become richer, and the poor have become poorer; and the vessel of the state is driven between the Scylla and Charybdis of anarchy and despotism.
A Defence of Poetry (1821) **Shelley, Percy Bysshe** (1792–1822) English poet, dramatist and essayist

81 The British Bourgeoisie
Is not born,
And does not die,
But, if it is ill,
It has a frightened look in its eyes.
'At the House of Mrs Kinfoot' (1921) **Sitwell, Sir Osbert** (1892–1969) English poet and writer

82 The state is a machine in the hands of the ruling class for suppressing the resistance of its class enemies.
Foundations of Leninism (1924) **Stalin, Joseph** (1879–1953) Soviet Communist leader

83 It is impossible for one class to appreciate the wrongs of another.
In Anthony and Gage, *History of Woman Suffrage* (1881) **Stanton, Elizabeth Cady** (1815–1902) US suffragist, abolitionist, feminist, editor and writer

84 The rich take their time, the rich marry late so that property will be divided little and late, while the poor rush to marry and divide the little pay that one gets.
For Love Alone (1944) **Stead, Christina** (1902–1983) Australian writer

85 Okie use' ta mean you was from Oklahoma. Now it means you're a dirty son-of-a-bitch. Okie means you're scum. Don't mean nothing itself, it's the way they say it.
The Grapes of Wrath (1939) **Steinbeck, John** (1902–1968) US writer

86 They have learnt nothing, and forgotten nothing.

Attr. **Talleyrand, Charles-Maurice de** (1754–1838) French statesman, memoirist and prelate. Comment on exiled French aristocrats

87 The charm of Britain has always been the ease with which one can move into the middle class.
The Observer, (1974) **Thatcher, Margaret** (1925–) English Conservative Prime Minister

88 The ship follows Soviet custom: it is riddled with class distinctions so subtle, it takes a trained Marxist to appreciate them.
The Great Railway Bazaar (1975) **Theroux, Paul** (1941–) US writer

89 I am seeking to rescue the poor stockinger, the Luddite cropper, the 'obsolete' handloom weaver, the 'utopian' artisan, and even the deluded follower of Joanna Southcott, from the enormous condescension of posterity.
The Making of the English Working Class, quoted in *The Guardian* **Thompson, E.P.** (1924–1993) English historian

90 Too long, that some may rest,
Tired millions toil unblest.
'New National Anthem' **Watson, Sir William** (1858–1936) English poet

91 The mistake in voting Labour, as 13.5 million people so foolishly did in 1997, was that it gave the wrong sort of people ideas above themselves.
The Observer, (1999) **Waugh, Auberon** (1939–) English writer and critic

92 For generations the British bourgeoisie have spoken of themselves as gentlemen, and by that they have meant, among other things, a self-respecting scorn of irregular perquisites. It is the quality that distinguishes the gentleman from both the artist and the aristocrat.
Decline and Fall (1928) **Waugh, Evelyn** (1903–1966) English writer and diarist

93 If property had simply pleasures, we could stand it; but its duties make it unbearable. In the interest of the rich we must get rid of it.
The Fortnightly Review, (1891)

94 Really, if the lower orders don't set us a good example, what on earth is the use of them? They seem, as a class, to have absolutely no sense of moral responsibility.
The Importance of Being Earnest (1895)

95 Cecily: When I see a spade I call it a spade. Gwendolen: I am glad to say that I have never seen a spade. It is obvious that our social spheres have been widely different.
The Importance of Being Earnest (1895) **Wilde, Oscar** (1854–1900) Irish poet, dramatist, writer, critic and wit

96 Everybody should have an equal chance – but they shouldn't have a flying start.
The Observer, (1963) **Wilson, Harold** (1916–1995) English Labour Prime Minister

97 I have no concern for the common man except that he should not be so common.
No Laughing Matter (1967) **Wilson, Sir Angus** (1913–1991) English author

98 Reluctant though one may be to admit it, the entire British aristocracy is seamed and honeycombed with immorality. If you took a pin and jabbed it down anywhere in the pages of Debrett's Peerage you would find it piercing the name of someone with a conscience as tender as a sunburned neck.
Mulliner Nights, (1933) **Wodehouse, P.G.** (1903–1950) English humorist and writer

99 There's what being in the working-class is all about – how to get out of it.
Sydney Morning Herald, (1982) **Wran, Neville Kenneth** (1926–) Australian lawyer and politician
See also democracy; language; money and wealth; society

COMMUNISM

1 Russian Communism is the illegitimate child of Karl Marx and Catherine the Great.
The Observer, (1956) **Attlee, Clement** (1883–1967) English statesman and Prime Minister

2 Its relationship to democratic institutions is that of the death watch beetle – it is not a Party, it is a conspiracy.
Attr. **Bevan, Aneurin** (1897–1960) Welsh Labour politician, miner and orator. Of the Communist Party

3 Beware, for the time may be short. A shadow has fallen across the scenes so lately lighted by the Allied victory. Nobody knows what Soviet Russia and its Communist international organization intend to do in the immediate future. From Stettin in the Baltic to Trieste in the Adriatic an Iron Curtain has descended across the Continent.
Speech, Fulton, Missouri, (March 1946) **Churchill, Sir Winston** (1874–1965) English Conservative Prime Minister

4 What is a communist? One who hath yearnings
For equal division of unequal earnings.
Epigram, (1850) **Elliott, Ebenezer** (1781–1849) English poet and merchant

5 The history of all hitherto existing society is the history of class struggles.
The Communist Manifesto (1848)

6 A spectre is haunting Europe – the spectre of Communism.
The Communist Manifesto (1848) **Engels, Friedrich** (1820–1895) German socialist and political philosopher

7 Men are made by nature unequal. It is vain, therefore, to treat them as if they were equal.
Short Studies on Great Subjects (1877) **Froude, James Anthony** (1818–1894) English historian and scholar

8 We are for our own people. We want to see them happy, healthy and wise, drawing strength from cooperation with the peoples of other lands, but also contributing their full share to the general well-being. Not a broken-down pauper and mendicant, but a strong, living partner in the progressive advancement of civilization.
The Case for Communism (1949) **Gallacher, William** (1881–1965) Scottish Communist politician

9 That all men are equal is a proposition to which, at ordinary times, no sane human being has ever given his assent.

Proper Studies (1927) **Huxley, Aldous** (1894–1963) English writer, poet and critic

10 Those who wait for that must wait until a shrimp learns to whistle.
Attr. **Khrushchev, Nikita** (1894–1971) Russian statesman and Premier of the USSR. On the possibility that the Soviet Union might one day reject communism

11 Communism is Soviet power plus the electrification of the whole country.
Report at the Congress of Soviets, (1920)
Lenin, V.I. (1870–1924) Russian revolutionary, Marxist theoretician and first leader of the USSR

12 Every Communist must grasp the truth. Political power grows out of the barrel of a gun.
Speech, (1938) **Mao Tse-Tung** (1893–1976) Chinese Communist leader

13 What I did that was new was prove ... that the class struggle necessarily leads to the dictatorship of the proletariat.
Letter, (1852) **Marx, Karl** (1818–1883) German political philosopher and economist; founder of Communism

14 I have here in my hand a list of two hundred and five people that were known to the Secretary of State as being members of the Communist Party and who nevertheless are still working and shaping the policy of the State Department.
Speech, Wheeling, West Virginia, (February 9, 1950)

15 It makes me sick, sick, sick way down inside.
In Lewis, *The Fifties* (1978) Of someone alleged to have communist sympathies

16 It looks like a duck, walks like a duck, and quacks like a duck.
Attr. On how to spot a communist **McCarthy, Joseph** (1908–1957) US Republican politician

17 The trouble with Communism is the Communists, just as the trouble with Christianity is the Christians.
Life, (1946) **Mencken, H.L.** (1880–1956) US writer, critic, philologist and satirist

18 All animals are equal, but some animals are more equal than others.
Animal Farm (1945) **Orwell, George** (1903–1950) English writer and critic

19 Communism is like prohibition, it's a good idea but it won't work.
Weekly Articles (1981) **Rogers, Will** (1879–1935) US humorist, actor, rancher, writer and wit

20 Nature has no cure for this sort of madness, though I have known a legacy from a rich relative work wonders.
Law, Life and Letters (1927) **Smith, F.E.** (1872–1930) English politician and Lord Chancellor. On Bolshevism

21 For us in Russia, communism is a dead dog, while for many people in the West, it is still a living lion.
The Listener, (1979) **Solzhenitsyn, Alexander** (1918–) Russian writer, dramatist and historian

22 The party is the rallying-point for the best elements of the working class.
Attr. **Stalin, Joseph** (1879–1953) Soviet Communist leader

23 Communism continued to haunt Europe as a spectre – a name men gave to their own fears and blunders. But the crusade against Communism was even more imaginary than the spectre of Communism.
The Origins of the Second World War (1961) **Taylor, A.J.P.** (1906–1990) English historian, writer, broadcaster and lecturer

24 Lenin's method leads to this: the party organization at first substitutes itself for the party as a whole. Then the central committee substitutes itself for the party organization, and finally a single dictator substitutes himself for the central committee.
In N. McInnes, *The Communist Parties of Western Europe* **Trotsky, Leon** (1879–1940) Russian revolutionary and Communist theorist
See also russia; socialism

COMPASSION

1 Blessed are the merciful: for they shall
obtain mercy.
Matthew, 5:7 **The Bible (King James Version)**

2 Can I see another's woe,
And not be in sorrow too?
Can I see another's grief,
And not seek for kind relief?
'On Another's Sorrow', *Songs of Innocence*
(1789) **Blake, William** (1757–1827) English poet,
engraver, painter and mystic

3 But for the grace of God there goes John
Bradford.
Attr. **Bradford, John** (c.1510–1555) English
Protestant martyr and writer. Remark on
criminals going to the gallows

4 Then gently scan your brother man,
Still gentler sister woman;
Tho' they may gang a kennin wrang,
To step aside is human.
'Address to the Unco Guid' (1786) **Burns,
Robert** (1759–1796) Scottish poet and
songwriter

5 For pitee renneth soone in gentil herte.
The Canterbury Tales (1387) **Chaucer, Geoffrey**
(c.1340–1400) English poet, public servant and
courtier

6 The dimensions of this mercy are above my
thoughts. It is, for aught I know, a
crowning mercy.
Letter to William Lenthall, (1651) **Cromwell,
Oliver** (1599–1658) English general, statesman
and Puritan leader

7 Compassion and love are not mere
luxuries. As the source of both inner and
external peace, they are fundamental to the
continued survival of our species.
The Times, June 1999 **Dalai Lama** (1935–)
Spiritual and temporal leader of Tibet

8 Clemency is also a revolutionary measure.
Speech, (1793) **Desmoulins, Camille** (1760–
1794) French pamphleteer, orator and
revolutionary

9 We hand folks over to God's mercy, and
show none ourselves.
Adam Bede (1859) **Eliot, George** (1819–1880)
English writer and poet

10 He best can pity who has felt the woe.
Dione (1720) **Gay, John** (1685–1732) English
poet, dramatist and librettist

11 Our sympathy is cold to the relation of
distant misery.
Decline and Fall of the Roman Empire (1788)
Gibbon, Edward (1737–1794) English historian,
politician and memoirist

12 My own heart let me more have pity on; let
Me live to my sad self hereafter kind,
Charitable; not live this tormented mind
With this tormented mind tormenting yet.
'My own Heart let me more have Pity on'
(c.1885) **Hopkins, Gerard Manley** (1844–1889)
English Jesuit priest, poet and classicist

13 She was a machine-gun riddling her
hostess with sympathy.
Mortal Coils (1922) **Huxley, Aldous** (1894–1963)
English writer, poet and critic

14 Compassion is not a sloppy, sentimental
feeling for people who are underprivileged
or sick … it is an absolutely practical belief
that, regardless of a person's background,
ability or ability to pay, he should be
provided with the best that society has to
offer.
Maiden speech, House of Commons, (1970)
Kinnock, Neil (1942–) Welsh Labour
politician

15 Give me your tired, your poor,
Your huddled masses yearning to breathe
free.
'The New Colossus' (1883); verse inscribed on
the Statue of Liberty **Lazarus, Emma** (1849–
1887) US poet and translator

16 To show pity is felt to be a sign of scorn,
because one has obviously stopped being
an object of fear as soon as one is pitied.
Human, All too Human (1886) **Nietzsche,
Friedrich Wilhelm** (1844–1900) German
philosopher, critic and poet

17 Pity is but one remove from love.
The History of Sir Charles Grandison (1754)
Richardson, Samuel (1689–1761) English
novelist

18 The quality of mercy is not strain'd;
It droppeth as the gentle rain from heaven
Upon the place beneath. It is twice blest:
It blesseth him that gives and him that
takes.
The Merchant of Venice, IV.i

19 Is there no pity sitting in the clouds
That sees into the bottom of my grief?
Romeo and Juliet, III.v **Shakespeare, William**
(1564–1616) English dramatist, poet and actor

20 Any man of humane sentiments ... would
have been prompted to offer his services to
the forlorn stranger: but ... our hero was
devoid of all these infirmities of human
nature.
The Adventures of Ferdinand Count Fathom (1753)
Smollett, Tobias (1721–1771) Scottish writer,
satirist, historian, traveller and physician

21 Brothers in humanity who live after us,
don't let your hearts be hardened against
us, for, if you take pity on us poor souls,
God will be more likely to have mercy on
you. But pray to God that he may be
willing to absolve us all!
'Ballad of the Hanged Men' (1462) **Villon,
François** (1431–1485)

22 No stranger to misery myself, I am
learning to befriend the wretched.
Aeneid **Virgil** (70–19 BC) Roman poet

23 And remember Mother's practical ethics:
*one can drown in compassion if one answers
every call it's another way of suicide.*
The Eye of the Storm (1973) **White, Patrick**
(1912–1990) English-born Australian writer
and dramatist

24 Anybody can sympathise with the
sufferings of a friend, but it requires a very
fine nature to sympathise with a friend's
success.
'The Soul of Man under Socialism' (1881)

25 I can sympathise with everything, except
suffering.
The Picture of Dorian Gray (1891) **Wilde, Oscar**
(1854–1900) Irish poet, dramatist, writer, critic
and wit
See also charity; forgiveness; goodness;
kindness; suffering; virtue

COMPUTERS

1 The computer can do more work faster
than a human because it doesn't have to
answer the phone.
Attr. **Adams, Joey** (1911– 1999) US comedian
and author

2 Any given program, when running, is
obsolete.
Laws of Computer Programming, I

3 Any given program costs more and takes
longer.
Laws of Computer Programming, II

4 If a program is useful, it will have to be
changed.
Laws of Computer Programming, III

5 If a program is useless, it will have to be
documented.
Laws of Computer Programming, IV

6 Any program will expand to fill available
memory.
Laws of Computer Programming, V

7 The value of a program is proportional to
the weight of its output.
Laws of Computer Programming, VI

8 Program complexity grows until it exceeds
the capabilities of the programmer who
must maintain it.
Laws of Computer Programming, VII

9 Any non-trivial program contains at least
one bug.
Laws of Computer Programming, VIII

10 Undetectable errors are infinite in variety,
in contrast to detectable errors, which by
definition are limited.
Laws of Computer Programming, IX

11 Adding manpower to a late software
project makes it later.
Laws of Computer Programming, X

12 If a computer cable has one end, then it
has another.
Lyall's Conjecture

13 A program is a spell cast over a computer,
turning input into error messages.

14 Applying computer technology is simply finding the right wrench to pound in the correct screw.

15 Artificial Intelligence is the study of how to make real computers act like the ones in movies.

16 Computers are not intelligent. They only think they are.

17 I speak BASIC to clients, 1-2-3 to management, and mumble to myself.

18 Intel has announced its next chip: the Repentium.

19 Press any key … no, no, no, NOT THAT ONE!

20 Putting a computer in front of a child and expecting it to teach him is like putting a book under his pillow, only more expensive.

21 There are two ways to write error-free programs. Only the third one works.

22 WARNING: Keyboard Not Attached. Press F10 to Continue.

23 What goes up must come down. Ask any system administrator.
Anonymous

24 The danger from computers is not that they will eventually get as smart as men, but we will meanwhile agree to meet them halfway.
Attr. **Avishai, Bernard** Canadian-Israeli professor, journalist and writer

25 The world has arrived at an age of cheap complex devices of great reliability, and something is bound to come of it.
Attr. **Bush, Vannevar** (1890–1974) US engineer and physicist

26 The Internet is an élite organisation; most of the population of the world has never even made a phone call.
The Observer Review, (1996) **Chomsky, Noam** (1928–) US linguist and political critic

27 In the information society, nobody thinks. We expect to banish paper, but we actually banish thought.
Jurassic Park (1991) **Crichton, Michael** (1942–) US writer

28 If the automobile had followed the same development cycle as the computer, a Rolls-Royce would today cost $100, get one million miles to the gallon, and explode once a year, killing everyone inside.
Attr. **Cringely, Robert X.** (1953–) US computer journalist and author

29 Personally, I rather look forward to a computer program winning the world chess championship. Humanity needs a lesson in humility.
Attr. **Dawkins, Richard** (1941–) English biologist and author

30 I am afraid it is a non-starter. I cannot even use a bicycle pump.
The Times, (1999) **Dench, Judi** (1934–) English actress. When asked whether she uses e-mail

31 Surfing on the Internet is like sex; everyone boasts about doing more than they actually do. But in the case of the Internet, it's a lot more.
Attr. **Fasulo, Tom** US entomologist and writer

32 The past twenty years have been an incredible adventure for me. It started on a day when, as a college sophomore, I stood in Harvard Square with my friend Paul Allen and pored over the description of a kit computer in *Popular Electronics* magazine.
Attr. **Gates, Bill** (1955–) US businessman; co-founder of Microsoft Corporation

33 The killer application will not be a shrink-wrapped program that sells in millions. The killer app will be a Web site that touches millions of people and helps them to do what they want to do.
Attr. **Gerstner, Lou** (1942–) US business executive; Chairman of IBM

34 *Cyberspace*: A consensual hallucination experienced daily by billions of legitimate operators, in every nation.
Neuromancer (1984) **Gibson, William** (1948–) US writer

35 I think computer viruses should count as life. I think it says something about human nature that the only form of life we have created so far is purely destructive. We've created life in our own image.

Attr. **Hawking, Stephen** (1942–) English theoretical physicist

36 Any sufficiently advanced bug is indistinguishable from a feature.
Attr. **Kulawiec, Rich**

37 I have a spelling checker
It came with my PC;
It plainly marks four my revue
Mistakes I cannot sea.
I've run this poem threw it,
I'm sure your pleased too no,
Its letter perfect in it's weigh,
My checker tolled me sew.
Attr. **Minor, Janet** US poet

38 There's so much darn porn out there, I never got out of the house.
The Times, (1999) **Nicholson, Jack** (1937–) US actor. Explaining why he disconnected his home computer from the Internet

39 I think giving this computer to the last Luddite is ridiculous. It's like giving a Porsche to someone who just discovered the bicycle.
Attr. **Ondaatje, Michael** (1943–) Canadian writer. Comment after accepting a computer at the Wang International Festival of Authors; the author writes with a fountain pen

40 The OED database is one of the wonders of the modern world – to paraphrase Christopher Marlowe, 'infinite riches in a little ROM'.
The Times Literary Supplement, (1992) **Segal, Erich** (1937–) US academic

41 Looking at the proliferation of personal web pages on the net, it looks like very soon everyone on earth will have 15 Megabytes of fame.
Attr. **Siriam, M.G.**

42 Why is it drug addicts and computer aficionados are both called users?
Attr. **Stoll, Clifford** US author

43 C makes it easy to shoot yourself in the foot. C++ makes it harder, but when you do, it blows away your whole leg.
Attr. **Stroustrup, Bjarne** (1950–) Danish computer scientist

44 I think there's a world market for about five computers.
In Martin Moskovits, *Science and Society*, (1995) **Watson, Thomas J.** (1874–1956) Founder of IBM. On the prospects for desktop computers

45 We've all heard that a million monkeys banging on a million typewriters will eventually reproduce the entire works of Shakespeare. Now, thanks to the Internet, we know this is not true.
Mail on Sunday, (1997) **Wilensky, Robert** (1951–) US professor

46 Never trust a computer you can't throw out a window.
Attr. **Wozniak, Steve** (1950–) Co-founder of Apple Computers

THE COUNTRY

1 Shooting is a popular sport in the countryside … Unlike many other countries, the outstanding characteristic of the sport has been that it is not confined to any one class.
The Northern Ireland Tourist Board, (1969) **Anonymous**

2 The city dweller who passes through a country town, and imagines it sleepy and apathetic is very far from the truth: it is watchful as the jungle.
The Pilgrimage (1961) **Broderick, John** (1927–) Irish writer

3 I nauseate walking; 'tis a country diversion, I loathe the country.
The Way of the World (1700) **Congreve, William** (1670–1729) English dramatist

4 God made the country, and man made the town.
The Task (1785)

5 Detested sport,
That owes its pleasures to another's pain.
The Task (1785) Of hunting **Cowper, William** (1731–1800) English poet, hymn writer and letter writer

6 Our farmers round, well pleased with constant gain,
Like other farmers, flourish and complain.

The Parish Register (1807) **Crabbe, George** (1754–1832) English poet, clergyman, surgeon and botanist

7 It is my belief, Watson, founded upon my experience, that the lowest and vilest alleys of London do not present a more dreadful record of sin than does the smiling and beautiful countryside.
'Copper Beeches' (1892) **Doyle, Sir Arthur Conan** (1859–1930) Scottish writer and war correspondent

8 A time there was, ere England's griefs began,
When every rood of ground maintained its man;
For him light labour spread her wholesome store,
Just gave what life required, but gave no more.
His best companions, innocence and health;
And his best riches, ignorance of wealth.
The Deserted Village (1770) **Goldsmith, Oliver** (c.1728–1774) Irish dramatist, poet and writer

9 There is nothing good to be had in the country, or, if there is, they will not let you have it.
The Round Table (1817)

10 When I am in the country, I wish to vegetate like the country.
Table-Talk (1822) **Hazlitt, William** (1778–1830) English writer and critic

11 There are few who would not rather be taken in adultery than in provincialism.
Antic Hay (1923) **Huxley, Aldous** (1894–1963) English writer, poet and critic

12 To find these abominations on the walls of Highland hotels, among people of such delicacy in other things, is peculiarly revolting.
Scottish Journey **Muir, Edwin** (1887–1959) Scottish poet, critic, translator and writer. On hunting trophies

13 Most of their discourse was about hunting, in a dialect I understand very little.
Diary, November 1663 **Pepys, Samuel** (1633–1703) English diarist, naval administrator and politician

14 The country habit has me by the heart,
For he's bewitched for ever who has seen,
Not with his eyes but with his vision,
Spring
Flow down the woods and stipple leaves with sun.
'Winter' (1926)

15 Those who have never dwelt in tents have no idea either of the charm or of the discomfort of a nomadic existence. The charm is purely romantic, and consequently very soon proves to be fallacious.
Twelve Days (1928) **Sackville-West, Vita** (1892–1962) English poet and novelist

16 It is a place with only one post a day ... In the country I always fear that creation will expire before tea-time.
In H. Pearson, *The Smith of Smiths* (1934)

17 I have no relish for the country; it is a kind of healthy grave.
Letter to Miss G. Harcourt, (1838) **Smith, Sydney** (1771–1845) English clergyman, essayist, journalist and wit

18 In the highlands, in the country places,
Where the old plain men have rosy faces,
And the young fair maidens
Quiet eyes.
Songs of Travel (1896) **Stevenson, Robert Louis** (1850–1894) Scottish writer, poet and essayist

19 Tell me a man's a fox-hunter, and I loves him at once.
Handley Cross (1843)

20 Three things I never lends – my 'oss, my wife, and my name.
Hillingdon Hall (1845) **Surtees, R.S.** (1805–1864) English writer

21 This bread I break was once the oat,
This wine upon a foreign tree
Plunged in its fruit;
Man in the day or wind at night
Laid the crops low, broke the grape's joy.
'This bread I break' (1936) **Thomas, Dylan** (1914–1953) Welsh poet, writer and radio dramatist

22 O happy are farmers, too happy if they knew their blessings.
Georgics **Virgil** (70–19 BC) Roman poet

23 Anybody can be good in the country.
The Picture of Dorian Gray (1891)

24 The English country gentleman galloping
after a fox – the unspeakable in full pursuit
of the uneatable.
A Woman of No Importance (1893) **Wilde, Oscar**
(1854–1900) Irish poet, dramatist, writer, critic
and wit
See also birds; cities; garden; nature

COURAGE

1 I looked along the line; it was enough to
assure me. The steady determined scowl of
my companions assured my heart and gave
me determination.
In Richardson, *Fighting Spirit: Psychological
Factors in War* (1978) The words of a soldier in
the Peninsular War

2 Never share a foxhole with anyone braver
than you are.
Anonymous

3 I count him braver who overcomes his
desires than him who overcomes his
enemies.
In Stobaeus, *Florilegium* **Aristotle** (384–322 BC)
Greek philosopher

4 Courage is the thing. All goes if courage
goes.
Address, St Andrews University, (1922) **Barrie,
Sir J.M.** (1860–1937) Scottish dramatist and
writer

5 The schoolboy, with his satchel in his hand,
Whistling aloud to bear his courage up.
'The Grave' (1743) **Blair, Robert** (1699–1746)
Scottish poet

6 The weak in courage is strong in cunning.
The Marriage of Heaven and Hell (c.1790–1793)
Blake, William (1757–1827) English poet,
engraver, painter and mystic

7 No coward soul is mine,
No trembler in the world's storm-troubled
sphere:
I see Heaven's glories shine,
And faith shines equal, arming me from
fear.
'Last Lines' (1846) **Brontë, Emily** (1818–1848)
English poet and writer

8 'I'm very brave generally,' he went on in a
low voice: 'only to-day I happen to have a
headache.'
Through the Looking-Glass (*and What Alice
Found There*) (1872) **Carroll, Lewis** (1832–1898)
English writer and photographer

9 Down these mean streets a man must go
who is not himself mean, who is neither
tarnished nor afraid.
Atlantic Monthly (1944) **Chandler, Raymond**
(1888–1959) US crime writer

10 To see what is right and not to do it is want
of courage.
Analects **Confucius** (c.550–c.478 BC) Chinese
philosopher and teacher of ethics

11 Courage is the price that Life exacts for
granting peace.
'Courage' (1927) **Earhart, Amelia** (1898–1937)
US aviator

12 If thy heart fails thee, climb not at all.
In Fuller, *The history of the Worthies of England*
(1662) **Elizabeth I** (1533–1603) Queen of
England. Upon seeing the line 'Fain would I
climb, yet fear I to fall' written on a window
pane

13 To stand upon the ramparts and die for
our principles is heroic, but to sally forth to
battle and win for our principles is
something more than heroic.
Speech, (1928) **Roosevelt, Franklin Delano**
(1882–1945) US Democrat President

14 Wherever valour true is found,
True modesty will there abound.
The Yeoman of the Guard (1888) **Gilbert, W.S.**
(1836–1911) English dramatist, humorist and
librettist

15 Grace under pressure.
Attr. **Hemingway, Ernest** (1898–1961) US
author. Definition of 'guts'

16 The important thing when you are going to
do something brave is to have someone on
hand to witness it.
The Observer, (1980) **Howard, Michael** (1922–)
English historian and writer

17 It is better to die on your feet than to live
on your knees.

Speech, Paris, (1936) **Ibárruri, Dolores ('La Pasionaria')** (1895–1989) Basque Communist leader

18 Courage without conscience is a wild beast.
Speech, (1882) **Ingersoll, Robert G.** (1833–1899) US lawyer, soldier and writer

19 It takes moral courage to grieve, but it takes religious courage to rejoice.
Attr. by Jonathan Sacks in *The Times*, (1998) **Kierkegaard, Søren** (1813–1855) Danish philosopher

20 It takes a good deal of physical courage to ride a horse. This, however, I have. I get it at about forty cents a flask, and take it as required.
Literary Lapses (1910) **Leacock, Stephen** (1869–1944) English-born Canadian humorist, writer and economist

21 Courage! I have shown it for years; think you I shall lose it at the moment when my sufferings are to end?
Attr. **Marie-Antoinette** (1755–1793) Queen of France. Remark on the way to the guillotine, 16 October 1793

22 Want of courage is want of sense.
The Tragic Comedians **Meredith, George** (1828–1909) English writer, poet and critic

23 As for moral courage, he said he had very rarely encountered two o'clock in the morning courage; that is, the courage of the unprepared.
Mémorial de Sainte Hélène **Napoleon I** (1769–1821) French emperor

24 Courage – or putting it more accurately, lack of fear – is a result of discipline. By an act of will, a man refuses to think of the reasons for fear, and so concentrates entirely on winning the battle.
The Independent, (1994) **Nixon, Richard** (1913–1994) US Republican politician and President

25 The stubborn spear-men still made good
Their dark impenetrable wood,
Each stepping where his comrade stood,
The instant that he fell.
Marmion (1808) **Scott, Sir Walter** (1771–1832) Scottish writer and historian

26 Cowards die many times before their deaths:
The valiant never taste of death but once.
Julius Caesar, II.ii

27 Courage mounteth with occasion.
King John, II.i

28 *Macbeth*: If we should fail?
Lady Macbeth: We fail!
But screw your courage to the sticking place,
And we'll not fail.
Macbeth, I.vii **Shakespeare, William** (1564–1616) English dramatist, poet and actor

29 My valour is certainly going! – it is sneaking off! – I feel it oozing out as it were at the palms of my hands!
The Rivals (1775) **Sheridan, Richard Brinsley** (1751–1816) Irish dramatist, politician and orator

30 The three-o'-clock in the morning courage, which Bonaparte thought was the rarest.
Walden (1854) **Thoreau, Henry David** (1817–1862) US essayist, social critic and writer

31 Courage is often lack of insight, whereas cowardice in many cases is based on good information.
Attr. **Ustinov, Sir Peter** (1921–2004) English actor, director, dramatist, writer and raconteur

32 'Tisn't life that matters! 'Tis the courage you bring to it.
Fortitude (1913) **Walpole, Sir Hugh** (1884–1941) New Zealand-born English writer
See also patriotism; war

COURTSHIP

1 If you want to win her hand,
Let the maiden understand
That's she's not the only pebble on the beach.
'You're Not the Only Pebble on the Beach' **Braisted, Harry** (19th century) Songwriter

2 Better be courted and jilted
Than never be courted at all.
'The Jilted Nymph' (1843) **Campbell, Thomas** (1777–1844) Scottish poet, ballad writer and journalist

3 Would you gain the tender Creature?
Softly, gently, kindly treat her;
Suff'ring is the Lover's Part.
Beauty by Constraint possessing,
You enjoy but half the Blessing,
Lifeless Charms, without the Heart.
Acis and Galatea (1718) **Gay, John** (1685–1732)
English poet, dramatist and librettist

4 She whom I love is hard to catch and
conquer,
Hard, but O the glory of the winning were
she won!
'Love in the Valley' (1883) **Meredith, George**
(1828–1909) English writer, poet and critic

5 I court others in verse: but I love thee in
prose:
And they have my whimsies, but thou hast
my heart.
'A Better Answer' (1718) **Prior, Matthew** (1664–
1721) English poet and diplomat

6 Your brother and my sister no sooner met
but they look'd;
no sooner look'd but they lov'd;
no sooner lov'd but they sigh'd;
no sooner sigh'd but they ask'd one
another the reason;
no sooner knew the reason but they sought
the remedy –
and in these degrees have they made a pair
of stairs to marriage,
which they will climb incontinent, or else
be incontinent before marriage.
As You Like, It V.ii

7 Women are angels, wooing:
Things won are done; joy's soul lies in the
doing.
That she belov'd knows nought that knows
not this:
Men prize the thing ungain'd more than it
is.
Troilus and Cressida, I.ii **Shakespeare, William**
(1564–1616) English dramatist, poet and actor
See also love; marriage; men and women;
passion; sex

CRIME

1 Perhaps it is the only crime in which the
victim becomes the accused and, in reality,
it is she who must prove her good
reputation, her mental soundness, and her
impeccable propriety.
Sisters in Crime (1975) **Adler, Freda** (1934–) US
educator and writer. On rape

2 No punishment has ever possessed
enough power of deterrence to prevent the
commission of crimes.
*Eichmann in Jerusalem: A Report on the Banality
of Evil* (1963) **Arendt, Hannah** (1906–1975)
German-born US theorist

3 Opportunity makes a thief.
Letter to Essex, (1598) **Bacon, Francis** (1561–
1626) English philosopher, essayist, politician
and courtier

4 I am laughing to think what risks you take
to try to find money in a desk by night
where the legal owner can never find any
by day.
Attr. **Balzac, Honoré de** (1799–1850) French
writer. Remark made on waking to find a
burglar in his room

5 It is not inconceivable that a man might
find freedom and identity by killing his
oppressor. But as a Chicagoan, I am rather
skeptical about this. Murderers are not
improved by murdering.
'A World Too Much With Us' (1975) **Bellow,
Saul** (1915–2005) Canadian-born US Jewish
writer

6 Even nowadays a man can't step up and kill
a woman without feeling just a bit
unchivalrous.
Attr. **Benchley, Robert** (1889–1945) US essayist,
humorist and actor

7 Whoso sheddeth man's blood, by man
shall his blood be shed.
Genesis, 9:6 **The Bible (King James Version)**

8 Labour is the party of law and order in
Britain today. Tough on crime and tough
on the causes of crime.
Speech at the Labour Party Conference, (1993)
Blair, Tony (1953–) British Labour Prime
Minister. Speech as Shadow Home Secretary

9 The mafia is rational, it wants to reduce homicides to the minimum.
Hell (1992) **Bocca, Giorgio** (1920–) Italian writer

10 When you've got nothing, being a great thief or a respected fighter really counts for something.
Interview, *The Big Issue,* (May 1996)

11 Society has a choice: it either has a prison system based on punitive measures or one that rehabilitates. Do people want to sleep with a shotgun under their bed and go shopping in an armoured van, or do they want to live in a safer, fairer community?
Interview, *The Big Issue,* (May 1996) **Boyle, Jimmy** (1944–) Scottish gangster

12 Ye're a vera clever chiel, man, but ye wad be nane the waur o' a hanging.
In Lockhart, *Life of Scott* **Braxfield, Lord** (1722–1799) Scottish judge. To an eloquent culprit at the bar

13 What is robbing a bank compared with founding a bank?
The Threepenny Opera (1928) **Brecht, Bertolt** (1898–1956) German dramatist

14 In other countries poverty is a misfortune – with us it is a crime.
England and the English (1833) **Bulwer-Lytton, Edward** (1803–1873) English novelist, dramatist, poet and politician

15 How many crimes committed simply because their authors could not endure being wrong!
The Fall, (1956) **Camus, Albert** (1913–1960) Algerian-born French writer

16 I've been accused of every death except the casualty list of the World War.
In Allsop, *The Bootleggers* (1961)

17 They can't collect legal taxes from illegal money.
In Kobler, *Capone* (1971) Objecting to the US Bureau of Internal Revenue claiming large sums in unpaid back tax **Capone, Al** (1899–1947) Chicago gangster

18 Stolen sweets are best.
The Rival Fools (1709) **Cibber, Colley** (1671–1757) English actor, dramatist and poet

19 Mordre wol out, that se we day by day.
The Canterbury Tales (1387) **Chaucer, Geoffrey** (c.1340–1400) English poet, public servant and courtier

20 Thieves respect property; they merely wish the property to become their property that they may more perfectly respect it.
Attr. **Chesterton, G.K.** (1874–1936) English writer, poet and critic

21 He that first cries out stop thief, is often he that has stolen the treasure.
Love for Love (1695) **Congreve, William** (1670–1729) English dramatist

22 If a man once indulges himself in murder, very soon he comes to think little of robbing; and from robbing he comes next to drinking and sabbath-breaking, and from that to incivility and procrastination.
'Murder Considered as One of the Fine Arts' (1839) **De Quincey, Thomas** (1785–1859) English writer

23 Necessity makes an honest man a knave.
Serious Reflections of Robinson Crusoe (1720) **Defoe, Daniel** (c.1661–1731) English writer and critic

24 I haven't committed a crime. What I did was fail to comply with the law.
Attr. **Dinkins, David** (1927–) US politician; Mayor of New York 1989–1993. Answering accusations that he failed to pay his taxes

25 'I should have more faith,' he said; 'I ought to know by this time that when a fact appears opposed to a long train of deductions it invariably proves to be capable of bearing some other interpretation.'
A Study in Scarlet (1887)

26 Singularity is almost invariably a clue. The more featureless and commonplace a crime is, the more difficult it is to bring it home.
The Adventures of Sherlock Holmes (1892), 'The Boscombe Valley Mystery'

27 You know my method. It is founded upon the observance of trifles.
The Adventures of Sherlock Holmes (1892), 'The Boscombe Valley Mystery'

28 You will remember, Watson, how the dreadful business of the Abernetty family was first brought to my notice by the depth which the parsley had sunk into the butter upon a hot day.
The Return of Sherlock Holmes (1905), 'The Adventure of the Six Napoleons'

29 All other men are specialists, but his specialism is omniscience.
His Last Bow (1917) **Doyle, Sir Arthur Conan** (1859–1930) Scottish writer and war correspondent

30 Macavity, Macavity, there's no one like Macavity,
There never was a Cat of such deceitfulness and suavity.
He always has an alibi, and one or two to spare:
At whatever time the deed took place –
MACAVITY WASN'T THERE!
'Macavity: the Mystery Cat' (1939) **Eliot, T.S.** (1888–1965) US-born British poet, verse dramatist and critic

31 As there is a use In medicine for poisons, so the world cannot move without rogues.
Conduct of Life (1860) **Emerson, Ralph Waldo** (1803–1882) US poet, essayist, transcendentalist and teacher

32 Crime expands according to our willingness to put up with it.
Attr. **Farber, Barry** (1859–1930)

33 Crimes, like virtues, are their own rewards.
The Inconstant (1702) **Farquhar, George** (1678–1707) Irish dramatist

34 The long and distressing controversy over capital punishment is very unfair to anyone meditating murder.
The Sunday Times, (1957) **Fisher, Geoffrey** (1887–1972) Archbishop of Canterbury

35 Punishment is not for revenge, but to lessen crime and reform the criminal.
Journal entry **Fry, Elizabeth** (1780–1845) English social and prison reformer

36 Crime is naught but misdirected energy.
Anarchism (1910) **Goldman, Emma** (1869–1940) US anarchist

37 I have often noticed that a bribe ... has that effect – it changes a relation. The man who offers a bribe gives away a little of his own importance; the bribe once accepted, he becomes the inferior, like a man who has paid for a woman.
The Comedians (1966)

38 Catholics and Communists have committed great crimes, but at least they have not stood aside, like an established society, and been indifferent. I would rather have blood on my hands than water like Pilate.
The Comedians (1966) **Greene, Graham** (1904–1991) English writer and dramatist

39 Were it possible to compel the prison warders of this past age to produce for our inspection a 'typical' transported convict, they would show us, not the countryman who snared rabbits, but the Londoner who stole spoons.
Australia (1930) **Hancock, Sir William Keith** (1898–1988) Australian historian

40 By the sympathy of your human hearts for sin ye shall scent out all the places – whether in church, bedchamber, street, field or forest – where crime has been committed, and shall exult to behold the whole earth one stain of guilt, one mighty blood spot.
Young Goodman Brown (1835) **Hawthorne, Nathaniel** (1804–1864) US allegorical writer

41 A burglar who respects his art always takes his time before taking anything else.
Makes the Whole World Kin **Henry, O.** (1862–1910) US short-story writer

42 Stolen sweets are always sweeter,
Stolen kisses much completer,
Stolen looks are nice in chapels,
Stolen, stolen, be your apples.
'Song of Fairies Robbing an Orchard' (1830) **Hunt, Leigh** (1784–1859) English writer, poet and literary editor

43 If we want to abolish the death penalty, let our friends the murderers take the first step.
Les Guêpes (1849) **Karr, Alphonse** (1808–1890) French writer and editor

44 If poverty is the mother of crime, lack of intelligence is its father.
Les caractères ou les moeurs de ce siècle (1688) **La Bruyère, Jean de** (1645–1696) French satirist

45 Murder, like talent, seems occasionally to run in families.
The Physiology of Common Life (1859) **Lewes, G.H.** (1817–1878) English writer, philosopher, critic and scientist

46 Death by drunken driving is a socially acceptable form of homicide.
San José Mercury, (April 1981) **Lightner, Candy** (1946–) US estate agent and founder of MADD (Mothers Against Drunk Driving)

47 Ye diners-out from whom we guard our spoons.
Letter to Hannah Macaulay, (1831) **Macaulay, Lord** (1800–1859) English Liberal statesman, essayist and poet

48 I had the thief's sickness ... I had a thieving crisis. How much meaning there can be in a word! I went along for a few days feeling disgusted and restless, until one morning I suddenly remembered: kleptomaniac. And I felt innocent.
Roman Tales (1954) **Moravia, Alberto** (1907–1990) Italian writer

49 Small habits, well pursued betimes,
May reach the dignity of crimes.
Florio (1786) **More, Hannah** (1745–1833) English poet, dramatist and religious writer

50 Murderers are really very agreeable clients. I do think murderers get a very bad press.
The Observer, (1999) **Mortimer, John** (1923–) English lawyer, dramatist and writer

51 The mountain sheep are sweeter,
But the valley sheep are fatter;
We therefore deemed it meeter
To carry off the latter.
The Misfortunes of Elphin (1823) **Peacock, Thomas Love** (1785–1866) English writer and poet

52 Murder is the most brutal form of censorship.
The Observer, (1995) **Pinter, Harold** (1930–) English dramatist, poet and screenwriter. On the execution of Nigerian writer Ken Saro-Wiwa

53 One murder made a villain,
Millions a hero.
'Death' (1759) **Porteus, Beilby** (1731–1808) English religious writer

54 Crime has its degrees, as virtue does.
Phèdre (1677) **Racine, Jean** (1639–1699) French tragedian and poet

55 A man who will steal for me will steal from me.
In Hagedorn, Roosevelt in the Bad Lands (1921) **Roosevelt, Theodore** (1858–1919) US Republican President. Dismissing a cowboy who had put Roosevelt's brand on a steer belonging to a neighbouring ranch

56 We're barking mad about crime in this country. We have an obsession with believing the worst, conning ourselves that there was a golden age – typically forty years before the one we're living in.
Radio Times, (1993) **Ross, Nick** (1947–) British broadcaster

57 Kill one man, and you are a murderer. Kill millions of men, and you are a conqueror. Kill them all, and you are a god.
Thoughts of a Biologist (1939) **Rostand, Jean** (1894–1977) French biologist

58 Crime has nothing to do with movies or guns, or TV. It has to do with Washington not creating an environment where one of the parents stays home to bring up children, so they point the finger at Hollywood.
The Observer, (1999) **Schwarzenegger, Arnold** (1947–) Austrian-born US film actor

59 Murder most foul, as in the best it is;
But this most foul, strange, and unnatural.
Hamlet, I.v

60 Why, Hal, 'tis my vocation, Hal; 'tis no sin for a man to labour in his vocation.
Henry IV, Part 1, I.ii Of stealing

61 The robb'd that smiles steals something from the thief.
Othello, I.iii **Shakespeare, William** (1564–1616) English dramatist, poet and actor

62 There is no satisfaction in hanging a man who does not object to it.

The Man of Destiny (1898) **Shaw, George Bernard** (1856–1950) Irish socialist, writer, dramatist and critic

63 When people come and talk to you of their aspirations, before they leave you had better count your spoons.
Afterthoughts (1931) **Smith, Logan Pearsall** (1865–1946) US-born British epigrammatist, critic and writer

64 A clever theft was praiseworthy amongst the Spartans; and it is equally so amongst Christians, provided it be on a sufficiently large scale.
Social Statics (1850) **Spencer, Herbert** (1820–1903) English philosopher and journalist

65 We haven't used our power only for doing bad things. I myself personally wounded the head of the local Communist party after the police asked us for help.
Newsweek, (1992) **Takayama, Tokutaro** (1928–2003) Kyoto mob boss defending the reputation of Japan's yakuza following the attack on film director Juzo Itami

66 Divorce? Never. But murder often!
Attr. **Thorndike, Dame Sybil** (1882–1976) English actress. Replying to a query as to whether she had ever considered divorce during her long marriage to Sir Lewis Casson

67 Upon my soul, I don't know, unless it was because she had such thick legs.
In W.C. Hazlitt, *Wainewright's Essays* (1880) **Wainewright, Thomas Griffiths** (1794–1847) On being asked by a caller at Newgate prison how he could have the barbarity to poison such a 'fair, innocent and trusting creature' as his sister-in-law Helen Abercromby

68 I came to the conclusion many years ago that almost all crime is due to the repressed desire for aesthetic expression.
Decline and Fall (1928) **Waugh, Evelyn** (1903–1966) English writer and diarist

69 Other sins only speak; murder shrieks out.
The Duchess of Malfi (1623) **Webster, John** (c.1580–c.1625) English dramatist

70 'Did you hear that fearful cry?'
'Ah! I 'eerd somethink.'
'There's murder going on – a woman, I think.'
'Dessay. It's Sat'dy night.'
No 5 John Street (1899) **Whiteing, Richard** (1840–1928) English journalist and novelist

71 A community is infinitely more brutalised by the habitual employment of punishment than it is by the occasional occurrence of crime.
'The Soul of Man under Socialism' (1891) **Wilde, Oscar** (1854–1900) Irish poet, dramatist, writer, critic and wit
See also guilt; judgement; justice and injustice; law; prison; right and wrong

CRITICISM

1 The only tastes worth having are acquired tastes.
Attr. **Adair, Gilbert** (1944–) English author and critic

2 Idly inquisitive tribe of grammarians, who dig up the poetry of others by the roots ... Get away, bugs that secretly bite the eloquent.
Greek Anthology **Antiphanes of Macedonia** (fl. 360 BC) Greek comic dramatist

3 I am bound by my own definition of criticism: a disinterested endeavour to learn and propagate the best that is known and thought in the world.
Essays in Criticism (1865) **Arnold, Matthew** (1822–1888) English poet, critic, essayist and educationist

4 Once upon a time I thought there was an old man with a grey beard somewhere who knew the truth, and if I was good enough, naturally he would tell me that this was it. That person doesn't exist, but that's who I write for. The great critic in the sky.
In Ingersoll, *Margaret Atwood: Conversations* (1990) **Atwood, Margaret** (1939–) Canadian writer, poet and critic

5 One cannot review a bad book without showing off.

The Dyer's Hand and Other Essays (1963) **Auden, W.H.** (1907–1973) English poet, essayist, critic, teacher and dramatist

6 This is the kind of show that gives pornography a bad name.
Attr. **Barnes, Clive** (1927–) English journalist and critic. On *Oh, Calcutta!* (1969)

7 I will try to account for the degree of my aesthetic emotion. That, I conceive, is the function of the critic.
Art (1914) **Bell, Clive** (1881–1964) English art critic

8 There is no point in seeing a man reduced to hysterical panic if hysterical panic is his forte.
The Guardian **Billington, Michael** (1939–) Guardian theatre critic. On Kenneth Williams in the farce *Signed and Sealed*

9 Tallulah Bankhead barged down the Nile last night and sank. As the Serpent of the Nile she proves to be no more dangerous than a garter snake.
In *Current Biography* (1941) **Brown, John Mason** (1900–1969) US critic. On Tallulah Bankhead's performance as Shakespeare's Cleopatra in 1937

10 He who discommendeth others obliquely commendeth himself.
Christian Morals (1716) **Browne, Sir Thomas** (1605–1682) English physician, author and antiquary

11 So, when a new book comes his way,
By someone still alive to-day,
Our Honest John, with right good will,
Sharpens his pencil for the kill.
'A Reviewer' **Bullet, Gerald** (1893–1958) English writer, poet and critic

12 I know how foolish critics can be, being one myself.
The Observer, (1980) **Burgess, Anthony** (1917–1993) English writer, linguist and composer

13 Talking it over, we agreed that Blake was no good because he learnt Italian at over 60 to study Dante, and we knew Dante was no good because he was so fond of Virgil, and Virgil was no good because Tennyson ran him, and as for Tennyson – well, Tennyson goes without saying.

The Note-Books of Samuel Butler (1912) **Butler, Samuel** (1835–1902) English writer, painter, philosopher and scholar

14 A man must serve his time to every trade
Save censure – critics all are ready made.
Take hackney'd jokes from Miller, got by rote,
With just enough of learning to misquote.
English Bards and Scotch Reviewers (1809)
Byron, Lord (1788–1824) English poet, satirist and traveller

15 The barrenest of all mortals is the sentimentalist.
Critical and Miscellaneous Essays (1839) **Carlyle, Thomas** (1795–1881) Scottish historian, biographer, critic, and essayist

16 A great deal of contemporary criticism reads to me like a man saying: 'Of course I do not like green cheese; I am very fond of brown sherry.'
All I Survey (1933) **Chesterton, G.K.** (1874–1936) English writer, poet and critic

17 Though by whim, envy, or resentment led,
They damn those authors whom they never read.
The Candidate (1764) **Churchill, Charles** (1731–1764) English poet, political writer and clergyman

18 I do not resent criticism, even when, for the sake of emphasis, it parts for the time with reality.
Speech, (1941) **Churchill, Sir Winston** (1874–1965) English Conservative Prime Minister

19 That passage is what I call the sublime dashed to pieces by cutting too close with the fiery four-in-hand round the corner of nonsense.
Table Talk (1835), 20 January 1834

20 Reviewers are usually people who would have been poets, historians, biographers, etc., if they could; they have tried their talents at one or at the other, and have failed; therefore they turn critics.
Seven Lectures on Shakespeare and Milton (1856)
Coleridge, Samuel Taylor (1772–1834) English poet, philosopher and critic

21 The biggest critics of my books are people who never read them.

Attr. **Collins, Jackie** (1937–) English-born US popular novelist

22 Too nicely Jonson knew the critic's part,
Nature in him was almost lost in Art.
'Verses Addressed to Sir Thomas Hanmer'
(1743) **Collins, William** (1721–1759) English poet and clergyman

23 I cannot take seriously the criticism of someone who doesn't know how to use a semicolon.
Attr. **Conran, Shirley** (1932–) English writer.
On Julie Burchill

24 Surprise me.
The Journals of Jean Cocteau (1956) **Diaghilev, Sergei** (1872–1929) Russian arts impresario.
Reply after Jean Cocteau's accusation that he rarely gave praise or encouragement

25 This shows how much easier it is to be critical than to be correct.
Speech, (1860)

26 You know who the critics are? The men who have failed in literature and art.
Lothair (1870)

27 Cosmopolitan critics, men who are the friends of every country save their own.
Speech, (1877) **Disraeli, Benjamin** (1804–1881) English statesman and writer

28 Confound those who have made our comments before us.
In St Jerome, *Commentaries on Ecclesiastes*
Donatus, Aelius (fl. 4th century AD) Roman Latin grammarian and teacher. Donatus was a commentator on texts

29 The critic, one would suppose, if he is to justify his existence, should endeavour to discipline his personal prejudices and cranks – tares to which we are all subject – and compose his differences with as many of his fellows as possible, in the common pursuit of true judgement.
'The Function of Criticism' (1923) **Eliot, T.S.**
(1888–1965) US-born British poet, verse dramatist and critic

30 He played the King as though under momentary apprehension that someone else was about to play the ace.

Attr. **Field, Eugene** (1850–1895) US columnist, children's poet, translator and humorist. Of Creston Clarke as King Lear

31 A good critic is one who tells of his own soul's adventures among masterpieces.
La Vie Littéraire (1888) **France, Anatole** (1844–1924) French writer and critic

32 I sometimes think
His critical judgement is so exquisite
It leaves us nothing to admire except his opinion.
The Dark is Light Enough (1954) **Fry, Christopher** (1907–2005) English verse dramatist, theatre director and translator

33 Backward ran sentences until reeled the mind.
More in Sorrow (1958) **Gibbs, Wolcott** (1902–1958) US humorist. Parody of *Time* magazine style

34 For there is an upstart Crow, beautified with our feathers, that with his Tyger's heart wrapt in a Player's hyde, supposes he is as well able to bombast out a blanke verse as the best of you: and being an absolute Iohannes fac totum, is in his owne conceit the onely Shake-scene in a countrey.
Greenes Groats-Worth of witte bought with a million of Repentance (1592) **Greene, Robert** (1558–1592) English dramatist and poet. Of Shakespeare

35 Asking a working writer what he thinks about critics is like asking a lamp-post how it feels about dogs.
The Sunday Times Magazine, (1977) **Hampton, Christopher** (1946–) English dramatist

36 When I read something saying I've not done anything as good as *Catch 22* I'm tempted to reply, 'who has?'
The Times, (1993) **Heller, Joseph** (1923–1999) US writer

37 What is a modern poet's fate?
To write his thoughts upon a slate;
The critic spits on what is done,
Gives it a wipe – and all is gone.
In Hallam Tennyson, *Alfred Lord Tennyson, A Memoir* (1897) **Hood, Thomas** (1799–1845) English poet, editor and humorist

38 Oh, for an hour of Herod!
   In Birkin, *J. M. Barrie and the Lost Boys* **Hope,
   Anthony** (1863–1933) English writer, dramatist
   and lawyer. On the first night of J. M. Barrie's
   play *Peter Pan*

39 Parodies and caricatures are the most
   penetrating of criticisms.
   Point Counter Point (1928) **Huxley, Aldous**
   (1894–1963) English writer, poet and critic

40 We must grant the artist his subject, his
   idea, his donnée: our criticism is applied
   only to what he makes of it.
   Partial Portraits (1888) **James, Henry** (1843–
   1916) US-born British writer, critic and letter
   writer

41 Particulars are not to be examined till the
   whole has been surveyed.
   The Plays of William Shakespeare (1765), *Preface*

42 Sir, there is no settling the point of
   precedency between a louse and a flea.
   In Boswell, *The Life of Samuel Johnson* (1791)
   Replying to Maurice Morgann who asked him
   whether Derrick or Smart was the better poet

43 The man who is asked by an author what
   he thinks of his work, is put to the torture,
   and is not obliged to speak the truth.
   In Boswell, *The Life of Samuel Johnson* (1791) Of
   literary criticism

44 Shakespeare never had six lines together
   without a fault. Perhaps you may find
   seven, but this does not refute my general
   assertion.
   In Boswell, *The Life of Samuel Johnson* (1791)

45 You may abuse a tragedy, though you
   cannot write one. You may scold a
   carpenter who has made you a bad table,
   though you cannot make a table. It is not
   your trade to make tables.
   In Boswell, *The Life of Samuel Johnson* (1791)
   Johnson, Samuel (1709–1784) English
   lexicographer, poet, critic, conversationalist
   and essayist

46 In the arts, the critic is the only
   independent source of information. The
   rest is advertising.
   Newsweek, (1973) **Kael, Pauline** (1919–2001) US
   film critic

47 The pleasure of criticizing takes away from
   us the pleasure of being moved by some
   very fine things.
   Les caractères ou les moeurs de ce siècle (1688) **La
   Bruyère, Jean de** (1645–1696) French satirist

48 Fleas know not whether they are upon the
   body of a giant or upon one of ordinary
   size.
   Imaginary Conversations (1824)

49 He who first praises a good book
   becomingly, is next in merit to the author.
   Imaginary Conversations (1824–1829) **Landor,
   Walter Savage** (1775–1864) English poet and
   writer

50 When I read Shakespeare I am struck with
   wonder
   That such trivial people should muse and
   thunder
   In such lovely language.
   Pansies (1929) **Lawrence, D.H.** (1885–1930)
   English writer, poet and critic

51 His verse exhibits ... something that is
   rather like Keats' vulgarity with a Public
   School accent.
   New Bearings in English Poetry (1932) Of Rupert
   Brooke

52 The Sitwells belong to the history of
   publicity rather than of poetry.
   New Bearings in English Poetry (1932) **Leavis,
   F.R.** (1895–1978) English critic, lecturer and
   writer

53 Coughing in the theatre is not a respiratory
   ailment. It is a criticism.
   The Street Where I Live (1978) **Lerner, Alan Jay**
   (1918–1986) US lyricist and screenwriter

54 Miss Hunnicutt's Viola was not Patience
   on a Monument – it was a monument of
   patience.
   Levin, Bernard (1928–2004) English critic. On
   Gayle Hunnicutt as Viola in *Twelfth Night*

55 A wise skepticism is the first attribute of a
   good critic.
   Among My Books **Lowell, James Russell** (1819–
   1891) US poet, editor, abolitionist and
   diplomat

56 I have never found in a long experience of
   politics that criticism is ever inhibited by
   ignorance.

Attr. **Macmillan, Harold** (1894–1986) British Conservative Prime Minister

57 I was so long writing my review that I never got around to reading the book.
Attr. **Marx, Groucho** (1895–1977) US comedian

58 People ask you for criticism, but they only want praise.
Of Human Bondage (1915) **Maugham, William Somerset** (1874–1965) English writer, dramatist and physician

59 Who reads
Incessantly, and to his reading brings not
A spirit and judgment equal or superior
(And what he brings, what needs he elsewhere seek)
Uncertain and unsettl'd still remains,
Deep verst in books and shallow in himself.
Paradise Regained (1671) **Milton, John** (1608–1674) English poet, libertarian and pamphleteer

60 The lot of critics is to be remembered by what they failed to understand.
Impressions and Opinions (1891) **Moore, George** (1852–1933) Irish writer, dramatist and critic

61 … the slaves, who are so cordial and upbeat about having their lives and property gentrified in 1776 that you fear for the entire future of the blues.
Review of the film *The Patriot* in the *San Francisco Examiner*, (2000) **Morris, Wesley** (1975–) US film critic

62 A bad review is even less important than whether it is raining in Patagonia.
The Times, (1989) **Murdoch, Iris** (1919–1999) Irish-born British writer, philosopher and dramatist

63 Kipling is a Jingo imperialist, he is morally insensitive and aesthically disgusting.
Horizon, (1942)

64 Prolonged, indiscriminate reviewing of books … not only involves praising trash … but constantly inventing reactions towards books about which one has no spontaneous feelings whatever.
Shooting an Elephant (1950) **Orwell, George** (1903–1950) English writer and critic

65 This is not a novel to be tossed aside lightly. It should be thrown with great force.
In Gaines, *Wit's End*

66 Tonstant Weader fwowed up.
On A. A. Milne's *The House at Pooh Corner* in her column 'Constant Reader' **Parker, Dorothy** (1893–1967) US writer, poet, critic and wit

67 Nor in the Critic let the Man be lost.
Good-nature and good-sense must ever join;
To err is human, to forgive, divine.
An Essay on Criticism (1711)

68 Some praise at morning what they blame at night;
But always think the last opinion right.
An Essay on Criticism (1711)

69 Whoever thinks a faultless piece to see,
Thinks what ne'er was, nor is, nor e'er shall be.
An Essay on Criticism (1711)

70 Turn what they will to Verse, their toil is vain,
Critics like me shall make it Prose again.
The Dunciad (1742) **Pope, Alexander** (1688–1744) English poet, translator and editor

71 Your works will be read after Shakespeare and Milton are forgotten – and not till then.
In Meissen, *Quotable Anecdotes* **Porson, Richard** (1759–1808) English scholar. Giving his opinion of Southey's poems

72 Donsmanship … 'the art of criticizing without actually listening'.
Lifemanship (1950) **Potter, Stephen** (1900–1969) English writer, critic and lecturer

73 They will review a book by a writer much older than themselves as if it were an over-ambitious essay by a second-year student … It is the little dons I complain about, like so many corgis trotting up, hoping to nip your ankles.
Outcries and Asides **Priestley, J.B.** (1894–1984) English writer, dramatist and critic

74 The best is the best, though a hundred judges have declared it so.

Oxford Book of English Verse (1900) **Quiller-Couch, Sir Arthur ('Q')** (1863–1944) English man of letters

75 I am sitting in the smallest room in my house. I have your review in front of me. In a moment it will be behind me.
In Slonimsky, *The Lexicon of Musical Invective*
Reger, Max (1873–1916) German composer, conductor, teacher and pianist. Letter written to Rudolf Louis in response to his criticism of Reger's *Sinfonietta*, 1906

76 Very good, but it has its longueurs.
Rivaroliana **Rivarol, Antoine de** (1753–1801) French writer and wit. On a couplet by a mediocre poet

77 But whether thus submissively or not, at least be sure that you go to the author to get at his meaning, not to find yours.
Sesame and Lilies (1865) **Ruskin, John** (1819–1900) English art critic, philosopher and reformer

78 You don't expect me to know what to say about a play when I don't know who the author is, do you? ... If it's by a good author, it's a good play, naturally. That stands to reason.
Fanny's First Play (1911)

79 A dramatic critic ... leaves no turn unstoned.
New York Times, (1950) **Shaw, George Bernard** (1856–1950) Irish socialist, writer, dramatist and critic

80 Pay no attention to what the critics say. No statue has ever been put up to a critic.
Attr. **Sibelius, Jean** (1865–1957) Finnish composer

81 I never read a book before reviewing it; it prejudices a man so.
In Pearson, *The Smith of Smiths* (1934) **Smith, Sydney** (1771–1845) English clergyman, essayist, journalist and wit

82 Unless the bastards have the courage to give you unqualified praise, I say ignore them.
In J.K. Galbraith, *A Life in Our Times* (1981) **Steinbeck, John** (1902–1968) US writer. On critics

83 Of all the cants which are canted in this canting world, – though the cant of hypocrites may be the worst, – the cant of criticism is the most tormenting!
Tristram Shandy (1759–1767) **Sterne, Laurence** (1713–1768) Irish-born English writer and clergyman

84 I had another dream the other day about music critics. They were small and rodent-like with padlocked ears, as if they had stepped out of a painting by Goya.
The Evening Standard, (1969) **Stravinsky, Igor** (1882–1971) Russian composer and conductor

85 So, naturalists observe, a flea
Hath smaller fleas that on him prey;
And these have smaller fleas to bite 'em,
And so proceed ad infinitum.
Thus every poet, in his kind,
Is bit by him that comes behind.
'On Poetry' (1733) **Swift, Jonathan** (1667–1745) Irish satirist, poet, essayist and cleric

86 A critic is a person who will slit the throat of a skylark to see what makes it sing.
Synge, J.M. (1871–1909) Irish dramatist

87 The Cigarette Girl certainly made me gasp in amazement, it is so unbelievably bad. ... The dialogue is putrid, the acting early marionette, the evening disastrous.
On *The Cigarette Girl* by William Douglas Home, (1962)

88 With his full mane of curly hair and dressed in a gold-encrusted tightly fitting mini-skirted costume, he struck me as more of an overweight elf than the savage conqueror of Asia.
On Albert Finney in *Tamberlaine*, (1976)
Thirkell, Arthur English theatre critic

89 A good drama critic is one who perceives what is happening in the theatre of his time. A great drama critic also perceives what is not happening.
Tynan Right and Left (1967)

90 A critic is a man who knows the way but can't drive the car.
New York Times Magazine, (1966) **Tynan, Kenneth** (1927–1980) English drama critic, producer and essayist

91 Persons attempting to find a motive in this narrative will be prosecuted; persons attempting to find a moral in it will be banished; persons attempting to find a plot in it will be shot.
The Adventures of Huckleberry Finn (1884), Introduction

92 I can live for two months on a good compliment.
Attr. **Twain, Mark** (1835–1910) US humorist, writer, journalist and lecturer

93 I do not think this poem will reach its destination.
Attr. **Voltaire** (1694–1778) French philosopher, dramatist, poet, historian writer and critic. Reviewing Rousseau's poem 'Ode to Posterity'

94 As far as criticism is concerned, we don't resent that unless it is absolutely biased, as it is in most cases.
The Observer, (1969) **Vorster, John** (1915–1983) South African Nationalist politician, Prime Minister and President

95 You shouldn't say it is not good. You should say, you do not like it; and then, you know, you're perfectly safe.
In Seitz, *Whistler Stories* (1913) **Whistler, James McNeill** (1834–1903) US painter, etcher and pamphleteer

96 No publisher should ever express an opinion of the value of what he publishes. That is a matter entirely for the literary critic to decide … A publisher is simply a useful middle-man. It is not for him to anticipate the verdict of criticism.
Letter in *St James's Gazette,* (1890)

97 The man who sees both sides of a question is a man who sees absolutely nothing at all.
'The Critic as Artist' (1891)

98 I saw the only rational method of art criticism I have ever come across … 'Please do not shoot the pianist. He is doing his best.' The mortality among pianists in that place is marvellous.
'Impressions of America' (1906) On a notice at a dancing saloon **Wilde, Oscar** (1854–1900) Irish poet, dramatist, writer, critic and wit

99 I saw it at a disadvantage – the curtain was up.

In Whiteman, *Come to Judgement* **Winchell, Walter** (1897–1972) US drama critic, columnist and broadcaster. Referring to a show starring Earl Carroll
See also acting; art; cynicism; judgement; spite; theatre and dance; writing

CULTURE

1 The men of culture are the true apostles of equality.
Culture and Anarchy (1869)

2 Culture being a pursuit of our total perfection by means of getting to know, on all the matters which most concern us, the best which has been thought and said in the world.
Culture and Anarchy (1869)

3 Culture, the acquainting ourselves with the best that has been known and said in the world, and thus the history of the human spirit.
Literature and Dogma **Arnold, Matthew** (1822–1888) English poet, critic, essayist and educationist

4 I wish I could bring Stonehenge to Nyasaland to show there was a time when Britain had a savage culture.
The Observer, (1963) **Banda, Dr Hastings** (1905–1997) Malawian politician and President

5 If culture means anything, it means knowing what value to set upon human life; it's not somebody with a mortarboard reading Greek. I know a lot of facts, history. That's not culture. Culture is the openness of the individual psyche … to the news of being.
The Glasgow Herald, (1985) **Bellow, Saul** (1915–2005) Canadian-born US Jewish writer

6 No man ever looks at the world with pristine eyes. He sees it edited by a definite set of customs and institutions and ways of thinking.
Patterns of Culture (1934) **Benedict, Ruth** (1887–1948) US anthropologist

7 The great law of culture is: let each become all that he was created capable of being.

'Jean Paul Friedrich Richter' (1839) **Carlyle, Thomas** (1795–1881) Scottish historian, biographer, critic, and essayist

8 The highest possible stage in moral culture is when we recognize that we ought to control our thoughts.
The Descent of Man (1871) **Darwin, Charles** (1809–1882) English naturalist

9 Creative culture is infinitely porous – it absorbs influences from all over the world.
Maclean's, (1991) **Frye, Northrop** (1912–1991) Canadian critic and academic

10 When I hear the word 'culture' ... I take the safety-catch off my Browning!
Schlageter (1933) **Johst, Hanns** (1890–1978) Hermann Goering paraphrased this in a speech a few years later

11 Decadent cultures usually fall in the end, and robust cultures rise to replace them. Our own cultural supermarket may eventually be subject to a takeover bid: the most likely challenger being, surely, Islam.
Sunday Telegraph, (1993) **Kenny, Mary** (1944–) Irish writer and broadcaster

12 Two half-truths do not make a truth, and two half-cultures do not make a culture.
The Ghost in the Machine (1961) **Koestler, Arthur** (1905–1983) British writer, essayist and political refugee

13 We are all children of our environment – the good no less than the bad, – products of that particular group of habits, customs, traditions, ways of looking at things, standards of right and wrong, which chance has presented to our still growing and expanding consciousness.
Hurrish (1886) **Lawless, Emily** (1845–1913) Irish novelist and poet

14 Culture isn't something that comes with one's race or sex. It comes only through experience; there isn't any other way to acquire it. And in the end everyone's culture is different, because everyone's experience is different.
The New Yorker, (1992) **Menand, Louis** (1953–) US writer

15 In a statesman so-called 'culture' is, after all, a useless luxury.

Il Populo d'Italia, (1919) **Mussolini, Benito** (1883–1945) Italian fascist dictator

16 All my wife has ever taken from the Mediterranean – from that whole vast intuitive culture – are four bottles of Chianti to make into lamps, and two china condiment donkeys labelled Sally and Peppy.
Equus (1973) **Shaffer, Peter** (1926–) English dramatist

17 What is a highbrow? He is a man who has found something more interesting than women.
New York Times, (1932) **Wallace, Edgar** (1875–1932) English writer and dramatist

18 Culture is an instrument wielded by teachers to manufacture teachers, who, in their turn, will manufacture teachers.
The Need for Roots (1949) **Weil, Simone** (1909–1943) French philosopher, essayist and mystic

19 Mrs Ballinger is one of the ladies who pursue Culture in bands, as though it were dangerous to meet it alone.
Xingu and Other Stories (1916) **Wharton, Edith** (1862–1937) US writer
See also class; custom; humanity and human nature; society

CUSTOM

1 What custom hath endear'd
We part with sadly, though we prize it not.
Basil (1798) **Baillie, Joanna** (1762–1851) Scottish dramatist and poet

2 Custom reconciles us to everything.
A Philosophical Enquiry into the Origin of our Ideas of the Sublime and Beautiful (1757) **Burke, Edmund** (1729–1797) Irish-born British statesman and philosopher

3 Habit with him was all the test of truth,
'It must be right: I've done it from my youth.'
The Borough (1810) **Crabbe, George** (1754–1832) English poet, clergyman, surgeon and botanist

4 Custom, that unwritten law,
By which the people keep even kings in awe.

Circe (1677) **Davenant, Charles** (1656–1714) English politician and dramatist

5 Custom, then, is the great guide of human life.
Philosophical Essays Concerning Human Understanding (1748) **Hume, David** (1711–1776) Scottish philosopher and political economist

6 Habit is the enormous fly-wheel of society, its most precious conservative agent.
Principles of Psychology (1890) **James, William** (1842–1910) US psychologist and philosopher

7 Custom calls me to't.
What custom wills, in all things should we do't.
Coriolanus II.iii

8 It is a custom
More honour'd in the breach than the observance.
Hamlet, I.iv

9 How use doth breed a habit in a man!
The Two Gentlemen of Verona, V.iv **Shakespeare, William** (1564–1616) English dramatist, poet and actor

10 There's nothing like being used to a thing.
The Rivals (1775) **Sheridan, Richard Brinsley** (1751–1816) Irish dramatist, politician and orator

11 Not choice
But habit rules the unreflecting herd.
'Grant that by this unsparing hurricane' (1822)
Wordsworth, William (1770–1850) English poet
See also culture; humanity and human nature; manners

CYNICISM

1 The lion and the calf shall lie down together but the calf won't get much sleep.
Without Feathers (1976) **Allen, Woody** (1935–)
US film director, writer, actor and comedian

2 A Jewish doctor who hates the sight of blood.
In Leo Rosten, *The Joys of Yiddish* (1968)
Anonymous Definition of a psychoanalyst

3 God is on everyone's side … And, in the final analysis, he is on the side of those who have plenty of money and large armies.
The Lark (1953) **Anouilh, Jean** (1910–1987)
French dramatist and screenwriter

4 Miracles do not happen.
Literature and Dogma (1883 edition) **Arnold, Matthew** (1822–1888) English poet, critic, essayist and educationist

5 Only mediocrity can be trusted to be always at its best.
In S.N. Behrman, *Conversations with Max* **Beerbohm, Sir Max** (1872–1956) English satirist, cartoonist, critic and essayist

6 *Patience*: A minor form of despair, disguised as a virtue.
The Cynic's Word Book (1906)

7 *Out-of-Doors*: That part of one's environment upon which no government has been able to collect taxes.
The Devil's Dictionary (1911)

8 *Contempt*: The feeling of a prudent man for an enemy who is too formidable safely to be oppoosed.
The Enlarged Devil's Dictionary (1961)

9 *Cynic*: A blackguard whose faulty vision sees things as they are, not as they ought to be.
The Enlarged Devil's Dictionary (1961)

10 *Exile*: One who serves his country by residing abroad, yet is not an ambassador.
The Enlarged Devil's Dictionary (1961)

11 *Flatter*: To impress another with a sense of one's own merit.
The Enlarged Devil's Dictionary (1961)

12 *Please*: To lay the foundation for a superstructure of imposition.
The Enlarged Devil's Dictionary (1961) **Bierce, Ambrose** (1842–c.1914) US writer, verse writer and soldier

13 Superstition is the religion of feeble minds.
Reflections on the Revolution in France (1790)
Burke, Edmund (1729–1797) Irish-born British statesman and philosopher

14 You know what charm is: a way of getting the answer yes without having asked any clear question.
The Fall (1956) **Camus, Albert** (1913–1960) Algerian-born French writer

15 Psychiatry's chief contribution to philosophy is the discovery that the toilet is the seat of the soul.
Perspectives (1966) **Chase, Alexander** (1926–) US journalist and author

16 After all, the cynicism of real life can't be outdone by any literature: one glass won't get someone drunk when he's already had a whole barrel.
Letter to M.V. Kiseleva, (1887) **Chekhov, Anton** (1860–1904) Russian writer, dramatist and doctor

17 All charming people have something to conceal, usually their total dependence on the appreciation of others.
Enemies of Promise (1938) **Connolly, Cyril** (1903–1974) English literary editor, writer and critic

18 A cynic is just a man who found out when he was about ten that there wasn't any Santa Claus, and he's still upset.
Attr. **Cozzens, James Gould** (1903–1978) US writer

19 There is a hook in every benefit, that sticks in his jaws that takes that benefit, and draws him whither the benefactor will.
Sermon, (c.1625) **Donne, John** (1572–1631) English poet

20 My dear Monsieur, know that every flatterer lives at the expense of the one who listens to him.
Fables, 'Le corbeau et le renard' **La Fontaine, Jean de** (1621–1695) French poet and fabulist

21 It doesn't do a man any good, daylight. It means up and doing, and that means up to no good.
The best life is led horizontal.
Thor, with Angels (1949) **Fry, Christopher** (1907–2005) English verse dramatist, theatre director and translator

22 A cynic is not merely one who reads bitter lessons from the past, he is one who is prematurely disappointed in the future.

On the Contrary (1962) **Harris, Sydney J.** (1917–1986) US journalist

23 Cynicism is an unpleasant way of saying the truth.
The Little Foxes (1939) **Hellman, Lillian** (1907–1984) US dramatist and screenwriter

24 Never make a decision. Let someone else make it and then if it turns out to be the wrong one, you can disclaim it, and if it is the right one you can abide by it.
The Hughes Legacy: Scramble for the Billion (1976) **Hughes, Howard** (1905–1976) US millionaire industrialist, aviator and film producer

25 It takes a clever man to turn cynic, and a wise man to be clever enough not to.
Attr. **Hurst, Fannie** (1889–1968) US writer and playwright

26 Is not a Patron, my Lord, one who looks with unconcern on a man struggling for life in the water, and, when he has reached ground, encumbers him with help? The notice which you have been pleased to take of my labours, had it been early, had been kind; but it has been delayed till I am indifferent, and cannot enjoy it; till I am solitary, and cannot impart it; till I am known, and do not want it.
Letter to Lord Chesterfield, (1755) **Johnson, Samuel** (1709–1784) English lexicographer, poet, critic, conversationalist and essayist

27 I don't believe in principles. Principles are only excuses for what we want to think or what we want to do.
The Adventures of Sylvia Scarlett (1918) **Mackenzie, Sir Compton** (1883–1972) Scottish writer and broadcaster

28 I think that's what they call professional courtesy.
Attr. **Mankiewicz, Herman J.** (1897–1953) US journalist and screenwriter. Commenting on the fact that he had not been harmed when swimming in shark-infested waters

29 Please accept my resignation. I don't want to belong to any club that would have me as a member.
Groucho and Me (1959) **Marx, Groucho** (1895–1977) US comedian

30 Cynicism is intellectual dandyism.
The Egoist (1879) **Meredith, George** (1828–1909)
English writer, poet and critic

31 He who is ridden by a conscience
Worries about a lot of nonscience;
He without benefit of scruples
His fun and income soon quadruples.
'Reflection on the Fallibility of Nemesis'
(1940) **Nash, Ogden** (1902–1971) US poet

32 The man who makes no mistakes does not
usually make anything.
Speech, (1899) **Phelps, E.J.** (1822–1900) US
lawyer and diplomat

33 Without money, honour is no more than a
disease.
Les Plaideurs (1668) **Racine, Jean** (1639–1699)
French tragedian and poet

34 For all men would be cowards if they durst.
'A Satire Against Reason and Mankind' (1679)
Rochester, Earl of (1647–1680) English poet,
satirist, courtier and libertine

35 She didn't believe in anything; only her
scepticism kept her from being an atheist.
Words (1964) **Sartre, Jean-Paul** (1905–1980)
French philosopher, writer, dramatist and
critic

36 Your virginity, your old virginity, is like one
of our French wither'd pears: it looks ill, it
eats drily.
All's Well That Ends Well, I.i **Shakespeare,
William** (1564–1616) English dramatist, poet
and actor

37 There are two kinds of statistics, the kind
you look up and the kind you make up.
Death of a Doxy **Stout, Rex** (1886–1975) US
crime writer

38 I will either take a large sleeping tablet and
sleep through the whole thing, or become
a waiter for the night. After all, monks are
born to serve.
The Times, (1999) **Sutch, Dom Antony** (1950–)
English Benedictine monk and headmaster.
Comment on his plans for the millennium

39 The cross of the Legion of Honour has
been conferred upon me. However, few
escape that distinction.
A Tramp Abroad (1880) **Twain, Mark** (1835–
1910) US humorist, writer, journalist and
lecturer

40 Charm is the great English blight. It does
not exist outside these damp islands. It
spots and kills anything it touches. It kills
love, it kills art.
Brideshead Revisited (1945) **Waugh, Evelyn**
(1903–1966) English writer and diarist

41 *Cecil Graham*: What is a cynic?
Lord Darlington: A man who knows the
price of everything and the value of
nothing.
Lady Windermere's Fan (1892)

42 One would have to have a heart of stone to
read the death of Little Nell without
laughing.
In H. Pearson, *Lives of the Wits* In a lecture on
Dickens **Wilde, Oscar** (1854–1900) Irish poet,
dramatist, writer, critic and wit

43 We have to distrust each other. It's our
only defence against betrayal.
Camino Real (1953) **Williams, Tennessee** (1911–
1983) US dramatist and writer
See also criticism; spite

DANGER

1 Danger (the spurre of all great mindes) is
ever
The curbe to your tame spirits.
Revenge of Bussy D'Ambois (1613) **Chapman,
George** (c.1559–c.1634) English poet, dramatist
and translator

2 When we conquer without danger our
triumph is without glory.
Le Cid (1637) **Corneille, Pierre** (1606–1684)
French dramatist, poet and lawyer

3 Always to islanders danger
Is what comes over the sea.
Collected Poems 1933–1973 (1974) **Curnow, Allen**
(1911–2001) New Zealand poet and editor

4 In skating over thin ice, our safety is in our
speed.
'Prudence' (1841)

5 As soon as there is life there is danger.

Society and Solitude (1870) **Emerson, Ralph Waldo** (1803–1882) US poet, essayist, transcendentalist and teacher

6 How, like a moth, the simple maid,
Still plays about the flame!
The Beggar's Opera (1728) **Gay, John** (1685–1732) English poet, dramatist and librettist

7 Our God and soldier we alike adore,
Just at the brink of ruin, not before:
The danger past, both are alike requited;
God is forgotten, and our soldier slighted.
Epigram **Jordan, Thomas** (c.1612–1685) English poet and actor

8 There are dragons in the wings of the world.
The Guardian, (1995) **MacCarthy, Cormac** (1933–) US writer

9 What I have to do, I have to catch everybody if they start to go over the cliff – I mean if they're running and they don't look where they're going I have to come out from somewhere and catch them ... I'd just be the catcher in the rye and all.
The Catcher in the Rye (1951) **Salinger, J.D.** (1919–) US writer

10 We are dancing on a volcano.
Remark made before July Revolution, (1830) **Salvandy, Narcisse Achille** (1795–1856) French statesman and man of letters

11 Look back, and smile at perils past.
The Bridal of Triermain (1813), Introduction **Scott, Sir Walter** (1771–1832) Scottish writer and historian

12 Out of this nettle, danger, we pluck this flower, safety.
Henry IV, Part 1, II.iii **Shakespeare, William** (1564–1616) English dramatist, poet and actor

13 The bright face of danger.
'The Lantern-Bearers' (1892) **Stevenson, Robert Louis** (1850–1894) Scottish writer, poet and essayist

14 I heard the bullets whistle, and believe me, there is something charming in the sound.
In P. Boller, *Presidential Anecdotes* **Washington, George** (1732–1799) US general, statesman and President

DEATH

1 See in what peace a Christian can die.
Dying words **Addison, Joseph** (1672–1719) English essayist, poet, playwright and statesman

2 I am dying with the help of too many physicians.
Attr. **Alexander the Great** (356–323 BC) Macedonian king and conquering army commander

3 It's not that I'm afraid to die. I just don't want to be there when it happens.
Without Feathers (1976)

4 I don't want to achieve immortality through my work ... I want to achieve it by not dying.
Attr. **Allen, Woody** (1935–) US film director, writer, actor and comedian

5 Dying was apparently a weaning process; all the attachments to familiar people and objects have to be undone.
Kinflicks (1976) **Alther, Lisa** (1944–) US novelist

6 Most of the people who walk after me will be children; make the beat keep time with little steps.
In R. Godden, *Hans Christian Andersen* (1955) **Andersen, Hans Christian** (1805–1875) Danish writer and dramatist. Of the music to be played at his funeral

7 Enjoy life. There's plenty of time to be dead.
Anonymous

8 Dying is nothing. So start by living. It's less fun and it lasts longer.
Roméo et Jeannette (1946) **Anouilh, Jean** (1910–1987) French dramatist and screenwriter

9 This is the last time I will take part as an amateur.
Attr. **Auber, Daniel François Esprit** (1782–1871) French opera composer. Remark made at a funeral

10 Men fear death as children fear to go in the dark; and as that natural fear in children is increased with tales, so is the other.
Essays (1625)

11 I do not believe that any man fears to be dead, but only the stroke of death.
The Remaines of ... Lord Verulam (1648)

12 I have often thought upon death, and I find it the least of all evils.
The Remaines of ... Lord Verulam (1648) **Bacon, Francis** (1561–1626) English philosopher, essayist, politician and courtier

13 I acknowledge the cold truth of her death for perhaps the first time. She is truly gone, forever out of reach, and I have become my own judge.
Imaginary Crimes (1982) **Ballantyne, Sheila** (1936–) US writer. Of the character's mother

14 The end is when all things return to unity, that is to say, God.
Louis Lambert (1832)

15 What does farewell mean, unless one is dying? But is death itself a farewell?
Louis Lambert (1832) **Balzac, Honoré de** (1799–1850) French writer

16 To die will be an awfully big adventure.
Peter Pan (1904) **Barrie, Sir J.M.** (1860–1937) Scottish dramatist and writer

17 O Death, old captain, the time has come! Let us weigh anchor!
Les Fleurs du mal (1857), 'Le Voyage' **Baudelaire, Charles** (1821–1867) French poet, translator and critic

18 *Clov:* Do you believe in the life to come?
Hamm: Mine was always that.
Endgame (1958) **Beckett, Samuel** (1906–1989) Irish dramatist, writer and poet

19 If thou wilt ease thine heart
Of love and all its smart,
Then sleep, dear, sleep ...
But wilt thou cure thine heart
Of love and all its smart,
Then die, dear, die.
Death's Jest Book (1850) **Beddoes, Thomas Lovell** (1803–1849) English poet and dramatist

20 Faith, Sir, we are here today and gone tomorrow.
The Lucky Chance (1687) **Behn, Aphra** (1640–1689) English dramatist, writer, poet, translator and spy

21 There was sun enough for lazing upon beaches,
There was fun enough for far into the night.
But I'm dying now and done for,
What on earth was all the fun for?
For I'm old and ill and terrified and tight.
'Sun and Fun' (1954) **Betjeman, Sir John** (1906–1984) English poet laureate

22 I am become death, the destroyer of worlds.
Quoted by J. Robert Oppenheimer on seeing the first nuclear explosion **Bhagavadgita**

23 The last enemy that shall be destroyed is death.
I Corinthians, 15:26

24 O death, where is thy sting? O grave, where is thy victory?
I Corinthians, 15:55 **The Bible (King James Version)**

25 Though boys throw stones at frogs in sport, the frogs do not die in sport, but in earnest.
Quoted by Plutarch **Bion** (fl. 280 BC) Greek poet

26 When Death to either shall come, –
I pray it be first to me.
'When Death to Either Shall Come' **Bridges, Robert** (1844–1930) English poet, dramatist, essayist and doctor

27 I lingered round them, under that benign sky: watched the moths fluttering among the heath and harebells; listened to the soft wind breathing through the grass; and wondered how anyone could ever imagine unquiet slumbers for the sleepers in that quiet earth.
Wuthering Heights (1847), last lines **Brontë, Emily** (1818–1848) English poet and writer

28 Oh! Death will find me long before I tire Of watching you; and swing me suddenly Into the shade and loneliness and mire Of the last land!
'Oh! Death will find me' (1909) **Brooke, Rupert** (1887–1915) English poet

29 We all labour against our own cure, for death is the cure of all diseases.
Religio Medici (1643)

30 He forgets that he can die who complains of misery – we are in the power of no calamity while death is in our own.
Religio Medici (1643)

31 I am not so much afraid of death, as ashamed thereof; 'tis the very disgrace and ignominy of our natures, that in a moment can so disfigure us that our nearest friends, wife, and children, stand afraid and start at us.
Religio Medici (1643)

32 The long habit of living indisposeth us for dying.
Hydriotaphia: Urn Burial (1658)

33 They carried them out of the world with their feet forward.
Hydriotaphia: Urn Burial (1658)

34 With rich flames, and hired tears, they solemnized their obsequies.
Hydriotaphia: Urn Burial (1658) **Browne, Sir Thomas** (1605–1682) English physician, author and antiquary

35 Euthanasia is a long, smooth-sounding word, and it conceals its danger as long, smooth words do, but the danger is there, nevertheless.
The Child Who Never Grew (1950) **Buck, Pearl S.** (1892–1973) US writer and dramatist

36 What Cato did, and Addison approved Cannot be wrong.
Attr. **Budgell, Eustace** (1686–1737) English writer. Lines found on his desk after his suicide

37 Tears are sometimes an inappropriate response to death. When a life has been lived completely honestly, completely successfully, or just completely, the correct response to death's perfect punctuation mark is a smile.
The Independent, (1989) **Burchill, Julie** (1960–) English writer

38 I would rather sleep in the southern corner of a little country church-yard, than in the tomb of the Capulets. I should like, however, that my dust should mingle with kindred dust.

Letter to Matthew Smith, (1750) **Burke, Edmund** (1729–1797) Irish-born British statesman and philosopher

39 O death, the poor man's dearest friend, The kindest and the best!
'Man was made to Mourn, a Dirge' (1784) **Burns, Robert** (1759–1796) Scottish poet and song writer

40 It costs a lot of money to die comfortably.
The Note-Books of Samuel Butler (1912)

41 When you have told anyone you have left him a legacy the only decent thing to do is to die at once.
In Festing Jones, Samuel Butler: A Memoir **Butler, Samuel** (1835–1902) English writer, painter, philosopher and scholar

42 It is important what you still have planned at the end. It shows the extent of injustice in your death.
The Human Province (1973) **Canetti, Elias** (1905–1994) Bulgarian-born English writer, dramatist and critic

43 Having journeyed through many peoples and over many a sea I come, my brother, for these sad funeral rites, that I may present to you a last gift in death and vainly address your dumb ashes, since fortune has taken you from me – alas, poor brother cruelly snatched from me – but now accept these offerings which by our parents' custom have been handed down as a funeral gift, bedewed with many fraternal tears, and for all time, my brother, hail and farewell.
Carmina

44 Now he goes along the shadowy path, there, from which they say no one returns.
Carmina **Catullus** (84–c.54 BC) Roman poet

45 Well, now: there's a remedy for everything, except death.
Don Quixote (1615) **Cervantes, Miguel de** (1547–1616) Spanish writer and dramatist

46 He had been, he said, a most unconscionable time dying; but he hoped that they would excuse it.
In Macaulay, The History of England (1849) **Charles II** (1630–1685) King of Great Britain and Ireland

47 This world nys but a thurghfare ful of wo,
And we been pilgrymes, passynge to and
fro.
Deeth is an ende of every worldly soore.
The Canterbury Tales (1387) **Chaucer, Geoffrey**
(c.1340–1400) English poet, public servant and
courtier

48 One does not learn how to die by killing
others.
Memoirs (1826–1841) **Chateaubriand, François-
René** (1768–1848) French writer and statesman

49 It seems perfectly simple and inevitable,
like lying down after a long day's work.
Prison letter to his wife **Childers, Erskine** (1870–
1922) English writer and historian; Irish
revolutionary. Writing about his imminent
execution

50 Pale death, the grand physician, cures all
pain;
The dead rest well who lived for joys in
vain.
'Child Harold' (1841) **Clare, John** (1793–1864)
English rural poet; died in an asylum

51 And when life's sweet fable ends,
Soul and body part like friends;
No quarrels, murmurs, no delay;
A kiss, a sigh, and so away.
'Temperance' (1652) **Crashaw, Richard** (c.1612–
1649) English religious poet

52 There is no hope of death for these souls,
and their lost life is so low, that they are
envious of any other kind.
Divina Commedia (1307) **Dante Alighieri** (1265–
1321) Italian poet

53 I have never killed a man, but I have read
many obituaries with a lot of pleasure.
Medley **Darrow, Clarence** (1857–1938) US
lawyer, reformer and writer

54 'If you don't go to other men's funerals,' he
told Father stiffly, 'they won't go to yours.'
Life with Father (1935), 'Father plans' **Day,
Clarence Shepard** (1874–1935) US essayist and
humorist

55 Mum, you would have loved the way you
went!
one moment, at a barbecue in the garden
– the next, falling out of your chair,
hamburger in one hand,
and a grandson yelling.
'Going' (1970) **Dawe, (Donald) Bruce** (1930–)
Australian poet

56 What argufies pride and ambition?
Soon or late death will take us in tow:
Each bullet has got its commission,
And when our time's come we must go.
'Each Bullet has its Commission' **Dibdin,
Charles** (1745–1814) English songwriter,
dramatist and actor

57 I heard a Fly buzz – when I died …
With Blue – uncertain stumbling Buzz –
Between the light – and me –
And then the Windows failed – and then
I could not see to see.
'I heard a Fly buzz – when I died' (c.1862)

58 Because I could not stop for Death –
He kindly stopped for me –
The Carriage held but just Ourselves –
And Immortality.
'Because I could not stop for Death' (c.1863)

59 This quiet Dust was Gentlemen and Ladies
And Lads and Girls –
Was laughter and ability and Sighing
And Frocks and Curls.
'This quiet Dust was Gentlemen and Ladies'
(c.1864) **Dickinson, Emily** (1830–1886) US poet

60 I bet you a hundred bucks he ain't in here.
Attr. **Dillingham, Charles Bancroft** (1868–
1934) US theatrical producer. Said at the
funeral of Harry Houdini, the escapologist,
while carrying his coffin

61 Think then, my soul, that death is but a
groom,
Which brings a taper to the outward room.
Of the Progress of the Soul (1612)

62 One short sleep past, we wake eternally,
And death shall be no more; death, thou
shalt die.
Holy Sonnets (1609–1617)

63 It comes equally to us all, and makes us all
equal when it comes.

LXXX Sermons (1640) On death **Donne, John** (1572–1631) English poet

64 Remember me when I am dead
And simplify me when I'm dead.
'Simplify me when I'm dead' (1941) **Douglas, Keith** (1920–1944) English war poet

65 They are not long, the weeping and the laughter,
Love and desire and hate:
I think they have no portion in us after
We pass the gate.
They are not long, the days of wine and roses;
Out of a misty dream
Our path emerges for a while, then closes
Within a dream.
'Vitae Summa Brevis Spem Nos Vetat Incohare Longam' (1896) **Dowson, Ernest** (1867–1900) English poet

66 Death, in itself, is nothing; but we fear,
To be we know not what, we know not where.
Aureng-Zebe (1675)

67 A man may be capable, as Jack Ketch's wife said of his servant, of a plain piece of work, a bare hanging; but to make a malefactor die sweetly was only belonging to her husband.
Of Satire (1693) Sarcastic reference to Jack Ketch, executioner, 1663–1686, who was notorious for his barbarity **Dryden, John** (1631–1700) English poet, satirist, dramatist and critic

68 Unto the deid gois all Estatis,
Princis, prelatis, and potestatis,
Baith rich and poor of all degree:
Timor Mortis conturbat me.
'Lament for the Makaris' (1834) **Dunbar, William** (c.1460–c.1525) Scottish poet, satirist and courtier

69 The bodies of those that made such a noise and tumult when alive, when dead, lie as quietly among the graves of their neighbours as any others.
Works (1834) **Edwards, Jonathan** (1703–1758) US theologian and philosopher

70 In every parting there is an image of death.
Scenes of Clerical Life (1858) **Eliot, George** (1819–1880) English writer and poet

71 Webster was much possessed by death
And saw the skull beneath the skin;
And breastless creatures under ground
Leaned backward with a lipless grin.
'Whispers of Immortality' (1920) **Eliot, T.S.** (1888–1965) US-born British poet, verse dramatist and critic

72 I have no pain, dear mother, now;
But oh! I am so dry:
Just moisten poor Jim's lips once more;
And, mother, do not cry!
'The Collier's Dying Child' **Farmer, Edward** (c.1809–1876) English poet and writer

73 It hath been often said, that it is not death, but dying, which is terrible.
Amelia (1751) **Fielding, Henry** (1707–1754) English writer, dramatist and journalist

74 Strange, is it not? that of the myriads who
Before us pass'd the door of Darkness through,
Not one returns to tell us of the Road,
Which to discover we must travel too.
The Rubáiyát of Omar Khayyám (1879) **Fitzgerald, Edward** (1809–1883) English poet, translator and letter writer

75 Death hath so many doors to let out life.
The Custom of the Country (1647) **Fletcher, John** (1579–1625) English dramatist

76 Death destroys a man; the idea of Death saves him.
Howard's End (1910) **Forster, E.M.** (1879–1970) English writer, essayist and literary critic

77 But in this world nothing can be said to be certain, except death and taxes.
Letter to Jean Baptiste Le Roy, (1789) **Franklin, Benjamin** (1706-1790) US statesman, scientist, political critic and printer

78 I'm told he makes a very handsome corpse, and becomes his coffin prodigiously.
The Good Natur'd Man (1768) **Goldsmith, Oliver** (c.1728–1774) Irish dramatist, poet and writer

79 There are nearly as many human beings alive as ever lived up to the start of this century. Soon, the Greek catchword for death – joining the majority – will cease to be accurate.

The Observer, (1998) **Gray, John** (1948–) British academic

80 A dead woman bites not.
Oral tradition, (1587) **Gray, Patrick** (d. 1612) Scottish courtier, ambassador at the court of Elizabeth I of England. Advocating the execution of Mary, Queen of Scots

81 The boast of heraldry, the pomp of pow'r,
And all that beauty, all that wealth e'er gave,
Awaits alike th' inevitable hour,
The paths of glory lead but to the grave.
'Elegy Written in a Country Churchyard' (1751) **Gray, Thomas** (1716–1771) English poet and scholar

82 Suicide is an act of narcissistic manipulation and deep hostility.
The Observer Review, (1995) **Greer, Germaine** (1939–) Australian feminist, critic, English scholar and writer

83 They're dying just the same in station homesteads
they're dying in Home Beautiful apartments
in among their lovely Danish furniture
on and across the furniture they're dying
spewing blood or stiffening dry and seeming never
to have been alive.
Black Bagatelles (1978) **Hall, Rodney** (1935–) US poet and writer

84 When the chilled dough of his flesh went in an oven
not unlike those he fuelled all his life,
I thought of his cataracts ablaze with Heaven
and radiant with the sight of his dead wife,
light streaming from his mouth to shape her name,
'not Florence and not Flo but always Florrie'.
Continuous (1981) **Harrison, Tony** (1937–) English poet

85 Grieve not that I die young. Is it not well
To pass away ere life hath lost its brightness?
'Swan Song' **Hastings, Lady Flora** (1806–1839) Scottish poet

86 We sometimes congratulate ourselves at the moment of waking from a troubled dream; it may be so the moment after death.
American Notebooks **Hawthorne, Nathaniel** (1804–1864) US allegorical writer

87 He had decided to live forever or die in the attempt.
Catch-22 (1961) **Heller, Joseph** (1923–1999) US writer

88 It's funny the way most people love the dead. Once you're dead, you're made for life.
In *Rolling Stone,* (1976) **Hendrix, Jimi** (1942–1970) US rock singer, songwriter and guitarist

89 Madam Life's a piece in bloom
Death goes dogging everywhere:
She's the tenant of the room,
He's the ruffian on the stair.
Echoes (1877) **Henley, William Ernest** (1849–1903) English poet, dramatist and critic

90 One doth but breakfast here, another dines, he that liveth longest doth but sup; we must all go to bed in another world.
Horae Succisivae (1631) **Henshaw, Bishop Joseph** (1603–1679) English churchman and writer

91 Death is still working like a mole,
And digs my grave at each remove.
The Temple (1633) **Herbert, George** (1593–1633) English poet and priest

92 Gather ye Rose-buds while ye may,
Old Time is still a-flying:
And this same flower that smiles today,
Tomorrow will be dying.
Hesperides (1648) **Herrick, Robert** (1591–1674) English poet, royalist and clergyman

93 Death is nothing at all. It does not count. I have only slipped away into the next room. Nothing has happened. Everything remains exactly as it was. I am I, and you are you, and the old life that we lived so fondly together is untouched, unchanged. Whatever we were to each other, that we are still. Call me by the old familiar name. Speak of me in the easy way which you always used. Put no difference into your tone. Wear no forced air of solemnity or sorrow. Laugh as we always laughed at the

little jokes that we enjoyed together. Play, smile, think of me, pray for me. Let my name be ever the household word that it always was. Let it be spoken without an effort, without the ghost of a shadow upon it. Life means all that it ever meant. It is the same as it ever was. There is absolute and unbroken continuity. What is death but a negligible accident? Why should I be out of mind because I am out of sight? I am but waiting for you, for an interval, somewhere very near, just round the corner. All is well.
Facts of the Faith (1919) **Holland, Canon Henry Scott** (1847–1918) English cleric, Professor of Divinity and Christian social reformer

94 Pale Death strikes with impartial foot at the cottages of the poor and the turrets of kings.
Odes **Horace** (65–8 BC) Roman poet

95 Death … It's the only thing we haven't succeeded in completely vulgarizing.
Eyeless in Gaza (1936) **Huxley, Aldous** (1894–1963) English writer, poet and critic

96 And if there be no meeting past the grave,
If all is darkness, silence, yet 'tis rest.
Be not afraid ye waiting hearts that weep;
For still He giveth His beloved sleep,
And if an endless sleep He wills, so best.
Lines on the grave of her husband, (1895) **Huxley, Henrietta** (1825–1915) English writer and poet; wife of T.H. Huxley

97 To kill a human being is, after all, the least injury you can do him.
Complete Tales (1867) **James, Henry** (1843–1916) US-born British writer, critic and letter writer

98 He will not, whither he is now gone, find much difference, I believe, either in the climate or the company.
In Piozzi, *Anecdotes of the Late Samuel Johnson* (1786) Of a Jamaican gentleman, then lately dead

99 An odd thought strikes me: – we shall receive no letters in the grave.
In Boswell, *The Life of Samuel Johnson* (1791)

100 Depend upon it, Sir, when a man knows he is to be hanged in a fortnight, it concentrates his mind wonderfully.
In Boswell, *The Life of Samuel Johnson* (1791)

101 It matters not how a man dies, but how he lives. The act of dying is not of importance, it lasts so short a time.
In Boswell, *The Life of Samuel Johnson* (1791)

102 Sir, executions are intended to draw spectators. If they do not draw spectators, they don't answer their purpose.
In The Economist, (1993) **Johnson, Samuel** (1709–1784) English lexicographer, poet, critic, conversationalist and essayist

103 Death only this mysterious truth unfolds,
The mighty soul, how small a body holds.
Satires **Juvenal** (c.60–130) Roman verse satirist and Stoic

104 Darkling I listen; and, for many a time
I have been half in love with easeful Death,
Call'd him soft names in many a musèd rhyme,
To take into the air my quiet breath;
Now more than ever seems it rich to die,
To cease upon the midnight with no pain,
While thou art pouring forth thy soul abroad
In such an ecstasy!
'Ode to a Nightingale' (1819) **Keats, John** (1795–1821) English poet

105 Oh, how quickly the glory in this world passes away.
De Imitatione Christi (1892) **Kempis, Thomas à** (c.1380–1471) German mystic, monk and writer

106 At this twelfth hour of unrelenting summer
I think of those whose ready mouths are stopped,
I remember those who crouch in narrow graves,
I weep for those whose eyes are full of sand.
Two Offices of a Sentry (1942) **Keyes, Sidney** (1922–1943) English poet and soldier

107 Sleep on, my Love, in thy cold bed,
Never to be disquieted!
My last good night! Thou wilt not wake
Till I thy fate shall overtake:
Till age, or grief, or sickness must
Marry my body to that dust
It so much loves; and fill the room
My heart keeps empty in thy tomb.
Stay for me there; I will not fail
To meet thee in that hollow vale …
But hark! My pulse like a soft drum
Beats my approach, tells thee I come.

'Exequy upon his Wife' (1651) **King, Bishop Henry** (1592–1669) English royal chaplain, poet and sermonist

108 I could not look on Death, which being known,
Men led me to him, blindfold and alone.
The Years Between (1919)

109 I've just read that I am dead. Don't forget to delete me from your list of subscribers.
Attr. To a magazine which incorrectly reported his death **Kipling, Rudyard** (1865–1936) Indian-born British poet and writer

110 Hitherto man had to live with the idea of death as an individual; from now onward mankind will have to live with the idea of its death as a species.
Attr. **Koestler, Arthur** (1905–1983) British writer, essayist and political refugee. Of the atomic bomb

111 Watching the peaceful death of a human being reminds us of a falling star; one of a million lights in a vast sky that flares up for a brief moment only to disappear into the endless night forever.
On Death and Dying (1969) **Kübler-Ross, Elisabeth** (1926–)

112 Death does not take the wise man by surprise, he is always prepared to leave.
'La Mort et le mourant' **La Fontaine, Jean de** (1621–1695) French poet and fabulist

113 Gone before
To that unknown and silent shore.
'Hester' (1803) **Lamb, Charles** (1775–1834) English essayist, critic and letter writer

114 Death stands above me, whispering low
I know not what into my ear;
Of his strange language all I know
Is, there is not a word of fear.
Epigrams (1853)

115 I strove with none; for none was worth my strife;
Nature I loved, and next to Nature, Art;
I warmed both hands before the fire of life;
It sinks, and I am ready to depart.
'Finis' **Landor, Walter Savage** (1775–1864) English poet and writer

116 The anaesthetic from which none come round.
'Aubade' (1988) **Larkin, Philip** (1922–1985) English poet, writer and librarian. On death

117 The dead don't die. They look on and help.
Letter to J. Middleton Murry, (1923)

118 Now it is autumn and the falling fruit
and the long journey towards oblivion –
Have you built your ship of death,
O have you?
O build your ship of death, for you will need it.
Last Poems (1932), 'The Ship of Death'
Lawrence, D.H. (1885–1930) English writer, poet and critic

119 I detest life-insurance agents; they always argue that I shall someday die, which is not so.
Literary Lapses (1910) **Leacock, Stephen** (1869–1944) English-born Canadian humorist, writer and economist

120 I am one of those unfortunates to whom death is less hideous than explanations.
Welcome to All This **Lewis, D.B. Wyndham** (1891–1969) British writer and biographer

121 What has this bugbear death to frighten man
If souls can die as well as bodies can?
De Rerum Natura

122 And since the man who is not, feels not woe,
(For death exempts him, and wards off the blow,
Which we, the living, only feel and bear,)
What is there left for us in death to fear?
When once that pause of life has come between
'Tis just the same as we had never been.
De Rerum Natura **Lucretius** (c.95–55 BC) Roman philosopher

123 No one who could come back from death would be able to tell you anything about it, because we do not experience it. We come out of the dark and go into the dark, and in between we have experiences, but beginning and end, birth and death, are not experienced by us, they have no subjective character.
The Magic Mountain (1924)

124 Instead of going to church you should go to a funeral when you wish to be uplifted. The people have got good black clothes on, they take their hats off, look at the coffin and are serious and reverent, and no-one dares make bad jokes.
The Magic Mountain (1924) **Mann, Thomas** (1875–1955) German writer and critic

125 The grave's a fine and private place,
But none I think do there embrace.
'To His Coy Mistress' (1681) **Marvell, Andrew** (1621–1678) English poet and satirist

126 Either he's dead or my watch has stopped.
A Day at the Races (film, 1937) **Marx, Groucho** (1895–1977) US comedian

127 Death opens unknown doors. It is most grand to die.
Pompey the Great (1910) **Masefield, John** (1878–1967) English poet, writer and critic

128 Death has a thousand doors to let out life: I shall find one.
A Very Woman (1634) **Massinger, Philip** (1583–1640) English dramatist and poet

129 Dying is a very dull, dreary affair. And my advice to you is to have nothing whatever to do with it.
In R. Maugham, *Escape from the Shadows* (1972) **Maugham, William Somerset** (1874–1965) English writer, dramatist and physician

130 Death devours all lovely things:
Lesbia with her sparrow
Shares the darkness, – presently
Every bed is narrow.
'Passer Mortuus Est' (1921)

131 Down, down, down into the darkness of the grave
Gently they go, the beautiful, the tender, the kind;
Quietly they go, the intelligent, the witty, the brave.
I know. But I do not approve. And I am not resigned.
'Dirge without Music' (1928) **Millay, Edna St Vincent** (1892–1950) US poet and dramatist

132 Why should I go? She won't be there.
Attr. **Miller, Arthur** (1915–2005) US dramatist and screenwriter. When asked if he would attend Marilyn Monroe's funeral

133 Methought I saw my late espoused Saint
Brought to me like Alcestis from the grave
...
But O as to embrace me she enclin'd,
I wak'd, she fled, and day brought back my night.
'Methought I saw my late espoused Saint' (1658) **Milton, John** (1608–1674) English poet, libertarian and pamphleteer

134 Gracious dying is a huge, macabre and expensive joke on the American public.
The American Way of Death (1963)

135 I have nothing against undertakers personally. It's just that I wouldn't want one to bury my sister.
Attr. in *Saturday Review*, (1964) **Mitford, Jessica** (1917–1996) English writer

136 One dies only once, and then for such a long time!
Le Dépit Amoureux (1656) **Molière** (1622–1673) French dramatist, actor and director

137 One should always have one's boots on and be ready to leave.
Essais (1580)

138 I want death to find me planting my cabbages, but caring little for it, and even less for my imperfect garden.
Essais (1580) **Montaigne, Michel de** (1533–1592) French essayist and moralist

139 I can't think of a more wonderful thanksgiving for the life I have had than that everyone should be jolly at my funeral.
TV interview, shown after his death in August 1979 **Mountbatten of Burma, First Earl** (1900–1979) English admiral and statesman

140 Oh well, no matter what happens, there's always death.
Attr. **Napoleon I** (1769–1821) French emperor

141 Even of death Christianity has made a terror which was unknown to the gay calmness of the Pagan.
Views and Opinions (1895) **Ouida** (1839–1908) English writer and critic

142 What passing-bells for these who die as cattle?
Only the monstrous anger of the guns.
Only the stuttering rifles' rapid rattle
Can patter out their hasty orisons.

'Anthem for Doomed Youth' (1917) **Owen, Wilfred** (1893–1918) English poet

143 How can they tell?
Parker, Dorothy (1893–1967) US writer, poet, critic and wit. On being told that US President Calvin Coolidge was dead

144 We shall die alone.
Pensées (1670) **Pascal, Blaise** (1623–1662) French philosopher and scientist. *(On mourra seul)*

145 Death is the only grammatically correct full-stop ...
'Schoolboy' (1990)

146 Between himself and the grave his parents stand,
monuments that will crumble.
'Schoolboy' (1990)

147 Death does not necessarily diminish us, it also deepens our awareness of what it means to be alive.
'Grave gossip' **Patten, Brian** (1946–) British poet

148 Memory and habit are the harbingers of death.
Note conjointe sur M. Descartes (1914) **Péguy, Charles** (1873–1914) French Catholic socialist, poet and writer

149 I went out to Charing Cross, to see Major-General Harrison hanged, drawn and quartered; which was done there, he looking as cheerful as any man could do in that condition.
Diary, (1660) **Pepys, Samuel** (1633–1703) English diarist, naval administrator and politician

150 I am curious to see what happens in the next world to one who dies unshriven.
Attr. **Perelman, S.J.** (1904–1979) US humorist, writer and dramatist. Giving his reasons for refusing to see a priest as he lay dying

151 It is the overtakers who keep the undertakers busy.
The Observer, (1963) **Pitts, William** (1900–1980) English chief constable

152 Dying
Is an art, like everything else.
I do it exceptionally well.

'Lady Lazarus' (1963) **Plath, Sylvia** (1932–1963) US poet, writer and diarist

153 I mount! I fly!
O Grave! where is thy victory?
O Death! where is thy sting?
'The Dying Christian to his Soul' (1730)

154 Go, like the Indian, in another life
Expect thy dog, thy bottle, and thy wife.
Essay on Man, IV (1734) **Pope, Alexander** (1688–1744) English poet, translator and editor

155 It is better to die young than to outlive all one loved, and all that rendered one lovable.
The Confessions of an Elderly Gentleman (1836) **Power, Marguerite, Countess of Blessington** (1789–1849) English writer

156 They buried him, but all through the night of mourning, in lighted windows, his books arranged three by three kept watch like angels with outspread wings and seemed, for him who was no more, the symbol of his resurrection.
La Prisonnière (1923) **Proust, Marcel** (1871–1922) French writer and critic

157 I am going to seek a great perhaps ...
Bring down the curtain, the farce is played out.
Attr. **Rabelais, François** (c.1494–c.1553) French monk, physician, satirist and humanist. Last words

158 O eloquent, just and mighty Death! ... thou hast drawn together all the far-stretched greatness, all the pride, cruelty, and ambition of man, and covered it all over with these two narrow words, *Hic jacet.*
The History of the World (1614)

159 So the heart be right, it is no matter which way the head lies.
In W. Stebbing, *Sir Walter Raleigh* (1891) Reply when asked which way he would like to lay his head on the block

160 Only we die in earnest, that's no jest.
'On the Life of Man' **Raleigh, Sir Walter** (c.1552–1618) English courtier, explorer, military commander, poet, historian and essayist

161 I shall have more to say when I am dead.
The Three Taverns (1920) **Robinson, Edwin Arlington** (1869–1935) US poet

162 Holy Moses! Have a look!
Flesh decayed in every nook.
Some rare bits of brain lie here,
Mortal loads of beef and beer.
'Lines on Westminster Abbey' **Ros, Amanda** (1860–1939) Irish novelist and poet

163 O Death, where is thy sting?
Thy victory, O Grave?
Philosophies (1910) **Ross, Sir Ronald** (1857–1932) Indian-born British physician

164 O Earth, lie heavily upon her eyes;
Seal her sweet eyes weary of watching, Earth.
'Rest' (1862) **Rossetti, Christina** (1830–1894) English poet

165 I do not see them here; but after death God knows I know the faces I shall see,
Each one a murdered self, with low last breath.
'I am thyself, – what hast thou done to me?'
'And I – and I – thyself', (lo! each one saith,)
'And thou thyself to all eternity!'
The House of Life **Rossetti, Dante Gabriel** (1828–1882) English poet, painter, translator and letter writer

166 Death is the privilege of human nature,
And life without it were not worth our taking.
The Fair Penitent (1703) **Rowe, Nicholas** (1674–1718) English dramatist

167 Waldo is one of those people who would be enormously improved by death.
Beasts and Super-Beasts (1914) **Saki** (1870–1916) Burmese-born British writer

168 Dear World, I am leaving you because I am bored. I am leaving you with your worries. Good luck.
Suicide note **Sanders, George** (1906–1972) Russian-born British film actor

169 I hate victims who respect their executioners.
Les Séquestrés d'Altona (1960) **Sartre, Jean-Paul** (1905–1980) French philosopher, writer, dramatist and critic

170 Stumbling along the trench in the dusk, dead men and living lying against the sides of the trenches – one never knew which were dead and which living. Dead and living were nearly one, for death was in all our hearts.
Diary, April 1917 **Sassoon, Siegfried** (1886–1967) English poet and writer

171 After your death you will be what you were before your birth.
Parerga and Paralipomena (1851)

172 Every separation gives a foretaste of death, – and every reunion a foretaste of resurrection.
Parerga und Paralipomena (1851) **Schopenhauer, Arthur** (1788–1860) German philosopher

173 And come he slow, or come he fast,
It is but Death who comes at last.
Marmion (1808)

174 His morning walk was beneath the elms in the churchyard; 'for death,' he said, 'had been his next-door neighbour for so many years, that he had no apology for dropping the acquaintance.'
A Legend of Montrose (1819) **Scott, Sir Walter** (1771–1832) Scottish writer and historian

175 I have a rendezvous with Death,
At some disputed barricade,
At midnight in some flaming town.
'I Have a Rendezvous with Death' (1916) **Seeger, Alan** (1888–1916) US poet

176 Anyone can take away a man's life, but no one his death; to this a thousand doors lie open.
Phoenissae

177 For him death grippeth right hard by the crop
That know of all, but to himself, alas
Doth die unknown, dazed with dreadful face.
Thyestes **Seneca** (c.4 BC–AD 65) Roman philosopher, poet, dramatist, essayist, rhetorician and statesman

178 I find death so terrible that I hate life more for leading me towards it than for the thorns encountered on the way.
Letter to Mme de Grignan, (1672) **Sévigné, Marquise de** (1626–1696) French letter writer

179 The dead are surprised by too many
friends.
Sunday Telegraph, (1993) **Shakespeare, Nicholas**
(1957–) English writer

180 If thou and nature can so gently part,
The stroke of death is as a lover's pinch,
Which hurts and is desir'd.
Antony and Cleopatra, V.ii

181 Fear no more the heat o' th' sun
Nor the furious winter's rages;
Thou thy worldly task hast done,
Home art gone, and ta'en thy wages.
Golden lads and girls all must,
As chimney-sweepers, come to dust.
Cymbeline, IV.ii

182 O, that this too too solid flesh would melt,
Thaw, and resolve itself into a dew!
Or that the Everlasting had not fix'd
His canon 'gainst self-slaughter! O God!
God!
How weary, stale, flat, and unprofitable,
Seem to me all the uses of this world!
Hamlet, I.ii

183 To be, or not to be – that is the question;
Whether 'tis nobler in the mind to suffer
The slings and arrows of outrageous
fortune,
Or to take arms against a sea of troubles,
And by opposing end them?
Hamlet, III.i

184 This fell sergeant Death
Is strict in his arrest.
Hamlet, V.ii

185 Men must endure
Their going hence, even as their coming
hither:
Ripeness is all.
King Lear, V.ii

186 Nothing in his life
Became him like the leaving it: he died
As one that had been studied in his death
To throw away the dearest thing he ow'd
As 'twere a careless trifle.
Macbeth, I.iv

187 Dar'st thou die?
The sense of death is most in
apprehension;
And the poor beetle that we tread upon
In corporal sufferance finds a pang as great
As when a giant dies.
Measure For Measure, III.i

188 The weariest and most loathed worldly life
That age, ache, penury, and imprisonment,
Can lay on nature is a paradise
To what we fear of death.
Measure For Measure, III.i

189 I shall despair. There is no creature loves
me;
And if I die no soul will pity me:
And wherefore should they, since that I
myself
Find in myself no pity to myself?
Richard III, V.iii

190 Out, alas! she's cold;
Her blood is settled, and her joints are stiff.
Life and these lips have long been
separated.
Death lies on her like an untimely frost
Upon the sweetest flower of all the field.
Romeo and Juliet IV.v

191 No longer mourn for me when I am dead
Than you shall hear the surly sullen bell
Give warning to the world that I am fled
From this vile world, with vilest worms to
dwell.
Sonnet 71

192 He that dies pays all debts.
The Tempest, III.ii **Shakespeare, William** (1564–
1616) English dramatist, poet and actor

193 Life levels all men: death reveals the
eminent.
Man and Superman (1903) **Shaw, George
Bernard** (1856–1950) Irish socialist, writer,
dramatist and critic

194 Death is the veil which those who live call
life:
They sleep, and it is lifted.
Prometheus Unbound (1820) **Shelley, Percy
Bysshe** (1792–1822) English poet, dramatist
and essayist

195 Beneath a church-yard yew
Decay'd and worn with age,
At dusk of eve methought I spy'd
Poor Slender's ghost, that whimpering cry'd
O sweet, O sweet Anne Page!
'Slender's Ghost' **Shenstone, William** (1714–1763) English poet, essayist and letter writer

196 Even good people achieve their rebirth in the Land of Perfect Bliss; then how much more so should the case be with evil persons!
Tannishō (c.1290) **Shinran** (1173–1263) Japanese Buddhist and writer

197 How little room
Do we take up in death that living know
No bounds!
The Wedding (1629)

198 The glories of our blood and state
Are shadows, not substantial things;
There is no armour against fate;
Death lays his icy hand on kings:
Sceptre and crown
Must tumble down,
And in the dust be equal made
With the poor crooked scythe and spade.
The Contention of Ajax and Ulysses (1659) **Shirley, James** (1596–1666) English poet and dramatist

199 Dead seamen, gone in search of the same landfall,
Whether as enemies they fought,
Or fought with us, or neither; the sand joins them together,
Enlisted on the other front.
'Beach Burial' (1942) **Slessor, Kenneth** (1901–1971) Australian poet and journalist

200 If there wasn't death, I think you couldn't go on.
The Observer, (1969) **Smith, Stevie** (1902–1971) English poet and writer

201 I cannot forgive my friends for dying; I do not find these vanishing acts of theirs at all amusing.
Afterthoughts (1931) **Smith, Logan Pearsall** (1865–1946) US-born British epigrammatist, critic and writer

202 Death must be distinguished from dying, with which it is often confused.
In H. Pearson, *The Smith of Smiths* (1934) **Smith, Sydney** (1771–1845) English clergyman, essayist, journalist and wit

203 Death is one of two things. Either it is nothingness, and the dead have no consciousness of anything; or, as people say, it is a change and migration of the soul from this place to another.
Attr. in Plato, *Apology* **Socrates** (469–399 BC) Athenian philosopher

204 Death is not the worst thing; rather, when one who craves death cannot attain even that wish.
Electra **Sophocles** (496–406 BC) Greek dramatist

205 My name is Death: the last best friend am I.
Carmen Nuptiale (1816) **Southey, Robert** (1774–1843) English poet, essayist, historian and letter writer

206 Poor soul, very sad; her late husband, you know, a very sad death – eaten by missionaries – poor soul!
In William Hayter, *Spooner* (1977) **Spooner, William** (1844–1930) English churchman and university warden

207 Old and young, we are all on our last cruise.
Virginibus Puerisque (1881) **Stevenson, Robert Louis** (1850–1894) Scottish writer, poet and essayist

208 It's not the first time I have died in Coventry.
The Times, (1999) **Swarbrick, Dave** (1941–) English folk musician. On reading his obituary in the *Daily Telegraph*

209 You think, as I ought to think, that it is time for me to have done with the world, and so I would if I could get into a better before I was called into the best, and not die here in a rage, like a poisoned rat in a hole.
Letter to Bolingbroke, (1729) **Swift, Jonathan** (1667–1745) Irish satirist, poet, essayist and cleric

210 Row upon row with strict impunity
The headstones yield their names to the
element.
'Ode to the Confederate Dead' (1926) **Tate,
Allen** (1899–1979) US poet

211 Do we indeed desire the dead
Should still be near us at our side?
Is there no baseness we would hide?
No inner vileness that we dread?
In Memoriam A. H. H. (1850)

212 Nor at all can tell
Whether I mean this day to end myself,
Or lend an ear to Plato where he says,
That men like soldiers may not quit the
post
Allotted by the Gods.
'Lucretius' (1868) **Tennyson, Alfred, Lord**
(1809–1892) English lyric poet

213 I, born of flesh and ghost, was neither
A ghost nor man, but mortal ghost.
And I was struck down by death's feather.
'Before I knocked' (1933)

214 Though they go mad they shall be sane,
Though they sink through the sea they
shall rise again;
Though lovers be lost love shall not;
And death shall have no dominion.
'And death shall have no dominion' (1936)

215 Do not go gentle into that good night,
Old age should burn and rave at close of
day;
Rage, rage against the dying of the light.
'Do Not Go Gentle into that Good Night'
(1952) **Thomas, Dylan** (1914–1953) Welsh poet,
writer and radio dramatist

216 One world at a time.
Attr. **Thoreau, Henry David** (1817–1862) US
essayist, social critic and writer. On being
asked his opinion of the hereafter

217 Go and try to disprove death. Death will
disprove you, and that's all there is to it!
Fathers and Sons (1862)

218 Death is an old jest but it comes to
everyone.
In Jennifer Johnston, *The Old Jest* **Turgenev,
Ivan** (1818–1883) Russian writer and dramatist

219 All say, 'How hard it is to die' – a strange
complaint to come from the mouths of
people who have had to live.
Pudd'nhead Wilson's Calendar (1894)

220 Whoever has lived long enough to find out
what life is, knows how deep a debt of
gratitude we owe to Adam, the first great
benefactor of our race. He brought death
into the world.
Pudd'nhead Wilson (1894)

221 The report of my death was an
exaggeration.
Cable, (1897) **Twain, Mark** (1835–1910) US
humorist, writer, journalist and lecturer

222 In fact we do not try to picture the afterlife,
nor is it ourselves in our nervous tics and
optical flecks that we wish to perpetuate; it
is the self as the window on the world that
we can't bear to think of shutting.
Self-Consciousness: Memoirs (1989) **Updike,
John** (1932–) US writer, poet and critic

223 Dear, beauteous death! the Jewel of the
Just,
Shining nowhere, but in the dark;
What mysteries do lie beyond thy dust;
Could man outlook that mark!
Silex Scintillans (1650–1655) **Vaughan, Henry**
(1622–1695) Welsh poet and physician

224 We owe respect to the living; we owe
nothing but truth to the dead.
'Première Lettre sur Oedipe' (1785) **Voltaire**
(1694–1778) French philosopher, dramatist,
poet, historian, writer and critic

225 There's no repentance in the grave.
Divine Songs for Children (1715) **Watts, Isaac**
(1674–1748) English hymn writer, poet and
minister

226 I know death hath ten thousand several
doors
For men to take their exits.
The Duchess of Malfi (1623)

227 O, that it were possible,
We might but hold some two days'
conference
With the dead!
The Duchess of Malfi (1623) **Webster, John**
(c.1580–c.1625) English dramatist

228 Every death, even the cruellest,
drowns in Nature's complete indifference.
We are the only ones who bestow a value
on our lives.
*The Hunting Down and Murder of Jean Paul
Marat* (1964) **Weiss, Peter** (1916–1982) German
dramatist, painter and film producer

229 My dear – the people we should have been
seen dead with.
Times Literary Supplement, (1982) **West, Dame
Rebecca** (1892–1983) English writer, critic and
feminist. Cable sent to Noël Coward after
learning they had both been on a Nazi death
list

230 Has anyone supposed it lucky to be born?
I hasten to inform him or her it is just as
lucky to die, and I know it.
'Song of Myself' (1855)

231 Beautiful that war and all its deeds of
carnage must in time be utterly lost,
That the hands of the sisters Death and
Night incessantly softly wash again, and
ever again, this soil'd world;
For my enemy is dead, a man as divine as
myself is dead,
I look where he lies white-faced and still in
the coffin – I draw near,
Bend down and touch lightly with my lips
the white face in the coffin.
'Reconciliation' (1865) **Whitman, Walt** (1819–
1892) US poet and writer

232 All her bright golden hair
Tarnished with rust,
She that was young and fair
Fallen to dust.
'Requiescat' (1881) **Wilde, Oscar** (1854–1900)
Irish poet, dramatist, writer, critic and wit

233 The solution of the problem of life is seen
in the vanishing of the problem.
Tractatus Logico-Philosophicus (1922)
Wittgenstein, Ludwig (1889–1951) Austrian
philosopher

234 Dead! and ... never called me mother.
East Lynne (stage adaptation, 1874) **Wood, Mrs
Henry** (1814–1877) English writer and editor

235 Death marshals up his armies round us
now.
Their footsteps crowd too near.
Lock your warm hand above the chilling
heart
and for a time I live without my fear.
Grope in the night to find me and
embrace,
for the dark preludes of the drums begin,
and round us, round the company of
lovers,
death draws his cordons in.
'The Company of Lovers' (1946) **Wright,
Judith** (1915–2000) Australian poet, critic and
writer

236 Nor dread nor hope attend
A dying animal;
A man awaits his end
Dreading and hoping all.
'Death' (1933) **Yeats, W.B.** (1865–1939) Irish
poet, dramatist, editor, writer and senator

237 Life is the desert, life the solitude;
Death joins us to the great majority.
The Revenge (1721)

238 All men think all men Mortal, but
themselves.
Night-Thoughts on Life, Death and Immortality
(1742–1746) **Young, Edward** (1683–1765) English
poet, dramatist, satirist and clergyman
See also absence; epitaphs; grief; last words;
sleep; the soul; time

DECEPTION

1 It is not only fine feathers that make fine
birds.
Fables

2 The lamb that belonged to the sheep
whose skin the wolf was wearing began to
follow the wolf in the sheep's clothing.
'The Wolf in Sheep's Clothing'

3 Appearances are often deceiving.
'The Wolf in Sheep's Clothing' **Aesop**
(6th century BC) Legendary Greek writer of
fables

4 It is the wisdom of the crocodiles, that
shed tears when they would devour.

'Of Wisdom for a Man's Self' (1625) **Bacon, Francis** (1561–1626) English philosopher, essayist, politician and courtier

5 It is impossible that a man who is false to his friends and neighbours should be true to the public.
Maxims Concerning Patriotism (1750) **Berkeley, Bishop George** (1685–1753) Irish philosopher and scholar

6 Beware of false prophets, which come to you in sheep's clothing, but inwardly they are ravening wolves.
Matthew, 7:15 **The Bible (King James Version)**

7 Their sighin, cantin, grace-proud faces, Their three-mile prayers, an' hauf-mile graces.
'To the Rev. John M'Math' (1785) **Burns, Robert** (1759–1796) Scottish poet and songwriter

8 It wasn't a woman who betrayed Jesus with a kiss.
The Savage Pilgrimage (1932) **Carswell, Catherine** (1879–1946) Scottish writer

9 The carl spak oo thing, but he thoghte another.
The Canterbury Tales (1387)

10 The smylere with the knyf under the cloke.
The Canterbury Tales (1387) **Chaucer, Geoffrey** (c.1340–1400) English poet, public servant and courtier

11 We ought to see far enough into a hypocrite to see even his sincerity.
Heretics (1905) **Chesterton, G.K.** (1874–1936) English writer, poet and critic

12 Says he, 'I am a handsome man, but I'm a gay deceiver.'
Love Laughs at Locksmiths (1808) **Colman, the Younger, George** (1762–1836) English dramatist and Examiner of Plays

13 Man was by Nature Woman's cully made: We never are, but by ourselves, betrayed.
The Old Bachelor (1693) **Congreve, William** (1670–1729) English dramatist

14 Necessity hath no law. Feigned necessities, imaginary necessities … are the greatest cozenage that men can put upon the Providence of God, and make pretences to break known rules by.
Speech to Parliament, (1654) **Cromwell, Oliver** (1599–1658) English general, statesman and Puritan leader

15 There is a great deal of wishful thinking in such cases; it is the easiest thing of all to deceive one's self.
Olynthiac **Demosthenes** (c.384–322 BC) Athenian statesman and orator

16 With affection beaming in one eye, and calculation shining out of the other.
Martin Chuzzlewit (1844) **Dickens, Charles** (1812–1870) English writer

17 Flattery wearis ane furrit gown, And falsett with the lord does roun, And truth stands barrit at the dure.
'Into this World May None Assure' (1834 edition) **Dunbar, William** (c.1460–c.1525) Scottish poet, satirist and courtier

18 Experience teaches you that the man who looks you straight in the eye, particularly if he adds a firm handshake, is hiding something.
Enter, Conversing **Fadiman, Clifton** (1904–1999) US writer, editor and broadcaster

19 To cheat a man is nothing; but the woman must have fine parts indeed who cheats a woman!
The Beggar's Opera (1728) **Gay, John** (1685–1732) English poet, dramatist and librettist

20 I have laughed in bitterness and agony of heart, at the contrast between what I seem and what I am!
The Scarlet Letter (1850) **Hawthorne, Nathaniel** (1804–1864) US allegorical writer

21 It was beautiful and simple as all truly great swindles are.
'The Octopus Marooned' (1908) **Henry, O.** (1862–1910) US short-story writer

22 You will eat (You will eat)
Bye and bye (Bye and bye)
In that glorious land above the sky (Way up
high)
Work and pray (Work and pray)
Live on hay (Live on hay)
You'll get pie in the sky when you die
(That's a lie).
'The Preacher and the Slave', *song*, (1911) **Hill,
Joe** (1879–1914) Swedish-born US songwriter
and workers' organizer

23 It is a double pleasure to trick the trickster.
Fables, 'Le coq et le renard' **La Fontaine, Jean
de** (1621–1695) French poet and fabulist

24 You can fool some of the people all of the
time, and all of the people some of the
time, but you cannot fool all of the people
all the time.
Attr. **Lincoln, Abraham** (1809–1865) US
statesman and President

25 Deceive boys with toys, but men with
oaths.
In Plutarch, *Parallel Lives*, 'Lysander' **Lysander**
(d. 395 BC) Spartan admiral

26 Hypocrisy is the most difficult and nerve-
racking vice that any man can pursue; it
needs an unceasing vigilance and a rare
detachment of spirit. It cannot, like
adultery or gluttony, be practised at spare
moments; it is a whole-time job.
Cakes and Ale (1930) **Maugham, William
Somerset** (1874–1965) English writer,
dramatist and physician

27 For neither Man nor Angel can discern
Hypocrisie, the onely evil that walks
Invisible, except to God alone.
Paradise Lost (1667) **Milton, John** (1608–1674)
English poet, libertarian and pamphleteer

28 O what a tangled web we weave,
When first we practise to deceive!
Marmion (1808) **Scott, Sir Walter** (1771–1832)
Scottish writer and historian

29 O villain, villain, smiling, damned villain!
My tables – meet it is I set it down
That one may smile, and smile, and be a
villain.
Hamlet, I.v

30 False face must hide what the false heart
doth know.
Macbeth, I.vii

31 An evil soul producing holy witness
Is like a villain with a smiling cheek,
A goodly apple rotten at the heart.
O, what a goodly outside falsehood hath!
The Merchant of Venice, I.iii

32 All that glisters is not gold,
Often have you heard that told.
The Merchant of Venice, II.vii

33 So may the outward shows be least
themselves;
The world is still deceiv'd with ornament.
The Merchant of Venice, III.ii

34 Roses have thorns, and silver fountains
mud;
Clouds and eclipses stain both moon and
sun,
And loathsome canker lives in sweetest
bud.
All men make faults.
Sonnet 35

35 Though I am not naturally honest, I am so
sometimes by chance.
The Winter's Tale, IV.iv **Shakespeare, William**
(1564–1616) English dramatist, poet and actor

36 In the matter of interest we are wary as
serpents, subtle as foxes, vigilant as the
birds of the night, rapacious as kites,
tenacious as grappling-hooks and the
weightiest anchors, and, above all, false
and hypocritical as a thin crust of ice
spread upon the face of a deep, smooth,
and dissembling pit.
XXV Sermons Preached at Golden Grove (1653)
Taylor, Bishop Jeremy (1613–1667) English
divine and writer

37 You can fool too many of the people too
much of the time.
The New Yorker, (1939)

38 It is not so easy to fool little girls today as it
used to be.
Fables for Our Time (1940) **Thurber, James**
(1894–1961) US humorist, writer and
dramatist

39 Who may deceive a lover?
Aeneid **Virgil** (70–19 BC) Roman poet

40 Glories, like glow-worms, afar off shine bright,
But, looked too near, have neither heat nor light.
The Duchess of Malfi (1623) **Webster, John** (c.1580–c.1625) English dramatist

41 I hope that you have not been leading a double life, pretending to be wicked and being really good all the time. That would be hypocrisy.
The Importance of Being Earnest (1895) **Wilde, Oscar** (1854–1900) Irish poet, dramatist, writer, critic and wit
See also appearance; guilt; lies; realism; secrets

DEMOCRACY

1 Remember, democracy never lasts long. It soon wastes, exhausts, and murders itself. There never was a democracy yet that did not commit suicide.
The Works of John Adams (1856), letter, (1814) **Adams, John** (1735–1826) US lawyer, diplomat and President

2 I don't know exactly what democracy is. But we need more of it.
Chinese student during protests in Tianamen Square, Beijing, (1989)

3 Democracy is mob rule, but with income taxes.
Anonymous

4 Democracy means government by discussion but it is only effective if you can stop people talking.
Speech, (1957) **Attlee, Clement** (1883–1967) English statesman and Prime Minister

5 The trouble in modern democracy is that men do not approach to leadership until they have lost the desire to lead anyone.
The Observer, (1934) **Beveridge, William Henry** (1879–1963) British economist and social reformer

6 One man shall have one vote.

The People's Barrier Against Undue Influence (1780) **Cartwright, John** (1740–1824) English political reformer

7 Democracy means government by the uneducated, while aristocracy means government by the badly educated.
New York Times, (1931)

8 You can never have a revolution in order to establish a democracy. You must have a democracy in order to have a revolution.
Tremendous Trifles **Chesterton, G.K.** (1874–1936) English writer, poet and critic

9 Many forms of government have been tried, and will be tried in this world of sin and woe. No one pretends that democracy is perfect or all-wise. Indeed, it has been said that democracy is the worst form of Government except all those other forms that have been tried from time to time.
Speech, (1947) **Churchill, Sir Winston** (1874–1965) English Conservative Prime Minister

10 There is one safeguard, which is an advantage and security for all, but especially to democracies, against despots. What is it? Distrust.
Philippics **Demosthenes** (c.384–322 BC) Athenian statesman and orator

11 Democracy is the name we give the people whenever we need them.
L'habit vert **Flers, Marquis de** (1872–1927) and **Caillavet, Arman de** (1869–1915) French playwrights

12 Correct! You said it! Scandal is the manure of democracy.
Accidental Death of an Anarchist (1974) **Fo, Dario** (1926–) Italian playwright and actor

13 So Two cheers for Democracy: one because it admits variety and two because it permits criticism. Two cheers are quite enough: there is no occasion to give three. Only Love the Beloved Republic deserves that.
Two Cheers for Democracy (1951) **Forster, E.M.** (1879–1970) English writer, essayist and literary critic

14 The most dangerous foe to truth and freedom in our midst is the compact majority. Yes, the damned, compact liberal majority.
An Enemy of the People (1882) **Ibsen, Henrik** (1828–1906) Norwegian writer, dramatist and poet

15 Democracy is only an experiment in government, and it has the obvious disadvantage of merely counting votes instead of weighing them.
Possible Recovery? (c.1922) **Inge, William Ralph** (1860–1954) English divine, writer and teacher

16 The right of election is the very essence of the constitution.
Letters (1769–1771) **Junius** (1769–1772) Pen-name of anonymous author of letters criticizing ministers of George III

17 No man is good enough to govern another man without that other's consent.
Speech, (1854)

18 The ballot is stronger than the bullet.
Speech, (1856) **Lincoln, Abraham** (1809–1865) US statesman and President

19 You don't arrange elections if you are going to lose them.
The Guardian, (1999) **Lissouba, Pascal** (1931–) President of Congo Brazzaville

20 Thus our democracy was, from an early period, the most aristocratic, and our aristocracy the most democratic in the world.
History of England (1849) **Macaulay, Lord** (1800–1859) English Liberal statesman, essayist and poet

21 Man's capacity for justice makes democracy possible, but man's inclination to injustice makes democracy necessary.
The Children of Light and the Children of Darkness (1944) **Niebuhr, Reinhold** (1892–1971) US Protestant theologian and writer

22 We enjoy a constitution that does not follow the customs of our neighbours; we are rather an example to them than they to us. Our government is called a democracy because power is in the hands not of the few but of the many.

In Thucydides, *Histories* **Pericles** (c.495–429) Athenian statesman, general, orator and cultural patron

23 An institution in which the whole is equal to the scum of all the parts.
Pot Shots from Pegasus **Preston, Keith** (1884–1927) US poet, writer and teacher. Of democracy

24 We must be the great arsenal of democracy.
Radio broadcast, (1940) **Roosevelt, Franklin Delano** (1882–1945) US Democrat President

25 One must admit one is powerless in the face of the political inevitability of this new order in history: universal suffrage.
Letter to Joseph Mazzini, (1848) **Sand, George** (1804–1876) French writer and dramatist

26 Magna Charter was ... the cause of Democracy in England, and thus a Good Thing for everyone (except the Common People).
1066 And All That (1930) **Sellar, Walter** (1898–1951) and **Yeatman, Robert Julian** (1897–1968) British writers

27 Democracy substitutes election by the incompetent many for appointment by the corrupt few.
Man and Superman (1903)

28 Our political experiment of democracy, the last refuge of cheap misgovernment.
Man and Superman (1903), Epistle Dedicatory **Shaw, George Bernard** (1856–1950) Irish socialist, writer, dramatist and critic

29 I sought the image of democracy, in order to learn what we have to fear and to hope from its progress.
De la Démocratie en Amérique (1840) **Tocqueville, Alexis de** (1805–1859) French historian, politician, lawyer and memoirist

30 The people's government, made for the people, made by the people, and answerable to the people.
Speech, (1830) **Webster, Daniel** (1782–1852) US statesman, orator and lawyer

31 Democracy means simply the bludgeoning of the people by the people for the people.

The Fortnightly Review, (1891) **Wilde, Oscar** (1854–1900) Irish poet, dramatist, writer, critic and wit

32 Knowledge – Zzzzzp! Money – Zzzzzp! – Power! That's the cycle democracy is built on!
The Glass Menagerie (1945) **Williams, Tennessee** (1911–1983) US dramatist and writer

33 The world must be made safe for democracy.
Speech, (1917) **Wilson, Woodrow** (1856–1924) US Democrat President
See also class; government

DESIRE

1 Man's desires are limited by his perceptions; none can desire what he has not perceiv'd.
There is No Natural Religion (c.1788)

2 The desire of Man being Infinite the possession is Infinite and himself Infinite.
There is No Natural Religion (c.1788)

3 Those who restrain desire, do so because theirs is weak enough to be restrained.
The Marriage of Heaven and Hell (c.1790–1793)

4 Abstinence sows sand all over
The ruddy limbs & flaming hair
But Desire Gratified
Plants fruits of life & beauty there.
'Abstinence sows sand all over' (c.1793) **Blake, William** (1757–1827) English poet, engraver, painter and mystic

5 My desires only are, and I shall be happy therein, to be but the last man, and bring up the rear in heaven.
Religio Medici (1643) **Browne, Sir Thomas** (1605–1682) English physician, author and antiquary

6 O, she is the antidote to desire.
The Way of the World (1700) **Congreve, William** (1670–1729) English dramatist

7 Thus when we fondly flatter our desires, Our best conceits do prove the greatest liars.
The Barrons' Wars (1603) **Drayton, Michael** (1563–1631) English poet

8 Some say the world will end in fire,
Some say in ice.
From what I've tasted of desire,
I hold with those who favour fire,
But if it had to perish twice,
I think I know enough of hate
To say that for destruction ice
Is also great
And would suffice.
'Fire and Ice' (1923) **Frost, Robert** (1874–1963) US poet

9 The desire of the moth for the star.
In Ellmann, *James Joyce* (1958) **Joyce, James** (1882–1941) Irish writer. Commenting on the interruption of a music recital when a moth flew into the singer's mouth

10 The depth and dream of my desire,
The bitter paths wherein I stray –
Thou knowest Who hast made the Fire,
Thou knowest Who hast made the Clay.
Life's Handicap (1888) **Kipling, Rudyard** (1865–1936) Indian-born British poet and writer

11 Not all that you want and ought not to have is forbidden to you,
Not all that you want and are allowed to want
Is acceptable.
Vanishing Trick (1976) **Patten, Brian** (1946–) British poet

12 Desire makes everything blossom; possession makes everything wither and fade.
Les Plaisirs et les Jours (1896)

13 There is nothing like desire for preventing the things one says from bearing any resemblance to what one has in mind.
Le Côté de Guermantes (1921) **Proust, Marcel** (1871–1922) French writer and critic

14 Why should a man whose blood is warm within
Sit like his grandsire cut in alabaster?
The Merchant of Venice, I.i **Shakespeare, William** (1564–1616) English dramatist, poet and actor

15 There are two tragedies in life. One is to lose your heart's desire. The other is to gain it.
Man and Superman (1903) **Shaw, George Bernard** (1856–1950) Irish socialist, writer, dramatist and critic

16 The stoical scheme of supplying our wants, by lopping off our desires, is like cutting off our feet when we want shoes.
Thoughts on Various Subjects (1711) **Swift, Jonathan** (1667–1745) Irish satirist, poet, essayist and cleric

17 The delight that consumes the desire,
The desire that outruns the delight.
'Dolores' (1866) **Swinburne, Algernon Charles** (1837–1909) English poet, critic, dramatist and letter writer
See also courtship; hope; love; men and women; passion; sex

DESTINY

1 Things are where things are, and, as fate has willed,
So shall they be fulfilled.
Agamemnon (trans. Browning) **Aeschylus** (525–456 BC) Greek dramatist and poet

2 Each man is the architect of his own destiny.
In Sallust, *Ad Caesarem* **Appius Claudius Caecus** (4th–3rd century BC) Roman censor

3 Yet they, believe me, who await
No gifts from chance, have conquered fate.
'Resignation' (1849) **Arnold, Matthew** (1822–1888) English poet, critic, essayist and educationist

4 That 'all that happens, happens as it should', if you observe carefully, you will find to be the case.
Meditations

5 Whatever may happen to you was prepared for you from all eternity; and the thread of causes was spinning from eternity both your being and this which is happening to you.
Meditations

6 Nothing happens to any thing which that thing is not made by nature to bear.
Meditations

7 All things from eternity are of similar forms and come round in a circle.
Meditations **Aurelius, Marcus** (121–180) Roman emperor and Stoic philosopher

8 If a man look sharply, and attentively, he shall see Fortune: for though she be blind, yet she is not invisible.
Essays (1625) **Bacon, Francis** (1561–1626) English philosopher, essayist, politician and courtier

9 Nothing more certain than incertainties;
Fortune is full of fresh variety:
Constant in nothing but inconstancy.
'The Shepherd's Content' (1594) **Barnfield, Richard** (1574–1627) English poet

10 What do I know of man's destiny? I could tell you more about radishes.
Six Residua (1978) **Beckett, Samuel** (1906–1989) Irish dramatist, writer and poet

11 Fate is not an eagle, it creeps like a rat.
The House in Paris (1935) **Bowen, Elizabeth** (1899–1973) Irish writer

12 We are puppets on strings worked by unknown forces; we ourselves are nothing, nothing!
Danton's Death (1835) **Büchner, Georg** (1813–1837) German playwright

13 The best-laid schemes o' mice an' men
Gang aft agley,
An' lea'e us nought but grief an' pain,
For promis'd joy!
'To a Mouse' (1785) **Burns, Robert** (1759–1796) Scottish poet and songwriter

14 The die is cast.
In Suetonius, *Lives of the Caesars* **Caesar, Gaius Julius** (c.102–44 BC) Roman statesman, historian and army commander. Remark on crossing the Rubicon

15 We make our friends, we make our enemies; but God makes our next-door neighbour.
Heretics (1905) **Chesterton, G.K.** (1874–1936) English writer, poet and critic

16 Which brings me to my conclusion upon Free Will and Predestination, namely – let the reader mark it – that they are identical.
My Early Life (1930)

17 I felt as if I were walking with destiny, and that all my past life had been but a preparation for this hour and this trial.
The Gathering Storm **Churchill, Sir Winston** (1874–1965) English Conservative Prime Minister

18 I feel that I am reserved for some end or other.
In Gleig, *The Life of Robert, First Lord Clive* (1848) **Clive, Lord** (1725–1774) English general, statesman and Indian administrator. Said when his pistol failed to go off twice, in his attempt to commit suicide

19 Whom the gods wish to destroy they first call promising.
Enemies of Promise (1938) **Connolly, Cyril** (1903–1974) English literary editor, writer and critic

20 We have no reliable guarantee that the afterlife will be any less exasperating than this one, have we?
Blithe Spirit (1941) **Coward, Sir Noël** (1899–1973) English dramatist, actor, producer and composer

21 Believe in fate, but lean forward where fate can see you.
Attr. **Crisp, Quentin** (1908–1999) English writer, publicist and model

22 The best of men cannot suspend their fate: The good die early, and the bad die late.
'Character of the late Dr S. Annesley' (1697) **Defoe, Daniel** (c.1661–1731) English writer and critic

23 Relations are made by fate, friends by choice.
Malheur et pitié (1803) **Delille, Abbé Jacques** (1738–1813) French poet and translator

24 Everything is ephemeral, both that which remembers and that which is remembered.
Meditations **Aurelius, Marcus** (121–180) Roman emperor and Stoic philosopher

25 I can enjoy her while she's kind;
But when she dances in the wind,
And shakes the wings, and will not stay,
I puff the prostitute away.
Sylvae (1685) **Dryden, John** (1631–1700) English poet, satirist, dramatist and critic. Of Fortune

26 'Character', says Novalis, in one of his questionable aphorisms – 'character is destiny.'
The Mill on the Floss (1860)

27 Among all forms of mistake, prophecy is the most gratuitous.
Middlemarch (1872) **Eliot, George** (1819–1880) English writer and poet

28 The bitterest tragic element in life to be derived from an intellectual source is the belief in a brute Fate or Destiny.
Natural History of Intellect (1893) **Emerson, Ralph Waldo** (1803–1882) US poet, essayist, transcendentalist and teacher

29 'Tis all a Chequer-board of Nights and Days
Where Destiny with Men for Pieces plays:
Hither and thither moves, and mates, and slays,
And one by one back in the Closet lays.
The Rubáiyát of Omar Khayyám (1859)

30 The Moving Finger writes; and, having writ,
Moves on: nor all thy Piety nor Wit
Shall lure it back to cancel half a Line,
Nor all thy Tears wash out a Word of it.
The Rubáiyát of Omar Khayyám (1859)
Fitzgerald, Edward (1809–1883) English poet, translator and letter writer

31 Tempt not the stars, young man, thou canst not play
With the severity of fate.
The Broken Heart (1633) **Ford, John** (c.1586–c.1640) English dramatist and poet

32 Chance might be God's pseudonym when He does not want to sign his name.
Le Jardin d'Epicure (1894) **France, Anatole** (1844–1924) French writer and critic

33 'Tis a gross error, held in schools,
That Fortune always favours fools.
Fables (1738) **Gay, John** (1685–1732) English poet, dramatist and librettist

34 Do not look back. And do not dream about the future, either. It will neither give you back the past, nor satisfy your other daydreams. Your duty, your reward – your destiny – are here and now.
Markings (1965) **Hammarskjöld, Dag** (1905–1961) Swedish statesman, Secretary-General of the United Nations

35 When good befalls a man he calls it Providence, when evil fate.
Vagabonds (1909) **Hamsun, Knut** (1859–1952) Norwegian novelist

36 There once was a man who said, 'Damn!
It is borne in upon me I am
An engine that moves
In predestinate grooves,
I'm not even a bus, I'm a tram.'
'Limerick' (1905) **Hare, Maurice Evan** (1886–1967) English limerick writer

37 I go the way that Providence bids me go with the certainty of a sleepwalker.
Speech, Munich, (1936) **Hitler, Adolf** (1889–1945) German Nazi dictator, born in Austria

38 You and I have been physically given two hands and two legs and half-decent brains. Some people have not been born like that for a reason. The karma is working from another lifetime. I have nothing to hide about that. It is not only people with disabilities. What you sow, you have to reap.
The Times, (1999) **Hoddle, Glenn** (1957–) English footballer and coach

39 Do not ask – it is forbidden to know – what end the gods have in store for me or for you.
Odes **Horace** (65–8 BC) Roman poet

40 Some people are so fond of ill-luck that they run half-way to meet it.
Wit and Opinions of Douglas Jerrold (1859) **Jerrold, Douglas William** (1803–1857) English dramatist, writer and wit

41 Blind Fortune still
Bestows her gifts on such as cannot use them.
Every Man out of His Humour (1599) **Jonson, Ben** (1572–1637) English dramatist and poet

42 Immortality is the only thing which doesn't tolerate being postponed.
Sayings and Contradictions (1909) **Kraus, Karl** (1874–1936) Austrian scientist, critic and poet

43 Fate keeps on happening.
Gentlemen Prefer Blondes (1925) **Loos, Anita** (1893–1981) US writer and screenwriter

44 He never would believe that Providence had sent a few men into the world ready booted and spurred to ride, and millions ready saddled and bridled to be ridden.
History of England (1849) **Macaulay, Lord** (1800–1859) English Liberal statesman, essayist and poet. Of Rumbold

45 Fortune, like a woman, is friendly to the young, because they show her less respect, they are more daring and command her with audacity.
The Prince (1532) **Machiavelli** (1469–1527) Florentine statesman, political theorist and historian

46 A throw of the dice will never eliminate chance.
Title of work, (1897) **Mallarmé, Stéphane** (1842–1898) French poet

47 Now and then
there is a person born
who is so unlucky
that he runs into accidents
which started out to happen
to somebody else.
archys life of mehitabel (1933) **Marquis, Don** (1878–1937) US columnist, satirist and poet

48 Chance is always powerful. Let your hook be always cast. In the pool where you least expect it, will be fish.
Attr. **Ovid** (43 BC–AD 18) Roman poet

49 It costs me never a stab nor squirm
To tread by chance upon a worm.
'Aha, my little dear,' I say,
'Your clan will pay me back one day.'
Sunset Gun, 'Thoughts for a Sunshiny Morning' **Parker, Dorothy** (1893–1967) US writer, poet, critic and wit

50 The only certainty is that nothing is certain.
Attr. **Pliny the Elder** (AD 23–79) Roman scholar

51 We may become the makers of our fate when we have ceased to pose as its prophets.
The Observer, (1975) **Popper, Sir Karl** (1902–1994) Austrian-born British philosopher

52 Sow an act, and you reap a habit. Sow a habit, and you reap a character. Sow a character, and you reap a destiny.
Attr. **Reade, Charles** (1814–1884) English novelist and dramatist

53 I don't believe in chance encounters.
Martereau **Sarraute, Nathalie** (1900–1999) French novelist

54 Fate shuffles the cards and we play.
'Aphorisms for Wisdom' (1851) **Schopenhauer, Arthur** (1788–1860) German philosopher

55 Let us sit and mock the good housewife Fortune from her wheel, that her gifts may henceforth be bestowed equally.
As You Like It, I.ii

56 A man that Fortune's buffets and rewards Hast ta'en with equal thanks; and blest are those
Whose blood and judgment are so well comeddled
That they are not a pipe for Fortune's finger
To sound what stop she please.
Hamlet, III.ii

57 O God! that one might read the book of fate,
And see the revolution of the times
Make mountains level, and the continent,
Weary of solid firmness, melt itself
Into the sea.
Henry IV, Part 2, III.i

58 Men at some time are masters of their fates:
The fault, dear Brutus, is not in our stars,
But in ourselves, that we are underlings.
Julius Caesar, I.ii

59 Fortune is merry,
And in this mood will give us any thing.
Julius Caesar, III.ii

60 There is a tide in the affairs of men
Which, taken at the flood, leads on to fortune;
Omitted, all the voyage of their life
Is bound in shallows and in miseries.
Julius Caesar, IV.iii.

61 As flies to wanton boys are we to th' gods –
They kill us for their sport.
King Lear, IV.i

62 Methinks I am a prophet new inspir'd,
And thus expiring do foretell of him:
His rash fierce blaze of riot cannot last,
For violent fires soon burn out themselves;
Small showers last long, but sudden storms are short;
He tires betimes that spurs too fast betimes.
Richard II, II.i

63 Since brass, nor stone, nor earth, nor boundless sea,
But sad mortality o'ersways their power,
How with this rage shall beauty hold a plea,
Whose action is no stronger than a flower?
Sonnet 65 **Shakespeare, William** (1564–1616) English dramatist, poet and actor

64 Each of us as he receives his private trouncings at the hands of fate is kept in good heart by the moth in his brother's parachute, and the scorpion in his neighbour's underwear.
A Resounding Tinkle (1958) **Simpson, N.F.** (1919–) English dramatist

65 We have to believe in free will. We've got no choice.
The Times, (1982) **Singer, Isaac Bashevis** (1904–1991) Polish-born US Yiddish writer

66 I have met with so many axidents, suprisals, and terrifications, that I am in a pafeck fantigo, and I believe I shall never be my own self again.
The Expedition of Humphry Clinker (1771) **Smollett, Tobias** (1721–1771) Scottish writer, satirist, historian, traveller and physician

67 Every Man is the Maker of his own Fortune.
The Tatler, 52, (1709) **Steele, Sir Richard** (1672–1729) Irish-born English writer, dramatist and politician

68 Fortune favours the brave.
Phormio **Terence** (c.190–159 BC) Carthaginian-born Roman dramatist

69 It is certain because it is impossible.
De Carne Christi **Tertullian** (c.AD 160–c.225) Carthaginian theologian

70 An elegant sufficiency, content, Retirement, rural quiet, friendship, books.
The Seasons (1746) **Thomson, James** (1700–1748) Scottish poet and dramatist

71 Hardly have I succeeded in reaching a definite position or in stopping at a familiar point of view, when fate drags me down from it.
Attr. **Turgenev, Ivan** (1818–1883) Russian writer and dramatist

72 Man is the shuttle, to whose winding quest
And passage through these looms
God order'd motion, but ordain'd no rest.
Silex Scintillans (1650–1655) **Vaughan, Henry** (1622–1695) Welsh poet and physician

73 Fortune's a right whore:
If she give aught, she deals it in small parcels,
That she may take away all at one swoop.
The White Devil (1612)

74 We are merely the stars' tennis-balls, struck and bandied,
Which way please them.
The Duchess of Malfi (1623) **Webster, John** (c.1580–c.1625) English dramatist
See also belief; faith

THE DEVIL

1 During the intervals [between dances] the devil is busy; yes, very busy, as sad experience proves, and on the way home in the small hours of the morning, he is busier still.
Statement on all-night dances, by Irish bishops, quoted in *Irish Catholic*, (1933)
Anonymous

2 All diseases of Christians are to be ascribed to demons; chiefly do they torment freshly-baptized Christians, yea, even the guiltless new-born infants.
Attr. **Augustine, Saint** (354–430) Numidian-born Christian theologian and philosopher

3 My dear brothers, never forget when you hear the progress of the Enlightenment praised, that the Devil's cleverest ploy is to persuade you that he doesn't exist.
Attr. **Baudelaire, Charles** (1821–1867) French poet, translator and critic

4 Through envy of the devil came death into the world.
Apocrypha, Wisdom of Solomon, 2:24

5 Resist the devil, and he will flee from you.
James, 4:7

6 Be sober, be vigilant; because your adversary the devil, as a roaring lion, walketh about, seeking whom he may devour.
Peter, 5:8 **The Bible (King James Version)**

7 Truly My Satan thou art but a Dunce
And dost not know the Garment from the Man.
Every Harlot was a Virgin once
Nor canst thou ever change Kate into Nan.
For the Sexes: The Gates of Paradise (c.1810) **Blake, William** (1757–1827) English poet, engraver, painter and mystic

8 Thus the devil played at chess with me, and yielding a pawn, thought to gain a queen of me, taking advantage of my honest endeavours.
Religio Medici (1643) **Browne, Sir Thomas** (1605–1682) English physician, author and antiquary

9 The devil's most devilish when respectable.
Aurora Leigh (1857) **Browning, Elizabeth Barrett** (1806–1861) English poet; wife of Robert Browning

10 An apology for the devil: it must be remembered that we have heard only one side of the case; God has written all the books.
The Note-Books of Samuel Butler (1912) **Butler, Samuel** (1835–1902) English writer, painter, philosopher and scholar

11 Sarcasm I now see to be, in general, the language of the Devil.

Sartor Resartus (1834) **Carlyle, Thomas** (1795–1881) Scottish historian, biographer, critic, and essayist

12 His jacket was red and his breeches were
blue,
And there was a hole where the tail came
through ...
'The Devil's Thoughts' (1799)

13 From his brimstone bed at break of day
A walking the Devil is gone,
To visit his snug little farm the Earth,
And see how his stock goes on ...
'The Devil's Thoughts' (1799) **Coleridge,
Samuel Taylor** (1772–1834) English poet,
philosopher and critic

14 The Devil watches all opportunities.
The Old Bachelor (1693) **Congreve, William**
(1670–1729) English dramatist

15 Wherever God erects a house of prayer,
The Devil always builds a chapel there;
And 'twill be found, upon examination,
The latter has the largest congregation.
The True-Born Englishman (1701) **Defoe, Daniel**
(c.1661–1731) English writer and critic

16 I think if the devil doesn't exist, and man
has created him, he has created him in his
own image and likeness.
The Brothers Karamazov (1880) **Dostoevsky,
Fyodor** (1821–1881) Russian writer

17 He did not see any reason why the devil
should have all the good tunes.
In Broome, *The Rev. Rowland Hill* (1881) **Hill,
Rowland** (1744–1833) English preacher and
hymn writer. Referring to his writing of
hymns

18 The devil is an optimist if he thinks he can
make people worse than they are.
In Thomas Szasz, *Anti-Freud: Karl Kraus's
Criticism of Psychoanalysis and Psychiatry* (1976)
Kraus, Karl (1874–1936) Austrian scientist,
critic and poet

19 It is no good casting out devils. They
belong to us, we must accept them and be
at peace with them.
'The Reality of Peace' (1936) **Lawrence, D.H.**
(1885–1930) English writer, poet and critic

20 The ancient prince of hell
Hath risen with purpose fell;
Strong mail of craft and power
He weareth in this hour;
On earth is not his fellow.
Hymn, (c.1527–1528; trans. Carlyle) **Luther,
Martin** (1483–1546) German Protestant
theologian and reformer

21 Here we may reign secure, and in my
choice
To reign is worth ambition though in Hell:
Better to reign in Hell, then serve in
Heav'n.
Paradise Lost (1667)

22 Abasht the Devil stood,
And felt how awful goodness is.
Paradise Lost (1667) **Milton, John** (1608–1674)
English poet, libertarian and pamphleteer

23 Courage, my friend, the devil is dead.
The Cloister and the Hearth (1861) **Reade,
Charles** (1814–1884) English novelist and
dramatist

24 Marry, he must have a long spoon that
must eat with the devil.
The Comedy of Errors, IV.iii

25 What, can the devil speak true?
Macbeth, I.iii

26 The devil can cite Scripture for his purpose.
The Merchant of Venice, I.iii **Shakespeare,
William** (1564–1616) English dramatist, poet
and actor

27 Is the devil to have all the passions as well
as all the good tunes?
Man and Superman (1903) **Shaw, George
Bernard** (1856–1950) Irish socialist, writer,
dramatist and critic

28 The devil, depend upon it, can sometimes
do a very gentlemanly thing.
New Arabian Nights (1882) **Stevenson, Robert
Louis** (1850–1894) Scottish writer, poet and
essayist

29 There is a dreadful Hell,
And everlasting pains;
There sinners must with devils dwell
In darkness, fire and chains.
Divine Songs for Children (1715) **Watts, Isaac**
(1674–1748) English hymn writer, poet and
minister

30 We are each our own devil, and we make
This world our hell.
The Duchess of Padua (1883) **Wilde, Oscar**
(1854–1900) Irish poet, dramatist, writer, critic
and wit
See also evil; God; religion; sin

DISABILITY

1 Cunning is the dark sanctuary of
incapacity.
Letter to his godson and heir (to be delivered
after his own death) **Chesterfield, Lord** (1694–
1773) English politician and letter writer

2 No, Sir, because I have time to think before
I speak, and don't ask impertinent
questions.
In Sir Francis Darwin, *Reminiscences of My
Father's Everyday Life* **Darwin, Erasmus** (1731–
1802) Dutch scholar and humanist. Reply
when asked whether he found his stammer
inconvenient

3 I don't think there is a distinction between
the body and soul. Which means that
although I may take pride in my
intelligence, I have to accept that the
disability is also part of me and not
something I can blame on a poor body I
happened to pick up at an auction.
Interview in *The Times*, (1998) **Hawking,
Stephen** (1942–) English theoretical physicist

4 Does it matter? – losing your legs? …
For people will always be kind,
And you need not show that you mind
When others come in after hunting
To gobble their muffins and eggs.
Does it matter? – losing your sight? …
There's such splendid work for the blind;
And people will always be kind,
As you sit on the terrace remembering
And turning your face to the light.
'Does it Matter?' (1917) **Sassoon, Siegfried**
(1886–1967) English poet and writer
See also health; suffering

DREAMS

1 Dreams and predictions of astrology …
ought to serve but for winter talk by the
fireside.
Essays (1625) **Bacon, Francis** (1561–1626)
English philosopher, essayist, politician and
courtier

2 If there were dreams to sell,
What would you buy?
Some cost a passing bell;
Some a light sigh,
That shakes from Life's fresh crown
Only a roseleaf down.
If there were dreams to sell,
Merry and sad to tell,
And the crier rung the bell,
What would you buy?
'Dream-Pedlary' (1851) **Beddoes, Thomas
Lovell** (1803–1849) English poet and dramatist

3 And he dreamed, and behold a ladder set
up on the earth, and the top of it reached
to heaven: and behold the angels of God
ascending and descending on it.
Genesis, 28:12

4 I will pour out my spirit upon all flesh; and
your sons and your daughters shall
prophesy, your old men shall dream
dreams, your young men shall see visions.
Joel, 2:28 **The Bible (King James Version)**

5 That children dream not in the first half
year, that men dream not in some
countries, are to me sick men's dreams,
dreams out of the ivory gate, and visions
before midnight.
In S. Wilkin (ed.), *Sir Thomas Browne's Works*
(1835) **Browne, Sir Thomas** (1605–1682)
English physician, author and antiquary

6 I dreamt that I dwelt in marble halls,
With vassals and serfs at my side.
The Bohemian Girl (1843) **Bunn, Alfred** (1796–
1860) English theatrical manager, librettist
and poet

7 Even in dreams doing good is not wasted.
Life is a Dream (1636)

8 For I see, since I am asleep, that I dream
while I am awake.
Life is a Dream (1636) **Calderón de la Barca,
Pedro** (1600–1681) Spanish dramatist and poet

9 I do not know whether I was then a man dreaming I was a butterfly, or whether I am now a butterfly dreaming I am a man.
Chuang Tse (1889) **Chuang Tse** (c.369–286 BC) Chinese philosopher

10 Dr Chandra, will I dream?
2001, A Space Odyssey (film, 1969) **Clarke, Arthur C.** (1917–) English writer. Voice of computer HAL 2000

11 Egypt's might is tumbled down
Down a-down the deeps of thought;
Greece is fallen and Troy town,
Glorious Rome hath lost her crown,
Venice' pride is nought.
But the dreams their children dreamed
Fleeting, unsubstantial, vain
Shadowy as the shadows seemed
Airy nothing, as they deemed,
These remain.
Poems (1894), 'Egypt's Might is Tumbled Down' **Coleridge, Mary** (1861–1907) British novelist and poet, great-niece of Samuel Taylor Coleridge

12 If a man could pass through Paradise in a dream, and have a flower presented to him as a pledge that his soul had really been there, and if he found that flower in his hand when he awoke – Aye, and what then?
Anima Poetae (1816) **Coleridge, Samuel Taylor** (1772–1834) English poet, philosopher and critic

13 So, if I dream I have you, I have you, For, all our joys are but fantastical.
Elegies (c.1600) **Donne, John** (1572–1631) English poet

14 With thousand such enchanting dreams, that meet
To make sleep not so sound, as sweet.
Hesperides (1648) **Herrick, Robert** (1591–1674) English poet, royalist and clergyman

15 No one should negotiate their dreams. Dreams must be free to flee and fly high. No government, no legislature, has a right to limit your dreams. You should never agree to surrender your dreams.
In *Playboy*, (1969) **Jackson, Jesse** (1941–) US clergyman and civil rights leader

16 All men dream: but not equally. Those who dream by night in the dusty recesses of their minds wake in the day to find that it was vanity; but the dreamers of the day are dangerous men, for they may act their dream with open eyes, to make it possible.
The Seven Pillars of Wisdom (1926) **Lawrence, T.E.** (1888–1935) British soldier, archaeologist, translator and writer; known as 'Lawrence of Arabia'

17 Nobody dast blame this man. A salesman is got to dream, boy. It comes with the territory.
Death of a Salesman (1949) **Miller, Arthur** (1915–2005) US dramatist and screenwriter

18 Those who have compared our life to a dream were, by chance, more right than they thought ... We are awake while sleeping, and sleeping while awake.
Essais (1580) **Montaigne, Michel de** (1533–1592) French essayist and moralist

19 Sink then dreamer into what might have been!
'Lethargy' **Patten, Brian** (1946–) British poet

20 They who dream by day are cognizant of many things which escape those who dream only by night.
Eleonora (1841)

21 All that we see or seem
Is but a dream within a dream.
'A Dream within a Dream' (1849) **Poe, Edgar Allan** (1809–1849) US poet, writer and editor

22 The hope I dreamed of was a dream,
Was but a dream; and now I wake,
Exceeding comfortless, and worn, and old,
For a dream's sake.
'Mirage' (1862) **Rossetti, Christina** (1830–1894) English poet

23 Only dreaming is of interest. What is life, without dreams? And I love the Far-away Princess.
La Princesse Lointaine (1895) **Rostand, Edmond** (1868–1918) French poet and dramatist

24 I have had dreams, and I've had nightmares. I overcame the nightmares because of my dreams.
Reader's Digest, (1980) **Salk, Jonas** (1914–1995) US virologist

25 O God, I could be bounded in a nutshell
and count myself a king of infinite space,
were it not that I have bad dreams.
Hamlet, II.ii

26 To die, to sleep;
To sleep, perchance to dream. Ay, there's
the rub;
For in that sleep of death what dreams may
come,
When we have shuffled off this mortal coil,
Must give us pause.
Hamlet, III.i

27 O, I have pass'd a miserable night,
So full of fearful dreams, of ugly sights,
That, as I am a Christian faithful man,
I would not spend another such a night
Though 'twere to buy a world of happy
days –
So full of dismal terror was the time!
Richard III, I.iv

28 Weary with toil, I haste me to my bed,
The dear repose for limbs with travel tired;
But then begins a journey in my head
To work my mind when body's work's
expired.
Sonnet 27

29 We are such stuff
As dreams are made on; and our little life
Is rounded with a sleep.
The Tempest, IV.i **Shakespeare, William** (1564–
1616) English dramatist, poet and actor

30 Looking into a dream is like looking into
the interior of a watch; you see the
processes at work by which results are
obtained. A man thus becomes his own
eavesdropper, he plays the spy on himself.
Hope and fear, and the other passions, are
all active; but the activity is uncontrolled by
the will, and in remembering dreams one
has the somewhat peculiar feeling of being
one's own spiritual anatomist.
On Dreams and Dreaming **Smith, Alexander**
(1830–1867) Scottish poet and writer

31 I dream for a living.
Time, (1985) **Spielberg, Steven** (1947–) US film
director and producer

32 Dreams are true while they last, and do we
not live in dreams?

'The Higher Pantheism' (1867) **Tennyson,
Alfred, Lord** (1809–1892) English lyric poet

33 Dreams come true; without that possibility,
nature would not incite us to have them.
Self-Consciousness: Memoirs (1989) **Updike,
John** (1932–) US writer, poet and critic

34 Two gates the silent house of Sleep adorn;
Of polished ivory this, that of transparent
horn:
True visions through transparent horn
arise;
Through polished ivory pass deluding lies.
Aeneid **Virgil** (70–19 BC) Roman poet

35 In dreams begins responsibility.
Responsibilities (1914) **Yeats, W.B.** (1865–1939)
Irish poet, dramatist, editor, writer and
senator
See also fantasy; imagination; sleep

DRINK, DRUGS AND DEBAUCHERY

1 I'm so holy that when I touch wine, it turns
into water.
Attr. in Compton Miller, *Who's Really Who*
(1983) **Aga Khan III** (1877–1957) Leader of
Ismaili Muslims. Justifying his liking for
alcohol

2 George Best, do you think, if you hadn't
had to do all that running around on a
football field, you wouldn't have got so
thirsty?
The Mrs Merton Show, (1995) **Aherne, Caroline**
(1963–) English comedian. As spoof chat-
show hostess, Mrs Merton to George Best,
Irish footballer renowned for his excessive
drinking

3 If all be true that I do think,
There are five reasons we should drink;
Good wine – a friend – or being dry –
Or lest we should be by and by –
Or any other reason why.
'Five Reasons for Drinking' (1689) **Aldrich,
Henry** (1647–1710) English scholar, divine and
composer of songs

4 A dusty thudding in his head made the scene before him beat like a pulse. His mouth had been used as a latrine by some small creature of the night and then as its mausoleum.
Lucky Jim (1958) **Amis, Kingsley** (1922–1995) English writer, poet and critic

5 It possesses many advantages over morphine ... it is not hypnotic and there is no danger of acquiring the habit.
Boston Medical Journal, (1900) The new drug in question was heroin

6 Choose Life, Not Drugs.
Scottish Health Education Council, *1980s*

7 The prospect that they could wreck their sex lives might just make them stop and think.
The British Medical Association, in *The Times,* (1999) On claims that smoking can make men impotent

8 Bring us in no browne bred, for that is made of brane,
Nor bring us in no white bred, for therein is no gane,
But bring us in good ale!
'Bring us in Good Ale'

9 I feel no pain dear mother now
But oh, I am so dry!
O take me to a brewery
And leave me there to die.
Parody of Edward Farmer, 'The Collier's Dying Child'

10 LSD melts your mind, not in your hand.

11 Reality is a crutch for people who can't handle drugs.
Anonymous

12 I am resolved to die in a tavern, so that wine will be very near to my dying mouth. Then the bands of angels will chant with greater joy 'May God forgive this drinker.'
The Confession of Golias **Archpoet of Cologne** (fl. c.1205) Poet

13 Many find it easier to abstain totally than to use moderation.
On the Good of Marriage **Augustine, Saint** (354–430) Numidian-born Christian theologian and philosopher

14 Let's not quibble! I'm the foe of moderation, the champion of excess. If I may lift a line from a die-hard whose identity is lost in the shuffle, 'I'd rather be strongly wrong than weakly right'.
Tallulah (1952)

15 Cocaine isn't habit-forming. I know, because I've been taking it for years.
Attr. **Bankhead, Tallulah** (1903–1968) US actress

16 *Fletcher:* I'd like to warn you, gentlemen, that this should be sipped delicately like a fine liqueur. It shouldn't be gulped down by the mugful. If you do that you will lose the flavour and the bouquet. You will also loose your power of speech.
Porridge, (1976) **Barker, Ronnie** (1929–2005) English comedian and scriptwriter. Fletcher launches his home-brewed hooch in Slade Prison

17 For when the wine is in, the wit is out.
Catechism (1560) **Becon, Thomas** (1512–1567) English Protestant divine

18 I only take a drink on two occasions – when I'm thirsty and when I'm not.
In McCann, *The Wit of Brendan Behan* **Behan, Brendan** (1923–1964) Irish dramatist, writer and Republican

19 There is no hangover on earth like the single malt hangover. It roars in the ears, burns in the stomach and sizzles in the brain like a short circuit. Death is the easy way out.
The Observer, (1991) **Bell, Ian** Scottish journalist

20 Strong Brother in God and last Companion: Wine.
Short Talks with the Dead and Others (1926) **Belloc, Hilaire** (1870–1953) English writer of verse, essayist and critic; Liberal MP

21 So who's in a hurry?
Attr. **Benchley, Robert** (1889–1945) US essayist, humorist and actor. Reply when asked if he realized that drinking was a slow death

22 It would be port if it could.
Attr. **Bentley, Richard** (1662–1742) English classical scholar. Of claret

23 *Debauchee*: One who has so earnestly pursued pleasure that he has had the misfortune to overtake it.
The Cynic's Word Book (1906) **Bierce, Ambrose** (1842–c.1914) US writer, verse writer and soldier

24 The shortest way out of Manchester is notoriously a bottle of Gordon's gin.
The Treasury of Humorous Quotations **Bolitho, William** (1890–1930) South African-born British writer

25 Good ale, the true and proper drink of Englishmen. He is not deserving of the name of Englishman who speaketh against ale, that is good ale.
Lavengro (1851) **Borrow, George** (1803–1881) English writer and linguist

26 All I can say is that drugs are a retreat. Artistic people are by nature so volatile, and if you're highly strung, which I am, you're vulnerable.
Attr. (1992) **Boy George** (1961–) English pop star, born George O'Dowd

27 When you stop drinking, you have to deal with this marvelous personality that started you drinking in the first place.
Table Money (1986) **Breslin, Jimmy** (1930–) US talk show host and columnist

28 I should like a great lake of ale
For the King of Kings.
The Feast of St Brigid of Kildare **Brigid of Kildare** (453–523) Irish abbess

29 Most British statesmen have either drunk too much or womanized too much. I never fell into the second category.
The Observer, (1974) **Brown, George** (1914–1985) English Conservative politician

30 I smoke 10 to 15 cigars a day: at my age I have to hold on to something.
Attr. **Burns, George** (1896–1996) US comedian

31 Freedom and whisky gang thegither,
Tak aff your dram!
'The Author's Earnest Cry and Prayer' (1786) **Burns, Robert** (1759–1796) Scottish poet and songwriter

32 Junk is the ideal product ... the ultimate merchandise. No sales talk necessary. The client will crawl through a sewer and beg to buy.
Naked Lunch (1959) **Burroughs, William S.** (1914–1999) US writer

33 I may not here omit those two main plagues, and common dotages of human kind, wine and women, which have infatuated and besotted myriads of people. They go commonly together.
Anatomy of Melancholy (1621) **Burton, Robert** (1577–1640) English clergyman and writer

34 Man, being reasonable, must get drunk;
The best of life is but intoxication:
Glory, the grape, love, gold, in these are sunk
The hopes of all men, and of every nation.
Don Juan (1824) **Byron, Lord** (1788–1824) English poet, satirist and traveller

35 The heart which grief hath canker'd
Hath one unfailing remedy – the Tankard.
'Beer' (1861)

36 How they who use fusees
All grow by slow degrees
Brainless as chimpanzees,
Meagre as lizards:
Go mad, and beat their wives;
Plunge (after shocking lives)
Razors and carving knives
Into their gizzards.
'Ode to Tobacco' (1861) **Calverley, C.S.** (1831–1884) English poet, parodist, scholar and lawyer

37 Under a bad cloak there is often a good drinker.
Don Quixote (1615) **Cervantes, Miguel de** (1547–1616) Spanish writer and dramatist

38 Alcohol is like love: the first kiss is magic, the second is intimate, the third is routine. After that you just take the girl's clothes off.
The Long Good-bye (1953) **Chandler, Raymond** (1888–1959) US crime writer

39 I gave up smoking at the age of 11. I had one or two strong ones behind the chicken run at school.
The Times, (1998) **Charles, Prince of Wales** (1948–) Son and heir of Elizabeth II and Prince Philip

40 For dronkenesse is verray sepulture
Of mannes wit and his discrecioun.
The Canterbury Tales (1387) **Chaucer, Geoffrey**
(c.1340–1400) English poet, public servant and
courtier

41 And Noah he often said to his wife when
he sat down to dine,
'I don't care where the water goes if it
doesn't get into the wine.'
The Flying Inn (1914) **Chesterton, G.K.** (1874–
1936) English writer, poet and critic

42 I should never be allowed out in private.
In B. Roberts, *Randolph: a Study of Churchill's
Son* (1984) **Churchill, Randolph** (1911–1968)
English journalist and writer. In a letter to a
hostess after ruining her dinner party with
one of his displays of drunken rudeness

43 I must point out that my rule of life
prescribed as an absolutely sacred rite
smoking cigars and also the drinking of
alcohol before, after, and if need be during
all meals and in the intervals between
them.
Triumph and Tragedy Said during a lunch with
the Arab leader Ibn Saud, when he heard that
the king's religion forbade smoking and
alcohol

44 And you, madam, are ugly. But I shall be
sober in the morning.
Attr. To Bessie Braddock MP who told him he
was drunk **Churchill, Sir Winston** (1874–1965)
English Conservative Prime Minister

45 He said later that the greatest pleasure he
ever knew in the world was when his eyes
met the eyes of a mate over the top of two
foaming glasses of beer.
In Search of Henry Lawson (1987) **Clark,
Manning** (1915–1991) Australian historian. Of
the Australian writer Henry Lawson

46 No man has a right to inflict the torture of
bad wine upon his fellow-creatures.
The Peripatetic Philosopher (1867–1870) **Clarke,
Marcus** (1846–1881) English-born Australian
writer

47 A well-balanced person has a drink in each
hand.
Gullible's Travels **Connolly, Billy** (1942–)
Scottish comedian and actor

48 One whisky is all right; two is too much;
three is too few.
A Taste of Scotch (1989) **Cooper, Derek** (1925–)
Scottish food writer and broadcaster.
Highland saying

49 All you need is love, love
or, failing that, alcohol.
Cope, Wendy (1945–) English poet. Variation
on a Lennon and McCartney song

50 Apart from cheese and tulips, the main
product of the country [Holland] is
advocaat, a drink made from lawyers.
The Sanity Inspector (1974) **Coren, Alan** (1938–)
British humorist, writer and broadcaster

51 Pernicious weed! whose scent the fair
annoys,
Unfriendly to society's chief joys,
Thy worst effect is banishing for hours
The sex whose presence civilizes ours.
'Conversation' (1782)

52 The pipe, with solemn interposing puff,
Makes half a sentence at a time enough;
The dozing sages drop the drowsy strain,
Then pause, and puff – and speak, and
pause again.
'Conversation' (1782) **Cowper, William** (1731–
1800) English poet, hymn writer and letter
writer

53 Lo! the poor toper whose untutor'd sense,
Sees bliss in ale, and can with wine
dispense;
Whose head proud fancy never taught to
steer,
Beyond the muddy ecstasies of beer.
Inebriety (1774) **Crabbe, George** (1754–1832)
English poet, clergyman, surgeon and
botanist

54 *Sam*: What will you have, Norm?
Norm: Well, I'm in a gambling mood,
Sammy. I'll take a glass of whatever comes
out of that tap.
Sam: Oh, looks like beer, Norm.
Norm: Call me Mister Lucky!
NBCTV's *Cheers*, (1985) **Danson, Ted** (1947–)
and **Wendt, George** (1948–) US actors

55 It is most absurdly said, in popular
language, of any man, that he is disguised
in liquor; for, on the contrary, most men
are disguised by sobriety.

Confessions of an English Opium Eater (1822)

56 Thou hast the keys of Paradise, oh just, subtle, and mighty opium!
Confessions of an English Opium Eater (1822) **De Quincey, Thomas** (1785–1859) English writer

57 Then trust me, there's nothing like drinking
So pleasant on this side the grave;
It keeps the unhappy from thinking,
And makes e'en the valiant more brave.
'Nothing like Grog' **Dibdin, Charles** (1745–1814) English songwriter, dramatist and actor

58 It's my opinion, sir, that this meeting is drunk, sir.
The Pickwick Papers (1837)

59 Bring in the bottled lightning, a clean tumbler, and a corkscrew.
Nicholas Nickleby (1839) **Dickens, Charles** (1812–1870) English writer

60 'I rather like bad wine,' said Mr Mountchesney; 'one gets so bored with good wine.'
Sybil (1845) **Disraeli, Benjamin** (1804–1881) English statesman and writer

61 Come quickly, I am tasting stars!
Attr. **Dom Pérignon** (c.1638–1715) Benedictine monk. On discovering champagne

62 A little monograph on the ashes of one hundred and forty different varieties of pipe, cigar, and cigarette tobacco.
'The Boscombe Valley Mystery' (1892) **Doyle, Sir Arthur Conan** (1859–1930) Scottish writer and war correspondent

63 There is wan thing an' on'y wan thing to be said in favour iv dhrink, an' that is that it has caused manny a lady to be loved that otherwise might've died single.
Mr Dooley Says (1910) **Dunne, Finley Peter** (1867–1936) US writer

64 No other human being, no woman, no poem or music, book or painting can replace alcohol in its power to give man the illusion of real creation.
Practicalities (1987) **Duras, Marguerite** (1914–1996) French author and filmmaker

65 I have known many persons who turned their gold into smoke, but you are the first to turn smoke into gold.
In Chamberlin, *The Sayings of Queen Elizabeth* (1923) **Elizabeth I** (1533–1603) Queen of England. To Sir Walter Raleigh

66 It was a brilliant affair; water flowed like champagne.
Attr. **Evarts, William Maxwell** (1818–1901) US lawyer and statesman. Of a dinner given by US President and temperance advocate Rutherford B. Hayes

67 I have fed purely upon ale; I have eat my ale, drank my ale, and I always sleep upon ale.
The Beaux' Stratagem (1707) **Farquhar, George** (1678–1707) Irish dramatist

68 They say that drinking interferes with your sex life. I figure it's the other way around
Attr. **Fields, W.C.** (1880–1946) US comedian and film actor

69 Drink! for you know not whence you came, nor why:
Drink! for you know not why you go, nor where.
The Rubáiyát of Omar Khayyám (1859)

70 And much as Wine has play'd the Infidel, And robb'd me of my Robe of Honour – Well,
I often wonder what the Vintners buy
One half so precious as the Goods they sell.
The Rubáiyát of Omar Khayyám (1859)

71 Here with a Loaf of Bread beneath the Bough,
A Flask of Wine, a Book of Verse – and Thou
Beside me singing in the Wilderness –
And Wilderness is Paradise enow.
The Rubáiyát of Omar Khayyám (1859) **Fitzgerald, Edward** (1809–1883) English poet, translator and letter writer

72 First you take a drink, then the drink takes a drink, then the drink takes you.
In Jules Feiffer, *Ackroyd* **Fitzgerald, F. Scott** (1896–1940) US writer

73 And he that will go to bed sober,
Falls with the leaf still in October.

The Bloody Brother (1616) **Fletcher, John** (1579–1625) English dramatist

74 Bacchus hath drowned more men than Neptune.
Gnomologia, (1732) **Fuller, Thomas** (1654–1734) English churchman and antiquary

75 He could take nothing for dinner but a partridge, with an imperial pint of champagne.
The Man of Property (1906) **Galsworthy, John** (1867–1933) English writer and dramatist

76 Whether we can afford it or no, we must have superfluities.
Polly (1729) **Gay, John** (1685–1732) English poet, dramatist and librettist

77 The domestic use of tea is a powerful champion able to encounter alcoholic drink in a fair field and throw it in a fair fight.
Budget speech, (1882) **Gladstone, William** (1809–1898) English statesman and reformer

78 Let school-masters puzzle their brain,
With grammar, and nonsense, and learning,
Good liquor, I stoutly maintain,
Gives genius a better discerning.
She Stoops to Conquer (1773) **Goldsmith, Oliver** (c.1728–1774) Irish dramatist, poet and writer

79 *Homer:* To alcohol! The cause of – and solution to – all life's problems!
The Simpsons, TV cartoon series **Groening, Matt** (1954–) US cartoonist. In an episode scripted by John Schwartzelder

80 *Woody:* How would a beer feel, Mr Peterson?
Norm: Pretty nervous if I was in the room.
NBCTV's *Cheers* **Harrelson, Woody** (1961–) and **Wendt, George** (1948–) US actors

81 Licker talks mighty loud w'en it git loose fum de jug.
Uncle Remus (1881) **Harris, Joel Chandler** (1848–1908) US author

82 What a blessing this smoking is! perhaps the greatest that we owe to the discovery of America.
Friends in Council (1859) **Helps, Sir Arthur** (1813–1875) English historian and writer

83 Drink not the third glasse, – which thou canst not tame
When once it is within thee.
The Temple (1633) **Herbert, George** (1593–1633) English poet and priest

84 For any ceremonial purposes the otherwise excellent liquid, water, is unsuitable in colour and other respects.
Uncommon Law (1935) **Herbert, Sir A.P.** (1890–1971) English humorist, writer, dramatist and politician

85 If you think dope is for kicks and for thrills, you're out of your mind. There are more kicks to be had in a good case of paralytic polio or by living in an iron lung.
Lady Sings the Blues (1956) **Holiday, Billie** (1915–1959) US singer

86 Man wants but little drink below,
But wants that little strong.
'A Song of other Days' (1848) **Holmes, Oliver Wendell** (1809–1894) US physician, poet, writer and scientist

87 Firm and erect the Caledonian stood,
Old was his mutton, and his claret good;
Let him drink port, an English statesman cried –
He drank the poison and his spirit died.
In Mackenzie, *An Account of the Life and Writings of John Home, Esq.* (1822) **Home, John** (1722–1808) Scottish clergyman and dramatist

88 Our country has deliberately undertaken a great social and economic experiment, noble in motive and far-reaching in purpose.
Letter to Senator Borah, (1928) **Hoover, Herbert Clark** (1874–1964) US Republican statesman and President. On the Eighteenth Amendment, enacting Prohibition

89 Oh many a peer of England brews
Livelier liquor than the Muse,
And malt does more than Milton can
To justify God's ways to man.
Ale, man, ale's the stuff to drink
For fellows whom it hurts to think.
A Shropshire Lad (1896) **Housman, A.E.** (1859–1936) English poet and scholar

90 Real ale is an odd concept, linked more to an imagined real pub with real fire and real bread and cheese, as much as to a scientific definition of a brewing process.
New Statesman and Society, (1989) **Howkins, Alun** (1947–) British historian and writer

91 It is difficult to speak about proper beer, because its friends (just like the friends of G.K. Chesterton) are its worst enemies. 'Real ale' fans are just like train-spotters – only drunk.
The Spectator, (1992) **Howse, Christopher**

92 They who drink beer will think beer.
The Sketch Book (1820) **Irving, Washington** (1783–1859) US writer and diplomat

93 My idea of a fine wine was one that merely stained my teeth without stripping the enamel.
Falling Towards England (Unreliable Memoirs II) **James, Clive** (1939–) Australian-born, UK-based TV critic and presenter

94 A custom loathesome to the eye, hateful to the nose, harmful to the brain, dangerous to the lungs, and in the black, stinking fume thereof, nearest resembling the horrible Stygian smoke of the pit that is bottomless.
A Counterblast to Tobacco (1604)

95 Herein is not only a great vanity, but a great contempt of God's good gifts, that the sweetness of man's breath, being a good gift of God, should be wilfully corrupted by this stinking smoke.
A Counterblast to Tobacco (1604)

96 A branch of the sin of drunkenness, which is the root of all sins.
A Counterblast to Tobacco (1604) **James VI of Scotland and I of England** (1566–1625) King of Scotland from 1567 and of England from 1603

97 If merely 'feeling good' could decide, drunkenness would be the supremely valid human experience.
Varieties of Religious Experience (1902) **James, William** (1842–1910) US psychologist and philosopher

98 Come, let me know what it is that makes a Scotchman happy!

In Boswell, *Journal of a Tour to the Hebrides* (1785) Calling for a gill of whisky

99 Claret is the liquor for boys; port for men; but he who aspires to be a hero must drink brandy.
In Boswell, *The Life of Samuel Johnson* (1791)

100 Wine gives a man nothing. It neither gives him knowledge nor wit; it only animates a man, and enables him to bring out what a dread of the company has repressed.
In Boswell, *The Life of Samuel Johnson* (1791)

101 He said that few people had intellectual resources sufficient to forgo the pleasures of wine. They would not otherwise contrive to fill the interval between dinner and supper.
In Boswell, *The Life of Samuel Johnson* (1791)

102 A man who exposes himself when he is intoxicated, has not the art of getting drunk.
In Boswell, *The Life of Samuel Johnson* (1791) **Johnson, Samuel** (1709–1784) English lexicographer, poet, critic, conversationalist and essayist

103 Ods me, I marvel what pleasure or felicity they have in taking their roguish tobacco. It is good for nothing but to choke a man, and fill him full of smoke and embers.
Every Man in His Humour (1598)

104 I do hold it, and will affirm it before any prince in Europe, to be the most sovereign and precious weed that ever the earth rendered to the use of man.
Every Man in His Humour (1598)

105 Neither do thou lust after that tawney weed tobacco.
Bartholomew Fair (1614) **Jonson, Ben** (1572–1637) English dramatist and poet

106 I was blue mouldy for the want of that pint. Declare to God I could hear it hit the pit of my stomach with a click.
Ulysses (1922) **Joyce, James** (1882–1941) Irish writer

107 The Finns have a very different alcohol culture from other European countries. Basically, it's nothing to do with socialising – it's about getting drunk.

Daily Mail, (1996) **Junell, Thomas** Host of Finland's seaborne drinking championships

108 Every form of addiction is a bad thing, irrespective of whether it is to alcohol, morphine or idealism.
Memories, Dreams, Thoughts (1962) **Jung, Carl Gustav** (1875–1961) Swiss psychiatrist and pupil of Freud

109 In the 1960s it was almost compulsory to drink vodka.
The Times, (1998) **Kamprad, Ingvar** (1926–) Swedish businessman; founder of IKEA. Putting his alcohol problems down to frequent business trips to Poland

110 Souls of poets dead and gone,
What Elysium have ye known,
Happy field or mossy cavern,
Choicer than the Mermaid Tavern?
Have ye tippled drink more fine
Than mine host's Canary wine?
'Lines on the Mermaid Tavern' (1818)

111 O for a beaker full of the warm South,
Full of the true, the blushful Hippocrene,
With beaded bubbles winking at the brim,
And purple-stainèd mouth;
That I might drink, and leave the world unseen;
And with thee fade away into the forest dim.
'Ode to a Nightingale' (1819) **Keats, John** (1795–1821) English poet

112 Even though a number of people have tried, no one has yet found a way to drink for a living.
Poor Richard (1963) **Kerr, Jean** (1923–2003) US writer and dramatist

113 And a woman is only a woman, but a good cigar is a Smoke.
'The Betrothed' (1886) **Kipling, Rudyard** (1865–1936) Indian-born British poet and writer

114 It is now proved beyond doubt that smoking is one of the leading causes of statistics.
Attr. **Knebel, Fletcher** (1911–1993) US journalist and author

115 This very night I am going to leave off tobacco! Surely there must be some other world in which this unconquerable purpose shall be realized. The soul hath not her generous aspirings implanted in her in vain.
Letter to Thomas Manning, (1815)

116 Dr Parr ... asked him, how he had acquired his power of smoking at such a rate? Lamb replied, 'I toiled after it, sir, as some men toil after virtue.'
In Talfourd, *Memoirs of Charles Lamb* (1892)

117 May my last breath be drawn through a pipe and exhaled in a pun.
In Wintle and Kenin, *Dictionary of Biographical Quotations* **Lamb, Charles** (1775–1834) English essayist, critic and letter writer

118 Frenchmen drink wine just like we used to drink water before Prohibition.
In R.E. Drennan, *Wit's End* **Lardner, Ring** (1885–1933) US humorist and writer

119 Just a wee deoch-an-doruis
Before we gang awa' ...
If y' can say
It's a braw brecht moonlecht necht,
Yer a' recht, that's a'.
Song, (1912) **Lauder, Sir Harry** (1870–1950) Scottish music-hall entertainer

120 Beer makes you feel as you ought to feel without beer.
In David Low, *Low's Autobiography* **Lawson, Henry** (1867–1922) Australian writer and poet

121 You'd be surprised how much fun you can have sober. When you get the hang of it.
In *Days of Wine and Roses* (film, 1962) **Lemmon, Jack** (1925–2001) US actor

122 Death by drunken driving is a socially acceptable form of homicide.
San José Mercury, (April 1981) **Lightner, Candy** (1946–) US estate agent and founder of MADD (Mothers Against Drunk Driving)

123 'You ain't got any tobacco,' he said scornfully to Bunyip Bluegum. 'I can see that at a glance, You're one of the non-smoking sort, all fur and feathers.'
The Magic Pudding (1918) **Lindsay, Norman** (1879–1969) Australian artist and writer

124 We are fighting Germany, Austria, and drink, and so far as I can see the greatest of these deadly foes is drink.
Speech, (1915) **Lloyd George, David** (1863–1945) British Liberal statesman. To a deputation of ship owners urging a campaign for prohibition during the First World War

125 Love makes the world go round? Not at all. Whisky makes it go round twice as fast.
Whisky Galore (1947) **Mackenzie, Sir Compton** (1883–1972) Scottish writer and broadcaster

126 I've smoked two joints in my life. Someone handed me cocaine at a party in a dish with a gold spoon. I thought it was Sweet 'n' Low and put it in my coffee.
Attr. **Maclaine, Shirley** (1934–) US actress

127 If die I must, let me die drinking in an inn.
De Nugis Curialium (1182) **Map, Walter** (c.1140– c.1209) Welsh clergyman and writer

128 I feel sorry for people who don't drink. When they wake up in the morning, that's the best they are going to feel all day.
Attr.

129 You're not drunk if you can lie on the floor without holding on.
Attr. **Martin, Dean** (1917–1995) US film actor and singer

130 I was T.T. until prohibition.
Attr. **Marx, Groucho** (1895–1977) US comedian

131 I've made it a rule never to drink by daylight and never to refuse a drink after dark.
New York Post, (1945) **Mencken, H.L.** (1880– 1956) US writer, critic, philologist and satirist

132 Give us the luxuries of life, and we will dispense with its necessities.
In Oliver Wendell Holmes, *Autocrat of the Breakfast Table* (1857–1858) **Motley, John Lothrop** (1814–1877) US diplomat and historian

133 Candy
Is dandy
But liquor
Is quicker.
'Reflections on Ice-Breaking' (1931) **Nash, Ogden** (1902–1971) US poet

134 This vice brings in one hundred million francs in taxes every year. I will certainly forbid it at once – as soon as you can name a virtue that brings in as much revenue.
In Hoffmeister, *Anekdotenschatz* **Napoleon III** (1808–1873) French emperor. On being asked to ban smoking

135 God grant me the serenity to accept the things I cannot change, the courage to change the things I can, and the wisdom to distinguish the one from the other.
Prayer adopted by Alcoholics Anonymous, attributed to but not accepted by Niebuhr **Niebuhr, Reinhold** (1892–1971) US Protestant theologian and writer

136 When things go wrong and will not come right,
Though you do the best you can,
When life looks black as the hour of night –
A PINT OF PLAIN IS YOUR ONLY MAN.
At Swim-Two-Birds (1939) **O'Brien, Flann** (1911–1966) Irish novelist and journalist

137 I can honestly say, all the bad things that ever happened to me were directly attributed to drugs and alcohol. I mean, I would never urinate at the Alamo at nine o'clock in the morning dressed in a woman's evening dress sober.
MTV News, (1992) **Osbourne, Ozzy** (1948–) English rock musician and TV personality

138 A torchlight procession marching down your throat.
Attr. **O'Sullivan, John L.** (1813–1895) US editor and diplomat. Of whisky

139 Milk of the elderly.
The Globe and Mail, (1988) **Osler, Sir William** (1849–1919) Canadian physician. His description of alcohol

140 Too much and too little wine. Give him none, he cannot find truth; give him too much, the same.
Pensées, (1670) **Pascal, Blaise** (1623–1662) French philosopher and scientist

141 There are two reasons for drinking; one is, when you are thirsty, to cure it; the other, when you are not thirsty, to prevent it ... Prevention is better than cure.
Melincourt (1817) **Peacock, Thomas Love** (1785– 1866) English writer and poet

142 In vino veritas. *(Wine brings out the truth)*
Historia Naturalis **Pliny the Elder** (AD 23–79)
Roman scholar

143 It is WRONG to do what everyone else
does – namely, to hold the wine list just
out of sight, look for the second cheapest
claret on the list, and say, 'Number 22,
please'.
One-Upmanship (1952)

144 A good general rule is to state that the
bouquet is better than the taste, and vice
versa.
One-Upmanship (1952) **Potter, Stephen** (1900–
1969) English writer, critic and lecturer

145 There are better things in life than alcohol,
but it makes up for not having them.
Attr. **Pratchett, Terry** (1948–) English author
and humorist

146 I hate a man with a memory at a drinking
bout.
Greek **Proverb**

147 I drink for the thirst to come.
Gargantua (1534)

148 No noble man ever hated good wine.
Gargantua (1534)

149 Getting up in the morning is no pleasure;
Drinking in the morning is the best.
Gargantua (1534) **Rabelais, François** (c.1494–
c.1553) French monk, physician, satirist and
humanist

150 Stars who debauch themselves, get
addicted to drugs then kick them get all
the praise. Wouldn't you think that people
who have never been addicted should be
praised all the more?
The Observer Review, (1996) **Richard, Cliff**
(1940–) English singer

151 No doubt you will urge the British Legion
to drop their Poppy appeal in case
everyone starts taking opium.
Roddick, Anita (1942–) British
businesswoman, founder of The Body Shop.
Response to criticism from Tory MP Ann
Widdecombe that The Body Shop's new
hemp-derived products will attract youth to
cannabis

152 Drunkenness is temporary suicide: the
happiness that it brings is merely negative,
a momentary cessation of unhappiness.
The Conquest of Happiness (1930) **Russell,
Bertrand** (1872–1970) English philosopher,
mathematician, essayist and social reformer

153 No, thank you, I was born intoxicated.
In L. Copeland, *10,000 Jokes, Toasts, and Stories*
Russell, George William (1867–1935) Irish
poet. Refusing a drink that was offered him

154 It is the unbroken testimony of all history
that alcoholic liquors have been used by
the strongest, wisest, handsomest, and in
every way best races of all times.
Attr. **Saintsbury, George** (1845–1933) English
critic and historian

155 By insisting on having your bottle pointing
to the north when the cork is being drawn,
and calling the waiter Max, you may induce
an impression on your guests which hours
of laboured boasting might be powerless
to achieve. For this purpose, however, the
guests must be chosen as carefully as the
wine.
The Chronicles of Clovis (1911) **Saki** (1870–1916)
Burmese-born British writer

156 'My doctor has always told me to smoke.
He explains himself thus: 'Smoke, my
friend. If you don't, someone else will
smoke in your place.'
Mémoires d'un amnésique (1924) **Satie, Erik**
(1866–1925) French composer

157 'Tis not the drinking that is to be blamed,
but the excess.
Table Talk (1689) **Selden, John** (1584–1654)
English historian, jurist and politician

158 Drunkenness doesn't create vices, but it
brings them to the fore.
Letters to Lucilius, (100 AD) **Seneca** (c.4 BC–AD
65) Roman philosopher, poet, dramatist,
essayist, rhetorician and statesman

159 Drink, sir, is a great provoker of three
things – nose-painting, sleep, and urine.
Lechery, sir, it provokes, and unprovokes: it
provokes the desire, but it takes away the
performance.
Macbeth, II.iii

160 They are as sick that surfeit with too much as they that starve with nothing. It is no mean happiness, therefore, to be seated in the mean: superfluity comes sooner by white hairs, but competency lives longer.
The Merchant of Venice, I.ii

161 I have very poor and unhappy brains for drinking; I could well wish courtesy would invent some other custom of entertainment.
Othello, II.iii

162 I hate ingratitude more in a man
Than lying, vainness, babbling drunkenness,
Or any taint of vice whose strong corruption
Inhabits our frail blood.
Twelfth Night, III.iv **Shakespeare, William** (1564–1616) English dramatist, poet and actor

163 I'm only a beer teetotaller, not a champagne teetotaller.
Candida (1898)

164 Alcohol is a very necessary article … It enables Parliament to do things at eleven at night that no sane person would do at eleven in the morning.
Major Barbara (1907) **Shaw, George Bernard** (1856–1950) Irish socialist, writer, dramatist and critic

165 A man may surely be allowed to take a glass of wine by his own fireside.
In Moore, *Memoirs of the Life of Sheridan* (1825) At a coffee house, during the fire which destroyed his Drury Lane theatre, 1809

166 Well, then, my stomach must just digest in its waistcoat.
In L. Harris, *The Fine Art of Political Wit* (1965) On being warned that his drinking would destroy the coat of his stomach **Sheridan, Richard Brinsley** (1751–1816) Irish dramatist, politician and orator

167 Smoking kills. If you're killed, you've lost a very important part of your life.
Remark, quoted in *The Observer*, (1998) **Shields, Brooke** (1965–) US film actress

168 Another little drink wouldn't do us any harm.

'Scotch Rhapsody' (1922) **Sitwell, Dame Edith** (1887–1964) English poet, anthologist, critic and biographer

169 But I'm not so think as you drunk I am.
'Ballade of Soporific Absorption' (1931) **Squire, Sir J.C.** (1884–1958) English poet, critic, writer and editor

170 Fifteen men on the dead man's chest
Yo-ho-ho, and a bottle of rum!
Drink and the devil had done for the rest –
Yo-ho-ho, and a bottle of rum!
Treasure Island (1883) **Stevenson, Robert Louis** (1850–1894) Scottish writer, poet and essayist

171 I can not eat but little meat,
My stomach is not good;
But sure I think, that I can drink
With him that wears a hood.
Though I go bare, take ye no care,
I am nothing a-cold:
I stuff my skin, so full within,
Of jolly good ale and old.
Gammer Gurton's Needle, song **Stevenson, William** (c.1546–1575) English scholar

172 Back and side go bare, go bare,
Both foot and hand go cold;
But, belly, God send thee good ale enough,
Whether it be new or old.
Gammer Gurton's Needle, song **Still, John** (c.1543–c.1608) English clergyman

173 Whipping and abuse are like laudanum; you have to double the dose as the sensibilities decline.
Uncle Tom's Cabin (1852) **Stowe, Harriet Beecher** (1811–1896) US writer and reformer

174 Champagne certainly gives one werry gentlemanly ideas, but for a continuance, I don't know but I should prefer mild hale.
Jorrocks's Jaunts and Jollities (1838) **Surtees, R.S.** (1805–1864) English writer

175 We were to do more business after dinner; but after dinner is after dinner – an old saying and a true, 'much drinking, little thinking'.
Journal to Stella, (1711) **Swift, Jonathan** (1667–1745) Irish satirist, poet, essayist and cleric

176 There are two things that will be believed of any man whatsoever, and one of them is that he has taken to drink.

Penrod (1914) **Tarkington, Booth** (1869–1946)
US writer and dramatist

177 My view is that the golden rule in life is
never to have too much of anything.
Andria **Terence** (c.190–159 BC) Carthaginian-
born Roman dramatist

178 Yes, there's never enough.
Daily Mail, (1996) **Thatcher, Denis** (1915–2003)
English businessman, husband of Margaret
Thatcher. Reply to someone who asked if he
had a drinking problem

179 An alcoholic is someone you don't like who
drinks as much as you do.
Attr. **Thomas, Dylan** (1914–1953) Welsh poet,
writer and radio dramatist

180 I smoked my first cigarette and kissed my
first woman on the same day. I have never
had time for tobacco since.
The Observer, (1946) **Toscanini, Arturo** (1867–
1957) Italian conductor

181 I've done it a hundred times!
Attr. **Twain, Mark** (1835–1910) US humorist,
writer, journalist and lecturer. Saying how
easy it is to give up smoking

182 The superfluous, a very necessary thing.
Le Mondain (1736) **Voltaire** (1694–1778) French
philosopher, dramatist, poet, historian, writer
and critic

183 Never turn down a drink, unless it is of
local manufacture.
The Times, (1999) **Walden, George** (1939–)
British Conservative politician and diplomat.
Advice for those travelling with the Queen

184 I prefer temperance hotels – although they
sell worse kinds of liquor than any other
kind of hotels.
Attr. **Ward, Artemus** (1834–1867) US humorist,
journalist, editor and lecturer

185 A cigarette is the perfect type of a perfect
pleasure. It is exquisite, and it leaves one
unsatisfied. What more can one want?
The Picture of Dorian Gray (1891)

186 Moderation is a fatal thing, Lady
Hunstanton. Nothing succeeds like excess.
A Woman of No Importance (1893)

187 I have made an important discovery ... that
alcohol, taken in sufficient quantities,
produces all the effects of intoxication.
Attr. **Wilde, Oscar** (1854–1900) Irish poet,
dramatist, writer, critic and wit

188 I hadn't the heart to touch my breakfast. I
told Jeeves to drink it himself.
My Man Jeeves (1919) **Wodehouse, P.G.** (1881–
1975) English humorist and writer

189 It took a lot of bottle for Tony Adams to
own up.
Attr. **Wright, Ian** (1963–) English footballer.
On his Arsenal teammate's alcoholism

190 Your lips, on my own, when they printed
'Farewell',
Had never been soiled by the 'beverage of
hell';
But they come to me now with the
bacchanal sign,
And the lips that touch liquor must never
touch mine.
'The lips that touch liquor must never touch
mine' (c.1870) **Young, George W.** (1846–1919)
British writer

DUTY

1 Straight is the line of Duty
Curved is the line of Beauty
Follow the first and thou shalt see
The second ever following thee.
Anonymous

2 Fear God, and keep his commandments:
for this is the whole duty of man.
Ecclesiastes, 12:13 **The Bible (King James
Version)**

3 *Duty*: That which sternly impels us in the
direction of profit, along the line of desire.
The Enlarged Devil's Dictionary (1967) **Bierce,
Ambrose** (1842–c.1914) US writer, verse writer
and soldier

4 From a very early age, I had imbibed the
opinion, that it was every man's duty to do
all that lay in his power to leave his country
as good as he had found it.
Political Register, (1832) **Cobbett, William** (1762–
1835) English politician, reformer, writer,
farmer and army officer

5 Do your duty, and put yourself into the hands of the gods.
Horace (1640) **Corneille, Pierre** (1606–1684) French dramatist, poet and lawyer

6 She, stirred somewhat beyond her wont, and taking as her text the three words which have been used so often as the inspiring trumpet-calls of men – the words God, Immortality, Duty – pronounced, with terrible earnestness, how inconceivable was the first, how unbelievable the second, and yet how peremptory and absolute the third. Never, perhaps, have sterner accents affirmed the sovereignty of impersonal and unrecompensing Law.
In F.W.H. Myers, *George Eliot* (1881) **Eliot, George** (1819–1880) English writer and poet

7 So nigh is grandeur to our dust,
So near is God to man,
When Duty whispers low, Thou must,
The youth replies, I can.
May-Day (1867) **Emerson, Ralph Waldo** (1803–1882) US poet, essayist, transcendentalist and teacher

8 When I'm not thank'd at all, I'm thank'd enough,
I've done my duty, and I've done no more.
Tom Thumb the Great (1731) **Fielding, Henry** (1707–1754) English writer, dramatist and journalist

9 Duty is what no one else will do at the moment.
Offshore **Fitzgerald, Penelope** (1916–2000) English novelist

10 The question is, had he not been a thing of beauty,
Would she be swayed by quite as keen a sense of duty?
The Pirates of Penzance (1880) **Gilbert, W.S.** (1836–1911) English dramatist, humorist and librettist

11 You can, for you ought to!
'An eighth' (1796); *written with Schiller* **Goethe** (1749–1832) German poet, writer, dramatist and scientist

12 No personal consideration should stand in the way of performing a public duty.
Note on letter, (1875) **Grant, Ulysses S.** (1822–1885) US President, general and memoirist

13 I slept, and dreamed that life was Beauty;
I woke, and found that life was Duty.
'Beauty and Duty' (1840) **Hooper, Ellen Sturgis** (1816–1841) US poet and hymn writer

14 What's a man's first duty? The answer's brief: To be himself.
Peer Gynt (1867) **Ibsen, Henrik** (1828–1906) Norwegian writer, dramatist and poet

15 It is our first duty to serve society, and, after we have done that, we may attend wholly to the salvation of our own souls. A youthful passion for abstracted devotion should not be encouraged.
In Boswell, *The Life of Samuel Johnson* (1791) **Johnson, Samuel** (1709–1784) English lexicographer, poet, critic, conversationalist and essayist

16 Duty then is the sublimest word in our language. Do your duty in all things. You cannot do more. You should never wish to do less.
Inscription in the Hall of Fame **Lee, Robert E.** (1807–1870) US general

17 Let us have faith that right makes might; and in that faith let us to the end, dare to do our duty as we understand it.
Speech, (1860) **Lincoln, Abraham** (1809–1865) US statesman and President

18 If we believe a thing to be bad, and if we have a right to prevent it, it is our duty to try to prevent it and to damn the consequences.
Speech, (1909) **Milner, Alfred** (1854–1925) British statesman and colonial administrator

19 England expects every man to do his duty.
In Southey, *The Life of Nelson* (1860) **Nelson, Lord** (1758–1805) English admiral. Nelson's last signal at the Battle of Trafalgar, 1805

20 A thing of duty is a boy for ever.
Attr. **O'Brien, Flann** (1911–1966) Irish novelist and journalist. Commenting on the fact that policemen always seem to look young

21 Sir, I have quarrelled with my wife; and a man who has quarrelled with his wife is absolved from all duty to his country.

Nightmare Abbey (1818) **Peacock, Thomas Love** (1785–1866) English writer and poet

22 Our first duty is towards the people of this country, to maintain their interests and their rights; our second duty is to all humanity.
Speech, (1896) **Salisbury, Lord** (1830–1903) English Conservative Prime Minister

23 O good old man, how well in thee appears
The constant service of the antique world,
When service sweat for duty, not for meed!
Thou art not for the fashion of these times,
Where none will sweat but for promotion,
And having that do choke their service up
Even with the having.
As You Like It, II.iii

24 Every subject's duty is the King's; but every subject's soul is his own.
Henry V, IV.i **Shakespeare, William** (1564–1616) English dramatist, poet and actor

25 When a stupid man is doing something he is ashamed of, he always declares that it is his duty.
Caesar and Cleopatra (1901) **Shaw, George Bernard** (1856–1950) Irish socialist, writer, dramatist and critic

26 There is no duty we so much underrate as the duty of being happy.
Virginibus Puerisque (1881) **Stevenson, Robert Louis** (1850–1894) Scottish writer, poet and essayist

27 O hard, when love and duty clash!
The Princess (1847) **Tennyson, Alfred, Lord** (1809–1892) English lyric poet

28 To persevere in one's duty and be silent is the best answer to calumny.
Moral Maxims **Washington, George** (1732–1799) US general, statesman and President

29 Duty is what one expects of others, it is not what one does oneself.
A Woman of No Importance (1893) **Wilde, Oscar** (1854–1900) Irish poet, dramatist, writer, critic and wit
See also patriotism; war

THE EAST

1 Nothing and no one can destroy the Chinese people. They are relentless survivors. They are the oldest civilized people on earth. Their civilization passes through phases but its basic characteristics remain the same. They yield, they bend to the wind, but they never break.
China, Past and Present (1972) **Buck, Pearl S.** (1892–1973) US writer and dramatist

2 He probably doesn't understand what he's looking at but he's reluctant to ask, because this is Japan and the student doesn't ask questions but waits to be told by the teacher.
A Circle Round The Sun – A Foreigner in Japan

3 ... Japan is like a quicksand – the more one tries to get out of it, the more it sucks one in – or a maze without a centre – a sphinx without a riddle – or like Peer Gynt's onion, peel away the layers one after another and in the end all there is left is mush and tears.
A Circle Round The Sun – A Foreigner in Japan
Hodson, Peregrine British author and journalist

4 The Japanese are described as 'the most nostalgic people on earth,' but I think possibly the remark applies to all island people, who have the spirit of adventure, but also the feeling of being secure on a small place among the waters.
Mirror, (1938) **Hyde, Robin** (1906–1939) New Zealand writer

5 Mao had managed to turn the people into the ultimate weapon of dictatorship. That was why under him there was no real equivalent of the KGB in China. There was no need. In bringing out and nourishing the worst in people, Mao had created a moral wasteland and a land of hatred.
Wild Swans (1991) **Jung Chang** (1952–) Chinese author

6 The ability of the Japanese to assimilate Western technology and science with astonishing rapidity after the Meiji Restoration was due, at least in part, to their education under Confucianism; Western rationalist thinking was not entirely foreign.

'Why Has Japan Succeeded?', quoted in Created in
Japan **Morishima, Michio** (1923–2004)
Japanese economist

7 Whereas Americans and Europeans often
develop complex, large-scale solutions to
problems, the Japanese constantly pare
down and reduce the complexity of
products and ideas to the barest
minimum. They streamline the design,
reduce the number of parts, and simplify
the inner workings and moving parts. The
influence of Zen and haiku poetry are often
evident in the simplicity and utility of
Japanese designs.
Made in Japan (1986) **Morita, Akio** (1921–1999)
Japanese businessman, chief executive of
Sony

8 To enter any Japanese social system you
must first get past the sign on the front
door, which invariably says, 'By
introduction only'. If you want to know
how the business climate is for outsiders in
Japan, meet Kochan the master sushi-chef.
He hides his fish so that he can refuse
service to strangers. When a customer
walks in without the proper introduction,
Kochan shakes his head and claims,
absurdly, that he is fresh out of everything.
Business Magazine, (1992)

9 ... Japan's social and economic systems
conspire, not against foreigners, but
against newcomers.
Business Magazine, (1992) **Rauch, Jonathan**
(1960–) US journalist

10 China, though it may perhaps stand still,
does not seem to go backwards.
Wealth of Nations (1776) **Smith, Adam** (1723–
1790) Scottish economist, philosopher and
essayist

11 There must be something in the Japanese
character that saves them from the despair
Americans feel in similar throes of
consuming. The American, gorging
himself on merchandise, develops a sense
of guilty self-consciousness; if the Japanese
have these doubts they do not show them.
Perhaps hesitation is not part of the
national character, or perhaps the ones
who hesitate are trampled by the crowds of

shoppers – that natural selection that
capitalist society practises against the
reflective.
The Great Railway Bazaar (1975)

12 It is with a kind of perverse pride that the
Japanese point out how expensive their
country has become. But this is as much a
measure of wealth as of inflation.
The Great Railway Bazaar (1975)

13 Outside the Nichigeki Music Hall, the
Japanese men who had watched with
fastidious languor and then so
enthusiastically applauded the savage
eroticism that could enjoy no encore –
baring their teeth as they did so – these
men, as I say, bowed deeply to one
another, murmured polite farewells to their
friends, linked arms with their wives with
the gentleness of old-fashioned lovers,
and, in the harsh lights of the street,
smiled, looking positively cherubic.
The Great Railway Bazaar (1975) **Theroux, Paul**
(1941–) US writer

EDUCATION

1 A teacher affects eternity; he can never tell
where his influence stops.
The Education of Henry Adams (1907) **Adams,
Henry** (1838–1918) US historian and
memoirist

2 The truth of it is, learning ... makes a silly
man ten thousand times more
insufferable, by supplying variety of matter
to his impertinence, and giving him an
opportunity of abounding in absurdities.
The Man of the Town **Addison, Joseph** (1672–
1719) English essayist, poet, playwright and
statesman

3 I wish I could have a little tape-and-
loudspeaker arrangement sewn into the
binding of this magazine, to be triggered
off by the light reflected from the reader's
eyes on to this part of the page, and set to
bawl out at several bels: MORE WILL
MEAN WORSE.

Encounter, (1960) **Amis, Kingsley** (1922–1995) English writer, poet and critic. On 'the delusion' that thousands of young people were capable of benefiting from university but had somehow failed to find their way there

4 You do not report daily that the sun rose in the east. So why report annually that the National Union of Teachers is opposed to reform of the education system?
Letter to the editor in *The Times,* (1999)

5 He left us as he came to us, fired with enthusiasm.
The Times, (1998) Headmaster's reference for a teacher he dismissed **Anonymous**

6 And yet, in the schoolroom more than any other place, does the difference of sex, if there is any, need to be forgotten.
In Theodore Stanton and Harriet Stanton Blatch (eds), *Elizabeth Cady Stanton* (1922) **Anthony, Susan B.** (1820–1906) US reformer, feminist and abolitionist

7 The roots of education are bitter, but the fruit is sweet.
In Diogenes Laertius, *Lives of Philosophers* **Aristotle** (384–322 BC) Greek philosopher

8 Of right and wrong he taught
Truths as refin'd as ever Athens heard;
And (strange to tell!) he practis'd what he preach'd.
The Art of Preserving Health (1744)

9 Much had he read,
Much more had seen; he studied from the life,
And in th' original perus'd mankind.
The Art of Preserving Health (1744) **Armstrong, Dr John** (1709–1779) Scottish physician, poet and writer

10 There is no such whetstone, to sharpen a good wit and encourage a will to learning, as is praise.
The Scholemaster (1570)

11 I said ... how, and why, young children were sooner allured by love, than driven by beating, to attain good learning.
The Scholemaster (1570) **Ascham, Roger** (1515–1568) English scholar, educationist and archer

12 A professor is one who talks in someone else's sleep.
Attr. **Auden, W.H.** (1907–1973) English poet, essayist, critic, teacher and dramatist

13 Universities incline wits to sophistry and affectation.
Valerius Terminus of the Interpretation of Nature (1603)

14 Reading maketh a full man; conference a ready man; and writing an exact man.
Essays (1625)

15 Crafty men contemn studies; simple men admire them; and wise men use them.
'Of Studies' (1625)

16 Studies serve for delight, for ornament, and for ability.
'Of Studies' (1625)

17 Read not to contradict and confute, nor to believe and take for granted, nor to find talk and discourse, but to weigh and consider.
'Of Studies' (1625) **Bacon, Francis** (1561–1626) English philosopher, essayist, politician and courtier

18 I read Shakespeare and the Bible and I can shoot dice. That's what I call a liberal education.
Attr. **Bankhead, Tallulah** (1903–1968) US actress

19 Most higher education is devoted to affirming the traditions and origins of an existing elite and transmitting them to new members.
Composing a Life (1989) **Bateson, Mary Catherine** (1939–) US anthropologist and writer

20 Not that I had any special reason for hating school ... I was a modest, good-humoured boy. It is Oxford that has made me insufferable.
More (1899) **Beerbohm, Sir Max** (1872–1956) English satirist, cartoonist, critic and essayist

21 Time is a great teacher, but unfortunately it kills all its pupils.
Attr. **Berlioz, Hector** (1803–1869) French composer; founder of modern orchestration

22 *Education*: That which discloses to the wise and disguises from the foolish their lack of understanding.
The Cynic's Word Book (1906)

23 *Learning*: The kind of ignorance distinguishing the studious.
The Devil's Dictionary (1911) **Bierce, Ambrose** (1842–c.1914) American writer, verse writer and soldier

24 Ask me my three main priorities for Government, and I tell you: education, education and education.
Speech at the Labour Party Conference, (1996) **Blair, Tony** (1953–) British Labour Prime Minister

25 The schoolmaster is abroad, and I trust more to him, armed with his primer, than I do to the soldier in full military array, for upholding and extending the liberties of his country.
Speech, (1828)

26 Education makes a people easy to lead, but difficult to drive; easy to govern, but impossible to enslave.
Attr. **Brougham, Lord Henry** (1778–1868) Scottish politician, abolitionist and journalist

27 Education is a wonderful thing. If you couldn't sign your name you'd have to pay cash.
Starting From Scratch (1988) **Brown, Rita Mae** (1944–) US writer and poet

28 To live for a time close to great minds is the best kind of education.
Memory Hold the Door **Buchan, John** (1875–1940) Scottish writer, lawyer and Conservative politician

29 Learning will be cast into the mire, and trodden down under the hoofs of the swinish multitude.
Reflections on the Revolution in France (1790) **Burke, Edmund** (1729–1797) Irish-born British statesman and philosopher

30 It were better to perish than to continue schoolmastering.
In Wilson, Carlyle Till Marriage (1923) **Carlyle, Thomas** (1795–1881) Scottish historian, biographer, critic, and essayist

31 'We called him Tortoise because he taught us,' said the Mock Turtle angrily. 'Really you are very dull!'
Alice's Adventures in Wonderland (1865)

32 'Reeling and Writhing, of course, to begin with,' the Mock Turtle replied; 'and then the different branches of Arithmetic – Ambition, Distraction, Uglification, and Derision.'
Alice's Adventures in Wonderland (1865)

33 The Drawling-master was an old conger-eel, that used to come once a week: he taught Drawling, Stretching, and Fainting in Coils.
Alice's Adventures in Wonderland (1865)

34 'That's the reason they're called lessons,' the Gryphon remarked: 'because they lessen from day to day.'
Alice's Adventures in Wonderland (1865) **Carroll, Lewis** (1832–1898) English writer and photographer

35 Wear your learning, like your watch, in a private pocket; and do not pull it out and strike it merely to show you have one. If you are asked what o'clock it is, tell it; but do not proclaim it hourly and unasked like the watchman.
Letter to his son, (1748) **Chesterfield, Lord** (1694–1773) English politician and letter writer

36 Education is simply the soul of a society as it passes from one generation to another.
The Observer, (1924) **Chesterton, G.K.** (1874–1936) English writer, poet and critic

37 Headmasters have powers at their disposal with which Prime Ministers have never yet been invested.
My Early Life (1930) **Churchill, Sir Winston** (1874–1965) English Conservative Prime Minister

38 This curious, and, to my mind, objectionable feature of English education was maintained solely in order that parents could get their children out of the house.
Another Part of the Wood (1974) **Clark, Lord Kenneth** (1903–1983) English art historian. On boarding schools

39 Education is casting false pearls before real swine.

Attr. **Cody, Henry John** (1868–1951) Anglican churchman

40 Examinations are formidable even to the best prepared, for the greatest fool may ask more than the wisest man can answer.
Lacon (1820) **Colton, Charles Caleb** (c.1780–1832) English clergyman and satirist

41 Learning without thought is labour lost; thought without learning is perilous.
Analects

42 The scholar who cherishes the love of comfort, is not fit to be deemed a scholar.
Analects **Confucius** (c.550–c.478 BC) Chinese philosopher and teacher of ethics

43 Aye, 'tis well enough for a servant to be bred at an University. But the education is a little too pedantic for a gentleman.
Love for Love (1695) **Congreve, William** (1670–1729) English dramatist

44 The ape-like virtues without which no one can enjoy a public school.
Enemies of Promise (1938) **Connolly, Cyril** (1903–1974) English literary editor, writer and critic

45 I can say that anyone who, like me, has been educated in English public schools and served in the ranks of the British Army is quite at home in a Third World prison.
Newsweek, (1991) **Cooper, Roger** British hostage in Iran. After five years in an Iranian prison

46 I've over-educated myself in all the things I shouldn't have known at all.
Mild Oats (1931) **Coward, Sir Noël** (1899–1973) English dramatist, actor, producer and composer

47 If you are going to be any good, you have got to like the little swine.
Attr. **Darling, Sir James** (1899–1995) Australian educationist

48 The most strenuous efforts of the most committed educationalists in the years since my boyhood have been quite unable to make a school into anything but a school, which is to say a jail with educational opportunities.

The Cunning Man (1994) **Davies, Robertson** (1913–1995) Canadian playwright, writer and critic

49 We lov'd the doctrine for the teacher's sake.
'Character of the late Dr S. Annesley' (1697) **Defoe, Daniel** (c.1661–1731) English writer and critic

50 EDUCATION. – At Mr Wackford Squeer's Academy, Dotheboys Hall, at the delightful village of Dotheboys, near Greta Bridge in Yorkshire, Youth are boarded, clothed, booked, furnished with pocket-money, provided with all necessaries, instructed in all languages, living and dead, mathematics, orthography, geometry, astronomy, trigonometry, the use of the globes, algebra, single stick (if required), writing, arithmetic, fortification, and every other branch of classical literature. Terms, twenty guineas per annum. No extras, no vacations, and diet unparalleled.
Nicholas Nickleby (1839)

51 Now, what I want is, Facts. Teach these boys and girls nothing but Facts. Facts alone are wanted in life. Plant nothing else, and root out everything else … Stick to Facts, sir!
Hard Times (1854) **Dickens, Charles** (1812–1870) English writer

52 Education is something that tempers the young and consoles the old, gives wealth to the poor and adorns the rich.
In Diogenes Laertius, *Lives of Eminent Philosophers* **Diogenes (the Cynic)** (c.400–325 BC) Greek ascetic philosopher

53 Upon the education of the people of this country the fate of this country depends.
Speech, (1874) **Disraeli, Benjamin** (1804–1881) English statesman and writer

54 By education most have been misled;
So they believe, because they so were bred.
The priest continues what the nurse began,
And thus the child imposes on the man.
The Hind and the Panther (1687) **Dryden, John** (1631–1700) English poet, satirist, dramatist and critic

55 If education cannot help separate truth from falsehood, beauty from vulgarity, right from wrong, then what can it teach us?
Atlantic Monthly, (1991) **D'Souza, Dinesh** (1961–) US author

56 I pay the schoolmaster, but 'tis the schoolboys that educate my son.
Journals **Emerson, Ralph Waldo** (1803–1882) US poet, essayist, transcendentalist and teacher

57 After Cambridge – unemployment. No one wanted much to know.
Good degrees are good for nothing in the business world below.
'The Sentimental Education' **Ewart, Gavin** (1916–1995) English poet

58 Charming women can true converts make, We love the precepts for the teacher's sake.
The Constant Couple (1699) **Farquhar, George** (1678–1707) Irish dramatist

59 Public schools are the nurseries of all vice and immorality.
Joseph Andrews (1742) **Fielding, Henry** (1707–1754) English writer, dramatist and journalist

60 The most devilish thing is 8 times 8 and 7 times 7 it is what nature itselfe cant endure.
In Esdaile, *Journals, Letters and Verses* (1934) **Fleming, Marjory** (1803–1811) Scottish child diarist

61 For as the old saying is,
When house and land are gone and spent
Then learning is most excellent.
Taste (1752) **Foote, Samuel** (1720–1777) English actor, dramatist and wit

62 They go forth into it [the world] with well-developed bodies, fairly developed minds, and undeveloped hearts.
Abinger Harvest (1936) **Forster, E.M.** (1879–1970) English writer, essayist and literary critic. Of public schoolboys

63 To the University of Oxford I acknowledge no obligation; and she will as cheerfully renounce me for a son, as I am willing to disclaim her for a mother. I spent fourteen months at Magdalen College: they proved the fourteen months the most idle and unprofitable of my whole life.
Memoirs of My Life and Writings (1796) **Gibbon, Edward** (1737–1794) English historian, politician and memoirist

64 I had left civilisation behind and entered a savage country of strange customs and inexplicable cruelties: a country in which I was a foreigner and a suspect, quite literally a hunted creature, known to have dubious associates.
Was not my father the headmaster? I was like the son of a quisling in a country under occupation.
A Sort of Life (1971) **Greene, Graham** (1904–1991) English writer and dramatist

65 There's more learning than is taught in books.
The Jester **Gregory, Lady Isabella Augusta** (1852–1932) Irish dramatist, writer and translator

66 I will not call my teacher 'Hot Cakes'.
I will not yell 'She's dead' during roll call.
A burp is not an answer.
I will not torment the emotionally frail.
I will not Xerox my butt.
I will not belch the National Anthem.
The Simpsons, TV cartoon series **Groening, Matt** (1954–) US cartoonist. Bart's blackboard lines

67 It is better to be able neither to read nor write than to be able to do nothing else.
The Edinburgh Magazine, (1818) **Hazlitt, William** (1778–1830) English writer and critic

68 Education made us what we are.
De l'esprit (1758) **Helvétius, Claude Adrien** (1715–1771) French philosopher

69 The solemn foolery of scholarship for scholarship's sake.
The Perennial Philosophy (1945) **Huxley, Aldous** (1894–1963) English writer, poet and critic

70 Some experience of popular lecturing had convinced me that the necessity of making things plain to uninstructed people was one of the very best means of clearing up the obscure corners of one's own mind.
Man's Place in Nature (1894)

71 Try to learn something about everything and everything about something.

Memorial stone **Huxley, T.H.** (1825–1895) English biologist, Darwinist and agnostic

72 In a growing number of countries everyone has a qualified right to attend a university ... The result is the emergence of huge caravanserais ... where higher education is doled out rather like gruel in a soup kitchen.
The Spectator, (1996) **Johnson, Paul** (1928–) British editor and writer

73 Example is always more efficacious than precept.
Rasselas (1759)

74 All intellectual improvement arises from leisure.
In Boswell, *The Life of Samuel Johnson* (1791)

75 It is no matter what you teach them [children] first, any more than what leg you shall put into your breeches first.
In Boswell, *The Life of Samuel Johnson* (1791)

76 There is now less flogging in our great schools than formerly, but then less is learned there; so that what the boys get at one end they lose at the other.
In Boswell, *The Life of Samuel Johnson* (1791)
Johnson, Samuel (1709–1784) English lexicographer, poet, critic, conversationalist and essayist

77 Man is the only creature which must be educated.
On Pedagogy (1803) **Kant, Immanuel** (1724–1804) German idealist philosopher

78 Corporal punishment is as humiliating for him who gives it as for him who receives it; it is ineffective besides. Neither shame nor physical pain have any other effect than a hardening one.
The Century of the Child (1909) **Key, Ellen** (1849–1926) Swedish feminist, writer and lecturer

79 Education is what most people receive, many pass on and few actually have.
Pro domo et mundo (1912) **Kraus, Karl** (1874–1936) Austrian scientist, critic and poet

80 ... that is what learning is. You suddenly understand something you've understood all your life, but in a new way.

The Four-Gated City (1969) **Lessing, Doris** (1919–) British writer, brought up in Zimbabwe

81 We think them verray naturall fules,
That lernis ouir mekle at the sculis.
'Complaynt to the King' **Lindsay, Sir David** (c.1490–1555) Scottish poet and satirist

82 I doubt whether the student can do a greater work for his nation in this grave moment in its history than to detach himself from its preoccupations, refusing to let himself be absorbed by distractions about which, as a scholar, he can do almost nothing.
The Scholar in a Troubled World (1932) **Lippmann, Walter** (1889–1974) Canadian sociologist

83 Four times, under our educational rules, the human pack is shuffled and cut – at eleven-plus, sixteen-plus, eighteen-plus and twenty-plus – and happy is he who comes top of the deck on each occasion, but especially the last. This is called Finals, the very name of which implies that nothing of importance can happen after it. The British postgraduate student is a lonely forlorn soul ... for whom nothing had been real since the Big Push.
Changing Places (1975)

84 Rummidge ... had lately suffered the mortifying fate of most English universities of its type (civic redbrick): having competed strenuously for fifty years with two universities chiefly valued for being old, it was, at the moment of drawing level, rudely overtaken in popularity and prestige by a batch of universities chiefly valued for being new.
Changing Places (1975)

85 Universities are the cathedrals of the modern age. They shouldn't have to justify their existence by utilitarian criteria.
Nice Work **Lodge, David** (1935–) English writer, satirist and literary critic

86 When you educate a man you educate an individual; when you educate a woman you educate a whole family.
Address at women's college **McIver, Charles D.** (1860–1906) US educationist

87 The reason universities are so full of
knowledge is that the students come with
so much and they leave with so little.
Antigonish Review, (1988) **McLuhan, Marshall**
(1911–1980) Canadian communications
theorist

88 I don't know, Ma'am, why they make all
this fuss about education; none of the
Pagets can read or write, and they get on
well enough.
Attr. **Melbourne, Lord** (1779–1848) English
statesman. To the Queen

89 ... the right path of a vertuous and noble
Education, laborious indeed at the first
ascent, but else so smooth, so green, so
full of goodly prospect, and melodious
sounds on every side, that the harp of
Orpheus was not more charming.
Of Education: To Master Samuel Hartlib (1644)
Milton, John (1608–1674) English poet,
libertarian and pamphleteer

90 We teachers can only help the work going
on, as servants wait upon a master.
The Absorbent Mind **Montessori, Maria** (1870–
1952) Italian doctor and educationist

91 The ratio of literacy to illiteracy is constant,
but nowadays the illiterates can read and
write.
The Observer, (1979) **Moravia, Alberto** (1907–
1990) Italian writer

92 Bryn Mawr had done what a four-year dose
of liberal education was designed to do:
unfit her for eighty per cent of useful work
of the world.
Song of Solomon (1977) **Morrison, Toni** (1931–)
US writer

93 'Casting Out Fear' ought to be the motto
over every school door.
The Problem Child (1926) **Neil, A.S.** (1883–1973)
Scottish educational reformer

94 A university is an *alma mater,* knowing her
children one by one, not a foundry, or a
mint, or a treadmill.
Attr. **Newman, John Henry, Cardinal** (1801–
1890) English Cardinal, theologian and poet

95 Earnestness is just stupidity sent to
college.

Attr. in *The Observer,* (1996) **O'Rourke, P.J.**
(1947–) US writer

96 Probably the Battle of Waterloo was won
on the playing-fields of Eton, but the
opening battles of all subsequent wars
have been lost there.
The Lion and the Unicorn (1941) **Orwell, George**
(1903–1950) English writer and critic

97 Add the fact that to have diligently studied
the liberal arts refines behaviour and does
not allow it to be savage.
Epistulae Ex Ponto **Ovid** (43 BC–AD 18) Roman
poet

98 It is the function of a liberal university not
to give the right answers, but to ask right
questions.
'Women and Creativity' (1969) **Ozick, Cynthia**
(1928–) US writer

99 The death of the grammar schools – those
public schools without the sodomy –
resulted in state education relinquishing its
role of nurturing bright young working
class kids.
Arena, (1989) **Parsons, Tony** (1953–) British
journalist and author

100 Before playtime let us consider the
possibilities of getting stoned on milk.
Grinning Jack (1990) **Patten, Brian** (1946–)
British poet

101 He was sent, as usual, to a public school,
where a little learning was painfully beaten
into him, and from thence to the
university, where it was carefully taken out
of him.
Nightmare Abbey (1818) **Peacock, Thomas Love**
(1785–1866) English writer and poet

102 King Alfred's parents paid for their children
to be taught next to nothing. When utopia
was nationalized, state-school parents got
the same service for free.
Times Literary Supplement, (1998) **Phillips,
Melanie** (1951–) English journalist. Reviewing
a book on King Alfred School, a progressive
co-educational independent school, described
as an experiment in Fabian utopianism

103 Let no one ignorant of mathematics enter
here.

Attr. **Plato** (c.429–347 BC) Greek philosopher. Inscription written over the entrance to the Academy

104 A little learning is a dangerous thing;
Drink deep, or taste not the Pierian spring:
There shallow draughts intoxicate the brain,
And drinking largely sobers us again.
An Essay on Criticism (1711) **Pope, Alexander** (1688–1744) English poet, translator and editor

105 He rang'd his tropes, and preach'd up patience;
Back'd his opinion with quotations.
'Paulo Purganti and his Wife' (1709) **Prior, Matthew** (1664–1721) English poet

106 Every school needs a debating society far more than it needs a computer. For a free society, it is essential.
In Kamm and Lean (eds), *A Scottish Childhood* (1985) **Rifkind, Malcolm** (1946–) Scottish barrister and Conservative politician

107 Instead of giving money to found colleges to promote learning, why don't they pass a constitutional amendment prohibiting anybody from learning anything? If it works as good as the Prohibition one did, why, in five years we would have the smartest race of people on earth.
Attr. **Rogers, Will** (1879–1935) US humorist, actor, rancher, writer and wit

108 One is only curious in proportion to one's level of education.
Émile ou De l'éducation (1762) **Rousseau, Jean-Jacques** (1712–1778) Swiss-born French philosopher, educationist and essayist

109 To make your children capable of honesty is the beginning of education.
Time and Tide by Weare and Tyne (1867) **Ruskin, John** (1819–1900) English art critic, philosopher and reformer

110 But, good gracious, you've got to educate him first. You can't expect a boy to be vicious till he's been to a good school.
Reginald in Russia (1910) **Saki** (1870–1916) Burmese-born British writer

111 Scholars, however, as a rule study with the aim of being able to teach and write. That is why their heads are like a stomach and intestines from which food passes out again undigested.
Parerga und Paralipomena (1851) **Schopenhauer, Arthur** (1788–1860) German philosopher

112 I tellt ye
I tellt ye.
Scotched, 'Scotch Education' **Scott, Alexander** (1920–1989) Scottish poet

113 All men who have turned out worth anything have had the chief hand in their own education.
Letter to J.G. Lockhart, (1830) **Scott, Sir Walter** (1771–1832) Scottish writer and historian

114 Though loaded firearms were strictly forbidden at St Trinian's to all but Sixth-Formers … one or two of them carried automatics acquired in the holidays, generally the gift of some indulgent relative.
The Terror of St Trinian's (1952) **Searle, Ronald William Fordham** (1920–) English cartoonist

115 Education is when you read the fine print. Experience is what you get if you don't.
Attr. **Seeger, Pete** (1919–) US singer and songwriter

116 Do not on any account attempt to write on both sides of the paper at once.
1066 And All That (1930) **Sellar, Walter** (1898–1951) and **Yeatman, Robert Julian** (1897–1968) British writers

117 Even while they teach, men learn.
Epistulae Morales **Seneca** (c.4 BC–AD 65) Roman philosopher, poet, dramatist, essayist, rhetorician and statesman

118 He who can, does. He who cannot, teaches.
Man and Superman (1903) **Shaw, George Bernard** (1856–1950) Irish socialist, writer, dramatist and critic

119 My education takes place during the holidays from Eton.
Who's Who (1929) **Sitwell, Sir Osbert** (1892–1969) English writer

120 Education is what survives when what has been learned has been forgotten.
New Scientist, (1964)

121 Indeed one of the ultimate advantages of an education is simply coming to the end of it.
The Technology of Teaching (1968) **Skinner, B.F.** (1904–1990) US psychologist

122 There are no public institutions for the education of women, and there is accordingly nothing useless, absurd, or fantastical in the common course of their education.
Wealth of Nations (1776)

123 Several of those learned societies have chosen to remain ... the sanctuaries in which exploded systems and obsolete prejudices found shelter and protection, after they had been hunted out of every other corner of the world.
Wealth of Nations (1776) Of universities **Smith, Adam** (1723–1790) Scottish economist, philosopher and essayist

124 To me education is a leading out of what is already there in the pupil's soul. To Miss Mackay it is a putting in of something that is not there, and that is not what I call education, I call it intrusion.
The Prime of Miss Jean Brodie (1961)

125 Give me a girl at an impressionable age, and she is mine for life.
The Prime of Miss Jean Brodie (1961)

126 Art and religion first; then philosophy; lastly science. That is the order of the great subjects of life, that's their order of importance.
The Prime of Miss Jean Brodie (1961) **Spark, Muriel** (1918–2006) Scottish writer, poet and dramatist

127 Education has for its object the formation of character.
Social Statics (1850) **Spencer, Herbert** (1820–1903) English philosopher and journalist

128 I am the Dean of Christ Church, Sir:
There's my wife; look well at her.
She's the Broad and I'm the High;
We are the University.

In Hiscock (ed.), *The Balliol Rhymes* (1939)
Spring-Rice, Cecil Arthur (1859–1918) English diplomat and hymn writer

129 When I was in junior high school, the teachers voted me the student most likely to end up in the electric chair.
Attr. **Stallone, Sylvester** (1946–) US actor

130 The truth of it is, the first rudiments of education are given very indiscreetly by most parents.
The Tatler, 173 **Steele, Sir Richard** (1672–1729) Irish-born English writer, dramatist and politician

131 Today we enjoy a social structure which offers equal opportunity in education. It is indeed regrettably true that there is no equal opportunity to take advantage of the equal opportunity.
Still More Commonplace (1973) **Stocks, Mary, Baroness** (1891–1975) English educationist, broadcaster and biographer

132 The King, observing with judicious eyes,
The state of both his universities,
To Oxford sent a troop of horse, and why?
That learned body wanted loyalty;
To Cambridge books, as very well discerning,
How much that loyal body wanted learning.
Epigram on George I's donation of Bishop Ely's Library to Cambridge University **Trapp, Joseph** (1679–1747) English poet, pamphleteer, translator and clergyman

133 Education ... has produced a vast population able to read but unable to distinguish what is worth reading.
English Social History (1942) **Trevelyan, G.M.** (1876–1962) English historian and writer

134 He must have known me had he seen me as he was wont to see me, for he was in the habit of flogging me constantly. Perhaps he did not recognize me by my face.
Autobiography (1883) **Trollope, Anthony** (1815–1882) English writer, traveller and post office official. Of his headmaster

135 Education: the path from cocky ignorance to miserable uncertainty.
Attr. **Twain, Mark** (1835–1910) US author and wit

136 The Founding Fathers in their wisdom decided that children were an unnatural strain on parents. So they provided jails called schools, equipped with tortures called an education.
The Centaur (1963) **Updike, John** (1932–) US writer, poet and critic

137 The English have an enormous nostalgia for school. There is no other country in the world where you see elderly gentleman dressed like schoolboys.
The Observer, (1998)

138 People at the top of the tree are those without qualifications to detain them at the bottom.
Attr. **Ustinov, Sir Peter** (1921–2004) English actor, director, dramatist, writer and raconteur

139 We schoolmasters must temper discretion with deceit.
Decline and Fall (1928)

140 I expect you'll be becoming a schoolmaster, sir. That's what most of the gentlemen does, sir, that gets sent down for indecent behaviour.
Decline and Fall (1928)

141 'We class schools, you see, into four grades: Leading School, First-rate School, Good School, and School. Frankly', said Mr Levy, 'School is pretty bad.'
Decline and Fall (1928)

142 That's the public-school system all over. They may kick you out, but they never let you down.
Decline and Fall (1928)

143 Assistant masters came and went ... Some liked little boys too little and some too much.
A Little Learning (1964) **Waugh, Evelyn** (1903–1966) English writer and diarist

144 The battle of Waterloo was won on the playing fields of Eton.
Attr. **Wellington, Duke of** (1769–1852) Irish-born British military commander and statesman

145 'I dunno,' Arthur said. 'I forget what I was taught. I only remember what I've learnt.'

The Solid Mandala (1966) **White, Patrick** (1912–1990) English-born Australian writer and dramatist

146 Everybody who is incapable of learning has taken to teaching.
'The Decay of Lying' (1889)

147 Education is an admirable thing, but it is well to remember from time to time that nothing that is worth knowing can be taught.
'The Critic as Artist' (1891)

148 In examinations the foolish ask questions that the wise cannot answer.
The Chameleon, (1894) **Wilde, Oscar** (1854–1900) Irish poet, dramatist, writer, critic and wit

149 For every person wishing to teach there are thirty not wanting to be taught.
And Now All This (1932) **Yeatman, Robert Julian** (1897–1968) English writer
See also class; intelligence; knowledge

EGOISM

1 Against whom?
Attr. **Adler, Alfred** (1870–1937) Austrian psychiatrist and psychologist. On hearing that an egocentric had fallen in love

2 Conceit spoils the finest genius. There is not much danger that real talent or goodness will be overlooked long; even if it is, the consciousness of possessing and using it well should satisfy one.
Little Women (1869) **Alcott, Louisa May** (1832–1888) US writer

3 I want to get out with my greatness intact.
The Observer, (1974) Announcing his retirement

4 I'm the greatest golfer. I just have not played yet.
Attr.

5 I am the greatest.
Catchphrase **Ali, Muhammad** (1942–) US heavyweight boxer

6 My name is George Nathaniel Curzon, I am a most superior person.
The Masque of Balliol (c.1870) **Anonymous**

7 It was prettily devised of Aesop, 'The fly sat upon the axletree of the chariot-wheel and said, what a dust do I raise.'
'Of Vain-Glory' (1625) **Bacon, Francis** (1561–1626) English philosopher, essayist, politician and courtier

8 I know I am God because when I pray to him I find I'm talking to myself.
The Ruling Class (1968) **Barnes, Peter** (1931–) English dramatist

9 To give an accurate and exhaustive account of that period would need a far less brilliant pen than mine.
Attr. **Beerbohm, Sir Max** (1872–1956) English satirist, cartoonist, critic and essayist

10 Vanity of vanities, saith the Preacher, vanity of vanities; all is vanity.
Ecclesiastes, 1:2 **The Bible (King James Version)**

11 *Egoist*: A person of low taste, more interested in himself than in me.
The Cynic's Word Book (1906) **Bierce, Ambrose** (1842–c.1914) US writer, verse writer and soldier

12 It's 'Damn you, Jack – I'm all right!' with you chaps.
The Brassbounder (1910) **Bone, Sir David** (1874–1959) Scottish novelist and sailor

13 If ever he went to school without any boots it was because he was too big for them.
Remark, (1949) **Bulmer-Thomas, Ivor** (1905–1993) English writer and politician. Of Harold Wilson

14 The advantage of doing one's praising for oneself is that one can lay it on so thick and exactly in the right places.
The Way of All Flesh (1903) **Butler, Samuel** (1835–1902) English writer, painter, philosopher and scholar

15 Someone said of a great egotist: 'He would burn your house down to cook himself a couple of eggs.'
Caractères et anecdotes **Chamfort, Nicolas** (1741–1794) French writer

16 The greatest of faults, I should say, is to be conscious of none.
On Heroes, Hero-Worship, and the Heroic in History **Carlyle, Thomas** (1795–1881) Scottish historian, biographer, critic, and essayist

17 He sicken'd at all triumphs but his own.
The Rosciad (1761) **Churchill, Charles** (1731–1764) English poet, political writer and clergyman. Of Thomas Franklin, Professor of Greek, Cambridge

18 O happy Rome, born when I was consul!
In Juvenal, Satires **Cicero** (106–43 BC) Roman orator, statesman, essayist and letter writer

19 An autobiography is an obituary in serial form with the last instalment missing.
The Naked Civil Servant (1968) **Crisp, Quentin** (1908–1999) English writer, publicist and model

20 I grew intoxicated with my own eloquence.
Contarini Fleming (1832)

21 Every day when he looked into the glass, and gave the last touch to his consummate toilette, he offered his grateful thanks to Providence that his family was not unworthy of him.
Lothair (1870) **Disraeli, Benjamin** (1804–1881) English statesman and writer

22 Yes, once – many, many years ago. I thought I had made a wrong decision. Of course, it turned out that I had been right all along. But I was wrong to have thought that I was wrong.
Attr. **Dulles, John Foster** (1888–1959) US statesman and lawyer. Reply when asked if he had ever been wrong

23 We are so vain that we are even concerned about the opinion of those people who are of no concern to us.
Aphorisms (1880) **Ebner-Eschenbach, Marie von** (1830–1916) Austrian writer

24 He was like a cock, who thought the sun had risen to hear him crow.
Adam Bede (1859)

25 I've never any pity for conceited people, because I think they carry their comfort about with them.
The Mill on the Floss (1860) **Eliot, George** (1819–1880) English writer and poet

26 If you wish in this world to advance
Your merits you're bound to enhance,
You must stir it and stump it,
And blow your own trumpet,
Or, trust me, you haven't a chance!

Ruddigore (1887) **Gilbert, W.S.** (1836–1911) English dramatist, humorist and librettist

27 As for disappointing them, I should not so much mind; but I can't abide to disappoint myself.
She Stoops to Conquer (1773) **Goldsmith, Oliver** (c.1728–1774) Irish dramatist, poet and writer

28 I am always prepared to recognize that there can be two points of view – mine, and one that is probably wrong.
In Trengove, *John Grey Gorton* **Gorton, John Grey** (1911– 2002) Australian parliamentarian

29 'Should I call myself an egoist?' Miss Johnstone mused. 'Others have called me so. They merely meant I did not care for them.'
Simonetta Perkins (1925) **Hartley, L.P.** (1895–1972) English writer and critic

30 Well, I don't want to be any more egotistical than possible. I have total confidence in my ability.
In Thomson and Butel, *The World According to Hawke* **Hawke, Bob** (1929–) Australian Premier. On first entering Parliament, 1979

31 A dominant personality doesn't believe in its own will. All it needs is the inability to recognise the existence of anybody else's.
Falling Towards England **James, Brian** (1892–1972) Australian writer

32 Conceit is the finest armour a man can wear.
Idle Thoughts of an Idle Fellow (1886) **Jerome, Jerome K.** (1859–1927) English writer and dramatist

33 Go climb the Alps, ambitious fool,
To please the boys, and be a theme at school.
Satires **Juvenal** (c.60–130) Roman verse satirist and Stoic

34 Every man has three characters: that which he exhibits, that which he has, and that which he thinks he has.
Attr. **Karr, Alphonse** (1808–1890) French writer and editor

35 Shyness is just egotism out of its depth.
The Observer, (1988) **Keith, Penelope** (1940–) English actress

36 It's only when you abandon your ambitions that they become possible.
Australian, (1983) **Keneally, Thomas** (1935–) Australian writer and screenwriter

37 Frankly, I am beautiful, famous and gorgeous.
Scotland on Sunday, (1998) **Kournikova, Anna** (1981–) Russian tennis player

38 We rarely think people have good sense unless they agree with us.
Maximes (1678)

39 If we had no faults of our own, we should not take so much pleasure in noticing them in others.
Maximes (1678) **La Rochefoucauld** (1613–1680) French writer

40 I have made a little scale, supposing myself to receive the following various accessions of dignity from the king, who is the fountain of honour – As at first, 1, Mr C. Lamb; – 10th, Emperor Lamb; 11th Pope Innocent, higher than which is nothing but the Lamb of God.
Letter to Thomas Manning, (1810)

41 How I like to be liked, and what I do to be liked!
Letter to D. Wordsworth, (1821) **Lamb, Charles** (1775–1834) English essayist, critic and letter writer

42 Has God then forgotten what I have done for him?
Attr. **Louis XIV** (1638–1715) King of France. On hearing of the French defeat at Malplaquet

43 In ... the book of Egoism, it is written, Possession without obligation to the object possessed approaches felicity.
The Egoist (1879) **Meredith, George** (1828–1909) English writer, poet and critic

44 Error has never even come close to my mind.
Remark, (1848) **Metternich, Prince Clement** (1773–1859) Austrian statesman

45 In the defiance of fashion is the beginning of character.
The Boy who Stole the Funeral (1979) **Murray, Les A.** (1938–) Australian poet and writer

46 The affair between Margot Asquith and Margot Asquith will live as one of the prettiest love stories in all literature.
New Yorker, (1927) **Parker, Dorothy** (1893–1967) US writer, poet, critic and wit. Reviewing Asquith's *Lay Sermons*

47 The egoist does not tolerate egoism.
Meditations of a Parish Priest (1886) **Roux, Joseph** (1834–1886) French priest and epigrammatist

48 I charge thee, fling away ambition:
By that sin fell the angels. How can man then,
The image of his Maker, hope to win by it?
Henry VIII, III.ii

49 I have no spur
To prick the sides of my intent, but only
Vaulting ambition, which o'er-leaps itself,
And falls on th' other.
Macbeth, I.vii

50 He that loves to be flattered is worthy o' th' flatterer.
Timon of Athens, I.i **Shakespeare, William** (1564–1616) English dramatist, poet and actor

51 I never apologise.
Arms and the Man (1898)

52 With the single exception of Homer, there is no eminent writer, not even Sir Walter Scott, whom I can despise so entirely as I despise Shakespeare when I measure my mind against his ... it would positively be a relief to me to dig him up and throw stones at him.
Dramatic Opinions and Essays (1906)

53 What really flatters a man is that you think him worth flattering.
John Bull's Other Island (1907)

54 I often quote myself. It adds spice to the conversation.
Reader's Digest, (1943) **Shaw, George Bernard** (1856–1950) Irish socialist, writer, dramatist and critic

55 I have often wished I had time to cultivate modesty ... But I am too busy thinking about myself.
The Observer, (1950)

56 Would you please substitute Dame Edith for Dr Sitwell. The Queen has honoured my poetry by making me a Dame, so that is now my name.
Letter to G. Singleton, (1955) **Sitwell, Dame Edith** (1887–1964) English poet, anthologist, critic and biographer

57 And he that strives to touch the starres,
Oft stombles at a strawe.
The Shepheardes Calender (1579) **Spenser, Edmund** (c.1522–1599) English poet

58 I suppose flattery hurts no one – that is, if he doesn't inhale.
Meet the Press, TV broadcast, (1952) **Stevenson, Adlai** (1900–1965) US lawyer, statesman and United Nations ambassador

59 The time was out of joint, and he was only too delighted to have been born to set it right.
Eminent Victorians (1918) **Strachey, Lytton** (1880–1932) English biographer and critic. Of Hurrell Froude

60 The individual ego asserts itself strongly in the West. In the East, there is no ego. The ego is non-existent and, therefore, there is no ego to be crucified.
Mysticism Christian and Buddhist (1957) **Suzuki, D.T.** (1870–1966) Japanese Buddhist scholar and main interpreter of Zen to the West

61 If a woman like Eva Peron with no ideals can get that far, think how far I can go with all the ideals that I have.
The Sunday Times, (1980) **Thatcher, Margaret** (1925–) English Conservative Prime Minister

62 He would like to destroy his old diaries and to appear before his children and the public only in his patriarchal robes. His vanity is enormous!
A Diary of Tolstoy's Wife (1860–1891) **Tolstoy, Sophie** (1844–1919) Russian diarist; wife of Leo Tolstoy. Of Tolstoy

63 As for conceit, what man will do any good who is not conceited? Nobody holds a good opinion of a man who has a low opinion of himself.
Orley Farm (1862) **Trollope, Anthony** (1815–1882) English writer, traveller and post office official

64 All my life I always wanted to be somebody. Now I see that I should have been more specific.
Attr. **Wagner, Jane** (1935–) US writer and director

65 If I ever felt inclined to be timid as I was going into a room full of people, I would say to myself, 'You're the cleverest member of one of the cleverest families in the cleverest class of the cleverest nation in the world, why should you be frightened?'
In Russell, *Portraits from Memory* (1956) **Webb, Beatrice** (1858–1943) English writer and reformer

66 Isn't it? I know in my case I would grow intolerably conceited.
In Pearson, *The Man Whistler* **Whistler, James McNeill** (1834–1903) US painter, etcher and pamphleteer. Replying to the pointed observation that it was as well that we do not see ourselves as others see us

67 Do I contradict myself?
Very well then I contradict myself,
(I am large, I contain multitudes).
'Song of Myself' (1855) **Whitman, Walt** (1819–1892) US poet and writer

68 I am the only person in the world I should like to know thoroughly.
Lady Windermere's Fan (1892) **Wilde, Oscar** (1854–1900) Irish poet, dramatist, writer, critic and wit
See also pride; self

EMANCIPATION OF WOMEN

1 Men their rights and nothing more; women their rights and nothing less.
Motto of The Revolution, (1868)

2 There never will be complete equality until women themselves help to make laws and elect lawmakers.
The Arena, (1897) **Anthony, Susan B.** (1820–1906) US reformer, feminist and abolitionist

3 Women are young at politics, but they are old at suffering; soon they will learn that through politics they can prevent some kinds of suffering.

My Two Countries (1923) **Astor, Nancy, Viscountess** (1879–1964) US-born British Conservative politician and hostess

4 Feminism is the theory: lesbianism is the practice.
Attr. in Amazons, *Bluestockings and Crones: A Feminist Dictionary* **Atkinson, Ti-Grace** (c.1938–) US feminist

5 I'm not a member of the weaker sex.
In Simon Rose, *Classic Film Guide* (1995) **Bacall, Lauren** (1924–) US film actress

6 Patience is one of those 'feminine' qualities which have their origin in our oppression but should be preserved after our liberation.
Marie-Claire, (1976) **Beauvoir, Simone de** (1908–1986) French writer, feminist critic and philosopher

7 I don't want to hear about ironing. I don't want to smell the iron. Why? I regard it as a badge of servitude.
The Times, (1998) **Binchy, Maeve** (1940–) Irish novelist

8 Had I been in anything inferior to him, he would not have hated me so thoroughly, but I knew all that he knew, and, what was worse, he suspected that I kept the padlock of silence on mental wealth in which he was no sharer.
The Professor (1857) **Brontë, Charlotte** (1816–1855) English writer

9 Uncle Harry was an early feminist ... Our family would often recount how, at a race-meeting in Ayr, he threw himself under a suffragette.
Are You Looking at Me, Jimmy? **Brown, Arnold** Scottish comedian

10 The freedom that women were supposed to have found in the Sixties largely boiled down to easy contraception and abortion; things to make life easier for men, in fact.
Born again Cows (1986)

11 A good part – and definitely the most fun part – of being a feminist is about frightening men.
Time Out, (1989) **Burchill, Julie** (1960–) English writer

12 Fascism recognises women as part of the life force of the country, laying down a division of duties between the two sexes, without putting obstacles in the way of those women who by their intellectual gifts reach the highest positions.
Italian Women, Past and Present (1937)
Castellani, Maria (fl. 1930s) Italian educator and writer

13 Convent girls never leave the church, they just become feminists. I learned that in Australia.
Turtle Beach (1981) **D'Alpuget, Blanche** (1944–) Australian writer

14 Patriarchy is itself the prevailing religion of the entire planet, and its essential message is necrophilia.
Gyn/Ecology: the Metaethics of Radical Feminism (1979) **Daly, Mary** (1928–) US feminist and theologian

15 Mateship is an informal male-bonding institution involving powerful subliminal homosexuality. Indeed some of its most ardent intellectual celebrants are slowly coming to see that mateship is deeply antipathetic to women.
The Real Matilda ... (1976) **Dixson, Miriam Joyce** (1930–)

16 We imagined, in our ignorance, that we might be novelists and philosophers... We did not know that our professors had a system of beliefs and convictions that designated us as an inferior gender class, and that that system of beliefs and convictions was virtually universal – the cherished assumption of most of the writers, philosophers, and historians we were so ardently studying.
Our Blood: Prophecies and Discourses on Sexual Politics (1976) **Dworkin, Andrea** (1946–2005) US writer and feminist

17 It's a cover for lesbian homosexuality.
Daily Mail, (1993) **Fairbairn, Sir Nicholas** (1933–1995) Scottish Conservative MP and barrister. On feminism

18 The 'feminine' woman is forever static and childlike. She is like the ballerina in an old-fashioned music box, her unchanging features tiny and girlish, her voice tinkly, her body stuck on a pin, rotating in a spiral that will never grow.
Backlash: The Undeclared War Against American Women (1991) **Faludi, Susan** (1959–) US writer and feminist

19 If the women's movement can be summed up in a single phrase, it is 'the right to choose'.
Women, Sex and Pornography (1980)

20 Women's Liberationists are both right and wrong when they say that rape is not about sex but about power: for men, sex is power, unless culture corrects biology.
Women, Sex and Pornography (1980) **Faust, Beatrice Eileen** (1939–) Australian writer and feminist

21 When modern woman discovered the orgasm it was (combined with modern birth control) perhaps the biggest single nail in the coffin of male dominance.
In Morgan, *The Descent of Woman* (1972) **Figes, Eva** (1932–) German-born British writer and critic

22 A man has every season while a woman only has the right to spring. That disgusts me.
Daily Mail, (1989) **Fonda, Jane** (1937–) US actress and political activist

23 It is men who face the biggest problems in the future, adjusting to their new and complicated role.
Attr. **Ford, Anna** (1943–) English television newscaster and reporter

24 The extension of women's privileges is the basic principle of all social progress.
Théorie des Quatre Mouvements (1808) **Fourier, François Charles Marie** (1772–1837) French social theorist

25 I hope there will come a day when you, daughter mine, or your daughter, can truly afford to say 'I'm not a feminist. I'm a person' – and a day, not too far away, I hope, when I can stop fighting for women and get onto other matters that interest me now.

Letter to her daughter, in *Cosmopolitan,* (1978)
Friedan, Betty (1921–2006) US feminist leader and writer

26 Gay men generally are in significant ways, perhaps in all important ways, more loyal to masculinity and male-supremacy than other men. The gay rights movement may be the fundamentalism of the global religion which is patriarchy.
In Julie Burchill, *Sex and Sensibility* **Frye, Marilyn** (1934–) US feminist and writer

27 If women understand by emancipation the adoption of the masculine role then we are lost indeed.
The Female Eunuch (1970) **Greer, Germaine** (1939–) Australian feminist, critic, English scholar and writer

28 Feminists who still sleep with men are delivering their most vital energies to the oppressor.
Lesbian Nation: The Feminist Solution (1973)

29 Until all women are lesbians there will be no true political revolution.
Lesbian Nation: The Feminist Solution (1973)

30 No one should have to dance backwards all their life.
In Miles, *The Women's History of the World* (1988) **Johnston, Jill** (1929–) English-born US dancer, critic and feminist

31 If men could get pregnant, abortion would be a sacrament.
In Steinem, *The Verbal Karate of Florynce R. Kennedy, Esq.* (1973) **Kennedy, Florynce R.** (1916–2000) US lawyer, feminist and civil rights activist

32 The emancipation of women is practically the greatest egoistic movement of the nineteenth century, and the most intense affirmation of the right of the self that history has yet seen.
The Century of the Child (1909) **Key, Ellen** (1849–1926) Swedish feminist, writer and lecturer

33 That learning belongs not to the female character, and that the female mind is not capable of a degree of improvement equal to that of the other sex, are narrow and unphilosophical prejudices.

Essays, Moral and Literary (1782) **Knox, Vicesimus** (1752–1821) English churchman and writer

34 Women have no surnames of their own. Their names are literally sirnames. Women only have one name that is ours, our first or given name.
Dance on the Earth: A Memoir (1989) **Laurence, Margaret** (1926–1987) Canadian novelist

35 I believe that (in one form or another) castration may be the solution. And the feminization of the white European and American is already far advanced, coming in the wake of the war.
The Art of Being Ruled (1926) **Lewis, Wyndham** (1882–1957) US-born British painter, critic and writer

36 Above the titles of wife and mother, which, although dear, are transitory and accidental, there is the title human being, which precedes and out-ranks every other.
What Shall We Do with Our Daughters **Livermore, Mary Ashton** (c.1820–1905) US writer

37 I'm furious about the Women's Liberationists. They keep getting up on soapboxes and proclaiming that women are brighter than men. That's true, but it should be kept very quiet or it ruins the whole racket.
The Observer, (1973) **Loos, Anita** (1893–1981) US writer and screenwriter

38 How idiotic civilization is! Why be given a body if you have to keep it shut up in a case like a rare, rare fiddle?
Bliss and Other Stories (1920) **Mansfield, Katherine** (1888–1923) New Zealand writer

39 Is it to be understood that the principles of the Declaration of Independence bear no relation to half of the human race?
Society in America (1837) **Martineau, Harriet** (1802–1876) English writer

40 The most important thing women have to do is to stir up the zeal of women themselves.
Letter to Alexander Bain, (1869)

41 The principle which regulates the existing social relations between the two sexes – the legal subordination of one sex to the other – is wrong in itself, and now one of the chief hindrances to human improvement; and ... it ought to be replaced by a principle of perfect equality, admitting no power or privilege on the one side, nor disability on the other.
The Subjection of Women (1869) **Mill, John Stuart** (1806–1873) English philosopher, economist and reformer

42 The vote, I thought, means nothing to women. We should be armed.
In Erica Jong, *Fear of Flying* (1973) **O'Brien, Edna** (1936–) Irish writer and dramatist

43 *Fat is a Feminist Issue.*
Title of book, (1978) **Orbach, Susie** (1946–) US psychotherapist

44 Women and children first is an unscientific sentimentality which must be opposed.
The Observer, (1998) **Paglia, Camille** (1947–) US academic

45 We are here to claim our right as women, not only to be free, but to fight for freedom. It is our privilege, as well as our pride and our joy, to take some part in this militant movement, which, as we believe, means the regeneration of all humanity.
Speech, (1911) **Pankhurst, Dame Christabel** (1880–1958) English suffragette

46 We have taken this action, because as women ... we realize that the condition of our sex is so deplorable that it is our duty even to break the law in order to call attention to the reasons why we do so.
Speech in court, (1908)

47 Men made the moral code and they expect women to accept it.
Speech, (1913)

48 If civilization is to advance at all in the future, it must be through the help of women, women freed of their political shackles, women with full power to work their will in society.
My Own Story (1914)

49 Women had always fought for men, and for their children. Now they were ready to fight for their own human rights. Our militant movement was established.
My Own Story (1914) **Pankhurst, Emmeline** (1858–1928) English suffragette

50 When women's lib started I was the first to burn my bra and it took three days to put out the fire.
In Simon Rose, *Essential Film Guide* (1993) **Parton, Dolly** (1946–) US country and western singer

51 One day ... there will be the girl and the woman, whose name will no longer signify merely a contrast to masculinity, but something of value in itself, something in respect of which one thinks not of a complement and a limitation, but only of life and existence: the female person. This progress will make the experience of love ... become a relationship which is one of person to person, no longer one of man and wife. And this more human love ... will resemble one ... which consists in this, that two solitary people protect and limit and greet each other.
Letters to a Young Poet (1929) **Rilke, Rainer Maria** (1875–1926) Austrian poet, born in Prague

52 It is about a socialist, anti-family movement that encourages women to leave their husbands, kill their children, practice witchcraft and become lesbians.
The World Almanac and Book of Facts, (1993) **Robertson, Pat** (1930–) US fundamentalist Christian broadcaster and politician. On feminism

53 I'm a Roman Catholic and I take a dim view of 2,500 celibates shuffling back and forth to Rome to discuss birth control and not one woman to raise a voice.
The Toronto Star, (1975) **Sabia, Laura** (1903–1990) Canadian feminist writer

54 No woman can call herself free who does not own and control her own body.
In Rosalind Miles, *The Women's History of the World* (1988) **Sanger, Margaret** (1879–1966) US birth control activist

55 We don't sell our bodies. Housewives do that. What we do is rent our bodies for sexual services.
The Toronto Star, (1989) **Scott, Valerie** Canadian prostitute and feminist

56 Home is the girl's prison and the woman's workhouse.
Man and Superman (1903)

57 Give women the vote, and in five years there will be a crushing tax on bachelors.
Man and Superman (1903) **Shaw, George Bernard** (1856–1950) Irish socialist, writer, dramatist and critic

58 Every man, deep down, knows he's a worthless piece of shit.
In Bassnett, *Feminist Experiences: The Women's Movement in Four Cultures* (1986) **Solanas, Valerie** (1940–1998) US artist. SCUM (Society for Cutting Up Men) manifesto, 1968

59 We hold these truths to be self-evident, that all men and women are created equal.
'Declaration of Sentiments', (1848)

60 ... we still wonder at the stolid incapacity of all men to understand that woman feels the invidious distinctions of sex exactly as the black man does those of color, or the white man the more transient distinctions of wealth, family, position, place, and power; that she feels as keenly as man the injustice of disfranchisement.
In Anthony and Gage (eds), *History of Woman Suffrage* (1881)

61 Woman has been the great unpaid laborer of the world.
In Anthony and Gage (eds), *History of Woman Suffrage* (1881)

62 Womanhood is the great fact in her life; wifehood and motherhood are but incidental relations.
In Anthony and Gage (eds), *History of Woman Suffrage* (1881)

63 The prolonged slavery of woman is the darkest page in human history.
In Anthony and Gage (eds), *History of Woman Suffrage* (1881)

64 As to woman's subjection, on which both the canon and the civil law delight to dwell, it is important to note that equal dominion is given to woman over every living thing, but not one word is said giving man dominion over woman.
The Woman's Bible (1895) On Genesis **Stanton, Elizabeth Cady** (1815–1902) US suffragist, abolitionist, feminist, editor and writer

65 I don't believe in segregation of any kind, and I think men and women should unite to fight the battle. All the men I've known have been in favour of women's success.
Interview with Rodney Wetherell, first broadcast by Australian Broadcasting Commission, (1980) **Stead, Christina** (1902–1983) Australian writer

66 Some of us have become the men we wanted to marry.
The Observer, (1982) **Steinem, Gloria** (1934–) US writer and feminist activist

67 Wonderful women! Have you ever thought how much we all, and women especially, owe to Shakespeare for his vindication of women in these fearless, high-spirited, resolute and intelligent heroines?
Four Lectures on Shakespeare (1932) **Terry, Dame Ellen** (1847–1928) English actress, theatrical manager and memoirist

68 Why join a women's group to lobby government ministers when you can become a minister yourself?
Australian Women's Weekly, (1982) **Toner, Pauline Therese** (1935–1989) Australian politician. The credo of the first woman Minister in the history of the Victorian Parliament

69 I blame the women's movement for ten years in a boiler suit.
Attr. **Tweedie, Jill** (1936–1993) English journalist

70 God created men and women different – then let them remain each in their own position.
Letter to Sir Theodore Martin, (1870) **Victoria, Queen** (1819–1901) Queen of the United Kingdom

71 The thought could not be avoided that the best home for a feminist was in another person's lab.
The Double Helix (1968) **Watson, James Dewey** (1928–) US biologist

72 There has to be a halt in the gender war and feminism must extend its remit to include the rights of men.
The Observer debate on feminism, (1998) **Weldon, Fay** (1931–) British writer

73 People call me a feminist whenever I express sentiments that differentiate me from a doormat or a prostitute.
In Anne Stibbs (ed.), *Hell Hath No Fury* **West, Dame Rebecca** (1892–1983) English writer, critic and feminist

74 Women have always been the guardians of wisdom and humanity which makes them natural, but usually secret, rulers. The time has come for them to rule openly, but together with and not against men.
Bisexuality: A Study **Wolff, Charlotte** (1904–1986) German-born British psychiatrist and writer

75 The woman who has only been taught to please will soon find that her charms are oblique sunbeams, and that they cannot have much effect on her husband's heart when they are seen every day.
A Vindication of the Rights of Woman (1792)

76 I do not wish them to have power over men; but over themselves.
A Vindication of the Rights of Woman (1792) Of women

77 The divine right of husbands, like the divine right of kings, may, it is hoped, in this enlightened age, be contested without danger.
A Vindication of the Rights of Woman (1792) **Wollstonecraft, Mary** (1759–1797) English feminist, writer and teacher
See also men and women

ENGLAND

1 The Knight in the triumph of his heart made several reflections on the greatness of the British Nation; as, that one Englishman could beat three Frenchmen; that we cou'd never be in danger of Popery so long as we took care of our fleet; that the Thames was the noblest river in Europe; that London Bridge was a greater piece of work than any of the Seven Wonders of the World; with many other honest prejudices which naturally cleave to the heart of a true Englishman.
The Spectator, (May 1712) **Addison, Joseph** (1672–1719) English essayist, poet, playwright and statesman

2 The English instinctively admire any man who has no talent and is modest about it.
Attr. **Agate, James** (1877–1947) English drama critic and writer

3 The English – in England – are among the most tolerant bigots on earth.
The Times, (1999) **Anonymous** Introduction to a new Lonely Planet British phrasebook

4 Beautiful city! so venerable, so lovely, so unravaged by the fierce intellectual life of our century, so serene! ... whispering from her towers the last enchantments of the Middle Age ... home of lost causes, and forsaken beliefs, and unpopular names, and impossible loyalties!
Essays in Criticism (1865) Of Oxford

5 And that sweet city with her dreaming spires,
She needs not June for beauty's heightening.
'Thyrsis' (1866) Of Oxford **Arnold, Matthew** (1822–1888) English poet, critic, essayist and educationist

6 One has not great hopes from Birmingham. I always say there is something direful in the sound.
Emma (1816)

7 Oh! who can ever be tired of Bath?
Northanger Abbey (1818) **Austen, Jane** (1775–1817) English writer

8 Oxford is on the whole more attractive than Cambridge to the ordinary visitor; and the traveller is therefore recommended to visit Cambridge first, or to omit it altogether if he cannot visit both.
Baedeker's Great Britain (1887) **Baedeker, Karl** (1801–1859) German publisher of guidebooks

9 Of all nations in the world the English are perhaps the least a nation of pure philosophers.
The English Constitution (1867) **Bagehot, Walter** (1826–1877) English economist and political philosopher

10 He was born an Englishman and remained one for years.
The Hostage (1958) **Behan, Brendan** (1923–1964) Irish dramatist, writer and Republican

11 The royal navy of England hath ever been its greatest defence and ornament; it is its ancient and natural strength; the floating bulwark of the island.
Commentaries on the Laws of England (1765–1769) **Blackstone, Sir William** (1723–1780) English judge, historian and politician

12 England, ah, perfidious England, which the bulwarks of the sea rendered inaccessible to the Romans, the faith of the Saviour made landfall even there.
Oeuvres de Bossuet (1816) **Bossuet, Jacques-Bénigne** (1627–1704)

13 When you destroy a blade of grass
You poison England at her roots:
Remember no man's foot can pass
Where evermore no green life shoots.
'To Ironfounders and Others' (1912)
Bottomley, Gordon (1874–1948) English poet and verse dramatist

14 I like the English. They have the most rigid code of immorality in the world.
Eating People is Wrong (1954) **Bradbury, Malcolm** (1932–) English writer, critic and academic

15 England is the mother of Parliaments.
Speech, (1865) **Bright, John** (1811–1889) English Liberal politician and social reformer

16 If I should die, think only this of me:
That there's some corner of a foreign field
That is for ever England.

'The Soldier' (1914) **Brooke, Rupert** (1887–1915) English poet

17 All places, all airs make unto me one country; I am in England, everywhere, and under any meridian.
Religio Medici (1643) **Browne, Sir Thomas** (1605–1682) English physician, author and antiquary

18 Oh, to be in England
Now that April's there,
And whoever wakes in England
Sees, some morning, unaware,
That the lowest boughs and the brushwood sheaf
Round the elm-tree bole are in tiny leaf,
While the chaffinch sings on the orchard bough
In England – now!
'Home Thoughts, from Abroad' (1845)
Browning, Robert (1812–1889) English poet

19 The wish to spread those opinions that we hold conducive to our own welfare is so deeply rooted in the English character that few of us can escape its influence.
Erewhon (1872) **Butler, Samuel** (1835–1902) English writer, painter, philosopher and scholar

20 I am sure my bones would not rest in an English grave, or my clay mix with the earth of that country. I believe the thought would drive me mad on my deathbed, could I suppose that any of my friends would be base enough to convey my carcass back to your soil. I would not even feed your worms if I could help it.
Letter to John Murray, (1819)

21 The English winter – ending in July,
To recommence in August.
Don Juan (1824) **Byron, Lord** (1788–1824) English poet, satirist and traveller

22 Thirty millions, mostly fools.
Attr. **Carlyle, Thomas** (1795–1881) Scottish historian, biographer, critic, and essayist. When asked what the population of England was

23 He's an Anglo-Saxon Messenger – and those are Anglo-Saxon attitudes.

Through the Looking-Glass (and What Alice Found There) (1872) **Carroll, Lewis** (1832–1898) English writer and photographer

24 It is upon the Navy under the good Providence of God that the safety, honour, and welfare of this Realm do chiefly depend.
Preamble to Articles of War, 1652, in Callender, *The Naval Side of British History* (1924) **Charles II** (1630–1685) King of Great Britain and Ireland

25 There'll always be an England
While there's a country lane.
'There'll always be an England' (song, 1939) **Charles, Hughie** (1907–1995) Songwriter and composer

26 Smile at us, pay us, pass us; but do not quite forget.
For we are the people of England, that never have spoken yet.
Poems (1915), 'The Secret People' **Chesterton, G.K.** (1874–1936) English writer, poet and critic

27 Be England what she will,
With all her faults, she is my country still.
'The Farewell' (1764) **Churchill, Charles** (1731–1764) English poet, political writer and clergyman

28 I have never accepted what many people have kindly said, namely that I inspired the nation. It was the nation and the race dwelling all round the globe that had the lion's heart. I had the luck to be called upon to give the roar.
Speech at the Palace of Westminster, 1954, on his 80th birthday **Churchill, Sir Winston** (1874–1965) English Conservative Prime Minister

29 Well, the English have no family feelings. That is, none of the kind you mean. They have them, and one of them is that relations must cause no expense.
Parents and Children (1941) **Compton-Burnett, Dame Ivy** (1884–1969) English novelist

30 Is there in the world a climate more uncertain than our own? And, which is a natural consequence, is there any where a people more unsteady, more apt to discontent, more saturnine, dark and melancholic than our selves? Are we not of all people the most unfit to be alone, and most unsafe to be trusted with our selves?
Amendments of Mr Collier's False and Imperfect Citations (1698) **Congreve, William** (1670–1729) English dramatist

31 Mad dogs and Englishmen go out in the mid-day sun;
The Japanese don't care to, the Chinese wouldn't dare to;
Hindus and Argentines sleep firmly from twelve to one,
But Englishmen detest a Siesta …
In the mangrove swamps where the python romps
There is peace from twelve till two.
Even caribous lie around and snooze,
For there's nothing else to do.
In Bengal, to move at all
Is seldom, if ever done.
'Mad Dogs and Englishmen' (song, 1931) **Coward, Sir Noël** (1899–1973) English dramatist, actor, producer and composer

32 England, with all thy faults, I love thee still –
My country!
The Task (1785) **Cowper, William** (1731–1800) English poet, hymn writer and letter writer

33 A young girl, when asked how she would like to go to England, replied with great naïveté, 'I should be afraid to go, from the number of thieves there,' doubtless conceiving England to be a downright hive of such, that threw off its annual swarms to people the wilds of this colony.
Two Years in New South Wales (1827) **Cunningham, Peter Miller** (1789–1864) Surgeon-superintendent on convict ships

34 Your Roman-Saxon-Danish-Norman English.
The True-Born Englishman (1701) **Defoe, Daniel** (c.1661–1731) English writer and critic

35 There is in the Englishman a combination of qualities, a modesty, an independence, a responsibility, a repose, combined with an absence of everything calculated to call a blush into the cheek of a young person, which one would seek in vain among the Nations of the Earth.
Our Mutual Friend (1865) **Dickens, Charles** (1812–1870) English writer

36 But 'tis the talent of our English nation, Still to be plotting some new reformation.
Prologue at Oxford (1680) **Dryden, John** (1631–1700) English poet, satirist, dramatist and critic

37 It is not that the Englishman can't feel – it is that he is afraid to feel. He has been taught at his public school that feeling is bad form. He must not express great joy or sorrow, or even open his mouth too wide when he talks – his pipe might fall out if he did.
Abinger Harvest (1936) **Forster, E.M.** (1879–1970) English writer, essayist and literary critic

38 We've got to have rules and obey them. After all, we're not savages. We're English; and the English are best at everything. So we've got to do the right things.
Lord of the Flies (1954) **Golding, William** (1911–1993) English writer and poet

39 Answer was given that they were called Angles. But he remarked, 'They are well named, for they have the countenance of angels, and as such should be coheirs with the angels in heaven.'
In Bede, *Historia Ecclesiastica* (731) **Gregory I** (540–604) Pope and saint

40 All of Stratford, in fact, suggests powdered history – add hot water and stir and you have a delicious, nourishing Shakespeare.
With Malice Toward Some (1938)

41 ... the English think of an opinion as something which a decent person, if he has the misfortune to have one, does all he can to hide.
With Malice Toward Some (1938)

42 Living in England, provincial England, must be like being married to a stupid but exquisitely beautiful wife.

With Malice Toward Some (1938)

43 The attitude of the English ... toward English history reminds one a good deal of the attitude of a Hollywood director toward love.
With Malice Toward Some (1938) **Halsey, Margaret** (1910– 1997) US writer

44 The English (it must be owned) are rather a foul-mouthed nation.
Table-Talk (1822) **Hazlitt, William** (1778–1830) English writer and critic

45 The Englishman never enjoys himself except for a noble purpose.
Uncommon Law (1935) **Herbert, Sir A.P.** (1890–1971) English humorist, writer, dramatist and politician

46 Nobody has ever lost money by overestimating the superstitious credulity of an English jury.
Pictures of Perfection (1994) **Hill, Reginald** (1936–) British writer and playwright

47 England has two books: the Bible and Shakespeare. England made Shakespeare but the Bible made England.
Attr. **Hugo, Victor** (1802–1885) French poet, writer, dramatist and politician

48 It will be said of this generation that it found England a land of beauty and left it a land of beauty spots.
The Observer, (1953) **Joad, C.E.M.** (1891–1953) English popularizer of philosophy

49 When two Englishmen meet, their first talk is of the weather.
The Idler (1758–1760) **Johnson, Samuel** (1709–1784) English lexicographer, poet, critic, conversationalist and essayist

50 It is impossible to live in a country which is continually under hatches ... Rain! Rain! Rain!
Letter to J.H. Reynolds, (1818) **Keats, John** (1795–1821) English poet. Of Devon

51 'Tis the hard grey weather Breeds hard English men.
'Ode to the North-East Wind' (1854) **Kingsley, Charles** (1819–1875) English writer, poet, lecturer and clergyman

52 For Allah created the English mad – the
maddest of all mankind!
The Five Nations (1903) **Kipling, Rudyard** (1865–
1936) Indian-born British poet and writer

53 It was one of those places where the spirit
of aboriginal England still lingers, the old
savage England, whose last blood flows
still in a few Englishmen, Welshmen,
Cornishmen.
St Mawr (1925) **Lawrence, D.H.** (1885–1930)
English writer, poet and critic

54 The British, he thought, must be gluttons
for satire: even the weather forecast
seemed to be some kind of spoof,
predicting every possible combination of
weather for the next twenty-four hours
without actually committing itself to
anything specific.
Changing Places (1975) **Lodge, David** (1935–)
English writer, satirist and literary critic

55 Owing to the weather, English social life
must always have largely occurred either
indoors, or, when out of doors, in active
motion.
'Life Among The English' (1942) **Macaulay,
Dame Rose** (1881–1958) English writer

56 An acre in Middlesex is better than a
principality in Utopia.
Collected Essays (1843), 'Lord Bacon'

57 The history of England is emphatically the
history of progress.
'Sir James Mackintosh' (1843) **Macaulay, Lord**
(1800–1859) English Liberal statesman,
essayist and poet

58 England is … a country infested with
people who love to tell us what to do, but
who very rarely seem to know what's going
on.
England, Half English **MacInnes, Colin** (1914–
1976) English writer

59 Let wealth and commerce, laws and
learning die,
But leave us still our old nobility!
England's Trust (1841) **Manners, Lord** (1818–
1906) English Conservative politician and
writer

60 England is not all the world.

Said at her trial, (1586) **Mary, Queen of Scots**
(1542–1587) Daughter of James V, mother of
James VI and I; executed by Elizabeth I of
England

61 An Englishman, even if he is alone, forms
an orderly queue of one.
How to be an Alien (1946) **Mikes, George** (1912–
1987) Hungarian-born British writer

62 The English are busy; they don't have the
time to be polite.
Pensées et fragments inédits (1899) **Montesquieu,
Charles** (1689–1755) French philosopher and
jurist

63 England is a nation of shopkeepers.
In O'Meara, *Napoleon in Exile* (1822) **Napoleon
I** (1769–1821) Emperor of France

64 Let us pause to consider the English
Who when they pause to consider
themselves they get all reticently thrilled
and tinglish.
Englishmen are distinguished by their
traditions and ceremonials,
And also by their affection for their
colonies and their condescension to their
colonials.
'England Expects' (1929) **Nash, Ogden** (1902–
1971) US poet

65 The Englishman has all the qualities of a
poker except its occasional warmth.
Attr. **O'Connell, Daniel** (1775–1847) Irish
nationalist politician

66 England is not the jewelled isle of
Shakespeare's much-quoted passage, nor
is it the inferno depicted by Dr Goebbels.
More than either it resembles a family, a
rather stuffy Victorian family, with not
many black sheep in it but with all its
cupboards bursting with skeletons. It has
rich relations who have to be kow-towed to
and poor relations who are horribly sat
upon, and there is a deep conspiracy about
the source of the family income. It is a
family in which the young are generally
thwarted and most of the power is in the
hands of irresponsible uncles and
bedridden aunts. Still, it is a family … A
family with the wrong members in control.
'England, Your England' (1941) **Orwell,
George** (1903–1950) English writer and critic

67 To be born an Englishman – ah, what an easy conceit that builds in you, what a self-righteous nationalism, a secure xenophobia, what a pride in your ignorance. No other people speak so few languages. No other people – certainly not the Germans, Italians or French, and not even the multi-ethnic Americans – have an expression that is the equivalent of 'greasy foreign muck'. The noble, wisecracking savages depicted everywhere from *Eastenders* to *Boys from the Blackstuff* are exercises in nostalgia who no longer exist.
Arena, (1989) **Parsons, Tony** (1953–) British journalist and broadcaster

68 But Lord! to see the absurd nature of Englishmen, that cannot forbear laughing and jeering at everything that looks strange.
Diary, (1662) **Pepys, Samuel** (1633–1703) English diarist, naval administrator and politician

69 England has saved herself by her exertions, and will, as I trust, save Europe by her example.
Speech, (1805) **Pitt, William** (1759–1806) English politician and Prime Minister

70 This is the city of perspiring dreams.
The Glittering Prizes (1976) **Raphael, Frederic** (1931–) English author. Of Cambridge

71 Remember that you are an Englishman, and have consequently won first prize in the lottery of life.
In Ustinov, *Dear Me* (1977) **Rhodes, Cecil** (1853–1902) English imperialist, financier and South African statesman

72 The English people imagine themselves to be free, but they are wrong: it is only during the election of members of parliament that they are so.
Du Contrat Social (1762) **Rousseau, Jean-Jacques** (1712–1778) Swiss-born French philosopher, educationist and essayist

73 England is the paradise of individuality, eccentricity, heresy, anomalies, hobbies, and humours.
Soliloquies in England (1922) **Santayana, George** (1863–1952) Spanish-born US philosopher and writer

74 We [the English] seem as it were to have conquered and peopled half the world in a fit of absence of mind.
The Expansion of England (1883) **Seeley, Sir John Robert** (1834–1895) English historian, essayist and scholar

75 Pope Gregory ... made the memorable joke – 'Non Angli, sed Angeli' ('not Angels, but Anglicans').
1066 And All That (1930) **Sellar, Walter** (1898–1951) and **Yeatman, Robert Julian** (1897–1968) British writers

76 This royal throne of kings, this scept'red isle,
This earth of majesty, this seat of Mars,
This other Eden, demi-paradise,
This fortress built by Nature for herself
Against infection and the hand of war,
This happy breed of men, this little world,
This precious stone set in the silver sea,
Which serves it in the office of a wall,
Or as a moat defensive to a house,
Against the envy of less happier lands;
This blessed plot, this earth, this realm, this England.
Richard II, II.i **Shakespeare, William** (1564–1616) English dramatist, poet and actor

77 There is nothing so bad or so good that you will not find Englishmen doing it; but you will never find an Englishman in the wrong. He does everything on principle. He fights you on patriotic principles; he robs you on business principles; he enslaves you on imperial principles; he bullies you on manly principles; he supports his king on loyal principles and cuts off his king's head on republican principles.
The Man of Destiny (1898)

78 How can what an Englishman believes be heresy? It is a contradiction in terms.
Saint Joan (1924) **Shaw, George Bernard** (1856–1950) Irish socialist, writer, dramatist and critic

79 What a pity it is that we have no amusements in England but vice and religion!
In H. Pearson, *The Smith of Smiths* (1934) **Smith, Sydney** (1771–1845) English clergyman, essayist, journalist and wit

80 This land is blessed with a powerful mediocrity of mind. It has saved you from communism and from fascism.
The Observer, 1998, from a review of Jeremy Paxman's *The English* **Steiner, George** (1929–) French-born US writer and critic

81 The English enjoy themselves sadly, according to the custom of their country.
Memoirs (1638) **Sully, Duc de** (1559–1641) French statesman and financier

82 It is a commonplace that the characteristic virtue of Englishmen is their power of sustained practical activity, and their characteristic vice a reluctance to test the quality of that activity by reference to principles.
The Acquisitive Society (1921) **Tawney, R.H.** (1880–1962) British economic historian and Christian socialist

83 The national sport of England is obstacle-racing. People fill their rooms with useless and cumbersome furniture, and spend the rest of their lives trying to dodge it.
In Hesketh Pearson, *Beerbohm Tree* (1956) **Tree, Sir Herbert Beerbohm** (1853–1917) English actor and theatre manager

84 Victorian values ... were the values when our country became great.
Television interview, (1982) **Thatcher, Margaret** (1925–) English Conservative Prime Minister

85 I would like to live in Manchester, England. The transition between Manchester and death would be unnoticeable.
Attr.

86 The English are mentioned in the Bible: Blessed are the meek for they shall inherit the earth.
Pudd'nhead Wilson's Calendar (1894) **Twain, Mark** (1835–1910) US humorist, writer, journalist and lecturer

87 The gloomy Englishman, even in love, always wants to reason. We are more reasonable in France.
Les Originaux, Entrée des Diverses Nations **Voltaire** (1694–1778) French philosopher, dramatist, poet, historian, writer and critic

88 In England we have come to rely upon a comfortable time-lag of fifty years or a century intervening between the perception that something ought to be done and a serious attempt to do it.
The Work, Wealth and Happiness of Mankind (1931) **Wells, H.G.** (1866–1946) English writer

89 It's nae good blamin' it oan the English fir colonising us. Ah don't hate the English. They're just wankers. We can't even pick a decent vibrant, healthy culture to be colonised by.
Trainspotting (1994) **Welsh, Irvine** (1957–) Scottish novelist

90 I did a picture in England one winter and it was so cold I almost got married.
New York Times, (1956) **Winters, Shelley** (1920–2006) US actress

91 Those things which the English public never forgives – youth, power, and enthusiasm.
In R. Ross (ed.), *Collected Works of Oscar Wilde* (1908)

92 The English have a miraculous power of turning wine into water.
Attr. **Wilde, Oscar** (1854–1900) Irish poet, dramatist, writer, critic and wit

93 Those comfortably padded lunatic asylums which are known, euphemistically, as the stately homes of England.
The Common Reader (1925) **Woolf, Virginia** (1882–1941) English writer and critic

94 I travelled among unknown men
In lands beyond the sea;
Nor, England! did I know till then
What love I bore to thee.
'I travelled among unknown men' (1807)

95 Milton! thou shouldst be living at this hour:
England hath need of thee; she is a fen
Of stagnant waters: altar, sword, and pen,
Fireside, the heroic wealth of hall and bower,
Have forfeited their ancient English dower
Of inward happiness.

'Milton! thou shouldst be living at this hour'
(1807) **Wordsworth, William** (1770–1850)
English poet
See also Britain; cities: London; class;
patriotism

EPITAPHS

1 This is the grave of Mike O'Day
Who died maintaining his right of way.
His right was clear, his will was strong.
But he's just as dead as if he'd been wrong.
Epitaph

2 Sacred to the memory of
Captain Anthony Wedgwood
Accidentally shot by his gamekeeper
Whilst out shooting
'Well done thou good and faithful servant'.
Epitaph

3 Mary Ann has gone to rest,
Safe at last on Abraham's breast,
Which may be nuts for Mary Ann,
But is certainly rough on Abraham.
Epitaph

4 Here lies Will Smith – and, what's
something rarish,
He was born, bred, and hanged, all in the
same parish.
Epitaph

5 Here lies the body of Richard Hind,
Who was neither ingenious, sober, nor
kind.
Epitaph

6 Here lies the body of Mary Ann Lowder,
She burst while drinking a seidlitz powder.
Called from the world to her heavenly rest,
She should have waited till it effervesced.
Epitaph

7 Here lies a poor woman who always was
tired,
For she lived in a place where help wasn't
hired.
Her last words on earth were, Dear friends
I am going
Where washing ain't done nor sweeping
nor sewing,
And everything there is exact to my wishes,
For there they don't eat and there's no
washing of dishes …
Don't mourn for me now, don't mourn for
me never,
For I'm going to do nothing for ever and
ever.
Epitaph in Bushey churchyard

8 Here lie I by the chancel door;
They put me here because I was poor.
The further in, the more you pay,
But here lie I as snug as they.
Epitaph in Devon churchyard

9 Here lies my wife,
Here lies she;
Hallelujah!
Hallelujee!
Epitaph in Leeds churchyard

10 My sledge and anvil lie declined
My bellows too have lost their wind
My fire's extinct, my forge decayed,
And in the dust my vice is laid
My coals are spent, my iron's gone
My nails are drove, my work is done.
Epitaph in Nettlebed churchyard

11 Here lies a man who was killed by
lightning;
He died when his prospects seemed to be
brightening.
He might have cut a flash in this world of
trouble,
But the flash cut him, and he lies in the
stubble.
Epitaph, Torrington, Devon

12 Little Willy from his mirror
Licked the mercury right off,
Thinking in his childish error,
It would cure the whooping cough.
At the funeral his mother
Smartly said to Mrs Brown:
'Twas a chilly day for Willie
When the mercury went down.'
'Willie's Epitaph'

13 Stranger! Approach this spot with gravity!
John Brown is filling his last cavity.
Epitaph of a dentist

14 That we spent, we had:
That we gave, we have:
That we left, we lost.
Epitaph of the Earl of Devonshire

15 Lo, Huddled up, together Lye
   Gray Age, Grene youth, White Infancy.
   If Death doth Nature's Laws dispence,
   And reconciles All Difference
   Tis Fit, One Flesh, One House Should have
   One Tombe, One Epitaph, One Grave:
   And they that Liv'd and Lov'd Either,
   Should Dye and Lye and Sleep together.
   Good reader, whether go or stay
   Thou must not hence be Long Away.
   Epitaph of William Bartholomew (died 1662),
   his wife and some of their children, St John
   the Baptist, Burford

16 Here lies a child that took one peep of Life
   And viewed its endless troubles with
   dismay,
   Gazed with an anguish'd glance upon the
   strife
   And sickening at the sight flew fast away.
   What though for many the gate of Heaven
   is shut,
   It stands wide open for this little Butt.
   Epitaph on Allena Butt, who had died when
   only 6 weeks old

17 All who come my grave to see
   Avoid damp beds and think of me.
   Epitaph of Lydia Eason, St Michael's, Stoke

18 Rest in peace – until we meet again.
   Widow's epitaph for husband; in Mitford, *The
   American Way of Death*

19 The Sun himself cannot forget
   His fellow traveller.
   Wit's Recreations (1640) Of Sir Francis Drake

20 Warm summer sun shine kindly here:
   Warm summer wind blow softly here:
   Green sod above lie light, lie light:
   Good-night, Dear Heart: good-night,
   good-night.
   Memorial to Clorinda Haywood, St
   Bartholomew's, Edgbaston

21 Remember man, as thou goes by,
   As thou art now so once was I,
   As I am now so must thou be,
   Remember man that thou must die.
   Headstone in Straiton, Ayrshire

22 Reader, one moment stop and think,
   That I am in eternity, and you are on the
   brink.
   Tombstone inscription at Perth, Scotland

23 Here lies Fred,
   Who was alive and is dead;
   Had it been his father,
   I had much rather;
   Had it been his brother,
   Still better than another;
   Had it been his sister,
   No one would have missed her;
   Had it been the whole generation,
   Still better for the nation:
   But since 'tis only Fred,
   Who was alive and is dead, –
   There's no more to be said.
   In Horace Walpole, *Memoirs of George II* (1847)

24 Here lie I and my four daughters,
   Killed by drinking Cheltenham waters.
   Had we but stuck to Epsom salts,
   We wouldn't have been in these here
   vaults.
   'Cheltenham Waters'

25 God took our flower,
   Our little Nell;
   He thought He too
   Would like a smell.
   In Thomas Wood, *Cobbers*

26 From a subtle serpents Bite he cride
   our RoseBud cut he drup'd his head and
   died,
   He was his Fathers glorey
   And Mothers pride.
   Memorial to John Howorth, died 8 October
   1804 at 11 years of a snake-bite, St John's
   Churchyard, Wilberforce, New South Wales
   Anonymous

27 Here continueth to rot the body of Francis
   Chartres.
   First line of epitaph **Arbuthnot, John** (1667–
   1735) Scottish physician, pamphleteer and wit

28 Hereabouts died a very gallant gentleman,
   Captain L.E.G. Oates of the Inniskilling
   Dragoons. In March 1912, returning from
   the Pole, he walked willingly to his death in
   a blizzard, to try and save his comrades,
   beset by hardships.
   Epitaph on a cairn and cross erected in the
   Antarctic, (November 1912) **Atkinson,
   Surgeon-Captain E.L.** (1882–1929) English
   polar explorer, doctor and naval officer

29 Perfection, of a kind, was what he was
after,
And the poetry he invented was easy to
understand;
He knew human folly like the back of his
hand,
And was greatly interested in armies and
fleets;
When he laughed, respectable senators
burst with laughter,
And when he cried the little children died
in the streets.
Collected Poems, 1933–1938, 'Epitaph on a
Tyrant'

30 He disappeared in the dead of winter:
The brooks were frozen, the airports
almost deserted,
And snow disfigured the public statues;
The mercury sank in the mouth of the
dying day.
What instruments we have agree
The day of his death was a dark cold day.
Collected Poems, 1939–1947, 'In Memory of W.B.
Yeats'

31 To save your world you asked this man to
die:
Would this man, could he see you now, ask
why?
'Epitaph for the Unknown Soldier' (1955)
Auden, W.H. (1907–1973) English poet,
essayist, critic, teacher and dramatist

32 Though I've always considered Sir
Christopher Wren,
As an architect, one of the greatest of men;
And, talking of Epitaphs, – much I admire
his,
'Circumspice, si Monumentum requiris';
Which an erudite Verger translated to me,
'If you ask for his Monument, Sir-come-
spy-see!'
The Ingoldsby Legends (1840–1847), 'The
Cynotaph' **Barham, Rev. Richard Harris**
(**Thomas Ingoldsby**) (1788–1845) English
clergyman and comic poet

33 The waters were his winding sheet, the sea
was made his tomb;
Yet for his fame the ocean sea, was not
sufficient room.

The Encomion of Lady Pecunia (1598), 'To the
Gentlemen Readers' **Barnfield, Richard** (1574–
1627) English poet. In memory of Sir John
Hawkins

34 When I am dead, I hope it may be said:
'His sins were scarlet, but his books were
read.'
Sonnets and Verse (1923), 'On His Books' **Belloc,
Hilaire** (1870–1953) English writer of verse,
essayist and critic; Liberal MP

35 She sleeps alone at last.
Attr. **Benchley, Robert** (1889–1945) US essayist,
humorist and actor. Suggesting an epitaph for
an actress

36 They Sacrificed Everything Save Honour.
Inscription, (1964) **Blauveldt, Robert R.** On
the cairn dedicated to the memory of the
United Empire Loyalists, Tusket, Yarmouth
County, N.S.; words chosen by Blauveldt who
is of U.E.L. descent

37 A hundred canvasses and seven sons
He left, and never got a likeness once.
'Epitaph on a Portrait Painter' **Bray, John
Jefferson** (1912–1995) Australian lawyer and
poet

38 Underneath this sable hearse
Lies the subject of all verse,
Sidney's sister, Pembroke's mother;
Death! ere thou hast slain another,
Fair and learn'd, and good as she,
Time shall throw a dart at thee.
'Epitaph on the Countess of Pembroke' (1623)
Browne, William (c.1591–1643) English poet

39 His virtues were his arts.
Inscription on the statue of the Marquis of
Rockingham in Wentworth Park **Burke,
Edmund** (1729–1797) Irish-born British
statesman and philosopher

40 Here lie Willie Michie's banes:
O Satan, when ye tak him,
Gie him the schulin' o' your weans,
For clever Deils he'll mak them!
'Epitaph for William Michie. Schoolmaster of
Cleish Parish, Fifeshire' (1787) **Burns, Robert**
(1759–1796) Scottish poet and songwriter

41 With death doomed to grapple,
Beneath this cold slab, he
Who lied in the chapel
Now lies in the Abbey.
'Epitaph for William Pitt' (1820) **Byron, Lord**
(1788–1824) English poet, satirist and traveller

42 My friend, judge not me,
Thou seest I judge not thee.
Betwixt the stirrup and the ground
Mercy I asked, mercy I found.
Remains Concerning Britain (1605), 'Epitaph for
a Man Killed by Falling from His Horse'
Camden, William (1551–1623) English scholar,
antiquary and historian

43 So though a Virgin, yet a Bride
To every Grace, she justifi'd
A chaste Poligamie, and dy'd.
'Inscription on the Tomb of Lady Mary
Wentworth' (1640)

44 Here lyes a King, that rul'd, as he thought
fit
The Universal Monarchie of wit,
Here lyes two Flamens, and both those, the
best,
Apollo's first, at last, the true God's Priest.
'An Elegy upon the death of Doctor Donne'
(1640) **Carew, Thomas** (c.1595–1640) English
poet, musician and dramatist

45 For forty years she was the true and ever-
loving helpmate of her husband, and, by
act and word, unweariedly forwarded him
as none else could, in all of worthy that he
did or attempted. She died at London, 21st
April 1866, suddenly snatched away from
him, and the light of his life as if gone out.
In Hector C. Macpherson, *Thomas Carlyle*
(1896) **Carlyle, Thomas** (1795–1881) Scottish
historian, biographer, critic, and essayist.
Epitaph for Jane Welsh Carlyle in
Haddington Church

46 Here lies wise and valiant dust,
Huddled up, 'twixt fit and just:
Strafford, who was hurried hence
'Twixt treason and convenience.
He spent his time here in a mist,
A Papist, yet a Calvinist.
His Prince's nearest joy and grief;
He had, yet wanted, all relief:
The Prop and Ruin of the State,
The people's violent love and hate:

One in extremes lov'd and abhor'd.
Riddles lie here, or in a word,
Here lies blood; and let it lie
Speechless still, and never cry.
'Epitaph on the Earl of Strafford' (1647)
Cleveland, John (1613–1658) English poet

47 Ere sin could blight or sorrow fade,
Death came with friendly care:
The opening bud to Heaven convey'd
And bade it blossom there.
'Epitaph on an Infant' (1794) **Coleridge,
Samuel Taylor** (1772–1834) English poet,
philosopher and critic

48 Whoso maintains that I am humbled now
(Who wait the Awful Day) is still a liar;
I hope to meet my Maker brow to brow
And find my own the higher.
'Epitaph for a Reviewer' (1954) **Cornford,
Frances Crofts** (1886–1960) English poet and
translator

49 To these, whom Death again did wed,
This Grave's the second Marriage-Bed ...
Peace, good Reader, doe not weepe;
Peace, the Lovers are asleepe:
They (sweet Turtles) folded lye,
In the last knot that love could tye.
Steps to the Temple (1646), 'An Epitaph upon
Husband and Wife, which died, and were
buried together' **Crashaw, Richard** (c.1612–
1649) English religious poet

50 Now we lament one
Who danced on a plume of words,
Sang with a fountain's panache,
Dazzled like slate roofs in sun
After rain, was flighty as birds
And alone as a mountain ash.
The ribald, inspired urchin
Leaning over the lip
Of his world, as over a rock pool
Or a lucky dip,
Found everything brilliant and virgin.
'In Memory of Dylan Thomas' **Day Lewis, C.**
(1904–1972) Irish-born British academic,
writer and critic

51 Here lies he who neither feared nor
flattered any flesh.
Attr. **Douglas, James, Earl of Morton** (c.1516–
1581) Regent of Scotland. Said during the
burial of John Knox, 1572

52 Here lies my wife: here let her lie!
Now she's at rest, and so am I.
'Epitaph intended for his wife' **Dryden, John**
(1631–1700) English poet, satirist, dramatist
and critic

53 When my country takes her place among
the nations of the earth, then and not till
then, let my epitaph be written. I have
done.
Attr. **Emmet, Robert** (1778–1803) Irish patriot.
Before his execution

54 Under this stone, Reader, survey
Dead Sir John Vanbrugh's house of clay.
Lie heavy on him, Earth! for he
Laid many heavy loads on thee!
'Epitaph on Sir John Vanbrugh, Architect of
Blenheim Palace' (died 1726) **Evans, Abel**
(1679–1737) English churchman, poet and
satirist

55 On the whole, I'd rather be in Philadelphia.
His own epitaph **Fields, W.C.** (1880–1946) US
film actor

56 The body of
Benjamin Franklin, printer,
(Like the cover of an old book,
Its contents worn out,
And stript of its lettering and gilding)
Lies here, food for worms!
Yet the work itself shall not be lost,
For it will, as he believed, appear once
more
In a new
And more beautiful edition,
Corrected and amended
By its Author!
Epitaph for himself, (1728) **Franklin,
Benjamin** (1706–1790) US statesman, scientist,
political critic and printer

57 I would have written of me on my stone:
I had a lover's quarrel with the world.
'The Lesson for Today' (1942) **Frost, Robert**
(1874–1963) US poet

58 Here lies Nolly Goldsmith, for shortness
call'd Noll,
Who wrote like an angel, but talk'd like
poor Poll.
'Impromptu Epitaph on Goldsmith', (1774)
Garrick, David (1717–1779) English actor and
theatre manager

59 Green be the turf above thee,
Friend of my better days!
None knew thee but to love thee,
Nor named thee but to praise.
'On the Death of J.R. Drake' (1820) **Halleck,
Fitz-Greene** (1790–1867) US poet, satirist and
banker

60 Go tell those old men, safe in bed,
We took their orders and are dead.
'Inscription for Any War' **Hope, Alec (
Derwent)** (1907–2000) Australian poet and
critic. An ironic parody of the Greek epitaph
commemorating the Spartans who died at
Thermopylae in 480 BC *(see also Epitaphs,97)*

61 His foe was folly and his weapon wit.
Inscription on the tablet to W.S. Gilbert,
Victoria Embankment, London, (1915) **Hope,
Anthony** (1863–1933) British novelist

62 These, in the day when heaven was falling,
The hour when earth's foundations fled,
Followed their mercenary calling
And took their wages and are dead.
Their shoulders held the sky suspended;
They stood, and earth's foundations stay;
What God abandoned, these defended,
And saved the sum of things for pay.
Last Poems (1922) **Housman, A.E.** (1859–1936)
English poet and scholar

63 Within this circular idea
Call'd vulgarly a tomb,
The ideas and impressions lie
That constituted Hume.
Epitaph on his monument on Calton Hill,
Edinburgh **Hume, David** (1711–1776) Scottish
philosopher and political economist

64 And if there be no meeting past the grave,
If all is darkness, silence, yet 'tis rest.
Be not afraid ye waiting hearts that weep;
For still He giveth His beloved sleep,
And if an endless sleep He wills, so best.
Lines on the grave of her husband, 1895, in
Deighton, *Huxley, His Life and Work* (1904)
Huxley, Henrietta (1825–1915) English writer
and poet; wife of T.H. Huxley

65 Officious, innocent, sincere,
Of every friendless name the friend.
Yet still he fills affection's eye,
Obscurely wise, and coarsely kind.

In Boswell, *The Life of Samuel Johnson* (1791) On the death of Mr Levett

66 To Oliver Goldsmith, A Poet, Naturalist, and Historian, who left scarcely any style of writing untouched, and touched none that he did not adorn.
In Boswell, *The Life of Samuel Johnson* (1791)

67 In lapidary inscriptions a man is not upon oath.
In Boswell, *The Life of Samuel Johnson* (1791)
Johnson, Samuel (1709–1784) English lexicographer, poet, critic, conversationalist and essayist

68 O rare Ben Jonson.
Epitaph in Westminster Abbey

69 Rest in soft peace, and, ask'd, say here doth lye
Ben Jonson his best piece of poetrie.
Epigrams (1616), 'On My First Son'

70 Weep with me, all you that read
This little story:
And know for whom a tear you shed
Death's self is sorry.
'Twas a child that so did thrive
In grace and feature,
As Heaven and Nature seem'd to strive
Which own'd the creature.
Years he number'd scarce thirteen
When Fates turn'd cruel,
Yet three fill'd Zodiacs had he been
The stage's jewel;
And did act, what now we moan,
Old men so duly,
As sooth the Parcae thought him one,
He play'd so truly.
So, by error, to his fate
They all consented;
But viewing him since, alas, too late!
They have repented;
And have sought (to give new birth)
In baths to steep him;
But being so much too good for earth,
Heaven vows to keep him.
Epigrams (1616), 'An Epitaph on Salomon Pavy, a Child of Queen Elizabeth's Chapel' **Jonson, Ben** (1572–1637) English dramatist and poet

71 Over my dead body!

Attr. **Kaufman, George S.** (1889–1961) US scriptwriter, librettist and journalist.
Suggestion for his own epitaph

72 Here lies one whose name was writ in water.
Epitaph for himself **Keats, John** (1795–1821) English poet

73 I could not look on Death, which being known,
Men led me to him, blindfold and alone.
The Years Between (1919), 'Epitaphs – The Coward'

74 A Soldier of the Great War Known unto God.
Inscription on the graves of unidentified soldiers, (1919) **Kipling, Rudyard** (1865–1936) Indian-born British poet and writer

75 A man with God is always in the majority.
Inscription on the Reformation Monument, Geneva, Switzerland **Knox, John** (1505–1572) Scottish religious reformer

76 A citizen, first in war, first in peace, and first in the hearts of his countrymen.
Resolution adopted by Congress on the death of George Washington, (1799) **Lee, Henry** (1756–1818) US soldier and statesman

77 Here lies that peerless peer Lord Peter,
Who broke the laws of God and man and metre.
Epitaph for Patrick ('Peter'), Lord Robertson, (1890) **Lockhart, John Gibson** (1794–1854) Scottish writer, critic, and translator

78 To my true king I offer'd free from stain
Courage and faith; vain faith, and courage vain ...
By those white cliffs I never more must see,
By that dear language which I spake like thee,
Forget all feuds, and shed one English tear
O'er English dust. A broken heart lies here.
'A Jacobite's Epitaph' (1845) **Macaulay, Lord** (1800–1859) English Liberal statesman, essayist and poet

79 Here lie I, Martin Elginbrodde:
Hae mercy o' my soul, Lord God;
As I wad do, were I Lord God,
And you were Martin Elginbrodde.

David Elginbrod (1863) **MacDonald, George** (1824–1905) Scottish writer, poet and preacher

80 Who can foretell for what high cause
This Darling of the Gods was born! ...
Gather the flowers, but spare the buds.
'The Picture of Little T.C. in a Prospect of Flowers' (1681) **Marvell, Andrew** (1621–1678) English poet and satirist

81 If, after I depart this vale, you ever remember me and have thought to please my ghost, forgive some sinner and wink your eye at some homely girl.
Smart Set, 1921, Epitaph **Mencken, H.L.** (1880–1956) US writer, critic, philologist and satirist

82 Were there but a few hearts and intellects like hers this earth would already become the hoped-for heaven.
Epitaph for his wife, Harriet, (1859) **Mill, John Stuart** (1806–1873) English philosopher, economist and reformer

83 Here lies George Moore, who looked upon corrections as the one morality.
Conversation with Geraint Goodwin **Moore, George** (1852–1933) Irish writer, dramatist and critic. What he would like on his tombstone

84 Her name was Margaret Lucas, youngest daughter of Lord Lucas, earl of Colchester, a noble family, for all the brothers were valiant, and all the sisters virtuous.
Epitaph in Westminster Abbey; quoted by Joseph Addison **Newcastle, Margaret, Duchess of** (c.1624–1674) English poet, dramatist and woman of letters

85 Excuse my dust.
In Alexander Woollcott, *While Rome Burns* (1934) Her own epitaph

86 He lies below, correct in cypress wood, And entertains the most exclusive worms.
Not So Deep as a Well (1937), 'Epitaph for a Very Rich Man'

87 This is on me.
In J. Keats, *You Might As Well Live* (1970) Suggesting words for tombstone **Parker, Dorothy** (1893–1967) US writer, poet, critic and wit

88 Long night succeeds thy little day
Oh blighted blossom! can it be,
That this gray stone and grassy clay
Have closed our anxious care of thee?
In Henry Cole (ed.), *Works of Peacock* (1875) **Peacock, Thomas Love** (1785–1866) English writer and poet

89 Nature, and Nature's laws lay hid in night:
God said, Let Newton be! and all was light.
'Epitaph for Sir Isaac Newton' (1730)

90 Of manners gentle, of affections mild;
In wit, a man; simplicity, a child:
With native humour temp'ring virtuous rage,
Formed to delight at once and lash the age.
'Epitaph: On Mr. Gay in Westminster Abbey', (1733) **Pope, Alexander** (1688–1744) English poet, translator and editor

91 Nobles and heralds, by your leave,
Here lies what once was Matthew Prior;
The son of Adam and of Eve,
Can Bourbon or Nassau go higher?
'Epitaph' (1702) **Prior, Matthew** (1664–1721) English poet

92 Here lies our sovereign lord the King
Whose word no man relies on,
Who never said a foolish thing,
Nor ever did a wise one.
Epitaph written for Charles II (1706) **Rochester, Earl of** (1647–1680) English poet, satirist, courtier and libertine

93 O Earth, lie heavily upon her eyes;
Seal her sweet eyes weary of watching.
'Rest' (1862) **Rossetti, Christina** (1830–1894) English poet

94 Here sleeps the Silurist; the loved physician;
The face that left no portraiture behind;
The skull that housed white angels and had vision
Of daybreak through the gateways of the mind.
The Heart's Journey (1928) **Sassoon, Siegfried** (1886–1967) English poet and writer

95 Here lies one who might be trusted with untold gold, but not with unmeasured whisky.

Epitaph for his favourite servant, Tom Purdie **Scott, Sir Walter** (1771–1832) Scottish writer and historian

96 Good friend, for Jesu's sake forbear,
To dig the dust enclosed here.
Blest be the man that spares these stones,
And curst be he that moves my bones.
Attr. **Shakespeare, William** (1564–1616)
English dramatist, poet and actor. Epitaph on his tomb

97 Go, tell the Spartans, thou who passest by,
That here, obedient to their laws, we lie.
In Herodotus, *Histories* **Simonides** (c.556–468 BC) Greek poet and epigrammatist. Epitaph for the three hundred Spartans under Leonidas who died at Thermopylae in 480BC

98 No man knows my history.
Funeral sermon, written by himself **Smith, Joseph** (1805–1844) Founder of the Mormon Church

99 Under the wide and starry sky
Dig the grave and let me lie.
Glad did I live and gladly die,
And I laid me down with a will.
This be the verse you grave for me:
'Here he lies where he longed to be;
Home is the sailor, home from sea,
And the hunter home from the hill.'
Underwoods (1887), 'Requiem' **Stevenson, Robert Louis** (1850–1894) Scottish writer, poet and essayist

100 Now I've laid me down to die
I pray my neighbours not to pry
Too deeply into sins that I
Not only cannot here deny
But much enjoyed as time flew by.
In Halliwell, *The Filmgoer's Book of Quotes* (1973) **Sturges, Preston** (1898–1959) US film director and scriptwriter. Suggested epitaph for himself

101 But to the heavens that simple soule is fled:
Which left with such, as covet Christ to know,
Witnesse of faith, that never shall be ded:
Sent for our helth, but not received so.
Thus, for our gilte, this jewel have we lost:
The earth his bones, the heavens possesse his gost.
'Of the death of Sir T.W. [Thomas Wyatt]' **Surrey, Henry Howard, Earl of** (c.1517–1547) English poet, courtier and soldier

102 Where fierce indignation can no longer
tear his heart.
Epitaph

103 Poor Pope will grieve a month, and Gay
A week, and Arbuthnot a day.
St John himself will scarce forbear
To bite his pen, and drop a tear.
The rest will give a shrug, and cry,
'I'm sorry – but we all must die!' ...
Yet malice never was his aim;
He lash'd the vice, but spared the name;
No individual could resent,
Where thousands equally were meant ...
He gave the little wealth he had
To build a house for fools and mad;
And show'd, by one satiric touch,
No nation wanted it so much.
That kingdom he hath left a debtor,
I wish it soon may have a better.
'Verses on the Death of Dr. Swift' (1731) **Swift, Jonathan** (1667–1745) Irish satirist, poet, essayist and cleric

104 He snatched the lightning shaft from
heaven, and the sceptre from tyrants.
In A.N. de Condorcet, *Vie de Turgot* **Turgot, A.-R.-J.** (1727–1781) French economist and statesman. Inscription for a bust of Benjamin Franklin, who invented the lightning conductor

105 An excellent angler, and now with God.
The Compleat Angler (1653) **Walton, Izaak** (1593–1683) English writer

106 All her bright golden hair
Tarnished with rust,
She that was young and fair
Fallen to dust.
'Requiescat' (1881) **Wilde, Oscar** (1854–1900) Irish poet, dramatist, writer, critic and wit

107 Three years she grew in sun and shower,
Then Nature said, 'A lovelier flower
On earth was never sown;
This child I to myself will take;
She shall be mine, and I will make
A Lady of my own'.
'Three years she grew' (1800) **Wordsworth, William** (1770–1850) English poet

108 He first deceased; she for a little tried
To live without him: liked it not, and died.
'Death of Sir Albertus Moreton's Wife' (c.1610)
Wotton, Sir Henry (1568–1639) English
diplomat, traveller and poet

109 If you are looking for his memorial, look
around you.
Inscription written by his son, in St Paul's
Cathedral, London **Wren, Sir Christopher**
(1632–1723) English architect and
mathematician and astronomer. (Si
monumentum requiris, circumspice)

110 Swift has sailed into his rest;
Savage indignation there
Cannot lacerate his breast.
Imitate him if you dare,
World-besotted traveller; he
Served human liberty.
In the *Dublin Magazine*, 1931, 'Swift's Epitaph'

111 Under bare Ben Bulben's head
In Drumcliff churchyard Yeats is laid …
On limestone quarried near the spot
By his command these words are cut:
Cast a cold eye
On life, on death.
Horseman, pass by!
In *The Irish Times, Irish Independent*, and *Irish
Press*, 1939 (Yeats' epitaph) **Yeats, W.B.** (1865–
1939) Irish poet, dramatist, editor, writer and
senator
See also death; last words

EUROPE

1 Rome took all the vanity out of me; for
after seeing the wonders there, I felt too
insignificant to live, and gave up all my
foolish hopes in despair.
Little Women (1869) **Alcott, Louisa May** (1832–
1888) US writer

2 Europe and the United States together
invented representative democracy and
human rights. But Europe invented
fascism and communism all by itself.
The Observer, (June 1998) **Ascherson, Neal**
(1932–) Scottish journalist

3 Europe has what we do not have yet, a
sense of the mysterious and inexorable
limits of life, a sense, in a word, of tragedy.
And we have what they sorely need: a sense
of life's possibilities.
Attr. **Baldwin, James** (1924–1987) US writer,
dramatist, poet and civil rights activist

4 When you think of the defence of England
you no longer think of the chalk cliffs of
Dover. You think of the Rhine. That is
where our frontier lies today.
Speech, (1934) **Baldwin, Stanley** (1867–1947)
English Conservative statesman and Prime
Minister

5 To make peace in Europe possible, the last
representative of the pre-war generation
must die and take his pre-war mentality
into the grave with him.
Interview, (1929) **Benes, Eduard** (1884–1948)
Czechoslovak statesman

6 Streets flooded. Please advise.
Attr. **Benchley, Robert** (1889–1945) US essayist,
humorist and actor. Telegram sent on
arriving in Venice

7 If you open that Pandora's Box you never
know what Trojan 'orses will jump out.
In Sir Roderick Barclay, *Ernest Bevin and the
Foreign Office* (1975) **Bevin, Ernest** (1881–1951)
English trade union leader and politician. On
the Council of Europe

8 At the announcement of Moro's
kidnapping, Italy looked as if she had been
knocked out by a blow below the belt: she
doesn't understand what's happening; it
seems impossible to her that terrorism
could be so powerful.
We Terrorists (1985) After the kidnapping and
subsequent murder of Aldo Moro, Christian
Democrat Premier, May 1978

9 Are we then the most dishonest people? I
don't really think so: but probably we are
the most indifferent ones.
The Good and the Bad (1989) **Biagi, Enzo**
(1920–) Italian writer. On the Italians

10 Put the strongest possible military power, in other words as much blood and iron as possible, in the hands of the King of Prussia, and then he will be able to carry out the policy you want; this cannot be achieved with speeches and shooting-matches and songs; it can only be achieved by 'blood and iron'!
Speech, Prussian House of Deputies, (1886) **Bismarck, Prince Otto von** (1815–1898) First Chancellor of the German Reich

11 If we walk away from Kosovo ... it would be a betrayal of everything this nation stands for.
The Independent, (March 1999)

12 This is not a battle for territory, this is a battle for humanity.
Speech to Kosovan refugees, (May 1999) On the war in the Balkans

13 For every act of barbarity, every slaughter of the innocent, Slobodan Milosevic must be made to pay a higher and higher price.
The Times, (1999) On the war in Kosovo **Blair, Tony** (1953–) British Labour Prime Minister

14 Rome's just a city like anywhere else. A vastly overrated city, I'd say. It trades on belief just as Stratford trades on Shakespeare.
Inside Mr Enderby (1968) **Burgess, Anthony** (1917–1993) English writer, linguist and composer

15 I found Rome a city of bricks and left it a city of marble.
In Suetonius, *Lives of the Caesars* **Caesar, Augustus** (63 BC–AD 14) First Roman emperor

16 Venice is like eating an entire box of chocolate liqueurs in one go.
The Observer, (1961) **Capote, Truman** (1924–1984) US writer

17 That is what is so marvellous about Europe; the people long ago learned that space and beauty and quiet refuges in a great city, where children may play and old people sit in the sun, are of far more value to the inhabitants than real estate taxes and contractors' greed.
Fresh From the Laundry (1967) **Chase, Ilka** (1905–1978) US writer, broadcaster and actress

18 We must build a kind of United States of Europe.
Speech, Zurich, (September 1946) **Churchill, Sir Winston** (1874–1965) English Conservative Prime Minister

19 Rome, believe me, my friend, is like its own Monte Testaceo,
Merely a marvellous mass of broken and castaway wine-pots.
Amours de Voyage (1858) **Clough, Arthur Hugh** (1819–1861) English poet and letter writer

20 Europe should make a new West Berlin out of Bosnia.
Interview in *Süddeutsche Zeitung,* (1994) **Cohn-Bendit, Daniel** (1945–)

21 The hardest thing is to convince European citizens that even the most powerful nation is no longer able to act alone.
The Independent, (May 1994)

22 Europe is not just about material results, it is about spirit. Europe is a state of mind.
The Independent (May 1994) **Delors, Jacques** (1925–) French politician

23 Italy is pulling out her own rotten tooth, let all other Countries pull out their own.
Speech in Toronto, Canada, November 1993, reported in the magazine *EPOCA,* (1994) **Di Pietro, Antonio** (1947–) Speaking of 'Mani pulite', a nationwide Italian police investigation into political corruption held in the 1990's

24 When I search for man in the technique and style of Europe, I see only a succession of negations of man, and an avalanche of murders.
The Wretched of the Earth (1961) **Fanon, Frantz** (1925–1961) West Indian psychoanalyst and philosopher

25 Purity of race does not exist. Europe is a continent of energetic mongrels.
History of Europe (1935) **Fisher, H.A.L.** (1856–1940) English historian

26 For the first time in its history, Germany is fighting on the right side.
The Times, (June 1999) **Fischer, Joschka** (1948–) German politician. Commenting on the war in Serbia

27 This is a negation of God erected into a system of government.
Letter to Lord Aberdeen, (1851) Commenting on the regime of Ferdinand II, king of the Two Sicilies

28 We are part of the community of Europe, and we must do our duty as such.
Speech, (1888) **Gladstone, William** (1809–1898) English statesman and reformer

29 Brussels is madness. I will fight it from within.
The Times, (June 1994) **Goldsmith, James** (1933–1997) British business magnate and MEP

30 On whatever side we regard the history of Europe, we shall perceive it to be a tissue of crimes, follies, and misfortunes.
The Citizen of the World (1762) **Goldsmith, Oliver** (c.1728–1774) Irish dramatist, poet and writer

31 Going to Europe, someone had written, was about as final as going to heaven. A mystical passage to another life, from which no one returned the same.
The Transit of Venus (1980) **Hazzard, Shirley** (1931–) Australian writer

32 Their Europeanism is nothing but imperialism with an inferiority complex.
The Observer, (1962) **Healey, Denis** (1917–) English Labour politician. Of Conservatives

33 Nor would it be in the interests of the European Community that its enlargement should take place except with the full-hearted consent of the Parliament and people of the new member countries.
Speech to the Franco-British Chamber of Commerce, Paris, (1970) **Heath, Sir Edward** (1916–2005) English Conservative Prime Minister

34 For, you Germans, you too are
Poor in deed and rich in thoughts.
'To the Germans' (1798) **Hölderlin, Friedrich** (1770–1843) German poet

35 The smoke and wealth and noise of Rome.
Odes **Horace** (65–8 BC) Roman poet

36 I represent a party which does not yet exist: the party of revolution, civilization. This party will make the twentieth century. There will issue from it first the United States of Europe, then the United States of the World.
Written on the wall of the room in which Hugo died, Paris, (1885) **Hugo, Victor** (1802–1885) French poet, writer, dramatist and politician

37 How appallingly thorough these Germans always managed to be, how emphatic! In sex no less than in war – in scholarship, in science. Diving deeper than anyone else and coming up muddier.
Time Must Have a Stop (1944) **Huxley, Aldous** (1894–1963) English writer, poet and critic

38 Economic and political union … is the next step toward a United States of Europe.
Comment, (1990) **Kohl, Helmut** (1930–) German Chancellor. On plans for a single currency

39 Italy was born on that sombre evening at Donnafugata, she was indeed born in that forgotten village.
A bad fairy, however, whose name no one knew must have been there.
The Leopard (1958) **Lampedusa, Giuseppe Tomasi di** (1896–1957) Italian novelist

40 It is as if the life had retreated eastwards. As if the Germanic life were slowly ebbing away from contact with western Europe, ebbing to the deserts of the east.
A Letter from Germany (1924) **Lawrence, D.H.** (1885–1930) English writer, poet and critic

41 Tell me, is there a country besides Germany where you learn to turn up your nose rather than wipe it?
Aphorisms (Scrawlings) (1775–1776) **Lichtenberg, Georg** (1742–1799) German physicist, satirist and writer

42 Which faults do you attribute to the Italian male: First he's a bully. Second a victim, a product that cannot look after himself.
In E. Biagi, *La Geografia di Italia* (1975) **Lotti, Nilde** (1920–1999) Italian politician

43 The immense popularity of American movies abroad demonstrates that Europe is the unfinished negative of which America is the proof.
On the Contrary (1961)

44 When an American heiress wants to buy a man, she at once crosses the Atlantic. The only really materialistic people I have ever met have been Europeans.
On the Contrary (1961) **McCarthy, Mary** (1912–1989) US writer and critic

45 Italy is a geographical concept.
Letter, (1849) **Metternich, Prince Clement** (1773–1859) Austrian statesman

46 There's romance for you! There's the lust and dark wine of Venice! No wonder George Eliot's husband fell into the Grand Canal.
Venice (1960) **Morris, Jan** (1926–) Welsh travel writer

47 Incidentally, I've always heard what a practical people the Swiss are – I finally understood these comments when I found out how they dispose of their mercury batteries. They collect them, and then dump them down an abandoned mine shaft – in France!
Said at the Summit on the Environment, Toronto, (1989) **Nichol, Dave** Canadian businessman and environmentalist

48 In this pungent atmosphere of romantic nationalism and churlish xenophobia, I sometimes wonder if there are some among us who have failed to notice that the war with Germany has ended.
The Observer, (May 1996) **Nicholson, Sir Bryan** (1932–) British businessman. On the government's non-cooperation with Europe over the ban on exporting British beef

49 Roll up that map; it will not be wanted these ten years.
In Lord Stanhope, *Life of the Rt. Hon. William Pitt* (1862) **Pitt, William** (1759–1806) English politician and Prime Minister. Commenting on the map of Europe, after the Battle of Austerlitz, 1805

50 Though the latitude's rather uncertain, And the longitude also is vague, The persons I pity who know not the city, The beautiful city of Prague.
'The City of Prague' **Prowse, William Jeffrey** (1836–1870) English poet

51 Here we are again with both feet firmly planted in the air.
The Observer, (1973) **Scanlon, Hugh, Baron** (1913– 2004) British trade union leader. Referring to his union's attitude to the Common Market

52 It is a curious failing in the German people that they search in the clouds for what lies at their feet.
Parerga und Paralipomena (1851) **Schopenhauer, Arthur** (1788–1860) German philosopher

53 All that EC nonsense is beyond me.
The Mail on Sunday, (1996) **Soames, Nicholas** (1948–) English Conservative politician. Comment during a Commons debate, the topics of which included positive discrimination for women in the armed forces and a European Union directive on equality

54 What a bloody country! even the cheese has got holes in it!
Travesties (1975) **Stoppard, Tom** (1937–) British dramatist

55 Historians will one day look back and think it a curious folly that just as the Soviet Union was forced to recognize reality by dispersing power to its separate states and by limiting the powers of its central government, some people in Europe were trying to create a new artificial state by taking powers from national states and concentrating them at the centre.
Speech, (1994) **Thatcher, Margaret** (1925–) English Conservative Prime Minister

56 I am sick of all this horrid business of politics, and Europe in general, and I think you will hear of me going with the children to live in Australia, and to think of Europe as the Moon!

Letter to her daughter, the Princess Royal, (1859) **Victoria, Queen** (1819–1901) Queen of the United Kingdom
See also Britain; England; France; Ireland; Scotland

EVIL

1 Whenever God prepares evil for a man, He first damages his mind.
Scholiast on Sophocles

2 Honi soit qui mal y pense (*Evil be to him who evil thinks*)
Motto of the Order of the Garter **Anonymous**

3 It was as though in those last minutes he was summing up the lessons that this long course in human wickedness had taught us – the lesson of the fearsome, word-and-thought-defying banality of evil.
Eichmann in Jerusalem (1963) **Arendt, Hannah** (1906–1975) German-born US theorist. Of Eichmann

4 All punishment is mischief: all punishment in itself is evil.
An Introduction to the Principles of Morals and Legislation (1789) **Bentham, Jeremy** (1748–1832) English writer and philosopher

5 I have seen the wicked in great power, and spreading himself like a green bay tree.
Psalms, 37:35

6 Woe unto them that call evil good, and good evil.
Isaiah, 5:20

7 There is no peace, saith the Lord, unto the wicked.
Isaiah, 48:22

8 The heart is deceitful above all things, and desperately wicked.
Jeremiah, 17:9 **The Bible (King James Version)**

9 The fear of one evil often leads us into a greater one.
L'Art Poétique (1674) **Boileau-Despréaux, Nicolas** (1636–1711) French writer

10 The only thing necessary for the triumph of evil is for good men to do nothing.
Attr. **Burke, Edmund** (1729–1797) Irish-born British statesman and philosopher

11 The belief in a supernatural source of evil is not necessary; men alone are quite capable of every wickedness.
Under Western Eyes (1911) **Conrad, Joseph** (1857–1924) Polish-born British writer, sailor and explorer

12 All the goodness of a good egg cannot make up for the badness of a bad one.
The Making of a Newspaper Man **Dana, Charles Anderson** (1819–1897) US newspaper editor and reformer

13 The idea of evil is something on which the health of society depends. We have an obligation to name evil and oppose it in ourselves as well as in others.
The Guardian, (1995) **Delbanco, Andrew** (1952–) Writer and academic

14 There are no limits to human ingratitude.
No-one Writes to the Colonel (1961) **García Márquez, Gabriel** (1928–) Colombian author

15 Don't let us make imaginary evils, when you know we have so many real ones to encounter.
The Good Natur'd Man (1768) **Goldsmith, Oliver** (c.1728–1774) Irish dramatist, poet and writer

16 Familiarity with evil breeds not contempt but acceptance.
The Guardian, (1993) **Hattersley, Roy** (1932–) British Labour politician and writer

17 To great evils we submit, we resent little provocations.
Table-Talk (1822) **Hazlitt, William** (1778–1830) English writer and critic

18 But evil is wrought by want of Thought, As well as want of Heart!
'The Lady's Dream' (1844) **Hood, Thomas** (1799–1845) English poet, editor and humorist

19 Of two evils the lesser is always to be chosen.
De Imitatione Christi (1892) **Kempis, Thomas à** (c.1380–1471) German mystic, monk and writer

20 There is scarcely a single man clever enough to know all the evil he does.
Maximes (1678) **La Rochefoucauld** (1613–1680) French writer

21 If someone tells you he is going to make 'a realistic decision', you immediately understand that he has resolved to do something bad.
On the Contrary (1961) **McCarthy, Mary** (1912–1989) US writer and critic

22 Whatever is the first time persons hear evil, it is quite certain that good has been beforehand with them, and they have a something within them which tells them it is evil.
Parochial and Plain Sermons **Newman, John Henry, Cardinal** (1801–1890) English Cardinal, theologian and poet

23 Whoever struggles with monsters might watch that he does not thereby become a monster. When you stare into an abyss for a long time, the abyss also stares into you.
Beyond Good and Evil (1886) **Nietzsche, Friedrich Wilhelm** (1844–1900) German philosopher, critic and poet

24 Vice is a monster of so frightful mien, As, to be hated, needs but to be seen; Yet soon too oft, familiar with her face, We first endure, then pity, then embrace.
An Essay on Man (1733) **Pope, Alexander** (1688–1744) English poet, translator and editor

25 No man is justified in doing evil on the ground of expediency.
The Strenuous Life (1900) **Roosevelt, Theodore** (1858–1919) US Republican President

26 One can only overcome an evil by means of another evil.
Les Mouches (1943) **Sartre, Jean-Paul** (1905–1980) French philosopher, writer, dramatist and critic

27 Men's evil manners live in brass: their virtues
We write in water.
Henry VIII, IV.ii

28 The evil that men do lives after them;
The good is oft interred with their bones.
Julius Caesar, III.ii

29 How oft the sight of means to do ill deeds
Make deeds ill done!
King John, IV.i

30 Through tatter'd clothes small vices do appear;
Robed and furr'd gowns hide all.
King Lear, IV.vi

31 Oftentimes to win us to our harm,
The instruments of darkness tell us truths,
Win us with honest trifles, to betray's
In deepest consequence.
Macbeth, I.iii

32 If one good deed in all my life I did,
I do repent it from my very soul.
Titus Andronicus, V.iii **Shakespeare, William** (1564–1616) English dramatist, poet and actor

33 No evil can befall a good man either in life or death.
Attr. in Plato, *Apology* **Socrates** (469–399 BC) Athenian philosopher

34 This is man's role:
to try evil, and if the outcome be evil,
to ask humbly for forgiveness for the act of depravity.
Second Eclogue **Vega, Garcilaso de la** (c.1501–1536) Spanish poet

35 Whenever I'm caught between two evils, I take the one I've never tried.
Klondike Annie (film, 1936) **West, Mae** (1892–1980) US actress and scriptwriter

36 Wickedness is a myth invented by good people to account for the curious attractiveness of others.
The Chameleon, (1894) **Wilde, Oscar** (1854–1900) Irish poet, dramatist, writer, critic and wit

37 No man chooses evil because it is evil; he only mistakes it for happiness, the good he seeks.
A Vindication of the Rights of Men (1790) **Wollstonecraft, Mary** (1759–1797) English feminist, writer and teacher
See also the devil; sin

EXPERIENCE

1 The man who views the world at fifty the same as he did at twenty has wasted thirty years of his life.
Playboy, (1975) **Ali, Muhammad** (1942–) US heavyweight boxer

2 Experience is the comb that nature gives us when we are bald.
Anonymous

3 Experience is a good teacher, but she sends in terrific bills.
Naked Truth and Veiled Allusions (1902) **Antrim, Minna** (1861–1950) US writer

4 You should make a point of trying every experience once, excepting incest and folk-dancing.
Farewell My Youth (1943) **Bax, Sir Arnold** (1883–1953) English composer

5 You will think me lamentably crude: my experience of life has been drawn from life itself.
Zuleika Dobson (1911) **Beerbohm, Sir Max** (1872–1956) English satirist, cartoonist, critic and essayist

6 What is the price of Experience? do men buy it for a song?
Or wisdom for a dance in the street?
No, it is bought with the price
Of all that a man hath, his house, his wife, his children.
Wisdom is sold in the desolate market where none come to buy,
And in the wither'd field where the farmer plows for bread in vain.
Vala, or the Four Zoas **Blake, William** (1757–1827) English poet, engraver, painter and mystic

7 Experience isn't interesting till it begins to repeat itself – in fact, till it does that, it hardly is experience.
The Death of the Heart (1938)

8 No, it is not only our fate but our business to lose innocence, and once we have lost that, it is futile to attempt a picnic in Eden.
In R. Lehmann and others (eds.), *Orion III* (1946) **Bowen, Elizabeth** (1899–1973) Irish writer

9 Ay, ay, I have experience: I have a wife, and so forth.
The Way of the World (1700) **Congreve, William** (1670–1729) English dramatist

10 Experience is the child of Thought, and Thought is the child of Action. We cannot learn men from books.
Vivian Grey (1826) **Disraeli, Benjamin** (1804–1881) English statesman and writer

11 The years teach much which the days never know.
'Experience' (1844) **Emerson, Ralph Waldo** (1803–1882) US poet, essayist, transcendentalist and teacher

12 Experience teaches you that the man who looks you straight in the eye, particularly if he adds a firm handshake, is hiding something.
Enter, Conversing **Fadiman, Clifton** (1904–1999) US writer, editor and broadcaster

13 My difficulty is trying to reconcile my gross habits with my net income.
Attr. **Flynn, Errol** (1909–1959) US actor

14 Experience teaches slowly, and at the cost of mistakes.
Short Studies on Great Subjects (1877) **Froude, James Anthony** (1818–1894) English historian and scholar

15 The best way to suppose what may come, is to remember what is past.
Political, Moral and Miscellaneous Thoughts and Reflections (1750) **Halifax, Lord** (1633–1695) English politician, courtier, pamphleteer and epigrammatist

16 What experience and history teach us, however, is this, that peoples and governments have never learned anything from history.
Lectures on the Philosophy of History (1837) **Hegel, Georg Wilhelm** (1770–1831) German philosopher

17 A moment's insight is sometimes worth a life's experience.
The Professor at the Breakfast-Table (1860) **Holmes, Oliver Wendell** (1809–1894) US physician, poet, writer and scientist

18 Experience is not what happens to a man. It is what a man does with what happens to him.
Attr. **Huxley, Aldous** (1894–1963) English writer, poet and critic

19 Experience is never limited, and it is never complete; it is an immense sensibility, a kind of huge spider-web of the finest silken threads suspended in the chamber of consciousness, and catching every air-borne particle in its tissue.
Partial Portraits (1888) **James, Henry** (1843–1916) US-born British writer, critic and letter writer

20 Nothing ever becomes real till it is experienced – Even a Proverb is no proverb to you till your Life has illustrated it.
Letter to George and Georgiana Keats, (1819) **Keats, John** (1795–1821) English poet

21 Experience teaches
that it doesn't.
A World of Difference (1983) **MacCaig, Norman** (1910–1996) Scottish lecturer and poet

22 an optimist is a guy
that has never had
much experience.
archy and mehitabel (1927) **Marquis, Don** (1878–1937) US columnist, satirist and poet

23 A whale ship was my Yale College and my Harvard.
Moby Dick (1851) **Melville, Herman** (1819–1891) US writer and poet

24 We spend our lives in learning pilotage,
And grow good steersmen when the vessel's crank!
'The Wisdom of Eld' **Meredith, George** (1828–1909) English writer, poet and critic

25 We live and learn, but not the wiser grow.
'Reason' (1700) **Pomfret, John** (1667–1702) English poet and clergyman

26 You know, by the time you reach my age, you've made plenty of mistakes if you've lived your life properly.
The Observer, (1987) **Reagan, Ronald** (1911–2004) US actor, Republican statesman and president

27 We often discover what will do, by finding out what will not do; and probably he who never made a mistake never made a discovery.
Self-Help (1859) **Smiles, Samuel** (1812–1904) English writer

28 The only people who never make mistakes are those who have never taken a decision.
The Observer, (May 1999) **Straw, Jack** (1946–) English Labour politician and Home Secretary

29 The soul's dark cottage, batter'd and decay'd
Lets in new light through chinks that time has made;
Stronger by weakness, wiser men become,
As they draw nearer to their eternal home.
Leaving the old, both worlds at once they view,
That stand upon the threshold of the new.
'Of the Last Verses in the Book' (1685) **Waller, Edmund** (1606–1687) English poet and politician

30 'I dunno,' Arthur said. 'I forget what I was taught. I only remember what I've learnt.'
The Solid Mandala (1966) **White, Patrick** (1912–1990) English-born Australian writer and dramatist

31 *Dumby*: Experience is the name every one gives to their mistakes.
Cecil Graham: One shouldn't commit any.
Dumby: Life would be very dull without them.
Lady Windermere's Fan (1892) **Wilde, Oscar** (1854–1900) Irish poet, dramatist, writer, critic and wit
See also age; history; youth

EXPLORATION

1 They are ill discoverers that think there is no land, when they can see nothing but sea.
The Advancement of Learning (1605) **Bacon, Francis** (1561–1626) English philosopher, essayist, politician and courtier

2 I can't say I was ever lost, but I was bewildered once for three days.
Attr. **Boone, Daniel** (1734–1820) US pioneer. Reply on being asked if he had ever been lost

3 Polar exploration is at once the cleanest and most isolated way of having a bad time which has been devised.
The Worst Journey in the World (1922) **Cherry-Garrard, Apsley** (1886–1959) English explorer

4 Altho' the discoveries made in this Voyage are not great, yet I flatter myself that they are such as may merit the attention of their Lordships, and altho' I have failed in discovering the so much talk'd of southern Continent (which perhaps do not exist) and which I myself had so much at heart, yet I am confident that no part of the failure of such discovery can be laid at my Charge.
Letter, (1770) **Cook, Captain James** (1728–1779) English navigator. Of the *Endeavour* expedition

5 Of course I realized there was a measure of danger. Obviously I faced the possibility of not returning when first I considered going. Once faced and settled there really wasn't any good reason to refer to it.
20 Hours: 40 Minutes – Our Flight in the Friendship (1928) Of her flight in the 'Friendship'

6 Flying might not be all plain sailing, but the fun of it is worth the price.
The Fun of It (1932) **Earhart, Amelia** (1898–1937) US aviator

7 As far as I knew, he had never taken a photograph before, and the summit of Everest was hardly the place to show him how.
High Adventure Referring to Tenzing Norgay, his companion on the conquest of Mt Everest, 1953

8 There is precious little in civilization to appeal to a Yeti.
The Observer, (1960)

9 Well, we knocked the bastard off!
Nothing Venture, Nothing Win (1975) Remark after first ascent of Mt Everest, 1953

10 Mount Everest is now littered with junk from bottom to top.
The Observer, (1982) **Hillary, Sir Edmund** (1919–) New Zealand mountaineer, explorer and apiarist

11 Had I been a man I might have explored the Poles or climbed Mount Everest, but as it was my spirit found an outlet in the air.
In Margot Asquith (ed.), *Myself When Young* **Johnson, Amy** (1903–1941) English aviator

12 Because it is there.
New York Times, (1923) **Mallory, George Leigh** (1886–1924) Asked why he wished to climb Mt Everest

13 Nothing easier. One step beyond the pole, you see, and the north wind becomes a south one.
Attr. Explaining how he knew he had reached the North Pole

14 The Eskimo had his own explanation. Said he: 'The devil is asleep or having trouble with his wife, or we should never have come back so easily.'
The North Pole (1910) **Peary, Robert Edwin** (1856–1920) US Arctic explorer, admiral and writer

15 The sight of it gave me infinite pleasure, as it proved that I was in a civilized society.
Attr. **Park, Mungo** (1771–1806) Scottish explorer, writer and physician. Remark on finding a gibbet in an unexplored part of Africa

16 Had we lived, I should have had a tale to tell of the hardihood, endurance, and courage of my companions which would have stirred the heart of every Englishman. These rough notes and our dead bodies must tell the tale.
Message to the Public, (1912)

17 Great God! this is an awful place.
Journal, (1912) Of the South Pole

18 We took risks, we knew we took them; things have come out against us, and therefore we have no cause for complaint.
'The Last Message' in Scott's Last Expedition (1913) **Scott, Robert Falcon** (1868–1912) English naval officer and Antarctic explorer

19 This is the Law of the Yukon, that only the Strong shall thrive;
That surely the Weak shall perish, and only the Fit survive.
Dissolute, damned and despairful, crippled and palsied and slain,
This is the Will of the Yukon, –
Lo, how she makes it plain!
'The Law of the Yukon' (1907) **Service, Robert W.** (1874–1958) Canadian poet

20 Crossing Piccadilly Circus.
In Dunbar, *J.M. Barrie* **Thomson, Joseph** (1858–1895) Scottish explorer, geologist and writer. His reply when J.M. Barrie asked what was the most hazardous part of his expedition to Africa
See also travel

EYES

1 Let beam upon my inward view
Those eyes of deep, soft, lucent hue –
Eyes too expressive to be blue,
Too lovely to be grey.
'Faded Leaves' (1852) **Arnold, Matthew** (1822–1888) English poet, critic, essayist and educationist

2 There is a glare in some men's eyes which seems to say, 'Beware, I am dangerous; *Noli me tangere*.' Lord Brougham's face has this. A mischievous excitability is the most obvious expression of it. If he were a horse, nobody would buy him; with that eye no one could answer for his temper.
Historical Essays **Bagehot, Walter** (1826–1877) English economist and political philosopher

3 It needs no dictionary of quotations to remind me that the eyes are the windows of the soul.
Zuleika Dobson (1911) **Beerbohm, Sir Max** (1872–1956) English satirist, cartoonist, critic and essayist

4 If thine eye offend thee, pluck it out.
Matthew, 18:9 **The Bible (King James Version)**

5 Two lovely black eyes,
Oh, what a surprise!
Only for telling a man he was wrong.
Two lovely black eyes!
'Two Lovely Black Eyes' (song, 1886) **Coborn, Charles** (1852–1945) English comedian and singer

6 When she raises her eyelids she seems to be taking her clothes off at the same time.
Claudine Goes Away (1903) **Colette** (1873–1954) French writer

7 Two walking baths; two weeping motions;
Portable, and compendious oceans.

'Saint Mary Magdalene, or The Weeper' (1652) **Crashaw, Richard** (c.1612–1649) English religious poet

8 'Yes, I have a pair of eyes,' replied Sam, 'and that's just it. If they wos a pair o' patent double million magnifyin' gas microscopes of hextra power, p'raps I might be able to see through a flight o' stairs and a deal door; but bein' only eyes, you see my wision's limited.'
The Pickwick Papers (1837) **Dickens, Charles** (1812–1870) English writer

9 Love's tongue is in the eyes.
'Piscatory Eclogues' (1633) **Fletcher, Phineas** (1582–1650) English poet and clergyman

10 Sweet, be not proud of those two eyes,
Which Star-like sparkle in their skies ...
That Rubie which you weare,
Sunk from the tip of your soft eare,
Will last to be a precious Stone,
When all your world of Beautie's gone.
Hesperides (1648) **Herrick, Robert** (1591–1674) English poet, royalist and clergyman

11 So excuse me forgetting, but these things I do
You see I've forgotten, if they're green or they're blue
Anyway, the thing is, what I really mean
Yours are the sweetest eyes, I've ever seen.
'Your Song' (1971) **John, Elton** (1947–) English singer

12 Jeepers Creepers – where'd you get them peepers?
'Jeepers Creepers' (song, 1938) **Mercer, Johnny** (1909–1976) US lyricist and composer

13 Bright as the sun, her eyes the gazers strike,
And, like the sun, they shine on all alike.
The Rape of the Lock (1714)

14 Why has not Man a microscopic eye?
For this plain reason, Man is not a fly.
Say what the use, were finer optics giv'n,
T' inspect a mite, not comprehend the heav'n?
An Essay on Man (1733) **Pope, Alexander** (1688–1744) English poet, translator and editor

15 Free us, for we perish
In this ever-flowing monotony
Of ugly print marks, black
Upon white parchment.
'The Eyes' (1908) **Pound, Ezra** (1885–1972) US
poet

16 For where is any author in the world
Teaches such beauty as a woman's eye?
Love's Labour Lost, IV.iii

17 Men's eyes were made to look, and let
them gaze;
I will not budge for no man's pleasure, I.
Romeo and Juliet, III.i **Shakespeare, William**
(1564–1616) English dramatist, poet and actor

18 But I did not remove my glasses, for I had
not asked for her company in the first
place, and there is a limit to what one can
listen to with the naked eye.
Voices at Play (1961) **Spark, Muriel** (1918–2006)
Scottish writer, poet and dramatist

19 'I am half distracted, Captain Shandy,' said
Mrs Wadman, … 'a mote – or sand – or
something – I know not what, has got into
this eye of mine – do look into it.'… In
saying which, Mrs Wadman edged herself
close in beside my uncle Toby, … 'Do look
into it,' – said she … If thou lookest, uncle
Toby, in search of this mote one moment
longer – thou art undone.
Tristram Shandy (1759–1767)

20 An eye full of gentle salutations – and soft
responses – … whispering soft – like the
last low accents of an expiring saint … It
did my uncle Toby's business.
Tristram Shandy (1759–1767) **Sterne, Laurence**
(1713–1768) Irish-born English writer and
clergyman

21 Stop looking at me like that, or you'll wear
your eyes out.
La Bête Humaine (1889–1890) **Zola, Emile**
(1840–1902) French writer
See also appearance; beauty

FAILURE

1 The worst of failure of this kind is that it
spoils the market for more competent
performers.
Ego 7, (1944) **Agate, James** (1877–1947) English
drama critic and writer. On the failed attempt
to assassinate Hitler

2 We are all failures – at least, the best of us
are.
Rectorial address at St Andrew's University, (3
May 1922) **Barrie, Sir J.M.** (1860–1937) Scottish
dramatist and writer

3 Ever tried. Ever failed. No matter. Try
Again. Fail again. Fail better.
Worstward Ho (1984) **Beckett, Samuel** (1906–
1989) Irish dramatist, writer and poet

4 Because God put His adamantine fate
Between my sullen heart and its desire,
I swore that I would burst the Iron Gate,
Rise up, and curse Him on His throne of
fire.
'Failure' (1905–1908) **Brooke, Rupert** (1887–
1915) English poet

5 As always, victory finds a hundred fathers,
but defeat is an orphan.
Diary, (1942) **Ciano, Count Galeazzo** (1903–
1944) Italian politician

6 Dear Randolph, utterly unspoiled by
failure.
Attr. **Coward, Sir Noël** (1899–1973) English
dramatist, actor, producer and composer. On
Randolph Churchill

7 She knows there's no success like failure
And that failure's no success at all.
'Love Minus Zero/No Limit' (song, 1965)
Dylan, Bob (1941–) US singer and songwriter

8 If all else fails, immortality can always be
assured by spectacular error.
Attr. **Galbraith, J.K.** (1908–2006) Canadian-
born US economist, diplomat and writer

9 Despair is the price one pays for setting
oneself an impossible aim.
Heart of the Matter (1948) **Greene, Graham**
(1904–1991) English writer and dramatist

10 Half the failures in life arise from pulling in
one's horse as he is leaping.
Guesses at Truth (1827) **Hare, Augustus** (1792–
1834) English clergyman and writer

11 Examining one's entrails while fighting a
battle is a recipe for certain defeat.

The Observer, (1983) **Healey, Denis** (1917–)
English Labour politician

12 He was a self-made man who owed his
lack of success to nobody.
Catch-22 (1961) **Heller, Joseph** (1923–1999) US
writer

13 But man is not made for defeat ... A man
can be destroyed but not defeated.
The Old Man and the Sea (1952) **Hemingway,
Ernest** (1898–1961) US author

14 I would sooner fail than not be among the
greatest.
Letter to James Hessey, (1818) **Keats, John**
(1795–1821) English poet

15 Like all weak men he laid an exaggerated
stress on not changing one's mind.
Of Human Bondage (1915) **Maugham, William
Somerset** (1874–1965) English writer,
dramatist and physician

16 Show me a good loser and I'll show you a
loser.
The Observer, (1982) **Newman, Paul** (1925–) US
actor

17 Failure is not the only punishment for
laziness: there is also the success of others.
Journal, (1898) **Renard, Jules** (1864–1910)
French writer and dramatist

18 Here lies one who meant well, tried a little,
failed much: – surely that may be his
epitaph, of which he need not be ashamed.
Across the Plains (1892) **Stevenson, Robert
Louis** (1850–1894) Scottish writer, poet and
essayist

19 We are not interested in the possibilities of
defeat; they do not exist.
In Cecil, *Life of Robert, Marquis of Salisbury*
(1931) **Victoria, Queen** (1819–1901) Queen of
the United Kingdom. Said of the Boer War in
'Black Week', 1899

20 Never having been able to succeed in the
world, he took his revenge by speaking ill
of it.
Zadig, or Fate (1747) **Voltaire** (1694–1778) French
philosopher, dramatist, poet, historian, writer
and critic

21 When you are down and out something
always turns up – and it is usually the
noses of your friends.
New York Times, (1962) **Welles, Orson** (1915–
1985) US actor, director and producer

22 We women adore failures. They lean on us.
A Woman of No Importance (1893) **Wilde, Oscar**
(1854–1900) Irish poet, dramatist, writer, critic
and wit
See also success

FAITH

1 O how great and how glorious are those
sabbaths which the heavenly court for ever
celebrates!
Hymnus Paraclitensis **Abelard, Peter** (1079–
1142) French philosopher and teacher

2 Men can be attracted but not forced to the
faith. You may drive people to baptism,
(but) you won't move them one step
further in religion.
In Frank S. Mead, 12,000 *Religious Quotations*
(1989) **Alcuin** (735–804) English theologian,
scholar and educationist

3 Trust in Allah, but tie your camel.
Old Muslim Proverb

4 God be in my head,
And in my understanding;
God be in my eyes,
And in my looking;
God be in my mouth,
And in my speaking;
God be in my heart,
And in my thinking;
God be at my end,
And at my departing.
Sarum Missal **Anonymous**

5 The Sea of Faith
Was once, too, at the full, and round
earth's shore
Lay like the folds of a bright girdle furl'd.
But now I only hear
Its melancholy, long, withdrawing roar,
Retreating, to the breath
Of the night-wind, down the vast edges
drear
And naked shingles of the world.

'Dover Beach' (1867) **Arnold, Matthew** (1822–1888) English poet, critic, essayist and educationist

6 If a man will begin with certainties, he shall end in doubts; but if he will be content to begin with doubts, he shall end in certainties.
The Advancement of Learning (1605)

7 It is true, that a little philosophy inclineth man's mind to atheism; but depth in philosophy bringeth men's minds about to religion.
Essays (1625)

8 God never wrought miracles to convince atheism, because his ordinary works convince it.
Essays (1625)

9 I had rather believe all the fables in the legend, and the Talmud, and the Alcoran, than that this universal frame is without a mind.
Essays (1625) **Bacon, Francis** (1561–1626) English philosopher, essayist, politician and courtier

10 He did not think with the Caliph Omar Ben Adalaziz, that it was necessary to make a hell of this world to enjoy paradise in the next.
Vathek (1787) **Beckford, William** (1760–1844) English writer, collector and politician

11 A faith is something you die for; a doctrine is something you kill for: there is all the difference in the world.
The Observer, (1989) **Benn, Tony** (1925–) English Labour politician

12 How long halt ye between two opinions?
I Kings, 18:21

13 O come, let us sing unto the Lord; let us make a joyful noise to the rock of our salvation.
Let us come before his presence with thanksgiving, and make a joyful noise unto him with psalms.
For the Lord is a great God, and a great King above all gods.
In his hand are the deep places of the earth: the strength of the hills is his also.

The sea is his, and he made it: and his hands formed the dry land.
O come, let us worship and bow down: let us kneel before the Lord our maker.
Psalms, 95:1–6

14 The people that walked in darkness have seen a great light: they that dwell in the shadow of death, upon them hath the light shined.
Isaiah, 9:2

15 O thou of little faith, wherefore didst thou doubt?
Matthew, 14:31

16 Faith is the substance of things hoped for, the evidence of things not seen.
Hebrews, 11:1

17 Whom the Lord loveth he chasteneth.
Hebrews, 12:6

18 Faith without works is dead.
James, 2:20 **The Bible (King James Version)**

19 He who Doubts from what he sees
Will neer Believe do what you Please.
If the Sun & Moon should doubt,
Theyd immediately Go out.
'Auguries of Innocence' (c.1803) **Blake, William** (1757–1827) English poet, engraver, painter and mystic

20 Of course I don't believe in it. But I understand that it brings you luck whether you believe in it or not.
Attr. **Bohr, Niels Henrik David** (1885–1962) Danish nuclear physicist. Explaining why he had a horseshoe on his wall

21 I have known what the Greeks knew not: uncertainty.
The Garden of Paths which Diverge (1941) **Borges, Jorge Luis** (1899–1986) Argentinian writer, poet and librarian

22 What now? What next? All these questions. All these doubts. So few certainties. But then I have taken new comfort and refuge in the doctrine that advises one not to seek tranquillity in certainty, but in permanently suspended judgement.
Brazzaville Beach (1990) **Boyd, William** (1952–) Scottish writer

23 Lord, deliver me from myself.
Religio Medici (1643)

24 To believe only possibilities, is not faith,
but mere Philosophy.
Religio Medici (1643)

25 Were the happiness of the next world as
closely apprehended as the felicities of this,
it were a martyrdom to live.
Hydriotaphia: Urn Burial (1658)

26 All things began in order, so shall they end,
and so shall they begin again; according to
the ordainer of order and mystical
mathematics of the city of heaven.
The Garden of Cyrus (1658) **Browne, Sir
Thomas** (1605–1682) English physician,
author and antiquary

27 God answers sharp and sudden on some
prayers,
And thrusts the thing we have prayed for in
our face,
A gauntlet with a gift in't.
Aurora Leigh (1857) **Browning, Elizabeth
Barrett** (1806–1861) English poet; wife of
Robert Browning

28 All we have gained then by our unbelief
Is a life of doubt diversified by faith,
For one of faith diversified by doubt:
We called the chess-board white, – we call
it black.
'Bishop Blougram's Apology' (1855)

29 On the earth the broken arcs; in the
heaven, a perfect round.
'Abt Vogler' (1864) **Browning, Robert** (1812–
1889) English poet

30 An atheist is a man who has no invisible
means of support.
Attr. **Buchan, John** (1875–1940) Scottish writer,
lawyer and Conservative politician

31 I feel no need for any other faith than my
faith in human beings.
I Believe (1939) **Buck, Pearl S.** (1892–1973) US
writer and dramatist

32 I am still an atheist, thank God.
Attr. **Buñuel, Luis** (1900–1983) Spanish film
director

33 Then I saw there was a way to Hell, even
from the gates of heaven.

The Pilgrim's Progress (1678) **Bunyan, John**
(1628–1688) English preacher, pastor and
writer

34 Man is by his constitution a religious
animal; ... atheism is against, not only our
reason, but our instincts.
Reflections on the Revolution in France ... (1790)
Burke, Edmund (1729–1797) Irish-born British
statesman and philosopher

35 An atheist-laugh's a poor exchange
For Deity offended!
'Epistle to a Young Friend' (1786) **Burns,
Robert** (1759–1796) Scottish poet and
songwriter

36 That which is the foundation of all our
hopes and of all our fears; all our hopes
and fears which are of any consideration: I
mean a Future Life.
The Analogy of Religion (1736) **Butler, Bishop
Joseph** (1692–1752) English philosopher and
divine

37 My Lord, I do not believe. Help thou mine
unbelief.
Samuel Butler's Notebooks (1951) **Butler, Samuel**
(1835–1902) English writer, painter,
philosopher and scholar

38 Worship is transcendent wonder.
*On Heroes, Hero-Worship, and the Heroic in
History* **Carlyle, Thomas** (1795–1881) Scottish
historian, biographer, critic, and essayist

39 Reason is itself a matter of faith. It is an act
of faith to assert that our thoughts have
any relation to reality at all.
Orthodoxy (1908)

40 John Grubby, who was short and stout
And troubled with religious doubt,
Refused about the age of three
To sit upon the curate's knee.
Poems (1915) **Chesterton, G.K.** (1874–1936)
English writer, poet and critic

41 He prayeth best, who loveth best
All things both great and small;
For the dear God who loveth us,
He made and loveth all.
'The Rime of the Ancient Mariner' (1798), VII
Coleridge, Samuel Taylor (1772–1834) English
poet, philosopher and critic

42 Blind unbelief is sure to err,
And scan his work in vain;
God is his own interpreter,
And he will make it plain.
Olney Hymns (1779)

43 Prayer makes the Christian's armour
bright;
And Satan trembles when he sees
The weakest saint upon his knees.
Olney Hymns (1779), 29 **Cowper, William** (1731–
1800) English poet, hymn writer and letter
writer

44 Life without faith is an arid business.
Blithe Spirit (1941) **Coward, Sir Noël** (1899–1973)
English dramatist, actor, producer and
composer

45 A few honest men are better than
numbers.
Letter to Sir William Spring, (1643) **Cromwell,
Oliver** (1599–1658) English general, statesman
and Puritan leader

46 Through me one goes to the sorrowful city.
Through me one goes to eternal suffering.
Through me one goes among lost
people …
Abandon all hope, you who enter!
Divina Commedia (1307) **Dante Alighieri** (1265–
1321) Italian poet

47 I do not consider it an insult, but rather a
compliment to be called an agnostic. I do
not pretend to know where many ignorant
men are sure – that is all that agnosticism
means.
Speech, (1925) **Darrow, Clarence** (1857–1938)
US lawyer, reformer and writer. At the trial of
John Thomas Scopes for teaching Darwin's
theory of evolution in school

48 A wrong decision can make me very
miserable. But I have trust in God. If you
have this trust you don't have to worry, as
you don't have the sole responsibility.
Speech on his retirement, (1982) **Denning, Lord**
(1899–1999) English Master of the Rolls

49 This is the tragedy of a man who could not
make up his mind.
Introduction to the film Hamlet, (1948) **Dent,
Alan** (1905–1978) Scottish writer and critic

50 See this egg. It is with this that one
overturns all the schools of theology and all
the temples on earth.
Le Rêve de d'Alembert (1769)

51 Wandering in a vast forest at night, I have
only a faint light to guide me. A stranger
appears and says to me: 'My friend, you
should blow out your candle in order to
find your way more clearly.' This stranger is
a theologian.
Addition aux Pensées Philosophiques **Diderot,
Denis** (1713–1784) French philosopher,
encyclopaedist, writer and dramatist

52 Those who mumble do not pray.
Prayers grow like windless trees from
silence.
'Twelve Sheep' **Dutton, Geoffrey** (1922–1998)
Australian poet and writer

53 I am the doubter and the doubt,
And I the hymn the Brahmin sings.
'Brahma' (1867) **Emerson, Ralph Waldo** (1803–
1882) US poet, essayist, transcendentalist and
teacher

54 His doubts are better than most people's
certainties.
In Boswell, *The Life of Samuel Johnson* (1791)
Hardwicke, Philip Yorke, Earl of (1690–1764)
English judge and Lord Chancellor. Referring
to Dirleton's *Doubts*

55 And I said to a man who stood at the gate
of the year: 'Give me a light that I may
tread safely into the unknown.' And he
replied: 'Go out into the darkness and put
your hand into the hand of God. That shall
be to you better than a light, and safer than
a known way.'
The Desert (1908), 'God Knows' **Haskins,
Minnie Louise** (1875–1957) English teacher and
writer. Quoted by King George VI in his
Christmas broadcast, 1939

56 Good God, how much reverence can you
have for a Supreme Being who finds it
necessary to include such phenomena as
phlegm and tooth decay in His divine
system of Creation?
Catch-22, (1961) **Heller, Joseph** (1923–1999) US
author

57 The crib will always be more important than the Dome.
The Times, (1999) **Hume, Basil** (1923–1999) English Cardinal, Archbishop of Westminster. On millennium jamborees

58 Defined in psychological terms, a fanatic is a man who consciously overcompensates a secret doubt.
Proper Studies (1927) **Huxley, Aldous** (1894–1963) English writer, poet and critic

59 I am too much of a sceptic to deny the possibility of anything.
Letter to Herbert Spencer, (1886) **Huxley, T.H.** (1825–1895) English biologist, Darwinist and agnostic

60 All argument is against it; but all belief is for it.
In Boswell, *The Life of Samuel Johnson* (1791) **Johnson, Samuel** (1709–1784) English lexicographer, poet, critic, conversationalist and essayist. Of ghosts

61 Two men look out through the same bars: One sees the mud, and one the stars.
'A Cluster of Quiet Thoughts' (1896) **Langbridge, Frederick** (1849–1923) English religious writer

62 The modern pantheist not only sees the god in everything, he takes photographs of it.
St Mawr (1925) **Lawrence, D.H.** (1885–1930) English writer, poet and critic

63 Doubt everything at least once – even the proposition that two and two are four.
Miscellaneous Writings **Lichtenberg, Georg** (1742–1799) German physicist, satirist and writer

64 Teach us, good Lord, to serve Thee as Thou deservest:
To give and not to count the cost;
To fight and not to heed the wounds;
To toil and not to seek for rest;
To labour and not to ask for any reward
Save that of knowing that we do Thy will.
'Prayer for Generosity' **Loyola, St Ignatius** (1491–1556) Spanish soldier and founder of the Jesuits

65 The Puritans hated bear-baiting, not because it gave pain to the bear, but because it gave pleasure to the spectators.
History of England (1849) **Macaulay, Lord** (1800–1859) English Liberal statesman, essayist and poet

66 A hefty whaler, after some discussion with Marsden, remarked, 'Your religion teaches that if a man is hit on one cheek, he will turn the other.' And he hit Marsden on the right cheek. Marsden obediently offered his left cheek and received a second blow. 'Now,' he said, 'I have obeyed my Master's commands. What I do next, he left to my own judgement. Take this.' And knocked the man down.
From Mrs P.R. Woodhouse, oral tradition **Marsden, Samuel** (1792–1848) English-born Australian churchman. On Christianity

67 Faith, like a jackal, feeds among the tombs, and even from these dead doubts she gathers her most vital hope.
Attr. **Melville, Herman** (1819–1891) US writer and poet

68 Faith may be defined briefly as an illogical belief in the occurrence of the improbable.
Prejudices (1927) **Mencken, H.L.** (1880–1956) US writer, critic, philologist and satirist

69 Long is the way
And hard, that out of Hell leads up to Light.
Paradise Lost (1667) **Milton, John** (1608–1674) English poet, libertarian and pamphleteer

70 Ten thousand difficulties do not make one doubt.
Apologia pro Vita Sua (1864) **Newman, John Henry, Cardinal** (1801–1890) English Cardinal, theologian and poet

71 To understand God's thoughts we must study statistics, for these are the measure of his purpose.
Attr. **Nightingale, Florence** (1820–1910) English nurse

72 He was an embittered atheist (the sort of atheist who does not so much disbelieve in God as personally dislike Him).
Down and Out in Paris and London (1933) **Orwell, George** (1903–1950) English writer and critic

73 These are rogues that pretend to be of a religion now!
Well, all I say is, honest atheism for my money.
The Atheist (1683) **Otway, Thomas** (1652–1685) English dramatist and poet

74 You are never dedicated to something you have complete confidence in. No one is fanatically shouting that the sun is going to rise tomorrow. They know it's going to rise tomorrow. When people are fanatically dedicated to political or religious faiths or any other kind of dogmas or goals, it's always because these dogmas or goals are in doubt.
Zen and the Art of Motorcycle Maintenance (1974) **Pirsig, Robert** (1928–) US author

75 Order is Heav'n's first law.
Essay on Man (1734) **Pope, Alexander** (1688–1744) English poet, translator and editor

76 It has been said that the highest praise of God consists in the denial of Him by the atheist, who finds creation so perfect that he has no need of a creator.
Le Côté de Guermantes (1921) **Proust, Marcel** (1871–1922) French writer and critic

77 O Lord, if there is a Lord, save my soul, if I have a soul.
'A Sceptic's Prayer' **Renan, J. Ernest** (1823–1892) French philologist, writer and historian

78 I feel a feeling which I feel you all feel.
Sermon, (1885) **Ridding, Bishop George** (1828–1904) English headmaster and bishop

79 The worst moment for the atheist is when he is really thankful and has nobody to thank.
Attr. **Rossetti, Dante Gabriel** (1828–1882) English poet, painter, translator and letter writer

80 Doubt, it seems to me, is the central condition of a human being in the twentieth century.
The Observer, (1989) **Rushdie, Salman** (1947–) Indian-born English author

81 I was told that the Chinese say they would bury me by the Western Lake and build a shrine to my memory. I have some slight regret that this did not happen, as I might have become a god, which would have been very chic for an atheist.
The Autobiography of Bertrand Russell (1969) **Russell, Bertrand** (1872–1970) English philosopher, mathematician, essayist and social reformer

82 My atheism, like that of Spinoza, is true piety towards the universe.
Soliloquies in England (1922)

83 People who feel themselves to be exiles in this world are mightily inclined to believe themselves citizens of another.
Attr. **Santayana, George** (1863–1952) Spanish-born US philosopher and writer

84 Therapy seems to be about making people feel good about their weaknesses and inadequacies. Religion is to do with making people feel bad about their weaknesses and inadequacies. We are therefore in a condition of social and spiritual chaos. Therapy enhances that chaos.
The Times, (2000) **Scruton, Roger** (1930–) English philosopher and critic

85 I will burn, but this is a mere incident. We shall continue our discussion in eternity.
Attr. **Servetus, Michael** (1511–1553) Spanish theologian. Comment to the judges of the Inquisition after being condemned to be burned at the stake

86 I am just going to pray for you at St Paul's, but with no very lively hope of success.
In H. Pearson, *The Smith of Smiths* (1934) **Smith, Sydney** (1771–1845) English clergyman, essayist, journalist and wit. To Monkton Milnes

87 We feel and know by experience that we are eternal.
Ethics (1677) **Spinoza, Baruch** (1632–1677) Dutch philosopher and theologian

88 Our current obsession with creativity is the result of our continued striving for immortality in an era when most people no longer believe in an afterlife.

The Female Woman (1973) **Stassinopoulos, Arianna** (1950–) Greek writer

89 Great fires flare up in the wind, but little ones are blown out if they are not sheltered.
Introduction à la vie dévote (1609) **St Francis de Sales** (1567–1622) French bishop and theologian

90 Life is not all Beer and Skittles. The inherent tragedy of things works itself out from white to black and blacker, and the poor things of a day look ruefully on. Does it shake my cast iron faith? I cannot say it does. I believe in an ultimate decency of things; ay, and if I woke in hell, should still believe it!
Letter to Sidney Colvin, (1893) **Stevenson, Robert Louis** (1850–1894) Scottish writer, poet and essayist

91 One man's faith is another man's delusion.
Feet of Clay (1996) **Storr, Dr Anthony** (1920–2001) British writer and psychiatrist

92 There lives more faith in honest doubt, Believe me, than in half the creeds.
In Memoriam A. H. H. (1850)

93 For nothing worth proving can be proven, Nor yet disproven: wherefore thou be wise, Cleave ever to the sunnier side of doubt.
'The Ancient Sage' (1885) **Tennyson, Alfred, Lord** (1809–1892) English lyric poet

94 If this man is not faithful to his God, how can he be faithful to me, a mere man?
In E. Guérard, *Dictionnaire Encyclopédique* **Theodoric** (c.445–526) King of the Ostrogoths. Explaining why he had a trusted minister, who had said he would adopt his master's religion, beheaded

95 Let me lie down like a stone, O Lord, and rise up like new bread.
War and Peace (1868–1869) **Tolstoy, Leo** (1828–1910) Russian writer, essayist, philosopher and moralist

96 The hands are a sort of feet, which serve us in our passage towards Heaven, curiously distinguished into joints and fingers, and fit to be applied to any thing which reason can imagine or desire.

Meditations on the Six Days of Creation (1717) **Traherne, Thomas** (c.1637–1674) English religious writer and clergyman

97 The courage to believe in nothing.
Fathers and Sons (1862)

98 Whatever a man prays for, he prays for a miracle. Every prayer reduces itself to this: 'Great God, grant that twice two be not four.'
'Prayer' (1881) **Turgenev, Ivan** (1818–1883) Russian writer and dramatist

99 Cure yourself of the disease of worrying about how you appear to others. Concern yourself only with how you appear before God, concern yourself with the idea which God has of you.
Vida de Don Quijote y Sancho (1914)

100 A faith which does not doubt is a dead faith.
La agonía del cristianismo (1931) **Unamuno, Miguel de** (1864–1936) Spanish philosopher, poet and writer

101 When all desires that dwell within the human heart are cast away, then a mortal becomes immortal and here he attaineth to Brahman.
Katha Upanishad **Upanishads** (c.800–300 BC)

102 Is it any better in Heaven, my friend Ford, Than you found it in Provence?
'To Ford Madox Ford in Heaven' (1944) **Williams, William Carlos** (1883–1963) US poet, writer and paediatrician

103 By Night an Atheist half believes a God.
Night-Thoughts on Life, Death and Immortality (1742–1745) **Young, Edward** (1683–1765) English poet, dramatist, satirist and clergyman

104 Faith consists in believing what reason does not believe ... It is not enough that a thing may be possible for it to be believed.
Questions sur l'Encyclopédie (1770–1772) **Voltaire** (1694–1778) French philosopher, dramatist, poet, historian writer and critic
See also belief; God; religion

FAME

1 David and I haven't got that many friends. We could have our wedding in a postbox.
The Observer, (1999) **Adams, Victoria** (1974–) English pop singer, member of the Spice Girls. On her marriage to footballer David Beckham

2 Fame is a pearl many dive for and only a few bring up. Even when they do, it is not perfect, and they sigh for more, and lose better things in struggling for them.
Jo's Boys (1886)

3 It takes very little fire to make a great deal of smoke nowadays, and notoriety is not real glory.
Jo's Boys (1886) **Alcott, Louisa May** (1832–1888) US writer

4 A celebrity is a person who works hard all his life to become well known, and then wears dark glasses to avoid being recognized.
In Laurence Peter, *Quotations for Our Time* (1977) **Allen, Fred** (1894–1956) US vaudeville performer and comedian

5 He was a handsome, well-shaped man: very good company, and of a very ready and pleasant smooth wit.
Brief Lives (c.1693) **Aubrey, John** (1626–1697) English antiquary, folklorist and biographer. Of Shakespeare

6 My claim to literary fame is that I used to deliver meat to a woman who became T.S. Eliot's mother-in-law.
The Observer, 'Sayings of the Year', (1992) **Bennett, Alan** (1934–) English dramatist, actor and diarist

7 He's always backing into the limelight.
Attr. **Berners, Lord** (1883–1950) Of T.E. Lawrence

8 A prophet is not without honour, save in his own country, and in his own house.
Matthew, 13:57 **The Bible (King James Version)**

9 A sign of a celebrity is that his name is often worth more than his services.
The Image (1962)

10 The celebrity is a person who is known for his well-knownness.
The Image (1962) **Boorstin, Daniel** (1914–2004) US librarian, historian, lawyer and writer

11 Rejoice ye dead, where'er your spirits dwell,
Rejoice that yet on earth your fame is bright,
And that your names, remembered day and night,
Live on the lips of those who love you well.
'Ode to Music' (1896) **Bridges, Robert** (1844–1930) English poet, dramatist, essayist and doctor

12 Passion for fame; a passion which is the instinct of all great souls.
Speech on American Taxation (1774) **Burke, Edmund** (1729–1797) Irish-born British statesman and philosopher

13 I awoke one morning and found myself famous.
In Moore, *Letters and Journals of Lord Byron* (1830) **Byron, Lord** (1788–1824) English poet, satirist and traveller. Remark on the instantaneous success of *Childe Harold*

14 Fame, like water, bears up the lighter things, and lets the weighty sink.
Attr. **Calderón de la Barca, Pedro** (1600–1681) Spanish dramatist and poet

15 Know, Celia (since thou art so proud,)
'Twas I that gave thee thy renowne:
Thou had'st in the forgotten crowd
Of common beauties, liv'd unknowne,
Had not my verse exhal'd thy name,
And with it imped the wings of fame.
'Ingratefull Beauty Threatened' (1640) **Carew, Thomas** (c.1595–1640) English poet, musician and dramatist

16 I would much rather have men ask why I have no statue than why I have one.
In Plutarch, *Lives* **Cato the Elder** (234–149 BC) Roman statesman

17 Bogart's a helluva nice guy until 11.30 p.m. After that he thinks he's Bogart.
In Halliwell, *The Filmgoer's Book of Quotes* (1973) **Chasen, Dave** (1926–) Hollywood restaurateur

18 Mother told me a couple of years ago,
'Sweetheart, settle down and marry a rich
man.' I said, 'Mom, I am a rich man.'
The Observer Review, (1995) **Cher** (1946–) US
singer and actress

19 No man is a hero to his valet.
In *Lettres de Mlle Aïssé à Madame C* (1787)
Cornuel, Madame Anne-Marie Bigot de
(1605–1694) French society hostess

20 For fame is not achieved by sitting on
feather cushions or lying in bed.
Divina Commedia (1307) **Dante Alighieri** (1265–
1321) Italian poet

21 My address will soon be Annihilation. As
for my name you will find it in the
Pantheon of History.
Attr. **Danton, Georges** (1759–1794) French
revolutionary leader. Response to formal
questions during his trial in Paris, 2 April
1794

22 Fame creates its own standard. A guy who
twitches his lips is just another guy with a
lip twitch – unless he's Humphrey Bogart.
Yes I Can (1965) **Davis Jnr., Sammy** (1925–1990)
US actor, singer and dancer

23 I want to be the queen of people's hearts.
BBC *Panorama* interview, (1996) **Diana,
Princess of Wales** (1961–1997)

24 Fame is a food that dead men eat, –
I have no stomach for such meat.
'Fame is a Food' (1906) **Dobson, Henry Austin**
(1840–1921) English poet, essayist and
biographer

25 I was the only one there I never heard of.
In Lieberman, *3,500 Good Quotes for Speakers*
(1983) **Farber, Barry** (1859–1930) US
broadcaster and writer

26 If you would not be forgotten as soon as
you are dead, either write things worth
reading or do things worth writing.
Attr. **Franklin, Benjamin** (1706–1790) US
statesman, scientist, political critic and
printer

27 Many were the wit-combats betwixt him
and Ben Jonson, which two I behold like a
Spanish great galleon, and an English man
of war; Master Jonson (like the former) was
built far higher in learning; solid but slow
in his performances. Shakespeare was the
English man of war, lesser in bulk, but
lighter in sailing, could turn with all tides,
tack about and take advantage of all winds,
by the quickness of his wit and invention.
The History of the Worthies of England (1662)
Fuller, Thomas (1608–1661) English
churchman and antiquary. Comparing
Shakespeare and Ben Jonson

28 I was born at the age of twelve on a Metro-
Goldwyn-Mayer lot.
The Observer, (1951) **Garland, Judy** (1922–1969)
US film actress and singer

29 The deed is all, the glory is naught.
Faust (1832) **Goethe** (1749–1832) German poet,
writer, dramatist and scientist

30 What is fame? an empty bubble;
Gold? a transient, shining trouble.
'Solitude' (1755) **Grainger, James** (c.1721–1766)
Scottish poet, army surgeon and editor

31 Fame is a powerful aphrodisiac.
Radio Times, (1964) **Greene, Graham** (1904–
1991) English writer and dramatist

32 Popularity is a Crime from the Moment it
is sought; it is only a Virtue where Men
have it whether they will or no.
*Political, Moral and Miscellaneous Thoughts and
Reflections* (1750) **Halifax, Lord** (1633–1695)
English politician, courtier, pamphleteer and
epigrammatist

33 There were our own, there were the others.
Their deaths were like their lives, human
and animal.
There were no gods and precious few
heroes.
Elegies for the Dead in Cyrenaica (1948)
Henderson, Hamish (1919–2002) Scottish
folklorist, composer, translator and poet

34 I don't care what is written about me as
long as it isn't true.
In Cooper and Hartman, *Violets and Vinegar*
(1980) **Hepburn, Katharine** (1909–2003) US
actress

35 The ultimate stage of reputation would be to have a name so powerful in market terms it would sell anything. Well, the money would be nice, but I don't know yet if I'm ready for the irresponsibility.
In Winks (ed.), *Colloquium on Crime* (1986) **Hill, Reginald** (1936–) British writer and playwright

36 A name made great is a name destroyed.
In Taylor (ed.), *Sayings of the Jewish Fathers* (1877) **Hillel, 'The Elder'** (c.60 BC–c.10 AD) Jewish religious leader

37 Fame? It's glory in small change.
Ruy Blas (1838) **Hugo, Victor** (1802–1885) French poet, writer, dramatist and politician

38 I'm afraid of losing my obscurity. Genuineness only thrives in the dark. Like celery.
Those Barren Leaves (1925) **Huxley, Aldous** (1894–1963) English writer, poet and critic

39 Posthumous fame is not particularly attractive to me, but, if I am to be remembered at all, I would rather it should be as 'a man who did his best to help the people' than by any other title.
In L. Huxley, *Life and Letters of Thomas Henry Huxley* (1900) **Huxley, T.H.** (1825–1895) English biologist, Darwinist and agnostic. Remark to George Howell

40 Fame, like a wayward girl, will still be coy
To those who woo her with too slavish knees.
'On Fame (1)' (1819) **Keats, John** (1795–1821) English poet

41 The nice thing about being a celebrity is that, if you bore people, they think it's their fault.
Attr. **Kissinger, Henry** (1923–) German-born US Secretary of State

42 The best fame is a writer's fame: it's enough to get a table at a good restaurant, but not enough that you get interrupted when you eat.
The Observer, (1993) **Lebowitz, Fran** (1946–) US writer

43 I cried all the way to the bank.

Autobiography (1973) **Liberace, Wladziu Valentino** (1919–1987) US pianist and showman. Remark made after hostile criticism

44 I don't care what you say, for me or against me, but for heaven's sake say something about me.
In Thompson, *On Lips of Living Men* **Melba, Dame Nellie** (1861–1931) Australian opera singer. To the editor of the *Argus*

45 A celebrity is one who is known to many persons he is glad he doesn't know.
Attr. **Mencken, H.L.** (1880–1956) US writer, critic, philologist and satirist

46 In Hollywood now when people die they don't say, 'Did he leave a will?' but 'Did he leave a diary?'
The Observer, (1989) **Minnelli, Liza** (1946–) US actress, singer and dancer

47 Until you've lost your reputation, you never realize what a burden it was or what freedom really is.
Gone with the Wind (1936) **Mitchell, Margaret** (1900–1949) US author

48 I had the radio on.
Time, (1952) **Monroe, Marilyn** (1926–1962) US film actress and model. When asked if she really had nothing on during a calendar shoot

49 Fame and tranquillity cannot dwell under the same roof.
Essais (1580) **Montaigne, Michel de** (1533–1592) French essayist and moralist

50 'What are you famous for?'
'For nothing. I am just famous.'
The Flight from the Enchanter (1955) **Murdoch, Iris** (1919–1999) Irish-born British writer, philosopher and dramatist

51 If you have to tell them who you are, you aren't anybody.
In S. Harris, *Pieces of Eight* **Peck, Gregory** (1916–2003) US actor. On the fact that no-one in a crowded restaurant recognized him

52 For the whole earth is the sepulchre of famous men.
In Thucydides, *Histories* **Pericles** (c.495–429) Athenian statesman, general, orator and cultural patron

53 A man can be forgiven a lot if he can quote Shakespeare in an economic crisis.
Attr. **Philip, Prince, Duke of Edinburgh** (1921–) Greek-born consort of Queen Elizabeth II

54 What rage for fame attends both great and small!
Better be damned than mentioned not at all!
'To the Royal Academicians' (1782–1785) **Pindar, Peter (John Wolcot)** (1738–1819) English satirical poet

55 Then teach me, Heav'n! to scorn the guilty bays,
Drive from my breast that wretched lust of praise,
Unblemished let me live, or die unknown;
Oh grant an honest fame, or grant me none!
The Temple of Fame (1715) **Pope, Alexander** (1688–1744) English poet, translator and editor

56 It is better to be faithful than famous.
In Riis, *Theodore Roosevelt, the Citizen* **Roosevelt, Theodore** (1858–1919) US Republican President

57 There may have been disillusionments in the lives of the mediaeval saints, but they would scarcely have been better pleased if they could have foreseen that their names would be associated nowadays chiefly with racehorses and the cheaper clarets.
Reginald (1904) **Saki** (1870–1916) Burmese-born British writer

58 They didn't act like people and they didn't act like actors. It's hard to explain. They acted more like they knew they were celebrities and all. I mean they were good, but they were too good.
The Catcher in the Rye (1951) **Salinger, J.D.** (1919–) US writer

59 I've been offered titles, but I think they get one into disreputable company.
In Barrow, *Gossip* **Shaw, George Bernard** (1856–1950) Irish socialist, writer, dramatist and critic

60 People in high or in distinguished life ought to have a greater circumspection in regard to their most trivial actions. For instance, I saw Mr Pope ... to the best of my memory, he was picking his nose.
The Selected Works in Verse and Prose of William Shenstone (1770) **Shenstone, William** (1714–1763)

61 The only thing that endures is character. Fame and wealth – all that is illusion. All that endures is character.
The Guardian, (1995) **Simpson, O.J.** (1947–) US footballer and actor. Following his acquittal on murder charges

62 A pompous woman of his acquaintance, complaining that the head-waiter of a restaurant had not shown her and her husband immediately to a table, said 'We had to tell him who we were.' Gerald, interested, enquired, 'And who were you?'
Taken Care Of (1965) **Sitwell, Dame Edith** (1887–1964) English poet, anthologist, critic and biographer

63 One day I wrote her name upon the strand,
But came the waves and washed it away:
Agayne I wrote it with a second hand,
But came the tyde, and made my paynes his pray.
Vayne man, sayd she, that doest in vaine assay,
A mortall thing so to immortalize,
For I my selfe shall lyke to this decay,
And eek my name bee wyped out lykewize.
Not so, (quod I) let baser things devize
To dy in dust, but you shall live by fame:
My verse your vertues rare shall eternize,
And in the hevens wryte your glorious name.
Where whenas death shall all the world subdew,
Our love shall live, and later life renew.
Amoretti and Epithalamion (1595) **Spenser, Edmund** (c.1522–1599) English poet

64 The very weird religion of celebrity scares me. It's like people are creating fake heroes because they don't have any real ones. The politicians have failed us, religion has failed us, so who do people turn to? Celebrities. It is wrong.

Attr. (1992) **Stipe, Michael** (1960–) US rock musician, singer in REM

65 The desire for fame is the last thing to be put aside, even by the wise.
Histories **Tacitus** (AD c.56–c.120) Roman historian

66 I stopped believing in Santa Claus when I was six. Mother took me to see him in a department store and he asked for my autograph.
Attr. **Temple, Shirley** (1928–) US child actress and diplomat

67 There was worlds of reputation in it, but no money.
A Yankee at the Court of King Arthur (1889) **Twain, Mark** (1835–1910) US humorist, writer, journalist and lecturer

68 What, when drunk, one sees in other women, one sees in Garbo sober.
The Sunday Times, (1963) **Tynan, Kenneth** (1927–1980) English drama critic, producer and essayist

69 Celebrity is a mask that eats into the face.
Memoirs (1989) **Updike, John** (1932–) US writer, poet and critic

70 In the future everyone will be world famous for fifteen minutes.
Catalogue for an exhibition, (1968)

71 He is not our hero because he was perfect. He is our hero because he perfectly represented the damaged and beautiful soul of our time.
In Brandreth, *Great Theatrical Disasters* Of James Dean **Warhol, Andy** (c.1926–1987) US painter, graphic designer and filmmaker

72 Vain the ambition of kings
Who seek by trophies and dead things,
To leave a living name behind,
And weave but nets to catch the wind.
The Devil's Law-Case (1623) **Webster, John** (c.1580–c.1625) English dramatist

73 I wouldn't want Tiger's life, even if it does bring things like a $40 million Nike contract. It's not worth it. I can go out for a drink with my mates and no one bothers me, and that's how I like it. I would never want bodyguards, all that hassle.
Attr. **Westwood, Lee** (1973–) English golfer

74 There is only one thing in the world worse than being talked about, and that is not being talked about.
The Picture of Dorian Gray (1891)

75 I should be like a lion in a cage of savage Daniels.
Attr. Refusing to attend a function at a club whose members were hostile to him **Wilde, Oscar** (1854–1900) Irish poet, dramatist, writer, critic and wit
See also egoism; greatness

FAMILIES

1 Sir Walter, being strangely surprised and put out of his countenance at so great a table, gives his son a damned blow over the face. His son, as rude as he was, would not strike his father, but strikes over the face the gentleman that sat next to him and said 'Box about: 'twill come to my father anon.'
Brief Lives (c.1693) **Aubrey, John** (1626–1697) English antiquary, folklorist and biographer. Of Sir Walter Raleigh

2 They were a tense and peculiar family, the Oedipuses, weren't they?
Attr. **Beerbohm, Sir Max** (1872–1956) English satirist, cartoonist, critic and essayist

3 Mothers of large families (who claim to common sense)
Will find a Tiger well repays the trouble and expense.
The Bad Child's Book of Beasts (1896) **Belloc, Hilaire** (1870–1953) English writer of verse, essayist and critic; Liberal MP

4 Generations pass while some tree stands, and old families last not three oaks.
Hydriotaphia: Urn Burial (1658) **Browne, Sir Thomas** (1605–1682) English physician, author and antiquary

5 I believe that more unhappiness comes from this source than from any other – I mean from the attempt to prolong family connection unduly and to make people hang together artificially who would never naturally do so. The mischief among the

lower classes is not so great, but among the middle and upper classes it is killing a large number daily. And the old people do not really like it much better than the young.
The Note-Books of Samuel Butler (1912) **Butler, Samuel** (1835–1902) English writer, painter, philosopher and scholar

6 A branch of one of your antediluvian families, fellows that the flood could not wash away.
Love for Love (1695) **Congreve, William** (1670–1729) English dramatist

7 Accidents will occur in the best-regulated families.
David Copperfield (1850)

8 It is a melancholy truth that even great men have their poor relations.
Bleak House (1853) **Dickens, Charles** (1812–1870) English writer

9 Like all the best families, we have our share of eccentricities, of impetuous and wayward youngsters and of family disagreements.
Daily Mail, (1989) **Elizabeth II** (1926–) Queen of the United Kingdom

10 I felt for a moment that the whole Wilcox family was a fraud, just a wall of newspapers and motor-cars and golf-clubs, and that if it fell I should find nothing behind it but panic and emptiness.
Howard's End (1910) **Forster, E.M.** (1879–1970) English writer, essayist and literary critic

11 The awe and dread with which the untutored savage contemplates his mother-in-law are amongst the most familiar facts of anthropology.
The Golden Bough (1900) **Frazer, Sir James** (1854–1941) Scottish anthropologist and writer

12 Philosophers and politicians have agreed that the bonding together in family groups is both instinctive and necessary to human welfare – and therefore essential to the health of a society. The family is the microcosm.
Attr. in *The Times*, (May 1996) **Freud, Sigmund** (1856–1939) Austrian physicist; founder of psychoanalysis

13 I can trace my ancestry back to a protoplasmal primordial atomic globule. Consequently, my family pride is something inconceivable.
The Mikado (1885) **Gilbert, W.S.** (1836–1911) English dramatist, humorist and librettist

14 I was ever of opinion, that the honest man who married and brought up a large family, did more service than he who continued single, and only talked of population.
The Vicar of Wakefield (1766) **Goldsmith, Oliver** (c.1728–1774) Irish dramatist, poet and writer

15 A person may be indebted for a nose or an eye, for a graceful carriage or a voluble discourse, to a great-aunt or uncle, whose existence he has scarcely heard of.
London Magazine, (1821) **Hazlitt, William** (1778–1830) English writer and critic

16 Good families are generally worse than any others.
The Prisoner of Zenda (1894) **Hope, Anthony** (1863–1933) English writer, dramatist and lawyer

17 It has long been my belief that in times of great stress, such as a 4-day vacation, the thin veneer of family wears off almost at once, and we are revealed in our true personalities.
Raising Demons (1956) **Jackson, Shirley** (1919–1965) US novelist

18 Treasure your families – the future of humanity passes by way of the family.
Speech, (1982)

19 As the family goes, so goes the nation and so goes the whole world in which we live.
The Observer, (1986) **John Paul II** (1920–2005) Polish pope

20 Despair of peace as long as your mother-in-law is alive.
Satires **Juvenal** (c.60–130) Roman verse satirist and Stoic

21 A poor relation – is the most irrelevant thing in nature.
Last Essays of Elia (1833) **Lamb, Charles** (1775–1834) English essayist, critic and letter writer

22 Far from being the basis of the good
society, the family, with its narrow privacy
and tawdry secrets, is the source of all our
discontents.
BBC Reith Lecture, (1967) **Leach, Sir Edmund**
(1910–1989) English social anthropologist

23 She's leaving home after living alone for so
many years.
'She's Leaving Home' (song, 1967) **Lennon,
John** (1940–1980) and **McCartney, Paul**
(1942–) English rock musicians, songwriters,
peace campaigners and cultural icons

24 I don't know who my grandfather was; I
am much more concerned to know what
his grandson will be.
In Gross, *Lincoln's Own Stories* **Lincoln,
Abraham** (1809–1865) US statesman and
President

25 A group of closely related persons living
under one roof; it is a convenience, often a
necessity, sometimes a pleasure,
sometimes the reverse; but who first
exalted it as admirable, an almost religious
ideal?
The World My Wilderness (1950) **Macaulay,
Dame Rose** (1881–1958) English writer

26 The sink is the great symbol of the
bloodiness of family life. All life is bad, but
family life is worse.
As Far as You Can Go (1963) **Mitchell, Julian**
(1935–) English writer

27 There is scarcely any less trouble in
running a family than in governing an
entire state ... and domestic matters are no
less importunate for being less important.
Essais (1580) **Montaigne, Michel de** (1533–1592)
French essayist and moralist

28 I find myself surprised at how its realism
actually unites morality with – yes –
romance. It is that need that draws us to
nest in rows, separated by thin walls,
hoping to be tolerated and loved forever –
and to go on reproducing ourselves in
family patterns, handing on some misery
(perhaps), but untold happiness too.
The Times, (1996) **Mooney, Bel** (1946–) British
writer. On the need for family life

29 One would be in less danger
From the wiles of a stranger
If one's own kin and kith
Were more fun to be with.
'Family Court' (1931) **Nash, Ogden** (1902–1971)
US poet

30 It is indeed desirable to be well descended,
but the glory belongs to our ancestors.
On the Training of Children **Plutarch** (c.46–
c.120) Greek biographer and philosopher

31 Oh how hideous it is
To see three generations of one house
gathered together!
It is like an old tree with shoots,
And with some branches rotted and falling.
'Commission' (1916) **Pound, Ezra** (1885–1972)
US poet

32 For there is no friend like a sister
In calm or stormy weather;
To cheer one on the tedious way,
To fetch one if one goes astray,
To lift one if one totters down,
To strengthen whilst one stands.
'Goblin Market' (1862) **Rossetti, Christina**
(1830–1894) English poet

33 Who boasts his ancestry, praises others'
worth.
Hercules Furens, line 340 (trans. Milton) **Seneca**
(c.4 BC–AD 65) Roman philosopher, poet,
dramatist, essayist, rhetorician and statesman

34 A little more than kin, and less than kind.
Hamlet, I.i **Shakespeare, William** (1564–1616)
English dramatist, poet and actor

35 Our ancestors are very good kind of folks;
but they are the last people I should choose
to have a visiting acquaintance with.
The Rivals (1775) **Sheridan, Richard Brinsley**
(1751–1816) Irish dramatist, politician and
orator

36 At last incapable of further harm.
The lewd forefathers of the village sleep.
'If Gray had had to write his Elegy in the
Cemetery of Spoon River' **Squire, Sir J.C.**
(1884–1958) English poet, critic, writer and
editor

37 Nothing like blood, sir, in hosses, dawgs,
and men.
Vanity Fair (1848)

38 If a man's character is to be abused, say what you will, there's nobody like a relation to do the business.
Vanity Fair (1848) **Thackeray, William Makepeace** (1811–1863) Indian-born English writer

39 All happy families resemble one another, but every unhappy family is unhappy in its own way.
Anna Karenina (1877) **Tolstoy, Leo** (1828–1910) Russian writer, essayist, philosopher and moralist

40 It is no use telling me that there are bad aunts and good aunts. At the core they are all alike. Sooner or later, out pops the cloven hoof.
The Code of the Woosters (1938)

41 Unlike the male codfish which, suddenly finding itself the parent of three million five hundred thousand little codfish, cheerfully resolves to love them all, the British aristocracy is apt to look with a somewhat jaundiced eye on its younger sons.
In R. Usborne, *Wodehouse at Work to the End* (1976) **Wodehouse, P.G.** (1881–1975) English humorist and writer
See also birth; childhood and children; marriage; men and women; parenthood

FANTASY

1 Every man's life is a fairy-tale written by God's fingers.
Works (c.1843), Preface **Andersen, Hans Christian** (1805–1875) Danish writer and dramatist

2 Anno 1670, not far from Cirencester, was an apparition; being demanded whether a good spirit or a bad? returned no answer, but disappeared with a curious perfume and most melodious twang. Mr W. Lilly believes it was a fairy.
Miscellanies (1696) **Aubrey, John** (1626–1697) English antiquary, folklorist and biographer

3 Every time a child says 'I don't believe in fairies,' there is a little fairy somewhere that falls down dead.
Peter Pan (1904) **Barrie, Sir J.M.** (1860–1937) Scottish dramatist and writer

4 For my part, I have ever believed, and do now know, that there are witches.
Religio Medici (1643) **Browne, Sir Thomas** (1605–1682) English physician, author and antiquary

5 'I can't explain myself, I'm afraid, sir,' said Alice, 'because I'm not myself, you see.' 'I don't see,' said the Caterpillar.
Alice's Adventures in Wonderland (1865)

6 'There's no use trying,' she said: 'one can't believe impossible things.'
'I dare say you haven't had much practice,' said the Queen. 'When I was your age, I always did it for half an hour a day. Why, sometimes I've believed as many as six impossible things before breakfast.'
Through the Looking-Glass (and What Alice Found There) (1872)

7 They gave it me ... for an un-birthday present.
Through the Looking-Glass (and What Alice Found There) (1872) **Carroll, Lewis** (1832–1898) English writer and photographer

8 When fishes flew and forests walked
And figs grew upon thorn,
Some moment when the moon was blood
Then surely I was born.
With monstrous head and sickening cry
And ears like errant wings,
The devil's walking parody
On all four-footed things ...
Fools! For I also had my hour;
One far fierce hour and sweet:
There was a shout about my ears,
And palms before my feet.
The Wild Knight and Other Poems (1900)
Chesterton, G.K. (1874–1936) English writer, poet and critic

9 There was a pause – just long enough for an angel to pass, flying slowly.
Vainglory (1915) **Firbank, Ronald** (1886–1926) English writer

10 There are many reasons why novelists write, but they all have one thing in common – a need to create an alternative world.

The Sunday Times Magazine, (1977) **Fowles, John** (1926–2005) English writer

11 Superstition is the poetry of life.
'Literature and Language' (1823) **Goethe** (1749–1832) German poet, writer, dramatist and scientist

12 Reason has moons, but moons not hers,
Lie mirror'd on her sea,
Confounding her astronomers,
But, O! delighting me.
'Reason Has Moons' (1917) **Hodgson, Ralph** (1871–1962) English poet, illustrator and journalist

13 We soon learn that there is nothing mysterious or supernatural in the case, but that all proceeds from the usual propensity of mankind towards the marvellous, and that, though this inclination may at intervals receive a check from sense and learning, it can never be thoroughly extirpated from human nature.
'Of Miracles' (1748) **Hume, David** (1711–1776) Scottish philosopher and political economist

14 Castles in the air – they're so easy to take refuge in. So easy to build, too.
The Master Builder (1892) **Ibsen, Henrik** (1828–1906) Norwegian writer, dramatist and poet

15 I'm the Prophet of the Utterly Absurd,
Of the Patently Impossible and Vain.
'The Song of the Banjo' (1894)

16 The great, grey-green, greasy Limpopo River, all set about with fever-trees.
Just So Stories (1902), 'The Elephant's Child' **Kipling, Rudyard** (1865–1936) Indian-born British poet and writer

17 I guess I am a fantasy.
In Steinem, *Outrageous Acts and Everyday Rebellions* (1984) **Monroe, Marilyn** (1926–1962) US film actress and model

18 We live in a fantasy world, a world of illusion. The great task in life is to find reality.
The Times, (1983) **Murdoch, Iris** (1919–1999) Irish-born British writer, philosopher and dramatist

19 It is such a mysterious place, the land of tears.

The Little Prince (1943) **Saint-Exupéry, Antoine de** (1900–1944) French author and aviator

20 This rough magic
I here abjure – I'll break my staff,
Bury it certain fathoms in the earth,
And, deeper than did ever plummet sound
I'll drown my book.
The Tempest, V.i **Shakespeare, William** (1564–1616) English dramatist, poet and actor

21 Fairy-tales interest me as a manifestation of pure art, perhaps the very first instance of art detaching itself from real life, and also because – like pure art – they enhance reality, remaking it in their own likeness, separating good from evil, and bringing all fears and terrors to a happy conclusion.
A Voice From the Chorus (1973) **Tertz, Abram** (1925–1997) Russian writer and dissident

22 The boys are dreaming wicked or of the bucking ranches of the night and the jollyrodgered sea.
Under Milk Wood (1954) **Thomas, Dylan** (1914–1953) Welsh poet, writer and radio dramatist

23 Anyone who stares long enough into the distance is bound to be mistaken for a philosopher or mystic in the end.
Happy Valley (1939) **White, Patrick** (1912–1990) English-born Australian writer and dramatist

24 We had fed the heart on fantasies,
The heart's grown brutal from the fare.
'Meditations in Time of Civil War' (1928) **Yeats, W.B.** (1865–1939) Irish poet, dramatist, editor, writer and senator
See also dreams; imagination

FASHION

1 It is not only fine feathers that make fine birds.
'The Jay and the Peacock' **Aesop** (6th century BC) Legendary Greek writer of fables

2 A person and face, of strong, natural, sterling insignificance, though adorned in the first style of fashion.
Sense and Sensibility (1811) **Austen, Jane** (1775–1817) English writer

3 I never cared for fashion much, amusing little seams and witty little pleats: it was the girls I liked.
The Independent, (1990)

4 The avant-garde has gone to Tescos.
The Times, (1999) Commenting on dumbed-down 'Cool Britannia' **Bailey, David** (1938–) English photographer

5 Look, in particular, at the people who, like you, are making average incomes for doing average jobs – bank vice presidents, insurance salesman, auditors, secretaries of defense – and you'll realize they all dress the same way, essentially the way the mannequins in the Sears menswear department dress. Now look at the real successes, the people who make a lot more money than you – Elton John, Captain Kangaroo, anybody from Saudi Arabia, Big Bird, and so on. They all dress funny – and they all succeed. Are you catching on?
'How to Dress for Real Success' **Barry, Dave** (1947–) US columnist and journalist

6 Never in the history of fashion has so little material been raised so high to reveal so much that needs to be covered so badly.
Attr. **Beaton, Cecil** (1904–1980) English photographer. On the miniskirt

7 I think one of the reasons I'm popular again is because I'm wearing a tie. You have to be different.
Attr. **Bennett, Tony** (1926–) US singer

8 It's a terrible sign. It will be the death of this profession if designers start using real people on the catwalks and in their advertising.
Daily Mail, (1995) **Bongay, Amy** President of the Models Guild. Commenting on the fact that the fashion industry had begun to find supermodels too demanding

9 Clothes are our weapons, our challenges, our visible insults.
Nothing Sacred (1982) **Carter, Angela** (1940–1992) English writer

10 Fashion anticipates, and elegance is a state of mind.
In My Own Fashion (1987) **Cassini, Oleg** (1913–2006) French-born US fashion designer

11 A fashion for the young? That is a pleonasm: there is no fashion for the old.
In Haedrich, *Coco Chanel, Her Life, Her Secrets* (1971)

12 Fashion is architecture: it is a matter of proportions.
In Haedrich, *Coco Chanel, Her Life, Her Secrets* (1971)

13 Fashion is reduced to a question of hem lengths. Haute couture is finished because it's in the hands of men who don't like women.
In Madsen, *Coco Chanel* (1990) Remark at a press conference, 1967

14 These are clothes by a man who doesn't know women, never had one and dreams of being one.
Scotland on Sunday, (1995) On Dior's New Look **Chanel, Coco** (1883–1971) French couturier and perfumer

15 Fashion – a word which knaves and fools may use,
Their knavery and folly to excuse.
The Rosciad (1761) **Churchill, Charles** (1731–1764) English poet, political writer and clergyman

16 One had as good be out of the world, as out of the fashion.
Love's Last Shift (1696) **Cibber, Colley** (1671–1757) English actor, dramatist and poet

17 Never wear artistic jewellery; it ruins a woman's reputation.
Gigi (1944) **Colette** (1873–1954) French writer

18 I think the most important thing a woman can have – next to talent, of course, – is her hairdresser.
Esquire, (1957) **Crawford, Joan** (1908–1977) US film actress

19 I go to a better tailor than any of you and pay more for my clothes. The only difference is that you probably don't sleep in yours.
In E. Fuller, *2500 Anecdotes* **Darrow, Clarence** (1857–1938) US lawyer, reformer and writer

20 Any man may be in good spirits and good temper when he's well drest. There ain't much credit in that.

Martin Chuzzlewit (1844) **Dickens, Charles** (1812–1870) English writer

21 'Goodness,' he cried, 'if it is our clothes which fit us for this world, in what high esteem must we hold those who make them!'
The Two Countesses, 'Countess Muschi' (1884) **Ebner-Eschenbach, Marie von** (1830–1916) Austrian writer

22 I thought everyone must know that a short jacket is always worn with a silk hat at a private view in the morning.
In Sir P. Magnus, *Edward VII* **Edward VII** (1841–1910) King of the United Kingdom

23 Living blood and a passion of kindness does at last distinguish God's gentlemen from Fashion's.
'Manners' (1844)

24 The Frenchman invented the ruffle, the Englishman added the shirt.
English Traits (1856)

25 They think him the best dressed man, whose dress is so fit for his use that you cannot notice or remember to describe it.
English Traits (1856) Of the English

26 It is only when the mind and character slumber that the dress can be seen.
Letters and Social Aims (1875) **Emerson, Ralph Waldo** (1803–1882) US poet, essayist, transcendentalist and teacher

27 A lady, if undrest at Church, looks silly, One cannot be devout in dishabilly.
The Stage Coach (1704) **Farquhar, George** (1678–1707) Irish dramatist

28 The sense of being well-dressed gives a feeling of inward tranquillity which religion is powerless to bestow.
In R.W. Emerson, *Letters and Social Aims*, (1875) **Forbes, Miss C.F.** (1817–1911) English socialite and writer

29 The Cranford ladies' dress is very independent of fashion; as they observe, 'What does it signify how we dress here at Cranford, where everybody knows us?' And if they go from home, their reason is equally cogent, 'What does it signify how we dress here, where nobody knows us?'

Cranford (1853) **Gaskell, Elizabeth** (1810–1865) English writer

30 And, even while fashion's brightest arts decoy,
The heart distrusting asks, if this be joy.
The Deserted Village (1770) **Goldsmith, Oliver** (c.1728–1774) Irish dramatist, poet and writer

31 Those who make their dress a principal part of themselves, will, in general, become of no more value than their dress.
'On the Clerical Character' **Hazlitt, William** (1778–1830) English writer and critic

32 A sweet disorder in the dresse
Kindles in cloathes a wantonnesse:
A Lawne about the shoulders thrown
Into a fine distraction …
A winning wave (deserving Note)
In the tempestuous petticote:
A carelesse shooe-string, in whose tye
I see a wilde civility:
Doe more bewitch me, than when Art
Is too precise in every part.
'Delight in Disorder' (1648)

33 When as in silks my Julia goes,
Then, then (me thinks) how sweetly flowes
That liquefaction of her clothes.
Next, when I cast mine eyes and see
That brave Vibration each way free;
O how that glittering taketh me!
Hesperides (1648) **Herrick, Robert** (1591–1674) English poet, royalist and clergyman

34 Fine clothes are good only as they supply the want of other means of procuring respect.
In Boswell, *The Life of Samuel Johnson* (1791) **Johnson, Samuel** (1709–1784) English lexicographer, poet, critic, conversationalist and essayist

35 Still to be neat, still to be drest,
As you were going to a feast;
Still to be powder'd, still perfum'd,
Lady, it is to be presumed,
Though art's hid causes are not found,
All is not sweet, all is not sound.
Give me a look, give me a face,
That makes simplicity a grace;
Robes loosely flowing, hair as free:
Such sweet neglect more taketh me,
Than all the adulteries of art;
They strike mine eyes, but not my heart.

Epicoene (1609) **Jonson, Ben** (1572–1637) English dramatist and poet

36 Today I dressed to meet my father's eyes; yesterday it was for my husband's.
In Macrobius, *Saturnalia* **Julia the Elder** (39 BC –AD 14) Daughter of Roman emperor Augustus. On being complimented by her father on the modest dress she was wearing that day

37 The sock is a highly sensitive conjugal object.
The Observer, (1992) **Kaufman, Jean-Claude**

38 Isn't it grand! Isn't it fine!
Look at the cut, the style, the line!
The suit of clothes is altogether, but altogether it's altogether
The most remarkable suit of clothes that I have ever seen.
'The King's New Clothes' (song, 1952) **Loesser, Frank** (1910–1969) US songwriter and composer

39 Kissing your hand may make you feel very very good but a diamond and sapphire bracelet lasts forever.
Gentlemen Prefer Blondes (1925) **Loos, Anita** (1893–1981) US writer and screenwriter

40 Join a Highland regiment, me boy. The kilt is an unrivalled garment for fornication and diarrhoea.
Bugles and a Tiger **Masters, John** (1914–1983) English writer

41 There was a young belle of old Natchez
Whose garments were always in patchez.
When comment arose
On the state of her clothes,
She drawled, When Ah itchez, Ah scratchez!
I'm a Stranger Here Myself (1935)

42 Sure, deck your lower limbs in pants;
Yours are the limbs, my sweeting.
You look divine as you advance –
Have you seen yourself retreating?
'What's the Use?' (1940) **Nash, Ogden** (1902–1971) US poet

43 The pocket was the first instinct of humanity and was used long years before the human race had a trousers between them – the quiver for arrows is one example and the pocket of the kangaroo is another.
At Swim-Two-Birds (1939) **O'Brien, Flann** (1911–1966) Irish novelist and journalist

44 The only really firm rule of taste about cross dressing is that neither sex should ever wear anything they haven't yet figured out how to go to the bathroom in.
Modern Manners (1984) **O'Rourke, P.J.** (1947–) US writer

45 Brevity is the soul of lingerie.
In Woollcott, *While Rome Burns* (1934)

46 Where's the man could ease a heart,
Like a satin gown?
'The Satin Dress' (1937) **Parker, Dorothy** (1893–1967) US writer, poet, critic and wit

47 You'd be surprised how much it costs to look this cheap.
In Carole McKenzie, *Quotable Women* (1992)

48 How on earth did Gandhi manage to walk so far in flip-flops? I can't last ten minutes in mine.
Attr. **Parton, Dolly** (1946–) US country and western singer

49 I base most of my fashion taste on what doesn't itch.
It's Always Something (1989) **Radner, Gilda** (1946–1989) US actress and comedian

50 I was walking along, fists in my torn pockets; my overcoat also was entering the realm of the ideal.
'Ma Bohème' (1870) **Rimbaud, Arthur** (1854–1891) French poet

51 His shoes exhaled the right soupçon of harness-room; his socks compelled one's attention without losing one's respect.
The Chronicles of Clovis (1911) **Saki** (1870–1916) Burmese-born British writer

52 Fashion, the arbiter, and rule of right.
The Spectator, 478 **Steele, Sir Richard** (1672–1729) Irish-born English writer, dramatist and politician

53 No one knows how ungentlemanly he can look, until he has seen himself in a shocking bad hat.
Mr Facey Romford's Hounds (1865) **Surtees, R.S.** (1805–1864) English writer

54 She wears her clothes, as if they were thrown on with a pitchfork.
Polite Conversation (1738) **Swift, Jonathan** (1667–1745) Irish satirist, poet, essayist and cleric

55 The only man who really needs a tail coat is a man with a hole in his trousers.
The Observer, 'Shouts and Murmurs' **Taylor, John** (20th century)

56 Beware of all enterprises that require new clothes.
Walden (1854) **Thoreau, Henry David** (1817–1862) US essayist, social critic and writer

57 It is charming to totter into vogue.
Letter to George Selwyn, (1765) **Walpole, Horace** (1717–1797) English writer and politician

58 The tulip and the butterfly
Appear in gayer coats than I:
Let me be dressed fine as I will,
Flies, worms, and flowers, exceed me still.
'Against Pride in Clothes' (1715) **Watts, Isaac** (1674–1748) English hymn writer, poet and minister

59 I never saw so many shocking bad hats in my life.
In Fraser, *Words on Wellington* (1889) **Wellington, Duke of** (1769–1852) Irish-born British military commander and statesman. On seeing the first Reformed Parliament

60 You can say what you like about long dresses, but they cover a multitude of shins.
In J. Weintraub, *Peel Me a Grape* (1975) **West, Mae** (1892–1980) US actress and scriptwriter

61 Hats divide generally into three classes: offensive hats, defensive hats, and shrapnel.
Shouts and Murmurs (1963) **Whitehorn, Katherine** (1926–) English writer

62 A well-tied tie is the first serious step in life.
A Woman of No Importance (1893)

63 The only way to atone for being occasionally a little over-dressed is by being always absolutely over-educated.
The Chameleon, (1894) **Wilde, Oscar** (1854–1900) Irish poet, dramatist, writer, critic and wit

64 The Right Hon was a tubby little chap who looked as if he had been poured into his clothes and had forgotten to say 'When!'
Very Good, Jeeves (1930) **Wodehouse, P.G.** (1881–1975) English humorist and writer
See also appearance; society

FEAR

1 Let them hate, so long as they fear.
Atreus **Accius, Lucius** (170–86 BC) Roman poet

2 Fear ... is forward. No one is afraid of yesterday.
In Melissa Stein, *The Wit & Wisdom of Women* (1993) **Adler, Renata** (1938–) US film critic and writer

3 There are times when fear is good. It must keep its watchful place.
Eumenides **Aeschylus** (525–456 BC) Greek dramatist and poet

4 My life is passing in front of my eyes. The worst part is I'm driving a used car.
Manhattan Murder Mystery (film, 1993) **Allen, Woody** (1935–) US film director, writer, actor and comedian

5 The truly fearless think of themselves as normal.
Bluebeard's Egg (1986) **Atwood, Margaret** (1939–) Canadian writer, poet and critic

6 To suffering there is a limit; to fearing, none.
Essays (1625) **Bacon, Francis** (1561–1626) English philosopher, essayist, politician and courtier

7 Proust has pointed out that the predisposition to love creates its own objects: is this not true of fear?
Collected Impressions (1950) **Bowen, Elizabeth** (1899–1973) Irish writer

8 The only effect the atomic age has had on man had been to give him an underlying sense of nervous apprehension, which must also have been felt during the Black Death, and by the Christians under Diocletian.
Day of My Delight (1965) **Boyd, Martin a'Beckett** (1893–1972) Australian novelist

9 No passion so effectually robs the mind of all its powers of acting and reasoning as fear.
A Philosophical Enquiry into the Origin of our Ideas of the Sublime and Beautiful (1757)

10 The concessions of the weak are the concessions of fear.
Speech on Conciliation with America (1775) **Burke, Edmund** (1729–1797) Irish-born British statesman and philosopher

11 The fear of some divine and supreme powers, keeps men in obedience.
Anatomy of Melancholy (1621) **Burton, Robert** (1577–1640) English clergyman and writer

12 Fear has many eyes and can see things which are underground.
Don Quixote I (1605) **Cervantes, Miguel de** (1547–1616) Spanish writer and dramatist

13 When I look back on all these worries I remember the story of the old man who said on his deathbed that he had had a lot of trouble in his life, most of which had never happened.
Their Finest Hour **Churchill, Sir Winston** (1874–1965) English Conservative Prime Minister

14 If hopes were dupes, fears may be liars.
'Say Not the Struggle Naught Availeth' (1855) **Clough, Arthur Hugh** (1819–1861) English poet and letter writer

15 He has no hope who never had a fear.
'Truth' (1782) **Cowper, William** (1731–1800) English poet, hymn writer and letter writer

16 Nothing in life is to be feared, it is only to be understood. Now is the time to understand more, so that we may fear less.
Attr. **Curie, Marie** (1867–1934) Polish-born French physicist

17 I'm not frightened of the darkness outside. It's the darkness inside houses I don't like.
A Taste of Honey (1959) **Delaney, Shelagh** (1939–) English dramatist, screenwriter and writer

18 I am devilishly afraid, that's certain; but ... I'll sing, that I may seem valiant.
Amphitryon (1690) **Dryden, John** (1631–1700) English poet, satirist, dramatist and critic

19 Fear is an instructor of great sagacity, and the herald of all revolutions.
Essays, First Series (1841) **Emerson, Ralph Waldo** (1803–1882) US poet, essayist, transcendentalist and teacher

20 None but a coward dares to boast that he has never known fear.
Attr. **Foch, Ferdinand** (1851–1929) French marshal

21 Fear is the parent of cruelty.
Short Studies on Great Subjects (1877) **Froude, James Anthony** (1818–1894) English historian and scholar

22 The greatest mistake you can make in life is to be continually fearing you will make one.
Attr. **Hubbard, Elbert** (1856–1915) US printer, editor, writer and businessman

23 Tell proud Jove,
Between his power and thine there is no odds:
'Twas only fear first in the world made gods.
Sejanus (1603) **Jonson, Ben** (1572–1637) English dramatist and poet

24 Dread is a sympathetic antipathy and an antipathetic sympathy.
In W.H. Auden, *Kierkegaard* **Kierkegaard, Søren** (1813–1855) Danish philosopher

25 There are two kinds of adventurers: those who go truly hoping to find adventure and those who go secretly hoping they won't.
Blue Highways (1983) **Least-Heat Moon, William** (1939–) US author

26 Man is
   a great wall builder ...
   but the wall
   most impregnable
   has a moat
   flowing with fright
   around his heart.
   Sounds of a Cowhide Drum (1971) **Mtshali,
   Oswald** (1940–) South African poet

27 Terror of discovery and fear of reproval slip
   into our unconscious minds during infancy
   and remain there forever, always potent,
   usually unacknowledged.
   The Spectator, (1996) **Parris, Matthew** (1949–)
   British Conservative politician and journalist

28 Nothing in the affairs of men is worthy of
   great anxiety.
   Republic **Plato** (c.429–347 BC) Greek
   philosopher

29 The only thing we have to fear is fear itself.
   First Inaugural Address, (1933) **Roosevelt,
   Franklin Delano** (1882–1945) US Democrat
   President

30 To jealousy nothing is more frightful than
   laughter.
   Attr. **Sagan, Françoise** (1935–) French writer

31 Instinct is a great matter: I was now a
   coward on instinct.
   Henry IV, Part 1, II.iv

32 I have almost forgot the taste of fears.
   The time has been my senses would have
   cool'd
   To hear a night-shriek, and my fell of hair
   Would at a dismal treatise rouse and stir
   As life were in't. I have supp'd full with
   horrors;
   Direness, familiar to my slaughterous
   thoughts,
   Cannot once start me.
   Macbeth, V.v **Shakespeare, William** (1564–1616)
   English dramatist, poet and actor

33 There is only one universal passion: fear.
   The Man of Destiny (1898) **Shaw, George
   Bernard** (1856–1950) Irish socialist, writer,
   dramatist and critic

34 Still as he fled, his eye was backward cast,
   As if his feare still followed him behind.

The Faerie Queene (1596) **Spenser, Edmund**
(c.1522–1599) English poet

35 Curiosity will conquer fear even more than
   bravery will.
   The Crock of Gold (1912) **Stephens, James** (1882–
   1950) Irish poet and writer

36 Worrying is the most natural and
   spontaneous of all human functions. It is
   time to acknowledge this, perhaps even to
   learn to do it better.
   The Medusa and the Snail **Thomas, Lewis**
   (1913–1993) US pathologist and university
   administrator

37 Fear follows crime, and is its punishment.
   Sémiramis (1748) **Voltaire** (1694–1778) French
   philosopher, dramatist, poet, historian, writer
   and critic

38 Cowardly dogs bark loudest.
   The White Devil (1612) **Webster, John** (c.1580–
   c.1625) English dramatist
   See also guilt

FILM QUOTES

1 I object, your honour. This trial is a
  travesty. It's a travesty of a mockery of a
  sham of a mockery of a travesty of two
  mockeries of a sham.
  Bananas (film, 1971) As Fielding Mellish,
  reluctant dictator

2 I once stole a pornographic book that was
  printed in braille. I used to rub the dirty
  parts.
  Bananas (film, 1971) As Fielding Mellish,
  reluctant dictator

3 Not only is there no God, but try getting a
  plumber on weekends.
  Getting Even (film, 1971)

4 Is sex dirty? Only if it's done right.
  *Everything You Always Wanted to Know About
  Sex* (film, 1972)

5 I'm really a timid person – I was beaten up
  by Quakers.
  Sleeper (film, 1973)

6 If only God would give me some clear sign!
  Like making a large deposit in my name at
  a Swiss bank.

Without Feathers (1976)

7 The worst that can be said is that he's an under-achiever.
Love and Death (film, 1976) Of God

8 I was thrown out of NYU my freshman year for cheating in my metaphysics final. I looked into the soul of the boy sitting next to me.
Annie Hall (film, 1977)

9 Hey, don't knock masturbation! It's sex with someone I love.
Annie Hall (film, 1977)

10 It was the most fun I ever had without laughing.
Annie Hall (film, 1977) After sex

11 The last time I was inside a woman was when I went to the Statue of Liberty.
Crimes and Misdemeanors (film, 1989)

12 Showbusiness is dog eat dog. It's worse than dog eat dog. It's dog doesn't return other dog's phone calls.
Crimes and Misdemeanours (film, 1989)

13 Life doesn't imitate art. It imitates bad television.
Husbands and Wives (film, 1992)

14 I can't listen to that much Wagner. I start getting the urge to conquer Poland.
Manhattan Murder Mystery (film, 1993) **Allen, Woody** (1935–) US film director, writer, actor and comedian

15 NO DINOSAURS WERE HARMED IN THE MAKING OF THIS MOTION PICTURE
Ad-line, *The Flintstones*, (1994) **Anonymous**

16 The Irish are the niggers of Europe ... An' Dubliners are the niggers of Ireland ... An' the northside Dubliners are the niggers o' Dublin – Say it loud. I'm black an' I'm proud.
The Commitments (film, 1987) **Arkins, Robert** Irish actor. As Jimmy Rabbitte

17 C'est tellement simple, l'amour.
Les Enfants du Paradis (film, 1945) **Arletty** (1898–1992) French model and actress, born Leonie Bathiat. As Garance (*Love is so simple*)

18 This here's Miss Bonnie Parker. I'm Clyde Barrow. We rob banks.

Bonnie and Clyde (film, 1967) **Beatty, Warren** (1937–) US film actor. As Clyde Barrow to Faye Dunaway's Bonnie Parker

19 *Rick*: If that plane leaves the ground and you're not with him, you'll regret it – maybe not today, maybe not tomorrow, but soon, and for the rest of your life.
Ilsa: But what about us?
Rick: We'll always have Paris.
Casablanca (film, 1942) As Rick, to Ingrid Bergman's Ilsa Lund

20 I remember every detail. The Germans wore grey. You wore blue.
Casablanca (film, 1942) As Rick, to Ingrid Bergman's Ilsa Lund

21 Of all the gin joints in all the towns in all the world, she walks into mine.
Casablanca (film, 1942)

22 I don't mind if you don't like my manners. I don't like them myself. They're pretty bad. I grieve over them long winter evenings.
The Big Sleep (film, 1946) As Raymond Chandler's famous private eye, Philip Marlowe **Bogart, Humphrey** (1899–1957) US film actor

23 *Marlowe*: Speaking of horses ... you've got a touch of class, but I don't know how far you can go.
Vivian: A lot depends on who's in the saddle.
The Big Sleep (film, 1946) **Bogart, Humphrey** (1899–1957) US film actor, and **Bacall, Lauren** (1924–) US film actress

24 I don't want to waste another moment of my life without you in it.
Garden State (film, 2004) **Braff, Zach** (1975–) US actor and film director. As Andrew Largeman

25 *Woman in bar*: Hey, Johnny, what are you rebelling against?
Johnny: What've you got?
The Wild One (film, 1953)

26 I'm gonna make him an offer he can't refuse.
The Godfather (film, 1972) As Don Vito Corleone

27 Justice and law are distant cousins. They're not on speaking terms at all.
A Dry White Season (film, 1989) **Brando, Marlon** (1924–2004) US film actor

28 That's it, baby, if you've got it, flaunt it.
The Producers (film, 1968)

29 He who hesitates is poor.
The Producers (film, 1968) **Brooks, Mel** (1926–) US film actor and director

30 The old man was right, only the farmers won. We lost. We'll always lose.
The Magnificent Seven (film, 1960) **Brynner, Yul** (1915–1985) US actor. As Chris, leader of the Seven

31 It seems to me if they ain't got you one way they've got you another. So what's the answer? That's what I keep asking myself - what's it all about? Know what I mean?
Alfie (film, 1966) In the title role

32 So you're doing all right then, Eric. You're making good … Do you know, I'd almost forgotten what your eyes looked like. They're still the same. Piss holes in the snow.
Get Carter (film, 1971) As Jack Carter **Caine, Michael** (1933–) English film actor

33 *King Arthur*: The Lady of the Lake, her arm clad in the purest shimmering samite held aloft Excalibur from the bosom of the water, signifying by divine providence that I, Arthur, was to carry Excalibur. That is why I am your king.
Dennis the Peasant: Listen, strange women lyin' in ponds distributin' swords is no basis for a system of government. Supreme executive power derives from a mandate from the masses, not from some farcical aquatic ceremony.
Monty Python and The Holy Grail (film, 1975) **Chapman, Graham** (1941–1989) English comedian and scriptwriter, and **Palin, Michael** (1943–) English comedian and travel writer

34 I fart in your general direction! Your mother was a hamster and your father smells of elderberries.
Monty Python and the Holy Grail (film, 1975) **Cleese, John** (1939–) English comedian and scriptwriter. As French Knight insulting King Arthur (Graham Chapman) from the battlements

35 *Bond*: You expect me to talk?
Goldfinger: No, Mr Bond, I expect you to die.
Goldfinger (film, 1964) **Connery, Sean** (1930–) Scottish actor, and **Froebe, Gert** (1913–1988) German actor. Bond spars with his enemy

36 *Harry*: No man can be friends with a woman that he finds attractive. He always wants to have sex with her.
Sally: So you're saying that a man can be friends with a woman he finds unattractive.
Harry: No. You pretty much want to nail them too.
When Harry Met Sally (film, 1989) **Crystal, Billy** (1947–) US actor, and **Ryan, Meg** (1961–) US actress. Part of the dialogue that precipitates the movie's famous fake orgasm scene

37 Fasten your seat belts. It's going to be a bumpy night.
All About Eve (film, 1950) **Davis, Bette** (1908–1989) US actress. Margo's immortal line

38 Stay alive, no matter what occurs. I will find you. No matter how long it takes, no matter how far. I will find you.
Last of The Mohicans (film, 1992) **Day-Lewis, Daniel** (1957–) Anglo-Irish actor. As Hawkeye to Cora Munro (Madeleine Stowe)

39 I think you're a sexist, misogynist dinosaur. A relic of the Cold War, who's boyish charms, though wasted on me, obviously appealed to the young lady I sent out to evaluate you.
Goldeneye (film, 1995) **Dench, Judi** (1934–) English actress. As M in the new regime alongside Pierce Brosnan's Bond

40 Have you never met a woman who inspires you to love? Until your every sense is filled with her? You inhale her. You taste her. You see your unborn children in her eyes and know that your heart has at last found a home. Your life begins with her, and without her it must surely end.
Don Juan Di Marco (film, 1995) In the title role

41 We had two bags of grass, seventy-five pellets of mescaline, five sheets of high-powered blotter-acid, a salt-shaker half full of cocaine, and a whole galaxy of multi-coloured uppers, downers, screamers, laughers; also a quart of tequila, a quart of rum, a case of beer, a pint of raw ether, and two dozen amyls. But the only thing that worried me was the ether.
Fear and Loathing in Las Vegas (film, 1998) As Raoul Duke **Depp, Johnny** (1963–) US film actor

42 This whole world's wild at heart and weird on top.
Wild at Heart (film, 1990) **Dern, Laura** (1967–) US film actress

43 Greed, for lack of a better word, is good! Greed is right! Greed works! Greed clarifies, cuts through, and captures the essence of the evolutionary spirit. Greed, in all of its forms.
Wall Street (film, 1987) **Douglas, Michael** (1944–) US film actor. As Gordon Gekko, unscrupulous Wall Street financier

44 I love the smell of Napalm in the morning … smells like victory.
Apocalypse Now (film, 1977) **Duvall, Robert** (1931–) US film actor. As Colonel Killgore

45 I know what you're thinking, did he fire six shots or only five? To tell the truth in all this confusion I forgot myself. Now being that this is a .44 magnum, the most powerful handgun in the world and can take your head clean off, you have to ask yourself a question, do I feel lucky? Well do ya, punk?
Dirty Harry (film 1971) **Eastwood, Clint** (1930–) American actor and film director. Said by Eastwood to a wounded bank robber reaching for his shotgun

46 You should be kissed, and often, by someone who knows how.
Gone with the Wind (film, 1939) As Rhett Butler

47 Don't drink alone, Scarlett. People always find out and it ruins the reputation.
Gone With The Wind (film, 1939) As Rhett Butler **Gable, Clark** (1901–1960) US film actor

48 Gimme whisky … ginger ale on the side. And don't be stingy, baby.
Anna Christie (film, 1930) **Garbo, Greta** (1905–1990) Swedish actress. In the title role

49 Toto, I have a feeling we're not in Kansas anymore.
The Wizard of Oz (film, 1939) **Garland, Judy** (1922–1969) US singer and actress. As Dorothy, to the little white dog

50 That's a real badge, I'm a real cop, and this is a real firing gun.
Lethal Weapon (film, 1987) **Gibson, Mel** (1956–) Australian actor. As Riggs

51 Insanity runs in my family. It practically gallops.
Arsenic and Old Lace (film, 1944) **Grant, Cary** (1904–1986) English-born US film actor

52 In short, to recap it slightly in a clearer version, … the words of David Cassidy in fact, … while he was still with the Partridge family, … I think I love you, and … I-I just wondered if by any chance you wouldn't like to … No, no, no of course not .. I'm an idiot, he's not.
Four Weddings and a Funeral (film, 1994) **Grant, Hugh** (1960–) English film actor. As Charles, addressing Carrie (Andie McDowell)

53 We want the finest wines available to humanity. We want them here, and we want them now!
Withnail and I (film, 1987) As Withnail to Paul McGann's 'I'

54 Right, here's the plan. First, we go in there and get wrecked, then we eat a pork pie, then we drop some Surmontil-50's each. That way we'll miss out on Monday and come up smiling Tuesday morning.
Withnail And I (film, 1987) As Withnail to Paul McGann's 'I' **Grant, Richard E.** (1957–) English actor and writer

55 I would like if I may, to take you on a strange journey …
Rocky Horror Picture Show (film, 1975) **Gray, Charles** (1928–2000) English actor. Opening lines of movie

56 The force will be with you – always.
Star Wars (film, 1977) **Guinness, Sir Alec** (1914–2000) English actor. As Obi-Wan Kenobi

57 My mama always said, life was like a box of chocolates. You never know what you're gonna get.
Forrest Gump (film, 1994) **Hanks, Tom** (1956–) US film actor. In the title role

58 It is totally impossible to be well dressed in cheap shoes.
The Englishman's Suit, (film, 1994) **Hardy Amies, Sir Edward** (1909–2003) English royal couturier

59 I've seen things you wouldn't believe. Attack ships on fire off the shoulder of Orion. I watched C-beams glitter in the dark near the Tannhauser gate. All those moments will be lost in time, like tears in rain. Time to die.
Blade Runner (film, 1982) **Hauer, Rutger** (1944–) Dutch actor. Dying speech of replicant Roy Batty

60 Your eyes are full of hate, 41. That's good. Hate keeps a man alive.
Ben-Hur (film, 1959) **Hawkins, Jack** (1910–1973) English actor. As galley-master Quintus Arrius

61 If I'd been a ranch, they would have named me the Bar Nothing.
Gilda (film, 1946) **Hayworth, Rita** (1918–1987) US actress. In the title role

62 Nature, Mr Allnut, is what we are put in this world to rise above.
The African Queen (film, 1951) **Hepburn, Katharine** (1907–2003) US film actress. As Rose Sayer to Humphrey Bogart's Charlie Allnut

63 *Bernie*: Why is it that women always think they understand men better than men do?
Georgie: Maybe because they live with them.
The Country Girl (film, 1954) **Holden, William** (1918–1981) US actor, and **Kelly, Grace** (1929–1982) US actress and Princess of Monaco

64 I do wish we could chat longer but I'm having an old friend for dinner.
Silence of The Lambs (film, 1991) As Hannibal Lecter, obliquely informing Clarice that he had just murdered and eaten his old nemesis, Chilton

65 Well, Clarice, have the lambs stopped screaming?
Silence of The Lambs (film, 1991) As Hannibal Lecter

66 What is a sausage? A sausage is an indigestible balloon of decayed beef, riddled with tuberculosis. Eat and die! For I have seen many a repentant meat glutton, his body full of uric acid and remorse, his soul adrift on the raft in the ocean of poisonous slime.
The Road to Wellville (film, 1994) As John Harvey Kellogg, physician and nutritionist **Hopkins, Anthony** (1937–) Welsh film actor

67 If it's in focus, it's pornography. If it's out of focus, it's art.
The Year of Living Dangerously (film, 1982) **Hunt, Linda** (1945–) American actress. As Billy Hunt

68 Oh, Fred, I've been so foolish. I've fallen in love. I'm an ordinary woman, I didn't think such things could happen to ordinary people.
Brief Encounter (film, 1945) **Johnson, Celia** (1908–1982) English actress. As Laura Jesson returning to her husband, Fred

69 Look at her. I would die for her. I would kill for her. Either way, what bliss.
Addams Family Values (film, 1991) **Julia, Raoul** (1940–1994) US-based Puerto-Rican actor. Gomez Addams eulogizes his wife, Morticia

70 Back home everyone said I didn't have any talent. They might be saying the same thing over here, but it sounds better in French.
An American in Paris (film, 1951) **Kelly, Gene** (1912–1996) US film actor. As Jerry Mulligan

71 Mother, just because I wear trackies and play sports does not make me a lesbian!
Bend It Like Beckham (film, 2002) **Knightley, Keira** (1985–) English actress. As teenage footballer Jules

72 I like a girl in a bikini. No concealed weapons.
The Man with the Golden Gun (film, 1974) **Lee, Christopher** (1922–) English actor. As the villain, Scaramanga

73 After all, tomorrow is another day.
Gone with the Wind (1936) **Leigh, Vivien** (1913–1967) British film actress. As Scarlett O'Hara

74 There was no way in all the world I could have known that murder sometimes can smell like honeysuckle.
Double Indemnity (film, 1944) **MacMurray, Fred** (1908–1991) US film actor. Narrating as Walter Neff at the start of the film

75 Look at me: I worked my way up from nothing to a state of extreme poverty.
Monkey Business (film, 1931)

76 There's a man outside with a big black moustache.
– Tell him I've got one.
Horse Feathers (film, 1932)

77 You're a disgrace to our family name of Wagstaff, if such a thing is possible.
Horse Feathers (film, 1932)

78 You've got the brain of a four-year-old boy, and I bet he was glad to get rid of it.
Horse Feathers (film, 1932)

79 Remember, men, we're fighting for this woman's honour; which is probably more than she ever did.
Duck Soup (film, 1933)

80 My husband is dead.
– I'll bet he's just using that as an excuse.
I was with him to the end.
– No wonder he passed away.
I held him in my arms and kissed him.
– So it was murder!
Duck Soup (film, 1933) **Marx, Groucho** (1895–1977) US comedian

81 Of course I may bring a boyfriend home occasionally, but only occasionally, because I do think that one ought to go to the man's room if one can. I mean, it doesn't look so much as if one expected it, does it?
Cabaret (film, 1972) **Minnelli, Liza** (1946–) US actress. As Sally Bowles

82 Any girl who was a lady would not even think of having such a good time that she did not remember to hang on to her jewelry.
Gentlemen Prefer Blondes (1953)

83 You have got to be a Queen to get away with a hat like that.
Gentlemen Prefer Blondes (film, 1953) **Monroe, Marilyn** (1826–1962) US film actress

84 'What is the difference between marriage and prison?'
'In prison somebody else does the cooking.'
Love Hurts (film, 1990) **Newman, Andrea** (1938–) English author

85 Money won is twice as sweet as money earned.
The Color of Money (film, 1986) **Newman, Paul** (1925–) US film actor. As Eddie Felson

86 You make me want to be a better man.
As Good As It Gets (film, 1997) **Nicholson, Jack** (1937–) US film actor. As obnoxious writer Melvin Udall, to waitress Carol Connelly (Helen Hunt)

87 I see dead people.
The Sixth Sense (film, 1999) **Osment, Haley Joel** (1988–) US child actor. As child-psychic Cole Sear

88 When nine hundred years old you will reach, look as good you will not, mm?
The Return of the Jedi (film, 1983) **Oz, Frank** (1944–) US actor and film producer. As the voice of Yoda

89 Keep your friends close, but your enemies closer.
The Godfather, Part II (film, 1974) **Pacino, Al** (1940–) US film actor. As Michael Corleone

90 *Viola* (in disguise): Tell me how you love her, Will.
Shakespeare: Like a sickness and its cure together.
Shakespeare in Love (film, 1998) **Paltrow, Gwyneth** (1972–) US actress, and **Fiennes, Joseph** (1970–) English actor

91 A boy's best friend is his mother.
Psycho (film, 1960) As serial killer Norman Bates

92 Mother – what's the phrase? – isn't quite herself today.
Psycho (film, 1960) As Norman Bates **Perkins, Anthony** (1932–1992) US actor

93 *Will Graham*: I know that I'm not smarter than you.
Dr Hannibal Lecter: Then how did you catch me?
Will Graham: You had disadvantages.
Dr Hannibal Lecter: What disadvantages?
Will Graham: You're insane.
Manhunter (film, 1986) **Peterson, William L.** (1953–) US actor, and **Cox, Brian** (1946–) British actor

94 There is a pain beyond pain, an agony so intense, it shocks the mind into instant beauty.
The House of Wax (film, 1953) **Price, Vincent** (1911–1993) English horror-movie actor. As the demented scientist, Professor Jarod

95 Major Strasser has been shot. Round up the usual suspects.
Casablanca (film, 1942) **Rains, Claude** (1889–1967) British film actor

96 Wait, we cannot break bread with you. You have taken the land which is rightfully ours. Years from now my people will be forced to live in mobile homes on reservations. Your people will wear cardigans, and drink highballs. We will sell our bracelets by the roadsides, and you will play golf, and eat hot hors d'oeuvres. My people will have pain and degradation. Your people will have stick shifts. The gods of my tribe have spoken. They said do not trust the pilgrims, especially Sarah Miller. And for all of these reasons I have decided to scalp you and burn your village to the ground.
Addams Family Values (film, 1993) **Ricci, Christina** (1980–) US actress. As Wednesday Addams, ad-libbing as an American Indian during the summer camp play

97 To be with another woman, that is French. To be caught, that is American.
Dirty Rotten Scoundrels (film, 1988) **Rodgers, Anton** (1933–) English actor. As Inspector Andre

98 Remember; alcohol equals puke equals smelly mess equals nobody likes you.
The Wedding Singer (film, 1998) **Sandler, Adam** (1966–) US actor. In the main role of Robbie

99 You're gonna need a bigger boat!
Jaws (film, 1975) **Scheider, Roy** (1932–) US actor. As Martin Brody; seeing the shark for the first time

100 It profits a man nothing to give his soul for the whole world ... But for Wales!
A Man for all Seasons (film, 1966) **Scofield, Paul** (1922–) English actor. More accepts his betrayal in the film version of Robert Bolt's play

101 It is the only disease you don't look forward to being cured of.
Citizen Kane (film, 1941) **Sloane, Everett** (1909–1965) US film actor. Of death

102 I want to look good naked!
American Beauty (film, 1999) As Lester Burnham, explaining why he wants to go the gym

103 My job requires mostly masking my contempt for the assholes in charge, and, at least once a day, retiring to the men's room so I can jerk off while I fantasize about a life that doesn't so closely resemble Hell.
American Beauty (film, 1999) As the disaffected Lester Burnham

104 You're one to talk, you bloodless, money-grubbing freak.
American Beauty (film, 1999) Lester Burnham's response to criticism by his wife **Spacey, Kevin** (1959–) US actor

105 I found out what the secret to life is: friends. Best friends.
Fried Green Tomatoes at the Whistle Stop Café (film, 1991) **Tandy, Jessica** (1909–1994) US actress. As Ninny

106 I'm not living with you. We occupy the same cage, that's all.
Cat on a Hot Tin Roof (film, 1958) **Taylor, Elizabeth** (1932–) English-born Hollywood actress. As Maggie Pollitt, to Paul Newman as Brick

107 This is a free country, madam. We have a right to share your privacy in a public place.
Romanoff and Juliet (1956)

108 The great thing about history is that it is adaptable.
Romanoff and Juliet (1956) **Ustinov, Sir Peter** (1921–2004) English actor, director, dramatist, writer and raconteur

109 I have killed for my country, or whatever, and I don't feel good about it. Coz there's not enough reason, man, to feel a person die in your hands, or to see your best buddy get blown away.
Coming Home (film, 1978) **Voigt, Jon** (1938–) US actor. As paraplegic war veteran Luke Martin

110 Howard's End? Sounds filthy, doesn't it?
Educating Rita (film, 1983) **Walters, Julie** (1950–) English actress. As mature student Rita, in the film version of Willy Russell's stage play

111 The only thing I like integrated is my coffee.
Malcolm X (film, 1992) **Washington, Denzel** (1954–) US film actor

112 This is Ripley – last survivor of the *Nostromo* – signing off.
Alien (film, 1979) **Weaver, Sigourney** (1949–) US film actress

113 Human beings are a disease, a cancer of this planet; you are a plague and we are the cure.
The Matrix (film, 1999) **Weaving, Hugo** (1960–) New Zealand actor. As the cloned Agent Smith

114 I run a couple of newspapers. What do you do?
Citizen Kane, (film, 1941)

115 In Italy for thirty years under the Borgias they had warfare, terror, murder, bloodshed – they produced Michelangelo, Leonardo da Vinci and the Renaissance. In Switzerland they had brotherly love, five hundred years of democracy and peace, and what did they produce …? The cuckoo clock.
The Third Man (film, 1949) **Welles, Orson** (1915–1985) US actor, director and producer

116 'Goodness, what beautiful diamonds!' 'Goodness had nothing to do with it!'
Night after Night (film, 1932)

117 When I'm good I'm very good, but when I'm bad I'm better.
I'm No Angel (film, 1933)

118 A man in the house is worth two in the street.
Belle of the Nineties (film, 1934)

119 When women go wrong, men go right after them.
In Weintraub, *The Wit and Wisdom of Mae West* (1967) **West, Mae** (1892–1980) US actress and scriptwriter

120 Most of the men in this town think monogamy is some kind of wood.
The Mask (film, 1994) **Yasbeck, Amy** (1962–) US film actress. As Peggy Brandt

121 acting; cinema

FOOD

1 The difference between good cookery and bad cookery can scarcely be more strikingly shown than in the manner in which sauces are prepared and served.
Modern Cookery for Private Families (1845) **Acton, Eliza** (1799–1859) English cook and author

2 Is there much chicken in chickpeas?
Big Brother, Series 2, (2001)

3 What's in kidney beans?
Big Brother, Series 2, (2001) **Adams, Helen** (1978–) Big Brother contestant

4 One man's poison ivy is another man's spinach.
Attr. **Ade, George** (1866–1944) US fabulist and playwright

5 The infusion of a China plant sweetened with the pith of an Indian cane.
The Spectator, (1711) **Addison, Joseph** (1672–1719) English essayist, poet, playwright and statesman

6 I was summoned to see Lord Orr-Ewing and told that this was a most grave matter and must never be repeated.
The Times, (1999) **Anonymous** Catering manager of the House of Lords on what happened when the macaroons ran out

7 Hunger knows no friend but its feeder.
The Wasps **Aristophanes** (c.445–385 BC) Greek
playwright

8 Eating is our earliest metaphor, preceding
our consciousness of gender difference,
race, nationality, and language. We eat
before we talk.
*The CanLit Foodbook: From Pen to Palate – A
Collection of Tasty Literary Fare* (1987) **Atwood,
Margaret** (1939–) Canadian writer, poet and
critic

9 Good mashed potato is one of the great
luxuries of life and I don't blame Elvis for
eating it every night for the last year of his
life.
In Praise of the Potato (1989) **Bareham, Lindsey**
(1948–) Food critic and writer

10 Food is our common ground, a universal
experience.
Beard on Food (1974) **Beard, James** (1903–1985)
US chef and author

11 Better is a dinner of herbs where love is,
than a stalled ox and hatred therewith.
Proverbs, 15:17 **The Bible (King James Version)**

12 ... life without veal stock, pork fat, sausage,
organ meat, demi-glace, or even stinky
cheese is a life not worth living.
Kitchen Confidential, (2000) **Bourdain, Anthony**
(1956–) US author and chef

13 I'm a man
More dined against than dining.
In Betjeman, *Summoned by Bells* (1960) **Bowra,
Sir Maurice** (1898–1971) English scholar

14 My cooking is modern Scottish – if you
complain you get headbutted.
The Times, (1999) **Bradley, Chris** Scottish chef

15 The discovery of a new dish does more for
the happiness of mankind than the
discovery of a star.
Physiologie du Goût (1825)

16 Tell me what you eat and I will tell you
what you are.
Physiologie du Goût (1825) **Brillat-Savarin,
Anthelme** (1755–1826) French jurist and
gastronome

17 I am not a vegetarian because I love
animals; I am a vegetarian because I hate
plants.
Attr. **Brown, A. Whitney** (1952–) US comedian

18 So munch on, crunch on, take your
nuncheon,
Breakfast, supper, dinner, luncheon.
The Pied Piper of Hamelin **Browning, Robert**
(1812–1889) English poet

19 Fair fa' your honest sonsie face,
Great chieftan o' the puddin' race!
'To A Haggis' **Burns, Robert** (1759–1796)
Scottish poet

20 Beautiful Soup, so rich and green,
Waiting in a hot tureen!
Who for such dainties would not stoop?
Soup of the evening, beautiful Soup!
Alice's Adventures in Wonderland (1865) **Carroll,
Lewis** (1832–1898) English writer and
photographer

21 Soup is usually the only course served by
the butler.
In *The Guardian,* (2000) **Cartland, Barbara**
(1901–2000) English writer

22 Hunger is the best sauce in the world.
Don Quixote (1615) **Cervantes, Miguel de** (1547–
1616) Spanish writer and dramatist

23 Coffee is a cold dry food, suited to the
ascetic life and sedative of lust.
In G.L. Lewis (trans.), *The Balance of Truth*
(1957) **Chelebi, Katib** (1609–1657) Turkish
scholar

24 Tea, although an Oriental,
Is a gentleman at least;
Cocoa is a cad and coward,
Cocoa is a vulgar beast.
The Flying Inn (1914) **Chesterton, G.K.** (1874–
1936) English writer, poet and critic

25 A Waldorf salad? I think we're out of
Waldorfs.
Fawlty Towers, (1979) As Basil Fawlty

26 The English contribution to world cuisine –
the chip.
A Fish Called Wanda (film, 1988) **Cleese, John**
(1939–) British comedian, actor and writer

27 Who discovered we could get milk from cows, and what did he think he was doing at the time?
Connolly, Billy (1942–) Scottish comedian

28 Life is too short to stuff a mushroom.
Superwoman, (1975) **Conran, Shirley** (1932–) English writer and celebrity housewife

29 Gentlemen do not take soup at luncheon.
In Woodward, *Short Journey* (1942) **Curzon, Lord** (1859–1925) English statesman and scholar

30 Do you know what breakfast cereal is made of? It's made of all those little curly wooden shavings you find in pencil sharpeners!
Charlie and the Chocolate Factory (1964) **Dahl, Roald** (1916–1990) British writer

31 Delicious meals can, as everybody knows, be cooked with the sole aid of a blackened frying-pan over a primus stove, a camp fire, a gas-ring, or even a methylated spirit lamp.
French Country Cooking (1951)

32 Even more than long hours in the kitchen, fine meals require ingenious organization and experience which is a pleasure to acquire. A highly developed shopping sense is important, so is some knowledge of the construction of a menu with a view to the food in season, the manner of cooking, the texture and colour of the dishes to be served in relation to each other.
French Country Cooking (1951)

33 To eat figs off the tree in the very early morning, when they have been barely touched by the sun, is one of the exquisite pleasures of the Mediterranean.
Italian Food (1954) **David, Elizabeth** (1913–1992) British cookery writer

34 Though the potato is an excellent root, deserving to be brought into general use, yet it seems not likely that the use of it should ever be normal in the country.
The Case of the Labourers in Husbandry (1795) **Davies, David** (1742–1819) Welsh cleric

35 I figure if horses can eat green shit and be strong and run like motherfuckers, why shouldn't I?

In Ian Carr, *Miles Davis: a Critical Biography* (1982) **Davis, Miles** (1926–1991) US jazz musician. On vegetarianism

36 It's a very odd thing –
As odd as can be –
That whatever Miss T. eats
Turns into Miss T.
'Miss T' (1913) **De La Mare, Walter** (1873–1956) English poet

37 Gluttony is an emotional escape, a sign something is eating us.
Comfort me with Apples (1956) **De Vries, Peter** (1910–1993) US novelist

38 The whole Mediterranean, the sculpture, the palms, the gold beads, the bearded heroes, the wine, the ideas, the ships, the moonlight, the winged gorgons, the bronze men, the philosophers – all of it seems to rise in the sour, pungent taste of these black olives between the teeth. A taste older than meat, older than wine. A taste as old as cold water.
Prospero's Cell (1945) **Durrell, Lawrence** (1912–1990) Indian-born British poet and writer

39 For my part now, I consider supper as a turnpike through which one must pass, in order to get to bed.
In Boswell, *The Life of Samuel Johnson* (1791) **Edwards, Oliver** (1711–1791) English lawyer

40 When a man's stomach is full it makes no difference whether he is rich or poor.
Attr. **Euripides** (c.485–406 BC) Greek dramatist and poet

41 Cheese – milk's leap toward immortality.
Any Number Can Play (1957) **Fadiman, Clifton** (1904–1999) US writer, editor and broadcaster

42 The way to a man's heart is through his stomach.
Willis Parton **Fern, Fanny (Sara Payson Parton)** (1811–1872) US writer

43 Man is what he eats.
In Moleschott, *Lehre der Nahrungsmittel: Für das Volk* (1850) **Feuerbach, Ludwig** (1804–1872) German philosopher

44 To lengthen thy life, lessen thy meals.
Poor Richard's Almanac (1733) **Franklin, Benjamin** (1706–1790) US statesman, scientist, political critic and printer

45 He was a very valiant man who first
ventured on eating of oysters.
The History of the Worthies of England (1662)
Fuller, Thomas (1608–1661) English
churchman and antiquary

46 The French cook; we open tins.
Treasury of Humorous Quotations **Galsworthy,
John** (1867–1933) English writer and dramatist

47 Man cannot live by bread alone; he must
have peanut butter.
Inaugural address, (1881) **Garfield, James A.**
(1831–1881) US President

48 Many excellent cooks are spoiled by going
into the arts.
In Cournos, *Modern Plutarch* (1928) **Gauguin,
Paul** (1848–1903) French Post-Impressionist
painter

49 Cookery without meat is Macbeth without
murder.
Le Caprice, (2000) **Gill, A.A.** (1954–) Scottish
newspaper columnist

50 In my hungry fatigue, and shopping for
images, I went into the neon fruit
supermarket, dreaming of your
enumerations!
What peaches and what penumbras! Whole
families shopping at night! Aisles full of
husbands! Wives in the avocados, babies in
the tomatoes! – and you, Garcia Lorca,
what were you doing down by the
watermelons?
'A Supermarket in California' **Ginsberg, Allen**
(1926–1997) US poet. Addressing Walt
Whitman

51 *Marge*: Say Grace, Bart.
Bart: Dear God, we paid for all this food
ourselves, so thanks for nothing.
The Simpsons, TV cartoon series

52 *Groundskeeper Willie*: Get yer haggis right
here! Chopped heart and lungs, boiled in a
wee sheep's stomach! Tastes as good as it
sounds!
The Simpsons, TV cartoon series **Groening,
Matt** (1954–) US cartoonist

53 The best number for a dinner party is two:
myself and a damn good head waiter.

The Observer, (1965) **Gulbenkian, Nubar** (1896–
1972) British industrialist, diplomat and
philanthropist

54 When I make a feast,
I would my guests should praise it, not the
cooks.
Epigrams (1618) **Harington, Sir John** (1561–
1612) English courtier

55 You always want to garnish it when it's orf.
'Talkabout', (c.1960) **Harney, Bill** (1895–1962)
Australian writer. Advice on bush cooking

56 A cheerful look makes a dish a feast.
Jacula Prudentum (1640) **Herbert, George**
(1593–1633) English poet and priest

57 Bring porridge, bring sausage, bring fish,
for a start,
Bring kidneys, and mushrooms, and
partridges' legs,
But let the foundation be bacon and eggs.
In Catherine Brown, *Scottish Cookery* (1985)
Herbert, Sir A.P. (1890–1971) English
humorist, writer, dramatist and politician

58 Home-made dishes that drive one from
home.
Miss Kilmansegg and her Precious Leg (1840)
Hood, Thomas (1799–1845) English poet,
editor and humorist

59 Honest bread is very well – it's the butter
that makes the temptation.
The Cat's Paw (1930) **Jerrold, Douglas William**
(1803–1857) English dramatist, writer and wit

60 A hardened and shameless tea-drinker,
who has for twenty years diluted his meals
with only the infusion of this fascinating
plant; whose kettle has scarcely time to
cool; who with tea amuses the evening,
with tea solaces the midnight, and with tea
welcomes the morning.
Review in the *Literary Magazine,* (1757)

61 A cucumber should be well sliced, and
dressed with pepper and vinegar, and then
thrown out, as good for nothing.
In Boswell, *Journal of a Tour to the Hebrides*
(1785)

62 A man seldom thinks with more
earnestness of anything than he does of his
dinner.

In Piozzi, *Anecdotes of the Late Samuel Johnson* (1786)

63 A man is in general better pleased when he has a good dinner upon his table, than when his wife talks Greek.
In Hawkins, *Life of Samuel Johnson* (1787)

64 This was a good dinner enough, to be sure; but it was not a dinner to ask a man to.
In Boswell, *The Life of Samuel Johnson* (1791)

65 We could not have had a better dinner had there been a Synod of Cooks.
In Boswell, *The Life of Samuel Johnson* (1791)

66 I look upon it, that he who does not mind his belly will hardly mind anything else.
In Boswell, *The Life of Samuel Johnson* (1791) **Johnson, Samuel** (1709–1784) English lexicographer, poet, critic, conversationalist and essayist

67 When I makes tea I makes tea, as old mother Grogan said. And when I makes water I makes water … Begob, ma'am, says Mrs. Cahill, God send you don't make them in the one pot.
Ulysses (1922) **Joyce, James** (1882–1941) Irish writer

68 'Tis by his cleanliness a cook must please.
Art of Cookery (1708) **King, William** (1663–1712)

69 I hate a man who swallows it, affecting not to know what he is eating. I suspect his taste in higher matters.
Essays of Elia (1823) **Lamb, Charles** (1775–1834) English essayist, critic and letter writer. Of food

70 I shall dine late; but the dining-room will be well lighted, the guests few and select.
Imaginary Conversations (1853)

71 Good God, I forgot the violets!
In F. Muir, *An Irreverent Companion to Social History* (1976) Having thrown his cook out of an open window into the flowerbed below **Landor, Walter Savage** (1775–1864) English poet and writer

72 If you knew how meat was made, you'd probably lose your lunch. I'm from cattle country. That's why I became a vegetarian.
Attr. **Lang, K.D.** (1961–) Canadian singer

73 Food is an important part of a balanced diet.
Metropolitan Life (1978)

74 Bread that must be sliced with an axe is bread that is too nourishing.
Metropolitan Life (1978) **Lebowitz, Fran** (1950–) US satirist

75 Cuisine is when things taste like what they are.
Lecture, 'The Fine Art of Food', (1987) **Leith, Prue** (1940–) English cookery writer and businesswoman

76 And there is good fresh trout for supper. My mother used to put them on a hot stone over the fire, wrapped in breadcrumbs, butter, parsley and lemon rind, all bound about with the fresh leaves of leeks. If there is better food in heaven, I am in a hurry to be there.
How Green Was My Valley (1939) **Llewellyn, Richard** (1907–1983) Welsh novelist

77 This piece of cod passes all understanding.
In Robert Lutyens, *Sir Edwin Lutyens* (1942) **Lutyens, Sir Edwin Landseer** (1869–1944) English architect. Comment made in a restaurant

78 I prefer that the courses at our banquet should give pleasure to the guests rather than to the cooks.
Epigrammata **Martial** (c.AD 40–c.104) Spanish-born Latin epigrammatist and poet

79 At a dinner party one should eat wisely but not too well, and talk well but not too wisely.
A Writer's Notebook (1949) **Maugham, William Somerset** (1874–1965) English writer, dramatist and physician

80 Kissing don't last: cookery do!
The Ordeal of Richard Feverel (1859) **Meredith, George** (1828–1909) English writer, poet and critic

81 We may live without poetry, music and art;
We may live without conscience, and live without heart;
We may live without friends; we may live without books;
But civilized man cannot live without cooks.

'Lucile' (1860) **Meredith, Owen** (1831–1891) English statesman and poet

82 Chopsticks are one of the reasons the Chinese never invented custard.
Milligan, Spike (1918–2002) English comedian and writer

83 One should eat to live, not live to eat.
L'Avare (1669) **Molière** (1622–1673) French dramatist, actor and director

84 Isn't there another part of the matzo you can eat?
Attr. **Monroe, Marilyn** (1926–1962) US film actress and model. On having matzo balls for supper at Arthur Miller's parents' house

85 The embarrassing thing is that the salad dressing is out-grossing my films.
Attr. **Newman, Paul** (1925–) US actor. On his salad dressing company

86 Twenty-two years of tofu is a lot of time.
Attr. (1997) **Obis, Paul** Founder of *Vegetarian Times*. On his decision to start eating meat

87 We may find in the long run that tinned food is a deadlier weapon than the machine-gun.
The Road to Wigan Pier (1937) **Orwell, George** (1903–1950) English writer and critic

88 The food is so bad I couldn't wait to get home.
The Times (1998) **Paltrow, Gwyneth** (1973–) US actress. On British cuisine

89 The noblest of all dogs is the hot-dog; it feeds the hand that bites it.
Quotations for Our Time (1977) **Peter, Laurence J.** (1919–1990) Canadian educationist and writer

90 Strange to see how a good dinner and feasting reconciles everybody.
Diary, 1665 **Pepys, Samuel** (1633–1703) English diarist, naval administrator and politician

91 Never eat anything at one sitting that you can't lift.
Woman's Hour, (1992) **Piggy, Miss** Character from *The Muppets*

92 While there's tea there's hope.
The Second Mrs Tanqueray (1893) **Pinero, Sir Arthur Wing** (1855–1934) English dramatist

93 Ice cream is the most evocative of puddings. It brings back summer holidays and the bicycle bell call of the hokey-cokey man with his tricycle cart, and rushing down the garden path with grandpa's big mug to have it filled for the ice cream sodas which were invariably constructed in tall sundae glasses.
The New Times Cookbook **Poole, Shona Crawford** (1943–) Cookery writer

94 Fame is at best an unperforming cheat;
But 'tis substantial happiness, to eat.
'Prologue for Mr D'Urfey's Last Play' (1727) **Pope, Alexander** (1688–1744) English poet, translator and editor

95 What! Can't a fellow even enjoy a biscuit any more?
In Winchester, *Their Noble Lordships* **Portland, Sixth Duke of** (1857–1943) British aristocrat. On being told to reduce his expenses by dispensing with one of his two Italian pastry cooks

96 To the old saying that man built the house but woman made of it a 'home' might be added the modern supplement that woman accepted cooking as a chore but man has made of it a recreation.
Etiquette (1922) **Post, Emily** (1873–1960) US writer

97 Dinner at the Huntercombes' possessed 'only two dramatic features – the wine was a farce and the food a tragedy'.
A Dance to the Music of Time: The Acceptance World (1955) **Powell, Anthony** (1905–2000) English writer and critic

98 Our trouble is that we drink too much tea. I see in this the slow revenge of the Orient, which has diverted the Yellow River down our throats.
The Observer, (1949) **Priestley, J.B.** (1894–1984) English writer, dramatist and critic

99 Salads, and eggs, and lighter fare,
Tune the Italian spark's guitar.
And, if I take Dan Congreve right,
Pudding and beef make Britons fight.
Alma (1718) **Prior, Matthew** (1664–1721) English poet

100 Appetite comes with eating ... thirst goes with drinking.
Gargantua (1534) **Rabelais, François** (c.1494–c.1553) French monk, physician, satirist and humanist

101 We would not lead a pleasant life,
And 'twould be finished soon,
If peas were eaten with the knife,
And gravy with the spoon.
Eat slowly: only men in rags
And gluttons old in sin
Mistake themselves for carpet bags
And tumble victuals in.
'Stans puer ad mensam' (1923) **Raleigh, Sir Walter A.** (1861–1922) English scholar, critic and essayist

102 ... bannocks and a share of cheese
Will make a breakfast that a laird might please.
'The Gentle Shepherd' (1725) **Ramsay, Allan** (1686–1758) Scottish poet and dramatist

103 Great restaurants are, of course, nothing but mouth-brothels. There is no point in going to them if one intends to keep one's belt buckled.
The Sunday Times Magazine, (1977) **Raphael, Frederic** (1931–) English author

104 She wrenched from her brow a diamond and eyed it with contempt, took from her pocket a sausage and contemplated it with respect and affection.
Peg Woffington (1852) **Reade, Charles** (1814–1884) English novelist and dramatist

105 You can tell a lot about a fellow's character by the way he eats jelly beans.
Daily Mail, (1981) **Reagan, Ronald** (1911–2004) US actor, Republican statesman and President

106 The national dish of America is menus.
Robinson's Travels, BBC TV programme, (1977) **Robinson, Robert** (1927–) British broadcaster and presenter

107 The real crystallisation of Jewish cuisine took place in the 16th century, when the Jews were confined to ghettos by edict. It may seem surprising that interest in food should blossom in a ghetto, especially one devoted to religious worship; but people focused on their home life as an antidote

to the misery and degradation outside. Hospitality became a means of survival and the celebration of religious festivals ... made it possible to remain indifferent to the world outside the gates.
The Good Food Guide, (1985) **Roden, Claudia** Egyptian-born British cookery writer

108 Great eaters of meat are in general more cruel and ferocious than other men. The English are known for their cruelty.
Attr. **Rousseau, Paul Émile** (1929–2001) Agent-General in London for Saskatchewan

109 These citizens are always willing to bet that what Nicely-Nicely dies of will be over-feeding and never anything small like pneumonia, for Nicely-Nicely is known far and wide as a character who dearly loves to commit eating.
Take it Easy (1938) **Runyon, Damon** (1884–1946) US writer

110 The cook was a good cook, as cooks go; and as cooks go she went.
Reginald (1904)

111 Oysters are more beautiful than any religion ... There's nothing in Christianity or Buddhism that quite matches the sympathetic unselfishness of an oyster.
The Chronicles of Clovis (1911)

112 I believe I once considerably scandalized her by declaring that clear soup was a more important factor in life than a clear conscience.
Beasts and Super-Beasts (1914) **Saki** (1870–1916) Burmese-born British writer

113 The Milanese, be it remarked, are undoubtedly the best cooks in Italy.
The Thorough Good Cook **Sala, George Augustus** (1828–1895) English journalist

114 Mum only ever uses the cooker to light her fags off.
Absolutely Fabulous **Sawalha, Julia** (1968–) English actress. As Saffy Monsoon, Edina's strait-laced daughter

115 Man is a cooking animal.
St Ronan's Well (1823) **Scott, Sir Walter** (1771–1832) Scottish writer and historian

116 My advice if you insist on slimming: Eat as much as you like – just don't swallow it.
Daily Herald, (1962) **Secombe, Sir Harry** (1921–2001) Welsh comedian, actor and singer

117 'Tis an ill cook that cannot lick his own fingers.
Romeo and Juliet, IV.ii

118 Methinks sometimes I have no more wit than a Christian or an ordinary man has; but I am a great eater of beef, and I believe that does harm to my wit.
Twelfth Night, I.iii **Shakespeare, William** (1564–1616) English dramatist, poet and actor

119 There is no love sincerer than the love of food.
Man and Superman (1903) **Shaw, George Bernard** (1856–1950) Irish socialist, writer, dramatist and critic

120 There are two Italies – the one is the most sublime and lovely contemplation that can be conceived by the imagination of man; the other is the most degraded, disgusting and odious. What do you think? Young women of rank actually eat – you will never guess what – garlick!
Attr. **Shelley, Percy Bysshe** (1792–1822) English poet, dramatist and essayist

121 Cooking is about not cheating yourself of pleasure.
Slice of Life, BBC TV programme **Slater, Nigel** English food writer

122 I truly have tried and we had a microwave to heat things in the filming – but, actually, we mainly use it to keep the ashtrays in. I think it takes the soul out of food. Cooking is about ingredients being put together, and having time to amalgamate.
Interview, *The Times*, (1990)

123 If you look at France now, after *nouvelle cuisine* and all the rest, you find that they are going crazy about what they call *cuisine grandmère*: just like granny used to make. I suppose that's what I'm about.
Interview with Libby Purves, *The Times*, (1990)

124 A perfect chip should be (i) crisp on the outside, (ii) soft, almost melting, in the middle, and (iii) dry, which is to say not greasy, oily or soggy. It is relatively easy to cook soggy chips, but far more difficult to produce a beautifully dry, crisp and melting chip.
Complete Illustrated Cookery Course **Smith, Delia** (1941–) English food writer

125 Most London dinners evaporate in whispers to one's next-door neighbour. I make it a rule never to speak a word to mine, but fire across the table; though I broke it once … I turned suddenly round and said, 'Madam, I have been looking for a person who disliked gravy all my life; let us swear eternal friendship.'
In Holland, *A Memoir of the Reverend Sydney Smith* (1855)

126 Serenely full, the epicure would say,
Fate cannot harm me, I have dined today.
In Holland, *A Memoir of the Reverend Sydney Smith* (1855) From his recipe for salads

127 My idea of heaven is, eating pâté de foie gras to the sound of trumpets.
In H. Pearson, *The Smith of Smiths* (1934)

128 Thank God for tea! What would the world do without tea? How did it exist? I am glad I was not born before tea.
Attr. **Smith, Sydney** (1771–1845) English clergyman, essayist, journalist and wit

129 There is a fine stuffed chavender,
A chavender, or chub,
That decks the rural pavender,
The pavender, or pub,
Wherein I eat my gravender,
My gravender, or grub.
'The Chavender, or Chub' **St Leger, Warham** (1850–c.1915) Irish aristocrat

130 Many's the long night I [Ben Gunn] have dreamed of cheese – toasted mostly, and woke up again and here I were … You might not happen to have a piece of cheese about you now?
Treasure Island (1883) **Stevenson, Robert Louis** (1850–1894) Scottish writer, poet and essayist

131 He showed me his bill of fare to tempt me to dine with him; Poh, said I, I value not your bill of fare; give me your bill of company.
Journal to Stella, (1711)

132 He was a bold man that first eat an oyster.
Polite Conversation (1738) **Swift, Jonathan** (1667–1745) Irish satirist, poet, essayist and cleric

133 Here's your arsenic, dear.
And your weedkiller biscuit.
I've throttled your parakeet.
I've spat in the vases.
I've put cheese in the mouseholes.
Here's your – nice tea, dear.
Under Milk Wood (1954) **Thomas, Dylan** (1914–1953) Welsh poet, writer and radio dramatist

134 What makes food such a tyranny for women? A man may in times of crisis hit the bottle (or another person), but he rarely hits the fridge.
The Times, (1998) **Trollope, Joanna** (1943–) English novelist

135 The best coffee in Europe is Vienna coffee, compared to which all other coffee is fluid poverty.
Greatly Exaggerated **Twain, Mark** (1835–1910) US humorist, writer, journalist and lecturer

136 The most remarkable thing about my mother is that for 30 years she served nothing but leftovers. The original meal was never found.
The Observer, (1999) **Ullman, Tracey** (1959–) English comedian

137 No pudding and no fun!
Attr. **Victoria, Queen** (1819–1901) Queen of the United Kingdom

138 I think it must be so, for I have been drinking it for sixty-five years and I am not dead yet.
Attr. **Voltaire** (1694–1778) French philosopher, dramatist, poet, historian, writer and critic. On learning that coffee was considered a slow poison

139 I saw him even now going the way of all flesh, that is to say towards the kitchen.
Westward Hoe (1607) **Webster, John** (c.1580–c.1625) English dramatist

140 Dear Frank, we believe you; you have dined in every house in London – once.
Attr. **Wilde, Oscar** (1854–1900) Irish poet, dramatist, writer, critic and wit. Said to Frank Harris who was listing the houses he had dined at

141 The lunches of fifty-seven years had caused his chest to slip down to the mezzanine floor.
The Heart of a Goof (1926) **Wodehouse, P.G.** (1881–1975) English humorist and writer

142 For a long time I thought coq au vin meant love in a lorry.
Attr. **Wood, Victoria** (1953–) English comedienne

FOOLISHNESS

1 You can never underestimate the stupidity of the general public.
The Dilbert Future **Adams, Scott** (1957–) US cartoonist

2 Thinking to get all the gold that the goose could give in one go, he killed it, and opened it only to find – nothing.
'The Goose with the Golden Eggs' **Aesop** (6th century BC) Legendary Greek writer of fables

3 When I was a little boy, I had but a little wit,
'Tis a long time ago, and I have no more yet;
Nor ever ever shall, until that I die,
For the longer I live the more fool am I.
In *Wit and Mirth, an Antidote against Melancholy* (1684)

4 Never attribute to malice that which is adequately explained by stupidity.
Hanlon's Razor

5 Artificial Intelligence is no match for natural stupidity.
Anonymous

6 A fool bolts pleasure, then complains of moral indigestion.
Naked Truth and Veiled Allusions (1902) **Antrim, Minna** (1861–1950) US writer

7 Obstinate people may be subdivided into the opinionated, the ignorant, and the boorish.
Nicomachean Ethics **Aristotle** (384–322 BC) Greek philosopher

8 There's a sucker born every minute.
Attr. **Barnum, Phineas T.** (1810–1891) US showman and writer

9 I have known many an instance of a man writing a letter and forgetting to sign his name, but this is the only instance I have ever known of a man signing his name and forgetting to write the letter.
Attr. **Beecher, Henry Ward** (1813–1887) US clergyman, lecturer, editor and writer. On receiving a note containing only one word: 'Fool'

10 Ignorance is an evil weed, which dictators may cultivate among their dupes, but which no democracy can afford among its citizens.
Full Employment in a Full Society (1944) **Beveridge, William Henry** (1879–1963) British economist and social reformer

11 Answer a fool according to his folly.
Proverbs, 26:5

12 As a dog returneth to his vomit, so a fool returneth to his folly.
Proverbs, 26:11 **The Bible (King James Version)**

13 If the fool would persist in his folly he would become wise.
'Proverbs of Hell' (1793)

14 To generalize is to be an idiot.
In Gilchrist, *Life of Blake* **Blake, William** (1757–1827) English poet, engraver, painter and mystic

15 A fool always finds a greater fool to admire him.
L'Art poétique (1674) **Boileau-Despréaux, Nicolas** (1636–1711) French writer

16 That's a' your jargon o' your Schools,
Your Latin names for horns an' stools?
If honest Nature made you fools,
What sairs your grammers.
'First Epistle to Lapraik' (1785) **Burns, Robert** (1759–1796) Scottish poet and songwriter

17 He's an intermittent fool, full of lucid intervals.
Don Quixote (1615) **Cervantes, Miguel de** (1547–1616) Spanish writer and dramatist

18 Fools are more to be feared than the wicked.
Pensées de Christine, reine de Suede (1825) **Christina of Sweden** (1626–1689) Queen of Sweden

19 Ignorance and superstition ever bear a close and even a mathematical relation to each other.
Jack Tier **Cooper, James Fenimore** (1789–1851) US writer

20 A fool must now and then be right, by chance.
'Conversation' (1782) **Cowper, William** (1731–1800) English poet, hymn writer and letter writer

21 A fool … is a man who never tried an experiment in his life.
In a letter from Maria Edgeworth to Sophy Ruxton, (1792) **Darwin, Erasmus** (1731–1802) Dutch scholar and humanist

22 He'd be sharper than a serpent's tooth, if he wasn't as dull as ditch water.
Our Mutual Friend (1866) **Dickens, Charles** (1812–1870) English writer

23 Mr Kremlin himself was distinguished for ignorance, for he had only one idea, – and that was wrong.
Sybil (1845) **Disraeli, Benjamin** (1804–1881) English statesman and writer

24 I said I liked being half-educated; you were so much more surprised at everything when you were ignorant.
My Family and Other Animals (1956) **Durrell, Sir Gerald** (1925–1995) English writer and naturalist

25 When lovely woman stoops to folly and
Paces about her room again, alone,
She smoothes her hair with automatic hand,
And puts a record on the gramophone.
The Waste Land (1922) **Eliot, T.S.** (1888–1965) US-born British poet, verse dramatist and critic

26 One fool at least in every married couple.
Amelia (1751) **Fielding, Henry** (1707–1754)
English writer, dramatist and journalist

27 Experience keeps a dear school, but fools
will learn in no other.
Poor Richard's Almanac (1743) **Franklin,
Benjamin** (1706–1790) US statesman, scientist,
political critic and printer

28 In my time, the follies of the town crept
slowly among us, but now they travel faster
than a stage-coach.
She Stoops to Conquer (1773) **Goldsmith, Oliver**
(c.1728–1774) Irish dramatist, poet and writer

29 Half the world is laughing at the other half,
which shows how foolish everyone is.
Handbook-Oracle and the Art of Prudence (1647)

30 It is not the one who commits an act of
foolishness who is foolish, but the one
who, once such an act has been
committed, does not know how to cover it
up.
Handbook-Oracle and the Art of Prudence (1647)
Gracián, Baltasar (1601–1658) Spanish writer

31 Where ignorance is bliss,
'Tis folly to be wise.
'Ode on a Distant Prospect of Eton College'
(1742) **Gray, Thomas** (1716–1771) English poet
and scholar

32 Most Men make little other use of their
Speech than to give evidence against their
own Understanding.
'Of Folly and Fools' (1750) **Halifax, Lord** (1633–
1695) English politician, courtier,
pamphleteer and epigrammatist

33 The most unthinking person of all: the one
who only flicks through every book.
The Weight of the World. A Diary (1977) **Handke,
Peter** (1942–) Austrian playwright

34 I wish you would read a little poetry
sometimes. Your ignorance cramps my
conversation.
The Dolly Dialogues (1894) **Hope, Anthony**
(1863–1933) English writer, dramatist and
lawyer

35 Mix a little folly with your plans: it is sweet
to be silly at the right moment.
Odes **Horace** (65–8 BC) Roman poet

36 Fools are in a terrible, overwhelming
majority, all the wide world over.
An Enemy of the People (1882) **Ibsen, Henrik**
(1828–1906) Norwegian writer, dramatist and
poet

37 Talk to him of Jacob's ladder, and he would
ask the number of the steps.
Wit and Opinions of Douglas Jerrold (1859)
Jerrold, Douglas William (1803–1857) English
dramatist, writer and wit

38 Ignorance, madam, sheer ignorance.
In Boswell, *The Life of Samuel Johnson* (1791)
Johnson, Samuel (1709–1784) English
lexicographer, poet, critic, conversationalist
and essayist. Asked the reason for a mistake
in his *Dictionary*

39 Nothing in all the world is more dangerous
than sincere ignorance and conscientious
stupidity.
Strength to Love, (1963) **King, Martin Luther**
(1929–1968) US civil rights leader and Baptist
minister

40 There are people who speak one moment
before they think.
Les caractères ou les moeurs de ce siècle (1688) **La
Bruyère, Jean de** (1645–1696) French satirist

41 The ignorant man always loves that which
he cannot understand.
The Man of Genius (1894) **Lombroso, Cesare**
(1853–1909) Italian criminologist. (*L'uomo
ignorante ama ciò che non capisce*)

42 Nobody ever did anything very foolish
except from some strong principle.
Attr. **Melbourne, Lord** (1779–1848) English
statesman

43 As often as a study is cultivated by narrow
minds, they will draw from it narrow
conclusions.
Auguste Comte and Positivism (1865) **Mill, John
Stuart** (1806–1873) English philosopher,
economist and reformer

44 The greatest folly of all is wanting to busy
oneself in setting the world to rights.
Le Misanthrope (1666)

45 A knowledgeable fool is more foolish than
an ignorant fool.
Les Femmes savantes (1672) **Molière** (1622–1673)
French dramatist, actor and director

46 You English ... think we know damn
nothing but I tell you we know damn all.
The Cruel Sea (1951) **Monsarrat, Nicholas** (1910–
1979) English novelist

47 For Fools rush in where Angels fear to
tread.
An Essay on Criticism (1711)

48 Some have at first for Wits, then Poets
pass'd,
Turned Critics next, and proved plain fools
at last.
An Essay on Criticism (1711)

49 You beat your Pate, and fancy Wit will
come;
Knock as you please, there's nobody at
home.
'Epigram' (1732) **Pope, Alexander** (1688–1744)
English poet, translator and editor

50 Better be a fool than a knave.
Proverb

51 It isn't pollution that's harming the
environment. It's the impurities in our air
and water that are doing it.
Attr. **Quayle, Dan** (1947–) US Republican
politician and Vice President

52 Reason, an ignis fatuus of the mind,
Which leaving the light of nature, sense,
behind ...
Then Old Age, and Experience, hand in
hand,
Lead him to Death, and make him
understand,
After a search so painful, and so long,
That all his life he has been in the wrong.
Huddled in dirt the reasoning engine lies,
Who was so proud, so witty, and so wise.
'A Satire Against Reason and Mankind' (1679)
Rochester, Earl of (1647–1680) English poet,
satirist, courtier and libertine

53 The follies which a man regrets most in his
life are those which he didn't commit when
he had the opportunity.
A Guide to Men (1922) **Rowland, Helen** (1875–
1950) US writer

54 Gods themselves struggle in vain with
stupidity.

The Maid of Orleans (1801) **Schiller, Johann
Christoph Friedrich** (1759–1805) German
writer, dramatist, poet and historian

55 In the British aristocracy, the gene pool has
always had a shallow end.
The Observer, (1998) **Seitz, Raymond** (1940–)
US diplomat

56 The haste of a Fool is the slowest thing in
the World.
A True Widow (1679), III **Shadwell, Thomas**
(c.1642–1692) English writer and poet

57 He uses his folly like a stalking-horse, and
under the presentation of that he shoots
his wit.
As You Like It, V.iv **Shakespeare, William**
(1564–1616) English dramatist, poet and actor

58 A fool and his words are soon parted; a
man of genius and his money.
Essays on Men and Manners **Shenstone,
William** (1714–1763) English poet, essayist and
letter writer

59 What you don't know would make a great
book.
In Lady Holland, *Memoir* (1855) **Smith, Sydney**
(1771–1845) English clergyman, essayist,
journalist and wit

60 The ultimate result of shielding men from
the effects of folly, is to fill the world with
fools.
Essays (1891) **Spencer, Herbert** (1820–1903)
English philosopher and journalist

61 For God's sake give me the young man
who has brains enough to make a fool of
himself!
Virginibus Puerisque (1881)

62 It is better to be a fool than to be dead.
Virginibus Puerisque (1881) **Stevenson, Robert
Louis** (1850–1894) Scottish writer, poet and
essayist

63 This is the sublime and refined point of
felicity, called the possession of being well
deceived; the serene peaceful state of being
a fool among knaves.
A Tale of a Tub (1704)

64 'Tis an old maxim in the schools,
That vanity's the food of fools;
Yet now and then your men of wit
Will condescend to take a bit.
'Cadenus and Vanessa' (c.1712)

65 Hated by fools, and fools to hate,
Be that my motto and my fate.
'To Mr Delany' (1718) **Swift, Jonathan** (1667–
1745) Irish satirist, poet, essayist and cleric

66 Any fool can make a rule and every fool will
mind it.
Attr. **Thoreau, Henry David** (1817–1862) US
essayist, social critic and writer

67 The most powerful weapon of ignorance –
the diffusion of printed material.
War and Peace (1868–1869) **Tolstoy, Leo** (1828–
1910) Russian writer, essayist, philosopher
and moralist

68 A fool and his money be soon at debate.
Five Hundred Points of Good Husbandry (1557)
Tusser, Thomas (c.1524–1580) English writer,
poet and musician

69 It is a folly to expect men to do all that they
may reasonably be expected to do.
Apophthegms (1854) **Whately, Richard** (1787–
1863) English philosopher, theologian,
educationist and writer

70 There is no sin except stupidity.
Intentions (1891), 'The Critic as Artist'

71 Ignorance is like a delicate exotic fruit;
touch it, and the bloom is gone.
The Importance of Being Earnest (1895) **Wilde,
Oscar** (1854–1900) Irish poet, dramatist,
writer, critic and wit

72 Be wise with speed;
A fool at forty is a fool indeed.
Love of Fame, the Universal Passion (1728)
Young, Edward (1683–1765) English poet,
dramatist, satirist and clergyman
See also wisdom

FOOTBALL

1 Tell the Kraut to get his ass up front. We
don't pay a million for a guy to hang
around in defence.
Anonymous A New York Cosmos executive
questions Franz Beckenbauer's position

2 I've just seen Gary Lineker shake hands
with Jurgen Klinsmann – it's a wonder
Klinsmann hasn't fallen over.
Attr. (1990) **Atkinson, Ron** (1939–) English
football manager

3 I definitely want Brooklyn to be christened,
but I don't know into what religion yet.
Becks Talking, (2002) **Beckham, David** (1975–)
English footballer

4 Was I the fifth Beatle? Not really.
Book of Sports Quotes, (1979)

5 It's a pleasure to be standing up here. It's a
pleasure to be standing up.
Speech, (1999) On being named Footballer of
the Century

6 I spent a lot of money on booze, birds and
fast cars. The rest I just squandered.
Attr.

7 He wears a No. 10 jersey. I thought it was
his position but it turns out to be his IQ.
Attr. Of Paul Gascoigne

8 You may have heard this before, but I will
respect this liver. After all, it's not mine.
Attr. **Best, George** (1946–2005) Irish footballer

9 The great fallacy is that the game is first
and last about winning. It is nothing of the
kind. The game is about glory, it is about
doing things in style and with a flourish,
about going out and beating the lot, not
waiting for them to die of boredom.
Attr. **Blanchflower, Danny** (1926–1993) Irish
footballer

10 When the seagulls follow the trawler, it is
because they think sardines will be thrown
into the sea.
The Observer, (1995) **Cantona, Eric** (1966–)
French footballer. Commenting on the
interest taken by the press in the outcome of
his court case

11 I wouldn't say I was the best manager in the business, but I was in the top one.
Quoted in *The Rough Guide to Football* **Clough, Brian** (1935–2004) English football manager

12 Football's football. If that weren't the case it wouldn't be the game it is.
TV commentary **Crooks, Garth** (1958–) English footballer and TV pundit

13 They offered me a handshake of £10,000 to settle amicably. I told them that they would have to be a lot more amicable than that.
Docherty, Tommy (1928–) Scottish football manager

14 I get on a train and sit in second class and people think, 'tight bastard. Money he's got and he sits in second class.' So I think, '– them' and I go in first class and then they say, 'look at that –ing flash bastard in first class'.
Glasgow Herald, (1995) **Gascoigne, Paul** (1967–) English footballer

15 Football is an art more central to our culture than anything the Arts Council deigns to recognize.
Independent, (1996) **Greer, Germaine** (1939–) Australian feminist, critic, English scholar and writer

16 Super Caley Go Ballistic, Celtic Are Atrocious.
The Sun, (2000) **Hickson, Paul** English sports subeditor. Headline describing Celtic's 3-1 defeat by Inverness Caledonian Thistle

17 Every fan you ask will say he wants to see lively, open football. But what the fan really wants to see is his team win.
Attr. **Hill-Wood, Dennis** (1906–1982) Businessman and director of Arsenal FC

18 Jesus was a normal, run-of-the-mill sort of guy who had a genuine gift, just as Eileen has.
Quoted in *The Wrong Kind of Shirts* **Hoddle, Glenn** (1957–) English footballer and manager. On his faith healer, Eileen Drewery

19 Our performance today would not have been the best-looking bird but at least we got her in the taxi. She weren't the best-looking lady we ended up taking home but she was pleasant and very nice, so thanks very much and let's have a coffee.
The Guardian, (2003) **Holloway, Ian** (1963–) English football manager. On QPR's 3–0 victory over Chesterfield

20 Soccer in Japan is interesting, in Glasgow it's a matter of life and death.
Daily Mail, (1996) **Huistra, Peter** (1967–) Dutch footballer

21 Football has taken the place of religion in Scotland.
A Would-Be Saint **Jenkins, Robin** (1912–2005) Scottish novelist

22 You get bunches of players like you do bananas, though that is a bad comparison.
TV commentary

23 Argentina won't be at Euro 2000 because they're from South America.
TV commentary

24 Ardiles strokes the ball like it is part of his own anatomy.
RTE

25 Argentina are the second-best team in the world, and there's no higher praise than that.
Attr.

26 In some ways, cramp is worse than having a broken leg. But leukaemia is worse still. Probably.
Attr. **Keegan, Kevin** (1951–) English footballer and manager

27 That's great. Tell him he's Pelé and get him back on.
Attr. **Lambie, John** (1940–) Scottish football manager. Upon discovering that dazed striker Colin McGlashan did not know who he was.

28 Being a woman is of special interest only to aspiring male transsexuals. To actual women, it is merely a good excuse not to play football.
Metropolitan Life (1978) **Lebowitz, Fran** (1946–) US writer

29 The goal was scored a little bit by the hand of God, another bit by the head of Maradona.
The Guardian, (1986) **Maradona, Diego** (1960–) Argentinian footballer. On his controversial goal against England in the 1986 World Cup

30 Soon there were bodies everywhere, blue with death ... I had come to photograph Platini and had ended up photographing war.
The Observer, (1989) **McCabe, Eamonn** (1948–) British newspaper photographer. On football

31 Oh, he's football crazy, he's football mad
And the football it has robbed him o' the wee bit o' sense he had.
And it would take a dozen skivvies, his clothes to wash and scrub,
Since our Jock became a member of that terrible football club.
'Football Crazy' (song, 1960) **McGregor, Jimmie** (1932–) Scottish folk singer

32 Please don't call me arrogant, but I'm European champion, and I think I'm a special one.
Announcing himself in The Premiership

33 I think he is one of these people who is a voyeur. He likes to watch other people. There are some guys who, when they are at home, have a big telescope to see what happens in other families. He speaks, speaks, speaks about Chelsea.
Attr. (2005) These badly-chosen words started The Christmas Card Wars with Arsenal manager Arsene Wenger **Mourinho, Jose** (1963–) Portuguese football manager

34 Win or die.
Quoted in *The Final Whistle* (1938) **Mussolini, Alberto** (1883–1945) Italian fascist dictator. Mussolini's pre-match telegram before the 1938 World Cup Final had the desired effect: Italy won

35 Crowds of drunk, usually disappointed men are, I think, quite a frightening spectre for a woman. When they happen to be got up like some savage hybrid of Calum Kennedy, Papa Smurf and Chewbacca, I think a full-blown phobia is perfectly understandable.
The Sunday Times, (1999) **Nicol, Patricia** English journalist. On Scottish football fans

36 Women are around all the time but World Cups come only every four years.
The Times, (1998) **Osgood, Peter** (1947–2006) English footballer

37 And now the worst news of all. Gay men are getting interested in football ... What a catastrophe. One became homosexual to get away from this sort of thing.
The Times, (1998) **Parris, Matthew** (1949–) British Conservative politician and journalist

38 Internationally, football has become a substitute for war.
The Sunday Times, (2000) **Paxman, Jeremy** (1950–) English journalist, writer and broadcaster

39 You've won the World Cup once, now go out and win it again.
Attr. (1966) **Ramsey, Alf** (1920–1999) England football manager. Famously exhorting England after a last-gasp German equalizer forced extra time in the 1966 World Cup Final

40 I couldn't settle in Italy – it was like living in a foreign country.
Attr. **Rush, Ian** (1961–) English footballer

41 Some people think football is a matter of life and death. I don't like that attitude. I can assure them it is much more serious than that.
Remark on BBC TV, (1981)

42 When people come to assess my career, I do not want them to judge me on victories or defeats. I want them to say: he played the game, he was fair, he didn't cheat the players or the crowd. If I never cheated them, I never cheated anybody.
Attr. **Shankly, Bill** (1913–1981) Scottish football manager and philosopher

43 Football and cookery are the two most important subjects in the country.
The Observer, (1997) **Smith, Delia** (1941–) English food writer. On her appointment as a director of Norwich City football club

44 How could I carry out a policy where I won't sign a Catholic but I'll go home and live with one?

In Kenny MacDonald, *Scottish Football Quotations* (1994) **Souness, Graeme** (1953–) Scottish footballer and coach

45 It's a tremendous honour. I'm going to have a banana to celebrate.
Radio interview, (1991) On being voted Footballer of the Year

46 If a Frenchman goes on about seagulls, trawlers and sardines, he's called a philosopher. I'd just be called a short Scottish bum talking crap.
Attr. Referring to a quote by Eric Cantona (*see football*, 11) **Strachan, Gordon** (1957–) Scottish footballer and manager

47 Football … causeth fighting, brawling, contention, quarrel picking, murder, homicide and great effusion of blood, as daily experience teacheth.
Anatomy of Abuses (1583) **Stubbes, Philip** (c.1555–1610) English Puritan pamphleteer and writer

48 They want us to be a nodding dog in the back of their car.
Rothmans Football Yearbook, 2002–03 **Taylor, Gordon** (1944–) English footballer, chief executive of the Professional Footballer's Association. Bemoaning the attitude of the Premier League

49 Other nations have history. We have football.
The Spectator, (1996) **Viera, Ondino** Uruguayan football manager
See also sport and games

FORGIVENESS

1 You ought certainly to forgive them as a Christian, but never to admit them in your sight, or allow their names to be mentioned in your hearing.
Pride and Prejudice (1813) **Austen, Jane** (1775–1817) English writer

2 Father, forgive them; for they know not what they do.
Luke, 23:34 **The Bible (King James Version)**

3 Good, to forgive;
Best, to forget!
Living, we fret;
Dying, we live.
La Saisiaz (1878) **Browning, Robert** (1812–1889) English poet

4 I shall be an autocrat: that's my job. And the good Lord will forgive me: that's his job.
Attr. **Catherine the Great** (1729–1796) Empress of Russia

5 Once a woman has forgiven her man, she must not reheat his sins for breakfast.
Marlene Dietrich's ABC (1962) **Dietrich, Marlene** (1901–1992) German-born US actress and singer

6 Forgiveness to the injured does belong;
But they ne'er pardon, who have done the wrong.
The Conquest of Granada (1670) **Dryden, John** (1631–1700) English poet, satirist, dramatist and critic

7 Forgive, O Lord, my little jokes on Thee
And I'll forgive Thy great big one on me.
'Cluster of Faith' (1962) **Frost, Robert** (1874–1963) US poet

8 Well, Polly; as far as one woman can forgive another, I forgive thee.
The Beggar's Opera (1728) **Gay, John** (1685–1732) English poet, dramatist and librettist

9 We should forgive our enemies, but only after they have been hanged first.
Attr. **Heine, Heinrich** (1797–1856) German lyric poet, essayist and journalist

10 Always forgive your enemies – but never forget their names.
Attr. **Kennedy, Robert F.** (1925–1968) US Attorney General and Democrat politician

11 The time for the healing of the wounds has come.
Speech at his inauguration as President of South Africa, (1994)

12 True reconciliation does not consist in merely forgetting the past.
Speech, (1996) **Mandela, Nelson** (1918–) South African statesman and President

13 Teach me to feel another's Woe,
To hide the Fault I see;
That Mercy I to others show,
That Mercy show to me.
'The Universal Prayer' (1738) **Pope, Alexander**
(1688–1744) English poet, translator and editor

14 Time hath, my lord, a wallet at his back,
Wherein he puts alms for oblivion,
A great-siz'd monster of ingratitudes.
Those scraps are good deeds past, which
are devour'd
As fast as they are made, forgot as soon
As done.
Troilus and Cressida, III.iii **Shakespeare,
William** (1564–1616) English dramatist, poet
and actor

15 If you strike a child, take care that you
strike it in anger, even at the risk of
maiming it for life. A blow in cold blood
neither can nor should be forgiven.
Man and Superman (1903) **Shaw, George
Bernard** (1856–1950) Irish socialist, writer,
dramatist and critic

16 Beautiful that war and all its deeds of
carnage must in time be utterly lost,
That the hands of the sisters Death and
Night incessantly softly wash again, and
ever again, this soil'd world;
For my enemy is dead, a man as divine as
myself is dead,
I look where he lies white-faced and still in
the coffin – I draw near,
Bend down and touch lightly with my lips
the white face in the coffin.
'Reconciliation' (1865) **Whitman, Walt** (1819–
1892) US poet and writer

17 Only the dead can be forgiven;
But when I think of that my tongue's a
stone.
'A Dialogue of Self and Soul' (1933) **Yeats,
W.B.** (1865–1939) Irish poet, dramatist, editor,
writer and senator
See also compassion; virtue

FRANCE

1 The overall impression from the British
and the Germans is that they love France
itself but would rather that the French
didn't live there.
Anonymous Paris Chamber of Commerce
spokesman commenting on the results of a
tourist survey

2 France, famed in all great arts, in none
supreme.
'To a Republican Friend' (1849) **Arnold,
Matthew** (1822–1888) English poet, critic,
essayist and educationist

3 Everybody's talking French. I don't
understand.
The Times, (1998) **Boycott, Geoffrey** (1940–)
English cricketer. During his trial in Grasse,
France

4 The whole territory of Gaul is divided into
three parts.
De Bello Gallico **Caesar, Gaius Julius** (c.102–
44 BC) Roman statesman, historian and army
commander

5 France was long a despotism tempered by
epigrams.
History of the French Revolution (1837) **Carlyle,
Thomas** (1795–1881) Scottish historian,
biographer, critic, and essayist

6 The Almighty in His infinite wisdom did
not see fit to create Frenchmen in the
image of Englishmen.
Speech, House of Commons, (December 1942)
Churchill, Sir Winston (1874–1965) English
Conservative Prime Minister

7 There's always something fishy about the
French.
Conversation Piece (1934) **Coward, Sir Noël**
(1899–1973) English dramatist, actor, producer
and composer

8 One can only unite the French under the
threat of danger. One cannot simply bring
together a nation that produces 265 kinds
of cheese.
Speech, (1951)

9 When I want to know what France thinks, I
ask myself.

Attr. **De Gaulle, Charles** (1890–1970) French general and statesman

10 France, mother of arts, of arms, and of laws.
Les Regrets (1558) **Du Bellay, Joachim** (1522–1560) French poet

11 The more foreigners I saw, the more I loved my native land.
Du Belloy, P.-L.B. (1727–1775) French poet

12 Paris is the paradise of the easily-impressed – the universal provincial mind.
In Burchill, *Sex and Sensibility* (1992) **Elms, Robert** (1959–) English writer and broadcaster

13 The words Liberté, Egalité, Fraternité rimming their coins might well be replaced by the slogan 'It can be arranged'.
The Zoo Gang (1971) **Gallico, Paul** (1897–1976) US author and scriptwriter

14 Weep not for little Léonie
Abducted by a French Marquis!
Though loss of honour was a wrench
Just think how it's improved her French.
More Ruthless Rhymes for Heartless Homes (1930) **Graham, Harry** (1874–1936) English writer

15 The last time I saw Paris,
Her heart was warm and gay,
I heard the laughter of her heart in ev'ry street café.
'The Last Time I Saw Paris' (song, 1940) **Hammerstein II, Oscar** (1895–1960) US lyricist

16 If you are lucky enough to have lived in Paris as a young man, then wherever you go for the rest of your life, it stays with you, for Paris is a moveable feast.
A Moveable Feast (1964) **Hemingway, Ernest** (1898–1961) US author

17 Paris is well worth a mass.
Attr. **Henri IV** (1553–1610) King of France

18 You think when you have slain me you will conquer France, but that you will never do. Though there were a hundred thousand God-dammees more in France than there are, they will never conquer that kingdom.
Attr. **Joan of Arc** (c.1412–1431) French patriot and martyr

19 What I gained by being in France was learning to be better satisfied with my own country.
In Boswell, *The Life of Samuel Johnson* (1791)

20 A Frenchman must be always talking, whether he knows anything of the matter or not; an Englishman is content to say nothing, when he has nothing to say.
In Boswell, *The Life of Samuel Johnson* (1791) **Johnson, Samuel** (1709–1784) English lexicographer, poet, critic, conversationalist and essayist

21 Cities are only human. And I had begun to see Paris for the bitch she is: a stunning transvestite – vain, narrow-minded and all false charm.
Daily Mail, (1996) **Kurtz, Irma** (1935–) English writer and 'agony aunt'

22 I do not like this word bomb. It is not a bomb; it is a device which is exploding.
Attr. **Le Blanc, Jacques** French ambassador to New Zealand. Describing France's nuclear testing, 1995

23 Let them eat cake.
Attr. **Marie-Antoinette** (1755–1793) Queen of France. On being told the people had no bread to eat

24 France has more need of me than I have need of France.
Speech, (1813) **Napoleon I** (1769–1821) French emperor

25 There's something Vichy about the French.
In Marsh, *Ambrosia and Small Beer* **Novello, Ivor** (1893–1951) Welsh actor, composer, songwriter and dramatist

26 What is not clear is not French.
Discours sur l'Universalité de la Langue Française (1784) **Rivarol, Antoine de** (1753–1801) French writer and wit

27 Allons, enfants de la patrie,
Le jour de gloire est arrivé!
'La Marseillaise', (1792) **Rouget de Lisle, Claude-Joseph** (1760–1836) French composer.
(*Let us go, children of this land, the day of glory has arrived!*)

28 That sweet enemy, France.

Astrophel and Stella (1591) **Sidney, Sir Philip** (1554–1586) English poet, critic, soldier, courtier and diplomat

29 French art, if not sanguinary, is usually obscene.
In *Home Life with Herbert Spencer* (1906) **Spencer, Herbert** (1820–1903) English philosopher and journalist

30 They are a loyal, a gallant, a generous, an ingenious, and good tempered people as is under heaven – if they have a fault, they are too serious.
A Sentimental Journey (1768) **Sterne, Laurence** (1713–1768) Irish-born English writer and clergyman. Of the French

31 The French want no-one to be their superior. The English want inferiors. The Frenchman constantly looks above him with anxiety. The Englishman looks beneath him with complacency. On either side it is pride, but understood in a different manner.
Voyage en Angleterre et en Irlande de 1835 (1835) **Tocqueville, Alexis de** (1805–1859) French historian, politician, lawyer and memoirist

32 I do not dislike the French from the vulgar antipathy between neighbouring nations, but for their insolent and unfounded airs of superiority.
Letter, (1787) **Walpole, Horace** (1717–1797) English writer and politician

33 France is a country where the money falls apart in your hands and you can't tear the toilet paper.
In Halliwell, *Filmgoer's Book of Quotes* (1973) **Wilder, Billy** (1906–2002) Austrian-born US fllm director, producer and screenwriter
See also Europe

FREEDOM

1 A day, an hour of virtuous liberty
Is worth a whole eternity in bondage.
Cato (1713) **Addison, Joseph** (1672–1719) English essayist, poet, playwright and statesman

2 For so long as but a hundred of us remain alive, we will in no way yield ourselves to the dominion of the English. For it is not for glory, nor riches, nor honour that we fight, but for Freedom only, which no good man lays down but with his life.
Declaration of Arbroath, (1320) **Anonymous** Declaration sent to Pope John XXII by the Scottish barons

3 Where we are free to act, we are also free not to act, and where we are able to say No, we are also able to say Yes.
Nicomachean Ethics **Aristotle** (384–322 BC) Greek philosopher

4 Remember that to change your mind and follow someone who puts you right is to be none the less free than you were before.
Meditations **Aurelius, Marcus** (121–180) Roman emperor and Stoic philosopher

5 There is a wind of nationalism and freedom blowing round the world, and blowing as strongly in Asia as elsewhere.
Speech, London, (4 December 1934) **Baldwin, Stanley** (1867–1947) English Conservative statesman and Prime Minister

6 A! fredome is a noble thing!
Fredome mayss man to haiff liking;
Fredome all solace to man giffio:
He levys at ess that frely levys!
The Bruce (1375) **Barbour, John** (c.1316–1395) Scottish poet, churchman and scholar

7 Only reason can convince us of those three fundamental truths without a recognition of which there can be no effective liberty: that what we believe is not necessarily true; that what we like is not necessarily good; and that all questions are open.
Civilisation (1928) **Bell, Clive** (1881–1964) English art critic

8 As to the evil which results from censorship, it is impossible to measure it, because it is impossible to tell where it ends.
On Liberty of the Press and Public Discussion **Bentham, Jeremy** (1748–1832) English writer and philosopher

9 Liberty is liberty, not equality or fairness or justice or culture, or human happiness or a quiet conscience.
Four Essays on Liberty (1969)

10 Rousseau asks why it is that man, who was born free, is nevertheless everywhere in chains; one might as well ask, says Maistre, why it is that sheep, who are born carnivorous, nevertheless everywhere nibble grass. Men are not born for freedom, nor for peace.
'The Counter-Enlightenment' **Berlin, Isaiah** (1909–1997) English philosopher

11 He who binds to himself a joy
Does the winged life destroy;
But he who kisses the joy as it flies
Lives in eternity's sun rise.
'Eternity' (c.1793), from 'The Rossetti Manuscript' **Blake, William** (1757–1827) English poet, engraver, painter and mystic

12 Everybody favours free speech in the slack moments when no axes are being ground.
New York World, (1926) **Broun, Heywood** (1888–1939) US journalist

13 Oppression makes the wise man mad.
Luria (1846) **Browning, Robert** (1812–1889) English poet

14 The humblest citizen of all the land, when clad in the armour of a righteous cause is stronger than all the hosts of error.
Speech, Chicago, (1896) **Bryan, William Jennings** (1860–1925) US Democrat politician and editor

15 The only liberty I mean, is a liberty connected with order; that not only exists along with order and virtue, but which cannot exist at all without them.
Speech, (1774)

16 Freedom and not servitude is the cure of anarchy; as religion, and not atheism, is the true remedy for superstition.
Speech on Conciliation with America (1775)

17 Abstract liberty, like other mere abstractions, is not to be found.
Speech on Conciliation with America (1775)

18 Liberty, too, must be limited in order to be possessed.
Letter to the Sheriffs of Bristol on the Affairs of America (1777) **Burke, Edmund** (1729–1797) Irish-born British statesman and philosopher

19 Yet, Freedom! yet thy banner, torn, but flying,
Streams like the thunder-storm against the wind.
Childe Harold's Pilgrimage (1812–18) **Byron, Lord** (1788–1824) English poet, satirist and traveller

20 Taxation and representation are inseparable ... whatever is a man's own, is absolutely his own; no man hath a right to take it from him without his consent either expressed by himself or representative; whoever attempts to do it, attempts an injury; whoever does it, commits a robbery; he throws down and destroys the distinction between liberty and slavery.
Speech, House of Lords, (1766) **Camden, Lord** (1714–1794) English lawyer and Lord Chancellor. Arguing that the British parliament had no right to tax the Americans

21 But what is Freedom? Rightly understood,
A universal licence to be good.
'Liberty' (1833) **Coleridge, Hartley** (1796–1849) English poet and writer

22 With what deep worship I have still adored
The spirit of divinest Liberty.
'France' (1798)

23 For what is freedom, but the unfettered use
Of all the powers which God for use had given?
'The Destiny of Nations' **Coleridge, Samuel Taylor** (1772–1834) English poet, philosopher and critic

24 Perfect freedom is reserved for the man who lives by his own work and in that work does what he wants to do.
Speculum Mentis (1924) **Collingwood, R.G.** (1889–1943) English philosopher and archaeologist

25 Liberty was ever the tradition of my fathers, and, among us, no person avails, but rather reason.
In Brendan Lehane, *Early Celtic Christianity* (1994) **Columbanus, Saint** (c.543–615) Irish missionary and abbot. To the Pope

26 Apostles of Freedom are ever idolised when dead, but crucified when alive.

Workers Republic, (1898) **Connolly, James** (1868–1916) Irish labour leader

27 Freedom has a thousand charms to show, That slaves, howe'er contented, never know.
Table Talk (1782) **Cowper, William** (1731–1800) English poet, hymn writer and letter writer

28 The condition upon which God hath given liberty to man is eternal vigilance; which condition if he break, servitude is at once the consequence of his crime, and the punishment of his guilt.
Speech, (1790) **Curran, John Philpot** (1750–1817) Irish judge, orator, politician and reformer

29 Men will never be free until the last king is strangled with the entrails of the last priest.
Dithyrambe sur la Fête des Rois **Diderot, Denis** (1713–1784) French philosopher, encyclopaedist, writer and dramatist

30 Freedom is the recognition of necessity.
In Mackay, *The Harvest of a Quiet Eye* (1977) **Engels, Friedrich** (1820–1895) German socialist and political philosopher

31 I gave my life for freedom – This I know: For those who bade me fight had told me so.
'The Souls' (1917) **Ewer, William Norman** (1885–1976) English journalist

32 Whilst we strive
To live most free,
we're caught in our own toils.
The Lover's Melancholy (1629) **Ford, John** (c.1586–c.1640) English dramatist and poet

33 The moment the slave resolves that he will no longer be a slave, his fetters fall. He frees himself and shows the way to others. Freedom and slavery are mental states.
Non-Violence in Peace and War (1949) **Gandhi, Mohandas** (1869–1948) Indian political leader

34 O Freedom, what liberties are taken in thy name!
In Sagittarius and D. George, *Perpetual Pessimist* (1963) **George, Dan** (1899–1982) Canadian Indian chief

35 The first of earthly blessings, independence.

Memoirs of My Life and Writings (1796) **Gibbon, Edward** (1737–1794) English historian, politician and memoirist

36 Censorship is never over for those who have experienced it. It is a brand on the imagination that affects the individual who has suffered it, forever.
Lecture, (June 1990) **Gordimer, Nadine** (1923–) South African writer

37 When the people contend for their Liberty, they seldom get any thing by their Victory but new Masters.
Political, Moral and Miscellaneous Thoughts and Reflections (1750)

38 Power is so apt to be insolent and Liberty to be saucy, that they are very seldom upon good Terms.
Political, Moral and Miscellaneous Thoughts and Reflections (1750) **Halifax, Lord** (1633–1695) English politician, courtier, pamphleteer and epigrammatist

39 The love of liberty is the love of others; the love of power is the love of ourselves.
Political Essays (1819) **Hazlitt, William** (1778–1830) English writer and critic

40 The history of the world is none other than the progress of the consciousness of freedom.
Philosophy of History **Hegel, Georg Wilhelm** (1770–1831) German philosopher

41 Give me liberty, or give me death!
Speech, (1775) **Henry, Patrick** (1736–1799) US lawyer, orator and statesman

42 Only very slowly and late have men come to realize that unless freedom is universal it is only extended privilege.
Century of Revolution (1961) **Hill, Christopher** (1912–2003) English historian

43 When people are free to do as they please, they usually imitate each other.
The Passionate State of Mind (1955) **Hoffer, Eric** (1902–1983) US writer, philosopher and longshoreman

44 Who then is free? The wise man who commands himself, whom neither poverty nor death nor chains can terrify, who is strong enough to defy his passions and to despise distinctions, a man who is complete in himself, polished and well-rounded.
Satires **Horace** (65–8 BC) Roman poet

45 As political and economic freedom diminish, sexual freedom tends compensatingly to increase.
Brave New World (1932) **Huxley, Aldous** (1894–1963) English writer, poet and critic

46 The enemies of Freedom do not argue; they shout and they shoot.
End of an Age (1948) **Inge, William Ralph** (1860–1954) English divine, writer and teacher

47 The bird, the beast, the fish eke in the sea, They live in freedom everich in his kind; And I a man, and lackith liberty.
The Kingis Quair **James I of Scotland** (1394–1437) King of Scotland

48 The tree of liberty must be refreshed from time to time with the blood of patriots and tyrants. It is its natural manure.
Letter to W.S. Smith, (1787) **Jefferson, Thomas** (1743–1826) US Democrat statesman and President

49 How is it that we hear the loudest yelps for liberty among the drivers of negroes?
Taxation No Tyranny (1775) **Johnson, Samuel** (1709–1784) English lexicographer, poet, critic, conversationalist and essayist

50 It's often better to be in chains than to be free.
The Trial (1925) **Kafka, Franz** (1883–1924) Czech-born German-speaking writer

51 People hardly ever make use of the freedom they have, for example, the freedom of thought; instead they demand freedom of speech as a compensation.
In *The Faber Book of Aphorisms* (1962) **Kierkegaard, Søren** (1813–1855) Danish philosopher

52 Free at last, free at last, thank God Almighty, we are free at last!
Speech, (1963)

53 … And I've looked over, and I've seen the promised land. I may not get there with you, but I want you to know tonight that we as a people will get to the promised land. So I'm happy tonight. I'm not worried about anything. I'm not fearing any man.
Speech in Memphis, (1968) Speech given the day before King was assassinated **King, Martin Luther** (1929–1968) US civil rights leader and Baptist minister

54 Freedom's just another word for nothing left to lose.
'Me and Bobby McGee' (song, 1969) **Kristofferson, Kris** (1936–) US singer and film actor

55 So long as the state exists there is no freedom. When there is freedom there will be no state.
The State and Revolution (1917)

56 It is true that liberty is precious – so precious that it must be rationed.
In Sidney and Beatrice Webb, *Soviet Communism* (1936) **Lenin, V.I.** (1870–1924) Russian revolutionary, Marxist theoretician and first leader of the USSR

57 Those who deny freedom to others, deserve it not for themselves.
Speech, (1856)

58 I leave you, hoping that the lamp of liberty will burn in your bosoms, until there shall no longer be a doubt that all men are created free and equal.
Speech, (1858)

59 In giving freedom to the slave, we assure freedom to the free – honourable alike in what we give and what we preserve.
Speech, (1862) **Lincoln, Abraham** (1809–1865) US statesman and President

60 Freedom is always and exclusively freedom for the one who thinks differently.
The Russian Revolution (1922, trans. 1961) **Luxemburg, Rosa** (1871–1919) German revolutionary

61 Many politicians of our time are in the habit of laying it down as a self-evident proposition, that no people ought to be free till they are fit to use their freedom. The maxim is worthy of the fool in the old story, who resolved not to go into the water till he had learnt to swim. If men are to wait for liberty till they become wise and good in slavery, they may indeed wait for ever.
Collected Essays (1843)

62 There is only one cure for the evils which newly acquired freedom produces; and that is freedom.
Collected Essays (1843) **Macaulay, Lord** (1800–1859) English Liberal statesman, essayist and poet

63 No free man shall be taken or imprisoned or dispossessed, or outlawed or exiled, or in any way destroyed, nor will we go upon him, nor will we send against him, except by the lawful judgement of his peers or by the law of the land.
Clause 39 **Magna Carta** (1215)

64 You can't separate peace from freedom because no one can be at peace unless he has his freedom.
Malcolm X Speaks, (1965) **Malcolm X** (1925–1965) US black leader

65 I have fought against white domination, and I have fought against black domination. I have cherished the ideal of a democratic and free society in which all persons will live together in harmony and with equal opportunities. It is an ideal which I hope to live for and achieve. But, if needs be, it is an ideal for which I am prepared to die.
Statement in the dock, (1964)

66 A sudden access of psychological freedom often turns from sheer excitement to deep panic.
The Man Who Dreamed of Tomorrow (1980)

67 I cannot and will not give any undertaking at a time when I, and you, the people, are not free. Your freedom and mine cannot be separated.
Message to a rally in Soweto, (1985)

68 Never, never and never again shall it be that this beautiful land will again experience the oppression of one by another and suffer the indignity of being the skunk of the world.
Inauguration speech, (1994)

69 Let there be justice for all. Let there be peace for all. Let there be bread, water and salt for all. Let freedom reign. The sun shall never set on so glorious a human achievement.
Independent on Sunday, (14 May 1994) **Mandela, Nelson** (1918–) South African statesman and President

70 Recognition of the suffering inflicted on peoples by their own leaders is undermining the idea of absolute national sovereignty, just as recognition of the unacceptability of domestic violence undermined the idea of absolute patriarchal rights in the family.
Scotland on Sunday, (1992) **McMillan, Joyce** (1952–) Scottish critic

71 I am not aware that any community has a right to force another to be civilized.
On Liberty (1859)

72 If all mankind minus one, were of one opinion, and only one person were of the contrary opinion, mankind would be no more justified in silencing that one person, than he, if he had the power, would be justified in silencing mankind.
On Liberty (1859)

73 Liberty consists in doing what one desires.
On Liberty (1859)

74 The liberty of the individual must be thus far limited; he must not make himself a nuisance to other people.
On Liberty (1859)

75 The sole end for which mankind are warranted, individually or collectively, in interfering with the liberty of action of any of their number, is self-protection.
On Liberty (1859)

76 We can never be sure that the opinion we are endeavouring to stifle is a false opinion; and if we were sure, stifling it would be an evil still.
On Liberty (1859)

77 Whatever crushes individuality is despotism, by whatever name it may be called.
On Liberty (1859) **Mill, John Stuart** (1806–1873) English philosopher, economist and reformer

78 Give me the liberty to know, to utter, and to argue freely according to conscience, above all liberties.
Areopagitica (1644)

79 None can love freedom heartilie, but good men; the rest love not freedom, but licence.
The Tenure of Kings and Magistrates (1649) **Milton, John** (1608–1674) English poet, libertarian and pamphleteer

80 Freedom is the right to do whatever the laws permit.
De l'esprit des lois (1748) **Montesquieu, Charles** (1689–1755) French philosopher and jurist

81 There are freedoms; freedom has never existed.
Speech, (1923) **Mussolini, Benito** (1883–1945) Italian fascist dictator

82 I sometimes think that the price of liberty is not so much eternal vigilance as eternal dirt.
The Road to Wigan Pier (1937) **Orwell, George** (1903–1950) English writer and critic

83 What we suffragettes aspire to be when we are enfranchised is ambassadors of freedom to women in other parts of the world, who are not so free as we are.
Speech, (1915) **Pankhurst, Dame Christabel** (1880–1958) English suffragette

84 Necessity is the plea for every infringement of human freedom. It is the argument of tyrants; it is the creed of slaves.
Speech, (1783) **Pitt, William** (1759–1806) English politician and Prime Minister

85 We must plan for freedom, and not only for security, if for no other reason than that only freedom can make security secure.
The Open Society and its Enemies (1945) **Popper, Sir Karl** (1902–1994) Austrian-born British philosopher

86 In their rules there was only this one clause: 'Do what you will.'
Gargantua (1534) **Rabelais, François** (c.1494–c.1553) French monk, physician, satirist and humanist. Referring to the fictional Abbey of Thélème

87 Intellectual freedom cannot exist without political freedom; political freedom cannot exist without economic freedom; a free mind and a free market are corollaries.
For the New Intellectual **Rand, Ayn** (1905–1982) Russian-born US writer

88 I favour the Civil Rights act of 1964, and it must be enforced at gunpoint if necessary.
Attr. (1965) **Reagan, Ronald** (1911–2002) US actor, later US President

89 O liberty! O liberty! how many crimes are committed in your name!
In Lamartine, *Histoire des Girondins* (1847) **Roland, Madame** (1754–1793) French revolutionary and writer. Remark on mounting the scaffold

90 In the future days, which we seek to make secure, we look forward to a world founded upon four essential human freedoms. The first is freedom of speech and expression – everywhere in the world. The second is freedom of every person to worship God in his own way – everywhere in the world. The third is freedom from want ... The fourth is freedom from fear.
Address, (1941) **Roosevelt, Franklin Delano** (1882–1945) US Democrat President

91 Man was born free, and everywhere he is in chains.
Du Contrat Social (1762) **Rousseau, Jean-Jacques** (1712–1778) Swiss-born French philosopher, educationist and essayist

92 Once freedom has exploded in the soul of a man, the gods have no more power over him.
The Flies (1943)

93 Man is condemned to be free.
Existentialism and Humanism **Sartre, Jean-Paul** (1905–1980) French philosopher, writer, dramatist and critic

94 I must have liberty
Withal, as large a charter as the wind,
To blow on whom I please.
As You Like It, II.vii **Shakespeare, William**
(1564–1616) English dramatist, poet and actor

95 The golden rule is that there are no golden rules.
Man and Superman (1903)

96 Liberty means responsibility. That is why most men dread it.
Man and Superman (1903) **Shaw, George Bernard** (1856–1950) Irish socialist, writer, dramatist and critic

97 I love liberty, but hope that it can be so managed that I shall have soft beds, good dinners, fine linen, etc., for the rest of my life. I am too old to fight or to suffer.
Letter to J.A. Murray, (3rd January, 1830) **Smith, Sydney** (1771–1845) English clergyman, essayist, journalist and wit

98 You took my freedom away long ago and you can't give it back to me because you haven't got it yourself.
The First Circle (1968)

99 You only have power over people as long as you don't take everything away from them. But when you've robbed a man of everything he's no longer in your power – he's free again.
The First Circle (1968) **Solzhenitsyn, Alexander** (1918–) Russian writer, dramatist and historian

100 My definition of a free society is a society where it is safe to be unpopular.
Speech, Detroit, (1952)

101 A hungry man is not a free man.
Speech, (1962) **Stevenson, Adlai** (1900–1965) US lawyer, statesman and United Nations ambassador

102 Strict censorship cannot be maintained without terrorism.
Index on Censorship, (1996) **Stromme, Sigmund** (1946–) Norwegian publisher

103 Sometimes you've got to let everything go … purge yourself. If you are unhappy with anything … whatever is bringing you down, get rid of it. Because you'll find that when you're free, your true creativity, your true self comes out.
I, Tina (1986) **Turner, Tina** (1938–) US singer

104 It is by the goodness of God that in our country we have those three unspeakably precious things: freedom of speech, freedom of conscience, and the prudence never to practise either of them.
Following the Equator (1897) **Twain, Mark** (1835–1910) US humorist, writer, journalist and lecturer

105 All human beings are born free and equal in dignity and rights.
Article 1 **Universal Declaration of Human Rights**

106 Liberty was born in England from the quarrels of tyrants.
Lettres philosophiques (1734)

107 I disapprove of what you say, but I will defend to the death your right to say it.
Attr. **Voltaire** (1694–1778) French philosopher, dramatist, poet, historian, writer and critic

108 Liberty, when it begins to take root, is a plant of rapid growth.
Letter, (1788) **Washington, George** (1732–1799) US general, statesman and President

109 Am I not a man and a brother?
Motto adopted by Anti-Slavery Society **Wedgwood, Josiah** (1730–1795) English potter, manufacturer and pamphleteer

110 He who would be free – must not conform.
The Fortnightly Review, (1891) **Wilde, Oscar** (1854–1900) Irish poet, dramatist, writer, critic and wit

111 Freedom is an indivisible word. If we want to enjoy it, and fight for it, we must be prepared to extend it to everyone, whether they are rich or poor, whether they agree with us or not, no matter what their race or the colour of their skin.
One World (1943) **Willkie, Wendell** (1892–1944) US lawyer, industrialist and Republican politician

112 The history of liberty is a history of
resistance.
Speech, (1912) **Wilson, Woodrow** (1856–1924)
US Democrat President

FRIENDSHIP

1 One friend in a lifetime is much; two are
many; three are hardly possible. Friendship
needs a certain parallelism of life, a
community of thought, a rivalry of aim.
The Education of Henry Adams (1918)

2 A friend in power is a friend lost.
The Education of Henry Adams (1918) **Adams,
Henry** (1838–1918) US historian and
memoirist

3 Friendships, in general, are suddenly
contracted; and therefore it is no wonder
they are easily dissolved.
*Interesting Anecdotes, Memoirs, Allegories, Essays,
and Poetical Fragments* (1794) **Addison, Joseph**
(1672–1719) English essayist, poet, playwright
and statesman

4 On being asked what is a friend, he said 'A
single soul dwelling in two bodies.'
In Diogenes Laertius, *Lives of Philosophers*
Aristotle (384–322 BC) Greek philosopher

5 There was a wonderful consimility of
phansey between him and Mr John
Fletcher, which caused that dearness of
friendship between them ... They lived
together on the Bank side, not far from the
Playhouse, both bachelors; lay together;
had one wench in the house between
them, which they did so admire; the same
clothes and cloak, &c.; between them.
Brief Lives (c.1693) **Aubrey, John** (1626–1697)
English antiquary, folklorist and biographer.
Of Francis Beaumont

6 It is the worst solitude, to have no true
friendships.
The Advancement of Learning (1605)

7 A false friend is more dangerous than an
open enemy.
A Letter of Advice ... to the Duke of Buckingham
(1616)

8 This communicating of a man's self to his
friend works two contrary effects; for it
redoubleth joys, and cutteth griefs in
halves.
Essays (1625) **Bacon, Francis** (1561–1626)
English philosopher, essayist, politician and
courtier

9 From quiet homes and first beginning,
Out to the undiscovered ends,
There's nothing worth the wear of winning,
But laughter and the love of friends.
Verses (1910) **Belloc, Hilaire** (1870–1953)
English writer of verse, essayist and critic;
Liberal MP

10 Yea, mine own familiar friend, in whom I
trusted, which did eat of my bread, hath
lifted up his heel against me.
Psalms, 41:9

11 Be not forgetful to entertain strangers: for
thereby some have entertained angels
unawares.
Hebrews, 13:2

12 Forsake not an old friend; for the new is
not comparable to him; a new friend is as
new wine; when it is old, thou shalt drink it
with pleasure.
Apocrypha, Ecclesiasticus

13 A faithful friend is a sturdy shelter: he that
has found one has found a treasure. There
is nothing so precious as a faithful friend,
and no scales can measure his excellence.
Apocrypha, Ecclesiasticus **The Bible (King James
Version)**

14 *Antipathy*: The sentiment inspired by one's
friend's friend.
The Enlarged Devil's Dictionary (1961) **Bierce,
Ambrose** (1842–c.1914) US writer, verse writer
and soldier

15 I've noticed your hostility towards him ... I
ought to have guessed you were friends.
The History Man (1975) **Bradbury, Malcolm**
(1932–) English writer, critic and academic

16 I'm wary of him. We're friends.
Mother Courage and her Children (1941) **Brecht,
Bertolt** (1898–1956) German dramatist

17 Love is like the wild rose-briar,
Friendship like the holly-tree,
The holly is dark when the rose-briar
blooms
But which will bloom most constantly?
'Love and Friendship' **Brontë, Emily** (1818–
1848) English poet and writer

18 There is no man so friendless but what he
can find a friend sincere enough to tell him
disagreeable truths.
What Will He Do With It? (1857) **Bulwer-Lytton,
Edward** (1803–1873) English novelist and
politician

19 Friendship is Love without his wings.
'L'amitié est l'amour sans ailes' (1806) **Byron,
Lord** (1788–1824) English poet satirist and
traveller

20 Give me the avowed, erect and manly foe;
Firm I can meet, perhaps return the blow;
But of all plagues, good Heaven, thy wrath
can send,
Save me, oh, save me, from the candid
friend.
'New Morality' (1821) **Canning, George** (1770–
1827) English Prime Minister, orator and poet

21 Two may talk together under the same roof
for many years, yet never really meet; and
two others at first speech are old friends.
Mackinac and Lake Stories, 'Marianson'
Catherwood, Mary (1847–1901)

22 Tell me the company you keep, and I'll tell
you who you are.
Don Quixote, II (1615) **Cervantes, Miguel de**
(1547–1616) Spanish writer and dramatist

23 Life becomes useless and insipid when we
have no longer either friends or enemies.
Pensées de Christine, reine de Suede (1825)
Christina of Sweden (1626–1689) Queen of
Sweden

24 Greatly his foes he dreads, but more his
friends;
He hurts me most who lavishly
commends.
'The Apology, addressed to the Critical
Reviewers' (1761) **Churchill, Charles** (1731–
1764) English poet, political writer and
clergyman

25 My true friends have always given me that
supreme proof of devotion, a spontaneous
aversion for the man I loved.
Break of Day (1928) **Colette** (1873–1954) French
writer

26 At any time you might act for my good.
When people do that, it kills something
precious between them.
Manservant and Maidservant (1947) **Compton-
Burnett, Dame Ivy** (1884–1969) English
novelist

27 Have no friends not equal to yourself.
Analects **Confucius** (c.550–c.478 BC) Chinese
philosopher and teacher of ethics

28 Acquaintance I would have, but when't
depends
Not on the number, but the choice of
friends.
Essays in Verse and Prose (1668) **Cowley,
Abraham** (1618–1667) English poet and
dramatist

29 Change your friends.
Attr. **De Gaulle, Charles** (1890–1970) French
general and statesman. Replying to Jacques
Soustelle's complaint that he was being
attacked by his own friends

30 Friendships begin with liking or gratitude
– roots that can be pulled up.
Daniel Deronda (1876) **Eliot, George** (1819–
1880) English writer and poet

31 The only reward of virtue is virtue; the only
way to have a friend is to be one.
'Friendship' (1841)

32 A friend may well be reckoned the
masterpiece of Nature.
'Friendship' (1841)

33 A friend is a person with whom I may be
sincere. Before him I may think aloud.
'Friendship' (1841)

34 Let the soul be assured that somewhere in
the universe it should rejoin its friend, and
it would be content and cheerful alone for
a thousand years.
'Friendship' (1841) **Emerson, Ralph Waldo**
(1803–1882) US poet, essayist,
transcendentalist and teacher

35 It is not so much our friends' help that helps us as the confident knowledge that they will help us.
Attr. **Epicurus** (341–270 BC) Greek philosopher and teacher

36 One single minute of reconciliation is worth more than an entire life of friendship.
One Hundred Years of Solitude (1968) **García Márquez, Gabriel** (1928–) Colombian author

37 A woman's friendship ever ends in love.
Dione (1720)

38 An open foe may prove a curse,
But a pretended friend is worse.
Fables (1727) **Gay, John** (1685–1732) English poet, dramatist and librettist

39 All his faults are such that one loves him still the better for them.
The Good Natur'd Man (1768)

40 Friendship is a disinterested commerce between equals; love, an abject intercourse between tyrants and slaves.
The Good Natur'd Man (1768) **Goldsmith, Oliver** (c.1728–1774) Irish dramatist, poet and writer

41 I have no trouble with my enemies. I can take care of my enemies all right. But my damn friends … They're the ones that keep me walking the floor nights!
Autobiography (1946) **Harding, Warren G.** (1865–1923) US statesman and Republican President

42 But love is lost, the way of friendship's gone,
Though David had his Jonathan, Christ his John.
The Temple (1633), 'The Church-Porch' **Herbert, George** (1593–1633) English poet and priest

43 Friendship is tested in the thick years of success rather than in the thin years of struggle.
In Green, *A Dictionary of Contemporary Quotations* (1982) **Humphries, Barry** (1934–) Australian entertainer

44 The endearing elegance of female friendship.

Rasselas (1759)

45 Friendship is not always the sequel of obligation.
The Lives of the Most Eminent English Poets (1779–1781)

46 How few of his friends' houses would a man choose to be at when he is sick.
In Boswell, *The Life of Samuel Johnson* (1791)

47 If a man does not make new acquaintance as he advances through life, he will soon find himself left alone. A man, Sir, should keep his friendship in constant repair.
In Boswell, *The Life of Samuel Johnson* (1791) **Johnson, Samuel** (1709–1784) English lexicographer, poet, critic, conversationalist and essayist

48 Friends are God's apology for relations.
In Ingrams, *God's Apology* (1977) **Kingsmill, Hugh** (1889–1949) English critic and writer

49 In the misfortunes of our closest friends, we always find something which is not displeasing to us.
Maximes (1665)

50 There is more shame in distrusting one's friends than in being deceived by them.
Maximes (1678) **La Rochefoucauld** (1613–1680) French writer

51 Friendship is unnecessary, like philosophy, like art. … It has no survival value; rather it is one of those things that give value to survival.
The Four Loves (c.1936) **Lewis, C.S.** (1898–1963) Irish-born English academic, writer and critic

52 Friendships that are acquired with money, and not through greatness and nobility of character, are paid for but not secured, and prove unreliable just when they are needed.
The Prince **Machiavelli** (1469–1527) Florentine statesman, political theorist and historian

53 We read that we ought to forgive our enemies; but we do not read that we ought to forgive our friends.
In Bacon, *Apophthegms* (1625) **Medici, Cosimo de'** (1389–1464) Member of Medici family, rulers of Tuscany and Florence

54 People who need people are the luckiest people in the world.
'People Who Need People' (song, 1964) **Merrill, Bob** (1921–1998) US songwriter

55 If I am pressed to say why I loved him, I feel it can only be explained by replying: 'Because it was he; because it was me.'
Essais (1580) **Montaigne, Michel de** (1533–1592) French essayist and moralist. Of his friend Étienne de la Boétie

56 True friendship's laws are by this rule express'd,
Welcome the coming, speed the parting guest.
The Odyssey (1726)

57 How often are we to die before we go quite off this stage? In every friend we lose a part of ourselves, and the best part.
Letter to Swift, (1732) **Pope, Alexander** (1688–1744) English poet, translator and editor

58 Friends share all things.
In Diogenes Laertius, *Lives of Eminent Philosophers* **Pythagoras** (6th century BC) Greek philosopher and mathematician

59 Was never eye, did see that face,
Was never ear, did hear that tongue,
Was never mind, did mind his grace,
That ever thought the travel long –
But eyes, and ears, and ev'ry thought,
Were with his sweet perfections caught.
'An Elegy, or Friend's Passion, for his Astrophill' (1593) **Roydon, Matthew** (fl. 1580–1622) English poet

60 To like and dislike the same things, this in the end is the basis of true friendship.
Catiline **Sallust** (86–c.34 BC) Roman historian and statesman

61 Old friends are best. King James used to call for his old shoes; they were easiest for his feet.
Table Talk (1689) **Selden, John** (1584–1654) English historian, jurist and politician

62 Give me that man
That is not passion's slave, and I will wear him
In my heart's core, ay, in my heart of heart,
As I do thee.
Hamlet, III.ii

63 Friendship is constant in all other things
Save in the office and affairs of love.
Much Ado About Nothing, II.i

64 I count myself in nothing else so happy
As in a soul rememb'ring my good friends.
Richard II, II.iii **Shakespeare, William** (1564–1616) English dramatist, poet and actor

65 I cannot forgive my friends for dying; I do not find these vanishing acts of theirs at all amusing.
Afterthoughts (1931)

66 I might give my life for my friend, but he had better not ask me to do up a parcel.
Afterthoughts (1931) **Smith, Logan Pearsall** (1865–1946) US-born British epigrammatist, critic and writer

67 I like familiarity. In me it does not breed contempt. Only more familiarity.
Dale Carnegie's Scrapbook **Stein, Gertrude** (1874–1946) US writer, dramatist, poet and critic

68 In all distresses of our friends,
We first consult our private ends;
While nature, kindly bent to ease us,
Points out some circumstance to please us –
Some great misfortune to portend,
No enemy can match a friend.
'Verses on the Death of Dr. Swift' (1731) **Swift, Jonathan** (1667–1745) Irish satirist, poet, essayist and cleric

69 Enemies publish themselves. They declare war. The friend never declares his love.
Journal, (1856) **Thoreau, Henry David** (1817–1862) US essayist, social critic and writer

70 The holy passion of Friendship is of so sweet and steady and loyal and enduring a nature that it will last through a whole lifetime, if not asked to lend money.
Pudd'nhead Wilson's Calendar (1894)

71 The proper office of a friend is to side with you when you are in the wrong. Nearly anybody will side with you when you are in the right.
Attr. **Twain, Mark** (1835–1910) US humorist, writer, journalist and lecturer

72 Whenever a friend succeeds, a little something in me dies.
The Sunday Times Magazine, (1973) **Vidal, Gore** (1925–) US writer, critic and poet

73 Be courteous to all, but intimate with few, and let those few be well tried before you give them your confidence. True friendship is a plant of slow growth, and must undergo and withstand the shocks of adversity before it is entitled to the appellation.
Letter, (1783) **Washington, George** (1732–1799) US general, statesman and President

74 We cherish our friends not for their ability to amuse us, but for our ability to amuse them.
Attr. **Waugh, Evelyn** (1903–1966) English writer and diarist

75 I no doubt deserved my enemies, but I don't believe I deserved my friends.
In Bradford, *Biography and the Human Heart* **Whitman, Walt** (1819–1892) US poet and writer

76 I have lost friends, some by death ... others through sheer inability to cross the street.
The Waves (1931) **Woolf, Virginia** (1882–1941) English writer and critic

77 We flatter those we scarcely know,
We please the fleeting guest,
And deal full many a thoughtless blow
To those who love us best.
'Life's Scars' (1917) **Wilcox, Ella Wheeler** (1850–1919) US poet and writer

78 Always we'd have the new friend meet the old
And we are hurt if either friend seem cold.
In the *English Review,* (1918)

79 Think where man's glory most begins and ends,
And say my glory was I had such friends.
'The Municipal Gallery Revisited' (1937) **Yeats, W.B.** (1865–1939) Irish poet, dramatist, editor, writer and senator

THE FUTURE

1 I don't know what the future may hold, but I know who holds the future.
In Andrew Young, *A Way Out of No Way* (1994) **Abernathy, Ralph** (1926–1990) US religious and civil rights leader

2 Always remember that the future comes one day at a time.
Sketches From Life **Acheson, Dean** (1893–1971) US Democrat politician

3 'We are always doing,' says he, 'something for Posterity, but I would fain see Posterity do something for us.'
The Spectator, (August 1714) **Addison, Joseph** (1672–1719) English essayist, poet, playwright and statesman

4 Men must pursue things which are just in present, and leave the future to the divine Providence.
The Advancement of Learning (1605) **Bacon, Francis** (1561–1626) English philosopher, essayist, politician and courtier

5 He who asks fortune-tellers the future unwittingly forfeits an inner intimation of coming events that is a thousand times more exact than anything they may say.
One-Way Street (1928) **Benjamin, Walter** (1892–1940) German writer, philosopher and critic

6 The people who live in the past must yield to the people who live in the future. Otherwise the world would begin to turn the other way round.
Attr. **Bennett, Arnold** (1867–1931) English writer, dramatist and journalist

7 The future ain't what it used to be.
Attr. **Berra, Yogi** (1925–) US baseball player

8 *Future*: That period of time in which our affairs prosper, our friends are true and our happiness is assured.
The Cynic's Word Book (1906) **Bierce, Ambrose** (1842–c.1914) US writer, verse writer and soldier

9 You can never plan the future by the past.
Letter to a Member of the National Assembly (1791) **Burke, Edmund** (1729–1797) Irish-born British statesman and philosopher

10 The future is the only kind of property that the masters willingly concede to slaves.
The Rebel (1951) **Camus, Albert** (1913–1960) Algerian-born French writer

11 The empires of the future are empires of the mind.
Speech, (1943) **Churchill, Sir Winston** (1874–1965) English Conservative Prime Minister

12 Often do the spirits
Of great events stride on before the events,
And in to-day already walks to-morrow.
'Death of Wallenstein' (1800) **Coleridge, Samuel Taylor** (1772–1834) English poet, philosopher and critic

13 Study the past, if you would divine the future.
Analects **Confucius** (c.550–c.478 BC) Chinese philosopher and teacher of ethics

14 I don't give a hoot about posterity. Why should I worry about what people think of me when I'm dead as a doornail anyway?
Present Laughter (1943) **Coward, Sir Noël** (1899–1973) English dramatist, actor, producer and composer

15 I still lived in the future – a habit which is the death of happiness.
The Naked Civil Servant (1968) **Crisp, Quentin** (1908–1999) English writer, publicist and model

16 What we anticipate seldom occurs; what we least expected generally happens.
Henrietta Temple (1837)

17 He seems to think that posterity is a pack-horse, always ready to be loaded.
Speech, House of Commons, (1862) **Disraeli, Benjamin** (1804–1881) English statesman and writer

18 I have learned to live each day as it comes, and not to borrow trouble by dreading tomorrow. It is the dark menace of the future that makes cowards of us.
Dorothy Dix, Her Book (1926) **Dix, Dorothy** (1870–1951) US writer

19 I never think of the future. It comes soon enough.
Interview, (1930) **Einstein, Albert** (1879–1955) German-born US mathematical physicist

20 I have seen the future and it sucks.
Pictures of Perfection (1994) **Hill, Reginald** (1936–) British writer and playwright

21 In the twentieth century, war will be dead, the scaffold will be dead, hatred will be dead, frontier boundaries will be dead, dogmas will be dead; man will live. He will possess something higher than all these – a great country, the whole earth, and a great hope, the whole heaven.
The Future of Man **Hugo, Victor** (1802–1885) French poet, writer, dramatist and politician

22 The future is purchased by the present.
Attr. **Johnson, Samuel** (1709–1784) English lexicographer, poet, critic, conversationalist and essayist

23 The Future is something which everyone reaches at the rate of sixty minutes an hour, whatever he does, whoever he is.
The Screwtape Letters (1942) **Lewis, C.S.** (1898–1963) Irish-born English academic, writer and critic

24 You don't fight hand-to-hand with the past. The future conquers it because it swallows it. If it leaves part of it outside, it is lost.
The Rebellion of the Masses (1930) **Ortega y Gasset, José** (1883–1955) Spanish philosopher

25 If you want a picture of the future, imagine a boot stamping on a human face – for ever.
Nineteen Eighty-Four (1949) **Orwell, George** (1903–1950) English writer and critic

26 The future bears a resemblance to the past, only more so.
The Popcorn Report (1991) **Popcorn, Faith** (1947–) US management consultant

27 What we call our future is the shadow which our past throws in front of us.
À l'ombre des jeunes filles en fleurs (1918) **Proust, Marcel** (1871–1922) French writer and critic

28 The future will be better tomorrow.
Attr. **Quayle, Dan** (1947–) US Republican politician and Vice President

29 What has posterity done for us?
Speech, (1780) **Roche, Sir Boyle** (1743–1807) Irish politician

30 Common men can show astonishing fortitude in chasing jam tomorrow. Jam today, and men aren't at their most exciting: jam tomorrow, and one often sees them at their noblest.
The Two Cultures and the Scientific Revolution (1959) **Snow, C.P.** (1905–1980) English writer, critic, physicist and public administrator. On industrialization

31 I have seen the future; and it works.
Letter to Marie Howe, (1919) **Steffens, Lincoln** (1866–1936) US political analyst and writer. Remark after visiting Russia in 1919

32 The future is made of the same stuff as the present.
On Science, Necessity, and the Love of God **Weil, Simone** (1909–1943) French philosopher, essayist and mystic

33 One thousand years more. That's all *Homo sapiens* has before him.
In H. Nicolson, *Diary* **Wells, H.G.** (1866–1946) English writer

34 The future is called 'perhaps', which is the only possible thing to call the future. And the important thing is not to allow that to scare you.
Attr. **Williams, Tennessee** (1911–1983) US dramatist and writer
See also destiny; hope; time

GARDEN

1 I value my garden more for being full of blackbirds than of cherries, and very frankly give them fruit for their songs.
The Spectator, (1712) **Addison, Joseph** (1672–1719) English essayist, poet, playwright and statesman

2 Gardening is not a rational act.
Bluebeard's Egg (1986) **Atwood, Margaret** (1939–) Canadian writer, poet and critic

3 God Almighty first planted a garden; and, indeed, it is the purest of human pleasures. It is the greatest refreshment to the spirits of man; without which, buildings and palaces are but gross handiworks.

'Of Gardens' (1625) **Bacon, Francis** (1561–1626) English philosopher, essayist, politician and courtier

4 A garden is a lovesome thing, God wot!
'My Garden' (1893) **Brown, Thomas Edward** (1830–1897) Manx poet, teacher and curate

5 I try to express in a physical form what I feel on an inner level. I think a garden should delight the eye, warm the heart and feed the soul.
Attr. **Charles, Prince of Wales** (1948–) Son and heir of Elizabeth II and Prince Philip

6 It is only when you start to plant a garden – probably after fifty – that you realize that something important happens every day.
The Opinionated Gardener, (1988) **Charlesworth, Geoffrey** Garden writer

7 God the first garden made, and the first city Cain.
'The Garden' (1668) **Cowley, Abraham** (1618–1667) English poet and dramatist

8 Here is a brighter garden,
Where not a frost has been;
In its unfading flowers
I hear the bright bee hum;
Prithee, my brother,
Into my garden come!
'There Is Another Sky'; lines in a letter to her brother Austin, (17th October 1851) **Dickinson, Emily** (1830–1886) US poet

9 ...the one smell that is more heart-racingly beautiful than the scent of any plant, and impossible to capture or contain within a garden, is the smell of warm, dusty soil immediately after a light shower of rain.
The Sensuous Garden (1997)

10 You do not need to know anything about a plant to know that it is beautiful.
The Sensuous Garden (1997) **Don, Montagu (Monty)** (1955–) English garden writer and TV presenter

11 What is a weed? A plant whose virtues have not yet been discovered.
Fortune of the Republic (1878) **Emerson, Ralph Waldo** (1803–1882) US poet, essayist, transcendentalist and teacher

12 Daisies smell-less, yet most quaint,
And sweet thyme true,
Primrose first born child of Ver,
Merry Springtime's Harbinger.
Two Noble Kinsmen (with Shakespeare, 1634)
Fletcher, John (1579–1625) English dramatist

13 The best time to take cuttings is when no
one is looking.
Attr. **Flowerdew, Bob** English organic
gardener

14 Sowe Carrets in your Gardens, and humbly
praise God for them, as for a singular and
great blessing.
*Profitable Instructions for the Manuring, Sowing
and Planting of Kitchen Gardens* (1599) **Gardiner,
Richard** (b. c.1533) English writer

15 The kiss of the sun for pardon,
The song of the birds for mirth,
One is nearer God's Heart in a garden
Than anywhere else on earth.
'God's Garden' (1913) **Gurney, Dorothy** (1858–
1932) English poet

16 No garden can really be too small to hold a
peony. Had I but four square feet of
ground at my disposal, I would plant a
peony in the center and proceed to
worship.
Peonies in the Little Garden, (1923) **Harding, Mrs
Edward** English garden writer

17 Of all human activities, apart from the
procreation of children, gardening is the
most optimistic and hopeful. The gardener
is by definition one who plans for and
believes and trusts in a future, whether in
the short or long term.
Through the Garden Gate **Hill, Susan** (1942–)
English author

18 A garden is to be enjoyed and should
satisfy the mind and not only the eye of the
beholder.
Quoted in *A Gardener's Bouquet of Quotations,*
(1993) **Hobhouse, Penelope** (1929–) English
garden writer

19 The Dahlia's first duty in life is to flaunt
and to swagger and to carry gorgeous
blooms well above its leaves, and on no
account to hang its head.
Wood and Garden, (1889)

20 The love of gardening is a seed once sown
that never dies.
Quoted in *Gardener's Companion* **Jekyll,
Gertrude** (1843–1932) English garden designer
and writer

21 A single flower could impress you with
more gorgeousness than one hundred
such.
'Japan the Beautiful and I' (1968) **Kawabata,
Yasunari** (1899–1972) Japanese novelist

22 Oh, Adam was a gardener, and God who
made him sees
That half a proper gardener's work is done
upon his knees,
So when your work is finished, you can
wash your hands and pray
For the Glory of the Garden, that it may
not pass away!
And the Glory of the Garden it shall never
pass away!
Songs written for C.R.L. Fletcher's *A History of
England* (1911) **Kipling, Rudyard** (1865–1936)
Indian-born British poet and writer

23 Here at the fountain's sliding foot,
Or at some fruit-tree's mossy root,
Casting the body's vest aside,
My soul into the boughs does glide.
'The Garden' (1681)

24 Annihilating all that is made
to a green thought in a green shade.
'The Garden' (1681)

25 I have a garden of my own,
But so with roses overgrown,
And lilies, that you would it guess
To be a little wilderness.
'The Nymph Complaining for the Death of
her Fawn' (1681) **Marvell, Andrew** (1621–1678)
English poet and satirist

26 And add to these retired leisure,
That in trim gardens takes his pleasure.
'Il Penseroso' (1645) **Milton, John** (1608–1674)
English poet, libertarian and pamphleteer

27 My neighbour asked if he could borrow my
lawnmower and I told him of course so
long as he didn't take it out of my garden.
Attr. **Morecambe, Eric** (1926–1984) English
comedian

28 Gertrude Jekyll, like Monet, was a painter
with poor eyesight, and their gardens – his
at Giverny in the Seine valley, hers in
Surrey – had resemblances that may have
sprung from this condition. Both loved
plants that foamed and frothed over walls
and pergolas, spread in tides beneath
trees; both saw flowers in islands of
coloured light – an image the normal eye
captures only by squinting.
Green Thoughts, (1981) **Perenyi, Eleanor**
(1920–) Hungarian-born English garden
writer

29 Every time I talk to a savant I feel quite sure
that happiness is no longer a possibility.
Yet when I talk to my gardener, I'm
convinced of the opposite.
Attr. **Russell, Bertrand** (1872–1970) English
philosopher, mathematician, essayist and
social reformer

30 'Tis in ourselves that we are thus or thus.
Our bodies are our gardens to the which
our wills are gardeners.
Othello, I.iii **Shakespeare, William** (1564–1616)
English dramatist, poet and actor

31 Won't you come into the garden? I would
like my roses to see you.
Attr. **Sheridan, Richard Brinsley** (1751–1816)
Irish dramatist, politician and orator

32 A weed is simply a plant that you don't
want.
The Observer, (1983) **Simmons, John** (1937–)
English gardener and curator

33 Come into the garden, Maud,
For the black bat, night, has flown,
Come into the garden, Maud,
I am here at the gate alone;
And the woodbine spices are wafted
abroad,
And the musk of the rose is blown.
Maud (1855) **Tennyson, Alfred, Lord** (1809–
1892) English lyric poet

34 Nothing grows in our garden, only
washing. And babies.
Under Milk Wood (1954) **Thomas, Dylan** (1914–
1953) Welsh poet, writer and radio dramatist

35 We may think we are tending our garden,
but of course, in many different ways, it is
the garden and the plants that are
nurturing us.
A Little History of British Gardening **Uglow,
Jenny** English author

36 'That is well said,' replied Candide, 'but we
must cultivate our garden.'
Candide (1759) **Voltaire** (1694–1778) French
philosopher, dramatist, poet, historian, writer
and critic

37 What a man needs in gardening is a cast-
iron back, with a hinge in it.
My Summer in a Garden, (1871) **Warner, Charles
Dudley** (1829–1900) US author
See also birds; nature

GENIUS

1 A genius is one who can do anything
except make a living.
Attr. **Adams, Joey** (1911–1999) US comedian
and author

2 It takes people a long time to learn the
difference between talent and genius,
especially ambitious young men and
women.
Little Women (1869)

3 Talent isn't genius and no amount of
energy can make it so. I want to be great,
or nothing. I won't be a commonplace
dauber, so I don't intend to try any more.
Little Women (1869) **Alcott, Louisa May** (1832–
1888) US writer

4 The difference between genius and
stupidity is that genius has its limits.
Anonymous

5 No amount of genius can overcome a
preoccupation with detail.
Levy's Eighth Law **Anonymous**

6 So we have the Philistine of genius in
religion – Luther; the Philistine of genius
in politics – Cromwell; the Philistine of
genius in literature – Bunyan.
Mixed Essays (1879) **Arnold, Matthew** (1822–
1888) English poet, critic, essayist and
educationist

7 I have known no man of genius who had not to pay, in some affliction or defect either physical or spiritual, for what the gods had given him.
And Even Now (1920) **Beerbohm, Sir Max** (1872–1956) English satirist, cartoonist, critic and essayist

8 Since when was genius found respectable?
Aurora Leigh (1857) **Browning, Elizabeth Barrett** (1806–1861) English poet; wife of Robert Browning

9 Everyone is born a genius, but the process of living de-geniuses them.
New York Post, (1968) **Buckminster Fuller, Richard** (1895–1983) US architect and engineer

10 Genius is merely a greater aptitude for patience.
In Hérault de Séchelles, *Voyage à Montbar* (1803) **Buffon, Comte de** (1707–1788) French naturalist

11 Genius ... has been defined as a supreme capacity for taking trouble ... It might be more fitly described as a supreme capacity for getting its possessors into pains of all kinds, and keeping them therein so long as the genius remains.
The Note-Books of Samuel Butler (1912) **Butler, Samuel** (1835–1902) English writer, painter, philosopher and scholar

12 'Genius' (which means transcendent capacity of taking trouble, first of all).
History of Frederick the Great (1858–1865) **Carlyle, Thomas** (1795–1881) Scottish historian, biographer, critic, and essayist

13 Genius is of no country.
The Rosciad (1761) **Churchill, Charles** (1731–1764) English poet, political writer and clergyman

14 I believe Shakespeare was not a whit more intelligible in his own day than he is now to an educated man, except for a few local allusions of no consequence. He is of no age – nor of any religion, or party or profession. The body and substance of his works came out of the unfathomable depths of his own oceanic mind: his observation and reading, which was considerable, supplied him with the drapery of his figures.

Table Talk (1835) **Coleridge, Samuel Taylor** (1772–1834) English poet, philosopher and critic

15 Mediocrity knows nothing higher than itself, but talent instantly recognizes genius.
The Valley of Fear (1914) **Doyle, Sir Arthur Conan** (1859–1930) Scottish writer and war correspondent

16 Genius is one per cent inspiration and ninety-nine per cent perspiration.
Life, (1932) **Edison, Thomas Alva** (1847–1931) US inventor and industrialist

17 To believe your own thought, to believe that what is true for you in your private heart is true for all men, – that is genius.
Essays, First Series (1841)

18 When Nature has work to be done, she creates a genius to do it.
Lecture, 1841, 'Method of Nature' **Emerson, Ralph Waldo** (1803–1882) US poet, essayist, transcendentalist and teacher

19 Taste is the feminine of genius.
Letter to J.R. Lowell, (1877) **Fitzgerald, Edward** (1809–1883) English poet, translator and letter writer

20 True Genius walks along a line, and, perhaps, our greatest pleasure is in seeing it so often near falling, without being ever actually down.
The Bee (1759) **Goldsmith, Oliver** (c.1728–1774) Irish dramatist, poet and writer

21 I'm the artist formerly known as Beck. I have a genius wig. When I put that wig on, then the true genius emerges. I don't have enough hair to be a genius. I think you have to have hair going everywhere.
Attr. **Hansen, Beck** (1970–) US musician and songwriter; real name Bek Campbell

22 Rules and models destroy genius and art.
'Thoughts on Taste' (1818) **Hazlitt, William** (1778–1830) English writer and critic

23 Unless one is a genius, it is best to aim at being intelligible.
The Dolly Dialogues (1894) **Hope, Anthony** (1863–1933) English writer, dramatist and lawyer

24 Gift, like genius, I often think, only means an infinite capacity for taking pains.
Work amongst Working Men, (1870) **Hopkins, Jane Ellice** (1836–1904) English social reformer and writer

25 One machine can do the work of fifty ordinary men. No machine can do the work of one extraordinary man.
A Thousand and One Epigrams (1911) **Hubbard, Elbert** (1856–1915) US printer, editor, writer and businessman

26 Whatever question there may be of his talent, there can be none, I think, of his genius. It was a slim and crooked one; but it was eminently personal. He was imperfect, unfinished, inartistic; he was worse than provincial – he was parochial.
Of Thoreau Hawthorne (1879) **James, Henry** (1843–1916) US-born British writer, critic and letter writer

27 The true genius is a mind of large general powers, accidentally determined to some particular direction.
The Lives of the Most Eminent English Poets (1779–1781) **Johnson, Samuel** (1709–1784) English lexicographer, poet, critic, conversationalist and essayist

28 He was not of an age, but for all time!
'To the Memory of My Beloved, the Author, Mr William Shakespeare' (1623)

29 Soul of the Age!
The applause! delight! the wonder of our stage!
My Shakespeare, rise; I will not lodge thee by
Chaucer, or Spenser, or bid Beaumont lie
A little further, to make thee a room:
Thou art a monument, without a tomb,
And art alive still, while thy book doth live,
And we have wits to read, and praise to give.
'To the Memory of My Beloved, the Author, Mr William Shakespeare' (1623) **Jonson, Ben** (1572–1637) English dramatist and poet

30 A man of genius makes no mistakes. His errors are volitional and are the portals of discovery.
Ulysses (1922) **Joyce, James** (1882–1941) Irish writer

31 So I do believe ... that works of genius are the first things in this world.
Letter to George and Tom Keats, (13 January 1818) **Keats, John** (1795–1821) English poet

32 ... probably the greatest concentration of talent and genius in this house, except for perhaps those times when Thomas Jefferson ate alone.
New York Times, (1962) **Kennedy, John F.** (1917–1963) US Democrat President. At a dinner held at the White House for Nobel prizewinners

33 Genius does what it must, and Talent does what it can.
'Last Words of a Sensitive Second-Rate Poet' (1868) **Meredith, Owen** (1831–1891) English statesman and poet

34 Shakespeare – the nearest thing in incarnation to the eye of God.
Kenneth Harris Talking To: 'Sir Laurence Olivier' **Olivier, Sir Laurence** (1907–1989) English actor and director

35 The way in which the man of genius rules is by persuading an efficient minority to coerce an indifferent and self-indulgent majority.
Liberty, Equality and Fraternity (1873) **Stephen, Sir James Fitzjames** (1829–1894) English judge and essayist

36 The Jews have produced only three originative geniuses: Christ, Spinoza, and myself.
In Mellow, *Charmed Circle* (1974) **Stein, Gertrude** (1874–1946) US writer, dramatist, poet and critic

37 When a true genius appears in the world, you may know him by this sign, that the dunces are all in confederacy against him.
Thoughts on Various Subjects (1711)

38 Good God! what a genius I had when I wrote that book.
In Sir Walter Scott, *Works of Swift* (1824) Of *A Tale of a Tub* **Swift, Jonathan** (1667–1745) Irish satirist, poet, essayist and cleric

39 A genius with the IQ of a moron.
The Observer, (1989) **Vidal, Gore** (1925–) US writer, critic and poet. Of Andy Warhol

40 The most amazing and effective inventions are not those which do most honour to the human genius.
Lettres philosophiques (1734) **Voltaire** (1694–1778) French philosopher, dramatist, poet, historian, writer and critic

41 One of the greatest geniuses that ever existed, Shakespeare, undoubtedly wanted taste.
Letter to Christopher Wren, (1764) **Walpole, Horace** (1717–1797) English writer and politician

42 Do you want to know the great tragedy of my life? I have put all of my genius into my life; all I've put into my works is my talent.
In Gide, *Oscar Wilde* (1910) Spoken to André Gide

43 I have nothing to declare except my genius.
In Harris, *Oscar Wilde* (1918) At the New York Customs **Wilde, Oscar** (1854–1900) Irish poet, dramatist, writer, critic and wit
See also greatness; intelligence; knowledge

GLOBAL AFFAIRS

1 New Zealanders are the most balanced people in the world – they have a chip on each shoulder.
A regular joke during his New Zealand tour, (1978) **Allen, Dave** (1936–2005) Irish comedian and television personality

2 Nations touch at their summits.
The English Constitution, (1867) **Bagehot, Walter** (1826–1877) English economist and political philosopher

3 His Majesty's Government views with favour the establishment in Palestine of a national home for the Jewish people.
'The Balfour Declaration', (1917) **Balfour, A.J.** (1848–1930) British Conservative Prime Minister

4 Let us not be deceived – we are today in the midst of a cold war.
Speech, (1947) **Baruch, Bernard** (1870–1965) US financier, government advisor and writer

5 The greatest military alliance in the world is becoming 'the gang that cannot shoot straight'.

Speech, House of Commons, (May 1999) **Bell, Martin** (1938–) English war correspondent and politician. Comment on NATO's accidental bombing of the Chinese Embassy in Belgrade

6 I consider the power of the German Empire ... to be more than that of an honest broker.
Speech, Reichstag, (1878) **Bismarck, Prince Otto von** (1815–1898) First Chancellor of the German Reich. Describing Germany's role in peace negotiations

7 Nations, like men, have their infancy.
Letters on Study and Use of History (1752) **Bolingbroke, Henry** (1678–1751) English statesman, historian and actor

8 Slavery they can have anywhere. It is a weed that grows in every soil.
Speech on Conciliation with America (1775) **Burke, Edmund** (1729–1797) Irish-born British statesman and philosopher

9 South Africa, renowned both far and wide
For politics and little else beside:
Where, having torn the land with shot and shell,
Our sturdy pioneers as farmers dwell,
And, 'twixt the hours of strenuous sleep, relax
To shear the fleeces or to fleece the blacks.
The Wayzgoose (1928) **Campbell, Roy** (1901–1957) South African poet and journalist

10 The day of small nations has long passed away. The day of Empires has come.
Speech, Birmingham, (1904) **Chamberlain, Joseph** (1836–1914) English politician

11 We do not covet anything from any nation except their respect.
Broadcast to the French people, (October 1940) **Churchill, Sir Winston** (1874–1965) English Conservative Prime Minister

12 People who come to this country and commit terrorist activities cannot expect to have a short holiday at the expense of our government and return home as heroes.

In Michael King, *Death of the Rainbow Warrior* (1986) **Davison, Sir Ronald Keith** (1920–) New Zealand judge. Giving judgement in the trial of Alain Mafart and Dominique Prieur, two French agents charged with manslaughter and wilful damage over the bombing of the Greenpeace vessel *Rainbow Warrior*

13 Colonies do not cease to be colonies because they are independent.
Speech, House of Commons, (1863) **Disraeli, Benjamin** (1804–1881) English statesman and writer

14 I was an expert on migration problems.
Attr. (1961) **Eichmann, Adolf** (1906–1962) Lieutenant Colonel in the SS. The man who put the final solution into place euphemistically describes his role

15 Saddam Hussein is not fit to have a finger on the nuclear trigger. And once we stop to think, nor is anyone else.
The Times, (1999) **Foot, Michael** (1913–) British Labour politician

16 I think it would be an excellent idea.
Attr. **Gandhi, Mohandas** (1869–1948) Indian political leader. When asked what he thought of Western civilization

17 The social progress, order, security and peace of each country are necessarily connected with the social progress, order, security and peace of all other countries.
Encyclical letter, (April 1963) **John XXIII** (1881–1963) Italian pope

18 If we cannot now end our differences, at least we can help make the world safe for diversity.
Speech, (1963)

19 The war against hunger is truly mankind's war of liberation.
Speech, (4 June 1963) **Kennedy, John F.** (1917–1963) US Democrat President

20 Take up the White Man's burden –
Send forth the best ye breed –
Go, bind your sons to exile
To serve your captives' need;
To wait in heavy harness
On fluttered folk and wild –
Your new-caught, sullen peoples,
Half devil and half child …

By all ye cry or whisper,
By all ye leave or do,
The silent, sullen peoples
Shall weigh your Gods and you.
'The White Man's Burden' (1899) **Kipling, Rudyard** (1865–1936) Indian-born British poet and writer

21 The great nations have always acted like gangsters, and the small nations like prostitutes.
The Guardian, (1963) **Kubrick, Stanley** (1928–1999) US screenwriter, producer and director

22 The statesmen of the world who boast and threaten that they have Doomsday weapons are far more dangerous, and far more estranged from 'reality', than many of the people on whom the label 'psychotic' is affixed.
The Divided Self (1960) **Laing, R.D.** (1927–1989) Scottish psychiatrist, psychoanalyst and poet

23 We are an enemy of the nuclear threat and we are an enemy of testing nuclear weapons in the South Pacific. New Zealand did not buy into this fight. France put agents into New Zealand. France put spies into New Zealand. France lets off bombs in the Pacific. France puts its President in the Pacific to crow about it.
In Michael King, *Death of the Rainbow Warrior* (1986) **Lange, David Russell** (1942–) New Zealand Prime Minister. A statement released during the investigations into the bombing of the Greenpeace vessel *Rainbow Warrior*, in 1985

24 Ah well! I am their leader, I really should be following them!
In E. de Mirecourt, *Histoire Contemporaine* (1857) **Ledru-Rollin, Alexandre Auguste** (1807–1874) French lawyer and politician. Trying to force his way through a mob during the 1848 revolution, of which he was one of the chief instigators.

25 The reluctant obedience of distant provinces generally costs more than it the territory is worth.
Collected Essays (1843), 'War of the Succession in Spain' **Macaulay, Lord** (1800–1859) English Liberal statesman, essayist and poet

26 Through its imperialist system Britain brought about untold suffering of millions of people. And this is an historical fact. To be able to admit this would increase the respect, you know, which we have for British institutions.
The Guardian, (1990) **Mandela, Nelson** (1918–) South African statesman and President

27 Imperialism is a paper tiger.
Quotations from Chairman Mao Tse-Tung **Mao Tse-Tung** (1893–1976) Chinese Communist leader

28 The hydrogen bomb is history's exclamation point. It ends an age-long sentence of manifest violence.
Attr. **McLuhan, Marshall** (1911–1980) Canadian communications theorist

29 We intend to remain alive. Our neighbours want to see us dead. This is not a question that leaves much room for compromise.
Reader's Digest, (1971)

30 Pessimism is a luxury that a Jew can never allow himself.
The Observer, (1974) **Meir, Golda** (1898–1978) Russian-born Israeli stateswoman and Prime Minister

31 Cricket civilizes people and creates good gentlemen. I want everyone to play cricket in Zimbabwe; I want ours to be a nation of gentlemen.
The Sunday Times, (1984) **Mugabe, Robert** (1924–) President of Zimbabwe

32 We knew the world would not be the same.
In Giovanitti and Freed, *The Decision to Drop the Bomb* (1965) **Oppenheimer, J. Robert** (1904–1967) US nuclear physicist. On the consequences of the first atomic test

33 Diplomacy is letting someone else have your way.
The Observer, (1965) **Pearson, Lester B.** (1897–1972) Canadian diplomat and politician

34 There is always something new out of Africa.
Historia Naturalis **Pliny the Elder** (AD 23–79) Roman scholar

35 Providence has given to the French the empire of the land, to the English that of the sea, and to the Germans that of – the air!
In Thomas Carlyle, 'Jean Paul Friedrich Richter' (1827) **Richter, Jean Paul Friedrich** (1763–1825) German humorist

36 Diplomacy is the art of saying 'nice doggy' until you can find a rock.
Attr. **Rogers, Will** (1879–1935) US humorist, actor, rancher, writer and wit

37 Imperialism, sane Imperialism, as distinguished from what I may call wild-cat Imperialism, is nothing but this – a larger patriotism.
Speech at a City Liberal Club dinner, (1899) **Rosebery, Earl of** (1847–1929) English statesman

38 We're eye-ball to eye-ball and the other fellow just blinked.
Remark, (1962) **Rusk, Dean** (1909–1994) US politician and diplomat. Of the Cuban missile crisis

39 The South African Police would leave no stone unturned to see that nothing disturbed the even tenor of their lives.
Indecent Exposure (1973) **Sharpe, Tom** (1928–) English writer

40 There is no evil in the atom; only in men's souls.
Speech, Hartford, Connecticut, (1952)

41 As the girl said, 'A kiss on the wrist feels good, but a diamond bracelet lasts forever.'
Address to Chicago Council on Foreign Relations **Stevenson, Adlai** (1900–1965) US lawyer, statesman and United Nations ambassador

42 The hand that signed the paper felled a city;
Five sovereign fingers taxed the breath,
Doubled the globe of death and halved a country;
These five kings did a king to death ...
The hand that signed the treaty bred a fever,
And famine grew, and locusts came;
Great is the hand that holds dominion over Man by a scribbled name.

'The hand that signed the paper' (1936)
Thomas, Dylan (1914–1953) Welsh poet, writer
and radio dramatist

43 No annihilation without representation.
Attr. **Toynbee, Arnold** (1889–1975) British
historian. Urging the need for a greater
British influence in the United Nations
Organization, 1947

44 When the white missionaries came to
Africa they had the Bible, and we had the
land. They said, 'Let us pray.' We closed
our eyes. When we opened them we had
the Bibles and they had the land.
Attr. **Tutu, Archbishop Desmond** (1931–)
South African cleric and statesman

45 To conquer is not to convince.
Speech, (1936) **Unamuno, Miguel de** (1864–
1936) Spanish philosopher, poet and writer.
Of Franco's supporters

46 A diplomat these days is nothing but a
head-waiter who's allowed to sit down
occasionally.
Romanoff and Juliet (1956) **Ustinov, Sir Peter**
(1921–2004) English actor, director, dramatist,
writer and raconteur

47 Today when science has perfected the
techniques of destruction, nuclear warfare
could mean the immediate annihilation of
what we know as civilisation, followed by a
slow infection of those who inhabit the less
directly involved surface of this globe – as
it revolves in space – swathed in its
contaminated shroud.
Speech to public meeting on nuclear
disarmament, Melbourne, (1981) **White,
Patrick** (1912–1990) English-born Australian
writer and dramatist

48 No nation is fit to sit in judgement upon
any other nation.
Speech, (1915) **Wilson, Woodrow** (1856–1924)
US Democrat President

49 An ambassador is an honest man sent to
lie abroad for the good of his country.
Written in an album, (1606) **Wotton, Sir
Henry** (1568–1639) English diplomat, traveller
and poet
See also politics; war; the world

GOD

1 The gods help those who help themselves.
'Hercules and the Waggoner' **Aesop**
(6th century BC) Legendary Greek writer of
fables

2 Even God is deprived of this one thing
only: the power to undo what has been
done.
In Aristotle, *Nicomachean Ethics* **Agathon**
(c.445–400 BC) Athenian poet

3 God doesn't believe in the easy way.
Attr. **Agee, James** (1909–1955) US novelist and
poet

4 God is working His purpose out as year
succeeds to year,
God is working His purpose out and the
time is drawing near;
Nearer and nearer draws the time, the time
that shall surely be,
When the earth shall be filled with the
glory of God as the waters cover the sea.
Hymn **Ainger, A.C.** (1841–1919) English writer,
lecturer and preacher

5 Man thinks, God directs.
Epistles **Alcuin** (735–804) English theologian,
scholar and educationist

6 What gets God by nobiscum? Nothing He.
What get we?
Sermon 9, Of the Nativity (c.1614) **Andrewes,
Bishop Lancelot** (1555–1626) English
churchman

7 Dear Sir,
Your astonishment's odd:
I am always about in the Quad.
And that's why the tree
Will continue to be,
Since observed by Yours faithfully, God.
Reply to Ronald Knox, 'There was once a
man' *(see God, 48)* **Anonymous**

8 For people who are hungry and inactive,
God can only appear in the form of work
and food.
The Little Rich Boy (1961) **Asturias, Miguel
Angel** (1899–1974) Guatemalan writer and poet

9 Thou hast created us for Thyself, and our
heart is restless till it finds rest in Thee.

Confessions (397–398) **Augustine, Saint** (354–430) Numidian-born Christian theologian and philosopher

10 If the concept of God has any validity or any use, it can only be to make us larger, freer, and more loving. If God cannot do this, then it is time we got rid of Him.
The Fire Next Time (1963) **Baldwin, James** (1924–1987) US writer, dramatist, poet and civil rights activist

11 Suppose you saw the Lord in glory continually before you; When you are hearing, praying, talking, jesting, eating, drinking, and when you are tempted to wilful sin: Suppose you saw the Lord stand over you, as verily as you see a man! Would you be godly or ungodly after it? As sure as you live, and see one another, God always seeth you.
'The Life of Faith' (1660) **Baxter, Richard** (1615–1691) English Nonconformist clergyman

12 In the beginning God created the heaven and the earth.
And the earth was without form, and void; and darkness was upon the face of the deep. And the Spirit of God moved upon the face of the waters.
And God said, Let there be light: and there was light.
Genesis, 1:1–3

13 For the Lord seeth not as man seeth: for man looketh on the outward appearance, but the Lord looketh on the heart.
I Samuel, 16:7

14 God is our refuge and strength, a very present help in trouble.
Therefore will not we fear, though the earth be removed, and though the mountains be carried into the midst of the sea.
Psalms, 46:1–2

15 God is a Spirit: and they that worship him must worship him in spirit and in truth.
John, 4:24 **The Bible (King James Version)**

16 The pride of the peacock is the glory of God.
'Proverbs of Hell' (c.1793) **Blake, William** (1757–1827) English poet, engraver, painter and mystic

17 A God who allowed us to prove his existence would be an idol.
'If you believe it, you have it' (1931)

18 In all important questions, man has learned to cope without recourse to God as a working hypothesis.
Letter to a friend, (1944) **Bonhoeffer, Dietrich** (1906–1945) German theologian, executed by the Nazis

19 God is like a skilful Geometrician.
Religio Medici (1643) **Browne, Sir Thomas** (1605–1682) English physician, author and antiquary

20 God's gifts put man's best gifts to shame.
Sonnets from the Portuguese (1850)

21 God answers sharp and sudden on some prayers,
And thrusts the thing we have prayed for in our face,
A gauntlet with a gift in't.
Aurora Leigh (1857) **Browning, Elizabeth Barrett** (1806–1861) English poet; wife of Robert Browning

22 'There is no God,' the wicked saith,
'And truly it's a blessing,
For what he might have done with us
It's better only guessing.'
Dipsychus (1865) **Clough, Arthur Hugh** (1819–1861) English poet and letter writer

23 God moves in a mysterious way
His wonders to perform;
He plants his footsteps in the sea,
And rides upon the storm.
Olney Hymns (1779) **Cowper, William** (1731–1800) English poet, hymn writer and letter writer

24 Imagine the Lord talking French! Aside from a few odd words in Hebrew, I took it completely for granted that God had never spoken anything but the most dignified English.
Life with Father (1935) **Day, Clarence Shepard** (1874–1935) US essayist and humorist

25 It is the final proof of God's omnipotence that he need not exist in order to save us.
The Mackerel Plaza (1958) **De Vries, Peter** (1910–1993) US novelist

26 Batter my heart, three person'd God; for, you
As yet but knock, breathe, shine, and seek to mend –
I, like an usurpt town, to another due,
Labour to admit you, but Oh, to no end –
Take me to you, imprison me, for I
Except you enthrall me, never shall be free,
Nor ever chaste, except you ravish me.
Holy Sonnets (1609–1617) **Donne, John** (1572–1631) English poet

27 It's not God that I don't accept, Alyosha, only I most respectfully return the ticket to Him.
The Brothers Karamazov (1879–1880) **Dostoevsky, Fyodor** (1821–1881) Russian writer

28 I have too much respect for the idea of God to make it responsible for such an absurd world.
Chronique des Pasquier (1948) **Duhamel, Georges** (1884–1966) French writer, poet, dramatist and physician

29 If God were suddenly condemned to live the life which he had inflicted on men, He would kill Himself.
Pensées d'album (1847) **Dumas, Alexandre (Fils)** (1824–1895) French dramatist, novelist and critic

30 God is an inhuman concept.
The Marriage of Mr Mississippi (1951) **Dürrenmatt, Friedrich** (1921–1990) Swiss dramatist and writer

31 The Lord God is crafty but he is not spiteful.
Inscription in the Mathematical Institute at Princeton **Einstein, Albert** (1879–1955) German-born US mathematical physicist

32 God is an unutterable Sigh in the Human Heart, said the old German mystic. And therewith said the last word.
Impressions and Comments (1914) **Ellis, Havelock** (1859–1939) English sexologist and essayist

33 God is a circle whose centre is everywhere and whose circumference is nowhere.
Attr. **Empedocles** (c.490–c.430 BC) Greek philosopher and poet

34 At bottom God is nothing more than an exalted father.
Totem and Taboo (1919) **Freud, Sigmund** (1856–1939) Austrian physicist; founder of psychoanalysis

35 God, to me, it seems,
is a verb
not a noun,
proper or improper.
No More Secondhand God (1963) **Fuller, Richard Buckminster** (1895–1983) US architect and engineer

36 I do not feel obliged to believe that the same God who has endowed us with sense, reason, and intellect has intended us to forgo their use.
Attr. **Galilei, Galileo** (1564–1642) Italian scientist

37 Cruelty is the first of God's attributes.
The Counterfeiters **Gide, André** (1869–1951) French writer, critic, dramatist and poet

38 God is love, but get it in writing.
Attr. **Gypsy Rose Lee** (1914–1970) US stripper, actress and author

39 The Creator ... has a special preference for beetles.
Lecture, (1951) **Haldane, J.B.S.** (1892–1964) British biochemist, geneticist and popularizer of science. Reply when asked what inferences could be drawn about the nature of God from a study of his works

40 God will forgive me. It is his profession.
In Meissner, *H H Erinnerungen* (1856) **Heine, Heinrich** (1797–1856) German lyric poet, essayist and journalist. Last words

41 The earth may shake, the pillars of the world may tremble under us, the countenance of the heaven may be appalled, the sun may lose his light, the moon her beauty, the stars their glory; but concerning the man that trusteth in God ... what is there in the world that shall change his heart, overthrow his faith, alter his affection towards God, or the affection of God to him?
Of the Laws of Ecclesiasticall Politie (1593) **Hooker, Richard** (c.1554–1600) English theologian and churchman

42 I'd like to thank God for fucking up my life and at the same time not existing, quite a special skill.
The Independent, (1993) **Hughes, Sean** (1966–) Irish comedian

43 God is a good fellow, but His mother's against him.
Wodwo (1967) **Hughes, Ted** (1930–1998) English poet

44 Operationally, God is beginning to resemble not a ruler but the last fading smile of a cosmic Cheshire cat.
Religion without Revelation (1957) **Huxley, Sir Julian Sorell** (1887–1975) English biologist and Director-General of UNESCO

45 Many people believe that they are attracted by God, or by Nature, when they are only repelled by man.
More Lay Thoughts of a Dean (1931) **Inge, William Ralph** (1860–1954) English divine, writer and teacher

46 If you don't find a God by five o'clock this afternoon you must leave the college.
Attr. **Jowett, Benjamin** (1817–1893) English scholar, translator, essayist and priest. Responding to a conceited young student's assertion that he could find no evidence for a God

47 For man proposes, but God disposes.
De Imitatione Christi (1892) **Kempis, Thomas à** (c.1380–1471) German mystic, monk and writer

48 There was once a man who said 'God
Must think it exceedingly odd
If He finds that this tree
Continues to be
When there's no one around in the Quad'
In *The Complete Limerick Book* (1924), 'There was once a man' **Knox, Ronald** (1888–1957) British clergyman

49 God seems to have left the receiver off the hook, and time is running out.
The Ghost in the Machine (1961) **Koestler, Arthur** (1905–1983) British writer, essayist and political refugee

50 What God does, He does well.
Fables, 'Le gland et la citrouille'

51 Help yourself, and heaven will help you.
Fables, 'Le Chartier embourbé' **La Fontaine, Jean de** (1621–1695) French poet and fabulist

52 I have no need of that hypothesis.
In E. Bell, *Men of Mathematics* **Laplace, Pierre-Simon, Marquis de** (1749–1827) French mathematician and astronomer. Reply when asked by Napoleon why he had made no reference to God in his book about the universe, *Mécanique céleste*

53 Though the mills of God grind slowly, yet they grind extremely small;
Though his patience makes him tarry, with exactness grinds He all.
Epigrams (1653), no. 638 **Logau, Friedrich von** (1605–1655) German epigrammatist

54 Whatever your heart clings to and relies upon, that is really your God.
Large Catechism (1529)

55 A strong castle is our God,
A good defence and weapon.
Hymn, first extant version, *Rauscher's Hymnal* (1531) **Luther, Martin** (1483–1546) German Protestant theologian and reformer

56 Whatever may be God's future, we cannot forget His past.
Is Life Worth Living? **Mallock, William Hurrell** (1849–1923) English poet and theological writer

57 It takes a long while for a naturally trustful person to reconcile himself to the idea that after all God will not help him.
Notebooks (1956)

58 God is the immemorial refuge of the incompetent, the helpless, the miserable. They find not only sanctuary in His arms, but also a kind of superiority, soothing to their macerated egos; He will set them above their betters.
Notebooks (1956) **Mencken, H.L.** (1880–1956) US writer, critic, philologist and satirist

59 If triangles created a god, they would give him three sides.
Lettres persanes (1721) **Montesquieu, Charles** (1689–1755) French philosopher and jurist

60 Did not God
Sometimes withhold in mercy what we ask,
We should be ruined at our own request.

Moses in the Bulrushes (1782) **More, Hannah** (1745–1833) English poet, dramatist and religious writer

61 God is dead! Heaven is empty – Weep, children, you no longer have a father.
'Le Christ aux Oliviers' **Nerval, Gérard de** (1808–1855) French poet and writer

62 God is dead: but men's natures are such that for thousands of years yet there will perhaps be caves in which his shadow will be seen.
The Gay Science (1887) **Nietzsche, Friedrich Wilhelm** (1844–1900) German philosopher, critic and poet

63 God and the doctor we alike adore
But only when in danger, not before;
The danger o'er, both are alike requited,
God is forgotten, and the Doctor slighted.
Epigrams **Owen, John** (c.1560–1622) Welsh epigrammatist and teacher

64 I cannot forgive Descartes; in all his philosophy he did his best to dispense with God. But he could not avoid making Him set the world in motion with a flick of His finger; after that he had no more use for God.
Pensées (1670) **Pascal, Blaise** (1623–1662) French philosopher and scientist

65 One, on God's side, is a majority.
Lecture, (1859) **Phillips, Wendell** (1811–1884) US reformer

66 God is really only another artist. He invented the giraffe, the elephant, and the cat. He has no real style. He just goes on trying other things.
In Françoise Gilot and Carlton Lake, *Life with Picasso* (1964) **Picasso, Pablo** (1881–1973) Spanish painter, sculptor and graphic artist

67 Nor God alone in the still calm we find,
He mounts the storm, and walks upon the wind.
An Essay on Man (1733)

68 All are but parts of one stupendous whole,
Whose body Nature is, and God the soul.
An Essay on Man (1733) **Pope, Alexander** (1688–1744) English poet, translator and editor

69 Our Father which art in heaven, stay there; and as for us, we shall stay on earth.
Paroles (1946) **Prévert, Jacques** (1900–1977) French poet and screenwriter

70 God can stand being told by Professor Ayer and Marghanita Laski that He doesn't exist.
The Listener, (1965) **Priestley, J.B.** (1894–1984) English writer, dramatist and critic

71 God is absence. God is the solitude of man.
Le Diable et le Bon Dieu (1951) **Sartre, Jean-Paul** (1905–1980) French philosopher, writer, dramatist and critic

72 There's a divinity that shapes our ends,
Rough-hew them how we will.
Hamlet, V.ii **Shakespeare, William** (1564–1616) English dramatist, poet and actor

73 Beware of the man whose god is in the skies.
Man and Superman (1903) **Shaw, George Bernard** (1856–1950) Irish socialist, writer, dramatist and critic

74 God heard the embattled nations sing and shout
'Gott strafe England!' and 'God save the King!'
God this, God that, and God the other thing –
'Good God!' said God, 'I've got my work cut out.'
The Survival of the Fittest (1916) **Squire, Sir J.C.** (1884–1958) English poet, critic, writer and editor

75 Yet her conception of God was certainly not orthodox. She felt towards Him as she might have felt towards a glorified sanitary engineer; and in some of her speculations she seems hardly to distinguish between the Deity and the Drains.
'Florence Nightingale' (1918) **Strachey, Lytton** (1880–1932) English biographer and critic

76 The vilest thing must be less vile than Thou
From whom it had its being, God and Lord!
The City of Dreadful Night (1880) **Thomson, James** (1834–1882) Scottish poet and dramatist

77 I did not know that we had ever quarrelled.
Attr. **Thoreau, Henry David** (1817–1862) US
essayist, social critic and writer. On being
urged to make his peace with God

78 He who knows about depth knows about
God.
The Shaking of the Foundations (1962 edition)
Tillich, Paul (1886–1965) German theologian

79 There is in God (some say)
A deep, but dazzling darkness; as men here
Say it is late and dusky, because they
See not all clear;
O for that night! where I in him
Might live invisible and dim.
Silex Scintillans (1650–1655) **Vaughan, Henry**
(1622–1695) Welsh poet and physician

80 The true God, the mighty God, is the God
of ideas.
'The Bottle in the Sea', (1847) **Vigny, Alfred de**
(1797–1863) French writer

81 If God did not exist, it would be necessary
to invent him.
Epîtres, 'A l'auteur du livre des trois
imposteurs'

82 God is not on the side of the big battalions,
but of the best marksmen.
'The Piccini Notebooks' (c.1735–1750) **Voltaire**
(1694–1778) French philosopher, dramatist,
poet, historian, writer and critic

83 I think it pisses God off if you walk by the
color purple in a field somewhere and
don't notice it.
The Color Purple (film, 1985) **Walker, Alice**
(1944–) US writer and poet

84 Even God has become female. God is no
longer the bearded patriarch in the sky. He
has had a sex change and turned into
Mother Nature.
The Times, (1998) **Weldon, Fay** (1931–) British
writer

85 If you'll forgive me, that's an immoral
question!
Debate, Oxford Union **Wiesel, Elie** (1928–)
Romanian-born US writer. Replying to the
question 'Why did God allow the Holocaust
to happen?'

86 Had I but served God as diligently as I have
served the King, he would not have given
me over in my grey hairs.
In Cavendish, *Negotiations of Thomas Wolsey*
(1641) **Wolsey, Thomas, Cardinal** (c.1475–1530)
English Cardinal and statesman. Remark to
Sir William Kingston

87 Ethiopians say that their gods are snub-
nosed and black, Thracians that theirs have
light blue eyes and red hair.
In J.H. Lesher, *Xenophanes of Colophon* (1992)
Xenophanes (c.570–480 BC) Greek philosopher
and poet

88 A God all mercy, is a God unjust.
Night-Thoughts on Life, Death and Immortality
(1742–1745) **Young, Edward** (1683–1765) English
poet, dramatist, satirist and clergyman
See also belief; faith; religion

GOODNESS

1 Content thyself to be obscurely good.
When vice prevails, and impious men bear
sway,
The post of honour is a private station.
Cato (1713) **Addison, Joseph** (1672–1719)
English essayist, poet, playwright and
statesman

2 In all things the middle state is to be
praised. But it is sometimes necessary to
incline towards overshooting and
sometimes to shooting short of the mark,
since this is the easiest way of hitting the
mean and the right course.
Nicomachean Ethics

3 The good has been well said to be that at
which all things aim.
Nicomachean Ethics **Aristotle** (384–322 BC)
Greek philosopher

4 The inclination to goodness is imprinted
deeply in the nature of man: insomuch,
that if it issue not towards men, it will take
unto other living creatures.
'Of Goodness, and Goodness of Nature' (1625)
Bacon, Francis (1561–1626) English
philosopher, essayist, politician and courtier

5 The most melancholy of human reflections, perhaps, is that, on the whole, it is a question whether the benevolence of mankind does most good or harm.
Physics and Politics (1872) **Bagehot, Walter** (1826–1877) English economist and political philosopher

6 Men have never been good, they are not good, they never will be good.
Time, (1954) **Barth, Karl** (1886–1968) Swiss Protestant theologian

7 He who would do good to another must do it in Minute Particulars.
General Good is the plea of the Scoundrel hypocrite & flatterer.
Jerusalem (1804–1820) **Blake, William** (1757–1827) English poet, engraver, painter and mystic

8 This Ayrian Eightfold Path, that is to say: Right view, right aim, right speech, right action, right living, right effort, right mindfulness, right contemplation.
In Woodward, *Some Sayings of the Buddha*
Buddha (c.563–483 BC) Indian religious teacher; founder of Buddhism

9 When bad men combine, the good must associate; else they will fall, one by one, an unpitied sacrifice in a contemptible struggle.
Thoughts on the Cause of the Present Discontents (1770)

10 Good order is the foundation of all good things.
Reflections on the Revolution in France (1790)
Burke, Edmund (1729–1797) Irish-born British statesman and philosopher

11 Virtue and vice are like life and death or mind and matter: things which cannot exist without being qualified by their opposite.
The Way of All Flesh (1903)

12 When the righteous man turneth away from his righteousness that he hath committed and doeth that which is neither quite lawful nor quite right, he will generally be found to have gained in amiability what he has lost in holiness.

The Note-Books of Samuel Butler (1912) **Butler, Samuel** (1835–1902) English writer, painter, philosopher and scholar

13 The man of life upright,
Whose guiltlesse hart is free
From all dishonest deedes
Or thought of vanitie …
Good thoughts his onely friendes,
His wealth a well-spent age,
The earth his sober Inne
And quiet Pilgrimage.
A Booke of Ayres (1601) **Campion, Thomas** (1567–1620) English poet and composer

14 At any time you might act for my good. When people do that, it kills something precious between them.
Manservant and Maidservant (1947) **Compton-Burnett, Dame Ivy** (1884–1969) English novelist

15 True goodness springs from a man's own heart. All men are born good.
Analects **Confucius** (c.550–c.478 BC) Chinese philosopher and teacher of ethics

16 He tried the luxury of doing good.
Tales of the Hall (1819) **Crabbe, George** (1754–1832) English poet, clergyman, surgeon and botanist

17 No people do so much harm as those who go about doing good.
The Life and Letters of Mandell Creighton (1904) **Creighton, Mandell** (1843–1901) English churchman, historian and biographer

18 Good things, if they are short, are twice as good.
Attr. **Gracián, Baltasar** (1601–1658) Spanish writer

19 I expect to pass through this world but once; any good thing therefore that I can do, or any kindness that I can show to any fellow-creature, let me do it now; let me not defer or neglect it, for I shall not pass this way again.
Attr. **Grellet, Stephen** (1773–1855) French missionary

20 Good, but not religious-good.
Under the Greenwood Tree (1872) **Hardy, Thomas** (1840–1928) English writer and poet

21 That action is best, which procures the greatest happiness for the greatest numbers.
An Inquiry into the Original of our Ideas of Beauty and Virtue (1725) **Hutcheson, Francis** (1694–1746) Scottish philosopher

22 Be good, sweet maid, and let who can be clever;
Do lovely things, not dream them, all day long;
And so make Life, and Death, and that For Ever,
One grand sweet song.
'A Farewell. To C.E.G.' (1856) **Kingsley, Charles** (1819–1875) English writer, poet, lecturer and clergyman

23 Goodness does not more certainly make men happy than happiness makes them good.
Imaginary Conversations (1853) **Landor, Walter Savage** (1775–1864) English poet and writer

24 Men never do anything good except out of necessity.
Discourse **Machiavelli** (1469–1527) Florentine statesman, political theorist and historian

25 Much benevolence of the passive order may be traced to a disinclination to inflict pain upon oneself.
Vittoria (1866) **Meredith, George** (1828–1909) English writer, poet and critic

26 The good is the beautiful.
Lysis **Plato** (c.429–347 BC) Greek philosopher

27 He preferred to be rather than to seem good.
Catiline **Sallust** (86–c.34 BC) Roman historian and statesman. Of Cato

28 How far that little candle throws his beams!
So shines a good deed in a naughty world.
The Merchant of Venice, V.i **Shakespeare, William** (1564–1616) English dramatist, poet and actor

29 But my life now, my whole life, independently of anything that can happen to me, every minute of it is no longer meaningless as it was before, but has a positive meaning of goodness with which I have the power to invest it.
Anna Karenina (1875–77) **Tolstoy, Leo** (1828–1910) Russian writer, essayist, philosopher and moralist

30 The best is the enemy of the good.
'Art dramatique' (1770) **Voltaire** (1694–1778) French philosopher, dramatist, poet, historian, writer and critic

31 He was quite sure that he had been wronged. Not to be wronged is to forgo the first privilege of goodness.
Bealby (1915) **Wells, H.G.** (1866–1946) English writer

32 Do all the good you can,
By all the means you can,
In all the ways you can,
In all the places you can,
At all the times you can,
To all the people you can,
As long as ever you can.
Letters (1915) **Wesley, John** (1703–1791) English theologian and preacher

33 It is better to be beautiful than to be good. But … it is better to be good than to be ugly.
The Picture of Dorian Gray (1891) **Wilde, Oscar** (1854–1900) Irish poet, dramatist, writer, critic and wit

34 If all the good people were clever,
And all clever people were good,
The world would be nicer than ever
We thought that it possibly could.
But somehow, 'tis seldom or never
The two hit it off as they should;
The good are so harsh to the clever,
The clever so rude to the good.
'The Clever and the Good' ((1890) **Wordsworth, Dame Elizabeth** (1840–1932) English educationist and writer
See also charity; compassion; kindness; morality; virtue

GOVERNMENT

1 The danger is not that a particular class is unfit to govern. Every class is unfit to govern.
Letter to Mary Gladstone, (1881) **Acton, Lord** (1834–1902) English historian and moralist

2 There's nothing which cannot be made a mess of again by officials.
Der Spiegel, (1975) **Adenauer, Konrad** (1876–1967) German Chancellor

3 A conference is a gathering of important people who singly can do nothing, but together can decide that nothing can be done.
Attr. **Allen, Fred** (1894–1956) US vaudeville performer and comedian

4 There'll be no need for wind farms once the Welsh Assembly gets going. There will be enough hot air to keep the principality lit up night and day.
The Times, (1998) **Anonymous**

5 There is no such thing as the State
And no one exists alone.
Hunger allows no choice
To the citizen or the police;
We must love one another or die.
Collected Poems, 1939–1947, 'September 1, 1939'
Auden, W.H. (1907–1973) English poet, essayist, critic, teacher and dramatist

6 One to mislead the public; another to mislead the Cabinet, and the third to mislead itself.
In Alastair Horne, *The Price of Glory* (1962)
Asquith, Herbert (1852–1928) English Liberal statesman and Prime Minister. On the reason for the three sets of figures kept by the War Office

7 A severe though not unfriendly critic of our institutions said that 'the cure for admiring the House of Lords was to go and look at it.'
The English Constitution (1867)

8 It has been said that England invented the phrase, 'Her Majesty's Opposition'; that it was the first Government which made a criticism of administration as much a part of the polity as administration itself. This critical opposition is the consequence of Cabinet government.
The English Constitution (1867)

9 The Crown is, according to the saying, the 'fountain of honour'; but the Treasury is the spring of business.

The English Constitution (1867) **Bagehot, Walter** (1826–1877) English economist and political philosopher

10 It is with government as with medicine, its only business is the choice of evils. Every law is an evil, for every law is an infraction of liberty.
An Introduction to the Principles of Morals and Legislation (1789) **Bentham, Jeremy** (1748–1832) English writer and philosopher

11 The object of government in peace and in war is not the glory of rulers or of races, but the happiness of the common man.
Report on Social Insurance and Allied Services (1942) **Beveridge, William Henry** (1879–1963) British economist and social reformer

12 One law for the Lion & Ox is Oppression.
The Marriage of Heaven and Hell (c.1790–1793) **Blake, William** (1757–1827) English poet, engraver, painter and mystic

13 To tax and to please, no more than to love and to be wise, is not given to men.
Speech on American Taxation (1774)

14 All government, indeed every human benefit and enjoyment, every virtue, and every prudent act, is founded on compromise and barter.
Speech on Conciliation with America (1775)

15 In all forms of Government the people is the true legislator.
Tracts on the Popery Laws (1812) **Burke, Edmund** (1729–1797) Irish-born British statesman and philosopher

16 Good government could never be a substitute for government by the people themselves.
Speech, (1905) **Campbell-Bannerman, Sir Henry** (1836–1908) Scottish Liberal statesman

17 Surely of all 'rights of man', this right of the ignorant man to be guided by the wiser, to be, gently or forcibly, held in the true course by him, is the indisputablest.
Chartism (1839) **Carlyle, Thomas** (1795–1881) Scottish historian, biographer, critic, and essayist

18 I'm surprised that a government organization could do it that quickly.

In *Time*, (March 1979) **Carter, Jimmy** (1924–)
US Democrat President. Visiting Egypt in
1979, when told that it took only 20 years to
build the Great Pyramid

19 The duty of an opposition is to oppose.
In W.S. Churchill, *Lord Randolph Churchill*
(1906) **Churchill, Lord Randolph** (1849–1894)
English Conservative politician

20 Government is a trust, and the officers of
the government are trustees. And both the
trust and the trustees are created for the
benefit of the people.
Speech, (1829) **Clay, Henry** (1777–1852) US
statesman

21 An oppressive government is more to be
feared than a tiger.
Analects **Confucius** (c.550–c.478 BC) Chinese
philosopher and teacher of ethics

22 The State, in choosing men to serve it,
takes no notice of their opinions. If they be
willing faithfully to serve it, that satisfies.
Said before the Battle of Marston Moor, (1644)
Cromwell, Oliver (1599–1658) English general,
statesman and Puritan leader

23 When I first came into Parliament, Mr
Tierney, a great Whig authority, used
always to say that the duty of an
Opposition was very simple – it was, to
oppose everything, and propose nothing.
Speech, House of Commons, (1841) **Derby,
Earl of** (1799–1869) English politician;
Conservative Prime Minister

24 Whatever was required to be done, the
Circumlocution Office was beforehand
with all the public departments in the art of
perceiving – HOW NOT TO DO IT.
Little Dorrit (1857) **Dickens, Charles** (1812–1870)
English writer

25 No Government can be long secure
without a formidable opposition.
Coningsby (1844)

26 I believe that without party Parliamentary
government is impossible.
Speech, Manchester, (1872) **Disraeli, Benjamin**
(1804–1881) English statesman and writer

27 The world is disgracefully managed, one
hardly knows to whom to complain.

Vainglory (1915) **Firbank, Ronald** (1886–1926)
English writer

28 Governments never learn. Only people
learn.
The Observer, (1996) **Friedman, Milton** (1912–)
US economist

29 The principles of a free constitution are
irrecoverably lost, when the legislative
power is nominated by the executive.
Decline and Fall of the Roman Empire (1776–88)
Gibbon, Edward (1737–1794) English historian,
politician and memoirist

30 I don't think any writers since the
generation of Jean-Paul Sartre and Camus
in France have influenced a government.
Interview, *The Observer*, (1998) **Gordimer,
Nadine** (1923–) South African writer

31 It is not easy nowadays to remember
anything so contrary to all appearances as
that officials are the servants of the public;
and the official must try not to foster the
illusion that it is the other way round.
Plain Words **Gowers, Sir Ernest** (1880–1966)
English civil servant, champion of plain
language

32 Well, fancy giving money to the
Government!
Might as well have put it down the drain.
Fancy giving money to the Government!
Nobody will see the stuff again.
Well, they've no idea what money's for –
Ten to one they'll start another war.
I've heard a lot of silly things, but, Lor'!
Fancy giving money to the Government!
'Too Much!' **Herbert, Sir A.P.** (1890–1971)
English humorist, writer, dramatist and
politician

33 The only way to erect such a common
power, as may be able to defend them
from the invasion of foreigners, and the
injuries of one another … is, to confer all
their power and strength upon one man,
or upon one assembly of men, that may
reduce all their wills, by plurality of voices,
unto one will.
Leviathan (1651) **Hobbes, Thomas** (1588–1679)
English political philosopher

34 Brute force without judgement collapses under its own weight.
Odes **Horace** (65–8 BC) Roman lyric poet and satirist

35 Nothing appears more surprising to those, who consider human affairs with a philosophical eye, than the easiness with which the many are governed by the few; and the implicit submission, with which men resign their own sentiments and passions to those of their rulers.
Essays, Moral, Political, and Literary (1742) **Hume, David** (1711–1776) Scottish philosopher and political economist

36 Official dignity tends to increase in inverse ratio to the importance of the country in which the office is held.
Beyond the Mexique Bay (1934) **Huxley, Aldous** (1894–1963) English writer, poet and critic

37 A man may build himself a throne of bayonets, but he cannot sit upon it.
Philosophy of Plotinus (1923) **Inge, William Ralph** (1860–1954) English divine, writer and teacher

38 I will govern according to the common weal, but not according to the common will.
Remark, (1621) **James VI of Scotland and I of England** (1566–1625) King of Scotland from 1567 and of England from 1603

39 When a man assumes a public trust, he should consider himself as public property.
Remark, (1807) **Jefferson, Thomas** (1743–1826) US Democrat statesman and President

40 I would not give half a guinea to live under one form of government rather than another. It is of no moment to the happiness of an individual.
In Boswell, *The Life of Samuel Johnson* (1791) **Johnson, Samuel** (1709–1784) English lexicographer, poet, critic, conversationalist and essayist

41 Always remember that if a civil servant had the ability to ... correctly foresee the demand situation for any product he would not be working for the government for long. He would shortly be sitting in the south of France with his feet in a bucket of champagne!
Economics Made Easy **Kelly, Bert** (1912–1997) Australian politician

42 The important thing for government is not to do things which individuals are doing already, and to do them a little better or a little worse; but to do those things which at present are not done at all.
'The End of Laissez-Faire' (1926) **Keynes, John Maynard** (1883–1946) English economist

43 To govern is to make choices.
Maximes et réflexions (1812) **Lévis, Duc de** (1764–1830) French writer and soldier

44 The Commons, faithful to their system, remained in a wise and masterly inactivity.
Vindiciae Gallicae (1791) **Mackintosh, Sir James** (1765–1832) Scottish philosopher, historian, lawyer and politician

45 Each country has the government it deserves.
Letter, (1811) **Maistre, Joseph de** (1753–1821) French diplomat and political philosopher

46 Rulers have no authority from God to do mischief.
A Discourse Concerning Unlimited Submission and Non-Resistance to the Higher Powers (1750) **Mayhew, Jonathan** (1720–1766) US clergyman and pamphleteer

47 The only thing that saves us from bureaucracy is its inefficiency. An efficient bureaucracy is the greatest threat to freedom.
Time, (1979) **McCarthy, Eugene** (1916–2005) US politician

48 Bureaucracy, the rule of no one, has become the modern form of despotism.
The New Yorker **McCarthy, Mary** (1912–1989) US writer and critic

49 An administrator in a bureaucratic world is a man who can feel big by merging his non-entity with an abstraction. A real person in touch with real things inspires terror in him.
Letter to Ezra Pound, (1951) **McLuhan, Marshall** (1911–1980) Canadian communications theorist

50 The worst government is the most moral. One composed of cynics is often very tolerant and human. But when fanatics are on top there is no limit to oppression.
Notebooks (1956) **Mencken, H.L.** (1880–1956) US writer, critic, philologist and satirist

51 The single most exciting thing you encounter in government is competence, because it's so rare.
New York Times, (1976) **Moynihan, Daniel** (1927–2003) US academic and politician

52 Feeling good about government is like looking on the bright side of any catastrophe. When you quit looking on the bright side, the catastrophe is still there.
Parliament of Whores (1991)

53 Giving money and power to the government is like giving whiskey and car keys to teenage boys.
Attr. **O'Rourke, P.J.** (1947–) US writer

54 Understood as a central consolidated power, managing and directing the various general interests of the society, all government is evil, and the parent of evil … The best government is that which governs least.
United States Magazine and Democratic Review, 1837, Introduction **O'Sullivan, John L.** (1813–1895) US editor and diplomat

55 Government, even in its best state, is but a necessary evil; in its worst state, an intolerable one. Government, like dress, is the badge of lost innocence; the palaces of kings are built upon the ruins of the bowers of paradise.
Common Sense (1776)

56 Lay then the axe to the root, and teach governments humanity. It is their sanguinary punishments which corrupt mankind.
The Rights of Man (1791)

57 Man is not the enemy of Man, but through the medium of a false system of government.
The Rights of Man (1791) **Paine, Thomas** (1737–1809) English-born US political theorist and pamphleteer

58 The British, being brought up on team games, enter their House of Commons in the spirit of those who would rather be doing something else. If they cannot be playing golf or tennis, they can at least pretend that politics is a game with very similar rules.
Parkinson's Law (1958) **Parkinson, C. Northcote** (1909–1993) English political scientist and historian

59 Never trust governments absolutely, and always do what you can to prevent them from doing too much harm.
The Limits of Government **Passmore, John Arthur** (1914–2004) Australian philosopher and academic

60 A parliament can do any thing but make a man a woman, and a woman a man.
Quoted in speech made by his son, the Fourth Earl, (1648) **Pembroke, Second Earl of** (c.1534–1601) Welsh courtier

61 Tyranny comes from no other form of government but democracy.
Republic **Plato** (c.429–347 BC) Greek philosopher

62 Governments don't retreat, they simply advance in another direction.
The Observer, (1981) **Rippon, Geoffrey** (1924–1997) English Conservative politician

63 If this government was an individual, it would be locked up in the interests of public safety.
Speech, Labour Party Conference, (1993) **Robertson, George** (1946–) Scottish Labour statesman; Secretary General of NATO. On John Major's government

64 Any institution which does not suppose the people good, and the magistrate corruptible, is a vicious one.
Déclaration des Droits de l'homme (1793), Article 25 **Robespierre, Maximilien** (1758–1794) French revolutionary

65 I don't make jokes – I just watch the government and report the facts.
Attr. **Rogers, Will** (1879–1935) US humorist, actor, rancher, writer and wit

66 Government and cooperation are in all things the laws of life; anarchy and competition, the laws of death.
Unto this Last (1862) **Ruskin, John** (1819–1900) English art critic, philosopher and reformer

67 Women are false in countries where men are tyrants. Violence everywhere leads to deception.
Paul et Virginie (1788) **Saint-Pierre, Bernardin de** (1737–1814) French author

68 A difficulty for every solution.
Attr. **Samuel, Lord** (1870–1963) English Liberal statesman, philosopher and administrator. Referring to the Civil Service

69 The working of great institutions is mainly the result of a vast mass of routine, petty malice, self interest, carelessness, and sheer mistake. Only a residual fraction is thought.
The Crime of Galileo **Santayana, George** (1863–1952) Spanish-born US philosopher and writer

70 Bureaucracy is not an obstacle to democracy but an inevitable complement to it.
Capitalism, Socialism and Democracy (1942) **Schumpeter, Joseph A.** (1883–1950) US economist

71 There is no art which one government sooner learns of another than that of draining money from the pockets of the people.
Wealth of Nations (1776) **Smith, Adam** (1723–1790) Scottish economist, philosopher and essayist

72 The Republican form of government is the highest form of government; but because of this it requires the highest type of human nature – a type nowhere at present existing.
Essays (1891) **Spencer, Herbert** (1820–1903) English philosopher and journalist

73 Government by postponement is bad enough, but it is far better than government by desperation.
The Observer, (1953) **Stevenson, Adlai** (1900–1965) US lawyer, statesman and United Nations ambassador

74 I heartily accept the motto, 'That government is best which governs least'; and I should like to see it acted up to more rapidly and systematically. Carried out, it finally amounts to this, which I also believe, – 'That government is best which governs not at all.'
Civil Disobedience (1849) **Thoreau, Henry David** (1817–1862) US essayist, social critic and writer

75 You don't have power if you surrender all your principles – you have office.
Attr. **Todd, Ron** (1927–) British trade union leader

76 A fainéant government is not the worst government that England can have. It has been the great fault of our politicians that they have all wanted to do something.
Phineas Finn (1869) **Trollope, Anthony** (1815–1882) English writer, traveller and post office official

77 There is something about a bureaucrat that does not like a poem.
Sex, Death and Money (1968) **Vidal, Gore** (1925–) US writer, critic and poet

78 In governments there must be both shepherds and butchers.
'The Piccini Notebooks' **Voltaire** (1694–1778) French philosopher, dramatist, poet, historian, writer and critic

79 Our supreme governors, the mob.
Letter to Sir Horace Mann, (1743) **Walpole, Horace** (1717–1797) English writer and politician

80 Mankind, when left to themselves, are unfit for their own government.
Letter, (1786) **Washington, George** (1732–1799) US general, statesman and President

81 You must build your House of Parliament upon the river: so ... that the populace cannot exact their demands by sitting down round you.
In Fraser, *Words on Wellington* (1889) **Wellington, Duke of** (1769–1852) Irish-born British military commander and statesman
See also democracy; communism; monarchy and royalty; politics; socialism

GREATNESS

1 Mrs Asquith remarked indiscreetly that if Kitchener was not a great man, he was, at least, a great poster.
In Sir Philip Magnus, *Kitchener: Portrait of an Imperialist* (1958) **Asquith, Margot** (1864–1945) Scottish political hostess and writer

2 All rising to great place is by a winding stair.
'Of Great Place' (1625) **Bacon, Francis** (1561–1626) English philosopher, essayist, politician and courtier

3 Great men are but life-sized. Most of them, indeed, are rather short.
Attr. **Beerbohm, Sir Max** (1872–1956) English satirist, cartoonist, critic and essayist

4 Great men are the guide-posts and landmarks in the state.
Speech on American Taxation (1774) **Burke, Edmund** (1729–1797) Irish-born British statesman and philosopher

5 What millions died – that Caesar might be great!
Pleasures of Hope (1799) **Campbell, Thomas** (1777–1844) Scottish poet, ballad writer and journalist

6 The Hero can be Poet, Prophet, King, Priest or what you will, according to the kind of world he finds himself born into.
'The Hero as Poet' (1841)

7 No great man lives in vain. The History of the world is but the Biography of great men.
'The Hero as Divinity' (1841)

8 No sadder proof can be given by a man of his own littleness than disbelief in great men.
On Heroes, Hero-Worship, and the Heroic in History **Carlyle, Thomas** (1795–1881) Scottish historian, biographer, critic, and essayist

9 It is notoriously known through the universal world that there be nine worthy and the best that ever were. That is to wit three paynims, three Jews, and three Christian men. As for the paynims they were ... the first Hector of Troy ... the second Alexander the Great; and the third Julius Caesar ... As for the three Jews ... the first was Duke Joshua ... the second David, King of Jerusalem; and the third Judas Maccabaeus.... And sith the said Incarnation... was first the noble Arthur.... The second was Charlemagne or Charles the Great ... and the third and last was Godfrey of Bouillon.
In Malory, *Le Morte d'Arthur* (1485) **Caxton, William** (c.1421–1491) First English printer

10 They're only truly great who are truly good.
Revenge for Honour (1654) **Chapman, George** (c.1559–c.1634) English poet, dramatist and translator

11 The superior man is satisfied and composed; the mean man is always full of distress.
Analects **Confucius** (c.550–c.478 BC) Chinese philosopher and teacher of ethics

12 True greatness consists in being master of one's self.
The Life and Adventures of Robinson Crusoe (1719) **Defoe, Daniel** (c.1661–1731) English writer and critic

13 A man of destiny knows that beyond this hill lies another and another. The journey is never complete.
The Observer, (1994) **De Klerk, F.W.** (1936–) South African politician and President

14 He was the man who of all modern, and perhaps ancient poets, had the largest and most comprehensive soul ... He was naturally learn'd; he needed not the spectacles of books to read Nature: he looked inwards, and found her there ... He is many times flat, insipid; his comic wit degenerating into clenches, his serious swelling into bombast. But he is always great.
Essay of Dramatic Poesy (1668) **Dryden, John** (1631–1700) English poet, satirist, dramatist and critic. Of Shakespeare

15 It is easy in the world to live after the world's opinion; it is easy in solitude after our own; but the great man is he who, in the midst of the crowd, keeps with perfect sweetness the independence of solitude.
Essays, First Series (1841)

16 Nothing great was ever achieved without enthusiasm.
Essays, First Series (1841)

17 A foolish consistency is the hobgoblin of little minds, adored by little statesmen and philosophers and divines. With consistency a great soul has simply nothing to do.
Essays, First Series (1841)

18 Is it so bad, then, to be misunderstood? Pythagoras was misunderstood, and Socrates, and Jesus, and Luther, and Copernicus, and Galileo, and Newton, and every pure and wise spirit that ever took flesh. To be great is to be misunderstood.
Essays, First Series (1841) **Emerson, Ralph Waldo** (1803–1882) US poet, essayist, transcendentalist and teacher

19 Tyndall, I must remain plain Michael Faraday to the last; and let me now tell you, that if I accepted the honour which the Royal Society desires to confer upon me, I would not answer for the integrity of my intellect for a single year.
In J. Tyndall, *Faraday as a Discoverer* (1868) **Faraday, Michael** (1791–1867) English chemist and physicist. On being offered the Presidency of the Royal Society

20 Greatness consists in bringing all manner of mischief on mankind, and goodness in removing it from them.
Jonathan Wild (1743) **Fielding, Henry** (1707–1754) English writer, dramatist and journalist

21 The world cannot live at the level of its great men.
The Golden Bough (1900) **Frazer, Sir James** (1854–1941) Scottish anthropologist and writer

22 On earth there is nothing great but man; in man there is nothing great but mind.
Lectures on Metaphysics and Logic (1859) **Hamilton, Sir William** (1788–1856) Scottish metaphysical philosopher. Quoting Phavorinus

23 The glory of great men must always be measured by the means they have used to obtain it.
Maximes (1678) **La Rochefoucauld** (1613–1680) French writer

24 The final test of a leader is that he leaves behind him in other men the conviction and the will to carry on.
New York Herald Tribune, (1945) **Lippmann, Walter** (1889–1974) Canadian sociologist

25 The heights by great men reached and kept
Were not attained by sudden flight,
But they, while their companions slept,
Were toiling upward in the night.
'The Ladder of Saint Augustine' (1850) **Longfellow, Henry Wadsworth** (1807–1882) US poet and writer

26 The worth of a State, in the long run, is the worth of the individuals composing it.
On Liberty (1859) **Mill, John Stuart** (1806–1873) English philosopher, economist and reformer

27 A man whose errors take ten years to correct is quite a man.
Attr. **Oppenheimer, J. Robert** (1904–1967) US nuclear physicist. Of Albert Einstein

28 The high sentiments always win in the end, leaders who offer blood, toil, tears and sweat always get more out of their followers than those who offer safety and a good time. When it comes to the pinch, human beings are heroic.
Horizon, (1941) **Orwell, George** (1903–1950) English writer and critic

29 Only real greatness can be so misplaced and so untimely.
Doctor Zhivago (1958) **Pasternak, Boris** (1890–1960) Russian poet and novelist

30 Wondrous close is the hero to those who die young.
Duino Elegies (1923) **Rilke, Rainer Maria** (1875–1926) Austrian poet, born in Prague

31 The soul and body rive not more in parting
Than greatness going off.
Antony and Cleopatra, IV.xiii

32 His legs bestrid the ocean; his rear'd arm
Crested the world. His voice was propertied
As all the tuned spheres, and that to friends;
But when he meant to quail and shake the orb,
He was as rattling thunder. For his bounty,
There was no winter in't; an autumn 'twas

That grew the more by reaping. His delights
Were dolphin-like: they show'd his back above
The element they liv'd in. In his livery
Walk'd crowns and crownets; realms and islands were
As plates dropp'd from his pocket.
Antony and Cleopatra, V.i

33 Rightly to be great
Is not to stir without great argument,
But greatly to find quarrel in a straw,
When honour's at the stake.
Hamlet, IV.iv

34 Thou wouldst be great;
Art not without ambition, but without
The illness should attend it. What thou wouldst highly,
That wouldst thou holily; wouldst not play false,
And yet wouldst wrongly win.
Macbeth, I.v

35 Be not afraid of greatness. Some are born great, some achieve greatness, and some have greatness thrust upon 'em.
Twelfth Night, II.v **Shakespeare, William** (1564–1616) English dramatist, poet and actor

36 Who shoots at the midday sun, though he be sure he shall never hit the mark, yet as sure he is he shall shoot higher than who aims but at a bush.
New Arcadia (1590) **Sidney, Sir Philip** (1554–1586) English poet, critic, soldier, courtier and diplomat

37 I think continually of those who were truly great.
The names of those who in their lives fought for life
Who wore at their hearts the fire's centre.
Born of the sun they travelled a short while towards the sun,
And left the vivid air signed with their honour.
'I think continually of those who were truly great' (1933) **Spender, Sir Stephen** (1909–1995) English poet, editor, translator and diarist

38 'My Lord,' a certain nobleman is said to have observed, after sitting next to Richard Bentley at dinner, 'that chaplain of yours is a very extraordinary man.' Stillingfleet agreed, adding, 'Had he but the gift of humility, he would be the most extraordinary man in Europe.'
In R.J. White, *Dr Bentley* **Stillingfleet, Edward** (1635–1699) British theologian and author

39 Keep away from people who try to belittle your ambitions. Small people always do that, but the really great make you feel that you, too, can become great.
Attr. **Twain, Mark** (1835–1910) US humorist, writer, journalist and lecturer

40 They who cannot perform great things themselves may yet have a satisfaction in doing justice to those who can.
Attr. **Walpole, Horace** (1717–1797) English writer and politician

41 A man went looking for America and couldn't find it anywhere.
On being advised not to join the overcrowded legal profession

42 There is always room at the top.
Attr. **Webster, Daniel** (1782–1852) US statesman, orator and lawyer

43 I believe I forgot to tell you I was made a Duke.
Postscript to a letter to his nephew, (1814) **Wellington, Duke of** (1769–1852) Irish-born British military commander and statesman
See also egoism; fame; genius

GRIEF

1 Strew on her roses, roses,
And never a spray of yew.
In quiet she reposes:
Ah! would that I did too.
'Requiescat' (1853) **Arnold, Matthew** (1822–1888) English poet, critic, essayist and educationist

2 We met ... Dr Hall in such very deep mourning that either his mother, his wife, or himself must be dead.
Letter to Cassandra Austen, (1799) **Austen, Jane** (1775–1817) English writer

3 But woman's grief is like a summer storm,
Short as it violent is.
Plays on the Passions (1798) **Baillie, Joanna**
(1762–1851) Scottish dramatist and poet

4 When we attend the funerals of our friends
we grieve for them, but when we go to
those of other people it is chiefly our own
deaths that we mourn for.
Thoughts in a Dry Season (1978) **Brenan, Gerald**
(1894–1987) English writer

5 Cold in the earth – and fifteen wild
Decembers,
From those brown hills, have melted into
spring ...
Sweet Love of youth, forgive if I forget thee
While the World's tide is bearing me
along:
Sterner desires and darker hopes beset me,
Hopes which obscure but cannot do thee
wrong! ...
But when the days of golden dreams had
perished,
And even Despair was powerless to
destroy,
Then did I learn how existence could be
cherished,
Strengthened, and fed without the aid of
joy ...
Once drinking deep of that divinest
anguish,
How could I seek the empty world again?
'Remembrance' (1845) **Brontë, Emily** (1818–
1848) English poet and writer

6 I tell you, hopeless grief is passionless.
Sonnets, 'Grief' (1844) **Browning, Elizabeth
Barrett** (1806–1861) English poet; wife of
Robert Browning

7 Dark tree, still sad when others' grief is
fled,
The only constant mourner o'er the dead!
'The Giaour' (1813) **Byron, Lord** (1788–1824)
English poet, satirist and traveller. Of a
cypress tree

8 Grief is itself a med'cine.
'Charity' (1782) **Cowper, William** (1731–1800)
English poet, hymn writer and letter writer

9 'In shuttered rooms let others grieve,
And coffin thought in speech of lead;
I'll tie my heart upon my sleeve:
It is the Badge of Men,' he said.
'The Badge of Men' (1891) **Davidson, John**
(1857–1909) Scottish writer

10 Grief never mended no broken bones, and
as good people's wery scarce, what I says
is, make the most on 'em.
Sketches by Boz (1836) **Dickens, Charles** (1812–
1870) English writer

11 The Bustle in a House
The Morning after Death
Is solemnest of industries
Enacted upon Earth.
'The Bustle in a House' (c.1866) **Dickinson,
Emily** (1830–1886) US poet

12 I've heard them lilting, at our yowe-
milking,
Lasses a' lilting before the dawn o' day;
But now they are moaning on ilka green
loaning –
The Flowers of the Forest are a' wede away.
'The Flowers of the Forest' (1756) **Elliot, Jean**
(1727–1805) Scottish lyricist

13 There are people who have an appetite for
grief; pleasure is not strong enough and
they crave pain.
In *The Faber Book of Aphorisms* (1962) **Emerson,
Ralph Waldo** (1803–1882) US poet, essayist,
transcendentalist and teacher

14 They are the silent griefs which cut the
heart-strings.
The Broken Heart (1633) **Ford, John** (c.1586–
c.1640) English dramatist and poet

15 Bombazine would have shown a deeper
sense of her loss.
Cranford (1853) **Gaskell, Elizabeth** (1810–1865)
English writer

16 His eyes are quickened so with grief,
He can watch a grass or leaf
Every instant grow.
'Lost Love' (1921) **Graves, Robert** (1895–1985)
English poet, writer, critic, translator and
mythologist

17 Thar was na solace mycht his sobbing ces,
Bot cryit ay, with caris cald and kene,
'Quhar art thow gane, my luf Erudices?'

'Orpheus and Eurydice' (1508) **Henryson, Robert** (c.1425–1505) Scottish poet

18 No worst, there is none. Pitched past pitch of grief,
More pangs will, schooled at forepangs, wilder wring.
Comforter, where, where is your comforting?
'No Worst, there is None' (1885) **Hopkins, Gerard Manley** (1844–1889) English Jesuit priest, poet and classicist

19 Grief and disappointment give rise to anger, anger to envy, envy to malice, and malice to grief again, until the whole circle be completed.
A Treatise of Human Nature (1739) **Hume, David** (1711–1776) Scottish philosopher and political economist

20 Grief is a species of idleness.
Letter to Mrs. Thrale, (1773) **Johnson, Samuel** (1709–1784) English lexicographer, poet, critic, conversationalist and essayist

21 Sorrow, the great idealizer.
Attr. **Lowell, James Russell** (1819–1891) US poet, editor, abolitionist and diplomat

22 What we call mourning is perhaps not so much grief that it is impossible to see our dead return to life as grief that we are quite unable to wish to do so.
The Magic Mountain (1924) **Mann, Thomas** (1875–1955) German writer and critic

23 In these flashing revelations of grief's wonderful fire, we see all things as they are; and though when the electric element is gone, the shadows once more descend, and the false outlines of objects again return; yet not with their former power to deceive.
In Lewis Wolpert, *Malignant Sadness* (1999) **Melville, Herman** (1819–1891) US writer and poet

24 The heart could never speak
But that the Word was spoken.
We hear the heart break
Here with hearts unbroken.
Time, teach us the art
That breaks and heals the heart.
'The heart could never speak' (1960) **Muir, Edwin** (1887–1959) Scottish poet, critic, translator and writer

25 Happiness alone is beneficial for the body, but it is grief that develops the powers of the mind.
Le Temps retrouvé (1926) **Proust, Marcel** (1871–1922) French writer and critic

26 When I am dead, my dearest,
Sing no sad songs for me;
Plant thou no roses at my head,
Nor shady cypress tree:
Be the green grass above me
With showers and dewdrops wet;
And if thou wilt, remember,
And if thou wilt, forget.
'Song: When I am Dead' (1862) **Rossetti, Christina** (1830–1894) English poet

27 From perfect grief there need not be
Wisdom or even memory:
One thing then learnt remains to me, –
The woodspurge has a cup of three.
'The Woodspurge' (1870) **Rossetti, Dante Gabriel** (1828–1882) English poet, painter, translator and letter writer

28 Nothing becomes so offensive so quickly as grief. When fresh it finds someone to console it, but when it becomes chronic, it is ridiculed, and rightly.
Attr. **Seneca** (c.4 BC–AD 65) Roman philosopher, poet, dramatist, essayist, rhetorician and statesman

29 Indeed the tears live in an onion that should water this sorrow.
Antony and Cleopatra, I.ii

30 The big round tears
Cours'd one another down his innocent nose
In piteous chase.
As You Like It, II.i

31 Great griefs, I see, med'cine the less.
Cymbeline, IV.ii

32 But to persever
In obstinate condolement is a course
Of impious stubbornness; 'tis unmanly grief;
It shows a will most incorrect to heaven,
A heart unfortified, a mind impatient.
Hamlet I.ii

33 Grief fills the room up of my absent child,
Lies in his bed, walks up and down with
me,
Puts on his pretty looks, repeats his words,
Remembers me of all his gracious parts,
Stuffs out his vacant garments with his
form;
Then have I reason to be fond of grief.
King John, III.iv

34 Howl, howl, howl, howl! O, you are men of
stones!
Had I your tongues and eyes, I'd use them
so
That heaven's vault should crack. She's
gone for ever.
King Lear, V.iii

35 What, man! Ne'er pull your hat upon your
brows;
Give sorrow words. The grief that does not
speak
Whispers the o'erfraught heart and bids it
break.
Macbeth, IV.iii

36 Every one can master a grief but he that
has it.
Much Ado About Nothing, III.ii

37 What's gone and what's past help
Should be past grief.
The Winter's Tale, III.ii **Shakespeare, William**
(1564–1616) English dramatist, poet and actor

38 Ah, woe is me! Winter is come and gone,
But grief returns with the revolving year.
Adonais (1821) **Shelley, Percy Bysshe** (1792–
1822) English poet, dramatist and essayist

39 The World is full of all sorts of sorrows and
miseries – and I think it is better never to
have been born – but when evils have
happened turn away your mind from them
as soon as you can to everything of good
which remains. Most people grieve as if
grief were a duty or a pleasure, but all who
can control it should control it – and
remember that these renovations of
sorrows are almost the charter and
condition under which life is held.

Letter to Lady Holland, (November 1819)
Smith, Sydney (1771–1845) English clergyman,
essayist, journalist and wit. Written in
response to the death of one of Lady
Holland's children

40 The bitterest tears shed over graves are for
words left unsaid and deeds left undone.
Little Foxes (1866) **Stowe, Harriet Beecher**
(1811–1896) US writer and reformer

41 Death has made
His darkness beautiful with thee.
In Memoriam A. H. H. (1850)

42 I sometimes hold it half a sin
To put in words the grief I feel;
For words, like Nature, half reveal
And half conceal the Soul within.
But, for the unquiet heart and brain,
A use in measured language lies;
The sad mechanic exercise,
Like dull narcotics, numbing pain.
In Memoriam A. H. H. (1850) **Tennyson, Alfred,
Lord** (1809–1892) English lyric poet

43 It is one of the mysteries of our nature that
man, all unprepared, can receive a
thunder-stroke like that and live. There is
but one reasonable explanation of it. The
intellect is stunned by the shock and but
gropingly gathers the meaning of the
words. The power to realize their full
import is mercifully lacking.
Autobiography **Twain, Mark** (1835–1910) US
humorist, writer, journalist and lecturer. On
receiving news of the death of a loved one

44 When lilacs last in the dooryard bloom'd,
And the great stars early droop'd in the
western sky in the night,
I mourn'd, and yet shall mourn with ever-
returning spring.
'When lilacs last in the dooryard bloom'd'
(1865) **Whitman, Walt** (1819–1892) US poet and
writer

45 Surprised by joy – impatient as the Wind
I turned to share the transport – Oh! with
whom
But thee, deep buried in the silent tomb.
'Surprised by joy' (1815) **Wordsworth, William**
(1770–1850) English poet
See also absence; death; suffering

GUILT

1 Conscience is what hurts when everything else feels so good.
Anonymous

2 It is quite gratifying to feel guilty if you haven't done anything wrong: how noble! Whereas it is rather hard and certainly depressing to admit guilt and to repent.
Eichmann in Jerusalem: A Report on the Banality of Evil (1963) **Arendt, Hannah** (1906–1975) German-born US theorist

3 Our gratitude to most benefactors is the same as our feeling for dentists who have pulled our teeth. We acknowledge the good they have done and the evil from which they have delivered us, but we remember the pain they occasioned and do not love them very much.
Maximes et pensées (1796) **Chamfort, Nicolas** (1741–1794) French writer

4 Better to stand ten thousand sneers than one abiding pang, such as time could not abolish, of bitter self-reproach.
Confessions of an English Opium Eater (1822) **De Quincey, Thomas** (1785–1859) English writer

5 We need never be ashamed of our tears.
Great Expectations (1861) **Dickens, Charles** (1812–1870) English writer

6 For all guilt is avenged on earth.
Wilhelm Meister's Apprentice Years (1796) **Goethe** (1749–1832) German poet, writer, dramatist and scientist

7 When lovely woman stoops to folly
And finds too late that men betray,
What charm can soothe her melancholy,
What art can wash her guilt away?
The only art her guilt to cover,
To hide her shame from every eye,
To give repentance to her lover
And wring his bosom – is to die.
The Vicar of Wakefield (1766) **Goldsmith, Oliver** (c.1728–1774) Irish dramatist, poet and writer

8 Mental torture is more readily endured, alas, than physical pain; and if I were forced to choose between a bad conscience and an aching tooth, I would settle for the bad conscience.
Letter on the French Stage (1837) **Heine, Heinrich** (1797–1856) German lyric poet, essayist and journalist

9 This be your wall of brass, to have nothing on your conscience, no reason to grow pale with guilt.
Epistles **Horace** (65–8 BC) Roman poet

10 The chief punishment is this: that no guilty man is acquitted in his own judgement.
Satires **Juvenal** (c.60–130) Roman verse satirist and Stoic

11 'But I'm not guilty,' said K., 'there's been a mistake. How can a man be guilty anyway.'
The Trial (1925) **Kafka, Franz** (1883–1924) Czech-born German-speaking writer

12 Guilt is of course not an emotion in the Celtic countries, it is simply a way of life – a kind of gleefully painful social anaesthetic.
So I am Glad (1995) **Kennedy, A.L.** (1965–) Scottish novelist

13 We would often be ashamed of our finest actions if the world could see the motives behind them.
Maximes (1678) **La Rochefoucauld** (1613–1680) French writer

14 You will put on a dress of guilt
and shoes with broken high ideals.
'Comeclose and Sleepnow' (1967) **McGough, Roger** (1937–) English poet and teacher

15 Conscience is the inner voice that warns us somebody may be looking.
A Mencken Chrestomathy (1949) **Mencken, H.L.** (1880–1956) US writer, critic, philologist and satirist

16 Saints should always be judged guilty until they are proved innocent.
Shooting an Elephant (1950) **Orwell, George** (1903–1950) English writer and critic

17 Life without industry is guilt.
'The Relation of Art to Morals' (1870) **Ruskin, John** (1819–1900) English art critic, philosopher and reformer

18 But with the morning cool repentance came.
Rob Roy (1817) **Scott, Sir Walter** (1771–1832) Scottish writer and historian

19 Thus conscience does make cowards of us
all;
And thus the native hue of resolution
Is sicklied o'er with the pale cast of
thought.
Hamlet, III.i

20 My words fly up, my thoughts remain
below.
Words without thoughts never to heaven
go.
Hamlet, III.iii

21 Well, I'll repent, and that suddenly, while I
am in some liking; I shall be out of heart
shortly, and then I shall have no strength
to repent.
Henry IV, Part 1, III.iii

22 Suspicion always haunts the guilty mind:
The thief doth fear each bush an officer.
Henry VI, Part 3, V.vi

23 A peace above all earthly dignities,
A still and quiet conscience.
Henry VIII, III.ii

24 And then it started like a guilty thing
Upon a fearful summons.
Macbeth, I.i

25 Will all great Neptune's ocean wash this
blood
Clean from my hand? No; this my hand
will rather
The multitudinous seas incarnadine,
Making the green one red.
Macbeth, II.ii

26 Out, damned spot! out, I say! One, two;
why then 'tis time to do't. Hell is murky.
Fie, my lord, fie! a soldier, and afeard?
What need we fear who knows it, when
none can call our pow'r to account? Yet
who would have thought the old man to
have had so much blood in him?
Macbeth, V.i

27 Here's the smell of the blood still. All the
perfumes of Arabia will not sweeten this
little hand. Oh, oh, oh!
Macbeth, V.i

28 He prays but faintly and would be denied.
Richard II, V.iii

29 My conscience hath a thousand several
tongues,
And every tongue brings in a several tale,
And every tale condemns me for a villain.
Richard III, V.iii

30 Conscience is but a word that cowards use,
Devis'd at first to keep the strong in awe.
Richard III, V.iii **Shakespeare, William** (1564–
1616) English dramatist, poet and actor

31 Societies need to have one illness which
becomes identified with evil, and attaches
blame to its 'victims'.
AIDS and Its Metaphors (1989) **Sontag, Susan**
(1933–) US critic and writer

32 Oh, I wish that God had not given me what
I prayed for! It was not so good as I
thought.
Heidi (1880–1881) **Spyri, Johanna** (1827–1901)
Swiss writer

33 What hangs people ... is the unfortunate
circumstance of guilt.
The Wrong Box (1889) **Stevenson, Robert Louis**
(1850–1894) Scottish writer, poet and essayist
See also crime; fear

HAPPINESS

1 Smile, it confuses people.
The Dilbert Principle **Adams, Scott** (1957–) US
cartoonist

2 The important question is not, what will
yield to man a few scattered pleasures, but
what will render his life happy on the whole
amount.
*Interesting Anecdotes, Memoirs, Allegories, Essays,
and Poetical Fragments* (1794) **Addison, Joseph**
(1672–1719) English essayist, poet, playwright
and statesman

3 One swallow does not make a summer,
neither does one fine day; similarly one day
or brief time of happiness does not make a
person entirely happy.
Nicomachean Ethics **Aristotle** (384–322 BC)
Greek philosopher

4 'Live with the gods'
But he is living with the gods who
constantly shows them that his soul is
satisfied with what is assigned to him.

Meditations **Aurelius, Marcus** (121–180) Roman emperor and Stoic philosopher

5 Why not seize the pleasure at once? How often is happiness destroyed by preparation, foolish preparation!
Emma (1816)

6 Perfect happiness, even in memory, is not common.
Emma (1816) **Austen, Jane** (1775–1817) English writer

7 ... this sacred truth – that the greatest happiness of the greatest number is the foundation of morals and legislation.
Works **Bentham, Jeremy** (1748–1832) English writer and philosopher. Quoting Francis Hutcheson

8 Happiness is good health – and a bad memory.
In Simon Rose, *Classic Film Guide* (1995) **Bergman, Ingrid** (1915–1982) Swedish actress

9 Happy is the man who fears the Lord, who is only too willing to follow his orders.
Psalms, 111:1 **The Bible (Vulgate)**

10 Nothing is miserable unless you think it so; conversely, every lot is happy to one who is content with it.
De Consolatione Philosophiae **Boethius** (c.475–524) Roman statesman, scholar and philosopher

11 The secret of happiness is to admire without desiring. And that is not happiness.
Aphorisms (1930) **Bradley, F.H.** (1846–1924) English philosopher

12 Certainly there is no happiness within this circle of flesh, nor is it in the optics of these eyes to behold felicity; the first day of our Jubilee is death.
Religio Medici (1643) **Browne, Sir Thomas** (1605–1682) English physician, author and antiquary

13 One moment may with bliss repay Unnumber'd hours of pain.
'The Ritter Bann' **Campbell, Thomas** (1777–1844) Scottish poet, ballad writer and journalist

14 Happiness is a mystery like religion, and should never be rationalized.
Heretics (1905) **Chesterton, G.K.** (1874–1936) English writer, poet and critic

15 We ne'er can be
Made happy by compulsion.
'The Three Graves' (1809) **Coleridge, Samuel Taylor** (1772–1834) English poet, philosopher and critic

16 True contentment depends not on what we have; a tub was large enough for Diogenes, but a world was too little for Alexander.
Lacon (1820) **Colton, Charles Caleb** (c.1780–1832) English clergyman and satirist

17 Domestic happiness, thou only bliss
Of Paradise that has surviv'd the fall!
The Task (1785) **Cowper, William** (1731–1800) English poet, hymn writer and letter writer

18 Happiness is too many things these days for anyone to wish it on anyone lightly. So let's just wish each other a bileless New Year and leave it at that.
The Private Eye, the Cowboy and the Very Naked Girl (1968) **Crist, Judith** (1922–) US film critic and writer

19 For all the happiness mankind can gain
Is not in pleasure, but in rest from pain.
The Indian Emperor (1665)

20 Happy the man, and happy he alone,
He, who can call to-day his own:
He who, secure within, can say,
Tomorrow do thy worst, for I have lived to-day.
Sylvae (1685) **Dryden, John** (1631–1700) English poet, satirist, dramatist and critic

21 The happiest women, like the happiest nations, have no history.
The Mill on the Floss (1860) **Eliot, George** (1819–1880) English writer and poet

22 To fill the hour, – that is happiness.
Essays, Second Series (1844) **Emerson, Ralph Waldo** (1803–1882) US poet, essayist, transcendentalist and teacher

23 Here with a Loaf of Bread beneath the
Bough,
A Flask of Wine, a Book of Verse – and
Thou
Beside me singing in the Wilderness –
And Wilderness is Paradise enow.
The Rubáiyát of Omar Khayyám (1859)
Fitzgerald, Edward (1809–1883) English poet,
translator and letter writer

24 Whoever is happy will make others happy,
too.
The Diary of Anne Frank (1947) **Frank, Anne**
(1929–1945) Jewish diarist; died in Nazi
concentration camp

25 Be in general virtuous, and you will be
happy.
'On Early Marriages' **Franklin, Benjamin**
(1706–1790) US statesman, scientist, political
critic and printer

26 The idea of always being at peace, always
being blissfully happy, is scary. Anyone in a
placid state is just going to vegetate.
In *The Observer*, (1999) **Heller, Joseph** (1923–
1999) US writer

27 You would not rightly call the man who has
many possessions happy; he more rightly
deserves to be called happy who knows
how to use the gifts of the gods wisely, and
can endure the hardship of poverty, and
who fears dishonour more than death.
Odes **Horace** (65–8 BC) Roman poet

28 The supreme happiness in life is the
conviction that we are loved.
Attr. **Hugo, Victor** (1802–1885) French poet,
writer, dramatist and politician

29 Happiness is like coke – something you get
as a by-product in the process of making
something else.
Point Counter Point (1928)

30 Stability isn't nearly so spectacular as
instability. And being contented has none
of the glamour of a good fight against
misfortune, none of the picturesqueness of
a struggle with temptation, or a fatal
overthrow by passion or doubt. Happiness
is never grand.
Brave New World (1932) **Huxley, Aldous** (1894–
1963) English writer, poet and critic

31 If you are foolish enough to be contented,
don't show it, but grumble with the rest.
Idle Thoughts of an Idle Fellow (1886) **Jerome,
Jerome K.** (1859–1927) English writer and
dramatist

32 There is nothing which has yet been
contrived by man, by which so much
happiness is produced as by a good tavern
or inn.
In Boswell, *The Life of Samuel Johnson* (1791)

33 That all who are happy, are equally happy,
is not true. A peasant and a philosopher
may be equally satisfied, but not equally
happy. Happiness consists in the
multiplicity of agreeable consciousness.
In Boswell, *The Life of Samuel Johnson* (1791)
Johnson, Samuel (1709–1784) English
lexicographer, poet, critic, conversationalist
and essayist

34 … because bliss is not an ideal of reason,
but of the powers of imagination.
Outline of the Metaphysics of Morals (1785)

35 Act in such a way that you will be worthy of
being happy.
Critique of Pure Reason (1787) **Kant, Immanuel**
(1724–1804) German idealist philosopher

36 It is a flaw
In happiness, to see beyond our bourn, –
It forces us in summer skies to mourn:
It spoils the singing of the nightingale.
'To J. H. Reynolds, Esq.' (1818) **Keats, John**
(1795–1821) English poet

37 Teach us Delight in simple things,
And Mirth that has no bitter springs.
Puck of Pook's Hill (1906), 'The Children's
Song' **Kipling, Rudyard** (1865–1936) Indian-
born British poet and writer

38 What vails your kingdome, and your rent,
And all your great treasure;
Without ye haif ane mirrie lyfe,
And cast aside all sturt, and stryfe.
Satyre of the Thrie Estaitis **Lindsay, Sir David**
(c.1490–1555) Scottish poet and satirist

39 Great joys, like griefs, are silent.
Holland's Leaguer (1632) **Marmion, Shackerley**
(1603–1639) English dramatist and poet

40 Ask yourself whether you are happy, and you cease to be so.
Autobiography (1873) **Mill, John Stuart** (1806–1873) English philosopher, economist and reformer

41 It is necessary to the happiness of man that he be mentally faithful to himself. Infidelity does not consist in believing, or in disbelieving, it consists in professing to believe what one does not believe.
The Age of Reason (1794) **Paine, Thomas** (1737–1809) English-born US political theorist and pamphleteer

42 If you want to be happy, pretend to be miserable.
Doctor Angélico's Papers (1911) **Palacio Valdés, Armando** (1853–1938) Spanish novelist

43 How happy is the blameless Vestal's lot? The world forgetting, by the world forgot.
'Eloisa to Abelard' (1717)

44 Oh Happiness! our being's end and aim!
Essay on Man (1734) **Pope, Alexander** (1688–1744) English poet, translator and editor

45 In Hollywood, if you don't have happiness, you send out for it.
In Colombo, *Colombo's Hollywood* **Reed, Rex** (1938–) US film and music critic and columnist

46 Had I been brighter, the ladies been gentler, the Scotch been weaker, had the gods been kinder, had the dice been hotter, this could have been a one-sentence story: Once upon a time I lived happily ever after.
Attr. **Rooney, Mickey** (1920–) US film actor

47 Happiness: a good bank account, a good cook, and a good digestion.
Treasury of Humorous Quotations **Rousseau, Jean-Jacques** (1712–1778) Swiss-born French philosopher, educationist and essayist

48 What is that wall that always rises up between human beings and their most intimate desire, their frightening will to be happy? ... Is it a nostalgia nurtured from childhood?
Le Garde du coeur (1968) **Sagan, Françoise** (1935–2004) French writer

49 If you want to understand the meaning of happiness, you must see it as a reward and not as a goal.
Carnets **Saint-Exupéry, Antoine de** (1900–1944) French author and aviator

50 One is happy as a result of one's own efforts, once one knows the necessary ingredients of happiness – simple tastes, a certain degree of courage, self denial to a point, love of work, and, above all, a clear conscience. Happiness is no vague dream, of that I now feel certain.
Correspondence **Sand, George** (1804–1876) French writer and dramatist

51 Happiness is the only sanction of life; where happiness fails, existence remains a mean and lamentable experience.
The Life of Reason (1905–1906) **Santayana, George** (1863–1952) Spanish-born US philosopher and writer

52 Joy, fair ray of the gods,
Daughter of Elysium,
Dazzled we enter,
Heavenly one, thy shrine.
Against thy charms join together
What custom has harshly divided,
All men become brothers,
Under thy gentle wing.
'To Joy' (revised 1803); set to music by Beethoven in the last movement of his Ninth Symphony **Schiller, Johann Christoph Friedrich** (1759–1805) German writer, dramatist, poet and historian

53 O, how bitter a thing it is to look into happiness through another man's eyes!
As You Like It, V.ii

54 I swear 'tis better to be lowly born
And range with humble livers in content
Than to be perk'd up in a glist'ring grief
And wear a golden sorrow.
Henry VIII, II.iii **Shakespeare, William** (1564–1616) English dramatist, poet and actor

55 We have no more right to consume happiness without producing it than to consume wealth without producing it.
Candida (1898)

56 A lifetime of happiness! No man alive could bear it: it would be hell on earth.

Man and Superman (1903) **Shaw, George Bernard** (1856–1950) Irish socialist, writer, dramatist and critic

57 Mankind are always happy for having been happy, so that if you make them happy now, you make them happy twenty years hence by the memory of it.
Sketches of Moral Philosophy (1849)

58 This great spectacle of human happiness.
Essays (1877) **Smith, Sydney** (1771–1845) English clergyman, essayist, journalist and wit

59 Until a man dies, be careful to call him not happy but lucky.
In Herodotus, *Histories* **Solon** (c.638–c.559 BC) Athenian statesman, reformer and poet

60 What more felicitie can fall to creature,
Than to enjoy delight with libertie.
Complaints (1591) **Spenser, Edmund** (c.1522–1599) English poet

61 Martial, the things for to attain
The happy life be these, I find:
The riches left, not got with pain;
The fruitful ground, the quiet mind;
The equal friend; no grudge nor strife;
No charge or rule nor governance;
Without disease the healthful life;
The household of continuance.
'The Happy Life' (1547) **Surrey, Henry Howard, Earl of** (c.1517–1547) English poet, courtier and soldier

62 Happiness is an imaginary condition, formerly often attributed by the living to the dead, now usually attributed by adults to children, and by children to adults.
The Second Sin (1973) **Szasz, Thomas** (1920–) Hungarian-born US psychiatrist and writer

63 If you want to be happy, be.
Attr. **Tolstoy, Leo** (1828–1910) Russian writer, essayist, philosopher and moralist

64 Contentment is a sleepy thing
If it in death alone must die;
A quiet mind is worse than poverty,
Unless it from enjoyment spring!
'Of Contentment' **Traherne, Thomas** (c.1637–1674) English religious writer and clergyman

65 I would rather sit on a pumpkin and have it all to myself than be crowded on a velvet cushion.

Walden (1854) **Thoreau, Henry David** (1817–1862) US essayist, social critic and writer

66 I can't quite explain it, but I don't believe one can ever be unhappy for long provided one does just exactly what one wants to and when one wants to.
Decline and Fall (1928) **Waugh, Evelyn** (1903–1966) English writer and diarist

67 I don't believe in happiness: why should we expect to be happy? In such a world as this, depression is rational, rage reasonable.
The Observer, (1995) **Weldon, Fay** (1931–) British writer

68 Happiness is no laughing matter.
Apophthegms (1854) **Whately, Richard** (1787–1863) English philosopher, theologian, educationist and writer

69 Happy is he, who, caring not for Pope, Consul, or King, can sound himself to know
The destiny of Man, and live in hope.
Sonnets Dedicated to Liberty and Order (1807) **Wordsworth, William** (1770–1850) English poet

70 The hell with it. Who never knew
the price of happiness will not be happy.
'Lies' (1955) **Yevtushenko, Yevgeny** (1933–) Russian poet
See also humour; pleasure

HATRED

1 Let them hate provided that they fear.
Atreus **Accius, Lucius** (170–86 BC) Roman poet

2 Who despises all, displeases all.
Liber Consolationis **Albertano of Brescia** (c.1190–c.1270) Jurist, philosopher and politician

3 Severity breedeth fear, but roughness breedeth hate. Even reproofs from authority ought to be grave, and not taunting.
'Of Great Place' (1625) **Bacon, Francis** (1561–1626) English philosopher, essayist, politician and courtier

4 It does not matter much what a man hates provided that he hates something.

Notebooks **Butler, Samuel** (1835–1902) English writer, painter, philosopher and scholar

5 Now hatred is by far the longest pleasure; Men love in haste, but they detest at leisure.
Don Juan (1824) **Byron, Lord** (1788–1824) English poet, satirist and traveller

6 Everybody hates me because I'm so universally liked.
The Vale of Laughter (1967) **De Vries, Peter** (1910–1993) US novelist

7 I hate all that don't love me, and slight all that do.
The Constant Couple (1699) **Farquhar, George** (1678–1707) Irish dramatist

8 I am free of all prejudice. I hate everyone equally.
Attr. **Fields, W.C.** (1880–1946) US film actor

9 I never hated a man enough to give him his diamonds back.
The Observer, (1957) **Gabor, Zsa-Zsa** (1919–) Hungarian-born US actress

10 Violent antipathies are always suspicious, and betray a secret affinity.
Table-Talk (1822)

11 We can scarcely hate any one that we know.
Table-Talk (1825)

12 The dupe of friendship, and the fool of love; have I not reason to hate and to despise myself? Indeed I do; and chiefly for not having hated and despised the world enough.
The Plain Speaker (1826) **Hazlitt, William** (1778–1830) English writer and critic

13 If we hate a person, we hate something in our image of him that lies within ourselves. What is not within ourselves doesn't upset us.
Demian (1919) **Hesse, Hermann** (1877–1962) German novelist and poet

14 Passionate hatred can give meaning and purpose to an empty life.
Attr. **Hoffer, Eric** (1902–1983) US writer, philosopher and longshoreman

15 He [Mao Zedong] was, it seemed to me, really a restless fight promoter by nature and good at it. He understood ugly human instincts such as envy and resentment, and knew how to mobilize them for his ends. He ruled by getting people to hate each other.
Wild Swans (1991) **Jung Chang** (1952–) Chinese author

16 Any kiddie in school can love like a fool, But hating, my boy, is an art.
Happy Days (1933) **Nash, Ogden** (1902–1971) US poet

17 Always give your best, never get discouraged, never be petty. Always remember, others may hate you, but those who hate you don't win unless you hate them, and then you destroy yourself.
Farewell speech to his staff, (1974) **Nixon, Richard** (1913–1994) US Republican politician and President

18 Sacred Heart of the Crucified Jesus, take away our hearts o' stone … an' give us hearts o' flesh! … Take away this murdherin' hate … an' give us Thine own eternal love!
Juno and the Paycock (1924) **O'Casey, Sean** (1880–1964) Irish dramatist

19 In hatred as in love, we grow like the thing we brood upon. What we loathe, we graft into our very soul.
The Mask of Apollo (1966) **Renault, Mary** (1905–1983) English novelist

20 Any man who hates dogs and babies can't be all bad.
Speech, (1939) **Rosten, Leo** (1908–1997) Polish-born US social scientist, writer and humorist. Of W.C. Fields; often attributed to him

21 Few people can be happy unless they hate some other person, nation or creed.
Attr. **Russell, Bertrand** (1872–1970) English philosopher, mathematician, essayist and social reformer

22 I never saw a richer company or to speak my mind a finer people. The worst of them is the bitter and envenomed dislike which they have to each other; their factions have been so long envenomed and have so little ground to fight their battle in that they are like people fighting with daggers in a hogshead.

Letter to Joanna Baillie, (1825) **Scott, Sir Walter** (1771–1832) Scottish writer and historian

23 And Sleep shall obey me,
And visit thee never,
And the Curse shall be on thee
For ever and ever.
The Curse of Kehama (1810) **Southey, Robert** (1774–1843) English poet, essayist, historian and letter writer

24 I have ever hated all nations, professions and communities, and all my love is towards individuals … But principally I hate and detest that animal called man; although I heartily love John, Peter, Thomas, and so forth.
Letter to Pope, (1725) **Swift, Jonathan** (1667–1745) Irish satirist, poet, essayist and cleric

25 It is part of human nature to hate those whom you have injured.
Agricola **Tacitus** (AD c.56–c.120) Roman historian

26 It were treason to our love
And a sin to God above
One iota to abate
Of a pure impartial hate.
'Indeed, Indeed I Cannot Tell' (1852) **Thoreau, Henry David** (1817–1862) US essayist, social critic and writer
See also anger; love; spite

HEALTH

1 We 'need' cancer because, by the very fact of its incurability, it makes all other diseases, however virulent, not cancer.
Myths and Memories (1986) **Adair, Gilbert** (1944–) English author and critic

2 It could be said that the Aids pandemic is a classic own-goal scored by the human race against itself.
Remark, (1988) **Anne, the Princess Royal** (1950–) Daughter of Elizabeth II

3 Coughs and sneezes spread diseases.
Ministry of Health, (c.1942)

4 Don't Die of Ignorance.
Department of Health AIDS campaign, (1987)
Anonymous

5 Nor bring, to see me cease to live,
Some doctor full of phrase and fame,
To shake his sapient head and give
The ill he cannot cure a name.
'A Wish' (1867) **Arnold, Matthew** (1822–1888) English poet, critic, essayist and educationist

6 Sciatica: he cured it, by boiling his buttock.
Brief Lives (c.1693) **Aubrey, John** (1626–1697) English antiquary, folklorist and biographer

7 Across the wires the electric message came:
'He is no better, he is much the same.'
Attr. **Austin, Alfred** (1835–1913) English poet and journalist. On the illness of the Prince of Wales

8 The remedy is worse than the disease.
'Of Seditions and Troubles' (1625) **Bacon, Francis** (1561–1626) English philosopher, essayist, politician and courtier

9 Physicians of the Utmost Fame
Were called at once; but when they came
They answered, as they took their Fees,
'There is no Cure for this Disease.'
Cautionary Tales (1907) **Belloc, Hilaire** (1870–1953) English writer of verse, essayist and critic; Liberal MP

10 'Ye can call it influenza if ye like,' said Mrs Machin. 'There was no influenza in my young days. We called a cold a cold.'
The Card (1911) **Bennett, Arnold** (1867–1931) English writer, dramatist and journalist

11 A merry heart doeth good like a medicine.
Proverbs, 17:22

12 Physician, heal thyself.
Luke, 4:23 **The Bible (King James Version)**

13 I'm anorexic really. Anorexic people look in the mirror and think they look fat. And so do I.
Attr. **Brand, Jo** (1957–) English comedienne

14 I reckon being ill as one of the great pleasures of life, provided one is not too ill and is not obliged to work till one is better.
The Way of All Flesh (1903) **Butler, Samuel** (1835–1902) English writer, painter, philosopher and scholar

15 The two best exercises in the world are making love and dancing. But a simple one is to stand on tiptoe.
Cartland, Barbara (1901–2000) English writer

16 If many remedies are suggested for a disease, that means the disease is incurable.
The Cherry Orchard (1904) **Chekhov, Anton** (1860–1904) Russian writer, dramatist and doctor

17 Thousands upon thousands of persons have studied disease. Almost no one has studied health.
Let's Eat Right to Keep Fit (1954) **Davis, Adelle** (1904–1974) US nutritionist and author

18 Not to be healthy ... is one of the few sins that modern society is willing to recognise and condemn.
The Cunning Man (1994) **Davies, Robertson** (1913–1995) Canadian playwright, writer and critic

19 Better to hunt in fields, for health unbought,
Than fee the doctor for a nauseous draught.
The wise, for cure, on exercise depend;
God never made his work, for man to mend.
Epistles (1700) **Dryden, John** (1631–1700) English poet, satirist, dramatist and critic

20 A person seldom falls sick, but the bystanders are animated with a faint hope that he will die.
Conduct of Life (1860) **Emerson, Ralph Waldo** (1803–1882) US poet, essayist, transcendentalist and teacher

21 I find the medicine worse than the malady.
The Lover's Progress (1623) **Fletcher, John** (1579–1625) English dramatist

22 Exercise is bunk. If you are healthy, you don't need it: if you are sick you shouldn't take it.
Attr. **Ford, Henry** (1863–1947) US car manufacturer

23 I am so changed that my oldest creditors would hardly know me.

Quoted by Byron in a letter to John Murray, (1817) **Fox, Henry Stephen** (1791–1846) English diplomat. Remark after an illness

24 I can mix a Margarita in five seconds.
The Times, (1998) **Fox, Michael** (1961–) US actor. Joking about the tremors caused by Parkinson's disease

25 He's the best physician that knows the worthlessness of the most medicines.
Poor Richard's Almanac (1733) **Franklin, Benjamin** (1706–1790) US statesman, scientist, political critic and printer

26 If you resolve to give up smoking, drinking and loving, you don't actually live longer; it just seems longer.
The Observer, (1964) **Freud, Clement** (1924–) British Liberal politician, broadcaster and writer

27 Much of the world's work, it has been said, is done by men who do not feel quite well. Marx is a case in point.
The Age of Uncertainty **Galbraith, J.K.** (1908–2006) Canadian-born US economist, diplomat and writer

28 Dr Winchester well remembered that he had a salary to receive, and only forgot that he had a duty to perform.
Memoirs of My Life and Writings (1796) **Gibbon, Edward** (1737–1794) English historian, politician and memoirist

29 Never admit the pain,
Bury it deep;
Only the weak complain,
Complaint is cheap.
The Wild Swan (1930) **Gilmore, Dame Mary** (1865–1962) Australian poet and journalist

30 The doctor found, when she was dead, –
Her last disorder mortal.
'Elegy on Mrs Mary Blaize' (1759) **Goldsmith, Oliver** (c.1728–1774) Irish dramatist, poet and writer

31 Any man who goes to a psychiatrist should have his head examined.
In Zierold, *Moguls* (1969) **Goldwyn, Samuel** (1882–1974) Polish-born US film producer

32 Like cures like.

Motto of homeopathic medicine
Hahnemann, C.F.S. (1755–1843) German physician and founder of homeopathy

33 Hungry Joe collected lists of fatal diseases and arranged them in alphabetical order so that he could put his finger without delay on any one he wanted to worry about.
Catch-22 (1961) **Heller, Joseph** (1923–1999) US writer

34 Life is short, science is so long to learn, opportunity is elusive, experience is dangerous, judgement is difficult.
Aphorisms (c.415 BC) Of medicine

35 For extreme illnesses extreme remedies are most fitting.
Aphorisms **Hippocrates** (c.460–357 BC) Greek physician

36 For that old enemy the gout
Had taken him in toe!
Comic Melodies (1830) **Hood, Thomas** (1799–1845) English poet, editor and humorist

37 Some physiologists will have it that the stomach is a mill; – others, that it is a fermenting vat; – others again that it is a stew-pan; – but in my view of the matter, it is neither a mill, a fermenting vat, nor a stew-pan – but a stomach, gentlemen, a stomach.
Hunter, William (1718–1783) Scottish anatomist and physician

38 Whenever I feel like exercise, I lie down until the feeling passes.
In Jarman, *The Guinness Dictionary of Sports Quotations* (1990) **Hutchins, Robert M.** (1899–1977)

39 I suppose one has a greater sense of intellectual degradation after an interview with a doctor than from any human experience.
In Leon Edel (ed.), *The Diary of Alice James*, (1890) **James, Alice** (1848–1892) US diarist

40 For in the case of nutrition and health, just as in the case of education, the gentleman in Whitehall really does know better what is good for people than the people know themselves.
The Socialist Case (1947) **Jay, Douglas** (1907–1996) British economist and writer

41 It is incident to physicians, I am afraid, beyond all other men, to mistake subsequence for consequence.
In Boswell, *The Life of Samuel Johnson* (1791) **Johnson, Samuel** (1709–1784) English lexicographer, poet, critic, conversationalist and essayist

42 Your prayers should be for a healthy mind in a healthy body.
Satires **Juvenal** (c.60–130) Roman verse satirist and Stoic

43 The kind of doctor I want is one who when he's not examining me is home studying medicine.
In Howard Teichmann, *George S. Kaufman: An Intimate Portrait* (1972) **Kaufman, George S.** (1889–1961) US scriptwriter, librettist and journalist

44 One of the most difficult things to contend with in a hospital is the assumption on the part of the staff that because you have lost your gall bladder you have also lost your mind.
Please Don't Eat the Daisies (1957) **Kerr, Jean** (1923–2003) US writer and dramatist

45 Doctors allow us to die; charlatans kill us.
Les caractères ou les moeurs de ce siècle (1688) **La Bruyère, Jean de** (1645–1696) French satirist

46 How sickness enlarges the dimensions of a man's self to himself!
Last Essays of Elia (1833) **Lamb, Charles** (1775–1834) English essayist, critic and letter writer

47 I am only half there when I am ill, and so there is only half a man to suffer. To suffer in one's whole self is so great a violation, that it is not to be endured.
Letter to Catherine Carswell, (1916) **Lawrence, D.H.** (1885–1930) English writer, poet and critic

48 *Drumm:* I asked him if he had the results of the x-rays. He took me into his surgery ... He gave me one of those looks of his, redolent of the cemetery, and said that I should buy day-returns from now on instead of season tickets.
A Life (1986) **Leonard, Hugh** (1926–) Irish dramatist and screenwriter

49 So then Dr Froyd said that all I needed was to cultivate a few inhibitions and get some sleep.
Gentlemen Prefer Blondes (1925) **Loos, Anita** (1893–1981) US writer and screenwriter

50 It is not to live but to be healthy that makes a life.
Epigrammata **Martial** (c.AD 40–c.104) Spanish-born Latin epigrammatist and poet

51 Well, better a semi-colon than a full stop!
In Coleman, *The Heart of James McAuley* (1980) **McAuley, James Philip** (1917–1976) Australian poet and critic. After his first cancer operation; to a friend

52 If the nineteenth century was the age of the editorial chair, ours is the century of the psychiatrist's couch.
Understanding Media (1964) **McLuhan, Marshall** (1911–1980) Canadian communications theorist

53 While we were talking about what could make one happy, I said to him: *Sanitas sanitatum et omnia sanitas.*
In *Ménagiana* (1693) **Ménage, Gilles** (1613–1692) French lexicographer. Part of a conversation with Jean-Louis Guez de Balzac

54 He's an expeditious man, who likes to hurry his patients along; and when you have to die, he gets it over with quicker than anyone else.
Monsieur de Pourceaugnac (1670) **Molière** (1622–1673) French dramatist, actor and director

55 I think it is considerate of me to have taken on the disease, thus protecting the remaining 99,999 Screen Actors' Guild members from this fate.
The Times, (1999) **Moore, Dudley** (1935–2002) English comedian and actor. On his brain disease, said to affect only one in 100,000 people

56 A cough is something that you yourself can't help, but everybody else does on purpose just to torment you.
You Can't Get There From Here (1957) **Nash, Ogden** (1902–1971) US poet

57 The only exercise I get these days is from walking behind the coffins of friends who took too much exercise.

The Observer, 'Sayings of the Year', (1998) **O'Toole, Peter** (1932–) English actor

58 No flowers, please, just caviare.
The Times, (1999) **Paterson, Jennifer** (1928–1999) British chef and writer. Request from her hospital bed

59 There must be quite a few things a hot bath won't cure, but I don't know many of them.
The Bell Jar (1963) **Plath, Sylvia** (1932–1963) US poet, writer and diarist

60 For years I have let dentists ride roughshod over my teeth: I have been sawed, hacked, chopped, whittled, bewitched, bewildered, tattooed, and signed on again; but this is cuspid's last stand.
Crazy Like a Fox (1944)

61 I've got Bright's disease and he's got mine.
Attr. **Perelman, S.J.** (1904–1979) US humorist, writer and dramatist

62 Confront disease at its onset.
Satires **Persius Flaccus, Aulus** (AD 34–62) Roman satirical poet

63 Mankind is responsible for tuberculosis. What an ignorant civilization has introduced, an educated civilization can remove.
Attr. **Philip, Sir Robert** (1857–1939) British physician

64 As soon as he ceased to be mad he became merely stupid. There are maladies we must not seek to cure because they alone protect us from others that are more serious.
Le Côté de Guermantes (1921) **Proust, Marcel** (1871–1922) French writer and critic

65 Show him death, and he'll be content with fever.
Russian **Proverb**

66 Physicians of all men are most happy; what good success soever they have, the world proclaimeth, and what faults they commit, the earth covereth.
Hieroglyphics of the Life of Man (1638) **Quarles, Francis** (1592–1644) English poet, writer and royalist

67 First they get on, then they get honour, then they get honest.

In David Ogilvy, *Confessions of an Advertising Man* (1963) **Rolleston, Sir Humphrey** (1862–1944) English physician. Of physicians

68 There are so many things to complain of in this household that it would never have occurred to me to complain of rheumatism.
The Chronicles of Clovis (1911) **Saki** (1870–1916) Burmese-born British writer

69 Diseases desperate grown
By desperate appliance are reliev'd,
Or not at all.
Hamlet, IV.iii **Shakespeare, William** (1564–1616) English dramatist, poet and actor

70 Optimistic lies have such immense therapeutic value that a doctor who cannot tell them convincingly has mistaken his profession.
Misalliance (1914) **Shaw, George Bernard** (1856–1950) Irish socialist, writer, dramatist and critic

71 Noble deeds and hot baths are the best cures for depression.
I Capture the Castle (1948) **Smith, Dodie** (1896–1990) English novelist

72 I am better in health … and drinking nothing but London water, with a million insects in every drop. He who drinks a tumbler of London water has literally in his stomach more animated beings than there are men, women, and children on the face of the globe.
Letter to Countess Grey, (1834)

73 I am convinced digestion is the great secret of life.
Letter to Arthur Kinglake, (1837)

74 If you hear of sixteen or eighteen pounds of human flesh, they belong to me. I look as if a curate has been taken out of me.
Letter to Lady Carlisle, (1844) On his convalescent diet **Smith, Sydney** (1771–1845) English clergyman, essayist, journalist and wit

75 Illness is the night-side of life, a more onerous citizenship. Everyone who is born holds dual citizenship, in the kingdom of the well and in the kingdom of the sick. Although we all prefer to use only the good passport, sooner or later each of us is obliged, at least for a spell, to identify ourselves as citizens of that other place.
Illness as Metaphor (1978) **Sontag, Susan** (1933–) US critic and writer

76 In home-sickness you must keep moving – it is the only disease that does not require rest.
The Bourgeois (1901) **Stacpoole, H. de Vere** (1863–1951) Irish writer and physician

77 Even if the doctor does not give you a year, even if he hesitates about a month, make one brave push and see what can be accomplished in a week.
Virginibus Puerisque (1881) **Stevenson, Robert Louis** (1850–1894) Scottish writer, poet and essayist

78 We are so fond of one another, because our ailments are the same.
Journal to Stella, 1711

79 I row after health like a waterman, and ride after it like a postboy, and find little success.
Attr. **Swift, Jonathan** (1667–1745) Irish satirist, poet, essayist and cleric

80 Our body is a machine for living. It is geared towards it, it is its nature. Let life go on in it unhindered and let it defend itself, it will be more effective than if you paralyse it by encumbering it with remedies.
War and Peace (1869) **Tolstoy, Leo** (1828–1910) Russian writer, essayist, philosopher and moralist

81 Make hunger thy sauce, as a medicine for health.
Five Hundred Points of Good Husbandry (1557) **Tusser, Thomas** (c.1524–1580) English writer, poet and musician

82 Look to your health; and if you have it, praise God, and value it next to a good conscience; for health is the second blessing that we mortals are capable of; a blessing money cannot buy.
The Compleat Angler (1653) **Walton, Izaak** (1593–1683) English writer

83 Physicians are like kings – they brook no contradiction.
The Duchess of Malfi (1623) **Webster, John** (c.1580–c.1625) English dramatist

84 They brought her to the city
And she faded slowly there –
Consumption has no pity
For blue eyes and golden hair.
'The Dying Girl' **Williams, Richard D'Alton**
(1822–1862) Irish poet

85 He was meddling too much in my private
life.
Attr. **Williams, Tennessee** (1911–1983) US
dramatist and writer. Explaining why he had
stopped seeing his psychoanalyst

86 Most of the time we think we're sick, it's all
in the mind.
Look Homeward, Angel (1929) **Wolfe, Thomas**
(1900–1938) US novelist and dramatist
See also disability; suffering

HISTORY

1 History is the sum total of things that
could have been avoided.
Attr. **Adenauer, Konrad** (1876–1967) German
Chancellor

2 The lessons of the past are ignored and
obliterated in a contemporary antagonism
known as the generation gap.
New York Times, (1969) **Agnew, Spiro T.** (1918–
1996) US Vice President

3 I send you a kaffis of mustard seed, that
you may taste and acknowledge the
bitterness of my victory.
Letter to King Darius III **Alexander the Great**
(356–323 BC) Macedonian king and conquering
army commander

4 History, faced with courage, need not be
lived again.
Speech at the Inauguration of President
William Clinton, (1993) **Angelou, Maya**
(1928–) US writer, poet and dramatist

5 N.B. There will be very few Dates in this
History.
The History of England (1791)

6 Real solemn history, I cannot be interested
in … The quarrels of popes and kings, with
wars or pestilences, in every page; the men
all so good for nothing, and hardly any
women at all, it is very tiresome.
Northanger Abbey (1818)

7 History tells me nothing that does not
either vex or weary me; the men are all so
good for nothing, and hardly any women
at all.
Letter **Austen, Jane** (1775–1817) English writer

8 The whole history of civilization is strewn
with creeds and institutions which were
invaluable at first, and deadly afterwards.
Physics and Politics (1872) **Bagehot, Walter**
(1826–1877) English economist and political
philosopher

9 History does not repeat itself. Historians
repeat each other.
Attr. **Balfour, A.J.** (1848–1930) British
Conservative Prime Minister

10 The exact measure of the progress of
civilization is the degree in which the
intelligence of the common mind has
prevailed over wealth and brute force.
Address to The Historical Society, New York,
(1854) **Bancroft, George** (1800–1891) US
historian

11 When the history of the first half of this
century comes to be written – properly
written – it will be acknowledged the most
stupid and brutal in the history of
civilization.
Attr. **Beecham, Sir Thomas** (1879–1961)
English conductor and impresario

12 George the Third
Ought never to have occurred.
One can only wonder
At so grotesque a blunder.
More Biography (1929) **Bentley, Edmund
Clerihew** (1875–1956) English writer

13 That great dust-heap called 'history'.
Obiter Dicta (1884–1887) **Birrell, Augustine**
(1850–1933) English author and politician

14 I have read somewhere or other – in
Dionysius of Halicarnassus, I think – that
History is Philosophy teaching by
examples.
Letters on Study and Use of History (1752)

15 They maintained the dignity of history.
Letters on Study and Use of History (1752) Of
Thucydides and Xenophon **Bolingbroke,
Henry** (1678–1751) English statesman,
historian and actor

16 The king has been very good to me. He promoted me from a simple maid to be a marchioness. Then he raised me to be a queen. Now he will raise me to be a martyr.
Attr. **Boleyn, Anne** (1507–1536) Wife of Henry VIII and mother of Elizabeth I. Said on hearing that she was to be executed for adultery

17 History can show few benign mergings of people with people. Flame and blood is always the cement.
'The View from Orkney' **Brown, George MacKay** (1921–1996) Scottish novelist, poet and playwright

18 People will not look forward to posterity, who never look backward to their ancestors.
Reflections on the Revolution in France (1790) **Burke, Edmund** (1729–1797) Irish-born British statesman and philosopher

19 It has been said that though God cannot alter the past, historians can; it is perhaps because they can be useful to Him in this respect that He tolerates their existence.
Erewhon Revisited (1901) **Butler, Samuel** (1835–1902) English writer, painter, philosopher and scholar

20 I came, I saw, I conquered.
In Suetonius, *Lives of the Caesars* **Caesar, Gaius Julius** (c.102–44 BC) Roman statesman, historian and army commander. On his triumphant Pontic campaign (Veni, vidi, vici.)

21 History [is] a distillation of rumour.
History of the French Revolution (1837)

22 The three great elements of modern civilization, Gunpowder, Printing, and the Protestant Religion.
Critical and Miscellaneous Essays (1839)

23 There is no life of a man, faithfully recorded, but is a heroic poem of its sort, rhymed or unrhymed.
Critical and Miscellaneous Essays (1839)

24 History is the essence of innumerable biographies.
'On History' (1839)

25 Happy the people whose annals are blank in history-books!
History of Frederick the Great (1865) **Carlyle, Thomas** (1795–1881) Scottish historian, biographer, critic, and essayist

26 The history of every country begins in the heart of a man or a woman.
O Pioneers! (1913) **Cather, Willa** (1876–1947) US writer

27 Better than going to a play.
In A. Bryant, *King Charles II* (1931) **Charles II** (1630–1685) King of Great Britain and Ireland. On the debates in the House of Lords on Lord Ross's Divorce Bill, 1670

28 You ask, what is our aim? I can answer that in one word: victory at all costs, victory in spite of all terror, victory however long and hard the road may be; for without victory there is no survival.
Speech, House of Commons, (May 1940) **Churchill, Sir Winston** (1874–1965) English Conservative Prime Minister

29 History is the witness that testifies to the passing of time; it illumines reality, vitalizes memory, provides guidance in daily life, and brings us tidings of antiquity.
Pro Publio Sestio **Cicero** (106–43 BC) Roman orator, statesman, essayist and letter writer

30 If men could learn from history, what lessons it might teach us! But passion and party blind our eyes, and the light which experience gives is a lantern on the stern, which shines only on the waves behind us!
Table Talk (1835) **Coleridge, Samuel Taylor** (1772–1834) English poet, philosopher and critic

31 The dominion of the sea, as it is an ancient and undoubted right of the crown of England, so it is the best security of the land. The wooden walls are the best walls of this kingdom.
Speech in Star Chamber, (1635) **Coventry, Thomas** (1578–1640) English Attorney-General and politician

32 History shows that most of the positive or beneficial developments in human society have occurred as the result of care and compassion. Consider, for example, the abolition of the slave trade – ideals are the engine of progress.
The Times, (June 1999) **Dalai Lama** (1935–) Spiritual and temporal leader of Tibet

33 History is philosophy teaching from examples.
Ars Rhetorica **Dionysius of Halicarnassus** (fl. 30–7 BC) Greek historian

34 Read no history: nothing but biography, for that is life without theory.
Contarini Fleming (1832) **Disraeli, Benjamin** (1804–1881) English statesman and writer

35 I must have the gentleman to haul and draw with the mariner, and the mariner with the gentleman … I would know him, that would refuse to set his hand to a rope, but I know there is not any such here.
In Corbett, *Drake and the Tudor Navy* (1898) **Drake, Sir Francis** (c.1540–1596) English navigator

36 Plots, true or false, are necessary things, To raise up commonwealths and ruin kings.
Absalom and Achitophel (1681) **Dryden, John** (1631–1700) English poet, satirist, dramatist and critic

37 History is an endless repetition of the wrong way of living.
The Listener, (1978) **Durrell, Lawrence** (1912–1990) Indian-born British poet and writer

38 History teaches us that men and nations behave wisely once they have exhausted all other alternatives.
Speech, (1970) **Eban, Abba** (1915–2002) South African-born Israeli statesman and writer

39 The more rapidly a civilisation progresses, the sooner it dies for another to rise in its place.
The Dance of Life **Ellis, Havelock** (1859–1939) English sexologist and essayist

40 There is properly no history; only biography.

Essays, First Series (1841) **Emerson, Ralph Waldo** (1803–1882) US poet, essayist, transcendentalist and teacher

41 One intellectual excitement has, however, been denied me. Men wiser and more learned than I have discerned in history a plot, a rhythm, a predetermined pattern. These harmonies are concealed from me. I can see only one emergency following upon another as wave follows upon wave, only one great fact with respect to which, since it is unique, there can be no generalizations, only one safe rule for the historian: that he should recognize in the development of human destinies the play of the contingent and the unforeseen.
History of Europe (1935) **Fisher, H.A.L.** (1856–1940) English historian

42 History is more or less bunk. It's tradition. We don't want tradition. We want to live in the present and the only history that is worth a tinker's damn is the history we make today.
Chicago Tribune, (1916) **Ford, Henry** (1863–1947) US car manufacturer. Popularly remembered as 'History is bunk'

43 The historian must have … some conception of how men who are not historians behave. Otherwise he will move in a world of the dead.
Abinger Harvest (1936) **Forster, E.M.** (1879–1970) English writer, essayist and literary critic

44 In essence the Renaissance was simply the green end of one of civilization's hardest winters.
The French Lieutenant's Woman (1969) **Fowles, John** (1926–2005) English writer

45 The golden age never was the present age.
Poor Richard's Almanac (1750) **Franklin, Benjamin** (1706–1790) US statesman, scientist, political critic and printer

46 There's only one story, the story of your life.
In Ayre, *Northrop Frye: A Biography* (1989) **Frye, Northrop** (1912–1991) Canadian critic and academic

47 History ... is, indeed, little more than the register of the crimes, follies, and misfortunes of mankind.
Decline and Fall of the Roman Empire (1776–88)

48 If a man were called to fix the period in the history of the world during which the condition of the human race was most happy and prosperous, he would, without hesitation, name that which elapsed from the death of Domitian to the accession of Commodus.
Decline and Fall of the Roman Empire (1776–88) **Gibbon, Edward** (1737–1794) English historian, politician and memoirist

49 One of the evil results of the political subjection of one people by another is that it tends to make the subject nation unnecessarily and excessively conscious of its past ... It is to the past – the gorgeous imaginary past of those whose present is inglorious, sordid, and humiliating – it is to the delightful founded-on-fact romances of history that subject peoples invariably turn.
Jesting Pilate (1926) **Huxley, Aldous** (1894–1963) English writer, poet and critic

50 It takes a great deal of history to produce a little literature.
Hawthorne (1879) **James, Henry** (1843–1916) US-born British writer, critic and letter writer

51 Great abilities are not requisite for an Historian ... Imagination is not required in any high degree.
In Boswell, *The Life of Samuel Johnson* (1791) **Johnson, Samuel** (1709–1784) English lexicographer, poet, critic, conversationalist and essayist

52 History is a nightmare from which I am trying to awake.
Ulysses (1922) **Joyce, James** (1882–1941) Irish writer

53 Whether you like it or not, history is on our side.
Speech to Western ambassadors, (1956)

54 People talk about who won and who lost. Human reason won. Mankind won.
The Observer, (1962) Of the Cuban missile crisis **Khrushchev, Nikita** (1894–1971) Russian statesman and Premier of the USSR

55 States, like men, have their growth, their manhood, their decrepitude, their decay.
Imaginary Conversations (1876) **Landor, Walter Savage** (1775–1864) English poet and writer

56 History is littered with dead opinion polls.
The Independent, (1994) **Lang, Ian** (1940–) Scottish Conservative politician

57 One step forward, two steps back ... It happens in the lives of individuals, and it happens in the history of nations and in the development of parties.
One Step Forward, Two Steps Back (1904) **Lenin, V.I.** (1870–1924) Russian revolutionary, Marxist theoretician and first leader of the USSR

58 Every schoolboy knows who imprisoned Montezuma, and who strangled Atahualpa.
Collected Essays (1843), 'Lord Clive' **Macaulay, Lord** (1800–1859) English Liberal statesman, essayist and poet

59 History is too serious to be left to historians.
The Observer, (1961) **Macleod, Iain** (1913–1970) English Conservative politician and writer

60 The present cannot be revealed to people until it has become yesterday.
In Marchand, *Marshall McLuhan* (1989)

61 The hydrogen bomb is history's exclamation point. It ends an age-long sentence of manifest violence.
Attr. **McLuhan, Marshall** (1911–1980) Canadian communications theorist

62 In my end is my beginning.
Motto embroidered with her mother's emblem **Mary, Queen of Scots** (1542–1587) Daughter of James V, mother of James VI and I; executed by Elizabeth I of England. (*En ma fin git mon commencement*)

63 Hegel says somewhere that all great events and personalities in world history reappear in one way or another. He forgot to add: the first time as tragedy, the second as farce.
The Eighteenth Brumaire of Louis Napoleon (1852) **Marx, Karl** (1818–1883) German political philosopher and economist; founder of Communism

64 Noble values, in the end, are always overcome; history tells the story of their defeat over and over again.
Le Maître de Santiago (1947) **Montherlant, Henry de** (1896–1972) French novelist and dramatist

65 The conflict over the Falklands is a moment dislodged from its natural home in the late nineteenth century.
The Observer, (1982) **Morrow, Lance** (1939–) US political journalist

66 In Germany they first came for the Communists, and I didn't speak up because I wasn't a Communist. Then they came for the Jews, and I didn't speak up because I wasn't a Jew. Then they came for the trade unionists, and I didn't speak up because I wasn't a trade unionist. Then they came for the Catholics, and I didn't speak up because I was a Protestant. Then they came for me – and by that time no one was left to speak up.
Concise Dictionary of Religious Quotations
Niemöller, Martin (1892–1984) German Lutheran theologian

67 We need all of history in order to see if we can manage to escape from it and not fall back into it.
The Rebellion of the Masses (1930) **Ortega y Gasset, José** (1883–1955) Spanish philosopher

68 To a surprising extent the war-lords in shining armour, the apostles of the martial virtues, tend not to die fighting when the time comes. History is full of ignominious getaways by the great and famous.
'Who are the War Criminals?' (1941) **Orwell, George** (1903–1950) English writer and critic

69 There are only three men who have ever understood it: one was Prince Albert, who is dead; the second was a German professor, who became mad. I am the third – and I have forgotten all about it.
Attr. in Palmer, *Quotations in History*
Palmerston, Lord (1784–1865) British Prime Minister. Of the Schleswig-Holstein question

70 But what is history? It is the setting up, through the ages, of works which are consistently devoted to solving death and to overcoming it in the future.

Doctor Zhivago (1958) **Pasternak, Boris** (1890–1960) Russian poet and novelist

71 History's full of absurd mistakes.
King Arthur if he ever existed
would only have farted and excused himself
from the Round Table in a hurry.
Grinning Jack (1990) **Patten, Brian** (1946–) British poet

72 It is impossible to write ancient history because we do not have enough sources, and impossible to write modern history because we have far too many.
Clio **Péguy, Charles** (1873–1914) French Catholic socialist, poet and writer

73 I fear that as time goes on – great deeds no longer impress. In the age of the common man, decorations may be frowned upon.
In *The Times,* (2000) **Place, Basil Charles Godfrey** (1921–) English lieutenant; decorated with the Victoria Cross during the Second World War

74 There is no history of mankind, there are only many histories of all kinds of aspects of human life. And one of these is the history of political power. This is elevated into the history of the world.
The Open Society and its Enemies (1945) **Popper, Sir Karl** (1902–1994) Austrian-born British philosopher

75 I am not worth purchasing, but such as I am, the King of Great Britain is not rich enough to do it.
In W.B. Reed, *Life and Correspondence of Joseph Reed* (1847) **Reed, Joseph** (1741–1785) American Revolutionary statesman. Reply on being offered money to act on behalf of the British Crown

76 Even the Hooligan was probably invented in China centuries before we thought of him.
Reginald (1904)

77 The people of Crete unfortunately make more history than they can consume locally.
The Chronicles of Clovis (1911) **Saki** (1870–1916) Burmese-born British writer

78 Hansard is history's ear, already listening.
The Observer, (1949) **Samuel, Lord** (1870–1963)
English Liberal statesman, philosopher and
administrator

79 Progress, far from consisting in change,
depends on retentiveness. Those who
cannot remember the past are condemned
to repeat it.
The Life of Reason (1906)

80 Civilisation is perhaps approaching one of
those long winters that overtake it from
time to time. Romantic Christendom –
picturesque, passionate, unhappy episode
– may be coming to an end. Such a
catastrophe would be no reason for
despair.
Characters and Opinions in the United States
Santayana, George (1863–1952) Spanish-born
US philosopher and writer

81 The history of the world is its judgement.
'Resignation' (1786) **Schiller, Johann
Christoph Friedrich** (1759–1805) German
writer, dramatist, poet and historian

82 A historian is a prophet in reverse.
Athenäum – Fragmente

83 The beginning and end of history are
prophetic, they are no longer the object of
pure history.
Fragments on Literature and Poetry **Schlegel,
Friedrich von** (1772–1829) German critic and
philosopher

84 History is past politics, and politics present
history.
The Growth of British Policy (1895) **Seeley, Sir
John Robert** (1834–1895) English historian,
essayist and scholar. Quoting E.A. Freeman

85 The Cavaliers (Wrong but Wromantic) and
the Roundheads (Right but Repulsive).
1066 And All That (1930) **Sellar, Walter** (1898–
1951) and **Yeatman, Robert Julian** (1897–1968)
British writers

86 History shows that there are no invincible
armies.
Speech on the declaration of war on
Germany, (1941) **Stalin, Joseph** (1879–1953)
Soviet Communist leader

87 No one would have doubted his ability to
rule had he never been emperor.
Histories **Tacitus** (AD c.56–c.120) Roman
historian. Of the Emperor Galba

88 Lenin was the first to discover that
capitalism 'inevitably' caused war; and he
discovered this only when the First World
War was already being fought. Of course
he was right. Since every great state was
capitalist in 1914, capitalism obviously
'caused' the First World War; but just as
obviously it had 'caused' the previous
generation of Peace.
The Origins of the Second World War (1961)

89 He was what I often think is a dangerous
thing for a statesman to be – a student of
history; and like most of those who study
history, he learned from the mistakes of
the past how to make new ones.
The Listener, (1963) Of Napoleon III

90 History gets thicker as it approaches recent
times.
English History, 1914–1945 (1965)

91 All change in history, all advance, comes
from nonconformity. If there had been no
trouble-makers, no dissenters, we should
still be living in caves.
The Trouble-makers **Taylor, A.J.P.** (1906–1990)
English historian, writer, broadcaster and
lecturer

92 In the past, people did not cling to life
quite as much, and it was easier to breathe.
A Voice From the Chorus (1973) **Tertz, Abram**
(1925–1997) Russian writer and dissident

93 Progress was all right; only it went on too
long.
Attr. **Thurber, James** (1894–1961) US
humorist, writer and dramatist

94 Historians are like deaf people who go on
answering questions that no one has asked
them.
Attr.

95 History would be an excellent thing if only
it were true.
Attr. **Tolstoy, Leo** (1828–1910) Russian writer,
essayist, philosopher and moralist

96 In a serious struggle there is no worse cruelty than to be magnanimous at an inappropriate time.
The History of the Russian Revolution (1933) **Trotsky, Leon** (1879–1940) Russian revolutionary and Communist theorist

97 Indeed, history is nothing but a tableau of crimes and misfortunes.
L'Ingénu (1767)

98 The Holy Roman Empire was neither holy, nor Roman, nor an Empire.
Attr. **Voltaire** (1694–1778) French philosopher, dramatist, poet, historian, writer and critic

99 Anything but history, for history must be false.
Attr. **Walpole, Robert** (1676–1745) British statesman and first British Prime Minister. On being asked whether he would like to be read to

100 The past, at least, is secure.
Speech, (1830) **Webster, Daniel** (1782–1852) US statesman, orator and lawyer

101 ... truth can neither be apprehended nor communicated ... history is an art like all other sciences.
Truth and Opinion (1960) **Wedgwood, Cicely Veronica** (1910–1997) English historian

102 Human history becomes more and more a race between education and catastrophe.
The Outline of History (1920) **Wells, H.G.** (1866–1946) English writer

103 I do not intend to prejudge the past.
The Times, (1973) **Whitelaw, William** (1918–1999) English Conservative politician

104 I don't believe in accidents. There are only encounters in history. There are no accidents.
International Herald Tribune, (1992) **Wiesel, Elie** (1928–) Romanian-born US writer

105 To give an accurate description of what has never occurred is not merely the proper occupation of the historian, but the inalienable privilege of any man of parts and culture.
Intentions (1891), 'The Critic as Artist' **Wilde, Oscar** (1854–1900) Irish poet, dramatist, writer, critic and wit

106 The chapter of accidents is the longest chapter in the book.
Attr. **Wilkes, John** (1727–1797) English politician
See also experience

HOPE

1 Far away there in the sunshine are my highest aspirations. I may not reach them, but I can look up and see their beauty, believe in them, and follow where they lead.
Little Women (1869) **Alcott, Louisa May** (1832–1888) US writer

2 And the pale master on his spar-strewn deck
With anguish'd face and flying hair
Grasping the rudder hard,
Still bent to make some port he knows not where,
Still standing for some false, impossible shore.
'A Summer Night' (1852)

3 Still nursing the unconquerable hope,
Still clutching the inviolable shade.
'The Scholar-Gipsy' (1853)

4 The foot less prompt to meet the morning dew,
The heart less bounding at emotion new,
And hope, once crushed, less quick to spring again.
'Thyrsis' (1866) **Arnold, Matthew** (1822–1888) English poet, critic, essayist and educationist

5 Hope is a good breakfast, but it is a bad supper.
'Apophthegms' **Bacon, Francis** (1561–1626) English philosopher, essayist, politician and courtier

6 One of the things I learned the hard way was that it doesn't pay to get discouraged. Keeping busy and making optimism a way of life can restore your faith in yourself.
In Eleanor Harris, *The Real Story of Lucille Ball* (1954) **Ball, Lucille** (1911–1989) US actress and comedian

7 Pessimism, when you get used to it, is just as agreeable as optimism.

Things That Have Interested Me **Bennett, Arnold** (1867–1931) English writer, dramatist and journalist

8 Those who have much to hope and nothing to lose will always be dangerous.
Letter, (1777) **Burke, Edmund** (1729–1797) Irish-born British statesman and philosopher

9 Hope is the power of being cheerful in circumstances which we know to be desperate.
Heretics (1905) **Chesterton, G.K.** (1874–1936) English writer, poet and critic

10 Hopeless hope hopes on and meets no end,
Wastes without springs and homes without a friend.
'Child Harold' (1841) **Clare, John** (1793–1864) English rural poet; died in an asylum

11 Work without hope draws nectar in a sieve,
And hope without an object cannot live.
'Work Without Hope' (1828) **Coleridge, Samuel Taylor** (1772–1834) English poet, philosopher and critic

12 He that lives upon hope will die fasting.
Poor Richard's Almanac (1758) **Franklin, Benjamin** (1706–1790) US statesman, scientist, political critic and printer

13 He that lives in hope danceth without music.
Jacula Prudentum (1640) **Herbert, George** (1593–1633) English poet and priest

14 Not, I'll not, carrion comfort, Despair, not feast on thee;
Not untwist – slack they may be – these last strands of man
In me or, most weary, cry I can no more. I can;
Can something, hope, wish day come, not choose not to be.
'Carrion Comfort' (1885) **Hopkins, Gerard Manley** (1844–1889) English Jesuit priest, poet and classicist

15 We must rediscover the distinction between hope and expectation.
Deschooling Society (1971) **Illich, Ivan** (1926–2002) Austrian-born US educator, sociologist, writer and priest

16 Do not despair, not even about the fact that you do not despair.
Diary, (1913) **Kafka, Franz** (1883–1924) Czech-born German-speaking writer

17 Ay, on the shores of darkness there is light,
And precipices show untrodden green;
There is a budding morrow in midnight;
There is a triple sight in blindness keen.
'To Homer' (1818) **Keats, John** (1795–1821) English poet

18 Hope is the feeling you have that the feeling you have isn't permanent.
Finishing Touches (1973) **Kerr, Jean** (1923–2003) US writer and dramatist

19 There is wishful thinking in Hell as well as on earth.
The Screwtape Letters (1942) **Lewis, C.S.** (1898–1963) Irish-born English academic, writer and critic

20 If we see light at the end of the tunnel,
It's the light of the oncoming train.
'Since 1939' (1977) **Lowell, Robert** (1917–1977) US poet and writer

21 Since I gave up hope I feel so much better.
The Independent, (1994) **Osborne, John** (1929–1994) English dramatist and actor. A notice in his bathroom

22 Hope springs eternal in the human breast;
Man never Is, but always To be blest.
An Essay on Man (1733) **Pope, Alexander** (1688–1744) English poet, translator and editor

23 For hope is but a dream of those that wake.
Solomon (1718) **Prior, Matthew** (1664–1721) English poet

24 Every cloud has a silver lining.
Proverb

25 True hope is swift and flies with swallow's wings;
Kings it makes gods, and meaner creatures kings.
Richard III, V.ii **Shakespeare, William** (1564–1616) English dramatist, poet and actor

26 He who has never hoped can never despair.
Caesar and Cleopatra (1901) **Shaw, George Bernard** (1856–1950) Irish socialist, writer, dramatist and critic

27 A self-made man is one who believes in luck and sends his son to Oxford.
House of All Nations (1938) **Stead, Christina** (1902–1983) Australian writer

28 Where there's life, there's hope.
Heauton Timoroumenos **Terence** (c.190–159 BC) Carthaginian-born Roman dramatist

29 Everything is for the best in the best of all possible worlds.
Candide (1759) **Voltaire** (1694–1778) French philosopher, dramatist, poet, historian, writer and critic

30 I can endure my own despair,
But not another's hope.
'Song: Of All the Torments' **Walsh, William** (1663–1708) English critic, poet and politician

31 For what human ill does dawn not seem to be an alleviation?
The Bridge of San Luis Rey **Wilder, Thornton** (1897–1975) US author and playwright
See also desire; the future

HOUSE AND HOME

1 Home wasn't built in a day.
In G. Ace, *The Fine Art of Hypochondria* (1966) **Ace, Jane** (1905–1974) US comedian and radio personality

2 Housekeeping ain't no joke.
Little Women (1868) **Alcott, Louisa May** (1832–1888) US writer

3 The first pull on the cord ALWAYS sends the curtains in the wrong direction.
Boyle's Other Law **Anonymous**

4 What the New Yorker calls home would seem like a couple of closets to most Americans, yet he manages not only to live there but also to grow trees and cockroaches right on the premises.
New York Times, (1978) **Baker, Russell** (1925–) US writer

5 In fact, most home projects are impossible, which is why you should do them yourself. There is no point in paying other people to screw things up when you can easily screw them up yourself for far less money.

'The Taming of the Screw' **Barry, Dave** (1947–) US columnist and journalist

6 Few tasks are more like the torture of Sisyphus than housework, with its endless repetition ... The housewife wears herself out marking time: she makes nothing, simply perpetuates the present.
The Second Sex (1949)

7 The ideal of happiness has always taken material form in the house, whether cottage or castle; it stands for permanence and separation from the world.
The Second Sex (1949) **Beauvoir, Simone de** (1908–1986) French writer, feminist critic and philosopher

8 I was a stranger, and ye took me in: Naked, and ye clothed me: I was sick, and ye visited me: I was in prison, and ye came unto me.
Matthew, 25:35–36 **The Bible (King James Version)**

9 Show me a man who lives alone and has a perpetually clean kitchen, and eight times out of nine I'll show you a man with detestable spiritual qualities.
Tales of Ordinary Madness (1967) **Bukowski, Charles** (1920–1994) US writer and poet

10 What is more agreeable than one's home?
Ad Familiares **Cicero** (106–43 BC) Roman orator, statesman, essayist and letter writer

11 Home is home, though it be never so homely.
Paraemiologia Anglo-Latina (1639) **Clarke, John** (fl. 1639) English scholar

12 Resolve to free yourselves from the slavery of the tea and coffee and other slop-kettle.
Advice to Young Men (1829) **Cobbett, William** (1762–1835) English politician, reformer, writer, farmer and army officer

13 The house of everyone is to him as his castle and fortress, as well for his defence against injury and violence, as for his repose.
Semayne's Case **Coke, Sir Edward** (1552–1634) English judge, writer and politician

14 Now stir the fire, and close the shutters
   fast,
   Let fall the curtains, wheel the sofa round,
   And, while the bubbling and loud-hissing
   urn
   Throws up a steamy column, and the cups,
   That cheer but not inebriate, wait on each,
   So let us welcome peaceful ev'ning in.
   The Task (1785)

15 I crown thee king of intimate delights,
   Fire-side enjoyments, home-born
   happiness.
   The Task (1785) 'The Winter Evening' **Cowper,
   William** (1731–1800) English poet, hymn
   writer and letter writer

16 There was no need to do any housework at
   all. After the first four years the dirt doesn't
   get any worse.
   The Naked Civil Servant (1968) **Crisp, Quentin**
   (1908–1999) English writer, publicist and
   model

17 It is the personality of the mistress that the
   home expresses. Men are forever guests in
   our homes, no matter how much
   happiness they may find there.
   The House in Good Taste (1920) **De Wolfe, Elsie**
   (1865–1950) US interior designer

18 Cleaning your house while your kids are
   growing
   Is like shoveling the walk before it stops
   snowing.
   Phyllis Diller's Housekeeping Hints **Diller,
   Phyllis** (1917–1974) US comedian

19 Many a man who thinks to found a home
   discovers that he has merely opened a
   tavern for his friends.
   South Wind (1917) **Douglas, Norman** (1868–
   1952) Austrian-born Scottish writer

20 Well! some people talk of morality, and
   some of religion, but give me a little snug
   property.
   The Absentee (1812) **Edgeworth, Maria** (1767–
   1849) English-born Irish writer

21 A man builds a fine house; and now he has
   a master, and a task for life; he is to
   furnish, watch, show it, and keep it in
   repair, the rest of his days.

Society and Solitude (1870) **Emerson, Ralph
Waldo** (1803–1882) US poet, essayist,
transcendentalist and teacher

22 Charity and beating begins at home.
   Wit Without Money (c.1614) **Fletcher, John**
   (1579–1625) English dramatist

23 Keep the home fires burning while your
   hearts are yearning,
   Though your lads are far away, they dream
   of home.
   There's a silver lining through the dark
   cloud shining:
   Turn the dark cloud inside out, till the boys
   come home.
   'Keep the Home Fires Burning' (1914) **Ford,
   Lena** (1870–1916) US verse writer

24 Something there is that doesn't love a
   wall –
   My apple trees will never get across
   And eat the cones under his pines, I tell
   him.
   He only says, 'Good fences make good
   neighbours.'
   'Mending Wall' (1914) **Frost, Robert** (1874–
   1963) US poet

25 A house is no home unless it contains food
   and fire for the mind as well as for the
   body.
   Woman in the Nineteenth Century (1845) **Fuller,
   Margaret** (1810–1850)

26 There's nothing like a thorn twig for
   cletterin' dishes.
   Cold Comfort Farm (1932) **Gibbons, Stella**
   (1902–1989) English poet and novelist

27 I am so tired of housekeeping I dreamed I
   was being served up for my guests and
   awoke only when the knife was at my
   throat.
   In Mary-Lou Kohfeldt, *Lady Gregory* (1985)
   Gregory, Lady Isabella Augusta (1852–1932)
   Irish dramatist, writer and translator

28 What's the good of a home, if you are
   never in it?
   Diary of a Nobody (1894) **Grossmith, George**
   (1847–
   1912) English singer and comedian, and
   Grossmith, Weedon (1854–
   1919) English writer, painter and actor

29 Oh give me a home where the buffalo
roam,
Where the deer and the antelope play,
Where seldom is heard a discouraging
word
And the skies are not cloudy all day.
'Home on the Range' (song, c.1873) **Higley,
Brewster** (19th century) US songwriter

30 I want a house that has got over all of its
troubles; I don't want to spend the rest of
my life bringing up a young and
inexperienced house.
Attr. **Jerome, Jerome K.** (1859–1927) English
writer and dramatist

31 In violent and chaotic times such as these,
our only chance for survival lies in creating
our own little islands of sanity and order,
in making little havens of our homes.
Falling Bodies (1974) **Kaufman, Sue** (1926–) US
novelist

32 Not many sounds in life, and I include all
urban and all rural sounds, exceed in
interest a knock at the door.
'Valentine's Day' (1823) **Lamb, Charles** (1775–
1834) English essayist, critic and letter writer

33 A man's home may seem to be his castle
on the outside; inside, it is more often his
nursery.
Attr. **Luce, Clare Boothe** (1903–1987) US
diplomat, politician and writer

34 Gentlemen know that fresh air should be
kept in its proper place – out of doors –
and that, God having given us indoors and
out-of-doors, we should not attempt to do
away with this distinction.
Crewe Train (1926) **Macaulay, Dame Rose**
(1881–1958) English writer

35 What the nation must realize is that the
home, when both parents work, is non-
existent. Once we have honestly faced the
fact, we must act accordingly.
Washington Post, (1943) **Meyer, Agnes** (1887–
c.1970) US writer and social worker

36 The sober comfort, all the peace which
springs
From the large aggregate of little things;
On these small cares of daughter, wife, or
friend,
The almost sacred joys of home depend.

'Sensibility' (1782) **More, Hannah** (1745–1833)
English poet, dramatist and religious writer

37 If you want a golden rule that will fit
everybody, this is it: Have nothing in your
houses that you do not know to be useful,
or believe to be beautiful.
Hopes and Fears for Art (1882) **Morris, William**
(1834–1896) English poet, designer, craftsman,
artist and socialist

38 Housework is work directly opposed to the
possibility of human self-actualization.
Woman's Work: The Housewife, Past and Present
(1974) **Oakley, Ann** (1944–) British sociologist

39 Mid pleasures and palaces though we may
roam,
Be it ever so humble, there's no place like
home;
A charm from the skies seems to hallow us
there,
Which, seek through the world, is ne'er
met with elsewhere.
Home, home, sweet, sweet home!
There's no place like home! there's no
place like home!
'Home, Sweet Home' (song, 1823) **Payne, J.H.**
(1791–1852) US dramatist, poet and actor

40 The poorest man may in his cottage bid
defiance to all the forces of the Crown. It
may be frail – its roof may shake – the
wind may blow through it – the rain may
enter – but the King of England cannot
enter – all his force dares not cross the
threshold of the ruined tenement!
Speech, (c.1763) **Pitt, William** (1708–1778)
English politician and Prime Minister

41 'Home' is any four walls that enclose the
right person.
Reflections of a Bachelor Girl (1909) **Rowland,
Helen** (1875–1950) US writer

42 One's own surroundings mean so much to
one, when one is feeling miserable.
Selected Letters (1970) **Sitwell, Dame Edith**
(1887–1964) English poet, anthologist, critic
and biographer

43 Home is a place not only of strong
affections, but of entire unreserve; it is
life's undress rehearsal, its backroom, its
dressing room, from which we go forth to
more careful and guarded intercourse,
leaving behind us much debris of cast-off
and everyday clothing.
Little Foxes (1866) **Stowe, Harriet Beecher**
(1811–1896) US writer and reformer

44 Home is where you come to when you
have nothing better to do.
Vanity Fair, (1991) **Thatcher, Margaret** (1925–)
English Conservative Prime Minister

45 *Mr Pritchard*: I must dust the blinds and
then I must raise them.
Mrs Ogmore-Pritchard: And before you let
the sun in, mind it wipes its shoes.
Under Milk Wood (1954) **Thomas, Dylan** (1914–
1953) Welsh poet, writer and radio dramatist

46 I had three chairs in my house; one for
solitude, two for friendship, three for
society.
Walden (1854) **Thoreau, Henry David** (1817–
1862) US essayist, social critic and writer

47 I was seized by the stern hand of
Compulsion, that dark, unreasonable Urge
that impels women to clean the house in
the middle of the night.
Alarms and Diversions **Thurber, James** (1894–
1961) US humorist, writer and dramatist

48 It is a comfortable feeling to know that you
stand on your own ground. Land is about
the only thing that can't fly away.
The Last Chronicle of Barset (1867) **Trollope,
Anthony** (1815–1882) English writer, traveller
and post office official

49 Seek home for rest,
For home is best.
Five Hundred Points of Good Husbandry (1557)
Tusser, Thomas (c.1524–1580) English writer,
poet and musician

50 The tragedy of domesticity, that avalanche
of overcoats and boots.
The Aunt's Story (1948) **White, Patrick** (1912–
1990) English-born Australian writer and
dramatist
See also garden; families; travel

HUMANITY AND HUMAN NATURE

1 The age of great men is going; the epoch
of the ant-hill, of life in multiplicity, is
beginning.
Journal, (1851) **Amiel, Henri-Frédéric** (1821–
1881) Swiss philosopher and writer

2 Alone, alone, about a dreadful wood
Of conscious evil runs a lost mankind,
Dreading to find its Father.
'For the Time Being' (1945)

3 Man is a history-making creature who can
neither repeat his past nor leave it behind.
The Dyer's Hand (1963) **Auden, W.H.** (1907–
1973) English poet, essayist, critic, teacher and
dramatist

4 Human nature is so well disposed towards
those who are in interesting situations,
that a young person, who either marries or
dies, is sure of being kindly spoken of.
Emma (1816) **Austen, Jane** (1775–1817) English
writer

5 Nature is often hidden; sometimes
overcome; seldom extinguished.
Essays (1625)

6 There is in human nature generally more
of the fool than of the wise.
Essays (1625) **Bacon, Francis** (1561–1626)
English philosopher, essayist, politician and
courtier

7 Drinking when we're not thirsty and
making love all the time, madam, that is all
there is to distinguish us from other
animals.
Le Barbier de Seville (1775) **Beaumarchais** (1732–
1799) French dramatist

8 Mankind is divisible into two great classes:
hosts and guests.
Attr. **Beerbohm, Sir Max** (1872–1956) English
satirist, cartoonist, critic and essayist

9 We are in the position of savage men who
have been educated into believing there
are no mysteries.
The Independent, (1990) **Bellow, Saul** (1915–
2005) Canadian-born US Jewish writer

10 And God said, Let us make man in our image, after our likeness.
Genesis, 1:26

11 Man is born unto trouble, as the sparks fly upward.
Job, 5:7

12 Man that is born of a woman is of few days, and full of trouble.
Job, 14:1

13 As for man, his days are as grass: as a flower of the field, so he flourisheth.
Psalms, 103:15

14 All flesh is grass, and all the goodliness thereof is as the flower of the field.
Isaiah, 40:6 **The Bible (King James Version)**

15 Man was formed for society.
Commentaries on the Laws of England (1765–1769) **Blackstone, Sir William** (1723–1780) English judge, historian and politician

16 My favourite, I might say, my only study, is man.
The Bible in Spain (1843) **Borrow, George** (1803–1881) English writer and linguist

17 It is good to know what a man is, and also what the world takes him for. But you do not understand him until you have learnt how he understands himself.
Aphorisms (1930) **Bradley, F.H.** (1846–1924) English philosopher

18 No man can justly censure or condemn another, because indeed no man truly knows another.
Religio Medici (1643)

19 There is surely a piece of divinity in us, something that was before the elements, and owes no homage unto the sun.
Religio Medici (1643) **Browne, Sir Thomas** (1605–1682) English physician, author and antiquary

20 Every animal leaves traces of what it was; man alone leaves traces of what he created.
The Ascent of Man (1973) **Bronowski, Jacob** (1908–1974) British scientist, writer and TV presenter

21 The human heart is like Indian rubber: a little swells it, but a great deal will not burst it.

22 Man is a noble animal, splendid in ashes, and pompous in the grave.
Hydriotaphia: Urn Burial (1658) **Browne, Sir Thomas** (1605–1682) English physician, author and antiquary

23 We are puppets on strings worked by unknown forces; we ourselves are nothing, nothing!
Danton's Death (1835) **Büchner, Georg** (1813–1837) German playwright

24 The march of the human mind is slow.
Speech on Conciliation with America (1775) **Burke, Edmund** (1729–1797) Irish-born British statesman and philosopher

25 Man's inhumanity to man
Makes countless thousands mourn!
'Man was made to Mourn, a Dirge' (1784)
Burns, Robert (1759–1796) Scottish poet and songwriter

26 'Man wants but little here below' but likes that little good – and not too long in coming.
Further Extracts from the Note-Books of Samuel Butler (1934)

27 Man is the only animal that can remain on friendly terms with the victims he intends to eat until he eats them.
Samuel Butler's Notebooks (1951) **Butler, Samuel** (1835–1902) English writer, painter, philosopher and scholar

28 And when we think we lead, we are most led.
The Two Foscari (1821) **Byron, Lord** (1788–1824) English poet, satirist and traveller

29 I hate 'Humanity' and all such abstracts: but I love people. Lovers of 'Humanity' generally hate people and children, and keep parrots or puppy dogs.
Light on a Dark Horse (1951) **Campbell, Roy** (1901–1957) South African poet and journalist

30 It is very true that we seldom confide in those who are better than ourselves.
The Fall (1956)

31 A single sentence will suffice for modern man: he fornicated and read the papers.

The Fall (1956) **Camus, Albert** (1913–1960) Algerian-born French writer

32 Man, only – rash, refined, presumptuous man,
Starts from his rank, and mars creation's plan.
'Progress of Man' (1799) **Canning, George** (1770–1827) English Prime Minister, orator and poet

33 Man is a Tool-using Animal ... feeblest of bipeds! ... Without Tools he is nothing, with Tools he is all.
Sartor Resartus (1834) **Carlyle, Thomas** (1795–1881) Scottish historian, biographer, critic, and essayist

34 Man's chief end is to glorify God, and to enjoy him forever.
Question 1

35 All mankind by their fall lost communion with God, are under his wrath and curse, and so made liable to all the miseries in this life, to death itself, and to the pains of hell for ever.
Question 19

36 No mere man since the fall is able in this life perfectly to keep the commandments of God, but doth daily break them in thought, word, and deed.
Question 82, **Catechism** The Shorter Catechism, approved 1648 by the General Assembly of the Church of Scotland

37 Every man is as God made him, and often even worse.
Don Quixote (1615) **Cervantes, Miguel de** (1547–1616) Spanish writer and dramatist

38 I am for people. I can't help it.
The Observer, (1952) **Chaplin, Charlie** (1889–1977) English comedian, film actor, director and satirist

39 The true science and the true study of man is man.
De la Sagesse (1601) **Charron, Pierre** (1541–1603) French theologian and philosopher

40 Human beings have been endowed with reason and a creative power so that they can add to what thay have been given. But until now they have been not creative, but destructive. Forests are disappearing, rivers are drying up, wildlife is becoming extinct, the climate's being ruined and with every passing day the earth is becoming poorer and uglier.
Uncle Vanya (1897) **Chekhov, Anton** (1860–1904) Russian writer, dramatist and doctor

41 The human race, to which so many of my readers belong, has been playing at children's games from the beginning, and will probably do it till the end, which is a nuisance for the few people who grow up.
The Napoleon of Notting Hill (1904) **Chesterton, G.K.** (1874–1936) English writer, poet and critic

42 You don't have to teach people to be human. You have to teach them how to stop being inhuman.
Conversations with Eldridge Cleaver (1970) **Cleaver, Eldridge** (1935–1998) US civil rights leader

43 A Fall of some sort or other – the creation as it were, of the non-absolute – is the fundamental postulate of the moral history of man. Without this hypothesis, man is unintelligible; with it, every phenomenon is explicable.
Table-Talk (1835) **Coleridge, Samuel Taylor** (1772–1834) English poet, philosopher and critic

44 Man is an embodied paradox, a bundle of contradictions.
Lacon (1820) **Colton, Charles Caleb** (c.1780–1832) English clergyman and satirist

45 Men's natures are alike; it is their habits that carry them far apart.
Analects **Confucius** (c.550–c.478 BC) Chinese philosopher and teacher of ethics

46 Consider your origins: you were not made to live as brutes, but to pursue virtue and knowledge.
Divina Commedia (1307), 'Inferno' **Dante Alighieri** (1265–1321) Italian poet

47 Nature has left this tincture in the blood,
That all men would be tyrants if they could.
'The Kentish Petition' (1713) **Defoe, Daniel**
(c.1661–1731) English writer and critic

48 There are strings ... in the human heart
that had better not be wibrated.
Barnaby Rudge (1841) **Dickens, Charles** (1812–
1870) English writer

49 I'm Nobody! Who are you?
Are you – Nobody – Too?
Then there's a pair of us?
Don't tell! they'd advertise – you know!
'I'm Nobody! Who are you?' (c.1861)
Dickinson, Emily (1830–1886) US poet

50 Man is only truly great when he acts from
the passions.
Coningsby (1844)

51 Man, my Lord, is a being born to believe.
Speech, meeting of Society for Increasing
Endowments of Small Livings in the Diocese
of Oxford, (1864) Addressed to Bishop
Wilberforce **Disraeli, Benjamin** (1804–1881)
English statesman and writer

52 I got disappointed in human nature as well
and gave it up because I found it too much
like my own.
Fairy Tales of New York (1961) **Donleavy, J.P.**
(1926–) US-born Irish writer and dramatist

53 No man is an Island, entire of it self; every
man is a piece of Continent, a part of the
main; if a clod be washed away by the sea,
Europe is the less, as well as if a
promontory were, as well as if a manor of
thy friends or of thine own were; any man's
death diminishes me, because I am
involved in Mankind;
And therefore never send to know for
whom the bell tolls; it tolls for thee.
Devotions upon Emergent Occasions (1624)
Donne, John (1572–1631) English poet

54 Through the centuries we have sacrificed so
much for the state that it is now time for
the state to sacrifice itself for us.
Romulus the Great (1964) **Dürrenmatt,
Friedrich** (1921–1990) Swiss dramatist and
writer

55 There is a great deal of unmapped country
within us which would have to be taken
into account in an explanation of our gusts
and storms.
Daniel Deronda (1876) **Eliot, George** (1819–
1880) English writer and poet

56 Human kind
Cannot bear very much reality.
Four Quartets (1944) **Eliot, T.S.** (1888–1965) US-
born British poet, verse dramatist and critic

57 It is easy in the world to live after the
world's opinion; it is easy in solitude after
our own; but the great man is he who, in
the midst of the crowd, keeps with perfect
sweetness the independence of solitude.
'Self-Reliance' (1841) **Emerson, Ralph Waldo**
(1803–1882) US poet, essayist,
transcendentalist and teacher

58 Someone has somewhere commented on
the fact that millions long for immortality
who don't know what to do with
themselves on a rainy Sunday afternoon.
Anger in the Sky (1943) **Ertz, Susan** (1894–1985)
English writer

59 Man is a tool-making animal.
In Boswell, *The Life of Samuel Johnson* (1791)
Franklin, Benjamin (1706–1790) US statesman,
scientist, political critic and printer

60 Wild animals never kill for sport. Man is
the only one to whom the torture and
death of his fellow creatures is amusing in
itself.
Oceana, or England and her Colonies (1886)
Froude, James Anthony (1818–1894) English
historian and scholar

61 Over all the world
Men move unhoming, and eternally
Concerned: a swarm of bees who have lost
their queen.
Venus Unobserved (1950) **Fry, Christopher**
(1907–2005) English verse dramatist, theatre
director and translator

62 Man wants but little here below,
Nor wants that little long.
The Vicar of Wakefield (1766) **Goldsmith, Oliver**
(c.1728–1774) Irish dramatist, poet and writer

63 Man and man alone is, I believe, the
creator of all things and all ideas.

Attr. **Gorky, Maxim** (1868–1936) Russian writer, dramatist and revolutionary

64 Why be difficult when with a little extra effort you can make yourself impossible?
Anecdotes, Index Part I, *Grainger Collection*
Grainger, Percy (1882–1961) Australian composer and pianist

65 Oh wearisome Condition of Humanity!
Borne under one Law, to another, bound:
Vainely begot, and yet forbidden vanity,
Created sicke, commanded to be sound.
Mustapha (1609) **Greville, Fulke** (1554–1628) English poet, dramatist, biographer, courtier and politician

66 Our Vices and Virtues couple with one another, and get Children that resemble both their Parents.
'Of the World' (1750)

67 It is a general Mistake to think the Men we like are good for every thing, and those we do not, good for nothing.
Political, Moral and Miscellaneous Thoughts and Reflections (1750) **Halifax, Lord** (1633–1695) English politician, courtier, pamphleteer and epigrammatist

68 If there is a technological advance without a social advance, there is, almost automatically, an increase in human misery.
The Other America (1962) **Harrington, Michael** (1928–1989) US writer

69 Once she had loved her fellow human beings; she did not love them now, she had seen them do too many unpleasant things.
Facial Justice (1960) **Hartley, L.P.** (1895–1972) English writer and critic

70 Man is an intellectual animal, and therefore an everlasting contradiction to himself. His senses centre in himself, his ideas reach to the ends of the universe; so that he is torn in pieces between the two, without a possibility of its ever being otherwise.
Characteristics (1823) **Hazlitt, William** (1778–1830) English writer and critic

71 Man is God's image, but a poore man is Christ's stamp to boot.

The Temple (1633) **Herbert, George** (1593–1633) English poet and priest

72 Most human beings have an almost infinite capacity for taking things for granted.
Themes and Variations (1950) **Huxley, Aldous** (1894–1963) English writer, poet and critic

73 Sir, are you so grossly ignorant of human nature, as not to know that a man may be very sincere in good principles without having good practice?
In Boswell, *Journal of a Tour to the Hebrides* (1785)

74 Subordination tends greatly to human happiness. Were we all upon an equality, we should have no other enjoyment than mere animal pleasure.
In Boswell, *The Life of Samuel Johnson* (1791)
Johnson, Samuel (1709–1784) English lexicographer, poet, critic, conversationalist and essayist

75 We need more understanding of human nature, because the only real danger that exists is man himself ... We know nothing of man, far too little. His psyche should be studied because we are the origin of all coming evil.
BBC television interview, (1959) **Jung, Carl Gustav** (1875–1961) Swiss psychiatrist and pupil of Freud

76 Two things only the people anxiously desire: bread and circuses.
Satires **Juvenal** (c.60–130) Roman verse satirist and Stoic

77 No straight thing can ever be formed from timber as crooked as that from which humanity is made.
Idea for a General History with a Cosmopolitan purpose (1784)

78 Is man by nature morally good or evil?
Neither, for he is by nature not a moral being; he only becomes such when his reason is raised to the concepts of duty and law.
On Pedagogy (1803) **Kant, Immanuel** (1724–1804) German idealist philosopher

79 Scenery is fine – but human nature is finer.
Letter to Benjamin Bailey, (13 March 1818)

80 Upon the whole I dislike Mankind: whatever people on the other side of the question may advance they cannot deny that they are always surprised at hearing of a good action and never of a bad one.
Letter to Georgiana Keats, (13–28 January, 1820) **Keats, John** (1795–1821) English poet

81 I submit to you that if a man hasn't discovered something he will die for, he isn't fit to live.
Speech in Detroit, (June 23, 1963) **King, Martin Luther** (1929–1968) US civil rights leader and Baptist minister

82 It is difficult to love mankind unless one has a reasonable private income and when one has a reasonable private income one has better things to do than loving mankind.
In R. Ingrams, *God's Apology* (1977) **Kingsmill, Hugh** (1889–1949) English critic and writer

83 Most men spend the best part of their lives in making their remaining years unhappy.
Les charactères ou les moeurs de ce siècle (1688) **La Bruyère, Jean de** (1645–1696) French satirist

84 In most of mankind gratitude is merely a secret hope for greater favours.
Maximes (1678) **La Rochefoucauld** (1613–1680) French writer

85 The very best that is in the Jewish blood: a faculty for pure disinterestedness, and warm, physically warm love, that seems to make the corpuscles of the blood glow.
Kangaroo (1923)

86 Ideal mankind would abolish death, multiply itself million upon million, rear up city upon city, save every parasite alive, until the accumulation of mere existence is swollen to a horror.
St Mawr (1925)

87 Away with all ideals. Let each individual act spontaneously from the for ever incalculable prompting of the creative wellhead within him. There is no universal law.
Phoenix (1936) **Lawrence, D.H.** (1885–1930) English writer, poet and critic

88 Man, false man, smiling, destructive man.

Theodosius (1680) **Lee, Nathaniel** (c.1653–1692) English dramatist

89 Ships that pass in the night, and speak each other in passing;
Only a signal shown and a distant voice in the darkness;
So on the ocean of life we pass and speak one another,
Only a look and a voice; then darkness again and a silence.
Tales of a Wayside Inn (1863–1874) **Longfellow, Henry Wadsworth** (1807–1882) US poet and writer

90 God creates men, but they choose each other.
The Mandrake (1518)

91 Men sooner forget the death of their father than the loss of their possessions.
The Prince, (1532) **Machiavelli** (1469–1527) Florentine statesman, political theorist and historian

92 One must not dislike people ... because they are intransigent. For that could be only playing their own game.
Zoo (1938) **MacNeice, Louis** (1907–1963) Belfast-born poet, writer, radio producer, translator and critic

93 I'll give you my opinion of the human race. ... Their heart's in the right place, but their head is a thoroughly inefficient organ.
The Summing Up (1938)

94 I've always been interested in people, but I've never liked them.
The Observer, 'Sayings of the Week', (1949) **Maugham, William Somerset** (1874–1965) English writer, dramatist and physician

95 Man has never been the same since God died.
He has taken it very hard. Why, you'd think it was only yesterday,
The way he takes it.
Not that he says much, but he laughs much louder than he used to,
And he can't bear to be left alone even for a minute, and he can't
Sit still.
Conversation at Midnight (1937) **Millay, Edna St Vincent** (1892–1950) US poet and dramatist

96 Heav'n is for thee too high
To know what passes there; be lowlie wise:
Think onely what concerns thee and thy
being.
Paradise Lost (1667) **Milton, John** (1608–1674)
English poet, libertarian and pamphleteer

97 Nothing man does to the animal creation
is equal to the cruelties he commits on his
own kind.
The Seals **Monash, Sir John** (1865–1931)
Australian military commander

98 Man is quite insane. He wouldn't know
how to create a maggot, yet he creates
Gods by the dozen.
Essais (1580) **Montaigne, Michel de** (1533–1592)
French essayist and moralist

99 What? is man only a mistake made by God,
or God only a mistake made by man?
Twilight of the Idols (1889) **Nietzsche, Friedrich
Wilhelm** (1844–1900) German philosopher,
critic and poet

100 Man is the only creature that consumes
without producing.
Animal Farm (1945) **Orwell, George** (1903–1950)
English writer and critic

101 Man is only a reed, the feeblest thing in
nature; but he is a thinking reed.
Pensées (1670) **Pascal, Blaise** (1623–1662)
French philosopher and scientist

102 Man is a wolf to man.
Asinaria **Plautus, Titus Maccius** (c.254–184 BC)
Roman comic dramatist

103 Created half to rise, and half to fall;
Great lord of all things, yet a prey to all;
Sole judge of truth, in endless error hurl'd:
The glory, jest, and riddle of the world!
An Essay on Man (1733)

104 Know then thyself, presume not God to
scan;
The proper study of Mankind is Man.
Plac'd on this isthmus of a middle state,
A being darkly wise, and rudely great:
With too much knowledge for the Sceptic
side,
With too much weakness for the Stoic's
pride,
He hangs between; in doubt to act or rest,
In doubt to deem himself a God, or Beast;

In doubt his Mind or Body to prefer,
Born but to die, and reas'ning but to err;
Alike in ignorance, his reason such,
Whether he thinks too little or too much.
An Essay on Man (1733) **Pope, Alexander** (1688–
1744) English poet, translator and editor

105 When I carefully consider the curious
habits of dogs
I am compelled to conclude
That man is the superior animal.
When I consider the curious habits of man
I confess, my friend, I am puzzled.
'Meditatio' (1916) **Pound, Ezra** (1885–1972) US
poet

106 Man is the measure of all things.
In Plato, *Theaetetus* **Protagoras** (c.485–c.410 BC)
Greek philosopher

107 No man is born unto himself alone;
Who lives unto himself, he lives to none.
'Esther' (1621)

108 Man is Heaven's masterpiece.
Emblems (1635)

109 Man is man's A.B.C. There is none that can
Read God aright, unless he first spell Man.
Hieroglyphics of the Life of Man (1638) **Quarles,
Francis** (1592–1644) English poet, writer and
royalist

110 I wish I loved the Human Race;
I wish I loved its silly face;
I wish I liked the way it walks;
I wish I liked the way it talks;
And when I'm introduced to one,
I wish I thought What Jolly Fun!
'Wishes of an Elderly Man' (1923) **Raleigh, Sir
Walter A.** (1861–1922) English scholar, critic
and essayist

111 Human beings were invented by water as a
device for transporting itself from one
place to another.
Another Roadside Attraction (1971) **Robbins,
Tom** (1936–) US writer

112 Nature made man happy and good, but ...
society corrupts him and makes him
miserable.
Rousseau juge de Jean-Jacques **Rousseau, Jean-
Jacques** (1712–1778) Swiss-born French
philosopher, educationist and essayist

113 No human being, however great, or powerful, was ever so free as a fish.
The Two Paths (1859)

114 I hold it for indisputable, that the first duty of a State is to see that every child born therein shall be well housed, clothed, fed and educated, till it attain years of discretion.
Time and Tide by Weare and Tyne (1867) **Ruskin, John** (1819–1900) English art critic, philosopher and reformer

115 So there is no human nature, since there is no God to conceive it.
Existentialism and Humanism (1946)

116 It is always easy to obey, if one dreams of being in command.
Situations **Sartre, Jean-Paul** (1905–1980) French philosopher, writer, dramatist and critic

117 Man is honoured by his heart and not by his opinions.
Wallensteins Tod (1801) **Schiller, Johann Christoph Friedrich** (1759–1805) German writer, dramatist, poet and historian

118 No-one can escape from his individuality.
Parerga und Paralipomena (1851) **Schopenhauer, Arthur** (1788–1860) German philosopher

119 What a piece of work is a man! How noble in reason! how infinite in faculties! in form and moving, how express and admirable! in action, how like an angel! in apprehension, how like a god! the beauty of the world! the paragon of animals!
Hamlet, II.ii

120 Roses have thorns, and silver fountains mud;
Clouds and eclipses stain both moon and sun,
And loathsome canker lives in sweetest bud.
All men make faults.
Sonnet 35 **Shakespeare, William** (1564–1616) English dramatist, poet and actor

121 Man can climb to the highest summits; but he cannot dwell there long.
Candida (1898) **Shaw, George Bernard** (1856–1950) Irish socialist, writer, dramatist and critic

122 I presume you're mortal, and may err.
The Lady of Pleasure (1637) **Shirley, James** (1596–1666) English poet and dramatist

123 A lady asked me why, on most occasions, I wore black. 'Are you in mourning?'
'Yes.'
'For whom are you in mourning?'
'For the world.'
Taken Care Of (1965) **Sitwell, Dame Edith** (1887–1964) English poet, anthologist, critic and biographer

124 The salvation of mankind lies only in making everything the concern of everyone.
Nobel Lecture, (1970) **Solzhenitsyn, Alexander** (1918–) Russian writer, dramatist and historian

125 Of wonders there are many, but none more wonderful than man.
Antigone **Sophocles** (496–406 BC) Greek dramatist

126 I myself believe that the tendency towards obedience is one of the most sinister of human traits.
Feet of Clay (1996) **Storr, Dr Anthony** (1920–2001) British writer and psychiatrist

127 Man can be considered as a superior animal who produces philosophies and poems much as silkworms construct their cocoons and bees their hives.
La Fontaine and his Fables, (1860) **Taine, Hippolyte Adolphe** (1828–1893) French writer and philosopher

128 It is not the ape, nor the tiger in man that I fear, it is the donkey.
Attr. **Temple, William** (1881–1944) Anglican prelate, social reformer and writer

129 I am a man, I count nothing human indifferent to me.
Heauton Timoroumenos **Terence** (c.190–159 BC) Carthaginian-born Roman dramatist

130 Man is always both much worse and much better than is expected of him. The fields of good are just as limitless as the wastelands of evil.
A Voice From the Chorus (1973) **Tertz, Abram** (1925–1997) Russian writer and dissident

131 The finest qualities of our nature, like the bloom on fruits, can be preserved only by the most delicate handling. Yet we do not treat ourselves nor one another delicately.
Walden (1854) **Thoreau, Henry David** (1817–1862) US essayist, social critic and writer

132 Man is the Only Animal that Blushes. Or needs to.
Following the Equator (1897) **Twain, Mark** (1835–1910) US humorist, writer, journalist and lecturer

133 Man, because he is man, because he is conscious, is, in relation to the ass or to a crab, already a diseased animal. Consciousness is a disease.
The Tragic Sense of Life (1913) **Unamuno, Miguel de** (1864–1936) Spanish philosopher, poet and writer

134 A man is infinitely more complicated than his thoughts.
In Auden, *A Certain World* **Valéry, Paul** (1871–1945) French poet, mathematician and philosopher

135 If God has created us in his image, we have repaid him well.
Le Sottisier (c.1778) **Voltaire** (1694–1778) French philosopher, dramatist, poet, historian, writer and critic

136 I'd like to share a revelation that I've had during my time here. It came to me when I tried to classify your species. I realized that you're not actually mammals. Every mammal on this planet instinctively develops a natural equilibrium with the surrounding environment, but you humans do not. You move to an area, and you multiply, and multiply, until every natural resource is consumed. The only way you can survive is to spread to another area. There is another organism on this planet that follows the same pattern. A virus. Human beings are a disease, a cancer of this planet, you are a plague, and we are the cure.
The Matrix (film, 1999) **Wachowski, Andy** and **Wachowski, Larry** US film directors and screenwriters. Agent Smith to Morpheus

137 Instead of this absurd division into sexes they ought to class people as static and dynamic.
Decline and Fall (1928) **Waugh, Evelyn** (1903–1966) English writer and diarist

138 Most people are other people. Their thoughts are someone else's opinions, their lives a mimicry, their passions a quotation.
De Profundis (1897) **Wilde, Oscar** (1854–1900) Irish poet, dramatist, writer, critic and wit

139 We're all of us guinea pigs in the laboratory of God. Humanity is just a work in progress.
Camino Real (1953) **Williams, Tennessee** (1911–1983) US dramatist and writer

140 In the final analysis, humanity has only two ways out – either universal destruction or universal brotherhood.
'The Spirit of Elbe' (1966) **Yevtushenko, Yevgeny** (1933–) Russian poet
See also life; society

HUMOUR

1 Of course, it's very easy to be witty tomorrow, after you get a chance to do some research and rehearse your ad libs.
Attr. **Adams, Joey** (1911–1999) US comedian and author

2 The amount of energy spent laughing at a joke should be directly proportional to the hierarchical status of the joke teller.
Building a Better Life by Stealing Office Supplies: Dogbert's Big Book of Business (1991) **Adams, Scott** (1957–) US cartoonist

3 If we may believe our logicians, man is distinguished from all other creatures by the faculty of laughter. He has a heart capable of mirth, and naturally disposed to it.
The Spectator, (1712)

4 Mirth is like a flash of lightning that breaks through a gloom of clouds and glitters for a moment.
The Spectator, (1712) **Addison, Joseph** (1672–1719) English essayist, poet, playwright and statesman

5 I have a fine sense of the ridiculous, but no sense of humour.
Who's Afraid of Virginia Woolf? (1962) **Albee, Edward** (1928–) US dramatist

6 Few women care to be laughed at and men not at all, except for large sums of money.
The Norman Conquests (1975) **Ayckbourn, Alan** (1939–) English dramatist and theatre director

7 The marvellous thing about a joke with a double meaning is that it can only mean one thing.
Attr. **Barker, Ronnie** (1929–2005) English comedian

8 I make myself laugh at everything, for fear of having to cry.
Le Barbier de Seville (1775) **Beaumarchais** (1732–1799) French dramatist

9 The world would not be in such a snarl, had Marx been Groucho instead of Karl.
Attr. **Berlin, Irving** (1888–1989) Russian-born US musical and songwriter. Telegram message to Groucho Marx on his 71st birthday

10 I said of laughter, It is mad: and of mirth, What doeth it?
Ecclesiastes, 2:2 **The Bible (King James Version)**

11 Humour is by far the most significant activity of the human brain.
Daily Mail, (1990) **Bono, Edward de** (1933–) British physician and writer

12 Humour [is] something that thrives between man's aspirations and his limitations. There is more logic in humour than in anything else. Because, you see, humour is truth.
The Times, (1984) **Borge, Victor** (1909–2000) Danish-born US entertainer and pianist

13 It's a good deed to forget a poor joke.
The Observer, (1943) **Bracken, Brendan, First Viscount** (1901–1958) Irish journalist and Conservative politician

14 Humour comes from self-confidence. There's an aggressive element to wit.
Starting From Scratch (1988) **Brown, Rita Mae** (1944–) US writer and poet

15 A rich man's joke is always funny.
'The Doctor' (1887) **Brown, Thomas Edward** (1830–1897) Manx poet, teacher and curate

16 The most perfect humour and irony is generally quite unconscious.
Life and Habit (1877) **Butler, Samuel** (1835–1902) English writer, painter, philosopher and scholar

17 No man who has once heartily and wholly laughed can be altogether irreclaimably bad.
Sartor Resartus (1834) **Carlyle, Thomas** (1795–1881) Scottish historian, biographer, critic, and essayist

18 The most wasted of all days is the day one did not laugh.
Maximes et Pensées (1796) **Chamfort, Nicolas** (1741–1794) French writer

19 In my mind, there is nothing so illiberal and so ill-bred, as audible laughter … I am neither of a melancholy, nor a cynical disposition; and am as willing, and as apt, to be pleased as anybody; but I am sure that, since I have had the full use of my reason, nobody has ever heard me laugh.
Letter to his son, (1748) **Chesterfield, Lord** (1694–1773) English politician and letter writer

20 A joke's a very serious thing.
The Ghost (1763) **Churchill, Charles** (1731–1764) English poet, political writer and clergyman

21 Men will confess to treason, murder, arson, false teeth, or a wig. How many of them will own up to a lack of humour?
Essays **Colby, Frank Moore** (1865–1925) US editor, historian and economist

22 A total absence of humour makes life impossible.
Chance Acquaintances **Colette** (1873–1954) French writer

23 It is the business of a comic poet to paint the vices and follies of human kind. There is nothing more unbecoming a man of quality than to laugh; Jesu, 'tis such a vulgar expression of the passion!
The Double Dealer (1694) **Congreve, William** (1670–1729) English dramatist

24 There's terrific merit in having no sense of humour, no sense of irony, practically no sense of anything at all. If you're born with these so-called defects you have a very good chance of getting to the top.
In Ronald Bergan, *Beyond the Fringe ... and Beyond* (1989) **Cook, Peter** (1937–1995) English comedian and writer

25 A man who could make so vile a pun would not scruple to pick a pocket.
The Gentleman's Magazine, (1781) **Dennis, John** (1657–1734) English critic and dramatist

26 The trouble with Freud is that he never played the Glasgow Empire Saturday night after Rangers and Celtic had both lost.
TV interview, (1965) **Dodd, Ken** (1931–) English comedian, singer, entertainer and actor. Commenting on Freud's theory that a good joke will lead to great relief and elation

27 A thing well said will be wit in all languages.
Essay of Dramatic Poesy (1668) **Dryden, John** (1631–1700) English poet, satirist, dramatist and critic

28 A difference of taste in jokes is a great strain on the affections.
Daniel Deronda (1876) **Eliot, George** (1819–1880) English writer and poet

29 Comedy, like sodomy, is an unnatural act.
The Times, (1969) **Feldman, Marty** (1933–1982) English comedian

30 Comedy is medicine.
The Comedians (1979) **Griffiths, Trevor** (1935–) English dramatist

31 I would like to throw an egg into an electric fan.
Attr. **Herford, Oliver** (1863–1935) British-born US writer and illustrator. When asked if he really had no ambition beyond making people laugh

32 Laughter is nothing else but sudden glory arising from some sudden conception of some eminency in ourselves, by comparison with infirmity of others, or with our own formerly.
Human Nature (1650) **Hobbes, Thomas** (1588–1679) Political philosopher

33 Everything I've ever said will be credited to Dorothy Parker.
Attr. **Kaufman, George S.** (1889–1961) US scriptwriter, librettist and journalist

34 One must laugh before one is happy, for fear of dying without ever having laughed at all.
Les caractères ou les moeurs de ce siècle (1688) **La Bruyère, Jean de** (1645–1696) French satirist

35 It is a pistol let off at the ear; not a feather to tickle the intellect.
Last Essays of Elia (1833) **Lamb, Charles** (1775–1834) English essayist, critic and letter writer. Referring to the nature of a pun

36 The coarse joke proclaims that we have here an animal which finds its own animality either objectionable or funny.
Miracles (c.1936) **Lewis, C.S.** (1898–1963) Irish-born English academic, writer and critic

37 In its essence the purpose of satire – whether verse or prose – is aggression ... Satire has a great big blaring target. If successful, it blasts a great big hole in the centre.
'Note on Verse-Satire' **Lewis, Wyndham** (1882–1957) US-born British painter, critic and writer

38 A person reveals his character by nothing so clearly as the joke he resents.
Attr. **Lichtenberg, Georg** (1742–1799) German physicist, satirist and writer

39 Humour and knowledge are the two great hopes of our culture.
Reader's Digest, (1978) **Lorenz, Konrad** (1903–1989) Austrian zoologist and psychologist

40 It is a good thing to be laughed at. It is better than to be ignored.
That Was The Week That Was, BBC TV, (1962) **Macmillan, Harold** (1894–1986) British Conservative Prime Minister

41 I want to register a complaint. Do you know who sneaked into my room at three o'clock this morning? – Who? Nobody, and that's my complaint.
Monkey Business (film, 1931)

42 An amateur thinks it's funny if you dress a man up as an old lady, sit him in a wheelchair, and shove the wheelchair down a slope towards an approaching car. For a pro, it's got to be a real old lady.
Attr. **Marx, Groucho** (1895–1977) US comedian

43 Impropriety is the soul of wit.
The Moon and Sixpence (1919) **Maugham, William Somerset** (1874–1965) English writer, dramatist and physician

44 It's a strange job, making decent people laugh.
L'Ecole des Femmes (1662) **Molière** (1622–1673) French dramatist, actor and director

45 Satire should, like a polished razor keen, Wound with a touch that's scarcely felt or seen.
'To the Imitator of the First Satire of Horace' **Montagu, Lady Mary Wortley** (1689–1762) English letter writer, poet, traveller and introducer of smallpox inoculation

46 Good taste and humour ... are a contradiction in terms, like a chaste whore.
Time, (1953)

47 It is not for nothing that, in the English language alone, to accuse someone of trying to be funny is highly abusive.
Tread Softly (1966) **Muggeridge, Malcolm** (1903–1990) English writer

48 Whatever is funny is subversive, every joke is ultimately a custard pie ... A dirty joke is not ... a serious attack upon morality, but it is a sort of mental rebellion, a momentary wish that things were otherwise.
'The Art of Donald McGill' (1941) **Orwell, George** (1903–1950) English writer and critic

49 The important thing is to know when to laugh, or since laughing is somewhat undignified, to smile.
The Golden Bubble **Owen, Roderic** (1921–) English playwright and novelist

50 Laughter is pleasant, but the exertion is too much for me.
Nightmare Abbey (1818) **Peacock, Thomas Love** (1785–1866) English writer and poet

51 A pessimist is a man who looks both ways before crossing a one-way street.
Attr. **Peter, Laurence J.** (1919–1990) Canadian educationist and writer

52 True Wit is Nature to advantage dress'd, What oft was thought, but ne'er so well express'd.
An Essay on Criticism (1711) **Pope, Alexander** (1688–1744) English poet, translator and editor

53 Comedy, we may say, is society protecting itself – with a smile.
George Meredith (1926) **Priestley, J.B.** (1894–1984) English writer, dramatist and critic

54 He who laughs on Friday will cry on Sunday.
Les Plaideurs (1668) **Racine, Jean** (1639–1699) French tragedian and poet

55 Irony is humanity's sense of propriety.
Journal, (1892) **Renard, Jules** (1864–1910) French writer and dramatist

56 My routines come out of total unhappiness. My audiences are my group therapy.
Television program, BBC2, (23 February 1990) **Rivers, Joan** (1937–) US comedian

57 Everything is funny as long as it is happening to someone else.
The Illiterate Digest (1924)

58 A comedian can only last till he either takes himself serious or his audience takes him serious.
Newspaper article, (1931) **Rogers, Will** (1879–1935) US humorist, actor, rancher, writer and wit

59 People who have not got a sense of humour shoudn't ever be put in charge.
In *The Guardian,* (2000) **Runcie, Robert** (1921–2000) Archbishop of Canterbury 1980–1991

60 Ridicule often checks what is absurd, and fully as often smothers that which is noble.
Quentin Durward (1823) **Scott, Sir Walter** (1771–1832) Scottish writer and historian

61 And wit's the noblest frailty of the mind.
A True Widow (1679) **Shadwell, Thomas** (c.1642–1692) English poet, writer and playwright

62 A jest's prosperity lies in the ear
Of him that hears it, never in the tongue
Of him that makes it.
Love's Labour Lost, V.ii **Shakespeare, William**
(1564–1616) English dramatist, poet and actor

63 Anything said off the cuff has usually been
written on it first.
Attr. **Skelton, Robin** (1925–1997) British-born
Canadian writer and poet

64 An ounce of a man's own wit is worth a ton
of other people's.
Tristram Shandy (1759–1767)

65 I live in a constant endeavour to fence
against the infirmities of ill health, and
other evils of life, by mirth; being firmly
persuaded that every time a man smiles, –
but much more so, when he laughs, it adds
something to this Fragment of Life.
Tristram Shandy (1759–1767)

66 'Tis no extravagant arithmetic to say, that
for every ten jokes, – thou hast got a
hundred enemies.
Tristram Shandy (1759–1767) **Sterne, Laurence**
(1713–1768) Irish-born English writer and
clergyman

67 Nothing like a little judicious levity.
The Wrong Box (1889) **Stevenson, Robert Louis**
(1850–1894) Scottish writer, poet and essayist

68 Satire, by being levelled at all, is never
resented for an offence by any.
A Tale of a Tub (1704)

69 Satire is a kind of glass, wherein beholders
do generally discover everybody's face but
their own.
The Battle of the Books (1704)

70 Humour is odd, grotesque, and wild,
Only by affectation spoil'd;
'Tis never by invention got,
Men have it when they know it not.
'To Mr Delany' (1718) **Swift, Jonathan** (1667–
1745) Irish satirist, poet, essayist and cleric

71 Humour is emotional chaos remembered
in tranquillity.
Attr. **Thurber, James** (1894–1961) US
humorist, writer and dramatist

72 Humour is an element which the German
man has lost.

'What may Satire do – ?' (1973) **Tucholsky,
Kurt** (1890–1935) German satirist and writer

73 What a good thing Adam had. When he
said a good thing he knew nobody had
said it before.
Notebooks **Twain, Mark** (1835–1910) US
humorist, writer, journalist and lecturer

74 Laughter would be bereaved if snobbery
died.
The Observer, (1955) **Ustinov, Sir Peter** (1921–
2004) English actor, director, dramatist,
writer and raconteur

75 I love such mirth as does not make friends
ashamed to look upon one another next
morning.
The Compleat Angler (1653) **Walton, Izaak** (1593–
1683) English writer

76 To err is human, but it feels divine.
In Simon Rose, *Classic Film Guide* (1995) **West,
Mae** (1892–1980) US actress and scriptwriter

77 Laugh and the world laughs with you;
Weep, and you weep alone;
For the sad old earth must borrow its
mirth,
But has trouble enough of its own.
'Solitude' (1917) **Wilcox, Ella Wheeler** (1850–
1919) US poet and writer

78 She had a penetrating sort of laugh. Rather
like a train going into a tunnel.
The Inimitable Jeeves (1923) **Wodehouse, P.G.**
(1881–1975) English humorist and writer
See also happiness; pleasure

IDEAS

1 Nothing is more dangerous than an idea,
when you only have one idea.
Remarks on Religion (1938)

2 There are only two kinds of scholars; those
who love ideas and those who hate them.
In Alan L. Mackay, *The Harvest of a Quiet Eye*
(1977) **Alain (Emile-Auguste Chartier)** (1868–
1951) French philosopher, teacher and essayist

3 Every revolutionary idea – in science, politics, art, or whatever – evokes three stages of reaction in a hearer:
• It is completely impossible – don't waste my time.
• It is possible, but it is not worth doing.
• I said it was a good idea all along.
Anonymous

4 He has a brilliant mind until he makes it up.
In *The Wit of the Asquiths* **Asquith, Margot** (1864–1945) Scottish political hostess and writer. Of Sir Stafford Cripps

5 To us he is no more a person
Now but a climate of opinion.
In Memory of Sigmund Freud **Auden, W.H.** (1907–1973) English poet, essayist, critic, teacher and dramatist

6 He that will not apply new remedies must expect new evils; for time is the greatest innovator.
Essays (1625) **Bacon, Francis** (1561–1626) English philosopher, essayist, politician and courtier

7 One of the greatest pains to human nature is the pain of a new idea.
Physics and Politics (1872) **Bagehot, Walter** (1826–1877) English economist and political philosopher

8 It's the same each time with progress. First they ignore you, then they say you're mad, then dangerous, then there's a pause and then you can't find anyone who disagrees with you.
The Observer, (1991) **Benn, Tony** (1925–) English Labour politician

9 I prefer complexity to certainty, cheerful mysteries to sullen facts.
Address, University of Toronto, (1969) **Bissell, Claude T.** (1916–2000) Canadian writer

10 One can live in the shadow of an idea without grasping it.
The Heat of the Day (1949) **Bowen, Elizabeth** (1899–1973) Irish writer

11 His mind is open; yes, it is so open that nothing is retained; ideas simply pass through him.

Attr. **Bradley, F.H.** (1846–1924) English philosopher

12 Those Himalayas of the mind
Are not so easily possessed:
There's more than precipice and storm
Between you and your Everest.
Transitional Poem (1924), 'Those Himalayas of the Mind' **Day Lewis, C.** (1904–1972) Irish-born British academic, writer and critic

13 It has long been an axiom of mine that the little things are infinitely the most important.
The Adventures of Sherlock Holmes (1892), 'A Case of Identity' **Doyle, Sir Arthur Conan** (1859–1930) Scottish writer and war correspondent

14 My mind to me a kingdom is,
Such present joys therein I find,
That it excels all other bliss
That earth affords or grows by kind.
Though much I want which most would have,
Yet still my mind forbids to crave.
'In praise of a contented mind' (1588) **Dyer, Sir Edward** (c.1540–1607) English poet and courtier

15 What we call 'Progress' is the exchange of one nuisance for another nuisance.
Impressions and Comments (1914) **Ellis, Havelock** (1859–1939) English sexologist and essayist

16 It is a lesson which all history teaches wise men, to put trust in ideas, and not in circumstances.
Miscellanies (1856) **Emerson, Ralph Waldo** (1803–1882) US poet, essayist, transcendentalist and teacher

17 What progress we are making. In the Middle Ages they would have burned me. Now they are content with burning my books.
Letter, (1933) **Freud, Sigmund** (1856–1939) Austrian physicist; founder of psychoanalysis

18 When an idea is dead it is embalmed in a textbook.
In Boardman, *The Worlds of Patrick Geddes* (1978) **Geddes, Patrick** (1854–1932) Scottish biologist and sociologist

19 Many ideas grow better when transplanted into another mind than in the one where they sprang up.
In Bowen, *Yankee from Olympus* (1945) **Holmes, Oliver Wendell, Jr** (1841–1935) US jurist and judge

20 One can resist the invasion of an army; but one cannot resist the invasion of ideas.
Histoire d'un Crime (1852) **Hugo, Victor** (1802–1885) French poet, writer, dramatist and politician

21 It is better to entertain an idea than to take it home to live with you for the rest of your life.
Pictures from an Institution (1954) **Jarrell, Randall** (1914–1965) US poet, critic and translator

22 Sentimentality is a superstructure covering brutality.
Reflections

23 The least of things with a meaning is worth more in life than the greatest of things without it.
Modern Man in Search of a Soul **Jung, Carl Gustav** (1875–1961) Swiss psychiatrist and pupil of Freud

24 The power of vested interests is vastly exaggerated compared with the gradual encroachment of ideas. Not, indeed, immediately ... But, soon or late, it is ideas, not vested interests, which are dangerous for good or evil.
The General Theory of Employment, Interest and Money (1936) **Keynes, John Maynard** (1883–1946) English economist

25 'Dying for an idea,' again, sounds well enough, but why not let the idea die instead of you?
The Art of Being Ruled (1926) **Lewis, Wyndham** (1882–1957) US-born British painter, critic and writer

26 In general it is a good morning exercise for a researcher to destroy a favourite hypothesis every day before breakfast – it keeps him young.
On Aggression (1963) **Lorenz, Konrad** (1903–1989) Austrian zoologist and psychologist

27 Society goes on and on and on. It is the same with ideas.
Speech, (1935) **MacDonald, Ramsay** (1866–1937) Scottish Labour politician and Prime Minister

28 An idea isn't responsible for the people who believe in it.
New York Sun **Marquis, Don** (1878–1937) US columnist, satirist and poet

29 The human mind treats a new idea the way the body treats a strange protein – it rejects it.
Attr. **Medawar, Sir Peter** (1915–1987) British zoologist and immunologist

30 The great majority of those who speak of perfectibility as a dream, do so because they feel that it is one which would afford them no pleasure if it were realized.
Speech on Perfectibility (1828) **Mill, John Stuart** (1806–1873) English philosopher, economist and reformer

31 General notions are generally wrong.
Letter to her husband, Edward Wortley Montagu, (1710) **Montagu, Lady Mary Wortley** (1689–1762) English letter writer, poet, traveller and introducer of smallpox inoculation

32 The English way with ideas is not to kill them but to let them die of neglect.
The Observer, 'Sayings of the Year', (1998) **Paxman, Jeremy** (1950–) English journalist, writer and broadcaster

33 That's the classical mind at work, runs fine inside but looks dingy on the surface.
Zen and the Art of Motorcycle Maintenance (1974) **Pirsig, Robert** (1928–) US author

34 We haven't the money, so we've got to think!
In Bulletin of the Institute of Physics, (1962) **Rutherford, Ernest** (1871–1937) English physicist

35 For an idea ever to be fashionable is ominous, since it must afterwards be always old-fashioned.
Winds of Doctrine (1913) **Santayana, George** (1863–1952) Spanish-born US philosopher and writer

36 This creature Man, who in his own selfish affairs is a coward to the backbone, will fight for an idea like a hero.
Man and Superman (1903) **Shaw, George Bernard** (1856–1950) Irish socialist, writer, dramatist and critic

37 Ideas are like rabbits. You get a couple and learn how to handle them, and pretty soon you have a dozen.
Attr. **Steinbeck, John** (1902–1968) US writer

38 It is the nature of an hypothesis, when once a man has conceived it, that it assimilates every thing to itself as proper nourishment; and, from the first moment of your begetting it, it generally grows the stronger by every thing you see, hear, read, or understand. This is of great use.
Tristram Shandy (1759–1767) **Sterne, Laurence** (1713–1768) Irish-born English writer and clergyman

39 A psychiatrist is a man who goes to the Folies-Bergère and looks at the audience.
The Observer, (1961) **Stockwood, Mervyn** (1913–1995) English Anglican churchman

40 A nice man is a man of nasty ideas.
Thoughts on Various Subjects (1711) **Swift, Jonathan** (1667–1745) Irish satirist, poet, essayist and cleric

41 It is not normally our ideas which make us optimists or pessimists, but it is our optimism or our pessimism, which is perhaps of a physiological or pathological origin ... which makes our ideas.
The Tragic Sense of Life (1913) **Unamuno, Miguel de** (1864–1936) Spanish philosopher, poet and writer
See also imagination; opinions; thought

IDLENESS AND UNEMPLOYMENT

1 Of course I don't look busy, I did it right the first time.
The Dilbert Principle **Adams, Scott** (1957–) US cartoonist

2 Doing nothing gets pretty tiresome because you can't stop and rest.
Anonymous

3 Those who do nothing are never wrong.
Odes funambulesques **Banville, Théodore Faullain de** (1823–1891) French poet, lyricist and dramatist

4 What a terrible burden it is to have nothing to do!
Epitres (c.1690) **Boileau-Despréaux, Nicolas** (1636–1711) French writer

5 It is not only an offence against society to be seen in the streets flaunting the fact that one does not work like everyone else; it challenges the settled order of things, a threat that no right thinking New Zealander could tolerate. It makes one an object of suspicion, and more, an enemy.
Indirections: A Memoir 1909–1947 (1980) **Brasch, Charles Orwell** (1909–1973) New Zealand poet and editor. On walking on a weekday in Dunedin, 1938, when he was unemployed

6 I always like to have the morning well-aired before I get up.
In Macfarlane, *Reminiscences of a Literary Life* (1917) **Brummel, Beau** (1778–1840) English dandy and wit

7 *Liubov Andreevna*: Are you really still a student?
Trofimov: I shall probably be a student forever.
The Cherry Orchard (1904) **Chekhov, Anton** (1860–1904) Russian writer, dramatist and doctor

8 Idleness is only the refuge of weak minds, and the holiday of fools.
Letter to his son, (1749) **Chesterfield, Lord** (1694–1773) English politician and letter writer

9 We owe most of our great inventions and most of the achievements of genius to idleness – either enforced or voluntary.
The Moving Finger (1942) **Christie, Agatha** (1890–1976) English crime writer and playwright

10 Never less idle than when free from work, nor less lonely than when completely alone.
De Officiis **Cicero** (106–43 BC) Roman orator, statesman, essayist and letter writer

11 I make no secret of the fact that I would rather lie on a sofa than sweep beneath it. But you have to be efficient if you're going to be lazy.
Superwoman (1975) **Conran, Shirley** (1932–) English writer

12 How various his employments, whom the world
Calls idle.
The Task (1785) **Cowper, William** (1731–1800) English poet, hymn writer and letter writer

13 A state of idleness is the very dregs of life.
The Life and Adventures of Robinson Crusoe (1719) **Defoe, Daniel** (c.1661–1731) English writer and critic

14 There's many a one would be idle if hunger didn't pinch him; but the stomach sets us to work.
Felix Holt (1866) **Eliot, George** (1819–1880) English writer and poet

15 After Cambridge – unemployment. No one wanted much to know.
Good degrees are good for nothing in the business world below.
'The Sentimental Education' **Ewart, Gavin** (1916–1995) English poet

16 Says little, thinks less, and does – nothing at all, faith.
The Beaux' Stratagem (1707) **Farquhar, George** (1678–1707) Irish dramatist

17 'What'll we do with ourselves this afternoon?' cried Daisy, 'and the day after that, and the next thirty years?'
The Great Gatsby (1925) **Fitzgerald, F. Scott** (1896–1940) US writer

18 Unemployed at last!
Such is Life (1903) **Furphy, Joseph** (1843–1912) Australian writer and poet

19 Only a real lazybones can produce labour-saving inventions.
The Tin Drum (1959) **Grass, Günter** (1927–) German writer

20 For dole bread is bitter bread
Bitter bread and sour
There's grief in the taste of it
There's weevils in the flour.
'Weevils in the Flour' **Hewett, Dorothy** (1923–2002) Australian dramatist and poet

21 When a great many people are unable to find work, unemployment results.
In Boller, *Presidential Anecdotes* (1981) **Hoover, Herbert Clark** (1874–1964) US Republican President

22 It is impossible to enjoy idling thoroughly unless one has plenty of work to do.
Idle Thoughts of an Idle Fellow (1886)

23 George goes to sleep at a bank from ten to four each day, except Saturdays, when they wake him up and put him outside at two.
Three Men in a Boat (1889) **Jerome, Jerome K.** (1859–1927) English writer and dramatist

24 Every man is, or hopes to be, an idler.
The Idler (1758–1760)

25 If you are idle, be not solitary; if you are solitary, be not idle.
Letter to Boswell, (1779) **Johnson, Samuel** (1709–1784) English lexicographer, poet, critic, conversationalist and essayist

26 I was raised to feel that doing nothing was a sin. I had to learn to do nothing.
The Observer, (1998) **Joseph, Jenny** (1932–) British poet

27 Research! A mere excuse for idleness; it has never achieved, and will never achieve any results of the slightest value.
In Logan Pearsall Smith, *Unforgotten Years* **Jowett, Benjamin** (1817–1893) English scholar, translator, essayist and priest

28 Never be completely idle, but be either reading, or writing, or praying, or meditating, or working at something useful for the community.
De Imitatione Christi (1892) **Kempis, Thomas à** (c.1380–1471) German mystic, monk and writer

29 Wasting time is negative, but there is something positive about idleness.
Attr. **Lynes, J. Russel** (1910–1991) US art historian and author

30 The devil finds mischief still for hands that have not learnt how to be idle.
Livre sans nom: Twelve Reflections (1934) **Madan, Geoffrey** (1895–1947) English bibliophile

31 Without doubt machinery has greatly increased the number of well to do idlers.

Das Kapital (1867) **Marx, Karl** (1818–1883) German political philosopher and economist; founder of Communism

32 It was such a lovely day I thought it was a pity to get up.
Our Betters (1923) **Maugham, William Somerset** (1874–1965) English writer, dramatist and physician

33 I would live my life in nonchalance and insouciance
Were it not for making a living, which is rather a nouciance.
'Introspective Reflection' (1940) **Nash, Ogden** (1902–1971) US poet

34 She marked thee there,
Stretch'd on the rack of a too easy chair,
And heard thy everlasting yawn confess
The Pains and Penalties of idleness.
The Dunciad (1742) **Pope, Alexander** (1688–1744) English poet, translator and editor

35 To help the unemployed is not the same thing as dealing with unemployment.
The Observer, (1933) **Samuel, Lord** (1870–1963) English Liberal statesman, philosopher and administrator

36 No applications can be received here on Sundays, nor any business done during the remainder of the week.
Attr. in Morwood, *The Life and Works of Sheridan* (1985) **Sheridan, Richard Brinsley** (1751–1816) Irish dramatist, politician and orator. On a notice fixed to his door when he was a Secretary to the Treasury

37 The insupportable Labour of doing nothing.
The Spectator, 54, (1711) **Steele, Sir Richard** (1672–1729) Irish-born English writer, dramatist and politician

38 Extreme busyness, whether at school or college, kirk or market, is a symptom of deficient vitality; and a faculty for idleness implies a catholic appetite and a strong sense of personal identity.
Virginibus Puerisque (1881) **Stevenson, Robert Louis** (1850–1894) Scottish writer, poet and essayist

39 It is better to have loafed and lost than never to have loafed at all.

Fables for Our Time (1940) **Thurber, James** (1894–1961) US humorist, writer and dramatist

40 I am happiest when I am idle. I could live for months without performing any kind of labour, and at the expiration of that time I should feel fresh and vigorous enough to go right on in the same way for numerous more months.
Artemus Ward in London (1867) **Ward, Artemus** (1834–1867) US humorist, journalist, editor and lecturer

41 In works of labour, or of skill,
I would be busy too;
For Satan finds some mischief still
For idle hands to do.
Divine Songs for Children (1715) **Watts, Isaac** (1674–1748) English hymn writer, poet and minister
See also boredom; work

IMAGINATION

1 A lady's imagination is very rapid; it jumps from admiration to love, from love to matrimony, in a moment.
Pride and Prejudice (1813) **Austen, Jane** (1775–1817) English writer

2 Imagination is the highest kite that one can fly.
Lauren Bacall, By Myself **Bacall, Lauren** (1924–) US actress

3 For the imagination of man's heart is evil from his youth.
Genesis, 8:21 **The Bible (King James Version)**

4 What is now proved was once only imagin'd.
'Proverbs of Hell' (c.1793) **Blake, William** (1757–1827) English poet, engraver, painter and mystic

5 I imagine that everything is as I say it is, neither more or less, and I paint her in my imagination the way I want her to be.
Don Quixote (1605) **Cervantes, Miguel de** (1547–1616) Spanish writer and dramatist. Don Quixote of his lady, Dulcinea del Toboso

6 The most imaginative people are the most credulous, for them everything is possible.
Perspectives (1966) **Chase, Alexander** (1926–) US journalist and author

7 Fancy, on the contrary, has no other counters to play with, but fixities and definites. The fancy is indeed no other than a mode of memory emancipated from the order of time and space.
Biographia Literaria (1817)

8 The primary imagination I hold to be the living power and prime agent of all human perception, and as a repetition in the finite mind of the eternal act of creation in the infinite I AM. The secondary imagination … dissolves, diffuses, dissipates, in order to recreate; or where this process is rendered impossible, yet still at all events it struggles to idealize and to unify.
Biographia Literaria (1817) **Coleridge, Samuel Taylor** (1772–1834) English poet, philosopher and critic

9 Imagination is more important than knowledge.
On Science **Einstein, Albert** (1879–1955) German-born US mathematical physicist

10 He said he should prefer not to know the sources of the Nile, and that there should be some unknown regions preserved as hunting-grounds for the poetic imagination.
Middlemarch (1872) **Eliot, George** (1819–1880) English writer and poet

11 Were it not for imagination, Sir, a man would be as happy in the arms of a chambermaid as of a Duchess.
In Boswell, *The Life of Samuel Johnson* (1791) **Johnson, Samuel** (1709–1784) English lexicographer, poet, critic, conversationalist and essayist

12 Imagination is the eye of the soul.
Attr. **Joubert, Joseph** (1754–1824) French essayist

13 The Imagination may be compared to Adam's dream – he awoke and found it truth.
Letter to Benjamin Bailey, (22 November 1817)

14 I am certain of nothing but of the holiness of the Heart's affections and the truth of Imagination – What the imagination seizes as Beauty must be truth – whether it existed before or not.
Letter to Benjamin Bailey, (22 November 1817) **Keats, John** (1795–1821) English poet

15 His imagination resembled the wings of an ostrich. It enabled him to run, though not to soar.
'John Dryden' (1843) **Macaulay, Lord** (1800–1859) English Liberal statesman, essayist and poet

16 How many works of the imagination have been goaded into life by envy of an untalented contemporary's success.
An Answer from Limbo (1994) **Moore, Brian** (1921–1999) Irish writer

17 It will be found, in fact, that the ingenious are always fanciful, and the truly imaginative never otherwise than analytic.
The Murders in the Rue Morgue (1841) **Poe, Edgar Allan** (1809–1849) US poet, writer and editor

18 Where does imagination start
but from primeval images
in man's barbaric heart?
'Mopoke' **Robinson, Roland Edward** (1912–1992) Irish-born Australian poet

19 I don't know what imagination is, if not an unpruned, tangled kind of memory.
Letty Fox: Her Luck (1946) **Stead, Christina** (1902–1983) Australian writer

20 It is the spirit of the age to believe that any fact, no matter how suspect, is superior to any imaginative exercise, no matter how true.
French Letters: Theories of the New Novel **Vidal, Gore** (1925–) US writer, critic and poet
See also dreams; fantasy; ideas

INFIDELITY

1 I am proud to say that I have a very good eye at an Adultress, for tho' repeatedly assured that another in the same party was the She, I fixed upon the right one from the first.

Letter to Cassandra Austen, (1801) **Austen, Jane** (1775–1817) English writer

2 It is better to be unfaithful than faithful without wanting to be.
The Observer, (1968) **Bardot, Brigitte** (1934–) French actress

3 One cubic foot less of space and it would have constituted adultery.
Attr. **Benchley, Robert** (1889–1945) US essayist, humorist and actor. Comment on an office shared with Dorothy Parker

4 Merely innocent flirtation. Not quite adultery, but adulteration.
Don Juan (1824)

5 What men call gallantry, and gods adultery, Is much more common where the climate's sultry.
Don Juan (1824) **Byron, Lord** (1788–1824) English poet, satirist and traveller

6 I've looked on a lot of women with lust. I've committed adultery in my heart many times. God recognizes I will do this and forgives me.
Interview with *Playboy*, (1976) **Carter, Jimmy** (1924–) US Democrat statesman and President

7 Sara could commit adultery at one end and weep for her sins at the other, and enjoy both operations at once.
The Horse's Mouth (1944) **Cary, Joyce** (1888–1957) English novelist

8 I may commit adultery again if God moves me to it.
The Observer, (1980) **Dring, Philip** (1924–) US preacher

9 I say I don't sleep with married men, but what I mean is that I don't sleep with happily married men.
Attr. **Ekland, Britt** (1942–) Swedish actress

10 Adultery in your heart is committed not only when you look with excessive sexual desire at a woman who is not your wife, but also if you look in the same manner at your wife.
The Observer, (1990) **John Paul II** (1920–2005) Polish pope

11 I thought as long as he's Minister for Foreign Affairs I might as well give him one he'd never forget.
Melbourne Herald, (1979) **Maclaine, Shirley** (1934–) US actress. On her friendship with Andrew Peacock

12 You know, of course, that the Tasmanians, who never committed adultery, are now extinct.
The Bread-Winner **Maugham, William Somerset** (1874–1965) English writer, dramatist and physician

13 Madame, you must really be more careful. Suppose it had been someone else who found you like this.
In Wallechinsky, *The Book of Lists* (1977) **Richelieu, Duc de** (1766–1822) French courtier, soldier and Prime Minister. On discovering his wife with her lover

14 Adultery? Thou shalt not die:
Die for adultery! No:
The wren goes to't, and the small gilded fly
Does lecher in my sight.
Let copulation thrive.
King Lear, IV.vi **Shakespeare, William** (1564–1616) English dramatist, poet and actor
See also forgiveness; guilt; lies; marriage; men and women; revenge

INTELLIGENCE

1 An intellectual is a man who doesn't know how to park a bike.
Attr. **Agnew, Spiro T.** (1918–1996) US Vice President

2 He's very clever, but sometimes his brains go to his head.
Quoted by Baroness Asquith in TV programme, *As I Remember*, (30 April 1967) **Asquith, Margot** (1864–1945) Scottish political hostess and writer. On F.E. Smith

3 To the man-in-the-street, who, I'm sorry to say,
Is a keen observer of life,
The word intellectual suggests straight away
A man who's untrue to his wife.

Collected Poems, 1939–(1947) **Auden, W.H.** (1907–1973) English poet, essayist, critic, teacher and dramatist

4 The intelligent are to the intelligentsia what a gentleman is to a gent.
Attr. **Baldwin, Stanley** (1867–1947) English Conservative statesman and Prime Minister

5 I've been called many things, but never an intellectual.
Tallulah (1952) **Bankhead, Tallulah** (1903–1968) US actress

6 The intellectuals' chief cause of anguish are one another's works.
The House of Intellect (1959) **Barzun, Jacques** (1907–) French-born US historian, teacher and author

7 I'm not very clever, but I'm quite intelligent.
Attr. **Bogarde, Dirk** (1921–1999) British actor and writer

8 Intellectuals are people who believe that ideas are of more importance than values. That is to say, their own ideas and other people's values.
Thoughts in a Dry Season (1978) **Brenan, Gerald** (1894–1987) English writer

9 An intellectual? Yes. And never deny it. An intellectual = one who splits himself in two. I like that. I am happy to be both halves.
Carnets, 1935–1942 (1962) **Camus, Albert** (1913–1960) Algerian-born French writer

10 Hercule Poirot tapped his forehead. 'These little gray cells, it is "up to them" – as you say over here.'
The Mysterious Affair at Styles (1920) **Christie, Agatha** (1890–1976) English crime writer and playwright

11 His wit invites you by his looks to come, But when you knock it is never at home.
'Conversation' (1782) **Cowper, William** (1731–1800) English poet, hymn writer and letter writer

12 We know the human brain is a device to keep the ears from grating on one another.
Comfort me with Apples (1956) **De Vries, Peter** (1910–1993) US novelist

13 Staircase wit.
Paradoxe sur le Comédien (c.1778) **Diderot, Denis** (1713–1784) French philosopher, encyclopaedist, writer and dramatist. A retort which comes to mind too late

14 Common sense is the best distributed thing in the world, for we all think we possess a good share of it.
Discours de la Méthode (1637) **Descartes, René** (1596–1650) French philosopher and mathematician

15 I am a brain, Watson. The rest of me is a mere appendix.
The Case Book of Sherlock Holmes (1927) **Doyle, Sir Arthur Conan** (1859–1930) Scottish writer and war correspondent

16 The voice of the intellect is a soft one, but it does not rest till it has gained a hearing.
The Future of an Illusion **Freud, Sigmund** (1856–1939) Austrian physicist; founder of psychoanalysis

17 Why is there invariably something comic about intellectuals when they meet together in crowds?
Diary, (1948) **Frisch, Max** (1911–1991) Swiss dramatist, writer and architect

18 Let the scintillations of your wit be like the coruscations of summer lightning, lambent but innocuous.
Sermon at Rugby **Goulburn, Edward, Dean of Norwich** (1818–1897) English divine and teacher

19 Wit's an unruly engine, wildly striking Sometimes a friend, sometimes the engineer.
The Temple (1633) **Herbert, George** (1593–1633) English poet and priest

20 A generous and elevated mind is distinguished by nothing more certainly than an eminent degree of curiosity.
In Boswell, *The Life of Samuel Johnson* (1791) **Johnson, Samuel** (1709–1784) English lexicographer, poet, critic, conversationalist and essayist

21 The only means of strengthening one's intellect is to make up one's mind about nothing – to let the mind be a thoroughfare for all thoughts. Not a select party.
Letter to George and Georgiana Keats, (1819)
Keats, John (1795–1821) English poet

22 How reconcile this world of fact with the bright world of my imagining? My darkness has been filled with the light of intelligence, and behold, the outer day-light world was stumbling and groping in social blindness.
In Upton Sinclair (ed.), *The Cry for Justice* (1963)
Keller, Helen (1880–1968) US writer and educator of the blind and deaf

23 The height of cleverness is to be able to conceal it.
Maximes (1678)

24 One can be more astute than another, but not more astute than all the others.
Maximes (1678) **La Rochefoucauld** (1613–1680) French writer

25 The highest intellects, like the tops of mountains, are the first to catch and to reflect the dawn.
'Sir James Mackintosh' (1843) **Macaulay, Lord** (1800–1859) English Liberal statesman, essayist and poet

26 Every intellectual attitude is latently political.
The Observer, (1974) **Mann, Thomas** (1875–1955) German writer and critic

27 Wit is the epigram for the death of an emotion.
Human, All too Human (1886) **Nietzsche, Friedrich Wilhelm** (1844–1900) German philosopher, critic and poet

28 The more intelligence one has the more people one finds original. Commonplace people see no difference between men.
Penseés (1670) **Pascal, Blaise** (1623–1662) French philosopher and scientist

29 Intellect is invisible to the man who has none.
Aphorismen zur Lebensweisheit **Schopenhauer, Arthur** (1788–1860) German philosopher

30 Brevity is the soul of wit.
Hamlet, II.ii

31 Look, he's winding up the watch of his wit; by and by it will strike.
The Tempest, II.i

32 This fellow is wise enough to play the fool; And to do that well craves a kind of wit.
Twelfth Night, III.i **Shakespeare, William** (1564–1616) English dramatist, poet and actor

33 Eggheads of the world unite; you have nothing to lose but your yolks.
Attr. **Stevenson, Adlai** (1900–1965) US lawyer, statesman and United Nations ambassador

34 Families, when a child is born
Want it to be intelligent.
I, through intelligence,
Having wrecked my whole life,
Only hope the baby will prove
Ignorant and stupid.
Then he will crown a tranquil life
By becoming a Cabinet Minister.
In Waley, *170 Chinese Poems* **Su Tung-P'o (Su Shih)** (1036–1101) Chinese poet, painter and public official

35 Intelligence is quickness to apprehend as distinct from ability, which is capacity to act wisely on the thing apprehended.
Dialogues (1954) **Whitehead, A.N.** (1861–1947) English mathematician and philosopher
See also education; genius; knowledge; thought; wisdom

IRELAND

1 The foreman says, 'You must have an intelligence test.' The Irishman says, 'All right.' So the foreman says, 'What is the difference between joist and girder?' And the Irishman says, 'Joyce wrote *Ulysses* and Goethe wrote *Faust.*'
Retelling the only Irish joke he really liked, quoted in Gus Smith, *God's Own Comedian* **Allen, Dave** (1936–2005) Irish comedian and television personality

2 Not men and women in an Irish street
But Catholics and Protestants you meet.
Attr. **Allingham, William** (1824–1889) Irish poet and diarist

3 Today, we were unlucky, but remember, we only have to be lucky once – you will have to be lucky always.
IRA statement after the bombing of Conservative Party Conference in Brighton, (October 1984) **Anonymous**

4 Peace in Northern Ireland has to built on its divisions, not on a fiction of unity which does not yet exist.
The Observer, (1998) **Ascherson, Neal** (1932–) Scottish journalist

5 There are a few fortunate races that have been endowed with cheerfulness as their main characteristic, the Australian Aborigine and the Irish being among these.
The Passing of the Aborigines ... (1938) **Bates, Daisy May** (1863–1951) Irish-born journalist, anthropologist and reformer

6 *Pat*: He was an Anglo-Irishman.
Meg: In the blessed name of God, what's that?
Pat: A Protestant with a horse.
The Hostage (1958)

7 Other people have a nationality. The Irish and the Jews have a psychosis.
Richard's Cork Leg (1972)

8 The English and Americans dislike only some Irish – the same Irish that the Irish themselves detest, Irish writers – the ones that think.
Richard's Cork Leg (1972) **Behan, Brendan** (1923–1964) Irish dramatist, writer and Republican

9 They say there's bread and work for all,
And the sun shines always there:
But I'll not forget old Ireland,
Were it fifty times as fair.
'Lament of the Irish Emigrant' (1845) **Blackwood, Helen Selina** (1807–1867) English poet

10 For the great Gaels of Ireland
Are the men that God made mad,
For all their wars are merry,
And all their songs are sad.
Ballad of the White Horse (1911) **Chesterton, G.K.** (1874–1936) English writer, poet and critic

11 Not in vain is Ireland pouring itself all over the earth ... The Irish, with their glowing hearts and reverent credulity, are needed in this cold age of intellect and skepticism.
Letters from New York (1842) **Child, Lydia M.** (1802–1880) US writer, abolitionist and suffragist

12 The whole notion of holding a referendum on women's access to information is such a profound disgrace for a nation such as this that I ... apologise to Irish women on behalf of what has been predominantly a male-dominated, male-driven male disgrace.
The Irish Times, (1993) **Clare, Dr Anthony** (1942–) Irish professor, psychiatrist and broadcaster

13 We must not let the men of the past ruin the future of the children of Northern Ireland.
Daily Mail, (1996) **Clinton, William ('Bill')** (1946–) US Democrat President. On the IRA, shortly after they resumed their campaign of violence in February 1996

14 Think – what have I got for Ireland? Something which she has wanted these past seven hundred years. Will anyone be satisfied at the bargain? Will anyone? I tell you this – early this morning I signed my death warrant. I thought at the time how odd, how ridiculous – a bullet may just as well have done the job five years ago.
Letter to John O'Kane, (1921) **Collins, Michael** (1890–1922) Irish revolutionary leader. Said on signing the agreement with Great Britain, 1921, that established the Irish Free State; he was assassinated some months later

15 Red bricks in the suburbs, white horse on the wall,
Eyetalian marbles in the City Hall:
O stranger from England, why stand so aghast?
May the Lord in his mercy be kind to Belfast.
'Ballad to a Traditional Refrain' **Craig, Maurice James** (1919–) Poet and historian

16 Whenever I wanted to know what the Irish people wanted, I had only to examine my own heart and it told me straight off what the Irish people wanted.

Dáil Éireann, (1922)

17 … a land whose countryside would be bright with cosy homesteads, whose fields and villages would be joyous with the sounds of industry, with the romping of sturdy children, the contests of athletic youths and the laughter of comely maidens, whose firesides would be forums for the wisdom of serene old age.
Radio broadcast, St Patrick's Day, (1943) **De Valera, Eamon** (1882–1975) Irish statesman

18 A starving population, an absentee aristocracy, and an alien Church, and in addition the weakest executive in the world. That is the Irish question.
Speech, (1844) **Disraeli, Benjamin** (1804–1881) English statesman and writer

19 When my country takes her place among the nations of the earth, then and not till then, let my epitaph be written. I have done.
Attr. **Emmet, Robert** (1778–1803) Irish patriot. Before his execution

20 The Irish were not English. God had sent them to Canada to keep people from marrying Protestants.
Across the Bridge (1993) **Gallant, Mavis** (1922–) Canadian writer

21 Politics is the chloroform of the Irish people, or rather the hashish.
As I Was Going Down Sackville Street (1937) **Gogarty, Oliver St John** (1878–1957) Irish poet, dramatist, writer, politician and surgeon

22 The names of a land show the heart of the race;
They move on the tongue like the lilt of a song.
You say the name and I see the place –
Drumbo, Dungannon, or Annalong.
Barony, townland, we cannot go wrong.
'Ulster Names' **Hewitt, John** (1907–1987) Irish poet and museum and art gallery director

23 The Irish are a fair people; – they never speak well of one another.
In Boswell, *The Life of Samuel Johnson* (1791) **Johnson, Samuel** (1709–1784) English lexicographer, poet, critic, conversationalist and essayist

24 My intention was to write a chapter of the moral history of my country and I chose Dublin for the scene because that city seemed to me the centre of paralysis.
Letter to Grant Richards, (1905)

25 Ireland is the old sow that eats her farrow.
A Portrait of the Artist as a Young Man (1916)

26 We feel in England that we have treated you Irish rather unfairly. It seems history is to blame.
Ulysses (1922)

27 I am afraid I am more interested, Mr Connolly, in the Dublin street names than in the riddle of the universe.
Remark to Cyril Connolly **Joyce, James** (1882–1941) Irish writer

28 The problem with Ireland is that it's a country full of genius, but with absolutely no talent.
Interview in *The Times*, (1977) **Leonard, Hugh** (1926–) Irish dramatist and screenwriter

29 If we are pushed back, we will start again. If we are pushed back, we will start again. If we are pushed back a third time we will start again.
The Observer Review, (1996) **Major, John** (1943–) English Conservative Prime Minister. On the search for peace in Northern Ireland after the end of the IRA ceasefire in February 1996

30 Who here really believes that we can win the war through the ballot box? But will anyone here object if with a ballot box in this hand and an Armalite in this hand we take power in Ireland.
Provisional Sinn Féin Conference, (1981) **Morrison, Danny** (1950–) Irish Republican activist

31 An Irish Quaker is a fellow who prefers women to drink.
Attr. on Nigel Rees' BBC programme *Quote Unquote*, (1999) **O'Faolain, Sean** (1900–1991) Irish writer

32 How could we tolerate for all those years the deeds of a fascist organisation dedicated to torture and murder? What cowardice or connivance prevented us from speaking out against these atrocities? Were we any better than the denizens of Buchenwald who couldn't smell the smoke from the crematoria?
Letter to *The Irish Times* (June 1999) **O'Leary, Father Joseph** On the IRA, during the search for the bodies of the 'disappeared'

33 No man has a right to fix the boundary of the march of a nation: no man has a right to say to his country – thus far shalt thou go and no further.
Speech, (1885) **Parnell, Charles Stewart** (1846–1891) Irish nationalist politician

34 As the elected choice of the people of this part of our island I want to extend the hand of friendship and of love to both communities in the other part.
Inaugural speech as President, (1991) **Robinson, Mary** (1944–) President of Ireland 1990–1997

35 An Irishman's heart is nothing but his imagination.
John Bull's Other Island (1907)

36 If you want to bore an Irishman, play him an Irish melody, or introduce him to another Irishman.
In Holroyd, *Shaw* (1989) **Shaw, George Bernard** (1856–1950) Irish socialist, writer, dramatist and critic

37 Without a union with Great Britain, the inhabitants of Ireland are not likely for many ages to consider themselves as one people.
Wealth of Nations (1776) **Smith, Adam** (1723–1790) Scottish economist, philosopher and essayist

38 The moment the very name of Ireland is mentioned, the English seem to bid adieu to common feeling, common prudence, and to common sense, and to act with the barbarity of tyrants, and the fatuity of idiots.
Letters of Peter Plymley (1807) **Smith, Sydney** (1771–1845) English clergyman, essayist, journalist and wit

39 The lovely and lonely bride,
Whom we have wedded but never won.
'Ode on the Coronation of Edward VII' (1902) **Watson, Sir William** (1858–1935) English poet. Of Ireland

40 Behind Ireland fierce and militant, is Ireland poetic, passionate, remembering, idyllic, fanciful, and always patriotic.
'Popular Ballad Poetry of Ireland', (1889)

41 This blind bitter land.
The Green Helmet and Other Poems (1912) Of Ireland

42 We against whom you have done this thing are no petty people. We are one of the great stocks of Europe. We are the people of Burke; we are the people of Grattan; we are the people of Swift, the people of Emmett, the people of Parnell. We have created the most of the modern literature of this country. We have created the best of its political intelligence.
Speech to the Senate, (June 1925) From Yeats's speech on divorce, in which he stressed the contribution made by the Protestant minority to the literary and political life of Ireland

43 The Irish mind has still in country rapscallion or in Bernard Shaw an ancient, cold, explosive, detonating impartiality. The English mind, excited by its newspaper proprietors and its schoolmasters, has turned into a bed-hot harlot.
'Ireland after the Revolution' (1939) **Yeats, W.B.** (1865–1939) Irish poet, dramatist, editor, writer and senator

ISLAM

1 The proposition that Muslims are welcome in Britain if, and only if, they stop behaving like Muslims is incompatible with the principles of a free society.
The Independent, (1995) **Hattersley, Roy** (1932–) British Labour politician and writer

2 There is no doubt in this book.
Chapter 1 **Koran**

3 We cannot live in this country together with *The Satanic Verses* and Salman Rushdie. They will have to go.
The Independent, (1989) **Siddique, Dr Kalim**
See also belief; faith; God; religion

JUDGEMENT

1 Sir Roger told them, with the air of a man who would not give his judgement rashly, that much might be said on both sides.
The Spectator, (July 1711) **Addison, Joseph** (1672–1719) English essayist, poet, playwright and statesman

2 The judgement of the world is sure.
Contra Epistolam Parmeniani **Augustine, Saint** (354–430) Numidian-born Christian theologian and philosopher

3 His judgement of persons was penetrating, but its process was internal; no-one felt on good behaviour with a man who seemed always to be enjoying himself.
Trent's Last Case (1913)

4 Between what matters and what seems to matter, how should the world we know judge wisely?
Trent's Last Case (1913) **Bentley, Edmund Clerihew** (1875–1956) English writer

5 Judge not, that ye be not judged.
Matthew, 7:1

6 By their fruits ye shall know them.
Matthew, 7:20

7 He that is without sin among you, let him first cast a stone at her.
Luke, 8:7 **The Bible (King James Version)**

8 Let no one till his death
Be called unhappy. Measure not the work,
Until the day's out and the labour done.
Aurora Leigh (1857) **Browning, Elizabeth Barrett** (1806–1861) English poet; wife of Robert Browning

9 Perhaps your fear in passing judgement is greater than mine in receiving it.
Attr. **Bruno, Giordano** (1548–1600) Italian philosopher. Said to the cardinals who excommunicated him

10 Don't wait for the Last Judgement. It is taking place every day.
The Fall (1956) **Camus, Albert** (1913–1960) Algerian-born French writer

11 Appearances are not held to be a clue to the truth. But we seem to have no other.
Manservant and Maidservant (1947) **Compton-Burnett, Dame Ivy** (1884–1969) English novelist

12 Judgment drunk, and brib'd to lose his way,
Winks hard, and talks of darkness at noon-day.
'The Progress of Error' (1782) **Cowper, William** (1731–1800) English poet, hymn writer and letter writer

13 We cannot judge either of the feelings or of the characters of men with perfect accuracy, from their actions or their appearance in public; it is from their careless conversations, their half-finished sentences, that we may hope with the greatest probability of success to discover their real character.
Castle Rackrent (1800) **Edgeworth, Maria** (1767–1849) English-born Irish writer

14 The wisest men follow their own direction
And listen to no prophet guiding them.
None but the fools believe in oracles,
Forsaking their own judgement. Those who know,
Know that such men can only come to grief.
Iphigenia in Tauris **Euripides** (c.485–406 BC) Greek dramatist and poet

15 Then I shall remind you of the old verdict: the person under suspicion is better to be moving than at rest, for at rest one can, without knowing it, be in the balance being weighed together with one's sins.
The Trial (1914) **Kafka, Franz** (1883–1924) Czech-born German-speaking writer

16 None of us lives out, at every moment, all of our ideas; but one should judge human beings more by their excellence than by their weaknesses.
Lélia ou la vie de George Sand (1952) **Maurois, André** (1885–1967) French writer

17 It is a dangerous and serious presumption, and argues an absurd temerity, to condemn what we do not understand.
Essais (1580) **Montaigne, Michel de** (1533–1592) French essayist and moralist

18 The cobbler should not judge beyond his last.
Historia Naturalis **Pliny the Elder** (AD 23–79) Roman scholar

19 'Tis with our judgements as our watches, none
Go just alike, yet each believes his own.
An Essay on Criticism (1711) **Pope, Alexander** (1688–1744) English poet, translator and editor

20 What judgment shall I dread, doing no wrong?
The Merchant of Venice, IV.i **Shakespeare, William** (1564–1616) English dramatist, poet and actor
See also crime; justice and injustice; law; opinions; right and wrong

JUSTICE AND INJUSTICE

1 The price of justice is eternal publicity.
Things That Have Interested Me **Bennett, Arnold** (1867–1931) English writer, dramatist and journalist

2 I don't deserve this, but I have arthritis, and I don't deserve that either.
Attr. **Benny, Jack** (1894–1974) US comedian. Said on receiving an award

3 They have sown the wind, and they shall reap the whirlwind.
Hosea, 8:7 **The Bible (King James Version)**

4 We cannot for ever be content to acknowledge that in England justice is open to all – like the Ritz Hotel.
Independent on Sunday, (1994) **Bingham, Sir Thomas** (1933–) English Master of the Rolls. Discussing the rising costs of going to law

5 It is easy to be popular. It is not easy to be just.
Boston Globe, (1982) **Bird, Rose Elizabeth** (1936–1999) US Supreme Court judge

6 It is better that ten guilty persons escape than one innocent suffer.
Commentaries on the Laws of England (1765–1769) **Blackstone, Sir William** (1723–1780) English judge, historian and politician

7 The rain it raineth on the just
And also on the unjust fella:
But chiefly on the just, because
The unjust steals the just's umbrella.
In Sichel, *Sands of Time* (1923) **Bowen, Lord** (1835–1894) English judge and scholar

8 Something must be wrong with your world. Why
Is a price set on wickedness, and why is the good man
Attended by such harsh punishments?
Good Woman of Setzuan (1943) **Brecht, Bertolt** (1898–1956) German dramatist

9 There is, however, a limit at which forbearance ceases to be a virtue.
Observations on 'The Present State of the Nation' (1769) **Burke, Edmund** (1729–1797) Irish-born British statesman and philosopher

10 If you can't be just, be arbitrary.
Naked Lunch (1959) **Burroughs, William S.** (1914–1999) US writer

11 Justice is not to be taken by storm. She is to be wooed by slow advances.
The Growth of the Law (1924) **Cardozo, Benjamin** (1870–1938) US Supreme Court judge

12 When one has been threatened with a great injustice, one accepts a smaller as a favour.
Journal, (1855) **Carlyle, Jane Welsh** (1801–1866) Scottish letter writer, literary hostess and poet

13 'No! No!' said the Queen. 'Sentence first – verdict afterwards.'
Alice's Adventures in Wonderland (1865)

14 'I'll be judge, I'll be jury,' said cunning old Fury:
'I'll try the whole cause, and condemn you to death.'
Alice's Adventures in Wonderland (1865) **Carroll, Lewis** (1832–1898) English writer and photographer

15 Recompense injury with justice, and recompense kindness with kindness.
Analects **Confucius** (c.550–c.478 BC) Chinese philosopher and teacher of ethics

16 Trial by jury itself, instead of being a security to persons who are accused, will be a delusion, a mockery, and a snare.

Speech in the House of Lords, (1844) **Denman, Lord** (1779–1854) English politician and Lord Chief Justice

17 Justice is truth in action.
Speech, House of Commons, (1851) **Disraeli, Benjamin** (1804–1881) English statesman and writer

18 Juridical punishment for crime scares a criminal far less than law-makers think, partly because the criminal himself requires it morally.
Letter to Katkov, (1865) **Dostoevsky, Fyodor** (1821–1881) Russian writer

19 Justice is not a mincer but an agreement.
The Marriage of Mr Mississippi (1951)

20 Justice is something terrible.
Romulus the Great (1964) **Dürrenmatt, Friedrich** (1921–1990) Swiss dramatist and writer

21 Let there be justice though the world perish.
Ferdinand I, Emperor (1503–1564) Holy Roman emperor, king of Bohemia and Hungary

22 Thwackum was for doing justice, and leaving mercy to Heaven.
Tom Jones (1749) **Fielding, Henry** (1707–1754) English writer, dramatist and journalist

23 To disarm the strong and arm the weak would be to change a social order which I have been commissioned to preserve. Justice is the means whereby established injustices are sanctioned.
Crainquebille (1904) **France, Anatole** (1844–1924) French writer and critic

24 My object all sublime
I shall achieve in time –
To let the punishment fit the crime –
The punishment fit the crime.
The Mikado (1885) **Gilbert, W.S.** (1836–1911) English dramatist, humorist and librettist

25 I would remind you that extremism in the defence of liberty is no vice. And let me remind you also that moderation in the pursuit of justice is no virtue!
Speech, (1964) **Goldwater, Barry** (1909–1998) US presidential candidate and writer

26 Men are not hang'd for stealing Horses, but that Horses may not be stolen.
'Of Punishment' (1750) **Halifax, Lord** (1633–1695) English politician, courtier, pamphleteer and epigrammatist

27 'Justice' was done, and the President of the Immortals, in Aeschylean phrase, had ended his sport with Tess.
Tess of the D'Urbervilles (1891) **Hardy, Thomas** (1840–1928) English writer and poet

28 It is not merely of some importance but is of fundamental importance that justice should not only be done, but should manifestly and undoubtedly be seen to be done.
Rex v. Sussex Justices, (1923) **Hewart, Gordon** (1870–1943) English Liberal politician and Lord Chief Justice

29 The power of punishment is to silence, not to confute.
Sermons (1788)

30 The rod produces an effect which terminates in itself. A child is afraid of being whipped, and gets his task, and there's an end on't; whereas, by exciting emulation and comparisons of superiority, you lay the foundation of lasting mischief; you make brothers and sisters hate each other.
In Boswell, *The Life of Samuel Johnson* (1791) **Johnson, Samuel** (1709–1784) English lexicographer, poet, critic, conversationalist and essayist

31 The injustice done to an individual is sometimes of service to the public.
Letters (1769–1771) **Junius** (1769–1772) Penname of anonymous author of letters criticizing ministers of George III

32 Justice is the constant and perpetual wish to give to every one his due.
Institutes **Justinian, Emperor** (c.482–565) Byzantine emperor

33 You may raise the objection that it really is not a trial at all; you are quite right, for it is only a trial if I recognise it as such.
The Trial (1925) **Kafka, Franz** (1883–1924) Czech-born German-speaking writer

34 There never was such a thing as justice in the English laws but any amount of injustice to be had.
In *Overland*, (1981) **Kelly, Ned** (1855–1880) Australian outlaw and folk hero

35 Injustice anywhere is a threat to justice everywhere.
Letter from Birmingham Jail, (April 16, 1963) **King, Martin Luther** (1929–1968) US civil rights leader and Baptist minister

36 The love of justice in most men is no more than the fear of suffering injustice.
Maximes (1678) **La Rochefoucauld** (1613–1680) French writer

37 The probability that we may fail in the struggle ought not to deter us from the support of a cause we believe to be just.
Speech, (1859) **Lincoln, Abraham** (1809–1865) US statesman and President

38 To no one will we sell, to no one will we deny, or delay, right or justice.
Clause 40 **Magna Carta** (1215)

39 The object of punishment is prevention from evil; it never can be made impulsive to good.
Lectures and Reports on Education (1845) **Mann, Horace** (1796–1859) US educationist, politician and writer

40 Consider what you think justice requires, and decide accordingly. But never give your reasons; for your judgement will probably be right, but your reasons will certainly be wrong.
In Campbell, *Lives of the Chief Justices* (1849) **Mansfield, William Murray, Earl of** (1705–1793) Scottish judge. Advice given to a new colonial governor

41 Who thinks it just to be judged by a single error?
West with the Night (1942) **Markham, Beryl** (1902–1986) English aviator and writer

42 Injustice is relatively easy to bear: what stings is justice.
Attr. **Mencken, H.L.** (1880–1956) US writer, critic, philologist and satirist

43 Yet I shall temper so
Justice with Mercie.

Paradise Lost (1667) **Milton, John** (1608–1674) English poet, libertarian and pamphleteer

44 Here they have a man hanged, and then proceed to try him.
Monsieur de Pourceaugnac (1670) **Molière** (1622–1673) French dramatist, actor and director

45 The injustice of it is almost perfect! The wrong people going hungry, the wrong people being loved, the wrong people dying!
Look Back in Anger (1956) **Osborne, John** (1929–1994) English dramatist and actor

46 The taking of a Bribe or Gratuity, should be punished with as severe Penalties as the defrauding of the State.
Some Fruits of Solitude, in Reflections and Maxims relating to the Conduct of Humane Life (1693) **Penn, William** (1644–1718) English Quaker, founder of state of Pennsylvania

47 'It may well be,' said Cadfael, 'that our justice sees as in a mirror image, left where right should be, evil reflected back as good, good as evil, your angel as her devil. But God's justice, if it makes no haste, makes no mistakes.'
The Potter's Field (1989) **Peters, Ellis** (1913–1995) English writer

48 The hungry Judges soon the sentence sign, And wretches hang that jury-men may dine.
The Rape of the Lock (1714) **Pope, Alexander** (1688–1744) English poet, translator and editor

49 The judge is condemned when the guilty party is acquitted.
Sententiae **Publilius, Syrus** (1st century BC) Roman writer

50 Since twelve honest men have decided the cause,
And were judges of fact, though not judges of laws.
'The Honest Jury' (1729) **Pulteney, William, Earl of Bath** (1684–1764) English politician

51 Desert and reward, I can assure her, seldom keep company.
Clarissa (1747–1748) **Richardson, Samuel** (1689–1761) English novelist

52 If you give me six lines written by the most honest man, I will find something in them to hang him.
Attr. **Richelieu, Cardinal** (1585–1642) Prime Minister to Louis XIII, 1624–1642

53 We love justice greatly, and just men but little.
Meditations of a Parish Priest (1886) **Roux, Joseph** (1834–1886) French priest and epigrammatist

54 Two mothers-in-law.
Attr. **Russell, Lord John** (1792–1878) English Liberal Prime Minister and writer. When asked to describe a suitable punishment for bigamy

55 Prejudice is making a judgment before you have looked at the facts. Postjudice is making a judgment afterwards. Prejudice is terrible, in the sense that you commit injustices and you make serious mistakes. Postjudice is not terrible. You can't be perfect of course; you may make mistakes also. But it is permissible to make a judgment after you have examined the evidence. In some circles it is even encouraged.
'Skeptical Enquirer' Vol. 12 **Sagan, Carl** (1934–1996) US astrophysicist

56 There can be slain
No sacrifice to God more acceptable
Than an unjust and wicked king.
Hercules Furens **Seneca** (c.4 BC–AD 65) Roman philosopher, poet, dramatist, essayist, rhetorician and statesman

57 Use every man after his desert, and who shall scape whipping?
Hamlet, II.ii

58 Why, as a woodcock, to mine own springe, Osric;
I am justly kill'd with mine own treachery.
Hamlet, V.ii

59 What stronger breastplate than a heart untainted?
Thrice is he arm'd that hath his quarrel just;
And he but naked, though lock'd up in steel,
Whose conscience with injustice is corrupted.
Henry VI, Part 2, III.ii

60 Heaven is above all yet: there sits a Judge That no king can corrupt.
Henry VIII, III.i

61 Now, as fond fathers,
Having bound up the threat'ning twigs of birch,
Only to stick it in their children's sight
For terror, not to use, in time the rod
Becomes more mock'd than fear'd; so our decrees,
Dead to infliction, to themselves are dead;
And liberty plucks justice by the nose;
The baby beats the nurse, and quite athwart
Goes all decorum.
Measure For Measure, I.iii

62 Condemn the fault and not the actor of it!
Measure For Measure, II.ii **Shakespeare, William** (1564–1616) English dramatist, poet and actor

63 Only the actions of the just
Smell sweet, and blossom in their dust.
The Contention of Ajax and Ulysses (1659) **Shirley, James** (1596–1666) English poet and dramatist

64 Steven's mind was so tolerant that he could have attended a lynching every day without becoming critical.
The Jovial Ghosts (1933) **Smith, Thorne** (1892–1934) US humorous novelist

65 Curses are like young chickens, they always come home to roost.
The Curse of Kehama (1810) **Southey, Robert** (1774–1843) English poet, essayist, historian and letter writer

66 Between the possibility of being hanged in all innocence, and the certainty of a public and merited disgrace, no gentleman of spirit could long hesitate.
The Wrong Box (1889) **Stevenson, Robert Louis** (1850–1894) Scottish writer, poet and essayist

67 This is a British murder inquiry and some degree of justice must be seen to be more or less done.
Jumpers (1972) **Stoppard, Tom** (1937–) British dramatist

68 When justice has spoken, humanity must
have its turn.
Speech, (1793) **Vergniaud, Pierre** (1753–1793)
French politician and revolutionary

69 For Man's grim Justice goes its way,
And will not swerve aside:
It slays the weak, it slays the strong,
It has a deadly stride.
The Ballad of Reading Gaol (1898) **Wilde, Oscar**
(1854–1900) Irish poet, dramatist, writer, critic
and wit
See also crime; judgement; law; prison; right
and wrong

KINDNESS

1 They now knew that if there is one thing
which can always be desired and
sometimes obtained, it is human
tenderness.
The Plague (1947) **Camus, Albert** (1913–1960)
Algerian-born French writer

2 Recompense injury with justice, and
recompense kindness with kindness.
Analects **Confucius** (c.550–c.478 BC) Chinese
philosopher and teacher of ethics

3 I love thee for a heart that's kind –
Not for the knowledge in thy mind.
'Sweet Stay-at-Home' (1913) **Davies, William
Henry** (1871–1940) Welsh poet, writer and
tramp

4 True kindness presupposes the faculty of
imagining as one's own the suffering and
joy of others.
Attr. **Gide, André** (1869–1951) French writer,
critic, dramatist and poet

5 We must touch his weaknesses with a
delicate hand. There are some faults so
nearly allied to excellence, that we can
scarce weed out the vice without
eradicating the virtue.
The Good Natur'd Man (1768) **Goldsmith,
Oliver** (c.1728–1774) Irish dramatist, poet and
writer

6 It's no use trying to be clever – we are all
clever here; just try to be kind – a little
kind.
In Benson's *Commonplace Book* **Jackson, F.J.
Foakes** (1855–1941) English divine and church
historian. Advice given to a new don at Jesus
College, Cambridge

7 Always, Sir, set a high value on
spontaneous kindness. He whose
inclination prompts him to cultivate your
friendship of his own accord, will love you
more than one whom you have been at
pains to attach to you.
In Boswell, *The Life of Samuel Johnson* (1791)
Johnson, Samuel (1709–1784) English
lexicographer, poet, critic, conversationalist
and essayist

8 Beware of people you've been kind to.
Remark to John Morrison **Marshall, Alan
John** (1911–1968) Australian zoologist and
explorer

9 It is almost a definition of a gentleman to
say that he is one who never inflicts pain.
'Knowledge and Religious Duty' (1852)
Newman, John Henry, Cardinal (1801–1890)
English Cardinal, theologian and poet

10 I must be cruel, only to be kind.
Hamlet, III.iv

11 How far that little candle throws his
beams!
So shines a good deed in a naughty world.
The Merchant of Venice, V.i **Shakespeare,
William** (1564–1616) English dramatist, poet
and actor

12 I have always depended on the kindness of
strangers.
A Streetcar Named Desire (1947) **Williams,
Tennessee** (1911–1983) US dramatist and
writer

13 On that best portion of a good man's life;
His little, nameless, unremembered acts
Of kindness and of love.
'Lines composed a few miles above Tintern
Abbey' (1798) **Wordsworth, William** (1770–
1850) English poet
See also charity; compassion; goodness; virtue

KNOWLEDGE

1 They know enough who know how to learn.
The Education of Henry Adams (1918) **Adams, Henry** (1838–1918) US historian and memoirist

2 The passionate controversies of one era are viewed as sterile preoccupations by another, for knowledge alters what we seek as well as what we find.
Sisters in Crime (1975) **Adler, Freda** (1934–) US educator and writer

3 Old men are always young enough to learn with profit.
Agamemnon **Aeschylus** (525–456 BC) Greek dramatist and poet

4 Facts are stupid until brought into connection with some general law.
In Laurence J. Peter, *Peter's Quotations* (1977) **Agassiz, Louis** (1807–1873) Swiss-born US naturalist

5 I would rather excel in the knowledge of what is excellent, than in the extent of my power.
In Plutarch, *Lives* **Alexander the Great** (356–323 BC) Macedonian king and conquering army commander

6 All men naturally desire knowledge.
Metaphysics

7 Probable impossibilities are always to be preferred to improbable possibilities.
Poetics **Aristotle** (384–322 BC) Greek philosopher

8 Knowledge itself is power.
'Of Heresies' (1597)

9 Knowledge is a rich storehouse for the glory of the Creator and the relief of man's estate.
The Advancement of Learning (1605) **Bacon, Francis** (1561–1626) English philosopher, essayist, politician and courtier

10 Facts were never pleasing to him. He acquired them with reluctance and got rid of them with relief. He was never on terms with them until he had stood them on their heads.

The Greenwood Hat (1937) **Barrie, Sir J.M.** (1860–1937) Scottish dramatist and writer

11 First come I; my name is Jowett.
There's no knowledge but I know it.
I am Master of this college:
What I don't know isn't knowledge.
'The Masque of Balliol' (late 1870s) **Beeching, Rev. H.C.** (1859–1919) English theologian, poet and essayist

12 Of all that writ, he was the wisest bard, who spoke this mighty truth –
He that knew all that ever learning writ, Knew only this – that he knew nothing yet.
The Emperor of the Moon (1687) **Behn, Aphra** (1640–1689) English dramatist, writer, poet, translator and spy

13 He that increaseth knowledge increaseth sorrow.
Ecclesiastes, 1:18 **The Bible (King James Version)**

14 But facts are chiels that winna ding, And downa be disputed.
'A Dream' (1786) **Burns, Robert** (1759–1796) Scottish poet and songwriter

15 What is all knowledge too but recorded experience, and a product of history; of which, therefore, reasoning and belief, no less than action and passion, are essential materials?
Critical and Miscellaneous Essays (1839) **Carlyle, Thomas** (1795–1881) Scottish historian, biographer, critic, and essayist

16 The chapter of knowledge is very short, but the chapter of accidents is a very long one.
Letter to Solomon Dayrolles, (1753) **Chesterfield, Lord** (1694–1773) English politician and letter writer

17 I prefer tongue-tied knowledge to ignorant loquacity.
De Oratore **Cicero** (106–43 BC) Roman orator, statesman, essayist and letter writer

18 Grace is given of God, but knowledge is bought in the market.
The Bothie of Tober-na-Vuolich (1848) **Clough, Arthur Hugh** (1819–1861) English poet and letter writer

19 Knowledge is proud that he has learn'd so
much;
Wisdom is humble that he knows no more.
The Task (1785) **Cowper, William** (1731–1800)
English poet, hymn writer and letter writer

20 A man should keep his little brain attic
stocked with all the furniture that he is
likely to use, and the rest he can put away
in the lumber-room of his library, where he
can get it if he wants it.
The Adventures of Sherlock Holmes (1892) **Doyle,
Sir Arthur Conan** (1859–1930) Scottish writer
and war correspondent

21 There is no knowledge that is not power.
Society and Solitude (1870) **Emerson, Ralph
Waldo** (1803–1882) US poet, essayist,
transcendentalist and teacher

22 We do not need to be shoemakers to know
if our shoes fit, and just as little have we
any need to be professionals to acquire
knowledge of matters of universal interest.
The Philosophy of Right (1821) **Hegel, Georg
Wilhelm** (1770–1831) German philosopher

23 It is the province of knowledge to speak
and it is the privilege of wisdom to listen.
The Poet at the Breakfast-Table (1872) **Holmes,
Oliver Wendell** (1809–1894) US physician,
poet, writer and scientist

24 The saying that a little knowledge is a
dangerous thing is, to my mind, a very
dangerous adage. If knowledge is real and
genuine, I do not believe that it is other
than a very valuable possession however
infinitesimal its quantity may be. Indeed, if
a little knowledge is dangerous, where is
the man who has so much as to be out of
danger?
Science and Culture (1877) **Huxley, T.H.** (1825–
1895) English biologist, Darwinist and
agnostic

25 The fruit of the tree of knowledge always
drives man from some paradise or other.
Attr. **Inge, William Ralph** (1860–1954) English
divine, writer and teacher

26 The fatal futility of Fact.
Prefaces (1897) **James, Henry** (1843–1916) US-
born British writer, critic and letter writer

27 There was never an age in which useless
knowledge was more important than in
ours.
The Observer, (1951) **Joad, C.E.M.** (1891–1953)
English popularizer of philosophy

28 Integrity without knowledge is weak and
useless, and knowledge without integrity is
dangerous and dreadful.
Rasselas (1759)

29 If it rained knowledge, I'd hold out my
hand; but I would not give myself the
trouble to go in quest of it.
In Boswell, *The Life of Samuel Johnson* (1791)

30 In my early years I read very hard. It is a
sad reflection, but a true one, that I knew
almost as much at eighteen as I do now.
In Boswell, *The Life of Samuel Johnson* (1791)
Johnson, Samuel (1709–1784) English
lexicographer, poet, critic, conversationalist
and essayist

31 Knowledge enormous makes a God of me.
Hyperion. A Fragment (1818) **Keats, John** (1795–
1821) English poet

32 He knows the world and does not know
himself.
Fables **La Fontaine, Jean de** (1621–1695) French
poet and fabulist

33 For the scientific acquisition of knowledge
is almost as tedious as a routine
acquisition of wealth.
White Man's Saga **Linklater, Eric** (1899–1974)
Welsh-born Scottish writer and satirist

34 No man's knowledge here can go beyond
his experience.
Essay concerning Human Understanding (1690)
Locke, John (1632–1704) English philosopher

35 Knowledge advances by steps, and not by
leaps.
'History' (1828) **Macaulay, Lord** (1800–1859)
English Liberal statesman, essayist and poet

36 Of course, knowing a little is more
agreeable than knowing a lot.
Spanish Literature Programme (1934) **Menéndez
y Pelayo, Marcelino** (1856–1912)

37 Where there is much desire to learn, there
of necessity will be much arguing, much
writing, many opinions; for opinion in
good men is but knowledge in the making.
Areopagitica (1644)

38 The first and wisest of them all profess'd
To know this onely, that he nothing knew.
Paradise Regained (1671) **Milton, John** (1608–
1674) English poet, libertarian and
pamphleteer

39 Ah, what a fine thing it is, to know
something.
Le Bourgeois Gentilhomme (1671) **Molière** (1622–
1673) French dramatist, actor and director

40 Knowledge is power if you know it about
the right person.
In Cowan, *The Wit of Women* **Mumford, Ethel**
(1878–1940) US writer, dramatist and
humorist

41 Our knowledge can only be finite, while
our ignorance must necessarily be infinite.
Conjectures and Refutations (1963) **Popper, Sir
Karl** (1902–1994) Austrian-born British
philosopher

42 'Knowledge is power' is the finest idea ever
put into words.
Dialogues et fragments philosophiques (1876)
Renan, J. Ernest (1823–1892) French
philologist, writer and historian

43 His had been an intellectual decision
founded on his conviction that if a little
knowledge was a dangerous thing, a lot
was lethal.
Porterhouse Blue (1974) **Sharpe, Tom** (1928–)
English writer

44 Madam, a circulating library in a town is an
ever-green tree of diabolical knowledge! –
It blossoms through the year! – And
depend on it, Mrs Malaprop, that they who
are so fond of handling the leaves, will
long for the fruit at last.
The Rivals (1775) **Sheridan, Richard Brinsley**
(1751–1816) Irish dramatist, politician and
orator

45 Understanding everything makes one very
tolerant.
Corinne (1807) **Staël, Mme de** (1766–1817)
French writer, critic, memoirist and hostess

46 The desire of knowledge, like the thirst of
riches, increases ever with the acquisition
of it.
Tristram Shandy (1767) **Sterne, Laurence** (1713–
1768) Irish-born English writer and
clergyman

47 Beware you be not swallowed up in books!
An ounce of love is worth a pound of
knowledge.
In Southey, *Life of Wesley* (1820) **Wesley, John**
(1703–1791) English theologian and preacher
See also education; intelligence; wisdom

LANGUAGE

1 Time that is intolerant
Of the brave and innocent,
And indifferent in a week
To a beautiful physique,
Worships language and forgives
Everyone by whom it lives.
Collected Poems, (1939–1947) **Auden, W.H.**
(1907–1973) English poet, essayist, critic,
teacher and dramatist

2 Translation is at best an echo.
Lavengro (1851) **Borrow, George** (1803–1881)
English writer and linguist

3 Translations (like wives) are seldom strictly
faithful if they are in the least attractive.
Poetry Review, (1949) **Campbell, Roy** (1901–
1957) South African poet and journalist

4 With the persuasive language of a tear.
'The Times' (1764) **Churchill, Charles** (1731–
1764) English poet, political writer and
clergyman

5 Everybody has a right to pronounce foreign
names as he chooses.
The Observer, (1951)

6 This is the sort of English up with which I
will not put.
In Gowers, *Plain Words* (1948) **Churchill, Sir
Winston** (1874–1965) English Conservative
Prime Minister. Marginal comment on a
document

7 I don't hold with abroad and think that
foreigners speak English when our backs
are turned.

The Naked Civil Servant (1968) **Crisp, Quentin** (1908–1999) English writer, publicist and model

8 The liberation of language is rooted in the liberation of ourselves.
Beyond God The Father, Toward a Philosophy of Women's Liberation (1973) **Daly, Mary** (1928–) US feminist and theologian

9 There was no light nonsense about Miss Blimber ... She was dry and sandy with working in the graves of deceased languages. None of your live languages for Miss Blimber. They must be dead – stone dead – and then Miss Blimber dug them up like a Ghoul.
Dombey and Son (1848) **Dickens, Charles** (1812–1870) English writer

10 My country is the English language.
In Galt (ed.), *The Saturday Night Traveller* (1990) **Dobbs, Kildare** (1923–) Canadian writer

11 In language, the ignorant have prescribed laws to the learned.
Maxims (1830) **Duppa, Richard** (1770–1831) English artist and writer

12 We cannot judge either of the feelings or of the characters of men with perfect accuracy, from their actions or their appearance in public; it is from their careless conversations, their half-finished sentences, that we may hope with the greatest probability of success to discover their real character.
Castle Rackrent (1800) **Edgeworth, Maria** (1767–1849) English-born Irish writer

13 Correct English is the slang of prigs who write history and essays.
Middlemarch (1872) **Eliot, George** (1819–1880) English writer and poet

14 Language is fossil poetry.
'The Poet' (1844) **Emerson, Ralph Waldo** (1803–1882) US poet, essayist, transcendentalist and teacher

15 Write with the learned, pronounce with the vulgar.
Poor Richard's Almanac (1738) **Franklin, Benjamin** (1706–1790) US statesman, scientist, political critic and printer

16 Afrikaans sounds like Welsh with attitude and emphysema.
Gill, A.A. (1954–) Scottish newspaper columnist

17 Whoever is not acquainted with foreign languages knows nothing of his own.
On Art and Antiquity (1827) **Goethe** (1749–1832) German poet, writer, dramatist and scientist

18 The true use of speech is not so much to express our wants as to conceal them.
The Bee (1759) **Goldsmith, Oliver** (c.1728–1774) Irish dramatist, poet and writer

19 Let's have some new clichés.
The Observer, (1948) **Goldwyn, Samuel** (1882–1974) Polish-born US film producer

20 If one cannot discriminate between grammar and solecism, sequence and incoherency, sense and nonsense, one has no protection against falsehood, and believes all the lies one is told.
M. Manilii Astronomicon (1903) **Housman, A.E.** (1859–1936) English poet and scholar

21 In order to de-Anglicise ourselves we must at once arrest the decay of the language.
'The Necessity for de-Anglicising Ireland' (1892) **Hyde, Douglas** (1860–1949) Irish President

22 In his whole life man achieves nothing so great and so wonderful as what he achieved when he learned to talk.
Language (1904) **Jespersen, Otto** (1860–1943) Danish philologist

23 I have laboured to refine our language to grammatical purity, and to clear it from colloquial barbarisms, licentious idioms, and irregular combinations.
The Rambler (1750–1752)

24 I am not yet so lost in lexicography, as to forget that words are the daughters of the earth, and that things are the sons of heaven. Language is only the instrument of science, and words are but the signs of ideas: I wish, however, that the instrument might be less apt to decay, and that signs might be permanent, like the things which they denote.
A Dictionary of the English Language (1755)

25 Every quotation contributes something to the stability or enlargement of the language.
A Dictionary of the English Language (1755) Of citations of usage in a dictionary

26 Language is the dress of thought.
The Lives of the Most Eminent English Poets (1781)

27 I am always sorry when any language is lost, because languages are the pedigree of nations.
In Boswell, *Journal of a Tour to the Hebrides* (1785) **Johnson, Samuel** (1709–1784) English lexicographer, poet, critic, conversationalist and essayist

28 In all pointed sentences, some degree of accuracy must be sacrificed to conciseness.
'The Bravery of the English Common Soldier' (1760) **Jonson, Ben** (1572–1637) English dramatist and poet

29 The German language is the most profound one, German speech the most shallow.
By Night (1919) **Kraus, Karl** (1874–1936) Austrian scientist, critic and poet

30 Grammere, that grounde is of alle.
The Vision of William Concerning Piers the Plowman **Langland, William** (c.1330–c.1400) English poet

31 Language is a kind of human reason, which has its own internal logic of which man knows nothing.
The Savage Mind (1962) **Lévi-Strauss, Claude** (1908–) French anthropologist

32 The word I used was 'bloody' which, where I come from in Yorkshire, is practically the only surviving adjective.
The Times, (1999) **Lipman, Maureen** (1946–) English actress. After criticism for swearing on TV

33 Language tethers us to the world; without it we spin like atoms.
Moon Tiger (1987) **Lively, Penelope** (1933–) English novelist

34 The English Bible, a book which, if everything else in our language should perish, would alone suffice to show the whole extent of its beauty and power.

'John Dryden' (1843) **Macaulay, Lord** (1800–1859) English Liberal statesman, essayist and poet

35 A gentleman need not know Latin, but he should at least have forgotten it.
Attr. **Matthews, Brander** (1852–1929) US critic, lecturer, dramatist and writer

36 In England only uneducated people show off their knowledge; nobody quotes Latin or Greek authors in the course of conversation, unless he has never read them.
How to be an Alien (1946) **Mikes, George** (1912–1987) Hungarian-born British writer

37 *Moriarty:* How are you at Mathematics?
Harry Secombe: I speak it like a native.
The Goon Show **Milligan, Spike** (1918–2002) Irish comedian and writer

38 If the English language had been properly organized … then there would be a word which meant both 'he' and 'she', and I could write, 'If John or Mary comes heesh will want to play tennis,' which would save a lot of trouble.
The Christopher Robin Birthday Book **Milne, A.A.** (1882–1956) English writer, dramatist and poet

39 He mobilized the English language and sent it into battle to steady his fellow countrymen and hearten those Europeans upon whom the long dark night of tyranny had descended.
Broadcast, (1954) **Murrow, Edward R.** (1908–1965) US reporter and war correspondent. Of Churchill

40 English is a very adaptable language. And it's so transparent it can take on the tint of any country.
Radio conversation, (1968) **Narayan, R. K.** (1907–2001) Indian writer and translator

41 Yet all world languages die at last:
Greek of grammar and factions; Latin of clotted syntax and Renaissance purism;
French of bad admirals and over-subtle vowels;
English and Chinese of their written forms;
Russian of subject people's hate.
'Lingua Romana' **O'Connor, Mark** (1945–) Australian poet and dramatist

42 You know, she speaks eighteen languages.
And she can't say 'No' in any of them.
In J. Keats, *You Might As Well Live* (1970)
Parker, Dorothy (1893–1967) US writer, poet,
critic and wit. Of an acquaintance

43 The differences between the spoken or
written language and the other ones –
plastic or musical – are very profound, but
not to such an extent that they make us
forget that essentially they are all language:
expressive systems which possess a
significant power.
The Bow and the Lyre (1956) **Paz, Octavio** (1914–
1998) Mexican poet and critic

44 Strange the difference of men's talk!
Diary, 1659–60 **Pepys, Samuel** (1633–1703)
English diarist, naval administrator and
politician

45 I include 'pidgin-English' ... even though I
am referred to in that splendid language as
'Fella belong Mrs Queen'.
Speech, English-Speaking Union Conference,
Ottawa, (1958) **Philip, Prince, Duke of
Edinburgh** (1921–) Greek-born consort of
Queen Elizabeth II

46 Life is too short to learn German.
In Thomas Love Peacock, *Gryll Grange* (1861)
Porson, Richard (1759–1808) English scholar

47 U and Non-U. An Essay in Sociological
Linguistics.
In Nancy Mitford (ed.), *Noblesse Oblige* (1956)
Ross, Alan S.C. (1907–1980) British linguistics
scholar

48 The English have no respect for their
language, and will not teach their children
to speak it ... It is impossible for an
Englishman to open his mouth without
making some other Englishman hate or
despise him.
Pygmalion (1916)

49 If ever I utter an oath again may my soul be
blasted to eternal damnation!
Saint Joan (1924)

50 England and America are two countries
separated by the same language.
Reader's Digest, (1942) **Shaw, George Bernard**
(1856–1950) Irish socialist, writer, dramatist
and critic

51 An aspersion upon my parts of speech! ...
If I reprehend anything in this world, it is
the use of my oracular tongue, and a nice
derangement of epitaphs!
The Rivals (1775)

52 Egad, I think the interpreter is the hardest
to be understood of the two!
The Critic (1779) **Sheridan, Richard Brinsley**
(1751–1816) Irish dramatist, politician and
orator

53 I am the Roman Emperor, and am above
grammar.
Attr. **Sigismund** (1368–1437) King of Hungary,
Bohemia and Holy Roman Emperor.
Responding to criticism of his Latin

54 So now they have made our English
tongue, a gallimaufray or hodgepodge of al
other speches.
The Shepheardes Calender (1579) **Spenser,
Edmund** (c.1522–1599) English poet

55 They have exacted from all their members
a close, naked, natural way of speaking;
positive expressions; clear senses; a native
easiness: bringing all things as near the
mathematical plainness, as they can; and
preferring the language of artizans,
countrymen, and merchants, before that of
wits or scholars.
The History of the Royal Society (1667) **Sprat,
Thomas** (1635–1713) English bishop and writer.
Of the Royal Society

56 Language grows out of life, out of its needs
and experiences ... Language and
knowledge are indissolubly connected;
they are interdependent. Good work in
language presupposes and depends on a
real knowledge of things.
Speech, (1894) **Sullivan, Annie** (1866–1936) US
lecturer, writer and teacher

57 Nor do they trust their tongue alone,
But speak a language of their own;
Can read a nod, a shrug, a look,
Far better than a printed book;
Convey a libel in a frown,
And wink a reputation down.
'The Journal of a Modern Lady' (1729) **Swift,
Jonathan** (1667–1745) Irish satirist, poet,
essayist and cleric

58 A foreign swear-word is practically inoffensive except to the person who has learnt it early in life and knows its social limits.
Saint Jack **Theroux, Paul** (1941–) US writer

59 Man invented language in order to satisfy his deep need to complain.
In Pinker, *The Language Instinct* (1994) **Tomlin, Lily** (1939–) US actress

60 English is a simple, yet hard language. It consists entirely of foreign words pronounced wrongly.
Scraps (1973) **Tucholsky, Kurt** (1890–1935) German satirist and writer

61 Some of his words were not Sunday-school words.
A Tramp Abroad (1880)

62 A verb has a hard time enough of it in this world when it's all together. It's downright inhuman to split it up. But that's just what those Germans do. They take part of a verb and put it down here, like a stake, and they take the other part of it and put it away over yonder like another stake, and between these two limits they just shovel in German.
Address, (1900) **Twain, Mark** (1835–1910) US humorist, writer, journalist and lecturer

63 I am not like a lady at the court of Versailles, who said: 'What a great pity it is that the adventure at the tower of Babel should have produced the confusion of languages; if it weren't for that, everyone would always have spoken French.'
Letter to Catherine the Great, (1767)

64 A language is a dialect that has an army and a navy.
In Rosten, *The Joys of Yiddish* (1968) **Voltaire** (1694–1778) French philosopher, dramatist, poet, historian writer and critic

65 'Never forget, gentlemen,' he said, to his astonished hearers, as he held up a copy of the 'Authorised Version' of the Bible, 'never forget that this is not the Bible,' then, after a moment's pause, he continued, 'This, gentlemen, is only a translation of the Bible.'

In H. Solly, *These Eighty Years* (1893) **Whately, Richard** (1787–1863) English philosopher, theologian, educationist and writer. To a meeting of his diocesan clergy

66 Language ... is not an abstract construction of the learned, or of dictionary-makers, but is something arising out of the work, needs, ties, joys, affections, tastes, of long generations of humanity, and has its bases broad and low, close to the ground.
November Boughs (1888) **Whitman, Walt** (1819–1892) US poet and writer

67 We dissect nature along lines laid down by our native language ... Language is not simply a reporting device for experience but a defining framework for it.
In Hoyer (ed.), *New Directions in the Study of Language* (1964) **Whorf, Benjamin** (1897–1941) US anthropological linguist and engineer

68 Subjunctive to the last, he preferred to ask, 'And that, sir, would be the Hippodrome?'
While Rome Burns (1934), 'Our Mrs Parker' **Woollcott, Alexander** (1887–1943) US writer, drama critic and anthologist
See also class; words

LAST WORDS

1 See in what peace a Christian can die.
Attr. **Addison, Joseph** (1672–1719) English essayist, poet, playwright and statesman

2 I am dying with the help of too many physicians.
Attr. **Alexander the Great** (356–323 BC) Macedonian king and conquering army commander

3 Well, gentlemen, you are about to see a baked Appel.
Attr. **Appel, George** (d.1928) Executed in electric chair in New York

4 It's time for me to enjoy another pinch of snuff. Tomorrow my hands will be bound, so as to make it impossible.
Attr. **Bailly, Jean Sylvain** (1736–1793) French astronomer and politician. Reflection on the evening before his execution

5 Codeine ... bourbon.
Attr. **Bankhead, Tallulah** (1903–1968) US actress

6 How were the receipts today at Madison Square Garden?
Attr. **Barnum, Phineas T.** (1810–1891) US showman and writer

7 I can't sleep.
Attr. **Barrie, Sir J.M.** (1860–1937) Scottish dramatist and writer

8 Is everybody happy? I want everybody to be happy. I know I'm happy.
Attr. **Barrymore, Ethel** (1879–1959) US actress

9 Now comes the mystery.
Attr. **Beecher, Henry Ward** (1813–1887) US clergyman, lecturer, editor and writer

10 Friends applaud, the comedy is finished.
Attr. **Beethoven, Ludwig van** (1770–1827) German composer

11 Thank you, sister. May you be the mother of a bishop!
Attr. **Behan, Brendan** (1923–1964) Irish dramatist, writer and Republican. Remark from his deathbed to a nun who was nursing him

12 So little done. So much to do.
Attr. **Bell, Alexander Graham** (1847–1922) Scottish-born US inventor and educator of the deaf

13 If there is ever another war in Europe, it will come out of some damned silly thing in the Balkans.
Attr. **Bismarck, Prince Otto von** (1815–1898) First Chancellor of the German Reich. Remark made just before he died

14 I should never have changed from scotch to martinis.
In Simon Rose, *Classic Film Guide* (1995) **Bogart, Humphrey** (1899–1957) US film actor

15 Pop, pop, pop!
Bom, bom, bom!
Throughout the day
no time for memorandums now.
Go ahead!
Liberty and independence forever.

Last entry in his journal at the Alamo, (5 March 1836) **Crockett, Davy** (1786–1836) US statesman and soldier

16 Thou wilt show my head to the people: it is worth showing.
In Carlyle, *French Revolution* **Danton, Georges** (1759–1794) French revolutionary leader. Said as he mounted the scaffold, 5 April 1794

17 Even if I die in the service of this nation, I would be proud of it. Every drop of my blood, I am sure, will contribute to the growth of this nation and make it strong and dynamic.
Attr. **Gandhi, Indira** (1917–1984) Indian statesman and Prime Minister. Said 24 hours before she was assassinated

18 How is the Empire?
Attr. **George V** (1865–1936) King of the United Kingdom. To Lord Wigram, his secretary; sometimes quoted as his last words

19 Let's do it!
Attr. **Gillmore, Gary** (d.1977) Executed by firing squad, Utah

20 More light!
Attr. **Goethe** (1749–1832) German poet, writer, dramatist and scientist

21 May God have mercy upon this afflicted Kingdom.
Attr. **Graham, James, Marquis of Montrose** (1612–1650) Scottish Covenanter, soldier, poet and Royalist

22 I have loved righteousness and hated iniquity: therefore I die in exile.
In Bowden, *The Life and Pontificate of Gregory VII* (1840) **Gregory VII** (c.1020–1085) Italian pope

23 It is. But not as hard as farce.
Time, (1984) **Gwenn, Edmund** (1875–1959) English actor. Reply on his deathbed, when someone said to him, 'It must be very hard'

24 I only regret that I have but one life to lose for my country.
In Johnston, *Nathan Hale* (1974) **Hale, Nathan** (1755–1776) US soldier and revolutionary. Speech before he was executed by the British

25 Well, I've had a happy life.

In W.C. Hazlitt, *Memoirs of William Hazlitt* (1867) **Hazlitt, William** (1778–1830) English writer and critic

26 Only one man ever understood me. ... And he didn't understand me.
In B. Conrad, *Famous Last Words* (1962) **Hegel, Georg Wilhelm** (1770–1831) German philosopher. Said on his deathbed

27 God will forgive me. It is his profession.
In Meissner, *H H Erinnerungen* (1856) **Heine, Heinrich** (1797–1856) German lyric poet, essayist and journalist

28 Don't turn down the light, I'm afraid to go home in the dark.
In Leacock, 'The Amazing Genius of O. Henry', (1916) **Henry, O.** (1862–1910) US short-story writer. Attr. last words, quoting the song 'I'm Afraid to Go Home in the Dark'

29 I am about to take my last voyage, a great leap in the dark.
In Watkins, *Anecdotes of Men of Learning* (1808) **Hobbes, Thomas** (1588–1679) Political philosopher

30 If heaven had granted me five more years, I could have become a real painter.
In B. Conrad, *Famous Last Words* (1962) **Hokusai** (1760–1849) Japanese artist. Said on his deathbed

31 If Mr Selwyn calls, let him in: if I am alive I shall be very glad to see him, and if I am dead he will be very glad to see me.
Attr. **Holland, First Lord** (**Henry Fox**) (1705–1774) Said during his last illness

32 I know this beach like the back of my hand.
Sydney Morning Herald, (1967) **Holt, Harold Edward** (1908–1967) Australian statesman and Prime Minister

33 And now, in keeping with Channel 40's policy of always bringing you the latest in blood and guts, in living color, you're about to see another first – an attempted suicide.
Attr. **Hubbock, Chris** (d.1970) US newsreader. Before shooting herself during a broadcast

34 I am dying as fast as my enemies, if I have any, could wish, and as cheerfully as my best friends could desire.

Attr. **Hume, David** (1711–1776) Scottish philosopher and political economist

35 O holy simplicity!
In Zincgreff and Weidner, *Apothegmata* (1653) **Huss, Jan** (c.1370–1415) Bohemian religious reformer, preacher and martyr. At the stake, on seeing a peasant bringing wood

36 On the contrary!
Attr. **Ibsen, Henrik** (1828–1906) Norwegian writer, dramatist and poet. In response to his nurse's remark that he was feeling a little better

37 Let us cross over the river and rest in the shade.
Attr. **Jackson, Thomas (Stonewall)** (1824–1863) US general. Last words before being mistakenly shot by his own men

38 I am able to follow my own death step by step. Now I move softly towards the end.
The Guardian, (1963) **John XXIII** (1881–1963) Italian pope. Remark made two days before he died

39 I will be conquered; I will not capitulate.
In Boswell, *The Life of Samuel Johnson* (1791) **Johnson, Samuel** (1709–1784) English lexicographer, poet, critic, conversationalist and essayist. On his deathbed

40 I shall soon be laid in the quiet grave – thank God for the quiet grave – O! I can feel the cold earth upon me – the daisies growing over me – O for this quiet – it will be my first.
Attr. **Keats, John** (1795–1821) English poet

41 Ah well, I suppose it has come to this! ... Such is life!
Attr. **Kelly, Ned** (1855–1880) Australian outlaw and folk hero. On the scaffold, 11 November 1880

42 Be of good comfort, Master Ridley, and play the man. We shall this day light such a candle by God's grace in England, as (I trust) shall never be put out.
In Foxe, *Actes and Monuments* (1562–1563) **Latimer, Bishop Hugh** (c.1485–1555) English Protestant churchman. Said shortly before being put to death

43 Don't give up the ship.
Attr. **Lawrence, James** (1781–1813) US naval officer. Last words, during naval battle

44 It's all been rather lovely.
In *The Times*, (1983) **Le Mesurier, John** (1912–1983) English actor

45 Why are you weeping? Did you imagine that I was immortal?
Attr. **Louis XIV** (1638–1715) King of France. Noticing as he lay on his deathbed that his attendants were crying

46 I have not told half of what I saw.
In W. Durant, *The Story of Civilization* **Marco Polo** (c.1254–1324) Venetian traveller

47 Keep Paddy behind the big mixer.
Attr. **McAlpine, Sir Alfred** (1881–1944) Scottish building contractor

48 Do not hack me as you did my Lord Russell.
In Macaulay, *History of England* (1849) **Monmouth, Duke of** (1649–1685) Illegitimate son of Charles II. Words to his executioner

49 I hope the people of England will be satisfied. I hope my country will do me justice.
Attr. **Moore, General Sir John** (1761–1809) Scottish soldier

50 After his head was upon the block, he lifted it up again, and gently drew his beard aside, and said, This hath not offended the king.
In Francis Bacon, *Apophthegms New and Old* (1625) **More, Sir Thomas** (1478–1535) English statesman and humanist

51 I want to get Mumbo-Jumbo out of the world.
Attr. **Morris, William** (1834–1896) English poet, designer, craftsman, artist and socialist

52 Thank God, I have done my duty.
In Robert Southey, *The Life of Nelson* (1860) **Nelson, Lord** (1758–1805) English admiral. At the Battle of Trafalgar, 1805

53 What a great artist dies with me!
In Suetonius, *Lives of the Caesars*, 'Nero' **Nero** (37–68) Roman emperor

54 I knew it. I knew it. Born in a hotel room – and God damn it – died in a hotel room.
Attr. **O'Neill, Eugene** (1888–1953) US dramatist

55 I am just going outside, and may be some time.
In Captain Scott's diary **Oates, Captain Lawrence** (1880–1912) English Antarctic explorer

56 Die, my dear Doctor, that's the last thing I shall do!
Attr. **Palmerston, Lord** (1784–1865) British Prime Minister

57 Get my swan costume ready.
Attr. **Pavlova, Anna** (1881–1931) Russian ballet dancer

58 I am curious to see what happens in the next world to one who dies unshriven.
Attr. **Perelman, S.J.** (1904–1979) US humorist, writer and dramatist. Giving his reasons for refusing to see a priest as he lay dying

59 Greetings, we have won.
In Lucian, *'Pro Lapsu inter salutandum'* **Pheidippides** (d. 490 BC) Greek herald. After he had run to Athens with news of the Battle of Marathon

60 Drink to me.
Attr. **Picasso, Pablo** (1881–1973) Spanish painter, sculptor and graphic artist

61 I think I could eat one of Bellamy's veal pies.
Attr. **Pitt, William** (1759–1806) English politician and Prime Minister

62 Here am I, dying of a hundred good symptoms.
In Spence, *Anecdotes* **Pope, Alexander** (1688–1744) English poet, translator and editor

63 I am going to seek a great perhaps ... Bring down the curtain, the farce is played out.
Attr. **Rabelais, François** (c.1494–c.1553) French monk, physician, satirist and humanist

64 'Tis a sharp remedy, but a sure one for all ills.
Attr. **Raleigh, Sir Walter** (c.1552–1618) English courtier, explorer, military commander, poet, historian and essayist. On feeling the edge of the axe before his execution

65 I should desire that the last words which I should pronounce in this Academy, and from this place, might be the name of – Michael Angelo.
Discourses on Art, XV (1790) **Reynolds, Sir Joshua** (1723–1792) English portrait painter

66 So little done, so much to do!
In Lewis Mitchell, *Life of Rhodes* (1910) **Rhodes, Cecil** (1853–1902) English imperialist, financier and South African statesman

67 Put that bloody cigarette out!
In A. J. Langguth, *Life of Saki* **Saki** (1870–1916) Burmese-born British writer. Said to one of his men who had lit up; he was killed by a German sniper

68 Dear World, I am leaving you because I am bored. I feel I have lived long enough. I am leaving you with your worries in this sweet cesspool – good luck.
Suicide note **Sanders, George** (1906–1972) Russian-born British film actor

69 Lord take my soul, but the struggle continues.
The Observer, (1995) **Saro-Wiwa, Ken** (1941–1995) Nigerian author and environmental activist

70 Everybody has got to die, but I have always believed an exception would be made in my case. Now what?
Time, (1984) **Saroyan, William** (1908–1981) US writer and dramatist

71 At last I am going to be well!
Attr. **Scarron, Paul** (1610–1660) French dramatist, writer and poet

72 For God's sake look after our people.
Journal, (25 March 1912)

73 Had we lived, I should have had a tale to tell of the hardihood, endurance, and courage of my companions which would have stirred the heart of every Englishman. These rough notes and our dead bodies must tell the tale.
Message to the Public, (1912) **Scott, Robert Falcon** (1868–1912) English naval officer and Antarctic explorer

74 Nonsense, they couldn't hit an elephant at this dist–.

Attr. **Sedgwick, John** (1813–1864) US general. In response to a suggestion that he should not show himself over the parapet during the Battle of the Wilderness

75 Thy necessity is yet greater than mine.
In Sir Fulke Greville, *Life of Sir Philip Sidney* (1652) **Sidney, Sir Philip** (1554–1586) English poet, critic, soldier, courtier and diplomat. Offering his water-bottle, despite his own injuries, to a dying soldier on the battlefield near Zutphen, 1586

76 I'm losing.
The Times, (1998) **Sinatra, Frank** (1915–1998) US singer and actor

77 I believe we must adjourn this meeting to some other place.
Attr. **Smith, Adam** (1723–1790) Scottish economist, philosopher and essayist

78 No man knows my history.
Funeral sermon, written by himself **Smith, Joseph** (1805–1844) Founder of the Mormon Church

79 Crito, we owe a cock to Asclepius. Pay it and do not neglect it.
Attr. in Plato, *Phaedo* **Socrates** (469–399 BC) Athenian philosopher

80 Beautifully done.
In Collis, *Stanley Spencer* (1962) **Spencer, Sir Stanley** (1891–1959) English painter. Thanking the nurse who had given him his nightly injection, just before he died

81 Capital punishment: them without the capital get the punishment.
Attr. **Spenkelink, John** (d.1979) Executed in electric chair, Florida.

82 Just before she [Stein] died she asked, 'What is the answer?' No answer came. She laughed and said, 'In that case, what is the question?' Then she died.
In Sutherland, *Gertrude Stein* (1951) **Stein, Gertrude** (1874–1946) US writer, dramatist, poet and critic

83 If this is dying, then I don't think much of it.
In Michael Holroyd, *Lytton Strachey: A Critical Biography* (1968) **Strachey, Lytton** (1880–1932) English biographer and critic

84 Ah, a German and a genius! a prodigy, admit him!
Attr. **Swift, Jonathan** (1667–1745) Irish satirist, poet, essayist and cleric. Learning of the arrival of Handel

85 God bless ... God damn.
Attr. **Thurber, James** (1894–1961) US humorist, writer and dramatist

86 My prime of youth is but a frost of cares;
My feast of joy is but a dish of pain;
My crop of corn is but a field of tares;
And all my good is but vain hope of gain.
The day is past, and yet I saw no sun;
And now I live, and now my life is done.
'Elegy', written in the Tower of London before his execution **Tichborne, Chidiock** (c.1558–1586) English Catholic conspirator against Elizabeth I

87 Even in the valley of the shadow of death, two and two do not make six.
Attr. **Tolstoy, Leo** (1828–1910) Russian writer, essayist, philosopher and moralist. Refusing to reconcile himself with the Russian Orthodox Church as he lay dying

88 All right, then, I'll say it: Dante makes me sick.
Attr. **Vega Carpio, Félix Lope de** (1562–1635) Spanish dramatis and poet. On learning that he was about to die

89 Woe is me, I think I am becoming a god.
In Suetonius, *Lives of the Caesars* **Vespasian** (AD 9–79) Roman emperor

90 Either that wallpaper goes, or I do.
Time, (16 January 1984) **Wilde, Oscar** (1854–1900) Irish poet, dramatist, writer, critic and wit. As he lay dying in a drab Paris bedroom

91 I haven't got time to be tired.
Attr. **Wilhelm I, Kaiser** (1797–1888) King of Prussia and first Emperor of Germany. Said during his last illness

92 Now God be praised, I will die in peace.
In J. Knox, *Historical Journal of Campaigns* (1914 edition) **Wolfe, James** (1727–1759) English major-general
See also epitaphs; death

LAW

1 You have been acquitted by a Limerick jury and you may now leave the dock without any other stain on your character.
In Healy, *The Old Munster Circuit* **Adams, Richard** (1846–1908) Irish journalist, barrister and judge

2 That man is a creature who needs order yet yearns for change is the creative contradiction at the heart of the laws which structure his conformity and define his deviancy.
Sisters in Crime (1975) **Adler, Freda** (1934–) US educator and writer

3 In the strange heat all litigation brings to bear on things, the very process of litigation fosters the most profound misunderstandings in the world.
Reckless Disregard (1986) **Adler, Renata** (1938–) US film critic and writer

4 A gentleman haranguing on the perfection of our law, and that it was equally open to the poor and the rich, was answered by another, 'So is the London Tavern'.
Tom Paine's Jests (1794)

5 The law doth punish man or woman
That steals the goose from off the common,
But lets the greater felon loose,
That steals the common from the goose.
On enclosures, 18th Century **Anonymous**

6 Law is a bottomless pit.
The History of John Bull (c.1712) **Arbuthnot, John** (1667–1735) Scottish physician, pamphleteer and wit

7 One of the Seven was wont to say: 'That laws were like cobwebs; where the small flies were caught, and the great brake through.'
Apophthegms New and Old (1624) **Bacon, Francis** (1561–1626) English philosopher, essayist, politician and courtier

8 Lawyers are the only persons in whom ignorance of the law is not punished.
Attr. **Bentham, Jeremy** (1748–1832) English writer and philosopher

9 *Lawsuit*: A machine which you go into as a pig and come out as a sausage.
The Cynic's Word Book (1906) **Bierce, Ambrose** (1842–c.1914) US writer, verse writer and soldier

10 Laws are like sausages. It's better not to see them being made.
Attr. **Bismarck, Prince Otto von** (1815–1898) First Chancellor of the German Reich

11 President Bush was against abortion, but for capital punishment. Spoken like a true fisherman; throw them back, kill them when they're bigger.
Comic Relief, HBO, (1986) **Boosler, Elayne** (1952–) US comedienne

12 Let them bring me prisoners, and I'll find them law.
Attr. **Braxfield, Lord** (1722–1799) Scottish judge

13 People crushed by law have no hopes but from power. If laws are their enemies, they will be enemies to laws; and those who have much to hope and nothing to lose will always be dangerous more or less.
Letter to Charles James Fox, (1777)

14 Bad laws are the worst sort of tyranny.
Speech at Bristol (1780)

15 There is but one law for all, namely, that law which governs all law – the law of our Creator, the law of humanity, justice, equity, the law of nature, and of nations.
Speech, (1794)

16 Laws, like houses, lean on one another.
Tracts on the Popery Laws (1812) **Burke, Edmund** (1729–1797) Irish-born British statesman and philosopher

17 I'me asham'd the law is such an Ass.
Revenge for Honour (1654) **Chapman, George** (c.1559–c.1634) English poet, dramatist and translator

18 The good of the people is the chief law.
De Legibus **Cicero** (106–43 BC) Roman orator, statesman, essayist and letter writer

19 All we can do is to uphold the laws, all of us, without allowing the memory of justice to fade.
Waiting for the Barbarians (1980) **Coetzee, J.M.** (1940–) South African writer

20 He saw a Lawyer killing a viper
On a dunghill hard by his own stable;
And the Devil smiled, for it put him in mind
Of Cain and his brother, Abel ...
'The Devil's Thoughts' (1799) **Coleridge, Samuel Taylor** (1772–1834) English poet, philosopher and critic

21 Law and equity are two things which God hath joined, but which man hath put asunder.
Lacon (1820) **Colton, Charles Caleb** (c.1780–1832) English clergyman and satirist

22 The Law of England is a very strange one; it cannot compel anyone to tell the truth ... But what the Law can do is to give you seven years for not telling the truth.
In Walker-Smith, *Lord Darling* **Darling, Charles** (1849–1936) English judge and Conservative politician

23 To every subject of this land, however powerful, I would use Thomas Fuller's words over three hundred years ago, 'Be ye never so high, the law is above you'.
High Court ruling against the Attorney-General, (1977) **Denning, Lord** (1899–1999) English Master of the Rolls

24 As far as I am concerned the only proper place for lawyers in the NHS is on the operating table.
In *The Observer*, (1999) **Dobson, Frank** (1940–) English Labour politician. On growing litigation in the NHS

25 Good men must not obey the laws too well.
'Politics' (1844) **Emerson, Ralph Waldo** (1803–1882) US poet, essayist, transcendentalist and teacher

26 The law, in its majestic equality, forbids the rich as well as the poor to sleep under bridges, to beg in the streets, and to steal bread.
Le Lys Rouge (1894) **France, Anatole** (1844–1924) French writer and critic

27 All of us here know that there is no better way of exercising the imagination than the study of law. No poet has ever interpreted nature as freely as a lawyer interprets reality.
La Guerre de Troie n'aura pas lieu (1935) **Giraudoux, Jean** (1882–1944) French dramatist, poet, writer and satirist

28 If one were to study all the laws, one would have absolutely no time to break them.
'Experience and Life' **Goethe** (1749–1832) German poet, writer, dramatist and scientist

29 Laws grind the poor, and rich men rule the law.
'The Traveller' (1764) **Goldsmith, Oliver** (c.1728–1774) Irish dramatist, poet and writer

30 To me judges seem the well paid watch-dogs of Capitalism, making things safe and easy for the devil Mammon.
Letter to W.B. Yeats **Gonne, Maud** (1865–1953) Irish patriot and philanthropist

31 I know no method to secure the repeal of bad or obnoxious laws so effective as their stringent execution.
Inaugural Address, (1869) **Grant, Ulysses S.** (1822–1885) US President, Civil War general and memoirist

32 The Common Law of England has been laboriously built about a mythical figure – the figure of 'The Reasonable Man'.
Uncommon Law (1935) **Herbert, Sir A.P.** (1890–1971) English humorist, writer, dramatist and politician

33 An elderly pensioner on being sentenced to fifteen years' penal servitude cried 'Ah! my Lord, I'm a very old man, and I'll never do that sentence.' The judge replied 'Well try to do as much of it as you can.'
In Healy, *The Old Munster Circuitm* (1939) **Holmes, Hugh (Lord Justice Holmes)** (1840–1916) Irish judge

34 In this country, my Lords, ... the individual subject ... 'has nothing to do with the laws but to obey them'.
Speech, House of Lords, (1795) **Horsley, Bishop Samuel** (1733–1806) English bishop

35 I have considered myself bound to observe the law for the whole of my 66 years.

The Times, (1999) **Ingham, Sir Bernard** (1932–) Chief Press Secretary to Margaret Thatcher. Comment after being bound over to keep the peace by Croydon magistrates

36 I have come to regard the law courts not as a cathedral but rather as a casino.
The Guardian, (1977) **Ingrams, Richard** (1937–) British journalist and editor of *Private Eye*

37 Johnson observed, that 'he did not care to speak ill of any man behind his back, but he believed the gentleman was an attorney.'
In Boswell, *The Life of Samuel Johnson* (1791) **Johnson, Samuel** (1709–1784) English lexicographer, poet, critic, conversationalist and essayist

38 A lawyer is never entirely comfortable with a friendly divorce, any more than a good mortician wants to finish his job and then have the patient sit up on the table.
Time, (1961) **Kerr, Jean** (1923–2003) US writer and dramatist

39 Oh, Mr President, do not let so great an achievement suffer from any taint of legality.
Attr. **Knox, Philander Chase** (1853–1921) US lawyer and Republican politician. Reply when Theodore Roosevelt requested legal justification for US acquisition of the Panama Canal Zone

40 Wherever Law ends, Tyranny begins.
Second Treatise of Civil Government (1690) **Locke, John** (1632–1704) English philosopher

41 Good examples are borne out of good education, which is the outcome of good legislation; and good legislation is borne out of those uprisings which are unduly damned by so many people.
Discourse **Machiavelli** (1469–1527) Florentine statesman, political theorist and historian

42 I have forgotten more law than you ever knew, but allow me to say, I have not forgotten much.
Attr. **Maynard, Sir John** (1602–1690) English judge, politician and royalist. Reply to Judge Jeffreys' suggestion that he was so old he had forgotten the law

43 No brilliance is needed in the law. Nothing but common sense, and relatively clean finger nails.
A Voyage Round My Father (1971) **Mortimer, John** (1923–) English lawyer, dramatist and writer

44 Did you know that a peer condemned to death had the right to be hanged with a silken cord? A bit like insisting that the electric chair had to be Chippendale.
The Observer, (1999) **Mosley, Charles**

45 Laws were made to be broken.
Blackwood's Edinburgh Magazine, (1830) **North, Christopher** (1785–1854) Scottish poet, writer, editor and critic

46 A judge is not supposed to know anything about the facts of life until they have been presented in evidence and explained to him at least three times.
The Observer, (1961) **Parker, Hubert Lister** (1900–1972) English Lord Chief Justice

47 Let us consider the reason of the case. For nothing is law that is not reason.
In *Lord Raymond's Reports* (1765) **Powell, Sir John** (1645–1713) English judge

48 Necessity gives the law without itself recognizing any.
Sententiae **Publilius, Syrus** (1st century BC) Roman writer

49 A lawyer with his briefcase can steal more than a thousand men with guns.
The Godfather (1969) **Puzo, Mario** (1920–1999) US writer

50 To pass a law and not have it enforced is to authorize the very thing you wish to prohibit.
Mémoires **Richelieu, Cardinal** (1585–1642) Prime Minister to Louis XIII

51 Any law which violates the indefeasible rights of man is in essence unjust and tyrannical; it is no law.
Déclaration des Droits de l'homme (1793) **Robespierre, Maximilien** (1758–1794) French revolutionary

52 Laws are always useful to those who have possessions, and harmful to those who have nothing.
Du Contrat Social (1762) **Rousseau, Jean-Jacques** (1712–1778) Swiss-born French philosopher, educationist and essayist

53 *Mrs Bertram*: That sounds like nonsense, my dear.
Mr Bertram: May be so, my dear; but it may be very good law for all that.
Guy Mannering (1815) **Scott, Sir Walter** (1771–1832) Scottish writer and historian

54 Ignorance of the law excuses no man; not that all men know the law, but because 'tis an excuse every man will plead, and no man can tell how to confute him.
Table Talk (1689)

55 Every law is a contract between the king and the people and therefore to be kept.
Table Talk (1689) **Selden, John** (1584–1654) English historian, jurist and politician

56 There is a higher law than the Constitution.
Speech against Fugitive Slave Law, (1850) **Seward, William** (1801–1872) US statesman

57 We must not make a scarecrow of the law,
Setting it up to fear the birds of prey,
And let it keep one shape till custom make it
Their perch, and not their terror.
Measure for Measure, II.i

58 The law hath not been dead, though it hath slept.
Measure For Measure, II.ii

59 Still you keep o' th' windy side of the law.
Twelfth Night, III.iv **Shakespeare, William** (1564–1616) English dramatist, poet and actor

60 All men are anarchists with regard to laws which are against their consciences.
In London our worst anarchists are the magistrates, because many of them are so old and ignorant that when they are called upon to administer any law that is based on ideas or knowledge less than half a century old, they disagree with it, and naively set the example of violating it.
Major Barbara (1907), Preface **Shaw, George Bernard** (1856–1950) Irish socialist, writer, dramatist and critic

61 Laws are generally found to be nets of such a texture, as the little creep through, the great break through, and the middle-sized are alone entangled in.
Works in Verse and Prose (1764) **Shenstone, William** (1714–1763) English poet, essayist and letter writer

62 *Judge Willis*: What do you suppose I am on the Bench for, Mr Smith?
F.E. Smith: It is not for me to attempt to fathom the inscrutable workings of Providence.
In Birkenhead, *Frederick Elwin, Earl of Birkenhead* (1933)

63 Possibly not, My Lord, but far better informed.
In Birkenhead, *Life of F.E. Smith* (1959) To a judge who complained that he was no wiser at the end than at the start of one of Smith's cases **Smith, F.E.** (1872–1930) English politician and Lord Chancellor

64 Laws are like spider's webs, which hold firm when any light, yielding object falls upon them, while a larger thing breaks through them and escapes.
In Diogenes Laertius, *Lives of the Eminent Philosophers* **Solon** (c.638–c.559 BC) Athenian statesman, reformer and poet

65 There is an old saying: 'When a German falls over, he doesn't stand up, but looks about to see who is liable to pay him compensation.'
Scraps (1973) **Tucholsky, Kurt** (1890–1935) German satirist and writer
See also crime; judgement; justice and injustice

LIES

1 It is the patriotic duty of every man to lie for his country.
Attr. **Adler, Alfred** (1870–1937) Austrian psychiatrist and psychologist

2 We Catholics may lie and say we are Protestants when we are among the Protestants or we may lie when we are among the Huguenots and say we are Huguenots; and if we wish we can stoop so low as to say we are Jews when we are among the Jews if our lying would benefit the Catholic Church.
Jesuit oath **Anonymous**

3 It contains a misleading impression, not a lie. It was being economical with the truth.
The Observer, (1986) **Armstrong, Sir Robert** (1927–) English civil servant. Replying to an allegation in court that a letter he had written on behalf of the British Government had contained a lie

4 She tells enough white lies to ice a wedding cake.
Quoted by Lady Violet Bonham Carter in *The Listener,* (1953) **Asquith, Margot** (1864–1945) Scottish political hostess and writer. Of Lady Desborough

5 But it is not the lie that passeth through the mind, but the lie that sinketh in, and settleth in it, that doth the hurt.
'Of Truth' (1625) **Bacon, Francis** (1561–1626) English philosopher, essayist, politician and courtier

6 Matilda told such Dreadful Lies,
It made one Gasp and Stretch one's Eyes;
Her Aunt, who, from her Earliest Youth,
Had kept a Strict Regard for Truth,
Attempted to Believe Matilda:
The effort very nearly killed her.
'Matilda' (1907) **Belloc, Hilaire** (1870–1953) English writer of verse, essayist and critic; Liberal MP

7 … the lounging mirth of cracker-barrel men,
Snowed in by winter, spitting at the fire,
And telling the disreputable truth
With the sad eye that marks the perfect liar.
'Poem' **Benét, Stephen Vincent** (1898–1943) US poet

8 God is not a man, that he should lie.
Numbers, 23:19 **The Bible (King James Version)**

9 The English are polite by telling lies. The Americans are polite by telling the truth.
Stepping Westward (1965) **Bradbury, Malcolm** (1932–) English writer, critic and academic

10 Falsehood has a perennial spring.

Speech on American Taxation (1774) **Burke, Edmund** (1729–1797) Irish-born British statesman and philosopher

11 Any fool can tell the truth, but it requires a man of some sense to know how to lie well.
The Note-Books of Samuel Butler (1912) **Butler, Samuel** (1835–1902) English writer, painter, philosopher and scholar

12 And, after all, what is a lie? 'Tis but
The truth in masquerade.
Don Juan (1824) **Byron, Lord** (1788–1824) English poet, satirist and traveller

13 A lie can be half-way round the world before the truth has got its boots on.
Speech, (1976) **Callaghan, James** (1912–2005) English Labour statesman and Prime Minister

14 One needs a good memory after telling lies.
Le Menteur (1643) **Corneille, Pierre** (1606–1684) French dramatist, poet and lawyer

15 Better a noble lie than a miserable truth.
In Twigg, *Conversations with Twenty-four Canadian Writers* (1981) **Davies, Robertson** (1913–1995) Canadian playwright, writer and critic

16 The camera cannot lie. But it can be an accessory to untruth.
Attr. **Evans, Harold** (1928–) English journalist and newspaper editor

17 As ten millions of circles can never make a square, so the united voice of myriads cannot lend the smallest foundation to falsehood.
The Vicar of Wakefield (1766) **Goldsmith, Oliver** (c.1728–1774) Irish dramatist, poet and writer

18 Nobody is ever truthful about his own life. There are always ambiguities.
The Observer, (1981) **Grant, Cary** (1904–1986) English-born US film actor

19 You see, I always divide people into two groups. Those who live by what they know to be a lie, and those who live by what they believe, falsely, to be the truth.
The Philanthropist (1970) **Hampton, Christopher** (1946–) English dramatist

20 The stormie working soul spits lies and froth.
Dare to be true. Nothing can need a ly.
A fault which needs it most grows two thereby.
The Temple (1633) **Herbert, George** (1593–1633) English poet and priest

21 Whoever would lie usefully should lie seldom.
In Croker, *Memoirs of the Reign of George II* (1848) **Hervey, Lord** (1696–1743) English politican and memoirist

22 The broad mass of a people … falls victim to a big lie more easily than to a small one.
Mein Kampf (1925) **Hitler, Adolf** (1889–1945) German Nazi dictator, born in Austria

23 It's easy to make a man confess the lies he tells to himself; it's far harder to make him confess the truth.
Rogue Male (1939) **Household, Geoffrey** (1900–1988) English writer

24 The Christian religion not only was at first attended with miracles, but even at this day cannot be believed by any reasonable person without one. Mere reason is insufficient to convince us of its veracity: and whoever is moved by Faith to assent to it, is conscious of a continued miracle in his own person, which subverts all the principles of his understanding, and gives him a determination to believe what is most contrary to custom and experience.
Philosophical Essays Concerning Human Understanding (1748) **Hume, David** (1711–1776) Scottish philosopher and political economist

25 Take the saving lie from the average man and you take his happiness away, too.
The Wild Duck (1884) **Ibsen, Henrik** (1828–1906) Norwegian writer, dramatist and poet

26 The lie in the Soul is a true lie.
From the introduction to his translation (1871) of Plato's Republic **Jowett, Benjamin** (1817–1893) English scholar, translator, essayist and priest

27 Lying increases the creative faculties ... It is only in lies, wholeheartedly and bravely told, that human nature attains through words and speech the forbearance, the nobility, the romance, the idealism, that it falls so short of in fact and in deeds.
Vanity Fair, (1930) **Luce, Clare Boothe** (1903–1987) US diplomat, politician and writer

28 She's too crafty a woman to invent a new lie when an old one will serve.
The Constant Wife (1927) **Maugham, William Somerset** (1874–1965) English writer, dramatist and physician

29 He led a double life. Did that make him a liar? He did not feel a liar. He was a man of two truths.
The Sacred and Profane Love Machine (1974) **Murdoch, Iris** (1919–1999) Irish-born British writer, philosopher and dramatist

30 We need lies ... in order to live.
Fragments (1880–1889) **Nietzsche, Friedrich Wilhelm** (1844–1900) German philosopher, critic and poet

31 They've never learned to stand up and lie like white men.
The Weekend Guardian, (1993) **O'Rourke, P.J.** (1947–) US writer. On white South Africans

32 One always seems to be lying when one speaks to the police.
Les Chroniques du canard sauvage **Philippe, Charles-Louis** (1874–1909) French author

33 One of those telegrams of which M. de Guermantes had wittily fixed the formula: 'Cannot come, lie follows'.
Le Temps retrouvé (1926) **Proust, Marcel** (1871–1922) French writer and critic

34 A liar must have a good memory.
Institutio Oratoria, IV, 2, 91 **Quintilian** (c.35–c.100) Roman rhetorician

35 Was it a friend or foe that spread these lies?
Nay, who but infants question in such wise?
'Twas one of my most intimate enemies.
'Fragment' **Rossetti, Dante Gabriel** (1828–1882) English poet, painter, translator and letter writer

36 I have never but once succeeded in making George Moore tell a lie, that was by a subterfuge. 'Moore,' I said, 'do you always speak the truth?' 'No,' he replied. I believe this to be the only lie he had ever told.
The Autobiography of Bertrand Russell (1967–1969) **Russell, Bertrand** (1872–1970) English philosopher, mathematician, essayist and social reformer

37 A little inaccuracy sometimes saves tons of explanation.
The Square Egg (1924) **Saki** (1870–1916) Burmese-born British writer

38 Excellent, excellent, you can just hear the lies trickling out of his mouth.
Attr. Remark at the unveiling of a portrait of a colleague

39 Well, it certainly cured you, Mahaffy.
Attr. On hearing a colleague claiming to have been caned only once in his life, and that, for telling the truth **Salmon, George** (1819–1904) Provost of Trinity College, Dublin

40 A very honest woman, but something given to lie.
Antony and Cleopatra, V.ii

41 For my part, if a lie may do thee grace, I'll gild it with the happiest terms I have.
Henry IV, Part 1, V.iv

42 Lord, Lord, how subject we old men are to this vice of lying!
Henry IV, Part 2, III.ii **Shakespeare, William** (1564–1616) English dramatist, poet and actor

43 During the writing ... of this book, I realized that the public will believe anything – so long as it is not founded on truth.
Taken Care Of (1965) **Sitwell, Dame Edith** (1887–1964) English poet, anthologist, critic and biographer

44 This universal, compulsory, force-feeding with lies is now the most agonizing aspect of existence in our country – worse than all our material miseries, worse than any lack of civil liberties.
Letter to Soviet Leaders (1974)

45 In our country the lie has become not just a moral category but a pillar of the State. In recoiling from the lie we are performing a moral act, not a political act.
Interview in *Time* magazine, (1974)
Solzhenitsyn, Alexander (1918–) Russian writer, dramatist and historian

46 A lie is real; it aims at success. A liar is a realist.
Letty Fox: Her Luck (1946) **Stead, Christina** (1902–1983) Australian writer

47 A lie is an abomination unto the Lord, and a very present help in trouble.
Speech, Springfield, Illinois, (1951) **Stevenson, Adlai** (1900–1965) US lawyer, statesman and United Nations ambassador

48 The cruellest lies are often told in silence.
Virginibus Puerisque (1881) **Stevenson, Robert Louis** (1850–1894) Scottish writer, poet and essayist

49 He replied that I must needs be mistaken, or that I said the thing which was not. (For they have no word in their language to express lying or falsehood.)
Gulliver's Travels (1726)

50 I mean, you lie – under a mistake.
Polite Conversation (1738) **Swift, Jonathan** (1667–1745) Irish satirist, poet, essayist and cleric

51 A lie which is all a lie may be met and fought with outright,
But a lie which is part a truth is a harder matter to fight.
'The Grandmother' (1859) **Tennyson, Alfred, Lord** (1809–1892) English lyric poet

52 An experienced, industrious, ambitious, and often quite picturesque liar.
Private History of a Campaign that Failed (1885) **Twain, Mark** (1835–1910) US humorist, writer, journalist and lecturer

53 Father, I cannot tell a lie; I did it with my little hatchet.
Attr., probably apocryphal **Washington, George** (1732–1799) US general, statesman and President. On being accused of cutting down a cherry tree

54 The Social Contract is nothing more or less than a vast conspiracy of human beings to lie to and humbug themselves and one another for the general Good. Lies are the mortar that bind the savage individual man into the social masonry.
Love and Mr Lewisham (1900) **Wells, H.G.** (1866–1946) English writer
See also art; deception; guilt; truth; secrets

LIFE

1 It began in mystery, and it will end in mystery, but what a savage and beautiful country lies in between.
A Natural History of the Senses (1990)
Ackerman, Diane (1948–) US poet

2 The Answer to the Great Question Of … Life, the Universe and Everything … Is … Forty-two.
The Hitch Hiker's Guide to the Galaxy (1979)
Adams, Douglas (1952–2001) English writer

3 Chaos often breeds life, when order breeds habit.
The Education of Henry Adams (1918) **Adams, Henry** (1838–1918) US historian and memoirist

4 Sunday clears away the rust of the whole week.
The Spectator, 112, (July 1711) **Addison, Joseph** (1672–1719) English essayist, poet, playwright and statesman

5 I am one of those people who just can't help getting a kick out of life – even when it's a kick in the teeth.
A House Is Not a Home (1953) **Adler, Polly** (1900–1962) US brothel keeper

6 If you are in Rome, live in the Roman fashion; if you are elsewhere, live as they do there.
In Taylor, *Ductor Dubitantium* (1660) **Ambrose, Saint** (c.340–397) French-born churchman; writer of music and hymns

7 Every life is a profession of faith, and exercises an inevitable and silent influence.
Journal, (1852) **Amiel, Henri-Frédéric** (1821–1881) Swiss philosopher and writer

8 And now the end is near
And so I face the final curtain,
My friends, I'll say it clear,
I'll state my case of which I'm certain.
I've lived a life that's full, I've travelled each
and evr'y high-way
And more, much more than this, I did it
my way.
'My Way' (song, 1969) **Anka, Paul** (1941–) US
pop singer and songwriter

9 Once a job is fouled up, anything done to
improve it only makes it worse.
Finagle's Fourth Law

10 If anything can go wrong, it will.
'Murphy's Law', probably dating from the US
in the 1940s. A Captain E. Murphy of the
California Northrop aviation firm may have
formulated it

11 Live well. It is the greatest revenge.
The Talmud **Anonymous**

12 Just as at the Olympic games it is not the
handsomest or strongest men who are
crowned with victory but the successful
competitors, so in life it is those who act
rightly who carry off all the prizes and
rewards.
Nicomachean Ethics **Aristotle** (384–322 BC)
Greek philosopher

13 For most men in a brazen prison live,
Where, in the sun's hot eye,
With heads bent o'er their toil, they
languidly
Their lives to some unmeaning taskwork
give,
Dreaming of nought beyond their prison-
wall.
'A Summer Night' (1852)

14 Is it so small a thing
To have enjoy'd the sun,
To have liv'd light in the spring,
To have lov'd, to have thought, to have
done?
'Empedocles on Etna' (1852)

15 When we are asked further, what is
conduct? – let us answer: Three fourths of
life.
Literature and Dogma (1873) **Arnold, Matthew**
(1822–1888) English poet, critic, essayist and
educationist

16 Only God can tell the saintly from the
suburban,
Counterfeit values always resemble the
true;
Neither in Life nor Art is honesty
bohemian,
The free behave much as the respectable
do.
'New Year Letter' (1941) **Auden, W.H.** (1907–
1973) English poet, essayist, critic, teacher and
dramatist

17 Remember that no one loses any other life
than this which he now lives, nor lives any
other than this which he now loses.
Meditations **Aurelius, Marcus** (121–180) Roman
emperor and Stoic philosopher

18 But men must know, that in this theatre of
man's life it is reserved only for God and
angels to be lookers on.
The Advancement of Learning (1605) **Bacon,
Francis** (1561–1626) English philosopher,
essayist, politician and courtier

19 Nothing matters very much, and very few
things matter at all.
Attr. **Balfour, A.J.** (1848–1930) British
Conservative Prime Minister

20 The life of every man is a diary in which he
means to write one story, and writes
another; and his humblest hour is when he
compares the volume as it is with what he
vowed to make it.
Attr. **Barrie, Sir J.M.** (1860–1937) Scottish
dramatist and writer

21 We always find something, eh, Didi, to
give us the impression that we exist?
Waiting for Godot (1955) **Beckett, Samuel** (1906–
1989) Irish dramatist, writer and poet

22 When we compare the present life of man
with that time of which we have no
knowledge, it seems to me like the swift
flight of a lone sparrow through the
banqueting-hall where you sit in the winter
months ... This sparrow flies swiftly in
through one door of the hall, and out
through another ... Similarly, man appears
on earth for a little while, but we know
nothing of what went on before this life,
and what follows.

Ecclesiastical History **Bede, The Venerable** (673–735) English monk, historian and scholar

23 I wonder why dreams must be broken, idylls lost and love forgotten? The transience of life has always exasperated me.
My Life with Brendan Behan (1973) **Behan, Beatrice** (1931–1993) Wife of Brendan Behan

24 When one door closes another door opens; but we often look so long and so regretfully upon the closed door that we do not see the ones which open for us.
Attr. **Bell, Alexander Graham** (1847–1922) Scottish-born US inventor and educator of the deaf

25 Most things in life are moments of pleasure and a lifetime of embarrassment; photography is a moment of embarrassment and a lifetime of pleasure.
The Independent, (1989) **Benn, Tony** (1925–) English Labour politician

26 You know life ... it's rather like opening a tin of sardines. We are all of us looking for the key.
Beyond the Fringe (1962) **Bennett, Alan** (1934–) English dramatist, actor and diarist

27 One should not exaggerate the importance of trifles. Life, for instance, is much too short to be taken seriously.
Attr. **Bentley, Nicolas** (1907–1978) English publisher and artist

28 Life has taught me that it is not for our faults that we are disliked and even hated but for our qualities.
The Passionate Sightseer (1960) **Berenson, Bernard** (1865–1959) Lithuanian-born US art critic

29 Human life is mainly a process of filling in time until the arrival of death or Santa Claus.
Games People Play, (1964) **Berne, Eric** (1910–1970) US psychiatrist

30 Life, friends, is boring. We must not say so.
Dream Songs (1964) **Berryman, John** (1914–1972) US poet and author

31 I will give unto him that is athirst of the fountain of the water of life freely.

Revelation, 21:6 **The Bible (King James Version)**

32 For every thing that lives is holy, life delights in life.
America: a Prophecy (1793)

33 Without Contraries is no progression. Attraction and Repulsion, Reason and Energy, Love and Hate, are necessary to Human existence.
The Marriage of Heaven and Hell (c.1793) **Blake, William** (1757–1827) English poet, engraver, painter and mystic

34 What now? What next? All these questions. All these doubts. So few certainties. But then I have taken new comfort and refuge in the doctrine that advises one not to seek tranquillity in certainty, but in permanently suspended judgement.
Brazzaville Beach (1990) **Boyd, William** (1952–) Scottish writer

35 The best plans have always been wrecked by the narrow-mindedness of those who should carry them out.
Mother Courage and her Children (1941) **Brecht, Bertolt** (1898–1956) German dramatist

36 We should live as if we were going to live forever, yet at the back of our minds remember that our time is short.
Thoughts in a Dry Season (1978) **Brenan, Gerald** (1894–1987) English writer

37 Life, believe, is not a dream,
So dark as sages say;
Oft a little morning rain
Foretells a pleasant day!
'Life' (1846) **Brontë, Charlotte** (1816–1855) English writer

38 Life itself is but the shadow of death, and souls but the shadows of the living. All things fall under this name. The sun itself is but the dark *simulacrum*, and light but the shadow of God.
The Garden of Cyrus (1658)

39 The long habit of living indisposeth us for dying.
Hydriotaphia: Urn Burial (1658) **Browne, Sir Thomas** (1605–1682) English physician, author and antiquary

40 It's a great life if you don't weaken.
Mr Standfast (1919) **Buchan, John** (1875–1940)
Scottish writer, lawyer and Conservative
politician

41 He'll hae misfortunes great an' sma',
But ay a heart aboon them a'.
'There was a Lad' (1785)

42 The best-laid schemes o' mice an' men
Gang aft agley,
An' lea'e us nought but grief an' pain,
For promis'd joy!
'To a Mouse' (1785) **Burns, Robert** (1759–1796)
Scottish poet and songwriter

43 To live is like love, all reason is against it,
and all healthy instinct for it.
The Note-Books of Samuel Butler (1912)

44 Life is one long process of getting tired.
The Note-Books of Samuel Butler (1912) **Butler,
Samuel** (1835–1902) English writer, painter,
philosopher and scholar

45 The optimist proclaims that we live in the
best of all possible worlds; and the
pessimist fears this is true.
The Silver Stallion (1926) **Cabell, James Branch**
(1879–1958) US writer, poet, genealogist and
historian

46 Comedy is tragedy that happens to *other*
people.
Wise Children (1991) **Carter, Angela** (1940–1992)
English writer

47 In all my life, I have never repented but of
three things: that I trusted a woman with a
secret, that I went by sea when I might
have gone by land, and that I passed a day
in idleness.
In Pliny, *Naturalis Historia* **Cato the Elder**
(234–149 BC) Roman statesman

48 I say have patience, and shuffle the cards.
Don Quixote (1615) **Cervantes, Miguel de** (1547–
1616) Spanish writer and dramatist

49 Living is an illness to which sleep provides
relief every sixteen hours. It's a palliative.
Death is the remedy.
Maximes et pensées (1796) **Chamfort, Nicolas**
(1741–1794) French writer

50 Life is a tragedy when seen in close-up, but
a comedy in long-shot.
In *The Guardian*, Obituary, (1977) **Chaplin,
Charlie** (1889–1977) English comedian, film
actor, director and satirist

51 I like living. I have sometimes been wildly,
despairingly, acutely miserable, racked with
sorrow, but through it all I still know quite
certainly that just to be alive is a grand
thing.
An Autobiography (1977) **Christie, Agatha** (1890–
1976) English crime writer and playwright

52 And what is Life? – an hour glass on the
run
A mist retreating from the morning sun
A busy bustling still repeated dream
Its length? – A moment's pause, a
moment's thought
And happiness? A Bubble on the stream
That in the act of seizing shrinks to
nought.
'What is Life?' (1820)

53 If life had a second edition, how I would
correct the proofs.
Letter to a friend **Clare, John** (1793–1864)
English rural poet; died in an asylum

54 Life is falling sideways.
Opium (1930) **Cocteau, Jean** (1889–1963) French
dramatist, poet, film writer and director

55 *Coach Pantusso*: How's life treating you
Norm?
Norm: Like I ran over its dog.
NBCTV's *Cheers* **Colasanto, Nicholas** (1924–
1985) and **Wendt, George** (1948–) US actors

56 As regards plots I find real life no help at
all. Real life seems to have no plots.
In R. Lehmann et al., *Orion I* (1945) **Compton-
Burnett, Dame Ivy** (1884–1969) English
novelist

57 Everything is a dangerous drug to me
except reality, which is unendurable.
The Unquiet Grave (1944) **Connolly, Cyril** (1903–
1974) English literary editor, writer and critic

58 The fatal imperfection of all the gifts of life,
which makes of them a delusion and a
snare.
Victory (1915) **Conrad, Joseph** (1857–1924)
Polish-born British writer, sailor and explorer

59 Life is too short to stuff a mushroom.
Superwoman (1975) **Conran, Shirley** (1932–)
English writer

60 Life is a matter of passing the time
enjoyably. There may be other things in
life, but I've been too busy passing my time
enjoyably to think very deeply about them.
The Guardian, (1994) **Cook, Peter** (1937–1995)
English comedian and writer

61 You promise heavens free from strife,
Pure truth, and perfect change of will;
But sweet, sweet is this human life,
So sweet, I fain would breathe it still;
Your chilly stars I can forgo,
This warm kind world is all I know …
All beauteous things for which we live
By laws of space and time decay.
But Oh, the very reason why
I clasp them, is because they die.
'Mimnermus in Church' (1858) **Cory, William**
(1823–1892) English poet, teacher and writer

62 The most important thing in life is not the
winning but the taking part; the essential
thing is not conquering but fighting well.
Speech, (1908) **Coubertin, Pierre de** (1863–
1937) French educationist and sportsman

63 Variety's the very spice of life,
That gives all its flavour.
The Task (1785) **Cowper, William** (1731–1800)
English poet, hymn writer and letter writer

64 What is life? It is the flash of a firefly in the
night. It is the breath of a buffalo in the
wintertime. It is the little shadow which
runs across the grass and loses itself in the
sunset.
Last words **Crowfoot** (1821–1890) Blackfoot
warrior

65 We will now discuss in a little more detail
the struggle for existence.
The Origin of Species (1859) **Darwin, Charles**
(1809–1882) English naturalist

66 What is this life if, full of care,
We have no time to stand and stare?
Songs of Joy (1911) **Davies, William Henry**
(1871–1940) Welsh poet, writer and tramp

67 The essence of life is statistical
improbability on a colossal scale.

The Blind Watchmaker (1986) **Dawkins, Richard**
(1941–) English biologist and author

68 Next to knowing when to seize an
opportunity, the most important thing in
life is to know when to forgo an advantage.
Attr. **Disraeli, Benjamin** (1804–1881) English
statesman and writer

69 Yesternight the sun went hence,
And yet is here today,
He hath no desire nor sense,
Nor half so short a way:
Then fear not me,
But believe that I shall make
Speedier journeys, since I take
More wings and spurs than he.
Songs and Sonnets (1611) **Donne, John** (1572–
1631) English poet

70 Believe in life! Always human beings will
live and progress to greater, broader, and
fuller life.
Last message to the world, read at his funeral
Du Bois, William (1868–1963) US academic
and author

71 People do not live nowadays – they get
about ten percent out of life.
This Quarter Autumn, 'Memoirs' **Duncan,
Isadora** (1878–1927) US modern dance pioneer

72 Setting an example is not the main means
of influencing others, it is the only means.
Attr.

73 Only a life lived for others is a life
worthwhile.
'Defining Success' **Einstein, Albert** (1879–1955)
German-born US mathematical physicist

74 Life is good only when it is magical and
musical, a perfect timing and consent, and
when we do not anatomize it. You must
treat the days respectfully, you must be a
day yourself, and not interrogate it like a
college professor … You must hear the
bird's song without attempting to render it
into nouns and verbs.
Society and Solitude (1870)

75 Write it on your heart that every day is the
best day in the year. No man has learned
anything rightly until he knows that every
day is Doomsday.

Society and Solitude (1870) **Emerson, Ralph Waldo** (1803–1882) US poet, essayist, transcendentalist and teacher

76 Ah, fill the Cup: – what boots it to repeat
How Time is slipping underneath our Feet:
Unborn TOMORROW and dead YESTERDAY,
Why fret about them if TO-DAY be sweet!
The Rubáiyát of Omar Khayyám (1859)
Fitzgerald, Edward (1809–1883) English poet, translator and letter writer

77 So we beat on, boats against the current, borne back ceaselessly into the past.
The Great Gatsby (1925) **Fitzgerald, F. Scott** (1896–1940) US writer

78 Parents can only give good advice or put them on the right paths, but the final forming of a person's character lies in their own hands.
The Diary of Anne Frank (1947) **Frank, Anne** (1929–1945) Jewish diarist; died in Nazi concentration camp

79 Dost thou love life? Then do not squander time, for that's the stuff life is made of.
Poor Richard's Almanac (1746)

80 A little neglect may breed mischief – for want of a nail, the shoe was lost; for want of a shoe, the horse was lost; and for want of a horse the rider was lost.
Poor Richard's Almanac (1758)

81 But in this world nothing can be said to be certain, except death and taxes.
Letter to Jean Baptiste Le Roy, (1789) **Franklin, Benjamin** (1706–1790) US statesman, scientist, political critic and printer

82 This was life – my life – my career, my brilliant career! I was fifteen – fifteen! A few fleeting hours and I would be old as those around me. I looked at them as they stood there, weary, and turning down the other side of the hill of life. When young, no doubt they had hoped for, and dreamed of, better things – had even known them, but here they were. This had been their life; this was their career. It was, and in all probability would be, mine too. My life – my career – my brilliant career!
My Brilliant Career (1901) **Franklin, Miles** (1879–1954) Australian writer

83 What a minefield
Life is! One minute you're taking a stroll in the sun,
The next your legs and arms are all over the hedge.
There's no dignity in it.
A Yard of Sun (1970) **Fry, Christopher** (1907–2005) English verse dramatist, theatre director and translator

84 I am a passenger on the spaceship, Earth.
Operating Manual for Spaceship Earth (1969)
Fuller, Richard Buckminster (1895–1983) US architect and engineer

85 Life is a jest; and all things show it.
I thought so once; but now I know it.
'My Own Epitaph' (1720) **Gay, John** (1685–1732) English poet, dramatist and librettist

86 If there's a problem, you have to go out and solve it.
Live Aid, music concert, (1985) **Geldof, Bob** (1951–) Irish musician and anti-poverty activist

87 What is our life? a play of passion,
Our mirth the music of derision,
Our mothers' wombs the tiring houses be,
Where we are dressed for this short comedy ...
Only we die in earnest, that's no jest.
The First Set of Madrigals and Motets of Five Parts (1612) **Gibbons, Orlando** (1583–1625) English organist and composer of church music

88 That state is a state of Slavery in which a man does what he likes to do in his spare time and in his working time that which is required of him.
'Slavery and Freedom' (1929) **Gill, Eric** (1882–1940) English stonecarver, topographer and writer

89 Talent is formed in quiet retreat,
Character in the headlong rush of life.
Torquato Tasso (1790)

90 Grey, dear friend, is all theory,
And green the golden tree of life.
Faust (1808) **Goethe** (1749–1832) German poet, writer, dramatist and scientist

91 Life is mostly froth and bubble,
Two things stand like stone,
Kindness in another's trouble,
Courage in your own.
Ye Wearie Wayfarer (1866)

92 A little season of love and laughter,
Of light and life, and pleasure and pain,
And a horror of outer darkness after,
And dust returneth to dust again.
'The Swimmer' (1903) **Gordon, Adam Lindsay**
(1833–1870) Australian poet and ballad writer

93 'What do you think of it, Moon,
As you go?
Is Life much, or no?'
'O, I think of it, often think of it
As a show
God ought surely to shut up soon,
As I go.'
'To the Moon' (1917) **Hardy, Thomas** (1840–
1928) English writer and poet

94 Life is made up of marble and mud.
The House of the Seven Gables (1851) **Hawthorne,
Nathaniel** (1804–1864) US allegorical writer

95 Life is made up of sobs, sniffles, and
smiles, with sniffles predominating.
The Four Million (1906) **Henry, O.** (1862–1910)
US short-story writer

96 No arts; no letters; no society; and which is
worst of all, continual fear, and danger of
violent death; and the life of man, solitary,
poor, nasty, brutish, and short.
Leviathan (1651) **Hobbes, Thomas** (1588–1679)
Political philosopher

97 It shows hunger for life, like the Zen
parable of a man holding on to a tree root
over the edge of a cliff: below him rocks,
above him a tiger, and a black and white
mouse nibbling at the root: the man
notices a strawberry beside him and picks
it.
A Circle Round The Sun – A Foreigner in Japan
Hodson, Peregrine British author

98 Life is just one damned thing after
another.
Philistine, (1909) **Hubbard, Elbert** (1856–1915)
US printer, editor, writer and businessman

99 Most of one's life … is one prolonged
effort to prevent oneself thinking.

Mortal Coils (1922)

100 Consistency is contrary to nature, contrary
to life. The only completely consistent
people are the dead.
Do What You Will (1929)

101 Living is an art; and to practise it well, men
need, not only acquired skill, but also a
native tact and taste.
Texts and Pretexts (1932) **Huxley, Aldous** (1894–
1963) English writer, poet and critic

102 The chess-board is the world; the pieces
are the phenomena of the universe; the
rules of the game are what we call the laws
of Nature. The player on the other side is
hidden from us. We know that his play is
always fair, just, and patient. But we also
know, to our cost, that he never overlooks a
mistake, or makes the smallest allowance
for ignorance.
Macmillan's Magazine, (1868) **Huxley, T.H.**
(1825–1895) English biologist, Darwinist and
agnostic

103 Live all you can; it's a mistake not to. It
doesn't so much matter what you do in
particular, so long as you have your life. If
you haven't had that then what have you
had?
The Ambassadors (1903) **James, Henry** (1843–
1916) US-born British writer, critic and letter
writer

104 Life exists in the universe only because the
carbon atom possesses certain exceptional
properties.
The Mysterious Universe (1930) **Jeans, Sir James
Hopwood** (1877–1946) English mathematician,
physicist and astronomer

105 Human life is everywhere a state in which
much is to be endured, and little to be
enjoyed.
Rasselas (1759)

106 Life is a pill which none of us can bear to
swallow without gilding.
In Hester Lynch Piozzi, *Anecdotes of the Late
Samuel Johnson* (1786)

107 There are innumerable questions to which the inquisitive mind can in this state receive no answer: Why do you and I exist? Why was this world created? Since it was to be created, why was it not created sooner?
In Boswell, *The Life of Samuel Johnson* (1791)

108 Our tastes greatly alter. The lad does not care for the child's rattle, and the old man does not care for the young man's whore.
In Boswell, *The Life of Samuel Johnson* (1791)
Johnson, Samuel (1709–1784) English lexicographer, poet, critic, conversationalist and essayist

109 As far as we are able to understand, the only aim of human existence is to kindle a light in the darkness of mere being.
Memories, Dreams, Thoughts (1962) **Jung, Carl Gustav** (1875–1961) Swiss psychiatrist and pupil of Freud

110 There is a goal but no way of reaching it; what we call the way is hesitation.
Reflections on Sin, Sorrow, Hope and the True Way **Kafka, Franz** (1883–1924) Czech-born German-speaking writer

111 But this is human life: the war, the deeds,
The disappointment, the anxiety,
Imagination's struggles, far and nigh,
All human.
'Endymion' (1818)

112 I compare human life to a large Mansion of Many Apartments, two of which I can only describe, the doors of the rest being as yet shut upon me.
Letter to J.H. Reynolds, (3 May 1818)

113 A Man's life of any worth is a continual allegory.
Letter to George and Georgiana Keats, (1819)
Keats, John (1795–1821) English poet

114 Life can only be understood backwards; but it must be lived forwards.
Life **Kierkegaard, Søren** (1813–1855) Danish philosopher

115 Nothing to do but work,
Nothing to eat but food,
Nothing to wear but clothes
To keep one from going nude.
Nothing to breathe but air,
Quick as a flash 'tis gone;
Nowhere to fall but off,
Nowhere to stand but on!

'The Pessimist' **King, Benjamin** (1857–1894) US humorist

116 Life is indeed precious. And I believe the death penalty helps to affirm this fact.
Attr. **Koch, Ed** (1924–) Mayor of New York

117 All man's life among men is nothing more than a battle for the ears of others.
The Book of Laughter and Forgetting (1981)
Kundera, Milan (1929–) Czech writer and critic

118 There are only three events in a man's life; birth, life, and death; he is not aware of being born, he dies in suffering, and he forgets to live.
Les caractères ou les moeurs de ce siècle (1688) **La Bruyère, Jean de** (1645–1696) French satirist

119 No flowery path leads to glory.
'Les deux aventuriers et le talisman' **La Fontaine, Jean de** (1621–1695) French poet and fabulist

120 Oh, what an everyday affair life is!
Les complaintes (1885) **Laforgue, Jules** (1860–1887) French poet

121 If you take the game of life seriously, if you take your nervous system seriously, if you take your sense organs seriously, if you take the energy process seriously, you must turn on, tune in, and drop out.
Politics of Ecstasy (1968) **Leary, Timothy** (1920–1996) US writer and psychologist

122 Life is like a sewer. What you get out of it depends on what you put in.
An Evening Wasted with Tom Lehrer, Record album, (1953) **Lehrer, Tom** (1928–) US academic and songwriter

123 While I thought that I was learning how to live, I have been learning how to die.
Selections from the Notebooks of Leonardo da Vinci (1952 edition) **Leonardo da Vinci** (1452–1519) Italian artist

124 Yesterday I loved, today I suffer, tomorrow I shall die. Nonetheless I still think with pleasure, today and tomorrow, of yesterday.
'Song taken from the Spanish' **Lessing, Gotthold Ephraim** (1729–1781) German dramatist, critic and theologian

125 Term, holidays, term, holidays, till we leave school, and then work, work, work till we die.
Surprised by Joy (1955) **Lewis, C.S.** (1898–1963) Irish-born English academic, writer and critic

126 Life would be tolerable but for its amusements.
In Dictionary of National Biography **Lewis, Sir George Cornewall** (1806–1863) English Liberal politician and writer

127 Lives of great men all remind us
We can make our lives sublime,
And, departing, leave behind us
Footprints on the sands of time.
'A Psalm of Life' (1838)

128 Our ingress into the world
Was naked and bare;
Our progress through the world
Is trouble and care.
Tales of a Wayside Inn (1863–1874), 'The Student's Tale' **Longfellow, Henry Wadsworth** (1807–1882) US poet and writer

129 Some groups increase, others diminish, and in a short space the generations of living creatures are changed and like runners pass on the torch of life.
De Rerum Natura

130 For life is not confined to him or thee;
'Tis given to all for use, to none for property.
De Rerum Natura **Lucretius** (c.95–55 BC) Roman philosopher

131 We have learned the answers, all the answers:
It is the question that we do not know.
The Hamlet of A. Macleish (1935) **MacLeish, Archibald** (1892–1982) US poet and librarian

132 I am not yet born; O fill me
With strength against those who would freeze my
humanity, would dragoon me into a lethal automaton,
would make me a cog in a machine, a thing with
one face, a thing, and against all those who would dissipate my entirety, would blow me like thistledown hither and thither or hither and thither
like water held in the

hands would spill me.
Let them not make me a stone and let them not spill me.
Otherwise kill me.
'Prayer before Birth' (1944) **MacNeice, Louis** (1907–1963) Belfast-born poet, writer, radio producer, translator and critic

133 Life is a tragedy full of joy.
New York Times, (1979) **Malamud, Bernard** (1914–1986) US writer

134 Man does not only live his personal life as an individual, but also, consciously or unconsciously, the life of his era and of his contemporaries.
The Magic Mountain (1924) **Mann, Thomas** (1875–1955) German writer and critic

135 Hell hath no limits nor is circumscrib'd
In one self place, where we are is Hell,
And where Hell is, there must we ever be.
And to be short, when all the world dissolves,
And every creature shall be purified,
All places shall be hell that are not heaven.
Doctor Faustus (1604) **Marlowe, Christopher** (1564–1593) English poet and dramatist

136 Believe me, 'I shall live' is not the saying of a wise man. Tomorrow's life is too late: live today.
Epigrammata **Martial** (c.AD 40–c.104) Spanish-born Latin epigrammatist and poet

137 Life is too short to do anything for oneself that one can pay others to do for one.
The Summing Up (1938) **Maugham, William Somerset** (1874–1965) English writer, dramatist and physician

138 All good things which exist are the fruits of originality.
On Liberty (1859) **Mill, John Stuart** (1806–1873) English philosopher, economist and reformer

139 ... who overcomes
By force, hath overcome but half his foe.
Paradise Lost (1667) **Milton, John** (1608–1674) English poet, libertarian and pamphleteer

140 I've looked at life from both sides now
From win and lose and still somehow
It's life's illusions I recall
I really don't know life at all.

'Both Sides Now' (song, 1968) **Mitchell, Joni** (1943–) US singer and songwriter

141 What if the hokey-cokey really is what it's all about?
Attr. **Monkhouse, Bob** (1928–2003) English comedian

142 Living is both my job and my art.
Essais (1580)

143 The value of life does not lie in the number of years but in the use you make of them … Whether you have lived enough depends on your will, not on the number of your years.
Essais (1580) **Montaigne, Michel de** (1533–1592) French essayist and moralist

144 When I consider how my life is spent,
I hardly ever repent.
'Reminiscent Reflection' (1931) **Nash, Ogden** (1902–1971) US poet

145 Believe me! – the secret of gathering in the greatest fruitfulness and the greatest enjoyment from existence is living dangerously!
The Gay Science (1887) **Nietzsche, Friedrich Wilhelm** (1844–1900) German philosopher, critic and poet

146 I am going where life is more like life than it is here.
Cock-a-Doodle Dandy (1949)

147 A lament in one ear, maybe; but always a song in the other. And to me life is simply an invitation to live.
In Eileen O'Casey, *Eileen* **O'Casey, Sean** (1880–1964) Irish dramatist

148 My feeling about life is a curious kind of triumphant feeling about seeing it bleak, knowing it is so, and walking into it fearlessly because one has no choice.
Attr. **O'Keeffe, Georgia** (1887–1986) US artist

149 Living is strife and torment, disappointment and love and sacrifice, golden sunsets and black storms. I said that some time ago, and today I do not think I would add one word.
Los Angeles Times, (1978) **Olivier, Sir Laurence** (1907–1989) English actor and director

150 Our lives are merely strange dark interludes in the electric display of God the Father!
Strange Interlude (1928) **O'Neill, Eugene** (1888–1953) US dramatist

151 Life is a petty thing unless there is pounding within it an enormous desire to extend its boundaries. We live in proportion to the extent to which we yearn to live more.
The Dehumanization of Art (1925) **Ortega y Gasset, José** (1883–1955) Spanish philosopher

152 Every luxury was lavished on you – atheism, breast-feeding, circumcision. I had to make my own way.
Loot (1967) **Orton, Joe** (1933–1967) English dramatist and writer

153 When schemes are laid in advance, it is surprising how often the circumstances fit in with them.
Attr. **Osler, Sir William** (1849–1919) Canadian physician

154 Razors pain you;
Rivers are damp;
Acids stain you;
And drugs cause cramp.
Guns aren't lawful;
Nooses give;
Gas smells awful;
You might as well live.
'Résumé' (1937) **Parker, Dorothy** (1893–1967) US writer, poet, critic and wit

155 The last act is bloody, however delightful the rest of the play may be.
Pensées (1670) **Pascal, Blaise** (1623–1662) French philosopher and scientist

156 We pass –
And lit briefly by one another's light
Think the way we go is right.
'One another's light'

157 When I went out I stole an orange
It was a safeguard against imagining there was nothing
bright or special in the world.
'The stolen orange' **Patten, Brian** (1946–) British poet

158 You must consider this too, that we are born, each of us, not for ourselves alone but partly for our country, partly for our parents and partly for our friends.
Epistles, IX **Plato** (c.429–347 BC) Greek philosopher

159 What dire offence from am'rous causes springs,
What mighty contests rise from trivial things,
I sing.
The Rape of the Lock (1714) **Pope, Alexander** (1688–1744) English poet, translator and editor

160 Good-bye, I've barely said a word to you, it is always like that at parties, we never see the people, we never say the things we should like to say, but it is the same everywhere in this life. Let us hope that when we are dead things will be better arranged.
À la recherche du temps perdu, Sodome et Gomorrhe (1922)

161 It is seldom indeed that one parts on good terms, because if one were on good terms one would not part.
La Prisonnière (1923) **Proust, Marcel** (1871–1922) French writer and critic

162 Life begins at forty.
All's well that ends well.
The best things in life are free.
Life is just a bowl of cherries.
Life is sweet.
He that lives long suffers much.
Proverb

163 Man never found the deities so kindly
As to assure him that he'd live tomorrow.
Pantagruel (1532) **Rabelais, François** (c.1494–c.1553) French monk, physician, satirist and humanist

164 Life should be tamed with tenderness.
Journal, (1892) **Renard, Jules** (1864–1910) French writer and dramatist

165 The feeling of Sunday is the same everywhere, heavy, melancholy, standing still. Like when they say, 'As it was in the beginning, is now, and ever shall be, world without end.'
Voyage in the Dark (1934)

166 Next week, or next month, or next year I'll kill myself. But I might as well last out my month's rent, which has been paid up, and my credit for breakfast in the morning.
Good Morning, Midnight (1939) **Rhys, Jean** (1894–1979) West Indian-born English writer

167 And so we live and forever take our leave.
Duino Elegies (1923) **Rilke, Rainer Maria** (1875–1926) Austrian poet, born in Prague

168 Brief and powerless is Man's life; on him and all his race the slow, sure doom falls pitiless and dark.
Mysticism and Logic (1918) **Russell, Bertrand** (1872–1970) English philosopher, mathematician, essayist and social reformer

169 Fanaticism consists in redoubling your effort when you have forgotten your aim.
The Life of Reason (1906)

170 There is no cure for birth and death save to enjoy the interval.
Soliloquies in England (1922)

171 Life is not a spectacle or a feast; it is a predicament.
In Sagittarius and George, *The Perpetual Pessimist* **Santayana, George** (1863–1952) Spanish-born US philosopher and writer

172 So that's what Hell is. I'd never have believed it ... Do you remember, brimstone, the stake, the gridiron? ... What a joke! No need of a gridiron, Hell is other people.
In Camera (1944) **Sartre, Jean-Paul** (1905–1980) French philosopher, writer, dramatist and critic

173 We shall never learn to feel and respect our real calling and destiny, unless we have taught ourselves to consider every thing as moonshine, compared with the education of the heart.
Letter to J.G. Lockhart, (1825) **Scott, Sir Walter** (1771–1832) Scottish writer and historian

174 Live among men as if God beheld you; speak to God as if men were listening.
Epistles

175 Eternal law has arranged nothing better than this, that it has given us one way in to life, but many ways out.

Epistulae Morales **Seneca** (c.4 BC–AD 65) Roman philosopher, poet, dramatist, essayist, rhetorician and statesman

176 All the world's a stage,
And all the men and women merely players;
They have their exits and their entrances;
And one man in his time plays many parts.
As You Like It, II.vii

177 O gentlemen, the time of life is short!
To spend that shortness basely were too long.
Henry IV, Part 1, V.ii

178 Past and to come seems best; things present, worst.
Henry IV, Part 2, I.iii

179 To-morrow, and to-morrow, and to-morrow,
Creeps in this petty pace from day to day
To the last syllable of recorded time,
And all our yesterdays have lighted fools
The way to dusty death. Out, out, brief candle!
Life's but a walking shadow, a poor player,
That struts and frets his hour upon the stage,
And then is heard no more; it is a tale
Told by an idiot, full of sound and fury,
Signifying nothing.
Macbeth, V.v

180 The heavens themselves, the planets, and this centre,
Observe degree, priority, and place,
Insisture, course, proportion, season, form,
Office, and custom, in all line of order.
Troilus and Cressida, I.iii **Shakespeare, William** (1564–1616) English dramatist, poet and actor

181 Lift not the painted veil which those who live
Call Life.
'Sonnet' (1818) **Shelley, Percy Bysshe** (1792–1822) English poet, dramatist and essayist

182 We have the highest authority for believing that the meek shall inherit the Earth; though I have never found any particular corroboration of this aphorism in the records of Somerset House.

Contemporary Personalities (1924), 'Marquess Curzon' **Smith, F.E.** (1872–1930) English politician and Lord Chancellor

183 There are two things to aim at in life: first, to get what you want; and, after that, to enjoy it. Only the wisest of mankind achieve the second.
Afterthoughts (1931)

184 People say that life is the thing, but I prefer reading.
Afterthoughts (1931)

185 Yes, there is a meaning, at least for me, there is one thing that matters – to set a chime of words tinkling in the minds of a few fastidious people.
New Statesman, (1946) Contemplating whether life has any meaning, shortly before his death **Smith, Logan Pearsall** (1865–1946) US-born British epigrammatist, critic and writer

186 What is life but a veil of affliction?
The Expedition of Humphry Clinker (1771) **Smollett, Tobias** (1721–1771) Scottish writer, satirist, historian, traveller and physician

187 But now it is time to depart, for me to die and for you to go on living; but which of us has the better lot, is unknown to anyone but God.
Attr. in Plato, *Apology*

188 The unexamined life is not a life worth living for a human being.
Attr. in Plato, *Apology* **Socrates** (469–399 BC) Athenian philosopher

189 Live as long as you may, the first twenty years are the longest half of your life.
The Doctor (1812) **Southey, Robert** (1774–1843) English poet, essayist, historian and letter writer

190 Progress, therefore, is not an accident, but a necessity ... it is a part of nature.
Social Statics (1850) **Spencer, Herbert** (1820–1903) English philosopher and journalist

191 The history of our spiritual life is a continuing search for the unity between ourselves and the world.
The Philosophy of Freedom (1964) **Steiner, Rudolf** (1861–1925) Austrian philosopher and founder of anthroposophy

192 To love playthings well as a child, to lead
an adventurous and honourable youth, and
to settle when the time arrives, into a
green and smiling age, is to be a good
artist in life and deserve well of yourself
and your neighbour.
Virginibus Puerisque (1881)

193 But all that I could think of, in the darkness
and the cold,
Was that I was leaving home and my folks
were growing old.
Ballads (1890) **Stevenson, Robert Louis** (1850–
1894) Scottish writer, poet and essayist

194 Life is a gamble, at terrible odds – if it was
a bet, you wouldn't take it.
Rosencrantz and Guildenstern Are Dead (1967)
Stoppard, Tom (1937–) British dramatist

195 Psychiatrists classify a person as neurotic if
he suffers from his problems in living, and
a psychotic if he makes others suffer.
The Second Sin (1973) **Szasz, Thomas** (1920–)
Hungarian-born US psychiatrist and writer

196 Each person's life is lived as a series of
conversations.
The Observer, (1992) **Tannen, Deborah** (1945–)
US linguist and academic

197 As our life is very short, so it is very
miserable, and therefore it is well it is
short.
The Rule and Exercise of Holy Dying (1651)
Taylor, Bishop Jeremy (1613–1667) English
divine and writer

198 When all is done, human life is, at the
greatest and the best, but like a froward
child, that must be play'd with and
humoured a little to keep it quiet till it falls
asleep, and then the care is over.
Miscellanea, The Second Part (1690) **Temple, Sir
William** (1628–1699) English diplomat and
writer

199 Where there's life, there's hope.
Heauton Timoroumenos **Terence** (c.190–159 BC)
Carthaginian-born Roman dramatist

200 Ah! *Vanitas Vanitatum!* Which of us is
happy in this world? Which of us has his
desire? or, having it, is satisfied? – Come,
children, let us shut up the box and the
puppets, for our play is played out.

Vanity Fair (1847–1848) **Thackeray, William
Makepeace** (1811–1863) Indian-born English
writer

201 Oh, isn't life a terrible thing, thank God?
Under Milk Wood (1954) **Thomas, Dylan** (1914–
1953) Welsh poet, writer and radio dramatist

202 Our life is frittered away by detail ...
Simplify, simplify.
Walden (1854)

203 I wanted to live deep and suck out all the
marrow of life ... to drive life into a corner,
and reduce it to its lowest terms, and, if it
proved to be mean, why then to get the
whole and genuine meanness of it, and
publish its meanness to the world; or if it
were sublime, to know it by experience,
and be able to give a true account of it in
my next excursion.
Walden (1854) **Thoreau, Henry David** (1817–
1862) US essayist, social critic and writer

204 There is something about the unexpected
that moves us. As if the whole of existence
is paid for in some way, except for that one
moment, which is free.
Sacred Country **Tremain, Rose** (1951–) English
author

205 All say, 'How hard it is to die' – a strange
complaint to come from the mouths of
people who have had to live.
Pudd'nhead Wilson's Calendar (1894) **Twain,
Mark** (1835–1910) US humorist, writer,
journalist and lecturer

206 I am an optimist, unrepentant and
militant. After all, in order not to be a fool
an optimist must know how sad a place the
world can be. It is only the pessimist who
finds this out anew every day.
Dear Me (1977) **Ustinov, Sir Peter** (1921–2004)
English actor, director, dramatist, writer and
raconteur

207 In order to achieve great things we must
live as though we were never going to die.
Réflexions et Maximes (1746) **Vauvenargues,
Marquis de** (1715–1747) French soldier and
moralist

208 Live? The servants will do that for us.
Axel (1890) **Villiers de L'Isle-Adam, Philippe-
Auguste** (1838–1889) French poet and writer

209 People tend to think that life really does progress for everyone eventually, that people progress, but actually only some people progress. The rest of the people don't.
In C. Tate (ed.), *Black Women Writers at Work* (1983) **Walker, Alice** (1944–) US writer and poet

210 I tell you, we're in a blessed drainpipe, and we've got to crawl along it till we die.
Kipps: the Story of a Simple Soul (1905) **Wells, H.G.** (1866–1946) English writer

211 It is the essence of life that it exists for its own sake.
Nature and Life (1934) **Whitehead, A.N.** (1861–1947) English mathematician and philosopher

212 One can live for years sometimes without living at all, and then all life comes crowding into one single hour.
Vera, or The Nihilist (1880)

213 *Lord Illingworth*: The soul is born old but grows young. That is the comedy of life.
Mrs Allonby: And the body is born young and grows old. That is life's tragedy.
A Woman of No Importance (1893)

214 One's real life is so often the life that one does not lead.
'L'Envoi to Rose-Leaf and Apple-Leaf' **Wilde, Oscar** (1854–1900) Irish poet, dramatist, writer, critic and wit

215 Character is a by-product; it is produced in the great manufacture of daily duty.
Speech, (1915) **Wilson, Woodrow** (1856–1924) US Democrat President

216 I spent the afternoon musing on Life. If you come to think of it, what a queer thing Life is! So unlike anything else, don't you know, if you see what I mean.
My Man Jeeves (1919) **Wodehouse, P.G.** (1881–1975) English humorist and writer

217 I was thinking, and I was moved to pity that the whole of human life is so short – not one of this great number will be alive a hundred years from now.
In Herodotus, *Histories* **Xerxes** (c.519–465 BC) King of Persia. On surveying his army

218 When I think of all the books I have read, and of the wise words I have heard spoken, and of the anxiety I have given to parents and grandparents, and of the hopes that I have had, all life weighed in the scales of my own life seems to me preparation for something that never happens.
Autobiographies (1955) **Yeats, W.B.** (1865–1939) Irish poet, dramatist, editor, writer and senator

219 All the problems of the world are caused by people who do not listen.
The Observer, (1998) **Zeffirelli, Franco** (1923–) Italian film director

220 The only interest in living comes from believing in life, from loving life and using all the power of your intelligence to know it better.
Le Docteur Pascal (1893) **Zola, Emile** (1840–1902) French novelist
See also advice; death; humanity and human nature; time

LITERATURE

1 The best part of the fiction in many novels is the notice that the characters are purely imaginary.
In Jonathan Green, *The Cynic's Lexicon* (1984) **Adams, Franklin P.** (1881–1960) US writer, poet, translator and editor

2 A play is fiction and fiction is fact distilled into truth.
New York Times, (1966) **Albee, Edward** (1928–) US dramatist

3 Science fiction is no more written for scientists than ghost stories are written for ghosts.
Penguin Science Fiction (1961) **Aldiss, Brian** (1925–) English writer

4 Others abide our question. Thou art free. We ask and ask – Thou smilest and art still, Out-topping knowledge.
'Shakespeare' (1849)

5 Nothing has raised more questioning among my critics than these words – noble, the grand style ... I think it will be found that the grand style arises in poetry, when a noble nature, poetically gifted, treats with simplicity or with severity a serious subject.
On Translating Homer (1861) **Arnold, Matthew** (1822–1888) English poet, critic, essayist and educationist

6 Political history is far too criminal and pathological to be a fit subject of study for the young. All teachers know this. In consequence, they bowdlerize, but to bowdlerize political history is not to simplify but to falsify it. Children should acquire their heroes and villains from fiction.
A Certain World (1970) **Auden, W.H.** (1907–1973) English poet, essayist, critic, teacher and dramatist

7 One of Edward's Mistresses was Jane Shore, who has had a play written about her, but it is a tragedy and therefore not worth reading.
The History of England (1791)

8 'And what are you reading, Miss —?' 'Oh! it is only a novel!' replies the young lady; while she lays down her book with affected indifference, or momentary shame. It is only *Cecilia*, or *Camilla*, or *Belinda*; or, in short, only some work in which the greatest powers of the mind are displayed, in which the most thorough knowledge of human nature, the happiest delineation of its varieties, the liveliest effusions of wit and humour, are conveyed to the world in the best chosen language.
Northanger Abbey (1818) **Austen, Jane** (1775–1817) English writer

9 If you are a novelist of a certain type of temperament, then what you really want to do is re-invent the world. God wasn't too bad a novelist, except he was a Realist.
Attr. **Barth, John** (1930–) US writer

10 The cliché is dead poetry. English, being the language of an imaginative race, abounds in clichés, so that English literature is always in danger of being poisoned by its own secretions.
Thoughts in a Dry Season (1978) **Brenan, Gerald** (1894–1987) English writer

11 Dr Weiss, at forty, knew that her life had been ruined by literature.
A Start in Life (1981) **Brookner, Anita** (1928–) English writer

12 There, Shakespeare, on whose forehead climb
The crowns o' the world. Oh, eyes sublime,
With tears and laughters for all time!
A Vision of Poets (1844) **Browning, Elizabeth Barrett** (1806–1861) English poet; wife of Robert Browning

13 'Begin at the beginning,' the King said, very gravely, 'and go on till you come to the end: then stop.'
Alice's Adventures in Wonderland (1865) **Carroll, Lewis** (1832–1898) English writer and photographer

14 It does not matter that Dickens' world is not lifelike: it is alive.
Early Victorian Novelists (1934) **Cecil, Lord David** (1902–1986) English critic and writer

15 When I started out to write fiction I had the great disadvantage of having absolutely no talent for it ... If more than two people were on scene I couldn't keep one of them alive.
Letter to Paul Brooks, (1949) **Chandler, Raymond** (1888–1959) US crime writer

16 Tragedie is to seyn a certeyn storie,
As olde bookes maken us memorie,
Of hym that stood in greet prosperitee
And is yfallen out of heigh degree
Into myserie, and endeth wrecchedly.
The Canterbury Tales (1387) **Chaucer, Geoffrey** (c.1340–1400) English poet, public servant and courtier

17 The novel remains for me one of the few forms where we can record man's complexity and the strength and decency of his longings.
Accepting the National Book Award, (1958)

18 Literature has been the salvation of the damned, literature has inspired and guided lovers, routed despair and can perhaps in this case save the world.

In Susan Cheever, *Home before Dark* (1984)
Speech on receiving the National Medal for
Literature **Cheever, John** (1912–1982) US
novelist

19 Medicine is my lawful wife but literature is
my mistress. When I'm bored with one, I
spend the night with the other.
Letter to Suvorin, (1888) **Chekhov, Anton**
(1860–1904) Russian writer, dramatist and
doctor

20 It is the art in which the conquests of
woman are quite beyond controversy ...
The novel of the nineteenth century was
female.
The Victorian Age in Literature (1913)
Chesterton, G.K. (1874–1936) English writer,
poet and critic

21 Johnson's style was grand and Gibbon's
elegant; the stateliness of the former was
sometimes pedantic, and the polish of the
latter was occasionally finical. Johnson
marched to kettle-drums and trumpets;
Gibbon moved to flutes and hautboys:
Johnson hewed passages through the Alps,
while Gibbon levelled walks through parks
and gardens.
Random Records (1830) **Colman, the Younger,
George** (1762–1836) English dramatist and
Examiner of Plays

22 The Mandarin style ... is beloved by literary
pundits, by those who would make the
written word as unlike as possible to the
spoken one. It is the style of those writers
whose tendency is to make their language
convey more than they mean or more than
they feel.
Enemies of Promise (1938)

23 Literature is the art of writing something
that will be read twice; journalism what will
be grasped at once.
Attr. **Connolly, Cyril** (1903–1974) English
literary editor, writer and critic

24 When I want to read a novel I write one.
Attr. **Disraeli, Benjamin** (1804–1881) English
statesman and writer

25 Novels are as useful as Bibles, if they teach
you the secret, that the best of life is
conversation, and the greatest success is
confidence.

Conduct of Life (1860)

26 Every man is a borrower and a mimic, life
is theatrical and literature a quotation.
Society and Solitude (1870) **Emerson, Ralph
Waldo** (1803–1882) US poet, essayist,
transcendentalist and teacher

27 Ulysses is the strongest character in the
whole of ancient literature, Hamlet the
strongest character in the whole of modern
literature.
Letter to Louise Colet, (1853) **Flaubert,
Gustave** (1821–1880) French writer

28 That the story is the highest factor
common to all novels, and I wish that it
was not so, that it could be something
different – melody, or perception of the
truth, not this low atavistic form.
Aspects of the Novel (1927)

29 Yes – oh dear, yes – the novel tells a story.
Aspects of the Novel (1927) **Forster, E.M.** (1879–
1970) English writer, essayist and literary
critic

30 Nor can I do better, in conclusion, than
impress upon you the study of Greek
literature, which not only elevates above
the vulgar herd, but leads not infrequently
to positions of considerable emolument.
Christmas Day Sermon, Oxford Cathedral
Gaisford, Rev. Thomas (1779–1855) Dean of
Christ Church, Oxford

31 The romance of Tom Jones, that exquisite
picture of human manners, will outlive the
palace of the Escurial and the imperial
eagle of the house of Austria.
Memoirs of My Life and Writings (1796) **Gibbon,
Edward** (1737–1794) English historian,
politician and memoirist

32 National literature does not now have
much significance, it is time for the era of
world literature.
Gespräche mit Eckermann, (1827) **Goethe** (1749–
1832) German poet, writer, dramatist and
scientist

33 Historians tell stories of the past, novelists
stories of the present.
Journal **Goncourt, Edmond de** (1822–1896)
French novelist

34 Is it a book you would even wish your wife or your servants to read?
The Times, (1960) **Griffith-Jones, Mervyn** (1909–1979) English lawyer. At the trial of D.H. Lawrence's novel *Lady Chatterley's Lover*

35 He knew everything about literature except how to enjoy it.
Catch-22 (1961) **Heller, Joseph** (1923–1999) US writer

36 In serious works and ones that promise great things, one or two purple patches are often stitched in, to glitter far and wide.
Ars Poetica **Horace** (65–8 BC) Roman lyric poet and satirist

37 The aristocratic pleasure of displeasing is not the only delight that bad taste can yield. One can love a certain kind of vulgarity for its own sake.
Vulgarity in Literature (1930) **Huxley, Aldous** (1894–1963) English writer, poet and critic

38 Literature flourishes best when it is half a trade and half an art.
'The Victorian Age' (1922) **Inge, William Ralph** (1860–1954) English divine, writer and teacher

39 I remember once saying to Henry James, in reference to a novel of the type that used euphemistically to be called 'unpleasant': 'You know, I was rather disappointed; that book wasn't nearly as bad as I expected'; to which he replied, with his incomparable twinkle: 'Ah, my dear, the abysses are all so shallow.'
In Edith Wharton, *The House of Mirth* (1936)

40 What is character but the determination of incident? What is incident but the illustration of character?
Partial Portraits (1888)

41 The only obligation to which in advance we may hold a novel, without incurring the accusation of being arbitrary, is that it be interesting.
Partial Portraits (1888) **James, Henry** (1843–1916) US-born British writer, critic and letter writer

42 Classical quotation is the parole of literary men all over the world.

In Boswell, *The Life of Samuel Johnson* (1791) **Johnson, Samuel** (1709–1784) English lexicographer, poet, critic, conversationalist and essayist

43 Far too many relied on the classic formula of a beginning, a muddle, and an end.
New Fiction, (1978) **Larkin, Philip** (1922–1985) English poet, writer and librarian. Referring to modern novels

44 The novel is the one bright book of life.
Phoenix (1936)

45 I am a man, and alive … For this reason I am a novelist. And being a novelist, I consider myself superior to the saint, the scientist, the philosopher, and the poet, who are all great masters of different bits of man alive, but never get the whole hog.
Phoenix (1936) **Lawrence, D.H.** (1885–1930) English writer, poet and critic

46 Our American professors like their literature clear, cold, pure, and very dead.
Address to Swedish Academy, (1930) **Lewis, Sinclair** (1885–1951) US writer

47 Literature is mostly about having sex and not much about having children; life is the other way round.
The British Museum is Falling Down (1965) **Lodge, David** (1935–) English writer, satirist and literary critic

48 When once the itch of literature comes over a man, nothing can cure it but the scratching of a pen.
Handy Andy (1842) **Lover, Samuel** (1797–1868) Irish songwriter, painter, writer and dramatist

49 The suspense of a novel is not only in the reader, but in the novelist, who is intensely curious about what will happen to the hero.
Attr. **McCarthy, Mary** (1912–1989) US writer and critic

50 Literature and butterflies are the two sweetest passions known to man.
Radio Times, (1962)

51 A novelist is, like all mortals, more fully at home on the surface of the present than in the ooze of the past.

Strong Opinions (1973) **Nabokov, Vladimir** (1899–1977) Russian-born US writer, poet, translator and critic

52 But is there, I wonder, any such thing as 'pure' literature? Isn't it just a conception of people who look on writing as an escape from the living world? Perhaps a painter, or musician, can cut himself off, in his work, from what's going on around him, but a writer can't.
Fourteen Years ..., Journal entry, (1939) **Palmer, Nettie** (1885–1964) Australian literary critic

53 Great Literature is simply language charged with meaning to the utmost possible degree.
How to Read (1931)

54 Literature is news that STAYS news.
ABC of Reading (1934) **Pound, Ezra** (1885–1972) US poet

55 People think that because a novel's invented, it isn't true. Exactly the reverse is the case. Biography and memoirs can never be wholly true, since they cannot include every conceivable circumstance of what happened. The novel can do that.
Hearing Secret Harmonies (1975) **Powell, Anthony** (1905–2000) English writer and critic

56 Does it or does it not strike you as queer that the people who set you 'courses of study' in English Literature never include the Authorised Version, which not only intrinsically but historically is out and away the greatest book of English Prose? Perhaps they pay you the compliment of supposing that you are perfectly acquainted with it? ... I wonder.
On the Art of Writing (1916) **Quiller-Couch, Sir Arthur ('Q')** (1863–1944) English man of letters

57 Make 'em laugh; make 'em cry; make 'em wait.
Attr. **Reade, Charles** (1814–1884) English novelist and dramatist. Programme for a serial novel

58 Literature is where I go to explore the highest and lowest places in human society and in the human spirit, where I hope to find not absolute truth but the truth of the tale, of the imagination and of the heart.
The Observer, (1989)

59 Means of artistic expression that require large quantities of finance and sophisticated technology – films, plays, records – become, by virtue of that dependence, easy to censor and to control. But what one writer can make in the solitude of one room is something no power can easily destroy.
Index on Censorship, (1996) **Rushdie, Salman** (1947–) Indian-born English author

60 A myth is, of course, not a fairy story. It is the presentation of facts belonging to one category in the idioms appropriate to another. To explode a myth is accordingly not to deny the facts but to re-allocate them.
The Concept of Mind (1949) **Ryle, Gilbert** (1900–1976) English philosopher

61 Without remarking that the thing became a trumpet in his hands, say something relevant about Milton's sonnets.
In Stephen Potter, *The Muse in Chains* (1937) **Saintsbury, George** (1845–1933) English critic and historian. From an examination paper

62 If you really want to hear about it, the first thing you'll probably want to know is where I was born and what my lousy childhood was like, and how my parents were occupied and all before they had me, and all that David Copperfield kind of crap.
The Catcher in the Rye (1951) **Salinger, J.D.** (1919–) US writer

63 One cannot write a novel unless one has something to say about life, and I had nothing to say about it, because I knew nothing.
In Hone, *Dorothy L. Sayers: A Literary Biography* (1979) On *Whose Body?*, 1923, her first book

64 My impression is that I was thinking about writing a detective story, and that he walked in, complete with spats.
Harcourt Brace News, 1936, 'How I came to Invent the Character of Lord Peter' **Sayers, Dorothy L.** (1893–1957) English writer, dramatist and translator

65 But I must say to the Muse of fiction, as the Earl of Pembroke said to the ejected nun of Wilton, 'Go spin, you jade, go spin!'

Journal, (1826) **Scott, Sir Walter** (1771–1832) Scottish writer and historian

66 It is clear that a novel cannot be too bad to be worth publishing ... It certainly is possible for a novel to be too good to be worth publishing.
Plays Pleasant and Unpleasant (1898) **Shaw, George Bernard** (1856–1950) Irish socialist, writer, dramatist and critic

67 I hate Novels, and love Romances. The Praise of the best of the former, their being natural, as it is called, is to me their greatest Demerit.
Letter, (1772) **Sheridan, Richard Brinsley** (1751–1816) Irish dramatist, politician and orator

68 Their teacher had advised them not to read Tolstoy's novels, because they were very long and would only confuse the clear ideas which they had acquired from reading critical studies about him.
The First Circle (1968) **Solzhenitsyn, Alexander** (1918–) Russian writer, dramatist and historian

69 Your true lover of literature is never fastidious.
The Doctor (1812) **Southey, Robert** (1774–1843) English poet, essayist, historian and letterwriter

70 Besides Shakespeare and me, who do you think there is?
In Mellow, *Charmed Circle* (1974) **Stein, Gertrude** (1874–1946) US writer, dramatist, poet and critic. Speaking to a friend she considered knew little about literature

71 Romanticism is the art of presenting people with the literary works which are capable of giving them the greatest possible pleasure, in the present state of their customs and beliefs. Classicism, on the other hand, presents them with the literature that gave the greatest possible pleasure to their great-grandfathers.
Racine et Shakespeare (1823)

72 A novel is a mirror walking along a wide road.
Le Rouge et le Noir (1830) **Stendhal** (1783–1842) French writer, critic and soldier

73 Fiction gives us a second chance that life denies us.
New York Times, (1976) **Theroux, Paul** (1941–) US writer

74 Literature is written according to certain rules, but which rules?
Interview, Waterstones, Glasgow **Tolstoya, Tatyana** (1951–) Russian novelist

75 A novel is a static thing that one moves through; a play is a dynamic thing that moves past one.
Curtains (1961) **Tynan, Kenneth** (1927–1980) English drama critic, producer and essayist

76 Something that everybody wants to have read and nobody wants to read.
'The Disappearance of Literature' **Twain, Mark** (1835–1910) US humorist, writer, journalist and lecturer. Definition of a classic

77 In the dying world I come from quotation is a national vice. It used to be the classics, now it's lyric verse.
The Loved One (1948) **Waugh, Evelyn** (1903–1966) English writer and diarist

78 Movement, that problem of the visible arts, can be truly realized by Literature alone. It is Literature that shows us the body in its swiftness and the soul in its unrest.
'The Critic as Artist' (1891)

79 The good ended happily, and the bad unhappily. That is what Fiction means.
The Importance of Being Earnest (1895) **Wilde, Oscar** (1854–1900) Irish poet, dramatist, writer, critic and wit

80 Literature is the orchestration of platitudes
Time, (1953) **Wilder, Thornton** (1897–1975) US author and playwright

81 A woman must have money and a room of her own if she is to write fiction.
A Room of One's Own (1929)

82 Literature is strewn with the wreckage of men who have minded beyond reason the opinions of others.
A Room of One's Own (1929) **Woolf, Virginia** (1882–1941) English writer and critic

83 All folk literature, and all literature that keeps the folk tradition, delights in unbounded and immortal things.
'The Celtic Element in Literature' (1902)

84 We have no longer in any country a
literature as great as the literature of the
old world, and that is because the
newspapers, all kinds of second-rate books,
the preoccupation of men with all kinds of
practical changes, have driven the living
imagination out of this world.
'First Principles' (1904) **Yeats, W.B.** (1865–
1939) Irish poet, dramatist, editor, writer and
senator
See also art; books; criticism; poetry; theatre
and dance; writing

LOVE

1 Western wind, when wilt thou blow,
The small rain down can rain?
Christ, if my love were in my arms
And I in my bed again!
New Oxford Book of 16th-Century Verse (1991)

2 My lover looked like an eagle from the
distance, but alas
When he came nearer I saw that he was
nothing but a buzzard.
In John Robert Colombo (ed.), *Songs of the
Great Land*, 'Song of a Maiden Disappointed
in Love', Blackfoot poem

3 Let those love now, who never loved
before;
Let those who always loved, now love the
more.
Pervigilium Veneris **Anonymous**

4 Love is, above all else, the gift of oneself.
Ardèle ou la Marguerite (1949) **Anouilh, Jean**
(1910–1987) French dramatist and
screenwriter

5 In an upper room at midnight
See us gathered on behalf
Of love according to the gospel
Of the radio-phonograph.
Nones (1951), 'The Love Feast'

6 When it comes, will it come without warning
Just as I'm picking my nose?
Will it knock on my door in the morning,
Or tread in the bus on my toes?
Will it come like a change in the weather?
Will its greeting be courteous or rough?
Will it alter my life altogether?
O tell me the truth about love.
'Twelve Songs'

7 Stop all the clocks, cut off the telephone,
Prevent the dog from barking with a juicy
bone,
Silence the pianos and with muffled drum
Bring out the coffin, let the mourners
come.
He was my North, my South, my East and
West,
My working week and my Sunday rest,
My noon, my midnight, my talk, my song;
I thought that love would last for ever: I
was wrong.
'Twelve Songs' **Auden, W.H.** (1907–1973)
English poet, essayist, critic, teacher and
dramatist

8 I came to Carthage where a whole frying
pan full of abominable loves crackled about
me on every side. I was not in love yet, yet I
loved to be in love … I was looking for
something to love, in love with love itself.
Confessions (397–398) **Augustine, Saint** (354–430)
Numidian-born Christian theologian and
philosopher

9 All the privilege I claim for my own sex …
is that of loving longest, when existence or
when hope is gone.
Persuasion (1818) **Austen, Jane** (1775–1817)
English writer

10 They do best who, if they cannot but admit
love, yet make it keep quarter; and sever it
wholly from their serious affairs and
actions of life: for if it check once with
business, it troubleth men's fortunes, and
maketh men, that they can no ways be true
to their own ends.
'Of Love' (1625) **Bacon, Francis** (1561–1626)
English philosopher, essayist, politician and
courtier

11 It is easier to be a lover than a husband, for
the same reason that it is more difficult to
show a ready wit all day long than to
produce an occasional bon mot.
Attr. **Balzac, Honoré de** (1799–1850) French
writer

12 My flocks feed not, my ewes breed not,
My rams speed not, all is amiss:
Love is denying, Faith is defying,
Heart's renying, causer of this.
In Nicholas Ling (ed.), *England's Helicon* (1600)
Barnfield, Richard (1574–1627) English poet

13 Oh, what a dear ravishing thing is the beginning of an Amour!
The Emperor of the Moon (1687) **Behn, Aphra** (1640–1689) English dramatist, writer, poet, translator and spy

14 I don't know how to kiss, or I would kiss you. Where do the noses go?
For Whom The Bell Tolls, (1943) **Bergman, Ingrid** (1915–1982) Swedish-born Hollywood actress. As Maria, to Gary Cooper's Robert Jordan

15 Hell, madam, is to love no longer.
The Diary of a Country Priest (1936) **Bernanos, Georges** (1888–1948) French novelist and essayist

16 'Let us not speak, for the love we bear one another –
Let us hold hands and look.'
She, such a very ordinary little woman;
He, such a thumping crook;
But both, for a moment, little lower than the angels
In the teashop's ingle-nook.
New Bats in Old Belfries (1945) **Betjeman, Sir John** (1906–1984) English poet laureate

17 And Jacob served seven years for Rachel; and they seemed unto him but a few days, for the love he had to her.
Genesis, 29:20

18 Intreat me not to leave thee, or to return from following after thee: for whither thou goest, I will go; and where thou lodgest, I will lodge: thy people shall be my people, and thy God my God.
Ruth, 1:16–17

19 Greater love hath no man than this, that a man lay down his life for his friends.
John, 15:13

20 Love your enemies, bless them that curse you, do good to them that hate you, and pray for them which despitefully use you, and persecute you.
Matthew, 5:44

21 He that loveth not knoweth not God; for God is love.
I John, 4:8

22 Perfect love casteth out fear.
I John, 4:18 **The Bible (King James Version)**

23 Perhaps it was right to dissemble your love,
But – why did you kick me downstairs?
'An Expostulation' (1789) **Bickerstaffe, Isaac** (c.1733–c.1808) Irish dramatist and author of ballad operas

24 Children of the future Age,
Reading this indignant page:
Know that in a former time,
Love! sweet Love! was thought a crime.
'A Little Girl Lost' (1794)

25 Love seeketh not Itself to please,
Nor for itself hath any care;
But for another gives its ease,
And builds a Heaven in Hells despair.
'The Clod & the Pebble' (1794) **Blake, William** (1757–1827) English poet, engraver, painter and mystic

26 She was an Amazon. Her whole life was spent riding at breakneck speed towards the wilder shores of love.
The Wilder Shores of Love (1954) **Blanch, Lesley** (1907–) British biographer and travel writer. Of Jane Digby who was successively Lady Ellenborough, Baroness Venningen, Countess Theotoky and the wife of Sheik Abdul Medjuel El Mezrab

27 Who can give a law to lovers? Love is a greater law unto itself.
De Consolatione Philosophiae (c.522–524) **Boethius** (c.475–524) Roman statesman, scholar and philosopher

28 If you want to win her hand,
Let the maiden understand
That's she's not the only pebble on the beach.
'You're Not the Only Pebble on the Beach' **Braisted, Harry** (19th century) Songwriter

29 My heart was wandering in the sands,
A restless thing, a scorn apart;
Love set his fire in my hands,
I clasped the flame into my heart.
Poems (1914) **Brennan, Christopher** (1870–1932) Australian poet

30 I never liked the men I loved, and never loved the men I liked.

In Norman Katkov, *The Fabulous Fanny* (1952)
Brice, Fanny (1891–1951) US singer and comedian

31 Awake, my heart, to be loved, awake, awake!
'Awake, My Heart, To be Loved' (1890)

32 When first we met we did not guess
That Love would prove so hard a master.
'Triolet' (1890) **Bridges, Robert** (1844–1930)
English poet, dramatist, essayist and doctor

33 I thought when love for you died, I should die.
It's dead. Alone, most strangely, I live on.
'The Life Beyond' (1910) **Brooke, Rupert**
(1887–1915) English poet

34 How do I love thee? Let me count the ways.
Sonnets from the Portuguese (1850) **Browning,
Elizabeth Barrett** (1806–1861) English poet;
wife of Robert Browning

35 To be overtopped in anything else, I can
bear: but in the tests of generous love, I
defy all mankind!
Letter to Clarinda, (1788)

36 Ae fond kiss, and then we sever!
Ae fareweel, and then forever! ...
But to see her was to love her,
Love but her, and love for ever.
Had we never lov'd sae kindly,
Had we never lov'd sae blindly,
Never met – or never parted –
We had ne'er been broken-hearted.
'Ae Fond Kiss' (1791)

37 O Luve will venture in where it daur na
weel be seen!
'The Posie' (1792)

38 O, my luve's like a red, red, rose
That's newly sprung in June.
O, my luve's like the melodie,
That's sweetly play'd in tune.
'A Red Red Rose' (1794) **Burns, Robert** (1759–
1796) Scottish poet and songwriter

39 No chord, nor cable can so forcibly draw,
or hold so fast, as love can do with a
twined thread.
Anatomy of Melancholy (1621) **Burton, Robert**
(1577–1640) English clergyman and writer

40 For money has a power above
The stars and fate, to manage love.
Hudibras (1678)

41 All love at first, like generous wine,
Ferments and frets until 'tis fine;
But when 'tis settled on the lee,
And from th' impurer matter free,
Becomes the richer still the older,
And proves the pleasanter the colder.
Miscellaneous Thoughts **Butler, Samuel (poet)**
(1612–1680) English poet

42 God is Love, I dare say. But what a
mischievous devil Love is.
The Note-Books of Samuel Butler (1912)

43 'Tis better to have loved and lost than
never to have lost at all.
The Way of All Flesh (1903) **Butler, Samuel**
(1835–1902) English writer, painter,
philosopher and scholar

44 In her first passion woman loves her lover,
In all the others all she loves is love.
Don Juan (1824)

45 Even innocence itself has many a wile,
And will not dare to trust itself with truth,
And love is taught hypocrisy from youth.
Don Juan (1824) **Byron, Lord** (1788–1824)
English poet, satirist and traveller

46 Better be courted and jilted
Than never be courted at all.
'The Jilted Nymph' (1843) **Campbell, Thomas**
(1777–1844) Scottish poet, ballad writer and
journalist

47 But what a woman says to her eager lover,
she ought to write in the wind and the
running water.
Carmina **Catullus** (84–c.54 BC) Roman poet

48 In our life there is a single colour, as on an
artist's palette, which provides the
meaning of life and art. It is the colour of
love.
Newsweek, (1985) **Chagall, Marc** (1887–1985)
Russian-born French painter

49 Love, as it exists in society, is nothing more
than the exchange of two fantasies and the
contact of two skins.
Maximes et pensées (1796) **Chamfort, Nicolas**
(1741–1794) French writer

50 If grass can grow through cement, love can find you at every time in your life.
The Times, (1998) **Cher** (1946–) US singer and actress

51 Many a man has fallen in love with a girl in a light so dim he would not have chosen a suit by it.
Attr. **Chevalier, Maurice** (1888–1972) French singer and actor

52 Language has not the power to speak what love indites:
The soul lies buried in the ink that writes.
Attr. **Clare, John** (1793–1864) English rural poet; died in an asylum

53 Love and a cottage! Eh, Fanny! Ah, give me indifference and a coach and six!
The Clandestine Marriage (1766) **Colman, the Elder, George** (1732–1794) English dramatist and theatrical manager

54 In my conscience I believe the baggage loves me, for she never speaks well of me her self, nor suffers any body else to rail me.
The Old Bachelor (1693) **Congreve, William** (1670–1729) English dramatist

55 Friendship often ends in love; but love in friendship – never.
Lacon (1820) **Colton, Charles Caleb** (c.1780–1832) English clergyman and satirist

56 Romeo was, like, a gigolo who falls for this girl Juliet, who says, 'Look, if you've got the balls, put them on the table.'
The Observer, (1998) **DiCaprio, Leonardo** (1974–) US film actor

57 They say that love takes wit away from those who have it, and gives it to those who have none.
Paradoxe sur le Comédien (1830) **Diderot, Denis** (1713–1784) French philosopher, encyclopaedist, writer and dramatist

58 Latins are tenderly enthusiastic. In Brazil they throw flowers at you. In Argentina they throw themselves.
Newsweek, (1959) **Dietrich, Marlene** (1901–1992) German-born US actress and singer

59 Love built on beauty, soon as beauty dies.
Elegies (c.1595)

60 Who ever loves, if he do not propose
The right true end of love, he's one that goes
To sea for nothing but to make him sick.
Elegies (c.1600)

61 Just such disparity
As is 'twixt Air and Angels' purity,
'Twixt women's love and men's will ever be.
Songs and Sonnets (1611)

62 I wonder by my troth, what thou, and I
Did, till we lov'd?
Songs and Sonnets (1611)

63 Chang'd loves are but chang'd sorts of meat,
And when he hath the kernel eat,
Who doth not fling away the shell?
Songs and Sonnets (1611)

64 I am two fools, I know,
For loving, and for saying so,
In whining poetry.
'The Triple Fool' **Donne, John** (1572–1631) English poet

65 I am the Love that dare not speak its name.
'Two Loves' (1896) **Douglas, Lord Alfred** (1870–1945) English poet; intimate of Oscar Wilde

66 Since there's no help, come let us kiss and part,
Nay, I have done: you get no more of me,
And I am glad, yea glad with all my heart,
That thus so cleanly, I myself can free,
Shake hands for ever, cancel all our vows,
And when we meet at any time again,
Be it not seen in either of our brows,
That we one jot of former love retain;
Now at the last gasp of love's latest breath,
When his pulse failing, passion speechless lies,
When faith is kneeling by his bed of death,
And innocence is closing up his eyes,
Now if thou wouldst, when all have given him over,
From death to life, thou might'st him yet recover.
'Idea', 61 (1619) **Drayton, Michael** (1563–1631) English poet

67 Pains of love be sweeter far
Than all other pleasures are.
Tyrannic Love (1669)

68 For, Heaven be thanked, we live in such an age,
When no man dies for love, but on the stage.
Mithridates (1678) **Dryden, John** (1631–1700) English poet, satirist, dramatist and critic

69 Love is friendship plus sex.
Attr. **Ellis, Havelock** (1859–1939) English sexologist and essayist

70 When love grows diseased, the best thing we can do is put it to a violent death; I cannot endure the torture of a lingering and consumptive passion.
The Man of Mode (1676) **Etherege, Sir George** (c.1635–1691) English dramatist

71 Money is the sinews of love, as of war.
Love and a Bottle (1698) **Farquhar, George** (1678–1707) Irish dramatist

72 Vera, who had carefully educated herself in the arts of love, did not believe that this sacred art, whose purpose was to unite her not only with her lover but with the earth and the firmament, too, should take place in the Western manner which to her resembled nothing so much as a pair of drunken rickshaw coolies colliding briefly at some foggy crossroads at the dead of night.
The Singapore Grip (1979) **Farrell, J.G.** (1935–1979) English novelist

73 Love and scandal are the best sweeteners of tea.
Love in Several Masques (1728) **Fielding, Henry** (1707–1754) English writer, dramatist and journalist

74 Love is like linen; often chang'd, the sweeter.
Sicelides (1614) **Fletcher, Phineas** (1582–1650) English poet and clergyman

75 Love's pleasure only lasts a moment; love's sorrow lasts one's whole life long.
'Célestine' (1784) **Florian, Jean-Pierre Claris de** (1755–1794) French writer

76 Only connect! That was the whole of her sermon. Only connect the prose and the passion, and both will be exalted, and human love will be seen at its highest.
Howard's End (1910) **Forster, E.M.** (1879–1970) English writer, essayist and literary critic

77 The having made a young girl miserable may give you frequent bitter reflection; none of which can attend the making of an old woman happy.
On the Choice of a Mistress **Franklin, Benjamin** (1706–1790) US statesman, scientist, political critic and printer

78 Oh, the unholy mantrap of love!
The Lady's not for Burning (1949)

79 Try thinking of love, or something.
Amor vincit insomnia.
A Sleep of Prisoners (1951) **Fry, Christopher** (1907–2005) English verse dramatist, theatre director and translator

80 Would you gain the tender Creature?
Softly, gently, kindly treat her;
Suff'ring is the Lover's Part.
Beauty by Constraint possessing,
You enjoy but half the Blessing,
Lifeless Charms, without the Heart.
Acis and Galatea (1718)

81 Can Love be controll'd by advice?
Dione (1720)

82 Then nature rul'd, and love, devoid of art,
Spoke the consenting language of the heart.
The Captives (1724)

83 She who has never lov'd, has never liv'd.
The Beggar's Opera (1728)

84 Pretty Polly, say,
When I was away,
Did your fancy never stray
To some newer lover?
The Beggar's Opera (1728)

85 How happy could I be with either,
Were t'other dear charmer away!
The Beggar's Opera (1728) **Gay, John** (1685–1732) English poet, dramatist and librettist

86 Love has no other desire but to fulfil itself.
But if you love and must needs have
desires, let these be your desires:
To melt and be like the running brook that
sings its melody to the night.
To know the pain of too much tenderness.
To be wounded by your own
understanding of love;
And to bleed willingly and joyfully.
To wake at dawn with a winged heart and
give thanks for another day of loving;
To rest at the noon hour and meditate
love's ecstasy;
To return home at eventide with gratitude;
And then to sleep with a prayer for the
beloved in your heart and a song of praise
upon your lips ...
Love one another, but make not a bond of
love:
Let it be rather a moving sea between the
shores of your souls ...
Let each one of you be alone,
Even as the strings of the lute are alone
though they quiver with the same music ...
Stand together yet not too near together:
For the pillars of the temple stand apart,
And the oak tree and the cypress grow not
in each other's shadow.
The Prophet (1923) **Gibran, Kahlil** (1883–1931)
Lebanese poet, mystic and painter

87 It seemed to me pretty plain, that they had
more of love than matrimony in them.
The Vicar of Wakefield (1766) **Goldsmith, Oliver**
(c.1728–1774) Irish dramatist, poet and writer

88 Love is always a bit deceitful,
Truth always struggles with it,
We wait long for a woman worthy of it,
And we wait in vain.
In *Samara Gazette*, (1895) **Gorky, Maxim** (1868–
1936) Russian writer, dramatist and
revolutionary

89 It hath and schal ben evermor
That love is maister wher he wile.
'Confessio Amantis' (1390) **Gower, John**
(c.1330–1408) English poet

90 I'll be this abject thing no more;
Love, give me back my heart again.
'Adieu l'Amour'

91 O Love! thou bane of the most generous
souls!
Thou doubtful pleasure, and thou certain
pain.
'Heroic Love' **Granville, George** (1666–1735)
English poet, dramatist and politician

92 In love as in sport, the amateur status must
be strictly maintained.
Attr.

93 Down, wanton, down! Have you no shame
That at the whisper of Love's name,
Or Beauty's, presto! up you raise
Your angry head and stand at gaze?
'Down, Wanton, Down' **Graves, Robert** (1895–
1985) English poet, writer, critic, translator
and mythologist

94 Love, love, love – all the wretched cant of it,
masking egotism, lust, masochism, fantasy
under a mythology of sentimental
postures, a welter of self induced miseries
and joys, blinding and masking the
essential personalities in the frozen
gestures of courtship, in the kissing and
the dating and the desire, the compliments
and the quarrels which vivify its
barrenness.
The Female Eunuch (1970) **Greer, Germaine**
(1939–) Australian feminist, critic, English
scholar and writer

95 Love is a snowmobile racing across the
tundra and then suddenly it flips over,
pinning you underneath. At night, the ice
weasels come.
Attr. **Groening, Matt** (1954–) US cartoonist

96 'My heart, I want to ask you:
What is love? Tell me!' –
'Two souls with just one thought,
Two hearts with just one beat.'
The Son of the Wilderness, (1842) **Halm,
Friedrich** (1806–1871) Austrian dramatist and
poet

97 A lover without indiscretion is no lover at
all.
The Hand of Ethelberta (1876)

98 Love is lame at fifty years.
'The Revisitation' (1904) **Hardy, Thomas**
(1840–1928) English writer and poet

99 When we are young, she thought, we
worship romantic love for the wrong
reasons ... and, because of that,
subsequently repudiate it. Only later, and
for quite other reasons, we discover its true
importance. And by then it has become
tiring even to observe.
The Evening of a Holiday (1966) **Hazzard,
Shirley** (1931–) Australian writer

100 And in that dream I dreamt – how like you
this? –
Our first night years ago in that hotel
When you came with your deliberate kiss
To raise us towards the lovely and painful
Covenants of flesh; our separateness;
The respite in our dewy dreaming faces.
Field Work (1979) **Heaney, Seamus** (1939–)
Irish poet

101 Love is just another dirty lie. ... I know
about love. Love always hangs up behind
the bath-room door. It smells like lysol. To
hell with love.
To Have and Have Not (1937) **Hemingway,
Ernest** (1898–1961) US author

102 O that our love might take no end,
Or never had beginning took! ...
For where God doth admit the fair,
Think you that he excludeth Love?
'An Ode upon a Question moved, Whether
Love should continue for ever?' (1665)
Herbert, Edward (1583–1648) English
statesman, poet and philosopher

103 Love bade me welcome; yet my soul drew
back,
Guiltie of dust and sinne.
But quick-ey'd Love, observing me grow
slack
From my first entrance in,
Drew nearer to me, sweetly questioning
If I lack'd any thing ...
Love took my hand, and smiling did reply,
Who made the eyes but I?
The Temple (1633) **Herbert, George** (1593–1633)
English poet and priest

104 I wouldn't be too ladylike in love if I were
you.
'I Wouldn't be Too Ladylike' **Herbert, Sir A.P.**
(1890–1971) English humorist, writer,
dramatist and politician

105 Thou art my life, my love, my heart,
The very eyes of me:
And hast command of every part,
To live and die for thee.
Hesperides (1648)

106 You say, to me - wards your affection's
strong;
Pray love me little, so you love me long.
Hesperides (1648)

107 Give me a kiss, add to that kiss a score;
Then to that twenty, add an hundred more:
A thousand to that hundred: so kiss on,
To make that thousand up a million.
Treble that million, and when that is done,
Let's kiss afresh, as when we first begun.
Hesperides (1648)

108 Love is a circle that doth restlesse move
In the same sweet eternity of love.
Hesperides (1648) **Herrick, Robert** (1591–1674)
English poet, royalist and clergyman

109 My body turns to you as the earth turns.
O for such bitter need you've taken me,
To dub me lover, friend and enemy,
Take neither one can set the other free.
But still there is a loveliness that burns
That burns between us two so tenderly.
'There is a Loveliness that Burns' **Hewett,
Dorothy** (1923–2002) Australian dramatist and
poet

110 O, love, love, love!
Love is like a dizziness;
It winna let a poor body
Gang about his biziness!
'Love is Like a Dizziness' **Hogg, James** (1770–
1835) Scottish poet, ballad writer and writer

111 Now I go to films alone
watch a silent telephone
send myself a valentine
whisper softly 'I am mine'.
'Men, Who Needs Them' **Hudson, Louise**
(1958–) English poet and editor

112 So far I fallen was in loves dance,
That suddenly my wit, my countenance,
My heart, my will, my nature, and my
mind
Was changit right clean in another kind.
The Kingis Quair **James I of Scotland** (1394–
1437) King of Scotland

113 Love is like the measles; we all have to go through it.
Idle Thoughts of an Idle Fellow (1886) **Jerome, Jerome K.** (1859–1927) English writer and dramatist

114 Love's like the measles – all the worse when it comes late in life.
Wit and Opinions of Douglas Jerrold (1859) **Jerrold, Douglas William** (1803–1857) English dramatist, writer and wit

115 Drink to me only with thine eyes,
And I will pledge with mine;
Or leave a kiss upon the cup,
And I'll not look for wine.
The Forest (1616) **Jonson, Ben** (1572–1637) English dramatist and poet

116 Wouldest thou wit thy Lord's meaning in this thing? Wit it well: Love was his meaning. Who shewed it thee? Love. What shewed He thee? Love. Wherefore shewed it He? for Love … Thus was I learned that Love is our Lord's meaning.
Revelations of Divine Love (1393) **Juliana of Norwich** (c.1343–c.1429) English mystic

117 Love is, that you are the knife which I plunge into myself.
Letter to Milena Jesenká, (1920) **Kafka, Franz** (1883–1924) Czech-born German-speaking writer

118 I never was in love – yet the voice and the shape of a Woman has haunted me these two days.
Letter to J.H. Reynolds, (22 September 1818)

119 I long to believe in immortality … If I am destined to be happy with you here – how short is the longest Life. I wish to believe in immortality – I wish to live with you for ever.
Letter to Fanny Brawne, (July 1820)

120 I wish you could invent some means to make me at all happy without you. Every hour I am more and more concentrated in you; every thing else tastes like chaff in my Mouth.
Letter to Fanny Brawne, (1820) **Keats, John** (1795–1821) English poet

121 Love is moral even without legal marriage, but marriage is immoral without love.
'The Morality of Women' (1911) **Key, Ellen** (1849–1926) Swedish feminist, writer and lecturer

122 I'm past the seven-year itch. When you're loved for your flaws, that's when you feel really safe.
The Observer, (1998) **Kidman, Nicole** (1967–) Australian actress

123 There are very few people who are not ashamed of having loved one another once they have fallen out of love.
Maximes (1678)

124 If love is to be judged by most of its effects, it looks more like hatred than like friendship.
Maximes (1678) **La Rochefoucauld** (1613–1680) French writer

125 Only one being is missing, and your whole world is bereft of people.
Premières Méditations poétiques (1820) **Lamartine, Alphonse de** (1790–1869) French poet, historian, royalist and statesman

126 What will survive of us is love.
'An Arundel Tomb' (1964) **Larkin, Philip** (1922–1985) English poet, writer and librarian

127 I love a lassie, a bonnie, bonnie lassie,
She's as pure as a lily in the dell.
She's as sweet as the heather,
The bonnie, bloomin' heather,
Mary, my Scotch Blue-bell.
'I Love a Lassie' (Song) **Lauder, Sir Harry** (1870–1950) Scottish music-hall entertainer

128 I loved you, so I drew these tides of men into my hands
and wrote my will across the sky in stars
To earn you Freedom, the seven pillared worthy house,
that your eyes might be shining for me
When we came.
The Seven Pillars of Wisdom (1926) **Lawrence, T.E.** (1888–1935) British soldier, archaeologist, translator and writer; known as 'Lawrence of Arabia'

129 To give up another person's love is a mild suicide.
Tarr (1918) **Lewis, Wyndham** (1882–1957) US-born British painter, critic and writer

130 The best love affairs are those we never had.
Bohemians of the Bulletin (1965) **Lindsay, Norman** (1879–1969) Australian artist and writer

131 Love, in my bosom, like a bee,
Doth suck his sweet.
'Love, In My Bosom' (1590) **Lodge, Thomas** (1558–1625) English poet

132 When Love with unconfined wings
Hovers within my gates;
And my divine Althea brings
To whisper at the grates:
When I lie tangled in her hair,
And fettered to her eye;
The Gods, that wanton in the air,
Know no such liberty.
'To Althea, From Prison' (1649)

133 True; a new mistress now I chase,
The first foe in the field;
And with a stronger faith embrace
A sword, a horse, a shield.
Yet this inconstancy is such,
As you too shall adore;
I could not love thee (Dear) so much,
Lov'd I not honour more.
'To Lucasta, Going to the Wars' (1649)
Lovelace, Richard (1618–1658) English poet

134 Two souls with but a single thought,
Two hearts that beat as one.
Ingomar the Barbarian **Lovell, Maria** (1803–1877) English actress and playwright

135 How alike are the groans of love to those of the dying.
Under the Volcano (1947) **Lowry, Malcolm** (1909–1957) English writer and poet

136 Love is mor than gold or gret richesse.
'The Story of Thebes' (c.1420) **Lydgate, John** (c.1370–c.1451) English monk, poet and translator

137 It is very rarely that a man loves
And when he does it is nearly always fatal.
'The International Brigade' (1957)
MacDiarmid, Hugh (1892–1978) Scottish poet

138 My heart is a lonely hunter that hunts on a lonely hill.

'The Lonely Hunter' (1896) **MacLeod, Fiona (William Sharp)** (1855–1905) Scottish poet, novelist and dramatist

139 Where both deliberate, the love is slight;
Who ever loved that loved not at first sight?
Hero and Leander (1598), First Sestiad

140 Come live with me, and be my love,
And we will all the pleasures prove.
'The Passionate Shepherd to his Love'
Marlowe, Christopher (1564–1593) English poet and dramatist

141 Therefore the love which us doth bind,
But Fate so enviously debars,
Is the conjunction of the mind,
And opposition of the stars.
'The Definition of Love' (1681) **Marvell, Andrew** (1621–1678) English poet and satirist

142 The love that lasts the longest is the love that is never returned.
A Writer's Notebook (1949) **Maugham, William Somerset** (1909–1957) English author

143 Love me, and never leave me,
Love, nor ever deceive me,
And I shall always bless you
If I may undress you:
This I heard a lover say
To his sweetheart where they lay.
He, though he did undress her,
Did not always bless her;
She, though she would not leave him,
Often did deceive him;
Yet they loved, and when they died
They were buried side by side.
'Love Me and Never Leave Me' (1930)
McCuaig, Ronald (1908–1990) Australian journalist and poet

144 She whom I love is hard to catch and conquer,
Hard, but O the glory of the winning were she won!
'Love in the Valley' (1883) **Meredith, George** (1828–1909) English writer, poet and critic

145 I never heard
Of any true affection, but 'twas nipt
With care.
Blurt, Master-Constable (1602) **Middleton, Thomas** (c.1580–1627) English dramatist

146 This have I known always: Love is no more
Than the wide blossom which the wind assails,
Than the great tide that treads the shifting shore,
Strewing fresh wreckage gathered in the gales:
Pity me that the heart is slow to learn
What the swift mind beholds at every turn.
The Harp-Weaver and Other Poems (1923)
Millay, Edna St Vincent (1892–1950) US poet and dramatist

147 Nor jealousie
Was understood, the injur'd Lover's Hell.
Paradise Lost (1667) **Milton, John** (1608–1674)
English poet, libertarian and pamphleteer

148 Like all the very young we took it for granted that making love is child's play.
The Pursuit of Love (1945) **Mitford, Nancy** (1904–1973) English writer

149 One is easily taken in by what one loves.
Tartuffe (1664) **Molière** (1622–1673) French dramatist, actor and director

150 No, there's nothing half so sweet in life
As love's young dream.
Irish Melodies (1807) **Moore, Thomas** (1779–1852) Irish poet

151 Love is enough: though the world be a-waning,
And the woods have no voice but the voice of complaining.
'Love is Enough' (1872) **Morris, William** (1834–1896) English poet, designer, craftsman, artist and socialist

152 So that love is possible, God must be a person – In love, one endures more than at other times, one tolerates everything.
Der Antichrist (1888)

153 There is always some madness in love. But there is also always some reason in madness.
On Reading and Writing **Nietzsche, Friedrich Wilhelm** (1844–1900) German philosopher, critic and poet

154 Oh, shadows of love, inebriations of love, foretastes of love, trickles of love, but never yet the one true love.

Night (1972) **O'Brien, Edna** (1936–) Irish writer and dramatist

155 You who seek an end to love, love will yield to business: be busy, and you will be safe.
Remedia Amoris **Ovid** (43 BC–AD 18) Roman poet

156 Oh, life is a glorious cycle of song,
A medley of extemporanea;
And love is a thing that can never go wrong,
And I am Marie of Roumania.
Not So Deep as a Well (1937) **Parker, Dorothy** (1893–1967) US writer, poet, critic and wit

157 Two children playing by a stream
Two lovers walking in a dream
A married pair whose dream is o'er,
Two old folks who are quite a bore.
'Love's Four Ages' **Parnell, Anna** (1852–1911) Irish politician

158 So, till to-morrow eve, my Own, adieu!
Parting's well-paid with soon again to meet,
Soon in your arms to feel so small and sweet,
Sweet to myself that am so sweet to you!
The Unknown Eros (1877), 'The Azalea' **Patmore, Coventry** (1823–1896) English poet

159 Love, smeared across his face, like a road accident.
Grinning Jack (1990), 'Schoolboy' **Patten, Brian** (1946–) British poet

160 Have you ever been in love, me boys
Oh! have you felt the pain,
I'd rather be in jail, I would,
Than be in love again.
'The Garden where the Praties Grow' **Patterson, Johnny** (1840–1889) Irish musician and songwriter

161 What thing is love for (well I wot) love is a thing.
It is a prick, it is a sting,
It is a pretty, pretty thing;
It is a fire, it is a coal
Whose flame creeps in at every hole.
'The Hunting of Cupid' (c.1591) **Peele, George** (c.1558–c.1597) English dramatist and poet

162 And we knew all that stream,
And our two horses had traced out the
valleys;
Knew the low flooded lands squared out
with poplars,
In the young days when the deep sky
befriended.
And great wings beat above us in the
twilight,
And the great wheels in heaven
Bore us together ... surging ... and
apart ...
Believing we should meet with lips and
hands,
High, high and sure ... and then the
counter-thrust:
'Why do you love me? Will you always love
me?
But I am like the grass, I cannot love you.'
'Near Perigord' (1915) **Pound, Ezra** (1885–1972)
US poet

163 I court others in verse: but I love thee in
prose:
And they have my whimsies, but thou hast
my heart.
'A Better Answer' (1718) **Prior, Matthew** (1664–
1721) English poet

164 Water may be older than light, diamonds
crack in hot goat's blood, mountaintops
give off cold fire, forests appear in mid-
ocean, it may happen that a crab is caught
with the shadow of a hand on its back, that
the wind be imprisoned in a bit of knotted
string. And it may be that love sometimes
occurs without pain or misery.
The Shipping News (1993) **Proulx, E. Annie**
(1935–) US writer

165 There can be no peace of mind in love,
since the advantage one has secured is
never anything but a fresh starting-point
for further desires.
À l'ombre des jeunes filles en fleurs (1918)

166 *A pretentious lady*: What are your views on
love?
Mme Leroi: I often make love but I never
talk about it.
Le Côté de Guermantes (1921)

167 It is wrong to speak of making a bad choice
in love, since as soon as there is choice, it
can only be bad.

La Fugitive (1923) **Proust, Marcel** (1871–1922)
French writer and critic

168 Ah, I have loved him too much not to hate
him!
Andromaque (1667)

169 I loved you inconstant; what would I have
done had you been faithful?
Andromaque (1667) **Racine, Jean** (1639–1699)
French tragedian and poet

170 Now what is love? I pray thee, tell.
It is that fountain and that well,
Where pleasure and repentance dwell.
It is perhaps that saucing bell,
That tolls all in to heaven or hell:
And this is love, as I hear tell.
'A Description of Love' **Raleigh, Sir Walter**
(c.1552–1618) English courtier, explorer,
military commander, poet, historian and
essayist

171 That cordial drop heaven in our cup has
thrown
To make the nauseous draught of life go
down.
'A letter from Artemisa in the Town to Chloe
in the Country' (1679) **Rochester, Earl of**
(1647–1680) English poet, satirist, courtier and
libertine

172 Oh! she was good as she was fair.
None – none on earth above her!
As pure in thought as angels are,
To know her was to love her.
Jacqueline (1814)

173 But there are moments which he calls his
own,
Then, never less alone than when alone,
Those whom he loved so long and sees no
more,
Loved and still loves – not dead – but gone
before,
He gathers round him.
'Human Life' (1819) **Rogers, Samuel** (1763–
1855) English poet

174 My heart is like a singing bird
Whose nest is in a watered shoot;
My heart is like an apple-tree
Whose boughs are bent with thickset fruit;
My heart is like a rainbow shell
That paddles in a halcyon sea;
My heart is gladder than all these
Because my love is come to me.

'A Birthday' (1862) **Rossetti, Christina** (1830–1894) English poet

175 Of all forms of caution, caution in love is perhaps the most fatal to true happiness.
Marriage and Morals (1929) **Russell, Bertrand** (1872–1970) English philosopher, mathematician, essayist and social reformer

176 Every little girl knows about love. It is only her capacity to suffer because of it that increases.
Daily Express **Sagan, Françoise** (1935–) French writer

177 Experience shows us that love is not looking into one another's eyes but looking together in the same direction.
Wind, Sand and Stars (1939) **Saint-Exupéry, Antoine de** (1900–1944) French author and aviator

178 Romance at short notice was her speciality.
Beasts and Super-Beasts (1914) **Saki** (1870–1916) Burmese-born British writer

179 Liszt said to me today that God alone deserves to be loved. It may be true, but when one has loved a man it is very different to love God.
Intimate Journal (1929) **Sand, George** (1804–1876) French writer and dramatist

180 Luve is ane fervent fire,
Kendillit without desire;
Short pleisure, lang displeisure,
Repentence is the hire;
Ane puir treisure without meisure.
Luve is ane fervent fire.
'A Rondel of Luve' (c.1568) **Scott, Alexander** (c.1525–c.1584) Scottish poet

181 True love's the gift which God has given
To man alone beneath the heaven:
It is the secret sympathy,
The silver link, the silken tie,
Which heart to heart, and mind to mind,
In body and in soul can bind.
The Lay of the Last Minstrel (1805) **Scott, Sir Walter** (1771–1832) Scottish writer and historian

182 Why then should I seek farther store,
And still make love anew;
When change itself can give no more,
'Tis easy to be true.

'To Celia'

183 Love still has something of the Sea
From whence his Mother rose.
'Song: Love still has Something' **Sedley, Sir Charles** (c.1639–1701) English poet

184 Love means never having to say you're sorry.
Love Story (1970) **Segal, Erich** (1937–) US writer

185 *Cleopatra*: If it be love indeed, tell me how much.
Antony: There's beggary in the love that can be reckon'd.
Cleopatra: I'll set a bourn how far to be belov'd.
Antony: Then must thou needs find out new heaven, new earth.
Antony and Cleopatra, I.i

186 Eternity was in our lips and eyes,
Bliss in our brows' bent.
Antony and Cleopatra, I.iii

187 We that are true lovers run into strange capers.
As You Like It, II.iv

188 It is as easy to count atomies as to resolve the propositions of a lover.
As You Like It, III.ii

189 Men have died from time to time, and worms have eaten them, but not for love.
As You Like It, IV.i

190 Your brother and my sister no sooner met but they look'd;
no sooner look'd but they lov'd;
no sooner lov'd but they sigh'd;
no sooner sigh'd but they ask'd one another the reason;
no sooner knew the reason but they sought the remedy –
and in these degrees have they made a pair of stairs to marriage,
which they will climb incontinent, or else be incontinent before marriage.
As You Like, It V.ii

191 Doubt thou the stars are fire;
Doubt that the sun doth move;
Doubt truth to be a liar;
But never doubt I love.
Hamlet, II.ii

192 Love is blind, and lovers cannot see
The pretty follies that themselves commit.
The Merchant of Venice, II.vi

193 Love looks not with the eyes, but with the mind;
And therefore is wing'd Cupid painted blind.
A Midsummer Night's Dream, I.i

194 Ay me! for aught that I could ever read,
Could ever hear by tale or history,
The course of true love never did run smooth.
A Midsummer Night's Dream, I.i

195 I thank God, and my cold blood, I am of your humour for that: I had rather hear my dog bark at a crow than a man swear he loves me.
Much Ado About Nothing, I.i

196 My bounty is as boundless as the sea,
My love as deep: the more I give to thee,
The more I have, for both are infinite.
Romeo and Juliet, II.ii

197 Parting is such sweet sorrow
That I shall say good night till it be morrow.
Romeo and Juliet, II.ii

198 Love goes toward love as school-boys from their books;
But love from love, toward school with heavy looks.
Romeo and Juliet, II.ii

199 Let me not to the marriage of true minds
Admit impediments. Love is not love
Which alters when it alteration finds,
Or bends with the remover to remove.
Sonnet 116

200 When my love swears that she is made of truth,
I do believe her, though I know she lies.
Sonnet 138

201 Love's fire heats water, water cools not love.
Sonnet 154

202 Women are angels, wooing:
Things won are done; joy's soul lies in the doing.
That she belov'd knows nought that knows not this:
Men prize the thing ungain'd more than it is.
Troilus and Cressida, I.ii

203 To be wise and love
Exceeds man's might.
Troilus and Cressida, III.ii

204 This is the monstruosity in love, lady, that the will is infinite, and the execution confin'd; that the desire is boundless, and the act a slave to limit.
Troilus and Cressida, III.ii

205 Fie, fie, how wayward is this foolish love,
That like a testy babe will scratch the nurse,
And presently, all humbled, kiss the rod!
Two Gentlemen of Verona, I.ii

206 She never told her love,
But let concealment, like a worm i' th' bud,
Feed on her damask cheek. She pin'd in thought;
And with a green and yellow melancholy
She sat like Patience on a monument,
Smiling at grief. Was not this love indeed?
We men may say more, swear more, but indeed
Our shows are more than will; for still we prove
Much in our vows, but little in our love.
Twelfth Night, II.iv

207 Love sought is good, but given unsought is better.
Twelfth Night, III.i **Shakespeare, William**
(1564–1616) English dramatist, poet and actor

208 The fickleness of the women I love is only equalled by the infernal constancy of the women who love me.
The Philanderer (1898) **Shaw, George Bernard**
(1856–1950) Irish socialist, writer, dramatist and critic

209 Familiar acts are beautiful through love.
Prometheus Unbound (1820) **Shelley, Percy Bysshe** (1792–1822) English poet, dramatist and essayist

210 My true Love hathe my harte and I have his,
By just exchaunge one for the other given,
I holde his deare, and myne hee can not misse,
There never was a better Bargayne driven.
Old Arcadia (1581)

211 They love indeede who dare not say they love.
Astrophel and Stella (1591) **Sidney, Sir Philip**
(1554–1586) English poet, critic, soldier, courtier and diplomat

212 'Tis very surprising that love should act so inconsistent with itself, as to deprive its votaries of the use of their faculties, when they have most occasion for them.
The Adventures of Roderick Random (1748)
Smollett, Tobias (1721–1771) Scottish writer, satirist, historian, traveller and physician. On being tongue-tied when alone with one's object of desire

213 To be wise and eke to love,
Is graunted scarce to God above.
The Shepheardes Calender (1579), 'March'

214 So let us love, deare love, lyke as we ought,
Love is the lesson which the Lord us taught.
Amoretti, and Epithalamion (1595), Sonnet 68
Spenser, Edmund (c.1522–1599) English poet

215 When women are free, we'll see other emotions, no love. Love is a slave emotion, like a dog's.
For Love Alone (1944) **Stead, Christina** (1902–1983) Australian writer

216 Love, an' please your honour, is exactly like war, in this; that a soldier, though he has escaped three weeks complete o' Saturday night, – may nevertheless be shot through his heart on Sunday morning.
Tristram Shandy **Sterne, Laurence** (1713–1768) Irish-born English writer and clergyman

217 A woman despises a man for loving her, unless she returns his love.
Attr. **Stoddard, Elizabeth Drew** (1823–1902) US novelist and poet

218 The love of man is a weed of the waste places.
One may think of it as the spinifex of dry souls.
'The Land's Meaning' (1969) **Stow, Randolph** (1935–) Australian poet and novelist

219 Out upon it, I have loved
Three whole days together;
And am like to love three more
If it prove fair weather.
'A Poem with the Answer' (1659)

220 I prithee send me back my heart,
Since I cannot have thine
For if from yours you will not part,
Why then shouldst thou have mine? ...
But love is such a mystery,
I cannot find it out:
For when I think I'm best resolv'd
I then am in most doubt.
'Song' **Suckling, Sir John** (1609–1642) English poet and dramatist

221 If love were what the rose is,
And I were like the leaf,
Our lives would grow together
In sad or singing weather,
Blown fields or flowerful closes,
Green pleasure or grey grief.
'A Match' (1866) **Swinburne, Algernon Charles** (1837–1909) English poet, critic, dramatist and letter writer

222 Love is what makes the world go around – that and clichés.
Sydney Morning Herald, (1970) **Symons, Michael Brooke** (1945–) Australian journalist

223 In the Spring a young man's fancy lightly turns to thoughts of love.
'Locksley Hall' (1838)

224 I hold it true, whate'er befall;
I feel it, when I sorrow most;
'Tis better to have loved and lost
Than never to have loved at all.
In Memoriam A. H. H. (1850)

225 To love one maiden only, cleave to her,
And worship her by years of noble deeds,
Until they won her; for indeed I knew
Of no more subtle master under heaven
Than is the maiden passion for a maid,
Not only to keep down the base in man,
But teach high thought, and amiable words

And courtliness, and the desire of fame,
And love of truth, and all that makes a
man.
The Idylls of the King **Tennyson, Alfred, Lord**
(1809–1892) English lyric poet

226 Lovers' quarrels are the renewal of love.
Andria **Terence** (c.190–159 BC) Carthaginian-
born Roman dramatist

227 Some cynical Frenchman has said that
there are two parties to a love transaction;
the one who loves and the other who
condescends to be so treated.
Vanity Fair (1847–1848)

228 We love being in love, that's the truth on't.
The History of Henry Esmond (1852) **Thackeray,
William Makepeace** (1811–1863) Indian-born
English writer

229 Light breaks where no sun shines;
Where no sea runs, the waters of the heart
Push in their tides.
'Light breaks where no sun shines' (1934)
Thomas, Dylan (1914–1953) Welsh poet, writer
and radio dramatist

230 May I be looking at you when my last hour
has come, and as I die may I hold you with
my weakening hand.
Elegies **Tibullus** (c.54–19 BC) Roman poet

231 Love is God, and when I die it means that I,
a particle of love, shall return to the general
and eternal source.
War and Peace (1869)

232 All, everything that I understand, I
understand only because I love.
War and Peace (1869) **Tolstoy, Leo** (1828–1910)
Russian writer, essayist, philosopher and
moralist

233 If love is the answer, could you rephrase
the question?
Attr. **Tomlin, Lily** (1939–) US actress

234 I feel it in my fingers, I feel it in my toes.
Well, love is all around me, and so the
feeling grows.
'Love is all Around' (song, 1968) **The Troggs**
(1966–) UK pop group

235 Those who have courage to love should
have courage to suffer.
The Bertrams (1859)

236 Love is like any other luxury. You have no
right to it unless you can afford it.
The Way We Live Now (1875) **Trollope, Anthony**
(1815–1882) English writer, traveller and post
office official

237 Love conquers all: let us also yield to love.
Eclogues **Virgil** (70–19 BC) Roman poet

238 When one is in love one begins by
deceiving oneself. And one ends by
deceiving others.
A Woman of No Importance (1893)

239 Yet each man kills the thing he loves,
By each let this be heard,
Some do it with a bitter look,
Some with a flattering word,
The coward does it with a kiss,
The brave man with a sword!
The Ballad of Reading Gaol (1898) **Wilde, Oscar**
(1854–1900) Irish poet, dramatist, writer, critic
and wit

240 A mistress should be like a little country
retreat near the town, not to dwell in
constantly, but only for a night and away.
The Country Wife (1675) **Wycherley, William**
(c.1640–1716) English dramatist and poet

241 A pity beyond all telling
Is hid in the heart of love.
'The Pity of Love' (1892)

242 It seems to me that true love is a discipline,
and it needs so much wisdom that the love
of Solomon and Sheba must have lasted,
for all the silence of the Scriptures.
*Estrangement: Being some fifty Thoughts from a
Diary kept in the year nineteen hundred and nine*
(1926) **Yeats, W.B.** (1865–1939) Irish poet,
dramatist, editor, writer and senator
See also courtship; hatred; marriage; men and
women; passion; sex

MADNESS

1 We are all born mad. Some remain so.
Waiting for Godot (1955) **Beckett, Samuel** (1906–
1989) Irish dramatist, writer and poet

2 Only the insane take themselves quite
seriously.
Attr. **Beerbohm, Sir Max** (1872–1956) English
satirist, cartoonist, critic and essayist

3 The madman is not the man who has lost his reason. The madman is the man who has lost everything except his reason.
Orthodoxy (1908) **Chesterton, G.K.** (1874–1936) English writer, poet and critic

4 Dear Sir, – I am in a Madhouse and quite forget your name or who you are.
Letter, (1860) **Clare, John** (1793–1864) English rural poet; died in an asylum

5 There is only one difference between a madman and me. I am not mad.
The American, (1956) **Dali, Salvador** (1904–1989) Spanish painter and writer

6 Babylon in all its desolation is a sight not so awful as that of the human mind in ruins.
Letter to Thomas Raikes, (1835) **Davies, Scrope Berdmore** (c.1783–1852) English conversationalist

7 Great wits are sure to madness near alli'd, And thin partitions do their bounds divide.
Absalom and Achitophel (1681) **Dryden, John** (1631–1700) English poet, satirist, dramatist and critic

8 The place where optimism most flourishes is the lunatic asylum.
The Dance of Life **Ellis, Havelock** (1859–1939) English sexologist and essayist

9 Whom God wishes to destroy, he first makes mad.
Fragment **Euripides** (c.485–406 BC) Greek dramatist and poet

10 I saw the best minds of my generation destroyed by madness, starving hysterical naked.
Howl (1956) **Ginsberg, Allen** (1926–1997) US poet

11 Innocence is a kind of insanity.
The Quiet American (1955) **Greene, Graham** (1904–1991) English writer and dramatist

12 Orr was crazy and could be grounded. All he had to do was ask; and as soon as he did, he would no longer be crazy and would have to fly more missions … Yossarian was moved very deeply by the absolute simplicity of this clause of Catch-22 and let out a respectful whistle.
Catch-22 (1961) **Heller, Joseph** (1923–1999) US writer

13 I inherited a vile melancholy from my father, which has made me mad all my life, at least not sober.
In Boswell, *Journal of a Tour to the Hebrides* (1785)

14 If a madman were to come into this room with a stick in his hand, no doubt we should pity the state of his mind; but our primary consideration would be to take care of ourselves. We should knock him down first, and pity him afterwards.
In Boswell, *The Life of Samuel Johnson* (1791) **Johnson, Samuel** (1709–1784) English lexicographer, poet, critic, conversationalist and essayist

15 Show me a sane man and I will cure him for you.
The Observer, (1975) **Jung, Carl Gustav** (1875–1961) Swiss psychiatrist and pupil of Freud

16 Every one is more or less mad on one point.
Plain Tales from the Hills (1888)

17 The mad all are in God's keeping.
Kim (1901) **Kipling, Rudyard** (1865–1936) Indian-born British poet and writer

18 I am never better than when I am mad. Then methinks I am a brave fellow; then I do wonders. But reason abuseth me, and there's the torment, there's the hell.
The Spanish Tragedy (1592) **Kyd, Thomas** (1558–1594) English dramatist and poet

19 Schizophrenia cannot be understood without understanding despair.
The Divided Self (1960)

20 Madness need not be all breakdown. It may also be break-through. It is potential liberation and renewal as well as enslavement and existential death.
The Politics of Experience (1967) **Laing, R.D.** (1927–1989) Scottish psychiatrist, psychoanalyst and poet

21 The six weeks that finished last year and began this, your very humble servant spent very agreeably in a madhouse at Hoxton. I am got somewhat rational now, and don't bite anyone.

Letter to Coleridge, (1796) **Lamb, Charles** (1775–1834) English essayist, critic and letter writer

22 The mind's terror of the body has probably driven more men mad than ever could be counted.
The Plumed Serpent (1926) **Lawrence, D.H.** (1885–1930) English writer, poet and critic

23 They called me mad, and I called them mad, and damn them, they outvoted me.
In Porter, *A Social History of Madness* **Lee, Nathaniel** (c.1653–1692) English dramatist. Objecting to being confined in Bedlam

24 I can calculate the motion of heavenly bodies but not the madness of people.
Attr. **Newton, Sir Isaac** (1642–1727) English scientist and philosopher

25 If neurotic is wanting two mutually exclusive things at one and the same time, then I'm neurotic as hell. I'll be flying back and forth between one mutually exclusive thing and another for the rest of my days.
The Bell Jar (1963) **Plath, Sylvia** (1932–1963) US poet, writer and diarist

26 Men have called me mad; but the question is not yet settled, whether madness is or is not the loftiest intelligence – whether much that is glorious – whether all that is profound – does not spring from disease of thought – from moods of mind exalted at the expense of the general intellect.
Eleonora (1841) **Poe, Edgar Allan** (1809–1849) US poet, writer and editor

27 For Virtue's self may too much zeal be had; The worst of Madmen is a Saint run mad.
Imitations of Horace (1737–1738) **Pope, Alexander** (1688–1744) English poet, translator and editor

28 Neurosis has an absolute genius for malingering. There is no illness which it cannot counterfeit perfectly ... If it is capable of deceiving the doctor, how should it fail to deceive the patient?
Le Côté de Guermantes (1921)

29 Everything great in the world is done by neurotics; they alone founded our religions and composed our masterpieces.
Le Côté de Guermantes (1921) **Proust, Marcel** (1871–1922) French writer and critic

30 To define true madness,
What is't but to be nothing else but mad?
Hamlet, II.ii

31 And he repelled, a short tale to make,
Fell into a sadness, then into a fast,
Thence to a watch, thence into a weakness,
Thence to a lightness, and, by this declension,
Into the madness wherein now he raves
And all we mourn for.
Hamlet, II.ii

32 O, what a noble mind is here o'erthrown!
The courtier's, soldier's, scholar's, eye, tongue, sword;
Th' expectancy and rose of the fair state,
The glass of fashion and the mould of form,
Th' observ'd of all observers – quite, quite down!
Hamlet, III.i

33 O, let me not be mad, not mad, sweet heaven!
Keep me in temper; I would not be mad!
King Lear, I.v

34 Canst thou not minister to a mind diseas'd,
Pluck from the memory a rooted sorrow,
Raze out the written troubles of the brain,
And with some sweet oblivious antidote
Cleanse the stuff'd bosom of that perilous stuff
Which weighs upon the heart?
Macbeth, V.iii

35 It is the very error of the moon;
She comes more nearer earth than she was wont,
And makes men mad.
Othello, V.ii

36 Like madness is the glory of this life.
Timon of Athens, I.ii

37 O the fierce wretchedness that glory brings us!
Timon of Athens, IV.ii **Shakespeare, William** (1564–1616) English dramatist, poet and actor

38 O Lord, sir, when a heroine goes mad she always goes into white satin.
The Critic (1779) **Sheridan, Richard Brinsley** (1751–1816) Irish dramatist, politician and orator

39 I think for my part one half of the nation is mad – and the other not very sound.
The Adventures of Sir Launcelot Greaves (1762) **Smollett, Tobias** (1721–1771) Scottish writer, satirist, historian, traveller and physician

40 Psychiatrists classify a person as neurotic if he suffers from his problems in living, and a psychotic if he makes others suffer.
The Second Sin (1973)

41 If you talk to God, you are praying; if God talks to you, you have schizophrenia. If the dead talk to you, you are a spiritualist; if God talks to you, you are a schizophrenic.
The Second Sin (1973) **Szasz, Thomas** (1920–) Hungarian-born US psychiatrist and writer

42 He was sitting straight up in bed and rocking from side to side as though the bed were on a rough road; the knotted edges of the counterpane were his reins; his invisible horses stood in a shadow beyond the bedside candle. Over a white flannel nightshirt he was wearing a red waistcoat with walnut-sized brass buttons.
Portrait of the Artist as a Young Dog (1940) **Thomas, Dylan** (1914–1953) Welsh poet, writer and radio dramatist

43 Neurosis is the way of avoiding non-being by avoiding being.
The Courage to Be (1952) **Tillich, Paul** (1886–1965) German-born US philosopher and theologian

44 Men will always be mad and those who think they can cure them are the maddest of all.
Letter, (1762) **Voltaire** (1694–1778) French philosopher, dramatist, poet, historian, writer and critic

MANKIND

1 Nor should those be heeded who are wont to say 'The voice of the people is the voice of God', since popular uproar is always akin to madness.
Letter to Charlemagne **Alcuin** (735–804) English theologian, scholar and educationist

2 More than any other time in history, mankind faces a crossroads. One path leads to despair and utter hopelessness. The other, to total extinction. Let us pray we have the wisdom to choose correctly.
Side Effects **Allen, Woody** (1935–) US film director, writer, actor and comedian

3 The energies of our system will decay, the glory of the sun will be dimmed, and the earth, tideless and inert, will no longer tolerate the race which has for a moment disturbed its solitude. Man will go down into the pit, and all his thoughts will perish.
The Foundations of Belief (1895) **Balfour, A.J.** (1848–1930) British Conservative Prime Minister

4 One part of mankind is in prison; another is starving to death; and those of us who are free and fed are not awake. What will it take to rouse us?
Critical Enquiry (1975) 'A World Too Much With Us' **Bellow, Saul** (1915–2005) Canadian-born US Jewish writer

5 We have first raised a dust and then complain we cannot see.
A Treatise Concerning the Principles of Human Knowledge (1710) **Berkeley, Bishop George** (1685–1753) Irish philosopher and scholar

6 Injustice, poverty, slavery, ignorance – these may be cured by reform or revolution. But men do not live only by fighting evils. They live by positive goals, individual and collective, a vast variety of them, seldom predictable, at times incompatible.
'Political Ideas in the Twentieth Century' (1969) **Berlin, Isaiah** (1909–1997) English philosopher

7 Man has no Body distinct from his Soul for that called Body is a portion of Soul discernd by the five Senses, the chief inlets of Soul in this age.
The Marriage of Heaven and Hell (c.1790–1793)

8 Cruelty has a Human Heart
And Jealousy a Human Face,
Terror the Human Form Divine,
And Secrecy the Human Dress.
'A Divine Image' (c.1832) **Blake, William** (1757–1827) English poet, engraver, painter and mystic

9 The wickedness of the world is so great that you have to run your legs off so you don't get them stolen from you.
The Threepenny Opera (1928) **Brecht, Bertolt** (1898–1956) German dramatist

10 A race that binds
Its body in chains and calls them Liberty,
And calls each fresh link Progress.
'Titan and Avatar' **Buchanan, Robert Williams** (1841–1901) British poet, writer and dramatist

11 To complain of the age we live in, to murmur at the present possessors of power, to lament the past, to conceive extravagant hopes of the future, are the common dispositions of the greatest part of mankind.
Thoughts on the Cause of the Present Discontents (1770) **Burke, Edmund** (1729–1797) Irish-born British statesman and philosopher

12 He who despairs over an event is a coward, but he who holds hopes for the human condition is a fool.
The Rebel (1951) **Camus, Albert** (1913–1960) Algerian-born French writer

13 Man is a tool-using animal.
Sartor Resartus (1834) **Carlyle, Thomas** (1795–1881) Scottish historian, biographer, critic, and essayist

14 One may be optimistic, but one can't exactly be joyful at the prospect before us.
End of TV series, *Civilization* **Clark, Lord Kenneth** (1903–1983) English art historian

15 I confess freely to you, I could never look long upon a monkey, without very mortifying reflections.

Letter to Mr Dennis, (1695) **Congreve, William** (1670–1729) English dramatist

16 You shall judge of a man by his foes as well as by his friends.
Lord Jim (1900) **Conrad, Joseph** (1857–1924) Polish-born British writer, sailor and explorer

17 pity this busy monster, manunkind,
not. Progress is a comfortable disease.
1 x 1 (1944), no. 14 **Cummings, E. E.** (1894–1962) US poet, noted for his typography, and painter

18 Cruelty is like hope: it springs eternal.
The Observer, (1998) **Daniels, Dr Anthony**

19 The expression often used by Mr Herbert Spencer of the Survival of the Fittest is more accurate, and is sometimes equally convenient.
The Origin of Species (1859)

20 We must, however, acknowledge, as it seems to me, that man with all his noble qualities ... still bears in his bodily frame the indelible stamp of his lowly origin.
The Descent of Man (1871) **Darwin, Charles** (1809–1882) English naturalist

21 The evolution of the human race will not be accomplished in the ten thousand years of tame animals, but in the million years of wild animals, because man is and will always be a wild animal.
The Next Ten Million Years **Darwin, Charles Galton** (1887–1962) English physicist; grandson of Charles Darwin

22 Is man an ape or an angel? Now I am on the side of the angels.
Speech, (1864) **Disraeli, Benjamin** (1804–1881) English statesman and writer

23 Nor is the people's judgement always true:
The most may err as grossly as the few.
Absalom and Achitophel (1681) **Dryden, John** (1631–1700) English poet, satirist, dramatist and critic

24 Character is nature in the highest form. It is of no use to ape it, or to contend with it.
Essays, Second Series (1844) **Emerson, Ralph Waldo** (1803–1882) US poet, essayist, transcendentalist and teacher

25 Man's main task in life is to give *birth* to himself.
Man for Himself **Fromm, Erich** (1900–1980) US psychologist and philosopher

26 The land was ours before we were the land's.
'The Gift Outright' (1942) **Frost, Robert** (1874–1963) US poet

27 Wild animals never kill for sport. Man is the only one to whom the torture and death of his fellow creatures is amusing in itself.
Oceana, or England and her Colonies (1886) **Froude, James Anthony** (1818–1894) English historian and scholar

28 All that is human must retrograde if it does not advance.
Decline and Fall of the Roman Empire (1776–88) **Gibbon, Edward** (1737–1794) English historian, politician and memoirist

29 Man errs as long as he strives.
Faust (1808) **Goethe** (1749–1832) German poet, writer, dramatist and scientist

30 If human beings could be propagated by cutting, like apple trees, aristocracy would be biologically sound.
The Inequality of Man and Other Essays (1932) **Haldane, J.B.S.** (1892–1964) British biochemist, geneticist and popularizer of science

31 Some men are born mediocre, some men achieve mediocrity, and some men have mediocrity thrust upon them. With Major Major it had been all three.
Catch-22 (1961) **Heller, Joseph** (1923–1999) US writer

32 A man's conscience and his judgement is the same thing, and as the judgement, so also the conscience, may be erroneous.
Attr. **Hobbes, Thomas** (1588–1679) Political philosopher

33 Like Leaves on Trees the Race of Man is found,
Now green in Youth, now with'ring on the Ground,
Another Race the following Spring supplies,
They fall successive, and successive rise.
Iliad **Homer** (fl. c.8th century BC) Greek epic poet

34 The nations which have put mankind and posterity most in their debt have been small states – Israel, Athens, Florence, Elizabethan England.
Outspoken Essays: Second Series (1922) **Inge, William Ralph** (1860–1954) English divine, writer and teacher

35 Our civilization is founded on the shambles, and every individual existence goes out in a lonely spasm of helpless agony.
Varieties of Religious Experience (1902) **James, William** (1842–1910) US psychologist and philosopher

36 It is thus that mutual cowardice keeps us in peace. Were one half of mankind brave and one half cowards, the brave would be always beating the cowards. Were all brave, they would lead a very uneasy life; all would be continually fighting; but being all cowards, we go on very well.
In Boswell, *The Life of Samuel Johnson* (1791) **Johnson, Samuel** (1709–1784) English lexicographer, poet, critic, conversationalist and essayist

37 The ultimate measure of a man is not where he stands in moments of comfort and convenience, but where he stands at times of challenge and controversy.
Strength to Love, (1963) **King, Martin Luther** (1929–1968) US civil rights leader and Baptist minister

38 The human species, according to the best theory I can form of it, is composed of two distinct races, the men who borrow, and the men who lend.
Essays of Elia (1823) **Lamb, Charles** (1775–1834) English essayist, critic and letter writer

39 It is the hideous rawness of the world of men, the horrible desolating harshness of the advance of the industrial world upon the world of nature, that is so painful … If only we could learn to take thought for the whole world instead of for merely tiny bits of it.
Twilight in Italy (1916) **Lawrence, D.H.** (1885–1930) English writer, poet and critic

40 Character is like a tree and reputation like its shadow. The shadow is what we think of it; the tree is the real thing.
In Gross, *Lincoln's Own Stories* **Lincoln, Abraham** (1809–1865) US statesman and President

41 All men are liable to error; and most men are, in many points, by passion or interest, under temptation to it.
Essay concerning Human Understanding (1690) **Locke, John** (1632–1704) English philosopher

42 It is the nature of men to be bound by the benefits they confer as much as by those they receive.
The Prince (1532) **Machiavelli** (1469–1527) Florentine statesman, political theorist and historian

43 Mankind always sets itself only those problems it can solve; since, looking at the matter more closely, one will always find that the task itself arises only when the material conditions for its solution already exist or are at least in the process of formation.
A Contribution to the Critique of Political Economy (1859) **Marx, Karl** (1818–1883) German political philosopher and economist; founder of Communism

44 Men have an extraordinarily erroneous opinion of their position in nature; and the error is ineradicable.
A Writer's Notebook (1949) **Maugham, William Somerset** (1874–1965) English writer, dramatist and physician

45 Man is, I admit it, a mediocre creature.
Tartuffe (1664) **Molière** (1622–1673) French dramatist, actor and director

46 I teach you the Superman. Man is something that is to be surpassed.
Thus Spake Zarathustra **Nietzsche, Friedrich Wilhelm** (1844–1900) German philosopher, critic and poet

47 Men would be Angels, Angels would be Gods.
Aspiring to be Gods, if Angels fell,
Aspiring to be Angels, Men rebel.
An Essay on Man (1733)

48 Then say not man's imperfect, Heav'n in fault;
Say rather, Man's as perfect as he ought.
An Essay on Man (1733)

49 All Nature is but Art, unknown to thee;
All Chance, Direction which thou canst not see;
All Discord, Harmony, not understood;
All partial Evil, universal Good;
And, spite of Pride, in erring Reason's spite,
One truth is clear, 'Whatever is, is right.'
An Essay on Man (1733)

50 The People's Voice is odd,
It is, and it is not, the voice of God.
Imitations of Horace (1737–1738) **Pope, Alexander** (1688–1744) English poet, translator and editor

51 The true paradises are the paradises we have lost.
Le Temps retrouvé (1926) **Proust, Marcel** (1871–1922) French writer and critic

52 What vain, unnecessary things are men! How well we do without 'em!
'Fragment' (published 1953) **Rochester, Earl of** (1647–1680) English poet, satirist, courtier and libertine

53 The universe is so vast and so ageless that the life of one man can only be justified by the measure of his sacrifice.
Letter to his mother, (1940) **Rosewarne, V.A.** (1916–1940) English airman

54 I love mankind – it's people I can't stand.
Go Fly a Kite, Charlie Brown **Schulz, Charles** (1922–2000) US cartoonist

55 After all, for mankind as a whole there are no exports. We did not start developing by obtaining foreign exchange from Mars or the moon. Mankind is a closed society.
Small is Beautiful, A Study of Economics as if People Mattered (1973) **Schumacher, E.F.** (1911–1977) German-born British economist and essayist

56 Man, proud man,
Dress'd in a little brief authority,
Most ignorant of what he's most assur'd,
His glassy essence, like an angry ape,
Plays such fantastic tricks before high
heaven
As makes the angels weep.
Measure For Measure, II.ii **Shakespeare,
William** (1564–1616) English dramatist, poet
and actor

57 The reasonable man adapts himself to the
world: the unreasonable one persists in
trying to adapt the world to himself.
Therefore all progress depends on the
unreasonable man.
Man and Superman (1903) **Shaw, George
Bernard** (1856–1950) Irish socialist, writer,
dramatist and critic

58 If it is for mind that we are searching the
brain, then we are supposing the brain to
be much more than a telephone-exchange.
We are supposing it a telephone-exchange
along with the subscribers as well.
Man on his Nature **Sherrington, Sir Charles
Scott** (1857–1952) British neuroscientist

59 Evolution ... is – a change from an
indefinite, incoherent homogeneity, to a
definite coherent heterogeneity.
First Principles (1862)

60 It cannot but happen ... that those will
survive whose functions happen to be most
nearly in equilibrium with the modified
aggregate of external forces ... This
survival of the fittest implies multiplication
of the fittest.
The Principles of Biology (1864) **Spencer,
Herbert** (1820–1903) English philosopher and
journalist

61 A man's body and his mind ... are exactly
like a jerkin and a jerkin's lining; – rumple
the one, – you rumple the other.
Tristram Shandy (1759–1767) **Sterne, Laurence**
(1713–1768) Irish-born English writer and
clergyman

62 Oh, Vanity of vanities!
How wayward the decrees of Fate are;
How very weak the very wise,
How very small the very great!

'Vanitas Vanitatum' **Thackeray, William
Makepeace** (1811–1863) Indian-born English
writer

63 The mass of men lead lives of quiet
desperation.
Walden (1854) **Thoreau, Henry David** (1817–
1862) US essayist, social critic and writer

64 Once the people start to reason, all is lost.
Letter to Damilaville, (1766) **Voltaire** (1694–
1778) French philosopher, dramatist, poet,
historian, writer and critic

65 I was taught that the human brain was the
crowning glory of evolution so far, but I
think it's a very poor scheme for survival.
The Observer, (1987) **Vonnegut, Kurt** (1922–)
US author and journalist

66 That is men all over ... They will aim too
low. And achieve what they expect.
Voss (1957) **White, Patrick** (1912–1990) English-
born Australian writer and dramatist

67 A civilisation is a struggle to keep self-
control.
A Vision (1925) **Yeats, W.B.** (1865–1939) Irish
poet, dramatist, editor, writer and senator
See also global affairs; humanity and human
nature; the world

MANNERS

1 Who take their manners from the Ape,
Their habits from the Bear,
Indulge the loud unseemly jape,
And never brush their hair.
The Bad Child's Book of Beasts (1896) **Belloc,
Hilaire** (1870–1953) English writer of verse,
essayist and critic; Liberal MP

2 Comedies of manners swiftly become
obsolete when there are no longer any
manners.
Relative Values (1951) **Coward, Sir Noël** (1899–
1973) English dramatist, actor, producer and
composer

3 It is but the courteous exterior of a bigot.
Woman Suffrage and Sentiment **Eastman, Max**
(1883–1969) US writer, editor and critic. On
chivalry

4 Good manners are made up of petty
sacrifices.
'Social Aims' (1875) **Emerson, Ralph Waldo**
(1803–1882) US poet, essayist,
transcendentalist and teacher

5 To Americans English manners are far
more frightening than none at all.
Pictures from an Institution (1954) **Jarrell,
Randall** (1914–1965) US poet, critic and
translator

6 Man is the only animal that learns by being
hypocritical. He pretends to be polite and
then, eventually, he becomes polite.
Finishing Touches (1973) **Kerr, Jean** (1923–2003)
US writer and dramatist

7 Punctuality is the politeness of kings.
Attr. **Louis XVIII** (1755–1824) King of France

8 It's all right, Arthur. The white wine came
up with the fish.
Attr. **Mankiewicz, Herman J.** (1897–1953) US
journalist and screenwriter. After being sick at
the table of a fastidious host

9 Civility costs nothing and buys everything.
Letter to the Countess of Bute, (1756)
Montagu, Lady Mary Wortley (1689–1762)
English letter writer, poet, traveller and
introducer of smallpox inoculation

10 He is the very pine-apple of politeness!
The Rivals (1775) **Sheridan, Richard Brinsley**
(1751–1816) Irish dramatist, politician and
orator

11 Where etiquette prevents me from doing
things disagreeable to myself, I am a
perfect martinet.
Letters, To Lady Holland **Smith, Sydney** (1771–
1845) English clergyman, essayist, journalist
and wit

12 The gentle minde by gentle deeds is
knowne.
For a man by nothing is so well bewrayd,
As by his manners.
The Faerie Queene (1596) **Spenser, Edmund**
(c.1522–1599) English poet

13 Hail ye small sweet courtesies of life.
A Sentimental Journey (1768) **Sterne, Laurence**
(1713–1768) Irish-born English writer and
clergyman

14 The Japanese have perfected good manners
and made them indistinguishable from
rudeness.
The Great Railway Bazaar (1975) **Theroux, Paul**
(1941–) US writer

15 Good breeding consists in concealing how
much we think of ourselves and how little
we think of other persons.
Notebooks (1935) **Twain, Mark** (1835–1910) US
humorist, writer, journalist and lecturer

16 Manners are especially the need of the
plain. The pretty can get away with
anything.
The Observer, (1962) **Waugh, Evelyn** (1903–
1966) English writer and diarist

17 Manners maketh man.
Motto of Winchester College and New
College, Oxford **William of Wykeham** (1324–
1404) English prelate and statesman
See also class; society

MARRIAGE

1 Tomorrow our marriage will be 21 years
old! How many a storm has swept over it
and still it continues green and fresh and
throws out vigorous roots.
Attr. **Albert, Prince Consort** (1819–1861)
German-born husband of Queen Victoria

2 It was partially my fault that we got
divorced … I tended to place my wife
under a pedestal.
At a nightclub in Chicago, (1964) **Allen,
Woody** (1935–) US film director, writer, actor
and comedian

3 To marry a man out of pity is folly; and, if
you think you are going to influence the
kind of fellow who has 'never had a chance,
poor devil,' you are profoundly mistaken.
One can only influence the strong
characters in life, not the weak; and it is the
height of vanity to suppose that you can
make an honest man of anyone.
The Autobiography of Margot Asquith (1920)
Asquith, Margot (1864–1945) Scottish political
hostess and writer

4 I married beneath me – all women do.

Dictionary of National Biography **Astor, Nancy, Viscountess** (1879–1964) US-born British Conservative politician and hostess

5 Marriage is not
a house or even a tent
it is before that, and colder:
the edge of the forest, the edge
of the desert ...
the edge of the receding glacier
where painfully and with wonder
at having survived even
this far
we are learning to make fire.
Procedures for Underground (1970) **Atwood, Margaret** (1939–) Canadian writer, poet and critic

6 Matrimony, as the origin of change, was always disagreeable.
Emma (1816)

7 It is a truth universally acknowledged, that a single man in possession of a good fortune, must be in want of a wife.
Pride and Prejudice (1813)

8 Happiness in marriage is entirely a matter of chance.
Pride and Prejudice (1813) **Austen, Jane** (1775–1817) English writer

9 He that hath wife and children, hath given hostages to fortune; for they are impediments to great enterprises, either of virtue or mischief.
'Of Marriage and Single Life' (1625)

10 Wives are young men's mistresses, companions for middle age, and old men's nurses.
'Of Marriage and Single Life' (1625)

11 What is it then to have or have no wife,
But single thraldom, or a double strife?
The World (1629) **Bacon, Francis** (1561–1626) English philosopher, essayist, politician and courtier

12 Women – one half the human race at least – care fifty times more for a marriage than a ministry.
The English Constitution (1867) **Bagehot, Walter** (1826–1877) English economist and political philosopher

13 The fate of a marriage depends on the first night.
La Physiologie du mariage (1826) **Balzac, Honoré de** (1799–1850) French writer

14 My father argued sair – my mother didna speak,
But she looked in my face till my heart was like to break;
They gied him my hand but my heart was in the sea;
And so auld Robin Gray, he was gudeman to me.
'Auld Robin Gray' (1771) **Barnard, Lady Ann** (1750–1825) Scottish poet

15 I think weddings is sadder than funerals, because they remind you of your own wedding. You can't be reminded of your own funeral because it hasn't happened. But weddings always make me cry.
Richard's Cork Leg (1972) **Behan, Brendan** (1923–1964) Irish dramatist, writer and Republican

16 Being a husband is a whole-time job. That is why so many husbands fail. They cannot give their entire attention to it.
The Title (1918) **Bennett, Arnold** (1867–1931) English writer, dramatist and journalist

17 Women at marriage move from the status of female to that of neuter being.
The Future of Marriage **Bernard, Jessie** (1932–) US sociologist and writer

18 Therefore shall a man leave his father and his mother, and shall cleave unto his wife: and they shall be one flesh.
Genesis, 2:24

19 It is better to marry than to burn.
I Corinthians, 7:9 **The Bible (King James Version)**

20 Never marry a man who hates his mother, because he'll end up hating you.
The Observer, (1982) **Bennet, Jill** (1931–1990) English actress

21 Husband and wife are one, and that one is the husband.
In Miles, *The Women's History of the World* (1988) **Blackstone, Sir William** (1723–1780) English judge, historian and politician

22 One was never married, and that's his hell;
another is, and that's his plague.
Anatomy of Melancholy (1621) **Burton, Robert**
(1577–1640) English clergyman and writer

23 Though women are angels, yet wed-lock's
the devil.
'To Eliza' (1806)

24 Romances paint at full length people's
wooings,
But only give a bust of marriages:
For no one cares for matrimonial cooings.
There's nothing wrong in a connubial kiss:
Think you, if Laura had been Petrarch's
wife,
He would have written sonnets all his life?
Don Juan (1824) **Byron, Lord** (1788–1824)
English poet, satirist and traveller

25 Experience, though noon auctoritee
Were in this world, is right ynogh for me
To speke of wo that is in mariage.
The Canterbury Tales (1387) **Chaucer, Geoffrey**
(c.1340–1400) English poet, public servant and
courtier

26 Nuns and married women are equally
unhappy, if in different ways.
Pensées de Christine, reine de Suede (1825)
Christina of Sweden (1626–1689) Queen of
Sweden

27 The most happy marriage I can picture or
imagine to myself would be union of a deaf
man to a blind woman.
In Allsop, *Recollections* (1836) **Coleridge,
Samuel Taylor** (1772–1834) English poet,
philosopher and critic

28 Courtship to marriage, as a very witty
prologue to a very dull Play.
The Old Bachelor (1693) **Congreve, William**
(1670–1729) English dramatist

29 Daisy, Daisy, give me your answer, do!
I'm half crazy, all for the love of you!
It won't be a stylish marriage,
I can't afford a carriage,
But you'll look sweet upon the seat
Of a bicycle made for two!
'Daisy Bell' (song, 1892) **Dacre, Harry** (1860–
1922) English songwriter

30 The value of marriage is not that adults
produce children but that children produce
adults.
The Tunnel of Love (1954) **De Vries, Peter** (1910–
1993) US novelist

31 There were three of us in this marriage, so
it was a bit crowded.
BBC television interview, (1995) **Diana,
Princess of Wales** (1961–1997) Referring to the
Prince of Wales' relationship with Camilla
Parker-Bowles

32 I have always thought that every woman
should marry – and no man.
Lothair (1870)

33 Marriage is the greatest earthly happiness
when founded on complete sympathy.
Letter to Gladstone **Disraeli, Benjamin** (1804–
1881) English statesman and writer

34 There's only one way to have a happy
marriage and as soon as I learn what it is
I'll get married again.
Attr. **Eastwood, Clint** (1930–) US actor and
film director

35 A woman dictates before marriage in order
that she may have an appetite for
submission afterwards.
Middlemarch (1872) **Eliot, George** (1819–1880)
English writer and poet

36 It is a maxim that man and wife should
never have it in their power to hang one
another.
The Beaux' Stratagem (1707) **Farquhar, George**
(1678–1707) Irish dramatist

37 A man in love is incomplete until he has
married. Then he's finished.
Newsweek, (1960)

38 You mean apart from my own?
Attr. Her answer to the question 'How many
husbands have you had?'

39 Husbands are like fires. They go out when
unattended.
Newsweek, (1960) **Gabor, Zsa-Zsa** (1919–)
Hungarian-born US actress

40 Do you think your mother and I should
have liv'd comfortably so long together, if
ever we had been married?
The Beggar's Opera (1728)

41 *Polly*: Then all my sorrows are at an end.
Mrs Peachum: A mighty likely speech in truth, for a wench who is just married!
The Beggar's Opera (1728)

42 I am ready, my dear Lucy, to give you satisfaction – if you think there is any in marriage.
The Beggar's Opera (1728)

43 One wife is too much for most husbands to hear,
But two at a time there's no mortal can bear.
This way, and that way, and which way I will,
What would comfort the one, t'other wife would take ill.
The Beggar's Opera (1728) **Gay, John** (1685–1732) English poet, dramatist and librettist

44 Mr Mybug said that, by God, D.H. Lawrence was right when he had said there must be a dumb, dark, dull, bitter belly-tension between a man and a woman, and how else could this be achieved save in the long monotony of marriage?
Cold Comfort Farm (1932) **Gibbons, Stella** (1902–1989) English poet and novelist

45 I … chose my wife as she did her wedding gown, not for a fine glossy surface, but such qualities as would wear well.
The Vicar of Wakefield (1766) **Goldsmith, Oliver** (c.1728–1774) Irish dramatist, poet and writer

46 There are women whose infidelity is the only thing that still links them to their husbands.
Elles et toi (1948)

47 The others were only my wives. But you, my dear, will be my widow.
Attr. Responding to his fifth wife's jealousy of his previous wives **Guitry, Sacha** (1885–1957) Russian-born French actor, dramatist and film director

48 I shall tell the women what it is our sex complains of in the married state; and if they be disposed to satisfy us in this particular, all the other difficulties will easily be accommodated. If I be not mistaken, 'tis their love of dominion.

Essays, Moral, Political and Literary (1742) **Hume, David** (1711–1776) Scottish philosopher and political economist

49 Marriage has many pains, but celibacy has no pleasures.
Rasselas (1759)

50 Marriages would in general be as happy, and often more so, if they were all made by the Lord Chancellor … without the parties having any choice in the matter.
In Boswell, *The Life of Samuel Johnson* (1791)

51 It is so far from being natural for a man and a woman to live in a state of marriage that we find all the motives which they have for remaining in that connection, and the restraints which civilized society imposes to prevent separation, are hardly sufficient to keep them together.
In Boswell, *The Life of Samuel Johnson* (1791)

52 A gentleman who had been very unhappy in marriage married immediately after his wife died. Dr Johnson said, it was the triumph of hope over experience.
In Boswell, *The Life of Samuel Johnson* (1791) **Johnson, Samuel** (1709–1784) English lexicographer, poet, critic, conversationalist and essayist

53 The roaring of the wind is my wife and the Stars through the window pane are my Children. The mighty abstract Idea I have of Beauty in all things stifles the more divided and minute domestic happiness … the opinion I have of the generality of women – who appear to me as children to whom I would rather give a Sugar Plum than my time, forms a barrier against Matrimony which I rejoice in.
Letter to George and Georgiana Keats, (1818) **Keats, John** (1795–1821) English poet

54 I was at Hazlitt's marriage, and had like to have been turned out several times during the ceremony. Anything awful makes me laugh. I misbehaved once at a funeral.
Letter to Southey, (1815)

55 Nothing to me is more distasteful than that entire complacency and satisfaction which beam in the countenance of a new-married couple.

Essays of Elia (1823) **Lamb, Charles** (1775–1834) English essayist, critic and letter writer

56 Same old slippers,
Same old rice,
Same old glimpse of
Paradise.
'June Weddings' **Lampton, William James** (1859–1917) US poet and journalist

57 There are good marriages, but no delightful ones.
Maximes (1678) **La Rochefoucauld** (1613–1680) French writer

58 I'm getting married in the morning!
Ding dong! the bells are gonna chime.
Pull out the stopper!
Let's have a whopper!
But get me to the church on time!
My Fair Lady (1956) **Lerner, Alan Jay** (1918–1986) US lyricist and screenwriter

59 The men that women marry,
And why they marry them, will always be
A marvel and a mystery to the world.
Michael Angelo (1883) **Longfellow, Henry Wadsworth** (1807–1882) US poet and writer

60 It's true that I did get the girl, but then my grandfather always said, 'Even a blind chicken finds a few grains of corn now and then.'
Attr. **Lovett, Lyle** (1956–) US singer. On marrying actress Julia Roberts, 1994

61 So they were married – to be the more together –
And found they were never again so much together,
Divided by the morning tea,
By the evening paper,
By children and tradesmen's bills.
'Les Sylphides' (1941) **MacNeice, Louis** (1907–1963) Belfast-born poet, writer, radio producer, translator and critic

62 Being married six times shows a degree of optimism over wisdom, but I am incorrigibly optimistic.
The Observer, (1988) **Mailer, Norman** (1923–) US writer

63 Any one must see at a glance that if men and women marry those whom they do not love, they must love those whom they do not marry.
Society in America (1837)

64 I am in truth very thankful for not having married at all.
Harriet Martineau's Autobiography (1877) **Martineau, Harriet** (1802–1876) English writer

65 But I wasn't kissing her. I was whispering in her mouth.
In G. Marx and R. Anobile, *The Marx Brothers Scrapbook* (1974) **Marx, Chico** (1886–1961) US comedian. Explanation given when his wife caught him kissing a chorus girl

66 When married people don't get on they can separate, but if they're not married it's impossible. It's a tie that only death can sever.
The Circle (1921) **Maugham, William Somerset** (1874–1965) English writer, dramatist and physician

67 The moral regeneration of mankind will only really commence, when the most fundamental of the social relations [marriage] is placed under the rule of equal justice, and when human beings learn to cultivate their strongest sympathy with an equal in rights and cultivation.
The Subjection of Women (1869) **Mill, John Stuart** (1806–1873) English philosopher, economist and reformer

68 Flesh of Flesh,
Bone of my Bone thou art, and from thy State
Mine never shall be parted, weal or woe.
Paradise Lost (1667) **Milton, John** (1608–1674) English poet, libertarian and pamphleteer

69 Marriage, Agnès, is not a joke.
L'École des Femmes (1662) **Molière** (1622–1673) French dramatist, actor and director

70 Far from going together like a horse and carriage, love and marriage have been in opposition for years.
The Times, (1998) **Mooney, Bel** (1946–) English writer

71 Overheard or recorded, all marital conversation sounds as if someone must be joking, though usually no one is.
Birds of America (1998) **Moore, Lorrie** (1957–) US novelist

72 'Come, come', said Tom's father, 'at your time of life,
There's no longer excuse for thus playing the rake –
It is time you should think, boy, of taking a wife' –
'Why, so it is, father – whose wife shall I take?'
Miscellaneous Poems (1840), 'A Joke Versified' **Moore, Thomas** (1779–1852) Irish poet

73 It has been said that a bride's attitude towards her betrothed can be summed up in three words: Aisle. Altar. Hymn.
Upon My Word!, 'A Jug of Wine', with Dennis Norden **Muir, Frank** (1920–1998) English writer, humorist and broadcaster

74 Marriage is an insult and women should not touch it.
Attr. **Murray, Jenni** (1950–) English journalist and broadcaster

75 Women will only leave a marriage if it's unbearable, whereas men will split if they get a better offer.
The Observer, (1999) **Newman, Andrea** (1938–) English author

76 Marriage may often be a stormy lake, but celibacy is almost always a muddy horse-pond.
Melincourt (1817) **Peacock, Thomas Love** (1785–1866) English writer and poet

77 Strange to say what delight we married people have to see these poor fools decoyed into our condition.
Diary, (December 1665) **Pepys, Samuel** (1633–1703) English diarist, naval administrator and politician

78 She who ne'er answers till a Husband cools,
Or, if she rules him, never shows she rules;
Charms by accepting, by submitting sways,
Yet has her humour most, when she obeys.
'Epistle to a Lady' (1735) **Pope, Alexander** (1688–1744) English poet, translator and editor

79 Ane canna wive an' thrive baith in ae year.
A Collection of Scots Proverbs (1737) **Ramsay, Allan** (1686–1758) Scottish poet and dramatist

80 It doesn't much signify whom one marries, for one is sure to find next morning that it was someone else.
Recollections of the Table-Talk of Samuel Rogers (1856) **Rogers, Samuel** (1763–1855) English poet

81 It's confusing. I've had so many wives and so many children I don't know which house to go to first on Christmas.
New York Post, (1960) **Rooney, Mickey** (1920–) US film actor. On his frequent marriages

82 Never feel remorse for what you have thought about your wife; she has thought much worse things about you.
Le Mariage **Rostand, Jean** (1894–1977) French biologist

83 Before marriage, a man will lie awake thinking about something you said; after marriage, he'll fall asleep before you finish saying it.
In Cowan, *The Wit of Women* **Rowland, Helen** (1875–1950) US writer

84 Marrying off your daughter is a piece of business you may expect to do only once in a lifetime, and, bearing in mind that none of the losses are recoverable later, you should approach the matter with extreme caution.
The Japanese Family Storehouse (1688)

85 And why do people wilfully exhaust their strength in promiscuous living, when their wives are on hand from bridal night till old age – to be taken when required, like fish from a private pond.
The Japanese Family Storehouse (1688) **Saikaku, Ihara** (1642–1693) Japanese writer and poet

86 The Western custom of one wife and hardly any mistresses.
Reginald in Russia (1910)

87 A woman who takes her husband about with her everywhere is like a cat that goes on playing with a mouse long after she's killed it.
Attr. **Saki** (1870–1916) Burmese-born British writer

88 It takes two to make a marriage a success and only one a failure.
A Book of Quotations (1947) **Samuel, Lord** (1870–1963) English Liberal statesman, philosopher and administrator

89 Marriage is nothing but a civil contract.
Table Talk (1689) **Selden, John** (1584–1654) English historian, jurist and politician

90 'You will marry a boy I choose,' said Mrs Rupa Mehra firmly to her younger daughter.
A Suitable Boy (1993) **Seth, Vikram** (1952–) Indian author

91 A young man married is a man that's marr'd.
All's Well That Ends Well, II.iii

92 Men are April when they woo, December when they wed: maids are May when they are maids, but the sky changes when they are wives.
As You Like It, IV.i

93 Let still the woman take
An elder than herself; so wears she to him,
So sways she level in her husband's heart.
For, boy, however we do praise ourselves,
Our fancies are more giddy and unfirm,
More longing, wavering, sooner lost and won,
Than women's are.
Twelfth Night, II.iv

94 Thy husband is thy lord, thy life, thy keeper,
Thy head, thy sovereign; one that cares for thee,
And for thy maintenance commits his body
To painful labour both by sea and land.
The Taming of the Shrew, V.ii

95 Let me give light, but let me not be light,
For a light wife doth make a heavy husband.
The Merchant of Venice, V.i **Shakespeare, William** (1564–1616) English dramatist, poet and actor

96 It is a woman's business to get married as soon as possible, and a man's to keep unmarried as long as he can.
Man and Superman (1903)

97 Marriage is popular because it combines the maximum of temptation with the maximum of opportunity.
Man and Superman (1903)

98 Those who talk most about the blessings of marriage and the constancy of its vows are the very people who declare that if the chain were broken and the prisoners left free to choose, the whole social fabric would fly asunder. You cannot have the argument both ways. If the prisoner is happy, why lock him in? If he is not, why pretend that he is?
Man and Superman (1903) **Shaw, George Bernard** (1856–1950) Irish socialist, writer, dramatist and critic

99 'Tis safest in matrimony to begin with a little aversion.
The Rivals (1775)

100 You had no taste when you married me.
The School for Scandal (1777) **Sheridan, Richard Brinsley** (1751–1816) Irish dramatist, politician and orator

101 She cannot say just when
The cooking first began within her mind –
But here she knows ... like cakes or bread, a wife
Must lie content as if within a hand
And feel the teeth of time upon her life.
'Wife' **Simpson, Ronald Albert** (1929–) Australian poet

102 No time to marry, no time to settle down;
I'm a young woman, and I ain't done runnin' around.
'Young Woman's Blues' (song, 1927) **Smith, Bessie** (1894–1937) US singer

103 Married women are kept women, and they are beginning to find it out.
Afterthoughts (1931) **Smith, Logan Pearsall** (1865–1946) US-born British epigrammatist, critic and writer

104 It resembles a pair of shears, so joined that they cannot be separated; often moving in opposite directions, yet always punishing anyone who comes between them.
In Holland, *A Memoir of the Reverend Sydney Smith* (1855) **Smith, Sydney** (1771–1845) English clergyman, essayist, journalist and wit. On marriage

105 'My brother Toby,' quoth she, 'is going to be married to Mrs Wadman.'
'Then he will never,' quoth my father, 'be able to lie diagonally in his bed again as long as he lives.'
Tristram Shandy (1759–1767) **Sterne, Laurence** (1713–1768) Irish-born English writer and clergyman

106 Trusty, dusky, vivid, true,
With eyes of gold and bramble-dew,
Steel-true and blade-straight,
The great artificer
Made my mate.
'My Wife' (1896)

107 Times are changed with him who marries; there are no more by-path meadows, where you may innocently linger, but the road lies long and straight and dusty to the grave.
Virginibus Puerisque (1881)

108 Marriage is a step so grave and decisive that it attracts light-headed, variable men by its very awfulness.
Virginibus Puerisque (1881)

109 Marriage is like life in this – that it is a field of battle and not a bed of roses.
Virginibus Puerisque (1881)

110 Lastly (and this is, perhaps, the golden rule), no woman should marry a teetotaller, or a man who does not smoke.
Virginibus Puerisque (1881)

111 In marriage, a man becomes slack and selfish, and undergoes a fatty degeneration of his moral being.
Virginibus Puerisque (1881) **Stevenson, Robert Louis** (1850–1894) Scottish writer, poet and essayist

112 The reason why so few marriages are happy, is, because young ladies spend their time in making nets, not in making cages.
Thoughts on Various Subjects (1711)

113 What they do in heaven we are ignorant of; what they do not we are told expressly, that they neither marry, nor are given in marriage.
Thoughts on Various Subjects (1711) **Swift, Jonathan** (1667–1745) Irish satirist, poet, essayist and cleric

114 An ideal wife is any woman who has an ideal husband.
Attr. **Tarkington, Booth** (1869–1946) US writer and dramatist

115 He that loves not his wife and children, feeds a lioness at home and broods a nest of sorrows.
XXV Sermons Preached at Golden Grove (1653) **Taylor, Bishop Jeremy** (1613–1667) English divine and writer

116 And this I set down as a positive truth. A woman with fair opportunities, and without an absolute hump may marry whom she likes.
Vanity Fair (1847–1848)

117 Remember, it is as easy to marry a rich woman as a poor woman.
Pendennis (1848–1850) **Thackeray, William Makepeace** (1811–1863) Indian-born English writer

118 I do, and I also wash and iron them.
Times (Los Angeles), 1981 **Thatcher, Denis** (1915–2003) Businessman; husband of British Prime Minister Margaret Thatcher. Replying to the question 'Who wears the pants in this house?'

119 No man worth having is true to his wife, or can be true to his wife, or ever was, or ever will be so.
The Relapse, or Virtue in Danger (1696) **Vanbrugh, Sir John** (1664–1726) English dramatist and baroque architect

120 Marriage is the only adventure open to the cowardly.
Attr. **Voltaire** (1694–1778) French philosopher, dramatist, poet, historian, writer and critic

121 He is dreadfully married. He's the most married man I ever saw in my life.
Artemus Ward's Lecture (1869) **Ward, Artemus** (1834–1867) US humorist, journalist, editor and lecturer

122 Marriage is the waste-paper basket of the emotions.
In Bertrand Russell, *Autobiography* (1967) **Webb, Sidney** (1859–1947) English reformer, historian and socialist

123 ... the great wonderful construct which is marriage – a construct made up of a hundred little kindnesses, a thousand little bitings back of spite, tens of thousands of minor actions of good intent – this must not, as an institution, be brought down in ruins.
Splitting (1995) **Weldon, Fay** (1931–) British writer

124 If our divorce laws were improved, we could at least say that if marriage does nobody much good it does nobody any harm.
The Clarion **West, Dame Rebecca** (1892–1983) English writer, critic and feminist

125 The real drawback to marriage is that it makes one unselfish. And unselfish people are colourless.
The Picture of Dorian Gray (1891)

126 Twenty years of romance make a woman look like a ruin; but twenty years of marriage make her something like a public building.
A Woman of No Importance (1893)

127 There's nothing in the world like the devotion of a married woman. It's a thing no married man knows anything about.
Lady Windermere's Fan (1893)

128 I am not in favour of long engagements. They give people the opportunity of finding out each other's character before marriage, which I think is never advisable.
The Importance of Being Earnest (1895)

129 The amount of women in London who flirt with their own husbands is perfectly scandalous. It looks so bad. It is simply washing one's clean linen in public.
The Importance of Being Earnest (1895) **Wilde, Oscar** (1854–1900) Irish poet, dramatist, writer, critic and wit

130 The best part of married life is the fights. The rest is merely so-so.
The Matchmaker (1954) **Wilder, Thornton** (1897–1975) US author and playwright

131 All the unhappy marriages come from the husbands having brains. What good are brains to a man? They only unsettle him.

The Adventures of Sally (1920) **Wodehouse, P.G.** (1881–1975) English humorist and writer

132 A marriage is really a nonstop conversation.
All in the Family: A Survival Guide for Living and Loving in a Changing World **Wylie, Betty Jane** (1931–) Canadian writer
See also courtship; love; men and women; passion; sex

MEDIA

1 The BBC is full of men appointing men who remind them of themselves when young, so you get the same backgrounds, the same education, and the same programmes.
The Observer, (1993) **Bakewell, Joan** (1933–) British journalist and television presenter

2 The greatest thing that could happen to the state and the nation is when we can get rid of all the media. Then we could live in peace and tranquillity, and no one would know anything.
The Spectator, (1987) **Bjelke-Petersen, Sir Johannes** (1911–2005) Australian politician, Premier of Queensland

3 All my shows are great. Some of them are bad. But they are all great.
The Observer, (1975) **Grade, Lew** (1906–1994) Russian-born British film, TV and theatrical producer.

4 The idea that media is there to educate us, or to inform us, is ridiculous because that's about tenth or eleventh on their list.
Speech, (1987) **Hoffman, Abbie** (1936–1989) US political activist

5 The proliferation of radio and television channels has produced a wilderness of cave-dwellers instead of the promised global village.
The Times, (1992) **Howard, Philip** (1933–) English journalist

6 To have open government you need mature media. It is more difficult for people to discuss complex issues than it used to be because of the destructive power of the tabloids. The TV sound bite

also makes it impossible to communicate complex arguments. It is all black and white, cut and dried, yaa-boo.
Independent on Sunday, (1994) **Jackson, Robert** (1946–) English Conservative politician and writer

7 If it bleeds, it leads.
The Guardian, (1999) **Kavanau, Ted** CNN news editor. Statement of CNN editorial policy

8 The medium is the message. This is merely to say that the personal and social consequences of any medium … result from the new scale that is introduced into our affairs by each extension of ourselves or by any new technology.
Understanding Media (1964) **McLuhan, Marshall** (1911–1980) Canadian communications theorist

9 It is true that I am a low mean snake. But you could walk beneath me wearing a top hat.
The Guardian, (1999) **Murdoch, Rupert** (1931–) Australian-born publisher and international businessman. In reply to Ted Turner (*see below*)

10 I like photographers, you don't ask questions.
Speech to White House News Photographers Association, (1983) **Reagan, Ronald** (1911–2004) US actor, Republican statesman and President

11 It was in fact the combination of public service motive, sense of moral obligation, assured finance and the brute force of monopoly which enabled the BBC to make of broadcasting what no other country has made of it.
Into the Wind (1949) **Reith, Lord** (1889–1971) Scottish wartime minister, administrator, diarist and Director-General of the BBC

12 There was once a wicked lady called Circe, who was reputed to turn human beings into swine. The object of broadcasting should be the exact opposite.
In Hamish Keith and William Main (eds), *New Zealand Yesterdays: A Look at Our Recent Past* **Shelley, Sir James** As Director of Broadcasting

13 Social misery has inspired the comfortably-off with the urge to take pictures, the gentlest of predations, in order to document a hidden reality, that is, a reality hidden from them.
New York Review of Books, (1977) **Sontag, Susan** (1933–) US critic and writer

14 The media. It sounds like a convention of spiritualists.
Night and Day (1978) **Stoppard, Tom** (1937–) British dramatist

15 Murdoch's a schlockmeister. We're gonna squish Rupert like a bug.
The Guardian, (1999) After launch of Rupert Murdoch's Fox news in 1996

16 See we're gonna take the news and put it on satellite and then we're gonna beam it down to Russia, and we're gonna bring world peace and we're gonna get rich in the process!
The Guardian, (1999) CNN launch speech, 1980 **Turner, Ted** (1938–) US media tycoon

17 Quite small and ineffectual demonstrations can be made to look like the beginnings of a revolution if the cameraman is in the right place at the right time.
A Dictionary of Contemporary Quotations (1982) **Whitlam, Gough** (1916–) Australian Labor statesman and Prime Minister

18 Television contracts the imagination and radio expands it.
The Observer, (1984) **Wogan, Terry** (1926–) Irish radio and television presenter
See also news and newspapers; television

MEMORY

1 Nothing is more responsible for the good old days than a bad memory.
In William Cole and Louis Phillips, *Treasury of Humorous Quotations* (1996) **Adams, Franklin P.** (1881–1960) US writer, poet, translator and editor

2 Someday we'll look back on this and plow into a parked car.
The Dilbert Principle **Adams, Scott** (1957–) US cartoonist

3 Memory is the mother of all wisdom.
Prometheus Bound **Aeschylus** (525–456 BC)
Greek dramatist and poet

4 Four ducks on a pond,
A grass-bank beyond,
A blue sky of spring,
White clouds on the wing:
What a little thing
To remember for years –
To remember with tears.
'A Memory' (1888) **Allingham, William** (1824–1889) Irish poet and diarist

5 Memories are hunting horns whose sound
dies away in the wind.
'Cors de Chasse' (1913) **Apollinaire, Guillaume**
(1880–1918) French poet and writer

6 Ere the parting hour go by,
Quick, thy tablets, Memory!
'A Memory Picture' (1849)

7 And we forget because we must
And not because we will.
'Absence' (1852) **Arnold, Matthew** (1822–1888)
English poet, critic, essayist and educationist

8 There seems something more speakingly
incomprehensible in the powers, the
failures, the inequalities of memory, than
in any other of our intelligences.
Mansfield Park (1814) **Austen, Jane** (1775–1817)
English writer

9 A safe but sometimes chilly way of recalling
the past is to force open a crammed
drawer. If you are searching for anything in
particular you don't find it, but something
falls out at the back that is often more
interesting.
'To the Five – A Dedication' in *Peter Pan* (1902)

10 God gave us memories that we might have
roses in December.
Courage (1922) **Barrie, Sir J.M.** (1860–1937)
Scottish dramatist and writer

11 I have more memories than if I had lived
for a thousand years.
Les Fleurs du mal (1857) **Baudelaire, Charles**
(1821–1867) French poet, translator and critic

12 There is always something rather absurd
about the past.
Attr. **Beerbohm, Sir Max** (1872–1956) English
satirist, cartoonist, critic and essayist

13 Memories are like stones, time and
distance erode them like acid.
Goat Island (1946) **Betti, Ugo** (1892–1953)
Italian playwright

14 Rejoice ye dead, where'er your spirits dwell,
Rejoice that yet on earth your fame is
bright,
And that your names, remembered day
and night,
Live on the lips of those who love you well.
'Ode to Music' (1896) **Bridges, Robert** (1844–1930) English poet, dramatist, essayist and
doctor

15 What memory has in common with art is
the knack for selection, the taste for detail
… More than anything, memory resembles
a library in alphabetical disorder, and with
no collected works by anyone.
'In a Room and a Half' (1986) **Brodsky, Joseph**
(1940–1996) Russian poet, essayist, critic and
exile

16 But the iniquity of oblivion blindly
scattereth her poppy, and deals with the
memory of men without distinction to
merit of perpetuity.
Hydriotaphia: Urn Burial (1658)

17 Oblivion is a kind of Annihilation.
Christian Morals (1716) **Browne, Sir Thomas**
(1605–1682) English physician, author and
antiquary

18 The 'good old times' – all times when old
are good –
Are gone.
'The Age of Bronze' (1823) **Byron, Lord** (1788–1824) English poet, satirist and traveller

19 I cannot sing the old songs now!
It is not that I deem them low;
'Tis that I can't remember how
They go.
'Changed' (1872) **Calverley, C.S.** (1831–1884)
English poet, parodist, scholar and lawyer

20 To live in hearts we leave behind
Is not to die.
'Hallowed Ground' **Campbell, Thomas** (1777–1844) Scottish poet, ballad writer and
journalist

21 We can ask and ask but we can't have again
what once seemed ours forever – the way
things looked, that church alone in the
fields, a bed on a belfry floor, a loved face
… They'd gone, and you could only wait
for the pain to pass.
A Month in the Country (1980) **Carr, J.L.** (1912–
1994) English writer and publisher

22 'The horror of that moment,' the King went
on, 'I shall never, never forget!'
'You will, though,' the Queen said, 'if you
don't make a memorandum of it.'
*Through the Looking-Glass (and What Alice
Found There)* (1872) **Carroll, Lewis** (1832–1898)
English writer and photographer

23 The present is the funeral of the past,
And man the living sepulchre of life.
'The Past' (1845) **Clare, John** (1793–1864)
English rural poet; died in an asylum

24 But the past, the beautiful past striped with
sunshine, grey with mist, childish,
blooming with hidden joy, bruised with
sweet sorrow. … Ah! if only I could
resurrect one hour of that time, one alone
– but which one?
Paysages et portraits (1958) **Colette** (1873–1954)
French writer

25 In hours of bliss we oft have met;
They could not always last;
And though the present I regret
I'm grateful for the past.
'False though she be' **Congreve, William**
(1670–1729) English dramatist

26 The difference between false memories
and true ones is the same as for jewels: it is
always the false ones that look the most
real, the most brilliant.
The Secret Life of Salvador Dali (1948) **Dali,
Salvador** (1904–1989) Spanish painter and
writer

27 All human memory is fraught with sorrow
and trouble.
A Christmas Carol (1843) **Dickens, Charles**
(1812–1870) English writer

28 Nobody is forgotten when it is convenient
to remember him.
Attr.

29 When I meet a man whose name I can't
remember, I give myself two minutes;
then, if it is a hopeless case, I always say,
And how is the old complaint?
Attr.

30 Nobody is forgotten when it is convenient
to remember him.
Attr. **Disraeli, Benjamin** (1804–1881) English
statesman and writer

31 Nothing is so good as it seems
beforehand.
Silas Marner (1861) **Eliot, George** (1819–1880)
English writer and poet

32 How comforting it is, once or twice a year
To get together and forget the old times.
The Memory of War. Poems 1968–1982 (1983)
Fenton, James (1949–) English poet

33 Conductors should be back on the buses,
packets of salt back in the crisps, clockwork
back in clocks and levers back in pens.
The Observer, (1998) **Fitzgerald, Penelope**
(1916–2000) English author. Her hopes for the
New Year

34 The past is a foreign country: they do
things differently there.
The Go-Between (1953) **Hartley, L.P.** (1895–1972)
English writer and critic

35 Into my heart an air that kills
From yon far country blows:
What are those blue remembered hills,
What spires, what farms are those?
That is the land of lost content,
I see it shining plain,
The happy highways where I went
And cannot come again.
A Shropshire Lad (1896) **Housman, A.E.** (1859–
1936) English poet and scholar

36 It's not just what we inherit from our
mothers and fathers that haunts us. It's all
kinds of old defunct theories, all sorts of
old defunct beliefs, and things like that. It's
not that they actually live on in us; they are
simply lodged there, and we cannot get rid
of them. I've only to pick up a newspaper
and I seem to see ghosts gliding between
the lines.
Ghosts (1881) **Ibsen, Henrik** (1828–1906)
Norwegian writer, dramatist and poet

37 You can only predict things after they've
happened.
Rhinoceros (1959) **Ionesco, Eugene** (1912–1994)
Romanian-born French dramatist

38 Men more frequently require to be
reminded than informed.
The Rambler (1750–1752)

39 Nobody can write the life of a man, but
those who have eat and drunk and lived in
social intercourse with him.
In Boswell, *The Life of Samuel Johnson* (1791)
Johnson, Samuel (1709–1784) English
lexicographer, poet, critic, conversationalist
and essayist

40 All, all are gone, the old familiar faces.
'The Old Familiar Faces' **Lamb, Charles** (1775–
1834) English essayist, critic and letter writer

41 A mist of memory broods and floats,
The border waters flow;
The air is full of ballad notes
Borne out of long ago.
'Twilight on Tweed' (1905) **Lang, Andrew**
(1844–1912) Scottish poet, writer, mythologist
and anthropologist

42 Everyone complains of his memory;
nobody of his judgment.
Maximes (1678) **La Rochefoucauld** (1613–1680)
French writer

43 What did they know about memory? What
was it but another name for dry love and
barren longing?
In the Middle of the Fields (1967) **Lavin, Mary**
(1912–1996) Irish novelist

44 Human memory is a marvellous but
fallacious instrument ... The memories
which lie within us are not carved in stone;
not only do they tend to become erased as
the years go by, but often they change, or
even increase by incorporating extraneous
features.
The Drowned and the Saved (1988) **Levi, Primo**
(1919–1987) Italian writer, poet and chemist;
survivor of Auschwitz

45 So now it is vain for the singer to burst into
clamour
With the great black piano appassionato.
The glamour
Of childish days is upon me, my manhood
is cast
Down in the flood of remembrance, I weep
like a child for the past.
New Poems (1918), 'Piano' **Lawrence, D.H.**
(1885–1930) English writer, poet and critic

46 I never forget a face, but I'll make an
exception in your case.
The Guardian, (1965) **Marx, Groucho** (1895–
1977) US comedian

47 The past is still, for us, a place that is not
yet safely settled.
*The Faber Book of Contemporary Canadian Short
Stories* (1990) **Ondaatje, Michael** (1943–)
Canadian writer

48 Before the war, and especially before the
Boer War, it was summer all the year
round.
Coming Up for Air (1939) **Orwell, George** (1903–
1950) English writer and critic

49 And suddenly the memory came back to
me. The taste was that of the little piece of
madeleine which on Sunday mornings at
Combray ... my aunt Léonie used to give
me, after dipping it first in her cup of tea
or tisane.
Du côté de chez Swann (1913) **Proust, Marcel**
(1871–1922) French writer and critic

50 Come to me in the silence of the night;
Come in the speaking silence of a dream;
Come with soft rounded cheeks and eyes
as bright
As sunlight on a stream;
Come back in tears,
O memory, hope, love of finished years.
'Echo' (1862)

51 Remember me when I am gone away,
Gone far away into the silent land.
'Remember' **Rossetti, Christina** (1830–1894)
English poet

52 Look in my face; my name is Might-have-
been
I am also called No-more, Too-Late,
Farewell.

The House of Life (1881) **Rossetti, Dante Gabriel** (1828–1882) English poet, painter, translator and letter writer

53 Women and elephants never forget an injury.
Reginald (1904) **Saki** (1870–1916) Burmese-born British writer

54 To expect a man to retain everything that he has ever read is like expecting him to carry about in his body everything that he has ever eaten.
Parerga and Paralipomena (1851) **Schopenhauer, Arthur** (1788–1860) German philosopher

55 Praising what is lost
Makes the remembrance dear.
All's Well That Ends Well, V.iii

56 I can suck melancholy out of a song, as a weasel sucks eggs.
As You Like It, II.v

57 In sooth I know not why I am so sad.
It wearies me; you say it wearies you;
But how I caught it, found it, or came by it,
What stuff 'tis made of, whereof it is born,
I am to learn;
And such a want-wit sadness makes of me
That I have much ado to know myself.
The Merchant of Venice, I.i **Shakespeare, William** (1564–1616) English dramatist, poet and actor

58 Reminiscences make one feel so deliciously aged and sad.
The Irrational Knot (1905) **Shaw, George Bernard** (1856–1950) Irish socialist, writer, dramatist and critic

59 Illiterate him, I say, quite from your memory.
The Rivals (1775) **Sheridan, Richard Brinsley** (1751–1816) Irish dramatist, politician and orator

60 I remember your name perfectly, but I just can't think of your face.
Attr. **Spooner, William** (1844–1930) English churchman and university warden

61 I've a grand memory for forgetting, David.
Kidnapped (1886) **Stevenson, Robert Louis** (1850–1894) Scottish writer, poet and essayist

62 There are three things I always forget. Names, faces and – the third I can't remember.
Attr. **Svevo, Italo** (1861–1928) Italian writer

63 Tears, idle tears, I know not what they mean,
Tears from the depth of some divine despair
Rise in the heart, and gather to the eyes,
In looking on the happy Autumn-fields,
And thinking of the days that are no more.
The Princess (1847) **Tennyson, Alfred, Lord** (1809–1892) English lyric poet

64 The past is the only dead thing that smells sweet.
'Early One Morning' (1917) **Thomas, Edward** (1878–1917) English poet

65 But where are the snows of yesteryear?
Le Grand Testament (1461) **Villon, François** (1431–1485) French poet

66 Keep off your thoughts from things that are past and done;
For thinking of the past wakes regret and pain.
Resignation, translated from the Chinese of Po-Chü-I **Wain, John** (1925–1994) English poet, writer and critic
See also age; childhood and children; life

MEN AND WOMEN

1 A psychiatrist is a fellow who asks you a lot of expensive questions your wife asks for nothing.
Attr.

2 Never let a fool kiss you, or a kiss fool you.
Attr. **Adams, Joey** (1911–1999) US comedian and author

3 Three things have been difficult to tame: the oceans, fools and women. We may soon be able to tame the oceans; fools and women will take a little longer.
Attr. **Agnew, Spiro T.** (1918–1996) US Vice President

4 A gentleman is any man who wouldn't hit a woman with his hat on.
Attr. **Allen, Fred** (1894–1956) US vaudeville performer and comedian

5 Your experience will be a lesson to all of us
men to be careful not to marry ladies in
very high positions.
In A. Barrow, *International Gossip* (1983) **Amin,
Idi** (1925–2003) Ugandan dictator. Public
message to Lord Snowdon, when his marriage
to Princess Margaret broke up

6 A God, a God their severance ruled!
And bade betwixt their shores to be
The unplumb'd, salt, estranging sea.
'To Marguerite – Continued' (1852) **Arnold,
Matthew** (1822–1888) English poet, critic,
essayist and educationist

7 I do hope I shall enjoy myself with you … I
am parshial to ladies if they are nice I
suppose it is my nature. I am not quite a
gentleman but you would hardly notice it.
The Young Visiters (1919) **Ashford, Daisy** (1881–
1972) English child author

8 A divorce is like an amputation; you
survive, but there's less of you.
Time, (1973) **Atwood, Margaret** (1939–)
Canadian writer, poet and critic

9 There certainly are not so many men of
large fortune in the world as there are
pretty women to deserve them.
Mansfield Park (1814) **Austen, Jane** (1775–1817)
English writer

10 But the most ordinary cause of a single life,
is liberty; especially in certain self-pleasing
and humorous minds, which are so
sensible of every restraint as they will go
near to think their girdles and garters to be
bonds and shackles.
'Of Marriage and Single Life' (1625) **Bacon,
Francis** (1561–1626) English philosopher,
essayist, politician and courtier

11 Every man who is high up loves to think
that he has done it all himself; and the wife
smiles, and lets it go at that. It's our only
joke. Every woman knows that.
What Every Woman Knows (1908) **Barrie, Sir
J.M.** (1860–1937) Scottish dramatist and writer

12 A man would never get the notion of
writing a book on the peculiar situation of
the human male.
The Second Sex (1953) **Beauvoir, Simone de**
(1908–1986) French writer, feminist critic and
philosopher

13 It is not good that the man should be
alone; I will make him an help meet for
him.
Genesis, 2:18 **The Bible (King James Version)**

14 Mr Darwin … has failed to hold definitely
before his mind the principle that the
difference of sex, whatever it may consist
in, must itself be subject to natural
selection and to evolution.
The Sexes Throughout Nature (1875) **Blackwell,
Antoinette Brown** (1825–1921) US writer

15 Every modern male has, lying at the
bottom of his psyche, a large, primitive
being covered with hair down to his feet.
Making contact with this Wild Man is the
step the Eighties male or the Nineties male
has yet to take.
Iron John (1990) **Bly, Robert** (1926–) US writer

16 What's wrong with you men? Would hair
stop growing on your chest if you asked
directions somewhere?
*When You Look Like Your Passport Photo, It's
Time to Go Home* (1991) **Bombeck, Erma** (1927–
1996) US humorist and writer

17 Lord! Ye've little to complain o': ye may be
thankfu' ye're no married to her.
In Cockburn, *Memorials* (1856) **Braxfield, Lord**
(1722–1799) Scottish judge. To the butler who
gave up his place because Lady Braxfield was
always scolding him

18 It is probably true to say that the largest
scope for change still lies in men's attitude
to women, and in women's attitude to
themselves.
Lady into Woman (1953) **Brittain, Vera** (1893–
1970) English writer and pacifist

19 If homosexuality were the normal way, God
would have made Adam and Bruce.
New York Times, (1977) **Bryant, Anita** (1940–)
Australian feminist writer

20 Men have charisma; women have vital
statistics.
Sex and Sensibility (1992) **Burchill, Julie** (1960–)
English writer

21 For a' that, an' a' that,
It's comin yet for a' that,
That man to man the world o'er
Shall brithers be for a' that.

'A Man's a Man for a' that' (1795) **Burns, Robert** (1759–1796) Scottish poet and songwriter

22 The more I see of men, the less I like them. If I could but say so of women too, all would be well.
Journal, (1814)

23 Oh! too convincing – dangerously dear –
In woman's eye the unanswerable tear!
The Corsair (1814)

24 Man's love is of man's life a thing apart,
'Tis woman's whole existence.
Don Juan (1824) **Byron, Lord** (1788–1824) English poet, satirist and traveller

25 I was foretold, your rebell sex,
Nor love, nor pitty knew.
And with what scorne, you use to vex
Poore hearts, that humbly sue.
'A deposition from love' **Carew, Thomas** (c.1595–1640) English poet, musician and dramatist

26 An honest woman and a broken leg should be at home; and for a decent maiden, working is her holiday.
Don Quixote (1615) **Cervantes, Miguel de** (1547–1616) Spanish writer and dramatist

27 Women are much more like each other than men; they have, in truth, but two passions, vanity and love; these are their universal characteristics.
Letter to his son, (1749)

28 A man of sense only trifles with them, plays with them, humours and flatters them, as he does with a sprightly, forward child; but he neither consults them about, nor trusts them with, serious matters; though he often makes them believe that he does both.
Letter to his son, (1748) Of women

29 Have you found out that every woman is infallibly to be gained by every sort of flattery, and every man by one sort or other?
Letter to his son, (1752) **Chesterfield, Lord** (1694–1773) English politician and letter writer

30 Individually, men may present a more or less rational appearance, eating, sleeping and scheming. But humanity as a whole is changeful, mystical, fickle and delightful. Men are men, but Man is a woman.
The Napoleon of Notting Hill (1904) **Chesterton, G.K.** (1874–1936) English writer, poet and critic

31 I love men, not because they are men, but because they are not women.
Pensées de Christine, reine de Suede (1825) **Christina of Sweden** (1626–1689) Queen of Sweden

32 Women run everything. The only thing I've done within my house in the last twenty years is recognise Angola as an independent state.
Attr. **Clough, Brian** (1935–2004) English football manager

33 The man's desire is for the woman; but the woman's desire is rarely other than for the desire of the man.
Table Talk (1835) **Coleridge, Samuel Taylor** (1772–1834) English poet, philosopher and critic

34 I've never yet met a man who could look after me. I don't need a husband. What I need is a wife.
The Sunday Times, (1987) **Collins, Joan** (1933–) English actress and author

35 Man was by Nature Woman's cully made:
We never are, but by ourselves, betrayed.
The Old Bachelor (1693)

36 Heav'n has no rage, like love to hatred turned,
Nor Hell a fury, like a woman scorn'd.
The Mourning Bride (1697)

37 O the pious friendships of the female sex!
The Way of the World (1700)

38 A little disdain is not amiss; a little scorn is alluring.
The Way of the World (1700) **Congreve, William** (1670–1729) English dramatist

39 There is no fury like an ex-wife searching for a new lover.
The Unquiet Grave (1944)

40 The true index of a man's character is the health of his wife.
The Unquiet Grave (1944) **Connolly, Cyril** (1903–1974) English literary editor, writer and critic

41 There are so many kinds of awful men –
One can't avoid them all. She often said
She'd never make the same mistake again:
She always made a new mistake instead.
'Rondeau Redoublé' (1986)

42 The day he moved out was terrible –
That evening she went through hell.
His absence wasn't a problem
But the corkscrew had gone as well.
'Loss' (1992)

43 1. Don't see him. Don't phone or write a letter.
2. The easy way: get to know him better.
Attr. Two cures for love **Cope, Wendy** (1945–) English poet

44 Men and women belong to different species, and communication between them is a science still in its infancy.
Love and Marriage (1989) **Cosby, Bill** (1937–) US comedian, actor and author

45 Women tell men things that men are not very likely to find out for themselves.
In J. Madison Davis, *Conversations with Robertson Davies* (1989) **Davies, Robertson** (1913–1995) Canadian playwright, writer and critic

46 If a man does something silly, people say, isn't he silly? If a woman does something silly, people say, aren't women silly?
Attr. **Day, Doris** (1924–) US actress

47 When a diplomat says yes, he means perhaps. When he says perhaps he means no. When he says no, he is not a diplomat. When a lady says no, she means perhaps. When she says perhaps, she means yes. But when she says yes, she is no lady.
Speech at meeting of Magistrates Association, (14 October 1982) **Denning, Lord** (1899–1999) English Master of the Rolls. His views on the difference between a diplomat and a lady

48 The road to success is filled with women pushing their husbands along.
Epigram **Dewar, Lord Thomas Robert** (1864–1930) Scottish Conservative politician and writer

49 If men had to have babies, they would only ever have one each.
The Observer, (1984) **Diana, Princess of Wales** (1961–1997)

50 Take example by your father, my boy, and be wery careful o' widders all your life.
The Pickwick Papers (1837) **Dickens, Charles** (1812–1870) English writer

51 Men should be the ones who succeed. It makes me feel comfortable if men are the ones in control.
Daily Mail, (1995) **Dickinson, Angie** (1931–) US actress

52 The average man is more interested in a woman who is interested in him than he is in a woman – any woman – with beautiful legs.
News item, (1954)

53 Most women set out to try to change a man, and when they have changed him they do not like him.
Attr. **Dietrich, Marlene** (1901–1992) German-born US actress and singer

54 Never go to bed mad. Stay up and fight.
Phyllis Diller's Housekeeping Hints **Diller, Phyllis** (1917–1974) US comedian

55 It is rather ridiculous that a woman doing manual work is still seen as something to make a fuss about. It's clear from the people who come into the garden centre that it's the women who do the gardening.
Attr. **Dimmock, Charlie** (1966–) English gardener and TV presenter

56 Men are but children of a larger growth;
Our appetites as apt to change as theirs,
And full as craving too, and full as vain.
All for Love (1678) **Dryden, John** (1631–1700) English poet, satirist, dramatist and critic

57 Before they're plumbers or writers or taxi drivers or unemployed or journalists, men are men. Whether heterosexual or homosexual. The only difference is that some of them remind you of it as soon as you meet them, and others wait for a little while.
Practicalities (1987)

58 You have to be very fond of men. Very, very fond. You have to be very fond of them to love them. Otherwise they're simply unbearable.
Practicalities (1987) **Duras, Marguerite** (1914–1996) French author and filmmaker

59 Men love death. In everything they make, they hollow out a central place for death ... Men especially love murder. In art they celebrate it. In life, they commit it.
The Independent, (1992) **Dworkin, Andrea** (1946–2005) US writer and feminist

60 A clever woman has millions of born enemies – all stupid men.
Aphorisms (1880) **Ebner-Eschenbach, Marie von** (1830–1916) Austrian writer

61 I'm not denyin' the women are foolish: God Almighty made 'em to match the men.
Adam Bede (1859)

62 A man is seldom ashamed of feeling that he cannot love a woman so well when he sees a certain greatness in her: nature having intended greatness for men.
Middlemarch (1872) **Eliot, George** (1819–1880) English writer and poet

63 Men are what their mothers made them.
The Conduct of Life (1860) **Emerson, Ralph Waldo** (1803–1882) US poet, essayist, transcendentalist and teacher

64 When a woman behaves like a man, why doesn't she behave like a nice man?
The Observer, (1956) **Evans, Dame Edith** (1888–1976) English actress

65 Behind every great man is an exhausted woman.
The Independent, (1994) **Fairbairn, Lady Sam** Wife of Conservative MP Sir Nicholas Fairbairn

66 Most cases of rape are reported as an act of vengeance because the fellow has got himself another woman. Or guilt.
Daily Mail, (1993)

67 I can't say I've ever got visually, artistically or sexually excited by any of them. They all look as though they're from the Fifth Kiev Stalinist machine-gun parade.
Daily Mail, (1993) On women MPs **Fairbairn, Sir Nicholas** (1933–1995) Scottish Conservative MP and barrister

68 Here's how men think. Sex, work – and those are reversible, depending on age – sex, work, food, sports and lastly, begrudgingly, relationships. And here's how women think. Relationships, relationships, relationships, work, sex, shopping, weight, food.
Surrender the Pink (1990) **Fisher, Carrie** (1956–) US actress and writer

69 Mrs Browning's death is rather a relief to me, I must say: no more Aurora Leighs, thank God! A woman of real genius, I know; but what is the upshot of it all? She and her sex had better mind the kitchen and their children; and perhaps the poor: except in such things as little novels, they only devote themselves to what men do much better, leaving that which men do worse or not at all.
Letter to W.H. Thompson, (1861) **Fitzgerald, Edward** (1809–1883) English poet, translator and letter writer

70 I think men are intimidated by my independence and wonder what they have to offer me when I already have a house in Kensington and a career. Men of my generation still need to feel needed.
Daily Mail, (1995) **Francis, Clare** (1946–) English yachtswoman and writer

71 Men are clumsy, stupid creatures regarding little things, but in their right place they are wonderful animals.
My Brilliant Career (1901) **Franklin, Miles** (1879–1954) Australian writer

72 Whatever they may be in public life, whatever their relations with men, in their relations with women, all men are rapists, and that's all they are. They rape us with their eyes, their laws and their codes.
The Women's Room (1977) **French, Marilyn** (1929–) US writer and critic

73 Men weren't really the enemy – they were fellow victims suffering from an outmoded masculine mystique that made them feel unnecessarily inadequate when there were no bears to kill.
Christian Science Monitor, (1974) **Friedan, Betty** (1921–2006) US feminist leader and writer

74 A diplomat is a man who always remembers a woman's birthday but never remembers her age.
Attr. **Frost, Robert** (1874–1963) US poet

75 Never despise what it says in the women's magazines: it may not be subtle but neither are men.
The Observer, (1976) **Gabor, Zsa-Zsa** (1919–) Hungarian-born US actress

76 A man ... is so in the way in the house!
Cranford (1853) **Gaskell, Elizabeth** (1810–1865) English writer

77 Man may escape from rope and gun;
Nay, some have out-liv'd the doctor's pill:
Who takes a woman must be undone,
That basilisk is sure to kill.
The fly that sips treacle is lost in the sweets,
So he that tastes woman, woman, woman,
He that tastes woman, ruin meets.
The Beggar's Opera (1728)

78 I think, you must do like other widows – buy your self weeds, and be cheerful.
The Beggar's Opera (1728)

79 The comfortable estate of widowhood, is the only hope that keeps up a wife's spirits.
The Beggar's Opera (1728) **Gay, John** (1685–1732) English poet, dramatist and librettist

80 A man who is slovenly and untidy is considered normal. The woman who is either is a slut or a sloven or a slag.
The Times, (1999)

81 Women have very little idea of how much men hate them.
The Female Eunuch (1970)

82 A woman becomes the extension of a man's ego like his horse or his car.
The Female Eunuch (1970)

83 Probably the only place where a man can feel really secure is in a maximum security prison, except for the imminent threat of release.
The Female Eunuch (1970)

84 Mother is the dead heart of the family, spending father's earnings on consumer goods to enhance the environment in which he eats, sleeps and watches the television.
The Female Eunuch (1970) **Greer, Germaine** (1939–) Australian feminist, critic, English scholar and writer

85 When a man steals your wife, there is no better revenge than to let him keep her.
Elles et toi (1948) **Guitry, Sacha** (1885–1957) Russian-born French actor, dramatist and film director

86 The unpalatable truth is that a substantial proportion of women still accept the sexual division of labour which sees home-making as women's principal activity and income-earning as men's principal activity in life.
The Observer Review, (1996) **Hakim, Catherine** British sociologist

87 My mother said it was simple to keep a man, you must be a maid in the living room, a cook in the kitchen and a whore in the bedroom. I said I'd hire the other two and take care of the bedroom bit.
The Observer, (1985) **Hall, Jerry** (1956–) US fashion model and actress

88 I like to wake up feeling a new man.
In Simon Rose, *Classic Film Guide* (1995) **Harlow, Jean** (1911–1937) US film actress

89 If men knew how women pass the time when they are alone they'd never marry.
'Memoirs of a Yellow Dog' (1906) **Henry, O.** (1862–1910) US short-story writer

90 Gentlemen may remove any garment consistent with decency.
Ladies may remove any garment consistent with charm.
'Beneath the Arches' **Hewett, Dorothy** (1923–) Australian dramatist and poet

91 He created a man who was hard of head, blunt of speech, knew which side his bread was buttered on, and above all took no notice of women. Then God sent him forth to multiply in Yorkshire.
Pictures of Perfection (1994) **Hill, Reginald** (1936–) British writer and playwright

92 Man has his will, – but woman has her way.
The Autocrat of the Breakfast-Table (1858) **Holmes, Oliver Wendell** (1809–1894) US physician, poet, writer and scientist

93 The prevalence of men living alone has thus caused the coining of a new word in Australia: that word is 'baching'; and the word expresses vividly, if crudely, the ugly life it gives a name to.
God's Own Country: an Appreciation of Australia (1914) **Jacomb, C.E.** (b. 1888) British author

94 Jealousy is all the fun you think they had.
Fear of Flying (1973)

95 Men and women, women and men. It will never work.
Attr. **Jong, Erica** (1942–) US writer

96 Follow a shadow, it still flies you,
Seem to fly it, it will pursue:
So court a mistress, she denies you;
Let her alone, she will court you.
Say, are not women truly, then,
Styl'd but the shadows of us men?
The Forest (1616) **Jonson, Ben** (1572–1637) English dramatist and poet

97 Supposing ... a wife to be of a studious or argumentative turn, it would be very troublesome: for instance, – if a woman should continually dwell upon the subject of the Arian heresy.
In Boswell, *The Life of Samuel Johnson* (1791) **Johnson, Samuel** (1709–1784) English lexicographer, poet, critic, conversationalist and essayist

98 Years ago, manhood was an opportunity for achievement, and now it is a problem to be overcome.
The Book of Guys (1994) **Keillor, Garrison** (1942–) US writer and broadcaster

99 I believe that unarmed truth and unconditional love will have the final word in reality. That is why right, temporarily defeated, is stronger than evil triumphant.
Speech at Civil Rights March on Washington, (August 28 1963) **King, Martin Luther** (1929–1968) US civil rights leader and Baptist minister

100 Open and obvious devotion from any sort of man is always pleasant to any sort of woman.
Plain Tales from the Hills (1888)

101 Take my word for it, the silliest woman can manage a clever man; but it needs a very clever woman to manage a fool.
Plain Tales from the Hills (1888)

102 For a man he must go with a woman, which women don't understand –
Or the sort that say they can see it, they aren't the marrying brand.
'The Mary Gloster' (1894) **Kipling, Rudyard** (1865–1936) Indian-born British poet and writer

103 The First Blast of the Trumpet Against the Monstrous Regiment of Women.
Title of pamphlet, (1558)

104 To promote a Woman to bear rule, superiority, dominion or empire, above any Realm, Nation, or City, is repugnant to Nature; contumely to God, a thing most contrarious to his revealed will and approved ordinance; and finally it is the subversion of good Order, of all equity and justice.
'The First Blast of the Trumpet Against the Monstrous Regiment of Women', (1558) **Knox, John** (1505–1572) Scottish religious reformer

105 Quarrels would not last long if the fault were on one side only.
Maximes (1678) **La Rochefoucauld** (1613–1680) French writer

106 Man in every age has created woman in the image of his own desire.
In Neustater, *Hyenas in Petticoats: a Look at 20 Years of Feminism* (1989) **Laver, James** (1899–1975) English art, costume and design historian

107 There is no comradeship between men and women, none whatsoever, but rather a condition of battle, reserve, hostility.
Twilight in Italy (1916)

108 One realizes with horror, that the race of men is almost extinct in Europe. Only Christ-like heroes and woman-worshipping Don Juans, and rabid equality-mongrels.
Sea and Sardinia (1921)

109 I'm not sure if a mental relation with a woman doesn't make it impossible to love her. To know the mind of a woman is to end in hating her. Love means the pre-cognitive flow … it is the honest state before the apple.
Letter to Dr Trigant Burrow, (1927) **Lawrence, D.H.** (1885–1930) English writer, poet and critic

110 In my youth there were words you couldn't say in front of a girl; now you can't say 'girl'.
Sunday Telegraph, (1996) **Lehrer, Tom** (1928–) US humorist

111 Why can't a woman be more like a man? Men are so honest, so thoroughly square; Eternally noble, historically fair.
My Fair Lady (1956) **Lerner, Alan Jay** (1918–1986) US lyricist and screenwriter

112 She's the sort of woman who lives for others – you can tell the others by their hunted expression.
The Screwtape Letters (1942) **Lewis, C.S.** (1898–1963) Irish-born English academic, writer and critic

113 As unto the bow the cord is,
So unto the man is woman;
Though she bends him, she obeys him,
Though she draws him, yet she follows;
Useless each without the other!
The Song of Hiawatha (1855) **Longfellow, Henry Wadsworth** (1807–1882) US poet and writer

114 A bachelor lives like a king and dies like a beggar.
Attr. **Lowry, L.S.** (1887–1976) English painter

115 A man is only as old as the woman he feels.
Attr. **Marx, Groucho** (1895–1977) US comedian

116 Women want mediocre men, and men are working to be as mediocre as possible.
Quote Magazine, (1958) **Mead, Margaret** (1901–1978) US anthropologist, psychologist and writer

117 But it's the men who are attacking the women. If there's to be a curfew, let the men stay at home, not the women.
Attr. **Meir, Golda** (1898–1978) Russian-born Israeli stateswoman and Prime Minister. Replying to a member of her Cabinet who proposed a curfew on women after dark in response to a recent outbreak of assaults on women

118 Women hate revolutions and revolutionists. They like men who are docile, and well-regarded at the bank, and never late at meals.
Prejudices (1922)

119 Every normal man must be tempted, at times, to spit on his hands, hoist the black flag, and begin slitting throats.
Prejudices (1922)

120 Men have a much better time of it than women. For one thing, they marry later. For another thing, they die earlier.
A Mencken Chrestomathy (1949)

121 The only really happy people are married women and single men.
Attr. **Mencken, H.L.** (1880–1956) US writer, critic, philologist and satirist

122 I expect that Woman will be the last thing civilized by Man.
The Ordeal of Richard Feverel (1859) **Meredith, George** (1828–1909) English writer, poet and critic

123 One enlightened member said that in the past the Garrick Club excluded lunatics, gays and women: now the first two classes have been let in there's no conceivable reason to bar the third.
Attr. **Mortimer, John** (1923–) English lawyer, dramatist and writer

124 There are men I could spend eternity with. But not this life.
The Middle of the World (1981) **Norris, Kathleen** (1880–1966) US writer, pacifist and activist

125 A study in the *Washington Post* says that women have better verbal skills than men. I just want to say to the authors of that study: *Duh.*
Attr. **O'Brien, Conan** (1963–) US comedian

126 If civilisation had been left in female hands, we would still be living in grass huts.
Sex, Art and American Culture: Essays (1992) **Paglia, Camille** (1947–) US academic and writer

127 When a man stops being a god for his wife, he can be sure that he's now less than a man.
Doctor Angélico's Papers (1911) **Palacio Valdés, Armando** (1853–1938) Spanish novelist

128 Men seldom make passes
At girls who wear glasses.
Not So Deep as a Well (1937)

129 By the time you swear you're his,
Shivering and sighing,
And he vows his passion is
Infinite, undying –
Lady, make a note of this:
One of you is lying.
'Unfortunate Coincidence' (1937)

130 Oh, don't worry about Alan ... Alan will always land on somebody's feet.
In J. Keats, *You Might As Well Live* (1970) Said of her husband on the day their divorce became final **Parker, Dorothy** (1893–1967) US writer, poet, critic and wit

131 A woman is a foreign land,
Of which, though there he settle young,
A man will ne'er quite understand
The customs, politics, and tongue.
The Angel in the House (1854–1862) **Patmore, Coventry** (1823–1896) English poet

132 I don't think a prostitute is more moral than a wife, but they are doing the same thing.
The Observer, (1988) **Philip, Prince, Duke of Edinburgh** (1921–) Greek-born consort of Queen Elizabeth II

133 Men are gentle, honest and straightforward. Women are convoluted, deceptive and dangerous.
Attr. in *The Observer,* (1996) **Pizzey, Erin** (1939–) English writer and activist

134 Every woman adores a Fascist,
The boot in the face, the brute
Brute heart of a brute like you.
'Daddy' (1963) **Plath, Sylvia** (1932–1963) US poet, writer and diarist

135 Men, some to business, some to pleasure take;
But every Woman is at heart a rake:
Men, some to quiet, some to public strife;
But every lady would be queen for life.
'Epistle to a Lady' (1735) **Pope, Alexander** (1688–1744) English poet, translator and editor

136 Be to her virtues very kind;
Be to her faults a little blind;
Let all her ways be unconfin'd;
And clap your padlock – on her mind.
'An English Padlock' (1705) **Prior, Matthew** (1664–1721) English poet

137 I have sometimes regretted living so close to Marie – because I may be very fond of her, but I am not quite so fond of her company.
Sodome et Gomorrhe (1922) **Proust, Marcel** (1871–1922) French writer and critic

138 More and more it appears that, biologically, men are designed for short, brutal lives and women for long miserable ones.
The Observer, (1985) **Ramey, Estelle** (1917–) US physiologist, educator and feminist

139 How can I possibly dislike a sex to which Your Majesty belongs?
Attr. **Rhodes, Cecil** (1853–1902) English imperialist, financier and South African statesman. Replying to Queen Victoria who remarked that he disliked women

140 Women must come off the pedestal. Men put us up there to get us out of the way.
The Observer, (1920) **Rhondda, Viscountess** (1883–1958) English magazine editor and suffragette

141 I often want to cry. That is the only advantage women have over men – at least they can cry.
Good Morning, Midnight (1939) **Rhys, Jean** (1894–1979) West Indian-born English writer

142 Never trust a husband too far, nor a bachelor too near.

The Rubaiyat of a Bachelor (1925) **Rowland, Helen** (1875–1950) US writer

143 One of the greatest satisfactions for a man is when the woman he passionately desired and who obstinately refused to give herself to him ceases to be beautiful.
Notebooks (1834–1847) **Sainte-Beuve, Charles-Augustin** (1804–1869) French writer and critic

144 I admit it is better fun to punt than to be punted, and that a desire to have all the fun is nine-tenths of the law of chivalry.
Gaudy Night (1935) **Sayers, Dorothy L.** (1893–1957) English writer, dramatist and translator

145 Obedience is woman's earthly duty,
Harsh suffering is her sorry fate.
The Maid of Orleans (1801) **Schiller, Johann Christoph Friedrich** (1759–1805) German writer, dramatist, poet and historian

146 It is delightful to be a woman; but every man thanks the Lord devoutly that he isn't one.
The Story of an African Farm (1884) **Schreiner, Olive** (1855–1920) South African writer

147 The more I see of men the more I admire dogs.
Attr. **Sévigné, Marquise de** (1626–1696) French letter writer

148 The venom clamours of a jealous woman
Poisons more deadly than a mad dog's tooth.
The Comedy of Errors, V.i

149 She's beautiful, and therefore to be woo'd;
She is a woman, therefore to be won.
Henry VI, Part 1, V.iii

150 O heaven, were man
But constant, he were perfect!
The Two Gentlemen of Verona, V.iv **Shakespeare, William** (1564–1616) English dramatist, poet and actor

151 A man who has no office to go to – I don't care who he is – is a trial of which you can have no conception.
The Irrational Knot (1905)

152 I am a woman of the world, Hector; and I can assure you that if you will only take the trouble always to do the perfectly correct thing, and to say the perfectly correct thing, you can do just what you like.
Heartbreak House (1919) **Shaw, George Bernard** (1856–1950) Irish socialist, writer, dramatist and critic

153 How can a bishop marry? How can he flirt? The most he can say is, 'I will see you in the vestry after service.'
In Holland, *A Memoir of the Reverend Sydney Smith* (1855) **Smith, Sydney** (1771–1845) English clergyman, essayist, journalist and wit

154 Do you think it pleases a man when he looks into a woman's eyes and sees a reflection of the British Museum Reading Room?
In Cowan, *The Wit of Women* (1969) **Spark, Muriel** (1918–2006) Scottish writer, poet and dramatist

155 Men are uniformly more attentive to women of rank, family, and fortune, who least need their care, than to any other class.
In Anthony and Gage (eds), *History of Woman Suffrage* (1881) **Stanton, Elizabeth Cady** (1815–1902) US suffragist, abolitionist, feminist, editor and writer

156 Women dissemble their Passions better than Men, but ... Men subdue their Passions better than Women.
The Lover (1714) **Steele, Sir Richard** (1672–1729) Irish-born English writer, dramatist and politician

157 One day, an army of grey-haired women may quietly take over the earth.
Outrageous Acts and Everyday Rebellions (1984)

158 A woman needs a man like a fish needs a bicycle.
Attr. **Steinem, Gloria** (1934–) US writer and feminist activist

159 Long live love! Long live philandering!
A Sentimental Journey (1768) **Sterne, Laurence** (1713–1768) Irish-born English writer and clergyman

160 The most memorable is always the current one; the rest just merge into a sea of blondes.
Attr. **Stewart, Rod** (1945–) English rock singer. On his sexual partners

161 Thus finishing his grand survey,
The swain disgusted slunk away,
Repeating in his amorous fits,
'Oh! Celia, Celia, Celia shits!'
'The Lady's Dressing Room' (1732) **Swift, Jonathan** (1667–1745) Irish satirist, poet, essayist and cleric

162 Husbands' inertia at home has made its mark on the language. Wives refer to their menfolk with fond exasperation as 'oversize' trash – and males sheepishly apply the term to themselves. A more recent coinage tags retired husbands as 'wet leaves': no matter how you try to sweep them out the door, they stick to the spot where they landed.
Newsweek, (1990) **Takayama, Hideko** Japanese journalist

163 Man for the field and woman for the hearth:
Man for the sword and for the needle she:
Man with the head and woman with the heart:
Man to command and woman to obey;
All else confusion.
The Princess (1847)

164 Man is the hunter; woman is his game:
The sleek and shining creatures of the chase,
We hunt them for the beauty of their skins;
They love us for it, and we ride them down.
The Princess (1847) **Tennyson, Alfred, Lord** (1809–1892) English lyric poet

165 That dismal pleasure which the idea of sacrificing themselves gives to certain women.
Pendennis (1848–1850)

166 'Tis strange what a man may do, and a woman yet think him an angel.
The History of Henry Esmond (1852) **Thackeray, William Makepeace** (1811–1863) Indian-born English writer

167 I always say that if you want a speech made you should ask a man, but if you want something done you should ask a woman.
Speech to a townswomen's guild, (1982) **Thatcher, Margaret** (1925–) English Conservative Prime Minister

168 Gomer Owen who kissed her once by the pig-sty when she wasn't looking and never kissed her again although she was looking all the time.
Under Milk Wood (1954) **Thomas, Dylan** (1914–1953) Welsh poet, writer and radio dramatist

169 A man's bed is his resting-place, but a woman's is often her rack.
Further Fables for Our Time (1956) **Thurber, James** (1894–1961) US humorist, writer and dramatist

170 Don't trust your horse in the field, or your wife in the house.
The Kreutzer Sonata (1890) **Tolstoy, Leo** (1828–1910) Russian writer, essayist, philosopher and moralist

171 How I did respect you when you dared to speak the truth to me! Men don't know women, or they would be harder to them.
The Claverings (1867)

172 Men are so seldom really good. They are so little sympathetic. What man thinks of changing himself so as to suit his wife? And yet men expect that women shall put on altogether new characters when they are married, and girls think that they can do so.
Phineas Redux (1874) **Trollope, Anthony** (1815–1882) English writer, traveller and post office official

173 Women from time to time don't have it easy either. But we men have to shave.
Scraps (1973) **Tucholsky, Kurt** (1890–1935) German satirist and writer

174 When a man confronts catastrophe on the road, he looks in his purse – but a woman looks in her mirror.
The Left Lady (1926) **Turnbull, Margaret** (fl. 1920s–1942) Scottish-born US writer and dramatist

175 Scarce, sir. Mighty scarce.

Attr. **Twain, Mark** (1835–1910) US humorist, writer, journalist and lecturer. Responding to the question 'In a world without women what would men become?'

176 Sometimes I think if there was a third sex men wouldn't get so much as a glance from me.
Love Me Little (1957) **Vail, Amanda** (1921–1966) US writer

177 It is a sad feature of modern life that only women for the most part have time to write novels, and they seldom have much to write about.
The Observer, (1981)

178 It is one of the tragedies of our time to see women making a nuisance of themselves as welfare officers when they could be employed as nursery maids.
The Independent on Sunday, (1994) **Waugh, Auberon** (1939–2001) English writer and critic

179 This 'relationship' business is one big waste of time. It is just Mother Nature urging you to breed, breed, breed. Learn from nature. Learn from our friend the spider. Just mate once and then kill him.
Spectator, (1994) **Wax, Ruby** (1953–) US comedian

180 There's nothing sooner dry than women's tears.
The White Devil (1612) **Webster, John** (c.1580– c.1625) English dramatist

181 There is, of course, no reason for the existence of the male sex except that sometimes one needs help with moving the piano.
The Sunday Telegraph, (1970)

182 The man who is convinced that his mother was a fool.
The Clarion Defining an anti-feminist **West, Dame Rebecca** (1892–1983) English writer, critic and feminist

183 No nice men are good at getting taxis.
The Observer, (1977) **Whitehorn, Katherine** (1926–) English writer

184 Remember, Ginger Rogers did everything Fred Astaire did, but she did it backwards and in high heels.

Attr. **Whittlesey, Faith** (1939–) US diplomat

185 Whatever women do they must do twice as well as men to be thought half as good. Luckily, this is not difficult.
Canada Month, (1963) **Whitton, Charlotte** (1896–1975) Canadian writer

186 All women become like their mothers. That is their tragedy. No man does. That's his.
The Importance of Being Earnest (1895)

187 Men can be analysed, women ... merely adored.
An Ideal Husband (1895)

188 Women represent the triumph of matter over mind, just as men represent the triumph of mind over morals.
The Picture of Dorian Gray (1891) **Wilde, Oscar** (1854–1900) Irish poet, dramatist, writer, critic and wit

189 Men play the game; women know the score.
The Observer, (1982) **Woddis, Roger** British writer

190 Why are women ... so much more interesting to men than men are to women?
A Room of One's Own (1929)

191 It is the masculine values that prevail. Speaking crudely, football and sport are 'important'; the worship of fashion, the buying of clothes 'trivial'... This is an important book, the critic assumes, because it deals with war. This is an insignificant book because it deals with feelings of women in a drawing-room ... everywhere and much more subtly the difference of values persists.
A Room of One's Own (1929) **Woolf, Virginia** (1882–1941) English writer and critic

192 Well, a widow, I see, is a kind of sinecure.
The Plain Dealer (1677) **Wycherley, William** (c.1640–1716) English dramatist and poet
See also emancipation of women; humanity and human nature; love; marriage; sex; women

THE MILITARY

1 Any officer who shall behave in a scandalous manner, unbecoming the character of an officer and a gentleman shall ... be CASHIERED.
Articles of War **Anonymous** Definition of NAAFI

2 The boy who volunteered at seventeen At twenty-three is heavy on the booze.
'Returned Soldier' (1946) **Baxter, James K.** (1926–1972) New Zealand poet and playwright

3 It is the army that finally makes a citizen of you; without it, you still have a chance, however slim, to remain a human being.
'Less Than One' (1986) **Brodsky, Joseph** (1940–1996) Russian poet, essayist, critic and exile

4 The Guard dies and does not surrender.
Attr., Waterloo, (June 1815) **Cambronne, General** (1770–1842) French General

5 You may take the most gallant sailor, the most intrepid airman, or the most audacious soldier, put them at a table together – what do you get? The sum of their fears.
In Macmillan, *The Blast of War*. On the Chiefs of Staffs system, 1943

6 Don't talk to me about naval tradition. It's nothing but rum, sodomy and the lash.
In Gretton, *Former Naval Person* (1968) **Churchill, Sir Winston** (1874–1965) English Conservative Prime Minister

7 War is much too serious a thing to be left to the military.
In Suarez, *Sixty Years of French History: Clemenceau* **Clemenceau, Georges** (1841–1929) French Prime Minister and journalist

8 You must be ruthless, relentless, and remorseless! Sack the lot!
Letter, *The Times*, (1919) **Fisher, John Arbuthnot** (1841–1920) British admiral. On the ruinous cost of the Fleet and those responsible for it

9 An army, like a serpent, goes on its belly.
Attr. **Frederick the Great** (1712–1786) King of Prussia

10 Come cheer up, my lads! 'tis to glory we steer,
To add something more to this wonderful year;
To honour we call you, not press you like slaves,
For who are so free as the sons of the waves?
Heart of oak are our ships,
Heart of oak are our men:
We always are ready;
Steady, boys, steady;
We'll fight and we'll conquer again and again.
'Heart of Oak' (1759) **Garrick, David** (1717–1779) English actor and theatre manager

11 The ties that bound us together were of the most sacred nature: they had been gotten in hardship and baptised in blood.
Army Life: A Private's Reminiscence of the Civil War (1882) **Gerrish, Theodore** (1712–1786) US soldier

12 A standing army is like a standing member: an excellent assurance of domestic tranquillity but a dangerous temptation to foreign adventure.
The Observer, 'Soundbites', (1998) **Gerry, Elbridge** (1744–1814) US Vice President

13 Fortunately, the army has had much practice in ignoring impossible instructions.
The Boy Who Shot Down an Airship (1988) **Green, Michael** (1927–) English writer and playwright

14 I had examined myself pretty thoroughly and discovered that I was unfit for military service.
Catch-22 (1961) **Heller, Joseph** (1923–1999) US writer

15 *Ludendorff:* The English soldiers fight like lions.
Hoffman: True. But don't we know that they are lions led by donkeys.
In Falkenhayn, *Memoirs* **Hoffmann, Max** (1869–1927) German general. Referring to the performance of the British army in the First World War

16 National Service did the country a lot of good but it darned near killed the army.

Attr. **Hull, General Sir Richard** (1907–1989)

17 No man will be a sailor who has contrivance enough to get himself into a jail; for being in a ship is being in a jail, with the chance of being drowned … A man in a jail has more room, better food, and commonly better company.
In Boswell, *The Life of Samuel Johnson* (1791) **Johnson, Samuel** (1709–1784) English lexicographer, poet, critic, conversationalist and essayist

18 O, it's Tommy this, an' Tommy that, an' 'Tommy, go away';
But it's 'Thank you, Mister Atkins,' when the band begins to play …
Then it's Tommy this, an' Tommy that, an' 'Tommy 'ow's yer soul?'
But it's 'Thin red line of 'eroes' when the drums begin to roll …
For it's Tommy this, an' Tommy that, an' 'Chuck him out, the brute!'
But it's 'Saviour of 'is country' when the guns begin to shoot.
Barrack-Room Ballads and Other Verses (1892) **Kipling, Rudyard** (1865–1936) Indian-born British poet and writer

19 The conventional army loses if it does not win. The guerilla wins if he does not lose.
'Foreign Affairs', XIII (1969) **Kissinger, Henry** (1923–) German-born US Secretary of State

20 If you don't want to use the army, I should like to borrow it for a while. Yours respectfully, A. Lincoln.
Letter to General George B. McClellan during the US Civil War, (1862) **Lincoln, Abraham** (1809–1865) US statesman and President

21 These apparently rude and brutal natures comforted, encouraged, and reconciled each other to fate, with a tenderness and tact which was more moving than anything in life.
Her Privates We (1929) **Manning, Frederic** (1882–1935) Australian writer. Of the men in his battalion

22 No soldier can fight unless he is properly fed on beef and beer.
Attr. **Marlborough, Duke of** (1650–1722) English soldier

23 The Army works like this: if a man dies when you hang him, keep hanging him until he gets used to it.
Attr. **Milligan, Spike** (1918–2002) Irish comedian and writer

24 Leadership counts for something, of course, but it cannot succeed without the spirit, élan and morale of those led. Therefore I count myself the most fortunate of men in having been placed at the head of the finest fighting machine the world has ever known.
Argus, (1927)

25 A man of character in peace is a man of courage in war.
The Anatomy of Courage (1945) **Monash, Sir John** (1865–1931) Australian military commander

26 In my experience, I have always found that you cannot have an efficient ship unless you have a happy ship, and you cannot have a happy ship unless you have an efficient ship. That is the way I intend to start this commission, and that is the way I intend to go on – with a happy and an efficient ship.
Address to crew of HMS Kelly, (1939) **Mountbatten of Burma, First Earl** (1900–1979) English admiral and statesman

27 Then was seen with what a strength and majesty the British soldier fights.
History of the War in the Peninsula **Napier, Sir William** (1785–1860) British general and historian

28 An army marches on its stomach.
Attr. **Napoleon I** (1769–1821) French emperor

29 The army is the true nobility of our country.
Speech, (March 1855) **Napoleon III** (1808–1873) French emperor

30 Recollect that you must be a seaman to be an officer; and also, that you cannot be a good officer without being a gentleman.
In Southey, *The Life of Nelson* (1860) **Nelson, Lord** (1758–1805) English admiral. To his midshipmen

31 Our God and soldiers we alike adore
Ev'n at the brink of danger; not before:
After deliverance, both alike requited,
Our God's forgotten, and our soldiers
slighted.
'Of Common Devotion' (1632) **Quarles,
Francis** (1592–1644) English poet, writer and
royalist

32 And there's the outhouse poet,
anonymous:
Soldiers who wish to be a hero
Are practically zero
But whose who wish to be civilians
Jesus they run into millions.
'The Big Road' **Rosten, Norman** (1914–1995)
US poet and writer

33 Soldiers are citizens of death's gray land,
Drawing no dividend from time's
tomorrows …
Soldiers are dreamers; when the guns
begin
They think of firelit homes, clean beds, and
wives.
I see them in foul dug-outs, gnawed by
rats,
And in the ruined trenches, lashed with
rain,
Dreaming of things they did with balls and
bats.
'Dreamers' (1917) **Sassoon, Siegfried** (1886–
1967) English poet and writer

34 Napoleon's armies always used to march
on their stomachs, shouting: 'Vive
l'Intérieur!' and so moved about very
slowly.
1066 And All That (1930) **Sellar, Walter** (1898–
1951) and **Yeatman, Robert Julian** (1897–1968)
British writers

35 That in the captain's but a choleric word
Which in the soldier is flat blasphemy.
Measure For Measure, II.ii **Shakespeare,
William** (1564–1616) English dramatist, poet
and actor

36 You can always tell an old soldier by the
inside of his holsters and cartridge boxes.
The young ones carry pistols and
cartridges: the old ones, grub.
Arms and the Man (1898)

37 I never expect a soldier to think.
The Devil's Disciple (1901)

38 When the military man approaches, the
world locks up its spoons and packs off its
womankind.
Man and Superman (1903) **Shaw, George
Bernard** (1856–1950) Irish socialist, writer,
dramatist and critic

39 He was, above all, the first twentieth-
century general, a man with petrol in his
veins and a computer in his head.
Smithers, Alan Jack (1919–) Of Sir John
Monash, Australian military commander

40 'A soldier,' cried my uncle Toby,
interrupting the corporal, 'is no more
exempt from saying a foolish thing, Trim,
than a man of letters.' – 'But not so often,
and please your honour,' replied the
corporal.
Tristram Shandy (1759–1767) **Sterne, Laurence**
(1713–1768) Irish-born English writer and
clergyman

41 The chief attraction of military service has
been and will remain this compulsory and
irreproachable idleness.
War and Peace (1868–1869) **Tolstoy, Leo** (1828–
1910) Russian writer, essayist, philosopher
and moralist

42 I didn't fire him because he was a dumb
son of a bitch, although he was, but that's
not against the law for generals. If it was,
half to three-quarters of them would be in
gaol.
In Miller, *Plain Speaking* (1974) **Truman, Harry
S.** (1884–1972) US Democrat President. Of
General MacArthur

43 The French soldier is a civilian in disguise,
the German civilian is a soldier in disguise.
'Ocean of Pain' (1973) **Tucholsky, Kurt** (1890–
1935) German satirist and writer

44 As for being a General, well, at the age of
four with paper hats and wooden swords
we're all Generals. Only some of us never
grow out of it.
Romanoff and Juliet (1956) **Ustinov, Sir Peter**
(1921–2004) English actor, director, dramatist,
writer and raconteur

45 The army is a nation within the nation; it is one of the vices of our times.
The Military Condition, (1835) **Vigny, Alfred de** (1797–1863) French writer

46 In this country it is considered a good idea to kill an admiral from time to time, to encourage the others.
Candide (1759) **Voltaire** (1694–1778) French philosopher, dramatist, poet, historian, writer and critic. Referring to the execution of the British Admiral Byng for refusing to attack a French fleet

47 Discipline is the soul of an army. It makes small numbers formidable; procures success to the weak, and esteem to all.
Letter of Instructions to the Captains of the Virginia Regiments, (1759) **Washington, George** (1732–1799) US general, statesman and President

48 The mere scum of the earth.
In Stanhope, *Conversations with the Duke of Wellington* (1888) Of his troops

49 When I reflect upon the characters and attainments of some of the general officers of this army, and consider that these are the persons on whom I am to rely to lead columns against the French, I tremble; and as Lord Chesterfield said of the generals of his day, 'I only hope that when the enemy reads the list of their names, he trembles as I do.'
Letter to Torrens, (29 August 1810); usually quoted as 'I don't know what effect these men will have upon the enemy, but, by God, they frighten me.' **Wellington, Duke of** (1769–1852) Irish-born British military commander and statesman

50 The army ages men sooner than the law and philosophy; it exposes them more freely to germs, which undermine and destroy, and it shelters them more completely from thought, which stimulates and preserves.
Bealby (1915) **Wells, H.G.** (1866–1946) English writer
See also courage; war

MONARCHY AND ROYALTY

1 What a king, what a court, how fine a palace, what peace, what repose, what joy is there!
Hymnus Paraclitensis **Abelard, Peter** (1079–1142) French theologian and philosopher

2 The personality conveyed by the utterances which are put into her mouth is that of a priggish schoolgirl, captain of the hockey team, a prefect, and a recent candidate for confirmation. It is not thus that she will be able to come into her own as an independent and distinctive character.
National and English Review, (August 1958) **Altrincham, Lord (John Grigg)** (1924–2001) English columnist and writer. On Queen Elizabeth II's style when speaking in public

3 A monarchy is a merchantman which sails well, but will sometimes strike on a rock, and go to the bottom; a republic is a raft which will never sink, but then your feet are always in the water.
Attr. **Ames, Fisher** (1758–1808) US statesman and essayist

4 Bloody hell, Ma'am, what's he doing here?
Daily Mail, (1982) **Andrews, Elizabeth** Palace chaimbermaid. Said when an intruder was found in Queen Elizabeth II's bedroom

5 Most Gracious Queen, we thee implore
To go away and sin no more,
But if that effort be too great,
To go away at any rate.
Epigram on Queen Caroline, quoted in Lord Colchester's Diary, (1820)

6 Hark the herald angels sing
Mrs Simpson's pinched our king.
Quoted by Clement Attlee in a letter of 26 December (1938) **Anonymous**

7 An entire family of divorcees, and they're head of the Church of England. It's going to make the person out there wonder if it's all worth it.
Comment on the Royal Family, (1992) **Archer, Lord Jeffrey** (1940–) English Conservative politician and novelist

8 Royalty is a government in which the attention of the nation is concentrated on one person doing interesting actions. A Republic is a government in which that attention is divided between many, who are all doing uninteresting actions. Accordingly, so long as the human heart is strong and the human reason weak, royalty will be strong because it appeals to diffused feeling, and Republics weak because they appeal to the understanding.
The English Constitution (1867)

9 It has been said, not truly, but with a possible approximation to truth, 'that in 1802 every hereditary monarch was insane.'
The English Constitution (1867)

10 The best reason why Monarchy is a strong government is, that it is an intelligible government. The mass of mankind understand it, and they hardly anywhere in the world understand any other.
The English Constitution (1867)

11 The mystic reverence, the religious allegiance, which are essential to a true monarchy, are imaginative sentiments that no legislature can manufacture in any people.
The English Constitution (1867)

12 The sovereign has, under a constitutional monarchy such as ours, three rights – the right to be consulted, the right to encourage, the right to warn.
The English Constitution (1867)

13 The Monarchy gives now a vast strength to the entire Constitution, by enlisting on its behalf the credulous obedience of enormous masses.
The English Constitution (1867) **Bagehot, Walter** (1826–1877) English economist and political philosopher

14 Our cock won't fight.
In Frances Donaldson, *Edward VIII* (1974) **Beaverbrook, Lord** (1879–1964) Canadian-born British newspaper owner. Remark to Winston Churchill during the abdication crisis, 1936

15 The king never dies.
Commentaries on the Laws of England (1765–1769)

16 That the king can do no wrong, is a necessary and fundamental principle of the English constitution.
Commentaries on the Laws of England (1765–1769) **Blackstone, Sir William** (1723–1780) English judge, historian and politician

17 She was the People's Princess, and that is how she will stay ... in our hearts and in our memories forever.
The Times, (1997) **Blair, Tony** (1953–) British Labour Prime Minister. On hearing of the death of Diana, Princess of Wales, 31 August 1997

18 The time of absolute and exclusive national sovereignty has passed.
Scotland on Sunday, (1992) **Boutros-Ghali, Boutros** (1922–) Secretary General of the United Nations

19 She is Madonna crossed with Mother Theresa – a glorious totem of Western ideals.
Sex and Sensibility (1992) **Burchill, Julie** (1960–) English writer. Of Diana, Princess of Wales

20 Who will not sing God save the King
Shall hang as high's the steeple;
But while we sing God save the King,
We'll ne'er forget the People!
'Does Haughty Gaul Invasion Threat?' (1795) **Burns, Robert** (1759–1796) Scottish poet and songwriter

21 I wish that the Roman people had only one neck!
In Suetonius, *Lives of the Caesars* **Caligula** (AD 12–41) Roman emperor

22 'Hop in,' said the Queen Mother. In I piled
Between them to lie like a stick of wood.
I couldn't find a thing to say. My blood
Beat, but like rollers at the ebb of tide.
'I hope Your Majesties sleep well,' I lied.
A hand touched mine and the Queen said,
'I am
Most grateful to you, Jock. Please call me Ma'am.'
'The Australian Dream' (c.1965) **Campbell, David** (1915–1979) Australian poet, rugby player and wartime pilot

23 A king is an insult to every other man in the land.

Letter, (1887) **Carnegie, Andrew** (1835–1919) Scottish-born US millionaire and philanthropist

24 The one advantage about marrying a princess – or someone from a royal family – is that they do know what happens.
Attr. **Charles, Prince of Wales** (1948–) Son and heir of Elizabeth II and Prince Philip

25 I would rather hew wood than be a king under the conditions of the King of England.
Attr. **Charles X** (1757–1836) King of France

26 For in the end, mercy is the greatest sign by which the world may recognise a true king.
Cinna (1641) **Corneille, Pierre** (1606–1684) French dramatist, poet and lawyer

27 Her lunch.
Attr. **Coward, Sir Noël** (1899–1973) English dramatist, actor, producer and composer. Coward had been asked, while watching the 1953 Coronation of Queen Elizabeth II on TV, who the man was riding in a carriage with the portly Queen of Tonga

28 Wha the deil hae we got for a King, But a wee, wee German lairdie!
'The Wee, Wee German Lairdie' (1825) **Cunningham, Allan** (1784–1842) Scottish poet, reporter and biographer

29 Everyone likes flattery; and when you come to Royalty you should lay it on with a trowel.
Attr. To Matthew Arnold

30 No, it is better not. She would only ask me to take a message to Albert.
Attr. Asked if Queen Victoria should visit him during his last illness

31 Her Majesty is not a subject.
Attr. In answer to Gladstone's taunt that Disraeli could make a joke of any subject, including Queen Victoria

32 Your Majesty is the head of the literary profession.
Attr. To Queen Victoria **Disraeli, Benjamin** (1804–1881) English statesman and writer

33 I have found it impossible to carry the heavy burden of responsibility and to discharge my duties as King as I would wish to do without the help and support of the woman I love.
Abdication speech, (1936)

34 Perhaps one of the only positive pieces of advice that I was ever given was that supplied by an old courtier who observed: 'Only two rules really count. Never miss an opportunity to relieve yourself; never miss a chance to sit down and rest your feet.'
A King's Story (1951)

35 Now what do I do with this?
Attr. On receiving a large bill from a luxury hotel **Edward VIII** (later Duke of Windsor) (1894–1972) King of the United Kingdom; abdicated 11 December 1936

36 The chopper has changed my life as conclusively as that of Anne Boleyn.
Quoted in *The Guardian*, (2000) **Elizabeth, the Queen Mother** (1900–2002) Queen of the United Kingdom and mother of Elizabeth II. On her love of helicopters

37 I know I have the body of a weak and feeble woman, but I have the heart and stomach of a king, and of a king of England too; and think foul scorn that Parma or Spain, or any prince of Europe, should dare to invade the borders of my realm.
Speech, (1588) Of the approaching Armada

38 Though God hath raised me high, yet this I count the glory of my crown: that I have reigned with your loves.
The Golden Speech, (1601)

39 The daughter of debate, that eke discord doth sow.
In F. Chamberlin, *The Sayings of Queen Elizabeth* (1923) Of Mary Queen of Scots

40 The queen of Scots is lighter of a fair son, and I am but a barren stock.
In F. Chamberlin, *The Sayings of Queen Elizabeth* (1923)

41 I am your anointed Queen. I will never be by violence constrained to do anything. I thank God I am endued with such qualities that if I were turned out of the Realm in my petticoat I were able to live in any place in Christendome.
Speech, (1566) **Elizabeth I** (1533–1603) Queen of England

42 She's more royal than we are.
Attr., in *Sunday magazine*, (1985) **Elizabeth II** (1926–) Queen of the United Kingdom. Comment about Princess Michael of Kent

43 Do turn it off. So embarrassing unless one is there. Like hearing the Lord's Prayer when playing canasta.
The Guardian, (2000) On hearing the National Anthem on TV

44 The children will not leave unless I do. I shall not leave unless their father does, and the King will not leave the country in any circumstances whatever
Attr. On whether, after the bombing of Buckingham Palace, her children would leave England **Elizabeth, the Queen Mother** (1900–2002) Queen of the United Kingdom and mother of Elizabeth II

45 King Henry I being in Normandy, after some writers, fell from or with his horse, whereof he caught his death; but Ranulphe says he took a surfeit by eating of a lamprey, and thereof died.
The New Chronicles of England and France (1516) **Fabyan, Robert** (d.1513) English chronicler

46 There will soon be only five kings left – the Kings of England, Diamonds, Hearts, Spades and Clubs.
Attr. **Farouk I** (1920–1965) Last king of Egypt. Remark made to Lord Boyd-Orr, 1948

47 I am the emperor, and I want dumplings.
In E. Crankshaw, *The Fall of the House of Habsburg* (1963) **Ferdinand I, Emperor of Austria** (1793–1875)

48 What should I do? I think the best thing is to order a new stamp to be made with my face on it.
In H. Hoffmeister, *Anekdotenschatz* **Francis Joseph, Charles** (1887–1922) Emperor of Austria. On hearing of his accession to emperor

49 A crown is merely a hat that lets the rain in.
Remark on declining a formal coronation, (1740) **Frederick the Great** (1712–1786) King of Prussia

50 Born and educated in this country I glory in the name of Briton.
Speech, (1760) **George III** (1738–1820) King of Great Britain and Ireland

51 Today, 23 years ago, dear Grandmama died. I wonder what she would have thought of a Labour Government.
Diary, (22 January 1924) **George V** (1865–1936) King of the United Kingdom. Having just asked Ramsay MacDonald to form the first Labour Government

52 We're not a family; we're a firm.
Attr. in Lane, *Our Future King* **George VI** (1895–1952) King of the United Kingdom

53 The monarch is a person and a symbol. He makes power and state both intelligible and mysterious.
The Times, (1992) **Gilmour, Sir Ian** (1926–) Scottish Conservative politician

54 The tourists who come to our island take in the Monarchy along with feeding the pigeons in Trafalgar Square.
My Queen and I (1975) **Hamilton, William (Willie)** (1917–2000) British politician, teacher and antiroyalist

55 The king of France's horses are better housed than I am.
Attr. **Hanover, Ernst August, Elector of** (1629–1698) On seeing Louis XIV's stables at Versailles

56 The institution of monarchy is inherently silly.
The Times, (1998) **Hattersley, Roy** (1932–) British Labour politician and writer

57 It is my wish that in my kingdom there should be no peasant so poor that he cannot have a chicken in his pot every Sunday.
In Hardouin de Péréfixe, *Histoire du Roy Henry le Grand* (1681)

58 The wisest fool in Christendom.
Attr.; also attributed to Sully. Of James VI and I **Henri IV** (1553–1610) King of France

59 'Twixt Kings & Tyrants there's this
difference known;
Kings seek their Subjects good: Tyrants
their owne.
Hesperides (1648) **Herrick, Robert** (1591–1674)
English poet, royalist and clergyman

60 It cam' wi' a lass, and it'll gang wi' a lass.
Remark, (1542) **James V** (1512–1542) King of
Scotland. On the rule of the Stuart dynasty in
Scotland

61 There is not a single crowned head in
Europe whose talents or merit would
entitle him to to be elected a vestryman by
the people of any parish in America.
Attr. **Jefferson, Thomas** (1743–1826) US
Democrat statesman and President

62 The saddest of all Kings
Crown'd, and again discrown'd ...
Alone he rides, alone,
The fair and fatal king.
'By the Statue of King Charles I at Charing
Cross' (1895) **Johnson, Lionel** (1867–1902)
English poet and critic

63 They say princes learn no art truly, but the
art of horsemanship. The reason is, the
brave beast is no flatterer. He will throw a
prince as soon as his groom.
*Timber, or Discoveries made upon Men and
Matter* (1641) **Jonson, Ben** (1572–1637) English
dramatist and poet

64 He wrote that monarchs were divine,
And left a son who – proved they weren't!
Songs written for C.R.L. Fletcher's *A History of
England* (1911), 'James I' **Kipling, Rudyard**
(1865–1936) Indian-born British poet and
writer

65 George the First was always reckoned
Vile, but viler George the Second;
And what mortal ever heard
Any good of George the Third?
When from earth the Fourth descended
God be praised, the Georges ended!
The Atlas, (1855) **Landor, Walter Savage** (1775–
1864) English poet and writer

66 The Queen has lived for seventy years, for
seventy years and three;
And few have lived a flatter life, more
useless life than she;
She never said a clever thing or wrote a
clever line,
She never did a noble deed, in coming
times to shine;
And yet we read, and still we read, in every
magazine,
The praises of that woman whom the
English call 'the Queen',
Whom the English call 'the Queen',
Whom the English call 'the Queen' –
That dull and brainless woman whom the
English call 'the Queen'.
'The English Queen: A Birthday Ode' **Lawson,
Henry** (1867–1922) Australian writer and poet

67 A constitutional king must learn to stoop.
In Kelen, *The Mistress* **Leopold II** (1835–1909)
King of the Belgians. Instructing Prince
Albert, the heir apparent, to pick up some
papers from the floor

68 Every time I make an appointment, I make
a hundred men discontented and one
ungrateful.
In Voltaire, *Siècle de Louis XIV*

69 Ah, if I were not king, I should lose my
temper.
Attr.

70 I am the State.
Attr. (*L'État c'est moi*)

71 I almost had to wait.
Attr. **Louis XIV** (1638–1715) King of France

72 In order to keep his people united and
faithful, a prince must not be concerned
with being reputed as a cruel man.
The Prince (1532) **Machiavelli** (1469–1527)
Florentine statesman, political theorist and
historian

73 For though the whole world cannot shew
such another,
Yet we'd better by far have him than his
brother.
'The Statue in Stocks-Market' (1689) **Marvell,
Andrew** (1621–1678) English poet and satirist.
Of Charles II

74 For God's sake, ma'am, let's have no more of that. If you get the English people into the way of making kings, you'll get them into the way of unmaking them.
In Lord David Cecil, *Lord M.* (1954) **Melbourne, Lord** (1779–1848) English statesman. Advising Queen Victoria against granting Prince Albert the title of King Consort

75 He will go from resort to resort getting more tanned and more tired.
In Alistair Cooke, *Six Men* **Pegler, Westbrook** (1894–1969) US journalist. On the abdication of Edward VIII

76 Every king springs from a race of slaves, and every slave has had kings among his ancestors.
Theaetetus **Plato** (c.429–347 BC) Greek philosopher

77 What is a King? – a man condemn'd to bear
The public burden of the nation's care.
Solomon (1718) **Prior, Matthew** (1664–1721) English poet

78 A merry monarch, scandalous and poor.
'A Satire on King Charles II' (1697)

79 Here lies our sovereign lord the King
Whose word no man relies on,
Who never said a foolish thing,
Nor ever did a wise one.
Epitaph written for Charles II (1706) **Rochester, Earl of** (1647–1680) English poet, satirist, courtier and libertine

80 Kings and such like are just as funny as politicians.
In John Dos Passos, *Mr Wilson's War* (1963) **Roosevelt, Theodore** (1858–1919) US Republican President

81 Kings are but slaves of their rank,
They may not follow their own heart.
Maria Stuart (1800) **Schiller, Johann Christoph Friedrich** (1759–1805) German writer, dramatist, poet and historian

82 A king is a thing men have made for their own sakes, for quietness' sake. Just as in a family one man is appointed to buy the meat.
Table Talk (1689) **Selden, John** (1584–1654) English historian, jurist and politician

83 Charles II was always very merry and was therefore not so much a king as a Monarch.
1066 And All That (1930) **Sellar, Walter** (1898–1951) and **Yeatman, Robert Julian** (1897–1968) British writers

84 Uneasy lies the head that wears a crown.
Henry IV, Part 2, III.i

85 I think the King is but a man as I am: the violet smells to him as it doth to me.
Henry V, IV.i

86 We were not born to sue, but to command.
Richard II, I.i

87 For God's sake let us sit upon the ground
And tell sad stories of the death of kings:
How some have been depos'd, some slain in war,
Some haunted by the ghosts they have depos'd,
Some poison'd by their wives, some sleeping kill'd,
All murder'd – for within the hollow crown
That rounds the mortal temples of a king
Keeps Death his court.
Richard II, III.ii **Shakespeare, William** (1564–1616) English dramatist, poet and actor

88 The king reigns, and the people govern themselves.
Le National, (1830) **Thiers, Louis Adolphe** (1797–1877) French statesman and historian

89 If ever King George V were to set foot in Chicago
I'd punch him in the snoot.
Attr. **Thompson, William Hale 'Big Bill'** (1867–1944) US politician

90 All kings is mostly rapscallions.
The Adventures of Huckleberry Finn (1884)

91 The institution of monarchy in any form is an insult to the human race.
Notebook, (1888) **Twain, Mark** (1835–1910) US humorist, writer, journalist and lecturer

92 We are not amused.
Attr. in Holland, *Notebooks of a Spinster Lady* (1919) **Victoria, Queen** (1819–1901) Queen of the United Kingdom

93 Where to elect there is but one,
'Tis Hobson's choice, – take that or none.
England's Reformation (1630) **Ward, Thomas**
(1577–1639) English controversialist and poet

94 Here lies our mutton-loving King,
Whose word no man relies on,
Who never said a foolish thing,
And never did a wise one.
Wilmot, Charles, Earl of Rochester (1647–
1680) English writer and courtier, friend of
Charles II. On King Charles II

95 The monarchy is a labour-intensive
industry.
The Observer, (1977) **Wilson, Harold** (1916–1995)
English Labour Prime Minister

96 A little more willingness to bore, and much
less eagerness to entertain, would do the
monarchy no end of good in 1993.
The Sunday Telegraph, (1993)

97 Dull men do make the best kings.
Comment on BBC programme, *George VI –
The Reluctant King*, (1999) **Worsthorne, Sir
Peregrine** (1923–) English journalist

98 The king reigns, but does not govern.
Speech, Polish Parliament, (1605) **Zamoyski,
Jan** (1541–1605) Polish Chancellor and army
leader
See also government

MONEY AND WEALTH

1 The rich man has his motor car,
His country and his town estate.
He smokes a fifty-cent cigar
And jeers at Fate ...
Yet though my lamp burns low and dim,
Though I must slave for livelihood –
Think you that I would change with him?
You bet I would!
'The Rich Man' **Adams, Franklin P.** (1881–
1960) US writer, poet, translator and editor

2 The difference between playing the stock
market and the horses is that one of the
horses must win.
Reader's Digest, (1985) **Adams, Joey** (1911–1999)
US comedian and author

3 Wealth unused might as well not exist.
Attr. **Aesop** (6th century BC) Legendary Greek
writer of fables

4 I can't afford to waste my time making
money.
Attr. **Agassiz, Louis** (1807–1873) Swiss
naturalist. On lecturing for fees

5 People don't have fortunes left them in
that style nowadays; men have to work and
women to marry for money. It's a
dreadfully unjust world.
Little Women (1869) **Alcott, Louisa May** (1832–
1888) US writer

6 The almighty dollar is the only object of
worship.
Philadelphia Public Ledger, (1860)
Anonymous

7 Rich men's houses are seldom beautiful,
rarely comfortable, and never original. It is
a constant source of surprise to people of
moderate means to observe how little a big
fortune contributes to Beauty.
The Autobiography of Margot Asquith (1920)
Asquith, Margot (1864–1945) Scottish political
hostess and writer

8 A man who has a million dollars is as well
off as if he were rich.
Attr. **Astor, John Jacob** (1763–1848) German-
born US fur-trader and financier

9 An annuity is a very serious business; it
comes over and over every year, and there
is no getting rid of it.
Sense and Sensibility (1811)

10 A large income is the best recipe for
happiness I ever heard of. It certainly may
secure all the myrtle and turkey part of it.
Mansfield Park (1814) **Austen, Jane** (1775–1817)
English writer

11 Riches are a good handmaid, but the worst
mistress.
The Dignity and Advancement of Learning (1623)

12 And money is like muck, not good except it
be spread.
'Of Seditions and Troubles' (1625) **Bacon,
Francis** (1561–1626) English philosopher,
essayist, politician and courtier

13 Money, it turned out, was exactly like sex, you thought of nothing else if you didn't have it and thought of other things if you did.
Nobody Knows My Name (1961) **Baldwin, James** (1924–1987) US writer, dramatist, poet and civil rights activist

14 If you would know what the Lord God thinks of money, you have only to look at those to whom He gives it.
Attr. **Baring, Maurice** (1874–1945) English diplomat and writer

15 Pound notes are the best religion in the world.
The Wit of Brendan Behan (1968) **Behan, Brendan** (1923–1964) Irish dramatist, writer and Republican

16 Money speaks sense in a language all nations understand.
The Rover (1677) **Behn, Aphra** (1640–1689) English dramatist, writer, poet, translator and spy

17 Lord Finchley tried to mend the Electric Light
Himself. It struck him dead: And serve him right!
It is the business of the wealthy man
To give employment to the artisan.
More Peers (1911)

18 I'm tired of Love: I'm still more tired of Rhyme.
But Money gives me pleasure all the time.
Sonnets and Verse (1923) **Belloc, Hilaire** (1870–1953) English writer of verse, essayist and critic; Liberal MP

19 I don't trust a bank that would lend money to such a poor risk.
Attr. **Benchley, Robert** (1889–1945) US essayist, humorist and actor. Comment on being told his request for a loan had been granted

20 We've had our political democracy decapitated in the interests of the worship of money.
The Observer, (1999) **Benn, Tony** (1925–) English Labour politician

21 I've to prostitute myself to live comfortably and I see no point in money except to buy off anxiety. I don't want to be rich. I want to be unanxious.
Interview with Graham Lord, *Sunday Express,* (1974) **Betjeman, Sir John** (1906–1984) English poet laureate

22 Where your treasure is, there will your heart be also.
Matthew, 6:21

23 No man can serve two masters: – Ye cannot serve God and mammon.
Matthew, 6:24

24 It is easier for a camel to go through the eye of a needle, than for a rich man to enter into the kingdom of God.
Mark, 10:25

25 The love of money is the root of all evil.
I Timothy, 6:10 **The Bible (King James Version)**

26 Those who have some means think that the most important thing in the world is love. The poor know that it is money.
Thoughts in a Dry Season (1978) **Brenan, Gerald** (1894–1987) English writer

27 My first rule of consumerism is never to buy anything you can't make your children carry.
The Lost Continent (1989) **Bryson, Bill** (1951–) US travel writer

28 Put all your eggs in one basket, and then pay very close attention to that basket.
Attr. **Buffett, Warren** (1930–) US billionaire investment expert

29 If we command our wealth, we shall be rich and free: if our wealth commands us, we are poor indeed.
Two Letters on the Proposals for Peace with the Regicide Directory of France **Burke, Edmund** (1729–1797) Irish-born British statesman and philosopher

30 It has been said that the love of money is the root of all evil. The want of money is so quite as truly.
Erewhon (1872)

31 All progress is based upon a universal innate desire on the part of every organism to live beyond its income.
The Note-Books of Samuel Butler (1912) **Butler, Samuel** (1835–1902) English writer, painter, philosopher and scholar

32 The progress of human society consists … in … the better and better apportioning of wages to work.
Past and Present (1843) **Carlyle, Thomas** (1795–1881) Scottish historian, biographer, critic, and essayist

33 Surplus wealth is a sacred trust which its possessor is bound to administer in his lifetime for the good of the community.
The Gospel of Wealth **Carnegie, Andrew** (1835–1919) Scottish-born US millionaire and philanthropist

34 The saddest thing I can imagine is to get used to luxury.
My Autobiography (1964) **Chaplin, Charlie** (1889–1977) English comedian, actor, director and satirist

35 Where large sums of money are concerned, it is advisable to trust nobody.
Endless Night (1967) **Christie, Agatha** (1890–1976) English crime writer and playwright

36 It was said that he gave money away as silently as a waiter falling down a flight of stairs with a tray of glasses.
Gullible's Travels **Connolly, Billy** (1942–) Scottish comedian and actor. Of Andrew Carnegie

37 They hired the money, didn't they?
Remark, (1925) **Coolidge, Calvin** (1872–1933) US President. Of Allied war debts

38 But then one is always excited by descriptions of money changing hands. It's much more fundamental than sex.
Cards of Identity (1955) **Dennis, Nigel** (1912–1989) English writer, dramatist and critic

39 'It was as true,' said Mr Barkis, '… as taxes is. And nothing's truer than them.'
David Copperfield (1850)

40 Annual income twenty pounds, annual expenditure nineteen nineteen six, result happiness. Annual income twenty pounds, annual expenditure twenty pounds ought and six, result misery.
David Copperfield (1850) **Dickens, Charles** (1812–1870) English writer

41 Money doesn't talk, it swears.
'It's Alright, Ma (I'm Only Bleeding)' (song, 1965) **Dylan, Bob** (1941–) US singer and songwriter

42 Errors look so very ugly in persons of small means – one feels they are taking quite a liberty in going astray; whereas people of fortune may naturally indulge in a few delinquencies.
Scenes of Clerical Life (1858) **Eliot, George** (1819–1880) English writer and poet

43 Keep the change, my dear. I trod on a grape as I came in.
In B. Forbes, *Dame Edith Evans: Ned's Girl* (1977) **Evans, Dame Edith** (1888–1976) English actress. In Fortnum and Mason, to a salesgirl who insisted on giving her threepence change

44 In every well-governed state, wealth is a sacred thing; in democracies it is the only sacred thing.
Penguin Island (1908) **France, Anatole** (1844–1924) French writer and critic

45 Creditors have better memories than debtors.
Poor Richard's Almanac (1758) **Franklin, Benjamin** (1706–1790) US statesman, scientist, political critic and printer

46 There's no such thing as a free lunch.
Title of book **Friedman, Milton** (1912–) US economist

47 Wealth is not without its advantages, and the case to the contrary, although it has often been made, has never proved widely persuasive.
The Affluent Society (1958)

48 Economics is extremely useful as a form of employment for economists.
Attr.

49 Money differs from an automobile, a mistress or cancer in being equally important to those who have it and those who do not.
Attr. **Galbraith, J.K.** (1908–2006) Canadian-born US economist, diplomat and writer

50 If you can actually count your money you are not really a rich man.
In A. Barrow, *Gossip*

51 The meek shall inherit the earth, but not the mineral rights.
Attr. **Getty, John Paul** (1892–1976) US oil billionaire and art collector

52 There are three kinds of economist. Those who can count and those who can't.
The Observer Review, (1996) **George, Eddie** (1938–) Governor of the Bank of England

53 It is better to give than to lend, and it costs about the same.
Attr. **Gibbs, Sir Philip** (1877–1962) British journalist

54 As I walk along the Bois Bou-long,
With an independent air,
You can hear the girls declare,
'He must be a millionaire',
You can hear them sigh and wish to die,
You can see them wink the other eye
At the man who broke the bank at Monte Carlo.
'The Man who Broke the Bank at Monte Carlo', (1892) **Gilbert, Fred** (1850–1903) British songwriter

55 Finance is, as it were, the stomach of the country, from which all the other organs take their tone.
From an 1858 article, quoted in H.C.G. Matthew, *Gladstone 1809-1874* (1986) **Gladstone, William** (1809–1898) English statesman and reformer

56 They had been corrupted by money, and he had been corrupted by sentiment. Sentiment was the more dangerous, because you couldn't name its price. A man open to bribes was to be relied upon below a certain figure, but sentiment might uncoil in the heart at a name, a photograph, even a smell remembered.
The Heart of the Matter (1948) **Greene, Graham** (1904–1991) English writer and dramatist

57 It's a good thing to be able to take up your money in your hand and to think no more of it when it slips away from you than you would of a trout that would slip back into the stream.
Twenty-Five **Gregory, Lady Isabella Augusta** (1852–1932) Irish dramatist, writer and translator

58 I warn you there are going to be howls of anguish from the 80,000 people who are rich enough to pay over 75% on the last slice of their income.
Speech, Labour Party Conference, (1 October 1973) **Healey, Denis** (1917–) English Labour politician

59 When people talk about a wealthy man of my creed, they call him an Israelite; but if he is poor they call him a Jew.
MS. Papers **Heine, Heinrich** (1797–1856) German lyric poet, essayist and journalist

60 We don't pay taxes. Only the little people pay taxes.
Remark during her trial for tax evasion, (1989) **Helmsley, Leona** (1920–) Hotel tycoon

61 Prosperity is like the tide, being able to flood one shore only by ebbing from another.
Capricornia (1938), 16 **Herbert, Xavier** (1901–1984) Australian writer, poet and social critic

62 The only purpose in creating wealth like mine is to separate oneself from the riff-raff.
The Observer, (1998) **Hoogstraten, Nicholas van** English property developer. Banning ramblers who claimed their was a public right of way across his land

63 Make money: make it honestly if possible; if not, make it by any means.
Epistles **Horace** (65–8 BC) Roman lyric poet and satirist

64 Goddammit, I'm a billionaire.
Attr. **Hughes, Howard** (1905–1976) US millionaire industrialist, aviator and film producer. Response when called a 'paranoid, deranged millionaire' by a newspaper

65 We all know how the size of sums of money appears to vary in a remarkable way according as they are being paid in or paid out.
Essays of a Biologist **Huxley, Sir Julian Sorell** (1887–1975) English biologist and Director-General of UNESCO

66 Home life ceases to be free and beautiful as soon as it is founded on borrowing and debt.
A Doll's House (1879) **Ibsen, Henrik** (1828–1906) Norwegian writer, dramatist and poet

67 Man must choose whether to be rich in things or in the freedom to use them.
Deschooling Society (1971)

68 In a consumer society there are inevitably two kinds of slaves: the prisoners of addiction and the prisoners of envy.
Tools for Conviviality (1973) **Illich, Ivan** (1926–) Austrian-born US educator, sociologist, writer and priest

69 The almighty dollar, that great object of universal devotion throughout our land.
Wolfert's Roost (1855) **Irving, Washington** (1783–1859) US writer and diplomat

70 Excise. A hateful tax levied upon commodities.
A Dictionary of the English Language (1755)

71 There are few ways in which a man can be more innocently employed than in getting money.
In Boswell, *The Life of Samuel Johnson* (1791)

72 You never find people labouring to convince you that you may live very happily upon a plentiful fortune.
In Boswell, *The Life of Samuel Johnson* (1791)

73 Sir, the insolence of wealth will creep out.
In Boswell, *The Life of Samuel Johnson* (1791) **Johnson, Samuel** (1709–1784) English lexicographer, poet, critic, conversationalist and essayist

74 Academic economists have about the status and reliability of astrologers or the readers of Tarot cards. If the medical profession was as lacking in resources as the economics we would not have advanced very far beyond the provision of splints for broken arms.
In John Wilkes (ed.), *The Future of Work* **Jones, Barry Owen** (1932–) Australian politician

75 Where I'm from we don't trust paper. Wealth is what's here on the premises. If I open a cupboard and see, say, 30 cans of tomato sauce and a five-pound bag of rice, I get a little thrill of well-being – much more so than if I take a look at the quarterly dividend report from my mutual fund.
Attr. **Keillor, Garrison** (1942–) US writer and broadcaster

76 If you want to make money, go where the money is.
In A.M. Schlesinger Jr, *Robert Kennedy and his Times* (1978) **Kennedy, Joseph P.** (1888–1969) US businessman and diplomat

77 It is better that a man should tyrannize over his bank balance than over his fellow-citizens.
The General Theory of Employment, Interest and Money (1936)

78 But this long run is a misleading guide to current affairs. In the long run we are all dead. Economists set themselves too easy, too useless a task if in tempestuous seasons they can only tell us that when the storm is long past the ocean will be flat again.
A Tract on Monetary Reform (1923) **Keynes, John Maynard** (1883–1946) English economist

79 If we did not see it with our own eyes, could we ever imagine the extraordinary disproportion created between men by a larger or smaller degree of wealth?
Les caractères ou les moeurs de ce siècle (1688) **La Bruyère, Jean de** (1645–1696) French satirist

80 He said he considered £40,000 a year a moderate income – such a one as a man might jog on with.
In *The Creevey Papers* (1903) **Lambton, John, First Earl of Durham** (1792–1840) English statesman

81 Recognising that if you haven't got the money for something you can't have it – this is a concept that's vanished for many years.
Interview, *The Observer*, (1979) **Larkin, Philip** (1922–1985) English poet, writer and librarian

82 Money is our madness, our vast collective madness.
'Money-Madness' (1929) **Lawrence, D.H.** (1885–1930) English writer, poet and critic

83 For I don't care too much for money,
For money can't buy me love.
'Can't Buy Me Love' (song, 1964) **Lennon, John** (1940–1980) and Mcartney, Paul (1942–) English rock musicians, songwriters, peace campaigners and cultural icons

84 The working classes are never embarrassed about money – only the absence of it.
Comment, (1987) **Livingstone, Ken** (1945–) English Labour politician and Mayor of London

85 The Chancellor of the Exchequer is a man whose duties make him more or less of a taxing machine. He is intrusted with a certain amount of misery which it is his duty to distribute as fairly as he can.
Speech, (1870) **Lowe, Robert (Viscount Sherbrooke)** (1811–1892) English Liberal politician and lawyer

86 The best way to tell gold is to pass the nugget around a crowded bar, and ask them if it's gold. If it comes back, it's not gold.
Here's Another (1932) **Lower, Lennie** (1903–1947) Australian journalist

87 For that reason our Lord God commonly gives wealth to those coarse asses to whom he grants nothing else.
Table Talk (1531–1546) **Luther, Martin** (1483–1546) German Protestant theologian and reformer

88 We have heard it said that five per cent is the natural interest of money.
Collected Essays (1843) **Macaulay, Lord** (1800–1859) English Liberal statesman, essayist and poet

89 Men sooner forget the death of their father than the loss of their possessions.
The Prince (1532) **Machiavelli** (1469–1527) Florentine statesman, political theorist and historian

90 It is particularly vulgar to talk about one's money – whether one has lots of it, and boasts about it, or is broke, and says so. Now I myself cannot see why a man should not talk about his money. Everybody is interested in everybody else's finances, and it seems hypocrisy to hush the subject up in the drawing room – as if bank balances were found under gooseberry bushes.
'In Defence of Vulgarity' (1937)

91 Better authentic mammon than a bogus god.
Autumn Journal (1939) **MacNeice, Louis** (1907–1963) Belfast-born poet, writer, radio producer, translator and critic

92 I have enough money to last me the rest of my life, unless I buy something.
Jackie Mason's America **Mason, Jackie** (1934–) US comedian

93 Money is like a sixth sense without which you cannot make a complete use of the other five.
Of Human Bondage (1915) **Maugham, William Somerset** (1874–1965) English writer, dramatist and physician

94 A nation is not in danger of financial disaster merely because it owes itself money.
Attr. **Mellon, Andrew William** (1855–1937) US, banker, public official and art collector

95 Money can't buy friends, but you can get a better class of enemy.
Puckoon (1963) **Milligan, Spike** (1918–2002) Irish comedian and writer

96 For one person who dreams of making fifty thousand pounds, a hundred people dream of being left fifty thousand pounds.
If I May **Milne, A.A.** (1882–1956) English writer, dramatist and poet

97 Statistically you stand just as good a chance of winning the lottery if you don't buy a ticket.
The Times, (1998) **Monkhouse, Bob** (1928–2003) English comedian

98 But he died as many people like him could die tomorrow, running after money, and believing that there is nothing but money; then he was suddenly frozen by the fear of seeing what lies behind money.
Two Women (1957) **Moravia, Alberto** (1907–1990) Italian writer

99 Everyone knows that if money were abolished, fraud, theft, robbery, quarrels, brawls, seditions, murders, treasons, poisonings and a whole set of crimes which are avenged but not prevented by the hangman would at once die out. If money disappeared, so would fear, anxiety, worry, toil and sleepless nights. Even poverty, which seems to need money more than anything else, would vanish if money were entirely done away with.
Utopia (1516) **More, Sir Thomas** (1478–1535) English statesman and humanist

100 For the average European a job was an income, for the average Japanese it was a home.
Pictures From the Water Trade – An Englishman in Japan **Morley, John David** (1812–1870) British writer

101 In the midst of life we are in debt.
Altogether New Cynic's Calendar (1907) **Mumford, Ethel** (1878–1940) US writer, dramatist and humorist

102 He who is ridden by a conscience
Worries about a lot of nonscience;
He without benefit of scruples
His fun and income soon quadruples.
'Reflection on the Fallibility of Nemesis' (1940) **Nash, Ogden** (1902–1971) US poet

103 I am in an age group where it is rude to discuss money, and now it is all anyone cares about.
The Observer, (1999) **Nicholson, Jack** (1937–) US film actor

104 I'm going to spend, spend, spend, that's what I'm going to do.
In V. Nicholson and S. Smith, *I'm Going to Spend, Spend, Spend* **Nicholson, Vivian** (1936–) Reply when asked what she would do with the £152,000 she won on the pools in 1961

105 There are few things in this world more reassuring than an unhappy Lottery winner.
The Observer, (1998) **Parsons, Tony** (1953–) British journalist and author

106 Every time a thing is won,
Every time a thing is owned,
Every time a thing is possessed,
It vanishes.
Love Poems, 'Tristan, waking in his wood, panics' **Patten, Brian** (1946–) British poet

107 I bless God I do find that I am worth more than ever I yet was, which is £6,200, for which the Holy Name of God be praised!
Diary, (October 1666)

108 But it is pretty to see what money will do.
Diary, (March 1667) **Pepys, Samuel** (1633–1703) English diarist, naval administrator and politician

109 Water is best, but gold like fire blazing in the night shines more brightly than all other lordly wealth.
Olympian Odes **Pindar** (518–438 BC) Greek lyric poet

110 Money never remains just coins and pieces of paper. Money can be translated into the beauty of living, a support in misfortune, an education, or future security. It also can be translated into a source of bitterness.
Sylvia Porter's Money Book (1975) **Porter, Sylvia** (1913–1991) US financial journalist

111 You pays your money and you takes your choice.
(1846) **Punch**

112 Having money is rather like being a blond. It is more fun but not vital.
The Observer, (1986) **Quant, Mary** (1934–) English fashion designer

113 The more things accumulate the more life is wasted because they have to be purchased at the cost of life.
The Mustard Seed: Reflections on the Sayings of Jesus (1978) **Rajneesh, Bhagwan Shree** (1931–1990) Indian guru and teacher

114 Money is good for bribing yourself through the inconveniences of life.
In L. Ross, *Picture* **Reinhardt, Gottfried** (1911–1994) Austrian film producer

115 People say that money is not the key to happiness, but I always figured if you have enough money, you can have a key made.
Enter Talking (1986) **Rivers, Joan** (1937–) US comedian

116 Income tax has made more liars out of American people than golf.
The Illiterate Digest (1924) **Rogers, Will** (1879–1935) US humorist, actor, rancher, writer and wit

117 Always try to rub up against money, for if you rub up against money long enough, some of it may rub off on you.
Furthermore (1938) **Runyon, Damon** (1884–1946) US writer

118 Whereas it has long been known and declared that the poor have no right to the property of the rich, I wish it also to be known and declared that the rich have no right to the property of the poor.
Unto this Last (1862)

119 There is no wealth but life.
Unto this Last (1862) **Ruskin, John** (1819–1900) English art critic, philosopher and reformer

120 The dollar is Russia's national currency now, the rouble is just a sweetie paper. We've handed our sword to America.
Newsweek, (1994) **Rutskoi, Alexander** (1947–) Russian politician

121 All decent people live beyond their incomes nowadays, and those who aren't respectable live beyond other people's. A few gifted individuals manage to do both.
The Chronicles of Clovis (1911)

122 I'm living so far beyond my income that we might almost be said to be living apart.
Attr. **Saki** (1870–1916) Burmese-born British writer

123 I was on a basic £100,000 a year. You don't make many savings on that.
The Observer, (1987) **Saunders, Ernest** (1935–) English businessman

124 Wealth is like sea-water; the more we drink, the thirstier we become; and the same is true of fame.
Parerga and Paralipomena (1851) **Schopenhauer, Arthur** (1788–1860) German philosopher

125 The elegant simplicity of the three per cents.
In Campbell, *Lives of the Lord Chancellors* **Scott, William** (1745–1836) English judge and statesman

126 People will swim through shit if you put a few bob in it.
In Halliwell, *The Filmgoer's and Video Viewer's Companion* **Sellers, Peter** (1925–1980) English actor and comedian

127 I can get no remedy against this consumption of the purse; borrowing only lingers and lingers it out, but the disease is incurable.
Henry IV Part II, I.ii

128 Well, whiles I am a beggar, I will rail
And say there is no sin but to be rich;
And being rich, my virtue then shall be
To say there is no vice but beggary.
King John, II.i

129 Remuneration! O, that's the Latin word for three farthings.
Love's Labour Lost, III.i

130 If thou art rich, thou'rt poor;
For, like an ass whose back with ingots bows,
Thou bear'st thy heavy riches but a journey,
And Death unloads thee.
Measure For Measure, III.i **Shakespeare, William** (1564–1616) English dramatist, poet and actor

131 Money is indeed the most important thing in the world; and all sound and successful personal and national morality should have this fact for its basis.
The Irrational Knot (1905)

132 I am a Millionaire. That is my religion.
Major Barbara (1907)

133 The trouble, Mr Goldwyn, is that you are only interested in art and I am only interested in money.
In Johnson, *The Great Goldwyn* (1937) **Shaw, George Bernard** (1856–1950) Irish socialist, writer, dramatist and critic

134 My dear fellow, be reasonable; the sum you ask me for is a very considerable one, whereas I only ask you for twenty-five pounds.

Attr. After being refused a loan of £25 from a friend who asked him to repay the £500 he had already borrowed

135 It is not my interest to pay the principal, nor my principle to pay the interest.
Attr. To his tailor when he requested payment of a debt, or at least the interest on it
Sheridan, Richard Brinsley (1751–1816) Irish dramatist, politician and orator

136 I'm sorry to hear that, sir, you don't happen to have the shilling about you now, do you?
In L. Harris, *The Fine Art of Political Wit* (1965)
Sheridan, Tom (1775–1817) English poet. To his father, after learning that he was to be cut out of his will with a shilling

137 Nothing knits man to man ... like the frequent passage from hand to hand of cash.
'The Language of Art' **Sickert, Walter** (1860–1942) German-born British painter and writer

138 The rich only select from the heap what is most precious and agreeable. They consume little more than the poor, and in spite of their natural selfishness and rapacity ... they divide with the poor the produce of all their improvements. They are led by an invisible hand to make nearly the same distribution of the necessaries of life, which would have been made, had the earth been divided into equal portions among all its inhabitants.
The Theory of Moral Sentiments (1759)

139 With the greater part of rich people, the chief enjoyment of riches consists in the parade of riches, which in their eyes is never so complete as when they appear to possess those decisive marks of opulence which nobody can possess but themselves.
Wealth of Nations (1776)

140 In England the different poll-taxes never produced the sum which had been expected of them, or which, it was supposed, they might have produced, had they been exactly levied.
Wealth of Nations (1776) **Smith, Adam** (1723–1790) Scottish economist, philosopher and essayist

141 Eat with the rich, but go to the play with the Poor, who are capable of Joy.
Afterthoughts (1931)

142 It is the wretchedness of being rich that you have to live with rich people.
Afterthoughts (1931)

143 To suppose, as we all suppose, that we could be rich and not behave as the rich behave, is like supposing that we could drink all day and keep absolutely sober.
Afterthoughts (1931)

144 I love money; just to be in the room with a millionaire makes me less forlorn.
Afterthoughts (1931)

145 There are few sorrows, however poignant, in which a good income is of no avail.
Afterthoughts (1931) **Smith, Logan Pearsall** (1865–1946) US-born British epigrammatist, critic and writer

146 The schoolboy whips his taxed top – the beardless youth manages his taxed horse, with a taxed bridle, on a taxed road: – and the dying Englishman, pouring his medicine, which has paid seven per cent., into a spoon that has paid fifteen per cent. – flings himself back upon his chintz bed, which has paid twenty-two per cent. – and expires in the arms of an apothecary who has paid a licence of a hundred pounds for the privilege of putting him to death.
Edinburgh Review, (1820), 'America' **Smith, Sydney** (1771–1845) English clergyman, essayist, journalist and wit

147 I see that you are indifferent about money, which is a characteristic rather of those who have inherited their fortunes than of those who have acquired them; the makers of fortunes have a second love of money as a creation of their own, resembling the affection of authors for their own poems, or of parents for their children, besides that natural love of it for the sake of use and profit which is common to them and all men. And hence they are very bad company, for they can talk about nothing but the praises of wealth.
In Plato's *Republic* **Socrates** (469–399 BC) Athenian philosopher

148 Honours, like impressions upon coin, may give an ideal and local value to a bit of base metal; but Gold and Silver will pass all the world over without any other recommendation than their own weight.
Tristram Shandy (1759–1767) **Sterne, Laurence** (1713–1768) Irish-born English writer and clergyman

149 I have always treated money as the stuff with which one purchases time.
Attr. **Stoppard, Tom** (1937–) British dramatist

150 He was a gentleman who was generally spoken of as having nothing a-year, paid quarterly.
Mr Sponge's Sporting Tour (1853) **Surtees, R.S.** (1805–1864) English writer

151 If heaven had looked upon riches to be a valuable thing, it would not have given them to such a scoundrel.
Letter to Miss Vanhomrigh, (1720)

152 For God's sake, madam, don't say that in England for if you do, they will surely tax it.
In H. Pearson, *Lives of the Wits* (1962) Responding to Lady Carteret's admiration for the quality of the air in Ireland **Swift, Jonathan** (1667–1745) Irish satirist, poet, essayist and cleric

153 I am always fascinated by wealth makeovers for, like the 'before and after' style makeovers in women's magazines, I usually feel the subjects were better off before the advice was given.
Scotland on Sunday, (1999) **Swinson, Antonia** British novelist

154 By paying scarcely anybody people can manage, for a time at least, to make a great show with very little means.
Vanity Fair (1847–1848) **Thackeray, William Makepeace** (1811–1863) Indian-born English writer

155 Pennies do not come from heaven. They have to be earned here on earth.
The Sunday Telegraph, (1982) **Thatcher, Margaret** (1925–) English Conservative Prime Minister

156 I've been poor and I've been rich. Rich is better.
In Cowan, *The Wit of Women*

157 From birth to eighteen, a girl needs good parents. From eighteen to thirty-five, she needs good looks. From thirty-five to fifty-five, she needs a good personality. From fifty-five on, she needs good cash.
In Freedland, *Sophie* (1978) **Tucker, Sophie** (1884–1966) Russian-born US vaudeville singer

158 I'm only giving up nine months' earnings. It's not that big a deal.
The Guardian, (1999) **Turner, Ted** (1938–) US media tycoon. On donating $1 billion to the UN, 1997

159 A banker is a person who lends you his umbrella when the sun is shining and wants it back the minute it rains.
Attr. **Twain, Mark** (1835–1910) US humorist, writer, journalist and lecturer

160 The want of a thing is perplexing enough, but the possession of it is intolerable.
The Confederacy (1705) **Vanbrugh, Sir John** (1664–1726) English dramatist and baroque architect

161 I have had no real gratification or enjoyment of any sort more than my neighbor on the next block who is worth only half a million.
In B. Conrad, *Famous Last Words* (1961) **Vanderbilt, William H.** (1821–1885) US financier and railway magnate

162 Money does not smell.
In Suetonius, *Lives of the Caesars* **Vespasian** (AD 9–79) Roman emperor

163 There's a lot to be said for being *nouveau riche* and the Reagans mean to say it all.
The Observer, (1981) **Vidal, Gore** (1925–) US writer, critic and poet

164 O sacred hunger of pernicious gold! What bands of faith can impious lucre hold?
Aeneid **Virgil** (70–19 BC) Roman poet

165 Prosperity doth bewitch men, seeming clear;
As seas do laugh, show white, when rocks are near.
The White Devil (1612) **Webster, John** (c.1580–c.1625) English dramatist

166 Algebra and money are essentially levellers;
the first intellectually, the second
effectively.
Attr. **Weil, Simone** (1909–1943) French
philosopher, essayist and mystic

167 I don't 'old with Wealth. What is Wealth?
Labour robbed out of the poor.
Kipps: the Story of a Simple Soul (1905) **Wells,
H.G.** (1866–1946) English writer

168 Let us all be happy, and live within our
means, even if we have to borrow the
money to do it with.
'Science and Natural History' **Ward, Artemus**
(1834–1867) US humorist, journalist, editor
and lecturer

169 It is only by not paying one's bills that one
can hope to live in the memory of the
commercial classes.
The Chameleon, (1894) **Wilde, Oscar** (1854–1900)
Irish poet, dramatist, writer, critic and wit

170 You can be young without money but you
can't be old without it.
Cat on a Hot Tin Roof (1955) **Williams,
Tennessee** (1911–1983) US dramatist and
writer

171 It does not mean, of course, that the
pound here in Britain, in your pocket or
purse or in your bank, has been devalued.
Television broadcast, (1967)

172 One man's wage rise is another man's
price increase.
The Observer, (1970) **Wilson, Harold** (1916–
1995) English Labour Prime Minister

173 I don't owe a penny to a single soul – not
counting tradesmen, of course.
'Jeeves and the Hard-Boiled Egg' (1919)
Wodehouse, P.G. (1881–1975) English
humorist and writer

174 Pornography was the great vice of the
seventies; plutography – the graphic
depiction of the acts of the rich – is the
great vice of the eighties.
The Sunday Times Magazine, (1988) **Wolfe,
Tom** (1931–) US author and journalist

175 Please Lord, let me prove to you that
winning the lottery won't spoil me.
The Sunday Times, (2000) **Wood, Victoria**
(1953–) English comedian

176 Just what God would have done if he had
the money.
Attr. **Woollcott, Alexander** (1887–1943) US
writer, drama critic and anthologist. On being
shown round Moss Hart's elegant country
house and grounds

177 Income tax returns: the most imaginative
fiction written today.
Attr. **Wouk, Herman** (1915–) US novelist

178 I've got all the money I'll ever need – just
so long as I die by four o'clock.
Attr. **Youngman, Henry** (1906–1998) US
comedian
See also drink, drugs and debauchery; fame;
poverty; society

MORALITY

1 It is always easier to fight for one's
principles than to live up to them.
In Phyllis Bottome, *Alfred Adler: Apostle of
Freedom* (1939) **Adler, Alfred** (1870–1937)
Austrian psychiatrist and psychologist

2 People want to be amused, not preached
at, you know. Morals don't sell nowadays.
Little Women (1869) **Alcott, Louisa May** (1832–
1888) US writer

3 No morality can be founded on authority,
even if the authority were divine.
Essay on Humanism **Ayer, A.J.** (1910–1989)
English philosopher

4 I would rather be an opportunist and float
than go to the bottom with my principles
round my neck.
Attr. **Baldwin, Stanley** (1867–1947) English
Conservative statesman and Prime Minister

5 The great enemy of progressive ideals is
not the Establishment but the limitless
dullness of those who take them up.
To Jerusalem and Back: A Personal Account (1976)
Bellow, Saul (1915–2005) Canadian-born US
Jewish writer

6 Conventionality is not morality. Self-
righteousness is not religion. To attack the
first is not to assail the last. To pluck the
mask from the face of the Pharisee, is not
to lift an impious hand to the Crown of
Thorns.

Jane Eyre (1847) **Brontë, Charlotte** (1816–1855) English writer

7 Morality comes with sad wisdom of age. When the sense of curiosity has withered.
Attr. in *The Observer,* (1996) **Greene, Graham** (1904–1991) English writer and dramatist

8 I like a story with a bad moral ... all true stories have a coarse touch or a bad moral, depend upon't. If the story-tellers could ha' got decency and good morals from true stories, who'd have troubled to invent parables?
Under the Greenwood Tree (1872) **Hardy, Thomas** (1840–1928) English writer and poet

9 Dr Johnson's morality was as English an article as a beefsteak.
Our Old Home (1863) **Hawthorne, Nathaniel** (1804–1864) US allegorical writer

10 The quality of moral behaviour varies in inverse ratio to the number of human beings involved.
Grey Eminence (1941) **Huxley, Aldous** (1894–1963) English writer, poet and critic

11 We are perpetually moralists, but we are geometricians only by chance. Our intercourse with intellectual nature is necessary; our speculations upon matter are voluntary, and at leisure.
'Milton' **Johnson, Samuel** (1709–1784) English lexicographer, poet, critic, conversationalist and essayist

12 Your morals are like roads through the Alps. They make these hairpin turns all the time.
Fear of Flying (1973) **Jong, Erica** (1942–) US writer

13 Act in such a way that you treat humanity, both in your own person as well as in that of any other, at any time as an end withal, never merely as a means.
Outline of the Metaphysics of Morals (1785) **Kant, Immanuel** (1724–1804) German idealist philosopher

14 Morality is the tendency to throw out the bath along with the baby.
Pro domo et mundo (1912) **Kraus, Karl** (1874–1936) Austrian scientist, critic and poet

15 Morality which is based on ideas, or on an ideal, is an unmitigated evil.
Fantasia of the Unconscious (1922) **Lawrence, D.H.** (1885–1930) English writer, poet and critic

16 The time has come for all good men to rise above principle.
Attr. **Long, Huey** (1893–1935) US populist politician

17 We know of no spectacle so ridiculous as the British public in one of its periodical fits of morality.
'Moore's Life of Byron' (1843) **Macaulay, Lord** (1800–1859) English Liberal statesman, essayist and poet

18 You can't learn too soon that the most useful thing about a principle is that it can always be sacrificed to expediency.
The Circle (1921) **Maugham, William Somerset** (1874–1965) English writer, dramatist and physician

19 I can honestly say that I was never affected by the question of the success of an undertaking. If I felt it was the right thing to do, I was for it regardless of the possible outcome.
In Syrkin, *Golda Meir: Woman with a Cause* (1964) **Meir, Golda** (1898–1978) Russian-born Israeli stateswoman and Prime Minister

20 There is master-morality and slave-morality.
Beyond Good and Evil (1886)

21 Morality is the herd-instinct in the individual.
The Gay Science (1887) **Nietzsche, Friedrich Wilhelm** (1844–1900) German philosopher, critic and poet

22 One becomes moral as soon as one is unhappy.
À l'ombre des jeunes filles en fleurs (1918) **Proust, Marcel** (1871–1922) French writer and critic

23 When the Iroquois made a decision, they said, 'How does it affect seven generations in the future?'
New York Times Magazine, (1988) **Rifkin, Jeremy** (c.1860–1930) US bioethicist

24 We have, in fact, two kinds of morality side by side: one which we preach but do not practise, and another which we practise but seldom preach.
Sceptical Essays (1928) **Russell, Bertrand** (1872–1970) English philosopher, mathematician, essayist and social reformer

25 All universal moral principles are idle fancies.
The 120 Days of Sodom (1784) **Sade, Marquis de** (1740–1814) French soldier and writer

26 Without doubt the greatest injury of all was done by basing morals on myth. For, sooner or later, myth is recognized for what it is, and disappears. Then morality loses the foundation on which it has been built.
Romanes Lecture, (1947) **Samuel, Lord** (1870–1963) English Liberal statesman, philosopher and administrator

27 An Englishman thinks he is moral when he is only uncomfortable.
Man and Superman (1903) **Shaw, George Bernard** (1856–1950) Irish socialist, writer, dramatist and critic

28 Absolute morality is the regulation of conduct in such a way that pain shall not be inflicted.
'Prison Ethics' (1891) **Spencer, Herbert** (1820–1903) English philosopher and journalist

29 If your morals make you dreary, depend upon it, they are wrong.
Across the Plains (1892) **Stevenson, Robert Louis** (1850–1894) Scottish writer, poet and essayist

30 Moral indignation is jealousy with a halo.
The Wife of Sir Isaac Harman (1914) **Wells, H.G.** (1866–1946) English writer

31 The moral life of man forms part of the subject matter of the artist, but the morality of art consists in the perfect use of an imperfect medium.
The Picture of Dorian Gray (1891)

32 Morality is simply the attitude we adopt towards people whom we personally dislike.
An Ideal Husband (1895) **Wilde, Oscar** (1854–1900) Irish poet, dramatist, writer, critic and wit

33 Ethics does not treat of the world. Ethics must be a condition of the world, like logic.
In Auden, *A Certain World* **Wittgenstein, Ludwig** (1889–1951) Austrian philosopher
See also goodness; virtue

MUSIC

1 Music, the greatest good that mortals know,
And all of heaven we have below.
'Song for St Cecilia's Day' (1694) **Addison, Joseph** (1672–1719) English essayist, poet, playwright and statesman

2 The music teacher came twice a week to bridge the awful gap between Dorothy and Chopin.
Attr. **Ade, George** (1866–1944) US fabulist and playwright

3 The essence of pop is brilliant songs. The rest is sex, subversion, style and humour.
Attr. **Ant, Adam** (1954–) English pop star, stage name of Stuart Goddard

4 I do not mind what language an opera is sung in so long as it is a language I don't understand.
The Observer, (1955) **Appleton, Sir Edward Victor** (1892–1965) English physicist

5 A lotta cats copy the Mona Lisa, but people still line up to see the original.
Attr. **Armstrong, Louis** (1900–1971) US jazz trumpeter, singer and bandleader. When asked how he felt about people copying his style

6 Today what is not worth saying is made into a song.
Le Barbier de Seville (1775) **Beaumarchais** (1732–1799) French dramatist, essayist, watchmaker and spy

7 The musical equivalent of the towers of St Pancras station – neo-Gothic, you know.
In N. Cardus, *Sir Thomas Beecham* (1961) On Elgar's A Flat Symphony

8 The English may not like music – but they absolutely love the noise it makes.
In L. Ayre, *The Wit of Music* (1966)

9 Too much counterpoint; what is worse, Protestant counterpoint.
The Guardian, (1971) Of Bach

10 There are two golden rules for an orchestra: start together and finish together. The public doesn't give a damn what goes on in between.
In H. Atkins and A. Newman, *Beecham Stories* (1978)

11 He's a kind of musical Malcolm Sargent.
In H. Atkins and A. Newman, *Beecham Stories* (1978) On Herbert von Karajan

12 What can you do with it? – it's like a lot of yaks jumping about.
In H. Atkins and A. Newman, *Beecham Stories* (1978) On Beethoven's 7th Symphony

13 At a dinner given in honour of his seventieth birthday, when messages of congratulation from great musicians all over the world were being read out, he was heard to murmur, 'What, nothing from Mozart?'
In Patricia Young, *Great Performers*

14 In the first movement alone, I took note of six pregnancies and at least four miscarriages.
Attr. Of Bruckner's 7th Symphony

15 A musicologist is a man who can read music but can't hear it.
Attr.

16 Brass bands are all very well in their place – outdoors and several miles away.
Attr.

17 The sound of the harpsichord resembles that of a bird-cage played with toasting-forks.
Attr. **Beecham, Sir Thomas** (1879–1961) English conductor and impresario

18 When I composed that, I was conscious of being inspired by God Almighty. Do you think I can consider your puny little fiddle when He speaks to me?

Attr. **Beethoven, Ludwig van** (1770–1827) German composer. Said to a violinist complaining that a passage was unplayable

19 It is the best of all trades, to make songs, and the second best to sing them.
On Everything (1909) **Belloc, Hilaire** (1870–1953) English writer of verse, essayist and critic; Liberal MP

20 I'm not interested in having an orchestra sound like itself. I want it to sound like the composer.
New York Times, (1985) **Bernstein, Leonard** (1918–1990) US composer and conductor

21 The opera always loses money. That's as it should be. Opera has no business making money.
New York Times, (1959) **Bing, Rudolf** (1902–1997) Director of the New York Metropolitan Opera

22 You can't stop. Composing's not voluntary, you know. There's no choice, you're not free. You're landed with an idea and you have responsibility to that idea.
The Observer, (1996)

23 I get someone to write the programme notes. Then I know what the piece is about.
The Observer, (1996) **Birtwistle, Harrison** (1934–) English composer

24 Being a rock star is like having a sex change. People stare at you, follow you down the street shouting comments, they hustle you and touch you up. I now know what it must feel like to be a woman.
Attr. (1992) **Bono** (1960–) Irish rock musician, singer with U2; born Paul Hewson

25 For there is a music wherever there is a harmony, order or proportion; and thus far we may maintain the music of the spheres; for those well ordered motions, and regular paces, though they give no sound unto the ear, yet to the understanding they strike a note most full of harmony.
Religio Medici (1643) **Browne, Sir Thomas** (1605–1682) English physician, author and antiquary

26 All the delusive seduction of martial music.
Diary, (1802) **Burney, Fanny** (1752–1840) English diarist and novelist

27 How thankful we ought to feel that Wordsworth was only a poet and not a musician. Fancy a symphony by Wordsworth! Fancy having to sit it out! And fancy what it would have been if he had written fugues!
The Note-Books of Samuel Butler (1912) **Butler, Samuel** (1835–1902) English writer, painter, philosopher and scholar

28 When my enemies stop hissing, I shall know I'm slipping.
In Arianna Stassinopoulos, *Maria Callas* (1981) **Callas, Maria** (1923–1977) US opera singer

29 I am amazed at radio DJs today. I am firmly convinced that AM stands for Absolute Moron. I will not begin to tell you what FM stands for.
Attr. **Carrott, Jasper** (1945–) English comedian

30 If it wasn't for [pimps, prostitutes, hustlers, gangsters, and gamblers] there wouldn't be no jazz! They supported the club owners who bought the music. It wasn't the middle-class people who said 'Let's go hear Charlie Parker tonight.'
Jazz Forum, (1979) **Carter, Betty** (1929–1998) US singer

31 You're a blues person only when you're playing. But Negro blues men live the blues environment, eat soul food. Even hearing them talk can be like hearing the blues. Rock is like a battery that must always go back to blues to get recharged.
Newsweek, (18th March 1968) **Clapton, Eric** (1945–) English guitarist and songwriter

32 I cannot sing the old songs
I sang long years ago,
For heart and voice would fail me,
And foolish tears would flow.
'The Old Songs' (1865) **Claribel (Mrs C.A. Barnard)** (1840–1869) English ballad writer

33 I don't consider myself a pessimist. I think of a pessimist as someone who is waiting for it to rain. And I feel soaked to the skin.
The Observer, (1993) **Cohen, Leonard** (1934–) Canadian singer

34 Swans sing before they die 'twere no bad thing
Should certain persons die before they sing.

'Epigram on a Volunteer Singer' (1800) **Coleridge, Samuel Taylor** (1772–1834) English poet, philosopher and critic

35 All a musician can do is to get closer to the sources of nature, and so feel that he is in communion with the natural laws.
Interview, (1962) **Coltrane, John** (1926–1967) US jazz musician

36 Music has charms to soothe a savage breast.
The Mourning Bride (1697) **Congreve, William** (1670–1729) English dramatist

37 Extraordinary how potent cheap music is.
Private Lives (1930) **Coward, Sir Noël** (1899–1973) English dramatist, actor, producer and composer

38 I never thought that the music called 'jazz' was ever meant to reach just a small group of people, or become a museum thing locked under glass like all other dead things that were once considered artistic.
Miles (1989) **Davis, Miles** (1926–1991) US jazz musician

39 Music is the arithmetic of sounds as optics is the geometry of light.
Attr. **Debussy, Claude** (1862–1918) French composer and critic

40 What passion cannot Music raise and quell?
'A Song for St. Cecilia's Day' (1687) **Dryden, John** (1631–1700) English poet, satirist, dramatist and critic

41 And, from an open window, Mozart's strings
Encourage echoed songs,
Thrush-throats,
Thrush-wings.
Alluded nature, quoting from a quote,
Returns the symphony
To its wood-note.
Northlight (1988) **Dunn, Douglas** (1942–) Scottish poet

42 In writing songs I've learned as much from Cézanne as I have from Woody Guthrie.
In Clinton Heylin, *Dylan: Behind the Shades* (1991)

43 I knew that when I got into folk music it was more of a serious type thing. The songs were filled with more despair, more sadness, more triumph, more faith in the supernatural, much deeper feelings ... life is full of complexities, and rock and roll didn't reflect that.
In Clinton Heylin, *Dylan: Behind the Shades* (1991)

44 I like those people who come to see me now. They're not aware of my early days, but I'm glad of that. It lifts that burden of responsibility, of having to play everything exactly like it was on some certain record. I can't do that. Which way the wind is blowing, they're going to come out different every time.
New York Times, (1998)

45 Yeah, some of them are about ten minutes long, others five or six.
Interview On being asked if he could say something about his songs **Dylan, Bob** (1941–) US singer and songwriter

46 I would rather be a brilliant memory than a curiosity.
Attr. **Eames, Emma** (1865–1952) Chinese-born US opera singer. On giving up her operatic career at 47

47 Elvis is the dream gone wrong, that's why as a character he's so fascinating. His demise was such a public one. He was for a lot of people the definition of America, all its promise, all which it could achieve and all the freedom of the country.
The Edge (1961–) Irish rock star, guitarist with U2; born Dave Evans

48 I knew a very wise man who believed that ... if a man were permitted to make all the ballads, he need not care who should make the laws of a nation. And we find that most of the ancient legislators thought they could not well reform the manners of any city without the help of a lyric, and sometimes of a dramatic poet.
Letter to the Marquis of Montrose, (1704) **Fletcher, Andrew, of Saltoun** (1655–1716) Scottish politician and reformer

49 Beethoven's Fifth Symphony is the most sublime noise that ever penetrated into the ear of man.
Howard's End (1910) **Forster, E.M.** (1879–1970) English writer, essayist and literary critic

50 I'm singing in the rain, just singing in the rain;
What a wonderful feeling, I'm happy again.
'Singing in the Rain' (song, 1929) **Freed, Arthur** (1894–1973) US film producer and songwriter

51 We were none of us musical, though Miss Jenkyns beat time, out of time, by way of appearing to be so.
Cranford (1853) **Gaskell, Elizabeth** (1810–1865) English writer

52 I'm into pop because I want to get rich, get famous and get laid.
Attr. **Geldof, Bob** (1954–) Irish rock musician

53 I think the music is so marvelous – I really can't believe I wrote it.
Quoted by E. Jablonski in sleeve notes to the RCA Victor recording **Gershwin, George** (1898–1937) US composer and musician. On his opera *Porgy and Bess*

54 Blues is easy to play, but hard to feel.
In Charles Shaar Murray, *Crosstown Traffic* (1989) **Hendrix, Jimi** (1942–1970) US rock singer, songwriter and guitarist

55 Music helps not the tooth-ache.
Jacula Prudentum; or Outlandish Proverbs, Sentences & c. (1640) **Herbert, George** (1593–1633) English poet and priest

56 In just five years he had transformed popular music beyond recognition, making rock 'n' roll capable of seeing a great deal more than just Awopbopaloobop, and had been vilified, glorified, even deified for his trouble.
Behind The Shades (1991) **Heylin, Clinton** US music writer. Of Bob Dylan

57 Mom and Pop were just a couple of kids when they got married. He was eighteen, she was sixteen, and I was three.
Lady Sings the Blues (1956) The opening words of her autobiography

58 You can't copy anybody and end with anything. If you copy, it means you're working without any real feeling. No two people on earth are alike, and it's got to be that way in music or it isn't music.
Lady Sings the Blues (1956)

59 I can't stand to sing the same song the same way two nights in succession, let alone two years or ten years. If you can, then it ain't music, it's close-order drill or exercise or yodeling or something, not music.
Lady Sings the Blues (1956) **Holiday, Billie** (1915–1959) US singer

60 Never compose anything unless the not composing of it becomes a positive nuisance to you.
Letter to W.G. Whittaker **Holst, Gustav** (1874–1934) English composer

61 Since Mozart's day composers have learned the art of making music throatily and palpitatingly sexual.
Along the Road (1925) **Huxley, Aldous** (1894–1963) English writer, poet and critic

62 The more I think about it the more awful it is.
The Times, (1998) On audiences that want songs the Rolling Stones sang 30 years ago.

63 I think rock 'n' roll is all frivolity – it should be about pink satin suits and white socks.
Attr. **Jagger, Mick** (1943–) English rock musician

64 Of all musicians, flautists are most obviously the ones who know something we don't know.
The Jenguin Pennings, 'Flautists Flaunt Afflatus' **Jennings, Paul** (1918–1989) British humorous writer

65 The great thing about rock and roll is that someone like me can be a star.
The New York Times, (1992) **John, Elton** (1947–) English singer

66 Of music Dr Johnson used to say that it was the only sensual pleasure without vice.
In *European Magazine*, (1795) **Johnson, Samuel** (1709–1784) English lexicographer, poet, critic, conversationalist and essayist

67 Slow, slow, fresh fount, keep time with my salt tears:
Yet, slower, yet; O faintly, gentle springs:
List to the heavy part the music bears,
Woe weeps out her division, when she sings.
Cynthia's Revels (1600) **Jonson, Ben** (1572–1637) English dramatist and poet

68 I even think that sentimentally I am disposed to harmony. But organically I am incapable of a tune.
Essays of Elia (1823), 'A Chapter on Ears' **Lamb, Charles** (1775–1834) English essayist, critic and letter writer

69 There is delight in singing, tho' none hear Beside the singer.
'To Robert Browning' (1846) **Landor, Walter Savage** (1775–1864) English poet and writer

70 Oh, well, you play Bach your way. I'll play him his.
Attr. **Landowska, Wanda** (1877–1959) Polish-born US harpsichordist. Remark to a fellow musician

71 It is sobering to consider that when Mozart was my age he had already been dead for a year.
In N. Shapiro, *An Encyclopedia of Quotations about Music* **Lehrer, Tom** (1928–) US academic and songwriter

72 I can't listen to music too often. It affects your nerves; you want to say nice, stupid things and stroke the heads of people who could create such beauty while living in this vile hell. And now you must not stroke anyone's head – you might get your hand bitten off. You have to hit them on the head, without any mercy.
In Lev Trotsky, trans. M. Eastman, *The History of the Russian Revolution* (1933) **Lenin, V.I.** (1870–1924) Russian revolutionary, Marxist theoretician and first leader of the USSR. Remark made to Gorky, while listening to Beethoven

73 Those in the cheaper seats clap. The rest of you rattle your jewellery.
Remark, Royal Variety Performance, (15 November 1963)

74 Rock 'n' roll is the music that inspired me to play music. There is nothing conceptually better than rock 'n' roll. No group, be it the Beatles, Dylan or the Stones have ever improved on Whole Lotta Shakin' for my money. Or maybe, like our parents, that's my period and I'll dig it and never leave it.
Attr. (1969)

75 We're more popular than Jesus Christ now. I don't know which will go first. Rock and roll or Christianity.
The Beatles Illustrated Lyrics **Lennon, John** (1940–1980) English rock musician, peace campaigner and cultural icon

76 You write a hit the same way you write a flop.
Attr. **Lerner, Alan Jay** (1918–1986) US lyricist and screenwriter

77 Just because the songs are about reality, there's no reason for music to be boring or depressing. Music is about uplifting people, you know?
Attr. (1995) **MacGowan, Shane** (1957–) Irish singer

78 I'm anal retentive. I'm a workaholic. I have insomnia. And I'm a control freak. That's why I'm not married. Who could stand me?
In Christopher Andersen, *Madonna Unauthorized* (1991) **Madonna** (1958–) US singer and actress

79 If you're in jazz and more than ten people like you, you're labelled commercial.
Mann, Herbie (1930–2003) US jazz flautist, born Herbert Solomon

80 A rock 'n' roll group is a banding together of individuals for the purpose of achieving something that none of them can get on their own: money, fame, the right sound, something less easy to put into words.
Marcus, Greil (1945–) US rock journalist

81 Music-hall songs provide the dull with wit, just as proverbs provide them with wisdom.
A Writer's Notebook (1949) **Maugham, William Somerset** (1874–1965) English writer, dramatist and physician

82 Something touched me deep inside
The day the music died.
'American Pie' (song, 1972) **McLean, Don** (1945–) US singer. On the death of Buddy Holly

83 The first rule in opera is the first rule in life: see to everything yourself.
Melodies and Memories (1925) **Melba, Dame Nellie** (1861–1931) Australian opera singer

84 Opera in English is, in the main, just about as sensible as baseball in Italian.
Attr. **Mencken, H.L.** (1880–1956) US writer, critic, philologist and satirist

85 Going to the opera, like getting drunk, is a sin that carries its own punishment with it.
The Letters of Hannah More (1925) **More, Hannah** (1745–1833) English poet, dramatist and religious writer

86 Music is spiritual. The music business is not.
The Times, (1990) **Morrison, Van** (1945–) Irish singer

87 To the outside adult eye, Punk Rock is the weirdest, ugliest, nastiest, scariest, most thoroughly repulsive and flat-out incomprehensible variant on the Teenage Wasteland formula that they've ever seen.
Attr. (1977) **Murray, Charles Shaar** (1952–) English rock journalist

88 The most despairing songs are the most beautiful, and I know of immortal ones which are pure tears.
'La Nuit de mai' (1840) **Musset, Alfred de** (1810–1857) French dramatist and poet

89 I don't like country music, but I don't mean to denigrate those who do. And for the people who like country music, denigrate means 'put down'.
Newhart, Bob (1929–) US comedian

90 I sometimes wonder which would be nicer – an opera without an interval, or an interval without an opera.
In Heyworth (ed.), *Berlioz, Romantic and Classic* **Newman, Ernest** (1868–1959) English music critic and writer

91 They teach you there's a boundary line to music. But, man, there's no boundary line to art.

In Shapiro and Hentoff, *Hear Me Talkin' To Ya* (1955)

92 Music is your own experience, your thoughts, your wisdom. If you don't live it, it won't come out of your horn.
In Shapiro and Hentoff, *Hear Me Talkin' To Ya* (1955)

93 Any musician who says he is playing better either on tea, the needle, or when he is juiced, is a plain straight liar ... You can miss the most important years of your life, the years of possible creation.
In Shapiro and Hentoff, *Hear Me Talkin' To Ya* (1955) **Parker, Charlie** (1920–1955) US jazz musician and composer

94 When I first met Elvis, he had a million dollars worth of talent. Now he has a million dollars.
Parker, Colonel Tom (1909–1997) US musical impresario, manager of Elvis Presley

95 Those people on the stage are making such a noise I can't hear a word you're saying.
In L. Humphrey, *The Humor of Music* **Parker, Henry Taylor** (1867–1934) US music critic. Rebuking some talkative members of an audience, near whom he was sitting

96 Learning music by reading about it is like making love by mail.
Reader's Digest, (1988)

97 In opera, as with any performing art, to be in great demand and to command high fees you must be good of course, but you must also be famous. The two are different things.
Autobiography

98 You don't need any brains to listen to music.
Attr. **Pavarotti, Luciano** (1935–) Italian opera singer

99 Went to hear Mrs Turner's daughter ... play on the harpsichon; but, Lord! it was enough to make any man sick to hear her; yet was I forced to commend her highly.
Diary, (May 1663)

100 Music and women I cannot but give way to, whatever my business is.

Diary, (1666) **Pepys, Samuel** (1633–1703) English diarist, naval administrator and politician

101 I tried to resist his overtures, but he plied me with symphonies, quartets, chamber music and cantatas.
Crazy Like a Fox (1944), 'The Love Decoy' **Perelman, S.J.** (1904–1979) US humorist, writer and dramatist

102 My sole inspiration is a telephone call from a director.
Press interview, (1955) **Porter, Cole** (1891–1964) US composer and lyricist

103 Music begins to atrophy when it departs too far from the dance; ... poetry begins to atrophy when it gets too far from music.
ABC of Reading (1934) **Pound, Ezra** (1885–1972) US poet

104 The basic difference between classical music and jazz is that in the former the music is always greater than its performance – whereas the way jazz is performed is always more important than what is being played.
In Shapiro, *An Encyclopedia of Quotations about Music* **Previn, André** (1929–) German-born US conductor and composer

105 Michael Jackson's album was only called Bad because there wasn't enough room on the sleeve for Pathetic.
Attr. **Prince** (1958–) US singer and musician

106 The kind of opera that starts at six o'clock and after it has been going three hours, you look at your watch and it says 6.20.
In *The Frank Muir Book* (1976) **Randolph, David** (1914–) US conductor. On Parsifal

107 The Beatles are a Shakespeare for the 20th century.
The Times, (1999) **Reddington, Helen** Lecturer in commercial music

108 I've never been interested in writing pop songs. I don't consider myself part of pop music at all.
Reed, Lou (1942–) US rock star and songwriter

109 I'll grow old physically, but I won't grow old musically
Richard, Cliff (1940–) English pop star

110 I have already heard it. I had better not go: I will start to get accustomed to it and finally like it.
In Robert Craft and Igor Stavinsky, *Conversations with Stravinsky* (1959) **Rimsky-Korsakov, Nikolai** (1844–1908) Russian composer. Of Debussy's music

111 Berry Gordy taught me how to make my songs be a story, with a beginning, a middle, an end and a theme.
Robinson, Smokey (1940–) US singer and songwriter

112 Wagner has beautiful moments but awful quarters of an hour.
In E. Naumann, *Italienische Tondichter* (1883)

113 Give me a laundry-list and I will set it to music.
Attr. **Rossini, Gioacchino** (1792–1868) Italian composer

114 To be frank, Mr Epstein, we don't like your boys' sound – groups of guitarists are on the way out.
Attr. (1962) **Rowe, Dick** (d. 1986) English impresario, head of Decca Records. Commenting on the future of The Beatles in the record industry

115 Often I am still listening when the song has ended.
Les Saisons, 'Le Printemps' **Saint-Lambert, Jean François, Marquis de** (1716–1803) French poet

116 Music is essentially useless, as life is: but both have an ideal extension which lends utility to its conditions.
The Life of Reason (1905–1906) **Santayana, George** (1863–1952) Spanish-born US philosopher and writer

117 A genius! For thirty-seven years I've practised fourteen hours a day, and now they call me a genius!
Attr. **Sarasate (y Navascués), Pablo** (1844–1908) Spanish violinist and composer. On being hailed as a genius by a critic

118 Just a little more reverence, please, and not so much astonishment.

Attr. **Sargent, Sir Malcolm** (1895–1967) English conductor. Rehearsing a female chorus in 'For Unto Us a Child is Born' from Handel's *Messiah*

119 Everyone suddenly burst out singing;
And I was filled with such delight
As prisoned birds must find in freedom
Winging wildly across the white
Orchards and dark green fields; on – on –
and out of sight.
'Everyone Sang' (1919)

120 The song was wordless;
The singing will never be done.
'Everyone Sang' (1919) **Sassoon, Siegfried** (1886–1967) English poet and writer

121 The musician is perhaps the most modest of animals, but he is also the proudest. It is he who invented the sublime art of ruining poetry.
In Pierre-Daniel Templier, *Erik Satie*

122 To be played with both hands in the pocket.
Attr. Direction on one of his piano pieces **Satie, Erik** (1866–1925) French composer

123 The notes I handle no better than many pianists. But the pauses between the notes – ah, that is where the art resides.
Chicago Daily News, (1958)

124 I know two kinds of audience only – one coughing and one not coughing.
My Life and Music (1961)

125 The sonatas of Mozart are unique; they are too easy for children, and too difficult for artists.
In Nat Shapiro (ed.), *An Encyclopaedia of Quotations about Music* (1978)

126 When a piece gets difficult make faces.
Attr. Advice given to the pianist Vladimir Horowitz **Schnabel, Artur** (1882–1951) Austrian pianist and composer

127 My compositions spring from my sorrows. Those that give the world the greatest delight were born of my deepest griefs.
Diary, (1824) **Schubert, Franz** (1797–1828) Austrian composer

128 Originally, the function of songs was devotional, I think. Then in the balladeering centuries, they became a vehicle for the spreading of information, stories and opinions. Now in the 20th century they become a way of making money and achieving fame. I think the other two purposes are much better.
Scott, Mike (1958–) Scottish singer, mainly with The Waterboys

129 The way was long, the wind was cold,
The Minstrel was infirm and old;
His wither'd cheek, and tresses gray,
Seemed to have known a better day.
The Lay of the Last Minstrel (1805), Introduction
Scott, Sir Walter (1771–1832) Scottish writer and historian

130 I had rather be a kitten and cry mew
Than one of these same metre ballad-mongers.
Henry IV, Part 1, III.i

131 In sweet music is such art,
Killing care and grief of heart
Fall asleep or hearing die.
Henry VIII, III.i

132 Music oft hath such a charm
To make bad good and good provoke to harm.
Measure For Measure, IV.i

133 The man that hath no music in himself,
Nor is not mov'd with concord of sweet sounds,
Is fit for treasons, stratagems, and spoils;
The motions of his spirit are dull as night,
And his affections dark as Erebus.
Let no such man be trusted.
The Merchant of Venice, V.i

134 I have a reasonable good ear in music.
Let's have the tongs and the bones.
A Midsummer Night's Dream, IV.i

135 Now, divine air! now is his soul ravish'd. Is it not strange that sheeps' guts should hale souls out of men's bodies?
Much Ado About Nothing, II.iii

136 How sour sweet music is
When time is broke and no proportion kept!
So is it in the music of men's lives.
Richard II, V.v

137 If music be the food of love, play on,
Give me excess of it, that, surfeiting,
The appetite may sicken and so die.
That strain again! It had a dying fall.
Twelfth Night, I.i **Shakespeare, William** (1564–1616) English dramatist, poet and actor

138 Hell is full of musical amateurs: music is the brandy of the damned.
Man and Superman (1903)

139 At every one of those concerts in England you will find rows of weary people who are there, not because they really like classical music, but because they think they ought to like it.
Man and Superman (1903) **Shaw, George Bernard** (1856–1950) Irish socialist, writer, dramatist and critic

140 Just as my fingers on these keys
Make music, so the self-same sounds
On my spirit make a music, too.
Music is feeling, then, not sound.
And thus it is what I feel,
Here in this room, desiring you.
Thinking of your blue-shadowed silk,
Is music.
'Peter Quince at the Clavier' (1923)

141 For she was the maker of the song she sang.
The ever-hooded, tragic-gestured sea
Was merely a place by which she walked to sing.
'The Idea of Order at Key West' (1936)
Stevens, Wallace (1879–1955) US poet, essayist, dramatist and lawyer

142 Rachmaninov's immortalizing totality was his scowl. He was a six-and-a-half-foot-tall scowl.
In Igor Stravinsky and Robert Craft,
Conversations with Igor Stravinsky (1958)

143 He was the only pianist I have ever seen who did not grimace. That is a great deal.
In Igor Stravinsky and Robert Craft,
Conversations with Igor Stravinsky (1958) On Rachmaninov

144 My music is best understood by children and animals.
The Observer, (1961)

145 A good composer does not imitate; he steals.
In Yates, *Twentieth Century Music* (1967)
Stravinsky, Igor (1882–1971) Russian composer and conductor

146 We all have the same eight notes to work with.
Attr. **Sullivan, Sir Arthur** (1842–1900) English composer, particularly of operettas. Accused of plagiarism

147 Music that gentlier on the spirit lies,
Than tir'd eyelids upon tir'd eyes.
'The Lotos-Eaters' (1832) **Tennyson, Alfred, Lord** (1809–1892) English lyric poet

148 The cello is not one of my favourite instruments. It has such a lugubrious sound, like someone reading a will.
Attr. **Thomas, Irene** (1920–) English writer and broadcaster

149 Go, songs, for ended is our brief sweet play;
Go, children of swift joy and tardy sorrow:
And some are sung, and that was yesterday,
And some unsung, and that may be to-morrow.
'Envoy' (1913) **Thompson, Francis** (1859–1907) English poet

150 The rock music business is a cruel and shallow trench, a long plastic hallway where thieves and pimps run free, and good men lie like dogs. There is also a negative side.
Thompson, Hunter S. (1937–2005) US journalist and author

151 Rock & roll is about attitude. I couldn't care less about technique.
Attr. (1977) **Thunders, Johnny** (1952–1991) US rock star, guitarist in New York Dolls

152 After I die, I shall return to earth as a gatekeeper of a bordello and I won't let any of you – not a one of you – enter!
In Howard Taubman, *The Maestro: The Life of Arturo Toscanini* (1951) Rebuking an incompetent orchestra

153 Madame, there you sit with that magnificent instrument between your legs, and all you can do is scratch it!
Attr. Rebuking an incompetent woman cellist
Toscanini, Arturo (1867–1957) Italian conductor

154 I have been told that Wagner's music is better than it sounds.
Autobiography (1959 edition) **Twain, Mark** (1835–1910) US humorist, writer, journalist and lecturer

155 You just pick a chord, go twang, and you've got music.
Attr. **Vicious, Sid** (1957–1979) English punk singer

156 An unalterable and unquestioned law of the musical world required that the German text of French operas sung by Swedish artists should be translated into Italian for the clearer understanding of English speaking audiences.
The Age of Innocence (1920) **Wharton, Edith** (1862–1937) US writer

157 Lloyd Webber's music is everywhere, but so is Aids.
Attr. **Williamson, Malcolm** (1931–) Master of the Queen's Music

158 Will no one tell me what she sings? –
Perhaps the plaintive numbers flow
For old, unhappy, far-off things,
And battles long ago.
'The Reaper' (1807) **Wordsworth, William** (1770–1850) English poet

159 I made my song a coat
Covered with embroideries
Out of old mythologies
From heel to throat;
But the fools caught it,
Wore it in the world's eye
As though they'd wrought it.
Song, let them take it
For there's more enterprise
In walking naked.
Responsibilities (1914) **Yeats, W.B.** (1865–1939) Irish poet, dramatist, editor, writer and senator

160 I've written most of my best songs driving on a long journey scribbling lyrics on cigarette packets whilst steering.
Young, Neil (1945–) Canadian singer-songwriter

161 Rock journalism is people who can't write interviewing people who can't talk for people who can't read.
In Linda Botts, *Loose Talk* (1980)

162 A composer? What the fuck do they do? All the good music's already been written by people with wigs and stuff.
Attr. **Zappa, Frank** (1940–1993) US rock musician, songwriter and record producer
See also criticism

NATURE

1 Should the whole frame of nature round him break,
In ruin and confusion hurled,
He, unconcerned, would hear the mighty crack,
And stand secure amidst a falling world.
Translation of Horace, *Odes* **Addison, Joseph** (1672–1719) English essayist, poet, playwright and statesman

2 The study of Nature is intercourse with the Highest Mind. You should never trifle with Nature.
In Shulman and Asimov, *Isaac Asimov's Book of Science and Nature Quotations* (1988) **Agassiz, Louis** (1807–1873) Swiss-born US naturalist

3 O ye Northumbrian Shades, which overlook
The rocky pavement and the mossy falls
Of solitary Wensbeck's limpid streams;
How gladly I recall your well-known seats
Beloved of old, and that delightful time
When all alone, for many a summer's day,
I wandered through your calm recesses, led
In silence by some powerful hand unseen.
The Pleasures of Imagination (1744) **Akenside, Mark** (1721–1770) English poet

4 Nature first made him, and then smashed the mould.
Orlando furioso (1516) **Ariosto, Ludovico** (1474–1533) Italian poet

5 Five minutes on even the nicest mountain is awfully long.
Mountains **Auden, W.H.** (1907–1973) English poet, essayist, critic, teacher and dramatist

6 Into the ancient pond
A frog dives:
A sound of the water.
'Haru-no-Hi' ('Spring Days', 1686) **Bashó, Matsuo** (1644–1694) Japanese haiku poet

7 Nature is a temple in which living columns sometimes utter confused words. Man walks through it among forests of symbols, which watch him with knowing eyes.
Les Fleurs du mal (1857) **Baudelaire, Charles** (1821–1867) French poet, translator and critic

8 Of all man's works of art, a cathedral is greatest. A vast and majestic tree is greater than that.
Proverbs from Plymouth Pulpit, (1870) **Beecher, Henry Ward** (1813–1887) US clergyman, lecturer, editor and writer

9 And out of the ground made the Lord God to grow every tree that is pleasant to the sight, and good for food; the tree of life also in the midst of the garden, and the tree of knowledge of good and evil.
Genesis. 2:9

10 While the earth remaineth, seedtime and harvest, and cold and heat, and summer and winter, and day and night shall not cease.
Genesis, 8:22

11 For, lo, the winter is past, the rain is over and gone;
The flowers appear on the earth; the time of the singing of birds is come, and the voice of the turtle is heard in our land.
Song of Solomon, 2:11–12

12 The wind bloweth where it listeth.
John, 3:8 **The Bible (King James Version)**

13 There's the wind on the heath, brother; if I could only feel that, I would gladly live for ever.
Lavengro (1851) **Borrow, George** (1803–1881) English writer and linguist

14 Fire in the heavens, and fire along the hills, and fire made solid in the flinty stone, thick-mass'd or scatter'd pebble, fire that fills
the breathless hour that lives in fire alone.
Poems (1914) **Brennan, Christopher** (1870–1932) Australian poet

15 The day begins to droop, –
  Its course is done:
  But nothing tells the place
  Of the setting sun.
  'Winter Nightfall' (1925)

16 Man masters nature not by force but by
  understanding.
  Attr. **Bridges, Robert** (1844–1930) English poet,
  dramatist, essayist and doctor

17 Fish say, they have their stream and pond;
  But is there anything beyond? –
  One may not doubt that, somehow, good
  Shall come of water and of mud;
  And, sure, the reverent eye must see
  A purpose in liquidity.
  'Heaven' (1913) **Brooke, Rupert** (1887–1915)
  English poet

18 All things are artificial, for nature is the art
  of God.
  Religio Medici (1643) **Browne, Sir Thomas**
  (1605–1682) English physician, author and
  antiquary

19 Gie me ae spark o' Nature's fire,
  That's a' the learning I desire.
  'First Epistle to Lapraik' (1785)

20 Of a' the airts the wind can blaw
  I dearly like the west.
  'Of a' the Airts' (1788)

21 Ye banks and braes o' bonny Doon,
  How can ye bloom sae fresh and fair?
  How can ye chant, ye little birds,
  And I sae weary fu' o' care?
  'Ye Banks and Braes o' Bonny Doon' (1791)
  Burns, Robert (1759–1796) Scottish poet and
  songwriter

22 There is a pleasure in the pathless woods,
  There is a rapture on the lonely shore,
  There is society, where none intrudes,
  By the deep Sea, and music in its roar:
  I love not Man the less, but Nature more,
  From these our interviews, in which I steal
  From all I may be, or have been before,
  To mingle with the Universe, and feel
  What I can ne'er express, yet cannot all
  conceal.
  Childe Harold's Pilgrimage (1818) **Byron, Lord**
  (1788–1824) English poet, satirist and traveller

23 'Tis distance lends enchantment to the
  view,
  And robes the mountain in its azure hue.
  Pleasures of Hope (1799) **Campbell, Thomas**
  (1777–1844) Scottish poet, ballad writer and
  journalist

24 You mountains, you mountains, you see it
  all and still you have not fallen on top of
  us.
  The Human Province. Notes from 1942 to 1972
  (1973) **Canetti, Elias** (1905–1994) Bulgarian-
  born English writer, dramatist and critic

25 Under the philosophy that now seems to
  guide our destinies, nothing must get in
  the way of the man with the spray gun.
  The Silent Spring (1962)

26 As man proceeds towards his announced
  goal of the conquest of nature, he has
  written a depressing record of destruction,
  directed not only against the earth he
  inhabits but against the life that shares it
  with him.
  The Silent Spring (1962) **Carson, Rachel Louise**
  (1907–1964) US marine biologist and writer

27 I believe agriculture has lost its soul.
  Organic farming can put its soul back.
  The Times, (1998)

28 Since bees and wind don't obey any sort of
  rules, we shall soon have an
  unprecedented and unethical situation in
  which one farmer's crop will contaminate
  another's against his will.
  The Times, (1999)

29 Are we going to allow the industrialisation
  of l ife itself, redesigning the natural world
  for the sake of convenience and embarking
  on an Orwellian future? – Or should we be
  adopting a gentler, more considered
  approach, seeking always to work with the
  grain of Nature in making better, more
  sustainable use of what we have, for the
  long-term benefit of mankind as a whole?
  Daily Mail, (1999) **Charles, Prince of Wales**
  (1948–) Son and heir of Elizabeth II and
  Prince Philip

30 Human beings have been endowed with reason and a creative power so that they can add to what thay have been given. But until now they have been not creative, but destructive. Forests are disappearing, rivers are drying up, wildlife is becoming extinct, the climate's being ruined and with every passing day the earth is becoming poorer and uglier.
Uncle Vanya (1897) **Chekhov, Anton** (1860–1904) Russian writer, dramatist and doctor

31 Is ditchwater dull? Naturalists with microscopes have told me that it teems with quiet fun.
The Listener, (1936) **Chesterton, G.K.** (1874–1936) English writer, poet and critic

32 It can't be Nature, for it is not sense.
'The Farewell' (1764) **Churchill, Charles** (1731–1764) English poet, political writer and clergyman

33 Who, as he was a happy imitator of Nature, was a most gentle expresser of it. His mind and hand went together: And what he thought, he uttered with that easiness, that we have scarce received from him a blot.
Preface to the *First Folio Shakespeare,* (1623) **Condell, Henry** (d. 1627) English actor and editor of Shakespeare's plays

34 What better than a Wilderness, to liberate the mind.
In the Blood (1995) **Conn, Stewart** (1936–) Scottish poet. On John Muir, naturalist

35 The shadows now so long do grow,
That brambles like tall cedars show,
Molehills seem mountains, and the ant
Appears a monstrous elephant.
'Evening Quatrains' (1689) **Cotton, Charles** (1630–1687) English poet

36 Nature is but a name for an effect,
Whose cause is God.
The Task (1785) **Cowper, William** (1731–1800) English poet, hymn writer and letter writer

37 All my life through, the new sights of Nature made me rejoice like a child.
Pierre Curie **Curie, Marie** (1867–1934) Polish-born French physicist

38 What a book a devil's chaplain might write on the clumsy, wasteful, blundering, low, and horribly cruel works of nature!
Letter to J.D. Hooker, (1856)

39 I have called this principle, by which each slight variation, if useful, is preserved, by the term of Natural Selection.
The Origin of Species (1859)

40 It is interesting to contemplate an entangled bank, clothed with many plants of many kinds, with birds singing on the bushes, with various insects flitting about, and with worms crawling through the damp earth, and to reflect that these elaborately constructed forms, so different from each other, and dependent upon each other in so complex a manner, have all been produced by laws acting around us ... Growth with Reproduction; Inheritance ... Variability ... a Ratio of Increase so high as to lead to a Struggle for Life, and as a consequence to Natural Selection, entailing Divergence of Character and the Extinction of less-improved forms.
The Origin of Species (1859) **Darwin, Charles** (1809–1882) English naturalist

41 Of all the trees in England,
Oak, Elder, Elm, and Thorn,
The Yew alone burns lamps of peace
For them that lie forlorn.
'Trees' (1913) **De La Mare, Walter** (1873–1956) English poet

42 There came a Wind like a Bugle –
It quivered through the Grass.
'There came a Wind' (c.1883) **Dickinson, Emily** (1830–1886) US poet

43 There is nothing that God hath established in a constant course of nature, and which therefore is done every day, but would seem a Miracle, and exercise our admiration, if it were done but once.
LXXX Sermons (1640) **Donne, John** (1572–1631) English poet

44 And all small fowlys singis on the spray:
Welcum the lord of lycht and lamp of day.
Eneados (1553) **Douglas, Gavin** (c.1474–1522) Scottish poet and bishop

45 I am against nature. I don't dig nature at all. I think nature is very unnatural. I think the truly natural things are dreams, which nature can't touch with decay.
In Robert Shelton, *No Direction Home* (1986) **Dylan, Bob** (1941–) US singer and songwriter

46 When God wanted to create the horse, he said to the South Wind, 'I want to make a creature of you. Condense.'
Horses: Their Role in the History of Man (1987), 'The First Progenitor' **Edwards, Elwyn Hartley** (1927–) British horse expert. Translated from the writings of the Emir Abd-el-Kadr

47 Nature is full of freaks, and now puts an old head on young shoulders, and then a young heart beating under fourscore winters.
Society and Solitude (1870) **Emerson, Ralph Waldo** (1803–1882) US poet, essayist, transcendentalist and teacher

48 All Nature wears one universal grin.
Tom Thumb the Great (1731) **Fielding, Henry** (1707–1754) English writer, dramatist and journalist

49 The best remedy for those who are afraid, lonely or unhappy is to go outside, somewhere where they can be quiet, alone with the heavens, nature and God. Because only then does one feel that all is as it should be.
The Diary of Anne Frank (1947) **Frank, Anne** (1929–1945) Jewish diarist; died in Nazi concentration camp

50 The woods are lovely, dark and deep,
But I have promises to keep,
And miles to go before I sleep,
And miles to go before I sleep.
'Stopping by Woods on a Snowy Evening' (1923) **Frost, Robert** (1874–1963) US poet

51 Nothing endured at all, nothing but the land ... The land was forever, it moved and changed below you, but was forever.
Sunset Song (1932) **Gibbon, Lewis Grassic** (1901–1935) Scottish writer

52 Ill fares the land, to hastening ills a prey,
Where wealth accumulates, and men decay.

The Deserted Village (1770) **Goldsmith, Oliver** (c.1728–1774) Irish dramatist, poet and writer

53 Art is not essential where Nature is sufficient.
The Hero (1637) **Gracián, Baltasar** (1601–1658) Spanish writer

54 Children are dumb to say how hot the day is,
How hot the scent is of the summer rose.
'The Cool Web' (1927) **Graves, Robert** (1895–1985) English poet, writer, critic, translator and mythologist

55 Civilisation says, 'Nature belongs to man.'
The Indian says, 'No, man belongs to nature.'
Address at Norwich **Grey Owl** (1888–1938) English-born Canadian Indian imposter

56 There are grounds for cautious optimism that we may now be near the end of the search for the ultimate laws of nature.
A Brief History of Time: From the Big Bang to Black Holes (1988) **Hawking, Stephen** (1942–) English theoretical physicist

57 Oh that I were an Orenge-tree,
That busie plant!
Then should I ever laden be,
And never want
Some fruit for him that dressed me.
The Temple (1633), 'Employment' **Herbert, George** (1593–1633) English poet and priest

58 Glory be to God for dappled things ...
All things counter, original, spare, strange;
Whatever is fickle, freckled (who knows how?)
With swift, slow; sweet, sour; adazzle, dim;
He fathers-forth whose beauty is past change:
Praise him.
'Pied Beauty' (1877)

59 What would the world be, once bereft
Of wet and of wildness? Let them be left,
O let them be left, wildness and wet;
Long live the weeds and the wilderness yet.
'Inversnaid' (1881) **Hopkins, Gerard Manley** (1844–1889) English Jesuit priest, poet and classicist

60 You may drive out Nature with a pitchfork, but she always comes hurrying back.

Epistles **Horace** (65–8 BC) Roman lyric poet
and satirist

61 The cuckoo shouts all day at nothing
In leafy dells alone –
For nature, heartless, witless nature,
Will neither care nor know
What stranger's feet may find the meadow
And trespass there and go,
Nor ask amid the dews of morning
If they are mine or no.
Last Poems (1922) **Housman, A.E.** (1859–1936)
English poet and scholar

62 Nature is unforgiving; she will not agree to
withdraw her flowers, her music, her scents
or her rays of light before the
abominations of man.
Ninety-three (1874) **Hugo, Victor** (1802–1885)
French poet, writer, dramatist and politician

63 In nature there are neither rewards nor
punishments – there are consequences.
Some Reasons Why (1881) **Ingersoll, Robert G.**
(1833–1899) US lawyer, soldier and writer

64 I love trees revealed, the way
Light rinses fog from colours, opens out.
Collected Poems (1964), 'Edward Thomas in
Heaven' **Kavanagh, P.J.** (1931–) English poet

65 In drear-nighted December,
Too happy, happy tree,
Thy branches ne'er remember
Their green felicity.
'In drear-nighted December' (1817)

66 As when, upon a trancèd summer-night,
Those green-rob'd senators of mighty
woods,
Tall oaks, branch-charmèd by the earnest
stars,
Dream, and so dream all night without a
stir.
'Hyperion. A Fragment' (1818) **Keats, John**
(1795–1821) English poet

67 I think that I shall never see
A poem lovely as a tree ...
Poems are made by fools like me,
But only God can make a tree.
'Trees' (1914) **Kilmer, Alfred Joyce** (1886–1918)
US poet

68 It is a fine thing to be out on the hills
alone. A man could hardly be a beast or a
fool alone on a great mountain.
Diary, (1871) **Kilvert, Francis** (1840–1879)
English curate and diarist

69 Of all the trees that grow so fair,
Old England to adorn,
Greater are none beneath the Sun,
Than Oak, and Ash, and Thorn.
Puck of Pook's Hill (1906), 'A Tree Song'
Kipling, Rudyard (1865–1936) Indian-born
British poet and writer

70 Nature does not make progress by leaps
and bounds.
Philosophia Botanica **Linnaeus, Carl** (1707–1778)
Swedish botanist

71 Nature never makes excellent things for
mean or no uses.
Essay concerning Human Understanding (1690)
Locke, John (1632–1704) English philosopher

72 Towering arrogantly above all else, on the
crests and down the spurs, stood groups of
the kauri, the giant timber tree of New
Zealand, whose great grey trunks, like the
pillars in the ancient halls of Karnak, shot
up seventy and eighty feet without a knot
or branch, and whose colossal heads,
swelling up onto the sky, made a cipher of
every tree near.
The Story of a New Zealand River (1920) **Mander,
Jane** (1877–1949) New Zealand novelist. On
early North Auckland

73 It's a warm wind, the west wind, full of
birds' cries;
I never hear the west wind but tears are in
my eyes,
For it comes from the west lands, the old
brown hills,
And April's in the west wind, and daffodils.
'The West Wind' (1902)

74 I have seen dawn and sunset on moors and
windy hills
Coming in solemn beauty like slow old
tunes of Spain.
'Beauty' (1903) **Masefield, John** (1878–1967)
English poet, writer and critic

75 There's an old saying which goes: Once the
last tree is cut and the last river poisoned,
you will find you cannot eat your money.

The Globe and Mail, (1989) **McLean, Joyce** (1860–1904) Canadian writer

76 We are living beyond our means. As a people we have developed a life-style that is draining the earth of its priceless and irreplaceable resources without regard for the future of our children and people all around the world.
Redbook **Mead, Margaret** (1901–1978) US anthropologist, psychologist and writer

77 In those vernal seasons of the yeer, when the air is calm and pleasant, it were an injury and sullennesse against nature not to go out, and see her riches, and partake in her rejoycing with heaven and earth.
Of Education: To Master Samuel Hartlib (1644) **Milton, John** (1608–1674) English poet, libertarian and pamphleteer

78 Woodman, spare that tree!
Touch not a single bough!
In youth it sheltered me,
And I'll protect it now.
'Woodman, Spare That Tree' (1830) **Morris, George Pope** (1802–1864) US journalist

79 'Tis the last rose of summer
Left blooming alone;
All her lovely companions
Are faded and gone.
Irish Melodies (1807), 'Tis the Last Rose' **Moore, Thomas** (1779–1852) Irish poet

80 I think that I shall never see
A billboard lovely as a tree.
Indeed, unless the billboards fall
I'll never see a tree at all.
'Song of the Open Road' (1933) **Nash, Ogden** (1902–1971) US poet

81 Whence is it that nature doth nothing in vain; and whence arises all that Order and Beauty which we see in the World?
Opticks (1730)

82 Nature is very consonant and conformable to her self.
Opticks (1730) **Newton, Sir Isaac** (1642–1727) English scientist and philosopher

83 Men being absent, Africa is good.
'The Wild Doves at Louis Trichardt' (1960) **Plomer, William** (1903–1973) South African-born British writer and editor

84 The difference between a gun and a tree is a difference of tempo. The tree explodes every spring.
Criterion (1937) **Pound, Ezra** (1885–1972) US poet

85 Afar in the desert I love to ride,
With the silent Bush-boy alone by my side;
Away, away in the wilderness vast,
Where the white man's foot hath never passed …
Man is distant, but God is near.
African Sketches (1834) **Pringle, Thomas** (1789–1834) Scottish poet

86 Nature abhors a vacuum.
Gargantua (1534) **Rabelais, François** (c.1494–c.1553) French monk, physician, satirist and humanist

87 Who has seen the wind?
Neither you nor I:
But when the trees bow down their heads,
The wind is passing by.
'Who Has Seen the Wind?' (1872) **Rossetti, Christina** (1830–1894) English poet

88 What is there in a Cornish hedge
The broken herring-bone pattern of stones,
The gorse, the ragged rick,
The way the little elms are,
Sea-bent, sea-shorn
That so affects the heart?
'Cornish Landscape' **Rowse, A.L.** (1903–1997) English historian, writer and poet

89 Mountains are the beginning and the end of all natural scenery.
Modern Painters (1856)

90 There is really no such thing as bad weather, only different kinds of good weather.
Attr. **Ruskin, John** (1819–1900) English art critic, philosopher and reformer

91 The greater cats with golden eyes
Stare out between the bars.
Deserts are there, and different skies,
And night with different stars.
The King's Daughter (1929) **Sackville-West, Vita** (1892–1962) English poet and novelist

92 The fog comes
on little cat feet.
It sits looking over harbor and city
on silent haunches
and then moves on.
Chicago Poems (1916), 'Fog' **Sandburg, Carl**
(1878–1967) US poet, writer and song collector

93 There are moments in our life when we
accord a kind of love and touching respect
to nature in plants, minerals, the
countryside, as well as human nature in
children, in the customs of country folk
and the primitive world, not because it is
beneficial for our senses, and not because
it satisfies our understanding or taste
either ... but simply because it is nature.
'On Naive and Sentimental Poetry', (1795–
1796)

94 When Nature conquers, Art must then give
way.
Remark to Goethe **Schiller, Johann Christoph
Friedrich** (1759–1805) German writer,
dramatist, poet and historian

95 Where have all the flowers gone?
The girls have picked them every one.
Oh, when will you ever learn?
'Where Have All the Flowers Gone?' (song,
1961) **Seeger, Pete** (1919–) US folk singer and
songwriter

96 Take a straw and throw it up into the air,
you shall see by that which way the wind is.
Table Talk (1689), 'Libels' **Selden, John** (1584–
1654) English historian, jurist and politician

97 In nature's infinite book of secrecy
A little I can read.
Antony and Cleopatra, I.ii

98 Hark, hark! the lark at heaven's gate sings,
And Phoebus 'gins arise,
His steeds to water at those springs
On chalic'd flow'rs that lies;
And winking Mary-buds begin
To ope their golden eyes.
With everything that pretty bin,
My lady sweet, arise.
Cymbeline, II.iii

99 But look, the morn, in russet mantle clad,
Walks o'er the dew of yon high eastward
hill.
Hamlet, I.i

100 The glowworm shows the matin to be near,
And gins to pale his uneffectual fire.
Hamlet, I.v

101 There's rosemary, that's for remembrance;
pray you, love, remember. And there is
pansies, that's for thoughts.
Hamlet, IV.v

102 Summer's lease hath all too short a date.
Sonnet 18

103 In nature there's no blemish but the mind:
None can be call'd deform'd but the
unkind.
Twelfth Night, III.iv

104 This is an art
Which does mend nature – change it
rather; but
The art itself is nature.
The Winter's Tale, IV.iv **Shakespeare, William**
(1564–1616) English dramatist, poet and actor

105 Nature, who makes the perfect rose and
bird,
Has never made the full and perfect man.
City Poems (1857) **Smith, Alexander** (1830–1867)
Scottish poet and writer

106 There's a tree that grows in Brooklyn.
Some people call it the Tree of Heaven. No
matter where its seed falls, it makes a tree
which struggles to reach the sky.
A Tree Grows in Brooklyn (1943) **Smith, Betty**
(1896–1972) US writer

107 When you were a tadpole, and I was a fish,
In the Palaeozoic time,
And side by side in the ebbing tide
We sprawled through the ooze and slime.
'A Toast to a Lady' (1906) **Smith, Langdon**
(1858–1918) Scottish-born US naturalist and
poet

108 My political position is to be a spokesman
for wild nature. I take that as a primary
constituency.
The Real Work, Interviews and Talks 1964–1979
(1980) **Snyder, Gary** (1930–) US mystical poet

109 Calm was the day, and through the
trembling air
Sweet-breathing Zephyrus did softly play.
Prothalamion (1596) **Spenser, Edmund** (c.1522–
1599) English poet

110 God tempers the wind ... to the shorn
lamb.
A Sentimental Journey (1768), 'Maria' **Sterne,
Laurence** (1713–1768) Irish-born English
writer and clergyman

111 We will listen instead to the wind's text
Blown through the roof, or the thrush's
song
In the thick bush that proved him wrong,
Wrong from the start, for nature's truth
Is primary and her changing seasons
Correct out of a vaster reason
The vague errors of the flesh.
Song at the Year's Turning (1955) **Thomas, R.S.**
(1913–2000) Welsh poet

112 I frequently tramped eight or ten miles
through the deepest snow to keep an
appointment with a beech-tree, or a yellow
birch, or an old acquaintance among the
pines.
Walden (1854) **Thoreau, Henry David** (1817–
1862) US essayist, social critic and writer

113 Yet true it is, as cow chews cud,
And trees at spring do yield forth bud,
Except wind stands as never it stood,
It is an ill wind turns none to good.
Five Hundred Points of Good Husbandry (1557)
Tusser, Thomas (c.1524–1580) English writer,
poet and musician

114 The arch of sky and mightiness of storms
Have moved the spirit within me,
Till I am carried away
Trembling with joy.
In Rasmussen, *Intellectual Culture of the Igulik
Eskimos* (1929) **Uvavnuk** Inuit singer and
shaman

115 Know that the secret of the arts is to correct
nature.
Epîtres **Voltaire** (1694–1778) French
philosopher, dramatist, poet, historian, writer
and critic

116 Nature is usually wrong.
Mr Whistler's 'Ten O'Clock' (1885) **Whistler,
James McNeill** (1834–1903) US painter, etcher
and pamphleteer

117 Why are there trees I never walk under but
large and melodious thoughts descend
upon me?
Song of the Open Road, (1856)

118 Give me the splendid silent sun with all his
beams full-dazzling!
'Give me the splendid silent sun' (1865)

119 After you have exhausted what there is in
business, politics, conviviality, and so on –
have found that none of these finally
satisfy, or permanently wear – what
remains? Nature remains.
Specimen Days and Collect (1882) **Whitman,
Walt** (1819–1892) US poet and writer

120 I have learned
To look on nature, not as in the hour
Of thoughtless youth; but hearing often-
times
The still, sad music of humanity.
'Lines composed a few miles above Tintern
Abbey' (1798)

121 Nature never did betray
The heart that loved her.
'Lines composed a few miles above Tintern
Abbey' (1798)

122 One impulse from a vernal wood
May teach you more of man,
Of moral evil and of good,
Than all the sages can ...
Sweet is the lore which Nature brings;
Our meddling intellect
Misshapes the beauteous forms of things:
We murder to dissect.
'The Tables Turned' (1798)

123 A huge peak, black and huge,
As if with voluntary power instinct
Upreared its head.
The Prelude (1850) **Wordsworth, William** (1770–
1850) English poet
See also animals; art; garden; humanity and
human nature; the sea; the seasons

NEWS AND
NEWSPAPERS

1 Some newspapers are fit only to line the
bottom of bird cages.
Attr. **Agnew, Spiro T.** (1918–1996) US Vice
President

2 The Times is a tribal noticeboard.

Remark by a candidate for the editorship of the paper's Woman's Page in the 1960s
Anonymous

3 At least we're la crème de la scum.
The Observer, (1995) **Arnold, Harry** British journalist. Commenting on the news that the Queen had started to refer privately to royal reporters as 'scum'

4 The magnificent roaring of the young lions of the Daily Telegraph.
Essays in Criticism (1865) **Arnold, Matthew** (1822–1888) English poet, critic, essayist and educationist

5 Lady Middleton ... exerted herself to ask Mr Palmer if there was any news in the paper.
'No, none at all,' he replied, and read on.
Sense and Sensibility (1811) **Austen, Jane** (1775–1817) English writer

6 Frank Harris ... said ...: 'The fact is, Mr Balfour, all the faults of the age come from Christianity and journalism.' To which Arthur replied ... 'Christianity, of course ... but why journalism?'
In Margot Asquith, *Autobiography* (1920) **Balfour, A.J.** (1848–1930) British Conservative Prime Minister

7 Journalists say a thing that they know isn't true, in the hope that if they keep on saying it long enough it will be true.
The Title (1918) **Bennett, Arnold** (1867–1931) English writer, dramatist and journalist

8 Remember, son, many a good story has been ruined by over-verification.
Attr. **Bennett, James Gordon** (1795–1872) Scottish-born US editor. Advice to journalists

9 No news is good news; no journalists is even better.
Attr. **Bentley, Nicolas** (1907–1978) English publisher and artist

10 The lowest form of popular culture – lack of information, misinformation, disinformation, and a contempt for the truth or the reality of most people's lives – has overrun real journalism. Today, ordinary Americans are being stuffed with garbage.
The Guardian, (1992)

11 The failures of the press have contributed immensely to the emergence of a talk-show nation, in which public discourse is reduced to ranting and raving and posturing.
The Guardian, (1992) **Bernstein, Carl** (1944–) US journalist

12 I read the newspapers avidly. It is my one form of continuous fiction.
The Observer, (1960) **Bevan, Aneurin** (1897–1960) Welsh Labour politician, miner and orator

13 A newspaper is lumber made malleable. It is ink made into words and pictures. It is conceived, born, grows up and dies of old age in a day.
Quill, (1963)

14 The reporter is the daily prisoner of clocked facts ... On all working days, he is expected to do his best in one swift swipe at each story.
A Bishop's Confession (1981) **Bishop, Jim** (1907–1987) US author and journalist

15 I ran the paper [*Daily Express*] purely for propaganda, and with no other purpose.
In A.J.P. Taylor, *Beaverbrook* (1972) **Beaverbrook, Lord** (1879–1964) Canadian-born British newspaper owner

16 He made righteousness readable.
Attr. **Bone, James** (1872–1962) Scottish journalist. Referring to C.P. Scott, former editor of *The Manchester Guardian*

17 Reading someone else's newspaper is like sleeping with someone else's wife. Nothing seems to be precisely in the right place, and when you find what you are looking for, it is not clear then how to respond to it.
Stepping Westward (1965) **Bradbury, Malcolm** (1932–2000) English writer, critic and academic

18 Burke said there were Three Estates in Parliament; but, in the Reporters' Gallery yonder, there sat a Fourth Estate more important far than they all.
'The Hero as Man of Letters' (1841) **Carlyle, Thomas** (1795–1881) Scottish historian, biographer, critic, and essayist

19 It's not the world that's got so much worse but the news coverage that's got so much better.
Attr. **Chesterton, G.K.** (1874–1936) English writer, poet and critic

20 Thou god of our idolatry, the press ...
Thou fountain, at which drink the good and wise;
Thou ever-bubbling spring of endless lies;
Like Eden's dread probationary tree,
Knowledge of good and evil is from thee.
'The Progress of Error' (1782) **Cowper, William** (1731–1800) English poet, hymn writer and letter writer

21 A master-passion is the love of news.
The Newspaper (1785) **Crabbe, George** (1754–1832) English poet, clergyman, surgeon and botanist

22 I hesitate to say what the functions of the modern journalist may be; but I imagine that they do not exclude the intelligent anticipation of facts even before they occur.
Speech, (1898) **Curzon, Lord** (1859–1925) English statesman and scholar

23 When a dog bites a man that is not news, but when a man bites a dog that is news.
New York Sun, (1882) **Dana, Charles Anderson** (1819–1897) US newspaper editor and reformer

24 Good God, that's done it. He's lost us the tarts' vote.
Attr. **Devonshire, Duke of** (1895–1950) English politician. Referring to Stanley Baldwin's attack on newspaper proprietors

25 Ill news hath wings, and with the wind doth go,
Comfort's a cripple and comes ever slow.
The Barrons' Wars (1603) **Drayton, Michael** (1563–1631) English poet

26 Journalism without a moral position is impossible. Every journalist is a moralist. It's absolutely unavoidable.
Outside: Selected Writings (1984) **Duras, Marguerite** (1914–1996) French author and film-maker

27 Journalists are people who take in one another's washing and then sell it.

Plaque with Laurel (1937) **Eldershaw, M. Barnard** (1897–1987) Australian writer, critic and librarian

28 The press: slow dripping of water on mud; thought's daily bagwash, ironing out opinion,
scarifying the edges of ideas.
Collected Poems (1966) **Fairburn, A.R.D.** (1904–1957) New Zealand poet

29 A newspaper, which consists of just the same number of words, whether there be news in it or not ... may, likewise, be compared to a stagecoach, which performs constantly the same course, empty as well as full.
Tom Jones (1749) **Fielding, Henry** (1707–1754) English writer, dramatist and journalist

30 I regard the fact that I don't write for the newspapers as a source of happiness in my life. My purse suffers – but my conscience is glad of it.
Letter, (1866) **Flaubert, Gustave** (1821–1880) French writer

31 Journalism is a literary genre very similar to that of the novel, and has the great advantage that the reporter can invent things. And that is completely forbidden to the novelist.
Speech, (April 1994), reported in El País

32 Destructive journalism fosters the belief that politicians routinely evade the truth and break their promises. It creates a climate in which trust in society as a whole dissolves; in which difficulties are magnified beyond all proportion; in which no one is believed to act except for the most self-centred of motives.
The Spectator, (May 1996) **García Márquez, Gabriel** (1928–) Colombian author

33 If we had failed to pursue the facts as far as they led, we would have denied the public any knowledge of an unprecedented scheme of political surveillance and sabotage.
Washington Post, (1973) **Graham, Katherine** (1917–2001) US newspaper propietor; owner of the *Washington Post*. On Watergate coverage

34 Please remain. You furnish the pictures and I'll furnish the war.
Attr. in Winkler, *W.R. Hearst* (1928) **Hearst, William Randolph** (1863–1951) US newspaper proprietor. Instruction to artist Frederic Remington, who wished to return from peaceful Havana in spring 1898

35 Most journalists of my generation died early, succumbing to one or other of the two great killers in the craft – cirrhosis or terminal alimony.
National Review, (1974) **Hepworth, John** (1921–1995) Australian writer

36 *Editor*: a person employed by a newspaper whose business it is to separate the wheat from the chaff and to see that the chaff is printed.
A Thousand and One Epigrams (1911) **Hubbard, Elbert** (1856–1915) US printer, editor, writer and businessman

37 News is a genre as much as fiction or drama: it is a regime of visual authority, a coercive organization of images according to a stopwatch.
Daedalus, (1988) **Ignatieff, Michael** (1947–) Canadian writer and media personality

38 My own motto is publish and be sued.
BBC radio broadcast, (1977) **Ingrams, Richard** (1937–) British journalist and editor of *Private Eye*

39 Power without responsibility – the prerogative of the harlot throughout the ages.
Remark, quoted by Stanley Baldwin in 1931 **Kipling, Rudyard** (1865–1936) Indian-born British poet and writer. Referring to Lord Beaverbook's political standpoint vis-à-vis the *Daily Express*

40 To have no thoughts and be able to express them – that's what makes a journalist.
Pro domo et mundo (1912)

41 Journalist: a person without any ideas but with an ability to express them; a writer whose skill is improved by a deadline: the more time he has, the worse he writes.
In Thomas Szasz, *Anti-Freud: Karl Kraus's Criticism of Psychoanalysis and Psychiatry* (1976) **Kraus, Karl** (1874–1936) Austrian scientist, critic and poet

42 The man must have a rare recipe for melancholy, who can be dull in Fleet Street.
Letter to Thomas Manning, (1802)

43 Newspapers always excite curiosity. No one ever lays one down without a feeling of disappointment.
Last Essays of Elia (1833) **Lamb, Charles** (1775–1834) English essayist, critic and letter writer

44 I think it well to remember that, when writing for the newspapers, we are writing for an elderly lady in Hastings who has two cats of which she is passionately fond. Unless our stuff can successfully compete for her interest with those cats, it is no good.
In Claud Cockburn, *In Time of Trouble* (1957) **Lewis, Willmott** (1877–1950) English journalist

45 The London *Times* is one of the greatest powers in the world. In fact, I don't know anything which has much more power, except perhaps the Mississippi.
Remark to *Times* correspondent William Howard Russell, 1861 **Lincoln, Abraham** (1809–1865) US statesman and President

46 On the whole I would not say that our Press is obscene. I would say that it trembles on the brink of obscenity.
The Observer, (1963) **Longford, Lord** (1905–2001) English politician, social reformer and biographer

47 I became a journalist to come as close as possible to the heart of the world.
Esquire, (1983) **Luce, Henry R.** (1898–1967) US publisher and editor

48 Journalists are more attentive to the minute hand of history than to the hour hand.
In Tynan, *Curtains* (1961) **MacCarthy, Sir Desmond** (1878–1952) English critic

49 She couldn't edit a bus ticket.
Attr. **MacKenzie, Kelvin** (1946–) English editor. On Janet Street-Porter's appointment as editor of *Independent on Sunday*

50 Once a newspaper touches a story, the facts are lost forever, even to the protagonists.

The Presidential Papers (1976) **Mailer, Norman** (1923–) US writer

51 The art of newspaper paragraphing is to stroke a platitude until it purrs like an epigram.
In Anthony, *O Rare Don Marquis* (1962) **Marquis, Don** (1878–1937) US columnist, satirist and poet

52 A good newspaper, I suppose, is a nation talking to itself.
The Observer, (1961) **Miller, Arthur** (1915–2005) US dramatist and screenwriter

53 Family newspapers like ourselves gain great kudos leaving this muck alone.
Telegram sent to the Adelaide News, (1953) On the publication of the *Kinsey Report*, a survey of human sexual behaviour

54 I think the important thing is that there be plenty of newspapers with plenty of people controlling them so there can be choice.
Film interview, (1967) **Murdoch, Rupert** (1931–) Australian-born publisher and international businessman

55 A reporter is a man who has renounced everything in life but the world, the flesh, and the devil.
The Observer, (1931) **Murray, David** (1888–1962) British writer

56 All the news that's fit to print.
Motto of the *New York Times* **Ochs, Adolph S.** (1858–1935) US newspaper publisher and editor

57 We live under a government of men and morning newspapers.
Address: *The Press* **Phillips, Wendell** (1811–1884) US reformer

58 At ev'ry word a reputation dies.
The Rape of the Lock (1714) **Pope, Alexander** (1688–1744) English poet, translator and editor

59 The New Yorker will not be edited for the old lady from Dubuque.
Remark **Ross, Harold W.** (1892–1951) US editor. On founding *The New Yorker* in 1925

60 By office boys for office boys.

In Fyfe, *Northcliffe, an Intimate Biography* (1930) **Salisbury, Lord** (1830–1903) English Conservative Prime Minister. Of the *Daily Mail*

61 Comment is free, but facts are sacred.
Manchester Guardian, (1921) **Scott, C.P.** (1846–1932) English newspaper editor and Liberal politician

62 The nature of bad news infects the teller.
Antony and Cleopatra, I.ii

63 Though it be honest, it is never good
To bring bad news. Give to a gracious message
An host of tongues; but let ill tidings tell
Themselves when they be felt.
Antony and Cleopatra, II.v **Shakespeare, William** (1564–1616) English dramatist, poet and actor

64 The newspapers! Sir, they are the most villainous – licentious – abominable – infernal – Not that I ever read them – No – I make it a rule never to look into a newspaper.
The Critic (1779) **Sheridan, Richard Brinsley** (1751–1816) Irish dramatist, politician and orator

65 *Milne:* No matter now imperfect things are, if you've got a free press everything is correctable, and without it everything is conceivable.
Ruth: I'm with you on the free press. It's the newspapers I can't stand.
Night and Day (1978)

66 He's someone who flies around from hotel to hotel and thinks the most interesting thing about any story is the fact that he has arrived to cover it.
Night and Day (1978) Referring to foreign correspondents **Stoppard, Tom** (1937–) British dramatist

67 Freedom of the press in Britain is freedom to print such of the proprietor's prejudices as the advertisers don't object to.
In Driberg, *Swaff* (1974) **Swaffer, Hannen** (1879–1962) English writer

68 The only qualities essential for real success in journalism are rat-like cunning, a plausible manner, and a little literary ability.
The Sunday Times Magazine, (1969) **Tomalin, Nicholas** (1931–1973) English journalist

69 News is what a chap who doesn't care much about anything wants to read. And it's only news until he's read it. After that it's dead.
Scoop (1938) **Waugh, Evelyn** (1903–1966) English writer and diarist

70 Possible? Is anything impossible? Read the newspapers.
In Fraser, *Words on Wellington* (1889)

71 Publish and be damned.
Attr. Reply to a threat of blackmail by Harriette Wilson **Wellington, Duke of** (1769–1852) Irish-born British military commander and statesman

72 As for modern journalism, it is not my business to defend it. It justifies its own existence by the great Darwinian principle of the survival of the vulgarest.
Intentions (1891)

73 There is much to be said in favour of modern journalism. By giving us the opinions of the uneducated, it keeps us in touch with the ignorance of the community.
'The Critic as Artist' (1891) **Wilde, Oscar** (1854–1900) Irish poet, dramatist, writer, critic and wit

74 You cannot hope
to bribe or twist,
thank God! the
British journalist.
But, seeing what
the man will do
unbribed, there's
no occasion to.
'Over the Fire' (1930) **Wolfe, Humbert** (1886–1940) Italian-born British poet, critic and civil servant
See also media

NIGHT

1 The tropical night has the companionability of a Roman Catholic cathedral compared to the Protestant churches of the north, which let you in on business only.
Out of Africa (1937) **Blixen, Karen** (1885–1962) Danish novelist

2 Hunters and lovers see best in the dark.
'Night Fishing' **Dutton, Geoffrey** (1922–1998)

3 Awake! for Morning in the Bowl of Night
Has flung the Stone that puts the Stars to Flight:
And Lo! the Hunter of the East has caught
The Sultan's Turret in a Noose of Light.
The Rubáiyát of Omar Khayyám (1859) **Fitzgerald, Edward** (1809–1883) English poet, translator and letter writer

4 I have been one acquainted with the night.
I have walked out in rain – and back in rain.
I have outwalked the furthest city light.
I have looked down the saddest city lane.
I have passed by the watchman on his beat
And dropped my eyes, unwilling to explain.
'Acquainted with the Night' (1928) **Frost, Robert** (1874–1963) US poet

5 It is always darkest just before the day dawneth.
Pisgah Sight (1650) **Fuller, Thomas** (1608–1661) English churchman and antiquary

6 Night makes no difference 'twixt the Priest and Clark;
Jone as my Lady is as good i' th' dark.
Hesperides (1648), 'No Difference i' th' Dark' **Herrick, Robert** (1591–1674) English poet, royalist and clergyman

7 I wake and feel the fell of dark, not day.
What hours, O what black hours we have spent
This night!
'I wake and feel the fell of dark, not day' (c.1885) **Hopkins, Gerard Manley** (1844–1889) English Jesuit priest, poet and classicist

8 In the description of night in Macbeth, the beetle and the bat detract from the general idea of darkness, – inspissated gloom.

In Boswell, *The Life of Samuel Johnson* (1791)
Johnson, Samuel (1709–1784) English lexicographer, poet, critic, conversationalist and essayist

9 When the sun sets, shadows, that showed at noon
  But small, appear most long and terrible.
  Oedipus (1679) **Lee, Nathaniel** (c.1653–1692) English dramatist

10 The cares that infest the day
   Shall fold their tents, like the Arabs,
   And as silently steal away.
   'The Day is Done' (1844) **Longfellow, Henry Wadsworth** (1807–1882) US poet and writer

11 Night hath a thousand eyes.
   Love's Metamorphosis (1601) **Lyly, John** (c.1554–1606) English dramatist and politician

12 Sable-vested Night, eldest of things.
   Paradise Lost (1667) **Milton, John** (1608–1674) English poet, libertarian and pamphleteer

13 Lo! thy dread empire, Chaos! is restored;
   Light dies before thy uncreating word:
   Thy hand, great Anarch! lets the curtain fall;
   And universal darkness buries all.
   The Dunciad (1742) **Pope, Alexander** (1688–1744) English poet, translator and editor

14 Let's have one other gaudy night. Call to me
   All my sad captains; fill our bowls once more;
   Let's mock the midnight bell.
   Antony and Cleopatra, III.xiii

15 Night's swift dragons cut the clouds full fast;
   And yonder shines Aurora's harbinger,
   At whose approach ghosts, wand'ring here and there,
   Troop home to churchyards.
   A Midsummer Night's Dream, III.ii

16 Come, night; come, Romeo; come, thou day in night;
   For thou wilt lie upon the wings of night
   Whiter than new snow on a raven's back.
   Come, gentle night, come, loving, black-brow'd night,
   Give me my Romeo; and, when he shall die,

Take him and cut him out in little stars,
And he will make the face of heaven so fine
That all the world will be in love with night,
And pay no worship to the garish sun.
Romeo and Juliet, III.ii

17 *Juliet*: Wilt thou be gone? It is not yet near day;
   It was the nightingale, and not the lark,
   That pierc'd the fearfull hollow of thine ear;
   Nightly she sings on yond pomegranate tree.
   Believe me, love, it was the nightingale.
   Romeo: It was the lark, the herald of the morn,
   No nightingale. Look, love, what envious streaks
   Do lace the severing clouds in yonder east;
   Night's candles are burnt out, and jocund day
   Stands tiptoe on the misty mountain tops.
   I must be gone and live, or stay and die.
   Romeo and Juliet, III.v **Shakespeare, William** (1564–1616) English dramatist, poet and actor

18 How beautiful is the night!
   A dewy freshness fills the silent air;
   No mist obscures, nor cloud, nor speck, nor stain,
   Breaks the serene of heaven.
   Thalaba the Destroyer **Southey, Robert** (1774–1843) English poet, essayist, historian and letter writer

19 To begin at the beginning: It is spring, moonless night in the small town, starless and bible-black, the cobblestreets silent and the hunched, courters'-and-rabbits' wood limping invisible down to the sloe-black, slow, black, crowblack, fishingboat-bobbing sea.
   Under Milk Wood (1954) **Thomas, Dylan** (1914–1953) Welsh poet, writer and radio dramatist

20 Dear night! this world's defeat;
   The stop to busie fools; care's check and curb;
   The day of Spirits; my soul's calm retreat
   Which none disturb!
   Silex Scintillans (1650–1655), 'The Night' **Vaughan, Henry** (1622–1695) Welsh poet and physician

21 And down the long and silent street,
The dawn, with silver-sandalled feet,
Crept like a frightened girl.
'The Harlot's House' (1881) **Wilde, Oscar**
(1854–1900) Irish poet, dramatist, writer, critic
and wit

22 Night, sable Goddess! from her Ebon
throne,
In rayless Majesty, now stretches forth
Her leaden Scepter o'er a slumbering
world.
Night-Thoughts on Life, Death and Immortality
(1742–1746) **Young, Edward** (1683–1765) English
poet, dramatist, satirist and clergyman
See also nature; sleep

NURSERY RHYMES

(For sources, the reader is referred to the authoritative *Oxford Dictionary of Nursery Rhymes*)

1 As I was going to St Ives,
I met a man with seven wives.
Each wife had seven sacks,
Each sack had seven cats,
Each cat had seven kits:
Kits, cats, sacks, and wives,
How many were going to St Ives?
One or none.

2 Baa, baa, black sheep,
Have you any wool?
Yes, sir, yes, sir,
Three bags full;
One for the master,
And one for the dame,
And one for the little boy who lives down
the lane.

3 Bobby Shafto's gone to sea,
Silver buckles on his knee;
He'll come back and marry me,
Bonny Bobby Shafto!

4 Boys and girls come out to play,
The moon doth shine as bright as day.

5 Bye, baby bunting,
Daddy's gone a-hunting,
Gone to get a rabbit skin
To wrap the baby bunting in.

6 Cock a doodle doo!
My dame has lost her shoe,
My master's lost his fiddling stick,
And doesn't know what to do.

7 Come, let's to bed
Says Sleepy-head;
Tarry a while, says Slow;
Put on the pan;
Says Greedy Nan,
Let's sup before we go.

8 Curly locks, Curly locks,
Wilt thou be mine?
Thou shalt not wash dishes
Nor yet feed the swine;
But sit on a cushion
And sew a fine seam,
And feed upon strawberries,
Sugar and cream.

9 Ding, dong, bell,
Pussy's in the well.
Who put her in?
Little Johnny Green.
Who pulled her out?
Little Timmy Stout.

10 Doctor Foster went to Gloucester
In a shower of rain;
He stepped in a puddle,
Right up to his middle,
And never went there again.

11 Fee, fi, fo, fum,
I smell the blood of an Englishman;
Be he alive or be he dead,
I'll grind his bones to make my bread.

12 A frog he would a-wooing go,
Heigh ho! says Rowley,
Whether his mother would let him or no.
With a rowley, powley, gammon and
spinach,
Heigh ho! says Anthony Rowley.

13 Georgie Porgie, pudding and pie,
Kissed the girls and made them cry;
When the boys came out to play,
Georgie Porgie ran away.

14 Goosey, goosey gander,
Whither shall I wander?
Upstairs and downstairs
And in my lady's chamber.
There I met an old man
Who wouldn't say his prayers,
I took him by the left leg
And threw him down the stairs.

15 Here is the church, and here is the steeple;
Open the door and here are the people.

16 Hey diddle diddle,
The cat and the fiddle,
The cow jumped over the moon;
The little dog laughed
To see such sport,
And the dish ran away with the spoon.

17 Hickory, dickory, dock,
The mouse ran up the clock.
The clock struck one,
The mouse ran down,
Hickory, dickory, dock.

18 Hot cross buns!
Hot cross buns!
One a penny, two a penny,
Hot cross buns!

19 How many miles to Babylon?
Three score miles and ten.
Can I get there by candle-light?
Yes, and back again.

20 Humpty Dumpty sat on a wall,
Humpty Dumpty had a great fall.
All the king's horses,
And all the king's men,
Couldn't put Humpty together again.

21 I had a little nut tree,
Nothing would it bear
But a silver nutmeg
And a golden pear;
The King of Spain's daughter
Came to visit me,
And all for the sake
Of my little nut tree.

22 I had a little pony,
His name was Dapple Grey;
I lent him to a lady
To ride a mile away.
She whipped him, she lashed him,
She rode him though the mire;
I would not lend my pony now,
For all the lady's hire.

23 I love little pussy,
Her coat is so warm,
And if I don't hurt her,
She'll do me no harm.

24 I love sixpence, jolly little sixpence,
I love sixpence better than my life;
I spent a penny of it, I lent a penny of it,
And I took fourpence home to my wife.

25 I'm the king of the castle,
Get down, you dirty rascal!

26 I see the moon,
And the moon sees me;
God bless the moon,
And God bless me.

27 Jack and Jill went up the hill
To fetch a pail of water;
Jack fell down and broke his crown,
And Jill came tumbling after.

28 Jack Sprat could eat no fat,
His wife could eat no lean,
And so between them both, you see,
They licked the platter clean.

29 Ladybird, ladybird,
Fly away home,
Your house is on fire
And your children are gone.
All except one
And that's little Ann
And she has crept under
The warming pan.

30 Lavender's blue, dilly dilly,
Lavender's green;
When I am king, dilly dilly,
You shall be queen.

31 The lion and the unicorn
Were fighting for the crown;
The lion beat the unicorn
All around the town.

32 Little boy blue, come blow your horn,
The sheep's in the meadow, the cow's in
the corn.

33 Little Jack Horner
Sat in the corner,
Eating a Christmas pie;
He put in his thumb,
And pulled out a plum,
And said, What a good boy am I!

34 Little Miss Muffet
Sat on a tuffet,
Eating her curds and whey;
There came a big spider,
Who sat down beside her
And frightened Miss Muffet away.

35 Little Polly Flinders
Sat among the cinders,
Warming her pretty little toes;
Her mother came and caught her,
And whipped her little daughter
For spoiling her nice new clothes.

36 Little Tommy Tucker,
Sings for his supper:
What shall we give him?
White bread and butter.
How shall he cut it
Without a knife?
How will he be married
Without a wife?

37 London Bridge is falling down,
Falling down, falling down,
London Bridge is falling down,
My fair lady.

38 Mary had a little lamb,
Its fleece was white as snow;
And everywhere that Mary went
The lamb was sure to go.
It followed her to school one day,
That was against the rule;
It made the children laugh and play
To see a lamb at school.

39 Mary, Mary, quite contrary,
How does your garden grow?
With silver bells and cockle shells,
And pretty maids all in a row.

40 Monday's child is fair of face,
Tuesday's child is full of grace,
Wednesday's child is full of woe,
Thursday's child has far to go,
Friday's child is loving and giving,
Saturday's child works hard for a living,
And the child that is born on the Sabbath
day
Is bonny and blithe, and good and gay.

41 My mother said that I never should
Play with the gypsies in the wood;
If I did, she would say,
Naughty girl to disobey.

42 The north wind doth blow,
And we shall have snow,
And what will poor robin do then?
Poor thing.

43 O dear, what can the matter be?
Dear, dear, what can the matter be,
Oh, dear, what can the matter be?
Johnny's so long at the fair.
He promised he'd buy me a fairing should
please me,
And then for a kiss, oh! he vowed he would
tease me,
He promised he'd buy me a bunch of blue
ribbons
To tie up my bonny brown hair.

44 Oh! the grand old Duke of York
He had ten thousand men;
He marched them up to the top of the hill,
And he marched them down again.
And when they were up they were up,
And when they were down they were down,
And when they were only half way up,
They were neither up nor down.

45 Old King Cole
Was a merry old soul,
And a merry old soul was he;
He called for his pipe,
And he called for his bowl,
And he called for his fiddlers three.

46 Old Mother Hubbard
Went to the cupboard,
To fetch her poor dog a bone;
But when she came there
The cupboard was bare
And so the poor dog had none.

47 One, two, buckle my shoe;
Three, four, knock at the door;
Five, six, pick up sticks;
Seven, eight, lay them straight;
Nine, ten, big fat hen;
Eleven, twelve, dig and delve;
Thirteen, fourteen, maids a-courting;
Fifteen, sixteen, maids in the kitchen,
Seventeen, eighteen, maids in waiting;
Nineteen, twenty, my plate's empty!

48 Oranges and lemons,
Say the bells of St Clement's …
You owe me five farthings,
Say the bells of St Martin's.
When will you pay me?
Say the bells of Old Bailey.
When I grow rich
Say the bells of Shoreditch.
Pray, when will that be?
Say the bells of Stepney.
I'm sure I don't know
Says the great bell at Bow.
Here comes a candle to light you to bed,
Here comes a chopper to chop off your
head!

49 Pat-a-cake, pat-a-cake, baker's man,
Bake me a cake as fast as you can;
Pat it and prick it, and mark it with B,
Put it in the oven for baby and me.

50 Peter, Peter, pumpkin eater,
Had a wife and couldn't keep her;
He put her in a pumpkin shell
And there he kept her very well.

51 Peter Piper picked a peck of pickled pepper.
A peck of pickled pepper Peter Piper
picked.
If Peter Piper picked a peck of pickled
pepper,
Where's the peck of pickled pepper Peter
Piper picked?

52 Please to remember
The Fifth of November,
Gunpowder, treason and plot;
We know no reason
Why gunpowder treason
Should ever be forgot.

53 Polly put the kettle on,
Polly put the kettle on,
Polly put the kettle on,
We'll all have tea.
Sukey take it off again,
Sukey take it off again,
Sukey take it off again,
They've all gone away.

54 Pussy cat, pussy cat,
Where have you been?
I've been to London
To look at the queen.

Pussy cat, pussy cat,
What did you there?
I frightened a little mouse
Under her chair.

55 The Queen of Hearts
She made some tarts,
All on a summer's day;
The Knave of Hearts
He stole the tarts,
And took them clean away.

56 Rain, rain, go away,
Come again another day.

57 Ride a cock-horse to Banbury Cross,
To see a fine lady upon a white horse;
Rings on her fingers and bells on her toes,
She shall have music wherever she goes.

58 Ring-a-ring o' roses,
A pocket full of posies,
A-tishoo! A-tishoo!
We all fall down.

59 Rock-a-bye, baby, on the tree top,
When the wind blows the cradle will rock;
When the bough breaks the cradle will fall,
Down will come baby, cradle, and all.

60 Round and round the garden
Like a teddy bear;
One step, two step,
Tickle you under there!

61 Round and round the rugged rock
The ragged rascal ran.

62 Rub-a-dub-dub,
Three men in a tub,
And how do you think they got there?
The butcher, the baker,
The candlestick-maker.
They all jumped out of a rotten potato,
'Twas enough to make a man stare.

63 See-saw, Margery Daw,
Jacky shall have a new master;
Jacky shall have but a penny a day,
Because he can't work any faster.

64 Simple Simon met a pieman,
Going to the fair;
Says Simple Simon to the pieman,
Let me taste your ware.

65 Sing a song of sixpence,
A pocket full of rye;
Four and twenty blackbirds,
Baked in a pie.
When the pie was opened,
The birds began to sing;
Wasn't that a dainty dish,
To set before the king?
The king was in his counting-house,
Counting out his money;
The queen was in the parlour,
Eating bread and honey.
The maid was in the garden,
Hanging out the clothes,
When down came a blackbird
And pecked off her nose!

66 Solomon Grundy,
Born on Monday
Christened on Tuesday
Married on Wednesday
Took ill on Thursday
Worse on Friday
Died on Saturday
Buried on Sunday.
This is the end of Solomon Grundy.

67 Taffy was a Welshman, Taffy was a thief,
Taffy came to my house and stole a piece
of beef.

68 Tell tale, tit!
Your tongue shall be split,
And all the dogs in town
Shall have a little bit.

69 There was a crooked man, and he walked a
crooked mile,
He found a crooked sixpence against a
crooked stile;
He bought a crooked cat, which caught a
crooked mouse,
And they all lived together in a little
crooked house.

70 There was an old woman who lived in a
shoe,
She had so many children she didn't know
what to do.
She gave them some broth without any
bread,
She whipped them all soundly and put
them to bed.

71 Thirty days hath September,
April, June and November;
All the rest have thirty-one,
Excepting February alone;
And that has twenty-eight days clear
And twenty-nine in each leap year.

72 This is the horse and the hound and the
horn
That belonged to the farmer sowing his
corn,
That kept the cock that crowed in the
morn,
That waked the priest all shaven and shorn,
That married the man all tattered and torn,
That kissed the maiden all forlorn,
That milked the cow with the crumpled
horn,
That tossed the dog,
That worried the cat,
That killed the rat,
That ate the corn,
That lay in the house that Jack built.

73 This little pig went to market,
This little pig stayed at home,
This little pig had roast beef,
This little pig had none,
And this little pig cried, Wee-wee-wee-
wee-wee,
I can't find my way home.

74 Three blind mice, see how they run!
They all ran after the farmer's wife,
She cut off their tails with a carving knife,
Did ever you see such a thing in your life,
As three blind mice?

75 Three little kittens they lost their mittens,
And they began to cry.
Oh mother dear, we sadly fear
Our mittens we have lost.
What! lost your mittens,
You naughty kittens!
Then you shall have no pie.

76 Tinker,
Tailor,
Soldier,
Sailor,
Rich man,
Poor man,
Beggarman,
Thief.

77 Tom, he was a piper's son,
He learnt to play when he was young,
And all the tune that he could play
Was 'Over the hills and far away'.
Tom, Tom, the piper's son,
Stole a pig and away he run.
The pig was eat,
And Tom was beat,
And Tom went howling down the street.

78 The twelfth day of Christmas,
My true love sent to me
Twelve lords a-leaping,
Eleven ladies dancing,
Ten pipers piping,
Nine drummers drumming,
Eight maids a-milking,
Seven swans a-swimming,
Six geese a-laying,
Five gold rings,
Four calling birds,
Three French hens,
Two turtle doves, and
A partridge in a pear tree.

79 Two little dicky birds,
Sitting on a wall;
One named Peter,
The other named Paul,
Fly away, Peter!
Fly away, Paul!
Come back, Peter!
Come back, Paul!

80 Wee Willie Winkie runs through the town
Upstairs and downstairs and in his
nightgown,
Rapping at the window, crying through the
lock,
Are the children all in bed? It's past eight
o'clock.

81 What are little boys made of?
Frogs and snails
And puppy-dogs' tails,
That's what little boys are made of.
What are little girls made of?
Sugar and spice
And all things nice,
That's what little girls are made of.

82 What are young men made of ?
Sighs and leers,
And crocodile tears,
That's what young men are made of.

83 What are young women made of?
Ribbons and laces,
And sweet, pretty faces,
That's what young women are made of.

84 Where are you going to, my pretty maid?
I'm going a-milking, sir, she said.
What is your fortune, my pretty maid?
My face is my fortune, sir, she said.

85 Who killed Cock Robin?
I, said the Sparrow,
With my bow and arrow,
I killed Cock Robin.
Who saw him die?
I, said the Fly,
With my little eye,
I saw him die.
And all the birds of the air
Fell to sighing and sobbing,
When they heard the bell toll
For poor Cock Robin.

86 A wise old owl lived in an oak;
The more he saw the less he spoke;
The less he spoke the more he heard.
Why can't we all be like that wise old bird?
See also childhood and children

OPINIONS

1 I've never had a humble opinion. If you've
got an opinion, why be humble about it.
Scotland on Sunday, (1992) **Baez, Joan** (1941–)
US folk singer and songwriter

2 I could never divide my self from any man
upon the difference of an opinion, or be
angry with his judgment for not agreeing
with me in that, from which perhaps within
a few days I should dissent my self.
Religio Medici (1643) **Browne, Sir Thomas**
(1605–1682) English physician, author and
antiquary

3 I am always of the opinion with the
learned, if they speak first.
Incognita (1692) **Congreve, William** (1670–1729)
English dramatist

4 Tomorrow a stranger will say with masterly good sense precisely what we have thought and felt all the time, and we shall be forced to take with shame our own opinion from another.
'Self-Reliance' (1841) **Emerson, Ralph Waldo** (1803–1882) US poet, essayist, transcendentalist and teacher

5 They that approve a private opinion, call it opinion; but they that mislike it, heresy: and yet heresy signifies no more than private opinion.
Leviathan (1651) **Hobbes, Thomas** (1588–1679) Political philosopher

6 The superiority of one man's opinion over another's is never so great as when the opinion is about a woman.
The Tragic Muse (1890) **James, Henry** (1843–1916) US-born British writer, critic and letter writer

7 Error of opinion may be tolerated where reason is left free to combat it.
First inaugural address, (1801) **Jefferson, Thomas** (1743–1826) US Democrat statesman and President

8 New opinions are always suspected, and usually opposed, without any reason but because they are not already common.
Essay concerning Human Understanding (1690) **Locke, John** (1632–1704) English philosopher

9 Men are never so good or so bad as their opinions.
'Jeremy Bentham' (1830) **Mackintosh, Sir James** (1765–1832) Scottish philosopher, historian, lawyer and politician

10 Wrong opinions are like counterfeit coins, which are first minted by great wrongdoers, then spent by decent people who perpetuate the crime without knowing what they are doing.
Les soirées de Saint-Pétersbourg **Maistre, Joseph de** (1753–1821) French diplomat and political philosopher

11 What is merit? The opinion one man entertains of another.
In Carlyle, 'Shooting Niagara and After?' (1837) **Palmerston, Lord** (1784–1865) British Prime Minister

12 Do not look for opinions beyond your own.
Satires **Persius Flaccus, Aulus** (AD 34–62) Roman satirical poet

13 You are now sail'd into the north of my lady's opinion; where you will hang like an icicle on a Dutchman's beard.
Twelfth Night, III.ii **Shakespeare, William** (1564–1616) English dramatist, poet and actor

14 Opinion is ultimately determined by the feelings, and not by the intellect.
Social Statics (1850) **Spencer, Herbert** (1820–1903) English philosopher and journalist

15 All opinions, properly so called, are stages on the road to truth.
Virginibus Puerisque, 'Crabbed Age and Youth' **Stevenson, Robert Louis** (1850–1894) Scottish writer, poet and essayist

16 There are as many opinions as there are people: each has his own point of view.
Phormio **Terence** (c.190–159 BC) Carthaginian-born Roman dramatist

17 I submit to no man's opinion; I have opinions of my own.
Fathers and Sons (1862) **Turgenev, Ivan** (1818–1883) Russian writer and dramatist

18 It is difference of opinion that makes horse races.
Pudd'nhead Wilson's Calendar (1894) **Twain, Mark** (1835–1910) US humorist, writer, journalist and lecturer

19 Inconsistencies of opinion, arising from changes of circumstances, are often justifiable.
Speech, (1846) **Webster, Daniel** (1782–1852) US statesman, orator and lawyer

20 The more opinions you have, the less you see.
Attr. **Wenders, Wim** (1945–) German film director
See also ideas

PARENTHOOD

1 It's true that a child belongs to its father. But when a father beats his child, it seeks sympathy in its mother's hut. A man belongs to his fatherland when times are good and life is sweet. But when there is sorrow and bitterness he finds refuge in his motherland. Your mother is there to protect you. She is buried there. And that is why we say that mother is supreme.
Things Fall Apart (1958) **Achebe, Chinua** (1930–) Nigerian writer, poet and critic

2 What do girls do who haven't any mothers to help them through their troubles?
Little Women (1868) **Alcott, Louisa May** (1832–1888) US writer

3 And my parents finally realize that I'm kidnapped and they snap into action immediately: they rent out my room.
In Eric Lax, *Woody Allen* (1991)

4 My parents were very old world. They come from Brooklyn which is the heart of the old world. Their values in life are God, and carpeting.
In Adler and Feinman, *Woody Allen: Clown Prince of American Humor* **Allen, Woody** (1935–) US film director, writer, actor and comedian

5 It's a very boring time. I am not particularly maternal – it's an occupational hazard of being a wife.
TV interview, quoted in the *Daily Express*, (1981) **Anne, the Princess Royal** (1950–) Daughter of Elizabeth II. On pregnancy

6 You can fool all of the people some of the time, and some of the people all of the time, but you Can't Fool Mom.
Captain Penny's Law **Anonymous**

7 The joys of parents are secret, and so are their griefs and fears.
'Of Parents and Children' (1625) **Bacon, Francis** (1561–1626) English philosopher, essayist, politician and courtier

8 Seismic with laughter,
Gin and chicken helpless in her Irish hand,
Irresistible as Rabelais, but most tender for
The lame dogs and hurt birds that surround her.

'Sonnet: To My Mother' (1944) **Barker, George** (1913–1991) English poet and writer

9 Mother always said that honesty was the best policy, and money isn't everything. She was wrong about other things too.
Attr. **Barzan, Gerald** US humorist

10 It's frightening to think that you mark your children merely by being yourself. It seems unfair. You can't assume the responsibility for everything you do – or don't do.
Les Belles Images (1966) **Beauvoir, Simone de** (1908–1986) French writer, feminist critic and philosopher

11 It ought ... to enter into the domestic policy of any parent, to make her children feel that home is the happiest place in the world.
Mrs Beeton's Household Management (1861) **Beeton, Isabella** (1836–1865) British cookery writer

12 Never throw stones at your mother,
You'll be sorry for it when she's dead,
Never throw stones at your mother,
Throw bricks at your father instead.
The Hostage (1958) **Behan, Brendan** (1923–1964) Irish dramatist, writer and Republican

13 The fathers have eaten sour grapes, and the children's teeth are set on edge.
Ezekiel, 18:2 **The Bible (King James Version)**

14 My mother phones daily to ask, 'Did you just try to reach me?' When I reply, 'No', she adds, 'So, if you're not too busy, call me while I'm still alive,' and hangs up.
The 1992 Erma Bombeck Calendar **Bombeck, Erma** (1927–1996) US humorist and writer

15 Parents are the last people on earth who ought to have children.
Attr. **Butler, Samuel** (1835–1902) English writer, painter, philosopher and scholar

16 I love all my children, but some of them I don't like.
In *Woman*, (1977)

17 Sometimes when I look at my children I say to myself, 'Lillian, you should have stayed a virgin.'
Remark, (1980) **Carter, ('Miz') Lillian** (1902–1983) Mother of US President Jimmy Carter

18 As fathers commonly go, it is seldom a misfortune to be fatherless; and considering the general run of sons, as seldom a misfortune to be childless.
Attr. **Chesterfield, Lord** (1694–1773) English politician and letter writer

19 Investigations into paternity are forbidden.
Article 340 **Code Napoléon**

20 So for the mother's sake the child was dear, And dearer was the mother for the child.
'Sonnet to a Friend Who Asked How I felt When the Nurse First Presented My Infant to Me' (1797) **Coleridge, Samuel Taylor** (1772–1834) English poet, philosopher and critic

21 My father was an eminent button maker – but I had a soul above buttons – I panted for a liberal profession.
Sylvester Daggerwood: or New Hay at the Old Market (1795) **Colman, the Younger, George** (1762–1836) English dramatist and Examiner of Plays

22 Don't be too hard on parents. You may find yourself in their place.
Elders and Betters (1944) **Compton-Burnett, Dame Ivy** (1884–1969) English novelist

23 Fatherhood is pretending the present you love most is soap-on-the-rope.
Attr.

24 The truth is that parents are not really interested in justice. They just want quiet.
Fatherhood (1986) **Cosby, Bill** (1937–) US comedian, actor and author

25 And now she is like everyone else.
Attr. **De Gaulle, Charles** (1890–1970) French general and statesman. After the death of his retarded daughter Anne

26 There are times when parenthood seems nothing but feeding the mouth that bites you.
The Tunnel of Love **De Vries, Peter** (1910–1993) US novelist

27 Every baby born into the world is a finer one than the last.
Nicholas Nickleby (1839) **Dickens, Charles** (1812–1870) English writer

28 We spend the first twelve months of our children's lives teaching them to walk and talk, and the next twelve telling them to sit down and shut up.
Attr. **Diller, Phyllis** (1917–) US comedienne

29 My mother took too much, a great deal too much, care of me; she over-educated, over-instructed, over-dosed me with premature lessons of prudence: she was so afraid that I should ever do a foolish thing, or not say a wise one, that she prompted my every word, and guided my eyes, hearing with her ears, and judging with her understanding, till, at length, it was found out that I had no eyes, or understanding of my own.
Vivian (1812) **Edgeworth, Maria** (1767–1849) English-born Irish writer

30 As a single woman with a child, I would love to have a wife.
The Independent, (1994) **Ekland, Britt** (1942–) Swedish actress

31 Respect the child. Be not too much his parent. Trespass not on his solitude.
Attr. **Emerson, Ralph Waldo** (1803–1882) US poet, essayist, transcendentalist and teacher

32 A mother is not a person to lean on but a person to make leaning unnecessary.
Her Son's Wife (1926) **Fisher, Dorothy Canfield** (1879–1958) US writer

33 A mother is only brought unlimited satisfaction by her relation to a son; this is altogether the most perfect, the most free from ambivalence of all human relationships.
Freud on Women (1990) **Freud, Sigmund** (1856–1939) Austrian physicist; founder of psychoanalysis

34 Blaming mother is just a negative way of clinging to her still.
My Mother/My Self (1977) **Friday, Nancy** (1937–) US writer

35 Having one child makes you a parent; having two you are a referee.
Independent, (1989) **Frost, David** (1939–) English broadcaster

36 It takes a great deal of effort to separate a mother from her infant, and a fair amount to get a father to be involved with his.
The Great Disruption (1999) **Fukuyama, Francis** (1952–) US historian

37 Where yet was ever found a mother,
Who'd give her booby for another?
Fables (1727) **Gay, John** (1685–1732) English poet, dramatist and librettist

38 *Homer:* Yeah, sure, for you, a baby's all fun and games. For me it's diaper changes and midnight feedings.
Lisa: Doesn't Mom do all that stuff?
Homer: Yeah, but I have to hear about it.
The Simpsons, TV cartoon series **Groening, Matt** (1954–) US cartoonist

39 No, he was my father.
In C. Bowen, *Yankee from Olympus* (1945) **Holmes, Oliver Wendell, Jr** (1841–1935) US jurist and judge. In response to Andrew Lang's enquiring if he were the son of the celebrated Oliver Wendell Holmes

40 The old-time mother who used to wonder where her boy was now has a grandson who wonders where his mother is.
Attr. **Hubbard, Kin** (1868–1930) US humorist and journalist

41 Lying apart now, each in a separate bed,
He with a book, keeping the light on late,
She like a girl dreaming of childhood.
The Mind has Mountains (1966) **Jennings, Elizabeth** (1926–2001) English poet

42 Rest in soft peace, and, ask'd, say here doth lye
Ben Jonson his best piece of poetrie.
Epigrams (1616), 'On My First Son' **Jonson, Ben** (1572–1637) English dramatist and poet

43 The mother is the most precious possession of the nation, so precious that society advances its highest wellbeing when it protects the functions of the mother.
The Century of the Child (1909) **Key, Ellen** (1849–1926) Swedish feminist, writer and lecturer

44 They fuck you up, your mum and dad.
They may not mean to, but they do.
They fill you with the faults they had
And add some extra, just for you.
'This be the Verse' (1974) **Larkin, Philip** (1922–1985) English poet, writer and librarian

45 We have loved each other, almost with a husband and wife love, as well as filial and maternal … It has been rather terrible and has made me, in some respects, abnormal.
Attr. **Lawrence, D.H.** (1885–1930) English writer, poet and critic. On his relationship with his mother

46 At her best, she is … quietly receptive and intelligent in only a moderate, concrete way; she is of even temperament, almost always in control of her emotions. She loves her children completely and unambivalently. Most of us are not like her.
The Mother Knot (1976) **Lazarre, Jane** (1943–) US journalist

47 The parent who could see his boy as he really is, would shake his head and say: 'Willie is no good: I'll sell him.'
Essays and Literary Studies (1916) **Leacock, Stephen** (1869–1944) English-born Canadian humorist, writer and economist

48 I used to rush to the mirror every morning to see if I had bloomed, but all I did was swell. My ankles looked like flesh-coloured flares and my breasts were so huge they needed their own postcode.
The Daily Telegraph, (May 1999) **Lette, Kathy** (1959–) English novelist. On pregnancy

49 He reminds me of the man who murdered both his parents, and then, when sentence was about to be pronounced, pleaded for mercy on the grounds that he was an orphan.
In Gross, *Lincoln's Own Stories* **Lincoln, Abraham** (1809–1865) US statesman and President

50 By and large, mothers and housewives are the only workers who do not have regular time off. They are the great vacationless class.

Gift from the Sea (1955) **Lindbergh, Anne Morrow** (1906–2001) US aviator, poet and writer

51 Few misfortunes can befall a boy which bring worse consequences than to have a really affectionate mother.
A Writer's Notebook (1949) **Maugham, William Somerset** (1874–1965) English writer, dramatist and physician

52 Small things can pit the memory like a cyst:
Having seen other fathers greet their sons,
I put my childish face up to be kissed
After an absence. The rebuff still stuns
My blood. The poor man's embarrassment
At such a delicate proffer of affection
Cut like a saw. But home the lesson went:
My tenderness thenceforth escaped detection.
Collected Poems (1971) **McAuley, James Philip** (1917–1976) Australian poet and critic

53 Children aren't happy with nothing to ignore,
And that's what parents were created for.
Happy Days (1933) **Nash, Ogden** (1902–1971) US poet

54 More than in any other human relationship, overwhelmingly more, motherhood means being instantly interruptible, responsive, responsible.
Silences: When Writers Don't Write (1965) **Olsen, Tillie** (1913–) US writer

55 If you bungle raising your children, I don't think whatever else you do well matters very much.
In Theodore C. Sorenson, *Kennedy* (1965) **Onassis, Jacqueline Kennedy** (1929–1994) US First Lady

56 It's all any reasonable child can expect if the dad is present at the conception.
Entertaining Mr Sloane (1964) **Orton, Joe** (1933–1967) English dramatist and writer

57 Every man must define his identity against his mother. If he does not, he just falls back into her and is swallowed up.
Sex, Art, and American Culture (1992) **Paglia, Camille** (1947–) US academic and writer

58 Dear Mary, We all knew you had it in you.
In J. Keats, *You Might As Well Live* (1970) **Parker, Dorothy** (1893–1967) US writer, poet, critic and wit. Telegram sent to Mary Sherwood after her much-publicized pregnancy

59 What did my fingers do before they held him?
What did my heart do, with its love?
I have never seen a thing so clear.
His lids are like the lilac flower
And soft as a moth, his breath.
I shall not let go.
There is no guile or warp in him. May he keep so.
'Three Women: A Poem for Three Voices' (1962) **Plath, Sylvia** (1932–1963) US poet, writer and diarist. On seeing her newborn baby

60 All the same, you know parents – especially step-parents – are sometimes a bit of a disappointment to their children. They don't fulfil the promise of their early years.
A Buyer's Market **Powell, Anthony** (1905–2000) English writer and critic

61 Motherhood is a dead-end job. You've no sooner learned the skills than you are redundant.
Weekend Guardian, (1960) **Rayner, Claire** (1931–) English journalist

62 The role of mother is probably the most important career a woman can have.
The Times-Picayune, (1986) **Riley, Janet Mary** US lawyer, educator and civil rights activist

63 A Jewish man with parents alive is a fifteen-year-old boy, and will remain a fifteen-year-old boy until they die.
Portnoy's Complaint (1969) **Roth, Philip** (1933–) US writer

64 I once knew a chap who had a system of just hanging the baby on the clothes line to dry and he was greatly admired by his fellow citizens for having discovered a wonderful innovation on changing a diaper.
Short Takes (1946) **Runyon, Damon** (1884–1946) US writer

65 The fundamental defect of fathers is that they want their children to be a credit to them.

Attr. **Russell, Bertrand** (1872–1970) English philosopher, mathematician, essayist and social reformer

66 Get to know your parents. You never know when they'll be gone for good.
'Everybody's Free (To Wear Sunscreen)' (speech and song, 1997) **Schmich, Mary** US writer

67 No matter how old a mother is, she watches her middle-aged children for signs of improvement.
The Measure of My Days (1968) **Scott-Maxwell, Florida** (1884–1979) British writer

68 It is a wise father that knows his own child.
The Merchant of Venice, II.ii

69 *Paris*: Younger than she are happy mothers made.
Capulet: And too soon marr'd are those so early made.
Romeo and Juliet, I.ii

70 Thou art thy mother's glass, and she in thee
Calls back the lovely April of her prime.
Sonnet 3 **Shakespeare, William** (1564–1616) English dramatist, poet and actor

71 Parentage is a very important profession; but no test of fitness for it is ever imposed in the interest of the children.
Everybody's Political What's What (1944) **Shaw, George Bernard** (1856–1950) Irish socialist, writer, dramatist and critic

72 Parents learn a lot from their children about coping with life.
The Comforters (1957) **Spark, Muriel** (1918–2006) Scottish writer, poet and dramatist

73 In automobile terms, the child supplies the power but the parents have to do the steering.
Common Sense Book of Baby and Child Care (1946) **Spock, Dr Benjamin** (1903–1998) US paediatrician and psychiatrist

74 ... mothers of the race, the most important actors in the grand drama of human progress.
History of Woman Suffrage (1881) **Stanton, Elizabeth Cady** (1815–1902) US suffragist, abolitionist, feminist, editor and writer

75 A mother! What are we really? They all grow up whether you look after them or not.
The Man Who Loved Children (1940) **Stead, Christina** (1902–1983) Australian writer

76 I wish either my father or my mother, or indeed both of them, as they were in duty both equally bound to it, had minded what they were about when they begot me.
Tristram Shandy (1759–1767) **Sterne, Laurence** (1713–1768) Irish-born English writer and clergyman

77 Being a mother means you never want to take your clothes off on television again.
Attr. **Stubbs, Imogen** (1961–) English actress

78 Who ran to help me when I fell,
And would some pretty story tell,
Or kiss the place to make it well?
My Mother.
Original Poems for Infant Minds (1804) **Taylor, Jane** (1783–1824) English poet

79 How many a father have I seen,
A sober man, among his boys,
Whose youth was full of foolish noise.
In Memoriam A. H. H. (1850) **Tennyson, Alfred, Lord** (1809–1892) English lyric poet

80 No man is responsible for his father. That is entirely his mother's affair.
Alabaster Lamps (1925) **Turnbull, Margaret** (fl. 1920s–1942) Scottish-born US writer and dramatist

81 When I was a boy of 14 my father was so ignorant I could hardly stand to have the old man around. But when I got to be 21, I was astonished at how much he had learned in seven years.
In Mackay, *The Harvest of a Quiet Eye* (1977) **Twain, Mark** (1835–1910) US humorist, writer, journalist and lecturer

82 The young need old men. They need men who are not ashamed of age, not pathetic imitiations of themselves ... Parents are the bones on which children sharpen their teeth.
Dear Me (1977) **Ustinov, Sir Peter** (1921–2004) English actor, director, dramatist, writer and raconteur

83 The hand that rocks the cradle
Is the hand that rules the world.
'What Rules the World' (c.1865) **Wallace,
William Ross** (c.1819–1881) US lawyer and
poet

84 The explanation is quite simple. I wished to
be near my mother.
Attr. **Whistler, James McNeill** (1834–1903) US
painter, etcher and pamphleteer. Explaining
to a snobbish lady why he had been born in
such an unfashionable place as Lowell,
Massachusetts

85 To lose one parent may be regarded as a
misfortune … to lose both seems like
carelessness.
The Importance of Being Earnest (1895) **Wilde,
Oscar** (1854–1900) Irish poet, dramatist,
writer, critic and wit
See also childhood and children; families

PASSION

1 Admiration is a very short-lived passion
that immediately decays upon growing
familiar with its object, unless it be still fed
with fresh discoveries, and kept alive by a
perpetual succession of miracles rising into
view.
The Spectator, (1711) **Addison, Joseph** (1672–
1719) English essayist, poet, playwright and
statesman

2 It was too pathetic for the feelings of
Sophia and myself – we fainted alternately
on a sofa.
Love and Friendship (1791) **Austen, Jane** (1775–
1817) English writer

3 For one heate (all know) doth drive out
another,
One passion doth expell another still.
Monsieur D'Olive (1606) **Chapman, George**
(c.1559–c.1634) English poet, dramatist and
translator

4 One only does well what one loves doing.
Neither science nor conscience makes a
great cook. What use is application where
inspiration is what's needed?
Prisons et paradis (1932) **Colette** (1873–1954)
French writer

5 The man who is master of his passions is
Reason's slave.
In V.S. Pritchett (ed.), *Turnstile One* **Connolly,
Cyril** (1903–1974) English literary editor,
writer and critic

6 A naked thinking heart, that makes no
show,
Is to a woman, but a kind of ghost.
Songs and Sonnets (1611) **Donne, John** (1572–
1631) English poet

7 A man is to be cheated into passion, but to
be reasoned into truth.
Religio Laici (1682) **Dryden, John** (1631–1700)
English poet, satirist, dramatist and critic

8 Many a heart is aching, if you could read
them all,
Many the hopes that have vanished, after
the ball.
'After the Ball' (song, 1892) **Harris, Charles**
(1865–1930) US songwriter

9 We never remark any passion or principle
in others, of which, in some degree or
other, we may not find a parallel in
ourselves.
A Treatise of Human Nature (1739) **Hume,
David** (1711–1776) Scottish philosopher and
political economist

10 A man who has not gone through the hell
of his passions has never overcome them
either.
Memories, Dreams, Thoughts (1962) **Jung, Carl
Gustav** (1875–1961) Swiss psychiatrist and
pupil of Freud

11 We are sometimes moved by passion and
think it zeal.
De Imitatione Christi (1892) **Kempis, Thomas à**
(c.1380–1471) German mystic, monk and writer

12 The mind is always fooled by the heart.
Maximes (1678) **La Rochefoucauld** (1613–1680)
French writer

13 It is with our passions as it is with fire and
water, they are good servants, but bad
masters.
Translation of Aesop's *Fables* **L'Estrange, Sir
Roger** (1616–1704) English writer, royalist,
translator and politician

14 The secret anniversaries of the heart.
Sonnets (1877) **Longfellow, Henry Wadsworth** (1807–1882) US poet and writer

15 In tragic life, God wot,
No villain need be! Passions spin the plot:
We are betrayed by what is false within.
Modern Love (1862) **Meredith, George** (1828–1909) English writer, poet and critic

16 The ruling Passion, be it what it will,
The ruling Passion conquers Reason still.
'Epistle to Lord Bathurst' (1733)

17 In Men, we various Ruling Passions find,
In Women, two almost divide the kind;
Those, only fix'd, they first or last obey,
The Love of Pleasure, and the Love of Sway.
'Epistle to a Lady' (1735) **Pope, Alexander** (1688–1744) English poet, translator and editor

18 As a bathtub lined with white porcelain,
When the hot water gives out or goes tepid,
So is the slow cooling of our chivalrous passion,
O my much praised but-not-altogether-satisfactory lady.
'The Bath Tub' (1916) **Pound, Ezra** (1885–1972) US poet

19 The heart is a small thing, but desireth great matters.
It is not sufficient for a kite's dinner, yet the whole world is not sufficient for it.
Emblems (1635) **Quarles, Francis** (1592–1644) English poet, writer and royalist

20 It is no longer an ardour hidden in my veins: it's Venus in all her power fastening on her prey.
Phèdre (1677) **Racine, Jean** (1639–1699) French tragedian and poet

21 Three passions, simple but overwhelmingly strong, have governed my life: the longing for love, the search for knowledge, and unbearable pity for the suffering of mankind.
The Autobiography of Bertrand Russell (1967–1969) **Russell, Bertrand** (1872–1970) English philosopher, mathematician, essayist and social reformer

22 Passion, you see, can be destroyed by a doctor. It cannot be created.
Equus (1973) **Shaffer, Peter** (1926–) English dramatist

23 O, a kiss
Long as my exile, sweet as my revenge!
Now, by the jealous queen of heaven, that kiss
I carried from thee, dear, and my true lip
Hath virgin'd it e'er since.
The Comedy of Errors, V.iii

24 Touch me with noble anger,
And let not women's weapons, water-drops,
Stain my man's cheeks!
No, you unnatural hags,
I will have such revenges on you both
That all the world shall – I will do such things –
What they are yet I know not; but they shall be
The terrors of the earth.
You think I'll weep.
No, I'll not weep.
I have full cause of weeping; but this heart
Shall break into a hundred thousand flaws
Or ere I'll weep.
O fool, I shall go mad!
King Lear, II.iv

25 Trifles light as air
Are to the jealous confirmations strong
As proofs of holy writ.
Othello, III.iii

26 Present mirth hath present laughter;
What's to come is still unsure.
In delay there lies no plenty,
Then come kiss me, sweet and twenty;
Youth's a stuff will not endure.
Twelfth Night, II.iii **Shakespeare, William** (1564–1616) English dramatist, poet and actor

27 Having been in love, with one princess or other, almost all my life, and I hope I shall go on so till I die, being firmly persuaded, that if ever I do a mean action, it must be in some interval betwixt one passion and another.
A Sentimental Journey (1768) **Sterne, Laurence** (1713–1768) Irish-born English writer and clergyman

28 You have only to look these happy couples in the face, to see they have never been in love, or in hate, or in any other high passion all their days.
Virginibus Puerisque (1881) **Stevenson, Robert Louis** (1850–1894) Scottish writer, poet and essayist

29 Yes, I am a fatal man, Madame Fribsbi. To inspire hopeless passion is my destiny.
Pendennis (1848–50) **Thackeray, William Makepeace** (1811–1863) Indian-born English writer

30 The seas are quiet, when the winds give o'er:
So calm are we, when passions are no more.
'Of the Last Verses in the Book' (1596) **Waller, Edmund** (1606–1687) English poet and politician
See also love; marriage; sex

PATRIOTISM

1 What pity is it
That we can die but once to serve our country!
Cato (1713) **Addison, Joseph** (1672–1719) English essayist, poet, playwright and statesman

2 From distant climes, o'er widespread seas we come,
Though not with much éclat or beat of drum;
True patriots we; for be it understood,
We left our country for our country's good.
No private views disgraced our generous zeal,
What urged our travels was our country's weal;
And none will doubt but that our emigration
Has proved most useful to the British nation.
'Prologue' for the opening of the Playhouse, Sydney, (1796) **Barrington, George** (1755–c.1835) Irish pickpocket and writer; transported to Australia. Of convicts transported to Botany Bay

3 Standing, as I do, in view of God and eternity I realize that patriotism is not enough. I must have no hatred or bitterness towards anyone.
The Times, (1915) **Cavell, Edith** (1865–1915) English nurse, executed by the Germans. Said on the eve of her execution

4 They died to save their country and they only saved the world.
The Ballad of Saint Barbara and Other Verses (1922) **Chesterton, G.K.** (1874–1936) English writer, poet and critic

5 Our country! In her intercourse with foreign nations, may she always be in the right; but our country, right or wrong.
In Mackenzie, *Life of Decatur* (1846) **Decatur, Stephen** (1779–1820) US naval commander. Toast during a banquet, 1815

6 Never was patriot yet, but was a fool.
Absalom and Achitophel (1681) **Dryden, John** (1631–1700) English poet, satirist, dramatist and critic

7 'Twas for the good of my country that I should be abroad. – Anything for the good of one's country – I'm a Roman for that.
The Beaux' Stratagem (1707) **Farquhar, George** (1678–1707) Irish dramatist

8 I hate the idea of causes, and if I had to choose between betraying my country and betraying my friend, I hope I should have the guts to betray my country.
Two Cheers for Democracy (1951) **Forster, E.M.** (1879–1970) English writer, essayist and literary critic

9 Men, I am leaving Rome. If you want to carry on fighting the invader, come with me. I cannot promise you either honours or wages; I can only offer you hunger, thirst, forced marches, battles and death. If you love your country, follow me.
In Guerzoni, *Garibaldi* (1929) **Garibaldi, Giuseppe** (1807–1882) Italian soldier and patriot

10 That kind of patriotism which consists in hating all other nations.
Sylvia's Lovers (1863) **Gaskell, Elizabeth** (1810–1865) English writer

11 Such is the patriot's boast, where'er we roam,
His first best country ever is at home.
'The Traveller' (1764) **Goldsmith, Oliver** (c.1728–1774) Irish dramatist, poet and writer

12 I only regret that I have but one life to lose for my country.
In Johnston, *Nathan Hale* (1974) **Hale, Nathan** (1755–1776) US soldier and revolutionary. Speech before he was executed by the British

13 Without a sign, his Sword the brave Man draws,
And asks no Omen but his Country's Cause.
Iliad (trans. Pope) **Homer** (fl. c.8th century BC) Greek epic poet. Hector rejects ill omens

14 It is sweet and honourable to die for one's country.
Odes **Horace** (65–8 BC) Roman lyric poet and satirist. *(Dulce et decorum est pro patria mori)*

15 We don't want to fight, but, by jingo if we do,
We've got the ships, we've got the men, we've got the money too.
Music-hall song, (1878) **Hunt, G.W.** (1829–1904) British song writer and painter

16 It is better to be the widow of a hero than the wife of a coward.
Speech, Valencia, (1936) **Ibárruri, Dolores ('La Pasionaria')** (1895–1989) Basque Communist leader

17 Patriotism is the last refuge of a scoundrel.
In Boswell, *The Life of Samuel Johnson* (1791) **Johnson, Samuel** (1709–1784) English lexicographer, poet, critic, conversationalist and essayist

18 I would die for my country but I could never let my country die for me.
Speech, (1987) **Kinnock, Neil** (1942–) Welsh Labour politician. Of nuclear disarmament

19 The accent of one's native country remains in the mind and the heart, as it does in one's speech.
Réflexions ou Sentences et Maximes Morales (1678) **La Rochefoucauld** (1613–1680) French writer

20 These are the times that try men's souls. The summer soldier and the sunshine patriot will, in this crisis, shrink from the service of their country; but he that stands it now, deserves the love and thanks of men and women.
The Crisis (1776)

21 My country is the world, and my religion is to do good.
The Rights of Man (1791) **Paine, Thomas** (1737–1809) English-born US political theorist and pamphleteer

22 Patriots always talk of dying for their country, and never of killing for their country.
Attr. **Russell, Bertrand** (1872–1970) English philosopher, mathematician, essayist and social reformer

23 Our country, right or wrong! When right, to be kept right; when wrong, to be put right!
Speech, (1872) **Schurz, Carl** (1829–1906) German-born US lawyer, soldier, Republican politician and writer

24 Breathes there the man, with soul so dead, Who never to himself hath said,
This is my own, my native land!
Whose heart hath ne'er within him burned, As home his footsteps he hath turned, From wandering on a foreign strand!
The Lay of the Last Minstrel (1805) **Scott, Sir Walter** (1771–1832) Scottish writer and historian

25 True Patriotism is of no Party.
The Adventures of Sir Launcelot Greaves (1762) **Smollett, Tobias** (1721–1771) Scottish writer, satirist, historian, traveller and physician

26 I vow to thee, my country – all earthly things above –
Entire and whole and perfect, the service of my love.
'I Vow to Thee, My Country' (1918) **Spring-Rice, Cecil Arthur** (1859–1918) English diplomat and hymn writer

27 The land of my fathers. My fathers can have it.
In John Ackerman, *Dylan Thomas* (1991) **Thomas, Dylan** (1914–1953) Welsh poet, writer and radio dramatist. Referring to Wales

28 Patriotism to the Soviet State is a revolutionary duty, whereas patriotism to a bourgeois State is treachery.
In Fitzroy Maclean, *Disputed Barricade*
Trotsky, Leon (1879–1940) Russian revolutionary and Communist theorist

29 'Shoot if you must, this old grey head, But spare your country's flag,' she said.
'Barbara Frietchie' (1863) **Whittier, John Greenleaf** (1807–1892) US poet, abolitionist and journalist

30 Patriotism is the virtue of the vicious.
Attr. **Wilde, Oscar** (1854–1900) Irish poet, dramatist, writer, critic and wit
See also war

PEACE

1 Since wars begin in the minds of men, it is in the minds of men that the defences of peace must be constructed.
Constitution of UNESCO **Anonymous**

2 Pale Ebenezer thought it wrong to fight, But Roaring Bill (who killed him) thought it right.
'The Pacifist' (1938) **Belloc, Hilaire** (1870–1953) English writer of verse, essayist and critic; Liberal MP

3 They shall beat their swords into plowshares, and their spears into pruninghooks: nation shall not lift up sword against nation, neither shall they learn war any more.
Isaiah, 2:4

4 The peace of God, which passeth all understanding.
Philippians, 4:7 **The Bible (King James Version)**

5 *Peace:* In international affairs, a period of cheating between two periods of fighting.
The Cynic's Word Book (1906) **Bierce, Ambrose** (1842–c.1914) US writer, verse writer and soldier

6 Sweet Prince! the arts of peace are great, And no less glorious than those of war.
Poetical Sketches (1783) **Blake, William** (1757–1827) English poet, engraver, painter and mystic

7 Don't tell me that peace has broken out.
Mother Courage (1939) **Brecht, Bertolt** (1898–1956) German dramatist

8 Force is not a remedy.
Speech, (1880) **Bright, John** (1811–1889) English Liberal politician and social reformer

9 An unjust Peace is to be preferr'd before a just War.
Two Speeches made in the Rump Parliament
Butler, Samuel (poet) (1612–1680) English poet

10 This is the second time in our history that there has come back from Germany to Downing Street peace with honour. I believe it is peace for our time.
Speech, Downing Street, after Munich Agreement, 1938, in Feiling, *The Life of Neville Chamberlain* (1946) **Chamberlain, Neville** (1869–1940) English Conservative Prime Minister

11 The thing which is by far the best and most desirable for all who are sane and good and fortunate is 'peace with honour'.
Pro Sestio, 98 **Cicero** (106–43 BC) Roman orator, statesman, essayist and letter writer

12 It's a maxim not to be despised, 'Though peace be made, yet it's interest that keeps peace.'
Speech, (1654) **Cromwell, Oliver** (1599–1658) English general, statesman and Puritan leader

13 Lord Salisbury and myself have brought you back peace – but peace, I hope, with honour.
Speech, (1878) **Disraeli, Benjamin** (1804–1881) English statesman and writer

14 I am an absolute pacifist ... It is an instinctive feeling. It is a feeling that possesses me, because the murder of men is disgusting.
Interview, (1929)

15 Peace cannot be kept by force. It can only be achieved by understanding.
Notes on Pacifism **Einstein, Albert** (1879–1955) German-born US mathematical physicist

16 The peace we seek, founded upon decent trust and co-operative effort among nations, can be fortified, not by weapons of war but by wheat and by cotton, by milk and by wool, by meat and by timber and by rice. These are words that translate into every language on earth. These are needs that challenge this world in arms.
Speech, (1953)

17 I think that people want peace so much that one of these days governments had better get out of the way and let them have it.
Broadcast discussion, (1959) **Eisenhower, Dwight D.** (1890–1969) US President and general

18 I wanted to avoid violence. Non-violence is the first article of my faith. It is also the last article of my creed.
Speech, (1922)

19 An eye for an eye makes the whole world blind.
Attr. **Gandhi, Mohandas** (1869–1948) Indian political leader

20 I have many times asked myself whether there can be more potent advocates of peace upon earth through the years to come than this massed multitude of silent witnesses to the desolation of war.
Attr. **George V** (1865–1936) King of the United Kingdom. On the battlefield cemeteries in Flanders, 1922

21 'Peace upon earth!' was said. We sing it, And pay a million priests to bring it. After two thousand years of mass We've got as far as poison-gas.
'Christmas: 1924' (1928) **Hardy, Thomas** (1840–1928) English writer and poet

22 He that makes a good war, makes a good peace.
Jacula Prudentum; or Outlandish Proverbs, Sentences &c. (1640) **Herbert, George** (1593–1633) English poet and priest

23 Wisdom has taught us to be calm and meek,
To take one blow, and turn the other cheek;
It is not written what a man shall do
If the rude caitiff smite the other too!

'Non-Resistance' (1861) **Holmes, Oliver Wendell** (1809–1894) US physician, poet, writer and scientist

24 I feel like a man who is drinking a bitter but useful medicine.
The Observer Review, (1995) **Izetbegovic, Alija** (1865–1936) President of Bosnia. On signing the Balkan peace accord in Paris, December 1995

25 We love peace, as we abhor pusillanimity; but not peace at any price.
'Peace' (1859) **Jerrold, Douglas William** (1803–1857) English dramatist, writer and wit

26 Now we are in a period which I can characterize as a period of cold peace.
The Observer, (1949) **Lie, Trygve** (1896–1968) Norwegian politician and Secretary-General of the UN

27 Peace is indivisible.
Speech to League of Nations, (1936) **Litvinov, Maxim** (1876–1951) Soviet politician and diplomat

28 The peace that passeth all understanding.
Speech, (1938) **Mayhew, Christopher** (1915–1997) British parliamentarian and writer. On the Munich Agreement

29 The issues are the same. We wanted peace on earth, love, and understanding between everyone around the world. We have learned that change comes slowly.
The Observer, (1987) **McCartney, Paul** (1942–) English rock musician

30 Peace hath her victories
No less renowned than war.
'To the Lord General Cromwell' (1652) **Milton, John** (1608–1674) English poet, libertarian and pamphleteer

31 Nation shall speak peace unto nation.
Motto of BBC **Rendall, Montague John** (1862–1950) English schoolmaster

32 When peace has been broken anywhere, the peace of all countries everywhere is in danger.
Radio broadcast, (1939) **Roosevelt, Franklin Delano** (1882–1945) US Democrat President

33 If peace cannot be maintained with honour, it is no longer peace.

Speech, (1853) **Russell, Lord John** (1792–1878) English Liberal Prime Minister and writer

34 Making peace is harder than making war.
Address to Chicago Council on Foreign Relations, (1946) **Stevenson, Adlai** (1900–1965) US lawyer, statesman and United Nations ambassador

35 They create a desert, and call it peace.
Agricola **Tacitus** (AD c.56–c.120) Roman historian

36 But peace is ungrateful and never knows it only owes its continued existence to war.
To Arno Holz (1913) **Tucholsky, Kurt** (1890–1935) German satirist and writer

37 Let him who desires peace be prepared for war.
Epitoma Rei Militaris **Vegetius Renatus, Flavius** (fl. c.AD 375) Latin military writer

38 When will the world know that peace and propagation are the two most delightful things in it?
Letter to Sir Horace Mann, (1778) **Walpole, Horace** (1717–1797) English writer and politician

39 When you're at war you think about a better life; when you're at peace you think about a more comfortable one.
The Skin of Our Teeth (1942) **Wilder, Thornton** (1897–1975) US author and playwright

40 There is a price which is too great to pay for peace, and that price can be put in one word. One cannot pay the price of self-respect.
Speech, (1916)

41 It must be a peace without victory ... only a peace between equals can last.
Speech, (1917) **Wilson, Woodrow** (1856–1924) US Democrat President

42 And I shall have some peace there, for peace comes dropping slow,
Dropping from the veils of the morning to where the cricket sings;
There midnight's all a glimmer, and noon a purple glow,
And evening full of the linnet's wings.

In the *National Observer*, 1890, 'The Lake Isle of Innisfree' **Yeats, W.B.** (1865–1939) Irish poet, dramatist, editor, writer and senator
See also the military; war

PETS

1 Cruel, but composed and bland,
Dumb, inscrutable and grand,
So Tiberius might have sat,
Had Tiberius been a cat.
'Poor Matthias' **Arnold, Matthew** (1822–1888) English poet, critic, essayist and educationist

2 So if you want to know more about neutering and why it's best for you and your dog, give us a call.
The Observer, (2000) **Anonymous**
Advertisement for National Canine Defence League

3 You will find that the woman who is really kind to dogs is always one who has failed to inspire sympathy in men.
Zuleika Dobson (1911) **Beerbohm, Sir Max** (1872–1956) English satirist, cartoonist, critic and essayist

4 It's the one species I wouldn't mind seeing vanish from the face of the earth. I wish they were like the white rhino – six of them left in the Serengeti National Park, and all males.
Attr. **Bennett, Alan** (1934–) English dramatist, actor and diarist. On dogs

5 I once knew a man out of courtesy help a lame dog over a stile, and he for requital bit his fingers.
The Religion of Protestants (1637) **Chillingworth, William** (1602–1644) English theologian and scholar

6 Though, as we know, she was not fond of pets that must be held in the hands or trodden on, she was always attentive to the feelings of dogs, and very polite if she had to decline their advances.
Middlemarch (1872) **Eliot, George** (1819–1880) English writer and poet

7 The Naming of Cats is a difficult matter,
It isn't just one of your holiday games;
You may think at first I'm as mad as a
hatter
When I tell you a cat must have THREE
DIFFERENT NAMES ...
When you notice a cat in profound
meditation,
The reason, I tell you, is always the same:
His mind is engaged in a rapt
contemplation
Of the thought, of the thought, of the
thought of his name:
His ineffable effable
Effanineffable
Deep and inscrutable singular Name.
'The Naming of Cats' (1939) **Eliot, T.S.** (1888–
1965) US-born British poet, verse dramatist
and critic

8 I have noticed that what cats most
appreciate in a human being is not the
ability to produce food which they take for
granted – but his or her entertainment
value.
Rogue Male (1939) **Household, Geoffrey** (1900–
1988) English writer

9 To his dog, every man is Napoleon; hence
the constant popularity of dogs.
Attr. **Huxley, Aldous** (1894–1963) English
writer, poet and critic

10 When I observed he was a fine cat, saying,
'why yes, Sir, but I have had cats whom I
liked better than this'; and then as if
perceiving Hodge to be out of
countenance, adding, 'but he is a very fine
cat, a very fine cat indeed.'
In Boswell, *The Life of Samuel Johnson* (1791)
Johnson, Samuel (1709–1784) English
lexicographer, poet, critic, conversationalist
and essayist

11 We were regaled by a dogfight ... How odd
that people of sense should find any
pleasure in being accompanied by a beast
who is always spoiling conversation.
In Trevelyan, *Life and Letters of Macaulay* (1876)
Macaulay, Lord (1800–1859) English Liberal
statesman, essayist and poet

12 The great open spaces
where cats are cats.

archys life of mehitabel (1933) **Marquis, Don**
(1878–1937) US columnist, satirist and poet

13 When I play with my cat, who knows
whether she isn't amusing herself with me
more than I am with her?
Essais (1580) **Montaigne, Michel de** (1533–1592)
French essayist and moralist

14 Dogs, like horses, are quadrupeds. That is
to say, they have four rupeds, one at each
corner, on which they walk.
You Can't Have Your Kayak and Heat It, with
Dennis Norden **Muir, Frank** (1920–1998)
English writer, humorist and broadcaster

15 A door is what a dog is perpetually on the
wrong side of.
'A Dog's Best Friend Is His Illiteracy' (1952)
Nash, Ogden (1902–1971) US poet

16 Moving one paw out and yawning,
he closes his eyes. Everywhere
people are in despair. And he is dancing.
Collected Poems (1983) **Porter, Peter Neville
Frederick** (1929–) Australian-born British
poet

17 Let some of the tranquillity of the cat
Curl into me.
'The Creature in the Chair' **Rowbotham,
David Harold** (1924–) Australian journalist,
critic and poet

18 For I will consider my Cat Jeoffry.
For he is the servant of the Living God,
duly and daily serving Him.
For at the first glance of the glory of God in
the East he worships in his way.
For this is done by wreathing his body
seven times round with elegant quickness.
Jubilate Agno

19 For he counteracts the powers of darkness
by his electrical skin and glaring eyes.
For he counteracts the Devil, who is death,
by brisking about the life.
Jubilate Agno

20 For the English Cats are the best in
Europe.
Jubilate Agno **Smart, Christopher** (1722–1771)
English poet and translator

21 For though he had very little Latin beyond
'Cave canem,' he had, as a young dog,
devoured Shakespeare (in a tasty leather
binding).
One Hundred and One Dalmatians (1956) **Smith,
Dodie** (1896–1990) English novelist

22 Oh I am a cat that likes to
Gallop about doing good.
'The Galloping Cat' (1972) **Smith, Stevie**
(1902–1971) English poet and writer

23 That indefatigable and unsavoury engine of
pollution, the dog.
Letter to *The Times*, (1975) **Sparrow, John**
(1906–1992) English lawyer and writer

24 I loathe people who keep dogs. They are
cowards who haven't got the guts to bite
people themselves.
A Madman's Diary **Streatfield, Sir Geoffrey
Hugh Benbow** (1897–1978) British judge

25 Cats, no less liquid than their shadows,
Offer no angles to the wind.
They slip, diminished, neat, through
loopholes
Less than themselves.
Cats (1934) **Tessimond, A.S.J.** (1902–1962)
English poet
See also animals; birds

PHILOSOPHY

1 Philosophy: unintelligible answers to
insoluble problems.
In Bert Leston Taylor, *The So-Called Human
Race* (1922) **Adams, Henry** (1838–1918) US
historian and memoirist

2 Accept that some days you're the pigeon,
and some days you're the statue.
The Dilbert Principle

3 Needing someone is like needing a
parachute. If he isn't there the first time
you need him, chances are you won't be
needing him again.
The Dilbert Principle **Adams, Scott** (1957–) US
cartoonist

4 It was said of Socrates that he brought
philosophy down from heaven to inhabit
among men; and I shall be ambitious to
have it said of me that I have brought
philosophy out of closets and libraries,
schools and colleges, to dwell in clubs and
assemblies, at tea-tables and in coffee-
houses.
The Spectator, (March 1711) **Addison, Joseph**
(1672–1719) English essayist, poet, playwright
and statesman

5 Here's my Golden Rule for a tarnished age:
Be fair with others, but keep after them
until they're fair with you.
Connecticut College News, (1980) **Alda, Alan**
(1936–) US actor and director

6 Be all you can be.
Scottish Health Education Council, *1980s*

7 The probability of someone watching you
is proportional to the stupidity of your
action.
Hartley's First Law **Anonymous**

8 The principles of logic and metaphysics are
true simply because we never allow them
to be anything else.
Language, Truth and Logic (1936) **Ayer, A.J.**
(1910–1989) English philosopher

9 All good moral philosophy ... is but an
handmaid to religion.
The Advancement of Learning (1605) **Bacon,
Francis** (1561–1626) English philosopher,
essayist, politician and courtier

10 What men call superstition and prejudice
are but the crust of custom which by sheer
survival has shown itself proof against the
ravages and vicissitudes of its long life; to
lose it is to lose the shield that protects
men's national existence, their spirit, the
habits, memories, faith that have made
them what they are.
'The Counter-Enlightenment' **Berlin, Isaiah**
(1909–1997) English philosopher

11 I prefer complexity to certainty, cheerful
mysteries to sullen facts.
Address, University of Toronto, (1969) **Bissell,
Claude T.** (1916–2000) Canadian writer

12 We have stopped believing in progress.
What progress that is!

Ibarra, *Borges et Borges* **Borges, Jorge Luis** (1899–1986) Argentinian writer, poet and librarian

13 On a metaphysician: A blind man in a dark room – looking for a black hat – which isn't there.
Attr. **Bowen, Lord** (1835–1894) English judge and scholar

14 Metaphysics is the finding of bad reasons for what we believe upon instinct; but to find these reasons is no less an instinct.
Appearance and Reality (1893) **Bradley, F.H.** (1846–1924) English philosopher

15 He that wrestles with us strengthens our nerves, and sharpens our skill. Our antagonist is our helper.
Reflections on the Revolution in France (1790) **Burke, Edmund** (1729–1797) Irish-born British statesman and philosopher

16 The profoundest thoughts of the philosophers have something tricklike about them. A lot disappears in order for something to suddenly appear in the palm of the hand.
The Secret Heart of the Clock: Notes, Aphorisms, Fragments 1973–1985 (1991) **Canetti, Elias** (1905–1994) Bulgarian-born English writer, dramatist and critic

17 I am tempted to say about metaphysicians what Scalinger would say about the Basques: they are said to understand one another, but I don't believe a word of it.
Maximes et Pensées (1796) **Chamfort, Nicolas** (1741–1794) French writer

18 One is not superior merely because one sees the world in an odious light.
Attr. **Chateaubriand, François-René** (1768–1848) French writer and statesman

19 But somehow there is nothing so absurd that some philosopher has not said it.
De Divinatione **Cicero** (106–43 BC) Roman orator, statesman, essayist and letter writer

20 Our greatest glory is not in never falling, but in rising every time we fall.
Analects **Confucius** (c.550–c.478 BC) Chinese philosopher and teacher of ethics

21 'I am ruminating,' said Mr Pickwick, 'on the strange mutability of human affairs.'
'Ah, I see – in at the palace door one day, out at the window the next. Philosopher, sir?'
'An observer of human nature, sir,' said Mr Pickwick.
The Pickwick Papers (1837) **Dickens, Charles** (1812–1870) English writer

22 If you were to destroy in mankind the belief in immortality, not only love but every living force maintaining the life of the world would at once dry up. Moreover, nothing then would be immoral, everything would be lawful, even cannibalism.
The Brothers Karamazov (1879–1880) **Dostoevsky, Fyodor** (1821–1881) Russian writer

23 When nothing is sure, everything is possible.
The Middle Ground (1980) **Drabble, Margaret** (1939–) English writer

24 Whoever is faced with the paradoxical exposes himself to reality.
The Physicists (1962) **Dürrenmatt, Friedrich** (1921–1990) Swiss dramatist and writer

25 I have tried too in my time to be a philosopher; but, I don't know how, cheerfulness was always breaking in.
In Boswell, *The Life of Samuel Johnson* (1791) **Edwards, Oliver** (1711–1791) English lawyer

26 Everything should be made as simple as possible, but not simpler.
Attr. **Einstein, Albert** (1879–1955) German-born US mathematical physicist

27 Men are conservatives when they are least vigorous, or when they are most luxurious. They are conservatives after dinner. … when they hear music, or when they read poetry, they are radicals.
Essays, Second Series (1844)

28 Other world! There is no other world! Here or nowhere is the whole fact.
'Natural Religion' **Emerson, Ralph Waldo** (1803–1882) US poet, essayist, transcendentalist and teacher

29 Nice philosophy
May tolerate unlikely arguments,
But heaven admits no jest.
'Tis Pity she's a Whore (1633) **Ford, John** (c.1586–c.1640) English dramatist and poet

30 To a philosopher, no circumstance, however trifling, is too minute.
The Citizen of the World (1762)

31 This same philosophy is a good horse in the stable, but an errant jade on a journey.
The Good Natur'd Man (1768) **Goldsmith, Oliver** (c.1728–1774) Irish dramatist, poet and writer

32 Perhaps catastrophe is the natural human environment, and even though we spend a good deal of energy trying to get away from it, we are programmed for survival amid catastrophe.
Sex and Destiny (1984) **Greer, Germaine** (1939–) Australian feminist, critic, English scholar and writer

33 For your own safety is at stake, when your neighbour's wall catches fire.
Epistles **Horace** (65–8 BC) Roman lyric poet and satirist

34 Philosophers never balance between profit and honesty, because their decisions are general, and neither their passions nor imaginations are interested in the objects.
A Treatise of Human Nature (1739) **Hume, David** (1711–1776) Scottish philosopher and political economist

35 Finding bad reasons for what one believes for other bad reasons – that's philosophy.
Brave New World (1932) **Huxley, Aldous** (1894–1963) English writer, poet and critic

36 I doubt if the philosopher lives, or has ever lived, who could know himself to be heartily despised by a street boy without some irritation.
Evolution and Ethics (1893) **Huxley, T.H.** (1825–1895) English biologist, Darwinist and agnostic

37 There is only one thing a philosopher can be relied on to do, and that is to contradict other philosophers.
Attr. **James, William** (1842–1910) US psychologist and philosopher

38 I refute it thus.
In Boswell, *The Life of Samuel Johnson* (1791) **Johnson, Samuel** (1709–1784) English lexicographer, poet, critic, conversationalist and essayist. Kicking a stone in order to disprove Berkeley's theory of the non-existence of matter

39 A metaphysical need is only a need for death.
Diary (1912) **Kafka, Franz** (1883–1924) Czech-born German-speaking writer

40 Do not all charms fly
At the mere touch of cold philosophy?
There was an awful rainbow once in heaven:
We know her woof, her texture; she is given
In the dull catalogue of common things.
Philosophy will clip an Angel's wings.
'Lamia' (1819) **Keats, John** (1795–1821) English poet

41 Acting without design, occupying oneself without making a business of it, finding the great in what is small and the many in the few, repaying injury with kindness, effecting difficult things while they are easy, and managing great things in their beginnings: this is the method of Tao.
Tao Te Ching **Lao-Tzu** (c.604–531 BC) Chinese philosopher

42 In the information age, you don't teach philosophy as they did after feudalism. You perform it. If Aristotle were alive today he'd have a talk show.
Evening Standard, (1989) **Leary, Timothy** (1920–1996) US writer and psychologist

43 Good-bye now, Plato and Hegel,
The shop is closing down;
They don't want any philosopher-kings in England,
There ain't no universals in this man's town.
Autumn Journal (1939) **MacNeice, Louis** (1907–1963) Belfast-born poet, writer, radio producer, translator and critic

44 It's no use crying over spilt milk, because all the forces of the universe were bent on spilling it.

Of Human Bondage (1915) **Maugham, William Somerset** (1874–1965) English writer, dramatist and physician

45 A State which dwarfs its men, in order that they may be more docile instruments in its hands even for beneficial purposes – will find that with small men no great thing can really be accomplished.
On Liberty (1859) **Mill, John Stuart** (1806–1873) English philosopher, economist and reformer

46 The cry of equality pulls everyone down.
The Observer, (1987) **Murdoch, Iris** (1919–1999) Irish-born British writer, philosopher and dramatist

47 What I understand philosophers to be: a terrible explosive, in the presence of which everything is in danger.
Ecce Homo (1888) **Nietzsche, Friedrich Wilhelm** (1844–1900) German philosopher, critic and poet

48 Sexual pleasure seems to consist in a sudden discharge of nervous energy. Aesthetic enjoyment is a sudden discharge of allusive emotions. Similarly, philosophy is like a sudden discharge of intellectual activity.
Meditations on Quijote (1914) **Ortega y Gasset, José** (1883–1955) Spanish philosopher

49 To ridicule philosophy is truly to philosophize.
Pensées (1670) **Pascal, Blaise** (1623–1662) French philosopher and scientist

50 I saw it, but I did not realize it.
In L. Tharp, *The Peabody Sisters of Salem* **Peabody, Elizabeth** (1804–1894) US teacher and writer. Giving a Transcendentalist explanation for her accidentally walking into a tree

51 Unless either philosophers become kings in our states, or those who are now called kings and rulers become to a serious and sufficient degree philosophers ... there will be no fewer ills afflicting our states or indeed the whole of the human race.
Republic **Plato** (c.429–347 BC) Greek philosopher

52 Our civilization ... has not yet fully recovered from the shock of its birth – the transition from the tribal or 'closed society', with its submission to magical forces, to the 'open society' which sets free the critical powers of man.
The Open Society and its Enemies (1945) **Popper, Sir Karl** (1902–1994) Austrian-born British philosopher

53 Not only is there but one way of doing things rightly, but there is only one way of seeing them, and that is, seeing the whole of them.
The Two Paths (1859) **Ruskin, John** (1819–1900) English art critic, philosopher and reformer

54 Organic life, we are told, has developed gradually from the protozoon to the philosopher, and this development, we are assured, is indubitably an advance. Unfortunately it is the philosopher, not the protozoon, who gives us this assurance.
Mysticism and Logic (1918)

55 Matter ... a convenient formula for describing what happens where it isn't.
An Outline of Philosophy (1927)

56 It is undesirable to believe a proposition when there is no ground whatever for supposing it true.
Sceptical Essays (1928)

57 The point of philosophers is to start with something so simple as to seem not worth stating, and to end with something so paradoxical that no one will believe it.
Logic and Knowledge (1956)

58 There's a Bible on that shelf there. But I keep it next to Voltaire – poison and antidote.
In Harris and Callas, *Kenneth Harris Talking to Maria Callas [and others]* (1971) **Russell, Bertrand** (1872–1970) English philosopher, mathematician, essayist and social reformer

59 Philosophy is the replacement of category-habits by category-disciplines.
The Concept of Mind (1949) **Ryle, Gilbert** (1900–1976) English philosopher

60 You become responsible, for ever, for what you have tamed. You are responsible for your rose.
The Little Prince (1943)

61 Man's 'progress' is but a gradual discovery that his questions have no meaning.
The Wisdom of the Sands **Saint-Exupéry, Antoine de** (1900–1944) French author and aviator

62 No lesson seems to be so deeply inculcated by the experience of life as that you never should trust experts. If you believe the doctors, nothing is wholesome: if you believe the theologians, nothing is innocent: if you believe the soldiers, nothing is safe. They all require to have their strong wine diluted by a very large admixture of insipid common sense.
Letter to Lord Lytton, (1877) **Salisbury, Lord** (1830–1903) English Conservative Prime Minister

63 It is a great advantage for a system of philosophy to be substantially true.
The Unknowable (1923) **Santayana, George** (1863–1952) Spanish-born US philosopher and writer

64 I know perfectly well that I don't want to do anything; to do something is to create existence – and there is quite enough existence as it is.
Nausea (1938) **Sartre, Jean-Paul** (1905–1980) French philosopher, writer, dramatist and critic

65 There is only one innate error, and that is that we are here in order to be happy.
The World as Will and Idea (1859)
Schopenhauer, Arthur (1788–1860) German philosopher

66 Philosophy is nothing but discretion.
Table Talk (1689) **Selden, John** (1584–1654) English historian, jurist and politician

67 Adversity's sweet milk, philosophy.
As You Like It, II.i

68 What's in a name? That which we call a rose
By any other name would smell as sweet.
Romeo and Juliet, II.ii

69 There are more things in heaven and earth, Horatio,
Than are dreamt of in your philosophy.
Romeo and Juliet, III.ii

70 Sweet are the uses of adversity;
Which, like the toad, ugly and venomous,
Wears yet a precious jewel in his head.
Hamlet, I.v **Shakespeare, William** (1564–1616) English dramatist, poet and actor

71 Two things of opposite natures seem to depend
On one another, as a man depends
On a woman, day on night, the imagined
On the real.
'Notes Toward a Supreme Fiction' (1948)
Stevens, Wallace (1879–1955) US poet, essayist, dramatist and lawyer

72 To be honest, to be kind – to earn a little and to spend a little less, to make upon the whole a family happier for his presence, to renounce when that shall be necessary and not be embittered, to keep a few friends, but these without capitulation – above all, on the same grim condition, to keep friends with himself – here is a task for all that a man has of fortitude and delicacy.
Across the Plains (1892) **Stevenson, Robert Louis** (1850–1894) Scottish writer, poet and essayist

73 Philosophy! the lumber of the schools.
'Ode to Sir W. Temple' (1692) **Swift, Jonathan** (1667–1745) Irish satirist, poet, essayist and cleric

74 Nothing is worth discovering except that which has not yet existed.
La Vision du passé **Teilhard de Chardin, Pierre** (1881–1955) French Jesuit philosopher and palaeontologist

75 I find no hint throughout the universe
Of good or ill, of blessing or of curse;
I find alone Necessity Supreme.
The City of Dreadful Night (1880) **Thomson, James** (1834–1882) Scottish poet and dramatist

76 There are now-a-days professors of philosophy but not philosophers.
Walden (1854) **Thoreau, Henry David** (1817–1862) US essayist, social critic and writer

77 Taste is created from a thousand distastes.
Unsaid Things **Valéry, Paul** (1871–1945) French poet, mathematician and philosopher

78 In philosophy, we must distrust the things we understand too easily as well as the things we don't understand.
Lettres philosophiques (1734)

79 Superstition sets the whole world on fire; philosophy quenches the flames.
Dictionnaire philosophique (1764) **Voltaire** (1694–1778) French philosopher, dramatist, poet, historian, writer and critic

80 The safest general characterization of the European philosophical tradition is that it consists of a series of footnotes to Plato.
Process and Reality (1929)

81 Philosophy is the product of wonder.
Nature and Life (1934)

82 The systematic thought of ancient writers is now nearly worthless; but their detached insights are priceless.
Attr. **Whitehead, A.N.** (1861–1947) English mathematician and philosopher

83 Philosophy is not a theory but an activity.
Tractatus Logico-Philosophicus (1922)

84 Philosophy is a struggle against the bewitching of our minds by means of language.
Philosophical Investigations (1953) **Wittgenstein, Ludwig** (1889–1951) Austrian philosopher
See also ideas; thought

PLEASURE

1 A sip is the most that mortals are permitted from any goblet of delight.
Table Talk (1877) **Alcott, Bronson** (1799–1888) US educator, reformer and transcendentalist

2 'I am afraid,' replied Elinor, 'that the pleasantness of an employment does not always evince its propriety.'
Sense and Sensibility (1811)

3 One half of the world cannot understand the pleasures of the other.
Emma (1816) **Austen, Jane** (1775–1817) English writer

4 Pleasure only starts once the worm has got into the fruit, to become delightful happiness must be tainted with poison.
My Mother (1966) **Bataille, Georges** (1897–1962) French writer

5 Variety is the soul of pleasure.
The Rover (1677) **Behn, Aphra** (1640–1689) English dramatist, writer, poet, translator and spy

6 I am convinced that we have a degree of delight, and that no small one, in the real misfortunes and pains of others.
A Philosophical Enquiry into the Origin of our Ideas of the Sublime and Beautiful (1757) **Burke, Edmund** (1729–1797) Irish-born British statesman and philosopher

7 But pleasures are like poppies spread:
You seize the flow'r, its bloom is shed;
Or like the snow falls in the river,
A moment white – then melts for ever.
'Tam o' Shanter' (1790) **Burns, Robert** (1759–1796) Scottish poet and songwriter

8 There's not a joy the world can give like that it takes away.
'Stanzas for Music' (1815)

9 Though sages may pour out their wisdom's treasure,
There is no sterner moralist than Pleasure.
Don Juan (1824)

10 Pleasure's a sin, and sometimes sin's a pleasure.
Don Juan (1824) **Byron, Lord** (1788–1824) English poet, satirist and traveller

11 A man possesses nothing certainly save a brief loan of his own body: and yet the body of man is capable of much curious pleasure.
Jurgen (1919) **Cabell, James Branch** (1879–1958) US writer, poet, genealogist and historian

12 He seemed to indulge in all the usual pleasures without being a slave to any of them.
The Plague (1947) **Camus, Albert** (1913–1960) Algerian-born French writer

13 Summer's pleasures they are gone like to visions every one
And the cloudy days of autumn and of winter cometh on
I tried to call them back but unbidden they are gone
Far away from heart and eye and for ever far away.
'Remembrances' (1908) **Clare, John** (1793–1864) English rural poet; died in an asylum

14 The horrible pleasure of pleasing inferior people.
Amours de Voyage (1858) **Clough, Arthur Hugh** (1819–1861) English poet and letter writer

15 Remorse, the fatal egg by pleasure laid.
'The Progress of Error' (1782) **Cowper, William** (1731–1800) English poet, hymn writer and letter writer

16 The only safe pleasure for a parliamentarian is a bag of boiled sweets.
Listener, (1982) **Critchley, Julian** (1930–) English writer, broadcaster, journalist and politician

17 For present joys are more to flesh and blood
Than a dull prospect of a distant good.
The Hind and the Panther (1687) **Dryden, John** (1631–1700) English poet, satirist, dramatist and critic

18 A miss for pleasure, and a wife for breed.
'The Toilette' (1716) **Gay, John** (1685–1732) English poet, dramatist and librettist

19 The art of pleasing consists in being pleased.
The Round Table (1817) **Hazlitt, William** (1778–1830) English writer and critic

20 Look not on pleasures as they come, but go.
The Temple (1633) **Herbert, George** (1593–1633) English poet and priest

21 People must not do things for fun. We are not here for fun. There is no reference to fun in any Act of Parliament.
Uncommon Law (1935) **Herbert, Sir A.P.** (1890–1971) English humorist, writer, dramatist and politician

22 A pleasure so exquisite as almost to amount to pain.
Letter to Alexander Ireland, (1848) **Hunt, Leigh** (1784–1859) English writer, poet and literary editor

23 Pleasure is very seldom found where it is sought; our brightest blazes of gladness are commonly kindled by unexpected sparks.
The Idler (1758–1760)

24 If I had no duties, and no reference to futurity, I would spend my life in driving briskly in a post-chaise with a pretty woman.
In Boswell, *The Life of Samuel Johnson* (1791)

25 No man is a hypocrite in his pleasures.
In Boswell, *The Life of Samuel Johnson* (1791)

26 The great source of pleasure is variety.
The Lives of the Most Eminent English Poets (1779–1781) **Johnson, Samuel** (1709–1784) English lexicographer, poet, critic, conversationalist and essayist

27 Ever let the Fancy roam,
Pleasure never is at home.
'Fancy' (1819) **Keats, John** (1795–1821) English poet

28 The greatest pleasure I know, is to do a good action by stealth, and to have it found out by accident.
'Table Talk by the Late Elia' **Lamb, Charles** (1775–1834) English essayist, critic and letter writer

29 Sometimes something worth doing is worth overdoing.
CBS *Late Show,* (1994) **Letterman, David** (1947–) US talk show host

30 Fun is fun but no girl wants to laugh all of the time.
Gentlemen Prefer Blondes (1925) **Loos, Anita** (1893–1981) US writer and screenwriter

31 From the midst of the fountain of delights rises something bitter that is a torment even among the flowers.
De Rerum Natura **Lucretius** (c.95–55 BC) Roman philosopher

32 Let us roll our strength and all
Our sweetness up into one ball,
And tear our pleasures with rough strife
Thorough the iron gates of life:
Thus, though we cannot make our sun
Stand still, yet we will make him run.
'To His Coy Mistress' (1681) **Marvell, Andrew** (1621–1678) English poet and satirist

33 I would like to know if, after all, the greatest rule of all is not to please.
L'École des Femmes (1662)

34 Heaven forbids certain pleasures, it is true,
but one can arrive at certain compromises.
Tartuffe (1664) **Molière** (1622–1673) French
dramatist, actor and director

35 Then awake! the heavens look bright, my
dear;
'Tis never too late for delight, my dear;
And the best of all ways
To lengthen our days
Is to steal a few hours from the night, my
dear!
Irish Melodies (1807), 'The Young May Moon'
Moore, Thomas (1779–1852) Irish poet

36 After all, what is your hosts' purpose in
having a party? Surely not for you to enjoy
yourself; if that were their sole purpose,
they'd have simply sent champagne and
women over to your place by taxi.
Attr. **O'Rourke, P.J.** (1947–) US writer

37 Pleasures are ever in our hands or eyes,
And when in act they cease, in prospect
rise;
Present to grasp, and future still to find,
The whole employ of body and of mind.
An Essay on Man (1733) **Pope, Alexander** (1688–
1744) English poet, translator and editor

38 'Is there then no more?'
She cries. 'All this to love and rapture's
due;
Must we not pay a debt to pleasure too?'
'The Imperfect Enjoyment' (1680) **Rochester,
Earl of** (1647–1680) English poet, satirist,
courtier and libertine

39 Pleasure is nothing else but the
intermission of pain, the enjoyment of
something I am in great trouble for till I
have it.
Table Talk (1689) **Selden, John** (1584–1654)
English historian, jurist and politician

40 These violent delights have violent ends.
Romeo and Juliet, II.vi

41 No profit grows where is no pleasure ta'en;
In brief, sir, study what you most affect.
The Taming of the Shrew, I.i **Shakespeare,
William** (1564–1616) English dramatist, poet
and actor

42 I consider the world as made for me, not
me for the world: it is my maxim therefore
to enjoy it while I can, and let futurity shift
for itself.
The Adventures of Roderick Random (1748)
Smollett, Tobias (1721–1771) Scottish writer,
satirist, historian, traveller and physician

43 And painefull pleasure turnes to pleasing
paine.
The Faerie Queene (1596) **Spenser, Edmund**
(c.1522–1599) English poet

44 Each one's pleasure draws him on.
Eclogues **Virgil** (70–19 BC) Roman poet

45 All the things I really like to do are either
immoral, illegal, or fattening.
In Drennan, *Wit's End* (1973) **Woollcott,
Alexander** (1887–1943) US writer, drama critic
and anthologist
See also happiness; humour

POETRY

1 A poem records emotions and moods that
lie beyond normal language, that can only
be patched together and hinted at
metaphorically.
In Janet Sternburg, *The Writer on Her Work*
(1991) **Ackerman, Diane** (1948–) US poet

2 He delivers the meanest of his precepts
with a kind of grandeur, he breaks the
clods and tosses the dung about with an
air of gracefulness.
Essay on Virgil's Georgics (1697) Of Virgil

3 Nothing which is a phrase or saying in
common talk, should be admitted into a
serious poem.
Essay on Virgil's Georgics (1697)

4 The most complete, elaborate, and finisht
piece of all antiquity.
Essay on Virgil's Georgics (1697) Of The
Georgics

5 Our language sunk under him, and was
unequal to that greatness of soul which
furnished him with such glorious
conceptions.
The Spectator, (February 1712), 297 Of Milton

6 He more had pleas'd us, had he pleas'd us less.
Attr. Remark made of the poet Cowley
Addison, Joseph (1672–1719) English essayist, poet, playwright and statesman

7 The task of the poet is not to describe what actually happened, but the kind of thing that might happen according to probability or necessity ... For this reason poetry is something more philosophical and more worthy of serious attention than history.
Poetics, IX **Aristotle** (384–322 BC) Greek philosopher

8 He spoke, and loosed our heart in tears.
He laid us as we lay at birth
On the cool flowery lap of earth.
'Memorial Verses' (1850) Of Wordsworth

9 Wordsworth says somewhere that wherever Virgil seems to have composed 'with his eye on the object', Dryden fails to render him. Homer invariably composes 'with his eye on the object', whether the object be a moral or a material one: Pope composes with his eye on his style, into which he translates his object, whatever it is.
On Translating Homer (1861)

10 In poetry, no less than in life, he is 'a beautiful and ineffectual angel, beating in the void his luminous wings in vain'.
Essays in Criticism (1888) Quoting his own writing on Shelley

11 His expression may often be called bald ... but it is bald as the bare mountain tops are bald, with a baldness full of grandeur.
Essays in Criticism (1888) Of Wordsworth

12 A criticism of life under the conditions fixed for such a criticism by the laws of poetic truth and poetic beauty.
Essays in Criticism (1888) Of poetry **Arnold, Matthew** (1822–1888) English poet, critic, essayist and educationist

13 There is the view that poetry should improve your life. I think people confuse it with the Salvation Army.
International Herald Tribune, (1989)

14 I like poems you can tack all over with a hammer and there are no hollow places.

The Times, (1984) **Ashbery, John** (1927–)
English poet

15 He was so fair that they called him the lady of Christ's College.
Brief Lives (c.1693) **Aubrey, John** (1626–1697)
English antiquary, folklorist and biographer.
Of Milton

16 It is a sad fact about our culture that a poet can earn much more money writing or talking about his art than he can by practising it.
The Dyer's Hand (1963)

17 A poet's hope: to be,
like some valley cheese,
local, but prized elsewhere.
'Shorts II' **Auden, W.H.** (1907–1973) English poet, essayist, critic, teacher and dramatist

18 Poesy was ever thought to have some participation of divineness, because it doth raise and erect the mind, by submitting the shows of things to the desires of the mind; whereas reason doth buckle and bow the mind unto the nature of things.
The Advancement of Learning (1605) **Bacon, Francis** (1561–1626) English philosopher, essayist, politician and courtier

19 Poetic licence. There's no such thing.
Petit traité de poésie française **Banville, Théodore Faullain de** (1823–1891) French poet, lyricist and dramatist

20 The poet is like the prince of the clouds, who haunts the tempest and mocks at the archer. Exiled to the ground, an object of derision, his giant wings prevent him from walking.
Les Fleurs du mal (1857) **Baudelaire, Charles** (1821–1867) French poet, translator and critic

21 Poetry is a kind of ingenious nonsense.
In Spence, *Anecdotes* **Barrow, Isaac** (1630–1677) English divine

22 I agree with one of your reputable critics that a taste for drawing-rooms has spoiled more poets than ever did a taste for gutters.
The Mauve Decade (1926) **Beer, Thomas** (1889–1940) US writer

23 It is a pretty poem, Mr Pope, but you must not call it Homer.
In John Hawkins (ed.), *The Works of Samuel Johnson* (1787) **Bentley, Richard** (1662–1742) English scholar

24 Too many people in the modern world view poetry as a luxury, not a necessity like petrol. But to me it's the oil of life.
The Observer, (1974) **Betjeman, Sir John** (1906–1984) English poet laureate

25 The reason Milton wrote in fetters when he wrote of Angels & God, and at liberty when of Devils & Hell, is because he was a true Poet and of the Devil's party without knowing it.
'The Voice of the Devil' **Blake, William** (1757–1827) English poet, engraver, painter and mystic

26 At last came Malherbe, and, the first in France, gave poetry a proper rhythm.
L'Art Poétique (1674)

27 Be the subject lighthearted or sublime, sense always should agree with rhyme.
L'Art Poétique (1674) **Boileau-Despréaux, Nicolas** (1636–1711) French writer

28 Poetry is defined by its energies and its eloquence, not by the passport of the poet or the editor; or the name of the nationality. That way lie all the categories, the separations, the censorships that poetry exists to dispel.
Review of Seamus Heaney's An Open Letter, *The Irish Times*, (1983) **Boland, Eavan** (1944–) Irish poet and critic

29 I am obnoxious to each carping tongue, Who sayes my hand a needle better fits, A Poet's Pen, all scorne, I should thus wrong;
For such despight they cast on female wits: If what I doe prove well, it won't advance, They'll say it's stolne, or else, it was by chance.
'The Prologue' (1650) **Bradstreet, Anne** (c.1612–1672) English-born US poet

30 I never had the least thought or inclination of turning Poet till I once got heartily in love, and then rhyme and song were, in a manner, the spontaneous language of my head.

Attr. **Burns, Robert** (1759–1796) Scottish poet and songwriter

31 Nothing so difficult as a beginning
In poesy, unless perhaps the end.
Don Juan (1819–1824)

32 What is poetry? – The feeling of a Former world and Future.
Journal, (1821) **Byron, Lord** (1788–1824) English poet, satirist and traveller

33 I have nothing to say, I am saying it, and that is poetry.
Silence (1961) **Cage, John** (1912–1992) US composer and writer

34 If they had said the sun and the moon was gone out of the heavens it could not have struck me with the idea of a more awful and dreary blank in the creation than the words: Byron is dead.
Letter to Thomas Carlyle, (May 1824) **Carlyle, Jane Welsh** (1801–1866) Scottish letter writer, literary hostess and poet

35 A poet without love were a physical and metaphysical impossibility.
Critical and Miscellaneous Essays (1839)

36 The excellence of Burns is, indeed, among the rarest, … but … it is plain and easily recognised: his Sincerity, his indisputable air of Truth.
Critical and Miscellaneous Essays (1839)

37 Robert Burns never had the smallest chance to get into Parliament, much as Robert Burns deserved, for all our sakes, to have been found there.
Latter-Day Pamphlets (1850) **Carlyle, Thomas** (1795–1881) Scottish historian, biographer, critic, and essayist

38 I can explain all the poems that ever were invented – and a good many that haven't been invented just yet.
Through the Looking-Glass (and What Alice Found There) (1872)

39 'I can repeat poetry as well as other folk if it comes to that –'
'Oh, it needn't come to that!' Alice hastily said.
Through the Looking-Glass (and What Alice Found There) (1872) **Carroll, Lewis** (1832–1898) English writer and photographer

40 For the sacred poet ought to be chaste himself, but it is not necessary that his verses should be so.
Carmina **Catullus** (84–c.54 BC) Roman poet

41 A Poeme, whose subject is not truth, but things like truth.
Revenge of Bussy D'Ambois (1613) **Chapman, George** (c.1559–c.1634) English poet, dramatist and translator

42 A true poet scarcely worries about poetry, just as a gardener does not scent his roses.
Professional Secrets (1922) **Cocteau, Jean** (1889–1963) French dramatist, poet, film writer and director

43 Poetry is not the proper antithesis to prose, but to science. Poetry is opposed to science, and prose to metre.
Definitions of Poetry (1811)

44 That willing suspension of disbelief for the moment, which constitutes poetic faith.
Biographia Literaria (1817)

45 No man was ever yet a great poet, without being at the same time a profound philosopher.
Biographia Literaria (1817)

46 To read Dryden, Pope, etc., you need only count syllables; but to read Donne you must measure time, and discover the time of each word by the sense of passion.
The Friend (1818)

47 With Donne, whose muse on dromedary trots,
Wreathe iron pokers into true-love knots;
Rhyme's sturdy cripple, fancy's maze and clue,
Wit's forge and fire-blast, meaning's press and screw.
'On Donne's Poetry' (1818)

48 I wish our clever young poets would remember my homely definitions of prose and poetry; that is prose = words in their best order; poetry = the best words in the best order.
Table Talk (1835)

49 Poetry is certainly something more than good sense, but it must be good sense at all events; just as a palace is more than a house, but it must be a house, at least.

Table Talk (1835) **Coleridge, Samuel Taylor** (1772–1834) English poet, philosopher and critic

50 It is the business of a comic poet to paint the vices and follies of human kind.
The Double Dealer (1694) **Congreve, William** (1670–1729) English dramatist

51 I used to think all poets were Byronic –
Mad, bad and dangerous to know.
And then I met a few. Yes it's ironic –
I used to think all poets were Byronic.
They're mostly wicked as a ginless tonic
And wild as pension plans. Not long ago
I used to think all poets were Byronic –
Mad, bad and dangerous to know.
Making Cocoa for Kingsley Amis (1986)

52 I hardly ever tire of love or rhyme –
That's why I'm poor and have a rotten time.
'Variation on Belloc's 'Fatigue'' (1992) **Cope, Wendy** (1945–) English poet

53 A young Apollo, golden-haired,
Stands dreaming on the verge of strife,
Magnificently unprepared
For the long littleness of life.
'Youth' (1910) **Cornford, Frances Crofts** (1886–1960) English poet and translator. Of Rupert Brooke

54 But he (his musical finesse was such,
So nice his ear, so delicate his touch)
Made poetry a mere mechanic art;
And ev'ry warbler has his tune by heart.
Table Talk (1782) Of Pope

55 There is a pleasure in poetic pains
Which only poets know.
The Task (1785) **Cowper, William** (1731–1800) English poet, hymn writer and letter writer

56 After the erection of the Chinese Wall of Milton, blank verse has suffered not only arrest but retrogression.
'Christopher Marlowe' (1919)

57 Poetry is not a turning loose of emotion, but an escape from emotion; it is not the expression of personality, but an escape from personality.
'Tradition and the Individual Talent' (1919)

58 The business of the poet is not to find new emotions, but to use the ordinary ones and, in working them up into poetry, to express feelings which are not in actual emotions at all.
'Tradition and the Individual Talent' (1919)

59 Tennyson and Browning are poets, and they think; but they do not feel their thought as immediately as the odour of a rose. A thought to Donne was an experience; it modified his sensibility.
'The Metaphysical Poets' (1921)

60 In the seventeenth century a dissociation of sensibility set in, from which we have never recovered.
'The Metaphysical Poets' (1921) **Eliot, T.S.** (1888–1965) US-born British poet, verse dramatist and critic

61 We had this rather lugubrious man in a suit, and he read a poem – I think it was called *The Desert* – and first the girls got the giggles, and then I did, and then even the King. Such a gloomy man. Looked as though he worked in a bank, and we didn't understand a word.
Quoted in *The Guardian*, (2000) **Elizabeth, the Queen Mother** (1900–2002) Queen of the United Kingdom and mother of Elizabeth II. On a private reading by TS Eliot of *The Waste Land*

62 It is not metres, but a metre-making argument, that makes a poem.
Essays, Second Series (1844) **Emerson, Ralph Waldo** (1803–1882) US poet, essayist, transcendentalist and teacher

63 Good light verse is better than bad heavy verse any day of the week.
Penultimate Poems (1989) **Ewart, Gavin** (1916–1995) English poet

64 Poetry's a mere drug, Sir.
Love and a Bottle (1698) **Farquhar, George** (1678–1707) Irish dramatist

65 Everything one invents is true, you can be sure of that. Poetry is as exact a science as geometry.
Letter to Louise Colet, (1853) **Flaubert, Gustave** (1821–1880) French writer

66 A poem may be worked over once it is in being, but may not be worried into being.
Collected Poems (1939)

67 Poetry is a way of taking life by the throat.
In Sergeant, *Robert Frost: the Trial by Existence* (1960)

68 Poetry is what is lost in translation.
In Untermeyer, *Robert Frost: a Backward Look* (1964) **Frost, Robert** (1874–1963) US poet

69 Lord Byron is only great as a poet; as soon as he reflects, he is a child.
Gespräche mit Eckermann, (1825) **Goethe** (1749–1832) German poet, writer, dramatist and scientist

70 Rightly thought of there is poetry in peaches … even when they are canned.
The Madras House **Granville-Barker, Harley** (1877–1946) English actor and playwright

71 To be a poet is a condition rather than a profession.
Questionnaire in Horizon **Graves, Robert** (1895–1985) English poet, writer, critic, translator and mythologist

72 Far from the sun and summer-gale,
In thy green lap was Nature's Darling laid,
What time, where lucid Avon stray'd,
To him the mighty Mother did unveil
Her aweful face: The dauntless child
Stretch'd forth his little arms, and smiled.
'The Progress of Poesy' (1757) **Gray, Thomas** (1716–1771) English poet and scholar. On Shakespeare

73 Shelley and Keats were the last British poets who were at all up-to-date in their chemical knowledge.
Daedalus or Science and the Future (1924) **Haldane, J.B.S.** (1892–1964) British biochemist, geneticist and popularizer of science

74 Of course poets have morals and manners of their own, and custom is no argument with them.
The Hand of Ethelberta (1876)

75 If Galileo had said in verse that the world moved, the Inquisition might have let him alone.

In F.E. Hardy, *The Later Years of Thomas Hardy* (1930) **Hardy, Thomas** (1840–1928) English writer and poet

76 He talked on for ever; and you wished him to talk on for ever.
Lectures on the English Poets (1818) **Hazlitt, William** (1778–1830) English writer and critic. Of Coleridge

77 To forge a poem is one thing, to forge the uncreated conscience of the race, as Stephen Dedalus put it, is quite another and places daunting pressures and responsibilities on anyone who would risk the name of poet.
Preoccupations, Selected Prose 1968–(1978) **Heaney, Seamus** (1939–) Irish poet

78 The poetical language of an age should be the current language heightened.
Letter to Robert Bridges, (1879) **Hopkins, Gerard Manley** (1844–1889) English Jesuit priest, poet and classicist

79 Even when poetry has a meaning, as it usually has, it may be inadvisable to draw it out ... perfect understanding will sometimes almost extinguish pleasure.
'The Name and Nature of Poetry' (1933)

80 Experience has taught me, when I am shaving of a morning, to keep watch over my thoughts, because, if a line of poetry strays into my memory, my skin bristles so that the razor ceases to act.
'The Name and Nature of Poetry' (1933) **Housman, A.E.** (1859–1936) English poet and scholar

81 It's like the question of the authorship of the Iliad ... The author of that poem is either Homer or, if not Homer, somebody else of the same name.
Those Barren Leaves (1925) **Huxley, Aldous** (1894–1963) English writer, poet and critic

82 Dr Donne's verses are like the peace of God; they pass all understanding.
Attr. **James VI of Scotland and I of England** (1566–1625) King of Scotland from 1567 and of England from 1603

83 Some poetry seems to have been written on typewriters by other typewriters.

Attr. **Jarrell, Randall** (1914–1965) US poet, critic and translator

84 He [the poet] must write as the interpreter of nature, and the legislator of mankind, and consider himself as presiding over the thoughts and manners of future generations; as a being superior to time and place.
Rasselas (1759)

85 The business of a poet, said Imlac, is to examine, not the individual but the species ... he does not number the streaks of the tulip, or describe the different shades in the verdure of the forest.
Rasselas (1759) **Johnson, Samuel** (1709–1784) English lexicographer, poet, critic, conversationalist and essayist

86 Lawn Tennyson, gentleman poet.
Ulysses (1922) **Joyce, James** (1882–1941) Irish writer

87 A long Poem is a test of Invention which I take to be the Polar Star of Poetry, as Fancy is the Sails, and Imagination the Rudder.
Letter to Benjamin Bailey, (1817)

88 I think I shall be among the British Poets after my death.
Letter to George and Georgiana Keats, (1818)

89 We hate poetry that has a palpable design upon us – and if we do not agree, seems to put its hand in its breeches pocket. Poetry should be great and unobtrusive, a thing which enters into one's soul, and does not startle it or amaze it with itself, but with its subject.
Letter to J.H. Reynolds, (1818)

90 Poetry should surprise by a fine excess and not by Singularity – it should strike the Reader as a wording of his own highest thoughts, and appear almost a Remembrance ... Its touches of Beauty should never be half way, thereby making the reader breathless instead of content: the rise, the progress, the setting of imagery should, like the Sun, come naturally to him.
Letter to John Taylor, (27 February 1818)

91 If Poetry comes not as naturally as Leaves to a tree it had better not come at all.

Letter to John Taylor, (1818)

92 A Poet is the most unpoetical of anything in existence; because he has no Identity – he is continually informing and filling some other Body.
Letter to Richard Woodhouse, (1818)

93 I am ambitious of doing the world some good: if I should be spared, that may be the work of maturer years – in the interval I will assay to reach to as high a summit in Poetry as the nerve bestowed upon me will suffer.
Letter to Richard Woodhouse, (1818) **Keats, John** (1795–1821) English poet

94 When power narrows the areas of man's concern, poetry reminds him of the richness and diversity of his existence.
Speech, (1963) **Kennedy, John F.** (1917–1963) US Democrat President

95 God and I both knew what it meant once; now God alone knows.
Attr. **Klopstock, Friedrich** (1724–1803) German poet. Of one of his poems

96 Milton almost requires a solemn service of music to be played before you enter upon him.
Last Essays of Elia (1833) **Lamb, Charles** (1775–1834) English essayist, critic and letter writer

97 Past ruin'd Ilion Helen lives,
Alcestis rises from the shades;
Verse calls them forth; 'tis verse that gives Immortal youth to mortal maids.
'To Ianthe' (1831)

98 Prose on certain occasions can bear a great deal of poetry: on the other hand, poetry sinks and swoons under a moderate weight of prose.
Imaginary Conversations (1853) **Landor, Walter Savage** (1775–1864) English poet and writer

99 Deprivation is for me what daffodils were for Wordsworth.
The Observer, (1979)

100 I rather think poetry has given me up, which is a great sorrow to me, but not an enormous, crushing sorrow. It's rather like going bald.
The Observer, (1984)

101 I can't understand these chaps who go round American universities explaining how they write poems: it's like going round explaining how you sleep with your wife.
New York Times, (1986) **Larkin, Philip** (1922–1985) English poet, writer and librarian

102 The poet ranks far below the painter in the representation of visible things, and far below the musician in that of invisible things.
Selections from the Notebooks of Leonardo da Vinci (1952) **Leonardo da Vinci** (1452–1519) Italian artist

103 It is a better and a wiser thing to be a starved apothecary than a starved poet; so back to the shop Mr John, back to 'plasters, pills, and ointment boxes'.
Blackwood's Magazine, (1818), Review of Keats's Endymion **Lockhart, John Gibson** (1794–1854) Scottish writer, critic, and translator

104 Walt Whitman who laid end to end words never seen in each other's company before outside of a dictionary.
Changing Places (1975) **Lodge, David** (1935–) English writer, satirist and literary critic

105 Not even for a moment, beautiful old Walt Whitman, have I stopped seeing your beard full of butterflies.
Poeta en Nueva York (1929–30) **Lorca, Federico García** (1899–1936) Spanish poet and dramatist

106 Poem me no poems.
Poetry Review, (1963) **Macaulay, Dame Rose** (1881–1958) English writer

107 Perhaps no person can be a poet, or can even enjoy poetry, without a certain unsoundness of mind.
Collected Essays (1843)

108 As civilization advances, poetry almost necessarily declines.
Collected Essays (1843) **Macaulay, Lord** (1800–1859) English Liberal statesman, essayist and poet

109 Poetry like politics maun cut
The cackle and pursue real ends,
Unerringly as Lenin, and to that
Its nature better tends.

'Second Hymn to Lenin' (1935) **MacDiarmid, Hugh** (1892–1978) Scottish poet

110 A Poem should be palpable and mute
As a globed fruit,
Dumb
As old medallions to the thumb,
Silent as the sleeve-worn stone
Of casement ledges where the moss has grown –
A poem should be wordless
As the flight of birds …
A poem should not mean
But be.
'Ars poetica' (1926) **MacLeish, Archibald** (1892–1982) US poet and librarian

111 Poetry is a comforting piece of fiction set to more or less lascivious music.
Prejudices (1919–1927) **Mencken, H.L.** (1880–1956) US writer, critic, philologist and satirist

112 … poetry, 'The Cinderella of the Arts.'
In Hope Stoddard, *Famous American Women*, 'Harriet Monroe' **Monroe, Harriet** (1860–1936) US poet and editor

113 I've never read a political poem that's accomplished anything. Poetry makes things happen, but rarely what the poet wants.
International Herald Tribune, (1988) **Nemerov, Howard** (1920–1991) US poet, novelist and critic

114 All the poet can do today is to warn.
That is why the true Poets must be truthful.
Quoted in *Poems* (1963) **Owen, Wilfred** (1893–1918) English poet

115 When in public poetry should take off its clothes and wave to the nearest person in sight; it should be seen in the company of thieves and lovers rather than that of journalists and publishers.
'Prose poem towards a definition of itself'

116 It should guide all those who are safe into the middle of busy roads and leave them there.
'Prose poem towards a definition of itself'
Patten, Brian (1946–) British poet

117 Poetry is nothing but time, ceaselessly creative rhythm.

The Bow and the Lyre (1956) **Paz, Octavio** (1914–1998) Mexican poet and critic

118 Being a poet is not an ambition of mine.
It is my way of being alone.
The Guardian of Flocks (1914) **Pessoa, Fernando** (1888–1935) Portuguese poet

119 Poets utter great and wise things which they do not themselves understand.
Republic **Plato** (c.429–347 BC) Greek philosopher

120 Poets, like painters, thus, unskill'd to trace
The naked nature and the living grace,
With gold and jewels cover ev'ry part,
And hide with ornaments their want of art.
An Essay on Criticism (1711)

121 Sir, I admit your gen'ral Rule
That every Poet is a Fool;
But you yourself may serve to show it,
That every Fool is not a Poet.
'Epigram from the French' (1732) **Pope, Alexander** (1688–1744) English poet, translator and editor

122 Come, my songs, let us speak of perfection –
We shall get ourselves rather disliked.
'Salvationists' (1916)

123 And give up verse, my boy,
There's nothing in it.
Hugh Selwyn Mauberley (1920) **Pound, Ezra** (1885–1972) US poet

124 Of all the literary scenes
Saddest this sight to me:
The graves of little magazines
Who died to make verse free.
'The Liberators' **Preston, Keith** (1884–1927) US poet, writer and teacher

125 The few bad poems which occasionally are created during abstinence are of no great interest.
The Sexual Revolution **Reich, Wilhelm** (1897–1957) Austrian-born US psychiatrist

126 It is a perfectly possible means of overcoming chaos.
Science and Poetry (1926) **Richards, I.A.** (1893–1979) English critic, linguist, poet and teacher. Of poetry

127 A sonnet is a moment's monument, –
Memorial from the Soul's eternity
To one dead deathless hour.
The House of Life (1881) **Rossetti, Dante Gabriel**
(1828–1882) English poet, painter, translator
and letter writer

128 For ne'er
Was flattery lost on poet's ear:
A simple race! they waste their toil
For the vain tribute of a smile.
The Lay of the Last Minstrel (1805), IV **Scott, Sir
Walter** (1771–1832) Scottish writer and
historian

129 Your monument shall be my gentle verse,
Which eyes not yet created shall o'er-read;
And tongues to be your being shall
rehearse,
When all the breathers of this world are
dead.
You still shall live, such virtue hath my pen,
Where breath most breathes, even in the
mouths of men.
Sonnet 81 **Shakespeare, William** (1564–1616)
English dramatist, poet and actor

130 Poetry lifts the veil from the hidden beauty
of the world, and makes familiar objects be
as if they were not familiar.
A Defence of Poetry (1821)

131 Poets are ... the trumpets which sing to
battle and feel not what they inspire ...
Poets are the unacknowledged legislators
of the world.
A Defence of Poetry (1821) **Shelley, Percy Bysshe**
(1792–1822) English poet, dramatist and
essayist

132 There have been many most excellent
poets that have never versified, and now
swarm many versifiers that need never
answer to the name of poets.
The Defence of Poesie (1595)

133 Nature never set foorth the earth inso rich
Tapistry as diverse Poets have done ... her
world is brasen, the Poets only deliver a
golden.
The Defence of Poesie (1595)

134 Though I will not wish unto you the Ass's
eares of Midas, nor to be driven by a Poet's
verses as Bubonax was, to hang himselfe,
nor to be rimed to death as is said to be
done in Ireland; yet thus much Curse I
must send you in the behalfe of all Poets,
that while you live, you live in love, and
never get favour, for lacking skill of a
Sonet, and when you die, your memorie
die from the earth for want of an Epitaphe.
The Defence of Poesie (1595) **Sidney, Sir Philip**
(1554–1586) English poet, critic, soldier,
courtier and diplomat

135 My poems are hymns of praise to the glory
of Life.
Selected Poems (1952) **Sitwell, Dame Edith**
(1887–1964) English poet, anthologist, critic
and biographer

136 Poetry is like fish: if it's fresh, it's good; if
it's stale, it's bad; and if you're not certain,
try it on the cat.
Attr. **Sitwell, Sir Osbert** (1892–1969) English
writer

137 People sometimes divide others into those
you laugh at and those you laugh with. The
young Auden was someone you could
laugh-at-with.
Address at W.H. Auden's memorial service,
Oxford, (1973) **Spender, Sir Stephen** (1909–
1995) English poet, editor, translator and
diarist

138 Poetry is the mother of superstition.
The History of the Royal Society (1667) **Sprat,
Thomas** (1635–1713) English bishop and writer

139 But Shelley had a hyper-thyroid face.
'Ballade of the Glandular Hypothesis' **Squire,
Sir J.C.** (1884–1958) English poet, critic, writer
and editor

140 Poetry is the supreme fiction, madame.
'A High-Toned Old Christian Woman' (1923)
Stevens, Wallace (1879–1955) US poet, essayist,
dramatist and lawyer

141 Whitman, like a large shaggy dog, just
unchained, scouring the beaches of the
world and baying at the moon.
Familiar Studies of Men and Books (1882)
Stevenson, Robert Louis (1850–1894) Scottish
writer, poet and essayist

142 Then, rising with Aurora's light,
The Muse invoked, sit down to write;
Blot out, correct, insert, refine,
Enlarge, diminish, interline ...
As learned commentators view
In Homer more than Homer knew.
'On Poetry' (1733)

143 Say, Britain, could you ever boast, –
Three poets in an age at most?
Our chilling climate hardly bears
A sprig of bays in fifty years.
'On Poetry' (1733) **Swift, Jonathan** (1667–1745)
Irish satirist, poet, essayist and cleric

144 These poems, with all their crudities,
doubts, and confusions, are written for the
love of Man and in praise of God, and I'd
be a damn' fool if they weren't.
Collected Poems (1952) **Thomas, Dylan** (1914–
1953) Welsh poet, writer and radio dramatist

145 Poetry is nothing but healthy speech.
Journal, (1841)

146 I do not perceive the poetic and dramatic
capabilities of an anecdote or story which is
told me, its significance, till some time
afterwards ... We do not enjoy poetry
unless we know it to be poetry.
Journal, (1856) **Thoreau, Henry David** (1817–
1862) US essayist, social critic and writer

147 My poems mean what people take them to
mean.
Variety (1924)

148 A poem is never finished, only abandoned.
In Auden, *A Certain World* **Valéry, Paul** (1871–
1945) French poet, mathematician and
philosopher

149 Poetry is to prose as dancing is to walking.
BBC broadcast, (1976) **Wain, John** (1925–1994)
English poet, writer and critic

150 Poets lose half the praise they should have
got,
Could it be known what they discreetly
blot.
'On Roscommon's Translation of Horace'
Waller, Edmund (1606–1687) English poet and
politician

151 Why do we need a Poet Laureate at all? We
might as well still retain a Court Jester or a
Royal Food Taster.

Comment following the death of Poet
Laureate Ted Hughes, (November 1998)
Waterhouse, Keith (1929–) English journalist
and author

152 I hate the whole race ... There is no
believing a word they say – your
professional poets, I mean – there never
existed a more worthless set than Byron
and his friends for example.
Attr. **Wellington, Duke of** (1769–1852) Irish-
born British military commander and
statesman

153 He found in stones the sermons he had
already hidden there.
The Nineteenth Century, (1889) Of Wordsworth

154 There seems to be some curious
connection between piety and poor
rhymes.
In Lucas, *A Critic in Pall Mall* (1919) **Wilde,
Oscar** (1854–1900) Irish poet, dramatist,
writer, critic and wit

155 I would venture to guess that Anon, who
wrote so many poems without signing
them, was often a woman.
A Room of One's Own (1929) **Woolf, Virginia**
(1882–1941) English writer and critic

156 I have said that poetry is the spontaneous
overflow of powerful feelings: it takes its
origin from emotion recollected in
tranquillity: the emotion is contemplated
till, by a species of reaction, the tranquillity
gradually disappears, and an emotion,
kindred to that which was before the
subject of contemplation, is gradually
produced, and does itself actually exist in
the mind.
Lyrical Ballads (1802)

157 The Poet writes under one restriction only,
namely, that of the necessity of giving
pleasure to a human Being possessed of
that information which may be expected
from him, not as a lawyer, a physician, a
mariner, an astronomer or a natural
philosopher, but as a Man.
Lyrical Ballads (1802)

158 Milton! thou shouldst be living at this
hour:
England hath need of thee; she is a fen
Of stagnant waters: altar, sword, and pen,
Fireside, the heroic wealth of hall and
bower,
Have forfeited their ancient English dower
Of inward happiness ...
Thy soul was like a star, and dwelt apart.
'Milton! thou shouldst be living at this hour'
(1807) **Wordsworth, William** (1770–1850)
English poet

159 I see a schoolboy when I think of him,
With face and nose pressed to a sweet-
shop window,
For certainly he sank into his grave
His senses and his heart unsatisfied,
And made – being poor, ailing and
ignorant,
Shut out from all the luxury of the world,
The coarse-bred son of a livery-stable
keeper –
Luxuriant song.
The Wild Swans at Coole, Other Verses and a Play
(1917) Of Keats

160 We make out of the quarrel with others,
rhetoric; but of the quarrel with ourselves,
poetry.
'Anima Hominis' (1917)

161 He is all blood, dirt and sucked sugar stick.
In D. Wellesley (ed.), *Letters on Poetry from W.B.
Yeats to Dorothy Wellesley* (1940) Referring to
Wilfred Owen

162 The poet finds and makes his mask in
disappointment, the hero in defeat.
'Anima Hominis' **Yeats, W.B.** (1865–1939) Irish
poet, dramatist, editor, writer and senator

163 I think poetry should be alive. You should
be able to dance it.
The Sunday Times, (1987) **Zephaniah, Benjamin**
(1958–) English poet
See also books; criticism; literature; writing

POLITICAL SLOGANS

1 A bayonet is a weapon with a worker at
each end.
Pacifist movement, (1940)

2 All power to the Soviets.
Petrograd workers, (1917)

3 All the way with LBJ.
US Democratic Presidential campaign, (1960)

4 Are we downhearted? No!
First World War, based on remark of Joseph
Chamberlain

5 Ban the bomb.
Current from 1953 onwards

6 Better red than dead.
British nuclear disarmament movement

7 Black is beautiful.
US civil rights movement, (1966)

8 Careless talk costs lives.
British Ministry of Information, Second
World War

9 Compassionate Conservatism.
George W. Bush Presidential campaign,
(2000)

10 Dig for victory.
Ministry of Agriculture, (1939)

11 England Expects – Scotland's Oil.
Scottish National Party, (1973)

12 The family that prays together stays
together.
Devised by Al Scalpone for the Roman
Catholic Family Rosary Crusade, (1947)

13 Flower Power.
Hippy slogan, 1960s

14 Hey, hey LBJ, how many kids did you kill
today?
Anti-Vietnam War slogan, 1960s

15 I like Ike.
US button badge, first used in 1947, to
support Eisenhower

16 In your heart you know he's right.
Goldwater Presidential campaign, (1964)

17 Is your journey really necessary?
Second World War

18 It's morning again in America.
Ronald Reagan's 1984 Presidential election
campaign

19 Keep Britain tidy.
British government, 1950s

20 Labour isn't working.
Conservative Party slogan, 1978–79 With a
poster showing a long queue outside an
unemployment office

21 Liberty! Equality! Brotherhood!
French Revolution, (1793)

22 Make love, not war.
Common in the mid-1960s

23 New Labour, new danger.
Conservative Party slogan, 1996

24 No taxation without representation.
In use before the American War of
Independence, (1775–1783)

25 One realm, one people, one leader.
Nazi Party, (1934)

26 Out of the closets and into the streets.
Gay Liberation movement, US (c.1969)

27 Power to the People.
Black Panther movement, (1969)

28 Strength through joy.
German Labour Front, (1933)

29 Ulster will fight, and Ulster will be right.
Ulster Volunteers opposed to Irish Home
Rule, (1913–1914), from a letter by Lord
Randolph Churchill, (1886)

30 Votes for Women.
Suffragette Movement, 1905, in Emmeline
Pankhurst, *My Own Story* (1914)

31 Would you buy a used car from this man?
Campaign slogan directed against Richard
Nixon, (1968)

32 Your King and Country need you.
First World War
See also government; politics; war

POLITICS

1 Being an MP is the sort of job all working-
class parents want for their children –
clean, indoors and no heavy lifting.
The Observer, (1994) **Abbott, Diane** (1953–)
British Labour politician

2 He told us he was going to take crime out
of the streets. He did. He took it into the
damn White House.
Abernathy, Ralph (1926–1990) US religious
and civil rights leader. On Richard Nixon

3 I will undoubtedly have to seek what is
happily known as gainful employment,
which I am glad to say does not describe
holding public office.
Time, (1952) On retiring to private life

4 Controversial proposals, once accepted,
soon become hallowed.
Speech, Independence, Missouri, (1962)
Acheson, Dean (1893–1971) US Democrat
politician

5 Anyone who is capable of getting
themselves made President should on no
account be allowed to do the job.
The Hitch Hiker's Guide to the Galaxy (1979)
Adams, Douglas (1952–2001) English writer

6 The trouble with this country is that there
are too many politicians who believe, with
a conviction based on experience, that you
can fool all of the people all of the time.
Nods and Becks (1944) **Adams, Franklin P.**
(1881–1960) US writer, poet, translator and
editor

7 We have to work to make the Omagh
bombing the last violent incident in our
country. The violence we have seen must
be a thing of the past, over, done with and
gone.
The Times, (1998)

8 If no one votes for us, then we'll disappear.
The Observer, (1998) Comment after the
referendum on the Good Friday peace
proposals **Adams, Gerry** (1948–) President of
Sinn Féin

9 Elections are won by men and women
chiefly because most people vote against
somebody rather than for somebody.

In Colin Jarman, *The Guinness Book of Poisonous Quotes* **Adams, Franklin P.** (1881–1960) US writer, poet, translator and editor

10 Practical politics consists in ignoring facts.
The Education of Henry Adams (1918)

11 Politics, as a practice, whatever its professions, has always been the systematic organization of hatreds.
The Education of Henry Adams (1918) **Adams, Henry** (1838–1918) US historian and memoirist

12 The art of politics consists in knowing precisely when it is necessary to hit an opponent slightly below the belt.
Attr. **Adenauer, Konrad** (1876–1967) German Chancellor

13 To some extent, if you've seen one city slum you've seen them all.
Election speech, Detroit, (October 1968) **Agnew, Spiro T.** (1918–1996) US Vice President

14 If John Major was drowning, his whole life would pass in front of him and he wouldn't be in it.
On stage, (1991) **Allen, Dave** (1936–2005) Irish comedian and television personality

15 You have sat too long here for any good you have been doing. Depart, I say, and let us have done with you. In the name of God, go!
Speech, House of Commons, (May 1940) **Amery, Leo** (1873–1955) English statesman. To Neville Chamberlain, quoting Cromwell's words when he dismissed the Rump of the Long Parliament in 1653

16 The Liberal Democrats are now so firmly in bed with the Labour Party that they have become little more than a shapeless lump under the Government's duvet.
The Observer, (May 1999) **Ancram, Michael** (1945–) English Conservative politician

17 The Labour Party has decided to renounce its principles, its policies and its past.
The Spectator, (May 1996) **Anderson, Bruce** (1838–1918) British journalist. Of Tony Blair's New Labour

18 Oh, my dear, I know just how you feel. I'm a Jehovah's Witness.
The Observer, (1998) Pensioner's response to Juliet Peck when she introduced herself as the local Conservative candidate

19 It would have been nice if the Foreign Secretary had had an ethical domestic policy as well.
The Times, (1999) Comment on Robin Cook in a letter to *The Times*

20 An MP, convicted of making a false election expenses return, has been ordered to do community service. Isn't that what MPs are supposed to do?
The Times, (1999)

21 MPs, ministers or otherwise, do not resign because of their integrity. They do so because they have been found out.
Letter to *The Times*, (1999)

22 Capitalism is the exploitation of man by man. Communism is the complete opposite.
Described by Laurence J. Peter as a 'Polish proverb'

23 Anarchy may not be the best form of government, but it's better than no government at all.
Anonymous

24 He warns the heads of parties against believing their own lies.
The Art of Political Lying (1712) **Arbuthnot, John** (1667–1735) Scottish physician, pamphleteer and wit

25 Truthfulness has never been counted among the political virtues, and lies have always been regarded as justifiable tools in political dealings.
Crises of the Republic (1972) **Arendt, Hannah** (1906–1975) German-born US theorist

26 Blessed is the state in which those in power have moderate and sufficient means since where some are immoderately wealthy and others have nothing, the result will be extreme democracy or absolute oligarchy, or a tyranny may result from either of these extremes.
Politics

27 Man is by nature a political animal.
Politics

28 Inferiors agitate in order that they may be equal and equals that they may be superior. Such is the state of mind which creates party strife.
Politics

29 The final association composed of several villages is the city state; it has now reached the limit of virtual self-sufficiency, and so while it comes into existence for the sake of life, it exists for the good life.
Politics **Aristotle** (384–322 BC) Greek philosopher

30 It is extremely frustrating to hear someone else singing snatches of our song but doing it so completely out of tune.
The Times, (1999) **Ashdown, Paddy** (1941–) Former leader of the UK Liberal Democrats. On Labour's 1999 Budget

31 He [a politician] always has his arm round your waist and his eye on the clock.
As I Remember, (1967)

32 He couldn't see a belt without hitting below it.
As I Remember, (1967) Of Lloyd George **Asquith, Margot** (1864–1945) Scottish political hostess and writer

33 Our researchers into Public Opinion are content
That he held the proper opinions for the time of year;
When there was peace, he was for peace; when there was war, he went.
Collected Poems, (1939–1947) **Auden, W.H.** (1907–1973) English poet, essayist, critic, teacher and dramatist

34 From politics, it was an easy step to silence.
Northanger Abbey (1818) **Austen, Jane** (1775–1817) English writer

35 A constitutional statesman is in general a man of common opinions and uncommon abilities.
Historical Essays, 'The Character of Sir Robert Peel' (1856)

36 No man has come so near our definition of a constitutional statesman – the powers of a first-rate man and the creed of a second-rate man.
Historical Essays, 'The Character of Sir Robert Peel' (1856) Of Sir Robert Peel

37 No real English gentleman, in his secret soul, was ever sorry for the death of a political economist.
'The First Edinburgh Reviewers' (1858) **Bagehot, Walter** (1826–1877) English economist and political philosopher

38 A group of politicians deciding to dump a President because his morals are bad is like the Mafia getting together to bump off the Godfather for not going to church on Sunday.
New York Times, (1974) **Baker, Russell** (1925–) US writer. On the impeachment of President Nixon

39 We wish, in a word, equality – equality in fact as corollary, or rather, as primordial condition of liberty. From each according to his faculties, to each according to his needs; that is what we wish sincerely and energetically.
In J. Morrison Davidson, *The Old Order and the New* (1890) **Bakunin, Mikhail** (1814–1876) Russian anarchist and writer. Anarchist declaration, Lyon, 1870

40 A lot of hard-faced men who look as if they had done very well out of the war.
Of the House of Commons, 1918

41 I met Curzon in Downing Street, from whom I got the sort of greeting a corpse would give to an undertaker.
Remark, (1933) On becoming Prime Minister

42 You will find in politics that you are much exposed to the attribution of false motives. Never complain and never explain.
To Harold Nicolson, (21 July 1943), quoting Disraeli

43 Then comes Winston with his hundred-horse-power mind and what can I do?
In G.M. Young, *Stanley Baldwin* (1952) On Churchill

44 There are three groups that no British Prime Minister should provoke: the Vatican, the Treasury and the miners.
Attr. **Baldwin, Stanley** (1867–1947) English Conservative statesman and Prime Minister

45 I thought he was a young man of promise; but it appears he is a young man of promises.
In Winston Churchill, *My Early Life* (1930) **Balfour, A.J.** (1848–1930) British Conservative Prime Minister. Comment on Winston Churchill in 1899

46 She is a petty-minded xenophobe who struts around the world interfering and lecturing in an arrogant and high-handed manner.
Banks, Tony (1943–2006) Labour MP and Sports Minister. On Margaret Thatcher

47 One of these days a British Prime Minister will have the guts to call an election with the cry 'This is a comparatively unimportant time in our nation's history.'
The New Yorker, (1992) **Barnes, Julian** (1946–) English author

48 A political leader must keep looking over his shoulder all the time to see if the boys are still there. If they aren't still there, he's no longer a political leader.
New York Times, (1965) **Baruch, Bernard** (1870–1965) US financier, government advisor and writer

49 You don't have to fool all the people all of the time; you just have to fool enough to get elected.
In Lieberman, *3,500 Good Quotes for Speakers* (1983) **Barzan, Gerald** US humorist

50 Here richly, with ridiculous display, The Politician's corpse was laid away.
While all of his acquaintances sneered and slanged.
I wept: for I had longed to see him hanged.
'Epitaph on the Politician Himself' **Belloc, Hilaire** (1870–1953) French-born English writer; Liberal MP

51 Judges are guided by the law; politicians by expediency.
El país, (1994) **Belloch, Juan Alberto** (1950–) Spanish politician

52 When I think of Cool Britannia, I think of old people dying of hypothermia.
The Observer, (1998) **Benn, Tony** (1925–) English Labour politician

53 We started off trying to set up a small anarchist community, but people wouldn't obey the rules.
Getting On (1972) **Bennett, Alan** (1934–) English dramatist, actor and diarist

54 Mr Lloyd George spoke for a hundred and seventeen minutes, in which period he was detected only once in the use of an argument.
Things That Have Interested Me (1921–1925) **Bennett, Arnold** (1867–1931) English writer, dramatist and journalist

55 When their lordships asked Bacon How many bribes he had taken He had at least the grace To get very red in the face.
Baseless Biography (1939) **Bentley, Edmund Clerihew** (1875–1956) English writer

56 Listening to a speech by Chamberlain is like paying a visit to Woolworths; everything in its place and nothing over sixpence.
In *Tribune,* (1937)

57 This island is almost made of coal and surrounded by fish. Only an organizing genius could produce a shortage of coal and fish at the same time.
Speech, Blackpool, (1945)

58 No amount of cajolery, and no attempts at ethical or social seduction, can eradicate from my heart a deep burning hatred for the Tory Party ... So far as I am concerned they are lower than vermin.
Speech, (1948)

59 We know what happens to people who stay in the middle of the road. They get run over.
The Observer, (1953)

60 If you carry this resolution and follow out all its implications and do not run away from it you will send a Foreign Secretary, whoever he may be, naked into the conference chamber.

Speech, (1957) Opposing unilateral nuclear disarmament

61 He is a man suffering from petrified adolescence.
In Brome, *Aneurin Bevan*. On Churchill

62 Fascism is not in itself a new order of society. It is the future refusing to be born.
Attr. **Bevan, Aneurin** (1897–1960) Welsh Labour politician, miner and orator

63 My policy is to be able to take a ticket at Victoria Station and go anywhere I damn well please.
Spectator, (1951) On foreign policy

64 Not while I'm alive, he ain't.
In M. Foot, *Aneurin Bevan 1945–60* (1975) When told that another Labourite was 'his own worst enemy' **Bevin, Ernest** (1881–1951) English trade union leader and politician

65 *Nepotism*: Appointing your grandfather to office for the good of the party.
The Enlarged Devil's Dictionary (1961) **Bierce, Ambrose** (1842–c.1914) US writer, verse writer and soldier

66 For the second time the Prime Minister has got rid of a Chancellor of the Exchequer who tried to get expenditure under control. Once is more than enough.
Letter to *The Times*, (1962) **Birch, Nigel** (1906–1981) British financier and Conservative politician

67 Politics is the art of the possible.
Remark, (1863)

68 Politics is not a precise science.
Speech, Prussian House of Deputies, (1863)

69 Politics is not a science ... but an art.
Speech, Reichstag, (1884) **Bismarck, Prince Otto von** (1815–1898) First Chancellor of the German Reich

70 Our motives were more social than political as it was a good way to meet boys.
The Times, (1999) **Blair, Cherie** (1954–) English barrister. Comment on her reasons for joining the Labour Party

71 When I became leader of the Labour Party, I was determined to put Labour's relations with business on a new footing.

Inside Labour

72 I want Britain to be a stake-holder economy where everyone has a chance to get on and succeed, where there is a clear sense of national purpose and where we leave behind some of the battles between Left and Right which really are not relevant in the new global economy of today.
Speech in Singapore, 1996

73 It marks the end of a something-for-nothing welfare state.
The Times, (1999) On his plan to reform the welfare state **Blair, Tony** (1953–) British Labour Prime Minister

74 *Andrea*: Unhappy the country that has no heroes! ...
Galileo: No. Unhappy the country that needs heroes.
Life of Galileo (1938–1939) **Brecht, Bertolt** (1898–1956) German dramatist

75 This party of two is like the Scotch terrier that was so covered with hair that you could not tell which was the head and which was the tail.
Speech, House of Commons, (1866)

76 He is a self-made man, and worships his creator.
Remark, (c.1868) Of Disraeli **Bright, John** (1811–1889) English Liberal politician and social reformer

77 Politics are usually the executive expression of human immaturity.
The Rebel Passion (1964) **Brittain, Vera** (1893–1970) English writer and pacifist

78 Dictators needed a talking cinema to twist nations round their fingers: remove the sound from Mussolini and you are left with a puffing bullfrog.
The Times, (1992) **Brown, Geoff** (1949–) Film critic and writer

79 He has the jovial garrulity and air of witty indiscretion that shows he intends to give nothing away.
Loose Talk (1979) **Brown, Tina** (1953–) English journalist and editor. Of Richard Crossman

80 I worship the quicksand he walks in.
Attr. **Buchwald, Art** (1925–) US humorist. Of Richard Nixon

81 Mr Blair cannot take a joke – or deliver one. He is, after all, leading a Government that is to humour what Lucretia Borgia was to cordon-bleu cooking.
The Times, (2000) **Buckland, Chris**

82 Green politics, in the final analysis, is so popular with the rich because it contains no race or class analysis at all; politics with everything but the glow of involvement taken out.
Sex and Sensibility (1992) **Burchill, Julie** (1960–) English writer

83 The US presidency is a Tudor monarchy plus telephones.
In Plimpton (ed.), *Writers at Work* (1977) **Burgess, Anthony** (1917–1993) English writer, linguist and composer

84 Your representative owes you, not his industry only, but his judgement; and he betrays, instead of serving you, if he sacrifices it to your opinion.
Speech to the Electors of Bristol, (1774)

85 The use of force alone is but temporary. It may subdue for a moment; but it does not remove the necessity of subduing again: and a nation is not governed, which is perpetually to be conquered.
Speech on Conciliation with America (1775)

86 The people never give up their liberties but under some delusion.
Speech, (1784)

87 The conduct of a losing party never appears right: at least it never can possess the only infallible criterion of wisdom to vulgar judgments – success.
Letter to a Member of the National Assembly (1791) **Burke, Edmund** (1729–1797) Irish-born British statesman and philosopher

88 That's Anthony for you – half mad baronet, half beautiful woman.
Attr. **Butler, R.A.** (1902–1982) Indian-born British Conservative politician. On Sir Anthony Eden, who had been described as the offspring of a mad baronet and a beautiful woman

89 The healthy stomach is nothing if not conservative. Few radicals have good digestions.

The Note-Books of Samuel Butler (1912) **Butler, Samuel** (1835–1902) English writer, painter, philosopher and scholar

90 Either back us or sack us.
Speech, Labour Party Conference, (1977) **Callaghan, James** (1912–2005) English Labour statesman and Prime Minister

91 I well recall the time when, for forty days and forty nights, you held the destiny of Australia in the hollow of your head.
In Fred Daly, *The Politician who Laughed* **Calwell, Arthur Augustus** (1894–1973) Australian Labour politician. To Arthur Fadden, in the House of Representatives

92 An honest politician is one who, when he is bought, will stay bought.
Remark **Cameron, Simon** (1799–1889) US statesman and newspaper editor

93 He had all the virtues of a Scottish Presbyterian, but none of the vices.
The Guardian, (1994) **Campbell, Menzies** (1941–) Scottish politician, leader of the UK Liberal Democrats. Of John Smith, leader of the Labour Party

94 Politics and the fate of mankind are shaped by men without ideals and without greatness. Men who have greatness within them don't concern themselves with politics.
Notebooks, (1935–1942) **Camus, Albert** (1913–1960) Algerian-born French writer

95 All reform except a moral one will prove unavailing.
Critical and Miscellaneous Essays (1839)

96 A witty statesman said, you might prove anything by figures.
Chartism (1839) **Carlyle, Thomas** (1795–1881) Scottish historian, biographer, critic, and essayist

97 The rule is, jam to-morrow and jam yesterday – but never jam to-day.
Through the Looking-Glass (and What Alice Found There) (1872) **Carroll, Lewis** (1832–1898) English writer and photographer

98 Anarchists who love God always fall for Spinoza because he tells them that God doesn't love them. This is just what they need. A poke in the eye. To a real anarchist a poke in the eye is better than a bunch of flowers. It makes him see stars.
The Horse's Mouth (1944) **Cary, Joyce** (1888–1957) English novelist

99 An army of lions led by asses.
In R.H. Croll, *I Recall ...* **Champion, Henry Hyde** (1859–1928) Australian politician. On the Labour Party of his day

100 I remain just one thing, and one thing only – and that is a clown. It places me on a far higher plane than any politician.
The Observer, (1960) **Chaplin, Charlie** (1889–1977) English comedian, film actor, director and satirist

101 What would the man of 1938 have said of the Prime Minister of 1944?
Churchill: The End of Glory (1993) **Charmley, John** (1955–) English historian

102 Make him a bishop, and you will silence him at once.
Attr. **Chesterfield, Lord** (1694–1773) English politician and letter writer. When asked what could be done to control the evangelical preacher George Whitefield

103 Sometimes you have to learn how to give the right answer to the wrong question.
Remark, (1994) **Christopher, Warren** (1925–) US statesman

104 An old man in a hurry.
Speech, (1886) Of Gladstone

105 For the purposes of recreation he has selected the felling of trees, and we may usefully remark that his amusements, like his politics, are essentially destructive ... The forest laments in order that Mr Gladstone may perspire.
Speech, (1884) Of Gladstone **Churchill, Lord Randolph** (1849–1894) English Conservative politician

106 He is one of those orators of whom it was well said, 'Before they get up they do not know what they are going to say; when they are speaking, they do not know what they are saying; and when they sit down, they do not know what they have said'.
Speech, House of Commons, (December 1912) Of Lord Charles Beresford

107 So they told me how Mr Gladstone read Homer for fun, which I thought served him right.
My Early Life (1930)

108 I remember, when I was a child, being taken to the celebrated Barnum's circus, which contained an exhibition of freaks and monstrosities, but the exhibit ... which I most desired to see was the one described as 'The Boneless Wonder'. My parents judged that that spectacle would be too revolting and demoralising for my youthful eyes, and I have waited 50 years to see the boneless wonder sitting on the Treasury Bench.
Speech, House of Commons, (January 1931) Of Ramsey MacDonald

109 Dictators ride to and fro upon tigers which they dare not dismount. And the tigers are getting hungry.
While England Slept (1936)

110 I have never seen a human being who more perfectly represented the modern conception of a robot.
The Second World War (1948–1954) Referring to the Soviet statesman Molotov

111 On the night of the tenth of May 1940, at the outset of this mighty battle, I acquired the chief power in the State, which henceforth I wielded in ever-growing measure for five years and three months of world war, at the end of which time, all our enemies having surrendered unconditionally or being about to do so, I was immediately dismissed by the British electorate from all further conduct of their affairs.
The Second World War (1948–1954)

112 He is a modest man who has a good deal to be modest about.

In *Chicago Sunday Tribune Magazine of Books*, (1954) Of Clement Attlee **Churchill, Sir Winston** (1874–1965) English Conservative Prime Minister

113 There are no true friends in politics. We are all sharks circling and waiting, for traces of blood to appear in the water.
Diary, (1990)

114 He is so ambitious that he squeaks when he walks, and cannot manage to smile at any colleague inferior in rank in case he compromises himself in some way.
Diaries – Into Politics, 2000 On Conservative Education Secretary John Patten **Clark, Alan** (1928–1999) British Conservative politician, historian and diarist

115 What we believe in is what works.
The Times, (1999) **Clinton, William ('Bill')** (1946–) US Democrat President

116 In politics, what begins in fear usually ends in folly.
Table Talk (1835) **Coleridge, Samuel Taylor** (1772–1834) English poet, philosopher and critic

117 I would walk over my grandmother if necessary to get Nixon re-elected!
Born Again (1976) **Colson, Charles** (1931–) US political aide. To campaign staff, 1972

118 Love our principle, order our foundation, progress our goal.
Système de politique positive **Comte, Auguste** (1798–1857) French philosopher and mathematician

119 Either none of mankind possesses genuine rights, or everyone shares them equally; whoever votes against another's rights, whatever his religion, colour or sex, forswears his own.
In Vansittart (ed.), *Voices of the Revolution* (1989) **Condorcet, Antoine-Nicolas de** (1743–1794) French mathematician and academician

120 The people may be made to follow a course of action, but they may not be made to understand it.
Analects **Confucius** (c.550–c.478 BC) Chinese philosopher and teacher of ethics

121 Governments in a capitalist society are but committees of the rich to manage the affairs of the capitalist class.
Irish Worker, (1914) **Connolly, James** (1868–1916) Irish labour leader

122 The British public has always displayed a healthy cynicism of MPs. They have taken it for granted that MPs are self-serving impostors and hypocrites who put party before country and self before party.
The Guardian, (1995) **Crewe, Ivor** (1945–) British political scientist. Testimony at the Nolan inquiry into standards in public life

123 Humming, Hawing and Hesitation are the three Graces of contemporary Parliamentary oratory.
Westminster Blues, (1985) **Critchley, Julian** (1930–2000) English MP

124 We now are, as we always have been, decidedly and conscientiously attached to what is called the Tory, and which might with more propriety be called the Conservative, party.
Quarterly Review, (1830) **Croker, John Wilson** (1780–1857) Irish politician and dramatist. First use of the phrase 'the Conservative Party'

125 a politician is an arse upon which everyone has sat except a man.
1 x 1 (1944), no. 10 **Cummings, E. E.** (1894–1962) US poet, noted for his typography, and painter

126 ... like the silver plate on a coffin.
Quoted by Daniel O'Connell, *Hansard*, (1835) **Curran, John Philpot** (1750–1817) Irish judge, orator, politician and reformer. Of Sir Robert Peel's smile

127 Ah, poor Bob. It's very sad; he would rather make a point than make a friend.
In Howard Beale, *This Inch of Time* ... **Curtin, John** (1885–1945) Australian Prime Minister. Of R.G. Menzies

128 Not even a public figure. A man of no experience. And of the utmost insignificance.
In Harold Nicolson, *Curzon: The Last Phase* **Curzon, Lord** (1859–1925) English statesman and scholar. Referring to Stanley Baldwin on his appointment as Prime Minister

129 When I was a boy I was told that anybody could become President. I'm beginning to believe it.
In Irving Stone, *Clarence Darrow for the Defence* (1941) **Darrow, Clarence** (1857–1938) US lawyer, reformer and writer

130 Christ in this country would quite likely have been arrested under the Suppression of Communism Act.
The Observer, (1963) **De Blank, Joost** (1908–1968) Dutch-born British churchman. Of South Africa

131 As usual, I have against me the bourgeois, the officers and the diplomatists, and for me only the people who take the Metro.
The Observer, (1967)

132 I have come to the conclusion that politics are too serious a matter to be left to the politicians.
Attr.

133 In order to become the master, the politician poses as the servant.
Attr.

134 Since a politician never believes what he says, he is quite surprised to be taken at his word.
Attr. **De Gaulle, Charles** (1890–1970) French general and statesman

135 The Conservatives are the weakest among the intellectual classes: as is natural.
Letter to Disraeli **Derby, Earl of** (1799–1869) English politician; Conservative Prime Minister

136 I dreamt that I was making a speech in the House. I woke up, and by Jove I was!
In Churchill, *Thought and Adventures* **Devonshire, Duke of** (1895–1950) English politician

137 This must be the first time in history that a separatist party has deliberately tried to conceal its sole purpose for existing from the electorate.
The Times, (1999) **Dewar, Donald** (1937–2000) Scottish Labour politician; First Minister of Scotland. Comment on the SNP's election manifesto

138 I think ... that it is the best club in London.
Our Mutual Friend (1865) **Dickens, Charles** (1812–1870) English writer. Of the House of Commons

139 I am dead: dead, but in the Elysian fields.
In Monypenny and Buckle, *Life of Disraeli* (1920) Said to a fellow peer when moving on to the House of Lords

140 A man may speak very well in the House of Commons, and fail very completely in the House of Lords. There are two distinct styles requisite: I intend, in the course of my career, if I have time, to give a specimen of both.
The Young Duke (1831)

141 The practice of politics in the East may be defined by one word – dissimulation.
Contarini Fleming (1832)

142 Though I sit down now, the time will come when you will hear me.
Maiden Speech in the House of Commons, (1837)

143 A Conservative government is an organized hypocrisy.
Speech, (1845)

144 It seems to me a barren thing this Conservatism – an unhappy cross-breed, the mule of politics that engenders nothing.
Coningsby (1844)

145 A sound Conservative government ... Tory men and Whig measures.
Coningsby (1844)

146 Conservatism discards Prescription, shrinks from Principle, disavows Progress: having rejected all respect for antiquity, it offers no redress for the present, and makes no preparation for the future.
Coningsby (1844)

147 A majority is always the best repartee.
Tancred (1847)

148 Finality is not the language of politics.
Speech, (1859)

149 A sophistical rhetorician, inebriated with the exuberance of his own verbosity.
Speech, (1878) Of Gladstone

150 There are three kinds of lies: lies, damned lies and statistics.
Attr. **Disraeli, Benjamin** (1804–1881) English statesman and writer

151 There are two problems in my life. The political ones are insoluble and the economic ones are incomprehensible.
Speech, (1964) **Douglas-Home, Sir Alec** (1903–1995) Scottish statesman

152 Everybody is always in favour of general economy and particular expenditure.
The Observer, (1956) **Eden, Anthony** (1897–1977) English Conservative Prime Minister

153 An empty stomach is not a good political adviser.
Cosmic Religion (1931) **Einstein, Albert** (1879–1955) German-born US mathematical physicist

154 There is one thing about being President – nobody can tell you when to sit down.
The Observer, (1953)

155 Every gun that is made, every warship launched, every rocket fired signifies, in the final sense, a theft from those who hunger and are not fed, those who are cold and are not clothed. This world in arms is not spending money alone. It is spending the sweat of its labourers, the genius of its scientists, the hopes of its children.
Speech, (1953) **Eisenhower, Dwight D.** (1890–1969) US Republican President and general

156 In the modern world the intelligence of public opinion is the one indispensable condition of social progress.
Speech, (1869) **Eliot, Charles W.** (1834–1926) President of Harvard University

157 An election is coming. Universal peace is declared, and the foxes have a sincere interest in prolonging the lives of the poultry.
Felix Holt (1866) **Eliot, George** (1819–1880) English writer and poet

158 The state is not abolished, it dies away.
Anti-Dühring (1878) **Engels, Friedrich** (1820–1895) German socialist and political philosopher

159 As I took my seat it was said by political pundits that 'a chill ran along the Labour back benches looking for a spine to run up'.
Attr. **Ewing, Winnie** (1929–) Scottish Nationalist politician. On entering Westminster after winning a 1967 by-election for the SNP

160 Industrial relations are like sexual relations. It's better between two consenting parties.
Guardian Weekly, (1976) **Feather, Vic, Baron** (1906–1976) English trade unionist

161 Hell, I never vote for anybody. I always vote against.
In Taylor, *W. C. Fields: His Follies and Fortunes* (1950) **Fields, W.C.** (1880–1946) US film actor

162 Politics is the art of human happiness.
History of Europe (1935) **Fisher, H.A.L.** (1856–1940) English historian

163 He had the misleading air of open-hearted simplicity that people have come to demand of their politicians.
The Hundredth Door (1950) **Foley, Rae** (1900–1978) US writer

164 A Royal Commission is a broody hen sitting on a china egg.
Speech, House of Commons, (1964) **Foot, Michael** (1913–) British Labour politician

165 I guess it proves that in America anyone can be President.
In Reeves, *A Ford Not a Lincoln*. Referring to his own appointment as President

166 I am a Ford, not a Lincoln. My addresses will never be as eloquent as Lincoln's. But I will do my best to equal his brevity and plain speaking.
Speech, published in *Washington Post*, (1973) On taking the vice-presidential oath **Ford, Gerald R.** (1913–) US Republican President

167 Marxism exists in nineteenth-century thought in the same way as a fish exists in water; that is, it stops breathing anywhere else.
In Eribon, *Michel Foucault* (1989) **Foucault, Michel** (1926–1984) French philosopher. In 1966, when *Les Mots et les choses* appeared, he was attacked for this remark

168 To be absolutely honest, what I feel really bad about is that I don't feel worse. There's the ineffectual liberal's problem in a nutshell.
The Observer, (1965) **Frayn, Michael** (1933–) English dramatist and writer

169 I never dared be radical when young
For fear it would make me conservative when old.
'Precaution' (1936)

170 A liberal is a man too broadminded to take his own side in a quarrel.
Attr. **Frost, Robert** (1874–1963) US poet

171 All terrorists, at the invitation of the Government, end up with drinks at the Dorchester.
Letter to *The Guardian*, (1977) **Gaitskell, Hugh** (1906–1963) English Labour politician

172 Few things are as immutable as the addiction of political groups to the ideas by which they have once won office.
The Affluent Society (1958)

173 There are times in politics when you must be on the right side and lose.
The Observer, (1968)

174 Politics is not the art of the possible. It consists in choosing between the disastrous and the unpalatable.
Ambassador's Journal (1969) **Galbraith, J.K.** (1908–2006) Canadian-born US economist, diplomat and writer

175 My profession does not allow me to go swanning around buying pints of milk. I wouldn't be of sufficient service to my constituents if I went into shops.
The Independent, (1994) **Garel-Jones, Tristan** (1941–) English Conservative politician

176 The Vice-Presidency isn't worth a pitcher of warm piss.
Attr. **Garner, John Nance** (1868–1937) US politician

177 Corruption, the most infallible symptom of constitutional liberty.
Decline and Fall of the Roman Empire (1776–88) **Gibbon, Edward** (1737–1794) English historian, politician and memoirist

178 I think one of the great problems we have in the Republican Party is that we don't encourage you to be nasty. We encourage you to be neat, obedient, loyal and faithful and all those Boy Scout words, which would be great around a campfire but are lousy in politics.
Attr. **Gingrich, Newt** (1943–) US Republican politician

179 Whoever can conquer the street will one day conquer the state, for every form of power politics and any dictatorship-run state has its roots in the street.
Speech to Nazi party congress, Nuremburg, Germany, (1927) **Goebbels, Joseph** (1897–1945) Nazi politician

180 You've got to vote for someone. It's a shame, but it's got to be done.
Detroit News, (1988) **Goldberg, Whoopi** (1949–) US actress

181 I have nothing against Nick's wife or his family but I think it is time he spent more time with them.
Sunday Telegraph, (1990) **Goodhart, Sir Philip** (1925–) British Conservative politician. On Conservative politician Nicholas Ridley

182 The Conservative establishment has always treated women as nannies, grannies and fannies.
The Observer, (1998) **Gorman, Theresa** (1931–) English Conservative politician

183 A politician is a fellow who will lay down your life for his country.
Attr. **Guinan, Texas** (1884–1933) Canadian actress

184 If Roland Rat were appointed to Northern Ireland, I would tell people to work with him. But I would still point out that he is a rat.
In *The Observer*, (1999) **Hague, William** (1961–) English politician; leader of the Conservative Party. Commenting on Peter Mandelson's new appointment in Northern Ireland

185 As of now, I am in charge at the White House.
The Times, (1981) **Haig, Alexander** (1924–) US army officer and politician. Statement after an assassination attempt on President Reagan

186 A very weak-minded fellow, I'm afraid, and, like the feather pillow, bears the marks of the last person who has sat on him!
Letter to his wife, (14 January 1918) **Haig, Douglas** (1861–1928) Scottish military commander. Of Lord Derby

187 A great party is not to be brought down because of a squalid affair between a woman of easy virtue and a proved liar.
Interview, BBC TV, (1963) On the Profumo affair

188 When I'm sitting on the Woolsack in the House of Lords I amuse myself by saying 'Bollocks' sotto voce to the bishops.
The Observer, (1985) **Hailsham, Quintin Hogg, Baron** (1907–2001) English Conservative politician and Lord Chancellor

189 No man can be a politician, except he be first a historian or a traveller; for except he can see what must be, or what may be, he is no politician.
The Commonwealth of Oceana (1656)
Harrington, James (1611–1677)

190 In politics, being ridiculous is more damaging than being extreme.
The Observer, (1996)

191 Politicians are entitled to change their minds. But when they adjust their principles some explanation is necessary.
The Observer, (March 1999)

192 If the Labour Party does not aspire to reduce class disparities in life expectation, it is hard to describe the purpose of its existence.
The Observer, (1999) **Hattersley, Roy** (1932–) British Labour politician and writer

193 Ideology is a special way of relating to the world. It offers human beings the illusion of an identity, of dignity, and of morality, while making it easier for them to part with it.
Living in Truth (1987) **Havel, Václav** (1936–) Czech President

194 Conservative party policy is not unlike a Wagner opera. It is not always as bad as it sounds.

The Observer, 'Sayings of the Year', (December 1998) **Hayes, Jerry** (1953–) English conservative politician

195 Like being savaged by a dead sheep.
Speech, (1978) On Geoffrey Howe's attack on his Budget proposals

196 For the past few months she has been charging about like some bargain basement Boadicea.
The Observer, (1982) Of Margaret Thatcher

197 She approaches the problems of our country with all the one-dimensional subtlety of a comic strip.
Of Margaret Thatcher

198 It is a good thing to follow the first law of holes; if you are in one, stop digging.
The Observer, (1988)

199 A statesman is a dead politician. I'm in the home of the living dead – the House of Lords.
The Sunday Times, (2000) **Healey, Denis** (1917–) English Labour politician

200 The unpleasant and unacceptable face of capitalism.
Speech, House of Commons, (1973) On the Lonrho affair (involving tax avoidance)

201 That would be difficult.
The Times, (1999) At a photocall when Baroness Thatcher said to him, 'You should be on my right.' **Heath, Sir Edward** (1916–2005) English Conservative Prime Minister

202 The plural of conscience is conspiracy.
The Independent, (1992) **Henderson, Arthur** (1863–1935) Scottish politician

203 Having a little inflation is like being a little pregnant.
Attr. **Henderson, Leon** (1895–1986) US economist

204 I cannot and will not cut my conscience to fit this year's fashions, even though I long ago came to the conclusion that I was not a political person and could have no comfortable place in any political group.
Letter to the US House of Representatives Committee on Un-American Activities, (1952)
Hellman, Lillian (1907–1984) US dramatist and screenwriter

205 The only things in the middle of the road
are yellow lines and dead armadillos.
Attr. **Hightower, Jim** (1933–) Texan
agriculture commissioner

206 All propaganda has to be popular and has
to accommodate itself to the
comprehension of the least intelligent of
those whom it seeks to reach.
Mein Kampf (1925)

207 The art of leadership... consists in
consolidating the attention of the people
against a single adversary and taking care
that nothing will split up that attention.
Mein Kampf (1925)

208 What is essential is the formation of the
political will of the entire nation: that is the
starting point for political actions.
Speech, (1932) **Hitler, Adolf** (1889–1945)
German Nazi dictator, born in Austria

209 Peter Mandelson is someone who can
skulk in broad daylight.
The Observer, (1998)

210 Reagan was probably the first modern
president to treat the post as a part-time
job, one way of helping to fill the otherwise
blank days of retirement.
America (1990) **Hoggart, Simon** (1946–)
British journalist

211 He that goeth about to persuade a
multitude, that they are not so well
governed as they ought to be, shall never
want attentive and favourable hearers.
Of the Laws of Ecclesiasticall Politie (1593)
Hooker, Richard (c.1554–1600) English
theologian and churchman

212 Politicians cannot help being clowns.
Political activity is essentially absurd. The
hopes held for it can be high, the results
tragic, but the political art itself must lack
dignity: it can never match our ideals of
how such things should be done.
The Legend of King O'Malley

213 Politics is both fraud and vision.
The Legend of King O'Malley **Horne, Donald
Richmond** (1921–2005) Australian novelist

214 There are no such things as good
politicians and bad politicians. There are
only politicians, which is to say, they all
have personal axes to grind, and all too
rarely are they honed for the public good.
Laughing All the Way (1973) **Howar, Barbara**
(1934–) US television correspondent and
writer

215 It's rather like sending in your opening
batsman only for them to find that their
bats have been broken by the team captain.
Howe, Sir Geoffrey (1926–) British
Conservative politician. Resigning from
Margaret Thatcher's Cabinet

216 Wherever they pass, they the fascists sow
death and desolation.
Speeches and Articles (1938) **Ibárruri, Dolores
('La Pasionaria')** (1895–1989) Basque
Communist leader

217 I am against government by crony.
Remark, (1946) **Ickes, Harold L.** (1874–1952)
US politician. On his resignation as Secretary
of the Interior after a dispute with President
Truman

218 People have said to me that your first week
in the Commons is like your first week at
school. My school was never like this.
People told you what to do, they were less
friendly, and there were more girls.
The List, (1992) Describing her first
impressions of being the new MP for
Hampstead and Highgate

219 My only political ambition is to be re-
elected.
Attr. On career aspirations, 1997 **Jackson,
Glenda** (1936–) English actress and Labour
politician

220 President Robbins was so well adjusted to
his environment that sometimes you could
not tell which was the environment and
which was President Robbins.
Pictures from an Institution (1954) **Jarrell,
Randall** (1914–1965) US poet, critic and
translator

221 We haven't said they're all hopeless, but
quite a few of them are.
The Times (1998) On her fellow members of
the House of Lords

222 When I gave my big speech on the Lords, the longest letter I received was from a lady who wanted to know where I had bought my blouse.
The Times, (1999) **Jay, Margaret, Baroness** English Labour politician; leader of the House of Lords

223 To win, a candidate must be standing on the right street corner at the right time when a street-car is going in the right direction, and must have the right amount of change in their pockets.
The Independent on Sunday, (1992) **Jeffe, Sherry Bebitch** US political analyst. A definition of the street-car theory of American politics

224 Breaking the mould of British politics.
Attr. **Jenkins, Roy** (1920–2003) Welsh politician and writer. Used in connection with the SDP

225 If you're in politics and you can't tell when you walk into a room who's for you and who's against you, then you're in the wrong line of work.
In B. Mooney, *The Lyndon Johnson Story* (1956)

226 Gerry Ford is so dumb that he can't fart and chew gum at the same time.
In R. Reeves, *A Ford, Not a Lincoln* (1975) Correct version of the frequently misquoted: 'He couldn't walk and chew gum at the same time' **Johnson, Lyndon Baines** (1908–1973) US Democrat President

227 Politics are now nothing more than a means of rising in the world.
In Boswell, *The Life of Samuel Johnson* (1791)

228 Why, Sir, most schemes of political improvement are very laughable things.
In Boswell, *The Life of Samuel Johnson* (1791) **Johnson, Samuel** (1709–1784) English lexicographer, poet, critic, conversationalist and essayist

229 We spend more on welfare without achieving well-being, while creating dangerous levels of dependency.
Speech to Oxford Union, (1975) **Joseph, Sir Keith** (1918–1994) English Conservative politician

230 There is a holy mistaken zeal in politics as well as in religion. By persuading others, we convince ourselves.
Letters (1769–1771) **Junius** (1769–1772) Pen-name of anonymous author of letters criticizing ministers of George III

231 Can a soufflé rise twice?
ABC television, (1987) **Keating, Paul** (1944–) Australian Premier. On Andrew Peacock's ambitions to become leader of the Liberal Party following the 1987 elections

232 Militarism … is one of the chief bulwarks of capitalism, and the day that militarism is undermined, capitalism will fail.
The Story of My Life (1902) **Keller, Helen** (1880–1968) US writer and educator of the blind and deaf

233 Voting Tory is like being in trouble with the police. You'd rather the neighbours didn't know.
Speech, Liberal Democrat Conference, (1994)

234 Paddy Ashdown is the only party leader to be a trained killer. Although, to be fair, Mrs Thatcher was self-taught.
The Observer, (1998) **Kennedy, Charles** (1959–) Former Leader of the UK Liberal Democrats

235 People here may be sharply divided over the Reagan administration's politics – but they admire Ronald Reagan for not getting involved in them.
Kennedy, Edward (1932–) US Senator

236 I have no political ambitions for myself or my children.
Quoted in an obituary, (18 November 1969) **Kennedy, Joseph P.** (1888–1969) US financier and diplomat

237 One fifth of the people are against everything all the time.
The Observer, (1964) **Kennedy, Robert F.** (1925–1968) US Attorney General and Democrat politician

238 There are the Trade Unionists, once the oppressed, now the tyrants, whose selfish and sectional pretensions need to be bravely opposed.
'Liberalism and Labour' (1926)

239 This goat-footed bard, this half-human visitor to our age from the hag-ridden magic and enchanted woods of Celtic antiquity.
Essays and Sketches in Biography (1933) Of Lloyd George

240 Practical men, who believe themselves to be quite exempt from any intellectual influences, are usually the slaves of some defunct economist. Madmen in authority, who hear voices in the air, are distilling their frenzy from some academic scribbler of a few years back.
The General Theory of Employment, Interest and Money (1936)

241 When he's alone in a room, there's nobody there.
As I Remember, (1967) When asked what happened when Lloyd George was alone in a room **Keynes, John Maynard** (1883–1946) English economist

242 Politicians are the same everywhere. They promise to build a bridge even when there's no river.
Remark to journalists in the USA, (1960) **Khrushchev, Nikita** (1894–1971) Russian statesman and Premier of the USSR

243 The grotesque chaos of a Labour council – a Labour council – hiring taxis to scuttle around a city handing out redundancy notices to its own workers.
Speech, Labour Party Conference, Bournemouth, (1985) **Kinnock, Neil** (1942–) Welsh Labour politician. Attacking militant members in Liverpool

244 Even a paranoid can have enemies.
Time, (1977)

245 Foreign policy should not be confused with missionary work.
London Review of Books, (1992) **Kissinger, Henry** (1923–) German-born US Secretary of State

246 He [Labouchere] did not object, he once said, to Gladstone's always having the ace of trumps up his sleeve, but only to his pretence that God had put it there.
In Curzon, *Modern Parliamentary Eloquence* (1913) **Labouchere, Henry** (1831–1912)

247 Party loyalty brings the greatest of men down to the petty level of the masses.
Les caractères ou les moeurs de ce siècle (1688) **La Bruyère, Jean de** (1645–1696) French satirist

248 He looked at me as if I was a side dish he hadn't ordered.
In A.K. Adams, *The Home Book of Humorous Quotations* **Lardner, Ring** (1885–1933) US humorist and writer. Referring to W.H. Taft, US President 1909–1913

249 I must follow them; I am their leader.
In E.T. Raymond, *Mr Balfour* **Law, Bonar** (1858–1923) Canadian-born British statesman and Conservative MP

250 He had grown up in a country run by politicians who sent the pilots to man the bombers to kill the babies to make the world safe for children to grow up in.
The Lathe of Heaven (1971) **Le Guin, Ursula** (1929–) US author

251 Under capitalism we have a state in the proper sense of the word, that is, a special machine for the suppression of one class by another.
The State and Revolution (1917) **Lenin, V.I.** (1870–1924) Russian revolutionary, Marxist theoretician and first leader of the USSR

252 Inflation in the Sixties was a nuisance to be endured, like varicose veins or French foreign policy.
The Pendulum Years (1970)

253 It is truth not sufficiently appreciated that any political proposal which commends itself to both front benches of the House of Commons is at best useless and at worst against the public interest; one which also appeals to both main parties' back benches is likely to be a constitutional outrage and certain to be seriously damaging to the people's liberty, prosperity or both.
The Times, (1984) **Levin, Bernard** (1928–2004) English critic and writer

254 Conservatism is not, never has been, and never will be, solely about the free market.
The Times, (1999) **Lilley, Peter** (1943–) English Conservative politician

255 Politics is a marathon, not a sprint.
New Statesman, (1997)

256 Being an MP is not really a job for grown-ups – you are wandering around looking for and making trouble.
The Guardian, (2000) **Livingstone, Ken** (1945–) British Labour politician and Mayor of London

257 The House of Lords is not the watchdog of the constitution: it is Mr Balfour's poodle. It fetches and carries for him. It barks for him. It bites anybody that he sets it on to! Speech, House of Commons, (1908)

258 When they circumcised Herbert Samuel they threw away the wrong bit.
Attr. in *The Listener,* (1978)

259 The Right Honourable gentleman has sat so long on the fence that the iron has entered his soul.
Speech in Parliament, of Sir John Simon

260 He saw foreign policy through the wrong end of a municipal drainpipe.
In Harris, *The Fine Art of Political Wit* Of Neville Chamberlain **Lloyd George, David** (1863–1945) British Liberal statesman

261 He looks as if he had been weaned on a pickle.
Crowded Hours (1933) **Longworth, Alice Roosevelt** (1884–1980) US writer. Of John Calvin Coolidge, US President 1923–1929

262 It was like a bunch of 11-year-olds at their first secondary school.
The Independent, (1992) **Lynne, Liz** (1948–) English politician. On the behaviour of MPs

263 The first time you meet Winston Churchill you see all his faults and the rest of your life you spend in discovering his virtues.
In Christopher Hassall, *Edward Marsh* **Lytton, Lady Constance** (1869–1923) British suffragette and writer

264 In every age the vilest specimens of human nature are to be found among demagogues.
History of England (1849)

265 The object of oratory alone is not truth, but persuasion.
'Essay on Athenian Orators' (1898) **Macaulay, Lord** (1800–1859) English Liberal statesman, essayist and poet

266 Tony Blair has pushed moderation to extremes.
The Observer, (1996) **MacLennan, Robert** (1936–) Scottish politician

267 He enjoys prophesying the imminent fall of the capitalist system, and is prepared to play a part, any part, in its burial, except that of mute.
Speech, House of Commons, (1934) Of Aneurin Bevan

268 Forever poised between a cliché and an indiscretion.
Newsweek, (1956) On the life of a Foreign Secretary

269 Let's be frank about it; most of our people have never had it so good.
Speech, (1957)

270 When you're abroad you're a statesman: when you're at home you're just a politician.
Speech, South African Parliament, (1958)

271 The most striking of all the impressions I have formed since I left London a month ago is of the strength of this African national consciousness. The wind of change is blowing through this continent.
Speech, (1960), written by Sir David Hunt

272 As usual the Liberals offer a mixture of sound and original ideas. Unfortunately none of the sound ideas is original and none of the original ideas is sound.
The Observer, (1961)

273 If people want a sense of purpose they should get it from their archbishop. They should certainly not get it from their politicians.
In Fairlie, *The Life of Politics* (1968)

274 Selling the family silver.
Speech, House of Lords, (1986) Referring to privatization of profitable nationalized industries **Macmillan, Harold** (1894–1986) British Conservative Prime Minister

275 We now have the worst of both worlds – not just inflation on the one side or stagnation on the other side, but both of them together. We have a sort of 'stagflation' situation.

Speech, (1965) **Macleod, Iain** (1913–1970)
English Conservative politician and writer

276 People with vision usually do more harm than good.
The Economist, (1993)

277 For those people who may suggest that at the moment the Conservative Party has its back to the wall, I would simply say we will do precisely what the British nation has done all through its history when it had its back to the wall: turn round and fight for the things it believes.
The Observer, (1996) Commenting on his party's disastrous results in local government elections **Major, John** (1943–) English Conservative Prime Minister

278 You show me a capitalist, I'll show you a bloodsucker.
Malcolm X Speaks, (1965) **Malcolm X** (1925–1965) US black leader

279 Population, when unchecked, increases in a geometrical ratio. Subsistence only increases in an arithmetical ratio.
Essay on the Principle of Population (1798) **Malthus, Thomas Robert** (1766–1834) English political economist

280 The struggle is my life.
Letter from underground, (1961) **Mandela, Nelson** (1918–) South African statesman and President

281 When was the last time you heard of a Tory Minister resigning to spend more time with his mortgage?
The Observer, (1999) **Mandelson, Peter** (1953–) English Labour politican. On the difference between New Labour and the Conservatives

282 All reactionaries are paper tigers.
Quotations from Chairman Mao Tse-Tung **Mao Tse-Tung** (1893–1976) Chinese Communist leader

283 Not every problem someone has with his girlfriend is necessarily due to the capitalist mode of production.
The Listener **Marcuse, Herbert** (1898–1979) German-born US philosopher

284 They see nothing wrong in the rule, that to the victor belong the spoils of the enemy.

Speech, (1832) **Marcy, William** (1786–1857) US Democrat politician. On the politicians of New York

285 Today's ministers are a bit like actors in a huge, dark theatre, initially delighted at the absence of heckling or booing, but beginning uneasily to ask themselves whether anyone is still watching.
The Observer, (1999) **Marr, Andrew** (1959–) Scottish journalist. On political apathy under New Labour

286 Capitalist production creates, with the inexorability of a law of nature, its own negation.
Das Kapital (1867) **Marx, Karl** (1818–1883) German political philosopher and economist; founder of Communism

287 Ambition, in a private man a vice,
Is, in a prince, the virtue.
The Bashful Lover (1636) **Massinger, Philip** (1583–1640) English dramatist and poet

288 If my friend cannot ride two horses – what's he doing in the bloody circus?
In G. McAllister, *James Maxton: the Portrait of a Rebel* (1935) On a man proposing that the ILP should no longer be affiliated to the Labour Party

289 Sit down, man. You're a bloody tragedy.
Said to Ramsay MacDonald when he made his last speech in Parliament **Maxton, James** (1885–1946) Scottish Labour leader

290 Being in politics is like being a football coach. You have to be smart enough to understand the game and dumb enough to think it's important.
Interview, (1968) **McCarthy, Eugene** (1916–2005) US politician, lecturer and writer

291 If modern civilisation had any meaning it was displayed in the fight against Fascism.
In Seldes, *The Great Quotations* (1960) **McKenney, Ruth** (1911–1972) US writer

292 Here, indeed, was his one really notable talent. He slept more than any other President, whether by day or by night ... Nero fiddled, but Coolidge only snored ... He had no ideas, and he was not a nuisance.

American Mercury, (1933) **Mencken, H.L.** (1880–1956) US writer, critic, philologist and satirist. On President Calvin Coolidge

293 A Prime Minister exercises his greatest public influence by creating a public impression of himself, hoping all the time that the people will be generous rather than just.
In Mayer and Nelson, *Australian Politics: A Third Reader*

294 If I were the Archangel Gabriel, madam, I'm afraid you would not be in my constituency.
In Robinson, *The Wit of Sir Robert Menzies* (1966) In answer to a woman shouting, 'I wouldn't vote for you if you were the Archangel Gabriel' **Menzies, Sir Robert** (1894–1978) Australian statesman

295 A party of order or stability, and a party of progress or reform, are both necessary elements of a healthy state of political life.
On Liberty (1859)

296 ... mere conformers to commonplace, or time-servers for truth, whose arguments on all great subjects are meant for their hearers, and are not those which have convinced themselves.
On Liberty (1859)

297 Whatever crushes individuality is despotism, by whatever name it may be called.
On Liberty (1859)

298 The Conservatives ... being by the law of their existence the stupidest party.
Considerations on Representative Government (1861) **Mill, John Stuart** (1806–1873) English philosopher, economist and reformer

299 One day the don't-knows will get in, and then where will we be?
Attr. **Milligan, Spike** (1918–2002) Irish comedian and writer. Remark made about a pre-election poll

300 A children's crusade led by the early middle-aged.
The Observer, (1998) Description of New Labour

301 An ermine-lined dustbin, an up-market geriatric home with a faint smell of urine.
On the House of Lords **Mitchell, Austin** (1934–) English Labour politician

302 Cette femme Thatcher! Elle a les yeux de Caligule, mais elle a la bouche de Marilyn Monroe.
Mitterand, Francois (1916–1996) French President. On Margaret Thatcher *(That woman Thatcher! She has the eyes of Caligula, but the mouth of Marilyn Monroe)*

303 They had one advantage over all the other parties. They knew they were loonies.
In *The Observer,* (1999) **Moore, Patrick** (1923–) British astronomer, writer and broadcaster. On the Monster Raving Loony Party

304 I'm not going to re-arrange the furniture on the deck of the Titanic.
Attr. **Morton, Rogers** (1914–1979) US government official. Refusing to make any last-ditch attempts to rescue President Ford's re-election campaign, 1976

305 I am not, and never have been, a man of the right. My position was on the left and is now in the centre of politics.
Letter to *The Times,* (1968)

306 Before the organization of the Blackshirt movement free speech did not exist in this country.
In *New Statesman, This England* **Mosley, Sir Oswald** (1896–1980) British founder of the British Union of Fascists

307 This is Africa. This isn't Little Puddleton-in-the-Marsh. They behave differently. They think nothing of sticking tent poles up each other's what-not and doing filthy beastly things to each other. It does happen. I'm afraid.
The Sunday Times, (2000) **Mugabe, Robert** (1924–) President of Zimbabwe. On violence against white farm owners

308 Macmillan seemed, in his very person, to embody the national decay he supposed himself to be confuting. He exuded a flavour of moth-balls.
Tread Softly For You Tread on My Jokes (1966)

309 He was not only a bore; he bored for England.

Tread Softly For You Tread on My Jokes (1966) Of Anthony Eden **Muggeridge, Malcolm** (1903–1990) English writer

310 Fascism is not an article for export.
Article in the German press, (1932)

311 For us fascists, frontiers, all frontiers, are sacred. We do not dispute them: we defend them.
Speech to the Lower House, (1938), In Seldes, *Sawdust Caesar*

312 Fascism is a religion; the twentieth century will be known in history as the century of Fascism.
On Hitler's seizing power **Mussolini, Benito** (1883–1945) Italian fascist dictator

313 I still love you, but in politics there is no heart, only head.
Attr. **Napoleon I** (1769–1821) Emperor of France and king of Italy. To Josephine in 1809, on divorcing her for reasons of state

314 I do not have to forgive my enemies, I have had them all shot.
Attr. **Narváez, Ramón María** (1800–1868) Spanish general and politician. On his deathbed, when asked by a priest if he forgave his enemies

315 There can be no whitewash at the White House.
The Observer, (1973)

316 Defeat doesn't finish a man – quit does. A man is not finished when he's defeated. He's finished when he quits.
In William Safire, *Before the Fall* (1975)

317 I let down my friends, I let down my country. I let down our system of government.
The Observer, (1977)

318 When the President does it, that means it is not illegal.
TV interview with David Frost, (May 1977) **Nixon, Richard** (1913–1994) US Republican politician and President

319 I cannot be a good Catholic; I cannot go to heaven; and if a man is to go to the devil, he may as well go thither from the House of Lords as from any other place on earth.

In Henry Best, *Personal and Literary Memorials* (1829) **Norfolk, Lord** (1746–1815) English Whig politician

320 If I saw Mr Haughey buried at midnight at a cross-roads, with a stake driven through his heart – politically speaking – I should continue to wear a clove of garlic round my neck, just in case.
The Observer, (1982) **O'Brien, Conor Cruise** (1917–) Irish journalist

321 I will be sad, if I look up or down after my death and don't see my son asleep on the same benches on which I slept.
The Observer, (1998) **Onslow, Lord** (1938–) English Conservative politician. Opposing plans to reform the House of Lords

322 I'm convinced that the present form of capitalism will make way for another one which will be more human and less speculative.
El País, (1994) **Ortega Spottorno, José** (1916–2002) Spanish journalist and publisher

323 No book is genuinely free from political bias. The opinion that art should have nothing to do with politics is itself a political attitude.
'Why I Write' (1946)

324 In our time, political speech and writing are largely the defence of the indefensible.
Shooting an Elephant (1950) **Orwell, George** (1903–1950) English writer and critic

325 Taxation without representation is tyranny.
Attr. **Otis, James** (1725–1783) US lawyer, politician and pamphleteer

326 It was on this issue, the nuclear defence of Britain, on which I left the Labour Party, and on this issue I am prepared to stake my entire political career.
The Observer, (1986) **Owen, Dr David** (1938–) English politician

327 Never lose your temper with the Press or the public is a major rule of political life.
Unshackled (1959) **Pankhurst, Dame Christabel** (1880–1958) English suffragette

328 The argument of the broken pane of glass is the most valuable argument in modern politics.

Attr. **Pankhurst, Emmeline** (1858–1928) English suffragette

329 How could they tell?
In Keats, *You Might As Well Live* (1970) **Parker, Dorothy** (1893–1967) US writer, poet, critic and wit. Response to news that President Calvin Coolidge had died

330 It is now known ... that men enter local politics solely as a result of being unhappily married.
Parkinson's Law (1958)

331 The man who is denied the opportunity of taking decisions of importance begins to regard as important the decisions he is allowed to take.
Parkinson's Law (1958) **Parkinson, C. Northcote** (1909–1993) English political scientist and historian

332 Being an MP feeds your vanity and starves your self-respect.
The Times, (1994)

333 Bishops are the unguided missiles of the Upper Chamber – unguided by human agency, anyway: you can never know what a bishop is about to say because all too often he does not know himself.
The Times, (1998) On the House of Lords

334 To call it toadying would be to invite a group libel action from toads.
The Times, (1998) On a particularly sycophantic question to Prime Minister Tony Blair from John Hatton MP **Parris, Matthew** (1949–) British Conservative politician and journalist

335 By liberalism I don't mean the creed of any party or any century. I mean a generosity of spirit, a tolerance of others, an attempt to comprehend otherness, a commitment to the rule of law, a high ideal of the worth and dignity of man, a repugnance for authoritarianism and a love of freedom.
Lecture on South Africa at Yale University, (1973) **Paton, Alan** (1903–1988) South African writer

336 Cecil Parkinson, you're director of a fertilizer company. How deep is the mess you're in?

The BBC's General Election results programme, (1997) Paxman's first question to former Conservative Party chairman on the night of New Labour's landslide victory

337 Didn't you feel a fraud accepting the Nobel Peace Prize?
BBC radio programme *Start the Week*, (1999) Interview with Henry Kissinger **Paxman, Jeremy** (1950–) English journalist, writer and broadcaster

338 A Sympathizer would seem to imply a certain degree of benevolent feeling. Nothing of the kind. It signifies a ready-made accomplice in any species of political villainy.
Gryll Grange (1861) **Peacock, Thomas Love** (1785–1866) English writer and poet

339 It is the rulers of the state, if anybody, who may lie in dealing with citizens or enemies, for reasons of state.
Republic **Plato** (c.429–347 BC) Greek philosopher

340 A statesman is a politician who places himself at the service of a nation. A politician is a statesman who places the nation at his service.
The Observer, (1973) **Pompidou, Georges** (1911–1974) French statesman, Premier and President

341 Coffee, which makes the politician wise, And see through all things with his half-shut eyes.
The Rape of the Lock (1712)

342 Party-spirit, which at best is but the madness of many for the gain of a few.
Letter to Edward Blount, (1714) **Pope, Alexander** (1688–1744) English poet, translator and editor

343 Above any other position of eminence, that of Prime Minister is filled by fluke.
The Observer, (1987) **Powell, Enoch** (1912–1998) English politician and scholar

344 We're in danger of loving ourselves to death.
The Observer, (1994) During a debate between Prescott, Tony Blair and Margaret Beckett at the time of the contest for the Labour leadership

345 The Green Belt is a Labour achievement, and we intend to build on it.
The Observer, 'Sayings of the Year', (1998)

346 There were security reasons and my wife does not like to have her hair blown about. Any more stupid questions?
In *The Times*, (1999) Reply when asked why he had taken a chauffeur-driven car on a 300-yard trip to the Labour Party Conference
Prescott, John (1938–) English Labour politician

347 He is racist, he's homophobic, he's xenophobic and he's a sexist. He's the perfect Republican candidate.
Press, Bill (1940–) US political commentator. On Pat Buchanan

348 A number of anxious dwarfs trying to grill a whale.
Outcries and Asides **Priestley, J.B.** (1894–1984) English writer, dramatist and critic. Of politicians

349 One word sums up probably the responsibility of any vice president, and that one word is 'to be prepared'.
Attr. **Quayle, Dan** (1947–) US Republican politician and Vice President

350 A British Prime Minister in command of a parliamentary majority is an elected dictator with vastly more domestic power than an American President.
The Observer, (1999) **Rawnsley, Andrew** (1962–) British broadcaster and journalist

351 Politics is supposed to be the second oldest profession. I have come to understand that it bears a very close resemblance to the first.
Remark at a conference, (1977)

352 What makes you think I'd be happy about that?
Time, (1981) When told by an aide that the Government was running normally, after an attempt to assassinate him

353 Please assure me that you are all Republicans!
In Boller, *Presidential Anecdotes* (1981) To the surgeons about to operate on him after he was wounded in an assassination attempt

354 Politics is not a bad profession. If you succeed there are many rewards, if you disgrace yourself you can always write a book.
Attr. **Reagan, Ronald** (1911–2004) US actor, Republican statesman and President

355 Remember this, Griffin. The revolution eats its own. Capitalism re-creates itself.
Cocksure (1968) **Richler, Mordecai** (1931–2001) Canadian novelist

356 England elects a Labour Government. When a man goes in for politics over here, he has no time to labour, and any man that labours has no time to fool with politics. Over there politics is an obligation; over here it's a business.
Autobiography of Will Rogers (1949)

357 The more you read ... about this Politics thing, you got to admit that each party is worse than the other.
Autobiography of Will Rogers (1949) **Rogers, Will** (1879–1935) US humorist, actor, rancher, writer and wit

358 I have spent many years of my life in opposition and I rather like the role.
Letter to Bernard Baruch, (1952) **Roosevelt, Eleanor** (1884–1962) US writer and lecturer

359 I ask you to judge me by the enemies I have made.
The Observer, (1932)

360 We have always known that heedless self-interest was bad morals; we know now that it is bad economics.
First Inaugural Address, (1933)

361 A radical is a man with both feet firmly planted in the air.
Radio broadcast, (1939) **Roosevelt, Franklin Delano** (1882–1945) US Democrat President

362 The most successful politician is he who says what everybody is thinking most often and in the loudest voice.
In Andrews, *Treasury of Humorous Quotations* **Roosevelt, Theodore** (1858–1919) US Republican President

363 The collection of prejudices which is called political philosophy is useful provided that it is not called philosophy.

The Observer, (1962)

364 Not a gentleman; dresses too well.
In Alistair Cooke, *Six Men* (1977) Of Anthony
Eden **Russell, Bertrand** (1872–1970) English
philosopher, mathematician, essayist and
social reformer

365 Washington could not tell a lie; Nixon
could not tell the truth; Reagan cannot tell
the difference.
The Observer, (1987)

366 Would you buy a second-hand car from
this man?
Said of President Nixon **Sahl, Mort** (1927–)
Canadian-born US comedian

367 The present Colonial Secretary Iain
Macleod has been too clever by half. I
believe he is a very fine bridge player. It is
not considered immoral, or even bad form
to outwit one's opponent at bridge. It
almost seems to me as if the Colonial
Secretary, when he abandoned the sphere
of bridge for the sphere of politics, brought
his bridge technique with him.
Speech, House of Lords, (1961) **Salisbury,
Fifth Marquess of** (1893–1972)

368 Members rise from CMG (known
sometimes in Whitehall as 'Call Me God')
to the KCMG ('Kindly Call Me God') to ...
the GCMG ('God Calls Me God').
The Anatomy of Britain (1962) **Sampson,
Anthony** (1926–2004) British writer. Of the
Civil Service

369 Capitalism inevitably and by virtue of the
very logic of its civilization creates,
educates and subsidizes a vested interest in
social unrest.
Capitalism, Socialism and Democracy (1942)

370 Economic progress, in capitalist society,
means turmoil.
Capitalism, Socialism and Democracy (1942)
Schumpeter, Joseph A. (1883–1950) US
economist

371 As minister I accept the responsibility but
not the blame.
In Richard Long, *Dominion* (1984) **Semple,
Robert** (1873–1955) New Zealand Labour
politician. Allegedly said on the occasion of
the Fordell tunnel botch, 1944

372 He knows nothing; and he thinks he knows
everything. That points clearly to a political
career.
Major Barbara (1907)

373 Whether you think Jesus was God or not,
you must admit that he was a first-rate
political economist.
Androcles and the Lion (1915) **Shaw, George
Bernard** (1856–1950) Irish socialist, writer,
dramatist and critic

374 We are the masters at the moment, and
not only at the moment, but for a very long
time to come.
Speech, House of Commons, (1946); usually
quoted as 'We are the masters now.'
Shawcross, Lord (1902–2003) English Labour
politician

375 Conscience has no more to do with
gallantry than it has with politics.
The Duenna (1775)

376 Mr Speaker, I said the honourable member
was a liar it is true and I am sorry for it.
The honourable member may place the
punctuation where he pleases.
On being asked to apologize for calling a
fellow MP a liar

377 The Right Honourable Gentleman is
indebted to his memory for his jests, and
to his imagination for his facts.
Speech, House of Commons. Reply to Mr
Dundas **Sheridan, Richard Brinsley** (1751–
1816) Irish dramatist, politician and orator

378 I would not for a million dollars subject
myself and family to the ordeal of a
political canvass and afterwards to a four
years' service in the White House.
Letter to his brother, (1884) **Sherman, William
Tecumseh** (1820–1891) US Civil War general

379 Most Conservatives believe that a creche is
something that happens between two
Range Rovers in Tunbridge Wells.
The Independent, (September 1993) **Shorten,
Caroline** British Liberal Democrat politician

380 Jimmy Carter had the air of a man who had
never taken any decisions in his life. They
had always taken him.
The Sunday Times, (1978) **Simon, Guy** (1944–)

381 ... to state as clearly as may be what means lie ready to develop a property-owning democracy, to bring the industrial and economic status of the wage-earner abreast of his political and educational, to make democracy stable and four-square.
Article in the *Spectator*, (1923) **Skelton, Noel** (1880–1935) Scottish Unionist politician

382 Winston Churchill has devoted the best years of his life to preparing his impromptu speeches.
Attr. **Smith, F.E.** (1872–1930) English politician and Lord Chancellor

383 The longest running farce in the West End.
Remark to foreign press, (1973) On the House of Commons

384 If the fence is strong enough I'll sit on it.
The Observer, (1974) **Smith, Sir Cyril** (1928–) British liberal politician

385 Tory and Whig in turns shall be my host, I taste no politics in boil'd and roast.
Letters, To John Murray, (1834) **Smith, Sydney** (1771–1845) English clergyman, essayist, journalist and wit

386 You won the elections. But I won the count.
The Guardian, (1977) **Somoza, Anastasio** (1925–1980) President of Nicaragua

387 It is, I think, good evidence of life after death.
The Listener, (1978) **Soper, Donald** (1903–1998) Methodist churchman and writer. On the quality of debate in the House of Lords

388 Every communist has a fascist frown, every fascist a communist smile.
The Girls of Slender Means **Spark, Muriel** (1918–2006) English novelist

389 If Her Majesty stood for Parliament – if the Tory Party had any sense and made Her its leader instead of that grammar school twit Heath – us Tories, mate, would win every election we went in for.
Till Death Do Us Part, television programme **Speight, Johnny** (1920–1998) English screenwriter

390 Go back to your constituencies and prepare for government!

Speech to party conference, (1981)

391 I sense that the British electorate is now itching to break out once and for all from the discredited straight-jacket of the past.
The Times, (1987) **Steel, Sir David** (1938–) English politician

392 I will make a bargain with the Republicans. If they will stop telling lies about Democrats, we will stop telling lies about them.
Speech, (1952)

393 He said that he was too old to cry, but it hurt too much to laugh.
Speech, (1952) Said after losing an election, quoting a story told by Abraham Lincoln

394 We hear the Secretary of State boasting of his brinkmanship – the art of bringing us to the edge of the abyss.
Speech, Hartford, Connecticut, (1956)

395 Needs to be dragged kicking and screaming into the twentieth century.
In K. Tynan, *Curtains* (1961) Of the Republican Party

396 A politician is a statesman who approaches every question with an open mouth.
In Harris, *The Fine Art of Political Wit* **Stevenson, Adlai** (1900–1965) US lawyer, statesman and United Nations ambassador

397 Politics is perhaps the only profession for which no preparation is thought necessary.
Familiar Studies of Men and Books (1882)

398 These are my politics: to change what we can; to better what we can; but still to bear in mind that man is but a devil weakly fettered by some generous beliefs and impositions; and for no word however sounding, and no cause however just and pious, to relax the stricture of these bonds.
The Dynamiter (1885) **Stevenson, Robert Louis** (1850–1894) Scottish writer, poet and essayist

399 The House of Lords, an illusion to which I have never been able to subscribe – reponsibility without power, the prerogative of the eunuch throughout the ages.
Lord Malquist and Mr Moon (1966) **Stoppard, Tom** (1937–) British dramatist

400 *Jack Straw*: We are in Iraq for one reason only – to help the elected Iraqi government build a secure, democratic and stable nation.
Walter Wolfgang: That's a lie – and you know it.
Labour Party Conference, (2005) **Straw, Jack** (1946–) British politician, and **Wolfgang, Walter** (1923–) German-born English Labour party member and peace activist. Exchange at the 2005 Labour Party Conference that led to the forced and physical ejection of octogenarian Wolfgang

401 Is it really good for policy-makers to act as if everything has its price, and as if policies should be judged chiefly by their effects in delivering material benefits to selfish citizens? … It does not ask those individuals whether they also have other values which are not revealed by their shopping.
Capitalism, Socialism and the Environment (1976)

402 People can't change the way they use resources without changing their relations with one another. … How to conserve is usually a harder question than whether, or what, to conserve.
Capitalism, Socialism and the Environment (1976)
Stretton, Hugh (1924–) Australian political scientist and historian

403 These unhappy people were proposing schemes for persuading monarchs to choose favourites upon the score of their wisdom, capacity and virtue; of teaching ministers to consult the public good; of rewarding merit, great abilities and eminent services; of instructing princes to know their true interest by placing it on the same foundation with that of their people; of choosing for employments persons qualified to exercise them; with many other wild impossible chimeras, that never entered before into the heart of man to conceive, and confirmed in me the old observation, that there is nothing so extravagant and irrational which some philosophers have not maintained for truth.
Gulliver's Travels (1726) **Swift, Jonathan** (1667–1745) Irish satirist, poet, essayist and cleric

404 Well, I have one consolation. No candidate was ever elected ex-president with such a large majority!
Attr. **Taft, William Howard** (1857–1930) US Republican politician and President. Referring to his disastrous defeat in the 1912 presidential election

405 I hope Mrs Thatcher will go until the turn of the century looking like Queen Victoria.
The Observer, (1987) **Tebbitt, Norman** (1931–) English Conservative politician

406 Reality hasn't really intervened in my mother's life since the seventies.
Daily Mail, (1996) **Thatcher, Carol** (1953–) English writer and broadcaster; daughter of Margaret Thatcher

407 Let our children grow tall, and some taller than others if they have it in them to do so.
Speech, US tour, (1975)

408 Britain is no longer in the politics of the pendulum, but of the ratchet.
Speech, (1977)

409 U-turn if you want to. The lady's not for turning.
Speech, (1980)

410 I don't mind how much my Ministers talk – as long as they do what I say.
The Observer, (1980)

411 If you are going from A to B you do not always necessarily go in a straight line.
The Observer, (1980)

412 No one would have remembered the Good Samaritan if he'd only had good intentions. He had money as well.
The Observer, (1980)

413 Victorian values … were the values when our country became great.
Television interview, (1982)

414 I think I have become a bit of an institution – you know, the sort of thing people expect to see around the place.
The Observer, (1987)

415 We have become a grandmother.
The Observer, (1989)

416 I don't understand Cool Britannia. I believe in Rule Britannia.

The Observer, (1998) **Thatcher, Margaret**
(1925–) English Conservative Prime Minister

417 While I'd rather be right than president, at
any time I'm ready to be both.
In A. Whitman, *Come to Judgment* **Thomas,
Norman M.** (1884–1968) US Presbyterian
minister and writer. Referring to his lack of
success in presidential campaigns

418 Greater love hath no man than this, that he
lay down his friends for his life.
Speech, (1962) **Thorpe, Jeremy** (1929–)
English Liberal politician. Remark on
Macmillan's Cabinet purge, 1962

419 A new world demands a new political
science.
De la démocratie en Amérique (1835–1840)
Tocqueville, Alexis de (1805–1859) French
historian, politician, lawyer and memoirist

420 It has been the great fault of our politicians
that they have all wanted to do something.
Phineas Finn (1869)

421 It is the necessary nature of a political party
in this country to avoid, as long as it can be
avoided, the consideration of any question
which involves a great change ... The best
carriage horses are those which can most
steadily hold back against the coach as it
trundles down the hill.
Phineas Redux (1874) **Trollope, Anthony** (1815–
1882) English writer, traveller and post office
official

422 All the president is, is a glorified public
relations man who spends his time
flattering, kissing and kicking people to get
them to do what they are supposed to do
anyway.
Letter to his sister, (1947)

423 You don't set a fox to watching the
chickens just because he has a lot of
experience in the hen house.
Speech, (1960) Referring to Vice President
Nixon's nomination for President

424 If you can't stand the heat, get out of the
kitchen.
Mr Citizen (1960)

425 A statesman is a politician who's been dead
ten or fifteen years.

Attr. **Truman, Harry S.** (1884–1972) US
Democrat President

426 For the Church in any country to retreat
from politics is nothing short of heresy.
Christianity is political or it is not
Christianity.
The Observer, (1994) **Tutu, Archbishop
Desmond** (1931–) South African churchman
and anti-apartheid campaigner

427 The radical invents the views. When he has
worn them out, the conservative adopts
them.
Notebooks (1935) **Twain, Mark** (1835–1910) US
humorist, writer, journalist and lecturer

428 To conquer is not to convince.
Speech, (1936) **Unamuno, Miguel de** (1864–
1936) Spanish philosopher, poet and writer

429 I can take no allegiance to a flag if I don't
know who's holding it.
Dear Me (1977)

430 When Mrs Thatcher says she has a
nostalgia for Victorian values I don't think
she realises that 90 per cent of her
nostalgia would be satisfied in the Soviet
Union.
The Observer, (1987)

431 I could never bear to be a politician. I
couldn't bear to be right all the time.
The Observer, (1998) **Ustinov, Sir Peter** (1921–
2004) English actor, director, dramatist,
writer and raconteur

432 Politics is the art of preventing people from
becoming involved in affairs which concern
them.
As Such 2 (1943) **Valéry, Paul** (1871–1945) French
poet, mathematician and philosopher

433 The danger to the country, to Europe, to
her vast Empire, which is involved in
having all these great interests entrusted to
the shaking hand of an old, wild, and
incomprehensible man of 82, is very great!
Letter to Lord Lansdowne, (1892) On
Gladstone's last appointment as Prime
Minister

434 He speaks to Me as if I was a public
meeting.

In G.W.E. Russell, *Collections and Recollections* (1898) Of Gladstone **Victoria, Queen** (1819–1901) Queen of the United Kingdom

435 Any American who is prepared to run for President should automatically, by definition, be disqualified from ever doing so.
Attr. **Vidal, Gore** (1925–) US writer, critic and poet

436 Patriots are not supposed to make fools of their own people.
The Times, (1996) On John Major's policy of non-cooperation with Europe over the export ban on British beef

437 I suspect there is a link between the indiscretions of politicians and the nature of their work.
The Observer, (1998) On the Ron Davies affair **Walden, George** (1939–) British Conservative politician and diplomat

438 All those men have their price.
In Coxe, *Memoirs of Sir Robert Walpole* (1798) **Walpole, Robert** (1676–1745) British statesman and first British Prime Minister. Of fellow-parliamentarians

439 It's very hard to be in awe of politicians.
The Times, (1998) **Wark, Kirsty** (1955–) Scottish journalist and broadcaster

440 A newspaper poll found that fewer than one in twenty people could explain the government's third way. Some thought it was a religious cult, others a sexual position, and one man asked if it were a plan to widen the M25.
The Observer, (1998)

441 If John Prescott remains in office much longer, cars will have to be preceded by a man walking in front of them singing the Red Flag.
In The Observer, (1999)

442 I cannot bring myself to vote for a woman who has been voice-trained to speak to me as though my dog had just died.
Commenting on Margaret Thatcher's delivery **Waterhouse, Keith** (1929–) English journalist and author

443 The art of politics is to make more friends than enemies.
Remark to S. Murray-Smith **Waten, Judah Leon** (1911–1985) Australian novelist

444 The staid conservative,
Came-over-with-the-Conqueror type of mind.
'A Study in Contrasts' (1905) **Watson, Sir William** (1858–1936) English poet

445 Politicians can forgive almost anything in the way of abuse; they can forgive subversion, revolution, being contradicted, exposed as liars, even ridiculed, but they can never forgive being ignored.
The Observer **Waugh, Auberon** (1939–2001) English journalist

446 Simply a radio personality who outlived his prime.
In Christopher Sykes, *Evelyn Waugh* **Waugh, Evelyn** (1903–1966) English writer and diarist. Of Winston Churchill

447 Until this moment, Senator, I think I never really gauged your cruelty or your recklessness ... Have you no sense of decency, sir, at long last? Have you left no sense of decency?
New York Times, (1954) **Welch, Joseph** (1890–1960) US attorney. Denouncing Senator Joseph McCarthy during the Army-McCarthy Congressional Hearings

448 Consumer capitalism has eaten up the Church, the state, trade unions, extended families, everywhere that people learn morality.
The Observer, (1998) **Welsh, Irvine** (1957–) Scottish novelist

449 Margaret Thatcher's great strength seems to be the better people know her, the better they like her. But, of course, she has one great disadvantage – she is a daughter of the people and looks trim, as the daughters of the people desire to be. Shirley Williams has such an advantage over her because she's a member of the upper-middle class and can achieve that kitchen-sink-revolutionary look that one cannot get unless one has been to a really good school.

Interview, *The Sunday Times*, (1976) **West, Dame Rebecca** (1892–1983) English writer, critic and feminist

450 It is a pity, as my husband says, that more politicians are not bastards by birth instead of vocation.
The Observer, (1964) **Whitehorn, Katherine** (1926–) English writer

451 I am not prepared to go about the country stirring up apathy.
Attr. **Whitelaw, William** (1918–1999) English Conservative politician

452 He has something of the night about him.
The Sunday Times, (1997) **Widdecombe, Ann** (1947–) English Conservative politician. Of Michael Howard as candidate for the Conservative leadership. Howard was Widdecombe's boss at the time

453 For Hon. Members opposite the deterrent is a phallic symbol. It convinces them that they are men.
The Observer, (1964) **Wigg, George Edward Cecil, Baron** (1900–1983) English politician. On nuclear weapons

454 A week is a long time in politics.
Remark, (1964)

455 He immatures with age.
Attr., BBC programme, (1995) Of Tony Benn

456 Hence the practised performances of latter-day politicians in the game of musical daggers: never be left holding the dagger when the music stops.
The Governance of Britain

457 The Labour Party is like a stage-coach. If you rattle along at great speed everybody inside is too exhilarated or too seasick to cause any trouble. But if you stop everybody gets out and argues about where to go next.
In L. Smith, *Harold Wilson, The Authentic Portrait* **Wilson, Harold** (1916–1995) English Labour Prime Minister

458 Politics is the entertainment branch of industry.
Attr. **Zappa, Frank** (1940–1993) US rock musician, songwriter and record producer
See also communism; democracy; government; monarchy and royalty; socialism

POVERTY

1 I should love to be poor, as long as I was excessively poor! Anything in excess is quite delightful.
Ring Round the Moon (1948) **Anouilh, Jean** (1910–1987) French dramatist and screenwriter

2 Poverty is an anomaly to rich people. It is very difficult to make out why people who want dinner do not ring the bell.
Literary Studies (1879) **Bagehot, Walter** (1826–1877) English economist and political philosopher

3 Now that the Social Security Secretary has defined poverty by reference to 32 factors, what word will we use for a serious lack of money?
In *The Observer*, (1999) **Baker, Kenneth, Lord** (1934–) English Conservative politician

4 Come away; poverty's catching.
The Rover (1677) **Behn, Aphra** (1640–1689) English dramatist, writer, poet, translator and spy

5 The poor always ye have with you.
John, 12:8 **The Bible (King James Version)**

6 Is this a holy thing to see,
In a rich and fruitful land,
Babes reducd to misery,
Fed with cold and usurous hand?
'Holy Thursday' (1794) **Blake, William** (1757–1827) English poet, engraver, painter and mystic

7 All things they have in common being so poor,
And their one fear, Death's shadow at the door.
Each sundown makes them mournful, each sunrise
Brings back the brightness in their failing eyes.
The Waggoner and Other Poems (1920) **Blunden, Edmund** (1896–1974) English poet

8 This Submerged Tenth – is it, then, beyond the reach of the nine-tenths in the midst of whom they live?

In Darkest England (1890) **Booth, General William** (1829–1912) English founder of the Salvation Army

9 In those days our Lord could demand that men love their neighbour, because they'd had enough to eat. Nowadays it's different.
Mother Courage and her Children (1941) **Brecht, Bertolt** (1898–1956) German dramatist

10 The poor are the negroes of Europe.
Maximes et Pensées (1796) **Chamfort, Nicolas** (1741–1794) French writer

11 For of fortunes sharpe adversitee
The worste kynde of infortune is this,
A man to han ben in prosperitee,
And it remembren, whan it passed is.
Troilus and Criseyde, III **Chaucer, Geoffrey** (c.1340–1400) English poet, public servant and courtier

12 To be poor and independent is very nearly an impossibility.
Advice to Young Men (1829) **Cobbett, William** (1762–1835) English politician, reformer, writer, farmer and army officer

13 He found it inconvenient to be poor.
'Charity' (1782) **Cowper, William** (1731–1800) English poet, hymn writer and letter writer. Of a burglar

14 The murmuring poor, who will not fast in peace.
The Newspaper (1785) **Crabbe, George** (1754–1832) English poet, clergyman, surgeon and botanist

15 The only thing that hurts more than paying an income tax is not having to pay an income tax.
Attr. **Dewar, Lord Thomas Robert** (1864–1930) Scottish Conservative politician and writer

16 Gif thou has micht, be gentle and free;
And gif thou stands in povertie,
Of thine awn will to it consent;
And riches sall return to thee:
He has eneuch that is content.
'Of Content' (1834 edition) **Dunbar, William** (c.1460–c.1525) Scottish poet, satirist and courtier

17 'Tis still my maxim, that there is no scandal like rags, nor any crime so shameful as poverty.

The Beaux' Stratagem (1707) **Farquhar, George** (1678–1707) Irish dramatist

18 It is only the poor who pay cash, and that not from virtue, but because they are refused credit.
In J.R. Solly, *A Cynic's Breviary* **France, Anatole** (1844–1924) French writer and critic

19 Necessity never made a good bargain.
Poor Richard's Almanac (1735) **Franklin, Benjamin** (1706–1790) US statesman, scientist, political critic and printer

20 No, Sir, tho' I was born and bred in England, I can dare to be poor, which is the only thing now-a-days men are asham'd of.
Polly (1729) **Gay, John** (1685–1732) English poet, dramatist and librettist

21 I'm not interested in the bloody system! Why has he no food? Why is he starving to death?
In Care, *Sayings of the Eighties* (1989) **Geldof, Bob** (1954–) Irish rock musician

22 Only the poor will help the poor.
Legends from Benson's Valley (1963) **Hardy, Frank** (1917–1994) Australian writer

23 Clothes make the poor invisible … America has the best-dressed poverty the world has ever known.
The Other America (1962) **Harrington, Michael** (1928–1989) US writer

24 Those that die by famine die by inches.
An Exposition of the Old and New Testament (1706) **Henry, Matthew** (1662–1714) English Nonconformist minister

25 Whoever is poor may lie to himself – that is his right.
Perhaps his only right.
A Child of our Time (1938) **Horváth, Ödön von** (1901–1938) German-Hungarian writer

26 It is easy enough to say that poverty is no crime. No; if it were men wouldn't be ashamed of it. It is a blunder, though, and is punished as such. A poor man is despised the whole world over.
Idle Thoughts of an Idle Fellow (1886) **Jerome, Jerome K.** (1859–1927) English writer and dramatist

27 This mournful truth is ev'rywhere
confess'd,
Slow rises worth by poverty depress'd.
London: A Poem (1738)

28 A man, doubtful of his dinner, or
trembling at a creditor, is not much
disposed to abstracted meditation, or
remote enquiries.
The Lives of the Most Eminent English Poets
(1781) **Johnson, Samuel** (1709–1784) English
lexicographer, poet, critic, conversationalist
and essayist

29 Rarely they rise by virtue's aid, who lie
Plung'd in the depths of helpless poverty.
Satires

30 Nothing is harder to bear about luckless
poverty than the way it exposes men to
ridicule.
Satires **Juvenal** (c.60–130) Roman verse satirist
and Stoic

31 Few, save the poor, feel for the poor.
'The Poor' **Landon, Letitia Elizabeth** (1802–
1838) English poet

32 You cannot feed the hungry on statistics.
Speech, (1904) **Lloyd George, David** (1863–
1945) British Liberal statesman. Advocating
Tariff Reform

33 Respectable means rich, and decent means
poor. I should die if I heard my family
called decent.
Crotchet Castle (1831) **Peacock, Thomas Love**
(1785–1866) English writer and poet

34 ... the forgotten man at the bottom of the
economic pyramid.
Radio broadcast, (1932)

35 I see one-third of a nation ill-housed, ill-
clad, ill-nourished.
Second Inaugural Address, (1937) **Roosevelt,
Franklin Delano** (1882–1945) US Democrat
President

36 We don't have to look as far as Ethiopia to
find the darkness of disease, death and
disaster. It is on our doorsteps.
Quoted in *The Guardian,* (2000) **Runcie,
Robert** (1921–2000) Archbishop of Canterbury
1980–1991

37 'No one has ever said it,' observed Lady
Caroline, 'but how painfully true it is that
the poor have us always with them!'
Attr. **Saki** (1870–1916) Burmese-born British
writer

38 I can't give away my old clothes to the
poor. They have enough to put up with
without the added humiliation of wearing
last season.
Absolutely Fabulous **Saunders, Jennifer** (1958–)
English comedienne and writer. As her own
creation, Edina Monsoon

39 The art of our necessities is strange
That can make vile things precious.
King Lear, III.ii **Shakespeare, William** (1564–
1616) English dramatist, poet and actor

40 If you are going to have doctors you had
better have doctors well off; just as if you
are going to have a landlord you had better
have a rich landlord. Taking all the round
of professions and occupations, you will
find that every man is the worse for being
poor; and the doctor is a specially
dangerous man when poor.
The Socialist Criticism of the Medical Profession
(1909) **Shaw, George Bernard** (1856–1950) Irish
socialist, writer, dramatist and critic

41 A hole is the accident of a day, but a darn is
premeditated poverty.
Dictionary of National Biography (1897) **Shuter,
Edward** (1728–1776) English actor and wit.
Explaining why he did not mend his stocking

42 Poverty, though it does not prevent the
generation, is extremely unfavourable to
the rearing of children. The tender plant is
produced, but in so cold a soil and so
severe a climate, soon withers and dies.
Wealth of Nations (1776) **Smith, Adam** (1723–
1790) Scottish economist, philosopher and
essayist

43 Poverty is no disgrace to a man, but it is
confoundedly inconvenient.
In J. Potter Briscoe (ed.), *Sydney Smith* (1900)
Smith, Sydney (1771–1845) English clergyman,
essayist, journalist and wit

44 Hark ye, Clinker, you are a most notorious
offender. You stand convicted of sickness,
hunger, wretchedness, and want.

The Expedition of Humphry Clinker (1771)
Smollett, Tobias (1721–1771) Scottish writer, satirist, historian, traveller and physician

45 The poor are our brothers and sisters ... people in the world who need love, who need care, who have to be wanted.
Time, (1975)

46 I think it is very beautiful for the poor to accept their lot, to share it with the passion of Christ. I think the world is being much helped by the suffering of the poor people.
Attr. **Teresa, Mother** (1910–1997) Catholic missionary in India

47 There were times my pants were so thin I could sit on a dime and tell if it was heads or tails.
In Swindell, *Spencer Tracy* **Tracy, Spencer** (1900–1967) US film actor. Of leaner times in his life

48 There's a proud array of soldiers –
what do they round your door?
They guard our master's granaries
from the thin hands of the poor.
'The Famine Years' **Wilde, Lady Jane** (1826–1896) Irish poet and society hostess, mother of Oscar Wilde

49 We are often told that the poor are grateful for charity. Some of them are, no doubt, but the best amongst the poor are never grateful. They are ungrateful, discontented, disobedient, and rebellious. They are quite right to be so.
'The Soul of Man under Socialism' (1891)
Wilde, Oscar (1854–1900) Irish poet, dramatist, writer, critic and wit
See also money and wealth

POWER

1 Power tends to corrupt, and absolute power corrupts absolutely. Great men are almost always bad men ... There is no worse heresy than that the office sanctifies the holder of it.
Letter to Bishop Mandell Creighton, (1887)
Acton, Lord (1834–1902) English historian and moralist

2 I am more and more convinced that man is a dangerous creature and that power, whether vested in many or a few, is ever grasping, and like the grave, cries 'Give, give.'
Letter to John Adams, (1775) **Adams, Abigail** (1744–1818) US letter writer and wife of President John Adams

3 Power always thinks it has a great soul and vast views beyond the comprehension of the weak.
The Works of John Adams (1856), letter to his wife Abigail Adams, (1780) **Adams, John** (1735–1826) US lawyer, diplomat and President

4 Generally, nobody behaves decently when they have power.
Radio Times, (1992) **Amis, Kingsley** (1922–1995) English writer, poet and critic

5 Power wears down the man who doesn't have it.
In Biagi, *The Good and the Bad* (1989)
Andreotti, Giulio (1919–) Italian statesman and Prime Minister

6 Concepts such as truth, justice, compassion are often the only bulwarks which stand against ruthless power.
Index on Censorship, (1994) **Aung San Suu Kyi, Daw** (1945–) Burmese political leader

7 Men in great place are thrice servants: servants of the sovereign or state, servants of fame, and servants of business ... It is a strange desire to seek power and to lose liberty.
'Of Great Place' (1625) **Bacon, Francis** (1561–1626) English philosopher, essayist, politician and courtier

8 He did not care in which direction the car was travelling, so long as he remained in the driver's seat.
New Statesman, (1963) **Beaverbrook, Lord** (1879–1964) Canadian-born British newspaper owner. Of Lloyd George

9 The weak have one weapon: the errors of those who think they are strong.
The Observer, (1962) **Bidault, Georges** (1899–1983) French statesman

10 Those who have been once intoxicated with power, and have derived any kind of emolument from it, even though but for one year, never can willingly abandon it.
Letter to a Member of the National Assembly (1791) **Burke, Edmund** (1729–1797) Irish-born British statesman and philosopher

11 Apart from the occasional saint, it is difficult for people who have the smallest amount of power to be nice.
In Care, *Sayings of the Eighties* (1989) **Clare, Dr Anthony** (1942–) Irish professor, psychiatrist and broadcaster

12 All ambitions are lawful except those which climb upward on the miseries or credulities of mankind.
A Personal Record (1912) **Conrad, Joseph** (1857–1924) Polish-born British writer, sailor and explorer

13 I expect that rape and murder, either separately or mixed together, fill the fantasies of most men and all stylists. They are the supreme acts of ascendancy over others; they yield the only moments when a man is certain beyond all doubt that his message has been received. Of the few who live out these dreams, some preface rape with murder so as to avoid embracing a partner who might criticize their technique.
In Guy Kettlehack (ed.), *The Wit and Wisdom of Quentin Crisp* **Crisp, Quentin** (1908–1999) English writer, publicist and model

14 I repeat ... that all power is a trust – that we are accountable for its exercise – that, from the people, and for the people, all springs, and all must exist.
Vivian Grey (1826) **Disraeli, Benjamin** (1804–1881) English statesman and writer

15 In the councils of government, we must guard against the acquisition of unwarranted influence, whether sought or unsought, by the military-industrial complex. The potential for the disastrous rise of misplaced power exists and will persist.
Farewell address, (17 January 1961) **Eisenhower, Dwight D.** (1890–1969) US President and general

16 I have several times suggested that what I call the 'Establishment' in this country is today more powerful than ever before. By the 'Establishment' I do not mean only the centres of official power – though they are certainly part of it – but rather the whole matrix of official and social relations within which power is exercised ... the 'Establishment' can be seen at work in the activities of, not only the Prime Minister, the Archbishop of Canterbury and the Earl Marshal, but of such lesser mortals as the Chairman of the Arts Council, the Director-General of the BBC, and even the editor of the Times Literary Supplement, not to mention dignitaries like Lady Violet Bonham-Carter.
Spectator, (1955) **Fairlie, Henry** (1924–1990) English journalist

17 Every uniform corrupts one's character.
Diary, (1948) **Frisch, Max** (1911–1991) Swiss dramatist, writer and architect

18 I have never been interested in any power except my own power in the theatre, which I love.
The Independent, (1994) **Gielgud, Sir John** (1904–2000) English actor

19 Guns will make us powerful; butter will only make us fat.
Broadcast, (1936) **Goering, Hermann** (1893–1946) Nazi leader and military commander

20 Fire and people do in this agree,
They both good servants, both ill masters be.
'An Inquisition upon Fame and Honour' (1633) **Greville, Fulke** (1554–1628) English poet, dramatist, biographer, courtier and politician

21 There is ... no other Fundamental, but that every Supream Power must be Arbitrary.
Political, Moral and Miscellaneous Thoughts and Reflections (1750) **Halifax, Lord** (1633–1695) English politician, courtier, pamphleteer and epigrammatist

22 Germany will either be a world power or will not exist at all.
Mein Kampf (1927) **Hitler, Adolf** (1889–1945) German Nazi dictator, born in Austria

23 The strongest man in the world is the man who stands alone.
An Enemy of the People (1882) **Ibsen, Henrik** (1828–1906) Norwegian writer, dramatist and poet

24 I want loyalty. I want him to kiss my ass in Macy's window at high noon and tell me it smells like roses. I want his pecker in my pocket.
In D. Halberstam, *The Best and the Brightest* (1972) **Johnson, Lyndon Baines** (1908–1973) US Democrat President

25 My opinion is, that power should always be distrusted, in whatever hands it is placed.
In Teignmouth, *Life of Sir W. Jones* (1835) **Jones, Sir William** (1746–1794) English orientalist, translator and jurist

26 Leadership is not about being nice. It's about being right and being strong.
Time, (1995) **Keating, Paul** (1944–) Australian Labor statesman and Prime Minister

27 The tyrant dies and his rule is over; the martyr dies and his rule begins.
Attr. **Kierkegaard, Søren** (1813–1855) Danish philosopher

28 Power is the ultimate aphrodisiac.
Attr. **Kissinger, Henry** (1923–) German-born US Secretary of State

29 The struggle of man against power is the struggle of memory against forgetting.
Attr. **Kundera, Milan** (1929–) Czech writer and critic

30 I looked around at the little fishes present and said, 'I'm the Kingfish.'
In A. Schlesinger Jr, *The Politics of Upheaval* (1961) **Long, Huey** (1893–1935) US populist politician

31 Power never takes a back step – only in the face of more power.
Malcolm X Speaks, (1965) **Malcolm X** (1925–1965) US black leader

32 The only purpose for which power can be rightfully exercised over any member of a civilized community, against his will, is to prevent harm to others. His own good, either physical or moral, is not sufficient warrant.
On Liberty (1859) **Mill, John Stuart** (1806–1873) English philosopher, economist and reformer

33 The new source of power is not money in the hands of a few but information in the hands of many.
Megatrends (1982) **Naisbitt, John** (1929–) US writer

34 When I want a peerage, I shall buy one like an honest man.
Attr. **Northcliffe, Lord** (1865–1922) Irish-born British newspaper proprietor

35 The sun does not set in my dominions.
In Schiller, *Don Carlos* (1787) **Philip II** (1527–1598) King of Spain

36 Unlimited power is apt to corrupt the minds of those who possess it.
Speech, House of Commons, (1770) **Pitt, William** (1708–1778) English politician and Prime Minister

37 Through obedience learn to command.
Leges **Plato** (c.429–347 BC) Greek philosopher

38 Get Place and Wealth, if possible, with Grace;
If not, by any means get Wealth and Place.
Imitations of Horace (1737–1738) **Pope, Alexander** (1688–1744) English poet, translator and editor

39 Fain would I climb, yet fear I to fall.
Attr. **Raleigh, Sir Walter** (c.1552–1618) English courtier, explorer, military commander, poet, historian and essayist. Written on a window-pane, and referring to his ambitions at the court of Elizabeth I

40 Such men as he be never at heart's ease
Whiles they behold a greater than themselves,
And therefore are they very dangerous.
Julius Caesar, I.ii Of Cassius

41 'Tis a common proof
That lowliness is young ambition's ladder,
Whereto the climber-upward turns his face;
But when he once attains the upmost round,
He then unto the ladder turns his back,
Looks in the clouds, scorning the base degrees
By which he did ascend.
Julius Caesar, II.i

42 The general's disdain'd
By him one step below, he by the next,
That next by him beneath; so every step,
Exampl'd by the first pace that is sick
Of his superior, grows to an envious fever
Of pale and bloodless emulation.
Troilus and Cressida, I.iii **Shakespeare, William**
(1564–1616) English dramatist, poet and actor

43 Titles distinguish the mediocre, embarrass
the superior, and are disgraced by the
inferior.
Man and Superman (1903) **Shaw, George
Bernard** (1856–1950) Irish socialist, writer,
dramatist and critic

44 'Knowledge is power' is the finest idea ever
put into words.
Dialogues et fragments philosophiques (1876)
Renan, J. Ernest (1823–1892) French
philologist, writer and historian

45 The megalomaniac differs from the
narcissist by the fact that he wishes to be
powerful rather than charming, and seeks
to be feared rather than loved. To this type
belong many lunatics and most of the
great men of history.
The Conquest of Happiness (1930) **Russell,
Bertrand** (1872–1970) English philosopher,
mathematician, essayist and social reformer

46 And thus, place, that great object which
divides the wives of aldermen, is the end of
half the labours of human life; and is the
cause of all the tumult and bustle, all the
rapine and injustice, which avarice and
ambition have introduced into this world.
The Theory of Moral Sentiments (1759) **Smith,
Adam** (1723–1790) Scottish economist,
philosopher and essayist

47 Power corrupts, but lack of power corrupts
absolutely.
The Observer, (1963) **Stevenson, Adlai** (1900–
1965) US lawyer, statesman and United
Nations ambassador

48 He aspired to power instead of influence,
and as a result forfeited both.
English History, 1914–1945 (1965) **Taylor, A.J.P.**
(1906–1990) English historian, writer,
broadcaster and lecturer. Of Lord Northcliffe

49 I'm extraordinarily patient provided I get
my own way in the end.
The Observer, (1983)

50 I love being at the centre of things.
Reader's Digest, (1984) **Thatcher, Margaret**
(1925–) English Conservative Prime Minister

51 Athens holds sway over all Greece; I
dominate Athens; my wife dominates me;
our newborn son dominates her.
Attr. **Themistocles** (c.528–462 BC) Athenian
soldier and statesman. Explaining his remark
that his young son ruled all Greece

52 God is always on the side of the big
battalions.
Attr. **Turenne, Henri, Vicomte** (1611–1675)
French marshal
See also government; monarchy and royalty;
politics

PRAISE

1 For as it is said of calumny, 'calumniate
boldly, for some of it will stick' so it may be
said of ostentation (except it be in a
ridiculous degree of deformity), 'boldly
sound your own praises, and some of them
will stick.'
Of the Dignity and Advancement of Learning
(1623) **Bacon, Francis** (1561–1626) English
philosopher, essayist, politician and courtier

2 Let us now praise famous men, and our
fathers that begat us.
Apocrypha, Ecclesiasticus, 44:1 **The Bible (King
James Version)**

3 *Eulogy:* Praise of a person who has either
the advantages of wealth and power, or the
consideration to be dead.
The Enlarged Devil's Dictionary (1961) **Bierce,
Ambrose** (1842–c.1914) US writer, verse writer
and soldier

4 Greatly his foes he dreads, but more his
friends;
He hurts me most who lavishly
commends.
'The Apology, addressed to the Critical
Reviewers' (1761) **Churchill, Charles** (1731–
1764) English poet, political writer and
clergyman

5 Praising all alike, is praising none.
'A Letter to a Lady' (1714) **Gay, John** (1685–1732) English poet, dramatist and librettist

6 All censure of a man's self is oblique praise. It is in order to shew how much he can spare.
In Boswell, *The Life of Samuel Johnson* (1791)

7 The applause of a single human being is of great consequence.
In Boswell, *The Life of Samuel Johnson* (1791) **Johnson, Samuel** (1709–1784) English lexicographer, poet, critic, conversationalist and essayist

8 Never praise a sister to a sister, in the hope of your compliments reaching the proper ears ... Sisters are women first, and sisters afterward; and you will find that you do yourself harm.
Plain Tales from the Hills (1888) **Kipling, Rudyard** (1865–1936) Indian-born British poet and writer

9 Refusal of praise reveals a desire to be praised twice over.
Maximes (1678) **La Rochefoucauld** (1613–1680) French writer

10 A single grateful thought raised to heaven is the most perfect prayer.
Minna von Barnhelm (1767) **Lessing, Gotthold Ephraim** (1729–1781) German dramatist, critic and theologian

11 They praise those works but they read something else.
Epigrammata **Martial** (c.AD 40–c.104) Spanish-born Latin epigrammatist and poet

12 Fondly we think we honour merit then, When we but praise ourselves in other men.
An Essay on Criticism (1711) **Pope, Alexander** (1688–1744) English poet, translator and editor

13 Ah! Madam, ... you know every thing in the world but your perfections, and you only know not those, because 'tis the top of perfection not to know them.
Incognita (1692) **Congreve, William** (1670–1729) English dramatist

14 Self-praise is no recommendation.
Proverb

15 I will praise any man that will praise me.
Antony and Cleopatra, II.vi **Shakespeare, William** (1564–1616) English dramatist, poet and actor

16 Yes, sir, puffing is of various sorts; the principal are, the puff direct, the puff preliminary, the puff collateral, the puff collusive, and the puff oblique, or puff by implication.
The Critic (1779) **Sheridan, Richard Brinsley** (1751–1816) Irish dramatist, politician and orator

17 Praise is the best diet for us, after all.
In Holland, *A Memoir of the Reverend Sydney Smith* (1855) **Smith, Sydney** (1771–1845) English clergyman, essayist, journalist and wit

18 He was a great patriot, a humanitarian, a loyal friend – provided, of course, that he really is dead.
Attr. **Voltaire** (1694–1778) French philosopher, dramatist, poet, historian, writer and critic. Giving a funeral oration

19 I can honestly say that I always look on Pauline as one of the nicest girls I was ever engaged to.
Thank You Jeeves (1934) **Wodehouse, P.G.** (1881–1975) English humorist and writer
See also egoism; pride

PRIDE

1 'Tis pride, rank pride, and haughtiness of soul;
I think the Romans call it stoicism.
Cato (1713) **Addison, Joseph** (1672–1719) English essayist, poet, playwright and statesman

2 Pride goeth before destruction, and an haughty spirit before a fall.
Proverbs, 16:18 **The Bible (King James Version)**

3 Proude as a pecocke.
The Life of Saint Werburge (1521) **Bradshaw, Henry** (d.1513) Monk and theologian

4 And the Devil did grin, for his darling sin Is pride that apes humility.
'The Devil's Thoughts' (1799) **Coleridge, Samuel Taylor** (1772–1834) English poet, philosopher and critic

5 I know my life's a pain and but a span,
  I know my sense is mock'd in every thing;
  And to conclude, I know myself a man,
  Which is a proud and yet a wretched thing.
  Nosce Teipsum (1599) **Davies, Sir John** (1569–
  1626) English poet and politician

6 It is difficult to be humble. Even if you aim
  at humility, there is no guarantee that
  when you have attained the state you will
  not be proud of the feat.
  John Wesley **Dobrée, Bonamy** (1891–1974)
  English academic, critic and editor

7 I know not whether I am proud,
  But this I know, I hate the crowd.
  'With an Album' **Landor, Walter Savage** (1775–
  1864) English poet and writer

8 Pride in your history is pride
  In living what your fathers died,
  Is pride in taking your own pulse
  And counting in you someone else.
  'Suite for recorders' (1966) **MacNeice, Louis**
  (1907–1963) Belfast-born poet, writer, radio
  producer, translator and critic

9 Pride, the never-failing vice of fools.
  An Essay on Criticism (1711) **Pope, Alexander**
  (1688–1744) English poet, translator and editor

10 Be modest! It is the kind of pride least
   likely to offend.
   Journal

11 There is false modesty, but there is no false
   pride.
   Journal **Renard, Jules** (1864–1910) French
   writer and dramatist

12 Honour pricks me on. Yea, but how if
   honour prick me off when I come on? How
   then? Can honour set to a leg? No. Or an
   arm? No. Or take away the grief of a
   wound? No. Honour hath no skill in
   surgery, then? No. What is honour? A
   word. What is in that word? Honour. What
   is that honour? Air. A trim reckoning! Who
   hath it? He that died o' Wednesday. Doth
   he feel it? No. Doth he hear it? No. 'Tis
   insensible, then? Yea, to the dead. But will
   it not live with the living? No. Why?
   Detraction will not suffer it. Therefore I'll
   none of it. Honour is a mere scutcheon.
   And so ends my catechism.
   Henry IV, Part 1, V.i

13 O world, how apt the poor are to be proud!
   Twelfth Night, III.i **Shakespeare, William**
   (1564–1616) English dramatist, poet and actor

14 But human pride
   Is skilful to invent most serious names
   To hide its ignorance.
   Queen Mab (1813) **Shelley, Percy Bysshe** (1792–
   1822) English poet, dramatist and essayist
   See also egoism; self

PRISON

1 I lived at Eton in the 1950s and know all
  about life in uncomfortable quarters.
  The Times, (1999) **Aitken, Jonathan** (1942–)
  English Conservative politician. On prison

2 Prisons are built with stones of Law,
  Brothels with bricks of Religion.
  The Marriage of Heaven and Hell (c.1790–1793)
  Blake, William (1757–1827) English poet,
  engraver, painter and mystic

3 *Visitor:* Ah, Bottomley, sewing?
  Bottomley: No, reaping.
  Attr. **Bottomley, Horatio William** (1860–1933)
  English journalist, politician and bankrupt.
  When spotted sewing mailbags during his
  imprisonment for misappropriation of funds

4 Prisoners and warders – we are all of one
  blood.
  They're much alike, except for a different
  coat
  And a different hat;
  And they all seem decent, kindly fellows
  enough
  As they work and chat:
  How can it be that men like this have been
  hanged
  By men like that?
  In O.E. Burton, *In Prison* (1945) **Dowling, Basil
  Cairns** (1777–1834) New Zealand poet and
  pacifist

5 When you have survived life in a
  concentration camp you have ceased to
  count yourself as a member of the human
  race. You will forever be outside the
  experience of the rest of mankind.
  In the *Daily Mail,* (1996) **Frank, Otto** (1889–
  1980) Dutch concentration camp survivor and
  father of Anne Frank

6 The black flower of civilized society, a
prison.
The Scarlet Letter (1850)

7 What other dungeon is so dark as one's
own heart! What jailer so inexorable as
one's self!
The House of the Seven Gables (1851) **Hawthorne,
Nathaniel** (1804–1864) US allegorical writer

8 The only thing I really mind about going to
prison is the thought of Lord Longford
coming to visit me.
Attr. **Ingrams, Richard** (1937–) British
journalist and editor of *Private Eye*. On the
prospect of going to jail, 1976

9 I would be the voyeur of myself. This
strategy I employed for the rest of my
captivity. I allowed myself to do and be and
say and think and feel all the things that
were in me, but at the same time could
stand outside observing and attempting to
understand.
An Evil Cradling **Keenan, Brian** (1950–) Irish
journalist and hostage in Lebanon

10 The worst survived – that is, the fittest; the
best all died.
The Drowned and the Saved (1988) **Levi, Primo**
(1919–1987) Italian writer, poet and chemist;
survivor of Auschwitz. Of the Nazi
concentration camps

11 Stone walls do not a prison make
Nor iron bars a cage;
Minds innocent and quiet take
That for an hermitage;
If I have freedom in my love,
And in my soul am free;
Angels alone, that soar above,
Enjoy such liberty.
'To Althea, From Prison' (1649) **Lovelace,
Richard** (1618–1658) English poet

12 The world itself is but a large prison, out of
which some are daily led to execution.
Attr. Said after his trial for treason, 1603

13 But now close kept, as captives wonted are:
That food, that heat, that light I find no
more;
Despair bolts up my doors, and I alone
Speak to dead walls, but those hear not my
moan.

Untitled poem **Raleigh, Sir Walter** (c.1552–
1618) English courtier, explorer, military
commander, poet, historian and essayist

14 So you put a man in jail because he can't
talk properly?
Vidas secas (Dry Lives, 1938) **Ramos, Graciliano**
(1892–1953) Brazilian writer

15 Forget the outside world. Life has different
laws in here. This is Campland, an invisible
country. It's not in the geography books, or
the psychology books or the history books.
This is the famous country where ninety-
nine men weep while one laughs.
The Love-Girl and the Innocent **Solzhenitsyn,
Alexander** (1918–) Russian writer, dramatist
and historian

16 Under a government which imprisons any
unjustly, the true place for a just man is
also a prison.
Civil Disobedience (1849) **Thoreau, Henry
David** (1817–1862) US essayist, social critic and
writer

17 Anyone who has been to an English public
school will always feel comparatively at
home in prison.
Decline and Fall (1928) **Waugh, Evelyn** (1903–
1966) English writer and diarist

18 I know not whether Laws be right,
Or whether Laws be wrong;
All that we know who lie in gaol
Is that the wall is strong;
And that each day is like a year,
A year whose days are long –
The vilest deeds like poison-weeds
Bloom well in prison-air;
It is only what is good in Man
That wastes and withers there:
Pale Anguish keeps the heavy gate
And the warder is Despair.
The Ballad of Reading Gaol (1898)

19 If this is the way Queen Victoria treats her
prisoners, she doesn't deserve to have any.
Attr. Complaining at having to wait in the
rain for transport to take him to prison
Wilde, Oscar (1854–1900) Irish poet,
dramatist, writer, critic and wit
See also crime; law; judgement; justice and
injustice

PROVERBS

1 Among the Ibo the art of conversation is regarded very highly and proverbs are the palm-oil with which words are eaten.
Things Fall Apart (1958) **Achebe, Chinua** (1930–) Nigerian writer, poet and critic

2 He that spareth his rod hateth his son.
Proverbs, 13:24 **The Bible (King James Version)**

3 Much matter decocted into a few words.
The History of the Worthies of England (1662) **Fuller, Thomas** (1608–1661) English churchman and antiquary. Definition of a proverb

4 Nothing is so useless as a general maxim.
Collected Essays (1843), 'Machiavelli' **Macaulay, Lord** (1800–1859) English Liberal statesman, essayist and poet

5 It is only one step from the sublime to the ridiculous.
In De Pradt, *Histoire de l'Ambassade dans le grand-duché de Varsovie en 1812* (1815) **Napoleon I** (1769–1821) Emperor of France and king of Italy

6 A proverb is one man's wit and all men's wisdom.
In R.J. Mackintosh, *Sir James Mackintosh* (1835) **Russell, Lord John** (1792–1878) English Liberal Prime Minister and writer

7 A bad workman always blames his tools.

8 A bird in the hand is worth two in the bush.

9 A cat has nine lives.

10 A cat may look at a king.

11 A fool and his money are soon parted.

12 A fool at forty is a fool indeed.

13 A friend in need is a friend indeed.

14 A good face is a letter of recommendation.

15 A good scare is worth more than good advice.

16 A guest always brings pleasure: if not the arrival, the departure.
Portuguese proverb

17 A hedge between keeps friendship green.

18 A judge knows nothing unless it has been explained to him three times.

19 A liar is worse than a thief.

20 A man can die but once.

21 A meal without flesh is like feeding on grass.

22 A tale never loses in the telling.

23 All are not saints that go to church.

24 All cats are grey in the dark.

25 All is fair in love and war.

26 All the world loves a lover.

27 All work and no play makes Jack a dull boy.

28 Although there exist many thousand subjects for elegant conversation, there are persons who cannot meet a cripple without talking about feet.
Chinese Proverb

29 An apple pie without some cheese is like a kiss without a squeeze.

30 An atheist is one point beyond the devil.

31 An hour in the morning is worth two in the evening.

32 Any publicity is good publicity.

33 Ask a silly question and you'll get a silly answer.

34 Ask no questions, and hear no lies.

35 Bad news travels fast.

36 Barking dogs seldom bite.

37 The beak of the goose is no longer than that of the gander.

38 Be happy while y'er leevin,
For y'er a lang time deid.
Scottish motto

39 Be not afraid of growing slowly, be afraid only of standing still.
Chinese Proverb

40 Beauty is only skin-deep.

41 Beauty is potent but money is omnipotent.

42 Believe nothing of what you hear, and only half of what you see.

43 Better a lie that heals than a truth that wounds.

44 Better be a fool than a knave.

45 Better be envied than pitied.

46 Better be safe than sorry.

47 Books and friends should be few but good.

48 Borrowed garments never fit well.

49 Bread is the staff of life.

50 Civility costs nothing.

51 Cold hands, warm heart.

52 Craft maun hae claes, but truth goes naked.
Scots proverb

53 Curiosity killed the cat.

54 Danger and delight grow on one stalk.

55 Death is the great leveller.

56 Doing is better than saying.

57 Don't put all your eggs in one basket.

58 Don't teach your grandmother to suck eggs.

59 Don't throw the baby out with the bathwater.

60 Don't wash your dirty linen in public.

61 Early to bed and early to rise, makes a man healthy, wealthy and wise.

62 Easier said than done.

63 East, west, home's best.

64 Empty vessels make the greatest sound.

65 Every man for himself and the devil take the hindmost.

66 Every month one should get drunk at least once.
French proverb

67 Every one is innocent until he is proved guilty.

68 Everything comes to him who waits.

69 Experience is the best teacher.

70 Experience is the mother of wisdom.

71 The eye is bigger than the belly.

72 Familiarity breeds contempt.

73 Fear of death is worse than death itself.

74 Fine feathers make fine birds.

75 Fine words butter no parsnips.

76 Fingers were made before forks, and hands before knives.

77 Fools build houses, and wise men buy them.

78 Forgive and forget.

79 From small beginnings come great things.

80 Go to bed with the lamb, and rise with the lark.

81 God could not be everywhere, so therefore he made mothers.
Jewish proverb

82 God helps them that help themselves.

83 Great oaks from little acorns grow.

84 Handsome is as handsome does.

85 Haste makes waste.

86 He that fights and runs away, may live to fight another day.

87 He travels fastest who travels alone.

88 He who sups with the devil should have a long spoon.

89 Health is better than wealth.

90 History repeats itself.

91 Home is where the heart is.

92 Hunger finds no fault with the cookery.

93 Hunger is the best sauce.

94 In love, there is always one who kisses, and one who offers his cheek.

95 If at first you don't succeed, try, try, try again.

96 If there's a hen or a goose, it's on the priest's table you'll find it.
Irish proverb

97 If you are patient in one moment of anger, you will escape a hundred days of sorrow.
Chinese Proverb

98 If you can't be good, be careful.

99 If you trust before you try, you may repent before you die.

100 Imitation is the sincerest form of flattery.

101 It is better to be born lucky than rich.

102 It is easy to be wise after the event.

103 Keep your mouth shut and your eyes open.

104 Knowledge is power.

105 Laugh and grow fat.

106 Laugh before breakfast, you'll cry before supper.

107 Laughter is brightest where food is best.

108 Laughter is the best medicine.

109 Lend only what you can afford to lose.

110 Long absent, soon forgotten.

111 Look before you leap.

112 Love conquers all.

113 Love is blind.

114 Love laughs at locksmiths.

115 Love me, love my dog.

116 Lucky at cards, unlucky in love.

117 Man fools himself. He prays for a long life, and he fears an old age.
Chinese saying

118 Many a true word is spoken in jest.

119 Many hands make light work.

120 Marriages are made in heaven.

121 Marry in haste, and repent at leisure.

122 Moderation in all things.

123 More haste, less speed.

124 Necessity is the mother of invention.

125 Never too late to learn.

126 Never put off till tomorrow what you can do today.

127 Ninety per cent of inspiration is perspiration.

128 No love like the first love.

129 No news is good news.

130 No time like the present.

131 None so deaf as those who will not hear.

132 Nothing succeeds like success.

133 Old habits die hard.

134 One good turn deserves another.

135 One who looks for a friend without faults will have none.

136 Opportunity seldom knocks twice.

137 Out of sight, out of mind.

138 Patience is a virtue.

139 Possession is nine points of the law.

140 Prevention is better than cure.

141 Punctuality is the politeness of princes.

142 Put off the evil hour as long as you can.

143 Revenge is a dish that tastes better cold.

144 Revenge is sweet.

145 Saying is one thing, and doing another.

146 Seeing is believing.

147 Sickness comes on horseback and departs on foot.
Dutch Proverb

148 Silence is golden.

149 Spare the rod and spoil the child.

150 Take care of the pence, and the pounds will take care of themselves.

151 Talk of the devil, and he is bound to appear.

152 The devil finds work for idle hands to do.

153 The devil is not so black as he is painted.

154 The devil looks after his own.

155 The early bird catches the worm.

156 The first day a guest, the second day a guest, the third day a calamity.

157 The full man doesn't understand the wants of the hungry.

158 The good die young.

159 The health of the salmon to you.
Irish toast

160 The nearer the bone the sweeter the flesh.

161 The reverse side also has a reverse side.
Japanese proverb

162 The road to a friend's house is never long.
Danish proverb

163 The road to hell is paved with good intentions.

164 There's no fool like an old fool.

165 There's no smoke without fire.

166 There's one law for the rich, and another for the poor.

167 There's only one pretty child in the world, and every mother has it.

168 There is honour among thieves.

169 There is much meat in God's storehouse.
Danish proverb

170 There will be sleeping enough in the grave.

171 Throw dirt enough, and some will stick.

172 Throw out a sprat to catch a mackerel.

173 Time is a great healer.

174 To change and to change for the better are two different things.
German proverb

175 To err is human; to forgive divine.

176 Travel broadens the mind.

177 True love never grows cold.

178 Truth is stranger than fiction.

179 Truth will out.

180 Vice is often clothed in virtue's habit.

181 Walls have ears.

182 What can't be cured, must be endured.

183 What you don't know can't hurt you.

184 When poverty comes in at the door, love flies out of the window.

185 When the cat's away, the mice will play.

186 With a Scotsman or a priest, don't begin a lawsuit.
See also advice

RACE

1 Bring on your tear gas, bring on your grenades, your new supplies of Mace, your state troopers and even your national guards. But let the record show we ain't going to be turned around.
And the Walls Came Tumbling Down (1989)

2 I'm sick and tired of black and white people of good intent giving aspirin to a society that is dying of a cancerous disease.
And the Walls Came Tumbling Down (1989)
Abernathy, Ralph (1926–1990) US religious and civil rights leader

3 The future is ... black.
The Observer, (1963) **Baldwin, James** (1924–1987) US writer, dramatist, poet and civil rights activist

4 The Anti-Semite is a man so absorbed in his subject that he loses interest in any matter unless he can give it some association with his delusion, for delusion it is. The Jew cannot help feeling superior, but he can help the expression of that superiority – at any rate he can modify such expression.
'The Jews' (1922) **Belloc, Hilaire** (1870–1953) English writer of verse, essayist and critic; Liberal MP

5 We wanted to remove him [the white man] from our table, strip the table of all the trappings put on it by him, decorate it in true African style, settle down and then ask him to join us if he liked.
Speech, (1971) **Biko, Steve** (1946–1977) Black South African civil rights leader; murdered in police custody

6 People who criticise Joh unfairly make me
angry. They call him 'a racist pig' in
Canberra. Joh's not a racist. Why, he's had
Aborigines working for him.
Woman's Day, (1975) **Bjelke-Petersen, Florence
Isabel** (1920–) Wife of Sir Johannes Bjelke-
Petersen, Premier of Queensland. On her
husband

7 Kafirs? (said Oom Schalk Lourens), Yes, I
know them. And they're all the same. I fear
the Almighty, and I respect His works, but I
could never understand why He made the
kafir and the rinderpest.
Mafeking Road (1947) **Bosman, Herman
Charles** (1905–1951) South African writer

8 Racism? But isn't it only a form of
misanthropy?
Less Than One (1986) **Brodsky, Joseph** (1940–
1996) Russian poet, essayist, critic and exile

9 I feel not in myself those common
antipathies that I can discover in others;
those national repugnances do not touch
me, nor do I behold with prejudice the
French, Italian, Spaniard, or Dutch; but
where I find their actions in balance with
my countrymen's, I honour, love and
embrace them in the same degree.
Religio Medici (1643) **Browne, Sir Thomas**
(1605–1682) English physician, author and
antiquary

10 There are many Wongs in the Chinese
community, but I have to say – and I am
sure that the honourable member for
Balaclava will not mind me doing so – that
'two Wongs do not make a White'.
Commonwealth Parliamentary Debates, (1947)
Calwell, Arthur Augustus (1894–1973)
Australian Labour politician. Defending the
deportation of a Chinese refugee who, Calwell
claimed, was not eligible to become a
permanent resident of Australia

11 Bigotry may be roughly defined as the
anger of men who have no opinions.
Heretics (1905) **Chesterton, G.K.** (1874–1936)
English writer, poet and critic

12 If you're not part of the solution, you're
part of the problem.
Attr. **Cleaver, Eldridge** (1935–1998) US black
leader and activist

13 Being a star has made it possible for me to
get insulted in places where the average
Negro could never hope to get insulted.
Yes I can (1965) **Davis Jnr., Sammy** (1925–1990)
US entertainer and singer

14 I suffer from an incurable disease – colour
blindness.
Attr. **De Blank, Joost** (1908–1968) Dutch-born
British churchman

15 All is race; there is no other truth.
Tancred (1847) **Disraeli, Benjamin** (1804–1881)
English statesman and writer

16 If my theory of relativity is proven
successful, Germany will claim me as a
German and France will declare that I am a
citizen of the world. Should my theory
prove untrue, France will say that I am a
German and Germany will declare that I
am a Jew.
Address, (c.1929) **Einstein, Albert** (1879–1955)
German-born US mathematical physicist

17 Is not the Turk a man and a brother?
Querela Pacis **Erasmus** (c.1466–1536) Dutch
scholar and humanist

18 For the black man there is only one
destiny. And it is white.
Black Skin, White Masks **Fanon, Frantz** (1925–
1961) West Indian psychoanalyst and
philosopher

19 The so-called white races are really pinko-
grey.
A Passage to India (1924) **Forster, E.M.** (1879–
1970) English writer, essayist and literary
critic

20 … to place before me soon a complete
proposal for the organisational, practical
and material preliminary measures which
have to be taken in order to bring about
the desired Final Solution to the Jewish
question.
Letter to Reinhard Heydrich, (1941) **Goebbels,
Joseph** (1897–1945) Nazi politician

21 The force of white men's wills, which
dispensed and withdrew life, imprisoned
and set free, fed or starved, like God
himself.
Six Feet of the Country (1956) **Gordimer, Nadine**
(1923–) South African writer

22 We are men, you and I.
King Solomon's Mines (1885) **Haggard, H. Rider** (1856–1925) English novelist. Umbopa to Quatermain

23 Whoever is not racially pure in this world is chaff.
Mein Kampf (1925) **Hitler, Adolf** (1889–1945) German Nazi dictator, born in Austria

24 I hear that melting-pot stuff a lot, and all I can say is that we haven't melted.
Playboy, (1969) **Jackson, Jesse** (1941–) US clergyman and civil rights leader

25 The old men running the industry just have not got a clue ... Britain is no longer totally a white place where people ride horses, wear long frocks and drink tea. The national dish is no longer fish and chips, it's curry.
The Observer, (1997) **Jean-Baptiste, Marianne** (1967–) English actress

26 I want to be the white man's brother, not his brother-in-law.
New York Journal – American, (1962)

27 Now, I say to you today my friends, even though we face the difficulties of today and tomorrow, I still have a dream. It is a dream deeply rooted in the American dream. I have a dream that one day this nation will rise up and live out the true meaning of its creed: – 'We hold these truths to be self-evident, that all men are created equal'.
Speech at civil rights march on Washington, (August 28, 1963)

28 I have a dream that my four little children will one day live in a nation where they will not be judged by the colour of their skin but by the content of their character.
Speech at civil rights march on Washington, (August 28, 1963)

29 We must learn to live together as brothers or perish together as fools.
Speech at St. Louis, (March 22, 1964) **King, Martin Luther** (1929–1968) US civil rights leader and Baptist minister

30 When old settlers say 'One has to understand the country', what they mean is, 'You have to get used to our ideas about the native.' They are saying, in effect, 'Learn our ideas, or otherwise get out; we don't want you.'
The Grass is Singing (1950) Referring to South Africa

31 When a white man in Africa by accident looks into the eyes of a native and sees the human being (which it is his chief preoccupation to avoid), his sense of guilt, which he denies, fumes up in resentment and he brings down the whip.
The Grass is Singing (1950) **Lessing, Doris** (1919–) British writer, brought up in Zimbabwe

32 I look at an ant and I see myself: a native South African, endowed by nature with a strength much greater than my size so I might cope with the weight of a racism that crushes my spirit.
Makeba, My Story (1987) **Makeba, Miriam** (1932–) South African singer

33 If you're born in America with a black skin, you're born in prison.
Interview, (June 1963)

34 We never made one step forward until world pressure put Uncle Sam on the spot ... It has never been out of any internal sense of morality or legality or humanism that we were allowed to advance.
Speech, (1964)

35 I believe in the brotherhood of all men, but I don't believe in wasting brotherhood on anyone who doesn't want to practise it with me.
Speech, (1964)

36 The Negro problem has ceased to be a Negro problem. It has ceased to be an American problem and has now become a world problem, a problem for all humanity.
Speech, Harvard Law School, (1964)

37 The soul of Africa is still reflected in the music played by the black man. In everything else we do we still are African in color, feeling, everything. And we will always be that whether we like it or not.

Speech, Harvard Law School, (1964) **Malcolm X** (1925–1965) US black leader

38 I have fought against white domination, and I have fought against black domination. I have cherished the ideal of a democratic and free society in which all persons will live together in harmony and with equal opportunities. It is an ideal which I hope to live for and achieve. But, if needs be, it is an ideal for which I am prepared to die.
Statement in the dock, (1964) **Mandela, Nelson** (1918–) South African statesman and President

39 God never made no difference between black, white, blue, pink or green. People is people, y'know.
Attr. **Marley, Bob** (1945–1981) Jamaican singer and cultural icon

40 Since my daughter is only half-Jewish, could she go into the water up to her knees?
The Observer, (1977) **Marx, Groucho** (1895–1977) US comedian. When excluded, on racial grounds, from a beach club

41 The evil of modern society isn't that it creates racism but that it creates conditions in which people who don't suffer from injustice seem incapable of caring very much about people who do.
The New Yorker, (1992) **Menand, Louis** (1952–) US writer

42 One of the things that makes a Negro unpleasant to white folk is the fact that he suffers from their injustice. He is thus a standing rebuke to them.
Notebooks (1956) **Mencken, H.L.** (1880–1956) US writer, critic, philologist and satirist

43 For anything I see, foreigners are fools.
In Boswell, *The Life of Samuel Johnson* (1791) **Meynell, Hugo** (1727–1780) Frequenter of London society, acquaintance of Dr Johnson

44 If there weren't any anti-semitism, I wouldn't think of myself as Jewish.
The Observer, (1995) **Miller, Arthur** (1915–2005) US dramatist and screenwriter

45 I'm not really a Jew; just Jew-ish, not the whole hog.

Beyond the Fringe (1961) **Miller, Jonathan** (1934–) English writer, director, producer and physician

46 Abroad is unutterably bloody and foreigners are fiends.
The Pursuit of Love (1945)

47 I loathe abroad, nothing would induce me to live there … and, as for foreigners, they are all the same, and they all make me sick.
The Pursuit of Love (1945) **Mitford, Nancy** (1904–1973) English writer

48 I trudge the city pavements
side by side with 'madam'
who shifts her handbag
from my side to the other.
Sounds of a Cowhide Drum (1971) **Mtshali, Oswald** (1940–) South African poet

49 I have one great fear in my heart, that one day when they whites are turned to loving, they will find we blacks are turned to hating.
Cry, the Beloved Country (1948)

50 It was on Wednesday 16 June 1976 that an era came to an end in South Africa. That was the day when black South Africans said to white, 'You can't do this to us any more.' It had taken three hundred years for them to say that.
Journey Continued (1988) **Paton, Alan** (1903–1988) South African writer

51 Africa is not the white man's country.
Turbott Wolfe (1926)

52 The warm heart of any human that saw the black man first not as a black but as a man.
Turbott Wolfe (1926) **Plomer, William** (1903-1973) South African-born British writer and editor

53 As I look ahead I am filled with foreboding. Like the Roman I seem to see 'the River Tiber foaming with much blood.'
Speech, Birmingham, (1968) **Powell, Enoch** (1912–1998) English politician and scholar. On race relations in Britain

54 When you are black you never really know what is inside another man's heart.
Attr. **Richards, Viv** (1952–) West Indian cricketer

55 The African is my brother – but he is my younger brother by several centuries.
The Observer, (1955) **Schweitzer, Albert** (1875–1965) French Protestant theologian, physician and musician

56 Hath not a Jew eyes? Hath not a Jew hands, organs, dimensions, senses, affections, passions, fed with the same food, hurt with the same weapons, subject to the same diseases, healed by the same means, warmed and cooled by the same winter and summer, as a Christian is? If you prick us, do we not bleed? If you tickle us, do we not laugh? If you poison us, do we not die? And if you wrong us, shall we not revenge? If we are like you in the rest, we will resemble you in that.
The Merchant of Venice, III.i **Shakespeare, William** (1564–1616) English dramatist, poet and actor

57 The only good Indian is a dead Indian.
Attr. **Sheridan, Philip Henry** (1831–1888) US general

58 Britain does not wish to be ruled by a conglomerate in Europe which includes Third World nations such as the Greeks and Irish, nor for that matter the Italians and French, whose standards of political morality are not ours, and never will be.
The Independent, (August 1990) **Sherman, Alfred** (1919–) British journalist

59 I don't believe in black majority rule in Rhodesia ... not in a thousand years.
Speech, (1976) **Smith, Ian** (1919–) Prime Minister of what was Rhodesia (now Zimbabwe)

60 The truth is that Mozart, Pascal, Boolean algebra, Shakespeare, parliamentary government, baroque churches, Newton, the emancipation of women, Kant, Marx, and Ballanchine ballets don't redeem what this particular civilization has wrought upon the world. The white race is the cancer of human history.
Attr. **Sontag, Susan** (1933–2004) US critic and writer

61 Bigotry tries to keep truth safe in its hand With a grip that kills it.
Fireflies (1928) **Tagore, Rabindranath** (1861–1941) Indian poet and philosopher

62 Youngsters of all races born here should be taught that British history is their history, or they will forever be foreigners holding British passports, and this kingdom will become a Yugoslavia.
Speech, Conservative Party Conference, (1997) **Tebbitt, Norman** (1931–) English Conservative politician

63 Where today are the Pequot? Where are the Narragansett, the Mohican, the Pokanoket, and many other once powerful tribes of our people? They have vanished before the avarice and the oppression of the White Man, as snow before a summer sun.
In Brown, *Bury My Heart at Wounded Knee* (1971) **Tecumseh** (d. 1812) Native American chief of the Shawnees

64 Modern Physics is an instrument of Jewry for the destruction of Nordic science ... True physics is the creation of the German spirit.
In Shirer, *The Rise and Fall of the Third Reich* (1960) **Tomaschek, Rudolphe** (b. c.1895) German scientist

65 It is very difficult now to find anyone in South Africa who ever supported apartheid.
The Observer, (1994) **Tutu, Archbishop Desmond** (1931–) South African churchman and anti-apartheid campaigner

66 I believe that the Jews have made a contribution to the human condition out of all proportion to their numbers: I believe them to be an immense people. Not only have they supplied the world with two leaders of the stature of Jesus Christ and Karl Marx, but they have even indulged in the luxury of following neither one nor the other.
Dear Me (1977) **Ustinov, Sir Peter** (1921–2004) English actor, director, dramatist, writer and raconteur

67 ... I too well know its truth, from experience, that whenever any poor Gipsies are encamped anywhere and crimes and robberies &c. occur, it is invariably laid to their account, which is shocking; and if they are always looked upon as vagabonds, how can they become good people?

Journal, (1836) **Victoria, Queen** (1819–1901) Queen of the United Kingdom

68 Ignorance, arrogance and racism have bloomed as Superior Knowledge in all too many universities.
In Search of our Mothers' Gardens (1983) **Walker, Alice** (1944–) US writer and poet

69 The law of dislike for the unlike will always prevail. And whereas the unlike is normally situated at a safe distance, the Jews bring the unlike into the heart of every milieu, and must there defend a frontier line as large as the world.
Speech, (1911) **Zangwill, Israel** (1864–1926) English writer and Jewish spokesman
See also freedom

REALISM

1 My reality check bounced.
The Dilbert Principle **Adams, Scott** (1957–) US cartoonist

2 Be content with your lot; one cannot be first in everything.
Attr. **Aesop** (6th century BC) Legendary Greek writer of fables

3 You will never make a crab walk straight.
Peace **Aristophanes** (c.445–385 BC) Greek playwright

4 We are much beholden to Machiavel and others, that write what men do, and not what they ought to do.
The Advancement of Learning (1605)

5 There is a superstition in avoiding superstition.
'Of Superstition' (1625) **Bacon, Francis** (1561–1626) English philosopher, essayist, politician and courtier

6 There are no things, only processes.
Attr. **Bohm, David** (1917–1992) US physicist

7 Reality is what I see, not what you see.
The Sunday Times Magazine, (1983) **Burgess, Anthony** (1917–1993) English writer, linguist and composer

8 They must be comfortable people who have leisure to think about going to heaven! My most constant and pressing anxiety is to keep out of bedlam, that's all.
Letters and Memorials of Jane Welsh Carlyle (1883) **Carlyle, Jane Welsh** (1801–1866) Scottish letter writer, literary hostess and poet

9 Look, your worship ... those things which you see over there are not giants, but windmills.
Don Quixote (1605) **Cervantes, Miguel de** (1547–1616) Spanish writer and dramatist

10 As far as the laws of mathematics refer to reality, they are not certain, and as far as they are certain, they do not refer to reality.
In Capra, *The Tao of Physics* (1975) **Einstein, Albert** (1879–1955) German-born US mathematical physicist

11 Human kind
Cannot bear very much reality.
Four Quartets (1944) **Eliot, T.S.** (1888–1965) US-born British poet, verse dramatist and critic

12 What is rational is real, and what is real is rational.
Basis of Legal Philosophy (1820) **Hegel, Georg Wilhelm** (1770–1831) German philosopher

13 Facts do not cease to exist because they are ignored.
Proper Studies (1927) **Huxley, Aldous** (1894–1963) English writer, poet and critic

14 If you cannot catch a bird of paradise, better take a wet hen.
Attr. **Khrushchev, Nikita** (1894–1971) Russian statesman and Premier of the USSR

15 Strive not, my soul, for an immortal life, but make the most of the possibilities open to you.
Pythian Odes **Pindar** (518–438 BC) Greek lyric poet

16 'Blessed is the man who expects nothing, for he shall never be disappointed,' was the ninth beatitude which a man of wit (who like a man of wit was a long time in gaol) added to the eighth.
Letter to William Fortescue, (1725) **Pope, Alexander** (1688–1744) English poet, translator and editor

17 O wretched fool,
That liv'st to make thine honesty a vice!
O monstrous world! Take note, take note,
O world,
To be direct and honest is not safe.
Othello, III.iii **Shakespeare, William** (1564–1616) English dramatist, poet and actor

18 As an old soldier I admit the cowardice: it's as universal as sea sickness, and matters just as little.
Man and Superman (1903) **Shaw, George Bernard** (1856–1950) Irish socialist, writer, dramatist and critic

19 I remember the way we parted,
The day and the way we met;
You hoped we were both broken-hearted,
And knew we should both forget …
And the best and the worst of this is
That neither is most to blame,
If you have forgotten my kisses
And I have forgotten your name.
'An Interlude' (1866) **Swinburne, Algernon Charles** (1837–1909) English poet, critic, dramatist and letter writer

20 Don't part with your illusions. When they are gone, you may still exist, but you have ceased to live.
Pudd'nhead Wilson's Calendar (1894) **Twain, Mark** (1835–1910) US humorist, writer, journalist and lecturer

21 The nineteenth century dislike of Realism is
the rage of Caliban seeing his own face in a glass.
The Picture of Dorian Gray (1891) **Wilde, Oscar** (1854–1900) Irish poet, dramatist, writer, critic and wit
See also deception

REBELLION

1 Rioting is at least as English as thatched cottages and honey still for tea.
The Observer, (1985) **Ascherson, Neal** (1932–) Scottish journalist

2 The defiance of established authority, religious and secular, social and political, as a world-wide phenomenon may well one day be accounted the outstanding event of the last decade.
Crises of the Republic (1972) **Arendt, Hannah** (1906–1975) German-born US theorist

3 Revolutions may spring from trifles, but their issues are far from trifling.
Politics, I **Aristotle** (384–322 BC) Greek philosopher

4 As for rioting, the old Roman way of dealing with that is always the right one; flog the rank and file, and fling the ringleaders from the Tarpeian rock.
Letter, (written before 1828) **Arnold, Thomas** (1795–1842) English historian and educator

5 In his chamber, weak and dying,
While the Norman Baron lay,
Loud, without, his men were crying,
'Shorter hours and better pay.'
'A Strike among the Poets' **Anonymous**

6 The parliament intended to have hanged him; and he expected no less, but resolved to be hanged with the Bible under one arm and Magna Carta under the other.
Brief Lives (c.1693), 'David Jenkins' **Aubrey, John** (1626–1697) English antiquary, folklorist and biographer

7 When I was a young man I felt within me a sentiment of rebellion. I used to challenge, to use a fashionable word, everything.
The Geography of Italy (1975) **Berlinguer, Enrico** (1922–1984) Italian political leader

8 Revolutions are celebrated when they are no longer dangerous.
The Guardian, (1989) **Boulez, Pierre** (1925–) French conductor and composer

9 Rebellion to tyrants is obedience to God.
In Randall, *Life of Jefferson* (1865) **Bradshaw, John** (1602–1659) English judge and republican

10 If there be any among those common objects of hatred I do contemn and laugh at, it is that great enemy of reason, virtue, and religion, the multitude; that numerous piece of monstrosity, which, taken asunder,

seem men, and the reasonable creatures of God, but, confused together, make but one great beast, and a monstrosity more prodigious than Hydra.
Religio Medici (1643) **Browne, Sir Thomas** (1605–1682) English physician, author and antiquary

11 Make the Revolution a parent of settlement, and not a nursery of future revolutions.
Reflections on the Revolution in France (1790) **Burke, Edmund** (1729–1797) Irish-born British statesman and philosopher

12 The timeless, surly patience of the serf
That moves the nearest to the naked earth
And ploughs down palaces, and thrones, and towers.
Adamastor (1930), 'The Serf' **Campbell, Roy** (1901–1957) South African poet and journalist

13 All modern revolutions have led to a reinforcement of the power of the State.
The Rebel (1951)

14 What is a rebel? A man who says no.
The Rebel (1951)

15 Every revolutionary ends as an oppressor or a heretic.
The Rebel (1951) **Camus, Albert** (1913–1960) Algerian-born French writer

16 All criticism is opposition. All opposition is counter-revolutionary.
In John Newhouse, 'Socialism of Death', *The New Yorker,* (1992) **Castro, Fidel** (1927–) President of Cuba

17 The scrupulous and the just, the noble, humane, and devoted natures, the unselfish and the intelligent may begin a movement – but it passes away from them. They are not the leaders of a revolution. They are its victims.
Under Western Eyes (1911) **Conrad, Joseph** (1857–1924) Polish-born British writer, sailor and explorer

18 I have been ever of opinion that revolutions are not to be evaded.
Coningsby (1844) **Disraeli, Benjamin** (1804–1881) English statesman and writer

19 No one can go on being a rebel too long without turning into an autocrat.
Balthazar (1958) **Durrell, Lawrence** (1912–1990) Indian-born British poet and writer

20 Come mothers and fathers,
Throughout the land
And don't criticize
What you can't understand.
Your sons and your daughters
Are beyond your command
Your old road is rapidly agin'.
Please get out of the new one
If you can't lend your hand
For the times they are a-changin'.
'The Times they are A-changin' (song, 1964) **Dylan, Bob** (1941–) US singer and songwriter

21 Here once the embattled farmers stood,
And fired the shot heard round the world.
Poems (1847) **Emerson, Ralph Waldo** (1803–1882) US poet, essayist, transcendentalist and teacher

22 God sent me to piss off the world.
'My Name Is' (song, 2000) **Eminem** (1972–) White US rap musician and songwriter; born Marshall Mathers

23 The proletariat has nothing to lose but its chains in this revolution. It has a world to win. Workers of the world, unite!
The Communist Manifesto (1848) **Engels, Friedrich** (1820–1895) German socialist and political philosopher

24 How much the greatest event it is that ever happened in the world! and how much the best!
Letter, (1789) **Fox, Charles James** (1749–1806) English statesman and abolitionist. On the fall of the Bastille

25 Is it possible that my people live in such awful conditions? ... I tell you, Mr Wheatley, that if I had to live in conditions like that I would be a revolutionary myself.
In MacNeill Weir, *The Tragedy of Ramsay MacDonald* (1938) **George V** (1865–1936) King of the United Kingdom. On hearing Mr Wheatley's life story

26 Acknowledge us, oh God, before the whole world. Give us also the right to our existence!

The Well of Loneliness (1928) **Hall, Radclyffe** (1883–1943) English writer and poet

27 The first thing revolutionaries of the left or right give up is their sense of humour. The second thing is other people's rights.
In Winks (ed.), *Colloquium on Crime* (1986) **Hill, Reginald** (1936–) British writer and playwright

28 The first duty of the revolutionary is to get away with it.
Speech, (1966)

29 Sacred cows make the best hamburger.
Attr. **Hoffman, Abbie** (1936–1989) US political activist

30 One of the unpardonable sins, in the eyes of most people, is for a man to go about unlabelled. The world regards such a person as the police do an unmuzzled dog, not under proper control.
Evolution and Ethics (1893) **Huxley, T.H.** (1825–1895) English biologist, Darwinist and agnostic

31 It is better to die on your feet than to live on your knees.
Speech, Paris, (1936) **Ibárruri, Dolores ('La Pasionaria')** (1895–1989) Basque Communist leader

32 A little rebellion, now and then, is a good thing, and as necessary in the political world as storms in the physical.
Letter to James Madison, (January 30, 1787) **Jefferson, Thomas** (1743–1826) US Democrat statesman and President

33 Every revolution evaporates, leaving behind only the slime of a new bureaucracy.
'The Great Wall of China' **Kafka, Franz** (1883–1924) Czech-born German-speaking writer

34 A riot is at bottom the language of the unheard.
Chaos or Community (1967) **King, Martin Luther** (1929–1968) US civil rights leader and Baptist minister

35 If you feed people with revolutionary slogans alone they will listen today, they will listen tomorrow, they will listen the day after that, but on the fourth day they will say 'To hell with you!'.

Attr. **Khrushchev, Nikita** (1894–1971) Russian statesman and Premier of the USSR

36 The allure of popular culture has always been its promise of a walk on the wild side.
Landesman, Cosmo British journalist

37 No, Sire, it is a revolution.
Remark, (1789) **La Rochefoucauld-Liancourt, Duc de** (1747–1827) French social reformer and writer. In reply to Louis XVI's question 'C'est une révolte?' on hearing of the fall of the Bastille

38 The substitution of the proletarian for the bourgeois state is impossible without a violent revolution.
The State and Revolution (1917) **Lenin, V.I.** (1870–1924) Russian revolutionary, Marxist theoretician and first leader of the USSR

39 The 'homo' is the legitimate child of the 'suffragette'.
The Art of Being Ruled (1926)

40 The revolutionary simpleton is everywhere.
Time and Western Man (1927) **Lewis, Wyndham** (1882–1957) US-born British painter, critic and writer

41 Usually when people are sad, they don't do anything. They just cry over their condition. But when they get angry, they bring about a change.
Malcolm X Speaks, (1965) **Malcolm X** (1925–1965) US black leader

42 Nine times out of ten a revolutionary is merely a climber with a bomb in his pocket.
New English Weekly, (1939) **Orwell, George** (1903–1950) English writer and critic

43 A share in two revolutions is living to some purpose.
In Eric Foner, *Tom Paine and Revolutionary America* (1976) **Paine, Thomas** (1737–1809) English-born US political theorist and pamphleteer

44 I have gone to war too ... I am going to fight capitalism even if it kills me. It is wrong that people like you should be comfortable and well fed while all around you people are starving.

In David Mitchell, *The Fighting Pankhursts*
Pankhurst, Sylvia (1882–1960) English
suffragette, pacifist and internationalist

45 Revolutions are not made; they come. A
revolution is as natural a growth as an oak,
It comes out of the past. Its foundations
are laid far back.
Speech in Congress, (1852) **Phillips, Wendell**
(1811–1884) US abolitionist politician

46 There is a homely old adage which runs,
'Speak softly and carry a big stick; you will
go far.'
Speech, (1903) **Roosevelt, Theodore** (1858–
1919) US Republican President

47 I know, and all the world knows, that
revolutions never go backward.
Speech at Rochester on the Irrepressible
Conflict, (1858) **Seward, William** (1801–1872)
US statesman

48 Rebellion lay in his way, and he found it.
Henry IV, Part 1, V.i

49 A little fire is quickly trodden out,
Which, being suffer'd, rivers cannot
quench.
Henry VI, Part 3, IV.viii

50 If you can look into the seeds of time
And say which grain will grow and which
will not,
Speak then to me, who neither beg nor
fear
Your favours nor your hate.
Macbeth, I.iii **Shakespeare, William** (1564–1616)
English dramatist, poet and actor

51 They are, in my mind, responsible for most
of the degeneration that has happened, not
only musically but also in the sense of
youth orientation and politically, too. They
are the people who made it first publicly
acceptable to spit in the eye of authority.
Sinatra, Frank (1915–1998) US actor and
singer. On The Beatles

52 My earliest memory is pretending to be
dead. My mum used to step over me while
I was laying on the kitchen floor.
Attr. (1993) **Siouxsie Sioux** (1957–) English
punk-rock singer

53 It is harder to rebel against love than
against authority.
Attr. **Storr, Dr Anthony** (1920–2000) British
writer and psychiatrist

54 He who has not lived during the years
around 1789 cannot know what is meant by
the joy of living.
In M. Guizot, *Mémoires pour servir à l'histoire de
mon temps* (1858) **Talleyrand, Charles-Maurice
de** (1754–1838) French statesman, memoirist
and prelate. Of the French Revolution

55 Where force is necessary, one should make
use of it boldly, resolutely, and right to the
end. But it is as well to know the
limitations of force; to know where to
combine force with manoeuvre, assault
with conciliation.
What Next? (1932)

56 The fundamental premise of a revolution is
that the existing social structure has
become incapable of solving the urgent
problems connected with the development
of the nation.
History of the Russian Revolution (1933)

57 Revolutions are always verbose.
History of the Russian Revolution (1933)

58 The revolution does not choose its paths, it
makes its first steps towards victory under
the belly of a Cossack's horse.
History of the Russian Revolution (1933)

59 Insurrection is an art, and like all arts it has
its laws.
History of the Russian Revolution (1933)

60 In a serious struggle there is no worse
cruelty than to be magnanimous at an
inappropriate time.
The History of the Russian Revolution (1933)
Trotsky, Leon (1879–1940) Russian
revolutionary and Communist theorist

61 To promise not to do a thing is the surest
way in the world to make a body want to
go and do that very thing.
The Adventures of Tom Sawyer (1876) **Twain,
Mark** (1835–1910) US humorist, writer,
journalist and lecturer

62 Revolutions have never succeeded unless
the establishment does three-quarters of
the work.

Dear Me (1977) **Ustinov, Sir Peter** (1921–2004)
English actor, director, dramatist, writer and
raconteur

63 There was reason to fear that the
Revolution, like Saturn, would eventually
devour all her children one by one.
In Lamartine, *Histoire des Girondins* (1847)
Vergniaud, Pierre (1753–1793) French
politician and revolutionary. Remark at his
trial, 1793

64 Nowadays we think of revolution not as the
solution to problems posed by current
developments but as a miracle which
releases us from the obligation to solve
these problems.
Oppression and Freedom (1955) **Weil, Simone**
(1909–1943) French philosopher, essayist and
mystic

65 Beginning reform is beginning revolution.
In Mrs Arbuthnot's Journal, (1830)
Wellington, Duke of (1769–1852) Irish-born
British military commander and statesman

66 Quite small and ineffectual demonstrations
can be made to look like the beginnings of
a revolution if the cameraman is in the
right place at the right time.
In Jonathon Green (ed.), *A Dictionary of
Contemporary Quotations* (1982) **Whitlam,
Gough** (1916–) Australian Labor statesman
and Prime Minister
See also government; politics; war

RELIGION

1 We have in England a particular
bashfulness in every thing that regards
religion.
The Spectator, 458, (August 1712) **Addison,
Joseph** (1672–1719) English essayist, poet,
playwright and statesman

2 Thus passes the glory of the world.
Spoken during the coronation of a new pope
(*Sic transit gloria mundi*)

3 There was a young man from Dijon,
Who had little, if any, religion.
He said, 'As for me,
I detest all three,
The Father, the Son, and the Pigeon.'
The Norman Douglas Limerick Book (1969)
Anonymous

4 The true meaning of religion is thus not
simply morality, but morality touched by
emotion.
Literature and Dogma (1873) **Arnold, Matthew**
(1822–1888) English poet, critic, essayist and
educationist

5 Bernard always had a few prayers in the
hall and some whiskey afterwards as he
was rarther pious but Mr Salteena was not
very addicted to prayers so he marched up
to bed.
The Young Visiters (1919) **Ashford, Daisy** (1881–
1972) English child author

6 I am a Catholic. As far as possible I go to
Mass every day. As far as possible I kneel
down and tell these beads every day. If you
reject me on account of my religion, I shall
thank God that he has spared me the
indignity of being your representative.
Speech, (1906)

7 Candidates should not attempt more than
six of these.
Suggested rider to the Ten Commandments
Belloc, Hilaire (1870–1953) English writer of
verse, essayist and critic; Liberal MP

8 I hope I never get so old I get religious.
Attr. **Bergman, Ingmar** (1918–) Swedish film
director

9 And the gates of this Chapel were shut,
And 'Thou shalt not' writ over the door ...
And Priests in black gowns were walking
their rounds,
And binding with briars my joys & desires.
'The Garden of Love' (1794) **Blake, William**
(1757–1827) English poet, engraver, painter and
mystic

10 There is always a danger in Judaism of
seeing history as a sort of poker game
played between Jews and God, in which the
presence of others is noted but not given
much importance.
The Observer, (1982) **Blue, Rabbi Lionel** (1930–)
English lecturer, writer and broadcaster

11 To Banbury came I, O profane one!
Where I saw a Puritane-one
Hanging of his cat on Monday
For killing of a mouse on Sunday.
Barnabee's Journal (1638) **Brathwaite, Richard**
(c.1588–1673) English poet and satirist

12 Religions are kept alive by heresies, which
are really sudden explosions of faith. Dead
religions do not produce them.
Thoughts in a Dry Season (1978) **Brenan, Gerald**
(1894–1987) English writer

13 But not so odd
As those who choose
A Jewish God,
But spurn the Jews.
*Reply to William Norman Ewer: How odd/Of
God/To choose/The Jews* **Browne, Cecil** (1932–)
US businessman

14 Persecution is a bad and indirect way to
plant religion.
Religio Medici (1643)

15 As for those wingy mysteries in divinity,
and airy subtleties in religion, which have
unhinged the brains of better heads, they
never stretched the *pia mater* of mine.
Methinks there be not impossibilities
enough in Religion for an active faith.
Religio Medici (1643)

16 At my devotion I love to use the civility of
my knee, my hat, and hand.
Religio Medici (1643)

17 There are many (questionless) canonized
on earth, that shall never be Saints in
Heaven.
Religio Medici (1643)

18 Men have lost their reason in nothing so
much as their religion, wherein stones and
clouts make martyrs.
Hydriotaphia: Urn Burial (1658) **Browne, Sir
Thomas** (1605–1682) English physician,
author and antiquary

19 Nothing is so fatal to religion as
indifference, which is, at least, half
infidelity.
Letter to William Smith, (1795) **Burke,
Edmund** (1729–1797) Irish-born British
statesman and philosopher

20 One religion is as true as another.
Anatomy of Melancholy (1621) **Burton, Robert**
(1577–1640) English clergyman and writer

21 To be at all is to be religious more or less.
The Note-Books of Samuel Butler (1912) **Butler,
Samuel** (1835–1902) English writer, painter,
philosopher and scholar

22 The king spoke to him [Lauderdale] to let
that Presbytery go, for it was not a religion
for gentlemen.
In Burnet, *The History of His Own Time* (1724)
Of Presbyterianism

23 He [Charles II] said once to myself, he was
no atheist, but he could not think God
would make a man miserable only for
taking a little pleasure out of the way. He
disguised his popery to the last.
In Burnet, *The History of His Own Time* (1724)
Charles II (1630–1685) King of Great Britain
and Ireland

24 Putting moral virtues at the highest, and
religion at the lowest, religion must still be
allowed to be a collateral security, at least,
to virtue; and every prudent man will
sooner trust to two securities than to one.
Letter to his son, (1750)

25 Religion is by no means a proper subject of
conversation in a mixed company ... It is
too awful and respectable a subject to
become a familiar one.
Letter to his godson, (c.1766) **Chesterfield,
Lord** (1694–1773) English politician and letter
writer

26 The Bible and the Bible only is the religion
of Protestants.
The Religion of Protestants (1637) **Chillingworth,
William** (1602–1644) English theologian and
scholar

27 Time consecrates; and what is grey with
age becomes religion.
Attr. **Coleridge, Samuel Taylor** (1772–1834)
English poet, philosopher and critic

28 Men will wrangle for religion; write for it;
fight for it; anything but – live for it.
Lacon (1820) **Colton, Charles Caleb** (c.1780–
1832) English clergyman and satirist

29 And of all plagues with which mankind are curst,
Ecclesiastic tyranny's the worst.
The True-Born Englishman (1701) **Defoe, Daniel** (c.1661–1731) English writer and critic

30 I do not know whether there are gods, but there ought to be.
In Tertullian, *Ad Nationes* **Diogenes** (c.400–325 BC) Greek philosopher

31 'Sensible men are all of the same religion.' 'And pray what is that?' inquired the prince. 'Sensible men never tell.'
Endymion (1880) **Disraeli, Benjamin** (1804–1881) English statesman and writer

32 It is no accident that the symbol of a bishop is a crook, and the sign of an archbishop is a double-cross.
Letter to *The Times*, (1977) **Dix, George Eglington** (1901–1952) English Anglican monk, historian and scholar

33 Yet dull religion teaches us content;
But when we ask it where that blessing dwells,
It points to pedant colleges and cells.
The Conquest of Granada (1670)

34 The Jews, a headstrong, moody, murmuring race
As ever tried the extent and stretch of grace,
God's pampered people, whom, debauched with ease,
No king could govern nor no God could please.
Gods they had tried of every shape and size
That godsmiths could produce or priests devise.
Absalom and Achitophel (1681) **Dryden, John** (1631–1700) English poet, satirist, dramatist and critic

35 Christian Science explains all cause and effect as mental, not physical.
Science and Health, with Key to the Scriptures (1875) **Eddy, Mary Baker** (1821–1910) US founder of Christian Science

36 The whole religious complexion of the modern world is due to the absence from Jerusalem of a lunatic asylum.

Impressions and Comments (1914) **Ellis, Havelock** (1859–1939) English sexologist and essayist

37 The religions we call false were once true.
'Character' (1866) **Emerson, Ralph Waldo** (1803–1882) US poet, essayist, transcendentalist and teacher

38 I have a Catholic soul, but a Lutheran stomach.
Of his failure to fast during Lent **Erasmus** (c.1466–1536) Dutch scholar and humanist

39 When I mention religion, I mean the Christian religion; and not only the Christian religion, but the Protestant religion; and not only the Protestant religion but the Church of England.
Tom Jones (1749) **Fielding, Henry** (1707–1754) English writer, dramatist and journalist

40 I hope I will be religious again but as for reganing my charecter I despare for it.
In Esdaile (ed.), *Journals, Letters and Verses* (1934) **Fleming, Marjory** (1803–1811) Scottish child diarist

41 My law-givers are Erasmus and Montaigne, not Moses and St Paul.
Two Cheers for Democracy (1951), 'What I Believe' **Forster, E.M.** (1879–1970) English writer, essayist and literary critic

42 The more the fruits of knowledge become accessible to men, the more widespread is the decline of religious belief.
The Future of an Illusion (1927)

43 Religion is an illusion and it derives its strength from the fact that it falls in with our instinctual desires.
New Introductory Lectures on Psychoanalysis (1933) **Freud, Sigmund** (1856–1939) Austrian physicist; founder of psychoanalysis

44 The various modes of worship, which prevailed in the Roman world, were all considered by the people as equally true; by the philosopher, as equally false; and by the magistrate, as equally useful.
Decline and Fall of the Roman Empire (1776–88) **Gibbon, Edward** (1737–1794) English historian, politician and memoirist

45 Cruelty is the first of God's attributes.
The Counterfeiters **Gide, André** (1869–1951)
French writer, critic, dramatist and poet

46 As I take my shoes from the shoemaker,
and my coat from the tailor, so I take my
religion from the priest.
In Boswell, *The Life of Samuel Johnson* (1791)
Goldsmith, Oliver (c.1728–1774) Irish
dramatist, poet and writer

47 Religion is a superstition that originated in
man's mental ability to solve natural
phenomena. The Church is an organized
institution that has always been a
stumbling block to progress.
What I Believe **Goldman, Emma** (1869–1940)
US anarchist

48 Those who marry God ... can become
domesticated too – it's just as hum-drum a
marriage as all the others.
A Burnt-Out Case (1961)

49 As a Roman Catholic I thank God for the
heretics. Heresy is only another word for
freedom of thought.
Attr. **Greene, Graham** (1904–1991) English
writer and dramatist

50 It is extremely difficult for a Jew to be
converted, for how can he bring himself to
believe in the divinity of – another Jew?
Attr. **Heine, Heinrich** (1797–1856) German
lyric poet, essayist and journalist

51 One man's theology is another man's belly
laugh.
Notebooks of Lazarus Long **Heinlein, Robert A.**
(1907–1988) US science fiction writer

52 Psychology is the theology of the 20th
century.
'Inhuman Race' **Hooton, Harry** (1908–1961)
Australian philosopher and poet

53 I do benefits for all religions. I'd hate to
blow the hereafter on a technicality.
In Simon Rose, *Classic Film Guide* (1995) **Hope,
Bob** (1903–2003) English-born US comedian

54 To become a popular religion, it is only
necessary for a superstition to enslave a
philosophy.
Outspoken Essays **Inge, William Ralph** (1860–
1954) English divine, writer and teacher

55 Religion's in the heart, not in the knees.
The Devil's Ducat (1830) **Jerrold, Douglas
William** (1803–1857) English dramatist, writer
and wit

56 It often happens that I wake at night and
begin to think about a serious problem and
decide I must tell the Pope about it. Then I
wake up completely and remember I am
the Pope.
Attr. **John XXIII** (1881–1963) Italian pope

57 Let there be no violence in religion.
Chapter 2 **Koran**

58 To the Puritan all things are impure, as
somebody says.
Etruscan Places (1932), 'Cerveteri' **Lawrence,
D.H.** (1885–1930) English writer, poet and
critic

59 Christianity will go. It will vanish and
shrink. I needn't argue about that. I'm
right and I'll be proved right. We're more
popular than Jesus now.
Interview in *The Evening Standard*, (4th March
1966) **Lennon, John** (1940–1980) English rock
musician, peace campaigner and cultural icon

60 Probably no invention came more easily to
man than Heaven.
Aphorisms **Lichtenberg, Georg** (1742–1799)
German physicist, satirist and writer

61 So potent a persuasion to evil was religion.
De Rerum Natura **Lucretius** (c.95–55 BC) Roman
philosopher

62 On the rich and the eloquent, on nobles
and priests, they looked down with
contempt: for they esteemed themselves
rich in a more precious treasure, and
eloquent in a more sublime language,
nobles by the right of an earlier creation,
and priests by the imposition of a mightier
hand.
Collected Essays (1843). Of the Puritans

63 Persecution produced its natural effect on
them. It found them a sect; it made them a
faction.
History of England (1849). Of Puritans and
Calvinists **Macaulay, Lord** (1800–1859) English
Liberal statesman, essayist and poet

64 Religion ... is the opium of the people.
A Contribution to the Critique of Hegel's Philosophy of Right (1844) **Marx, Karl** (1818–1883) German political philosopher and economist; founder of Communism

65 The number one book of the ages was written by a committee, and it was called The Bible.
In Halliwell, *The Filmgoer's Book of Quotes* (1973) **Mayer, Louis B.** (1885–1957) Russian-born US film executive. Comment to writers who had objected to changes in their work

66 Things have come to a pretty pass when religion is allowed to invade the sphere of private life.
In Russell, *Collections and Recollections* (1898) **Melbourne, Lord** (1779–1848) English statesman. On listening to an evangelical sermon

67 We must respect the other fellow's religion, but only in the sense and to the extent that we respect his theory that his wife is beautiful and his children smart.
Notebooks (1956) **Mencken, H.L.** (1880–1956) US writer, critic, philologist and satirist

68 Our religion was made to root out vices; it covers them up, nourishes them, incites them.
Essais (1580) **Montaigne, Michel de** (1533–1592) French essayist and moralist.

69 From the age of fifteen, dogma has been the fundamental principle of my religion: I know no other religion; I cannot enter into the idea of any other sort of religion; religion, as a mere sentiment, is to me a dream and a mockery.
Apologia pro Vita Sua (1864) **Newman, John Henry, Cardinal** (1801–1890) English Cardinal, theologian and poet

70 There's no reason to bring religion into it. I think we ought to have as great a regard for religion as we can, so as to keep it out of as many things as possible.
The Plough and the Stars (1926) **O'Casey, Sean** (1880–1964) Irish dramatist

71 As to religion, I hold it to be the indispensable duty of government to protect all conscientious professors thereof, and I know of no other business which government hath to do therewith.
Common Sense (1776) **Paine, Thomas** (1737–1809) English-born US political theorist and pamphleteer

72 I do not accept the word of the slanderous bachelor who lives on the bank of the Tiber.
Paisley, Rev. Ian (1926–) Northern Irish politican. On the Pope

73 Leading the Jewish people is not easy – we are a divided, obstinate, highly individualistic people who have cultivated faith, sharp wittedness and polemics to a very high level.
New York Times, (1986) **Peres, Shimon** (1923–) Israeli statesman and Prime Minister

74 I am temperamentally against clappy-and-happy, huggy-and-feely worship, which seems to reduce God to a puppet.
The Guardian, (2000) **Runcie, Robert** (1921–2000) Archbishop of Canterbury 1980–1091

75 Too much religion makes me go pop.
In M. Duggan, *Runcie: The Making of an Archbishop* (1983) **Runcie, Rosalind** (1932–) Wife of the Archbishop of Canterbury

76 Unlike Christianity, which preached a peace that it never achieved, Islam unashamedly came with a sword.
A History of the Crusades (1954) **Runciman, Sir Steven** (1903–2000) British scholar, historian and archaeologist

77 Religion is based ... mainly on fear ... fear of the mysterious, fear of defeat, fear of death. Fear is the parent of cruelty, and therefore it is no wonder if cruelty and religion have gone hand in hand ... My own view on religion is that of Lucretius. I regard it as a disease born of fear and as a source of untold misery to the human race. I cannot, however, deny that it has made some contributions to civilization. It helped in early days to fix the calendar, and it caused Egyptian priests to chronicle eclipses with such care that in time they became able to predict them. These two services I am prepared to acknowledge, but I do not know of any others.

Why I Am Not a Christian and Other Essays
Russell, Bertrand (1872–1970) English
philosopher, mathematician, essayist and
social reformer

78 Hunting people tend to be churchgoers on
a higher level than ordinary folk. One has a
religious experience in the field.
The Times, (1993) **Seal, Christopher** (1880–1954)
British churchman

79 These two words have undone the world.
Table Talk (1689) The two words are
'scrutamini scripturas' (*Let us look at the
Scriptures*)

80 For a priest to turn a man when he lies a-
dying, is just like one that has a long time
solicited a woman, and cannot obtain his
end; at length he makes her drunk, and so
lies with her.
Table Talk **Selden, John** (1584–1654) English
historian, jurist and politician

81 There is no religion without love, and
people may talk as much as they like about
their religion, but if it does not teach them
to be good and kind to man and beast, it is
all a sham.
Black Beauty (1877) **Sewell, Anna** (1820–1878)
English writer

82 'People differ in their discourse and
profession about these matters, but men of
sense are really but of one religion.' …
'Pray, my Lord, what religion is that which
men of sense agree in?' 'Madam,' says the
earl immediately, 'men of sense never tell
it.'
In Bishop Burnet's History of His Own Time
(1823) **Shaftesbury, Earl of** (1621–1683) English
statesman

83 There is only one religion, though there
are a hundred versions of it.
Plays Pleasant and Unpleasant (1898)

84 In heaven an angel is nobody in particular.
Man and Superman (1903)

85 I am a sort of collector of religions; and the
curious thing is that I find I can believe in
them all.
Major Barbara (1907)

86 I can't talk religion to a man with bodily
hunger in his eyes.
Major Barbara (1907) **Shaw, George Bernard**
(1856–1950) Irish socialist, writer, dramatist
and critic

87 Earth groans beneath religion's iron age,
And priests dare babble of a God of peace,
Even whilst their hands are red with
guiltless blood.
Queen Mab (1813) **Shelley, Percy Bysshe** (1792–
1822) English poet, dramatist and essayist

88 Just how many witnesses do they need
before Jehovah's trial starts?
Attr. **Shields, Tom** Scottish humorist and
diarist

89 Progress has its drawbacks, and they are
great and serious; but whatever its value
may be, unity in religious belief would
further it.
Liberty, Equality and Fraternity (1873) **Stephen,
Sir James Fitzjames** (1829–1894) English judge
and essayist

90 Whenever a man talks loudly against
religion, – always suspect that it is not his
reason, but his passions which have got the
better of his creed.
Tristram Shandy (1759–67) **Sterne, Laurence**
(1713–1768) Irish-born English writer and
clergyman

91 We have just enough religion to make us
hate, but not enough to make us love one
another.
Thoughts on Various Subjects (1711) **Swift,
Jonathan** (1667–1745) Irish satirist, poet,
essayist and cleric

92 You have told me, O God, to believe in
hell. But you have forbidden me to think,
with absolute certainty, of any man as
damned.
Le Milieu divin **Teilhard de Chardin, Pierre**
(1881–1955) French Jesuit philosopher and
palaeontologist

93 Protestant women may take the Pill.
Roman Catholic woman must keep taking
The Tablet.
The Guardian, (1990) **Thomas, Irene** (1920–
2001) English writer and broadcaster

94 Even in the valley of the shadow of death, two and two do not make six.
Attr. **Tolstoy, Leo** (1828–1910) Russian writer, essayist, philosopher and moralist. Refusing to reconcile himself with the Russian Orthodox Church as he lay dying

95 Religion is love; in no case is it logic.
My Apprenticeship (1926) **Webb, Beatrice** (1858–1943) English writer and reformer

96 Merit, indeed! ... We are come to a pretty pass if they talk of merit for a bishopric.
In C. Oman, *The Gascoyne Heiress* (1968) **Westmorland, John Fane, Tenth Earl of** (1759–1841)

97 So many gods, so many creeds,
So many paths that wind and wind,
While just the art of being kind
Is all the sad world needs.
'The World's Need' (1917) **Wilcox, Ella Wheeler** (1850–1919) US poet and writer

98 Religion does not help me. The faith that others give to what is unseen, I give to what one can touch, and look at.
De Profundis (1897) **Wilde, Oscar** (1854–1900) Irish poet, dramatist, writer, critic and wit

99 No one can worship God or love his neighbour on an empty stomach.
Speech, (1912) **Wilson, Woodrow** (1856–1924) US Democrat President

100 No Jew was ever fool enough to turn Christian unless he was a clever man.
Children of the Ghetto (1892)

101 Let us start a new religion with one commandment, 'Enjoy thyself'.
Children of the Ghetto (1892) **Zangwill, Israel** (1864–1926) English writer and Jewish spokesman
See also belief; Christianity; Christmas; the devil; faith; God; Islam

REVENGE

1 An eye for an eye leads only to more blindness.
Cat's Eye (1988) **Atwood, Margaret** (1939–) Canadian writer, poet and critic

2 A man that studieth revenge keeps his own wounds green.
'Of Revenge' (1625)

3 Revenge is a kind of wild justice, which the more man's nature runs to, the more ought law to weed it out.
'Of Revenge' (1625) **Bacon, Francis** (1561–1626) English philosopher, essayist, politician and courtier

4 Life for life,
Eye for eye, tooth for tooth, hand for hand, foot for foot,
Burning for burning, wound for wound, stripe for stripe.
Exodus, 21:23–25

5 Vengeance is mine; I will repay, saith the Lord.
Romans, 12:19 **The Bible (King James Version)**

6 The universe may perish, so long as I have my revenge.
La Mort d'Agrippine (1654) **Cyrano de Bergerac, Savinien de** (1619–1655) French writer

7 Revenge proves its own executioner.
The Broken Heart (1633) **Ford, John** (c.1586–c.1640) English dramatist and poet

8 But when our neighbours do wrong, we sometimes feel the fitness of making them smart for it, whether they have repented or not.
The Common Law (1881) **Holmes, Oliver Wendell** (1809–1894) US physician, poet, writer and scientist

9 Revenge, at first though sweet,
Bitter ere long back on itself recoils.
Paradise Lost (1667) **Milton, John** (1608–1674) English poet, libertarian and pamphleteer

10 Vengeance, deep-brooding o'er the slain, Had lock'd the source of softer woe.
The Lay of the Last Minstrel (1805) **Scott, Sir Walter** (1771–1832) Scottish writer and historian

11 Heat not a furnace for your foe so hot That it do singe yourself.
Henry VIII, I.i

12 Let's make us med'cines of our great revenge
To cure this deadly grief.
Macbeth, IV.iii

13 The rarer action is
In virtue than in vengeance.
The Tempest, V.*i* **Shakespeare, William** (1564–1616) English dramatist, poet and actor

14 Lord, confound this surly sister,
Blight her brow with blotch and blister,
Cramp her larynx, lung and liver,
In her guts a galling give her.
Let her live to earn her dinners
In Mountjoy with seedy sinners:
Lord, this judgement quickly bring,
And I'm your servant, J.M. Synge.
'The Curse' **Synge, J.M.** (1871–1909) Irish dramatist, poet and letter writer. To the sister of an enemy of the author who disapproved of *The Playboy of the Western World*
See also anger; spite

RIGHT AND WRONG

1 Where so many hours have been spent in convincing myself that I am right, is there not some reason to fear I may be wrong?
Sense and Sensibility (1811) **Austen, Jane** (1775–1817) English writer

2 It is better to be approximately right than precisely wrong.
Fortune, (1994) **Buffett, Warren** (1930–) US billionaire investment expert

3 The heart ay's the part ay
That makes us right or wrang.
'Epistle to Davie, a Brother Poet' (1785) **Burns, Robert** (1759–1796) Scottish poet and songwriter

4 The best things carried to excess are wrong.
The Rosciad (1761) **Churchill, Charles** (1731–1764) English poet, political writer and clergyman

5 Perhaps it is better to be irresponsible and right than to be responsible and wrong.
Party Political Broadcast, London, (1950) **Churchill, Sir Winston** (1874–1965) English Conservative Prime Minister

6 I had rather be right than be President.
Remark, (1839) **Clay, Henry** (1777–1852) US statesman

7 The innumerable multitude of Wrongs
By man on man inflicted.
'Religious Musings' (1796) **Coleridge, Samuel Taylor** (1772–1834) English poet, philosopher and critic

8 A noisy man is always in the right.
'Conversation' (1782) **Cowper, William** (1731–1800) English poet, hymn writer and letter writer

9 No law can be sacred to me but that of my nature. Good and bad are but names very readily transferable to that or this; the only right is what is after my own constitution, the only wrong what is against it.
Essays, First Series (1841) **Emerson, Ralph Waldo** (1803–1882) US poet, essayist, transcendentalist and teacher

10 I am willing to admit that I may not always be right, but I am never wrong.
Attr. **Goldwyn, Samuel** (1882–1974) Polish-born US film producer

11 I have loved righteousness and hated iniquity: therefore I die in exile.
In Bowden, *The Life and Pontificate of Gregory VII* (1840) **Gregory VII** (c.1020–1085) Italian pope. Last words

12 The pendulum of the mind swings between sense and nonsense, and not between what is right and what is wrong.
Memories, Dreams, Thoughts (1962) **Jung, Carl Gustav** (1875–1961) Swiss psychiatrist and pupil of Freud

13 It is not that you do wrong by design, but that you should never do right by mistake.
Letters (1769–1771) **Junius** (1769–1772) Pen-name of anonymous author of letters criticizing ministers of George III

14 Some say that the age of chivalry is past, that the spirit of romance is dead. The age of chivalry is never past, so long as there is a wrong left unredressed on earth.
In Mrs C. Kingsley, *Life* (1879) **Kingsley, Charles** (1819–1875) English writer, poet, lecturer and clergyman

15 When everyone is wrong, everyone is right.
La Gouvernante (1747) **La Chaussée, Nivelle de** (1692–1754) French sentimental dramatist

16 What is the greatest good and evil? – two ends of an invisible chain which come closer together the further they move apart.
Vadim (1834) **Lermontov, Mikhail** (1814–1841) Russian poet and writer

17 What I want is men who will support me when I am in the wrong.
In Lord David Cecil, *Lord M.* (1954) **Melbourne, Lord** (1779–1848) English statesman. Replying to someone who said he would support Melbourne so long as he was right

18 I think she must have been very strictly brought up, she's so desperately anxious to do the wrong thing correctly.
Reginald (1904) **Saki** (1870–1916) Burmese-born British writer

19 Some rise by sin, and some by virtue fall.
Measure for Measure, II.i

20 Virtue that transgresses is but patch'd with sin, and sin that amends is but patch'd with virtue.
Twelfth Night, I.v **Shakespeare, William** (1564–1616) English dramatist, poet and actor

21 Cruel he looks, but calm and strong, Like one who does, not suffers wrong.
Prometheus Unbound (1820) **Shelley, Percy Bysshe** (1792–1822) English poet, dramatist and essayist

22 Wrongdoing can only be avoided if those who are not wronged feel the same indignation at it as those who are.
Attr. **Solon** (c.638–c.559 BC) Athenian statesman, reformer and poet

23 One and the same thing can at the same time be good and bad, for example, music is good to the melancholy, bad to the mourner, and neither good nor bad to the deaf.
Ethics (1677) **Spinoza, Baruch** (1632–1677) Dutch philosopher and theologian

24 When Lord Copper was right he said, 'Definitely, Lord Copper'; when he was wrong, 'Up to a point'.
Scoop (1938) **Waugh, Evelyn** (1903–1966) English writer and diarist

25 No question is ever settled Until it is settled right.
'Settle the Question Right' (1917) **Wilcox, Ella Wheeler** (1850–1919) US poet and writer
See also judgement; morality

RUSSIA

1 An intelligent Russian once remarked to us, 'Every country has its own constitution; ours is absolutism moderated by assassination.'
In Munster, *Political Sketches of Europe* (1868) **Anonymous**

2 The bear does not change his spots.
The Times, (1999) **Burnham, Lord** (d. 2005) On Russian policy

3 I cannot forecast to you the action of Russia. It is a riddle wrapped in a mystery inside an enigma.
Broadcast, (October 1939) **Churchill, Sir Winston** (1874–1965) English Conservative Prime Minister

4 Any cook should be able to run the country.
In Alexander Solzhenitzyn, *The First Circle* (1968) **Lenin, V.I.** (1870–1924) Russian revolutionary, Marxist theoretician and first leader of the USSR

5 Russia has two generals in whom she can trust – Generals Janvier and Février.
Attr. **Nicholas I, Emperor** (1796–1855) Russian Emperor

6 Without large-scale outside aid, Russia may turn to a new despotism, which could be a far more dangerous threat to peace and freedom than the old Soviet totalitarianism.
Remark at a Washington conference, (1992) **Nixon, Richard** (1913–1994) US Republican politician and President. Urging more generous support for Russian leader Boris Yeltsin

7 You would need to be heartless not to regret the disintegration of the Soviet Union. You would need to be brainless to attempt to restore it.

The Scotsman, (2000) **Putin, Vladimir** (1952–)
President of Russia

8 My fellow Americans, I am pleased to tell
you that I have signed legislation to outlaw
Russia for ever. We begin bombing in five
minutes.
Audio recording, (1984) **Reagan, Ronald** (1911–
2004) US actor, Republican statesman and
President. During a microphone test prior to
a radio broadcast

9 The difference between our decadence and
the Russians' is that while theirs is brutal,
ours is apathetic.
The Observer, (1961) **Thurber, James** (1894–
1961) US humorist, writer and dramatist

10 In our country we are all great specialists in
the irrational but not yet great specialists in
the logical ... Today in Russia there are as
many sorcerers as militia men.
Interview, Waterstones, Glasgow **Tolstoya,
Tatyana** Russian novelist

11 From being a patriotic myth, the Russian
people have become a terrible reality.
History of the Russian Revolution (1933) **Trotsky,
Leon** (1879–1940) Russian revolutionary and
Communist theorist

12 When Mrs Thatcher says she has a
nostalgia for Victorian values I don't think
she realises that 90 per cent of her
nostalgia would be satisfied in the Soviet
Union.
The Observer, (1987) **Ustinov, Sir Peter** (1921–
2004) English actor, director, dramatist,
writer and raconteur

13 I am for the market, not for the bazaar.
The Times, (1992)

14 History will record that the twentieth
century essentially ended on 19–21 August
1991.
Article in *Newsweek*, (1994). Said after the
failure of the communist coup **Yeltsin, Boris**
(1931–) Russian statesman and President

15 No Jewish blood runs among my blood,
but I am as bitterly and hardly hated
by every anti-semite
as if I were a Jew. By this
I am a Russian.

'Babi Yar' (1961) **Yevtushenko, Yevgeny** (1933–)
Russian poet

16 The whole nation, I promise you, will
experience an orgasm next year.
In Newsweek, (1994) **Zhirinovsky, Vladimir**
(1946–) Russian politician
See also communism

SCIENCE

1 By studying the masters – not their pupils.
In E.T. Bell, *Men of Mathematics* (1937) **Abel,
Niels Henrik** (1809–1829) Norwegian
mathematician. Explaining how he had
become a great mathematician at such a
young age

2 Basic research is like shooting an arrow
into the air and, where it lands, painting a
target.
Nature, (1984) **Adkins, Homer** (1892–1949) US
chemist

3 Not only are all characters and scenes in
this book entirely fictitious; most of the
technical, medical and psychological data
are too. My working maxim here has been
as follows: I may not know much about
science but I know what I like.
Dead Babies (1975) **Amis, Martin** (1949–)
English writer

4 The limits of the possible can only be
defined by going beyond them into the
impossible.
Clarke's Second Law

5 No experiment is reproducible.
Wyszowski's Law

6 Multiplication is vexation,
Division is as bad;
The rule of three doth puzzle me,
And practice drives me mad.
Elizabethan rhyme **Anonymous**

7 Eureka!
In Vitruvius Pollio, *De Architectura* (*I've got it*)

8 Give me a place to stand, and I will move
the Earth.
In Poppus Alexander, *Collectio* **Archimedes**
(c.287–212 BC) Greek mathematician

9 Tranquillity Base here – the Eagle has landed.
TV coverage, (20 July 1969) **Armstrong, Neil** (1930–) US astronaut and first man on the moon. First words on lunar touch-down of space module during Apollo XI mission

10 Rather than have Physical Science the principal thing in my son's mind, I would rather have him think that the Sun went round the Earth, and the Stars were merely spangles set in a bright blue firmament.
In Alan L. Mackay, *The Harvest of a Quiet Eye* (1977) **Arnold, Thomas** (1795–1842) English historian and educator

11 When I find myself in the company of scientists, I feel like a shabby curate who has strayed by mistake into a drawing-room full of dukes.
The Dyer's Hand (1963)

12 The true men of action in our time, those who transform the world, are not the politicians and statesmen, but the scientists. Unfortunately, poetry cannot celebrate them, because their deeds are concerned with things, not persons and are, therefore, speechless.
The Dyer's Hand (1963) **Auden, W.H.** (1907–1973) English poet, essayist, critic, teacher and dramatist

13 What is algebra exactly; is it those three-cornered things?
Quality Street (1901) **Barrie, Sir J.M.** (1860–1937) Scottish dramatist and writer

14 The Microbe is so very small
You cannot make him out at all ...
Oh! let us never, never doubt
What nobody is sure about!
More Beasts for Worse Children (1897) **Belloc, Hilaire** (1870–1953) English writer of verse, essayist and critic; Liberal MP

15 An inventor is a person who makes an ingenious arrangement of wheels, levers and springs, and believes it civilization.
The Devil's Dictionary, (1958) **Bierce, Ambrose** (1842–c.1914) US writer, verse writer and soldier

16 Technology is so much fun but we can drown in our technology. The fog of information can drive out knowledge.

New York Times, (1983) **Boorstin, Daniel** (1914–2004) US librarian, historian, lawyer and writer

17 The world has achieved brilliance without conscience. Ours is a world of nuclear giants and ethical infants.
Speech, Armistice Day, (1948) **Bradley, Omar** (1893–1981) US general

18 The Heart of Man, we are told, is deceitful and desperately wicked. However that may be, it consists of four chambers, the right ventricle, the left ventricle, the left auricle, the right auricle.
The Anatomist (1931)

19 Eve and the apple was the first great step in experimental science.
Mr Bolfry (1943) **Bridie, James** (1888–1951) Scottish dramatist, writer and physician

20 Science has nothing to be ashamed of, even in the ruins of Nagasaki.
Science and Human Values

21 That is the essence of science: ask an impertinent question, and you are on the way to the pertinent answer.
The Ascent of Man (1973)

22 Physics becomes in those years the greatest collective work of science – no, more than that, the great collective work of art of the twentieth century.
The Ascent of Man (1973) **Bronowski, Jacob** (1908–1974) British scientist, writer and TV presenter

23 I have often admired the mystical way of Pythagoras, and the secret magic of numbers.
Religio Medici (1643) **Browne, Sir Thomas** (1605–1682) English physician, author and antiquary

24 I just invent, then wait until man comes around to needing what I've invented.
Time, (1964) **Buckminster Fuller, Richard** (1895–1983) US architect and engineer. On geodesic domes

25 To pursue science is not to disparage the things of the spirit. In fact, to pursue science rightly is to furnish the framework on which the spirit may rise.

Speech, (1953) **Bush, Vannevar** (1890–1974) US engineer and physicist

26 And the Social Science, – not a 'gay science', ... no, a dreary, desolate, and indeed quite abject and distressing one; what we might call ... the dismal science.
Latter-Day Pamphlets (1850) **Carlyle, Thomas** (1795–1881) Scottish historian, biographer, critic, and essayist. Of political economics

27 I happen to believe that this kind of genetic modification takes mankind into the realms that belong to God, and to God alone ... do we have the right to experiment with, and commercialise, the building blocks of life?
Daily Telegraph, (1998) **Charles, Prince of Wales** (1948–) Son and heir of Elizabeth II and Prince Philip. On genetically modified food crops

28 As soon as questions of will or decision or reason or choice of action arise, human science is at a loss.
Television interview, (1978) **Chomsky, Noam** (1928–) US linguist and political critic

29 Technology, sufficiently advanced, is indistinguishable from magic.
The Times, (1996)

30 When a distinguished but elderly scientist states that something is possible, he is almost certainly right. When he states that something is impossible, he is very probably wrong. (Clarke's First Law).
The New Yorker, (1969)

31 Any sufficiently advanced technology is indistinguishable from magic.
Technology and the Future **Clarke, Arthur C.** (1917–) English writer

32 Scientific thought is not an accompaniment or condition of human progress, but human progress itself.
Aims and Instruments of Scientific Thought (1872) **Clifford, William Kingdon** (1845–1879) English mathematician

33 Curse the scientists, and all science into the bargain.

In J.C. Beaglehole (ed.), *The Voyage of the Resolution* (1961) **Cook, Captain James** (1728–1779) English navigator. Following Cook's experiences with the natural historians on his second voyage

34 We have discovered the secret of life!
In Watson, *The Double Helix* (1968) **Crick, Francis** (1916–) British biologist. On the discovery of the structure of DNA, 1953

35 A virus is only doing its job.
Sunday Telegraph, (1992) **Cronenberg, David** (1943–) Canadian film director

36 After all, science is essentially international, and it is only through lack of the historical sense that national qualities have been attributed to it.
Memorandum, 'Intellectual Co-operation' **Curie, Marie** (1867–1934) Polish-born French physicist

37 I can see ... why a man who lives in Colorado is so anxious for all this nuclear activity to go on in Australia, an area famed among nuclear scientists for its lack of immediate proximity to their own residential areas.
Dagshead Revisited (1989) **Dagg, Fred** (1948–) Australian writer, actor and broadcaster

38 Our science has become terrible, our research dangerous, our knowledge fatal.
The Physicists (1962) **Dürrenmatt, Friedrich** (1921–1990) Swiss dramatist and writer

39 We used to think that if we knew one, we knew two, because one and one are two. We are finding that we must learn a great deal more about 'and'.
In Alan L. Mackay, *The Harvest of a Quiet Eye* (1977)

40 Science is an edged tool, with which men play like children, and cut their own fingers.
Attr. **Eddington, Sir Arthur** (1882–1944) English astronomer, physicist and mathematician

41 To invent, you need a good imagination and a pile of junk.
Attr. **Edison, Thomas Alva** (1847–1931) US inventor and industrialist

42 Why does this magnificent applied science which saves work and makes life easier bring us so little happiness? The simple answer runs: Because we have not yet learned to make sensible use of it.
Address, California Institute of Technology, (1931)

43 Science without religion is lame, religion without science is blind.
Science, Philosophy and Religion: a Symposium (1941)

44 If only I had known, I should have become a watchmaker.
New Statesman, (1965) Of his part in the development of the atom bomb

45 A theory can be proved by experiment; but no path leads from experiment to the birth of a theory.
In Alan L. Mackay, The Harvest of a Quiet Eye (1977)

46 When a man sits with a pretty girl for an hour, it seems like a minute. But let him sit on a hot stove for a minute – and it's longer than any hour. That's relativity.
Attr. Einstein, Albert (1879–1955) German-born US mathematical physicist

47 Invention breeds invention.
Society and Solitude (1870) Emerson, Ralph Waldo (1803–1882) US poet, essayist, transcendentalist and teacher

48 A line is length without breadth.
Elements Euclid (fl. c.300 BC) Greek mathematician

49 It may be a weed instead of a fish that, after all my labour, I may at last pull up.
Letter, (1831) Faraday, Michael (1791–1867) English chemist and physicist. On his scientific research

50 The time is overdue for adding the separation of state and science to the by now customary separation of state and church. Science is only one of the many instruments man has invented to cope with his surroundings. It is not the only one, it is not infallible, and it has become too powerful, too pushy, and too dangerous to be left on its own.

Against Method (1975) Feyerabend, Paul (1924–1994) Austrian philosopher

51 What is the use of a new-born child?
In Parton, Life and Times of Benjamin Franklin (1864) Franklin, Benjamin (1706–1790) US statesman, scientist, political critic and printer. On being asked the use of a new invention

52 Technology is the knack of so arranging the world that we do not experience it.
In Rollo May, The Cry for Myth Frisch, Max (1911–1991) Swiss dramatist, writer and architect

53 I've begun to believe that the reasonable
Is an invention of man, altogether in opposition
To the facts of creation.
The Firstborn (1945) Fry, Christopher (1907–2005) English verse dramatist, theatre director and translator

54 But it does move.
Attr. (1632) Galilei, Galileo (1564–1642) Italian scientist. Remark made after he was forced to withdraw his assertion that the Earth moved round the Sun

55 I could prove God statistically.
Attr. Gallup, George (1901–1984) US statistician and market research pioneer

56 The way to do research is to attack the facts at the point of greatest astonishment.
The Decline and Fall of Science Green, Celia (1935–) British philosopher and psychologist

57 Einstein – the greatest Jew since Jesus. I have no doubt that Einstein's name will still be remembered and revered when Lloyd George, Foch, and William Hohenzollern share with Charlie Chaplin that ineluctable oblivion which awaits the uncreative mind.
Daedalus or Science and the Future (1924) Haldane, J.B.S. (1892–1964) British biochemist, geneticist and popularizer of science

58 That's an amazing invention [the telephone], but who would ever want to use one of them?

Attr. **Hayes, Rutherford B.** (1822–1893) US President. After participating in a trial telephone conversation, 1876

59 An expert is a man who knows some of the worst errors that can be made in the subject in question and who therefore understands how to avoid them.
The Part and the Whole (1969)

60 Natural science does not simply describe and explain nature, it is part of the interplay between nature and ourselves.
Attr. **Heisenberg, Werner** (1901–1976) German theoretical physicist

61 Geometry ... is the only science that it hath pleased God hitherto to bestow on mankind.
Leviathan (1651) **Hobbes, Thomas** (1588–1679) Political philosopher

62 The world is moving so fast these days that the man who says it can't be done is generally interrupted by someone doing it.
Attr. **Hubbard, Elbert** (1856–1915) US printer, editor, writer and businessman

63 The great tragedy of Science – the slaying of a beautiful hypothesis by an ugly fact.
British Association Annual Report (1870)

64 Logical consequences are the scarecrows of fools and the beacons of wise men.
Nature, (1874), 'On the Hypothesis that Animals are Automata and its History'
Huxley, T.H. (1825–1895) English biologist, Darwinist and agnostic

65 Science should leave off making pronouncements: the river of knowledge has too often turned back on itself.
The Mysterious Universe (1930) **Jeans, Sir James Hopwood** (1877–1946) English mathematician, physicist and astronomer

66 Science may have found a cure for most evils; but it has found no remedy for the worst of them all – the apathy of human beings.
My Religion (1927) **Keller, Helen** (1880–1968) US writer and educator of the blind and deaf

67 Our scientific power has outrun our spiritual power. We have guided missiles and misguided men.

Strength to Love, (1963) **King, Martin Luther** (1929–1968) US civil rights leader and Baptist minister

68 In everything that relates to science, I am a whole Encyclopaedia behind the rest of the world.
Essays of Elia (1823) **Lamb, Charles** (1775–1834) English essayist, critic and letter writer

69 Water is H2O, hydrogen two parts, oxygen one,
but there is also a third thing, that makes it water
and nobody knows what it is.
Pansies (1929) **Lawrence, D.H.** (1885–1930) English writer, poet and critic

70 Science is all metaphor.
Interview, (1980) **Leary, Timothy** (1920–1996) US writer and psychologist

71 Those of our own-day scientists who stir the embers of fires that went out millions of years ago may believe their theories but can never know. It would be better for all of us if they said as much.
The Times, (1992) **Levin, Bernard** (1928–2004) British writer

72 We ought not to permit a cottage industry in the God business.
The Guardian, (1997) **Marchi, John** (1948–)
After Scottish scientists pioneered the cloning of a sheep, Dolly

73 Properly handled, GM crops have the potential to be more wildlife-friendly than the ones we have now.
The Scotsman, (May 1999) **May, Sir Robert** (1936–) British scientist; Chief Scientific Adviser to the UK government

74 In science, all facts, no matter how trivial or banal, enjoy democratic equality.
Attr. **McCarthy, Mary** (1912–1989) US writer and critic

75 Scientific discovery is a private event, and the delight that accompanies it, or the despair of finding it illusory does not travel.
Hypothesis and Imagination **Medawar, Sir Peter** (1915–1987) British zoologist and immunologist

76 Science without conscience is but death of the soul.
In Simcox, *Treasury of Quotations on Christian Themes* **Montaigne, Michel de** (1533–1592) French essayist and moralist

77 The place where we do our scientific work is a place of prayer.
In Alan L. Mackay, *The Harvest of a Quiet Eye* (1977) **Needham, Joseph** (1900–1995) British biochemist

78 If I have seen further it is by standing on the shoulders of giants.
Letter to Robert Hooke, (1675–76) **Newton, Sir Isaac** (1642–1727) English scientist and philosopher

79 The physicists have known sin; and this is a knowledge which they cannot lose.
Lecture, (1947) **Oppenheimer, J. Robert** (1904–1967) US nuclear physicist. On the consequences of the first atom bomb

80 In the field of observation, chance favours only the prepared mind.
Lecture, (1854)

81 There are no applied sciences, only applications of science.
Address, (1872) **Pasteur, Louis** (1822–1895) French chemist, bacteriologist and immunologist

82 I can imagine the night when waking from a nervous sleep
you find the telephone has dragged itself up the stairs one at a time
and sits mewing,
the electronic pet waiting for its bowl of words.
'I studied telephones constantly' **Patten, Brian** (1946–) British poet

83 I almost think it is the ultimate destiny of science to exterminate the human race.
Gryll Grange (1861) **Peacock, Thomas Love** (1785–1866) English writer and poet

84 Traditional scientific method had always been at the very best, 20-20 hindsight. It's good for seeing where you've been.
Zen and the Art of Motorcycle Maintenance (1974) **Pirsig, Robert** (1928–) US author

85 Science must begin with myths, and with the criticism of myths.
In C.A. Mace (ed.), *British Philosophy in the Mid-Century* (1957)

86 Science may be described as the art of systematic oversimplification.
The Observer, (1982) **Popper, Sir Karl** (1902–1994) Austrian-born British philosopher

87 Should we force science down the throats of those that have no taste for it? Is it our duty to drag them kicking and screaming into the twenty-first century? I am afraid that it is.
Speech, (1986) **Porter, Sir George** (1920–2002) English chemist

88 No, it is a very interesting number; it is the smallest number expressible as a sum of two cubes in two different ways.
Proceedings of the London Mathematical Society (1921) **Ramanujan, Srinivasa** (1887–1920) Indian mathematician. Reply to the mathematician, G.H. Hardy, who remarked that a cab's number – 1729 – was dull; the two ways are $1^3 + 12^3$, and $9^3 + 10^3$.

89 The machine threatens all achievement.
The Sonnets to Orpheus (1923) **Rilke, Rainer Maria** (1875–1926) Austrian poet, born in Prague

90 Science is for those who learn; poetry, for those who know.
Meditations of a Parish Priest (1886) **Roux, Joseph** (1834–1886) French priest and epigrammatist

91 The work of science is to substitute facts for appearances, and demonstration for impressions.
The Stones of Venice (1851) **Ruskin, John** (1819–1900) English art critic, philosopher and reformer

92 Pure mathematics consists entirely of assertions to the effect that, if such and such a proposition is true of anything, then such and such another proposition is true of that thing. It is essential not to discuss whether the first proposition is really true, and not to mention what the anything is, of which it is supposed to be true.
Mysticism and Logic (1918)

93 Mathematics may be defined as the subject in which we never know what we are talking about, nor whether what we are saying is true.
Mysticism and Logic (1918)

94 Mathematics, rightly viewed, possesses not only truth, but supreme beauty – a beauty cold and austere, like that of sculpture.
Mysticism and Logic (1918)

95 Machines are worshipped because they are beautiful, and valued because they confer power; they are hated because they are hideous, and loathed because they impose slavery.
Sceptical Essays (1928) **Russell, Bertrand** (1872–1970) English philosopher, mathematician, essayist and social reformer

96 Some fool in a laboratory might blow up the universe unawares.
In Mark Oliphant, *Rutherford Recollections of the Cambridge Days* (1972) **Rutherford, Ernest** (1871–1937) English physicist. Joking about the atom's enormous potential energy

97 In science it often happens that scientists say, 'You know that's a really good argument; my position is mistaken,' and then they would actually change their minds and you never hear that old view from them again. They really do it. It doesn't happen as often as it should, because scientists are human and change is sometimes painful. But it happens every day. I cannot recall the last time something like that happened in politics or religion.
Lecture, (1987) **Sagan, Carl** (1934–1996) US astrophysicist

98 The people – could you patent the sun?
Attr. **Salk, Jonas** (1914–1995) US virologist. On being asked who owned the patent on his antipolio vaccine

99 If all the arts aspire to the condition of music, all the sciences aspire to the condition of mathematics.
The Observer, (1928) **Santayana, George** (1863–1952) Spanish-born US philosopher and writer

100 If we hadn't put a man on the moon, there wouldn't be a Silicon Valley today.
US News & World Report, (1992) **Sculley, John** (1939–) US business executive

101 What would life be without arithmetic, but a scene of horrors.
Letters, To Miss – , (1835)

102 Science is his forte and omniscience is his foible.
In Isaac Todhunter, *William Whewell* (1876). Of William Whewell **Smith, Sydney** (1771–1845) English clergyman, essayist, journalist and wit

103 A good many times I have been present at gatherings of people who, by the standards of the traditional culture, are thought highly educated and who have with considerable gusto been expressing their incredulity at the illiteracy of scientists. Once or twice I have been provoked and have asked the company how many of them could describe the Second Law of Thermodynamics. The response was cold: it was also negative.
The Two Cultures and the Scientific Revolution (1959) **Snow, C.P.** (1905–1980) English writer, critic, physicist and public administrator

104 Science is organized knowledge.
Education (1861) **Spencer, Herbert** (1820–1903) English philosopher and journalist

105 I know a man who has a device for converting solar energy into food. Delicious stuff he makes with it, too. Being doing it for years ... It's called a farm.
Crisis in Abundance (1966) **Stenhouse, David** (1932–) English-born New Zealand zoologist and educationist. On the conservation of biological resources

106 Science is really in the business of disproving its current models or changing them to conform to new information. In essence, we are constantly proving our latest ideas are wrong.
Metamorphosis: Stages in a Life (1987) **Suzuki, David** (1936–) Japanese Buddhist scholar and main interpreter of Zen to the West

107 He put this engine to our ears, which made an incessant noise like that of a water-mill; and we conjecture it is either some unknown animal, or the god that he worships; but we are more inclined to the latter opinion.

Gulliver's Travels (1726) Describing a watch

108 He had been eight years upon a project for extracting sun-beams out of cucumbers, which were to be put into vials hermetically sealed, and let out to warm the air in raw inclement summers.
Gulliver's Travels (1726) **Swift, Jonathan** (1667–1745) Irish satirist, poet, essayist and cleric

109 Discovery consists of seeing what everybody has seen and thinking what nobody has thought.
In Good (ed.), *The Scientist Speculates* (1962) **Szent-Györgyi, Albert von** (1893–1986) Hungarian-born US biochemist

110 The highest wisdom has but one science – the science of the whole – and science explaining the whole creation and man's place in it.
War and Peace (1868–1869) **Tolstoy, Leo** (1828–1910) Russian writer, essayist, philosopher and moralist

111 The term Science should only be given to the collection of the recipes that are always successful. All the rest is literature.
Moralities, (1932) **Valéry, Paul** (1871–1945) French poet, mathematician and philosopher

112 The outcome of any serious research can only be to make two questions grow where only one grew before.
The Place of Science in Modern Civilization (1919) **Veblen, Thorstein** (1857–1929) US economist and sociologist

113 Nothing holds up the progress of science so much as the right idea at the wrong time.
Most Secret War (1978) **Vigneaud, Vincent de** (1901–1978) Canadian biochemist

114 Space travel is utter bilge.
In Martin Moskovits, *Science and Society,* (1995) **Woolley, Richard** (1906–1986) English astronomer. In 1956, one year before Sputnik

115 If it keeps up, man will atrophy all his limbs but the push-button finger.
New York Times Magazine, (1953) **Wright, Frank Lloyd** (1869–1959) US architect and writer

116 The airplane stays up because it doesn't have the time to fall.

Attr. **Wright, Orville** (1871–1948) US aircraft pioneer. Explaining the principles of powered flight

117 Duct tape is like the force. It has a light side, and a dark side, and it holds the universe together.
Attr. **Zwanzig, Carl** Scientist
See also computers; culture; genius; nature; universe

SCOTLAND

1 A day oot o' Aberdeen is a day oot o' life.
Traditional Scottish saying **Anonymous**

2 There are few more impressive sights in the world than a Scotsman on the make.
What Every Woman Knows (1908)

3 You've forgotten the grandest moral attribute of a Scotsman, Maggie, that he'll do nothing which might damage his career.
What Every Woman Knows (1908) **Barrie, Sir J.M.** (1860–1937) Scottish dramatist and writer

4 You must not look down on … Glasgow which gave the world the internal combustion engine, political economy, antiseptic and cerebral surgery, the balloon, the mariner's compass, the theory of Latent Heat, Tobias Smollett and James Bridie.
Letter to St John Ervine **Bridie, James** (1888–1951) Scottish dramatist, writer and physician

5 The devellysche dysposicion of a Scottysh man, not to love nor favour an Englishe man.
Letter to Thomas Cromwell, (1536)

6 Trust you no Skott.
Letter to Thomas Cromwell, (1536) **Boorde, Andrew** (c.1490–1549) English traveller, physician and writer

7 From scenes like these, old Scotia's grandeur springs
That makes her lov'd at home, rever'd abroad:
Princes and lords are but the breath of kings,
'An honest man's the noblest work of God.'
'The Cotter's Saturday Night' (1785)

8 The story of Wallace poured a Scottish prejudice in my veins which will boil along there till the flood-gates of life shut in eternal rest.
Letter to Dr Moore, (1787)

9 My heart's in the Highlands, my heart is not here,
My heart's in the Highlands a-chasing the deer,
A-chasing the wild deer and following the roe –
My heart's in the Highlands, wherever I go!
'My Heart's in the Highlands' (1790)

10 Scots, wha hae wi' Wallace bled,
Scots, wham Bruce has aften led,
Welcome to your gory bed
Or to victorie! …
Lay the proud usurpers low!
Tyrants fall in ev'ry foe!
Liberty's in every blow!
Let us do, or die!
'Scots, Wha Hae' (1793)

11 Contented wi' little and cantie wi' mair,
Whene'er I forgather wi' Sorrow and Care,
I gie them a skelp, as they're creepin alang,
Wi' a cog o' guid swats and an auld Scottish sang.
'Contented wi' Little and Cantie wi' Mair' (1794) **Burns, Robert** (1759–1796) Scottish poet and songwriter

12 Rarely have I been so pleased to leave a place.
Chronicle of a Book (1958) **Cernuda, Luis** (1902–1963) Spanish poet. On leaving Glasgow, where he had lived from 1939 to 1943

13 Had Cain been Scot, God would have changed his doom,
Nor forced him wander, but confined him home.
'The Rebel Scot' (1647) **Cleveland, John** (1613–1658) English poet

14 Scotland should be nothing less than equal with all the other nations of the world.
The Times, (1999) **Connery, Sean** (1930–) Scottish actor

15 The Irish are great talkers
Persuasive and disarming,
You can say lots and lots
Against the Scots –
But at least they're never charming!
The Complete Little Ones (1986) **Ewart, Gavin** (1916–1995) English poet

16 The Scottish Parliament, adjourned on 25th March 1707, is hereby reconvened.
Speech at the opening of the new Scottish Parliament, (12th May 1999) **Ewing, Winnie** (1929–) Scottish Nationalist politician

17 A desperate disease requires a dangerous remedy … one of my objects was to blow the Scots back again into Scotland.
Dictionary of National Biography **Fawkes, Guy** (1570–1606) English conspirator. On being asked by the King whether he regretted his proposed plot against Parliament and the royal family

18 It is difficult to imagine how, if Scotland's identity is stifled as a nation of five million in an economic and monetary union of 58 million, it will somehow have more influence, more authority and more status in a European Union of 371 million.
Speech, (1999) **Forsyth, Michael** (1954–) Scottish Conservative politician. Attacking Scottish National Party policy on Europe

19 I went to Scotland and found nothing there that looks like Scotland.
In Halliwell, *The Filmgoer's Book of Quotes* (1973) **Freed, Arthur** (1894–1973) US film producer and songwriter. Defending his decision to produce *Brigadoon* on the MGM lot

20 From the lone shieling of the misty island
Mountains divide us, and the waste of seas –
Yet still the blood is strong, the heart is Highland,
And we in dreams behold the Hebrides!
Fair these broad meads, these hoary woods are grand;
But we are exiles from our fathers' land.
Attr. in *Blackwood's Edinburgh Magazine,* (1829) **Galt, John** (1779–1839) Scottish writer and Canadian pioneer

21 In simmer, whan aa sorts foregether
   in Embro to the ploy,
   fowk seek out friens to hae a blether,
   or faes they'd fain annoy;
   smorit wi British Railways' reek
   frae Glesca or Glen Roy
   or Wick, they come to hae a week
   of cultivatit joy,
   or three,
   in Embro to the ploy.
   Selected Poems (1966) **Garioch, Robert** (1909–1981)

22 As sure as I'm a Scot
   A redshank Norland haggis-eater.
   Quoted in F. Marian McNeill, *The Scots Kitchen* (1929) **Halliday, J.** (1790–1867) Rustic bard

23 Courage is a quality Scots lack only when they become MPs. They should be twisting the lion's tail until it comes out by the roots.
   Daily Mail, (1996) **Hamilton, Ian** (1925–) Lawyer and Scottish Nationalist. On the performance of Scottish National Party MPs in Westminster

24 Oats. A grain, which in England is generally given to horses, but in Scotland supports the people.
   A Dictionary of the English Language (1755)

25 I know not whether it be not peculiar to the Scots to have attained the liberal without the manual arts, to have excelled in ornamental knowledge, and to have wanted not only the elegancies, but the conveniences of common life.
   A Journey to the Western Islands of Scotland (1775)

26 Seeing Scotland, Madam, is only seeing a worse England. It is seeing the flower fade away to the naked stalk.
   In Boswell, *The Life of Samuel Johnson* (1791)

27 Much may be made of a Scotchman, if he be caught young.
   In Boswell, *The Life of Samuel Johnson* (1791)

28 Norway, too, has noble wild prospects; and Lapland is remarkable for prodigious noble wild prospects. But, Sir, let me tell you, the noblest prospect which a Scotchman ever sees, is the high road that leads him to England!
   In Boswell, *The Life of Samuel Johnson* (1791)

29 Their learning is like bread in a besieged town: every man gets a little, but no man gets a full meal.
   In Boswell, *The Life of Samuel Johnson* (1791) Of the Scots

30 *Boswell*: I do indeed come from Scotland, but I cannot help it …
   Johnson: That, Sir, I find, is what a very great many of your countrymen cannot help.
   In Boswell, *The Life of Samuel Johnson* (1791) **Johnson, Samuel** (1709–1784) English lexicographer, poet, critic, conversationalist and essayist

31 Poor sister Scotland!
   Her doom is fell.
   She cannot find any more Stuarts to sell.
   Chamber Music (1907) **Joyce, James** (1882–1941) Irish writer

32 Lutherans are like Scottish people, only with less frivolity.
   The Independent, (1992) **Keillor, Garrison** (1942–) US writer and broadcaster

33 I have been trying all my life to like Scotchmen, and am obliged to desist from the experiment in despair.
   'Imperfect Sympathies' (1823) **Lamb, Charles** (1775–1834) English essayist, critic and letter writer

34 St Andrews by the Northern Sea,
   A haunted town it is to me!
   'Almae Matres' (1884) **Lang, Andrew** (1844–1912) Scottish poet, writer, mythologist and anthropologist

35 Glasgow is not a melting pot; it's closer to a chip pan in which you've attempted to boil cream, the ingredients have separated, and neither element is palatable.
   The Scotsman, (1999) **Lappin, Tom** Scottish journalist

36 Having little else to cultivate, they cultivated the intellect. The export of brains came to be their chief item of commerce.
   Humour (1935) **Leacock, Stephen** (1869–1944) English-born Canadian humorist, writer and economist. Of the Scots

37 Beautiful, glorious Scotland, has spoilt me for every other country!
Letter, (1869) in *The Mary Lincoln Letters* (1956) **Lincoln, Mary Todd** (1818–1882) Wife of US President Abraham Lincoln

38 While swordless Scotland, sadder than its psalms,
Fosters its sober youth on national alms
To breed a dull provincial discipline,
Commerce its god and golf its anodyne.
'Preamble to a Satire' **Linklater, Eric** (1899–1974) Welsh-born Scottish writer and satirist

39 In all my travels I have never met with any one Scotchman but what was a man of sense. I believe everybody of that country that has any, leaves it as fast as they can.
In Spence, *Anecdotes* (1858) **Lockier, Francis** (1667–1740) English churchman

40 A Scottish poet maun assume
The burden o' his people's doom,
And dee to brak' their livin' tomb.
A Drunk Man Looks at the Thistle (1926)

41 It's easier to lo'e Prince Charlie
Than Scotland – mair's the shame!
'Bonnie Prince Charlie' (1930)

42 The rose of all the world is not for me
I want for my part
Only the little white rose of Scotland
That smells sharp and sweet – and breaks the heart.
'The Little White Rose' **MacDiarmid, Hugh** (1892–1978) Scottish poet

43 Scotchmen seem to think it's a credit to them to be Scotch.
A Writer's Notebook (1949) **Maugham, William Somerset** (1874–1965) English writer, dramatist and physician

44 Beautiful city of Glasgow, I now conclude my muse,
And to write in praise of thee my pen does not refuse;
And, without fear of contradiction, I will venture to say
You are the second grandest city in Scotland at the present day.
'Glasgow' (1890) **McGonagall, William** (c.1830–1902) Scottish poet, tragedian and actor

45 I think it possible that all Scots are illegitimate, Scotsmen being so mean and Scotswomen so generous.
Scottish Journey (1935) **Muir, Edwin** (1887–1959) Scottish poet, critic, translator and writer

46 Better lo'ed ye canna be,
Will ye no come back again?
Lays from Strathearn (1846), 'Bonnie Charlie's now awa!' **Nairne, Carolina, Baroness** (1766–1845) Referring to Bonnie Prince Charlie

47 No Mc
Tavish
Was ever lavish.
'Genealogical Reflection' (1931) **Nash, Ogden** (1902–1971) US poet

48 England treats Scotland as if it was an island off the coast of West Africa in the 1830s.
Daily Mail, (1996) **Nicholson, Emma** British Liberal Democrat MEP

49 Minds like ours, my dear James, must always be above national prejudices, and in all companies it gives me true pleasure to declare, that, as a people, the English are very little indeed inferior to the Scotch.
Blackwood's Edinburgh Magazine, (1826) **North, Christopher** (1785–1854) Scottish poet, writer, editor and critic

50 Now there's an end of ane old song.
Remark, (1707) **Ogilvy, James** (1663–1730) Scottish politician and lawyer. On signing the Act of Union

51 There is nothing the Scots like better to hear than abuse of the English.
Attr. **Piccolomini, Enea** (1405–1464) Pope 1458–1464. Comment after a visit to Scotland in 1435

52 A Scots mist will weet an Englishman to the skin.
A Collection of Scots Proverbs (1737) **Ramsay, Allan** (1686–1758) Scottish poet

53 In Europe the big word is tolerance. Homosexuals are riding high in the media … and in Scotland, you can't believe how strong the homosexuals are.
The Guardian, (1999) **Robertson, Pat** (1930–) US fundamentalist Christian broadcaster and politician

54 There is not an anti-English bone in my body. I have forgotten more about English history than most Tory MPs ever learned.
The Observer, (1998) **Salmond, Alex** (1955–) Scottish nationalist politician

55 O Caledonia! stern and wild,
Meet nurse for a poetic child!
Land of brown heath and shaggy wood,
Land of the mountain and the flood,
Land of my sires! what mortal hand
Can e'er untie the filial band,
That knits me to thy rugged strand!
The Lay of the Last Minstrel (1805)

56 Still from the sire the son shall hear
Of the stern strife, and carnage drear,
Of Flodden's fatal field,
Where shiver'd was fair Scotland's spear,
And broken was her shield!
Marmion (1808)

57 We have become the caterpillars of the island, instead of its pillars.
Letter to the Editor of *The Edinburgh Weekly Journal*, (1826) Comment on the Union of Scotland with England in 1707 **Scott, Sir Walter** (1771–1832) Scottish writer and historian

58 It requires a surgical operation to get a joke well into a Scotch understanding. Their only idea of wit … is laughing immoderately at stated intervals.
In Holland, *A Memoir of the Reverend Sydney Smith* (1855)

59 That knuckle-end of England – that land of Calvin, oat-cakes, and sulphur.
In Holland, *A Memoir of the Reverend Sydney Smith* (1855). Of Scotland **Smith, Sydney** (1771–1845) English clergyman, essayist, journalist and wit

60 The Scots have a slight tincture of letters, with which they make a parade among people who are more illiterate than themselves; but they may be said to float on the surface of science, and they have made very small advances in the useful arts.
Humphry Clinker (1771) **Smollett, Tobias** (1721–1771) Scottish writer, satirist, historian, traveller and physician

61 It was Edinburgh that bred within me the conditions of exiledom; and what have I been doing since then but moving from exile to exile? It has ceased to be a fate, it has become a calling.
'What Images Return' **Spark, Muriel** (1918–2006) Scottish writer, poet and dramatist

62 Be it granted to me to behold you again in dying,
Hills of home! and to hear again the call;
Hear about the graves of the martyrs the peewees crying,
And hear no more at all.
Songs of Travel (1896) **Stevenson, Robert Louis** (1850–1894) Scottish writer, poet and essayist

63 The Scottish people will one day become extinct.
The Observer, (1998) **Vincent, John** English historian and journalist. On the falling birth rate in Scotland

64 In Scotland – well, you know what the Scots are like. They booze, they smoke and they eat anything that comes to hand.
Attr. **Witzel, Jean-Luc** French football agent. Comment before a France–Scotland football match

65 It is never difficult to distinguish between a Scotsman with a grievance and a ray of sunshine.
Blandings Castle and Elsewhere (1935) **Wodehouse, P.G.** (1881–1975) English humorist and writer

THE SEA

1 The ceaseless twinkling laughter of the waves of the sea.
Prometheus Bound **Aeschylus** (525–456 BC) Greek dramatist and poet

2 Sand-strewn caverns, cool and deep,
Where the winds are all asleep;
Where the spent lights quiver and gleam;
Where the salt weed sways in the stream;
Where the sea-beasts ranged all round
Feed in the ooze of their pasture-ground…
Where great whales come sailing by,
Sail and sail, with unshut eye,
Round the world for ever and aye.
'The Forsaken Merman' (1849)

3 The sea is calm to-night,
The tide is full, the moon lies fair
Upon the straits.
'Dover Beach' (1867) **Arnold, Matthew** (1822–1888) English poet, critic, essayist and educationist

4 Everywhere, the sea is a teacher of truth. I am not sure that the best thing I find in sailing is not this salt of reality ... There, sailing the sea, we play every part of life: control, direction, effort, fate; and there can we test ourselves and know our state.
Quoted by Libby Purves, *The Times*, (1998) **Belloc, Hilaire** (1870–1953) English writer of verse, essayist and critic; Liberal MP

5 They that go down to the sea in ships, that do business in great waters;
These see the works of the Lord, and his wonders in the deep.
Psalms, 107:23–24 **The Bible (King James Version)**

6 Whither, O splendid ship, thy white sails crowding,
Leaning across the bosom of the urgent West,
That fearest not sea rising, nor sky clouding,
Whither away, fair rover, and what thy quest?
'A Passer-by' (1890) **Bridges, Robert** (1844–1930) English poet, dramatist, essayist and doctor

7 Dark-heaving – boundless, endless, and sublime,
The image of eternity.
Childe Harold's Pilgrimage (1818)

8 Roll on, thou deep and dark blue Ocean – roll!
Ten thousand fleets sweep over thee in vain;
Man marks the earth with ruin – his control
Stops with the shore.
Childe Harold's Pilgrimage (1818) **Byron, Lord** (1788–1824) English poet, satirist and traveller

9 Now it is water I dream of,
... lifting
casually on a shore
where yellow lions come out
in the early morning
and stare out to sea.
Collected Poems 1947–1981 (1981) **Campbell, Alistair Te Ariki** (1925–) New Zealand poet

10 What are the wild waves saying
Sister, the whole day long,
That ever amid our playing,
I hear but their low lone song?
'What are the Wild Waves Saying' (song, 1850) **Carpenter, Joseph Edwards** (1813–1885)

11 In its mysterious past, it encompasses all the dim origins of life and receives in the end ... the dead husks of that same life. For all at last return to the sea – to Oceanus, the ocean river, like the ever-flowing stream of time, the beginning and the end.
The Sea Around Us (1951) **Carson, Rachel Louise** (1907–1964) US marine biologist and writer

12 The voice of the sea speaks to the soul. The touch of the sea is sensuous, enfolding the body in its soft, close embrace.
The Awakening (1899) **Chopin, Kate** (1851–1904) US writer

13 You can do far worse than putting it into a deep and well-flushed sea. As far as poisoning the fish is concerned, that's rubbish. The sewage has probably kept the poor fish alive.
The Times, (1992) **Clayton, Keith** (1928–) Professor of Environmental Sciences. Of sewage

14 The fair breeze blew, the white foam flew,
The furrow followed free;
We were the first that ever burst
Into that silent sea.
'The Rime of the Ancient Mariner' (1798)

15 As idle as a painted ship
Upon a painted ocean.
'The Rime of the Ancient Mariner' (1798)

16 Water, water, every where,
And all the boards did shrink;
Water, water, every where
Nor any drop to drink.

'The Rime of the Ancient Mariner' (1798)
Coleridge, Samuel Taylor (1772–1834) English poet, philosopher and critic

17 This could have occurred nowhere but in England, where men and sea interpenetrate, so to speak.
Youth (1902) **Conrad, Joseph** (1857–1924) Polish-born British writer, sailor and explorer

18 A wet sheet and a flowing sea,
A wind that follows fast
And fills the white and rustling sail
And bends the gallant mast.
'A Wet Sheet and a Flowing Sea' (1825)
Cunningham, Allan (1784–1842) Scottish poet, reporter and biographer

19 I want to know what it says ... The sea, Floy, what it is that it keeps on saying?
Dombey and Son (1848)

20 'People can't die, along the coast,' said Mr Peggotty, 'except when the tide's pretty nigh out. They can't be born, unless it's pretty nigh in – not properly born, till flood. He's a going out with the tide.'
David Copperfield (1850) **Dickens, Charles** (1812–1870) English writer

21 The sea is as deepe in a calme as in a storme.
Sermons **Donne, John** (1572–1631) English poet

22 A ship, an isle, a sickle moon –
With few but with how splendid stars
The mirrors of the sea are strewn
Between their silver bars.
The Golden Journey to Samarkand (1913)

23 The dragon-green, the luminous, the dark, the serpent-haunted sea.
The Golden Journey to Samarkand (1913) **Flecker, James Elroy** (1884–1915) English poet, orientalist and translator

24 The wine-dark sea.
Iliad **Homer** (fl. c.8th century BC) Greek epic poet

25 The snotgreen sea. The scrotumtightening sea.
Ulysses (1922) **Joyce, James** (1882–1941) Irish writer

26 It keeps eternal whisperings around Desolate shores, and with its mighty swell Gluts twice ten thousand caverns.
'On the Sea' (1817) **Keats, John** (1795–1821) English poet

27 What is a woman that you forsake her, And the hearth-fire and the home-acre, To go with the old grey Widow-maker?
'Harp Song of the Dane Women' (1906)

28 Oh, was there ever sailor free to choose, That didn't settle somewhere near the sea?
The Years Between (1919) **Kipling, Rudyard** (1865–1936) Indian-born British poet and writer

29 'Wouldst thou' – so the helmsman answered –
'Learn the secret of the sea?
Only those who brave its dangers
Comprehend its mystery!'
'The Secret of the Sea' (1904) **Longfellow, Henry Wadsworth** (1807–1882) US poet and writer

30 I must go down to the seas again, to the lonely sea and the sky,
And all I ask is a tall ship and a star to steer her by,
And the wheel's kick and the wind's song and the white sail's shaking,
And a grey mist on the sea's face and a grey dawn breaking ...
I must go down to the seas again, for the call of the running tide
Is a wild call and a clear call that may not be denied ...
I must go down to the seas again, to the vagrant gypsy life,
To the gull's way and the whale's way where the wind's like a whetted knife;
And all I ask is a merry yarn from a laughing fellow rover,
And a quiet sleep and a sweet dream when the long trick's over.
'Sea Fever' (1902) **Masefield, John** (1878–1967) English poet, writer and critic

31 You gentlemen of England
Who live at home at ease,
How little do you think
On the dangers of the seas.

In J.O. Halliwell (ed.), *Early Naval Ballads* (1841), 'The Valiant Sailors' **Parker, Martin** (c.1600–c.1656) English ballad writer

32 I have bathed in the Poem
Of the Sea, steeped in stars, milky,
Devouring the green azures.
'Le Bâteau ivre' (1870) **Rimbaud, Arthur** (1854–1891) French poet

33 The sea hath no king but God alone.
'The White Ship' **Rossetti, Dante Gabriel** (1828–1882) English poet, painter, translator and letter writer

34 It's no fish ye're buying – it's men's lives.
The Antiquary (1816) **Scott, Sir Walter** (1771–1832) Scottish writer and historian

35 I will go back to the great sweet mother,
Mother and lover of men, the sea.
I will go down to her, I and no other,
Close with her, kiss her and mix her with me ...
I shall sleep, and move with the moving ships,
Change as the winds change, veer in the tide;
My lips will feast on the foam of thy lips,
I shall rise with thy rising and with thee subside.
'The Triumph of Time' (1866) **Swinburne, Algernon Charles** (1837–1909) English poet, critic, dramatist and letter writer

36 'A man who is not afraid of the sea will soon be drownded,' he said, 'for he will be going out on a day he shouldn't. But we do be afraid of the sea, and we do only be drownded now and again.'
The Aran Islands (1907) **Synge, J.M.** (1871–1909) Irish dramatist, poet and letter writer

37 The great sea
Has set me adrift
It moves me as the weed in the river,
Earth and the great weather
Move me,
Have carried me away
And move my inward parts with joy.
In Rasmussen, *Intellectual Culture of the Igulik Eskimos* (1929) **Uvavnuk** Inuit singer and shaman

38 Only fools and passengers drink at sea.
The Observer, (1957) **Villiers, Alan John** (1903–1982) Australian naval commander

39 Eternal Father, strong to save,
Whose arm hath bound the restless wave,
... O hear us when we cry to Thee
For those in peril on the sea.
Hymn, (1869) **Whiting, William** (1825–1878) English teacher, poet and hymn writer

40 The sea! The sea!
Anabasis **Xenophon** (c.430–354 BC) Greek historian, essayist and military commander. The joyful cry of his soldiers after their long march (1000 miles) back to the Aegean from the centre of Persia
See also nature

THE SEASONS

1 Many human beings say that they enjoy the winter, but what they really enjoy is feeling proof against it.
Watership Down (1974) **Adams, Richard** (1920–) English writer

2 It was no summer progress. A cold coming they had of it, at this time of the year; just the worst time of the year to take a journey, and specially a long journey, in. The ways deep, the weather sharp, the days short, the sun farthest off in solstitio brumali, the very dead of Winter.
Sermon 15, *Of the Nativity* (1629) **Andrewes, Bishop Lancelot** (1555–1626) English churchman

3 What dreadful hot weather we have! It keeps me in a continual state of inelegance.
Letter, (1796) **Austen, Jane** (1775–1817) English writer

4 When men were all asleep the snow came flying,
In large white flakes falling on the city brown,
Stealthily and perpetually settling and loosely lying,
Hushing the latest traffic of the drowsy town ...
All night it fell, and when full inches seven

It lay in depth of its uncompacted lightness,
The clouds blew off from a high and frosty heaven;
And all woke either for the unaccustomed brightness
Of the winter dawning, the strange unheavenly glare ...
Or peering up from under the white-mossed wonder,
'O look at the trees!' they cried, 'O look at the trees!'
'London Snow' (1890) **Bridges, Robert** (1844–1930) English poet, dramatist, essayist and doctor

5 Sweet rain, bless our windy farm,
Stepping round in skirts of storm:
Amongst the broken clods the hare
Folds his ears like hands in prayer.
'Prayer for Rain' (c.1950) **Campbell, David** (1915–1979) Australian poet, rugby player and wartime pilot

6 The Summer hath his joyes,
And Winter his delights;
Though Love and all his pleasures are but toyes,
They shorten tedious nights.
The Third Booke of Ayres (1617) **Campion, Thomas** (1567–1620) English poet

7 Now Spring brings back her gentle warmth.
Carmina **Catullus** (84–c.54 BC) Roman poet

8 He who doesn't notice whether it is winter or summer is happy. I think that if I were in Moscow, I wouldn't notice what the weather was like.
The Three Sisters (1901) **Chekhov, Anton** (1860–1904) Russian writer, dramatist and doctor

9 Therefore all seasons shall be sweet to thee,
Whether the summer clothe the general earth
With greenness, or the redbreast sit and sing
Betwixt the tufts of snow on the bare branch
Of mossy apple-tree, while the nigh thatch
Smokes in the sun-thaw; whether the eave-drops fall
Heard only in the trances of the blast,

Or if the secret ministry of frost
Shall hang them up in silent icicles,
Quietly shining to the quiet moon.
'Frost at Midnight' (1798)

10 Summer has set in with its usual severity.
Letters of Charles Lamb (1888) **Coleridge, Samuel Taylor** (1772–1834) English poet, philosopher and critic

11 Our severest winter, commonly called the spring.
Letter to the Rev. W. Unwin, (1783) **Cowper, William** (1731–1800) English poet, hymn writer and letter writer

12 Snowy, Flowy, Blowy,
Showery, Flowery, Bowery,
Hoppy, Croppy, Droppy,
Breezy, Sneezy, Freezy.
'The Twelve Months' **Ellis, George** (1753–1815) West Indian-born British satirist and poet

13 A woman rang to say she'd heard there was a hurricane on the way – well don't worry, there isn't.
Sunday Telegraph, (1989) **Fish, Michael** (1944–) English meteorologist and weather presenter. Said during the weather forecast just prior to the storm of October 1987 which proved him disastrously wrong

14 This is the weather the cuckoo likes,
And so do I;
When showers betumble the chestnut spikes,
And nestlings fly:
And the little brown nightingale bills his best,
And they sit outside at 'The Travellers' Rest'.
'Weathers' (1922)

15 Every branch big with it,
Bent every twig with it;
Every fork like a white web-foot;
Every street and pavement mute:
Some flakes have lost their way, and grope back upward, when
Meeting those meandering down they turn and descend again.
'Snow in the Suburbs' (1925) **Hardy, Thomas** (1840–1928) English writer and poet

16 No sun – no moon!
No morn – no noon
No dawn – no dusk – no proper time of
day –
No warmth, no cheerfulness, no healthful
ease,
No comfortable feel in any member –
No shade, no shine, no butterflies, no
bees,
No fruits, no flowers, no leaves, no birds, –
November!
Whimsicalities (1844), 'No!'

17 I saw old Autumn in the misty morn
Stand shadowless like Silence, listening
To silence.
'Ode: Autumn' (1823) **Hood, Thomas** (1799–
1845) English poet, editor and humorist

18 Worshippe, ye that loveris been, this May,
For of your blisse the Kalendis are begun,
And sing with us, away, Winter, away!
Come, Summer, come the sweet seasoun
and sun.
The Kingis Quair **James I of Scotland** (1394–
1437) King of Scotland

19 Where are the songs of Spring? Ay, where
are they?
Think not of them, thou hast thy music
too.
'To Autumn' (1819)

20 Four seasons fill the measure of the year;
There are four seasons in the mind of man.
'The Human Seasons' (1818) **Keats, John**
(1795–1821) English poet

21 No one thinks of winter when the grass is
green!
Rewards and Fairies (1910), 'A St Helena
Lullaby' **Kipling, Rudyard** (1865–1936) Indian-
born British poet and writer

22 In a somer seson whan soft was the sonne.
*The Vision of William Concerning Piers the
Plowman* **Langland, William** (c.1330–c.1400)
English poet

23 Yes, I was right, spring and summer did
happen in Cambridge almost every year
(that mysterious 'almost' was singularly
pleasing).
The Real Life of Sebastian Knight (1941)
Nabokov, Vladimir (1899–1977) Russian-born
US writer, poet, translator and critic

24 Two evils, monstrous either one apart,
Possessed me, and were long and loath at
going:
A cry of Absence, Absence, in the heart,
And in the wood the furious winter
blowing –
Dear love, these fingers that had known
your touch,
And tied our separate forces first together,
Were ten poor idiot fingers not worth
much,
Ten frozen parsnips hanging in the
weather.
'Winter Remembered' (1945) **Ransom, John
Crowe** (1888–1974) US poet and critic

25 Spring has come again. The earth is like a
child who knows poems.
The Sonnets to Orpheus (1923) **Rilke, Rainer
Maria** (1875–1926) Austrian poet, born in
Prague

26 In the bleak mid-winter
Frosty wind made moan,
Earth stood hard as iron,
Water like a stone;
Snow had fallen, snow on snow,
Snow on snow,
In the bleak mid-winter,
Long ago.
'A Christmas Carol' (1875) **Rossetti, Christina**
(1830–1894) English poet

27 To be interested in the changing seasons
is, in this middling zone, a happier state of
mind than to be hopelessly in love with
spring.
Little Essays (1920) **Santayana, George** (1863–
1952) Spanish-born US philosopher and
writer

28 At Christmas I no more desire a rose
Than wish a snow in May's new-fangled
shows;
But like of each thing that in season grows.
Love's Labour's Lost, I.i

29 Shall I compare thee to a summer's day?
Thou art more lovely and more temperate.
Rough winds do shake the darling buds of
May,
And summer's lease hath all too short a
date.
Sonnet 18 **Shakespeare, William** (1564–1616)
English dramatist, poet and actor

30 Thank heavens, the sun has gone in, and I don't have to go out and enjoy it.
All Trivia (1933) **Smith, Logan Pearsall** (1865–1946) US-born British epigrammatist, critic and writer

31 Their wintry garment of unsullied snow
The mountains have put on.
The Poet's Pilgrimage (1816) **Southey, Robert** (1774–1843) English poet, essayist, historian and letter writer

32 Fresh spring the herald of love's mighty king,
In whose cote armour richly are displayd
All sorts of flowers the which on earth do spring
In goodly colours gloriously arrayd.
Amoretti, and Epithalamion (1595), Sonnet 70 **Spenser, Edmund** (c.1522–1599) English poet

33 I can never remember whether it snowed for six days and six nights when I was twelve or whether it snowed for twelve days and twelve nights when I was six.
A Child's Christmas in Wales (1954) **Thomas, Dylan** (1914–1953) Welsh poet, writer and radio dramatist

34 Spring is come home with her world-wandering feet.
And all things are made young with young desires.
'From the Night of Forebeing' (1913) **Thompson, Francis** (1859–1907) English poet

35 The comic almanacs give us dreadful pictures of January and February; but, in truth, the months which should be made to look gloomy in England are March and April. Let no man boast himself that he has got through the perils of winter till at least the seventh of May.
Doctor Thorne (1858) **Trollope, Anthony** (1815–1882) English writer, traveller and post office official

36 Sweet April showers
Do spring May flowers.
Five Hundred Points of Good Husbandry (1557) **Tusser, Thomas** (c.1524–1580) English writer, poet and musician

37 Everybody talks about the weather but nobody does anything about it.
Attr. **Twain, Mark** (1835–1910) US humorist, writer, journalist and lecturer

38 The way to ensure summer in England is to have it framed and glazed in a comfortable room.
Letter to William Cole, (1774) **Walpole, Horace** (1717–1797) English writer and politician
See also nature

SECRETS

1 Everything secret degenerates ... nothing is safe that does not show how it can bear discussion and publicity.
Attr. **Acton, Lord** (1834–1902) English historian and moralist

2 Ninety-two percent of the stuff told you in confidence you couldn't get anyone else to listen to.
Attr. **Adams, Franklin P.** (1881–1960) US writer, poet, translator and editor

3 No one ever confides a secret to one person only. No one destroys all copies of a document.
In Melissa Stein, *The Wit & Wisdom of Women* (1993) **Adler, Renata** (1936–) US film critic and writer

4 At last the secret is out, as it always must come in the end,
The delicious story is ripe to tell to the intimate friend;
Over the tea-cups and in the square the tongue has its desire;
Still waters run deep, my dear, there's never smoke without fire ...
For the clear voice suddenly singing, high up in the convent wall,
The scent of elder bushes, the sporting prints in the hall,
The croquet matches in summer, the handshake, the cough, the kiss,
There is always a wicked secret, a private reason for this.
Collected Poems, 1933–1938, 'Twelve Songs, VIII' **Auden, W.H.** (1907–1973) English poet, essayist, critic, teacher and dramatist

5 Love ceases to be a pleasure, when it ceases to be a secret.

The Lover's Watch (1686) **Behn, Aphra** (1640–1689) English dramatist, writer, poet, translator and spy

6 Brazenness and public liberties do much more harm to a woman's honour than secret wickedness.
Don Quixote (1615) **Cervantes, Miguel de** (1547–1616) Spanish writer and dramatist

7 Dear boy, I can hardly close the door.
The Observer, (1998) **Clark, Alan** (1928–1999) British Conservative politician, historian and diarist. On being asked whether he had any embarrassing skeletons in the cupboard

8 I know that's a secret, for it's whispered everywhere.
Love for Love (1695) **Congreve, William** (1670–1729) English dramatist

9 Secrets with girls, like loaded guns with boys,
Are never valued till they make a noise.
Tales of the Hall (1819) **Crabbe, George** (1754–1832) English poet, clergyman, surgeon and botanist

10 We never knows wot's hidden in each other's hearts; and if we had glass winders there, we'd need keep the shetters up, some on us, I do assure you!
Martin Chuzzlewit (1844) **Dickens, Charles** (1812–1870) English writer

11 For secrets are edged tools,
And must be kept from children and from fools.
Sir Martin Mar-All (1667) **Dryden, John** (1631–1700) English poet, satirist, dramatist and critic

12 Three may keep a secret, if two of them are dead.
Poor Richard's Almanac (1735) **Franklin, Benjamin** (1706–1790) US statesman, scientist, political critic and printer

13 It is a secret in the Oxford sense: you may tell it to only one person at a time.
Sunday Telegraph, (1977) **Franks, Oliver, Baron** (1905–1992) English diplomat, lecturer and banker

14 We dance round in a ring and suppose,
But the Secret sits in the middle and knows.

'The Secret Sits' (1942) **Frost, Robert** (1874–1963) US poet

15 Once the toothpaste is out of the tube, it is awfully hard to get it back in.
Hearings Before the Select Committee on Presidential Campaign Activities of US Senate: Watergate and Related Activities (1973) **Haldeman, H.R.** (1926–1993) US President Nixon's Chief of Staff. Comment to John Dean on the Watergate affair, 1973

16 But that I am forbid
To tell the secrets of my prison-house,
I could a tale unfold whose lightest word
Would harrow up thy soul, freeze thy young blood,
Make thy two eyes, like stars, start from their spheres,
Thy knotted and combined locks to part,
And each particular hair to stand an end,
Like quills upon the fretful porpentine.
But this eternal blazon must not be
To ears of flesh and blood. List, list, O, list!
Hamlet, I.v **Shakespeare, William** (1564–1616) English dramatist, poet and actor

17 A secret is a weapon and a friend. Man is God's secret, Power is man's secret, Sex is woman's secret.
The Crock of Gold (1912) **Stephens, James** (1882–1950) Irish poet and writer

18 There is no secret so close as that between a rider and his horse.
Mr Sponge's Sporting Tour (1853) **Surtees, R.S.** (1805–1864) English writer
See also deception; guilt; lies; silence

SELF

1 Resolve to be thyself; and know, that he,
Who finds himself, loses his misery!
'Self-Dependence' (1852) **Arnold, Matthew** (1822–1888) English poet, critic, essayist and educationist

2 Some thirty inches from my nose
The frontier of my Person goes,
And all the untilled air between
Is private pagus and demesne.
Stranger, unless with bedroom eyes
I beckon you to fraternize,
Beware of rudely crossing it;
I have no gun, but I can spit.

About the House,'Prologue: the Birth of Architecture' **Auden, W.H.** (1907–1973) English poet, essayist, critic, teacher and dramatist

3 This whatever this is that I am is flesh and spirit, and the ruling part.
Meditations **Aurelius, Marcus** (121–180) Roman emperor and Stoic philosopher

4 It is a poor centre of a man's actions, himself.
'Of Wisdom for a Man's Self' (1625) **Bacon, Francis** (1561–1626) English philosopher, essayist, politician and courtier

5 The tragedy of a man who has found himself out.
What Every Woman Knows (1908) **Barrie, Sir J.M.** (1860–1937) Scottish dramatist and writer

6 He who considers this as a slayer or he who thinks that this is slain, neither of these knows the Truth. For it does not slay, nor is it slain.
Ch. II **Bhagavadgita** On the Self

7 He is more myself than I am.
Wuthering Heights (1847) **Brontë, Emily** (1818–1848) English poet and writer

8 There is another man within me, that's angry with me, rebukes, commands, and dastards me.
Religio Medici (1643) **Browne, Sir Thomas** (1605–1682) English physician, author and antiquary

9 O wad some Power the giftie gie us
To see oursels as ithers see us!
It wad frae monie a blunder free us,
An' foolish notion:
What airs in dress an' gait wad lea'e us,
An' ev'n devotion!
'To a Louse' (1786) **Burns, Robert** (1759–1796) Scottish poet and songwriter

10 A certain inarticulate Self-consciousness dwells dimly in us ... Hence, too, the folly of that impossible precept, Know thyself; till it be translated into this partially possible one, Know what thou canst work at.
Sartor Resartus (1834) **Carlyle, Thomas** (1795–1881) Scottish historian, biographer, critic, and essayist

11 The proud, the cold untroubled heart of stone,
That never mused on sorrow but its own.
Pleasures of Hope (1799) **Campbell, Thomas** (1777–1844) Scottish poet, ballad writer and journalist

12 You have to believe in yourself, that's the secret. Even when I was in the orphanage, when I was roaming the street trying to find enough to eat, even then I thought of myself as the greatest actor in the world. I had to feel the exuberance that comes from utter confidence in yourself. Without it, you go down to defeat.
My Autobiography (1964) **Chaplin, Charlie** (1889–1977) English comedian, film actor, director and satirist

13 The spirit is the true self.
De Republica **Cicero** (106–43 BC) Roman orator, statesman, essayist and letter writer

14 'Know thyself' is a most superfluous direction. We can't avoid it. We can only hope that no one else knows.
A Family and a Fortune (1939) **Compton-Burnett, Dame Ivy** (1884–1969) English novelist

15 What the superior man seeks is in himself: what the small man seeks is in others.
Analects **Confucius** (c.550–c.478 BC) Chinese philosopher and teacher of ethics

16 I have always disliked myself at any given moment; the total of such moments is my life.
Enemies of Promise (1938) **Connolly, Cyril** (1903–1974) English literary editor, writer and critic

17 Everybody worships me, it's nauseating.
Present Laughter (1943) **Coward, Sir Noël** (1899–1973) English dramatist, actor, producer and composer

18 Vanity, like murder, will out.
The Belle's Stratagem (1780) **Cowley, Hannah** (1743–1809) English dramatist and poet

19 All sensible people are selfish, and nature is tugging at every contract to make the terms of it fair.

Conduct of Life (1860) **Emerson, Ralph Waldo** (1803–1882) US poet, essayist, transcendentalist and teacher

20 The one important thing I have learned over the years is the difference between taking one's work seriously and taking one's self seriously. The first is imperative and the second is disastrous.
Margot Fonteyn: Autobiography (1976) **Fonteyn, Margot** (1919–1991) English dancer

21 I do not know myself either, and may God protect me from that.
Gespräche mit Eckermann, (1829) **Goethe** (1749–1832) German poet, writer, dramatist and scientist

22 If I am not for myself who is for me; and being for my own self what am I? If not now when?
In Taylor (ed.), *Sayings of the Jewish Fathers* (1877) **Hillel, 'The Elder'** (c.60 BC–c.10 AD) Jewish religious leader

23 There's only one corner of the universe you can be certain of improving, and that's your own self.
Time Must Have a Stop (1944) **Huxley, Aldous** (1894–1963) English writer, poet and critic

24 Whenever I look inside myself I am afraid.
The Observer, (1942) **Joad, C.E.M.** (1891–1953) English popularizer of philosophy

25 Wherever an inferiority complex exists, there is a good reason for it. There is always something inferior there, although not just where we persuade ourselves that it is.
Interview, (1943) **Jung, Carl Gustav** (1875–1961) Swiss psychiatrist and pupil of Freud

26 The humble knowledge of thyself is a surer way to God than the deepest search after learning.
De Imitatione Christi (1892)

27 If you cannot mould yourself to such as you would wish, how can you expect others to be entirely to your liking?
De Imitatione Christi (1892) **Kempis, Thomas à** (c.1380–1471) German mystic, monk and writer

28 Self-interest speaks every kind of language, and plays every role, even that of disinterestedness.
Maximes (1678)

29 Self-love is the greatest flatterer of all.
Maximes (1678)

30 One would rather speak ill of oneself than not speak of oneself at all.
Maximes (1678) **La Rochefoucauld** (1613–1680) French writer

31 Not in the clamour of the crowded street,
Not in the shouts and plaudits of the throng,
But in ourselves, are triumph and defeat.
'The Poets' (1876) **Longfellow, Henry Wadsworth** (1807–1882) US poet and writer

32 He's been true to one party – an' thet is himself.
The Biglow Papers (1848) **Lowell, James Russell** (1819–1891) US poet, editor, abolitionist and diplomat

33 However much we reform our ways, grow a new self, we *are* our past; it lurks behind us, follows us, denounces us, tracks us down.
Ideas and the Novel (1980) **McCarthy, Mary** (1912–1989) US writer and critic

34 To have the courage of your excess – to find the limit of yourself.
Journal of Katherine Mansfield (1954) **Mansfield, Katherine** (1888–1923) New Zealand writer. On human limitations

35 We always took care of number one.
Scenes and Adventures in the Life of Frank Mildmay (1829) **Marryat, Frederick** (1792–1848) English naval officer and writer

36 I recognize that I am made up of several persons and that the person that at the moment has the upper hand will inevitably give place to another. But which is the real one? All of them or none?
A Writer's Notebook (1949) **Maugham, William Somerset** (1874–1965) English writer, dramatist and physician

37 The first rule in opera is the first rule in life: see to everything yourself.
Melodies and Memories (1925) **Melba, Dame Nellie** (1861–1931) Australian opera singer

38 We should look long and carefully at ourselves before we consider judging others.
Le Misanthrope (1666) **Molière** (1622–1673) French dramatist, actor and director

39 The greatest thing in the world is to know how to belong to oneself.
Essais (1580) **Montaigne, Michel de** (1533–1592) French essayist and moralist

40 Self is hateful.
Pensées (1670) **Pascal, Blaise** (1623–1662) French philosopher and scientist

41 I had – I have – nothing to say about myself, directly. I wouldn't know where to begin. Particularly since I often look at myself in the mirror and say 'Who the hell's that?'
Attr. **Pinter, Harold** (1930–) English dramatist, poet and screenwriter. On being asked why he did not include a character representing himself in *The Birthday Party*

42 He fell in love with himself at first sight and it is a passion to which he has always remained faithful. Self-love seems so often unrequited.
The Acceptance World (1955) **Powell, Anthony** (1905–2000) English writer and critic

43 I am always surprised when I am told that somebody likes me.
Instead of the Trees: A Final Chapter of Autobiography (1977) **Priestley, J.B.** (1894–1984) English writer, dramatist and critic

44 Man is not a solitary animal, and so long as social life survives, self-realization cannot be the supreme principle of ethics.
A History of Western Philosophy (1946) **Russell, Bertrand** (1872–1970) English philosopher, mathematician, essayist and social reformer

45 Vanity dies hard; in some obstinate cases it outlives the man.
Prince Otto **Stevenson, Robert Louis** (1850–1894) Scottish writer, poet and essayist

46 This above all – to thine own self be true, And it must follow, as the night the day, Thou canst not then be false to any man.
Hamlet, I.iii **Shakespeare, William** (1564–1616) English dramatist, poet and actor

47 It is easy – terribly easy – to shake a man's faith in himself. To take advantage of that to break a man's spirit is devil's work.
Candida (1898)

48 Don't fuss, my dear, I'm not unhappy. I am enjoying the enormous freedom of having found myself out and got myself off my mind; it is the beginning of hope and the end of hypocrisy.
On the Rocks **Shaw, George Bernard** (1856–1950) Irish socialist, writer, dramatist and critic

49 Why not be oneself? That is the whole secret of a successful appearance. If one is a greyhound, why try to look like a Pekingese?
'Why I look the way I do' (1955) **Sitwell, Dame Edith** (1887–1964) English poet, anthologist, critic and biographer

50 I have a little shadow that goes in and out with me,
And what can be the use of him is more than I can see.
A Children's Garden of Verses (1885), 'My Shadow' **Stevenson, Robert Louis** (1850–1894) Scottish writer, poet and essayist

51 I am always with myself, and it is I who am my own tormentor.
Memoirs of a Madman (1943) **Tolstoy, Leo** (1828–1910) Russian writer, essayist, philosopher and moralist

52 No man thinks there is much ado about nothing when the ado is about himself.
The Bertrams (1859)

53 Never think that you're not good enough yourself. A man should never think that. My belief is that in life people will take you very much at your own reckoning.
The Small House at Allington (1864) **Trollope, Anthony** (1815–1882) English writer, traveller and post office official

54 When people do not respect us we are sharply offended; yet deep down in his heart no man much respects himself.
Notebooks (1935) **Twain, Mark** (1835–1910) US humorist, writer, journalist and lecturer

55 I have never managed to escape being this thing, Myself.

The Eye of the Storm (1973) **White, Patrick** (1912–1990) English-born Australian writer and dramatist

56 Behold, I do not give lectures or a little charity,
When I give I give myself.
'Song of Myself' (1855) **Whitman, Walt** (1819–1892) US poet and writer

57 Other people are quite dreadful. The only possible society is oneself.
An Ideal Husband (1895) **Wilde, Oscar** (1854–1900) Irish poet, dramatist, writer, critic and wit
See also egoism; pride; solitude

SEX

1 Vasectomy means not ever having to say you're sorry.
Attr. **Adler, Larry** (1914–2001) US musician

2 The real stuff's inside. Whether you want your porn in black and white, full-colour litho, on film or on gramophone records and in any one of five languages, this is Stockholm's place for connoisseurs. There are no pictures of old slags and tattooed sailors here. The girls in the pictures are young and pretty and even the Great Danes are registered at the Swedish Kennel Club.
Snowball (1976) **Allbeury, Ted** (1917–2006) English crime writer

3 I finally had an orgasm, and then my doctor told me it was the wrong kind.
Attr. in *The Herald,* (1998)

4 I want to tell you a terrific story about oral contraception. I asked this girl to sleep with me and she said 'no'.
Attr. **Allen, Woody** (1935–) US film director, writer, actor and comedian

5 After coition every animal is sad.
Post-classical saying

6 Would you like to sin
With Elinor Glyn
On a tiger-skin?
Or would you prefer
To err with her
On some other fur?

Quoted in A. Glyn, *Elinor Glyn* (1955)

7 Every time you sleep with a boy you sleep with all his old girlfriends.
Government slogan, anti-Aids campaign, (1987) **Anonymous**

8 He loved a wench well: and one time getting up one of the maids of honour against a tree in a wood ('twas his first lady) who seemed at first boarding to be somewhat fearful of her honour, and modest, she cried, 'Sweet Sir Walter, what do you ask me? Will you undo me? Nay, sweet Sir Walter! Sir Walter!' At last as the danger and the pleasure at the same time grew higher, she cried in ecstasy, 'Swisser Swatter! Swisser Swatter!' She proved with child and I doubt not but this hero took care of them both, as also that the product was more than an ordinary mortal.
Brief Lives (c.1693) **Aubrey, John** (1626–1697) English antiquary, folklorist and biographer

9 The great and terrible step was taken. What else could you expect from a girl so expectant? 'Sex,' said Frank Harris, 'is the gateway to life.' So I went through the gateway in an upper room in the Café Royal.
Enid Bagnold's Autobiography (1969) **Bagnold, Enid** (1889–1981) English playwright

10 I'll come and make love to you at five o'clock. If I'm late start without me.
In Morgan, *Somerset Maugham* (1980) **Bankhead, Tallulah** (1903–1968) US actress. To an admirer

11 Love is just a system for getting someone to call you darling after sex.
Talking It Over (1991) **Barnes, Julian** (1946–) English novelist

12 Yes, I haven't had enough sex.
Time With Betjeman, BBC TV, (1983) **Betjeman, Sir John** (1906–1984) English poet laureate. When asked if he had any regrets

13 I'd rather have a cup of tea than go to bed with someone – any day.
Remark, variously expressed, (1983) **Boy George** (1961–) English singer

14 If God had meant us to have group sex, I guess he'd have given us all more organs.

Who Do You Think You Are? Stories and Parodies (1976) **Bradbury, Malcolm** (1932–2000) English writer, critic and academic

15 *Doctor*: But there the maids doe woe the Batchelors, and tis most probable, The wives lie uppermost.
Diana: That is a trim, upside-downe Antipodian tricke indeed.
The Antipodes (1638) **Brome, Richard** (c.1590–1652) English dramatist

16 I could be content that we might procreate like trees, without conjunction, or that there were any way to perpetuate the World without this trivial and vulgar way of coition.
Religio Medici (1643) **Browne, Sir Thomas** (1605–1682) English physician, author and antiquary

17 Sex, on the whole, was meant to be short, nasty and brutish. If what you want is cuddling, you should buy a puppy.
Sex and Sensibility (1992) **Burchill, Julie** (1960–) English writer

18 I don't mind where people make love, so long as they don't do it in the street and frighten the horses.
Attr. **Campbell, Mrs Patrick** (1865–1940) English actress

19 The right diet directs sexual energy into the parts that matter.
The Observer, (1981)

20 If a woman's going to leap into the bedroom waving a sex manual and demanding her rights to have 15 orgasms every five minutes, men are going to lose their pride and confidence. Do that to a man and he's finished.
The Guardian, (2000) **Cartland, Barbara** (1901–2000) English writer

21 She gave me a smile I could feel in my hip pocket.
Farewell, My Lovely (1940) **Chandler, Raymond** (1888–1959) US crime writer

22 The pleasure is momentary, the position ridiculous, and the expense damnable.
Attr. **Chesterfield, Lord** (1694–1773) English politician and letter writer

23 Politics gives guys so much power that they tend to behave badly around women. I hope I never get into that.
Said to a woman friend while a Rhodes scholar at Oxford

24 I did not have sexual relations with that woman.
Deposition in the Jones sexual harassment lawsuit, (17th January 1998) Referring to White House intern Monica Lewinsky **Clinton, William ('Bill')** (1946–) US Democrat President

25 A woman who has the divine gift of lechery will always make a superlative partner.
Attr. **Comfort, Alex** (1920–2000) British medical biologist and writer on sex

26 In the sex-war thoughtlessness is the weapon of the male, vindictiveness of the female.
The Unquiet Grave (1944) **Connolly, Cyril** (1903–1974) English literary editor, writer and critic

27 It's rather like teaching swimming from a book without ever having got wet oneself.
Disillusioned Decades: Ireland, 1966–87 (1987) **Coogan, Tim Pat** (1935–) Irish writer. Describing the rulings of the Catholic Church on matters of sexual morality

28 What is wrong with pornography is that it is a successful attempt to sell sex for more than it is worth.
In Kettlehack (ed.), *The Wit and Wisdom of Quentin Crisp* **Crisp, Quentin** (1908–1999) English writer, publicist and model

29 My message to the businessmen of this country when they go abroad on business is that there is one thing above all they can take with them to stop them catching Aids, and that is the wife.
The Observer, (1987) **Currie, Edwina** (1946–) English politician and writer

30 Sex that is not an evidence of a strong human tie is just like blowing your nose; it's not a celebration of a splendid relationship.
Interview, (1974) **Davies, Robertson** (1913–1995) Canadian playwright, writer and critic

31 Licence my roving hands, and let them go,
Before, behind, between, above, below.
O my America! my new-found-land,
My kingdom, safeliest when with one man
mann'd.
'To His Mistress Going to Bed' (c.1595)
Donne, John (1572–1631) English poet

32 No more about sex, it's too boring.
Tunc (1968) **Durrell, Lawrence** (1912–1990)
Indian-born British poet and writer

33 Intercourse as an act often expresses the
power men have over women.
Intercourse (1987)

34 Sex exists on both sides of the law but the
law itself creates the sides.
Intercourse (1987)

35 Seduction is often difficult to distinguish
from rape. In seduction, the rapist often
bothers to buy a bottle of wine.
The Independent, (1992) **Dworkin, Andrea**
(1946–2005) US writer and feminist

36 I say I don't sleep with married men, but
what I mean is that I don't sleep with
happily married men.
Attr. **Ekland, Britt** (1942–) Swedish actress

37 Women need a reason to have sex. Men
need a place.
When Harry Met Sally (film, 1989) **Ephron,
Nora** (1941–) US writer and screenwriter

38 Sex is a human activity like any other. It's a
natural urge, like breathing, thinking,
drinking, laughing, talking with friends,
golf. They are not crimes if you plan them
with someone other than your wife. Why
should sex be?
The Independent, (1992) **Fairbairn, Sir Nicholas**
(1933–1995) Scottish Conservative MP and
barrister

39 I couldn't believe it when I picked up a
newspaper and read that 82 per cent of
men would rather sleep with a goat than
me.
Attr. **Ferguson, Sarah** (1959–) Former Duchess
of York

40 A little of what people want is OK as long
as it's on the harmless end of the
spectrum. The more you try to ban it the
more it will grow.

The Times, (1998) **Ferman, James** (1930–2002)
Former director of the British Board of Film
Classification

41 He in a few minutes ravished this fair
creature, or at least would have ravished
her, if she had not, by a timely compliance,
prevented him.
Jonathan Wild (1743)

42 What is commonly called love, namely the
desire of satisfying a voracious appetite
with a certain quantity of delicate white
human flesh.
Tom Jones (1749) **Fielding, Henry** (1707–1754)
English writer, dramatist and journalist

43 People always lie about sex – to get sex,
during sex, after sex, about sex.
The Times, (1999) **Flynt, Larry** (1942–) US
publisher of *Hustler* magazine. Defending
President Bill Clinton

44 I really think that sex always looks kind of
funny in a movie.
Attr. **Friedkin, William** (1939–) US film
director

45 I gave coitus the red card for utilitarian
reasons: the displeasure, discomfort and
aggravation it caused outweighed any
momentary explosions of pleasure, ease or
solace.
Paperweight (1992)

46 A walk, a smile, a gait, a way of flicking the
hair away from the eyes, the manner in
which clothes encase the body, these can
be erotic, but I would be greatly in the debt
of the man who could tell me what could
ever be appealing about those damp, dark,
foul-smelling and revoltingly tufted areas
of the body that constitute the main dishes
in the banquet of love.
Paperweight (1992) **Fry, Stephen** (1957–) British
comedian and writer

47 For men, it is a notch on the belt; for
women, it is a chance to draw men into a
relationship of greater intimacy.
Lecture, (1997) **Fukuyama, Francis** (1952–) US
historian. Arguing that women were more
selective in choosing sexual partners than
men (he later excepted certain kinds of
seahorses and British women)

48 But oh, the farmyard world of sex!
The Madras House **Granville-Barker, Harley**
(1877–1946) English actor and playwright

49 No sex is better than bad sex.
Attr. **Greer, Germaine** (1939–) Australian
feminist, critic, English scholar and writer

50 As for me, it is my profession, I do not
pretend to anything better.
In Miles, *The Women's History of the World*
(1988) **Gwyn, Nell** (1650–1687) English actress
and mistress of Charles II. On prostitution

51 I feel sorry for Mick. Y'know sexual
promiscuity just leads to chaos.
The Sunday Times, (2000) **Hall, Jerry** (1956–)
US fashion model. On her recent divorce
from Mick Jagger

52 Seamed stockings aren't subtle but they
certainly do the job. You shouldn't wear
them when out with someone you're not
prepared to sleep with.
Sex Tips For Girls (1983) **Heimel, Cynthia** US
writer

53 Prostitution gives her an opportunity to
meet people. It provides fresh air and
wholesome exercise, and it keeps her out
of trouble.
Catch-22 (1961) **Heller, Joseph** (1923–1999) US
writer

54 Night makes no difference 'twixt the Priest
and Clark;
Jone as my Lady is as good i' th' dark.
Hesperides (1648) **Herrick, Robert** (1591–1674)
English poet, royalist and clergyman

55 I am happy now that Charles calls on my
bedchamber less frequently than of old. As
it is, I now endure but two calls a week and
when I hear his steps outside my door I lie
down on my bed, close my eyes, open my
legs and think of England.
Journal (1912) **Hillingdon, Lady Alice** (1857–
1940) English aristocrat

56 Girls in our town are too good for the Pill
But if you keep asking they probably will
Perhaps 'cause they like you, or else for the
thrill
And explain it away in the morning.
'Girls in our Town' (song) **Hudson, Bob**
(1946–) US comedian and songwriter

57 A million million spermatozoa,
All of them alive:
Out of their cataclysm but one poor Noah
Dare hope to survive.
'Fifth Philosopher's Song' (1918)

58 Mr Mercaptan went on to preach a brilliant
sermon on that melancholy sexual
perversion known as continence.
Antic Hay (1923)

59 Lady Capricorn, he understood, was still
keeping open bed.
Antic Hay (1923)

60 Real orgies are never so exciting as
pornographic books.
Point Counter Point (1928)

61 People will insist … on treating the *mons
Veneris* as though it were Mount Everest.
Eyeless in Gaza (1936)

62 'Bed,' as the Italian proverb succinctly puts
it, 'is the poor man's opera.'
Heaven and Hell (1956) **Huxley, Aldous** (1894–
1963) English writer, poet and critic

63 Some motorists view their cars as the
extension to their sexuality and driving
develops into a complicated mating ritual.
The Times, (1998) **Keane, Conrad** On 'Road
lust'

64 Never go to bed with anyone crazier than
yourself.
The Observer, (1999) **Kristofferson, Kris** (1936–)
US singer and film actor

65 Women complain about sex more often
than men. Their gripes fall into two major
categories: (1) Not enough (2) Too much.
Ann Landers Says Truth Is Stranger Than …
(1968) **Landers, Ann** (1918–2002) Famous
'agony aunt' and columnist

66 Sexual intercourse began
In nineteen sixty-three
(Which was rather late for me) –
Between the end of the Chatterley ban
And the Beatles' first LP.
'Annus Mirabilis' (1974) **Larkin, Philip** (1922–
1985) English poet, writer and librarian

67 It's all this cold-hearted fucking that is
death and idiocy.
The Plumed Serpent (1926)

68 'It is sex,' she said to herself. 'How wonderful sex can be, when men keep it powerful and sacred, and it fills the world! Like sunshine through and through one!'
Lady Chatterley's Lover (1928)

69 Pornography is the attempt to insult sex, to do dirt on it.
Phoenix (1936) **Lawrence, D.H.** (1885–1930) English writer, poet and critic

70 The 'homo' is the legitimate child of the 'suffragette'.
The Art of Being Ruled (1926) **Lewis, Wyndham** (1882–1957) US-born British painter, critic and writer

71 No sex without responsibility.
The Observer, (1954) **Longford, Lord** (1905–2001) English politician, social reformer and biographer

72 Sex appeal is fifty percent what you've got and fifty percent what people think you've got.
In Halliwell, *Filmgoer's Companion* (1984) **Loren, Sophia** (1934–) Italian actress

73 What is a promiscuous person? It's usually someone who is getting more sex than you are.
Playboy interview, (1985) **Lownes, Victor** (1928–) US businessman and Playboy executive

74 From the days of Eve women have always faced sexual facts with more courage and realism than men.
Literature in My Time (1933)

75 I told him [D.H. Lawrence] that if he was determined to convert the world to proper reverence for the sexual act ... he would always have to remember one handicap for such an undertaking – that except to the two people who are indulging in it the sexual act is a comic operation.
My Life and Times (1971) **Mackenzie, Sir Compton** (1883–1972) Scottish writer and broadcaster

76 The more sex becomes a non-issue in people's lives, the happier they are.
Attr. **Maclaine, Shirley** (1934–) US actress

77 Whoever named it necking was a poor judge of anatomy.
Attr.

78 Many years ago I chased a woman for almost two years, only to discover her tastes were exactly like mine: we were both crazy about girls.
Attr. **Marx, Groucho** (1895–1977) US comedian

79 It is now quite lawful for a Catholic woman to avoid pregnancy by a resort to mathematics, though she is still forbidden to resort to physics and chemistry.
Notebooks (1956) **Mencken, H.L.** (1880–1956) US writer, critic, philologist and satirist

80 Continental people have sex life; the English have hot-water bottles.
How to be an Alien (1946) **Mikes, George** (1912–1987) Hungarian-born British writer

81 Sex is one of the nine reasons for reincarnation ... The other eight are unimportant.
Big Sur and the Oranges of Hieronymus Bosch **Miller, Henry** (1891–1980) US writer

82 I like the girls who do,
I like the girls who don't;
I hate the girl who says she will
And then she says she won't.
But the girl that I like best of all
And I think you'll say I'm right –
Is the one who says she never has
But looks as though she ....
'Ere, listen
The Max Miller Blue Book, (1975) **Miller, Max** (1894–1963) English music-hall comedian

83 Contraceptives should be used on every conceivable occasion.
The Last Goon Show of All **Milligan, Spike** (1918–2002) Irish comedian and writer

84 Into thir inmost bower
Handed they went; and eas'd the putting off
These troublesom disguises which wee wear,
Strait side by side were laid, nor turned I weene
Adam from his fair Spouse, nor Eve the Rites
Mysterious of connubial Love refus'd:
Whatever Hypocrits austerely talk
Of puritie and place and innocence,
Defaming as impure what God declares
Pure, and commands to som, leaves free to all.

Paradise Lost (1667) **Milton, John** (1608–1674) English poet, libertarian and pamphleteer

85 This sort of thing may be tolerated by the French, but we are British – thank God. Speech, (1965) **Montgomery, Viscount** (1887–1976) English field marshal. Comment on a bill to relax the laws against homosexuals

86 An orgy looks particularly alluring seen through the mists of righteous indignation. *The Most of Malcolm Muggeridge* (1966)

87 The orgasm has replaced the Cross as the focus of longing and the image of fulfilment. *Tread Softly* (1966) **Muggeridge, Malcolm** (1903–1990) English writer

88 Home is heaven and orgies are vile But you need an orgy, once in a while. 'Home, Sweet Home' (1935) **Nash, Ogden** (1902–1971) US poet

89 Sex is between the ears as well as between the legs. *Mega-Nutrients for Your Nerves* **Newbold, H.L.** (1890–1971) US psychiatrist and writer

90 He felt that he could love this woman with the greatest brutality. The situation between them was electric. When he was in a room with her the only thing he could think of was sex. *A Journey to the Interior* (1945) **Newby, P.H.** (1918–1997) English writer and Director of the BBC

91 If couples need Viagra, they shouldn't be getting married in the first place. *The Times,* (1998) **Oddie, William** Editor of the *Catholic Herald*

92 There are a number of mechanical devices which increase sexual arousal, particularly in women. Chief among these is the Mercedes-Benz 380SL convertible. Attr. **O'Rourke, P.J.** (1947–) US writer

93 You were born with your legs apart. They'll send you to the grave in a Y-shaped coffin. *What the Butler Saw* (1969) **Orton, Joe** (1933–1967) English dramatist and writer

94 Pleasure in coupling is gross and brief. Once sated, desire begins to pall.

In A. Baehrens, *Poetae Latini Minores* **Petronius Arbiter** (d. AD 66) Roman satirist

95 On a sofa upholstered in panther skin Mona did research in original sin. 'Mews Flat Mona' (1960) **Plomer, William** (1903–1973) South African-born British writer and editor

96 No, no, for my virginity, When I lose that, says Rose, I'll die; Behind the elms last night, cry'd Dick, Rose, were you not extremely sick? 'A True Maid' (1718) **Prior, Matthew** (1664–1721) English poet

97 Obscenity is what happens to shock some elderly and ignorant magistrate. *Look* magazine **Russell, Bertrand** (1872–1970) English philosopher, mathematician, essayist and social reformer

98 Sex is something I really don't understand too hot. You never know where the hell you are. I keep making up these sex rules for myself, and then I break them right away. *The Catcher in the Rye* (1951) **Salinger, J.D.** (1919–) US writer

99 I have made love to ten thousand women. *Die Tat,* (1977) **Simenon, Georges** (1903–1989) Belgian writer. His wife later said: 'The true figure is no more than twelve hundred'

100 Someone asked Sophocles, 'How do you stand in matters of love? Are you still able to have sex with a woman?' 'Quiet, man,' he replied, 'I've left all that behind me very gladly, as if I'd escaped from a mad and savage master.' In Plato, *Republic* **Sophocles** (496–406 BC) Greek dramatist

101 Don't be daft. You don't get any pornography on there, not on the telly. Get filth, that's all. The only place you get pornography is in yer Sunday papers. *Till Death Do Us Part,* TV sitcom **Speight, Johnny** (1920–1998) English screenwriter

102 If the shoe doesn't fit, must we change the foot? *Outrageous Acts and Everyday Rebellions* (1984) **Steinem, Gloria** (1934–) US writer and feminist activist. On transsexualism

103 At length the candle's out, and now
All that they had not done they do:
What that is, who can tell?
But I believe it was no more
That thou and I have done before
With Bridget, and with Nell.
'A Ballad upon a Wedding' (1646) **Suckling, Sir John** (1609–1642) English poet and dramatist

104 Traditionally, sex has been a very private, secretive activity. Herein perhaps lies its powerful force for uniting people in a strong bond. As we make sex less secretive, we may rob it of its power to hold men and women together.
The Second Sin (1973)

105 Masturbation: the primary sexual activity of mankind. In the nineteenth century it was a disease; in the twentieth, it's a cure.
The Second Sin (1973) **Szasz, Thomas** (1920–) Hungarian-born US psychiatrist and writer

106 It was the kind of show where the girls are not auditioned – just measured.
Attr. **Thomas, Irene** (1920–2001) English writer and broadcaster

107 Surely you don't mean by unartificial insemination!
Attr. **Thurber, James** (1894–1961) US humorist, writer and dramatist. On being accosted at a party by a drunk woman who claimed she would like to have a baby by him

108 Being a sex symbol has to do with attitude, not looks. Most men think it's looks, most women know otherwise.
Attr. **Turner, Kathleen** (1954–) US actress

109 Oh, I think so, certainly. … I mean, there are few rational people in this world to whom the word 'fuck' is particularly diabolical or revolting or totally forbidden.
In Paul Ferris, *Sex and the British* (1993) **Tynan, Kenneth** (1927–1980) English drama critic, producer and essayist. When asked on live television if he would allow sexual intercourse on stage at the National Theatre

110 I was too polite to ask.
Forum, (1987) On being asked if his first sexual experience had been heterosexual or homosexual

111 I'm all for bringing back the birch, but only between consenting adults.
TV interview with David Frost When asked for his views about corporal punishment
Vidal, Gore (1925–) US writer, critic and poet

112 It is one of the superstitions of the human mind to have imagined that virginity could be a virtue.
'The Leningrad Notebooks' (c.1735–1750)

113 Once: a philosopher; twice: a pervert!
Attr. Turning down an invitation to an orgy, having attended one the previous night for the first time **Voltaire** (1694–1778) French philosopher, dramatist, poet, historian, writer and critic

114 All this fuss about sleeping together. For physical pleasure I'd sooner go to my dentist any day.
Vile Bodies (1930) **Waugh, Evelyn** (1903–1966) English writer and diarist

115 The mind can also be an erogenous zone.
Attr. **Welch, Raquel** (1940–) US actress

116 Reading about sex in yesterday's novels is like watching people smoke in old films.
The Guardian, (1989) **Weldon, Fay** (1931–) British writer

117 In my day, I would only have sex with a man if I found him extremely attractive. These days, girls seem to choose them in much the same way as they might choose to suck on a boiled sweet.
Independent, (1997) **Wesley, Mary** (1912–2002) English novelist

118 I didn't invent sex, I just rediscovered it, uncovered it, and gave it a couple of definitions that Mr Webster never thought of.
Attr. **West, Mae** (1893–1980) US actress and writer

119 God gave all men a penis and a brain, but only enough blood to run one at a time.
Attr. **Williams, Robin** (1952–) US comedian and actor

120 The tragedy of sexual intercourse is the perpetual virginity of the soul.
Attr. in Jeffares, *W.B. Yeats: Man and Poet* (1949) **Yeats, W.B.** (1865–1939) Irish poet, dramatist, editor, writer and senator

121 I've never taken advantage of one night stands. It's like treating sex like sneezing. Sex is a fairly disgusting sort of tufted, smelly-area kind of activity, which is too intimate to engage in with strangers.
Attr. (1995) **Yorke, Thom** (1968–) English rock musician, lead member of Radiohead
See also courtship; love; marriage; men and women; passion

SILENCE

1 Silence is the virtue of fools.
Of the Dignity and Advancement of Learning (1623) **Bacon, Francis** (1561–1626) English philosopher, essayist, politician and courtier

2 The din of cicadas
seeps into the rock;
the air rings with silence.
'Narrow Roads of Oku' (1703) **Bashó, Matsuo** (1644–1694) Japanese haiku poet

3 Under all speech that is good for anything there lies a silence that is better. Silence is deep as Eternity; speech is shallow as Time.
'Memoirs of the Life of Scott' (1839) **Carlyle, Thomas** (1795–1881) Scottish historian, biographer, critic, and essayist

4 Silence ruled this land. Out of silence mystery comes, and magic, and the delicate awareness of unreasoning things.
The Timeless Land (1941) **Dark, Eleanor** (1901–1985) Australian novelist

5 Speech is often barren; but silence also does not necessarily brood over a full nest. Your still fowl, blinking at you without remark, may all the while be sitting on one addled nest-egg; and when it takes to cackling, will have nothing to announce but that addled delusion.
Felix Holt (1866) **Eliot, George** (1819–1880) English writer and poet

6 Still-born Silence! thou that art Floodgate of the deeper heart.
'Invocation of Silence' (1653) **Flecknoe, Richard** (d. c.1678) Irish priest, poet and dramatist

7 Silence is become his mother tongue.

The Good Natur'd Man (1768) **Goldsmith, Oliver** (c.1728–1774) Irish dramatist, poet and writer

8 And silence, like a poultice, comes
To heal the blows of sound.
'The Music-Grinders' (1836) **Holmes, Oliver Wendell** (1809–1894) US physician, poet, writer and scientist

9 There is a silence where hath been no sound,
There is a silence where no sound may be,
In the cold grave – under the deep, deep sea,
Or in the wide desert where no life is found.
'Sonnet: Silence' (1823) **Hood, Thomas** (1799–1845) English poet, editor and humorist

10 Silence is as full of potential wisdom and wit as the unhewn marble of great sculpture.
Point Counter Point (1928) **Huxley, Aldous** (1894–1963) English writer, poet and critic

11 Calumnies are answered best with silence.
Volpone (1607) **Jonson, Ben** (1572–1637) English dramatist and poet

12 Silence is the safest policy for the man who distrusts himself.
Maximes (1678) **La Rochefoucauld** (1613–1680) French writer

13 Better to remain silent and be thought a fool than to speak out and remove all doubt.
Attr. **Lincoln, Abraham** (1809–1865) US statesman and President

14 If nothing else is left, one must scream. Silence is the real crime against humanity.
Hope Against Hope (1970) **Mandelstam, Nadezhda** (1899–1980) Russian writer, translator and teacher

15 Do not the most moving moments of our lives find us all without words?
Reader's Digest, (1958) **Marceau, Marcel** (1923–) French mime artist

16 The eternal silence of these infinite spaces terrifies me.
Pensées (1670) **Pascal, Blaise** (1623–1662) French philosopher and scientist

17 Silence more musical than any song.
'Rest' (1862) **Rossetti, Christina** (1830–1894)
English poet

18 'Tis visible silence, still as the hour-glass ...
Deep in the sun-searched growths the
dragon-fly
Hangs like a blue thread loosened from the
sky: –
So this winged hour is dropt to us from
above.
Oh! clasp we to our hearts, for deathless
dower,
This close-companioned inarticulate hour
When twofold silence was the song of love.
The House of Life (1881) **Rossetti, Dante Gabriel**
(1828–1882) English poet, painter, translator
and letter writer

19 Silence is the supreme contempt.
'Mes Poisons' **Sainte-Beuve, Charles-
Augustin** (1804–1869) French writer and critic

20 You get the impression that their normal
condition is silence and that speech is a
slight fever which attacks them now and
then.
Nausea (1938) **Sartre, Jean-Paul** (1905–1980)
French philosopher, writer, dramatist and
critic

21 He could be silent in seven languages.
Attr. **Schleiermacher, F.E.D.** (1768–1834)
German philosopher. Of a celebrated
philologist

22 Shallow brookes murmur moste,
Depe sylent slyde away.
Old Arcadia (1581), 'The Firste Eclogues'
Sidney, Sir Philip (1554–1586) English poet,
critic, soldier, courtier and diplomat

23 My personal hobbies are reading, listening
to music, and silence.
Attr. **Sitwell, Dame Edith** (1887–1964) English
poet, anthologist, critic and biographer

24 He has occasional flashes of silence, that
make his conversation perfectly delightful.
In Holland, *A Memoir of the Reverend Sydney
Smith* (1855) **Smith, Sydney** (1771–1845) English
clergyman, essayist, journalist and wit. Of
Macaulay

25 For words divide and rend;
But silence is most noble till the end.

Atalanta in Calydon (1865) **Swinburne,
Algernon Charles** (1837–1909) English poet,
critic, dramatist and letter writer

26 There are many sorts of noises, but there is
only one silence.
Scraps (1973) **Tucholsky, Kurt** (1890–1935)
German satirist and writer

27 Well-timed silence hath more eloquence
than speech.
Proverbial Philosophy (1838) **Tupper, Martin**
(1810–1889) English writer, lawyer and
inventor

28 The most wise speech
is not as holy as silence.
The Stupid Lady (1613) **Vega Carpio, Félix Lope
de** (1562–1635) Spanish dramatist and poet

29 Silence alone is great; all else is weakness
...
Perform with all your heart your long and
heavy task ...
Then, afterwards, as do I, suffer and die
without a word.
'The Death of the Wolf' (1843) **Vigny, Alfred
de** (1797–1863) French writer

30 Through the friendly silence of the
soundless moonlight.
Aeneid **Virgil** (70–19 BC) Roman poet

31 What can be said at all can be said clearly;
and whereof one cannot speak, thereon
one must keep silent.
Tractatus Logico-Philosophicus (1922)
Wittgenstein, Ludwig (1889–1951) Austrian
philosopher
See also secrets; solitude

SIN

1 Do not worry about avoiding temptation.
As you grow older it will avoid you.
Attr. **Adams, Joey** (1911–1999) US comedian
and author

2 All sin tends to be addictive, and the
terminal point of addiction is what is called
damnation.
A Certain World (1970) **Auden, W.H.** (1907–
1973) English poet, essayist, critic, teacher and
dramatist

3 Here's a rule I recommend. Never practice
two vices at once.
Tallulah (1952) **Bankhead, Tallulah** (1903–1968)
US actress

4 I am not over-fond of resisting temptation.
Vathek (1787) **Beckford, William** (1760–1844)
English writer, collector and politician

5 The Devil, having nothing else to do,
Went off to tempt My Lady Poltagrue.
My Lady, tempted by a private whim,
To his extreme annoyance, tempted him.
Sonnets and Verse (1923) **Belloc, Hilaire** (1870–
1953) English writer of verse, essayist and
critic; Liberal MP

6 Ye shall be as gods, knowing good and
evil.
Genesis, 3:5

7 Be sure your sin will find you out.
Numbers, 32:23

8 The wicked flee when no man pursueth:
but the righteous are bold as a lion.
Proverbs, 28:1

9 I am not come to call the righteous, but
sinners to repentance.
Matthew, 9:13

10 Joy shall be in heaven over one sinner that
repenteth, more than over ninety and nine
just persons, which need no repentance.
Luke, 15:7

11 He that is without sin among you, let him
first cast a stone.
John, 8:7

12 The wages of sin is death.
Romans, 6:23 **The Bible (King James Version)**

13 Shame is Pride's cloke.
The Marriage of Heaven and Hell (c.1790–1793)
Blake, William (1757–1827) English poet,
engraver, painter and mystic

14 Let heaven exist, even if my place be hell.
'The Library of Babel' (1941) **Borges, Jorge
Luis** (1899–1986) Argentinian writer, poet and
librarian. (*Que el cielo exista, aunque mi lugar
sea el infierno*)

15 A man, indeed, is not genteel when he gets
drunk; but most vices may be committed
very genteelly: a man may debauch his
friend's wife genteelly: he may cheat at
cards genteelly.
The Life of Samuel Johnson (1791) **Boswell,
James** (1740–1795) Scottish lawyer and writer

16 Good girls go to heaven, bad girls go
everywhere.
Attr. **Brown, Helen Gurley** (1922–) US writer
and editor. Promotional line for *Cosmopolitan*
magazine

17 Cowardice is, without a doubt, one of the
greatest sins.
The Master and Margarita (1967) **Bulgakov,
Mikhail** (1891–1940) Russian writer and
dramatist

18 One leak will sink a ship, and one sin will
destroy a sinner.
The Pilgrim's Progress (1678) **Bunyan, John**
(1628–1688) English preacher, pastor and
writer

19 An original something, fair maid, you
would win me
To write – but how shall I begin?
For I fear I have nothing original in me –
Excepting Original Sin.
'To a Young Lady, Who Asked Me to Write
Something Original for Her Album' (1843)
Campbell, Thomas (1777–1844) Scottish poet,
ballad writer and journalist

20 Thou shalt have one God only; who
Would be at the expense of two? ...
Thou shalt not kill; but need'st not strive
Officiously to keep alive.
Do not adultery commit;
Advantage rarely comes of it.
Thou shalt not steal; an empty feat,
When it's so lucrative to cheat ...
Thou shalt not covet; but tradition
Approves all forms of competition.
'The Latest Decalogue' (1862) **Clough, Arthur
Hugh** (1819–1861) English poet and letter
writer

21 Lukewarmness I account a sin
As great in love as in religion.
'The Request' (1647) **Cowley, Abraham** (1618–
1667) English poet and dramatist

22 Vice is its own reward.
The Naked Civil Servant (1968) **Crisp, Quentin** (1908–1999) English writer, publicist and model

23 Keep up appearances; there lies the test;
The world will give thee credit for the rest.
Outward be fair, however foul within;
Sin if thou wilt, but then in secret sin.
'Night' (1761) **Churchill, Charles** (1731–1764) English poet, political writer and clergyman

24 Even imperfection itself may have its ideal or perfect state.
'Murder Considered as One of the Fine Arts' (1839) **De Quincey, Thomas** (1785–1859) English writer

25 Wilt thou forgive that sin, where I begun,
Which is my sin, though it were done before?
Wilt thou forgive those sins through which I run
And do them still, though still I do deplore?
When thou hast done, thou hast not done,
For I have more.
'Hymn to God the Father' (1623) **Donne, John** (1572–1631) English poet

26 Thou strong seducer, opportunity!
The Conquest of Granada (1670)

27 Repentance is but want of power to sin.
Palamon and Arcite (1700) **Dryden, John** (1631–1700) English poet, satirist, dramatist and critic

28 Sin brought death, and death will disappear with the disappearance of sin.
Science and Health (1875) **Eddy, Mary Baker** (1821–1910) US founder of Christian Science

29 Show me a Wednesday wencher and a Sunday saint, and I'll show you a Roman Catholic.
The Legend of King O'Malley (1974) **Ellis, Bob** (1942–) Australian dramatist

30 Christianity has done a great deal for love by making a sin of it.
Le Jardin d'Epicure (1894) **France, Anatole** (1844–1924) French writer and critic

31 Deny yourself! You should deny yourself!
That is the eternal song.

Faust, I (1808), 'Studierzimmer' ('Study') **Goethe** (1749–1832) German poet, writer, dramatist and scientist

32 Ralph wept for the end of innocence, the darkness of man's heart, and the fall through the air of the true, wise friend called Piggy.
Lord of the Flies (1954) **Golding, William** (1911–1993) English writer and poet

33 The best way to get the better of temptation is just to yield to it.
Mystifications (1859) **Graham, Clementina Stirling** (1782–1877) Scottish writer, lyricist and translator

34 Don't tell my mother I'm living in sin,
Don't let the old folks know:
Don't tell my twin that I breakfast on gin,
He'd never survive the blow.
Laughing Ann (1925) **Herbert, Sir A.P.** (1890–1971) English humorist, writer, dramatist and politician

35 'You oughtn't to yield to temptation.'
'Well, somebody must, or the thing becomes absurd.'
The Dolly Dialogues (1894) **Hope, Anthony** (1863–1933) English writer, dramatist and lawyer

36 Men are not punished for their sins, but by them.
A Thousand and One Epigrams (1911) **Hubbard, Elbert** (1856–1915) US printer, editor, writer and businessman

37 Sin is behovely, but all shall be well and all shall be well and all manner of things shall be well.
Revelations of Divine Love (1393) **Juliana of Norwich** (c.1343–c.1429) English mystic

38 Count it the greatest sin to put life before honour, and for the sake of life to lose the reasons for living.
Satires **Juvenal** (c.60–130) Roman verse satirist and Stoic

39 It is so stupid of modern civilization to have given up believing in the devil when he is the only explanation of it.
Attr. **Knox, Ronald** (1888–1957) English Catholic priest and biblical translator

40 There's nothing so artificial as sinning nowadays. I suppose it once was real.
St Mawr (1925) **Lawrence, D.H.** (1885–1930) English writer, poet and critic

41 So blind am I to my mortal entanglement that I dare not call upon thee, Lord, for fear that thou wouldst take me away from my sin.
Christian Heraclitus (1613) **Quevedo y Villegas, Francisco Gómez de** (1580–1645) Spanish poet and writer

42 The worst sin towards our fellow creatures is not to hate them, but to be indifferent to them: that's the essence of inhumanity.
The Devil's Disciple (1901) **Roosevelt, Theodore** (1858–1919) US Republican President

43 At such an hour the sinners are still in bed resting up from their sinning of the night before, so they will be in good shape for more sinning a little later on.
Runyon à la carte (1944), 'The Idyll of Miss Sarah Brown' **Runyon, Damon** (1884–1946) US writer

44 There is no other hell for man than the stupidity and wickedness of his own kind.
Histoire de Juliette (1797) **Sade, Marquis de** (1740–1814) French soldier and writer

45 The flow'ry way that leads to the broad gate and the great fire.
All's Well That Ends Well, IV.v

46 Through tatter'd clothes small vices do appear;
Robed and furr'd gowns hide all.
King Lear, IV.vi

47 Plate sin with gold,
And the strong lance of justice hurtless breaks;
Arm it in rags, a pigmy's straw does pierce it.
King Lear, IV.vi

48 Angels are bright still, though the brightest fell.
Macbeth, IV.iii

49 Few love to hear the sins they love to act.
Pericles, I.i

50 Nothing emboldens sin so much as mercy.
Timon of Athens, III.v **Shakespeare, William** (1564–1616) English dramatist, poet and actor

51 They are written as if sin were to be taken out of man like Eve out of Adam – by putting him to sleep.
In J. Larwood, *Anecdotes of the Clergy* **Smith, Sydney** (1771–1845) English clergyman, essayist, journalist and wit. Of boring sermons

52 More people are flattered into virtue than bullied out of vice.
The Analysis of the Hunting Field (1846) **Surtees, R.S.** (1805–1864) English writer

53 I never wonder to see men wicked, but I often wonder to see them not ashamed.
Thoughts on Various Subjects (1711) **Swift, Jonathan** (1667–1745) Irish satirist, poet, essayist and cleric

54 You just wait, I'll sin till I blow up!
Under Milk Wood (1954) **Thomas, Dylan** (1914–1953) Welsh poet, writer and radio dramatist

55 Adam was but human – this explains it all. He did not want the apple for the apple's sake, he wanted it only because it was forbidden.
Pudd'nhead Wilson (1894) **Twain, Mark** (1835–1910) US humorist, writer, journalist and lecturer

56 The gates of Hell are open night and day;
Smooth the descent, and easy is the way:
But to return, and view the cheerful skies,
In this the task and mighty labour lies.
Aeneid **Virgil** (70–19 BC) Roman poet

57 It has been said that the great events of the world take place in the brain. It is in the brain, and the brain only, that the great sins of the world take place.
The Picture of Dorian Gray (1891)

58 The only way to get rid of a temptation is to yield to it.
The Picture of Dorian Gray (1891)

59 I couldn't help it. I can resist everything except temptation.
Lady Windermere's Fan (1892) **Wilde, Oscar** (1854–1900) Irish poet, dramatist, writer, critic and wit
See also the devil; evil; guilt; religion

SLEEP

1 Whilst Adam slept, Eve from his side arose:
Strange his first sleep should be his last
repose.
'The Consequence' **Anonymous**

2 The cool kindliness of sheets, that soon
Smooth away trouble; and the rough male
kiss of blankets.
'The Great Lover' (1914) **Brooke, Rupert** (1887–
1915) English poet

3 Sleep is a death, O make me try,
By sleeping what it is to die.
And as gently lay my head
On my grave, as now my bed.
Religio Medici (1643)

4 Sleep is in fine, so like death, I dare not
trust it without my prayers.
Religio Medici (1643)

5 Half our days we pass in the shadow of the
earth; and the brother of death exacteth a
third part of our lives.
Pseudodoxia Epidemica (1646)

6 Nor will the sweetest delight of gardens
afford much comfort in sleep; wherein the
dullness of that sense shakes hands with
delectable odours; and though in the bed
of Cleopatra, can hardly with any delight
raise up the ghost of a rose.
The Garden of Cyrus (1658) **Browne, Sir
Thomas** (1605–1682) English physician,
author and antiquary

7 Laugh and the world laughs with you;
snore and you sleep alone.
Inside Mr. Enderby (1963) **Burgess, Anthony**
(1917–1993) English writer, linguist and
composer

8 God bless whoever invented sleep, the
cloak that covers all human thoughts. It is
the food that satisfies hunger, the water
that quenches thirst, the fire that warms
cold, the cold that reduces heat, and, lastly,
the common currency which can buy
anything, the balance and compensating
weight that makes the shepherd equal to
the king, and the simpleton equal to the
sage.
Don Quixote (1615) **Cervantes, Miguel de** (1547–
1616) Spanish writer and dramatist

9 Oh sleep! it is a gentle thing
Beloved from pole to pole!
To Mary Queen the praise be given!
She sent the gentle sleep from Heaven,
That slid into my soul.
'The Rime of the Ancient Mariner' (1798)
Coleridge, Samuel Taylor (1772–1834) English
poet, philosopher and critic

10 Care-charmer Sleep, son of the sable
Night,
Brother to Death, in silent darkness born:
Relieve my anguish, and restore the light,
With dark forgetting of my care return
And let the day be time enough to mourn
The shipwreck of my ill adventured youth:
Let waking eyes suffice to wail their scorn,
Without the torment of the night's
untruth.
Delia (1592) **Daniel, Samuel** (1562–1619)
English poet, historian and dramatist

11 I met at eve the Prince of Sleep,
His was a still and lovely face,
He wandered through a valley steep,
Lovely in a lonely place.
'I Met at Eve' (1902) **De La Mare, Walter** (1873–
1956) English poet

12 Golden slumbers kiss your eyes,
Smiles awake you when you rise:
Sleep, pretty wantons, do not cry,
And I will sing a lullaby:
Rock them, rock them, lullaby.
'Patient Grissil' (1603) **Dekker, Thomas**
(c.1570–c.1632) English dramatist

13 'It would make any one go to sleep, that
bedstead would, whether they wanted to or
not.'
'I should think,' said Sam, ... 'poppies was
nothing to it.'
The Pickwick Papers (1837) **Dickens, Charles**
(1812–1870) English writer

14 The best cure for insomnia is to get a lot of
sleep.
Attr. **Fields, W.C.** (1880–1946) US film actor

15 Care-charming Sleep, thou easer of all
woes,
Brother to Death.

The Tragedy of Valentinian (1647) **Fletcher, John** (1579–1625) English dramatist

16 Sleep is when all the unsorted stuff comes flying out as from a dustbin upset in a high wind.
Pincher Martin (1956) **Golding, William** (1911–1993) English writer and poet

17 Great eaters and great sleepers are not capable of doing anything great.
Attr. **Henri IV** (1553–1610) King of France

18 'Bed,' as the Italian proverb succinctly puts it, 'is the poor man's opera.'
Heaven and Hell (1956) **Huxley, Aldous** (1894–1963) English writer, poet and critic

19 Now deep in my bed I turn
And the world turns on the other side.
'In the Night' **Jennings, Elizabeth** (1926–2001) English poet

20 O soft embalmer of the still midnight,
Shutting, with careful fingers and benign,
Our gloom-pleas'd eyes.
'To Sleep' (1819) **Keats, John** (1795–1821) English poet

21 Tell me what the role of wakefulness is, and then I shall explain the role of sleep.
Obituary, *The Times*, (1999) **Kleitman, Nathaniel** (1895–1999) US sleep scientist

22 O! it's nice to get up in the mornin',
But it's nicer to stay in bed.
Song, 1913 **Lauder, Sir Harry** (1870–1950) Scottish music-hall entertainer

23 Sleeping is no mean art: it is necessary to stay awake for it all day.
Thus Spake Zarathustra (1884) **Nietzsche, Friedrich Wilhelm** (1844–1900) German philosopher, critic and poet

24 Don't sleep too much. If you sleep three hours less each night for a year, you will have an extra month and a half to succeed in.
New York Times **Onassis, Aristotle** (1906–1975) Turkish-born Greek shipping magnate

25 How do people go to sleep? I'm afraid I've lost the knack. I might try busting myself smartly over the temple with the nightlight. I might repeat to myself, slowly and soothingly, a list of quotations beautiful from minds profound; if I can remember any of the damned things.
Here Lies (1939) **Parker, Dorothy** (1893–1967) US writer, poet, critic and wit

26 She fell asleep and slept the sleep of the just.
Abrégé de l'Histoire de Port Royal (1742) **Racine, Jean** (1639–1699) French tragedian and poet

27 Why do you lie with your legs ungainly huddled,
And one arm bent across your sullen, cold
Exhausted face? ...
You are too young to fall asleep for ever;
And when you sleep you remind me of the dead.
'The Dug-Out' (1918) **Sassoon, Siegfried** (1886–1967) English poet and writer

28 Weariness
Can snore upon the flint, when resty sloth
Finds the down pillow hard.
Cymbeline, III.vi

29 O sleep, O gentle sleep,
Nature's soft nurse, how have I frighted thee,
That thou no more wilt weigh my eyelids down,
And steep my senses in forgetfulness?
Why rather, sleep, liest thou in smoky cribs,
Upon uneasy pallets stretching thee,
And hush'd with buzzing night-flies to thy slumber,
Than in the perfum'd chambers of the great,
Under the canopies of costly state,
And lull'd with sound of sweetest melody?
Henry IV, Part 2, III.i

30 Methought I heard a voice cry 'Sleep no more;
Macbeth does murder sleep' – the innocent sleep,
Sleep that knits up the ravell'd sleave of care,
The death of each day's life, sore labour's bath,
Balm of hurt minds, great nature's second course,
Chief nourisher in life's feast.
Macbeth, II.ii

31 Not poppy, nor mandragora,
   Nor all the drowsy syrups of the world,
   Shall ever medicine thee to that sweet
   sleep
   Which thou owed'st yesterday.
   Othello, III.iii **Shakespeare, William** (1564–
   1616) English dramatist, poet and actor

32 Take thou of me smooth pillows, sweetest
   bed;
   A chamber deaf to noise and blind to light,
   A rosy garland and a weary head.
   Astrophel and Stella (1591)

33 Come, Sleepe, O Sleepe, the certaine knot
   of peace,
   The bathing place of wits, the balm of woe,
   The poore man's wealth, the prysoner's
   release,
   The indifferent Judge betweene the hie and
   lowe.
   Astrophel and Stella (1591) **Sidney, Sir Philip**
   (1554–1586) English poet, critic, soldier,
   courtier and diplomat

34 Thou hast been call'd, O Sleep! the friend
   of Woe,
   But 'tis the happy who have called thee so.
   The Curse of Kehama (1810) **Southey, Robert**
   (1774–1843) English poet, essayist, historian
   and letter writer

35 Sleep is the watering place of the soul to
   which it hastens at night to drink at the
   sources of life.
   In sleep we receive confirmation ... that we
   must go on living.
   A Voice From the Chorus (1973) **Tertz, Abram**
   (1925–1997) Russian writer and dissident

36 Sleeping as quiet as death, side by wrinkled
   side, toothless, salt and brown, like two old
   kippers in a box.
   Under Milk Wood (1954) **Thomas, Dylan** (1914–
   1953) Welsh poet, writer and radio dramatist

37 I have come to the borders of sleep,
   The unfathomable deep
   Forest where all must lose
   Their way, however straight,
   Or winding, soon or late;
   They cannot choose.
   'Lights Out' (1917) **Thomas, Edward** (1878–
   1917) English poet

38 A pleasing land of drowsyhead it was.
   The Castle of Indolence (1748) **Thomson, James**
   (1700–1748) Scottish poet and dramatist

39 There ain't no way to find out why a snorer
   can't hear himself snore.
   Tom Sawyer Abroad (1894) **Twain, Mark** (1835–
   1910) US humorist, writer, journalist and
   lecturer

40 I never quite forgave Mahaffy for getting
   himself suspended from preaching in the
   College Chapel. Ever since his sermons
   were discontinued, I suffer from insomnia
   in church.
   In Oliver St John Gregory, *As I Was Going
   Down Sackville Street* **Tyrrell, George** (1861–
   1909) Irish theologian

41 I haven't been to sleep for over a year.
   That's why I go to bed early. One needs
   more rest if one doesn't sleep.
   Decline and Fall (1928) **Waugh, Evelyn** (1903–
   1966) English writer and diarist

42 Tir'd nature's sweet Restorer, balmy Sleep!
   He, like the World, his ready visit pays
   Where Fortune smiles; the wretched he
   forsakes.
   Night-Thoughts on Life, Death and Immortality
   (1742–1746) **Young, Edward** (1683–1765) English
   poet, dramatist, satirist and clergyman
   See also death; dreams; night

SOCIALISM

1 The paradox at the moment is that the
  Labour Party is cheering the leader because
  they think he'll win. The City and the press
  are cheering him because they think he's
  going to destroy socialism.
  The Observer, (1995) **Benn, Tony** (1925–)
  English Labour politician. On Tony Blair

2 Why is it always the intelligent people who
  are socialists?
  Forty Years On (1969) **Bennett, Alan** (1934–)
  English dramatist, actor and diarist

3 The language of priorities is the religion of
  Socialism.
  Attr. **Bevan, Aneurin** (1897–1960) Welsh
  Labour politician, miner and orator

4 The trouble with half the Socialists is
they're suffering from vitamin deficiency.
Remark 1965, quoted in *The Guardian*, (2000)
Cartland, Barbara (1901–2000) English writer

5 The people's flag is deepest red;
It shrouded oft our martyred dead,
And ere their limbs grew stiff and cold,
Their heart's blood dyed its every fold.
Then raise the scarlet standard high!
Within its shade we'll live or die.
Tho' cowards flinch and traitors sneer,
We'll keep the red flag flying here.
'The Red Flag' (1889) **Connell, James M.** (1852–
1929) Irish-born writer of socialist songs and
poems

6 In the service of the people we followed
such a policy that socialism would not lose
its human face.
Attr. **Dubcek, Alexander** (1921–1992)
Czechoslovak statesman; First Secretary of the
Communist Party 1968–1969

7 There is nothing in Socialism that a little
age or a little money will not cure.
Attr. **Durant, Will** (1885–1982) US philosopher
and writer

8 We are all socialists now.
Attr. **Edward VIII**
(later Duke of Windsor) (1894–1972) King of
the United Kingdom; abdicated 11 December
1936. Quoting Sir William Harcourt

9 Since I was 16 I have held the view that the
Sermon on the Mount was a better
statement of democratic socialism than
Clause 4, either old or new.
The Observer, (1999) **Hattersley, Roy** (1932–)
British Labour politician and writer

10 Marxian Socialism must always remain a
portent to the historians of opinion – how
a doctrine so illogical and so dull can have
exercised so powerful and enduring an
influence over the minds of men, and,
through them, the events of history.
'The End of Laissez-Faire' (1926) **Keynes, John
Maynard** (1883–1946) English economist

11 The idea that there is a model Labour
voter, a blue-collar council house tenant
who belongs to a union and has 2.4
children, a five-year-old car and a holiday
in Blackpool, is patronizing and politically
immature.
Speech, (1986) **Kinnock, Neil** (1942–) Welsh
Labour politician

12 We shall now proceed to construct the
socialist order.
Speech, (1917)

13 Under socialism all will govern in turn and
will soon become accustomed to no one
governing.
The State and Revolution (1917) **Lenin, V.I.**
(1870–1924) Russian revolutionary, Marxist
theoretician and first leader of the USSR

14 They were a bloodthirsty lot, those
sentimentalists who wept for the sad lot of
the working classes.
Bohemians of the Bulletin (1965) **Lindsay,
Norman** (1879–1969) Australian artist and
writer. On Melbourne socialists

15 What is this, the sound and rumour? What
is this that all men hear,
Like the wind in hollow valleys when the
storm is drawing near,
Like the rolling on of ocean in the eventide
of fear?
'Tis the people marching on.
Chants for Socialists (1885), 'The March of the
Workers' **Morris, William** (1834–1896) English
poet, designer, craftsman, artist and socialist

16 To the ordinary working man, the sort you
would meet in any pub on Saturday night,
Socialism does not mean much more than
better wages and shorter hours and
nobody bossing you about.
The Road to Wigan Pier (1937)

17 As with the Christian religion, the worst
advertisement for Socialism is its
adherents.
The Road to Wigan Pier (1937) **Orwell, George**
(1903–1950) English writer and critic

18 Our object in the establishment of the state
is the greatest happiness of the whole, and
not that of any one class.
Republic **Plato** (c.429–347 BC) Greek
philosopher

19 Socialists treat their servants with respect
and then wonder why they vote
Conservative.
Lord Malquist and Mr Moon (1966) **Stoppard,
Tom** (1937–) British dramatist

20 To put it in the most shocking possible
language, socialism should cease to be the
factory-floor and chicken-battery party, and
become the hearth-and-home, do-it-
yourself party.
Capitalism, Socialism and the Environment (1976)
Stretton, Hugh (1924–) Australian political
scientist and historian

21 In place of the conception of the Power-
State we are led to that of the Welfare-
State.
Citizen and Churchman (1941) **Temple, William**
(1881–1944) Anglican prelate, social reformer
and writer

22 State socialism is totally alien to the British
character.
The Times, (1983) **Thatcher, Margaret** (1925–)
English Conservative Prime Minister

23 Socialism can arrive only by bicycle.
In Ivan Illich, *Energy and Equity* (1974) **Viera
Gallo, José Antonio** (1943–) Chilean politician

24 Many people consider the things which
government does for them to be social
progress, but they consider the things
government does for others as socialism.
Peter's Quotations **Warren, Earl** (1891–1974) US
lawyer and politician

25 He had one peculiar weakness; he had
faced death in many forms but he had
never faced a dentist. The thought of
dentists gave him just the same sick horror
as the thought of Socialism.
Bealby (1915) **Wells, H.G.** (1866–1946) English
writer

26 We are redefining and we are restating our
socialism in terms of the scientific
revolution ... the Britain that is going to be
forged in the white heat of this revolution
will be no place for restrictive practices or
out-dated methods on either side of
industry.
Speech, (1963) **Wilson, Harold** (1916–1995)
English Labour Prime Minister
See also communism; politics

SOCIETY

1 Every one carries his own inch-rule of
taste, and amuses himself by applying it,
triumphantly, wherever he travels.
The Education of Henry Adams (1918) **Adams,
Henry** (1838–1918) US historian and
memoirist

2 Civilization is a method of living, an
attitude of equal respect for all men.
Speech, Honolulu, (1933) **Addams, Jane** (1860–
1935) US sociologist and writer

3 For parlor use, the vague generality is a life
saver.
Attr.

4 To ensure peace of mind ignore the rules
and regulations.
Attr. **Ade, George** (1866–1944) US fabulist and
playwright

5 It is not only by the questions we have
answered that progress may be measured,
but also by those we are still asking.
Sisters in Crime (1975) **Adler, Freda** (1934–) US
educator and writer

6 Civilization degrades the many to exalt the
few.
Table Talk (1877) **Alcott, Bronson** (1799–1888)
US educator, reformer and transcendentalist

7 When you've got over the disgrace of the
single life, it's more airy.
Irish woman, quoted in broadcasts by Joyce
Grenfell **Anonymous**

8 A person who cannot live in society, or
does not need to because he is self-
sufficient, is either a beast or a god.
Politics **Aristotle** (384–322 BC) Greek
philosopher

9 This strange disease of modern life.
'The Scholar-Gipsy' (1853). On the present

10 Wandering between two worlds, one dead,
The other powerless to be born,
With nowhere yet to rest my head,
Like these, on earth I wait forlorn ...
Years hence, perhaps, may dawn an age,
More fortunate, alas! than we,
Which without hardness will be sage,
And gay without frivolity.

'The Grande Chartreuse' (1855) **Arnold, Matthew** (1822–1888) English poet, critic, essayist and educationist

11 Private faces in public places
Are wiser and nicer
Than public faces in private places.
The Orators (1932) **Auden, W.H.** (1907–1973) English poet, essayist, critic, teacher and dramatist

12 What is not good for the beehive, cannot be good for the bees.
Meditations **Aurelius, Marcus** (121–180) Roman emperor and Stoic philosopher

13 She was nothing more than a mere good-tempered, civil and obliging young woman; as such we could scarcely dislike her – she was only an Object of Contempt.
Love and Friendship (1791)

14 I do not want people to be very agreeable, as it saves me the trouble of liking them a great deal.
Letter, (1798)

15 It is happy for you that you possess the talent of flattering with delicacy. May I ask whether these pleasing attentions proceed from the impulse of the moment, or are the result of previous study?
Pride and Prejudice (1813)

16 For what do we live, but to make sport for our neighbours, and laugh at them in our turn?
Pride and Prejudice (1813)

17 Fine dancing, I believe, like virtue, must be its own reward.
Emma (1816)

18 The sooner every party breaks up the better.
Emma (1816)

19 'My idea of good company, Mr Elliot, is the company of clever, well-informed people, who have a great deal of conversation; that is what I call good company.' 'You are mistaken,' said he gently, 'that is not good company; that is the best.'
Persuasion (1818)

20 No moral system can rest solely on authority.

Humanist Outlook (1968) **Ayer, A.J.** (1910–1989) English philosopher

21 Man seeketh in society comfort, use, and protection.
The Advancement of Learning (1605)

22 If a man be gracious and courteous to strangers, it shews he is a citizen of the world.
Essays **Bacon, Francis** (1561–1626) English philosopher, essayist, politician and courtier

23 The most melancholy of human reflections, perhaps, is that, on the whole, it is a question whether the benevolence of mankind does most good or harm.
Physics and Politics (1872) **Bagehot, Walter** (1826–1877) English economist and political philosopher

24 I'm a second eleven sort of chap.
The Admirable Crichton (1902) **Barrie, Sir J.M.** (1860–1937) Scottish dramatist and writer

25 If you think squash is a competitive activity, try flower arrangement.
Talking Heads (1988) **Bennett, Alan** (1934–) English dramatist, actor and diarist

26 Good taste is better than bad taste, but bad taste is better than no taste.
The Observer, (1930) **Bennett, Arnold** (1867–1931) English writer, dramatist and journalist

27 The history of society is the history of the inventive labours that alter man, alter his desires, habits, outlook, relationships both to other men and to physical nature, with which man is in perpetual physical and technological metabolism.
Karl Marx (1978)

28 To belong to a given community, to be connected with its members by indissoluble and impalpable ties of a common language, historical memory, habit, tradition and feeling, is a basic human need no less natural than that for food or drink and security or procreation. One nation can understand and sympathize with the institutions of another only because it knows how much its own mean to itself. Cosmopolitanism is the shedding of all that makes one most human, most oneself.

'The Counter-Enlightenment' **Berlin, Isaiah** (1909–1997) Russian-born historian and political philisopher

29 Phone for the fish-knives, Norman
As Cook is a little unnerved;
You kiddies have crumpled the serviettes
And I must have things daintily served.
A Few Late Chrysanthemums (1954), 'How to get on in Society'

30 Gaily into Ruislip Gardens
Runs the red electric train,
With a thousand Ta's and Pardon's
Daintily alights Elaine –
Well cut Windsmoor flapping lightly,
Jacqmar scarf of mauve and green
Hiding hair which, Friday nightly,
Delicately drowns in Drene.
A Few Late Chrysanthemums (1954), 'Middlesex'
Betjeman, Sir John (1906–1984) English poet laureate

31 Scratch a pessimist, and you find often a defender of privilege.
The Observer, (1943) **Beveridge, William Henry** (1879–1963) British economist and social reformer

32 Talent, like beauty, to be pardoned, must be obscure and unostentatious.
Desultory Thoughts and Reflections (1839)
Blessington, Lady Marguerite (1789–1849) Irish-born writer and socialite

33 As soon as tradition has come to be recognized as tradition, it is dead.
The Closing of the American Mind (1987) **Bloom, Allan** (1930–1992) US academic and critic

34 The propriety of some persons seems to consist in having improper thoughts about their neighbours.
Aphorisms (1930) **Bradley, F.H.** (1846–1924) English philosopher

35 Violence is the repartee of the illiterate.
Punch, (1973) **Brien, Alan** (1925–) English writer

36 The wish to hurt, the momentary intoxication with pain, is the loophole through which the pervert climbs into the minds of ordinary men.

The Face of Violence (1954) **Bronowski, Jacob** (1908–1974) British scientist, writer and TV presenter

37 I think the reward for conformity is that everyone likes you except yourself.
Bingo **Brown, Rita Mae** (1944–) US writer and poet

38 People are broad-minded. They'll accept the fact that a person can be an alcoholic, a dope fiend, a wife beater and even a newspaperman, but if a man doesn't drive, there's something wrong with him.
Have I Ever Lied to You? (1968) **Buchwald, Art** (1925–) US humorist

39 These things [subject matter] are external to the man; style is the essence of man.
'Discours sur le Style' (1753) **Buffon, Comte de** (1707–1788) French naturalist

40 It is a general popular error to imagine the loudest complainers for the public to be the most anxious for its welfare.
Observations on 'The Present State of the Nation' (1769)

41 It is therefore our business carefully to cultivate in our minds, to rear to the most perfect vigour and maturity, every sort of generous and honest feeling that belongs to our nature. To bring the dispositions that are lovely in private life into the service and conduct of the commonwealth; so to be patriots, as not to forget we are gentlemen.
Thoughts on the Cause of the Present Discontents (1770)

42 Nobility is a graceful ornament to the civil order. It is the Corinthian capital of polished society.
Reflections on the Revolution in France and on the Proceedings in Certain Societies in London (1790)
Burke, Edmund (1729–1797) Irish-born British statesman and philosopher

43 In an affluent society most healthy women would like to have four healthy children.
Dominant Mammal (1970) **Burnet, Sir Frank Macfarlane** (1899–1985) Australian medical researcher

44 Nothing is so delicate as the reputation of a woman; it is at once the most beautiful and most brittle of all human things.
Evelina (1778)

45 Dancing? Oh, dreadful! How it was ever adopted in a civilized country I cannot find out; 'tis certainly a Barbarian exercise, and of savage origin.
Cecilia (1782) **Burney, Fanny** (1752–1840) English diarist and novelist

46 Whatever mitigates the woes or increases the happiness of others, this is my criterion of goodness; and whatever injures society at large, or any individual in it, this is my measure of iniquity.
Attr. **Burns, Robert** (1759–1796) Scottish poet and songwriter

47 The Public is an old woman. Let her maunder and mumble.
Attr. **Carlyle, Thomas** (1795–1881) Scottish historian, biographer, critic, and essayist

48 'If everybody minded their own business,' said the Duchess in a hoarse growl, 'the world would go round a deal faster than it does.'
Alice's Adventures in Wonderland (1865) **Carroll, Lewis** (1832–1898) English writer and photographer

49 There are only two lineages in the world, as a grandmother of mine used to say, the Haves and the Have-nots.
Don Quixote, II (1615) **Cervantes, Miguel de** (1547–1616) Spanish writer and dramatist

50 Custom has made dancing sometimes necessary for a young man; therefore mind it while you learn it, that you may learn to do it well, and not be ridiculous, though in a ridiculous act.
Letter to his son, (1746)

51 In the case of scandal, as in that of robbery, the receiver is always thought as bad as the thief.
Letter to his son, (1748) **Chesterfield, Lord** (1694–1773) English politician and letter writer

52 For all the churches you can build, and all the books you can export, will never do much good without what a gentleman in that Colony very appropriately called 'God's police' – wives and little children – good and virtuous women.
Emigration and Transportation Relatively Considered (1847) **Chisholm, Caroline** (1808–1877) English-born Australian humanitarian

53 Curious things, habits. People themselves never knew they had them.
Witness for the Prosecution (1953) **Christie, Agatha** (1890–1976) English crime writer and playwright

54 There is no finer investment for any community than putting milk into babies.
Radio broadcast, (March 1943) **Churchill, Sir Winston** (1874–1965) English Conservative Prime Minister

55 What times! What manners!
In *Catilinam* **Cicero** (106–43 BC) Roman orator, statesman, essayist and letter writer. (*O tempora! O mores!*)

56 The only living societies are those which are animated by inequality and injustice.
Conversations dans le Loir-et-Cher **Claudel, Paul** (1868–1955) French dramatist, poet and diplomat

57 Loving your neighbour as much as yourself is practically bloody impossible ... You might as well have a Commandment that states, 'Thou shalt fly'.
The Times, (1993) **Cleese, John** (1939–) British comedian, actor and writer

58 If the crowd has to choose someone to crucify, it will always save Barabbas.
Le Coq et l'Arlequin (1918) **Cocteau, Jean** (1889–1963) French dramatist, poet, film writer and director

59 Retired to their tea and scandal, according to their ancient custom.
The Double Dealer (1694)

60 She lays it on with a trowel.
The Double Dealer (1694)

61 They come together like the Coroner's Inquest, to sit upon the murdered reputations of the week.

The Way of the World (1700) **Congreve, William** (1670–1729) English dramatist

62 The terrorist and the policeman both come from the same basket.
The Secret Agent (1907) **Conrad, Joseph** (1857–1924) Polish-born British writer, sailor and explorer

63 The Act of God designation on all insurance policies; which means, roughly, that you cannot be insured for the accidents that are most likely to happen to you.
The Lady from Stalingrad Museum (1977) **Coren, Alan** (1938–) British humorist, writer and broadcaster

64 In human society the warmth is mainly at the bottom.
Age, (1986) **Counihan, Noel Jack** (1913–1986) Australian cartoonist and artist

65 No people do so much harm as those who go about doing good.
The Life and Letters of Mandell Creighton (1904) **Creighton, Mandell** (1843–1901) English churchman, historian and biographer

66 I became one of the stately homos of England.
The Naked Civil Servant (1968) **Crisp, Quentin** (1908–1999) English writer, publicist and model

67 It's not sex and drug advice these kids need, so much as help in acquiring a world view, in motivating them to take responsibility and enabling them to build proper relationships. But if you say that sort of thing to the social work agencies, they just turn off and say: 'Oh, those are moral issues – we can't be going into those.' But we have to! Otherwise, we shall simply be raising generations of animals, of Calibans.
Daily Mail, (1996) **Curry, George** English churchman. On the young people involved in the 1991 riots in Tyneside

68 Mr Podsnap settled that whatever he put behind him he put out of existence … Mr Podsnap had even acquired a peculiar flourish of his right arm in often clearing the world of its most difficult problems, by sweeping them behind him.
Our Mutual Friend (1865) **Dickens, Charles** (1812–1870) English writer

69 What Soft – Cherubic Creatures –
These Gentlewomen are –
One would as soon assault a Plush –
Or violate a Star –
Such Dimity Convictions –
A Horror so refined
Of freckled Human Nature –
Of Deity – ashamed.
'What Soft – Cherubic Creatures' (c.1862) **Dickinson, Emily** (1830–1886) US poet

70 Increased means and increased leisure are the two civilizers of man.
Speech, Manchester, (1872) **Disraeli, Benjamin** (1804–1881) English statesman and writer

71 But far more numerous was the herd of such
Who think too little and who talk too much.
Absalom and Achitophel (1681) **Dryden, John** (1631–1700) English poet, satirist, dramatist and critic

72 The rejection of authority can sometimes result, paradoxically, in an embrace of authoritarianism. Indeed, it can happen with insidious ease.
Atlantic Monthly, (1991) **D'Souza, Dinesh** (1961–) Indian-born US writer

73 Gossip is a sort of smoke that comes from the dirty tobacco-pipes of those who diffuse it: it proves nothing but the bad taste of the smoker.
Daniel Deronda (1876) **Eliot, George** (1819–1880) English writer and poet

74 Society everywhere is in conspiracy against the manhood of every one of its members.
'Self-Reliance' (1841)

75 The virtues of society are the vices of the saint.
Essays, First Series (1841) **Emerson, Ralph Waldo** (1803–1882) US poet, essayist, transcendentalist and teacher

76 Charming women can true converts make,
We love the precepts for the teacher's sake.
The Constant Couple (1699)

77 I believe they talked of me, for they
laughed consumedly.
The Beaux' Stratagem (1707) **Farquhar, George**
(1678–1707) Irish dramatist

78 I was one of the few guests who had
actually been invited. People were not
invited – they went there.
The Great Gatsby (1925)

79 I entertained on a cruising trip that was so
much fun that I had to sink my yacht to
make my guests go home.
The Crack-Up (1945) **Fitzgerald, F. Scott** (1896–
1940) US writer

80 For there is no such thing as a democratic
gentleman; the adjective and the noun are
hyphenated by a drawn sword.
Such is Life (1903) **Furphy, Joseph** (1843–1912)
Australian writer and poet

81 In the affluent society, no sharp distinction
can be made between luxuries and
necessaries.
The Affluent Society (1958) **Galbraith, J.K.** (1908–
2006) Canadian-born US economist, diplomat
and writer

82 No society can survive, no civilization can
survive, with 12-year-olds having babies,
with 15-year-olds killing each other, with
17-year-olds dying of Aids, with 18-year-
olds getting diplomas they can't read.
The Times, (1995) **Gingrich, Newt** (1943–) US
Republican politician

83 Diplomacy is to do and say
The nastiest thing in the nicest way.
The Reflex, (1927) **Goldberg, Isaac** (1887–1938)
US critic and writer

84 It is flattering some Men to endure them.
'Of Company' (1750) **Halifax, Lord** (1633–1695)
English politician, courtier, pamphleteer and
epigrammatist

85 If I had to give a definition of capitalism I
would say: the process whereby American
girls turn into American women.
Savages (1973) **Hampton, Christopher** (1946–)
English dramatist

86 'You left us in tatters, without shoes or
socks,
Tired of digging potatoes, and spudding
up docks;
And now you've gay bracelets and bright
feathers three!'–
'Yes: that's how we dress when we're
ruined,' said she.
'The Ruined Maid' (1866) **Hardy, Thomas**
(1840–1928) English writer and poet

87 The Gypsies are a litmus test not of
democracy but of civil society.
Attr. **Havel, Václav** (1936–) Czech President

88 I do not think there is anything deserving
the name of society to be found out of
London.
Table-Talk (1822)

89 There is not a more mean, stupid,
dastardly, pitiful, selfish, spiteful, envious,
ungrateful animal than the Public. It is the
greatest of cowards, for it is afraid of itself.
Table-Talk (1822) **Hazlitt, William** (1778–1830)
English writer and critic

90 The English pub is, we are told from
childhood, a unique institution. Nothing
'quite like it' exists anywhere else. That's
true. The pub uniquely represents, even in
metropolitan England, the precise
inequalities of gender, race and class that
construct our society. From the inclusive
white, male and proletarian 'public' of
many northern pubs to the parasitic blazer
and cotton dress 'locals' of the home
counties, our unique institution divides
our society and our social life.
New Statesman and Society, (1989) **Howkins,
Alun** (1947–) British historian and writer

91 We have really lost in our society the sense
of the sacredness of life.
The Observer Review, (1995) **Hume, Basil** (1923–
1999) English Cardinal, Archbishop of
Westminster. On the killing of London
headmaster Philip Lawrence

92 The majority has the might – more's the
pity – but it hasn't right ... The minority is
always right.
An Enemy of the People (1882)

93 People don't do such things!
Hedda Gabler (1890) Judge Brack, on Hedda
Gabler's suicide **Ibsen, Henrik** (1828–1906)
Norwegian writer, dramatist and poet

94 Any attempt to reform the university
without attending to the system of which it
is an integral part is like trying to do urban
renewal in New York City from the twelfth
storey up.
Deschooling Society (1971) **Illich, Ivan** (1926–)
Austrian-born US educator, sociologist, writer
and priest

95 A nation is a society united by a delusion
about its ancestry and by a common hatred
of its neighbours.
In Sagittarius and George, *The Perpetual
Pessimist* **Inge, William Ralph** (1860–1954)
English divine, writer and teacher

96 Few rich men own their own property. The
property owns them.
Address, (1896) **Ingersoll, Robert G.** (1833–
1899) US lawyer, soldier and writer

97 The permissive society has been allowed to
become a dirty phrase. A better phrase is
the civilized society.
Speech, (1969) **Jenkins, Roy** (1920–2003) Welsh
politician and writer

98 For me this is a vital litmus test: no
intellectual society can flourish where a Jew
feels even slightly uneasy.
The Sunday Times Magazine, (1977) **Johnson,
Paul** (1928–) British editor and writer

99 It is better that some should be unhappy
than that none should be happy, which
would be the case in a general state of
equality.
In Boswell, *The Life of Samuel Johnson* (1791)

100 Your levellers wish to level down as far as
themselves; but they cannot bear levelling
up to themselves.
In Boswell, *The Life of Samuel Johnson* (1791)

101 Questioning is not the mode of
conversation among gentlemen.
In Boswell, *The Life of Samuel Johnson* (1791)
Johnson, Samuel (1709–1784) English
lexicographer, poet, critic, conversationalist
and essayist

102 Yes to the market economy. No to the
market society.
The Observer, (1998) **Jospin, Lionel** (1937–)
French politician and Socialist Prime
Minister

103 It is much safer to be in a subordinate
position than in one of authority.
De Imitatione Christi (1892 ed.) **Kempis,
Thomas à** (c.1380–1471) German mystic, monk
and writer

104 Man is the only animal that learns by being
hypocritical. He pretends to be polite and
then, eventually, he becomes polite.
Finishing Touches (1973) **Kerr, Jean** (1923–2003)
US writer and dramatist

105 Over-great haste to repay an obligation is a
form of ingratitude.
Maximes (1678) **La Rochefoucauld** (1613–1680)
French writer

106 Is it progress if a cannibal uses knife and
fork?
Unkempt Thoughts (1962) **Lec, Stanislaw** (1909–
1966) Polish writer

107 If you haven't anything nice to say about
anyone, come and sit by me.
New York Times, (1980) **Longworth, Alice
Roosevelt** (1884–1980) US writer.
Embroidered on a cushion at her home in
Washington

108 The true snob never rests: there is always a
higher goal to attain, and there are, by the
same token, always more and more people
to look down upon.
Attr. **Lynes, J. Russel** (1910–1991) US writer

109 We enter into a covenant that we shall
build the society in which all South
Africans, both black and white, will be able
to walk tall, without any fear in their hearts,
assured of their inalienable right to human
dignity – a rainbow nation at peace with
itself and the world.
Inaugural Address, (1994) **Mandela, Nelson**
(1918–) South African statesman and
President

110 The only thing of weight that can be said against modern honour is that it is directly opposite to religion. The one bids you bear injuries with patience, the other tells you if you don't resent them, you are not fit to live.
The Fable of the Bees (1714) **Mandeville, Bernard** (1670–1733) Dutch-born British doctor and satirist

111 I don't think you want too much sincerity in society. It would be like a girder in a house of cards.
The Circle **Maugham, William Somerset** (1874–1965) English writer, dramatist and physician

112 The car has become the carapace, the protective and aggressive shell, of urban and suburban man.
Understanding Media (1964) **McLuhan, Marshall** (1911–1980) Canadian communications theorist

113 I have always thought complaints of ill-usage contemptible, whether from a seduced disappointed girl or a turned out Prime Minister.
In a letter from Emily Eden to Mrs Lister, (1834) **Melbourne, Lord** (1779–1848) English statesman. After his dismissal by William IV

114 A society made up of individuals who were all capable of original thought would probably be unendurable. The pressure of ideas would simply drive it frantic.
'Minority Report' (1956) **Mencken, H.L.** (1880–1956) US writer, critic, philologist and satirist

115 Protection, therefore, against the tyranny of the magistrate is not enough: there needs protection also against the tyranny of the prevailing opinion and feeling.
On Liberty (1859)

116 When society requires to be rebuilt, there is no use in attempting to rebuild it on the old plan.
Dissertations and Discussions (1859) **Mill, John Stuart** (1806–1873) English philosopher, economist and reformer

117 Policemen are numbered in case they get lost.
The Last Goon Show of All **Milligan, Spike** (1918–2002) Irish comedian and writer

118 Public scandal is what constitutes offence; to sin in secret is no sin at all.
Tartuffe (1664) **Molière** (1622–1673) French dramatist, actor and director

119 Traditionalists are pessimists about the future and optimists about the past.
Technics and Civilization (1934) **Mumford, Lewis** (1895–1990) US sociologist and writer

120 We felt that the police needed a label, a label other than that fear image that they carried in the community. So we used the pig as the rather low-lifed animal in order to identify the police. And it worked.
In Henry Hampton, *Voices of Freedom* (1990) **Newton, Huey P.** (1942–1989) US political activist

121 Question and answer is not a civilized form of conversation.
Clarissa Oakes (1992) **O'Brian, Patrick** (1914–2000) Irish writer

122 A cruel story runs on wheels, and every hand oils the wheels as they run.
Wisdom, Wit and Pathos, 'Moths' **Ouida** (1839–1908) English writer and critic

123 The public demands elocution rather than reason of those who address it … On matters of the greatest interest it craves to be excited or amused.
The Tale of the Ripe Scholar **Parkman, Francis** (1823–1893) US historian

124 And mighty proud I am (and ought to be thankful to God Almighty) that I am able to have a spare bed for my friends.
Diary, (August 1666) **Pepys, Samuel** (1633–1703) English diarist, naval administrator and politician

125 Censorship in the UK reveals a deeply conservative country still in thrall to its strict Protestant values.
Index on Censorship, (1996) **Pinter, Harold** (1930–) English dramatist, poet and screenwriter

126 *He*: Have you heard it's in the stars
Next July we collide with Mars?
She: Well, did you evah! What a swell party this is.

'Well, Did you Evah!' (song, 1956) from High Society **Porter, Cole** (1891–1964) US songwriter and composer

127 If I were asked to answer the following question: 'What is slavery?' and I replied in one word, 'Murder!' my meaning would be understood at once ... Why, then, to this other question: 'What is property?' may I not likewise answer 'Theft'?
Qu'est-ce que la propriété? (1840) **Proudhon, Pierre-Joseph** (1809–1865) French social reformer, anarchist and writer

128 His hatred of snobs was a derivative of his snobbishness, but made the simpletons (in other words, everyone) believe that he was immune from snobbishness.
Le Côté de Guermantes (1921) **Proust, Marcel** (1871–1922) French writer and critic

129 The poorest he that is in England hath a life to live as the greatest he.
Speech in Army debates, (1647) **Rainborowe, Thomas** (d. 1648) English parliamentarian and soldier

130 Civilization is the progress toward a society of privacy. The savage's whole existence is public, ruled by the laws of his tribe. Civilization is the process of setting man free from men.
The Fountainhead (1943) **Rand, Ayn** (1905–1982) Russian-born US writer

131 I come from suburbia – I don't ever want to go back. It's the one place in the world that's further away than anywhere else.
The Glittering Prizes (1976) **Raphael, Frederic** (1931–) English author

132 It is gentlemanly to get one's quotations very slightly wrong. In that way one unprigs oneself and allows the company to correct one.
In Cooper, *The Light of Common Day* (1959) **Ribblesdale, Lord** (1854–1925) British army officer and courtier

133 The men with the muck-rakes are often indispensable to the well-being of society; but only if they know when to stop raking the muck.
Speech, (1906) **Roosevelt, Theodore** (1858–1919) US Republican President

134 A free-loader is a confirmed guest. He is the man who is always willing to come to dinner.
Short Takes (1946) **Runyon, Damon** (1884–1946) US writer

135 When she inveighed eloquently against the evils of capitalism at drawing-room meetings and Fabian conferences she was conscious of a comfortable feeling that the system, with all its inequalities and iniquities, would probably last her time. It is one of the consolations of middle-aged reformers that the good they inculcate must live after them if it is to live at all.
Beasts and Super-Beasts (1914) **Saki** (1870–1916) Burmese-born British writer

136 The people will live on.
The learning and blundering people will live on.
The People, Yes (1936) **Sandburg, Carl** (1878–1967) US poet, writer and song collector

137 The greater part of humanity is far too weary and worn down by the struggle with want to rouse itself for a new and harder struggle with error.
On the Aesthetic Education of Man (1793–1795) **Schiller, Johann Christoph Friedrich** (1759–1805) German writer, dramatist, poet and historian

138 Society is no comfort
To one not sociable.
Cymbeline, IV:ii

139 Rumour is a pipe
Blown by surmises, jealousies, conjectures,
And of so easy and so plain a stop
That the blunt monster with uncounted heads,
The still-discordant wav'ring multitude,
Can play upon it.
Henry IV, Part 2, Induction **Shakespeare, William** (1564–1616) English dramatist, poet and actor

140 I have never sneered in my life. Sneering doesn't become either the human face or the human soul.
Pygmalion (1916) **Shaw, George Bernard** (1856–1950) Irish socialist, writer, dramatist and critic

141 Here is the whole set! a character dead at every word.
The School for Scandal (1777)

142 Tale-bearers are as bad as the tale-makers.
The School for Scandal (1777)

143 I'm called away by particular business. But I leave my character behind me.
The School for Scandal (1777) **Sheridan, Richard Brinsley** (1751–1816) Irish dramatist, politician and orator

144 A place for everything, and everything in its place. Order is wealth.
Thrift (1875) **Smiles, Samuel** (1812–1904) English writer

145 No society can surely be flourishing and happy, of which the far greater part of the members are poor and miserable.
Wealth of Nations (1776) **Smith, Adam** (1723–1790) Scottish economist, philosopher and essayist

146 Heat, Ma'am! It was so dreadful here, that I found there was nothing left for it but to take off my flesh and sit in my bones.
In Holland, *A Memoir of the Reverend Sydney Smith* (1855) Discussing the recent hot weather

147 One of the greatest pleasures in life is conversation.
Essays (1877) **Smith, Sydney** (1771–1845) English clergyman, essayist, journalist and wit

148 The painful ceremony of receiving and returning visits.
The Adventures of Peregrine Pickle (1751) **Smollett, Tobias** (1721–1771) Scottish writer, satirist, historian, traveller and physician

149 I am not an Athenian nor a Greek, but a citizen of the world.
Attr. in Plutarch, *On Exile*, 600 **Socrates** (469–399 BC) Athenian philosopher

150 No one can be perfectly free till all are free; no one can be perfectly moral till all are moral; no one can be perfectly happy till all are happy.
Social Statics (1850) **Spencer, Herbert** (1820–1903) English philosopher and journalist

151 I no more like people personally than I like dogs. When I meet them I am only apprehensive whether they will bite me, which is reasonable and sensible.
In Collis, *Stanley Spencer* (1962) **Spencer, Sir Stanley** (1891–1959) English painter

152 Man is a social animal.
Ethics (1677) **Spinoza, Baruch** (1632–1677) Dutch philosopher and theologian

153 We were in some little Time fixed in our Seats, and sat with that Dislike which People not too good-natured, usually conceive of each other at first Sight.
The Spectator, 132, (1711) **Steele, Sir Richard** (1672–1729) Irish-born English writer, dramatist and politician

154 So long as a man rides his hobby-horse peaceably and quietly along the King's highway, and neither compels you or me to get up behind him, – pray, Sir, what have either you or I to do with it?
Tristram Shandy (1759–1767) **Sterne, Laurence** (1713–1768) Irish-born English writer and clergyman

155 The only infallible rule we know is, that the man who is always talking about being a gentleman never is one.
Ask Mamma (1858)

156 These sort of boobies think that people come to balls to do nothing but dance; whereas everyone knows that the real business of a ball is either to look out for a wife, to look after a wife, or to look after somebody else's wife.
Mr Facey Romford's Hounds (1865) **Surtees, R.S.** (1805–1864) English writer

157 Promises and pie-crusts are made to be broken, they say.
Polite Conversation (1738) **Swift, Jonathan** (1667–1745) Irish satirist, poet, essayist and cleric

158 As long as men are men, a poor society cannot be too poor to find a right order of life, nor a rich society too rich to have need to seek it.
The Acquisitive Society (1921) **Tawney, R.H.** (1880–1962) British economic historian and Christian socialist

159 He who meanly admires mean things is a Snob.
The Book of Snobs (1848) **Thackeray, William Makepeace** (1811–1863) Indian-born English writer

160 Wherever a man goes, men will pursue him and paw him with their dirty institutions, and, if they can, constrain him to belong to their desperate oddfellow society.
Walden (1854) **Thoreau, Henry David** (1817–1862) US essayist, social critic and writer

161 For the most of us, if we do not talk of ourselves, or at any rate of the individual circles of which we are the centres, we can talk of nothing. I cannot hold with those who wish to put down the insignificant chatter of the world.
Framley Parsonage (1860) **Trollope, Anthony** (1815–1882) English writer, traveller and post office official

162 It is by the goodness of God that in our country we have those three unspeakably precious things: freedom of speech, freedom of conscience, and the prudence never to practise either of them.
Following the Equator (1897) **Twain, Mark** (1835–1910) US humorist, writer, journalist and lecturer

163 The able man is the one who makes mistakes according to the rules.
Bad Thoughts and Not So Bad **Valéry, Paul** (1871–1945) French poet, mathematician and philosopher

164 I was told I am a true cosmopolitan. I am unhappy everywhere.
The Guardian, (1968) **Vizinczey, Stephen** (1933–) Hungarian-born writer, editor and broadcaster

165 Associate yourself with men of good quality if you esteem your own reputation; for 'tis better to be alone than in bad company.
Rules of Civility and Decent Behaviour

166 Labour to keep alive in your breast that little spark of celestial fire, called conscience.
Rules of Civility and Decent Behaviour
Washington, George (1732–1799) US general, statesman and President

167 Pappenhacker says that every time you are polite to a proletarian you are helping to bolster up the capitalist system.
Scoop (1938)

168 Lady Peabury was in the morning room reading a novel; early training gave a guilty spice to this recreation, for she had been brought up to believe that to read a novel before luncheon was one of the gravest sins it was possible for a gentlewoman to commit.
Work Suspended (1942) **Waugh, Evelyn** (1903–1966) English writer and diarist

169 It is easier for a man to be loyal to his club than to his planet: the by-laws are shorter and he is personally acquainted with the other members.
One Man's Meat **White, E.B.** (1899–1985) US humorist and writer

170 The Life and Soul, the man who will never go home while there is one man, woman or glass of anything not yet drunk.
Sunday Best (1976)

171 A good listener is not someone who has nothing to say. A good listener is a good talker with a sore throat.
Attr. **Whitehorn, Katherine** (1926–) English writer

172 A little sincerity is a dangerous thing, and a great deal of it is absolutely fatal.
Intentions (1891), 'The Critic as Artist'

173 It is absurd to divide people into good and bad. People are either charming or tedious.
Lady Windermere's Fan (1892)

174 To be in it is merely a bore. But to be out of it simply a tragedy.
A Woman of No Importance (1893) Of society

175 You should study the Peerage, Gerald. It is the one book a young man about town should know thoroughly, and it is the best thing in fiction the English have ever done.
A Woman of No Importance (1893)

176 Questions are never indiscreet. Answers sometimes are.
An Ideal Husband (1895)

177 I have invented an invaluable permanent invalid called Bunbury, in order that I may be able to go down into the country whenever I choose.
The Importance of Being Earnest (1895)

178 Never speak disrespectfully of Society, Algernon. Only people who can't get into it do that.
The Importance of Being Earnest (1895)

179 It is very vulgar to talk like a dentist when one isn't a dentist. It produces a false impression.
The Importance of Being Earnest (1895)

180 The amount of women in London who flirt with their own husbands is perfectly scandalous. It looks so bad. It is simply washing one's clean linen in public.
The Importance of Being Earnest (1895)

181 In matters of grave importance, style, not sincerity, is the vital thing.
The Importance of Being Earnest (1895)

182 The man who can dominate a London dinner table can dominate the world.
Attr. **Wilde, Oscar** (1854–1900) Irish poet, dramatist, writer, critic and wit

183 There is something utterly nauseating about a system of society which pays a harlot 25 times as much as it pays its Prime Minister, 250 times as much as it pays its Members of Parliament, and 500 times as much as it pays some of its ministers of religion.
Speech, (1963) **Wilson, Harold** (1916–1995) English Labour Prime Minister. Referring to Christine Keeler

184 For her own breakfast she'll project a scheme,
Nor take her tea without a stratagem.
Love of Fame, the Universal Passion (1725–1728)
Young, Edward (1683–1765) English poet, dramatist, satirist and clergyman
See also class; humanity and human nature; manners

SOLITUDE

1 Yes! in the sea of life enisled,
With echoing straits between us thrown,
Dotting the shoreless watery wild,
We mortal millions live alone.
'To Marguerite – Continued' (1852)

2 This truth – to prove, and make thine own:
'Thou hast been, shalt be, art, alone.'
'Isolation. To Marguerite' (1857)

3 Friends who set forth at our side,
Falter, are lost in the storm,
We, we only are left!
'Rugby Chapel' (1867) **Arnold, Matthew** (1822–1888) English poet, critic, essayist and educationist

4 It had been hard for him that spake it to have put more truth and untruth together, in a few words, than in that speech: 'Whosoever is delighted in solitude is either a wild beast, or a god.'
'Of Friendship' (1625) **Bacon, Francis** (1561–1626) English philosopher, essayist, politician and courtier

5 I have been a stranger in a strange land.
Exodus, 2:22 **The Bible (King James Version)**

6 Who knows what true loneliness is – not the conventional word but the naked terror? To the lonely themselves it wears a mask.
Attr. **Conrad, Joseph** (1857–1924) Polish-born British writer, sailor and explorer

7 I praise the Frenchman, his remark was shrewd –
How sweet, how passing sweet, is solitude!
But grant me still a friend in my retreat,
Whom I may whisper – solitude is sweet.
'Retirement' (1782) **Cowper, William** (1731–1800) English poet, hymn writer and letter writer

8 No man will ever unfold the capacities of his own intellect, who does not at least checker his life with solitude.
Suspiria de Profundis (1845) **De Quincey, Thomas** (1785–1859) English writer

9 Solitude is a kind of freedom.
The Observer Review, (1995) **Eco, Umberto** (1932–) Italian critic and writer

10 I was never less alone than when by myself.
Memoirs of My Life and Writings (1796) **Gibbon, Edward** (1737–1794) English historian, politician and memoirist

11 Pray that your loneliness may spur you into finding something to live for, great enough to die for.
Diaries, (1951) **Hammarskjöld, Dag** (1905–1961) Swedish statesman, Secretary-General of the United Nations

12 Loneliness is to endure the presence of one who does not understand.
Attr. **Hubbard, Elbert** (1856–1915) US printer, editor, writer and businessman

13 Waits at the window, wearing the face that she keeps in a jar by the door
Who is it for? All the lonely people, where do they all come from?
All the lonely people, where do they all belong?
'Eleanor Rigby' (song, 1966) **Lennon, John** (1940–1980) and **McCartney, Paul** (1942–) English rock musicians, songwriters, peace campaigners and cultural icons

14 Solitude gives rise to what is original, to what is daringly and displeasingly beautiful, to poetry. Solitude however also gives rise to what is wrong, excessive, absurd and forbidden.
Death in Venice (1912) **Mann, Thomas** (1875–1955) German writer and critic

15 My heart shall be thy garden.
'The Garden' (1875) **Meynell, Alice** (1847–1922) English poet

16 We should keep for ourselves a little back shop, all our own, untouched by others, in which we establish our true freedom and chief place of seclusion and solitude.
Essais (1580) **Montaigne, Michel de** (1533–1592) French essayist and moralist

17 I often get lonely for unrealistic things: for something absolute.
The Observer, (1992) **O'Brien, Edna** (1936–) Irish writer and dramatist

18 Thus let me live, unseen, unknown;
Thus unlamented let me die;
Steal from the world, and not a stone
Tell where I lie.
'Ode on Solitude' (c.1700)

19 Happy the man, whose wish and care
A few paternal acres bound,
Content to breathe his native air,
In his own ground.
'Ode on Solitude' (c.1700) **Pope, Alexander** (1688–1744) English poet, translator and editor

20 To be an adult is to be alone.
Thoughts of a Biologist (1939) **Rostand, Jean** (1894–1977) French biologist

21 Loneliness is the poverty of self; solitude is the richness of self.
Mrs Stevens Hears the Mermaids Singing (1993) **Sarton, May** (1912–1995) US poet and writer

22 Alone ... The word is life endured and known.
It is the stillness where our spirits walk
And all but inmost faith is overthrown.
The Heart's Journey (1928) **Sassoon, Siegfried** (1886–1967) English poet and writer

23 Solitude is the fate of all outstanding minds: it will at times be deplored; but it will always be chosen as the lesser of two evils.
'Aphorisms for Wisdom' (1851) **Schopenhauer, Arthur** (1788–1860) German philosopher

24 She thought of the narrowness of the limits within which a human soul may speak and be understood by its nearest of mental kin, of how soon it reaches that solitary land of the individual experience in which no fellow footfall is ever heard.
The Story of an African Farm (1884) **Schreiner, Olive** (1855–1920) South African writer

25 I never found the companion that was so companionable as solitude.
Walden (1854) **Thoreau, Henry David** (1817–1862) US essayist, social critic and writer

26 Hear that lonesome whippoorwill?
He sounds too blue to fly.
The midnight train is whining low,
I'm so lonesome I could cry.
'I'm So Lonesome I Could Cry' (song, 1942) **Williams, Hank** (1923–1953) US country music singer
See also silence

THE SOUL

1 We cannot kindle when we will
The fire which in the heart resides,
The spirit bloweth and is still,
In mystery our soul abides.
'Morality' (1852) **Arnold, Matthew** (1822–1888)
English poet, critic, essayist and educationist

2 I have freed my soul.
'Epistle 371' **Bernard, Saint** (1091–1153) French
abbot and founder of the Cistercian order

3 What is a man profited, if he shall gain the
whole world, and lose his own soul?
Matthew, 16:26 **The Bible (King James
Version)**

4 It is the soul that sees; the outward eyes
Present the object, but the mind descries.
The Lover's Journey **Crabbe, George** (1754–1832)
English poet, clergyman, surgeon and
botanist

5 The Soul selects her own Society –
Then – shuts the Door –
To her divine Majority –
Present no more …
I've known her – from an ample nation –
Choose One –
Then – close the Valves of her attention –
Like Stone.
'The Soul selects her own Society' (c.1862)
Dickinson, Emily (1830–1886) US poet

6 Poor intricated soul! Riddling, perplexed,
labyrinthical soul!
LXXX Sermons (1640) **Donne, John** (1572–1631)
English poet

7 Dim, as the borrowed beams of moon and
stars
To lonely, weary, wandering travellers
Is reason to the soul.
Religio Laici (1682) **Dryden, John** (1631–1700)
English poet, satirist, dramatist and critic

8 When divine souls appear men are
compelled by their own self-respect to
distinguish them.
Journals **Emerson, Ralph Waldo** (1803–1882)
US poet, essayist, transcendentalist and
teacher

9 In the real dark night of the soul it is
always three o'clock in the morning.
The Crack-Up (1945) **Fitzgerald, F. Scott** (1896–
1940) US writer

10 Ah fleeting Spirit! wand'ring Fire,
That long hast warm'd my tender Breast,
Must thou no more this Frame inspire?
No more a pleasing, cheerful Guest?
'Ad Animam Suam' (trans. Pope) **Hadrian** (AD
76–138) Roman emperor and patron of the
arts

11 Death only this mysterious truth unfolds,
The mighty soul, how small a body holds.
Satires **Juvenal** (c.60–130) Roman verse satirist
and Stoic

12 A man should have the fine point of his
soul taken off to become fit for this world.
Letter to J.H. Reynolds, (1817) **Keats, John**
(1795–1821) English poet

13 The soul started at the knee-cap and ended
at the navel.
The Apes of Gods (1930) **Lewis, Wyndham**
(1882–1957) US-born British painter, critic and
writer

14 What has this bugbear death to frighten
man
If souls can die as well as bodies can?
De Rerum Natura **Lucretius** (c.95–55 BC) Roman
philosopher

15 The soul must feed on something for its
dreams,
In those brick suburbs, and there wasn't
much:
It can make do with little, so it seems.
'Wisteria' (1971) **McAuley, James Philip** (1917–
1976) Australian poet and critic

16 There is nothing the body suffers the soul
may not profit by.
Diana of the Crossways (1885) **Meredith, George**
(1828–1909) English writer, poet and critic

17 Strive not, my soul, for an immortal life,
but make the most of what is possible.
Pythian Odes **Pindar** (518–438 BC) Greek lyric
poet

18 Let us be persuaded ... to consider that the soul is immortal and capable of enduring all evil and all good, and so we shall always hold to the upward way and pursue justice with wisdom.
Republic **Plato** (c.429–347 BC) Greek philosopher

19 It is with narrow-souled people as with narrow-necked bottles: the less they have in them, the more noise they make in pouring it out.
Miscellanies (1727), 'Thoughts on Various Subjects' **Pope, Alexander** (1688–1744) English poet, translator and editor

20 Go, Soul, the body's guest,
Upon a thankless arrant:
Fear not to touch the best;
The truth shall be thy warrant:
Go, since I needs must die,
And give the world the lie.
'The Lie' (1608) **Raleigh, Sir Walter** (c.1552–1618) English courtier, explorer, military commander, poet, historian and essayist

21 O seasons, O castles! What soul is without faults?
'Ô saisons, ô châteaux' (1872) **Rimbaud, Arthur** (1854–1891) French poet

22 The soul of man, like unextinguished fire, Yet burns towards heaven with fierce reproach.
Prometheus Unbound (1820) **Shelley, Percy Bysshe** (1792–1822) English poet, dramatist and essayist

23 Most people sell their souls, and live with a good conscience on the proceeds.
Afterthoughts (1931) **Smith, Logan Pearsall** (1865–1946) US-born British epigrammatist, critic and writer

24 A man should feel confident concerning his soul, who in his life has rejected those pleasures and fineries that go with the body as being alien to him, considering them to result more in harm than in good, and has eagerly sought the pleasures that go with learning and adorned his soul with no alien but rather with its own proper refinements, moderation and justice and courage and freedom and truth; thus he awaits his journey to the world below, ready whenever fate calls him.
Attr. in Plato, *Phaedo* **Socrates** (469–399 BC) Athenian philosopher

25 I am positive I have a soul; nor can all the books with which materialists have pestered the world ever convince me to the contrary.
A Sentimental Journey (1768) **Sterne, Laurence** (1713–1768) Irish-born English writer and clergyman

26 The Manner whereby the Soul and Body are united, and how they are distinguished, is wholly unaccountable to us. We see but one Part, and yet we know we consist of two; and this is a Mystery we cannot comprehend, any more than that of the Trinity.
'On the Trinity' **Swift, Jonathan** (1667–1745) Irish satirist, poet, essayist and cleric

27 A little soul for a little bears up this corpse which is man.
'Hymn to Proserpine' (1866) **Swinburne, Algernon Charles** (1837–1909) English poet, critic, dramatist and letter writer

28 My soul, like to a ship in a black storm, Is driven, I know not whither.
The White Devil (1612) **Webster, John** (c.1580–c.1625) English dramatist

29 Our birth is but a sleep and a forgetting.
The Soul that rises with us, our life's Star,
Hath had elsewhere its setting,
And cometh from afar.
'Ode: Intimations of Immortality' (1807) **Wordsworth, William** (1770–1850) English poet
See also death; self

SPITE

1 If I had a head like yours, I'd have it circumcised.
In Gus Smith, *God's Own Comedian* **Allen, Dave** (1936–2005) Irish comedian and television personality

2 You have delighted us long enough.
Pride and Prejudice (1813)

3 I cannot anyhow continue to find people agreeable; I respect Mrs Chamberlayne for doing her hair well, but cannot feel a more tender sentiment. Miss Langley is like any other short girl, with a broad nose and wide mouth, fashionable dress and exposed bosom. Adam Stanhope is a gentleman-like man, but then his legs are too short and his tail too long.
Letter to her sister, Cassandra **Austen, Jane** (1775–1817) English writer

4 I like Frenchmen very much, because even when they insult you they do it so nicely.
Attr. **Baker, Josephine** (1906–1975) French dancer, singer and entertainer

5 The dullard's envy of brilliant men is always assuaged by the suspicion that they will come to a bad end.
Zuleika Dobson (1911) **Beerbohm, Sir Max** (1872–1956) English satirist, cartoonist, critic and essayist

6 I am not going to spend any time whatsoever in attacking the Foreign Secretary. Quite honestly I am beginning to feel extremely sorry for him. If we complain about the tune, there is no reason to attack the monkey when the organ grinder is present.
Speech, House of Commons, (1957) **Bevan, Aneurin** (1897–1960) Welsh Labour politician, miner and orator. Wishing to address Harold Macmillan, the Prime Minister, rather than Selwyn Lloyd, the Foreign Secretary, in the post-Suez debate

7 *Backbite*: To speak of a man as you find him when he can't find you.
The Enlarged Devil's Dictionary (1961) **Bierce, Ambrose** (1842–c.1914) US writer, verse writer and soldier

8 *Johnson*: Well, we had a good talk.
Boswell: Yes, Sir; you tossed and gored several persons.
The Life of Samuel Johnson (1791) **Boswell, James** (1740–1795) Scottish biographer

9 If there is anyone here whom I have not insulted, I beg his pardon.
Attr. **Brahms, Johannes** (1833–1897) German composer, pianist and conductor. Said on leaving a gathering of friends

10 I wish my deadly foe, no worse
Than want of friends, and empty purse.
'A Farewell to Town' (1577) **Breton, Nicholas** (c.1545–c.1626) English writer and poet

11 Who's your fat friend?
In Gronow, *Reminiscences* (1862) **Brummel, Beau** (1778–1840) English dandy and wit. Said of the Prince of Wales, 1813

12 An injury is much sooner forgotten than an insult.
Letter to his son, (1746) **Chesterfield, Lord** (1694–1773) English politician and letter writer

13 Who wit with jealous eye surveys,
And sickens at another's praise.
The Ghost (1763) **Churchill, Charles** (1731–1764) English poet, political writer and clergyman

14 You are all camphire and frankincense, all chastity and odour.
The Way of the World (1700) **Congreve, William** (1670–1729) English dramatist

15 He who allows himself to be insulted, deserves to be.
Héraclius (1646) **Corneille, Pierre** (1606–1684) French dramatist, poet and lawyer

16 I see – she's the original good time that was had by all.
In Halliwell, *Filmgoer's Book of Quotes* (1973) **Davis, Bette** (1908–1989) US film actress. Of a starlet

17 Your dexterity seems a happy compound of the smartness of an attorney's clerk and the intrigue of a Greek of the lower empire.
Attr. **Disraeli, Benjamin** (1804–1881) English statesman and writer. Speaking to Lord Palmerston

18 Fools may our scorn, not envy raise,
For envy is a kind of praise.
Fables (1727) **Gay, John** (1685–1732) English poet, dramatist and librettist

19 I shouldn't be sufficiently degraded in my own estimation unless I was insulted with a very considerable bribe.
The Mikado (1885) **Gilbert, W.S.** (1836–1911) English dramatist, humorist and librettist

20 The Scotch may be compared to a tulip planted in dung, but I never see a Dutchman in his own house, but I think of a magnificent Egyptian Temple dedicated to an ox.
Letter from Leyden to Rev. Thomas Contarine, (1754)

21 Here lies David Garrick, describe me who can,
An abridgment of all that was pleasant in man ...
On the stage he was natural, simple, affecting,
'Twas only that, when he was off, he was acting ...
He cast off his friends as a huntsman his pack,
For he knew, when he pleased, he could whistle them back.
'Retaliation' (1774) **Goldsmith, Oliver** (c.1728–1774) Irish dramatist, poet and writer

22 I am a poor man, but I would gladly give ten shillings to find out who sent me the insulting Christmas card I received this morning.
Diary of a Nobody (1894) **Grossmith, George** (1847–1912) English singer and comedian, and **Grossmith, Weedon** (1854–1919) English writer, painter and actor

23 The difference between us is that my family begins with me, whereas yours ends with you.
Attr. **Iphicrates** (419–353 BC) Athenian general. Responding to a descendant of Harmodius (an Athenian hero), who had mocked Iphicrates for being the son of a shoemaker

24 Of all the griefs that harrass the distress'd,
Sure the most bitter is a scornful jest;
Fate never wounds more deep the gen'rous heart,
Than when a blockhead's insult points the dart.
London: A Poem (1738)

25 A fellow who makes no figure in company, and has a mind as narrow as the neck of a vinegar cruet.
In Boswell, *Journal of a Tour to the Hebrides* (1785)

26 Sir, your wife, under pretence of keeping a bawdy-house, is a receiver of stolen goods.
In Boswell, *The Life of Samuel Johnson* (1791) To an abusive Thames waterman

27 Madam, before you flatter a man so grossly to his face, you should consider whether or not your flattery is worth his having.
In *Diary and Letters of Madame d'Arblay* (1842) Remark to Hannah More **Johnson, Samuel** (1709–1784) English lexicographer, poet, critic, conversationalist and essayist

28 I was implying that the Honourable Member was like a lizard on a rock – alive but looking dead.
Keating, Paul (1944–) Australian Prime Minister. On John Howard

29 What did I think of Titanic? I'd rather have been on it.
Review **Kruger, Miles** Cinema critic and theatre historian

30 We only admit our little faults to persuade others that we have no great ones.
Maximes (1678) **La Rochefoucauld** (1613–1680) French writer

31 Oozing charm from every pore,
He oiled his way around the floor.
My Fair Lady (1956) **Lerner, Alan Jay** (1918–1986) US lyricist and screenwriter

32 They made peace between us; we embraced, and since that time we have been mortal enemies.
Le Diable boiteux **Lesage, Alain-René** (1668–1747) French writer and dramatist

33 He was brilliant to the top of his army boots.
Attr. **Lloyd George, David** (1863–1945) English Liberal Prime Minister. Of Sir Douglas Haig

34 If Harold Wilson ever went to school without any boots, it was merely because he was too big for them.
Macmillan, Harold (1894–1986) British Prime Minister. Casting aspersions on Harold Wilson's claims of a poor upbringing

35 When I hear the name Richard Body I hear the sound of white coats flapping.
Attr. (1994) **Major, John** (1943–) British Conservative Prime Minister

36 I do not like you, Sabidius, and I cannot say why; all I can say is this: I do not like you.
Epigrammata **Martial** (c.AD 40–c.104) Spanish-born Latin epigrammatist and poet

37 People wish their enemies dead – but I do not; I say give them the gout, give them the stone!
In a letter from Horace Walpole to the Earl of Harcourt, (1778) **Montagu, Lady Mary Wortley** (1689–1762) English letter writer, poet, traveller and introducer of smallpox inoculation

38 He really deserves some sort of decoration – a medal inscribed 'For Vaguery in the Field'.
Look Back in Anger (1956) **Osborne, John** (1929–1994) English dramatist and actor

39 Who can refute a sneer?
Principles of Moral and Political Philosophy (1785) **Paley, Rev. William** (1743–1805) English theologian and philosopher

40 Where does she find them?
In Lyttelton Hart-Davis, *Letters* **Parker, Dorothy** (1893–1967) US writer, poet, critic and wit. Reply to the comment, 'Anyway, she's always very nice to her inferiors'

41 Ho! the honourable member for Bourke, who is believed to have committed every crime in the calendar, – except the one we could so easily have forgiven him – suicide.
In Wannan, *With Malice Aforethought* **Parkes, Sir Henry** (1815–1896) Australian politician, writer and poet. On William Nicholas Willis

42 He was a man of splendid abilities but utterly corrupt. Like rotten mackerel by moonlight, he shines and stinks.
Randolph, John, of Roanoke (1773–1833) US politician. On fellow-politician Edward Livingstone

43 If it's a boy, I'll call it after myself. If it's a girl I'll call it Victoria after our Queen. But if, as I strongly suspect, it's nothing but piss and wind, I'll call it after you.
In Humphrey McQueen, *Social Sketches of Australia* **Reid, Sir George Houstoun** (1845–1918) Australian politician. On being asked at a meeting, apropos of his stomach, 'What are you going to call it, George?'

44 Certain phrases stick in the throat, even if they offer nothing that is analytically improbable. 'A dashing Swiss officer' is one such.
Paris (1960) **Russell, John** (1919–) British art critic

45 I can't see that she could have found anything nastier to say if she'd thought it out with both hands for a fortnight.
Busman's Honeymoon (1937) **Sayers, Dorothy L.** (1893–1957) English writer, dramatist and translator

46 O, beware, my lord, of jealousy;
It is the green-ey'd monster which doth mock
The meat it feeds on.
Othello, III.iii **Shakespeare, William** (1564–1616) English dramatist, poet and actor

47 If it is abuse, – why one is always sure to hear of it from one damned good-natured friend or another!
The Critic (1779) **Sheridan, Richard Brinsley** (1751–1816) Irish dramatist, politician and orator

48 Come again when you can't stay so long.
In D. Welch, 'Sickert at St Peter's', *Horizon*, (1942) **Sickert, Walter** (1860–1942) German-born British painter and writer. To Denton Welch

49 I do not want Miss Mannin's feelings to be hurt by the fact that I have never heard of her ... At the moment I am debarred from the pleasure of putting her in her place by the fact that she has not got one.
In J. Pearson, *Façades* (1978) **Sitwell, Dame Edith** (1887–1964) English poet, anthologist, critic and biographer. On novelist Ethel Mannin

50 It proves what they say, give the public what they want to see and they'll come out for it.
Remark, (1958) **Skelton, Red** (1913–1997) US comedian. Commenting on the large crowds attending the funeral of Hollywood producer Harry Cohn

51 *Judge Willis*: You are extremely offensive, young man.
F.E. Smith: As a matter of fact, we both are, and the only difference between us is that I am trying to be, and you can't help it.
In Birkenhead, *Frederick Elwin, Earl of Birkenhead* (1933) **Smith, F.E.** (1872–1930) English politician and Lord Chancellor

52 Let the Dean and Canons lay their heads together and the thing will be done. (It being proposed to surround St Paul's with a wooden pavement.)
In H. Pearson, *The Smith of Smiths* (1934) **Smith, Sydney** (1771–1845) English clergyman, essayist, journalist and wit

53 Malice is like a game of poker or tennis; you don't play it with anyone who is manifestly inferior to you.
The Darkened Room **Spiel, Hilde** (1911–1990) Austrian writer

54 In Church your grandsire cut his throat;
To do the job too long he tarry'd,
He should have had my hearty vote,
To cut his throat before he marry'd.
'Verses on the Upright Judge' (1724) **Swift, Jonathan** (1667–1745) Irish satirist, poet, essayist and cleric

55 What time he can spare from the adornment of his person he devotes to the neglect of his duties.
In M.R. Bobbit, *With Dearest Love to All* (1960) **Thompson, William Hepworth** (1810–1886) English Greek scholar. Of Sir Richard Jebb, Professor of Greek at Cambridge

56 A man should not insult his wife publicly, at parties. He should insult her in the privacy of the home.
Thurber Country (1953) **Thurber, James** (1894–1961) US humorist, writer and dramatist

57 I admire him [Cecil Rhodes], I frankly confess it; and when his time comes I shall buy a piece of the rope for a keepsake.
Following the Equator (1897) **Twain, Mark** (1835–1910) US humorist, writer, journalist and lecturer

58 People always call it luck when you've acted more sensibly than they have.
Celestial Navigation (1974) **Tyler, Anne** (1941–) US novelist

59 Muggeridge, a garden gnome expelled from Eden, has come to rest as a gargoyle brooding over a derelict cathedral.
Tynan, Kenneth (1927–1980) English theatre critic. On Malcolm Muggeridge

60 A perfectly good second-class chemist, a Beta chemist ... she wasn't an interesting person, except as a conservative ... I would never, if I had amusing, interesting people staying, have thought of asking Margaret Thatcher.
Vaughan, Dame Janet (1899–1993) Pathologist, also tutor of Somerville College, Oxford. On former student Margaret Thatcher

61 I have never made but one prayer to God, a very short one: 'O Lord, make my enemies ridiculous.' And God granted it.
Letter to Damilaville, (1767) **Voltaire** (1694–1778) French philosopher, dramatist, poet, historian, writer and critic

62 To see him fumbling with our rich and delicate language is to experience all the horror of seeing a Sèvres vase in the hands of a chimpanzee.
The Tablet, (1951) **Waugh, Evelyn** (1903–1966) English author. On Stephen Spender

63 You have Van Gogh's ear for music.
Attr. **Wilder, Billy** (1906–2002) Austrian-born US film director, producer and screenwriter. Said to Cliff Osmond

64 That must depend on whether I embrace your lordship's principles or your mistress.
Attr. in Sir Charles Petrie, *The Four Georges* (1935) **Wilkes, John** (1727–1797) English radical, journalist and politician. Reply to Lord Sandwich, who had told him that he would die either on the gallows or of the pox

65 A shiver looking for a spine to run up.
Wilson, Harold (1916–1995) British Labour Prime Minister. Of Ted Heath, leader of the Opposition

66 He has a bungalow mind.
Wilson, Woodrow (1856–1924) US Democrat President. On Warren G. Harding, his successor as President
See also criticism

SPORT AND GAMES

1 It took me seventeen years to get three thousand hits in baseball. I did it in one afternoon on the golf course.
In Lee Green, *Sportswit* (1984) **Aaron, Hank** (1934–)

2 Champions aren't made in gyms. Champions are made from something they have deep inside them – a desire, a dream, a vision. They have to have the skill, and the will. But the will must be stronger than the skill.
The Greatest (1975)

3 It's just a job. Grass grows, birds fly, waves pound the sand. I beat people up.
The New York Times, (1977)

4 Fighting is not the answer to frustration and hate. It is a sport, not a philosophy of life.
Interview, *TV Guide* magazine, (1999)

5 Float like a butterfly, sting like a bee.
Catchphrase **Ali, Muhammad** (1942–) US heavyweight boxer

6 Professional football is no longer a game. It's a war. And it brings out the same primitive instincts that go back thousands of years.
The Observer, (1973) **Allison, Malcolm** (1927–) English footballer and coach

7 Illingworth (n) A measure of rich humbug, prob originating in Yorkshire. Used figuratively of person who claims credit for success but blames others for failure. Examples: any interview with the chairman of England's cricket selectors.
Private Eye, (1995) Raymond Illingworth was a former Yorkshire cricketer and chairman of England's cricket selectors

8 In affectionate Remembrance of ENGLISH CRICKET which died at the Oval on 29th August, 1882. Deeply lamented by a large circle of sorrowing Friends and Acquaintances R.I.P. N.B. – The body will be cremated, and the Ashes taken to Australia.
Sporting Times, (1882) The mock obituary which began the story of 'The Ashes'

9 Trousers may be worn by women on the course, but must be taken off upon entering the clubhouse.
Golf club rule, (1927)

10 Bodyline bowling has assumed such proportions as to menace the best interests of the game, making protection of the body by the batsmen the main consideration. This is causing intensely bitter feeling between the players as well as injury. In our opinion it is unsportsmanlike. Unless stopped at once it is likely to upset the friendly relationships existing between Australia and England.
Text of cable from Australian Cricket Board to MCC, following Adelaide Test, (1933) **Anonymous**

11 I never comment on referees and I'm not going to break the habit of a lifetime for that prat.
Sky Sports

12 He dribbles a lot and the opposition don't like it – you can see it over their faces.
Sky Sports **Atkinson, Ron** (1939–) English football coach and commentator

13 In the case of almost every sport one can think of, from tennis to billiards, golf to skittles, it was royalty or the aristocracy who originally developed, codified and popularised the sport, after which it was taken up by the lower classes.
The Spectator, (1996) **Archer, Mark** British journalist

14 Say that cricket has nothing to do with politics and you say that cricket has nothing to do with life.
Arlott, John (1914–1991) English cricket commentator

15 Perhaps it is idealistic to suppose that any minister might know their subject, but a passing interest is not beyond expectations.
Balding, Clare (1971–) English amateur jockey and TV sports presenter. Commenting on a lamentable performance by Richard Caborn, the new Minister for Sport, in her live sports quiz on *Radio 5 Live*, 2001

16 Playing snooker gives you firm hands and helps to build up character. It is the ideal recreation for dedicated nuns.
The Daily Telegraph, (1989) **Barbarito, Luigi** (1922–) Papal emissary. Commenting on a sponsored snooker competition at a convent

17 It's a pity to see Paris, the world capital of thinking, devoting so much interest to a game played with feet.
The Scotsman, (June 1998) **Bardot, Brigitte** (1934–) French actress. Comment on the 1998 World Cup, hosted by France

18 The commentary lost more that just Arlott's unassuming gravitas. When he retired, the commentary team lost much of its humanity.
On the death of John Arlott, 1991

19 Sport is something that does not matter, but is performed as if it did. In that contradiction lies its beauty.
The Spectator, (1996)

20 Showbiz brings us people who change their superficial appearance, but sport brings us people who ... change their bodies as we might change a shirt.
The Times, (1999) On the use of drugs in sport **Barnes, Simon** (1951–) English writer

21 Boxing is show business with blood.
Attr. (1915), quoted by Frank Bruno in 1991 **Belasco, David** (1853–1931) US theatre producer and playwright

22 I do love cricket – it's so very English.
Attr. **Bernhardt, Sarah** (1844–1923) French actress. Remark while watching a game of football

23 We forget that the nineteenth century often turned work into sport. We, in contrast, often turn sport into work.
Victorian Historical Journal, (1978) **Blainey, Geoffrey Norman** (1930–) Australian writer

24 The sort of place everyone should send his mother-in-law for a month, all expenses paid.
BBC Radio 2 interview, (March 1984) **Botham, Ian** (1955–) English cricketer. On Pakistan

25 A coach who suppresses natural instincts may find that he has lifted a poor player to a mediocre one but has reduced a potential genius to the rank and file.
Attr. **Bradman, Don** (1908–2001) Australian cricketer, generally believed to the best ever player

26 John Arlott has been that rarity, a man respected by the players as much as the public ... somehow Arlott's presence made you feel cricket was in good hands.
Another Day, Another Match, (1981) **Brain, Brian** (1940–) English county cricketer and chronicler

27 Sport strips away personality, letting the white bone of character shine through.
Sudden Death (1983) **Brown, Rita Mae** (1944–) US writer and poet

28 Life's too short for chess.
Our Boys **Byron, H.J.** (1834–1884) English dramatist and actor

29 The trouble with referees is that they just don't care which side wins.
The Guardian, (1980) **Canterbury, Tom** US basketball player

30 A game is exactly what is made of it by the character of the men playing it.
Good Days, (1934) **Cardus, Neville** (1889–1975) English cricket writer

31 A compliment to the English martial spirit.
The Times, (1998) **Clark, Alan** (1928–1999) English Conservative politican, historian and diarist. On football hooligans

32 That's the fastest time ever run – but it's not as fast as the world record.
In Fantoni, *Private Eye's Colemanballs (3)* (1986) **Coleman, David** (1926–) English sports commentator and broadcaster

33 I love fishing. It's like transcendental meditation with a punch-line.
Gullible's Travels **Connolly, Billy** (1942–) Scottish comedian and actor

34 I hate to lose more than I love to win. I hate to see the happiness on their faces when they beat me.
New York Times, (1977)

35 New Yorkers love it when you spill your
guts out there. Spill your guts at
Wimbledon and they make you stop and
clean it up.
The Guardian, (1984) **Connors, Jimmy** (1952–)
US tennis player

36 Sport is cut and dried. You always know
when you succeed ... You are not an actor:
you don't wonder 'did my performance go
down all right?' You've lost.
Remark **Davis, Steve** (1957–) English snooker
player

37 Kill the other guy before he kills you.
Motto **Dempsey, Jack** (1895–1983) US boxer

38 Yesterday at the racket court, sitting in the
gallery among strangers, the ball ... fell at
my feet. I picked it up, and observing a
young rifleman excessively stiff, I humbly
requested him to forward its passage into
the court, as I really had never thrown a
ball in my life.
Letter to his father, quoted by André Maurois
in *Disraeli: A Picture of the Victorian Age* (1927)
Disraeli, Benjamin (1804–1881) English
statesman and writer

39 Water creates a neurosis in golfers. The
very thought of this harmless fluid robs
them of their normal powers of rational
thought, turns their legs to jelly, and
produces a palsy of the upper limbs.
Dobereiner, Peter Golf writer

40 The soles of your feet tingle as you watch
and when he grins you're suddenly sharing
the feeling: the pure joy of hitting the ball.
Doust, Dudley English golf writer. On
watching the 20-year-old Seve Ballesteros

41 Nice guys finish last.
Attr. **Durocher, Leo** (1905–1991) US baseball
player and coach. Remark at a practice
ground, 1946

42 Any boxer who says he loves boxing is
either a liar or a fool. I'm not looking for
glory ... I'm looking for money. I'm
looking for readies.
The Times, (1993) **Eubank, Chris** (1966–)
British boxer

43 Lika an octopus falling out of a tree.

TV commentary. Commenting on Jim Furyk's
swing

44 I'm incensed by these guys. There are so
few willing to be gentlemen about this.
Here we have a woman willing to have a go
at this, and the last athlete to deliberately
put himself in this focus was Jesse Owens.
She doesn't have to prove anything to me.
She's the best woman ever to have played.
To have the guts to play the men and to
endure this mean-spirited stuff, God
Almighty, it's petty stuff.
Commenting on the opposition to Annika
Sorenstam's wish to play in a men's
tournament

45 The world's number one tennis player
spends 90% of his time winning, while the
world's number one golfer spends 90% of
his time losing. Golfers are great losers.
Attr. **Feherty, David** (1958–) Irish-born US-
based golfer and pundit

46 The bigger they come, the harder they fall.
Attr. **Fitzsimmons, Robert** (1862–1917) New
Zealand world champion boxer. Remark
before a boxing match, 1900

47 Exercise is bunk. If you are healthy, you
don't need it: if you are sick, you shouldn't
take it.
Attr. **Ford, Henry** (1863–1947) US car
manufacturer

48 Golf is deceptively simple, endlessly
complicated. A child can play it well, and a
grown man can never master it.
Attr. (1899) **Forgan, Robert** (1824–1900)
Scottish golf club manufacturer

49 I listened to a football coach who spoke
straight from the shoulder – at least I could
detect no higher origin in anything he
said.
Attr. **Fox, Dixon Ryan** US historian

50 The competitive spirit is an ethos which it
is the business of universities ... to subdue
and neutralise.
Paperweight (1992) **Fry, Stephen** (1957–) British
comedian and writer

51 This is a Test match. It's not Old
Reptonians versus Lymeswold, one off the
mark and jolly good show.

Press conference, (1984) **Gower, David** (1957–) English cricketer and TV presenter. Refusing to condemn the West Indies' short-pitched bowling

52 When I win the toss on a good pitch, I bat. When I win the toss on a doubtful pitch, I think about it a bit and then I bat. When I win the toss on a very bad pitch, I think about it a bit longer, and then I bat.
Grace, W.G. (1848–1915) Pioneering English cricketer

53 The only thing that Norwich didn't get was the goal that they finally got.
In Fantoni, *Private Eye's Colemanballs (2)* (1984)

54 The thing about sport, any sport, is that swearing is very much part of it.
Attr. **Greaves, Jimmy** (1940–) English footballer and television commentator

55 Extravagant hospitality, gifts and freebies have been part of the culture of the International Olympics Committee for years.
The Times, (1999) **Gummer, John** (1939–) English Conservative politician

56 Never hurry, never worry, and always remember to smell the flowers along the way.
Attr. **Hagen, Walter** (1892–1969) US golfer. On the game of golf

57 Bullfighting is the only art in which the artist is in danger of death and in which the degree of brilliance in the performance is left to the fighter's honour.
Death in the Afternoon (1932) **Hemingway, Ernest** (1898–1961) US author

58 Don't let's go to the dogs tonight
For mother will be there.
She-Shanties (1926), 'Don't Let's Go to the Dogs Tonight' **Herbert, Sir A.P.** (1890–1971) English humorist, writer, dramatist and politician

59 Winning is everything. The only ones who remember you when you come second are your wife and your dog.
The Sunday Times, (1994) **Hill, Damon** (1960–) English racing driver

60 It's more than a game. It's an institution.

Tom Brown's Schooldays (1857) **Hughes, Thomas** (1822–1896) English author. Of cricket

61 Sport is a loathsome and dangerous pursuit.
Sydney Morning Herald, (1982) **Humphries, Barry** (1934–) Australian entertainer

62 I admire the Australians' approach to the game; they have the utmost ability for producing that little extra, or instilling into the opposition an inferiority complex that can have, and has had, a crushing effect. Australians have no inhibitions.
Just My Story, (1956) **Hutton, Sir Leonard** (1916–1990) English cricketer

63 Blood sport is brought to its ultimate refinement in the gossip columns.
Remark, (1986) **Ingham, Sir Bernard** (1932–) English government press officer and writer

64 I always feel that the ball is too small.
The Times, (1998) **James, Mark** (1953–) British golfer. When asked how his sport could be improved

65 He is the most immeasurable of golf champions. ... it is partly because of the nobility he has brought to losing. And more than anything, it is true because of the pure, unmixed joy he has brought to trying.
Jenkins, Dan US golf writer. On Arnold Palmer

66 The only athletic sport I ever mastered was backgammon.
In W. Jerrold, *Douglas Jerrold* (1914) **Jerrold, Douglas William** (1803–1857) English dramatist, writer and wit

67 It is unbecoming for a cardinal to ski badly.
Attr. **John Paul II** (1920–2005) Polish pope. Replying to the suggestion that it was inappropriate for a cardinal to ski

68 I am sorry I have not learned to play at cards. It is very useful in life: it generates kindness and consolidates society.
In Boswell, *Journal of a Tour to the Hebrides* (1785)

69 Fly fishing may be a very pleasant amusement; but angling or float fishing I can only compare to a stick and a string, with a worm at one end and a fool at the other.
Attr. in Hawker, *Instructions to Young Sportsmen* (1859) **Johnson, Samuel** (1709–1784) English lexicographer, poet, critic, conversationalist and essayist

70 Palmer and Player played superbly, but Nicklaus played a game with which I'm not familiar.
After the 22-year-old Nicklaus won the 1962 US Open

71 I have never felt so lonely as on the golf course in the midst of the championship with thousands of people around.
Attr. **Jones, Bobby** (1902–1971) US golfer

72 Hazards are like spices that a designer sprinkles on a course to give it flavour.
Jones, Robert Trent (1906–2000) US golf course designer

73 It's really impossible for athletes to grow up. As long as you're playing, no one will let you. On the one hand, you're a child, still playing a game … But on the other hand, you're a superhuman hero that everyone dreams of being. No wonder we have such a hard time understanding who we are.
Billie-Jean (1982) **King, Billie-Jean** (1943–) US tennis player

74 Every Australian worships the Goddess of Sport with profound adoration, and there is no nation in the world which treats itself to so many holidays.
The Australian at Home (c.1895) **Kinglake, Edward** (1864–1935)

75 Man is a gaming animal. He must always be trying to get the better in something or other.
'Mrs Battle's Opinions on Whist' (1823) **Lamb, Charles** (1775–1834) English essayist, critic and letter writer

76 Golf is a thoroughly national game. It is as Scotch as haggis, cockie-leekie, high cheek-bones, or rowanberry jam.

In W. Pett Ridge (ed.), *Daily News, Lost Leaders*, (1889) **Lang, Andrew** (1844–1912) Scottish poet, writer, mythologist and anthropologist

77 St Andrews? I feel like I'm back visiting an old grandmother. She's crotchety and eccentric but also elegant. Anyone who doesn't fall in love with her has no imagination.
Lema, Tony (1934–1966) US golfer

78 Golf, perhaps through it's very slowness, can reach the most extraordinary heights of tenseness and drama.
Longhurst, Henry (1909–1978) English golfer and commentator

79 He can run, but he can't hide.
Attr. **Louis, Joe** (1914–1981) US champion boxer. Referring to the speed of an opponent, Billy Conn

80 Cricket – a game which the English, not being a spiritual people, have invented in order to give themselves some conception of eternity.
Bees in Some Bonnets (1979) **Mancroft, Lord** (1914–1987) English politician

81 The enigma with no variation.
Marks, Vic (1955–) English cricketer and radio commentator. On the talented but underachieving England cricketer Chris Lewis

82 Golf's three ugliest words: still your shot.

83 Never bet with anyone you meet on the first tee who has a deep suntan, a one iron in his bag, and squinty eyes.
Marr, Dave (1933–1997) US golfer and golf guru

84 I think I was the best baseball player I ever saw.
Newsweek, (1970) **Mays, Willie** (1931–) US baseball player

85 You cannot be serious.
Attr. **McEnroe, John** (1959–) US tennis player. To an umpire; this remark became a catchphrase in the early 1980s

86 How can you play cricket with a bloke and then not be allowed to sit in a railway carriage with him?

Attr. (1983) **McEwan, Ken** (1952–) South African cricketer. After West Indian cricketer Colin Croft was ejected from a whites-only section of a train during the West Indies rebel tour to South Africa

87 The gladiators and champions through the ages confirm quite clearly that aggressive competition is part of the human makeup. For the sport of professional boxing to be banned would be the most terrible error.
The Observer, (1994) **McGuigan, Barry** (1961–) British boxer

88 Few things are more deeply rooted in the collective imagination of the English than the village cricket match. It stirs a romantic illusion about the rustic way of life, it suggests a tranquil and unchanging order in an age of bewildering flux, and it persuades a lot of townsfolk that that is where they would rather be.
Best Loved Game, (1979)

89 This is of course, something much more considerable than a place where cricket of the highest calibre is played and watched. It is nothing less than an international institution as well, because of its history and because of what it represents.
Lord's, (1983) **Moorhouse, Geoffrey** English writer

90 Nobody ever beats Wales at rugby, they just score more points.
In Keating, *Caught by Keating* **Mourie, Graham** (1952–) New Zealand rugby player

91 Do you know the difference between involvement and commitment? Think of ham and eggs. The chicken is involved. The pig is committed.
The Observer, (1982)

92 The moment of victory is much too short to live for that and nothing else.
The Guardian, (1989) **Navratilova, Martina** (1956–) US tennis player

93 I didn't think you would miss it. But I wasn't going to give you the chance.
The Ryder Cup, (1969) **Nicklaus, Jack** (1940–) US golfer. Nicklaus conceded a missable putt to Tony Jacklin on the final green, thus halving their personal contest and the whole match

94 The love call of two pieces of sandpaper.
New Zealand Listener, (1984) **O'Reilly, Tony** (1936–) Irish entrepreneur and international rugby player. Commenting on the voice of Winston McCarthy, the noted rugby commentator

95 Serious sport has nothing to do with fair play. It is bound up with hatred, jealousy, boastfulness, disregard for all rules and sadistic pleasure in witnessing violence; in other words it is war minus the shooting.
Shooting an Elephant (1950) **Orwell, George** (1903–1950) English writer and critic

96 There is no way sport is so important that it can be allowed to damage the rest of your life.
Remark at the Olympic Games, (1984) **Ovett, Steve** (1955–) English athlete

97 The more I practise the luckier I get.
Attr. **Palmer, Arnold** (1929–) US golfer. Replying to an onlooker who observed that he was playing so well he must have plenty of luck on his side

98 This Test series has an epic grandeur capable of making all other big sporting events puny by comparison.
Parkinson, Michael (1935–) English writer and TV presenter. On the 2005 Ashes

99 Golf tips are like aspirin. One may do you good, but if you swallow the whole bottle you will be lucky to survive.
Penick, Harvey (1904–1995) US golf guru

100 I tend to believe that cricket is the greatest thing that God ever created on earth ... certainly greater than sex, although sex isn't too bad either.
Interview in *The Observer*, (1980) **Pinter, Harold** (1930–) English dramatist, poet and screenwriter

101 For when the One Great Scorer comes to mark against your name,
He marks – not that you won or lost – but how you played the Game.
'Alumnus Football' (1941) **Rice, Grantland** (1880–1954) US writer

102 Show me a good and gracious loser and I'll show you a failure.

Attr. **Rockne, Knut** (1888–1931) US football coach

103 The first time I played the Masters, I was so nervous I drank a bottle of rum before I teed off. I shot the happiest 83 of my life.
Rodríguez, Chi Chi (1935–) Puerto Rican golfer

104 I've got a feeling for the game of golf. I did very well on the course in Skegness, until I got stuck in one of the little wooden windmills.
As Rigsby in *Rising Damp*, TV series, (1970s) **Rossiter, Leonard** (1926–1985) English comic actor

105 A passion, an obsession, a romance, a nice acquaintanceship with trees, sand, and water.
Attr. **Ryan, Bob** (1946–) US golf writer and journalist. On the game of golf

106 I don't know who's ahead – it's either Oxford or Cambridge.
Radio commentary on the Boat Race, (1949) **Snagge, John** (1904–1996) British television broadcaster and commentator

107 My hoarse-sounding horn
Invites thee to the chase, the sport of kings;
Image of war, without its guilt.
The Chase (1735) **Somerville, William** (1675–1742) English poet

108 It was remarked to me … that to play billiards well was a sign of an ill-spent youth.
In Duncan, *Life and Letters of Spencer* (1908) **Spencer, Herbert** (1820–1903) English philosopher and journalist

109 If anyone were to ask us the question 'what class of useful men receive most abuse and least thanks for their service?' We should, without hesitation, reply, 'Cricket umpires'.
The Badminton Library - Cricket, (1904) **Steel, A.G.** (1858–1914) English cricket writer

110 If you don't get goosebumps when you walk into this place, you don't have a pulse.
Sutton, Hal (1958–) US golfer. On Augusta, perennial home of the US Masters

111 I wanted a play that would paint the full face of sensuality, rebellion and revivalism. In South Wales these three phenomena have played second fiddle only to the Rugby Union which is a distillation of all three.
Jackie the Jumper (1962) **Thomas, Gwyn** (1913–1981) Welsh writer, dramatist and teacher

112 Without rival, the ripest, the richest, the rip-roaringest individual performer on cricket's stage.
The Cricketer magazine, (1961) **Thomson, A.A.** English cricket writer. On Fred Trueman

113 Sport has always been an instrument for political strife.
Corriere della Sera, (1994) **Tosatti, Giorgio** Italian sports journalist

114 I've never had a coach in my life; when I can find one who can beat me, I'll listen.
Trevino, Lee (1939–) US golfer of Mexican descent

115 Losing is the great American sin.
Quoted in *The New York Times*, (1977) **Tunis, John** (1889–1975) US sportswriter

116 Golf is a good walk spoiled.
Attr. **Twain, Mark** (1835–1910) US humorist, writer, journalist and lecturer

117 To bowl fast is to revel in the glad animal action, to thrill in physical power and to enjoy a certain sneaking feeling of superiority over mortals who play the game.
A Typhoon Called Tyson, (1961) **Tyson, Frank** (1930–) English cricketer

118 Moderation is essential in all things, Madam, but never in my life have I failed to beat a teetotaller.
Attr. **Vardon, Harry** (1870–1937) English golfer and commentator

119 There's no secret. You just press the accelerator to the floor and steer left.
Attr. **Vukovich, Bill** (1918–1955) US racing driver. Explaining his success in the Indianapolis 500

120 As no man is born an artist, so no man is born an angler.
The Compleat Angler (1653)

121 We may say of angling as Dr Boteler said of strawberries: 'Doubtless God could have made a better berry, but doubtless God never did'; and so (if I might be judge) God never did make a more calm, quiet, innocent recreation than angling.
The Compleat Angler (1653) **Walton, Izaak** (1593–1683) English writer

122 Putting is really a game within a game.
Attr. **Watson, Tom** (1949–) US golfer

123 You've just dropped the World Cup.
The World Cup, (1999) **Waugh, Steve** (1965–) Australian cricketer. To South African fielder Herschelle Gibbs after Gibbs dropped a crucial catch in the World Cup match. Waugh went on to play a match-winning innings

124 I will not permit thirty men to travel four hundred miles to agitate a bag of wind.
In D. Wallechinsky, *The People's Almanac* **White, Andrew Dickson** (1832–1918) US educator and diplomat. Refusing to allow the Cornell football team to visit Michigan to play a match

125 The least thing upset him on the links. He missed short putts because of the uproar of the butterflies in the adjoining meadows.
The Clicking of Cuthbert (1922)

126 The man who can go into a patch of rough alone with the knowledge that only God is watching him, and play his ball where it lies, is the man who will serve you faithfully and well.
The Clicking of Cuthbert (1922)

127 While they were content to peck cautiously at the ball, he never spared himself in his efforts to do it a violent injury.
The Heart of a Goof (1926) **Wodehouse, P.G.** (1881–1975) English humorist and writer
See also football

SUCCESS

1 I never doubted my ability, but when you hear all your life you're inferior, it makes you wonder if the other guys have something you've never seen before. If they do, I'm still looking for it.
I Had a Hammer (1992) **Aaron, Hank** (1934–) US baseball player

2 Rockefeller once explained the secret of success. 'Get up early, work late – and strike oil.'
Attr. **Adams, Joey** (1911–1999) US comedian and author

3 'Tis not in mortals to command success, But we'll do more, Sempronius; we'll deserve it.
Cato (1713) **Addison, Joseph** (1672–1719) English essayist, poet, playwright and statesman

4 Anybody can win, unless there happens to be a second entry.
Attr. **Ade, George** (1866–1944) US fabulist and playwright

5 One's religion is whatever he is most interested in, and yours is Success.
The Twelve-Pound Look **Barrie, Sir J.M.** (1860–1937) Scottish dramatist and writer

6 The trouble with fulfilling your ambitions is you think you will be transformed into some sort of archangel and you're not. You still have to wash your socks.
The Times, (1999) **Bernières, Louis de** (1954–) English author

7 In real life, of course, it is the hare who wins. Every time. Look around you. And in any case it is my contention that Aesop was writing for the tortoise market … Hares have no time to read. They are too busy winning the game.
Hotel du Lac (1984) **Brookner, Anita** (1928–) English writer. On the myth of the tortoise and the hare

8 A minute's success pays the failure of years.
'Apollo and the Fates' (1887) **Browning, Robert** (1812–1889) English poet

9 If at first you succeed, quit trying.
In Janet Lowe, *Warren Buffet Speaks* **Buffett, Warren** (1930–) US billionaire investment expert

10 The only infallible criterion of wisdom to vulgar minds – success.
Letter to a Member of the National Assembly (1791)

11 Well is it known that ambition can creep as well as soar.
Third Letter ... on the Proposals for Peace with the Regicide Directory of France (1797) **Burke, Edmund** (1729–1797) Irish-born British statesman and philosopher

12 Made it, Ma! Top of the world!
White Heat (film, 1949) **Cagney, James** (1904–1986) US film actor

13 Success is the space one occupies in the newspaper. Success is one day's insolence.
The Secret Heart of the Clock: Notes, Aphorisms, Fragments 1973–1985 (1991) **Canetti, Elias** (1905–1994) Bulgarian-born English writer, dramatist and critic

14 Adversity is sometimes hard upon a man; but for one man who can stand prosperity, there are a hundred that will stand adversity.
On Heroes, Hero-Worship, and the Heroic in History (1841) **Carlyle, Thomas** (1795–1881) Scottish historian, biographer, critic, and essayist

15 Where he falls short, 'tis Nature's fault alone;
Where he succeeds, the merit's all his own.
The Rosciad (1761) **Churchill, Charles** (1731–1764) English poet, political writer and clergyman

16 In all things, success depends upon previous preparation, and without such preparation there is sure to be failure.
Analects **Confucius** (c.550–c.478 BC) Chinese philosopher and teacher of ethics

17 Success is counted sweetest
By those who ne'er succeed.
To comprehend a nectar
Requires sorest need.
'Success is counted sweetest' (c.1859) **Dickinson, Emily** (1830–1886) US poet

18 The clock which has stopped but has twice daily indicated the right time can years later look back on a long line of successes.
Aphorisms (1880) **Ebner-Eschenbach, Marie von** (1830–1916) Austrian writer

19 Who aimeth at the sky
Shoots higher much than he that means a tree.

The Temple (1633) **Herbert, George** (1593–1633) English poet and priest

20 Success – 'The bitch-goddess, Success,' in William James's phrase – demands strange sacrifices from those who worship her.
Proper Studies (1927)

21 Those who believe that they are exclusively in the right are generally those who achieve something.
Proper Studies (1927) **Huxley, Aldous** (1894–1963) English writer, poet and critic

22 The moral flabbiness born of the exclusive worship of the bitch-goddess success. That – with the squalid cash interpretation put on the word success – is our national disease.
Letter to H.G. Wells, (1906) **James, William** (1842–1910) US psychologist and philosopher

23 Patron. Commonly a wretch who supports with insolence, and is paid with flattery.
A Dictionary of the English Language (1755) **Johnson, Samuel** (1709–1784) English lexicographer, poet, critic, conversationalist and essayist

24 I have no political ambitions for myself or my children.
Quoted in an obituary, (18 November 1969) **Kennedy, Joseph P.** (1888–1969) US financier and diplomat

25 Talent is cheaper than table salt. What separates the talented individual from the successful one is a lot of hard work.
Independent on Sunday, (1996) **King, Stephen** (1947–) US writer

26 To succeed in the world we do all we can to appear successful.
Maximes (1678) **La Rochefoucauld** (1613–1680) French writer

27 If you would hit the mark, you must aim a little above it;
Every arrow that flies feels the attraction of earth.
'Elegiac Verse' (1880) **Longfellow, Henry Wadsworth** (1807–1882) US poet and writer

28 I could never tell where inspiration begins and impulse leaves off. I suppose the answer is in the outcome. If your hunch proves a good one, you were inspired; if it proves bad, you are guilty of yielding to thoughtless impulse.
West with the Night (1941) **Markham, Beryl** (1902–1986) English aviator and writer

29 Success can be wracking and reproachful, to you and those close to you. It can entangle you with legends that are consuming and all but impossible to live up to.
Voices in the Mirror (1990) **Parks, Gordon** (1912–2006) US photographer and film director

30 To burn always with this hard, gemlike flame, to maintain this ecstasy, is success in life.
Studies in the History of the Renaissance (1873) **Pater, Walter** (1839–1894) English critic, writer and lecturer

31 There are no secrets to success: don't waste time looking for them. Success is the result of perfection, hard work, learning from failure, loyalty to those for whom you work, and persistence.
Colin Powell (1989) **Powell, Colin** (1937–) US military leader

32 Great is the height that I must scale, but the prospect of glory gives me strength.
Elegies **Propertius, Sextus Aurelius** (c.50–c.15 BC) Roman poet

33 If we do not succeed, then we run the risk of failure.
Attr. **Quayle, Dan** (1947–) US Republican politician and Vice President

34 Is it possible to succeed without betrayal?
My Life and My Films (1974) **Renoir, Jean** (1894–1979) French film director

35 Success is a public affair. Failure is a private funeral.
Life Is a Banquet (1977) **Russell, Rosalind** (1911–1976) US actress

36 The only place where success comes before work is a dictionary.

Quoting one of his teachers in a BBC radio broadcast **Sassoon, Vidal** (1928–) English hairdresser

37 Who shoots at the midday sun, though he be sure he shall never hit the mark, yet as sure he is he shall shoot higher than who aims but at a bush.
New Arcadia (1590) **Sidney, Sir Philip** (1554–1586) English poet, critic, soldier, courtier and diplomat

38 Your success story is a bigger story than whatever you're trying to say on stage … Success makes life easier. It doesn't make living easier.
Q magazine, (1992) **Springsteen, Bruce** (1949–) US singer and songwriter

39 Is there anything in life so disenchanting as attainment?
New Arabian Nights (1882) **Stevenson, Robert Louis** (1850–1894) Scottish writer, poet and essayist

40 In these days a man is nobody unless his biography is kept so far posted up that it may be ready for the national breakfast-table on the morning after his demise.
Doctor Thorne (1858) **Trollope, Anthony** (1815–1882) English writer, traveller and post office official

41 A successful man is one who makes more money than his wife can spend. A successful woman is one who can find such a man.
Attr. **Turner, Lana** (1920–1995) US actress

42 The real power behind whatever success I have now was something I found within myself – something that's in all of us, I think, a little piece of God just waiting to be discovered.
I, Tina (1986) **Turner, Tina** (1938–) US singer

43 Whenever a friend succeeds, a little something in me dies.
The Sunday Times Magazine, (1973)

44 It is not enough to succeed. Others must fail.
In Irvine, *Antipanegyric for Tom Driberg* (1976) **Vidal, Gore** (1925–) US writer, critic and poet

45 To these success gives heart: they can because they think they can.
Aeneid **Virgil** (70–19 BC) Roman poet
See also failure; fame

SUFFERING

1 When suffering knocks at your door and you say there is no seat for him, he tells you not to worry because he has brought his own stool.
Arrow of God (1967) **Achebe, Chinua** (1930–) Nigerian writer, poet and critic

2 The manner in which one endures what must be endured is more important than the thing that must be endured.
Plain Speaking: An Oral Biography of Harry S. Truman **Acheson, Dean** (1893–1971) US Democrat politician

3 Three things one does not recover from – oppression that knows the backing of brute force,
poverty that knows the destitution of one's home,
and being deprived of children.
Somali poem **Anonymous**

4 About suffering they were never wrong, The Old Masters: how well they understood
Its human position; how it takes place
While someone else is eating or opening a window or just walking dully along.
'Musée des Beaux Arts' **Auden, W.H.** (1907–1973) English poet, essayist, critic, teacher and dramatist

5 One does not love a place the less for having suffered in it, unless it has all been suffering, nothing but suffering.
Persuasion (1818) **Austen, Jane** (1775–1817) English writer

6 It is a miserable state of mind to have few things to desire and many things to fear.
'Of Empire' (1625) **Bacon, Francis** (1561–1626) English philosopher, essayist, politician and courtier

7 Suffering isn't ennobling, recovery is.
New York Times, (1985) **Barnard, Christiaan** (1922–2001) South African surgeon

8 Nothing is miserable unless you think it so; conversely, every lot is happy to one who is content with it.
De Consolatione Philosophiae (c.524)

9 At every blow of fate, the worst kind of misfortune is to have been happy.
De Consolatione Philosophiae (c.524) **Boethius** (c.475–524) Roman statesman, scholar and philosopher

10 Unhappiness is best defined as the difference between our talents and our expectations.
The Observer, (1977) **Bono, Edward de** (1933–) British physician and writer

11 Oh dreadful is the check – intense the agony –
When the ear begins to hear and the eye begins to see;
When the pulse begins to throb, the brain to think again;
The soul to feel the flesh and the flesh to feel the chain!
'The Prisoner' (1846) **Brontë, Emily** (1818–1848) English novelist

12 For frequent tears have run
The colours from my life.
Sonnets from the Portuguese (1850) **Browning, Elizabeth Barrett** (1806–1861) English poet; wife of Robert Browning

13 Man's Unhappiness, as I construe, comes of his Greatness; it is because there is an Infinite in him, which with all his cunning he cannot quite bury under the Finite.
Sartor Resartus (1834) **Carlyle, Thomas** (1795–1881) Scottish historian, biographer, critic, and essayist

14 For of fortunes sharpe adversitee
The worste kynde of infortune is this,
A man to han ben in prosperitee,
And it remembren, whan it passed is.
Troilus and Criseyde **Chaucer, Geoffrey** (c.1340–1400) English poet, public servant and courtier

15 *Millamant*: I believe I gave you some pain.
Mirabel: Does that please you?
Millamant: Infinitely; I love to give pain.
The Way of the World (1700) **Congreve, William** (1670–1729) English dramatist

16 Telling one's sorrows often brings comfort.
Polyeucte (1643) **Corneille, Pierre** (1606–1684)
French dramatist, poet and lawyer

17 But misery still delights to trace
Its semblance in another's case.
'The Castaway' (1799) **Cowper, William** (1731–1800) English poet, hymn writer and letter writer

18 No sorrow is deeper than the remembrance of happiness when in misery.
Divina Commedia (1307) **Dante Alighieri** (1265–1321) Italian poet

19 After great pain, a formal feeling comes –
The Nerves sit ceremonious, like Tombs –
The stiff Heart questions was it He, that bore,
And Yesterday, or Centuries before? ...
This is the Hour of Lead –
Remembered, if outlived,
As Freezing persons, recollect the Snow –
First – Chill – then Stupor – then the letting go.
'After great pain, a formal feeling comes' (c.1862) **Dickinson, Emily** (1830–1886) US poet

20 It is only the women whose eyes have been washed clear with tears who get the broad vision that makes them little sisters to all the world.
Dorothy Dix, Her Book (1926) **Dix, Dorothy** (1870–1951) US writer

21 If there is no struggle, there is no progress.
Attr. **Douglass, Frederick** (c.1818–1895) US anti-slavery activist

22 Hell is oneself;
Hell is alone, the other figures in it
Merely projections. There is nothing to escape from
And nothing to escape to. One is always alone.
The Cocktail Party (1950) **Eliot, T.S.** (1888–1965) US-born British poet, verse dramatist and critic

23 Sadness, adieu, sadness, hello, you are engraved in the lines of the ceiling.
'Slightly Disfigured' (1932) **Éluard, Paul** (1895–1952) French poet

24 A moment of time may make us unhappy forever.
The Beggar's Opera (1728) **Gay, John** (1685–1732) English poet, dramatist and librettist

25 The least pain in our little finger gives us more concern and uneasiness, than the destruction of millions of our fellow-beings.
Edinburgh Review, (1829) **Hazlitt, William** (1778–1830) English writer and critic

26 The world breaks everyone and afterward many are strong at the broken places.
A Farewell to Arms (1929) **Hemingway, Ernest** (1898–1961) US author

27 How often does the evening cup of joy lead to sorrow in the morning!
Attr. **Hogg, James** (1770–1835) Scottish poet, ballad writer and writer

28 No worst, there is none. Pitched past pitch of grief,
More pangs will, schooled at forepangs, wilder wring.
Comforter, where, where is your comforting?
'No Worst, there is None' (1885) **Hopkins, Gerard Manley** (1844–1889) English Jesuit priest, poet and classicist

29 Let us suffer if we must, but let us suffer on the heights.
Contemplations (1856) **Hugo, Victor** (1802–1885) French poet, writer, dramatist and politician

30 There is no more miserable human being than one in whom nothing is habitual but indecision.
Principles of Psychology (1890) **James, William** (1842–1910) US psychologist and philosopher

31 I shall long to see the miseries of the world, since the sight of them is necessary to happiness.
Rasselas (1759)

32 There is no wisdom in useless and hopeless sorrow.
Letter to Mrs. Thrale, (1781)

33 Depend upon it that if a man talks of his misfortunes there is something in them that is not disagreeable to him; for where there is nothing but pure misery there never is any recourse to the mention of it.

In Boswell, *The Life of Samuel Johnson* (1791)
Johnson, Samuel (1709–1784) English
lexicographer, poet, critic, conversationalist
and essayist

34 Is there another Life? Shall I awake and
find all this a dream? There must be, we
cannot be created for this sort of suffering.
Letter to Charles Brown, (1820) **Keats, John**
(1795–1821) English poet

35 If you bear the cross willingly, it will bear
you.
De Imitatione Christi (1892) **Kempis, Thomas à**
(c.1380–1471) German mystic, monk and writer

36 The Two Ways: One is to suffer; the other
is to become a professor of the fact that
another suffered.
In W.H. Auden, *Kierkegaard* **Kierkegaard,
Søren** (1813–1855) Danish philosopher

37 We that did nothing study but the way
To love each other, with which thoughts
the day
Rose with delight to us, and with them set,
Must learn the hateful art, how to forget.
'The Surrender' (1651) **King, Bishop Henry**
(1592–1669) English royal chaplain; poet and
sermonist

38 One is never as unhappy as one thinks, or
as happy as one hopes to be.
Maximes (1664)

39 We are all strong enough to bear the
sufferings of others.
Maximes (1678) **La Rochefoucauld** (1613–1680)
French writer

40 The misfortunes hardest to bear are those
which never come.
'Democracy' (1887) **Lowell, James Russell**
(1819–1891) US poet, editor, abolitionist and
diplomat

41 There is little to choose morally between
beating up a man physically and beating
him up mentally.
On Moral Courage (1962) **Mackenzie, Sir
Compton** (1883–1972) Scottish writer and
broadcaster

42 Years ago a person, he was unhappy, didn't
know what to do with himself – he'd go to
church, start a revolution – something.
Today you're unhappy? Can't figure it out?
What is the salvation? Go shopping.
The Price (1968) **Miller, Arthur** (1915–2005) US
dramatist and screenwriter

43 A man who fears suffering is already
suffering from what he fears.
Essais (1580) **Montaigne, Michel de** (1533–1592)
French essayist and moralist

44 The only good things the world has left me
are the times that I have wept.
'Tristesse' (1841) **Musset, Alfred de** (1810–1857)
French dramatist and poet

45 We can't for a certainty tell
What mirth may molest us on Monday;
But, at least, to begin the week well,
Let us all be unhappy on Sunday.
Songs and Verses **Neaves, Lord Charles** (1800–
1876) English jurist

46 The thought of suicide is a great comfort:
it's a good way of getting through many a
bad night.
Beyond Good and Evil (1886) **Nietzsche,
Friedrich Wilhelm** (1844–1900) German
philosopher, critic and poet

47 What actually fills you with indignation as
regards suffering is not suffering in itself
but the pointlessness of suffering.
On the Genealogy of Morals (1881) **Nietzsche,
Friedrich Wilhelm** (1844–1900) German
philosopher, critic and poet

48 Sorrow is tranquillity remembered in
emotion.
Here Lies (1939) **Parker, Dorothy** (1893–1967)
US writer, poet, critic and wit

49 All the troubles of men are caused by one
single thing, which is their inability to stay
quietly in a room.
Pensées (1670) **Pascal, Blaise** (1623–1662)
French philosopher and scientist

50 I never knew any man in my life, who could
not bear another's misfortunes perfectly
like a Christian.
Miscellanies (1727) **Pope, Alexander** (1688–1744)
English poet, translator and editor

51 He's simply got the instinct for being
unhappy highly developed.
The Chronicles of Clovis (1911) **Saki** (1870–1916)
Burmese-born British writer

52 Blow, blow, thou winter wind,
Thou art not so unkind
As man's ingratitude …
Thy tooth is not so keen,
Freeze, freeze, thou bitter sky,
That dost not bite so nigh
As benefits forgot.
As You Like It, II.vii

53 When sorrows come, they come not single
spies,
But in battalions.
Hamlet, IV.v

54 The worst is not
So long as we can say 'This is the worst'.
King Lear, IV.i

55 In sooth I know not why I am so sad.
It wearies me; you say it wearies you;
But how I caught it, found it, or came by it,
What stuff 'tis made of, whereof it is born,
I am to learn;
And such a want-wit sadness makes of me
That I have much ado to know myself.
The Merchant of Venice, I.i

56 Misery acquaints a man with strange
bedfellows.
The Tempest, II.ii **Shakespeare, William** (1564–
1616) English dramatist, poet and actor

57 The secret of being miserable is to have
leisure to bother about whether you are
happy or not.
Misalliance (1914) **Shaw, George Bernard**
(1856–1950) Irish socialist, writer, dramatist
and critic

58 I'm for anything that can get you through
the night, be it prayer, tranquillizers or a
bottle of Jack Daniels.
Attr. in *The Herald*, (1998) **Sinatra, Frank** (1915–
1998) US singer and actor

59 Nothing begins and nothing ends
That is not paid with moan;
For we are born in others' pain,
And perish in our own.
'Daisy' (1913) **Thompson, Francis** (1859–1907)
English poet

60 He knew that people would be merciless
for the very reason that his heart was
lacerated. He felt that his fellow-man
would destroy him, as dogs kill some poor
cur maimed and howling with pain. He
knew that his only salvation lay in hiding
his wounds, and he had instinctively tried
to do this for two days, but now he no
longer had the strength to keep up the
unequal struggle.
Anna Karenina (1875–1877)

61 Pure and complete sorrow is just as
impossible as pure and complete joy.
War and Peace (1869) **Tolstoy, Leo** (1828–1910)
Russian writer, essayist, philosopher and
moralist

62 Tears fall in my heart as rain falls on the
city.
Romances sans paroles (1874) **Verlaine, Paul**
(1844–1896) French poet and autobiographer

63 I love the majesty of human suffering.
The Shepherd's House (1844) **Vigny, Alfred de**
(1797–1863) French writer

64 To lose a lover or even a husband or two
during the course of one's life can be
vexing. But to lose one's teeth is a
catastrophe.
A Little Night Music (1974) **Wheeler, Hugh**
(1912–1987) English-born US writer

65 For all sad words of tongue or pen,
The saddest are these: 'It might have been!'
'Maud Muller' (1854) **Whittier, John Greenleaf**
(1807–1892) US poet, abolitionist and
journalist

66 Where there is sorrow, there is holy
ground.
De Profundis (1897) **Wilde, Oscar** (1854–1900)
Irish poet, dramatist, writer, critic and wit

67 A useful … way of thinking about
depression is in terms of malignant
sadness. Sadness is to depression what
normal growth is to cancer.
Malignant Sadness (1999) **Wolpert, Lewis**
English biologist
See also disability; health; grief

TELEVISION

1 We are concerned to remind broadcasters that 9pm is a watershed, not a waterfall.
Broadcasting Standards Commission, in *The Times*, (1999) **Anonymous**

2 The BBC is full of men appointing men who remind them of themselves when young, so you get the same backgrounds, the same education, and the same programmes.
The Observer, (1993) **Bakewell, Joan** (1933–) British journalist and television presenter

3 Television is the first truly democratic culture – the first culture available to everybody and entirely governed by what the people want. The most terrifying thing is what people do want.
The New York Times, (30 September 1969) **Barnes, Clive** (1927–) English journalist and critic

4 Television has done more for the unification of Italy than Garibaldi and Cavour did; it has given us a communal custom and language.
The Good and the Bad (1989) **Biagi, Enzo** (1920–) Italian writer

5 There is a bias in television journalism. It is not against any particular party or point of view – it is a bias against *understanding*.
The Times, (1975) **Birt, John** (1944–) Former Director-General of the BBC

6 Every time you think television has hit its lowest ebb, a new … program comes along to make you wonder where you thought the ebb was.
Have I Ever Lied to You? (1968) **Buchwald, Art** (1925–) US humorist

7 Television is democracy at its ugliest.
Attr. **Chayefsky, Paddy** (1923–1981) US playwright and screenwriter

8 Television is more interesting than people. If it were not, we should have people standing in the corners of our rooms.
Attr. **Coren, Alan** (1938–) British humorist, writer and broadcaster

9 Television is for appearing on, not looking at.
Attr. **Coward, Sir Noël** (1899–1973) English dramatist, actor, producer and composer

10 If any reader of this book is in the grip of some habit of which he is deeply ashamed, I advise him not to give way to it in secret but to do it on television. No-one will pass him with averted gaze on the other side of the street. People will cross the road at the risk of losing their own lives in order to say 'We saw you on the telly'.
How to Become a Virgin **Crisp, Quentin** (1908–1999) English writer, publicist and model

11 Everything is being compressed into tiny tablets. You take a little pill of news every day – 23 minutes and that's supposed to be enough.
Newsweek, (1983) **Cronkite, Walter** (1916–) US broadcast journalist. Criticizing the quality of television news

12 The darkest spot in modern society is a small luminous screen.
Teachers, Writers, Celebrities **Debray, Régis** (1942–) French writer

13 Television doesn't present, as an ideal to aspire to, the superman but the everyman. Television puts forward, as an ideal, the absolutely average man.
Diario Minimo **Eco, Umberto** (1932–) Italian critic and writer

14 It is a medium of entertainment which permits millions of people to listen to the same joke at the same time, and yet remain lonesome.
Attr. **Eliot, T.S.** (1888–1965) US-born British poet, verse dramatist and critic

15 Let's face it, there are no plain women on television.
The Observer, (1979) **Ford, Anna** (1943–) English television newscaster and reporter

16 Television is an invention that permits you to be entertained in your living room by people you wouldn't have in your home.
Remark, (1971) **Frost, David** (1939–) English broadcaster

17 Television has raised writing to a new low.

Attr. **Goldwyn, Samuel** (1882–1974) Polish-born US film producer

18 Television exacerbates the concentration on personality and trivia at the expense of serious discussion and analysis, but its tendency to unbalance and to displace what really matters goes much further and is potentially very damaging to our lives and beliefs. It tends to destroy public trust.
The Spectator, (1996) **Hanson, Lord James** (1922–2004) English businessman

19 Television has brought murder back into the home – where it belongs.
The Observer, (1965)

20 Television has done much for psychiatry by spreading information about it, as well as contributing to the need for it.
Attr. **Hitchcock, Alfred** (1899–1980) English film director

21 Television – a medium. So called because it is neither rare nor well-done.
Attr. **Kovacs, Ernie** (1919–1962) US comedian

22 Television has proved that people will look at anything rather than each other.
Attr. **Landers, Ann** (1918–2002) Famous 'agony aunt' and columnist

23 Damned fine cup of coffee!
Twin Peaks, TV series (1989–91) **Lynch, David** (1947–) US film director. Frequent remark by Agent Dale Cooper

24 Television brought the brutality of war into the comfort of the living room. Vietnam was lost in the living rooms of America – not on the battle fields of Vietnam.
Montreal Gazette, (1975) **McLuhan, Marshall** (1911–1980) Canadian communications theorist

25 I find television very educating. Every time somebody turns on the set, I go into the other room and read a book.
Attr. **Marx, Groucho** (1895–1977) US comedian

26 I have had my TV aerials removed – it's the moral equivalent of a prostate operation.
In *Radio Times*, (1981) **Muggeridge, Malcolm** (1903–1990) English writer

27 Television is actually closer to reality than anything in books. The madness of TV is the madness of human life.
Sex, Art, and American Culture (1992) **Paglia, Camille** (1947–) US academic and writer

28 Television lies. All television lies. It lies persistently, instinctively and by habit ... A culture of mendacity surrounds the medium, and those who work there live it, breathe it and prosper by it ... I know of no area of public life – no, not even politics – more saturated by professional cynicism.
The Spectator, (1996) **Parris, Matthew** (1949–) British Conservative politician and journalist

29 It's through the spirit of television that the essence of the new power clearly shows itself.
From an essay in *Corriere della sera*, (1973) **Pasolini, Pier Paolo** (1922–1975) Italian film director

30 Television? The word is half Latin and half Greek. No good can come of it.
Attr. **Scott, C.P.** (1846–1932) English newspaper editor and Liberal politician

31 Men don't care what's on TV. They only care what else is on TV.
Attr. **Seinfeld, Jerry** (1955–) US comedian

32 Television won't last. It's a flash in the pan.
Attr. (1948) **Somerville, Mary** (1946–) English Radio broadcaster

33 A terminal blight has hit the TV industry nipping fun in the bud and stunting our growth. This blight is management – the dreaded Four M's: male, middle class, middle-aged and mediocre.
MacTaggart lecture, Edinburgh Television Festival, (1995) **Street-Porter, Janet** (1946–) English editor and writer

34 You know, it's just like having a licence to print your own money.
In R. Braddon, *Roy Thomson of Fleet Street* (1965) **Thomson, Roy** (1894–1976) Canadian-born English newspaper and television magnate. To an Edinburgh neighbour just after the opening of Scottish Television, which Thomson had founded, in 1957

35 I hate television. I hate it as much as peanuts. But I can't stop eating peanuts.
New York Herald Tribune, (1956) **Welles, Orson** (1915–1985) US actor, director and producer
See also acting; media

THEATRE AND DANCE

1 The reason why Absurdist plays take place in No Man's Land with only two characters is primarily financial.
Attr. **Adamov, Arthur** (1908–1970) Russian-born French political dramatist. Remark at the International Drama Conference, Edinburgh, 1963

2 A perfect tragedy is the noblest production of human nature.
The Spectator, (1711) **Addison, Joseph** (1672–1719) English essayist, poet, playwright and statesman

3 Theatre director: a person engaged by the management to conceal the fact that the players cannot act.
Attr. **Agate, James** (1877–1947) English drama critic and writer

4 A whole is that which has a beginning, a middle, and an end.
Poetics Of the dramatic form of tragedy

5 The plot is the first principle and, as it were, the soul of tragedy; character comes second.
Poetics

6 Tragedy, then, is the imitation of an action that is serious, has magnitude, and is complete in itself … through incidents arousing pity and fear it effects a catharsis of these and similar emotions.
Poetics **Aristotle** (384–322 BC) Greek philosopher

7 Pantomimes – the smell of oranges and wee-wee.
Attr. **Askey, Arthur** (1900–1982) English comic entertainer

8 The desires of the heart are as crooked as corkscrews,
Not to be born is the best for man;
The second-best is a formal order,
Thy dance's pattern; dance while you can.
Dance, dance, for the figure is easy,
The tune is catching and will not stop;
Dance till the stars come down from the rafters;
Dance, dance, dance till you drop.
Collected Poems, 1933–1938, 'Death's Echo'
Auden, W.H. (1907–1973) English poet, essayist, critic, teacher and dramatist

9 In my ballets, woman is first. Men are consorts. God made men to sing the praises of women. They are not equal to men: They are better.
Time (15 September 1980) **Balanchine, George** (1904–1983) Russian-born US choreographer

10 It's one of the tragic ironies of the theatre that only one man in it can count on steady work – the night watchman.
Tallulah (1952) **Bankhead, Tallulah** (1903–1968) US actress

11 In the theatre the audience want to be surprised – but by things that they expect.
Attr. **Bernard, Tristan** (1866–1947) French writer and dramatist

12 If it wasn't the feeling I get while performing, I think it would have been impossible for me to have continued as long as I have.
Chuck Berry: The Autobiography, (1987) **Berry, Chuck** (1926–) US musician

13 Let a single complete action, in one place, in one day, keep a full house till the end of the play.
L'Art Poétique (1674) **Boileau-Despréaux, Nicolas** (1636–1711) French writer

14 Tragedy is if I cut my finger. Comedy is if I walk into an open sewer and die.
The New Yorker, (1978) **Brooks, Mel** (1926–) US film actor and director

15 What the devil does the plot signify, except to bring in fine things?
The Rehearsal (1663) **Buckingham, Duke of** (1628–1687) English courtier and dramatist

16 'Do you come to the play without knowing what it is?' 'Oh, yes, sir, yes, very frequently. I have no time to read play-bills. One merely comes to meet one's friends, and show that one's alive.'
Evelina (1778) **Burney, Fanny** (1752–1840) English diarist and novelist

17 All tragedies are finish'd by a death,
All comedies are ended by a marriage.
Don Juan (1824) **Byron, Lord** (1788–1824) English poet, satirist and traveller

18 You know, I go to the theatre to be entertained ... I don't want to see plays about rape, sodomy and drug addiction ... I can get all that at home.
The Observer, cartoon caption, (1962) **Cook, Peter** (1937–1995) English comedian and writer

19 If they'd stuffed the child's head up the horse's arse, they would have solved two problems at once.
In N. Sherrin, *Cutting Edge, or, Back in the Knife Box Miss Sharp* (1984) On child star Bonnie Langford in a musical version of *Gone with the Wind* (1972) when a horse defecated on stage

20 Two things should be cut: the second act and the child's throat.
In D. Richards, *The Wit of Noël Coward* Comment on a child star, in a long-winded play

21 It made me feel that Albert had married beneath his station.
In D. Richards, *The Wit of Noël Coward* On a poor portrayal of Queen Victoria **Coward, Sir Noël** (1899–1973) English dramatist, actor, producer and composer

22 Farce is the essential theatre. Farce refined becomes high comedy: farce brutalized becomes tragedy.
Attr. **Craig, Sir Gordon** (1872–1966) English actor, artist and stage designer

23 [going about the country] preaching to the perverted.
Obituary, *The Times*, (1999) **Crisp, Quentin** (1908–1999) English writer, publicist and model. Description of his touring show

24 See how the rascals use me! They will not let my play run and yet they steal my thunder!
Attr. **Dennis, John** (1657–1734) English critic and dramatist. Remark at a production of *Macbeth*, which used his new technique for producing stage thunder

25 Ladies and gentlemen, it takes more than one to make a ballet.
The New Yorker **De Valois, Dame Ninette** (1898–1998) English ballerina and choreographer

26 Whenever that undecided Prince had to ask a question or state a doubt, the public helped him out with it – on the question whether 'twas nobler in the mind to suffer, some roared yes, and some no, and some inclining to both opinions said 'toss up for it'.
Great Expectations (1861) **Dickens, Charles** (1812–1870) English writer. On a performance of *Hamlet*

27 I have discovered the dance. I have discovered the art which has been lost for two thousand years.
My Life (1927) **Duncan, Isadora** (1878–1927) US modern dance pioneer

28 I saw Hamlet Prince of Denmark played: but now the old playe began to disgust this refined age.
Diary, (1661) **Evelyn, John** (1620–1706) English writer and diarist

29 Prologues precede the piece – in mournful verse;
As undertakers – walk before the hearse.
Prologue to Arthur Murphy's *The Apprentice* (1756) **Garrick, David** (1717–1779) English actor and theatre manager

30 We were as nearly bored as enthusiasm would permit.
In C. Hassall, *Biography of Edward Marsh* **Gosse, Sir Edmund** (1849–1928) English literary critic. Referring to one of Swinburne's plays

31 I'd rather go to the provinces where they still speak English and not Japanese.
Scotsman, (1992) **Guinness, Sir Alec** (1914–2000) British actor. Vowing never to perform again in the West End when he saw the blank faces of uncomprehending tourists

32 The trouble with nude dancing is that not everything stops when the music stops.
In *The Frank Muir Book* (1976) After the opening night of *Oh, Calcutta!*

33 Aren't all ballets sexy? I think they should be. I can think of nothing more kinky than a prince chasing a swan around all night.
In Jonathon Green (ed.), *A Dictionary of Contemporary Quotations* (1982) **Helpman, Sir Robert Murray** (1909–1986) Australian choreographer and director

34 What is drama but life with the dull bits cut out?
The Observer, (1960) **Hitchcock, Alfred** (1899–1980) English film director

35 We participate in a tragedy; at a comedy we only look.
The Devils of Loudun (1952) **Huxley, Aldous** (1894–1963) English writer, poet and critic

36 The stage but echoes back the public voice.
The drama's laws the drama's patrons give,
For we that live to please must please to live.
'Prologue at the Opening of Drury Lane' (1747) **Johnson, Samuel** (1709–1784) English lexicographer, poet, critic, conversationalist and essayist

37 Ladies and gentlemen, unless the play is stopped, the child cannot possibly go on.
Attr. **Kemble, John Philip** (1757–1823) English Shakespearian actor. Said during a play which was continually interrupted by a crying child

38 It doesn't stand up to huge intellectual scrutiny.
Attr. **Lloyd Webber, Andrew** (1948–) English composer. On the success of his *Phantom of the Opera*, 1995

39 An entertainer is a whole different thing, an entertainer to me doesn't necessarily deal with reality. It's someone who makes you forget. It's like a drug, it's euphoric and I think it has its place in the world. But that's not the only thing I do. I think I'm an educator – and I do think I'm an artist.
Attr. **Madonna** (1958–) US singer and actress

40 Although one may fail to find happiness in theatrical life, one never wishes to give it up after having once tasted its fruits. To enter the School of the Imperial Ballet is to enter a convent whence frivolity is banned, and where merciless discipline reigns.
In A.H. Franks (ed.), *Pavlova: A Biography* **Pavlova, Anna** (1881–1931) Russian ballet dancer

41 Political theatre is by definition subversive: anything else is only propaganda.
Review, *Sunday Times*, (1998) **Peter, John**

42 I've never regarded myself as the one authority on my plays just because I wrote the damned things.
The Observer, (1993) **Pinter, Harold** (1930–) English dramatist, poet and screenwriter

43 A nice, respectable, middle-class, middle-aged, maiden lady, with time on her hands and the money to help her pass it ... Let us call her Aunt Edna ... Aunt Edna is universal, and to those who might feel that all the problems of the modern theatre might be solved by her liquidation, let me add that ... she is also immortal.
Collected Plays (1953) **Rattigan, Terence** (1911–1977) English dramatist and screenwriter. Describing the typical theatregoer

44 Now do take my advice, and write a play – if any incident happens, remember, it is better to have written a damned play, than no play at all – it snatches a man from obscurity.
The Dramatist (1789) **Reynolds, Frederic** (1765–1841) English playwright

45 To play the lyre and dance more beautifully than a virtuous woman need.
Catiline **Sallust** (86–c.34 BC) Roman historian and statesman

46 Rehearsing a play is making the word flesh. Publishing a play is reversing the process.
Equus (1973) **Shaffer, Peter** (1926–) English dramatist

47 When you do dance, I wish you
A wave o' th' sea, that you might ever do
Nothing but that; move still, still so,
And own no other function.
The Winter's Tale, IV.iv **Shakespeare, William** (1564–1616) English dramatist, poet and actor

48 I quite agree with you, sir, but what can two do against so many?
Oxford Book of Literary Anecdotes Responding to a solitary boo amongst the mid-act applause at the first performance of *Arms and the Man* in 1894

49 You don't expect me to know what to say about a play when I don't know who the author is, do you? ... If it's by a good author, it's a good play, naturally. That stands to reason.
Fanny's First Play (1911)

50 An all-night sitting in a theatre would be at least as enjoyable as an all-night sitting in the House of Commons, and much more useful.
Saint Joan (1924) **Shaw, George Bernard** (1856–1950) Irish socialist, writer, dramatist and critic

51 What time is the next swan?
In W. Slezak, *What Time's the Next Swan?* (1962) **Slezak, Leo** (1873–1946) Austrian-born US tenor. When the mechanical swan left the stage without him during a performance of *Lohengrin*

52 The bad end unhappily, the good unluckily. That is what tragedy means.
Rosencrantz and Guildenstern Are Dead (1967)

53 I can do you blood and love without the rhetoric, and I can do you blood and rhetoric without the love and I can do you all three concurrent or consecutive but I can't do you love and rhetoric without the blood. Blood is compulsory – they're all blood you see.
Rosencrantz and Guildenstern Are Dead (1967)

54 We do on the stage the things that are supposed to happen off. Which is a kind of integrity, if you look on every exit being an entrance somewhere else.
Rosencrantz and Guildenstern Are Dead (1967) **Stoppard, Tom** (1937–) British dramatist

55 Her feet beneath her petticoat,
Like little mice, stole in and out,
As if they fear'd the light:
But O she dances such a way!
No sun upon an Easter-day
Is half so fine a sight.
'A Ballad upon a Wedding' (1646) **Suckling, Sir John** (1609–1642) English poet and dramatist

56 The composition of a tragedy requires testicles.
In a letter from Byron to John Murray, (1817) **Voltaire** (1694–1778) French philosopher, dramatist, poet, historian, writer and critic. When asked why no woman had ever written a tolerable tragedy

57 When I play on my fiddle in Dooney,
Folk dance like a wave of the sea …
For the good are always the merry,
Save by an evil chance,
And the merry love the fiddle,
And the merry love to dance.
In the *Bookman*, (1892)

58 All men are dancers and their tread
Goes to the barbarous clangour of a gong.
'Nineteen Hundred and Nineteen' (1921)

59 O chestnut-tree, great-rooted blossomer,
Are you the leaf, the blossom or the bole?
O body swayed to music, O brightening glance,
How can we know the dancer from the dance?
'Among School Children' (1927) **Yeats, W.B.** (1865–1939) Irish poet, dramatist, editor, writer and senator
See also acting; criticism; literature

THOUGHT

1 Thinking is seeing.
Louis Lambert (1832)

2 I prefer thought to action, ideas to events, meditation to movement.
Louis Lambert (1832) **Balzac, Honoré de** (1799–1850) French writer

3 Men of genius are not quick judges of character. Deep thinking and high imagining blunt that trivial instinct by which you and I size people up.
And Even Now (1920) **Beerbohm, Sir Max** (1872–1956) English satirist, cartoonist, critic and essayist

4 All the choir of heaven and furniture of earth – in a word, all those bodies which compose the mighty frame of the world – have not any subsistence without a mind.
A Treatise Concerning the Principles of Human Knowledge (1710) **Berkeley, Bishop George** (1685–1753) Irish philosopher and scholar

5 His Lordship says he will turn it over in what he is pleased to call his mind.
In Nash, *Life of Westbury* **Bethell, Richard** (1800–1873) English judge

6 *Brain*: An apparatus with which we think that we think.
The Cynic's Word Book (1906) **Bierce, Ambrose** (1842–c.1914) US writer, verse writer and soldier

7 Man's desires are limited by his perceptions; none can desire what he has not perceiv'd.
There is No Natural Religion (c.1788)

8 If the doors of perception were cleansed every thing would appear to man as it is, infinite.
The Marriage of Heaven and Hell (c.1790–1793)

9 One thought fills immensity.
The Marriage of Heaven and Hell (c.1790–1793) **Blake, William** (1757–1827) English poet, engraver, painter and mystic

10 The liberally educated person is one who is able to resist the easy and preferred answers, not because he is obstinate but because he knows others worthy of consideration.
The Closing of the American Mind (1987) **Bloom, Allan** (1930–1992) US academic and critic

11 The unconscious is the ocean of the unsayable, of what has been expelled from the land of language, removed as a result of ancient prohibitions.
The Literature Machine (1987) **Calvino, Italo** (1923–1985) Italian writer

12 There is a road from the eye to the heart that does not go through the intellect.
The Defendant (1901) **Chesterton, G.K.** (1874–1936) English writer, poet and critic

13 I think, therefore I am. (*Cogito, ergo sum*)
Discours de la Méthode (1637) **Descartes, René** (1596–1650) French philosopher and mathematician

14 The mind is a tool, a machine, moved by spiritual fire.
Letter to his brother, (1838) **Dostoevsky, Fyodor** (1821–1881) Russian writer

15 It is a capital mistake to theorize before one has data.
The Adventures of Sherlock Holmes (1892)

16 It is quite a three-pipe problem, and I beg that you won't speak to me for fifty minutes.
The Adventures of Sherlock Holmes (1892) **Doyle, Sir Arthur Conan** (1859–1930) Scottish writer and war correspondent

17 Beware when the great God lets loose a thinker on this planet. Then all things are at risk.
'Circles' (1841) **Emerson, Ralph Waldo** (1803–1882) US poet, essayist, transcendentalist and teacher

18 Give me, kind heav'n, a private station, A mind serene for contemplation.
Fables (1738) **Gay, John** (1685–1732) English poet, dramatist and librettist

19 Everything worth thinking has already been thought, our concern must only be to try to think it through again.
'Thought and Action' (1829) **Goethe** (1749–1832) German poet, writer, dramatist and scientist

20 People who jump to conclusions rarely alight on them.
The Observer, (1924) **Guedalla, Philip** (1889–1944) English historian, writer and lawyer

21 The most fluent talkers or most plausible reasoners are not always the justest thinkers.
Atlas (1830) **Hazlitt, William** (1778–1830) English writer and critic

22 The real problem in life is to have sufficient time to think.
The Observer, (1981) **Heath, Sir Edward** (1916–2005) English Conservative Prime Minister

23 A thought is often original, though you have uttered it a hundred times.
The Autocrat of the Breakfast-Table (1858) **Holmes, Oliver Wendell** (1809–1894) US physician, poet, writer and scientist

24 O the mind, mind has mountains; cliffs of fall
Frightful, sheer, no-man-fathomed.
'No Worst, there is None' (1885) **Hopkins, Gerard Manley** (1844–1889) English Jesuit priest, poet and classicist

25 Little minds are interested in the extraordinary; great minds in the commonplace.
A Thousand and One Epigrams (1911) **Hubbard, Elbert** (1856–1915) US printer, editor, writer and businessman

26 Thought must be divided against itself before it can come to any knowledge of itself.
Do What You Will (1929) **Huxley, Aldous** (1894–1963) English writer, poet and critic

27 Worry is interest paid on trouble before it is due.
The Observer, (1932) **Inge, William Ralph** (1860–1954) English divine, writer and teacher

28 A great many people think they are thinking when they are merely rearranging their prejudices.
Attr. **James, William** (1842–1910) US psychologist and philosopher

29 Whatever withdraws us from the power of our senses; whatever makes the past, the distant, or the future, predominate over the present, advances us in the dignity of thinking beings.
A Journey to the Western Islands of Scotland (1775)

30 That is the happiest conversation where there is no competition, no vanity, but a calm quiet interchange of sentiments.
In Boswell, *The Life of Samuel Johnson* (1791) **Johnson, Samuel** (1709–1784) English lexicographer, poet, critic, conversationalist and essayist

31 Between good sense and good taste there is the same difference as between cause and effect.
Les caractères ou les moeurs de ce siècle (1688) **La Bruyère, Jean de** (1645–1696) French satirist

32 The reason of the strongest is always the best.
Fables, 'Le loup et l'agneau' **La Fontaine, Jean de** (1621–1695) French poet and fabulist

33 Thoughts are not subject to duty.
On Worldly Authority (1523) **Luther, Martin** (1483–1546) German Protestant theologian and reformer

34 A new maxim is often a brilliant error.
Pensées et maximes **Malesherbes, Chrétien Guillaume de Lamoignonde** (1721–1794) French statesman

35 How many pessimists end up by desiring the things they fear, in order to prove that they are right.
Apostilles **Mallet, Robert** (1915–2002) French university rector, poet and writer

36 No great improvements in the lot of mankind are possible, until a great change takes place in the fundamental constitution of their modes of thought.
Autobiography (1873) **Mill, John Stuart** (1806–1873) English philosopher, economist and reformer

37 The trouble with specialists is that they tend to think in grooves.
The Descent of Woman **Morgan, Elaine** (1920–) Welsh writer

38 If I have done the public any service, it is due to patient thought.
Letter to Dr Bentley, (1713) **Newton, Sir Isaac** (1642–1727) English scientist and philosopher

39 Thinking is the desire to gain reality by means of ideas.
The Dehumanization of Art (1925) **Ortega y Gasset, José** (1883–1955) Spanish philosopher

40 The sublime and the ridiculous are often so nearly related, that it is difficult to class them separately. One step above the sublime, makes the ridiculous; and one step above the ridiculous, makes the sublime again.
The Age of Reason (1795) **Paine, Thomas** (1737–1809) English-born US political theorist and pamphleteer

41 Ideal conversation must be an exchange of thought, and not, as many of those who worry most about their shortcomings believe, an eloquent exhibition of wit or oratory.
Etiquette (1922) **Post, Emily** (1873–1960) US writer

42 You can't think rationally on an empty stomach, and a whole lot of people can't do it on a full one either.

Attr. **Reith, Lord** (1889–1971) Scottish wartime minister, administrator, diarist and Director-General of the BBC

43 People don't seem to realize that it takes time and effort and preparation to think. Statesmen are far too busy making speeches to think.
In Harris and Callas, *Kenneth Harris Talking To Maria Callas [and others]* (1971)

44 Many people would sooner die than think. In fact they do.
In Flew, *Thinking about Thinking* (1975) **Russell, Bertrand** (1872–1970) English philosopher, mathematician, essayist and social reformer

45 Thoughts which are born in front of everyone are like beautiful women who spend their lives at balls ... they have no colouring. Try to produce thoughts which have their natural colour, their true colour, which is red.
Notebooks, (1834–1847) **Sainte-Beuve, Charles-Augustin** (1804–1869) French writer and critic. On the habit of literary men and politicians of constantly improvising and expressing their thoughts in public

46 The mind is the guide and ruler of men's lives.
Jugurtha **Sallust** (86–c.34 BC) Roman historian and statesman

47 My thought is me: that is why I cannot stop. I exist by what I think ... and I can't prevent myself from thinking.
Nausea (1938) **Sartre, Jean-Paul** (1905–1980) French philosopher, writer, dramatist and critic

48 There is nothing either good or bad, but thinking makes it so.
Hamlet, II.ii **Shakespeare, William** (1564–1616) English dramatist, poet and actor

49 The man who listens to Reason is lost: Reason enslaves all whose minds are not strong enough to master her.
Man and Superman (1903) **Shaw, George Bernard** (1856–1950) Irish socialist, writer, dramatist and critic

50 Mrs Shelley was choosing a school for her son, and asked the advice of this lady, who gave for advice ... Just the sort of banality, you know, one does come out with: 'Oh, send him somewhere where they will teach him to think for himself!' ... Mrs Shelley answered: 'Teach him to think for himself? Oh, my God, teach him rather to think like other people!'
In Matthew Arnold, *Essays in Criticism* (1888) **Shelley, Mary Wollstonecraft** (1797–1851) English writer

51 A single word even may be a spark of inextinguishable thought.
A Defence of Poetry (1821) **Shelley, Percy Bysshe** (1792–1822) English poet, dramatist and essayist

52 I don't know any business you have to think at all – thought does not become a young woman.
The Rivals (1775) **Sheridan, Richard Brinsley** (1751–1816) Irish dramatist, politician and orator

53 We think so because other people think so, Or because – or because – after all we do think so,
Or because we were told so, and think we must think so,
Or because we once thought so, and think we still think so,
Or because having thought so, we think we will think so.
'Lines Composed in his Sleep' **Sidgwick, Henry** (1838–1900) English philosopher

54 I never could find any man who could think for two minutes together.
Sketches of Moral Philosophy (1849) **Smith, Sydney** (1771–1845) English clergyman, essayist, journalist and wit

55 Speech was given to man to disguise his thoughts.
Attr. **Talleyrand, Charles-Maurice de** (1754–1838) French statesman, memoirist and prelate

56 There are a thousand thoughts lying within a man that he does not know till he takes up the pen to write.

The History of Henry Esmond (1852) **Thackeray, William Makepeace** (1811–1863) Indian-born English writer

57 ... to cure the pain
Of the headache called thought in the brain.
'L'Ancien Régime' (1880) **Thomson, James** (1834–1882) Scottish poet and dramatist

58 Thinking is work.
After I Was Sixty: A Chapter of Autobiography
Thomson, Roy (1894–1976) Canadian-born English newspaper and television magnate

59 Disinterested intellectual curiosity is the life blood of real civilization.
English Social History (1942) **Trevelyan, G.M.** (1876–1962) English historian and writer

60 I must have a prodigious quantity of mind; it takes me as much as a week, sometimes, to make it up.
The Innocents Abroad (1869) **Twain, Mark** (1835–1910) US humorist, writer, journalist and lecturer

61 A gloss on Descartes: Sometimes I think: and sometimes I am.
The Faber Book of Aphorisms (1962) **Valéry, Paul** (1871–1945) French poet, mathematician and philosopher

62 Thinking is to me the greatest fatigue in the world.
The Relapse, or Virtue in Danger (1696) **Vanbrugh, Sir John** (1664–1726) English dramatist and baroque architect

63 And yet, as Angels in some brighter dreams
Call to the soul, when man doth sleep:
So some strange thoughts transcend our wonted theams,
And into glory peep.
Silex Scintillans (1650–1655), 'They Are All Gone' **Vaughan, Henry** (1622–1695) Welsh poet and physician

64 Great thoughts come from the heart.
Réflexions et Maximes (1746) **Vauvenargues, Marquis de** (1715–1747) French soldier and moralist

65 People use thought only to justify their injustices, and they use words only to disguise their thoughts.

Dialogues (1763) **Voltaire** (1694–1778) French philosopher, dramatist, poet, historian, writer and critic

66 The little girl had the makings of a poet in her who, being told to be sure of her meaning before she spoke, said: 'How can I know what I think till I see what I say?'
The Art of Thought (1926) **Wallas, Graham** (1858–1932) English political scientist

67 When people will not weed their own minds, they are apt to be overrun with nettles.
Letter to the Countess of Ailesbury, (1779) **Walpole, Horace** (1717–1797) English writer and politician

68 There's nothing of so infinite vexation As man's own thoughts.
The White Devil (1612) **Webster, John** (c.1580–c.1625) English dramatist

69 There's nothing like eavesdropping to show you that the world outside your head is different from the world inside your head.
The Matchmaker (1954) **Wilder, Thornton** (1897–1975) US author and playwright

70 Minds like beds always made up,
(more stony than a shore)
unwilling or unable.
Paterson (1958) **Williams, William Carlos** (1883–1963) US poet, writer and paediatrician

71 In order to draw a limit to thinking, we should have to be able to think both sides of this limit.
Tractatus Logico-Philosophicus (1922) **Wittgenstein, Ludwig** (1889–1951) Austrian philosopher
See also belief; ideas; intelligence; philosophy

TIME

1 Time wounds all heels.
In Goodman Ace, *The Fine Art of Hypochondria* (1966) **Ace, Jane** (1905–1974) US comedian and radio personality

2 Time brings all things to pass.
The Libation Bearers **Aeschylus** (525–456 BC) Greek dramatist and poet

3 The only things that start on time are those that you're late for.
Cayo's Law **Anonymous**

4 O let not Time deceive you,
You cannot conquer Time.
Collected Poems, (1933–1938) **Auden, W.H.** (1907–1973) English poet, essayist, critic, teacher and dramatist

5 Time is like a river made up of the things which happen, and its current is strong; no sooner does anything appear than it is carried away, and another comes in its place, and will be carried away too.
Meditations **Aurelius, Marcus** (121–180) Roman emperor and Stoic philosopher

6 He that will not apply new remedies, must expect new evils; for time is the greatest innovator.
'Of Innovations' (1625) **Bacon, Francis** (1561–1626) English philosopher, essayist, politician and courtier

7 Days and months are itinerants on an eternal journey; the years that pass by are also travellers.
'Narrow Roads of Oku' (1703) **Bashó, Matsuo** (1644–1694) Japanese haiku poet

8 *Vladimir:* That passed the time.
Estragon: It would have passed in any case.
Vladimir: Yes, but not so rapidly.
Waiting for Godot (1955) **Beckett, Samuel** (1906–1989) Irish dramatist, writer and poet

9 I am a sundial, and I make a botch
Of what is done far better by a watch.
Sonnets and Verse (1938) **Belloc, Hilaire** (1870–1953) English writer of verse, essayist and critic; Liberal MP

10 For a thousand years in thy sight are but as yesterday when it is past, and as a watch in the night.
Psalms, 90:4

11 To every thing there is a season, and a time to every purpose under the heaven:
A time to be born, and a time to die ...
A time to love, and a time to hate; a time of war, and a time of peace.
Ecclesiastes, 3:1–8 **The Bible (King James Version)**

12 To see a World in a Grain of Sand
And a Heaven in a Wild Flower
Hold Infinity in the palm of your hand
And Eternity in an hour.
'Auguries of Innocence' (c.1803) **Blake, William** (1757–1827) English poet, engraver, painter and mystic

13 Men talk of killing time, while time quietly kills them.
London Assurance (1841) **Boucicault, Dion** (1822–1890) Irish dramatist, actor and theatrical manager

14 Who can speak of eternity without a solecism, or think thereof without an ecstasy? Time we may comprehend, 'tis but five days elder than ourselves.
Religio Medici (1643)

15 The night of time far surpasseth the day, and who knows when was the equinox?
Hydriotaphia: Urn Burial (1658) **Browne, Sir Thomas** (1605–1682) English physician, author and antiquary

16 The illimitable, silent, never-resting thing called Time, rolling, rushing on, swift, silent, like an all-embracing ocean-tide, on which we and all the Universe swim like exhalations, like apparitions which are, and then are not.
'The Hero as Divinity' (1841) **Carlyle, Thomas** (1795–1881) Scottish historian, biographer, critic, and essayist

17 I recommend to you to take care of minutes; for hours will take care of themselves.
Letter to his son, (1747) **Chesterfield, Lord** (1694–1773) English politician and letter writer

18 'Time has too much credit,' said Bridget. 'I never agree with the compliments paid to it. It is not a great healer. It is an indifferent and perfunctory one. Sometimes it does not heal at all. And sometimes when it seems to, no healing has been necessary.'
Darkness and Day (1951) **Compton-Burnett, Dame Ivy** (1884–1969) English novelist

19 Time is the reef upon which all our frail mystic ships are wrecked.

Blithe Spirit (1941) **Coward, Sir Noël** (1899–1973) English dramatist, actor, producer and composer

20 It may be true that preoccupation with time has been the downfall of Western man, but it can also be argued that conjecture about eternity is a waste of time.
In Guy Kettlehack (ed.), *The Wit and Wisdom of Quentin Crisp* **Crisp, Quentin** (1908–1999) English writer, publicist and model

21 Our journey had advanced –
Our feet were almost come
To that odd Fork in Being's Road –
Eternity – by term.
'Our Journey had Advanced' (c.1862) **Dickinson, Emily** (1830–1886) US poet

22 Time is the great physician.
Henrietta Temple (1837) **Disraeli, Benjamin** (1804–1881) English statesman and writer

23 Time goes, you say? Ah no!
Alas, Time stays, we go.
'The Paradox of Time' (1877) **Dobson, Henry Austin** (1840–1921) English poet, essayist and biographer

24 We keep imagining eternity as an idea that can't be understood, as something enormous … instead of all that there will just be one little room, somewhat like a country bath-house, with spiders in all the corners – that's eternity.
Crime and Punishment (1865) **Dostoevsky, Fyodor** (1821–1881) Russian writer

25 The best way to fill time is to waste it.
Practicalities (1987) **Duras, Marguerite** (1914–1996) French author and film-maker

26 A day is a miniature eternity.
Journals **Emerson, Ralph Waldo** (1803–1882) US poet, essayist, transcendentalist and teacher

27 Come, fill the Cup, and in the Fire of Spring
The Winter Garment of Repentance fling:
The Bird of Time has but a little way
To fly – and Lo! the Bird is on the Wing.
The Rubáiyát of Omar Khayyám (1859) **Fitzgerald, Edward** (1809–1883) English poet, translator and letter writer

28 There is no past, present or future. Using tenses to divide time is like making chalk marks on water.
Faces in the Water (1961) **Frame, Janet** (1924–2004) New Zealand writer

29 Remember that time is money.
Advice to a Young Tradesman (1748) **Franklin, Benjamin** (1706–1790) US statesman, scientist, political critic and printer

30 How marvellous, wide and broad is my inheritance!
Time is my property, my estate is time.
Wilhelm Meister's Wandering Years (1821) **Goethe** (1749–1832) German poet, writer, dramatist and scientist

31 In my best social accent I addressed him. I said, 'It is most extraordinary weather for this time of year!' He replied, 'Ah, it isn't this time of year at all.'
It Isn't This Time of Year at All (1954) **Gogarty, Oliver St John** (1878–1957) Irish poet, dramatist, writer, politician and surgeon

32 Gather ye rosebuds while ye may,
Old Time is still a-flying;
And this same flower that smiles today
Tomorrow will be dying.
Hesperides (1648) **Herrick, Robert** (1591–1674) English poet, royalist and clergyman

33 Sometimes there's nothing but Sundays for weeks on end. Why can't they move Sunday to the middle of the week so you could put it in the OUT tray on your desk?
The Lion of Boaz-Jachin and Jachin-Boaz **Hoban, Russell** (1925–) US author

34 Time, you old gypsy man,
Will you not stay,
Put up your caravan,
Just for one day?
'Time, You Old Gypsy Man' (1917) **Hodgson, Ralph** (1871–1962) English poet, illustrator and journalist

35 The changing year and the passing hour that takes away genial day warns you not to build everlasting hopes.
Odes **Horace** (65–8 BC) Roman poet

36 Patience and time do more than force and rage.

Fables **La Fontaine, Jean de** (1621–1695) French poet and fabulist

37 What are days for?
Days are where we live
They come they wake us
Time and time over.
They are to be happy in;
Where can we live but days?
'Days' (1964) **Larkin, Philip** (1922–1985)
English poet, writer and librarian

38 Decades have a delusive edge to them.
They are not, of course, really periods at all,
except as any other ten years would be. But
we, looking at them, are caught by the
different name each bears, and give them
different attributes, and tie labels on them,
as if they were flowers in a border.
Told by an Idiot (1923) **Macaulay, Dame Rose**
(1881–1958) English writer

39 But at my back I always hear
Time's wingèd chariot hurrying near.
And yonder all before us lie
Deserts of vast eternity.
Thy beauty shall no more be found;
Nor, in thy marble vault, shall sound
My echoing song: then worms shall try
That long preserved virginity:
And your quaint honour turn to dust;
And into ashes all my lust.
The grave's a fine and private place,
But none I think do there embrace.
'To His Coy Mistress' (1681) **Marvell, Andrew**
(1621–1678) English poet and satirist

40 Yet while there is time, there is the
certainty of return.
Ring of Bright Water (1960) **Maxwell, Gavin**
(1914–1969) British writer and naturalist

41 Every age has a keyhole to which its eye is
pasted.
Attr. **McCarthy, Mary** (1912–1989) US writer
and critic

42 For tribal man space was the
uncontrollable mystery. For technological
man it is time that occupies the same role.
The Mechanical Bridge (1951) **McLuhan,
Marshall** (1911–1980) Canadian
communications theorist

43 'Twenty-three and a quarter minutes past,'
Uncle Matthew was saying furiously, 'in
precisely six and three-quarter minutes the
damned fella will be late.'
Love in a Cold Climate (1949) **Mitford, Nancy**
(1904–1973) English writer

44 Over the sound a ship so slow would pass
That in the black hill's gloom it seemed to
lie
The evening sound was smooth like
sunken glass
And time seemed finished ere the ship
passed by.
'Childhood' (1952) **Muir, Edwin** (1887–1959)
Scottish poet, critic, translator and writer

45 Wait for that wisest of counsellors, Time.
In Plutarch, *Life* **Pericles** (c.495–429) Athenian
statesman, general, orator and cultural patron

46 Time brings everything.
Greek Anthology **Plato** (c.429–347 BC) Greek
philosopher

47 Even such is Time, which takes in trust
Our youth, our joys, and all we have,
And pays us but with age and dust;
Who in the dark and silent grave,
When we have wandered all our ways,
Shuts up the story of our days.
Untitled poem (1618) **Raleigh, Sir Walter**
(c.1552–1618) English courtier, explorer,
military commander, poet, historian and
essayist. Written the night before his
execution

48 Ev'ry member of the force
Has a watch and chain, of course;
If you want to know the time,
Ask a P'liceman!
'Ask a P'liceman' (song, 1889) **Rogers, E.W.**
(1864–1913) English songwriter

49 Half our life is spent trying to find
something to do with the time we have
rushed through life trying to save.
New York Times, (1930) **Rogers, Will** (1879–1935)
US humorist, actor, rancher, writer and wit

50 Three o'clock is always too late or too early
for anything you want to do.
Nausea (1938) **Sartre, Jean-Paul** (1905–1980)
French philosopher, writer, dramatist and
critic

51 Ah! the clock is always slow;
It is later than you think.
'It is Later than You Think' (1921) **Service,
Robert W.** (1874–1958) Canadian poet

52 Th' inaudible and noiseless foot of Time.
All's Well That Ends Well, V.iii

53 But thoughts, the slaves of life, and life,
time's fool,
And time, that takes survey of all the world,
Must have a stop.
Henry IV, Part 1, V.iv

54 Come what come may,
Time and the hour runs through the
roughest day.
Macbeth, I.iii

55 Time's glory is to calm contending kings,
To unmask falsehood, and bring truth to
light.
'The Rape of Lucrece'

56 I wasted time, and now doth time waste
me.
Richard II, V.v

57 Time's thievish progress to eternity.
Sonnet 77 **Shakespeare, William** (1564–1616)
English dramatist, poet and actor

58 In reality, killing time is only the name for
another of the multifarious ways by which
time kills us.
'Milordo Inglese' (1958) **Sitwell, Sir Osbert**
(1892–1969) English writer

59 All through the night-time, clock talked to
clock,
In the captain's cabin, tock-tock-tock,
One ticked fast and one ticked slow,
And Time went over them a hundred years
ago.
'Five Visions of Captain Cook' (1931) **Slessor,
Kenneth** (1901–1971) Australian poet and
journalist

60 So passeth, in the passing of a day,
Of mortall life the leafe, the bud, the flowre,
Ne more doth flourish after first decay,
That earst was sought to decke both bed
and bowre,
Of many a Ladie, and many a Paramowre:
Gather therefore the Rose, whilest yet is
prime,

For soone comes age, that will her pride
deflowre:
Gather the Rose of love, whilest yet is time,
Whilest loving thou mayst loved be with
equall crime.
The Faerie Queene (1596) **Spenser, Edmund**
(c.1522–1599) English poet

61 Time: That which man is always trying to
kill, but which ends in killing him.
Definitions **Spencer, Herbert** (1820–1903)
English philosopher and journalist

62 Eternity's a terrible thought. I mean,
where's it all going to end?
Rosencrantz and Guildenstern Are Dead (1967)
Stoppard, Tom (1937–) British dramatist

63 Hurry! I never hurry. I have no time to
hurry.
Attr. **Stravinsky, Igor** (1882–1971) Russian
composer and conductor. Responding to his
publisher's request that he hurry his
completion of a composition

64 It is very strange ... that the years teach us
patience; that the shorter our time, the
greater our capacity for waiting.
A Wreath of Roses (1950) **Taylor, Elizabeth**
(1912–1975) English writer

65 Oh as I was young and easy in the mercy of
his means,
Time held me green and dying
Though I sang in my chains like the sea.
'Fern Hill' (1946) **Thomas, Dylan** (1914–1953)
Welsh poet, writer and radio dramatist

66 Time is but the stream I go a-fishing in.
Walden (1854)

67 As if you could kill time, without injuring
eternity.
Walden (1854) **Thoreau, Henry David** (1817–
1862) US essayist, social critic and writer

68 But time meanwhile is flying, flying
beyond recall.
Georgics **Virgil** (70–19 BC) Roman poet

69 Time, like an ever-rolling stream,
Bears all its sons away;
They fly forgotten, as a dream
Dies at the opening day.
The Psalms of David Imitated (1719) **Watts, Isaac**
(1674–1748) English hymn writer, poet and
minister

70 Though I am always in haste, I am never in a hurry.
Letter to Miss March, (1777) **Wesley, John** (1703–1791) English theologian and preacher

71 Procrastination is the Thief of Time.
Night-Thoughts on Life, Death and Immortality (1742–1746)

72 We take no note of Time
But from its Loss.
Night-Thoughts on Life, Death and Immortality (1742–1746) **Young, Edward** (1683–1765) English poet, dramatist, satirist and clergyman
See also age; change; death; life; memory

TRANSPORT

1 Clunk, click, every trip.
Road safety campaign promoting the use of seat belts, (1971) **Anonymous**

2 Flight by machines heavier than air is unpractical, and insignificant, if not utterly impossible.
New York Times, (1903) **Newcomb, Simon** (1835–1909) US astronomer and mathematician

3 People who spend most of their natural lives riding iron bicycles over the rocky roadsteads of this parish get their personalities mixed up with the personalities of their bicycles as a result of the interchanging of the atoms of each of them and you would be surprised at the number of people in these parts who nearly are half people and half bicycles.
The Third Policeman (1967) **O'Brien, Flann** (1911–1966) Irish novelist and journalist

4 Monsieur Garnevin goes up again tomorrow with an Umbrella Thing to hinder his Fall, he calls it for that Reason a Parachute. We shall see how it answers – taking so much money at such a Risk of breaking all his bones.
Letter to Lady Williams, (2 July 1802) **Piozzi, Hester Lynch (Mrs Henry Thrale)** (1741–1821) English writer. Of a balloonist exhibiting in London

5 After the first powerful plain manifesto
The black statement of pistons, without more fuss
But gliding like a queen, she leaves the station.
'The Express' (1933) **Spender, Sir Stephen** (1909–1995) English poet, editor, translator and diarist

6 I see no reason to suppose that these machines will ever force themselves into general use.
In J. Gere, *Geoffrey Madan's Notebooks* **Wellington, Duke of** (1769–1852) Irish-born British military commander and statesman. Referring to steam locomotives
See also exploration; travel

TRAVEL

1 When the plane you are on is late, the plane you want to transfer to is on time.
The Airplane Law

2 The strength of the turbulence is directly proportional to the temperature of your coffee.
Gunter's Second Law of Air Travel

3 When you are served a meal aboard an aircraft, the aircraft will encounter turbulence.
Gunter's First Law of Air Travel **Anonymous**

4 A wanderer is man from his birth.
He was born in a ship
On the breast of the river of Time.
'The Future'

5 And see all sights from pole to pole,
And glance, and nod, and bustle by;
And never once possess our soul
Before we die.
'A Southern Night' (1861) **Arnold, Matthew** (1822–1888) English poet, critic, essayist and educationist

6 The north focuses our anxieties. Turning to face north, we enter our own unconscious. Always, in retrospect, the journey north has the quality of dream.
Saturday Night, (1987), 'True North' **Atwood, Margaret** (1939–) Canadian writer, poet and critic

7 The earth is all the home I have,
The heavens my wide roof-tree.
'The Wandering Jew' (1867) **Aytoun, W.E.**
(1813–1865) Scottish poet, ballad writer and
satirist

8 Upon the upland road
Ride easy, stranger:
Surrender to the sky
Your heart of anger.
'High Country Weather' (1945) **Baxter, James
K.** (1926–1972) New Zealand poet and
playwright

9 I have done almost every human activity
inside a taxi which does not require main
drainage.
Punch, (1972) **Brien, Alan** (1925–) English
writer

10 Canadian trains did not rush and rock.
They pounded steadily along, every so
often giving a warning blast on their
sirens. I remember those sirens blowing in
the icy darkness of winter nights in Ottawa,
the most haunting sound, at once
melancholy and stirring, like the mourning
of some strange, sad beast.
A Memoir **Buchan, William** (1822–1888)

11 Travelling is the ruin of all happiness!
There's no looking at a building here after
seeing Italy.
Cecilia (1782) **Burney, Fanny** (1752–1840)
English diarist and novelist

12 The knowledge of the world is only to be
acquired in the world, and not in a closet.
Letter to his son, (1746) **Chesterfield, Lord**
(1694–1773) English politician and letter writer

13 Chesterton taught me this: the only way to
be sure of catching a train is to miss the
one before it.
In P. Daninos, Vacances à tous prix (1958), 'Le
supplice de l'heure' **Chesterton, G.K.** (1874–
1936) English writer, poet and critic

14 To argue that a car is simply a means of
conveyance is like arguing that Blenheim
Palace is simply a house.
Sunday Times, (1999) **Clarkson, Jeremy** (1960–)
English motoring journalist

15 From whatever place I write you will expect
that part of my 'Travels' will consist of
excursions in my own mind.
Satyrane's Letters (1809) **Coleridge, Samuel
Taylor** (1772–1834) English poet, philosopher
and critic

16 How much a dunce that has been sent to
roam
Excels a dunce that has been kept at home.
'The Progress of Error' (1782) **Cowper,
William** (1731–1800) English poet, hymn
writer and letter writer

17 Lord Dewar … made the famous epigram
about there being only two classes of
pedestrians in these days of reckless motor
traffic – the quick, and the dead.
In George Robey, *Looking Back on Life* **Dewar,
Lord Thomas Robert** (1864–1930) Scottish
Conservative politician and writer

18 Certain places seem to exist mainly
because someone has written about them.
The White Album (1979) **Didion, Joan** (1934–)
US writer

19 Too often travel, instead of broadening the
mind, merely lengthens the conversation.
The Literature of Gossip (1964) **Drew, Elizabeth**
(1887–1965) English-born US writer and critic

20 'Abroad', that large home of ruined
reputations.
Felix Holt (1866) **Eliot, George** (1819–1880)
English writer and poet

21 The first condition of understanding a
foreign country is to smell it.
Attr. **Eliot, T.S.** (1888–1965) US-born British
poet, verse dramatist and critic

22 Travelling is a fool's paradise. Our first
journeys discover to us the indifference of
places.
'Self-Reliance' (1841) **Emerson, Ralph Waldo**
(1803–1882) US poet, essayist,
transcendentalist and teacher

23 I find it hard to say, because when I was
there it seemed to be shut.
BBC radio, (1978) **Freud, Clement** (1924–)
British Liberal politician, broadcaster and
writer. On being asked his opinion of New
Zealand

24 I travel light; as light,
   That is, as a man can travel who will
   Still carry his body around because
   Of its sentimental value.
   The Lady's not for Burning (1949) **Fry,
   Christopher** (1907–2005) English verse
   dramatist, theatre director and translator

25 The Great Wall, I've been told, is the only
   man-made structure on earth that is visible
   from the moon. For the life of me I cannot
   see why anyone would go to the moon to
   look at it, when, with almost the same
   difficulty, it can be viewed in China.
   The Sunday Times Magazine **Galbraith, J.K.**
   (1908–2006) Canadian-born US economist,
   diplomat and writer

26 The real way to travel! Here today – in next
   week tomorrow! Villages skipped, towns
   and cities jumped – always somebody
   else's horizon! O bliss! O poop-poop! O
   my! O my!
   The Wind in the Willows (1908) **Grahame,
   Kenneth** (1859–1932) English author. Toad's
   reaction to the motor-car which destroyed his
   gypsy caravan

27 Give me the clear blue sky over my head,
   and the green turf beneath my feet, a
   winding road before me, and a three
   hours' march to dinner – and then to
   thinking! It is hard if I cannot start some
   game on these lone heaths.
   'On Going a Journey' (1822)

28 One of the pleasantest things in the world
   is going on a journey; but I like to go by
   myself.
   Table-Talk (1822) **Hazlitt, William** (1778–1830)
   English writer and critic

29 'Tis always morning somewhere in the
   world.
   Orion (1843) **Horne, Richard Henry** (1803–1884)
   English writer

30 A man who has not been in Italy, is always
   conscious of an inferiority, from his not
   having seen what it is expected a man
   should see. The grand object of travelling
   is to see the shores of the Mediterranean.

In Boswell, *The Life of Samuel Johnson* (1791)
Johnson, Samuel (1709–1784) English
lexicographer, poet, critic, conversationalist
and essayist

31 The Road is life.
   On the Road (1957) **Kerouac, Jack** (1922–1969)
   US writer and poet

32 Of all noxious animals, too, the most
   noxious is a tourist. And of all tourists, the
   most vulgar, ill-bred, offensive and
   loathsome is the British tourist.
   Diary, (1870) **Kilvert, Francis** (1840–1879)
   English curate and diarist

33 Down to Gehenna or up to the Throne,
   He travels the fastest who travels alone.
   'The Winners' (1888) **Kipling, Rudyard** (1865–
   1936) Indian-born British poet and writer

34 The great and recurrent question about
   abroad is, is it worth getting there?
   Attr. **Macaulay, Dame Rose** (1881–1958)
   English writer

35 Whenever I prepare for a journey I prepare
   as though for death. Should I never return,
   all is in order. That is what life has taught
   me.
   Journal of Katherine Mansfield (1954) **Mansfield,
   Katherine** (1888–1923) New Zealand writer

36 I saw the world as some sort of exchange
   scheme for my ideals, but the world
   deserves better than this. When you come
   across an alien culture you must not
   automatically respect it. You must
   sometimes pay it the compliment of hating
   it.
   'Last Months in Al Hamra' (1987) **Mantel,
   Hilary** (1952–) English writer

37 It is good to be out on the road, and going
   one knows not where,
   Going through meadow and village, one
   knows not whither nor why.
   'Tewkesbury Road' (1902) **Masefield, John**
   (1878–1967) English poet, writer and critic

38 A man travels the world over in search of
   what he needs and returns home to find it.
   The Brook Kerith (1916) **Moore, George** (1852–
   1933) Irish writer, dramatist and critic

39 Travel, which was once either a necessity or an adventure, has become very largely a commodity, and from all sides we are persuaded into thinking that it is a social requirement, too.
New York Times, (1985) **Morris, Jan** (1926–) Welsh travel writer

40 If you travel as much as we do, you appreciate how much more comfortable aircraft have become. Unless you travel in something called economy class, which sounds ghastly.
Comment during the Jubilee tour, (2002) **Philip, Prince, Duke of Edinburgh** (1921–) Greek-born consort of Queen Elizabeth II

41 A good holiday is one spent among people whose notions of time are vaguer than yours.
Attr. **Priestley, J.B.** (1894–1984) English writer, dramatist and critic

42 What is better than presence of mind in a railway accident? Absence of body.
(1849) **Punch**

43 There was a rocky valley between Buxton and Bakewell, ... divine as the vale of Tempe; you might have seen the gods there morning and evening, – Apollo and the sweet Muses of the Light ... You enterprised a railroad, ... you blasted its rocks away ... And now, every fool in Buxton can be at Bakewell in half-an-hour, and every fool in Bakewell at Buxton.
Praeterita (1889) **Ruskin, John** (1819–1900) English art critic, philosopher and reformer

44 Travel is the most private of pleasures. There is no greater bore than the travel bore. We do not in the least want to hear what he has seen in Hong-Kong.
Passenger to Tehran (1926) **Sackville-West, Vita** (1892–1962) English poet and novelist

45 Because there's no fourth class.
In Thomas, *Living Biographies of the Great Philosophers* **Santayana, George** (1863–1952) Spanish-born US philosopher and writer. On being asked why he always travelled third class

46 Whoe'er has travell'd life's dull round,
Where'er his stages may have been,
May sigh to think he still has found
The warmest welcome, at an inn.
'At an Inn at Henley' (1758) **Shenstone, William** (1714–1763) English poet, essayist and letter writer

47 The dark train shakes and plunges;
Bells cry out; the night-ride starts again.
Soon I shall look out into nothing but blackness,
Pale, windy fields. The old roar and knock of the rails
Melts into dull fury. Pull down the blind.
Sleep. Sleep.
Nothing but grey, rushing rivers of bush outside.
Gaslight and milk-cans. Of Rapptown I recall nothing else.
'The Night-Ride' **Slessor, Kenneth** (1901–1971) Australian poet and journalist

48 The beckoning counts, and not the clicking latch behind you.
Sunday Telegraph, (1993) **Stark, Dame Freya** (1893–1993) French-born traveller and writer

49 A man should know something of his own country too, before he goes abroad.
Tristram Shandy (1767)

50 I think there is a fatality in it – I seldom go to the place I set out for.
A Sentimental Journey (1768)

51 I pity the man who can travel from Dan to Beersheba, and cry, 'tis all barren.
A Sentimental Journey (1768)

52 The whole circle of travellers may be reduced to the following Heads:
Idle Travellers,
Inquisitive Travellers,
Lying Travellers,
Proud Travellers,
Vain Travellers,
Splenetic Travellers,
Then follow The Travellers of Necessity,
The delinquent and felonious Traveller,
The unfortunate and innocent Traveller,
The simple Traveller,
And last of all (if you please)
The Sentimental Traveller.

A Sentimental Journey (1768) **Sterne, Laurence** (1713–1768) Irish-born English writer and clergyman

53 For my part, I travel not to go anywhere, but to go. I travel for travel's sake. The great affair is to move.
Travels with a Donkey in the Cévennes (1879)

54 To travel hopefully is a better thing than to arrive, and the true success is to labour.
Virginibus Puerisque (1881)

55 But all that I could think of, in the darkness and the cold,
Was that I was leaving home and my folks were growing old.
'Christmas at Sea' (1890)

56 Let the blow fall soon or late,
Let what will be o'er me;
Give the face of earth around
And the road before me.
Wealth I seek not, hope nor love,
Nor a friend to know me;
All I seek, the heaven above
And the road below me.
Songs of Travel (1896)

57 Give to me the life I love,
Let the lave go by me,
Give the jolly heaven above
And the byway nigh me.
Bed in the bush with stars to see,
Bread I dip in the river –
There's the life for a man like me,
There's the life for ever.
Songs of Travel (1896) **Stevenson, Robert Louis** (1850–1894) Scottish writer, poet and essayist

58 I always love to begin a journey on Sundays, because I shall have the prayers of the church to preserve all that travel by land, or by water.
Polite Conversation (1738) **Swift, Jonathan** (1667–1745) Irish satirist, poet, essayist and cleric

59 Why do they always put mud into coffee on board steamers? Why does the tea generally taste of boiled boots?
The Kickleburys on the Rhine (1850) **Thackeray, William Makepeace** (1811–1863) Indian-born English writer

60 It is because we put up with bad things that hotel-keepers continue to give them to us.
Orley Farm (1862) **Trollope, Anthony** (1815–1882) English writer, traveller and post office official

61 We cannot bring ourselves to believe it possible that a foreigner should in any respect be wiser than ourselves. If any such point out to us our follies, we at once claim those follies as the special evidences of our wisdom.
Orley Farm (1862) **Trollope, Anthony** (1815–1882) English writer, traveller and post office official

62 They spell it Vinci and pronounce it Vinchy; foreigners always spell better than they pronounce.
The Innocents Abroad (1869)

63 You feel mighty free and easy and comfortable on a raft.
The Adventures of Huckleberry Finn (1884) **Twain, Mark** (1835–1910) US humorist, writer, journalist and lecturer

64 I've always thought a hotel ought to offer optional small animals ... I mean a cat to sleep on your bed at night, or a dog of some kind to act pleased when you come in. You ever notice how a hotel room feels so lifeless?
The Accidental Tourist (1985) **Tyler, Anne** (1941–) US novelist

65 Africa has always walked in my mind proudly upright, an African giant among the other continents, toes well dug into the final ocean of one hemisphere, rising to its full height in the greying skies of the other; head and shoulders broad, square and enduring, making light of the bagful of blue Mediterranean slung over its back as it marches patiently through time.
Flamingo Feather (1955) **Van der Post, Sir Laurens** (1906–1996) South African explorer and writer

66 Here we are in the Holy Land of Israel – a Mecca for tourists.
Attr. **Vine, David** English television commentator

67 I was told I am a true cosmopolitan. I am unhappy everywhere.
The Guardian, (1968) **Vizinczey, Stephen** (1933–) Hungarian-born writer, editor and broadcaster

68 There are only two emotions in a plane: boredom and terror.
The Times, (1985) **Welles, Orson** (1915–1985) US actor, director and producer

69 Commuter – one who spends his life
In riding to and from his wife;
A man who shaves and takes a train,
And then rides back to shave again.
Poems and Sketches, (1982) **White, E.B.** (1899–1985) US humorist and writer

70 I never travel without my diary. One should always have something sensational to read in the train.
The Importance of Being Earnest (1895) **Wilde, Oscar** (1854–1900) Irish poet, dramatist, writer, critic and wit
See also exploration; house and home; transport

TRUTH

1 The truth is often a terrible weapon of aggression. It is possible to lie, and even to murder, for the truth.
Problems of Neurosis (1929) **Adler, Alfred** (1870–1937) Austrian psychiatrist and psychologist

2 Every scientific truth goes through three states: first, people say it conflicts with the Bible; next, they say it has been discovered before; lastly, they say they always believed it.
In Shulman and Asimov, *Isaac Asimov's Book of Science and Nature Quotations* (1988) **Agassiz, Louis** (1807–1873) Swiss-born US naturalist

3 The truth which makes men free is for the most part the truth which men prefer not to hear.
A Time for Greatness (1942) **Agar, Herbert Sebastian** (1897–1980) US writer

4 There's a world of difference between truth and facts. Facts can obscure truth.
I Know Why the Caged Bird Sings (1970) **Angelou, Maya** (1928–) US writer, poet and dramatist

5 Plato is dear to me, but dearer still is truth.
Attr. **Aristotle** (384–322 BC) Greek philosopher.
Greek original attributed to Aristotle

6 Truth sits upon the lips of dying men.
'Sohrab and Rustum' (1853) **Arnold, Matthew** (1822–1888) English poet, critic, essayist and educationist

7 What a man had rather were true he more readily believes.
The New Organon (1620)

8 Some in their discourse desire rather commendation of wit, in being able to hold all arguments, than of judgement in discerning what is true.
'Of Discourse' (1625)

9 This same truth is a naked and open daylight, that doth not show the masques and mummeries and triumphs of the world half so stately and daintily as candlelights.
'Of Truth' (1625) **Bacon, Francis** (1561–1626) English philosopher, essayist, politician and courtier

10 A platitude is simply a truth repeated until people get tired of hearing it.
Attr. **Baldwin, Stanley** (1867–1947) English Conservative statesman and Prime Minister

11 It is unfortunate, considering that enthusiasm moves the world, that so few enthusiasts can be trusted to speak the truth.
Letter to Mrs Drew, (1891) **Balfour, A.J.** (1848–1930) British Conservative Prime Minister

12 Truth is the cry of all, but the game of the few.
Siris (1744) **Berkeley, Bishop George** (1685–1753) Irish philosopher and scholar

13 And ye shall know the truth, and the truth shall make you free.
John, 8:32

14 Great is Truth, and mighty above all things.
Apocrypha, I Esdras, 4:41 **The Bible (King James Version)**

15 Truth can never be told so as to be understood, and not be believ'd.
'Proverbs of Hell' (c.1793)

16 A truth that's told with bad intent
Beats all the Lies you can invent.
'Auguries of Innocence' (c.1803)

17 When I tell any Truth it is not for the sake of Convincing those who do not know it but for the sake of defending those who Do.
Public address, from the *Notebook*, (c.1810)

18 Always be ready to speak your mind, and a base man will avoid you.
Attr. **Blake, William** (1757–1827) English poet, engraver, painter and mystic

19 Truth lies within a little and certain compass, but error is immense.
Reflections upon Exile (1716)

20 Plain truth will influence half a score of men at most in a nation, or an age, while mystery will lead millions by the nose.
Letter, (1721)

21 They make truth serve as a stalking-horse to error.
Letters on Study and Use of History (1752) **Bolingbroke, Henry** (1678–1751) English statesman, historian and actor

22 Nobody speaks the truth when there's something they must have.
The House in Paris (1935) **Bowen, Elizabeth** (1899–1973) Irish writer

23 Truth exists; only lies are invented.
Day and Night, Notebooks (1952) **Braque, Georges** (1882–1963) French painter

24 For great is truth, and shall prevail.
The Crown and Glory of Christianity (1662) **Brooks, Thomas** (1608–1680) English Puritan divine

25 I have tried if I could reach that great resolution ... to be honest without a thought of Heaven or Hell.
Religio Medici (1643)

26 A man may be in as just possession of truth as of a city, and yet be forced to surrender.
Religio Medici (1643)

27 Many ... have too rashly charged the troops of error, and remain as trophies unto the enemies of truth.
Religio Medici (1643) **Browne, Sir Thomas** (1605–1682) English physician, author and antiquary

28 No man should break his word of honour.
The White Guard (1925) **Bulgakov, Mikhail** (1891–1940) Russian writer and dramatist

29 Make yourself an honest man and then you may be sure there is one rascal less in the world.
Attr. **Carlyle, Thomas** (1795–1881) Scottish historian, biographer, critic, and essayist

30 What I tell you three times is true.
'The Hunting of the Snark' (1876) **Carroll, Lewis** (1832–1898) English writer and photographer

31 Trouthe is the hyeste thyng that man may kepe.
The Canterbury Tales (1387) **Chaucer, Geoffrey** (c.1340–1400) English poet, public servant and courtier

32 You can only find truth with logic if you have already found truth without it.
The Man who was Orthodox **Chesterton, G.K.** (1874–1936) English writer, poet and critic

33 My experience of gentlemen's agreements is that, when it comes to the pinch, there are rarely enough bloody gentlemen about.
In Crisp, *Ben Chifley* (1960) **Chifley, Joseph Benedict** (1885–1951)

34 And diff'ring judgments serve but to declare
That truth lies somewhere, if we knew but where.
'Hope' (1782) **Cowper, William** (1731–1800) English poet, hymn writer and letter writer

35 Perjury is often bold and open. It is truth that is shamefaced – as, indeed, in many cases is no more than decent.
Scintillae Juris (1877)

36 Much truth is spoken, that more may be concealed.
Scintillae Juris (1877) **Darling, Charles** (1849–1936) English judge and Conservative politician

37 Tell all the Truth but tell it slant –
Success in Circuit lies
Too bright for our infirm Delight
The Truth's superb surprise.
'Tell all the Truth but tell it slant' (c.1868)
Dickinson, Emily (1830–1886) US poet

38 On a huge hill,
Cragged, and steep, Truth stands, and he
that will
Reach her, about must, and about must
go;
And what the hill's suddenness resists, win
so.
Satire, no. 3 (c.1594) **Donne, John** (1572–1631)
English poet

39 It is an old maxim of mine that when you
have excluded the impossible, whatever
remains, however improbable, must be the
truth.
'The Beryl Coronet' (1892) **Doyle, Sir Arthur
Conan** (1859–1930) Scottish writer and war
correspondent

40 I never saw any good that came of telling
truth.
Amphitryon (1690) **Dryden, John** (1631–1700)
English poet, satirist, dramatist and critic

41 Whenever two good people argue over
principles, both are always right.
Aphorisms (1880) **Ebner-Eschenbach, Marie
von** (1830–1916) Austrian writer

42 The truth is always libellous.
Sydney Morning Herald, (1981) **Finey, George**
(1895–1987) New Zealand cartoonist

43 I am one of the few honest people that I
have ever known.
The Great Gatsby (1926) **Fitzgerald, F. Scott**
(1896–1940) US writer

44 In an age of explanation one can always
choose varieties of truth.
Living in the Maniototo (1979) **Frame, Janet**
(1924–) New Zealand writer

45 There may always be another reality
To make fiction of the truth we think we've
arrived at.
A Yard of Sun (1970) **Fry, Christopher** (1907–
2005) English verse dramatist, theatre director
and translator

46 He who sees the truth, let him proclaim it,
without asking who is for it or who is
against it.
The Land Question (1881) **George, Henry** (1839–
1897) US economist, editor and lecturer

47 What probably distorts everything in life is
the fact that we are convinced we are
telling the truth because we are saying
what we think.
Toutes réflexions faites **Guitry, Sacha** (1885–1957)
Russian-born French actor, dramatist and
film director

48 Truth, like a torch, the more it's shook it
shines.
Discussions on Philosophy (1852) **Hamilton, Sir
William** (1788–1856) Scottish metaphysical
philosopher

49 Truth, when witty, is the wittiest of all
things.
Guesses at Truth (1827) **Hare, Augustus** (1792–
1834) English clergyman and writer

50 We have not passed that subtle line
between childhood and adulthood until we
move from the passive voice to the active
voice – that is, until we have stopped
saying 'It got lost', and say, 'I lost it'.
Attr. **Harris, Sydney J.** (1917–1986) US
journalist

51 Cynicism is an unpleasant way of saying
the truth.
The Little Foxes (1939) **Hellman, Lillian** (1907–
1984) US dramatist and screenwriter

52 In Prayer the Lips ne'er act the winning
part,
Without the sweet concurrence of the
Heart.
Noble Numbers (1647) **Herrick, Robert** (1591–
1674) English poet, royalist and clergyman

53 True and false are attributes of speech, not
of things. And where speech is not, there is
neither truth nor falsehood.
Leviathan (1651) **Hobbes, Thomas** (1588–1679)
Political philosopher

54 It is the customary fate of new truths to
begin as heresies and to end as
superstitions.
Science and Culture, and Other Essays (1881)

55 Irrationally held truths may be more harmful than reasoned errors.
Science and Culture, and Other Essays (1881) **Huxley, T.H.** (1825–1895) English biologist, Darwinist and agnostic

56 A man should never have his best trousers on when he goes out to battle for freedom and truth.
An Enemy of the People (1882) **Ibsen, Henrik** (1828–1906) Norwegian writer, dramatist and poet

57 It is always the best policy to speak the truth, unless of course you are an exceptionally good liar.
In *The Idler*, (1892) **Jerome, Jerome K.** (1859–1927) English writer and dramatist

58 Truth, Sir, is a cow which will yield such people no more milk, and so they are gone to milk the bull.
In Boswell, *The Life of Samuel Johnson* (1791) On sceptics

59 I have got no further than this: Every man has a right to utter what he thinks truth, and every other man has a right to knock him down for it. Martyrdom is the test.
In Boswell, *The Life of Samuel Johnson* (1791) **Johnson, Samuel** (1709–1784) English lexicographer, poet, critic, conversationalist and essayist

60 Honesty is praised and is left out in the cold. *(Probitas laudatur et alget)*
Satires **Juvenal** (c.60–130) Roman verse satirist and Stoic

61 I have never yet been able to perceive how any thing can be known for truth by consecutive reasoning – and yet it must be.
Letter to Benjamin Bailey, (22 November 1817) **Keats, John** (1795–1821) English poet

62 I am being frank about myself in this book. I tell of my first mistake on page 850.
The Observer, (1983) **Kissinger, Henry** (1923–) German-born US Secretary of State. On the second volume of his memoirs, *Years of Upheaval*

63 There are some circumstances in life where truth and simplicity are the best strategy in the world.
Les caractères ou les moeurs de ce siècle (1688) **La Bruyère, Jean de** (1645–1696) French satirist

64 A half truth in argument, like a half brick, carries better.
In Flesch, *The Book of Unusual Quotations* **Leacock, Stephen** (1869–1944) English-born Canadian humorist, writer and economist

65 Paradox with him was only Truth standing on its head to attract attention.
The Romantic 90s **Le Gallienne, Richard** (1866–1947) English writer and critic. Of Oscar Wilde

66 It is one thing to show a man that he is in an error, and another to put him in possession of truth.
Essay concerning Human Understanding (1690) **Locke, John** (1632–1704) English philosopher

67 New occasions teach new duties:
Time makes ancient good uncouth;
They must upward still, and onward, who would keep abreast of Truth.
'The Present Crisis' (1845) **Lowell, James Russell** (1819–1891) US poet, editor, abolitionist and diplomat

68 Honesty is a good thing but it is not profitable to its possessor unless it is kept under control.
'Archygrams' (1933) **Marquis, Don** (1878–1937) US columnist, satirist and poet

69 History teems with instances of truth put down by persecution … It is a piece of idle sentimentality that truth, merely as truth, has any inherent power denied to error, of prevailing against the dungeon and the stake.
On Liberty (1859) **Mill, John Stuart** (1806–1873) English philosopher, economist and reformer

70 Beholding the bright countenance of truth in the quiet and still air of delightfull studies.
The Reason of Church-government Urg'd against Prelaty (1642) **Milton, John** (1608–1674) English poet, libertarian and pamphleteer

71 I do not know what I may appear to the world, but to myself I seem to have been only a boy playing on the sea-shore, and diverting myself in now and then finding a smoother pebble or a prettier shell than ordinary, whilst the great ocean of truth lay all undiscovered before me.
In Brewster, *Memoirs of the Life, Writings, and Discoveries of Sir Isaac Newton* (1855) **Newton, Sir Isaac** (1642–1727) English scientist and philosopher

72 Let us begin by committing ourselves to the truth, to see it like it is and to tell it like it is, to find the truth, to speak the truth and live with the truth. That's what we'll do.
Nomination acceptance speech, (1968) **Nixon, Richard** (1913–1994) US Republican politician and President

73 For want of me the world's course will not fail:
When all its work is done, the lie shall rot;
The truth is great, and shall prevail,
When none cares whether it prevail or not.
The Unknown Eros (1877) **Patmore, Coventry** (1823–1896) English poet

74 But, my dearest Agathon, it is truth which you cannot contradict; you can easily contradict Socrates.
Symposium **Plato** (c.429–347 BC) Greek philosopher

75 A truth which is clearly understood can no longer be written with sincerity.
'Senancour c'est moi' **Proust, Marcel** (1871–1922) French writer and critic

76 Speak the truth, but leave immediately after.
From Slovenia **Proverb**

77 Your honesty is not to be based either on religion or policy. Both your religion and policy must be based on it. Your honesty must be based, as the sun is, in vacant heaven; poised, as the lights in the firmament, which have rule over the day and over the night.
Time and Tide by Weare and Tyne (1867) **Ruskin, John** (1819–1900) English art critic, philosopher and reformer

78 A truism is on that account none the less true.
A Book of Quotations (1947) **Samuel, Lord** (1870–1963) English Liberal statesman, philosopher and administrator

79 The truth is too simple, it must always be arrived at through complication.
Letter to Armand Barbès, (1867) **Sand, George** (1804–1876) French writer and dramatist

80 Truth lives on in deception.
On the Aesthetic Education of Man (1793–1795) **Schiller, Johann Christoph Friedrich** (1759–1805) German writer, dramatist, poet and historian

81 This above all – to thine own self be true,
And it must follow, as the night the day,
Thou canst not then be false to any man.
Hamlet, I.iii

82 O, while you live, tell truth, and shame the devil!
Henry IV, Part 1, III.i **Shakespeare, William** (1564–1616) English dramatist, poet and actor

83 My way of joking is to tell the truth. It's the funniest joke in the world.
John Bull's Other Island (1907)

84 All great truths begin as blasphemies.
Annajanska (1919) **Shaw, George Bernard** (1856–1950) Irish socialist, writer, dramatist and critic

85 It is the calling of great men, not so much to preach new truths, as to rescue from oblivion those old truths which it is our wisdom to remember and our weakness to forget.
Attr. **Smith, Sydney** (1771–1845) English clergyman, essayist, journalist and wit

86 A clear, attentive mind
Has no meaning but that
Which sees is truly seen.
Riprap (1959) **Snyder, Gary** (1930–) US mystical poet

87 If decade after decade the truth cannot be told, each person's mind starts to roam irretrievably. One's fellow countrymen become harder to understand than Martians.
Cancer Ward (1968)

88 When truth is discovered by someone else, it loses something of its attractiveness.
Candle in the Wind **Solzhenitsyn, Alexander** (1918–) Russian writer, dramatist and historian

89 It takes two to speak the truth, – one to speak, and another to hear.
A Week on the Concord and Merrimack Rivers (1849) **Thoreau, Henry David** (1817–1862) US essayist, social critic and writer

90 Matters of fact, which as Mr Budgell somewhere observes, are very stubborn things.
The Will of Matthew Tindal (1733) **Tindal, Matthew** (1657–1733) English deist and writer

91 There was things which he stretched, but mainly he told the truth.
The Adventures of Huckleberry Finn (1884)

92 When in doubt, tell the truth.
Pudd'nhead Wilson's New Calendar **Twain, Mark** (1835–1910) US humorist, writer, journalist and lecturer

93 I am very fond of truth, but not at all of martyrdom.
Letter to d'Alembert, (1776)

94 We owe respect to the living; to the dead we owe only truth.
Oeuvres, 'Premiere lettre sur Oedipe' **Voltaire** (1694–1778) French philosopher, dramatist, poet, historian, writer and critic

95 Honesty is the best policy, but he who is governed by that maxim is not an honest man.
Apophthegms (1854) **Whately, Richard** (1787–1863) English philosopher, theologian, educationist and writer

96 There are no whole truths; all truths are half-truths. It is trying to treat them as whole truths that plays the devil.
Dialogues (1954) **Whitehead, A.N.** (1861–1947) English mathematician and philosopher

97 If one tells the truth, one is sure, sooner or later, to be found out.
The Chameleon, (1894)

98 The truth is rarely pure and never simple. Modern life would be very tedious if it were either, and modern literature a complete impossibility!
The Importance of Being Earnest (1895)

99 A thing is not necessarily true because a man dies for it.
Sebastian Melmoth (1904) **Wilde, Oscar** (1854–1900) Irish poet, dramatist, writer, critic and wit

100 Words cannot be relied on to bury the truth. Even when the winners have rewritten history, where a language and civilization have been destroyed – the buried truth finds its way in from the margins.
The Observer, (2000) **Williams, Rowan** (1950–) Archbishop of Canterbury

101 If you do not tell the truth about yourself you cannot tell it about other people.
The Moment and Other Essays **Woolf, Virginia** (1882–1941) English writer and critic

102 The truth is more important than the facts.
In Simcox, *Treasury of Quotations on Christian Themes* **Wright, Frank Lloyd** (1869–1959) US architect and writer

103 I believe that in the end the truth will conquer.
In J.R. Green, *Short History of the English People* **Wycliffe, John** (c.1329–1384) English religious reformer. To the Duke of Lancaster, 1381

104 And of course the clear and certain truth no man has seen.
In J.H. Lesher, *Xenophanes of Colophon* (1992) **Xenophanes** (c.570–480 BC) Greek philosopher and historian

105 Truth is truth, and the truth will overcome the left, the right and the centre.
Interview in *Newsweek*, (1994) **Yeltsin, Boris** (1931–) Russian statesman and President

106 Truth is on the move and nothing can stop it.
In *La Vérité en marche* (1901) **Zola, Emile** (1840–1902) French writer. Article on the Dreyfus affair
See also deception; lies; realism

UNIVERSE

1 You may think it's a long way down the road to the chemist, but that's just peanuts to space.
The Hitch Hiker's Guide to the Galaxy (1979)

2 In the beginning the Universe was created. This has made a lot of people very angry and has been widely regarded as a bad move.
The Restaurant at the End of the Universe (1980) **Adams, Douglas** (1952–2001) English humorous writer and scriptwriter

3 The spacious firmament on high,
With all the blue ethereal sky,
And spangled heavens, a shining frame,
Their great Original proclaim.
The Spectator, (1712) **Addison, Joseph** (1672–1719) English essayist, poet, playwright and statesman

4 If the Lord Almighty had consulted me before embarking upon Creation, I should have recommended something simpler.
Attr. **Alfonso X** (1221–1284) Spanish monarch. On the Ptolemaic system of astronomy

5 That's one small step for a man, one giant leap for mankind.
New York Times, (1969) **Armstrong, Neil** (1930–) US astronaut and first man on the moon. On stepping on to the moon

6 The heavens declare the glory of God; and the firmament sheweth his handywork.
Psalms, 19:1 **The Bible (King James Version)**

7 Where star-cold and the dread of space in icy silence bind the main
I feel but vastness on my face
I sit, a mere incurious brain,
under some outcast satellite.
Poems (1914) **Brennan, Christopher** (1870–1932) Australian poet

8 Ye stars! which are the poetry of heaven!
Childe Harold's Pilgrimage (1812–18) **Byron, Lord** (1788–1824) English poet, satirist and traveller

9 The sentinel stars set their watch in the sky.

'The Soldier's Dream' **Campbell, Thomas** (1777–1844) Scottish poet, ballad writer and journalist

10 It is a mathematical fact that the casting of this pebble from my hand alters the centre of gravity of the Universe.
Sartor Resartus (1834)

11 I don't pretend to understand the Universe – it's a great deal bigger than I am ... People ought to be modester.
In D.A. Wilson and D. Wilson MacArthur, *Carlyle in Old Age* (1934) To William Allingham **Carlyle, Thomas** (1795–1881) Scottish historian, biographer, critic, and essayist

12 The cosmos is about the smallest hole that a man can hide his head in.
Orthodoxy (1908) **Chesterton, G.K.** (1874–1936) English writer, poet and critic

13 I am very interested in the universe – I am specializing in the universe and all that surrounds it.
Beyond the Fringe, (1962) **Cook, Peter** (1937–1995) English comedian and writer

14 Anyone informed that the universe is expanding and contracting in pulsations of eighty billion years has a right to ask, 'What's in it for me?'
The Glory of the Hummingbird (1974) **De Vries, Peter** (1910–1993) US novelist

15 They cannot scare me with their empty spaces
Between stars – on stars where no human race is.
I have it in me so much nearer home
To scare myself with my own desert places.
'Desert Places' (1936) **Frost, Robert** (1874–1963) US poet

16 This grand book, the universe, is written in the language of mathematics.
Quoted by Melvyn Bragg, *BBC radio,* (1999) **Galilei, Galileo** (1564–1642) Italian scientist

17 My own suspicion is that the universe is not only queerer than we suppose, but queerer than we can suppose.
Possible Worlds and Other Essays (1927) **Haldane, J.B.S.** (1892–1964) British biochemist, geneticist and popularizer of science

18 The sovereign brilliancy of Sirius pierced the eye with a steely glitter, the star called Capella was yellow, Aldebaran and Betelgueux shone with a fiery red. To persons standing alone on a hill during a clear midnight such as this, the roll of the world eastward is almost a palpable movement.
Far from the Madding Crowd (1874) **Hardy, Thomas** (1840–1928) English writer and poet

19 If we find the answer to that, it would be the ultimate triumph of human reason – for then we would know the mind of God.
A Brief History of Time (1988) **Hawking, Stephen** (1942–) English theoretical physicist. On the reason for the existence of the universe

20 This universe is not hostile, nor yet is it friendly. It is simply indifferent.
A Sensible Man's View of Religion (1932) **Holmes, Rev. John H.** (1879–1964) US Unitarian minister

21 Look at the stars! look, look up at the skies! Oh look at all the fire-folk sitting in the air! The bright boroughs, the circle-citadels there!
'The Starlight Night' (1877) **Hopkins, Gerard Manley** (1844–1889) English Jesuit priest, poet and classicist

22 The heaventree of stars hung with humid nightblue fruit.
Ulysses (1922) **Joyce, James** (1882–1941) Irish writer

23 I often looked up at the sky an' assed meself the question – what is the stars, what is the stars?
Juno and the Paycock (1924) **O'Casey, Sean** (1880–1964) Irish dramatist

24 Look how the floor of heaven
Is thick inlaid with patines of bright gold;
There's not the smallest orb which thou behold'st
But in his motion like an angel sings,
Still quiring to the young-ey'd cherubins.
The Merchant of Venice, V.i **Shakespeare, William** (1564–1616) English dramatist, poet and actor

25 With how sad steps O Moone thou clim'st the skyes,
How silently, and with how meane a face,
What may it be, that even in heavenly place,
That busie Archer his sharpe Arrowes tryes?
Astrophel and Stella (1591) **Sidney, Sir Philip** (1554–1586) English poet, critic, soldier, courtier and diplomat

26 And when the rising sun has first breathed on us with his panting horses, over there the glowing evening-star is lighting his late lamps.
Georgics **Virgil** (70–19 BC) Roman poet

27 But moon nor star-untidy sky
Could catch my eye as that star's eye;
For still I looked on that same star,
That fitful, fiery Lucifer,
Watching with mind as quiet as moss
Its light nailed to a burning cross.
'The Evening Star' (1922) **Young, Andrew John** (1885–1971) Scottish poet, churchman and botanist
See also night; science

VIRTUE

1 It's too bad I'm not as wonderful a person as people say I am, because the world could use a few people like that.
Attr. **Alda, Alan** (1936–) US actor

2 Moral virtues we acquire through practice like the arts.
Nicomachean Ethics

3 Moral virtue is the child of habit.
Nicomachean Ethics **Aristotle** (384–322 BC) Greek philosopher

4 Virtue is like a rich stone, best plain set.
'Of Beauty' (1625)

5 Prosperity doth best discover vice, but adversity doth best discover virtue.
Essays (1625), 'Of Adversity' **Bacon, Francis** (1561–1626) English philosopher, essayist, politician and courtier

6 Nothing is more unpleasant than a virtuous person with a mean mind.

Literary Studies (1879) **Bagehot, Walter** (1826–1877) English economist and political philosopher

7 Thou shalt love thy neighbour as thyself.
Leviticus, 19:18

8 Who can find a virtuous woman? for her price is far above rubies.
Proverbs, 31:10

9 Whatsoever things are true, whatsoever things are honest, whatsoever things are just, whatsoever things are pure, whatsoever things are lovely, whatsoever things are of good report; if there be any virtue, and if there be any praise, think on these things.
Philippians, 4:8 **The Bible (King James Version)**

10 To Mercy, Pity, Peace and Love
All pray in their distress,
And to these virtues of delight
Return their thankfulness.
Songs of Innocence (1789) **Blake, William** (1757–1827) English poet, engraver, painter and mystic

11 Whenever there are such great virtues, it's proof that something's fishy.
Mother Courage and her Children (1941) **Brecht, Bertolt** (1898–1956) German dramatist

12 There is no road or ready way to virtue.
Religio Medici (1643) **Browne, Sir Thomas** (1605–1682) English physician, author and antiquary

13 Virtue and vice are like life and death, or mind and matter: things which cannot exist without being qualified by their opposite.
The Way of All Flesh (1903) **Butler, Samuel** (1835–1902) English writer, painter, philosopher and scholar

14 My virtue's still far too small, I don't trot it out and about yet.
Claudine at School (1900) **Colette** (1873–1954) French writer

15 Virtue is not left to stand alone. He who practises it will have neighbours.
Analects

16 To be able to practise five things everywhere under heaven constitutes perfect virtue ... gravity, generosity of soul, sincerity, earnestness, and kindness.
Analects

17 Fine words and an insinuating appearance are seldom associated with true virtue.
Analects **Confucius** (c.550–c.478 BC) Chinese philosopher and teacher of ethics

18 For 'tis some virtue, virtue to commend.
'To Sir Godfrey Kneller' **Congreve, William** (1670–1729) English dramatist

19 Repentance is the virtue of weak minds.
The Indian Emperor (1665) **Dryden, John** (1631–1700) English poet, satirist, dramatist and critic

20 'Tis virtue, and not birth that makes us noble:
Great actions speak great minds, and such should govern.
The Prophetess (1647) **Fletcher, John** (1579–1625) English dramatist

21 The virtue which requires to be ever guarded, is scarce worth the sentinel.
The Vicar of Wakefield (1766) **Goldsmith, Oliver** (c.1728–1774) Irish dramatist, poet and writer

22 Innocence always calls mutely for protection, when we would be so much wiser to guard ourselves against it: innocence is like a dumb leper who has lost his bell, wandering the world meaning no harm.
The Quiet American (1955) **Greene, Graham** (1904–1991) English writer and dramatist

23 Purity is the feminine, Truth the masculine, of Honour.
Guesses at Truth (1827) **Hare, Augustus** (1792–1834) English clergyman and writer

24 The greatest offence against virtue is to speak ill of it.
London Weekly Review, (1828) **Hazlitt, William** (1778–1830) English writer and critic

25 Onely a sweet and vertuous soul,
Like season'd timber, never gives;
But though the whole world turn to coal,
Then chiefly lives.
The Temple (1633) **Herbert, George** (1593–1633) English poet and priest

26 Particulars, as everyone knows, make for virtue and happiness. Generalities are intellectually necessary evils.
Brave New World (1932) **Huxley, Aldous** (1894–1963) English writer, poet and critic

27 The one and only true nobility is virtue.
Satires **Juvenal** (c.60–130) Roman verse satirist and Stoic

28 To be discontented with the divine discontent, and to be ashamed with the noble shame, is the very germ and first upgrowth of all virtue.
Health and Education (1874) **Kingsley, Charles** (1819–1875) English writer, poet, lecturer and clergyman

29 Greater virtues are needed to sustain good fortune than bad.
Maximes (1678)

30 Hypocrisy is a homage that vice pays to virtue.
Maximes (1678) **La Rochefoucauld** (1613–1680) French writer

31 Virtue is the fount whence honour springs.
Tamburlaine the Great (1590) **Marlowe, Christopher** (1564–1593) English poet and dramatist

32 Patience, the beggar's virtue.
A New Way to Pay Old Debts (1633) **Massinger, Philip** (1583–1640) English dramatist and poet

33 Most men admire
Vertue, who follow not her lore.
Paradise Regained (1671) **Milton, John** (1608–1674) English poet, libertarian and pamphleteer

34 Virtue, in this world, should be accommodating.
Le Misanthrope (1666) **Molière** (1622–1673) French dramatist, actor and director

35 Virtue shuns ease as a companion. It needs a rough and thorny path.
Essais (1580) **Montaigne, Michel de** (1533–1592) French essayist and moralist

36 Let them see virtue and pine away for having lost it.
Satires **Persius Flaccus, Aulus** (AD 34–62) Roman satirical poet

37 Good-humour can prevail,
When airs, and flights, and screams, and scolding fail.
Beauties in vain their pretty eyes may roll;
Charms strike the sight, but merit wins the soul.
The Rape of the Lock (1714)

38 When men grow virtuous in their old age, they only make a sacrifice to God of the devil's leavings.
Miscellanies (1727) **Pope, Alexander** (1688–1744) English poet, translator and editor

39 My innocence is at last becoming a burden to me.
Andromaque (1667) **Racine, Jean** (1639–1699) French tragedian and poet

40 There's no room in my life for drugs, fights, divorce, adultery, sadism, unnecessary fuss and sex.
Daily Mail, (1996) **Richard, Cliff** (1940–) English singer

41 No one gossips about other people's secret virtues.
On Education, especially in early childhood (1926)

42 … the nuns who never take a bath without wearing a bathrobe all the time. When asked why, since no man can see them, the reply 'Oh, but you forget the good God.'
The Basic Writings of Bertrand Russell (1961) **Russell, Bertrand** (1872–1970) English philosopher, mathematician, essayist and social reformer

43 Tolerance is the virtue of the weak.
La nouvelle Justine (1797) **Sade, Marquis de** (1740–1814) French soldier and writer

44 Chaste as the icicle
That's curdied by the frost from purest snow,
And hangs on Dian's temple.
Coriolanus, V.iii

45 Assume a virtue, if you have it not.
That monster custom, who all sense doth eat,
Of habits devil, is angel yet in this.
Hamlet, III.iv

46 Though patience be a tired mare, yet she will plod.
Henry V, II.i

47 Men's evil manners live in brass: their
virtues
We write in water.
Henry VIII, IV.ii

48 Virtue is bold, and goodness never fearful.
Measure For Measure, III.i

49 They say best men are moulded out of
faults;
And, for the most, become much more the
better
For being a little bad.
Measure For Measure, V.i

50 Virtue? A fig!
'Tis in ourselves that we are thus or thus.
Our bodies are our gardens to the which
our wills are gardeners.
Othello, I.iii

51 How poor are they that have not patience!
What wound did ever heal but by degrees?
Othello, II.iii

52 Good name in man and woman, dear my
lord,
Is the immediate jewel of their souls:
Who steals my purse steals trash; 'tis
something, nothing;
'Twas mine, 'tis his, and has been slave to
thousands;
But he that filches from me my good name
Robs me of that which not enriches him
And makes me poor indeed.
Othello, III.iii

53 The purest treasure mortal times afford
Is spotless reputation; that away,
Men are but gilded loam or painted clay.
A jewel in a ten-times barr'd-up chest
Is a bold spirit in a loyal breast.
Mine honour is my life; both grow in one;
Take honour from me, and my life is done.
Richard II, I.i

54 Dost thou think, because thou art virtuous,
there shall be no more cakes and ale?
Twelfth Night, II.iii **Shakespeare, William**
(1564–1616) English dramatist, poet and actor

55 Self-denial is not a virtue: it is only the
effect of prudence on rascality.
Man and Superman (1903)

56 What is virtue but the Trade Unionism of
the married?
Man and Superman (1903) **Shaw, George
Bernard** (1856–1950) Irish socialist, writer,
dramatist and critic

57 Woman's virtue is man's greatest
invention.
Attr. **Skinner, Cornelia Otis** (1901–1979) US
actress

58 The world continues to offer glittering
prizes to those who have stout hearts and
sharp swords.
Rectorial Address, Glasgow University, (1923)
Smith, F.E. (1872–1930) English politician and
Lord Chancellor

59 The noble hart, that harbours vertuous
thought,
And is with child of glorious great intent,
Can never rest, untill it forth have brought
Th' eternall brood of glorie excellent.
The Faerie Queene (1596) **Spenser, Edmund**
(c.1522–1599) English poet

60 Will Honeycomb calls these over-offended
Ladies the outrageously virtuous.
The Spectator, 266, (1712) **Steele, Sir Richard**
(1672–1729) Irish-born English writer,
dramatist and politician

61 Vice and virtues are products like sulphuric
acid and sugar.
History of English Literature, (1863) **Taine,
Hippolyte Adolphe** (1828–1893) French writer
and philosopher

62 From yon blue heavens above us bent
The gardener Adam and his wife
Smile at the claims of long descent.
Howe'er it be, it seems to me,
'Tis only noble to be good.
Kind hearts are more than coronets,
And simple faith than Norman blood.
'Lady Clara Vere de Vere' (c.1835) **Tennyson,
Alfred, Lord** (1809–1892) English lyric poet

63 Not only humble but umble, which I look
upon to be the comparative, or, indeed,
superlative degree.
Doctor Thorne (1858) **Trollope, Anthony** (1815–
1882) English writer, traveller and post office
official

64 *Belinda*: Ay, but you know we must return good for evil.
Lady Brute: That may be a mistake in the translation.
The Provok'd Wife (1697) **Vanbrugh, Sir John** (1664–1726) English dramatist and baroque architect

65 It is amusing that the vice of chastity is made into a virtue; and it's an odd sort of chastity at that, which leads men straight to the sin of Onan, and girls to the fading of their colours.
Letter to M. Mariott, (1766) **Voltaire** (1694–1778) French philosopher, dramatist, poet, historian, writer and critic

66 Virtue knows to a farthing what it has lost by not having been vice.
In Kronenberger, *The Extraordinary Mr. Wilkes* (1974)

67 Tell me, ye divines, which is the most virtuous man, he who begets twenty bastards, or he who sacrifices an hundred thousand lives?
Letter to Sir Horace Mann, (1778) **Walpole, Horace** (1717–1797) English writer and politician

68 Good company and good discourse are the very sinews of virtue.
The Compleat Angler (1653) **Walton, Izaak** (1593–1683) English writer

69 Few men have virtue to withstand the highest bidder.
Moral Maxims **Washington, George** (1732–1799) US general, statesman and President

70 I used to be Snow White – but I drifted.
In J. Weintraub (ed.), *The Wit and Wisdom of Mae West* (1967) **West, Mae** (1892–1980) US actress and scriptwriter

71 Virtue is … frequently in the nature of an iceberg, the other parts of it submerged.
The Tree of Man (1955) **White, Patrick** (1912–1990) English-born Australian writer and dramatist

72 No woman is virtuous
who does not give herself to her lover
– forthwith.
Paterson (1946–1958) **Williams, William Carlos** (1883–1963) US poet, writer and paediatrician

73 Virtue is the roughest way,
But proves at night a bed of down.
'Upon the Imprisonment of the Earl of Essex' **Wotton, Sir Henry** (1568–1639) English diplomat, traveller and poet

74 Too long a sacrifice
Can make a stone of the heart.
'Easter, 1916' (1916) **Yeats, W.B.** (1865–1939) Irish poet, dramatist, editor, writer and senator
See also evil; goodness; morality

WAR

1 It is worse than immoral, it's a mistake.
Quoted on Alistair Cooke's radio programme *Letter from America* **Acheson, Dean** (1893–1971) US Democrat politician. Of the Vietnam war

2 It would be superfluous in me to point out to your lordship that this is war.
Dispatch to Earl Russell, (September 1863) **Adams, Charles Francis** (1807–1886) US politician

3 O God, if there be a God, save my soul, if I have a soul!
Prayer of a common soldier before the Battle of Blenheim **Anonymous**

4 Give them the cold steel, boys!
Attr. **Armistead, Lewis** (1817–1863) US general. Spoken at Gettysburg, 1863

5 But now in blood and battles was my youth,
And full of blood and battles is my age;
And I shall never end this life of blood.
'Sohrab and Rustum' (1853) **Arnold, Matthew** (1822–1888) English poet, critic, essayist and educationist

6 O Lord! thou knowest how busy I must be this day; if I forget thee, do not thou forget me.
Prayer before the Battle of Edgehill, (1642) **Astley, Sir Jacob** (1579–1652) English soldier and Royalist

7 We shall never sheath the sword which we have not lightly drawn until Belgium recovers in full measure all and more than she has sacrificed, until France is adequately secured against the menace of aggression, until the rights of the smaller nationalities of Europe are placed upon an unassailable foundation, and until the military domination of Prussia is wholly and finally destroyed.
Speech, (1914) **Asquith, Herbert** (1852–1928) English Liberal statesman and Prime Minister

8 O what is that sound which so thrills the ear
Down in the valley drumming, drumming?
Only the scarlet soldiers, dear,
The soldiers coming.
Collected Poems, (1933–1938) **Auden, W.H.** (1907–1973) English poet, essayist, critic, teacher and dramatist

9 How horrible it is to have so many people killed! – And what a blessing that one cares for none of them!
Letter to Cassandra Austen, (1811) **Austen, Jane** (1775–1817) English writer. Of the Battle of Albuera in 1811

10 It is better for aged diplomats to be bored than for young men to die.
Attr. **Austin, Warren Robinson** (1877–1962) First US ambassador to the UN. On being asked if he found long debates at the UN tiring

11 The desire for destruction is, at the same time, a creative desire.
In *Jahrbuch für Wissenschaft und Kunst,* (1842) **Bakunin, Mikhail** (1814–1876) Russian anarchist and writer

12 I think it is well also for the man in the street to realise that there is no power on earth that can protect him from being bombed. Whatever people may tell him, the bomber will always get through. The only defence is in offence, which means that you have to kill more women and children more quickly than the enemy if you want to save yourselves.
Speech, (1932) **Baldwin, Stanley** (1867–1947) English Conservative statesman and Prime Minister

13 All quiet along the Potomac to-night,
No sound save the rush of the river,
While soft falls the dew on the face of the dead –
The picket's off duty forever.
In *Harper's Magazine,* (1861), 'The Picket Guard' **Beers, Ethel Lynn** (1827–1879) US poet

14 Whatever happens, we have got
The Maxim Gun, and they have not.
Modern Traveller (1898) **Belloc, Hilaire** (1870–1953) English writer of verse, essayist and critic; Liberal MP

15 I have never understood this liking for war. It panders to instincts already catered for within the scope of any respectable domestic establishment.
Forty Years On (1969) **Bennett, Alan** (1934–) English dramatist, actor and diarist

16 Just for a word – 'neutrality', a word which in wartime has so often been disregarded, just for a scrap of paper – Great Britain is going to make war.
Letter, (1914) **Bethmann Hollweg, Theobald von** (1856–1921) German statesman

17 1. The position will be held, and the section will remain here until relieved.
2. The enemy cannot be allowed to interfere with the programme.
3. If the section cannot remain here alive, it will remain here dead, but in any case it will remain here.
4. Should any man, through shell shock or other cause, attempt to surrender, he will remain here dead.
5. Should all guns be blown out, the section will use Mills grenades, and other novelties.
6. Finally, the position, as stated, will be held.
An order issued by Bethune to his machine gun section in France, (13 March 1918) **Bethune, Frank Pogson** (1877–1942)

18 Gracious Lord, oh bomb the Germans.
Spare their women for Thy Sake,
And if that is not too easy
We will pardon Thy Mistake.
But, gracious Lord, whate'er shall be,
Don't let anyone bomb me.
Old Lights for New Chancels (1940) **Betjeman, Sir John** (1906–1984) English poet laureate

19 All they that take the sword shall perish with the sword.
Matthew, 26:52 **The Bible (King James Version)**

20 They shall grow not old, as we that are left grow old:
Age shall not weary them, nor the years condemn.
At the going down of the sun and in the morning
We will remember them.
'For the Fallen' (1914) **Binyon, Laurence** (1869–1943) English poet, art historian and critic

21 Put your trust in God, my boys, and keep your powder dry.
Oliver's Advice (1856) **Blacker, Valentine** (1778–1823) English lieutenant-colonel

22 The Falklands thing was a fight between two bald men over a comb.
Time, (1983) **Borges, Jorge Luis** (1899–1986) Argentinian writer, poet and librarian. On the Falklands War of 1982

23 It is magnificent, but it is not war. (*C'est magnifique mais ce n'est pas la guerre*)
Attr. **Bosquet, Pierre François Joseph** (1810–1861) French general. Remark on witnessing the Charge of the Light Brigade, 1854

24 The way to win an atomic war is to make certain it never starts.
The Observer, (1952)

25 The wrong war, at the wrong place, at the wrong time, and with the wrong enemy.
Senate inquiry, (1951) On General MacArthur's proposal to carry the Korean war into China **Bradley, Omar** (1893–1981) US general

26 War always finds a solution.
Mother Courage and her Children (1941)

27 There'll perhaps never be a perfect war where you could say that there was nothing wrong with it.
Mother Courage and her Children (1941)

28 It's too long since there's been a war here.
Mother Courage and her Children (1941) **Brecht, Bertolt** (1898–1956) German dramatist

29 The angel of death has been abroad throughout the land; you may almost hear the beating of his wings.
Speech, (1855) Referring to the Crimean War

30 My opinion is that the Northern States will manage somehow to muddle through.
Comment on the American Civil War **Bright, John** (1811–1889) English Liberal politician and social reformer

31 Now, God be thanked Who has matched us with His hour,
And caught our youth, and wakened us from sleeping …
Leave the sick hearts that honour could not move,
And half-men, and their dirty songs and dreary,
And all the little emptiness of love …
Naught broken save this body, lost but breath;
Nothing to shake the laughing heart's long peace there
But only agony, and that has ending;
And the worst friend and enemy is but Death.
'Peace' (1914)

32 Blow out, you bugles, over the rich Dead!
There's none of these so lonely and poor of old,
But, dying, has made us rarer gifts than gold.
These laid the world away; poured out the red
Sweet wine of youth, gave up the years to be
Of work and joy, and that unhoped serene,
That men call age; and those who would have been,
Their sons, they gave, their immortality.
'The Dead' (1914) **Brooke, Rupert** (1887–1915) English poet

33 The combat deepens. On, ye brave,
Who rush to glory, or the grave!
'Hohenlinden' **Campbell, Thomas** (1777–1844) Scottish poet, ballad writer and journalist

34 There they are cutting each other's throats, because one half of them prefer hiring their servants for life, and the other by the hour.
Attr. **Carlyle, Thomas** (1795–1881) Scottish historian, biographer, critic, and essayist. Referring to the American Civil War

35 How horrible, fantastic, incredible, it is that we should be digging trenches and trying on gas-masks here because of a quarrel in a far-away country between people of whom we know nothing.
Speech, (1938) On the annexation by Germany of the Sudetenland

36 In war, whichever side may call itself the victor, there are no winners, but all are losers.
Speech, Kettering, (1938)

37 We have resolved to finish it. It is the evil things we shall be fighting against – brute force, bad faith, injustice, oppression and persecution and against them I am certain that the right will prevail.
Radio broadcast, (3 September 1939)

38 This morning the British Ambassador in Berlin handed the German Government a final note, stating that, unless the British Government heard from them by eleven o'clock that they were prepared at once to withdraw their troops from Poland, a state of war would exist between us. I have to tell you now that no such undertaking has been received, and that consequently this country is at war with Germany.
Radio broadcast, (3 September 1939)
Chamberlain, Neville (1869–1940) English Conservative Prime Minister

39 One is left with the horrible feeling now that war settles nothing; that to win a war is as disastrous as to lose one!
An Autobiography (1977) **Christie, Agatha** (1890–1976) English crime writer and playwright

40 Those who can win a war well can rarely make a good peace and those who could make a good peace would never have won the war.
My Early Life (1930)

41 Never in the field of human conflict was so much owed by so many to so few.
Speech, (1940) On RAF pilots in the Battle of Britain

42 The battle of Britain is about to begin.
Speech, (July 1940)

43 Let us therefore brace ourselves to our duties, and so bear ourselves that, if the British Empire and its Commonwealth last for a thousand years, men will still say, 'This was their finest hour'.
Speech, (June 1940)

44 We shall not flag or fail. We shall go on to the end. We shall fight in France, we shall fight on the seas and oceans, we shall fight with growing confidence and growing strength in the air, we shall defend our island, whatever the cost may be, we shall fight on the beaches, we shall fight on the landing grounds, we shall fight in the fields and in the streets, we shall fight in the hills; we shall never surrender.
Speech, (June 1940)

45 This is not the end. It is not even the beginning of the end. But it is, perhaps, the end of the beginning.
Speech, Mansion House, (November 1942) On the Battle of Egypt

46 In war, resolution; in defeat, defiance; in victory, magnanimity; in peace, goodwill.
The Gathering Storm (1948)

47 Before Alamein we never had a victory. After Alamein we never had a defeat.
The Second World War (1948–1954)

48 When you have to kill a man it costs nothing to be polite.
The Second World War (1948–1954) On the ceremonial form of the declaration of war against Japan, 8 December 1941

49 Wars are not won by evacuations.
The Second World War (1948–1954) Referring to Dunkirk

50 No one can guarantee success in war, but only deserve it.
The Second World War (1948–1954)

51 Peace with Germany and Japan on our terms will not bring much rest ... As I observed last time, when the war of the giants is over the wars of the pygmies will begin.
The Second World War (1948–1954)

52 To jaw-jaw is better than to war-war.

Speech, Washington, (1954) **Churchill, Sir Winston** (1874–1965) English Conservative Prime Minister

53 The sinews of war, unlimited money.
Philippic

54 Laws are silent in war.
Pro Milone **Cicero** (106–43 BC) Roman orator, statesman, essayist and letter writer

55 The Americans have a proud and noble tradition of being utterly hopeless in warfare. They lost in Vietnam, they lost in Somalia, they lost in the Bay of Pigs, and though they won the Gulf war they managed to kill more British soldiers than the Iraqis.
The Sunday Times, (1999) **Clarkson, Jeremy** (1960–) English motoring journalist

56 War is nothing but a continuation of politics by other means.
On War (1834) **Clausewitz, Karl von** (1780–1831) German general and military philosopher

57 *Fawlty*: Is there something wrong?
Guest: Will you stop talking about the war.
Fawlty: Me? You started it.
Guest: We did not start it.
Fawlty: Yes you did – you invaded Poland.
Fawlty Towers (BBC TV, 1975) **Cleese, John** (1939–) British comedian, actor and writer. Addressing a German guest in the dining room

58 My home policy? I wage war. My foreign policy? I wage war. Always, everywhere, I wage war!
Speech to the Chamber of Deputies, (8 March 1918)

59 It is easier to make war than to make peace.
Speech, (1919)

60 We have won the war: now we have to win the peace, and it may be more difficult.
In D.R. Watson, *Georges Clemenceau: a Political Biography* (1974) To General Mordacq, 11 November 1918 **Clemenceau, Georges** (1841–1929) French Prime Minister and journalist

61 How long ago Hector took off his plume,
Not wanting that his little son should cry,
Then kissed his sad Andromache goodbye –
And now we three in Euston waiting-room.
'Parting in Wartime' (1948) **Cornford, Frances Crofts** (1886–1960) English poet and translator

62 War lays a burden on the reeling state,
And peace does nothing to relieve the weight.
'Expostulation' (1782)

63 To combat may be glorious, and success
Perhaps may crown us; but to fly is safe.
The Task (1785) **Cowper, William** (1731–1800) English poet, hymn writer and letter writer

64 A man-of-war is the best ambassador.
Attr. **Cromwell, Oliver** (1599–1658) English general, statesman and Puritan leader

65 There are no atheists in the foxholes.
In Romulo, *I Saw the Fall of the Philippines* (1943) **Cummings, William Thomas** (1903–1945) US priest

66 Come on, you sons of bitches! Do you want to live for ever?
Attr. **Daly, Dan** (1874–1937) Remark during Allied resistance at Belleau Wood, 1918

67 For I must go where lazy Peace
Will hide her drowsy head;
And, for the sport of Kings, increase
The number of the Dead.
'The Soldier Going to the Field' (1673) **D'Avenant, Sir William** (1606–1668)

68 All day, day after day, they're bringing them home,
they're picking them up, those they can find, and bringing them home,
they're bringing them in, piled on the hulls of Grants, in trucks, in convoys,
they're zipping them up in green plastic bags,
they're tagging them now in Saigon, in the mortuary coolness,
they're giving them names, they're rolling them out of
the deep-freeze lockers – on the tarmac at Tan Son Nhut
the noble jets are whining like hounds,
they are bringing them home …

telegrams tremble like leaves from a
wintering tree
and the spider grief swings in his bitter
geometry
– they're bringing them home, now, too
late, too early.
'Homecoming' (1971) **Dawe, (Donald) Bruce**
(1930–) Australian poet

69 War is the most exciting and dramatic
thing in life. In fighting to the death you
feel terribly relaxed when you manage to
come through.
The Observer, (1972) **Dayan, Moshe** (1915–81)
Israeli general and politician

70 All delays are dangerous in war.
Tyrannic Love (1669)

71 War is the trade of kings.
King Arthur (1691) **Dryden, John** (1631–1700)
English poet, satirist, dramatist and critic

72 'I see,' he said with emphasis, 'the faces of
the little children who have lost a father, as
they walk behind the coffin with roses in
their hands. I see the faces of good,
honest, decent people who have never
done wrong to anyone else, who have lost
a loved one, blown to bits by a terrorist
bomb. And of course I weep.'
The Observer, (1992) **Eames, Dr Robin** (1940–)
Referring to the Enniskillen bombing, 8
November 1987

73 We are not at war with Egypt. We are in
armed conflict.
Speech, (1956) **Eden, Anthony** (1897–1977)
English Conservative Prime Minister

74 I'm glad we've been bombed. It makes me
feel I can look the East End in the face.
Attr. **Elizabeth, the Queen Mother** (1900–
2002) Queen of the United Kingdom and
mother of Elizabeth II. After Buckingham
Palace was bombed during the Blitz in 1940

75 In many a war it has been the vanquished,
not the victor, who has carried off the
finest spoils.
The Soul of Spain (1908) **Ellis, Havelock** (1859–
1939) English sexologist and essayist

76 War is sweet to those who do not fight.
Adagia (1500) **Erasmus** (c.1466–1536) Dutch
scholar and humanist

77 I gave my life for freedom – This I know:
For those who bade me fight had told me
so.
Five Souls and Other Verses (1917) **Ewer, William
Norman** (1885–1976) English journalist

78 My centre is giving way, my right is
retreating; situation excellent. I shall attack.
Attr. **Foch, Ferdinand** (1851–1929) French
marshal. Dispatch during the Battle of the
Marne, 1914

79 I will go to my grave regretting the
photograph of me on an anti-aircraft gun,
which looks like I was trying to shoot at
American planes. It galvanised hostility.
The Sunday Times, (2000) **Fonda, Jane** (1937–)
US actress and political activist. On her visit
to Hanoi in support of the Viet Cong during
the Vietnam War

80 I detest war: it ruins conversation.
In Auden, *A Certain World* (1970) **Fontenelle,
Bernard** (1657–1757) French librettist,
philosopher and man of letters

81 Praise the Lord and pass the ammunition.
Attr. **Forgy, Howell** (1908–1983) US navy
chaplain. Remark at Pearl Harbour, 1941

82 There never was a good war, or a bad
peace.
Letter to Josiah Quincy, (1783) **Franklin,
Benjamin** (1706–1790) US statesman, scientist,
political critic and printer

83 Madam, I am the civilization they are
fighting to defend.
In Balsdon, *Oxford Now and Then* (1970)
Garrod, Heathcote William (1878–1960)
English scholar, academic and essayist. In
response to criticism that, during the First
World War, he was not fighting to defend
civilization

84 Mad, is he? Then I hope he will *bite* some
of my other generals.
In Wilson, *The Life and Letters of James Wolfe*
(1909) **George II** (1683–1760) King of Great
Britain and Ireland. Reply to the Duke of
Newcastle who complained that General
Wolfe was a madman

85 You've got to forget about this civilian.
Whenever you drop bombs, you're going
to hit civilians.

Speech, (1967) **Goldwater, Barry** (1909–1998) US presidential candidate and writer

86 One thing is clear; we are entering the first act of a world-wide tragedy.
Attr. (1914) **Gorky, Maxim** (1868–1936) Russian writer, dramatist and revolutionary. On Germany's declaration of war against Russia

87 Cowards in scarlet pass for men of war.
The She Gallants (1696) **Granville, George** (1666–1735) English poet, dramatist and politician

88 The boast of heraldry, the pomp of pow'r,
And all that beauty, all that wealth e'er gave,
Awaits alike th' inevitable hour,
The paths of glory lead but to the grave.
'Elegy Written in a Country Churchyard' (1751) **Gray, Thomas** (1716–1771) English poet and scholar

89 The lamps are going out all over Europe; we shall not see them lit again in our lifetime.
In *Twenty-five Years* **Grey, Edward, Viscount of Fallodon** (1862–1933) English statesman and writer. To a caller at the Foreign Office in August 1914

90 Every position must be held to the last man: there must be no retirement. With our backs to the wall, and believing in the justice of our cause, each one of us must fight on to the end.
Order to British forces on the Western Front, (1918) **Haig, Douglas** (1861–1928) Scottish military commander

91 Our ships have been salvaged and are retiring at high speed toward the Japanese fleet.
Radio message, (1944), following claims by the Japanese that most of the American Third Fleet had been sunk or were retiring **Halsey, Admiral W.F. ('Bull')** (1882–1959) US naval commander

92 I'm not allowed to say how many planes joined the raid but I counted them all out and I counted them all back.
BBC report, (1 May 1982) **Hanrahan, Brian** (1949–) English journalist. Reporting the British attack on Port Stanley airport, during the Falklands War

93 My argument is that War makes rattling good history; but Peace is poor reading.
The Dynasts (1903) **Hardy, Thomas** (1840–1928) English writer and poet

94 The Gulf War was like teenage sex. We got in too soon and we got out too soon.
Independent on Sunday, (1991) **Harkin, Thomas** (1939–)

95 The war situation has developed not necessarily to Japan's advantage.
Announcing Japan's surrender, (15 August 1945) **Hirohito, Emperor** (1901–1989) Emperor of Japan

96 In starting and waging a war it is not right that matters, but victory.
In Shirer, *The Rise and Fall of the Third Reich* (1960) **Hitler, Adolf** (1889–1945) German Nazi dictator, born in Austria. Said in 1939

97 Force, and fraud, are in war the two cardinal virtues.
Leviathan (1651) **Hobbes, Thomas** (1588–1679) Political philosopher

98 I believe in compulsory cannibalism. If people were forced to eat what they killed, there would be no more wars.
Attr. **Hoffman, Abbie** (1936–1989) US political activist

99 Older men declare war. But it is youth that must fight and die.
Speech, (1944) **Hoover, Herbert Clark** (1874–1964) US Republican President

100 The man that runs away
Lives to die another day.
A Shropshire Lad (1896) **Housman, A.E.** (1859–1936) English poet and scholar

101 Elevate them guns a little lower.
Attr. **Jackson, Andrew** (1767–1845) US President. Order given during the Battle of New Orleans, American War of Independence

102 From my mother's sleep I fell into the State,
And I hunched in its belly till my wet fur froze.
Six miles from earth, loosed from its dream of life,
I woke to black flak and the nightmare fighters.
When I died they washed me out of the turret with a hose.

'The Death of the Ball Turret Gunner' (1969) **Jarrell, Randall** (1914–1965) US poet, critic and translator

103 The first casualty when war comes is truth.
Speech, US Senate, (1917) **Johnson, Hiram** (1866–1945) US Republican politician

104 Long ones, backwards.
Quoted in his obituary, *The Sunday Times*, (1994) **Johnston, Brian** (1912–1994) British broadcaster. When asked by his commanding officer what steps he would take if he came across a German battalion

105 Waste of Blood, and waste of Tears,
Waste of youth's most precious years,
Waste of ways the saints have trod,
Waste of Glory, waste of God,
War!
'Waste' (1919) **Kennedy, G.A. Studdert** (1883–1929)

106 If I live, I mean to spend the rest of my life working for perpetual peace. I have seen war and faced artillery and know what an outrage it is against simple men.
Poems and Parodies **Kettle, Thomas** (1880–1916) Irish writer and academic

107 Formerly, a nation that broke the peace did not trouble to try and prove to the world that it was done solely from higher motives … Now war has a bad conscience. Now every nation assures us that it is bleeding for a human cause, the fate of which hangs in the balance of its victory … No nation will admit that it was only to insure its own safety that it declared war. No nation dares to admit the guilt of blood before the world.
War, Peace, and the Future (1916)

108 Everything, everything in war is barbaric …
But the worst barbarity of war is that it forces men collectively to commit acts against which individually they would revolt with their whole being.
War, Peace, and the Future (1916) **Key, Ellen** (1849–1926) Swedish feminist, writer and lecturer

109 Only lunatics or suicides, who themselves want to perish and to destroy the whole world before they die, could want an atomic war.

The Independent, (1992) **Khrushchev, Nikita** (1894–1971) Russian statesman and Premier of the USSR. Of the Cuban missile crisis

110 These were our children who died for our lands …
But who shall return us the children?
'The Children' (1917) **Kipling, Rudyard** (1865–1936) Indian-born British poet and writer

111 The most persistent sound which reverberates through men's history is the beating of war drums.
Janus: A Summing Up (1978) **Koestler, Arthur** (1905–1983) British writer, essayist and political refugee

112 Hail, ye indomitable heroes, hail!
Despite of all your generals ye prevail.
'The Crimean Heroes' **Landor, Walter Savage** (1775–1864) English poet and writer

113 To joy in conquest is to joy in the loss of human life.
Tao Te Ching **Lao-Tzu** (c.604–531 BC) Chinese philosopher

114 At first it was a giant column that soon took the shape of a supramundane mushroom.
New York Times, (1945) **Laurence, William L.** (1888–1977) US scientific journalist. Referring to the explosion of the first atomic bomb, over Hiroshima, 6 August 1945

115 I said in 1911 that if ever war arose between Great Britain and Germany it would not be due to inevitable causes, for I did not believe in inevitable war. I said it would be due to human folly.
Speech, House of Commons, (1914) **Law, Bonar** (1858–1923) Canadian-born British statesman and Conservative MP

116 We have all lost the war. All Europe.
The Ladybird (1923)

117 Loud peace propaganda makes war seem imminent.
Pansies (1929) **Lawrence, D.H.** (1885–1930) English writer, poet and critic

118 It is well that war is so terrible – we would grow too fond of it.
Remark after the Battle of Fredericksburg, (1862)

119 I should be trading on the blood of my men.
In M. Ringo, *Nobody Said It Better*. On refusing to write his memoirs **Lee, Robert E.** (1807–1870) Confederate general during US Civil War

120 This war, like the next war, is a war to end war.
Attr. **Lloyd George, David** (1863–1945) British Liberal statesman. Referring to the popular opinion that the First World War would be the last major war

121 I have never met anybody who wasn't against war. Even Hitler and Mussolini were, according to themselves.
In Jonathon Green (ed.), *A Dictionary of Contemporary Quotations* (1982) **Low, Sir David** (1891–1963) New Zealand-born British political cartoonist

122 And the softness of my body will be guarded from embrace
By each button, hook, and lace.
For the man who should loose me is dead,
Fighting with the Duke in Flanders,
In a pattern called a war.
Christ! What are patterns for?
Men, Women and Ghosts (1916), 'Patterns' **Lowell, Amy** (1874–1925) US poet

123 In war there is no substitute for victory.
Speech to Congress, (1951) **MacArthur, Douglas** (1880–1964) US general

124 He knew that the essence of war is violence, and that moderation in war is imbecility.
Collected Essays (1843) **Macaulay, Lord** (1800–1859) English Liberal statesman, essayist and poet. Of John Hampden

125 We hear war called murder. It is not: it is suicide.
The Observer, (1930) **MacDonald, Ramsay** (1866–1937) Scottish Labour politician and Prime Minister

126 And that is why all the armed prophets were victorious, whilst all the unarmed perished.
The Prince (1532) **Machiavelli** (1469–1527) Florentine statesman, political theorist and historian

127 Ever since the first World War there has been an inclination to denigrate the heroic aspect of man.
On Moral Courage (1962) **Mackenzie, Sir Compton** (1883–1972) Scottish writer and broadcaster

128 War is waged by men; not by beasts, or by gods. It is a peculiar human activity. To call it a crime against mankind is to miss half its significance; it is also the punishment of a crime.
Her Privates We (1929) **Manning, Frederic** (1882–1935) Australian writer

129 We are advocates of the abolition of war, we do not want war; but war can only be abolished through war, and in order to get rid of the gun it is necessary to take up the gun.
Quotations from Chairman Mao Tse-Tung **Mao Tse-Tung** (1893–1976) Chinese Communist leader

130 Accurs'd be he that first invented war!
Tamburlaine the Great (1590) **Marlowe, Christopher** (1564–1593) English poet and dramatist

131 No more bloody wars, no more bloody medals.
Attr. **Mary, Queen Consort** (1867–1953) Queen Consort of George V. Remark to soldier who had exclaimed 'No more bloody wars for me'

132 There's some say that we wan, some say that they wan,
Some say that nane wan at a', man;
But one thing I'm sure, that at Sheriffmuir
A battle there was which I saw, man:
And we ran, and they ran, and they ran, and we ran,
And we ran; and they ran awa', man!
In J. Woodfall Ebsworth (ed.), *Roxburghe Ballads* (1889) **McLennan, Murdoch** (fl. 1715) Scottish poet

133 I don't object to it's being called 'McNamara's War'... It is a very important war and I am pleased to be identified with it and do whatever I can to win it.
New York Times, (1964) On the war in Vietnam

134 We were wrong. We were terribly wrong.

Daily Telegraph, (1995) Speech on the 20th anniversary of the American withdrawal from Vietnam **McNamara, Robert** (1916–) US politician and Secretary of Defence

135 A leader who doesn't hesitate before he sends his nation into battle is not fit to be a leader.
I. and M. Shenker, *As Good as Golda* (1943) **Meir, Golda** (1898–1978) Russian-born Israeli stateswoman and Prime Minister

136 War will never cease until babies begin to come into the world with larger cerebrums and smaller adrenal glands.
Notebooks (1956) **Mencken, H.L.** (1880–1956) US writer, critic, philologist and satirist

137 You're not here to die for your country. You're here to make those — die for theirs.
Attr. **Michaelis, John H.** (1912–1985) US army officer. Said to the 27th Infantry (Wolfhound) Regiment during the Korean War

138 The earth itself will burn under the occupiers' feet.
The Times, (April 1999) **Milosevic, Slobodan** (1941–) Serbian political leader. Warning NATO of the consequences of invading Serbia

139 For what can Warr, but endless warr still breed.
'On the Lord Generall Fairfax at the siege of Colchester' (1648) **Milton, John** (1608–1674) English poet, libertarian and pamphleteer

140 Eternal peace is a dream, and not even a pleasant one; and war is an integral part of the way God has ordered the world ... Without war, the world would sink in the mire of materialism.
Letter to Dr J.K. Bluntschli, (1880) **Moltke, Helmuth von** (1800–1891) German field marshal

141 War is not a business in which one can take any pride or pleasure, or even pretend to. Its horror, its ghastly inefficiency, its unspeakable cruelty and misery has always appalled me, but there is nothing to do but to set one's teeth and stick it out as long as one can.
In Geoffrey Serle, *John Monash* (1982) **Monash, Sir John** (1865–1931) Australian military commander. In France, 1917

142 War hath no fury like a non-combatant.
Disenchantment (1922) **Montague, C.E.** (1867–1928) English writer and critic

143 An empire founded by war has to maintain itself by war.
Considérations sur les causes de la grandeur des Romains et de leur décadence (1734) **Montesquieu, Charles** (1689–1755) French philosopher and jurist

144 The US has broken the second rule of war. That is, don't go fighting with your land army on the mainland of Asia. Rule One is don't march on Moscow. I developed these two rules myself.
Speech, (1962) **Montgomery, Viscount** (1887–1976) English field marshal. On American policy in Vietnam

145 Sound, sound the clarion, fill the fife, Throughout the sensual world proclaim, One crowded hour of glorious life Is worth an age without a name.
'Verses written during the War, 1756–1763' (1791) **Mordaunt, Thomas Osbert** (1730–1809) British soldier

146 See, the conquering hero comes! Sound the trumpets, beat the drums!
Joshua (1748) **Morell, Thomas** (1703–1784) English scholar, librettist, editor and clergyman

147 It's the most beautiful battlefield I've ever seen.
Referring to the carnage at the Battle of Borodino, 1812

148 In war, three-quarters depends on matters of character and morale; the balance of manpower and equipment counts only for the remaining quarter.
Correspondance de Napoléon I (1854–1869)

149 Has he luck?
Question asked of potential officers **Napoleon I** (1769–1821) French emperor

150 I don't care for war, there's far too much luck in it for my liking.
In E. Crankshaw, *The Fall of the House of Habsburg* **Napoleon III** (1808–1873) French emperor. After the narrow and bloody French victory at Solferino, 1859

151 Victory is not a name strong enough for such a scene.
In Robert Southey, *The Life of Nelson* (1860) At the Battle of the Nile, 1798

152 Leave off action? Now, damn me if I do! ... I have only one eye – I have a right to be blind sometimes ... I really do not see the signal! ... Damn the signal!
In Southey, *The Life of Nelson* (1860) At the Battle of Copenhagen, 1801 **Nelson, Lord** (1758–1805) English admiral

153 The quickest way of ending a war is to lose it.
Polemic (1946) **Orwell, George** (1903–1950) English writer and critic

154 My subject is War, and the pity of War. The Poetry is in the pity.
Quoted in *Poems* (1963), Preface

155 If you could hear, at every jolt, the blood
Come gargling from the froth-corrupted lungs,
Obscene as cancer, bitter as the cud
Of vile, incurable sores on innocent tongues, –
My friend, you would not tell with such high zest
To children ardent for some desperate glory,
The old Lie: Dulce et decorum est
Pro patria mori.
'Dulce et decorum est' (1917)

156 What passing-bells for these who die as cattle?
Only the monstrous anger of the guns.
Only the stuttering rifles' rapid rattle
Can patter out their hasty orisons.
'Anthem for Doomed Youth' (1917) **Owen, Wilfred** (1893–1918) English poet

157 I could not give my name to aid the slaughter in this war, fought on both sides for grossly material ends, which did not justify the sacrifice of a single mother's son. Clearly I must continue to oppose it, and expose it, to all whom I could reach with voice or pen.
The Home Front **Pankhurst, Sylvia** (1882–1960) English suffragette, pacifist and internationalist

158 Untutored courage is useless in the face of educated bullets.
Cavalry Journal, (1922) **Patton, George S.** (1885–1945) US general

159 The object of war is not to die for your country, but to make the other bastard die for his.
Attr. **Patton, George S.** (1885–1945) US general

160 Out of that bungled, unwise war
An alp of unforgiveness grew.
'The Boer War' (1932) **Plomer, William** (1903–1973) South African-born British writer and editor

161 Don't fire until you see the whites of their eyes.
Attr. **Prescott, William** (1726–1795) Command given at the Battle of Bunker Hill, 1775

162 If we are victorious against the Romans in one more battle we shall be utterly ruined.
In Plutarch, *Lives* **Pyrrhus** (319–272 BC) King of Epirus and army commander. After a hard-won battle

163 The strength of a war waged without a good supply of money is as fleeting as a breath. Money is the sinews of battle.
Gargantua (1534) **Rabelais, François** (c.1494–c.1553) French monk, physician, satirist and humanist

164 War is, after all, the universal perversion. We are all tainted: if we cannot experience our perversion at first hand we spend our time reading war stories, the pornography of war; or seeing war films, the blue films of war; or titillating our senses with the imagination of great deeds, the masturbation of war.
The Custard Boys (1960) **Rae, John** (1931–) English educationist and writer

165 In a civil war, the general must know – and I'm afraid it's a thing rather of instinct than of practice – he must know exactly when to move over to the other side.
Not a Drum was Heard: The War Memoirs of General Gland (1959) **Reed, Henry** (1914–1986) English poet, radio dramatist and translator

166 I saw Major Johnstone, who is here to lay the bases of an American History. We discussed the right name of the war. I said that we called it now The War, but that this could not last. The Napoleonic War was The Great War. To call it The German War was too much flattery for the Boche. I suggested The World War as a shade better title, and finally we mutually agreed to call it The First World War in order to prevent the millennium folk from forgetting that the history of the world was the history of war.
Diary entry for 10 September 1918, published in *The First World War 1914–18* (1920) **Repington, Lieut-Col. Charles A'Court** (1858–1925)

167 You can't say civilization don't advance, however, for in every war they kill you a new way.
New York Times, (1929) **Rogers, Will** (1879–1935) US humorist, actor, rancher, writer and wit

168 More than an end to war, we want an end to the beginnings of all wars.
Speech, (1945) **Roosevelt, Franklin Delano** (1882–1945) US Democrat President

169 'Come cheer up, my lads, 'tis to glory we steer!'
As the soldier remarked whose post lay in the rear.
Untitled couplet (c.1845) **Rossetti, Christina** (1830–1894) English poet

170 We don't want to lose you but we think you ought to go.
'Your King and Country Want You' (song, 1914) **Rubens, Paul Alfred** (1875–1917) English dramatist and songwriter

171 You may reasonably expect a man to walk a tightrope safely for ten minutes; it would be unreasonable to do so without accident for two hundred years.
In Desmond Bagley, *The Tightrope Men* (1973) **Russell, Bertrand** (1872–1970) English philosopher, mathematician, essayist and social reformer. On the possibility of nuclear war between the USA and the USSR

172 The Russians on their left drew breath for a moment, and then in one grand line dashed at the Highlanders. The ground flies beneath their horses' feet; gathering speed at every stride, they dash on towards that thin red streak topped with a line of steel.
The Times, (1854) **Russell, William Howard** (1820–1907) English journalist. Reporting the charge of the Russian cavalry on Sir Colin Campbell's Highland infantry during the Crimean War

173 Every war is easy to begin but difficult to stop; its beginning and end are not in the control of the same person.
Jugurtha **Sallust** (86–c.34 BC) Roman historian and statesman

174 Pile the bodies high at Austerlitz and Waterloo.
Shovel them under and let me work –
I am the grass; I cover all.
Cornhuskers (1918), 'Grass'

175 Sometime they'll give a war and nobody will come.
The People, Yes (1936) **Sandburg, Carl** (1878–1967) US poet, writer and song collector

176 Safe with his wound, a citizen of life,
He hobbled blithely through the garden gate,
And thought: 'Thank God they had to amputate!'
'The One-Legged Man' (1916)

177 If I were fierce and bald and short of breath,
I'd live with scarlet Majors at the Base,
And speed glum heroes up the line to death …
And when the war is done and youth stone dead
I'd toddle safely home and die – in bed.
'Base Details' (1917)

178 I'd like to see a Tank come down the stalls,
Lurching to rag-time tunes, or 'Home, sweet Home,' –
And there'd be no more jokes in Music-halls
To mock the riddled corpses round Bapaume.
'Blighters' (1917)

179 The place was rotten with dead: green clumsy legs
High-booted, sprawled and grovelled along the saps
And trunks, face downward, in the sucking mud
Wallowed like trodden sandbags loosely filled;
And naked sodden buttocks, mats of hair,
Bulged, clotted heads slept in the plastering slime.
And then the rain began – the jolly old rain!
'Counter-Attack' (1917)

180 The simplicity that I see in some of the men is the one candle in my darkness. The one flower in all this arid sunshine.
Diary, (April 1918)

181 I am making this statement as an act of wilful defiance of military authority, because I believe that the War is being deliberately prolonged by those who have the power to end it … I have seen and endured the sufferings of the troops, and I can no longer be a party to prolong these sufferings for ends which I believe to be evil and unjust.
Memoirs of an Infantry Officer (1930) From the statement sent to his commanding officer, July 1917 **Sassoon, Siegfried** (1886–1967) English poet and writer

182 He is neither a strategist nor is he schooled in the operational arts, nor is he a tactician, nor is he a general. Other than that he's a great military man.
Attr. **Schwarzkopf, Norman** (1934–) US general. Describing Saddam Hussein of Iraq, 1991

183 When we, the Workers, all demand: 'What are we fighting for?' …
Then, then we'll end that stupid crime, that devil's madness – War.
'Michael' (1921) **Service, Robert W.** (1874–1958) Canadian poet

184 To th' wars, my boy, to th' wars!
He wears his honour in a box unseen
That hugs his kicky-wicky here at home,
Spending his manly marrow in her arms,
Which should sustain the bound and high curvet
Of Mars's fiery steed.
All's Well That Ends Well, II.iii

185 Let me have war, say I; it exceeds peace as far as day does night; it's spritely, waking, audible, and full of vent. Peace is a very apoplexy, lethargy; mull'd, deaf, sleepy, insensible; a getter of more bastard children than war's a destroyer of men.
Coriolanus, IV.v

186 Once more unto the breach, dear friends, once more;
Or close the wall up with our English dead.
In peace there's nothing so becomes a man
As modest stillness and humility;
But when the blast of war blows in our ears,
Then imitate the action of the tiger:
Stiffen the sinews, summon up the blood,
Disguise fair nature with hard-favour'd rage;
Then lend the eye a terrible aspect.
Henry V, III.i

187 We few, we happy few, we band of brothers;
For he to-day that sheds his blood with me
Shall be my brother.
Henry V, IV.iii **Shakespeare, William** (1564–1616) English dramatist, poet and actor

188 There is many a boy here today who looks on war as all glory, but, boys, it is all hell.
Speech, (1880) **Sherman, William Tecumseh** (1820–1891) US general

189 'And everybody praised the Duke,
Who this great fight did win.'
'But what good came of it at last?'
Quoth little Peterkin.
'Why that I cannot tell,' said he,
'But 'twas a famous victory.'
'The Battle of Blenheim' (1798) **Southey, Robert** (1774–1843) English poet, essayist, historian and letter writer

190 To win in Vietnam, we will have to exterminate a nation.
Dr Spock on Vietnam (1968) **Spock, Dr Benjamin** (1903–1998) US paediatrician and psychiatrist

191 The Pope! How many divisions has he got?

In W.S. Churchill, *The Gathering Storm* (1948) **Stalin, Joseph** (1879–1953) Soviet Communist leader. Reply to Laval, French Foreign Minister, who asked Stalin in 1935 to do something to encourage the Catholic religion in Russia in order to help him gain the support of the Pope

192 That's what you are. That's what you all are. All of you young people who served in the war. You are a lost generation.
In Hemingway, *A Moveable Feast* (1964) **Stein, Gertrude** (1874–1946) US writer, dramatist, poet and critic. Remark made in the 1920s

193 Fascism means war.
Slogan, (1930s) **Strachey, John St Loe** (1901–1963) English politician

194 I should try and come between them.
In Holroyd, *Lytton Strachey: A Critical Biography* (1968) **Strachey, Lytton** (1880–1932) English biographer and critic. Reply when asked by a tribunal what he, as a conscientious objector, would do if he saw a German soldier trying to rape his sister

195 To abolish shooting before you had abolished war was rather like flecking a speck of dust off the top of a midden.
Mrs Miniver, quoted in *The Times*, (1993) **Struther, Jan** (1901–1953) English writer

196 Hobbes clearly proves, that every creature Lives in a state of war by nature.
'On Poetry' (1733) **Swift, Jonathan** (1667–1745) Irish satirist, poet, essayist and cleric

197 The guerrilla fights the war of the flea, and his military enemy suffers the dog's disadvantages: too much to defend; too small, ubiquitous, and agile an enemy to come to grips with.
The War of the Flea **Taber, Robert** (20th century) US writer

198 War is much too serious to be left to the generals.
Attr. **Talleyrand, Charles-Maurice de** (1754–1838) French statesman, memoirist and prelate

199 A racing tipster who only reached Hitler's level of accuracy would not do well for his clients.

The Origins of the Second World War (1961) **Taylor, A.J.P.** (1906–1990) English historian, writer, broadcaster and lecturer

200 Could we have avoided the tragedy of Hiroshima? Could we have started the atomic age with clean hands? No one knows. No one can find out.
Teller, Edward (1908–2003) Hungarian-born US physicist

201 A mushroom of boiling dust up to 20,000 feet.
Attr. **Tibbet, Paul W.** (20th century) Description of atomic bomb explosion

202 The next war will be fought with atom bombs and the one after that with spears.
The Observer, (1946) **Urey, Harold** (1893–1981) US chemist

203 I see wars, dreadful wars, and the Tiber foaming with much blood.
Aeneid **Virgil** (70–19 BC) Roman poet

204 Ironically, the horrors of war have taught me that there are things that are worse than war, and against them determined and careful war should be waged, in the name of the innocent and the weak.
The Weekend Guardian, (1992) **Vulliamy, Ed** British journalist and author. A pacifist until the war in Bosnia forced him to change his convictions

205 When the war broke out she took down the signed photograph of the Kaiser and, with some solemnity, hung it in the menservants' lavatory; it was her one combative action.
Vile Bodies (1930)

206 Like German opera, too long and too loud.
Giving his opinions of warfare after the battle of Crete, 1941 **Waugh, Evelyn** (1903–1966) English writer and diarist

207 I lard pounding this, gentlemen; let's see who will pound longest.
In Sir Walter Scott, *Paul's Letters* (1816) Remark at Waterloo

208 I always say that, next to a battle lost, the greatest misery is a battle gained.
In Rogers, *Recollections* (1859)

209 All the business of war, and indeed all the business of life, is to endeavour to find out what you don't know by what you do; that's what I called 'guessing what was at the other side of the hill'.
The Croker Papers (1885)

210 It is not the business of generals to shoot one another.
Refusing permission to shoot at Napoleon during the Battle of Waterloo **Wellington, Duke of** (1769–1852) Irish-born British military commander and statesman

211 But bombs are unbelievable until they actually fall.
Riders in the Chariot (1961) **White, Patrick** (1912–1990) English-born Australian writer and dramatist

212 As long as war is regarded as wicked it will always have its fascination. When it is looked upon as vulgar, it will cease to be popular.
The Critic as Artist (1890) **Wilde, Oscar** (1854–1900) Irish poet, dramatist, writer, critic and wit

213 You will be home before the leaves have fallen from the trees.
Remark to troops leaving for the Front, (August 1914) **Wilhelm II, Kaiser** (1859–1941) German emperor

214 Once lead this people into war and they'll forget there ever was such a thing as tolerance.
In Dos Passos, *Mr Wilson's War* (1917) **Wilson, Woodrow** (1856–1924) US Democrat President

215 One to destroy, is murder by the law;
And gibbets keep the lifted hand in awe;
To murder thousands, takes a specious name,
War's glorious art, and gives immortal fame.
Night-Thoughts on Life, Death and Immortality **Young, Edward** (1683–1765) English poet, dramatist, satirist and clergyman
See also global affairs; the military; patriotism; peace; suffering

WISDOM

1 Even he who is wiser than the wise may err.
Fragments

2 It is a fine thing even for an old man to learn wisdom.
Fragments **Aeschylus** (525–456 BC) Greek dramatist and poet

3 One may learn wisdom even from one's enemies.
Birds **Aristophanes** (c.445–385 BC) Greek playwright

4 A wise man will make more opportunities than he finds.
'Of Ceremonies and Respects' (1625) **Bacon, Francis** (1561–1626) English philosopher, essayist, politician and courtier

5 The fear of the Lord is the beginning of wisdom.
Psalms, 111:10

6 Wisdom is the principal thing; therefore get wisdom: and with all thy getting get understanding.
Proverbs, 4:7

7 For ye suffer fools gladly, seeing ye yourselves are wise.
Paul, 3:67 **The Bible (King James Version)**

8 The road of excess leads to the palace of Wisdom.
'Proverbs of Hell' (1793)

9 I care not whether a Man is Good or Evil;
all that I care
Is whether he is a Wise Man or a Fool. Go! put off Holiness
And put on Intellect.
Jerusalem (1804–1820) **Blake, William** (1757–1827) English poet, engraver, painter and mystic

10 Ful wys is he that kan hymselven knowe!
The Canterbury Tales (1387) **Chaucer, Geoffrey** (c.1340–1400) English poet, public servant and courtier

11 For one word a man is often deemed to be wise, and for one word he is often deemed to be foolish. We should be careful indeed what we say.
Analects

12 The heart of the wise, like a mirror, should reflect all objects without being sullied by any.
Analects

13 Gravity is only the bark of wisdom's tree, but it preserves it.
Analects **Confucius** (c.550–c.478 BC) Chinese philosopher and teacher of ethics

14 Knowledge is proud that he has learn'd so much;
Wisdom is humble that he knows no more.
The Task (1785)

15 Knowledge dwells
In heads replete with thoughts of other men;
Wisdom in minds attentive to their own.
The Task (1785) **Cowper, William** (1731–1800) English poet, hymn writer and letter writer

16 Errors, like straws, upon the surface flow;
He who would search for pearls must dive below.
All for Love (1678) **Dryden, John** (1631–1700) English poet, satirist, dramatist and critic

17 Before God we are all equally wise – equally foolish.
Address, Sorbonne, Paris **Einstein, Albert** (1879–1955) German-born US mathematical physicist

18 The wise through excess of wisdom is made a fool.
Essays, Second Series (1844)

19 Now that is the wisdom of a man, in every instance of his labor, to hitch his wagon to a star, and see his chore done by the gods themselves.
Society and Solitude (1870) **Emerson, Ralph Waldo** (1803–1882) US poet, essayist, transcendentalist and teacher

20 With them the Seed of Wisdom did I sow,
And with mine own hand wrought to make it grow;
And this was all the Harvest that I reap'd –
'I came like Water, and like Wind I go'.
The Rubáiyát of Omar Khayyám (1859)
Fitzgerald, Edward (1809–1883) English poet, translator and letter writer

21 Many have been the wise speeches of fools, though not so many as the foolish speeches of wise men.
The Holy State and the Profane State (1642)
Fuller, Thomas (1608–1661) English churchman and antiquary

22 To have made a beginning is half of the business; dare to be wise.
Epistles **Horace** (65–8 BC) Roman lyric poet and satirist

23 Wisdom denotes the pursuing of the best ends by the best means.
An Inquiry into the Original of our Ideas of Beauty and Virtue (1725) **Hutcheson, Francis** (1694–1746) Scottish philosopher

24 He is no wise man who will quit a certainty for an uncertainty.
The Idler (1758–1760) **Johnson, Samuel** (1709–1784) English lexicographer, poet, critic, conversationalist and essayist

25 How often when they find a sage
As great as Socrates or Plato
They hand him hemlock for his wage
Or take him like a sweet potato.
Taking the Longer View **Marquis, Don** (1878–1937) US columnist, satirist and poet

26 What all the wise men promised has not happened, and what all the d—d fools said would happen has come to pass.
In H. Dunckley, *Lord Melbourne* (1890)
Melbourne, Lord (1779–1848) English statesman. Of Catholic emancipation

27 In action Wisdom goes by majorities.
The Ordeal of Richard Feverel (1859) **Meredith, George** (1828–1909) English writer, poet and critic

28 Each generation imagines itself to be more intelligent than the one that went before it, and wiser than the one that comes after it.
Attr. **Orwell, George** (1903–1950) English writer and critic

29 That man is wisest who, like Socrates, has realized that in truth his wisdom is worth nothing.
The Apology of Socrates **Plato** (c.429–347 BC) Greek philosopher

30 A man should never be ashamed to own he has been in the wrong, which is but saying, in other words, that he is wiser today than he was yesterday.
Miscellanies (1727) **Pope, Alexander** (1688–1744) English poet, translator and editor

31 Be wisely worldly, not worldly wise.
Emblems (1635) **Quarles, Francis** (1592–1644) English poet, writer and royalist

32 Nine-tenths of wisdom is being wise in time.
Speech, (1917) **Roosevelt, Theodore** (1858–1919) US Republican President

33 Wisely and slow; they stumble that run fast.
Romeo and Juliet, II:iii **Shakespeare, William** (1564–1616) English dramatist, poet and actor

34 Some folks are wise, and some are otherwise.
The Adventures of Roderick Random (1748) **Smollett, Tobias** (1721–1771) Scottish writer, satirist, historian, traveller and physician

35 No wise man ever wished to be younger.
Thoughts on Various Subjects (1711) **Swift, Jonathan** (1667–1745) Irish satirist, poet, essayist and cleric

36 The stupid neither forgive nor forget; the naive forgive and forget; the wise forgive but do not forget.
The Second Sin (1973) **Szasz, Thomas** (1920–) Hungarian-born US psychiatrist and writer

37 It is a characteristic of wisdom not to do desperate things.
Walden (1854) **Thoreau, Henry David** (1817–1862) US essayist, social critic and writer

38 It may almost be a question whether such wisdom as many of us have in our mature years has not come from the dying out of the power of temptation, rather than as the results of thought and resolution.
The Small House at Allington (1864) **Trollope, Anthony** (1815–1882) English writer, traveller and post office official

39 The wisest prophets make sure of the event first.
Letter to Thomas Walpole, (1785) **Walpole, Horace** (1717–1797) English writer and politician

40 And of all axioms this shall win the prize, — 'Tis better to be fortunate than wise.
The White Devil (1612) **Webster, John** (c.1580–c.1625) English dramatist

41 Wisdom doth live with children round her knees.
Sonnets Dedicated to Liberty and Order (1807)

42 Wisdom is oftimes nearer when we stoop Than when we soar.
The Excursion (1814) **Wordsworth, William** (1770–1850) English poet

43 Be wise today,'tis madness to defer.
Night-Thoughts on Life, Death and Immortality (1742–1746) **Young, Edward** (1683–1765) English poet, dramatist, satirist and clergyman
See also age; belief; ideas; intelligence; knowledge; philosophy; thought

WOMEN

1 Old-fashioned ways which no longer apply to changed conditions are a snare in which the feet of women have always become readily entangled.
Newer Ideals of Peace (1907) **Addams, Jane** (1860–1935) US sociologist and writer

2 I consider woman as a beautiful, romantic animal, that may be adorned with furs and feathers, pearls and diamonds, ores and silks.
Trial of the Petticoat

3 The woman that deliberates is lost.
Cato (1713) **Addison, Joseph** (1672–1719) English essayist, poet, playwright and statesman

4 Girls are so queer you never know what they mean. They say No when they mean Yes, and drive a man out of his wits for the fun of it.
Little Women (1869) **Alcott, Louisa May** (1832–1888) US writer

5 The weaker sex, to piety more prone.
Doomsday (1614) **Alexander, Sir William, Earl of Stirling** (c.1567–1640) Scottish poet and statesman

6 In particular, the State recognises that by her life within the home, woman gives to the State a support without which the common good cannot be achieved.
The Irish Constitution **Anonymous**

7 With women the heart argues, not the mind.
Merope (1858) **Arnold, Matthew** (1822–1888) English poet, critic, essayist and educationist

8 Women should not be enlightened or educated in any way. They should, in fact, be segregated as they are the cause of hideous and involuntary erections in holy men.
Attr. **Augustine, Saint** (354–430) Numidian-born Christian theologian and philosopher

9 Next to being married, a girl likes to be crossed in love a little now and then.
Pride and Prejudice (1813)

10 Where people wish to attach, they should always be ignorant. To come with a well-informed mind, is to come with an inability of administering to the vanity of others, which a sensible person would always wish to avoid. A woman especially, if she have the misfortune of knowing any thing, should conceal it as well as she can.
Northanger Abbey (1818)

11 In nine cases out of ten, a woman had better show more affection than she feels.
Letter **Austen, Jane** (1775–1817) English writer

12 One is not born a woman: one becomes a woman.
The Second Sex (1950) **Beauvoir, Simone de** (1908–1986) French writer, feminist critic and philosopher

13 Women who love the same man have a kind of bitter freemasonry.
Zuleika Dobson (1911) **Beerbohm, Sir Max** (1872–1956) English satirist, cartoonist, critic and essayist

14 The soft, unhappy sex.
The Wandering Beauty (c.1694) **Behn, Aphra** (1640–1689) English dramatist, writer, poet, translator and spy

15 And the rib, which the Lord God had taken from man, made he a woman.
Genesis, 2:22

16 All wickedness is but little to the wickedness of a woman.
Ecclesiasticus, 25:19 **The Bible (King James Version)**

17 All women born are so perverse
No man need boast their love possessing.
If nought seem better, nothing's worse:
All women born are so perverse.
From Adam's wife, that proved a curse
Though God had made her for a blessing,
All women born are so perverse
No man need boast their love possessing.
'Triolet' (1890) **Bridges, Robert** (1844–1930) English poet, dramatist, essayist and doctor

18 Auld nature swears, the lovely dears
Her noblest work she classes, O:
Her prentice han' she try'd on man,
An' then she made the lasses, O.
'Green Grow the Rashes' (1783) **Burns, Robert** (1759–1796) Scottish poet and songwriter

19 The souls of women are so small,
That some believe they've none at all.
Miscellaneous Thoughts **Butler, Samuel (poet)** (1612–1680) English poet

20 Brigands demand your money or your life; women require both.
Attr. **Butler, Samuel** (1835–1902) English writer, painter, philosopher and scholar

21 There is something to me very softening in the presence of a woman, – some strange influence, even if one is not in love with them – which I cannot at all account for, having no very high opinion of the sex.
Journal, (1814) **Byron, Lord** (1788–1824) English poet, satirist and traveller

22 It was a blonde. A blonde to make a bishop kick a hole in a stained glass window.
Farewell, My Lovely (1940) **Chandler, Raymond** (1888–1959) US crime writer

23 What is bettre than wisedoom? Womman. And what is bettre than a good womman? Nothyng.
The Canterbury Tales (1387) **Chaucer, Geoffrey** (c.1340–1400) English poet, public servant and courtier

24 Women don't forgive failure.
The Seagull (1896) **Chekhov, Anton** (1860–1904) Russian writer, dramatist and doctor

25 Women, then, are only children of a larger growth; they have an entertaining tattle and sometimes wit; but for solid, reasoning good-sense, I never in my life knew one that had it, or who reasoned or acted consequentially for four-and-twenty hours together.
Letter to his son, (1748) **Chesterfield, Lord** (1694–1773) English politician and letter writer

26 She [the elegant female] was maintaining the prime truth of woman, the universal mother: that if a thing is worth doing, it is worth doing badly.
What's Wrong with the World (1910) **Chesterton, G.K.** (1874–1936) English writer, poet and critic

27 Women are like tricks by slight of hand, Which, to admire, we should not understand.
Love for Love (1695)

28 Heav'n has no rage, like love to hatred turned,
Nor Hell a fury, like a woman scorn'd.
The Mourning Bride (1697) **Congreve, William** (1670–1729) English dramatist

29 Certain women should be struck regularly, like gongs.
Private Lives (1930) **Coward, Sir Noël** (1899–1973) English dramatist, actor, producer and composer

30 But what is woman? – only one of Nature's agreeable blunders.
Who's the Dupe? (1779) **Cowley, Hannah** (1743–1809) English dramatist and poet

31 Women never have young minds. They are born three thousand years old.
A Taste of Honey (1959) **Delaney, Shelagh** (1939–) English dramatist, screenwriter and writer

32 Women are like the Arts, forc'd unto none, Open to all searchers, unpriz'd if unknown.
Elegies (c.1595) **Donne, John** (1572–1631) English poet

33 I don't operate rationally. I think just like a woman.
The Times, (1999) **Dyson, James** (1947–) English inventor of the bagless vacuum cleaner

34 I should like to know what is the proper function of women, if it is not to make reasons for husbands to stay at home, and still stronger reasons for bachelors to go out.
The Mill on the Floss (1860)

35 A woman can hardly ever choose ... she is dependent on what happens to her. She must take meaner things, because only meaner things are within her reach.
Felix Holt (1866)

36 Half the sorrows of women would be averted if they could repress the speech they know to be useless; nay, the speech they have resolved not to make.
Felix Holt (1866) **Eliot, George** (1819–1880) English writer and poet

37 There's some diversion in a talking blockhead; and since a woman must wear chains, I would have the pleasure of hearing 'em rattle a little.
The Beaux' Stratagem (1707) **Farquhar, George** (1678–1707) Irish dramatist

38 The great question ... which I have not been able to answer, despite my thirty years of research into the feminine soul, is 'What does a woman want?'
In Robb, *Psychiatry in American Life* **Freud, Sigmund** (1856–1939) Austrian physicist; founder of psychoanalysis

39 Woman's mind
Oft' shifts her passions, like th' inconstant wind;
Sudden she rages, like the troubled main,
Now sinks the storm, and all is calm again.
Dione (1720)

40 I must have women. There is nothing unbends the mind like them.
The Beggar's Opera (1728) **Gay, John** (1685–1732) English poet, dramatist and librettist

41 Of all the plagues with which the world is curst,
Of every ill, a woman is the worst.
The British Enchanters **Granville, George** (1666–1735) English poet, dramatist and politician

42 The itemised telephone bill ranks up there with suspender belts, Sky Sports channels and *Loaded* magazine as inventions women could do without.
The Times, (1999) **Haran, Maeve** British writer and journalist

43 I've always thought there were only three kinds of women: wives, whores and mistresses.
Daily Mail, (1996) **Harman, Sir Jeremiah** (1930–) British High Court judge

44 He seldom errs
Who thinks the worst he can of womankind.
Douglas (1756) **Home, John** (1722–1808) Scottish clergyman and dramatist

45 A woman's whole life is a history of the affections.
The Sketch Book (1820) **Irving, Washington** (1783–1859) US writer and diplomat

46 These are rare attainments for a damsel, but pray tell me, can she spin?
Attr. **James 1 of Scotland** (1394–1437) King of Scotland. On being introduced to a young girl proficient in Latin, Greek, and Hebrew

47 Sir, a woman's preaching is like a dog's walking on his hinder legs. It is not done well; but you are surprised to find it done at all.
In Boswell, *The Life of Samuel Johnson* (1791) **Johnson, Samuel** (1709–1784) English lexicographer, poet, critic, conversationalist and essayist

48 'Tisn't beauty, so to speak, nor good talk necessarily. It's just IT. Some women'll stay in a man's memory if they once walked down a street.
Traffics and Discoveries (1904) **Kipling, Rudyard** (1865–1936) Indian-born British poet and writer

49 Can anything be more absurd than keeping women in a state of ignorance, and yet so vehemently to insist on their resisting temptation?
Liberal Education (1780) **Knox, Vicesimus** (1752–1821) English churchman and writer

50 I'd be equally as willing
For a dentist to be drilling
Than to ever let a woman in my life.
My Fair Lady (1956)

51 There is no greater fan of the opposite sex than me, and I have the bills to prove it.
Attr. **Lerner, Alan Jay** (1918–1986) US lyricist and screenwriter

52 She's the sort of woman who lives for others – you can always tell the others by their hunted expression.
The Screwtape Letters (1942) **Lewis, C.S.** (1898–1963) Irish-born English academic, writer and critic

53 So this gentleman said a girl with brains ought to do something with them besides think.
Gentlemen Prefer Blondes (1925) **Loos, Anita** (1893–1981) US writer and screenwriter

54 Women do not find it difficult nowadays to behave like men; but they often find it extremely difficult to behave like gentlemen.
Literature in My Time (1933) **Mackenzie, Sir Compton** (1883–1972) Scottish writer and broadcaster

55 You don't know a woman until you've met her in court.
The Observer, (1983) **Mailer, Norman** (1923–) US writer

56 Most women turn to salt, looking back.
In John Middleton Murry (ed.), *Journal of Katherine Mansfield* (1954) **Mansfield, Katherine** (1888–1923) New Zealand writer. On women's ambition

57 Like untun'd golden strings all women are Which long time lie untouch'd, will harshly jar.
Hero and Leander (1598) **Marlowe, Christopher** (1564–1593) English poet and dramatist

58 To get the whole world out of bed
And washed, and dressed, and warmed, and fed,
To work, and back to bed again,
Believe me, Saul, costs worlds of pain.
'The Everlasting Mercy' (1911) **Masefield, John** (1878–1967) English poet, writer and critic

59 A woman will always sacrifice herself if you give her the opportunity. It is her favourite form of self-indulgence.
The Circle (1921) **Maugham, William Somerset** (1874–1965) English writer, dramatist and physician

60 For those of us whose lives have been defined by others – by wifehood and motherhood – there is no individual achievement to measure, only the experience of life itself.
Private Faces/Public Places (1972) **McCarthy, Abigail** (1915–2001) US writer

61 When women kiss, it always reminds me of prize-fighters shaking hands.
Attr. **Mencken, H.L.** (1880–1956) US writer, critic, philologist and satirist

62 One tongue is sufficient for a woman.
Reply when asked if he would allow his daughters to learn foreign languages

63 O why did God,
Creator wise, that peopl'd highest Heav'n
With Spirits Masculine, create at last
This noveltie on Earth, this fair defect
Of Nature?
Paradise Lost (1667)

64 ... nothing lovelier can be found
In Woman, than to studie household good,
And good works in her Husband to promote.
Paradise Lost (1667) **Milton, John** (1608–1674) English poet, libertarian and pamphleteer

65 Disguise our bondage as we will,
'Tis woman, woman, rules us still.
Miscellaneous Poems (1840), 'Sovereign Woman'
Moore, Thomas (1779–1852) Irish poet

66 I want to walk through life instead of being dragged through it.
Attr. **Morissette, Alanis** (1974–) US singer

67 On the last day of his life Dan decided that women who haunted you were not those whom you had enjoyed or even known remotely well, but strangers who had at one time or another troubled you with the most transient flicker of desire.
Loser **Mulkerns, Val** (1925–) Irish writer

68 Women would rather be right than reasonable.
'Frailty, Thy Name is a Misnomer' (1942)
Nash, Ogden (1902–1971) US poet

69 Everything to do with women is a mystery, and everything to do with women has one solution: it's called pregnancy.
Thus Spake Zarathustra (1884) **Nietzsche, Friedrich Wilhelm** (1844–1900) German philosopher, critic and poet

70 Women (and I, in this Diary) have never separated sex from feeling, from love of the whole man.
Delta of Venus (1977) **Nin, Anaïs** (1903–1977) French-born US writer

71 I think any woman who becomes successful is demonised by the media because they can't possibly be attractive, intelligent, nice and genuine. It's just too scary for a woman to be all these things.
The Times, (1999) **Noble, Emma** (1971–) English model

72 Oh woman! lovely woman! Nature made thee
To temper man: we had been brutes without you;
Angels are painted fair, to look like you;
There's in you all that we believe of heav'n,
Amazing brightness, purity, and truth,
Eternal joy, and everlasting love.
Venice Preserv'd (1682) **Otway, Thomas** (1652–1685) English dramatist and poet

73 Whether they give or refuse, women are glad that they have been asked.
Ars Amatoria **Ovid** (43 BC–AD 18) Roman poet

74 There is no female Mozart because there is no female Jack the Ripper.
Attr. in *The Observer*, (1996) **Paglia, Camille** (1947–) US academic

75 The greatest glory of a woman is to be least talked about by men, in praise or blame.
In Thucydides, *Histories* **Pericles** (c.495–429) Athenian statesman, general, orator and cultural patron

76 Woman's at best a Contradiction still.
'Epistle to a Lady' (1735) **Pope, Alexander** (1688–1744) English poet, translator and editor

77 She wavers, she hesitates; in a word, she is a woman.
Athalie (1691) **Racine, Jean** (1639–1699) French tragedian and poet

78 Woman puts us back into communication with the eternal spring in which God looks at his reflection.
Souvenirs d'enfance et de jeunesse (1883) **Renan, J. Ernest** (1823–1892) French philologist, writer and historian

79 It takes a woman twenty years to make a man of her son, and another woman twenty minutes to make a fool of him.
Reflections of a Bachelor Girl (1909) **Rowland, Helen** (1875–1950) US writer

80 One needs only to see the way she is built to realise that woman is not intended for great mental labour.
Attr. **Schopenhauer, Arthur** (1788–1860) German philosopher

81 O Woman! in our hours of ease,
Uncertain, coy, and hard to please,
And variable as the shade
By the light quivering aspen made;
When pain and anguish wring the brow,
A ministering angel thou!
Marmion (1808)

82 Woman's faith, and woman's trust –
Write the characters in dust.
The Betrothed (1825) **Scott, Sir Walter** (1771–1832) Scottish writer and historian

83 Do you not know I am a woman? When I think, I must speak.
As You Like It, III.ii

84 Frailty, thy name is woman!
Hamlet, I.ii

85 She's beautiful, and therefore to be woo'd;
She is a woman, therefore to be won.
Henry VI, Part 1, V.iii

86 A woman mov'd is like a fountain troubled –
Muddy, ill-seeming, thick, bereft of beauty.
The Taming of the Shrew, V.ii **Shakespeare, William** (1564–1616) English dramatist, poet and actor

87 The truth is I worship women ... the kind who can use both intelligence and femininity. The woman must give the impression that she needs a man.
In Spada, *Streisand: The Intimate Biography* (1995) **Sharif, Omar** (1932–) Egyptian film actor

88 The fickleness of the women I love is only equalled by the infernal constancy of the women who love me.
The Philanderer (1898)

89 The one point on which all women are in furious secret rebellion against the existing law is the saddling of the right to a child with the obligation to become the servant of a man.
Getting Married (1911) **Shaw, George Bernard** (1856–1950) Irish socialist, writer, dramatist and critic

90 Here's to the maiden of bashful fifteen;
Here's to the widow of fifty;
Here's to the flaunting, extravagant quean;
And here's to the housewife that's thrifty.
Let the toast pass –
Drink to the lass –
I'll warrant she'll prove an excuse for the glass!
The School for Scandal (1777) **Sheridan, Richard Brinsley** (1751–1816) Irish dramatist, politician and orator

91 What will not woman, gentle woman, dare,
When strong affection stirs her spirit up?
Madoc (1805) **Southey, Robert** (1774–1843) English poet, essayist, historian and letter writer

92 It is clearly absurd that it should be possible for a woman to qualify as a saint with direct access to the Almighty while she may not qualify as a curate.
Attr. **Stocks, Mary, Baroness** (1891–1975) English educationist, broadcaster and biographer

93 The woman is so hard
Upon the woman.
The Princess (1847) **Tennyson, Alfred, Lord** (1809–1892) English lyric poet

94 Once a woman has given you her heart you can never get rid of the rest of her.

The Relapse, or Virtue in Danger (1696)
Vanbrugh, Sir John (1664–1726) English dramatist and baroque architect

95 The female woman is one of the greatest institooshuns of which this land can boste.
Artemus Ward, His Book (1862), 'Woman's Rights' **Ward, Artemus** (1834–1867) US humorist, journalist, editor and lecturer

96 There's no social differences – till women come in.
Kipps: the Story of a Simple Soul (1905) **Wells, H.G.** (1866–1946) English writer

97 Women have served all these centuries as looking-glasses possessing the magic and delicious power of reflecting the figure of man at twice its natural size.
A Room of One's Own (1929) **Woolf, Virginia** (1882–1941) English writer and critic

98 Scheherazade is the classical example of a woman saving her head by using it.
Attr. **Wynne-Tyson, Esme** (1898–1972) British actress and writer
See also emancipation of women; men and women

WORDS

1 … a habit the pleasure of which increases with practice, but becomes more irksome with neglect.
Letter to her daughter, (1808) **Adams, Abigail** (1744–1818) US letter writer and wife of President John Adams. Of letter-writing

2 'Whom are you?' said he, for he had been to night school.
Attr. **Ade, George** (1866–1944) US fabulist and playwright

3 Words are physic to the distempered mind.
Prometheus Bound **Aeschylus** (525–456 BC) Greek dramatist and poet

4 Lord, make my words sweet and reasonable. Some day I may have to eat them.
The Observer, (1998) **Ashdown, Paddy** (1941–) Former leader of the UK Liberal Democrats

5 Letters of thanks, letters from banks,
Letters of joy from girl and boy,
Receipted bills and invitations
To inspect new stock or to visit relations,
And applications for situations,
And timid lovers' declarations,
And gossip, gossip from all the nations.
Collected Poems, 1933–1938, 'Night Mail' **Auden, W.H.** (1907–1973) English poet, essayist, critic, teacher and dramatist

6 The ill and unfit choice of words wonderfully obstructs the understanding.
The New Organon (1620) **Bacon, Francis** (1561–1626) English philosopher, essayist, politician and courtier

7 The habit of common and continuous speech is a symptom of mental deficiency.
Literary Studies (1879) **Bagehot, Walter** (1826–1877) English economist and political philosopher

8 Man shall not live by bread alone, but by every word that proceedeth out of the mouth of God.
Matthew, 4:4 **The Bible (King James Version)**

9 We who deal in words must strive to keep language pure and wholesome; and it is hard work, as hard almost as digging a stony field with a blunt spade.
Time in a Red Coat (1984) **Brown, George MacKay** (1921–1996) Scottish novelist, poet and playwright

10 Obstinacy in a bad cause, is but constancy in a good.
Religio Medici (1643) **Browne, Sir Thomas** (1605–1682) English physician, author and antiquary

11 An orator is a man who says what he thinks and feels what he says.
Attr. **Bryan, William Jennings** (1860–1925) US Democrat politician and editor

12 Be not the slave of Words.
Sartor Resartus (1834)

13 Speech is human, silence is divine, yet also brutish and dead: therefore we must learn both arts.
Attr. **Carlyle, Thomas** (1795–1881) Scottish historian, biographer, critic, and essayist

14 It wasn't my finest hour. It wasn't even my
finest half hour.
The Washington Post, (1988) **Clinton, William
('Bill')** (1946–) US Democrat President.
Remembering an overlong speech

15 I am glad you came in to punctuate my
discourse, which I fear has gone on for an
hour without any stop at all.
Remak, 29 June 1833, published in *Table Talk*
(1835) **Coleridge, Samuel Taylor** (1772–1834)
English poet, philosopher and critic

16 Without knowing the force of words, it is
impossible to know men.
Analects **Confucius** (c.550–c.478 BC) Chinese
philosopher and teacher of ethics

17 A timid question will always receive a
confident answer.
Scintillae Juris (1877) **Darling, Charles** (1849–
1936) English judge and Conservative
politician

18 Until we learn the use of living words we
shall continue to be waxworks inhabited by
gramophones.
The Observer, (1929) **De La Mare, Walter** (1873–
1956) English poet

19 'Not to put too fine a point upon it' – a
favourite apology for plain-speaking with
Mr Snagsby.
Bleak House (1853) **Dickens, Charles** (1812–1870)
English writer

20 Sir, more than kisses, letters mingle souls.
'To Sir Henry Wotton' (1597–1598) **Donne,
John** (1572–1631) English poet

21 I am not an optimist but a meliorist.
In L. Housman, *A.E.H.* (1937) **Eliot, George**
(1819–1880) English writer and poet

22 Words strain,
Crack and sometimes break, under the
burden,
Under the tension, slip, slide, perish,
Decay with imprecision, will not stay in
place,
Will not stay still.
Four Quartets (1944) **Eliot, T.S.** (1888–1965) US-
born British poet, verse dramatist and critic

23 Words are also actions, and actions are a
kind of words.

'The Poet' (1844)

24 By necessity, by proclivity, – and by delight,
we all quote.
Letters and Social Aims (1875) **Emerson, Ralph
Waldo** (1803–1882) US poet, essayist,
transcendentalist and teacher

25 Grant me some wild expressions, Heavens,
or I shall burst ... Words, words or I shall
burst.
The Constant Couple (1699) **Farquhar, George**
(1678–1707) Irish dramatist

26 It was in the times, barbarous and gothic,
when words had a meaning; in those days,
writers would express thoughts.
La Vie Littéraire (1888) **France, Anatole** (1844–
1924) French writer and critic

27 Dialect words – those terrible marks of the
beast to the truly genteel.
The Mayor of Casterbridge (1886) **Hardy,
Thomas** (1840–1928) English writer and poet

28 Words are wise men's counters, they do
but reckon by them; but they are the
money of fools.
Leviathan (1651) **Hobbes, Thomas** (1588–1679)
Political philosopher

29 I am omniverbivorous by nature and
training. Passing by such words as are
poisonous, I can swallow most others, and
chew such as I cannot swallow.
The Autocrat of the Breakfast-Table (1858)
Holmes, Oliver Wendell (1809–1894) US
physician, poet, writer and scientist

30 I labour to be brief, and I become obscure.
Ars Poetica, line 25 **Horace** (65–8 BC) Roman
poet

31 Thanks to words, we have been able to rise
above the brutes; and thanks to words, we
have often sunk to the level of the demons.
Adonis and the Alphabet (1956)

32 Words can be like X-rays, if you use them
properly – they'll go through anything.
Brave New World (1932) **Huxley, Aldous** (1894–
1963) English writer, poet and critic

33 Summer afternoon – summer afternoon;
to me those have always been the two most
beautiful words in the English language.

In Edith Wharton, *A Backward Glance* (1934) **James, Henry** (1843–1916) US-born British writer, critic and letter writer

34 *Lexicographer*. A writer of dictionaries, a harmless drudge.
A Dictionary of the English Language (1755)

35 *Dull*. 8. To make dictionaries is dull work.
A Dictionary of the English Language (1755)

36 He that tries to recommend him by select quotations, will succeed like the pedant in Hierocles, who, when he offered his house to sale, carried a brick in his pocket as a specimen.
The Plays of William Shakespeare (1765)

37 In a man's letter his soul lies naked.
Quoted in *The Times* **Johnson, Samuel** (1709–1784) English lexicographer, poet, critic, conversationalist and essayist

38 Talking and eloquence are not the same: to speak, and to speak well, are two things.
Timber, or Discoveries made upon Men and Matter (1641) **Jonson, Ben** (1572–1637) English dramatist and poet

39 I fear those big words, Stephen said, which make us so unhappy.
Ulysses (1922) **Joyce, James** (1882–1941) Irish writer

40 Words are, of course, the most powerful drug used by mankind.
Speech, (1923) **Kipling, Rudyard** (1865–1936) Indian-born British poet and writer

41 I hate false words, and seek with care, difficulty, and moroseness, those that fit the thing.
Imaginary Conversations (1853)

42 How many verses have I thrown
Into the fire because the one
Peculiar word, the wantcd most,
Was irrevocably lost.
'Verses Why Burnt' **Landor, Walter Savage** (1775–1864) English poet and writer

43 The finest eloquence is that which gets things done; the worst is that which delays them.
Speech at Paris Peace Conference, (1919) **Lloyd George, David** (1863–1945) British Liberal statesman

44 Woord is but wynd; leff woord and tak the dede.
'Secrets of Old Philosophers' **Lydgate, John** (c.1370–c.1451) English monk, poet and translator

45 Nothing is so useless as a general maxim.
Collected Essays (1843), 'Machiavelli' **Macaulay, Lord** (1800–1859) English Liberal statesman, essayist and poet

46 Words are men's daughters, but God's sons are things.
Boulter's Monument (1745) **Madden, Samuel** (1686–1765) Irish writer

47 All words,
And no performance!
The Parliament of Love (1624) **Massinger, Philip** (1583–1640) English dramatist and poet

48 There are things to confess that enrich the world, and things that need not be said.
The Independent, (1988) **Mitchell, Joni** (1943–) Canadian singer and songwriter

49 That most delightful way of wasting time.
Critical Miscellanies (1886), 'Life of George Eliot' **Morley, John, 1st Viscount Morley** (1838–1923) British journalist, critic and statesman. Of letter-writing

50 Beware of the conversationalist who adds 'in other words'. He is merely starting afresh.
The Observer, (1964) **Morley, Robert** (1908–1992) British actor

51 The belief that words have a meaning of their own account is a relic of primitive word magic, and it is still a part of the air we breathe in nearly every discussion.
The Meaning of Meaning (1923) **Ogden, C.K.** (1889–1957) and **Richards, I.A** (1893–1979) English critics and poets

52 All letters, methinks, should be as free and easy as one's discourse, not studied as an oration, nor made up of hard words like a charm.
Letter to Sir William Temple, (1653) **Osborne, Dorothy (Lady Temple)** (1627–1695) English letter writer

53 You can lead a horticulture but you can't make her think.

In J. Keats, *You Might As Well Live* (1970) When challenged to compose a sentence using the word 'horticulture'

54 Check enclosed.
Giving her version of the two most beautiful words in the English language **Parker, Dorothy** (1893–1967) US writer, poet, critic and wit

55 He remembered too late on his thorny green bed,
Much that well may be thought cannot wisely be said.
Crotchet Castle (1831), 'The Priest and the Mulberry Tree' **Peacock, Thomas Love** (1785–1866) English writer and poet

56 A widely-read man never quotes accurately … Misquotation is the pride and privilege of the learned.
Common Misquotations (1937) **Pearson, Hesketh** (1887–1964) English biographer

57 Dr Johnson's sayings would not appear so extraordinary, were it not for his bow-wow way.
In Boswell, *The Life of Samuel Johnson* (1791) **Pembroke, Earl of** (1734–1794) English general

58 You've a sharp tongue in your head, Mr Essick. Look out it doesn't cut your throat.
The Rising Gorge **Perelman, S.J.** (1904–1979) US humorist, writer and dramatist

59 A word to the wise is enough.
Persa **Plautus, Titus Maccius** (c.254–184 BC) Roman comic dramatist

60 Words are like leaves; and where they most abound,
Much fruit of sense beneath is rarely found.
An Essay on Criticism (1711) **Pope, Alexander** (1688–1744) English poet, translator and editor

61 But words once spoke can never be recall'd.
Horace's Art of Poetry Made English (1680) **Roscommon, Fourth Earl of** (1633–1685) Irish translator and poet

62 There is a southern proverb, – fine words butter no parsnips.
A Legend of Montrose (1819) **Scott, Sir Walter** (1771–1832) Scottish writer and historian

63 Snivelling snufflebusters.
A Semple-ism, first recorded 1905 **Semple, Robert** (1873–1955) New Zealand politician. A favourite term of abuse for whingeing complainants or opponents

64 Conversation has a kind of charm about it, an insinuating and insidious something that elicits secrets from us just like love or liquor.
Epistles **Seneca** (c.4 BC–AD 65) Roman philosopher, poet, dramatist, essayist, rhetorician and statesman

65 Words may be false and full of Art,
Sighs are the natural language of the heart.
Psyche (1675) **Shadwell, Thomas** (c.1642–1692) English poet, writer and playwright

66 I do not much dislike the matter, but
The manner of his speech.
Antony and Cleopatra, II.ii

67 Men of few words are the best men.
Henry V, III.ii

68 He draweth out the thread of his verbosity finer than the staple of his argument.
Love's Labour Lost, V.i

69 But words are words: I never yet did hear
That the bruis'd heart was pierced through the ear.
Othello, I.iii **Shakespeare, William** (1564–1616) English dramatist, poet and actor

70 She's as headstrong as an allegory on the banks of the Nile.
The Rivals (1775)

71 You shall see them on a beautiful quarto page, where a neat rivulet of text shall murmur through a meadow of margin.
The School for Scandal (1777) **Sheridan, Richard Brinsley** (1751–1816) Irish dramatist, politician and orator

72 The latest definition of an optimist is one who fills up his crossword puzzle in ink.
The Observer, (1925) **Shorter, Clement King** (1857–1926) English writer and critic

73 How often misused words generate misleading thoughts.
Principles of Ethics (1879) **Spencer, Herbert** (1820–1903) English philosopher and journalist

74 The word bites like a fish.
Shall I throw it back, free
Arrowing to that sea
Where thoughts lash tail and fin?
Or shall I pull it in
To rhyme upon a dish?
'Word' **Spender, Sir Stephen** (1909–1995)
English poet, editor, translator and diarist

75 I have heard Will Honeycomb say, A
Woman seldom Writes her Mind but in
her Postscript.
The Spectator, 79, (1711) **Steele, Sir Richard**
(1672–1729) Irish-born English writer,
dramatist and politician

76 Rose is a rose is a rose, is a rose.
Sacred Emily (1913) **Stein, Gertrude** (1874–1946)
US writer, dramatist, poet and critic

77 'Tis known by the name of perseverance in
a good cause, – and of obstinacy in a bad
one.
Tristram Shandy (1759–67) **Sterne, Laurence**
(1713–1768) Irish-born English writer and
clergyman

78 Man is a creature who lives not upon bread
alone, but principally by catchwords.
Virginibus Puerisque (1881) **Stevenson, Robert
Louis** (1850–1894) Scottish writer, poet and
essayist

79 It's better to be quotable than to be honest.
The Guardian **Stoppard, Tom** (1937–) British
dramatist

80 Famous remarks are seldom quoted
correctly.
No Mean City (1944) **Strunsky, Simeon** (1879–
1948)

81 No, my dear, it is I who am surprised; you
are merely astonished.
Attr. **Webster, Noah** (1758–1843) US
lexicographer. Responding to his wife's
comment that she had been surprised to find
him embracing their maid

82 We should constantly use the most
common, little, easy words (so they are
pure and proper) which our language
affords.
In R. Southey, *Life of Wesley* (1820) **Wesley,
John** (1703–1791) English theologian and
preacher. On preaching to 'plain people'

83 There is no such thing as conversation. It is
an illusion. There are intersecting
monologues, that is all.
There is No Conversation (1935) **West, Dame
Rebecca** (1892–1983) English writer, critic and
feminist
See also language; writing

WORK

1 I will undoubtedly have to seek what is
happily known as gainful employment,
which I am glad to say does not describe
holding public office.
Attr. **Acheson, Dean** (1893–1971) US Democrat
politician. Remark made on leaving his post
as Secretary of State, 1952

2 I love deadlines. I like the wooshing sound
they make as they fly by.
Attr. **Adams, Douglas** (1952–2001) English
humorist and author

3 Your business clothes are naturally
attracted to staining liquids. This attraction
is strongest just before an important
meeting.
*Building a Better Life by Stealing Office Supplies:
Dogbert's Big Book of Business* (1991)

4 Be careful that what you write does not
offend anybody or cause problems within
the company. The safest approach is to
remove all useful information.
*Building a Better Life by Stealing Office Supplies:
Dogbert's Big Book of Business* (1991)

5 It is better for your career to do nothing,
than to do something and attract criticism.
*Building a Better Life by Stealing Office Supplies:
Dogbert's Big Book of Business* (1991)

6 In Japan, employees occasionally work
themselves to death. It's called Karoshi. I
don't want that to happen to anybody in
my department. The trick is to take a break
as soon as you see a bright light and hear
dead relatives beckon.
The Dilbert Principle (1996)

7 There's nothing more dangerous than a
resourceful idiot.
The Dilbert Principle **Adams, Scott** (1957–) US
cartoonist

8 Miracles can be made, but only by
sweating.
Corriere della Sera, (1994) **Agnelli, Giovanni**
(1921–2003) Italian industrialist

9 If it should exist, it doesn't.
Arnold's First Law of Documentation

10 If it does exist, it's out of date.
Arnold's Second Law of Documentation

11 The remaining work to finish in order to
reach your goal increases as the deadline
approaches.
Bove's Theorem

12 The Six Stages of Production:
• Wild Enthusiasm
• Total Confusion
• Utter Despair
• The Search for the Guilty
• The Persecution of the Innocent
• The Promotion of the Incompetent.
No project was ever completed on time
and within budget.
Cheops Law **Anonymous**

13 The more I want to get something done,
the less I call it work.
Illusions: Reflections of a Reluctant Messiah **Bach,
Richard** (1936–)

14 How can I take an interest in my work
when I don't like it?
Attr. **Bacon, Francis (artist)** (1909–1992) Irish-
born expressionist painter

15 I hold every man a debtor to his profession.
The Elements of Common Law (1596) **Bacon,
Francis** (1561–1626) English philosopher,
essayist, politician and courtier

16 The price one pays for pursuing any
profession or calling is an intimate
knowledge of its ugly side.
Nobody Knows My Name (1961) **Baldwin, James**
(1924–1987) US writer, dramatist, poet and
civil rights activist

17 I rather think of having a career of my own.
In Asquith, *Autobiography* (1920) **Balfour, A.J.**
(1848–1930) British Conservative Prime
Minister. On being asked whether he was
going to marry Margot Tennant

18 A servant's too often a negligent elf;
– If it's business of consequence do it
yourself!
The Ingoldsby Legends (1840–1847) **Barham,
Rev. Richard Harris** (1788–1845) English
clergyman and comic poet

19 Anyone can do any amount of work,
provided it isn't the work he is supposed to
be doing at the moment.
In Robert E. Drennan, *The Algonquin Wits*
(1968)

20 I do most of my work sitting down; that's
where I shine.
Attr. **Benchley, Robert** (1889–1945) US essayist,
humorist and actor

21 Habit of work is growing on me. I could
get into the way of going to my desk as a
man goes to whisky, or rather to chloral.
Journals (1932)

22 The test of a first-rate work, and a test of
your sincerity in calling it a first-rate work,
is that you finish it.
Things That Have Interested Me (1921–1925)
Bennett, Arnold (1867–1931) English writer,
dramatist and journalist

23 His was the sort of career that made the
Recording Angel think seriously about
taking up shorthand.
Attr. **Bentley, Nicolas** (1907–1978) English
publisher and artist

24 The labourer is worthy of his hire.
Luke, 10:7

25 If any would not work, neither should he
eat.
II Thessalonians, 3:10

26 The husbandman that laboureth must be
first partaker of the fruits.
II Timothy, 2:6 **The Bible (King James Version)**

27 *Plan:* To bother about the best method of
accomplishing an accidental result.
The Enlarged Devil's Dictionary (1961) **Bierce,
Ambrose** (1842–c.1914) US writer, verse writer
and soldier

28 To youth I have but three words of counsel
– work, work, work.
Attr. **Bismarck, Prince Otto von** (1815–1898)
First Chancellor of the German Reich

29 What is qualified? What have I been qualified for in my life? I haven't been qualified to be a mayor. I'm not qualified to be a songwriter. I'm not qualified to be a TV producer. I'm not qualified to be a successful businessman. And so, I don't know what qualified means. And I think people get too hung up on that in a way, you know?
Attr. **Bono, Sonny** (1935–1997) US singer-songwriter, businessman and politician

30 She felt weary and careworn, in the way one often does before the big job of work is tackled; that sense of premature or projected exhaustion that is the breeding-ground of all procrastination.
Brazzaville Beach (1990) **Boyd, William** (1952–) Scottish writer

31 All our talents increase in the using, and every faculty, both good and bad, strengthens by exercise.
The Tenant of Wildfell Hall (1848) **Brontë, Anne** (1820–1849) English writer and poet

32 We labour soon, we labour late,
To feed the titled knave, man,
And a' the comfort we're to get,
Is that ayont the grave, man.
'The Tree of Liberty' (1838) **Burns, Robert** (1759–1796) Scottish poet and songwriter

33 Every man's work, whether it be literature or music or pictures or architecture or anything else, is always a portrait of himself.
The Way of All Flesh (1903) **Butler, Samuel** (1835–1902) English writer, painter, philosopher and scholar

34 That was where certainty lay, in everyday work ... The essential thing was to do one's job well.
The Plague (1947) **Camus, Albert** (1913–1960) Algerian-born French writer

35 Be no longer a Chaos, but a World, or even Worldkin. Produce! Produce! Were it but the pitifullest infinitesimal fraction of a Product, produce it, in God's name! 'Tis the utmost thou hast in thee: out with it, then. Up, up! Whatsoever thy hand findeth to do, do it with thy whole might.
Sartor Resartus (1834)

36 Blessed is he who has found his work; let him ask no other blessedness.
Past and Present (1843)

37 Work is the grand cure of all the maladies and miseries that ever beset mankind.
Speech, (1886) **Carlyle, Thomas** (1795–1881) Scottish historian, biographer, critic, and essayist

38 Diligence is the mother of good fortune; and the goal of a good intention was never reached through its opposite, laziness.
Don Quixote (1615) **Cervantes, Miguel de** (1547–1616) Spanish writer and dramatist

39 The time has come, something huge is approaching us, a refreshing, powerful storm is brewing ... Soon it will blow away all the laziness, indifference, prejudice against work and decaying boredom from our society ... I'm going to work, and in some twenty-five or thirty years' time every one will be working. Every one!
The Three Sisters (1901) **Chekhov, Anton** (1860–1904) Russian writer, dramatist and doctor

40 You seem to have no real purpose in life and won't realize at the age of twenty-two that for a man life means work, and hard work if you mean to succeed.
Letter to Winston Churchill, (1897) **Churchill, Jennie Jerome** (1854–1921) US-born English hostess and author

41 For it is commonly said: 'hard tasks are pleasant when they are finished'.
De Finibus **Cicero** (106–43 BC) Roman orator, statesman, essayist and letter writer

42 He that would thrive
Must rise at five;
He that hath thriven
May lie till seven.
Paraemiologia Anglo-Latina (1639) **Clarke, John** (fl. 1639) English scholar

43 Petticoats up to the knees, or even, it might be, above them,
Matching their lily-white legs with the clothes that they trod in the wash-tub!
The Bothie of Tober-na-Vuolich (1848) **Clough, Arthur Hugh** (1819–1861) English poet and letter writer

44 Energy, brains and hard work made Hong Kong. If only a few of its people would come here.
Daily Mail, (1996) **Cluff, Algy** (1940–) British businessman. On the controversy over whether the inhabitants of Hong Kong should be allowed to enter Britain

45 Work, for the night is coming,
When man works no more.
Hymn, (1854) **Coghill, Anna Louisa** (1836–1907) Canadian poet and hymn writer

46 Work without hope draws nectar in a sieve,
And hope without an object cannot live.
'Work Without Hope' (1828) **Coleridge, Samuel Taylor** (1772–1834) English poet, philosopher and critic

47 Perfect freedom is reserved for the man who lives by his own work and in that work does what he wants to do.
Speculum Mentis (1924) **Collingwood, R.G.** (1889–1943) English philosopher, archaeologist and historian

48 Not a penny off the pay, not a minute on the day.
Speech, (1926) **Cook, A.J.** (1885–1931) English miners' leader

49 There is no right to strike against the public safety by anybody, anywhere, any time.
Telegram to the President of the American Federation of Labour, (1919) **Coolidge, Calvin** (1872–1933) US President. Of the Boston police strike

50 Work is much more fun than fun.
The Observer, (1963) **Coward, Sir Noël** (1899–1973) English dramatist, actor, producer and composer

51 It is better to wear out than to rust out.
In Horne, *The Duty of Contending for the Faith* (1786) **Cumberland, Bishop Richard** (1631–1718) English philosopher, divine and translator

52 One never notices what has been done; one can only see what remains to be done.
Letter to her brother, (1894) **Curie, Marie** (1867–1934) Polish-born French physicist

53 'My time is filched by toil and sleep;
My heart,' he thought, 'is clogged with dust;
My soul that flashed from out the deep,
A magic blade, begins to rust.'
'A Ballad of a Workman' (1894) **Davidson, John** (1857–1909) Scottish writer

54 This became a credo of mine ... attempt the impossible in order to improve your work.
Attr. **Davis, Bette** (1908–1989) US film actress

55 To do nothing and get something, formed a boy's ideal of a manly career.
Sybil (1845) **Disraeli, Benjamin** (1804–1881) English statesman and writer

56 'You're working class, right?'
'We would be if there was any work.'
The Commitments (film, 1991) **Doyle, Roddy** (1958–) Irish writer

57 People don't choose their careers; they are engulfed by them.
New York Times, (1959) **Dos Passos, John** (1896–1970) US writer

58 These works brought all these people here. Something must be done to find them work.
Speech, (1936) **Edward VIII** (later Duke of Windsor) (1894–1972) King of the United Kingdom; abdicated 11 December 1936. Of steel works in South Wales where 9,000 men had been made unemployed

59 One trouble with being efficient is that it makes everybody hate you so.
The Calgary Eye Opener (1916) **Edwards, Bob** (1864–1922)

60 If while you are in school, there is a shortage of qualified personnel in a particular field, then by the time you graduate with the necessary qualifications, that field's employment market is glutted.
Attr. **Emmons, Margaret**

61 Man is so made that he can only find relaxation from one kind of labour by taking up another.
The Crime of Sylvestre Bonnard (1881) **France, Anatole** (1844–1924) French writer and critic

62 The man who gives me employment, which I must have or suffer, that man is my master, let me call him what I will.
Social Problems (1884) **George, Henry** (1839–1897) US economist, editor and lecturer

63 There's a whining at the threshold
There's a scratching at the floor.
To work! To work! In Heaven's name!
The wolf is at the door.
Attr. **Gilman, Charlotte Perkins** (1860–1935) US writer, social reformer and feminist

64 O! Men with Mothers and Wives!
It is not linen you're wearing out,
But human creatures' lives! ...
Oh! God! that bread should be so dear,
And flesh and blood so cheap! ...
No blessed leisure for Love or Hope,
But only time for Grief!
'The Song of the Shirt' (1843) **Hood, Thomas** (1799–1845) English poet, editor and humorist

65 I like work; it fascinates me. I can sit and look at it for hours. I love to keep it by me: the idea of getting rid of it nearly breaks my heart.
Three Men in a Boat (1889) **Jerome, Jerome K.** (1859–1927) English writer and dramatist

66 The ugliest of trades have their moments of pleasure. Now, if I were a grave-digger, or even a hangman, there are some people I could work for with a great deal of enjoyment.
Wit and Opinions of Douglas Jerrold (1859) **Jerrold, Douglas William** (1803–1857) English dramatist, writer and wit

67 I have protracted my work till most of those whom I wished to please have sunk into the grave, and success and miscarriage are empty sounds; I therefore dismiss it with frigid tranquillity, having little to fear or hope from censure or praise.
In Boswell, *The Life of Samuel Johnson* (1791) **Johnson, Samuel** (1709–1784) English lexicographer, poet, critic, conversationalist and essayist

68 That one must do some work seriously and must be independent and not merely amuse oneself in life – this our mother has told us always, but never that science was the only career worth following.
In Mary Margaret McBride, *A Long Way from Missouri* **Joliot-Curie, Irène** (1897–1956) French nuclear physicist. Recalling the advice of her mother, Marie Curie

69 If you don't show up for work on Saturday, don't bother coming in on Sunday.
Attr. **Katzenberg, Jeffrey** (1951–) US film producer

70 We're really all of us bottomly broke. I haven't had time to work in weeks.
On the Road (1957) **Kerouac, Jack** (1922–1969) US writer and poet

71 For the last third of life there remains only work. It alone is always stimulating, rejuvenating, exciting and satisfying.
Diaries and Letters (1955) **Kollwitz, Käthe** (1867–1945) German painter, sculptor and graphic artist

72 Job insecurity is a state of mind.
The Observer Review, (1995) **Lang, Ian** (1940–) Scottish Conservative politician

73 Why should I let the toad work
Squat on my life?
Can't I use my wit as a pitchfork
And drive the brute off?
'Toads' (1955) **Larkin, Philip** (1922–1985) English poet, writer and librarian

74 The drop of rain maketh a hole in the stone, not by violence, but by oft falling.
Sermon preached before Edward VI, (1549) **Latimer, Bishop Hugh** (c.1485–1555) English Protestant churchman

75 The bond between a man and his profession is similar to that which ties him to his country; it is just as complex, often ambivalent, and in general it is understood completely only when it is broken ... by retirement in the case of a trade or profession.
Other People's Trades (1989) **Levi, Primo** (1919–1987) Italian writer, poet and chemist; survivor of Auschwitz

76 She did her work with the thoroughness of a mind that reveres details and never quite understands them.
Babbit (1922) **Lewis, Sinclair** (1885–1951) US writer

77 In an English ship, they say, it is poor grub, poor pay, and easy work; in an American ship, good grub, good pay, and hard work. And this is applicable to the working populations of both countries.
The People of the Abyss (1903) **London, Jack** (1876–1916) US writer, sailor, socialist and goldminer

78 Let us, then, be up and doing,
With a heart for any fate;
Still achieving, still pursuing,
Learn to labour and to wait.
'A Psalm of Life' (1838)

79 The heights by great men reached and kept
Were not attained by sudden flight,
But they, while their companions slept,
Were toiling upward in the night.
'The Ladder of Saint Augustine' (1850)
Longfellow, Henry Wadsworth (1807–1882) US poet and writer

80 No man is born into the world, whose work
Is not born with him; there is always work,
And tools to work withal, for those who will:
And blessèd are the horny hands of toil!
'A Glance Behind the Curtain' (1844) **Lowell, James Russell** (1819–1891) US poet, editor, abolitionist and diplomat

81 If politics is the art of the possible, research is surely the art of the soluble. Both are immensely practical-minded affairs.
New Statesman, (1964) **Medawar, Sir Peter** (1915–1987) British zoologist and immunologist

82 The unceasing labour of your life is to build the house of death.
Essais (1580) **Montaigne, Michel de** (1533–1592) French essayist and moralist

83 All their devices for cheapening labour simply resulted in increasing the burden of labour.
News from Nowhere (1891) **Morris, William** (1834–1896) English poet, designer, craftsman, artist and socialist

84 Another fact of life that will not have escaped you is that, in this country, the twenty-four-hour strike is like the twenty-four-hour flu. You have to reckon on it lasting at least five days.
You Can't Have Your Kayak and Heat It, 'Great Expectations', *with Dennis Norden* **Muir, Frank** (1920–1998) English writer, humorist and broadcaster

85 Work should begin with wine and generous joking,
And in the place of penalties for smoking
Let us have fines for platitudes and croaking.
Collected Poems (1934), 'To a Blonde Typist' **Neilson, John Shaw** (1872–1942) Australian poet

86 The rise in the total of those employed is governed by Parkinson's Law and would be much the same whether the volume of work were to increase, diminish or even disappear.
Parkinson's Law (1958)

87 Work expands so as to fill the time available for its completion.
Parkinson's Law (1958) **Parkinson, C. Northcote** (1909–1993) English political scientist and historian

88 In research the horizon recedes as we advance, and is no nearer at sixty than it was at twenty. As the power of endurance weakens with age, the urgency of the pursuit grows more intense – And research is always incomplete.
Isaac Casaubon (1875) **Pattison, Mark** (1813–1884)

89 Competence, like truth, beauty and contact lenses, is in the eye of the beholder.
The Peter Principle – Why Things Always Go Wrong (1969)

90 In a hierarchy every employee tends to rise to his level of incompetence.
The Peter Principle – Why Things Always Go Wrong (1969) **Peter, Laurence J.** (1919–1990) Canadian educationist and writer

91 I am self-employed.
Attr. **Philip, Prince, Duke of Edinburgh**
(1921–) Greek-born consort of Queen
Elizabeth II. Replying to a query as to what
nature of work he did

92 They say hard work never hurt anybody,
but I figure why take the chance.
Attr. **Reagan, Ronald** (1911–2004) US actor,
Republican statesman and President

93 If you have great talents, industry will
improve them: if you have but moderate
abilities, industry will supply their
deficiency.
Discourses on Art (1769) **Reynolds, Sir Joshua**
(1723–1792) English portrait painter

94 I was lucky to always have a work ethic.
Relationships end, men fail, but your work
will never let you down.
The Observer, (1998) **Rhodes, Zandra** (1940–)
English fashion designer

95 I wish to preach not the doctrine of ignoble
ease, but the doctrine of the strenuous life.
Speech, (1899)

96 No man needs sympathy because he has to
work … Far and away the best prize that
life offers is the chance to work hard at
work worth doing.
Address, (1903) **Roosevelt, Theodore** (1858–
1919) US Republican President

97 You will find it a very good practice always
to verify your references, sir!
Attr. **Routh, Martin Joseph** (1755–1854) English
divine and scholar

98 When you see what some girls marry, you
realize how they must hate to work for a
living.
Reflections of a Bachelor Girl (1909) **Rowland,
Helen** (1875–1950) US writer

99 Which of us … is to do the hard and dirty
work for the rest – and for what pay? Who
is to do the pleasant and clean work, and
for what pay?
Sesame and Lilies (1865)

100 Labour without joy is base. Labour without
sorrow is base. Sorrow without labour is
base. Joy without labour is base.
Time and Tide by Weare and Tyne (1867)

101 Life without industry is guilt, and industry
without art is brutality.
Lectures on Art (1870) **Ruskin, John** (1819–1900)
English art critic, philosopher and reformer

102 One of the symptoms of approaching
nervous breakdowns is the belief that one's
work is terribly important. If I were a
medical man, I should prescribe a holiday
to any patient who considered his work
important.
Attr. **Russell, Bertrand** (1872–1970) English
philosopher, mathematician, essayist and
social reformer

103 No! this right hand shall work it all off!
In Cockburn, *Memorials of His Time* (1856)
Scott, Sir Walter (1771–1832) Scottish writer
and historian. Refusing offers of help
following his bankruptcy in 1826

104 I earn that I eat, get that I wear; owe no
man hate, envy no man's happiness; glad
of other men's good, content with my
harm.
As You Like It, III.ii

105 Every good servant does not all
commands.
Cymbeline, V.i

106 If all the year were playing holidays,
To sport would be as tedious as to work;
But when they seldom come, they wish'd-
for come.
Henry IV, Part 1, I.ii

107 The labour we delight in physics pain.
Macbeth, II.iii **Shakespeare, William** (1564–
1616) English dramatist, poet and actor

108 A day's work is a day's work, neither more
nor less, and the man who does it needs a
day's sustenance, a night's repose, and due
leisure, whether he be painter or
ploughman.
An Unsocial Socialist (1887)

109 There are only two qualities in the world:
efficiency and inefficiency; and only two
sorts of people: the efficient and the
inefficient.
John Bull's Other Island (1907) **Shaw, George
Bernard** (1856–1950) Irish socialist, writer,
dramatist and critic

110 We know that you, the organized workers of the country, are our friends ... As for the rest, they do not matter a tinker's curse.
Speech at the Electrical Trades Union Conference, Margate, (1947) **Shinwell, Emanuel** (1884–1986) British Labour politician

111 It is the interest of every man to live as much at his ease as he can; and if his emoluments are to be precisely the same whether he does, or does not perform some very laborious duty, it is certainly his interest, at least as interest is vulgarly understood, either to neglect it altogether, or, if he is subject to some authority which will not suffer him to do this, to perform it in as careless and slovenly a manner as that authority will permit.
Wealth of Nations (1776) **Smith, Adam** (1723–1790) Scottish economist, philosopher and essayist

112 And when we're worn,
Hack'd, hewn with constant service, thrown aside
To rust in peace, or rot in hospitals.
The Loyal Brother (1682) **Southerne, Thomas** (1660–1746) Irish dramatist

113 Have you noticed, the last four strikes we've had, it's pissed down? It wouldn't be a bad idea to check the weather reports before they pull us out next time.
Till Death Do Us Part, television programme **Speight, Johnny** (1920–1998) English screenwriter

114 You will find as you grow older that the weight of rages will press harder and harder upon the employer.
In W. Hayter, *Spooner* (1977) **Spooner, William** (1844–1930) English churchman and university warden

115 Surely we should find it both touching and inspiriting, that in a field from which success is banished, our race should not cease to labour.
Across the Plains (1892) **Stevenson, Robert Louis** (1850–1894) Scottish writer, poet and essayist

116 And he gave it for his opinion, that whoever could make two ears of corn or two blades of grass to grow upon a spot of ground where only one grew before, would deserve better of mankind, and do more essential service to his country than the whole race of politicians put together.
Gulliver's Travels (1726) **Swift, Jonathan** (1667–1745) Irish satirist, poet, essayist and cleric

117 He didn't riot. He got on his bike and looked for work and he kept looking till he found it.
Speech, (1981) **Tebbitt, Norman** (1931–) English Conservative politician. Of his father who had grown up during the 1930s

118 An expert is a man who has made all the mistakes which can be made in a very narrow field.
Remark, (1972) **Teller, Edward** (1908–2003) Hungarian-born US physicist

119 For more than five years I maintained myself thus solely by the labor of my hands, and I found, that by working about six weeks in a year, I could meet all the expenses of living.
Walden (1854) **Thoreau, Henry David** (1817–1862) US essayist, social critic and writer

120 It's a recession when your neighbour loses his job; it's a depression when you lose your own.
The Observer, (1958) **Truman, Harry S.** (1884–1972) US Democrat President

121 Work consists of whatever a body is obliged to do.
The Adventures of Tom Sawyer (1876) **Twain, Mark** (1835–1910) US humorist, writer, journalist and lecturer

122 When man was put in the garden of Eden, he was put there to work; that proves that man was not born for rest. Let us work without reasoning – that is the only way to make life bearable.
Candide (1759)

123 Work keeps away those three great evils: boredom, vice, and poverty.
Candide (1759) **Voltaire** (1694–1778) French philosopher, dramatist, poet, historian, writer and critic

124 In works of labour, or of skill,
I would be busy too;
For Satan finds some mischief still
For idle hands to do.
'Against Idleness and Mischief' (1715) **Watts,
Isaac** (1674–1748) English hymn writer, poet
and minister

125 Everybody hates house-agents because
they have everybody at a disadvantage. All
other callings have a certain amount of
give and take; the house-agent simply
takes.
Kipps: the Story of a Simple Soul (1905) **Wells,
H.G.** (1866–1946) English writer

126 The best careers advice to give to the
young is 'Find out what you like doing best
and get someone to pay you for doing it.'
The Observer, (1975) **Whitehorn, Katherine**
(1926–) English writer

127 Work is the curse of the drinking classes.
In Pearson, *Life of Oscar Wilde* (1946) **Wilde,
Oscar** (1854–1900) Irish poet, dramatist,
writer, critic and wit

128 The intellect of man is forced to choose
Perfection of the life, or of the work.
'The Choice' (1933) **Yeats, W.B.** (1865–1939)
Irish poet, dramatist, editor, writer and
senator
See also idleness and unemployment

THE WORLD

1 Alexander wept on hearing from
Anaxarchus that there was an infinite
number of worlds ... 'Do you not think it
lamentable that with such an infinite
number, we have not yet conquered one?'
In Plutarch, *On the Tranquillity of the Mind*
Alexander the Great (356–323 BC) Macedonian
king and conquering army commander

2 Ah, love, let us be true
To one another! for the world, which seems
To lie before us like a land of dreams,
So various, so beautiful, so new,
Hath really neither joy, nor love, nor light,
Nor certitude, nor peace, nor help for pain;
And we are here as on a darkling plain
Swept with confused alarms of struggle
and flight
Where ignorant armies clash by night.
'Dover Beach' (1867) **Arnold, Matthew** (1822–
1888) English poet, critic, essayist and
educationist

3 This is a singularly ill-contrived world, but
not so ill-contrived as all that.
Attr. **Balfour, A.J.** (1848–1930) British
Conservative Prime Minister

4 Well, my deliberate opinion is – it's a jolly
strange world.
The Title (1918) **Bennett, Arnold** (1867–1931)
English writer, dramatist and journalist

5 The world is made of people who never
quite get into the first team and who just
miss the prizes at the flower show.
The Face of Violence (1954) **Bronowski, Jacob**
(1908–1974) British scientist, writer and TV
presenter

6 There is always a 'but' in this imperfect
world.
The Tenant of Wildfell Hall (1848) **Brontë, Anne**
(1820–1849) English writer and poet

7 For the world, I count it not an inn, but an
hospital, and a place, not to live, but to die
in.
Religio Medici (1643) **Browne, Sir Thomas**
(1605–1682) English physician, author and
antiquary

8 The world is made up for the most part of
fools and knaves.
'To Mr. Clifford, on his Humane Reason'
Buckingham, Duke of (1628–1687) English
courtier and dramatist

9 The world will, in the end, follow only
those who have despised as well as served
it.
The Note-Books of Samuel Butler (1912) **Butler,
Samuel** (1835–1902) English writer, painter,
philosopher and scholar

10 But the world is an old woman, and
mistakes any gilt farthing for a gold coin;
whereby being often cheated, she will
thenceforth trust nothing but the common
copper.
Sartor Resartus (1834) **Carlyle, Thomas** (1795–
1881) Scottish historian, biographer, critic,
and essayist

11 This world is bad enough, may-be,
We do not comprehend it;
But in one fact can all agree,
God won't, and we can't mend it.
Dipsychus (1865) **Clough, Arthur Hugh** (1819–1861) English poet and letter writer

12 How much can come
And much can go,
And yet abide the World!
'There came a Wind' (c.1883) **Dickinson, Emily** (1830–1886) US poet

13 What a fine comedy this world would be if one did not play a part in it!
Letters to Sophie Volland **Diderot, Denis** (1713–1784) French philosopher, encyclopaedist, writer and dramatist

14 Well, World, you have kept faith with me,
Kept faith with me;
Upon the whole you have proved to be
Much as you said you were.
'He Never Expected Much, A Consideration on My Eighty-Sixth birthday' (1928) **Hardy, Thomas** (1840–1928) English writer and poet

15 If the world were good for nothing else, it is a fine subject for speculation.
Characteristics (1823) **Hazlitt, William** (1778–1830) English writer and critic

16 The world is a fine place and worth the fighting for.
For Whom the Bell Tolls (1940) **Hemingway, Ernest** (1898–1961) US author

17 This world where much is to be done and little to be known.
In G.B. Hill (ed.), *Johnsonian Miscellanies* (1897) **Johnson, Samuel** (1709–1784) English lexicographer, poet, critic, conversationalist and essayist

18 In the struggle between you and the world, support the world.
Reflections on Sin, Sorrow, Hope and the True Way (1953) **Kafka, Franz** (1883–1924) Czech-born German-speaking writer

19 Call the world if you Please 'The vale of Soul-making'.
Letter to George and Georgiana Keats, (1819) **Keats, John** (1795–1821) English poet

20 One may not regard the world as a sort of metaphysical brothel for emotions.
Darkness at Noon (1940) **Koestler, Arthur** (1905–1983) British writer, essayist and political refugee

21 The world is becoming like a lunatic asylum run by lunatics.
The Observer, (1953) **Lloyd George, David** (1863–1945) British Liberal statesman

22 World is crazier and more of it than we think,
Incorrigibly plural. I peel and portion
A tangerine and spit the pips and feel
The drunkenness of things being various.
'Snow' (1935) **MacNeice, Louis** (1907–1963) Belfast-born poet, writer, radio producer, translator and critic

23 Ours is a world where people don't know what they want and are willing to go through hell to get it.
Treasury of Humorous Quotations **Marquis, Don** (1878–1937) US columnist, satirist and poet

24 Th' whole worl's in a terrible state o' chassis!
Juno and the Paycock (1924) **O'Casey, Sean** (1880–1964) Irish dramatist

25 The optimist thinks that this is the best of all possible worlds and the pessimist knows it.
Bulletin of Atomic Scientists, (1951) **Oppenheimer, J. Robert** (1904–1967) US nuclear physicist

26 All the world is queer save thee and me, and even thou art a little queer.
Attr. (1828) **Owen, Robert** (1771–1858) Welsh social and educational reformer. To W. Allen, on dissolving their business partnership

27 and I understood
how there is nothing complicated in the world
that is not of my own making.
'turning the pages' **Patten, Brian** (1946–) British poet

28 The world can survive very well without literature. But it can survive even more easily without man.

Situations **Sartre, Jean-Paul** (1905–1980)
French philosopher, writer, dramatist and
critic

29 The ae half of the warld thinks the tither
daft.
Redgauntlet (1824) **Scott, Sir Walter** (1771–1832)
Scottish writer and historian

30 O, how full of briers is this working-day
world!
As You Like It, I.iii

31 I hold the world but as the world,
Gratiano –
A stage, where every man must play a part,
And mine a sad one.
The Merchant of Venice, I.i

32 How many goodly creatures are there here!
How beauteous mankind is! O brave new
world
That has such people in't!
The Tempest, V.i **Shakespeare, William** (1564–
1616) English dramatist, poet and actor

33 Nothing is ever done in this world until
men are prepared to kill one another if it is
not done.
Major Barbara (1907) **Shaw, George Bernard**
(1856–1950) Irish socialist, writer, dramatist
and critic

34 I consider the world as made for me, not
me for the world: it is my maxim therefore
to enjoy it while I can, and let futurity shift
for itself.
The Adventures of Roderick Random (1748)
Smollett, Tobias (1721–1771) Scottish writer,
satirist, historian, traveller and physician

35 In my room, the world is beyond my
understanding;
But when I walk I see that it consists of
three or four hills and a cloud.
'Of the Surface of Things' (1923) **Stevens,
Wallace** (1879–1955) US poet, essayist,
dramatist and lawyer

36 The world is so full of a number of things,
I'm sure we should all be as happy as
kings.
A Child's Garden of Verses (1885), 'Happy
Thought' **Stevenson, Robert Louis** (1850–1894)
Scottish writer, poet and essayist

37 O world invisible, we view thee,
O world intangible, we touch thee,
O world unknowable, we know thee,
Inapprehensible, we clutch thee!
'The Kingdom of God' (1913) **Thompson,
Francis** (1859–1907) English poet

38 You never enjoy the world aright, till the
sea itself floweth in your veins, till you are
clothed with the heavens, and crowned
with the stars: and perceive yourself to be
the sole heir of the whole world, and more
than so, because men are in it who are
every one sole heirs as well as you. Till you
can sing and rejoice and delight in God, as
misers do in gold, and kings in sceptres,
you can never enjoy the world.
Centuries of Meditations **Traherne, Thomas**
(c.1637–1674) English religious writer and
clergyman

39 This world is a comedy to those that think,
and a tragedy to those that feel.
Letter to Anne, Countess of Upper Ossory,
(1776) **Walpole, Horace** (1717–1797) English
writer and politician

40 The world is full of care, much like unto a
bubble;
Women and care, and care and women,
and women and care and trouble.
Epigram (1647) **Ward, Nathaniel** (1578–1652)
English Puritan divine

41 The world is too much with us; late and
soon,
Getting and spending, we lay waste our
powers.
'The world is too much with us' (1807)

42 Not in Utopia – subterranean fields, –
Or some secreted island, Heaven knows
where!
But in the very world, which is the world
Of all of us, – the place where, in the end
We find our happiness, or not at all!
The Prelude (1850) **Wordsworth, William** (1770–
1850) English poet

43 When we meet, all the world to nothing we
shall laugh; and, in truth Sir this world is
worthy of nothing else.
Letter to Sir Edmund Bacon, (1614) **Wotton,
Sir Henry** (1568–1639) English diplomat,
traveller and poet

44 This pragmatical, preposterous pig of a
world.
The Exile, (1928) **Yeats, W.B.** (1865–1939) Irish
poet, dramatist, editor, writer and senator

45 To know the World, not love her, is thy
point;
She gives but little, nor that little long.
Night-Thoughts on Life, Death and Immortality
(1742–45) **Young, Edward** (1683–1765) English
poet, dramatist, satirist and clergyman
See also global affairs; nature; universe

WRITING

1 Having imagination, it takes you an hour
to write a paragraph that, if you were
unimaginative, would take you only a
minute. Or you might not write the
paragraph at all.
Attr. **Adams, Franklin P.** (1881–1960) US
writer, poet, translator and editor

2 Thus I live in the world rather as a
spectator of mankind, than as one of the
species, by which means I have made
myself a speculative statesman, soldier,
merchant, and artisan, without ever
meddling with any practical part in life.
The Spectator, (March 1711)

3 Authors have established it as a kind of
rule, that a man ought to be dull
sometimes; as the most severe reader
makes allowances for many rests and
nodding-places in a voluminous writer.
The Spectator, (July 1711)

4 I have but ninepence in ready money, but I
can draw for a thousand pounds.
In Boswell, *The Life of Samuel Johnson (1791)* Of
the difference between his conversational and
writing abilities **Addison, Joseph** (1672–1719)
English essayist, poet, playwright and
statesman

5 After being turned down by numerous
publishers, he decided to write for
posterity.
The Fable of the Bohemian who had Hard Luck
(1899) **Ade, George** (1866–1944) US fabulist
and playwright

6 Good writers define reality; bad ones
merely restate it. A good writer turns fact
into truth; a bad writer will, more often
than not, accomplish the opposite.
Saturday Review, (1966) **Albee, Edward** (1928–)
US dramatist

7 Why had I become a writer in the first
place? Because I wasn't fit for society; I
didn't fit into the system.
In Jon Winokur, *Writers on Writing (1990)*
Aldiss, Brian (1925–) English writer

8 Where were you fellows when the paper
was blank?
Attr. **Allen, Fred** (1894–1956) US vaudeville
performer and comedian. Remark to writers
who had heavily edited one of his scripts

9 To be more interested in the writer than
the writing is just eternal human vulgarity.
The Observer Review, (1996) **Amis, Martin**
(1949–) English writer. Of biography

10 Dryden and Pope are not classics of our
poetry, they are classics of our prose.
Essays in Criticism (1888)

11 He lacks the high seriousness of the great
classics, and therewith an important part of
their virtue.
Essays in Criticism (1888) Of Chaucer

12 People think that I can teach them style.
What stuff it all is! Have something to say,
and say it as clearly as you can. That is the
only secret of style.
In Russell, *Collections and Recollections (1898)*
Arnold, Matthew (1822–1888) English poet,
critic, essayist and educationist

13 He that will write well in any tongue, must
follow this counsel of Aristotle, to speak as
the common people do, to think as wise
men do; and so should every man
understand him, and the judgment of wise
men allow him.
Toxophilus (1545) **Ascham, Roger** (1515–1568)
English scholar, educationist and archer

14 Once upon a time I thought there was an
old man with a grey beard somewhere who
knew the truth, and if I was good enough,
naturally he would tell me that this was it.
That person doesn't exist, but that's who I
write for. The great critic in the sky.

In Earl G. Ingersoll (ed.), *Margaret Atwood: Conversations* (1990)

15 Writing ... is an act of faith: I believe it's also an act of hope, the hope that things can be better than they are.
Attr. **Atwood, Margaret** (1939–) Canadian writer, poet and critic

16 How these curiosities would be quite forgot, did not such idle fellows as I am put them down.
Brief Lives (c.1693)

17 When he killed a calf he would do it in high style, and make a speech.
Brief Lives (c.1693) Of Shakespeare **Aubrey, John** (1626–1697) English antiquary, folklorist and biographer

18 No poet or novelist wishes he were the only one who ever lived, but most of them wish they were the only one alive, and quite a number fondly believe their wish has been granted.
The Dyer's Hand (1963) **Auden, W.H.** (1907–1973) English poet, essayist, critic, teacher and dramatist

19 Let other pens dwell on guilt and misery.
Mansfield Park (1814)

20 We all talk Shakespeare, use his similes, and describe with his descriptions.
Mansfield Park (1814)

21 I think I may boast myself to be, with all possible vanity, the most unlearned and uninformed female who ever dared to be an authoress.
Letter to James Stanier Clarke, (1815)

22 ... the little bit (two inches wide) of ivory on which I work with so fine a brush, as produces little effect after much labour.
Letter, (1816) **Austen, Jane** (1775–1817) English writer

23 Writers, like teeth, are divided into incisors and grinders.
'The First Edinburgh Reviewers' (1858)

24 A man who has not read Homer is like a man who has not seen the ocean. There is a great object of which he has no idea.

Literary Studies (1879) **Bagehot, Walter** (1826–1877) English economist and political philosopher

25 Beryl is getting down to her new novel. She can't accept social engagements as they inevitably lead to getting tired and emotional.
The Observer, (1999) **Bainbridge, Beryl** (1934–) English novelist. Message on her answering machine

26 Only good girls keep diaries. Bad girls don't have the time.
Attr. **Bankhead, Tallulah** (1903–1968) US actress

27 That old yahoo George Moore ... His stories impressed me as being on the whole like gruel spooned up off a dirty floor.
Letter, (1914) **Barlow, Jane** (1860–1917) Irish novelist

28 I do loathe explanations.
My Lady Nicotine (1890) **Barrie, Sir J.M.** (1860–1937) Scottish dramatist and writer

29 The writer of originality, unless dead, is always shocking, scandalous; novelty disturbs and repels.
The Second Sex (1953) **Beauvoir, Simone de** (1908–1986) French writer, feminist critic and philosopher

30 If one yearns to live dangerously, is it not as dangerous to persist in the truth as to rush to the barricades? But then it is always more agreeable to play the role of a writer than to be a writer. A writer's life is solitary, often bitter. How pleasant it is to come out of one's room, to fly about the world, make speeches, and cut a swath.
Critical Enquiry, (1975)

31 With a novelist, like a surgeon, you have to get a feeling that you've fallen into good hands – someone from whom you can accept the anaesthetic with confidence.
The New York Times Book Review, (1977) **Bellow, Saul** (1915–2005) Canadian-born US Jewish writer

32 Work on good prose has three steps: a musical stage when it is composed, an architectonic one when it is built, and a textile one when it is woven.
One-Way Street (1928) **Benjamin, Walter** (1892–1940) German writer, philosopher and critic

33 We were put to Dickens as children but it never quite took. That unremitting humanity soon had me cheesed off.
The Old Country (1978) **Bennett, Alan** (1934–) English dramatist, actor and diarist

34 Prose is when all the lines except the last go on to the end. Poetry is when some of them fall short of it.
In Packe, *Life of John Stuart Mill* (1954) **Bentham, Jeremy** (1748–1832) English writer and philosopher

35 The art of Biography
Is different from Geography.
Geography is about Maps,
But Biography is about chaps.
Biography for Beginners (1905) **Bentley, Edmund Clerihew** (1875–1956) English writer

36 Writers as a rule don't make fighters, although I would hate to have to square up to Taki or Andrea Dworkin.
The Spectator, (1992) **Bernard, Jeffrey** (1932–1997) British columnist

37 *Plagiarize*: To take the thought or style of another writer whom one has never, never read.
The Enlarged Devil's Dictionary (1961) **Bierce, Ambrose** (1842–c.1914) US writer, verse writer and soldier

38 If I write four words, I shall strike out three.
Satires (1666)

39 He who does not know how to limit himself does not know how to write.
L'Art Poétique (1674) **Boileau-Despréaux, Nicolas** (1636–1711) French writer

40 Miller is not really a writer but a non-stop talker to whom someone has given a typewriter.
Thoughts in a Dry Season (1978) **Brenan, Gerald** (1894–1987) English writer. Of Henry Miller

41 The idea that it is necessary to go to a university in order to become a successful writer, or even a man or woman of letters (which is by no means the same thing), is one of those phantasies that surround authorship.
On Being an Author (1948) **Brittain, Vera** (1893–1970) English writer and pacifist

42 Novelists should never allow themselves to weary of the study of real life.
The Professor (1857)

43 One day, in the autumn of 1845, I accidentally lighted on a MS volume of verse in my sister Emily's handwriting ... I looked it over, and something more than surprise seized me, – a deep conviction that these were not common effusions, nor at all like the poetry women generally write. I thought them condensed and terse, vigorous and genuine. To my ear, they had also a peculiar music – wild, melancholy, and elevating.
Biographical notice **Brontë, Charlotte** (1816–1855) English novelist

44 No quailing, Mrs Gaskell! no drawing back!
Letter to Ellen Nussey, 1855, about her agreeing to write the life of Charlotte Brontë

45 Girls, do you know Charlotte has been writing a book, and it is much better than likely?
In Elizabeth Gaskell, *Life of Charlotte Brontë* (1857) **Brontë, Rev. Patrick** (1777–1861) English clergyman; father of the Brontës

46 Show me a writer, any writer, who hasn't suffered and I'll show you someone who writes in pastels as opposed to primary colors.
Starting From Scratch (1988) **Brown, Rita Mae** (1944–) US writer and poet

47 Listen, dear, you couldn't write fuck on a dusty venetian blind.
Attr. in *The Sunday Times Magazine*, 1984 **Browne, Coral** (1913–1991) English actress. To a Hollywood writer who had criticized the work of Alan Bennett

48 Beneath the rule of men entirely great
The pen is mightier than the sword.
Richelieu (1839) **Bulwer-Lytton, Edward** (1803–1873) English novelist and politician

49 Writing is more than anything a compulsion, like some people wash their hands thirty times a day for fear of awful consequences if they do not. It pays a whole lot better than this type of compulsion, but it is no more heroic.
Sex and Sensibility (1992) **Burchill, Julie** (1960–) English writer

50 The trouble began with Forster. After him it was considered ungentlemanly to write more than five or six novels.
The Guardian, (1989) **Burgess, Anthony** (1917–1993) English writer, linguist and composer

51 You praise the firm restraint with which they write –
I'm with you there, of course:
They use the snaffle and the curb all right,
But where's the bloody horse?
Adamastor (1930) **Campbell, Roy** (1901–1957) South African poet and journalist

52 Writing has laws of perspective, of light and shade just as painting does, or music. If you are born knowing them, fine. If not, learn them. Then rearrange the rules to suit yourself.
Writers at Work (1958) **Capote, Truman** (1924–1984) US writer

53 O thou who art able to write a Book, which once in the two centuries or oftener there is a man gifted to do, envy not him whom they name City-builder, and inexpressibly pity him whom they name Conqueror or City-burner!
Sartor Resartus (1834)

54 Literary men are ... a perpetual priesthood.
Critical and Miscellaneous Essays (1839)

55 A well-written Life is almost as rare as a well-spent one.
Critical and Miscellaneous Essays (1839)

56 A hoaryheaded and toothless baboon.
Collected Works (1871) On Ralph Waldo Emerson

57 After two weeks of blotching and blaring I have produced two clear papers.
Attr. **Carlyle, Thomas** (1795–1881) Scottish historian, biographer, critic, and essayist

58 As long as the plots keep arriving from outer space, I'll go on with my virgins.
New Yorker, (1976) **Cartland, Barbara** (1901–2000) English writer. On the publication of her 217th book

59 The worshipful father and first founder and embellisher of ornate eloquence in our English, I mean Master Geoffrey Chaucer.
Epilogue to Caxton's edition (c.1478) of Chaucer's translation of Boethius, *The Consolacion of Philosophie* **Caxton, William** (c.1421–1491) First English printer

60 If my books had been any worse I should not have been invited to Hollywood, and if they had been any better I should not have come.
Letter, (1945), to *Atlantic Monthly* editor, Charles W. Morton

61 Would you convey my compliments to the purist who reads your proofs and tell him or her that I write in a sort of broken-down patois which is something like the way a Swiss waiter talks, and that when I split an infinitive, God damn it, I split it so it will stay split.
Letter to Edward Weeks, his English publisher, (1947)

62 The more you reason the less you create.
Raymond Chandler Speaking (1962)

63 What greater prestige can a man like me (not too gifted, but very understanding) have than to have taken a cheap, shoddy and utterly lost kind of writing, and have made of it something that intellectuals claw each other about?
Raymond Chandler Speaking (1962)

64 A good story cannot be devised; it has to be distilled.
Raymond Chandler Speaking (1962) **Chandler, Raymond** (1888–1959) US crime writer

65 The original writer is not the one who refrains from imitating others, but the one who can be imitated by none.
The Beauties of Christianity (1802) **Chateaubriand, François-René** (1768–1848) French writer and statesman

66 I can't write without a reader. It's precisely like a kiss – you can't do it alone.
Christian Science Monitor, (1979)

67 Trust your editor, and you'll sleep on straw.
In Susan Cheever, *Home Before Dark* (1984)
Cheever, John (1912–1982) US novelist

68 If Shakespeare's genius had been cultivated, those beauties, which we so justly admire in him, would have been undisgraced by those extravagancies and that nonsense with which they are frequently accompanied.
Letter to his son, (1748) **Chesterfield, Lord** (1694–1773) English politician and letter writer

69 A good novel tells us the truth about its hero; but a bad novel tells us the truth about its author.
Heretics (1905)

70 Mr Shaw is (I suspect) the only man on earth who has never written any poetry.
Orthodoxy (1908)

71 Hardy went down to botanise in the swamp, while Meredith climbed towards the sun. Meredith became, at his best, a sort of daintily dressed Walt Whitman: Hardy became a sort of village atheist brooding and blaspheming over the village idiot.
The Victorian Age in Literature (1913)

72 Jane Austen was born before those bands which (we are told) protected woman from truth, were burst by the Brontës or elaborately untied by George Eliot. Yet the fact remains that Jane Austen knew much more about men than either of them.
The Victorian Age in Literature (1913)
Chesterton, G.K. (1874–1936) English writer, poet and critic

73 Men will forgive a man anything except bad prose.
Election speech, Manchester, (1906)
Churchill, Sir Winston (1874–1965) English Conservative Prime Minister

74 All writers are liars, and there is not the slightest chance that any writer will get into heaven.
Speech, Melbourne, (1987) **Clark, Manning** (1915–1991)

75 Victor Hugo ... a madman who thought he was Victor Hugo.
Opium (1930) **Cocteau, Jean** (1889–1963) French dramatist, poet, film writer and director

76 I believe the souls of five hundred Sir Isaac Newtons would go to the making up of a Shakespeare or a Milton.
Letter to Thomas Poole, (1801)

77 Until you understand a writer's ignorance, presume yourself ignorant of his understanding.
Biographia Literaria (1817)

78 When I was a boy, I was fondest of Aeschylus; in youth and middle-age I preferred Euripides; now in my declining years I prefer Sophocles. I can now at length see that Sophocles is the most perfect. Yet he never rises to the sublime simplicity of Aeschylus – a simplicity of design, I mean – nor diffuses himself in the passionate outpourings of Euripides.
Table Talk (1835)

79 The faults of great authors are generally excellences carried to an excess.
Miscellanies **Coleridge, Samuel Taylor** (1772–1834) English poet, philosopher and critic

80 Writers are too self-centred to be lonely.
Attr. **Condon, Richard** (1915–1996) US writer

81 An author arrives at a good style when his language performs what is required of it without shyness.
Enemies of Promise (1938)

82 He would not blow his nose without moralizing on conditions in the handkerchief industry.
The Evening Colonnade (1973) Of George Orwell

83 Better to write for yourself and have no public, than write for the public and have no self.
In Pritchett (ed.), *Turnstile One* **Connolly, Cyril** (1903–1974) English literary editor, writer and critic

84 Who often reads, will sometimes wish to write.
Tales (1812) **Crabbe, George** (1754–1832) English poet, clergyman, surgeon and botanist

85 Biography at its best is a form of fiction.
The Lyre of Orpheus (1988) **Davies, Robertson** (1913–1995) Canadian playwright, writer and critic

86 You need a skin as thin as a cigarette paper to write a novel and the hide of an elephant to publish it.
Meanjin, (1982) **Davison, Frank Dalby** (1893–1970) Australian writer

87 Years ago I used to think it was possible for a novelist to alter the inner life of the culture. Now bomb-makers and gunmen have taken that territory. They make raids on human consciousness. What writers used to do before we were all incorporated.
Mao II **Delillo, Don** (1936–) US author

88 I hold my inventive faculty on the stern condition that it must master my whole life, often have complete possession of me … and sometimes for months together put everything else away from me.
The Letters of Charles Dickens **Dickens, Charles** (1812–1870) English writer

89 Writers are always selling somebody out.
Slouching Towards Bethlehem (1968) **Didion, Joan** (1934–) US writer

90 An author who speaks about his own books is almost as bad as a mother who talks about her own children.
Speech at banquet given in Glasgow on his installation as Lord Rector, (1873)

91 We authors, Ma'am.
Said to Queen Victoria **Disraeli, Benjamin** (1804–1881) English statesman and writer

92 Writing is a socially acceptable form of schizophrenia.
In George Plimpton, *Writers at Work* (1988)

93 Writing is like driving at night in the fog. You can only see as far as your headlights, but you can make the whole trip that way.
In George Plimpton, *Writers at Work* (1988) **Doctorow, E. L.** (1931–) US writer

94 Our author by experience finds it true, 'Tis much more hard to please himself than you.
Aureng-Zebe (1675) **Dryden, John** (1631–1700) English poet, satirist, dramatist and critic

95 We can say of Shakespeare, that never has a man turned so little knowledge to such great account.
Lecture, (1942)

96 The common word exact without vulgarity, the formal word precise but not pedantic, the complete consort dancing together.
Sunday Telegraph, (1993) On his ideal of writing **Eliot, T.S.** (1888–1965) US-born British poet, verse dramatist and critic

97 Talent alone cannot make a writer. There must be a man behind the book.
'Goethe; or, the Writer' (1850)

98 When Shakespeare is charged with debts to his authors, Landor replies: 'Yet he was more original than his originals. He breathed upon dead bodies and brought them into life.'
Letters and Social Aims (1875)

99 Next to the originator of a good sentence is the first quoter of it.
Letters and Social Aims (1875) **Emerson, Ralph Waldo** (1803–1882) US poet, essayist, transcendentalist and teacher

100 Writing, Madam, is a mechanic part of wit; a gentleman should never go beyond a song or a billet.
The Man of Mode (1676) **Etherege, Sir George** (c.1635–1691) English Restoration dramatist

101 We prefer to believe that the absence of inverted commas guarantees the originality of a thought, whereas it may be merely that the utterer has forgotten its source.
Any Number Can Play (1957) **Fadiman, Clifton** (1904–1999) US writer, editor and broadcaster

102 It is always easier to proclaim rejection than to reject.
Les damnées de la terre (1961) **Fanon, Frantz** (1925–1961) West Indian psychoanalyst and philosopher. On 'native' writers trying to rid themselves of European influences

103 The writer's only responsibility is to his art … If a writer has to rob his mother, he will not hesitate; the 'Ode on a Grecian Urn' is worth any number of old ladies.
Paris Review, (1956)

104 The nicest old lady I ever met.
In E. Stone, *The Battle and the Books* (c.1964)
On Henry James

105 He has never been known to use a word
that might send the reader to the
dictionary.
Attr. Of Ernest Hemingway **Faulkner,
William** (1897–1962) US writer

106 To write it, it took three months; to
conceive it – three minutes; to collect the
data in it – all my life.
'The Author's Apology' (1920) **Fitzgerald, F.
Scott** (1896–1940) US writer. Referring to his
novel *This Side of Paradise*

107 Writing a novel is not merely going on a
shopping expedition across the border to
an unreal land: it is hours and years spent
in the factories, the streets, the cathedrals
of the imagination.
The Envoy from Mirror City (1985) **Frame, Janet**
(1924–) New Zealand writer

108 Writing free verse is like playing tennis
with the net down.
Address, (1935)

109 No tears in the writer, no tears in the
reader.
Collected Poems (1939) **Frost, Robert** (1874–1963)
US poet

110 I do wish I had the gift of writing. I really
think that it is the nicest way of making
money going.
Letter to Monica Sanderson, (c.1894)
Galsworthy, John (1867–1933) English writer
and dramatist

111 Journalism is a literary genre very similar
to that of the novel, and has the great
advantage that the reporter can invent
things. And that is completely forbidden to
the novelist.
Speech, (1994) **García Márquez, Gabriel**
(1928–) Colombian author

112 There's no greater bliss in life than when
the plumber eventually comes to unblock
your drains. No writer can give that sort of
pleasure.
The Observer, (1993) **Glendinning, Victoria**
(1937–) English writer

113 Novelists do not write as birds sing, by the
push of nature. It is part of the job that
there should be much routine and some
daily stuff on the level of carpentry.
'Rough Magic' lecture, (1977) **Golding,
William** (1911–1993) English writer and poet

114 As writers become more numerous, it is
natural for readers to become more
indolent.
The Bee (1759) **Goldsmith, Oliver** (c.1728–1774)
Irish dramatist, poet and writer

115 The tension between standing apart and
being fully involved; that is what makes a
writer.
Selected Stories (1975) **Gordimer, Nadine** (1923–)
South African writer

116 You must write for children just as you do
for adults, only better.
Attr. **Gorky, Maxim** (1868–1936) Russian
writer, dramatist and revolutionary

117 The remarkable thing about Shakespeare is
that he is really very good – in spite of all
the people who say he is very good.
The Observer, (1964) **Graves, Robert** (1895–1985)
English poet, writer, critic, translator and
mythologist

118 Any fool may write a most valuable book by
chance, if he will only tell us what he heard
and saw with veracity.
Letter to Horace Walpole, (1768) **Gray,
Thomas** (1716–1771) English poet and scholar

119 Biography, like big-game hunting, is one
of the recognized forms of sport, and it is
as unfair as only sport can be.
Supers and Supermen (1920)

120 The work of Henry James has always
seemed divisible by a simple dynastic
arrangement into three reigns: James I,
James II, and the Old Pretender.
Collected Essays (1920) **Guedalla, Philip** (1889–
1944) English historian, writer and lawyer

121 Wrong dressed out in pride, pomp, and
circumstance, has more attraction than
abstract right.
Characters of Shakespeare's Plays (1817)

122 He writes as fast as they can read, and he does not write himself down ... His works (taken together) are almost like a new edition of human nature. This is indeed to be an author! ... His worst is better than any other person's best.
The Spirit of the Age (1825). Of Sir Walter Scott **Hazlitt, William** (1778–1830) English writer and critic

123 If I had to give young writers advice, I would say don't listen to writers talking about writing or themselves.
New York Times, (1960) **Hellman, Lillian** (1907–1984) US dramatist and screenwriter

124 Prose is architecture, not interior decoration, and the Baroque is over.
Death in the Afternoon (1932)

125 And when you saw him he would take up a conversation interrupted three years before. It was nice to see a great writer in our time.
Green Hills of Africa (1935) Of James Joyce

126 Poor Faulkner. Does he really think big emotions come from big words? He thinks I don't know the ten-dollar words. I know them all right. But there are older and simpler and better words, and those are the ones I use.
In response to a jibe by William Faulkner *(see writing, 105)* **Hemingway, Ernest** (1898–1961) US author

127 The praise of ancient authors, proceeds not from the reverence of the dead, but from the competition, and mutual envy of the living.
Leviathan (1651) **Hobbes, Thomas** (1588–1679) Political philosopher

128 There are three things which the public will always clamour for, sooner or later: namely, Novelty, novelty, novelty.
Announcement of the 1836 version of *The Comic Annual* **Hood, Thomas** (1799–1845) English poet, editor and humorist

129 The progress of any writer is marked by those moments when he manages to outwit his own inner police system.
In Wendy Cope, *Making Cocoa for Kingsley Amis* (1986) **Hughes, Ted** (1930–1998) English poet

130 I am always at a loss to know how much to believe of my own stories.
Tales of a Traveller (1824) **Irving, Washington** (1783–1859) US writer and diplomat

131 I'll bet Shakespeare compromised himself a lot; anybody who's in the entertainment industry does to some extent.
In Jon Winokur, *Writers on Writing* (1990) **Isherwood, Christopher** (1904–1986) English novelist

132 It is the fate of those who toil at the lower employments of life ... to be exposed to censure, without hope of praise; to be disgraced by miscarriage, or punished for neglect ... Among these unhappy mortals is the writer of dictionaries ... Every other author may aspire to praise; the lexicographer can only hope to escape reproach.
A Dictionary of the English Language (1755)

133 The chief glory of every people arises from its authors.
A Dictionary of the English Language (1755)

134 The reciprocal civility of authors is one of the most risible scenes in the farce of life.
Life of Sir Thomas Browne (1756)

135 The only end of writing is to enable the readers better to enjoy life, or better to endure it.
Works (1787)

136 The greatest part of a writer's time is spent in reading, in order to write: a man will turn over half a library to make one book.
In Boswell, *The Life of Samuel Johnson* (1791)

137 No man was more foolish when he had not a pen in his hand, or more wise when he had.
In Boswell, *The Life of Samuel Johnson* (1791) Of Goldsmith

138 He was dull in a new way, and that made many people think him great.
In Boswell, *The Life of Samuel Johnson* (1791) Of Thomas Gray

139 Why, Sir, if you were to read Richardson for the story, your impatience would be so much fretted, that you would hang yourself. But you must read him for the sentiment, and consider the story as only giving occasion to the sentiment.
In Boswell, *The Life of Samuel Johnson* (1791)

140 Read over your compositions, and where ever you meet with a passage which you think is particularly fine, strike it out.
In Boswell, *The Life of Samuel Johnson* (1791)

141 A man may write at any time, if he will set himself doggedly to it.
In Boswell, *The Life of Samuel Johnson* (1791)

142 No man but a blockhead ever wrote, except for money.
In Boswell, *The Life of Samuel Johnson* (1791)

143 What is written without effort is in general read without pleasure.
In William Seward, *Biographia* (1799) **Johnson, Samuel** (1709–1784) English lexicographer, poet, critic, conversationalist and essayist

144 In small proportions we just beauties see;
And in short measures, life may perfect be.
The Underwood (1640) **Jonson, Ben** (1572–1637) English dramatist and poet

145 Authors are easy to get on with – if you're fond of children.
The Observer, (1949) **Joseph, Michael** (1897–1958) English publisher and writer

146 The incurable itch for writing takes hold of many and becomes chronic in their distempered brains.
Satires **Juvenal** (c.60–130) Roman verse satirist and Stoic

147 There is an old saying 'well begun is half done' – 'tis a bad one. I would use instead – 'Not begun at all until half done'.
Letter to B.R. Haydon, (10–11 May, 1817)

148 I have great reason to be content, for thank God I can read and perhaps understand Shakespeare to his depths.
Letter to John Taylor, (1818)

149 I have come to this resolution – never to write for the sake of writing or making a poem, but from running over with any little knowledge or experience which many years of reflection may perhaps give me; otherwise I will be dumb.
Letter to B.R. Haydon, (8 March 1819)

150 Shakespeare led a life of Allegory: his works are the comments on it.
Letter to George and Georgiana Keats, (1819)

151 I am convinced more and more day by day that fine writing is next to fine doing, the top thing in the world.
Letter to J. H. Reynolds, (1819) **Keats, John** (1795–1821) English poet

152 You are put up in Five-Star-Hotel land, when you come from One-Star-Hotel land – you can't even afford to go out of the door. So you go to the bookshop, you drink sour wine, you talk to people who don't want to talk to you, and you go back to your hotel room with a club sandwich, and watch a documentary on East Timor.
Sunday Herald, (1999) **Kennedy, A.L.** (1965–) Scottish novelist. On book promotion tours

153 A writer's ambition should be … to trade a hundred contemporary readers for ten readers in ten years' time and for one reader in a hundred years' time.
New York Times Book Review, (1951) **Koestler, Arthur** (1905–1983) British writer, essayist and political refugee

154 You must read all writers twice, both the good ones and the bad ones. You'll recognize the good ones and you'll unmask the others.
Sayings and Contradictions (1909) **Kraus, Karl** (1874–1936) Austrian scientist, critic and poet

155 Everything has been said already; we come too late after more than seven thousand years in which men have lived and thought.
Les caractères ou les moeurs de ce siècle (1688) **La Bruyère, Jean de** (1645–1696) French satirist

156 Mad, bad, and dangerous to know.
Journal, (1812) **Lamb, Lady Caroline** (1785–1828) English writer and poet. Of Byron

157 He says he never saw a man so happy in three wives as Mr Wordsworth is.
Letter to Sarah Hutchinson, (1816) **Lamb, Mary** (1764–1847) English prose writer. Of Henry Crabb Robinson

158 Clear writers, like clear fountains, do not seem so deep as they are; the turbid look the most profound.
Imaginary Conversations (1824) **Landor, Walter Savage** (1775–1864) English poet and writer

159 I like to write when I feel spiteful: it's like having a good sneeze.
Letter to Lady Cynthia Asquith, (1913) **Lawrence, D.H.** (1885–1930) English writer, poet and critic

160 Writing is like walking in a deserted street. Out of the dust in the street you make a mud pie.
Time, (1964) **Le Carré, John** (1931–) English writer

161 The trouble with Ian Fleming is that he gets off with women because he can't get on with them.
Borrowing a line from Elizabeth Bowen, quoted in J. Pearson, *The Life of Ian Fleming* (1966) **Lehmann, Rosamond** (1901–1990) English novelist

162 A good man fallen among Fabians.
In Arthur Ransome, *Six Weeks in Russia in 1919* (1919) **Lenin, V.I.** (1870–1924) Russian revolutionary, Marxist theoretician and first leader of the USSR. Of Bernard Shaw

163 The last gentleman in Europe.
Letters to the Sphinx (1930) **Leverson, Ada Beddington** (1862–1936) English writer. Of Oscar Wilde

164 So you're the little woman who wrote the book that made this great war!
Attr. **Lincoln, Abraham** (1809–1865) US statesman and President. On meeting Harriet Beecher Stowe

165 Every journalist has a novel in him, which is an excellent place for it.
Attr. **Lynes, J. Russel** (1910–1991) US writer

166 Biographers, translators, editors, all, in short, who employ themselves in illustrating the lives or writings of others, are peculiarly exposed to the Lues Boswelliana, or disease of admiration.
Collected Essays (1843) **Macaulay, Lord** (1800–1859) English Liberal statesman, essayist and poet

167 Our principal writers have nearly all been fortunate in escaping regular education.
The Observer, (1953) **MacDiarmid, Hugh** (1892–1978) Scottish poet

168 But my work is undistinguished
And my royalties are lean
Because I never am obscure
And not at all obscene.
'An Author's Lament' **MacManus, Michael** (1888–1951)

169 Better to write twaddle, anything, than nothing at all.
Attr. **Mansfield, Katherine** (1888–1923) New Zealand writer

170 Sentimentality is only sentiment that rubs you up the wrong way.
A Writer's Notebook (1949)

171 You don't just get a story ... You have to wait for it to come to you. I've never written a story in my life. The story has come to me and demanded to be written.
In Robin Maugham, *Conversation with Willie* (1978) **Maugham, William Somerset** (1874–1965) English writer, dramatist and physician

172 I write in order to attain that feeling of tension relieved and function achieved which a cow enjoys on giving milk.
The Delights of Reading **Mencken, H.L.** (1880–1956) US writer, critic, philologist and satirist

173 I'm a lousy writer; a helluva lot of people have got lousy taste.
In Jon Winokur, *Writers on Writing* (1990) **Metalious, Grace** (1924–1964) US writer; author of *Peyton Place*

174 The really great writers are people like Emily Brontë who sit in a room and write out of their limited experience and unlimited imagination.
New York Times, (1985) **Michener, James** (1907–1997) US writer

175 I have discovered that our great favourite, Miss Austen, is my country-woman ... with whom mamma before her marriage was acquainted. Mamma says that she was then the prettiest, silliest, most affected, husband-hunting butterfly she ever remembers.
Letter to Sir William Elford, (1815)

176 Perpendicular, precise and taciturn.
In *Life and Letters of Mary R. Mitford* (1870). Said of Jane Austen **Mitford, Mary Russell** (1787–1855) English writer

177 When you steal from one author, it's plagiarism; if you steal from many, it's research.
Attr. **Mizner, Wilson** (1876–1933) US writer, wit and dramatist

178 To be amused at what you read – that is the great spring of happy quotation.
A Writer's Notes on his Trade (1930) **Montague, C.E.** (1867–1928) English writer and critic

179 One could say of me that in this book I have only made up a bunch of other men's flowers, providing of my own only the string to tie them together.
Essais (1580) **Montaigne, Michel de** (1533–1592) French essayist and moralist

180 He lik'd those literary cooks
Who skim the cream of others' books;
And ruin half an author's graces
By plucking bon-mots from their places.
Attr. **More, Hannah** (1745–1833) English poet, dramatist and religious writer

181 If there's a book you really want to read but it hasn't been written yet, then you must write it.
Attr. **Morrison, Toni** (1931–) US writer

182 He looked, I decided, like a letter delivered to the wrong address.
Tread Softly For You Tread on My Jokes (1966) **Muggeridge, Malcolm** (1903–1990) English writer. Of Evelyn Waugh

183 Writing is like getting married. One should never commit oneself until one is amazed at one's luck.
The Black Prince (1989) **Murdoch, Iris** (1919–1999) Irish-born British writer, philosopher and dramatist

184 English literature's performing flea.
In P.G. Wodehouse, *Performing Flea* (1953) **O'Casey, Sean** (1880–1964) Irish dramatist. Of P.G. Wodehouse

185 Everywhere I go I'm asked if I think the university stifles writers. My opinion is that they don't stifle enough of them. There's many a bestseller that could have been prevented by a good teacher.
In Fitzgerald, *The Nature and Aim of Fiction* **O'Connor, Flannery** (1925–1964) US writer

186 A bedbug on which a sensitive man refuses to stamp because of the smell and squashiness.
Attr. in Larry Powell, 'The Discovery of a New Master, Roderic O'Conor', *Etudes Irlandaises*, (1933) **O'Conor, Roderic** (1860–1940) Irish artist. On Somerset Maugham

187 Good prose is like a window pane.
'Why I Write' (1946)

188 Never use a metaphor, simile or other figure of speech which you are used to seeing in print. Never use a long word where a short one will do. If it is possible to cut a word out, always cut it out. Never use the passive where you can use the active. Never use a foreign phrase, a scientific word or a jargon word if you can think of an everyday English equivalent. Break any of these rules sooner than say anything outright barbarous.
'Politics and the English Language' (1950). His rules for writing good English **Orwell, George** (1903–1950) English writer and critic

189 I have made this letter longer only because I have not had time to make it shorter.
Lettres Provinciales (1657)

190 The last thing one finds out when constructing a work is what to put first.
Pensées (1670)

191 When we see a natural style, we are quite surprised and delighted, for we expected to see an author and we find a man.
Pensées (1670) **Pascal, Blaise** (1623–1662) French philosopher and scientist

192 To write one's memoirs is to speak ill of everybody except oneself.

The Observer, (1946) **Pétain, Marshal** (1856–1951) French soldier and statesman

193 Writing is for me a completely private activity, a poem or a play, no difference ... What I write has no obligation to anything other than to itself.
Speech to student drama festival, (1962) **Pinter, Harold** (1930–) English dramatist, poet and screenwriter

194 True ease in writing comes from art, not chance,
As those move easiest who have learn'd to dance.
'Tis not enough no harshness gives offence,
The sound must seem an echo to the sense.
An Essay on Criticism (1711)

195 'Tis hard to say, if greater want of skill Appear in writing or in judging ill.
An Essay on Criticism (1711) **Pope, Alexander** (1688–1744) English poet, translator and editor

196 O God, O Venus, O Mercury, patron of thieves,
Lend me a little tobacco-shop,
or install me in any profession
Save this damn'd profession of writing,
where one needs one's brains all the time.
'The Lake Isle' (1916) **Pound, Ezra** (1885–1972) US poet

197 Comedy, we may say, is society protecting itself – with a smile.
George Meredith (1926) **Priestley, J.B.** (1894–1984) English writer, dramatist and critic

198 I don't think I am writing books for people too stupid to wear their baseball caps the right way round.
The Times, (1998) **Pratchett, Terry** (1948–) English writer

199 I wish thee as much pleasure in the reading, as I had in the writing.
Emblems (1635) **Quarles, Francis** (1592–1644) English poet, writer and royalist

200 Poor style reflects imperfect thought.
Journal, (1898)

201 The profession of letters is, after all, the only one in which one can make no money without being ridiculous.

Journal **Renard, Jules** (1864–1910) French writer and dramatist

202 In Hollywood the woods are full of people that learned to write but evidently can't read; if they could read their stuff, they'd stop writing.
The Autobiography of Will Rogers (1949) **Rogers, Will** (1879–1935) US humorist, actor, rancher, writer and wit

203 Choose an author as you choose a friend.
An Essay on Translated Verse (1684) **Roscommon, Fourth Earl of** (1633–1685) Irish translator and poet

204 Writers and politicians are natural rivals. Both groups try to make the world in their own images; they fight for the same territory.
The Observer, (1989) **Rushdie, Salman** (1947–) Indian-born English author

205 Thackeray settled like a meat-fly on whatever one had got for dinner, and made one sick of it.
Fors Clavigera (1871–1884) **Ruskin, John** (1819–1900) English art critic, philosopher and reformer

206 The writer, a free man addressing free men, has only one subject – freedom.
What Is Literature? **Sartre, Jean-Paul** (1905–1980) French philosopher, writer, dramatist and critic

207 But no one shall find me rowing against the stream. I care not who knows it – I write for the general amusement.
The Fortunes of Nigel (1822)

208 The Big Bow-Wow strain I can do myself like any now going; but the exquisite touch, which renders ordinary commonplace things and characters interesting, from the truth of the description and the sentiment, is denied to me.
Journal, (14 March 1826). On Jane Austen

209 The blockheads talk of my being like Shakespeare – not fit to tie his brogues.
Journal, (11 December 1826) **Scott, Sir Walter** (1771–1832) Scottish writer and historian

210 You write with ease, to show your
breeding;
But easy writing's vile hard reading.
'Clio's Protest' (1771)

211 All that can be said is, that two people
happened to hit on the same thought –
and Shakespeare made use of it first, that's
all.
The Critic (1779) **Sheridan, Richard Brinsley**
(1751–1816) Irish dramatist, politician and
orator

212 It is disappointing to report that George
Bernard Shaw appearing as George
Bernard Shaw is sadly miscast in the part.
Satirists should be heard and not seen.
Reviewing a Shaw play **Sherwood, Robert
Emmet** (1896–1955) US writer and dramatist

213 When I was a little boy they called me a liar
but now that I am a grown up they call me
a writer.
The Observer, (1983) **Singer, Isaac Bashevis**
(1904–1991) Polish-born US Yiddish writer

214 Byting my tongue and penne, beating my
selfe for spite:
'Foole,' saide My muse to mee, 'looke in
thy heart and write'.
Astrophel and Stella (1591) **Sidney, Sir Philip**
(1554–1586) English poet, critic, soldier,
courtier and diplomat

215 Writing is not a profession but a vocation
of unhappiness.
Writers at Work (1958) **Simenon, Georges**
(1903–1989) Belgian writer

216 I enjoyed talking to her, but thought
nothing of her writing. I considered her 'a
beautiful little knitter'.
Letter to G. Singleton, (1955) **Sitwell, Dame
Edith** (1887–1964) English poet, anthologist,
critic and biographer. Of Virginia Woolf

217 The principal benefit of publication is that
it clears work out of the mind finally, and
provides an impulse for new work.
Letter to Norman Lindsay, (1944) **Slessor,
Kenneth** (1901–1971) Australian poet and
journalist

218 No regime has ever loved great writers,
only minor ones.

219 *The First Circle* (1968) **Solzhenitsyn, Alexander**
(1918–) Russian writer, dramatist and
historian

219 If the public likes you, you're good.
Shakespeare was a common, down-to-
earth writer in his day.
In Jon Winokur, *Writers on Writing* (1990)
Spillane, Mickey (1918–) US author

220 I have often thought that a Story-teller is
born, as well as a Poet.
The Guardian, 42, (1713) **Steele, Sir Richard**
(1672–1729) Irish-born English writer,
dramatist and politician

221 The profession of book writing makes
horse racing seem like a solid, stable
business.
Quoted in *Newsweek*, (1962) **Steinbeck, John**
(1902–1968) US writer. Accepting the Nobel
prize for literature

222 Will there never come a season
Which shall rid us from the curse
Of a prose which knows no reason
And an unmelodious verse ...
When there stands a muzzled stripling,
Mute, beside a muzzled bore:
When the Rudyards cease from kipling
And the Haggards ride no more.
Lapsus Calami (1891) **Stephen, James Kenneth**
(1859–1892) English writer and poet

223 Writing, when properly managed, (as you
may be sure I think mine is) is but a
different name for conversation.
Tristram Shandy (1759–1767) **Sterne, Laurence**
(1713–1768) Irish-born English writer and
clergyman

224 Though we are mighty fine fellows
nowadays, we cannot write like Hazlitt.
Virginibus Puerisque (1881)

225 Of all my verse, like not a single line;
But like my title, for it is not mine,
That title from a better man I stole;
Ah, how much better, had I stol'n the
whole!
Underwoods (1887) **Stevenson, Robert Louis**
(1850–1894) Scottish writer, poet and essayist

226 Biographies are like anthologies, especially anthologies of poetry. One's eyes are magnetically directed to what ought to be there but isn't, as well as to what oughtn't to be there but is.
Still More Commonplace (1973) **Stocks, Mary, Baroness** (1891–1975) English educationist, broadcaster and biographer

227 You can only write about what bites you.
The Observer, (1984) **Stoppard, Tom** (1937–) British dramatist

228 I did not write it. God wrote it. I merely did his dictation.
Attr. **Stowe, Harriet Beecher** (1811–1896) US writer and reformer. Of *Uncle Tom's Cabin*

229 Proper words in proper places, make the true definition of a style.
Letter to a Young Gentleman Lately Entered Into Holy Orders (1720) **Swift, Jonathan** (1667–1745) Irish satirist, poet, essayist and cleric

230 William Congreve is the only sophisticated playwright England has produced; and like Shaw, Sheridan, and Wilde, his nearest rivals, he was brought up in Ireland.
Curtains (1961) **Tynan, Kenneth** (1927–1980) English drama critic, producer and essayist

231 Not that the story need be long, but it will take a long while to make it short.
Letter to Harrison Blake, (1857) **Thoreau, Henry David** (1817–1862) US essayist, social critic and writer

232 Three hours a day will produce as much as a man ought to write.
Autobiography (1883) **Trollope, Anthony** (1815–1882) English writer, traveller and post office official

233 As to the Adjective: when in doubt, strike it out.
Pudd'nhead Wilson's Calendar (1894) **Twain, Mark** (1835–1910) US humorist, writer, journalist and lecturer

234 American writers want to be not good but great; and so are neither.
Two Sisters (1970) **Vidal, Gore** (1925–) US writer, critic and poet

235 All styles are good except the tedious kind.
L'Enfant prodigue (1738)

236 If we do not find anything pleasant, we shall at least find something new.
Candide (1759) **Voltaire** (1694–1778) French philosopher, dramatist, poet, historian, writer and critic

237 Lord Rochester's poems have much more obscenity than wit, more wit than poetry, more poetry than politeness.
Catalogue of Royal and Noble Authors (1758)

238 The life of any man written under the direction of his family, did nobody honour.
Letter, (1778) **Walpole, Horace** (1717–1797) English writer and politician

239 It is a pity that Chawcer, who had geneyus, was so unedicated. He's the wuss speller I know of.
Artemus Ward in London (1867) **Ward, Artemus** (1834–1867) US humorist, journalist, editor and lecturer

240 Meanwhile you will write an essay on 'self-indulgence'. There will be a prize of half a crown for the longest essay, irrespective of any possible merit.
Decline and Fall (1928)

241 No writer before the middle of the 19th century wrote about the working classes other than as grotesque or as pastoral decoration. Then when they were given the vote certain writers started to suck up to them.
Paris Review, (1963)

242 I put the words down and push them a bit.
Obituary, *New York Times*, (11 April 1966)

243 I wouldn't give up writing about God at this stage if I was you. It would be like P.G. Wodehouse dropping Jeeves half-way through the Wooster series.
In Christopher Sykes, *Evelyn Waugh*. Remark to Graham Greene, who was planning to write a political novel **Waugh, Evelyn** (1903–1966) English writer and diarist

244 I think if you had ever written a book you were absolutely pleased with, you'd never write another. The same probably goes for having children.
The Guardian, (1991) **Weldon, Fay** (1931–) British writer

245 The thing his novel is about is always there. It is like a church lit but without a congregation to distract you, with every light and line focused on the high altar. And on the altar, very reverently placed, intensely there, is a dead kitten, an egg-shell, a bit of string.
Boon (1915) **Wells, H.G.** (1866–1946) English writer. Of Henry James

246 Style is the dress of thought; a modest dress,
Neat, but not gaudy, will true critics please.
'An Epistle to a Friend concerning Poetry' (1700) **Wesley, Samuel** (1662–1735) English churchman and poet

247 Just how difficult it is to write biography can be reckoned by anybody who sits down and considers just how many people know the real truth about his or her love affairs.
Vogue, (1952) **West, Dame Rebecca** (1892–1983) English writer, critic and feminist

248 The challenge for the writer is to adapt his ancient and difficult craft to a generation that is largely insensitive to its virtues and to a popular audience increasingly distracted by the pace, immediacy and materialism of contemporary life.
Speech, (1975) **Whitlam, Gough** (1916–) Australian Labor statesman and Prime Minister

249 Every great man has his disciples, but it is always Judas who writes the biography.
Attr. **Wilde, Oscar** (1854–1900) Irish poet, dramatist, writer, critic and wit

250 The nicest thing about quotes is that they give us a nodding acquaintance with the originator which is often socially impressive.
Acid Drops (1980) **Williams, Kenneth** (1926–1988) English actor and comedian

251 I am reading Henry James ... and feel myself as one entombed in a block of smooth amber.
Attr. **Woolf, Virginia** (1882–1941) English author

252 Never forget what I believe was observed to you by Coleridge, that every great and original writer, in proportion as he is great and original, must himself create the taste by which he is to be relished.
Letter to Lady Beaumont, (1807) **Wordsworth, William** (1770–1850) English poet

253 Bald heads forgetful of their sins,
Old, learned, respectable bald heads
Edit and annotate the lines
That young men, tossing on their beds,
Rhymed out in love's despair
To flatter beauty's ignorant ear.
All shuffle there; all cough in ink;
All wear the carpet with their shoes;
All think what other people think;
All know the man their neighbour knows.
Lord, what would they say
Did their Catullus walk that way?
In *Catholic Anthology* (1914–1915)

254 A good writer should be so simple that he has no faults, only sins.
The Death of Synge and other Passages from an Old Diary (1928)

255 She is magnificently ugly – deliciously hideous ... now in this vast ugliness resides a most powerful beauty which, in a very few minutes, steals forth and charms the mind.
Attr. Of George Eliot

256 It's not a writer's business to hold opinions.
Attr. **Yeats, W.B.** (1865–1939) Irish poet, dramatist, editor, writer and senator

257 Some, for renown, on scraps of learning dote,
And think they grow immortal as they quote.
Love of Fame, the Universal Passion (1725–1728) **Young, Edward** (1683–1765) English poet, dramatist, satirist and clergyman
See also criticism; literature; books

YOUTH

1 Let us be happy while we are young, for after carefree youth and careworn age, the earth will hold us also.
'Gaudeamus Igitur', (13th century)
Anonymous

2 Youth would be an ideal state if it came a little later in life.

The Observer, (1923) **Asquith, Herbert** (1852–1928) English Liberal statesman and Prime Minister

3 I've never understood why people consider youth a time of freedom and joy. It's probably because they have forgotten their own.
Ms, (1976) **Atwood, Margaret** (1939–) Canadian writer, poet and critic

4 Youth will be served, every dog has his day, and mine has been a fine one.
Lavengro (1851) **Borrow, George** (1803–1881) English writer and linguist

5 In the lexicon of youth, which Fate reserves For a bright manhood, there is no such word As – fail!
Richelieu (1839) **Bulwer-Lytton, Edward** (1803–1873) English novelist and politician

6 When I was young and irresponsible, I was young and irresponsible.
The Times, (1999) **Bush, George W.** (1946–) US Republican President. Reply when asked if he had experimented with drugs

7 Oh, talk not to me of a name great in story; The days of our youth are the days of our glory; And the myrtle and ivy of sweet two-and-twenty Are worth all your laurels, though ever so plenty.
'Stanzas Written on the Road between Florence and Pisa', (November 1821) **Byron, Lord** (1788–1824) English poet, satirist and traveller

8 Being 18 is like visiting Russia. You're glad you've had the experience but you'd never want to repeat it.
Comment 1978, quoted in *The Guardian*, (2000) **Cartland, Barbara** (1901–2000) English writer

9 Youth is something very new: twenty years ago no one mentioned it.
In Haedrich, *Coco Chanel, Her Life, Her Secrets* (1971) **Chanel, Coco** (1883–1971) French couturier and perfumer

10 I remember my youth and the feeling that will never come back any more – the feeling that I could last for ever, outlast the sea, the earth, and all men; the deceitful feeling that lures us on to perils, to love, to vain effort – to death; the triumphant conviction of strength, the heat of life in the handful of dust, that glow in the heart that with every year grows dim, grows cold, grows small, and expires – and expires, too soon, too soon – before life itself.
Youth (1902) **Conrad, Joseph** (1857–1924) Polish-born British writer, sailor and explorer

11 The young always have the same problem – how to rebel and conform at the same time. They have now solved this by defying their parents and copying one another.
The Naked Civil Servant (1968) **Crisp, Quentin** (1908–1999) English writer, publicist and model

12 Youth, what man's age is like to be doth show; We may our ends by our beginnings know.
'Of Prudence' (1668) **Denham, Sir John** (1615–1669) English poet, royalist and Surveyor-General

13 Youth is a blunder; Manhood a struggle; Old Age a regret.
Coningsby (1844)

14 Almost everything that is great has been done by youth.
Coningsby (1844)

15 The Youth of a Nation are the Trustees of Posterity.
Sybil (1845) **Disraeli, Benjamin** (1804–1881) English statesman and writer

16 Alas, that Spring should vanish with the Rose! That Youth's sweet-scented Manuscript should close! The Nightingale that in the Branches sang, Ah, whence, and whither flown again, who knows!
The Rubáiyát of Omar Khayyám (1859) **Fitzgerald, Edward** (1809–1883) English poet, translator and letter writer

17 Youth's the season made for joys, Love is then our duty.
The Beggar's Opera (1728) **Gay, John** (1685–1732) English poet, dramatist and librettist

18 Where young boys plan for what they will achieve and attain, young girls plan for whom they will achieve and attain.
Women and Economics (1898) **Gilman, Charlotte Perkins** (1860–1935) US writer, social reformer and feminist

19 No young man believes he shall ever die.
'On the Feeling of Immortality in Youth' (1827) **Hazlitt, William** (1778–1830) English writer and critic

20 Now that the April of your youth adorns The Garden of your face.
'Ditty in imitation of the Spanish Entre tantoque L'Avril' (1665) **Herbert, Edward** (1583–1648) English statesman, poet and philosopher

21 Youth will come here and beat on my door, and force its way in.
The Master Builder (1892) **Ibsen, Henrik** (1828–1906) Norwegian writer, dramatist and poet

22 People have this obsession. They want you to be like you were in 1969. They want you to, because otherwise their youth goes with you ... It's very selfish, but it's understandable.
The Observer, (1993) **Jagger, Mick** (1943–) English rock musician

23 Young men have more virtue than old men; they have more generous sentiments in every respect.
In Boswell, *The Life of Samuel Johnson* (1791) **Johnson, Samuel** (1709–1784) English lexicographer, poet, critic, conversationalist and essayist

24 Young men make great mistakes in life; for one thing, they idealize love too much.
Life and Letters of Benjamin Jowett (1897) **Jowett, Benjamin** (1817–1893) English scholar, translator, essayist and priest

25 When all the world is young, lad,
And all the trees are green;
And every goose a swan, lad,
And every lass a queen;
Then hey for boot and horse, lad,
And round the world away:
Young blood must have its course, lad,
And every dog his day.
Song from *The Water Babies* (1863), 'Young and Old' **Kingsley, Charles** (1819–1875) English writer, poet, lecturer and clergyman

26 I've always believed in the adage that the secret of eternal youth is arrested development.
Conversations with Alice Roosevelt Longworth **Longworth, Alice Roosevelt** (1884–1980) US writer

27 You ask for some details as to myself. I am poor – obscure – just eighteen years of age – with a rapacious appetite for everything and principles as light as my purse.
In O'Sullivan and Scott (eds), *The Collected Letters of Katherine Mansfield 1903–1917* (1984) **Mansfield, Katherine** (1888–1923) New Zealand writer. To a magazine editor

28 How lovely is youth, which is always slipping away! Let him be glad who will be so: for tomorrow has no certainty.
'Trionfo di Bacco ed Arianna' **Medici, Lorenzo de'** (1449–1492) Florentine ruler

29 In youth we are, but in age we seem.
Pierre (1852) **Melville, Herman** (1819–1891) US writer and poet

30 I keep looking back, as far as I can remember, and I can't think what it was like to feel young, really young.
Look Back in Anger (1956) **Osborne, John** (1929–1994) English dramatist and actor

31 Funky royals, coked-out old men and streaking BA stewardesses make me nostalgic for an age when people knew youth was just a stage you passed through, like acne.
The Observer, (1999) **Parsons, Tony** (1953–) British journalist and author

32 The atrocious crime of being a young man ... I shall neither attempt to palliate nor deny.
Speech, House of Commons, (1741)

33 I cannot give them my confidence; pardon me, gentlemen, confidence is a plant of slow growth in an aged bosom: youth is the season of credulity.
Speech, (1766) **Pitt, William** (1708–1778) English politician and Prime Minister

34 They have found that the fountain of youth
Is a mixture of gin and vermouth.
'The Fountain of Youth' (song, 1928) **Porter,
Cole** (1891–1964) US songwriter

35 How ruthless and hard and vile and right
the young are.
The Watcher on the Cast-iron Balcony (1963)
Porter, Hal (1911–1984) Australian writer,
dramatist and poet

36 I confess to pride in this coming
generation. You are working out your own
salvation; you are more in love with life;
you play with fire openly, where we did in
secret, and few of you are burned!
Address, (1926) **Roosevelt, Franklin Delano**
(1882–1945) US Democrat President

37 I was about half in love with her by the
time we sat down. That's the thing about
girls. Every time they do something pretty,
even if they're not much to look at, or even
if they're sort of stupid, you fall half in love
with them, and then you never know where
you are.
The Catcher in the Rye (1951) **Salinger, J.D.**
(1919–) US writer

38 I used to love sitting in the gutter with bare
feet, a chrome-studded chair, covered
leather jacket and filthy jeans. Eatin' chips.
People look at you with such disgust and
hate. It was terrific.
Bullshit & Jellybeans (1971) **Shadbolt, Tim**
(1932–) New Zealand novelist. On teenage
pleasures, c.1960

39 My salad days,
When I was green in judgment, cold in
blood,
To say as I said then.
Antony and Cleopatra, I.v

40 He capers, he dances, he has eyes of youth,
he writes verses, he speaks holiday, he
smells April and May.
The Merry Wives of Windsor, III.ii

41 Two lads that thought there was no more
behind
But such a day tomorrow as today,
And to be boy eternal.
The Winter's Tale, I.ii

42 I would there were no age between ten and
three and twenty, or that youth would sleep
out the rest; for there is nothing in the
between but getting wenches with child,
wronging the anciently, stealing, fighting.
The Winter's Tale, III.iii **Shakespeare, William**
(1564–1616) English dramatist, poet and actor

43 Youth, which is forgiven everything,
forgives itself nothing: age, which forgives
itself everything, is forgiven nothing.
Man and Superman (1903)

44 It's all that the young can do for the old, to
shock them and keep them up to date.
Fanny's First Play (1911) **Shaw, George Bernard**
(1856–1950) Irish socialist, writer, dramatist
and critic

45 The old know what they want; the young
are sad and bewildered.
'Last Words' (1933) **Smith, Logan Pearsall**
(1865–1946) US-born British epigrammatist,
critic and writer

46 Youth is the time to go flashing from one
end of the world to the other both in mind
and body; to try the manners of different
nations; to hear the chimes at midnight; to
see sunrise in town and country; to be
converted at a revival; to circumnavigate
the metaphysics, write halting verses, run a
mile to see a fire, and wait all day long in
the theatre to applaud *Hernani*.
Virginibus Puerisque (1881) **Stevenson, Robert
Louis** (1850–1894) Scottish writer, poet and
essayist

47 Young people ought not to be idle. It is
very bad for them.
The Times, (1984) **Thatcher, Margaret** (1925–)
English Conservative Prime Minister

48 Now as I was young and easy under the
apple boughs
About the lilting house and happy as the
grass was green …
Oh as I was young and easy in the mercy of
his means,
Time held me green and dying
Though I sang in my chains like the sea.
'Fern Hill' (1946)

49 Years and years and years ago, when I was a boy, when there were wolves in Wales, and birds the colour of red-flannel petticoats whisked past the harp-shaped hills ... when we rode the daft and happy hills bareback, it snowed and it snowed.
A Child's Christmas in Wales (1954) **Thomas, Dylan** (1914–1953) Welsh poet, writer and radio dramatist

50 Youth is a time when we find the books we give up but do not get over.
New York Times, (1966) **Trilling, Lionel** (1905–1975) US critic

51 He must have known me had he seen me as he was wont to see me, for he was in the habit of flogging me constantly. Perhaps he did not recognize me by my face.
Autobiography (1883) **Trollope, Anthony** (1815–1882) English writer, traveller and post office official. Of his headmaster

52 In youth alone, unhappy mortals live;
But oh! the mighty bliss is fugitive:
Discoloured sickness, anxious labours, come,
And age and death's inexorable doom.
Georgics **Virgil** (70–19 BC) Roman poet

53 In a harbour grene aslepe whereas I lay,
The byrdes sang swete in the middes of the day,
I dreamèd fast of mirth and play:
In youth is pleasure, in youth is pleasure.
'Lusty Juventus' **Wever, Robert** (fl. 1550) British poet

54 Youth, large, lusty, loving – youth full of grace, force, fascination,
Do you know that Old Age may come after you with equal grace, force, fascination?
'Youth, Day, Old Age and Night' (1855) **Whitman, Walt** (1819–1892) US poet and writer

55 The old-fashioned respect for the young is fast dying out.
The Importance of Being Earnest (1895) **Wilde, Oscar** (1854–1900) Irish poet, dramatist, writer, critic and wit

56 Generally young men are regarded as radicals. This is a popular misconception. The most conservative persons I ever met are college undergraduates.
Speech, (1905) **Wilson, Woodrow** (1856–1924) US Democrat President

57 Bliss was it in that dawn to be alive,
But to be young was very heaven.
The Prelude (1850) **Wordsworth, William** (1770–1850) English poet

58 In the Junes that were warmer than these are, the waves were more gay,
When I was a boy with never a crack in my heart.
'The Meditation of the Old Fisherman' (1886) **Yeats, W.B.** (1865–1939) Irish poet, dramatist, editor, writer and senator
See also age; childhood and children

Index